FOOD

AN AUTHORITATIVE AND VISUAL HISTORY
AND DICTIONARY OF THE FOODS OF THE WORLD

Waverley Root

SIMON AND SCHUSTER • NEW YORK

FRONTISPIECE. Severin Roesen (1815/20–c. 1872)
Still Life with Watermelon, oil on canvas.

Courtesy Elvehjem Museum of Art, Max W. Zabel Fund Purchase.

PUBLISHED BY SIMON AND SCHUSTER
A DIVISION OF GULF & WESTERN CORPORATION
SIMON & SCHUSTER BUILDING
ROCKEFELLER CENTER
1230 AVENUE OF THE AMERICAS
NEW YORK, NEW YORK 10020

DESIGNED BY EVE METZ
PICTURE EDITOR, VINCENT VIRGA

MANUFACTURED IN THE UNITED STATES OF AMERICA
PRINTED AND BOUND BY THE MURRAY PRINTING CO.
COLOR INSERT PRINTED LEHIGH PRESS
COMPOSITION BY MARYLAND LINOTYPE CO.

10 9 8 7 6 5 4 3 2 1

LIBRARY OF CONGRESS CATALOGING IN PUBLICATION DATA
Root, Waverley Lewis, 1903-
Food

Bibliography: p.
1. Food—Dictionaries. I. Title.
TX349.R58 641'.0321 80-14737
ISBN 0-671-22589-8

NOTE

The illustrations, gathered from many museums and galleries, libraries, institutions and private collections, offer an informal history of food in art, from early herbal to modern sculpture—food as fact and food as metaphor; food as labor, food as science, food as decoration; food for the body, the mind and the spirit.

In particular, we wish to thank The Metropolitan Museum of Art and The Botany Library of The Smithsonian Institution.

A

ALLEN, FRED: *Before food was invented, books about cooking were unknown.*

AA
stands for

aardvark, eaten in tropical Africa, and **aardwolf,** eaten in South Africa; and for **Aaron's rod,** otherwise the mullein.

AB
stands for

abata-kola, chewed for energy by West Africans; for **abavo,** described by Alexandre Dumas as a pumpkin which grows on a tree; for **abelmosk,** whose Arabic name means "father of musk"; for **abdelavis,** an Egyptian melon whose flesh, like the drink made from its seeds, quenches thirst, a useful quality in a fruit which persists in growing where the temperature is 105° F.; for the **Abe Lincoln apple,** a misguided patriotic attempt to hide the identity of the Red Astrachan; for **Aberdeen Angus,** prized Scotch beef critters, and **Abers,** prized French oysters; for **abessin,** a seed so called because it was eaten in Abyssinia; and for the **ablet,** a fish of such delicate taste that it responds to the lure of anise-perfumed flour scattered on the water—and then bites on a grub.

And **AB** also stands for

ABALONE. About four times during the winter an "ormering tide" uncovers the rocks surrounding the Channel Islands of Jersey and Guernsey. A decade ago, whenever this happened, banks, factories, stores and schools closed. The population, dressed in its oldest clothes, swarmed out en masse to pry ormers from the bared rocks with iron bars. A good haul per person during the two hours the tide stayed out was fourteen dozen—more if one had a boat. It was too good to last. In 1972 the government had to decree a completely closed season of three years to stave off the extinction of the ormer, a slow grower. Since 1975, restrictions have varied in function of the situation of the moment.

The ormer might reasonably be described as the object of a cult in the Channel Islands and also

ABALONE *shells are sacred vessels for the American Indian.*

in California, where it is called the abalone, and where there is no danger of gathering fourteen dozen. Indeed the amateur abalone hunter is lucky there to find any at all above the minimum size he is permitted to take, at the time of writing seven inches for the red abalone. The commercial catch is gathered by divers, for local consumption only. It is against the law to can them, dry them or ship them out of the state.

The abalone looks like a large, single-shelled clam with its open side glued against the rock; it is actually a sort of flattened snail. Californians tend to talk as though they had invented it, but there are in fact seventy-five species scattered widely throughout the world. Chinese and Japanese are its largest consumers; in Japan it is the principal prey of the famous diving girls. It is becoming scarce there too, because of the disinclination of modern Japanese daughters to succeed their mothers in this grueling occupation, as they did automatically in more heroic times.

The abalone resigns itself with the utmost reluctance to the duty of becoming edible. It must be pounded unmercifully to make it tender enough for human consumption and then cooked with watchful brevity, lest it pass the point of no return. Treated otherwise, it comes out rubbery and very nearly tasteless.

Abalone is a luxury in California and poor folks' food in Chile. Sea otters are fond of them.

AC
stands for

the **acacia**, which is not the source of acacia honey, and the **acanthus**, whose leaves are sometimes chewed and sometimes chiseled on the capitals of Corinthian columns; for the **accola**, a Maltese fish rich in oil, and the **acerola**, a Caribbean berry rich in vitamin C; for the **acha**, an African seed known popularly as "hungry rice," and the **ache**, a wild celery known popularly as "fool's-parsley"; for the **achanaca**, a cactus eaten by Peruvian Indians, and the **achiote**, a seed eaten by Mexican Indians; for the **acoho**, an edible hen which lays inedible eggs; for **acorns**, best eaten indirectly by man, in the form of pork, though they were consumed directly by pre-Columbian North American Indians who had no pigs; for the **acorn squash**, which Amerindians relished also; and for **acorus calamus**, an aphrodisiac rush known to the ancient Romans as "the plant of Venus."

AD
stands for

Adam's flannel, our second name for the mullein; for the **adana**, a sort of sturgeon fished by Italians from the Po, and the **addax**, a sort of antelope hunted by Africans in the desert; and for **adjab butter**, from the nut of a tree which grows in Gabon.

AE
stands for

the **aerial yam**, or air potato, which is relished by tropical Africans in blithe disregard of the detail that it is poisonous.

AF
stands for

the **African apricot**, which is not an apricot, and of which the seeds, not the fruit, are eaten; for the **African locust bean**, whose fermented seeds are used as a condiment in eastern Africa; and for the **African walnut**, which is the Boer bean unless it happens to be the almond wood.

AG
stands for

the **agami**, or trumpeter, a delicious domesticated bird used in tropical South America to ride herd on less disciplined poultry; for the **agar**, a Saharan tree which provides food for Tuareg men and assistance in time of need for repudiated Tuareg women; for **agar-agar**, which starts out as seaweed and ends up as gelatin; for the **agaric**, the most widely eaten cultivated mushroom in the world; for **agave**, the century plant, so called because it takes one hundred years to blossom in literature and ten in fact; for **agnus castus**, an anti-aphrodisiac so effective that, Pliny tells us, a few twigs under the bed will assure an uneventful night; and for the **agouti**, a tropical Latin-American cousin of the guinea pig, whose meat is said to be more succulent than that of rabbit.

AJ
stands for

aji, a hot chili which brought tears to the eyes of Christopher Columbus.

AK
stands for

akee, a favorite fruit in the Caribbean, imported from Africa by slaves, which looks like a peach and tastes like scrambled eggs.

AL
stands for

the **Alaska king crab**, whose leg span sometimes

reaches five feet; for a fish called **albacore** in the sea and tuna in the can; for **Albany beef**, which meant sturgeon in the days when there were still sturgeon in the Hudson; for the **albatross**, which, Coleridge to the contrary notwithstanding, ancient mariners in the days of sail killed for fresh meat; for the **Albemarle pippin**, an apple planted by Thomas Jefferson; for the **alberge**, a peach-apricot which the French Hellenist Paul-Louis Courrier compared to his wife because it was "dry and leathery"; for **alewives**, which pretend to be herring but aren't, and for **alexanders**, or horse parsley, abandoned in the eighteenth century in favor of celery; for **alfalfa**, eaten fresh by cows and in tablet form by natural-food addicts; for **algae**, which the Japanese eat today and we shall all eat tomorrow if the biochemists have their way; for **algarroba**, a bean-bearing tree which provides food for man and fodder for livestock in Africa and South America; for **alligator**, appreciated by Prince Achille Murat, but despised by Natchez Indians; for **aloes**, which provide protection from eclipses; for the **alpaca**, which Peruvians eat when the animal has become too old to work; for **alum**, which goes into baking powder; and for **alya**, fat from the tail of a sheep, so prized in the Middle East that a special race has been developed there with obese tails which have to be supported on little carts which the animals drag behind them.

And **AL** also stands for

ALLSPICE. As a youngster I assumed that the box marked "Allspice" in the family pantry contained a mixture of spices, which is perhaps the impression the word conveys to many. Not so. This seasoning is derived from a single source, the berry of the allspice tree, *Pimenta officinalis* or *Eugenia pimenta*, called in Jamaica bayberry and in some other Caribbean islands the Indian wood tree. It is a native of Central America and the West Indies, particularly abundant in Jamaica.

The name is accounted for by the fact that its taste and smell suggested to English-speaking people the mingled aromas of cinnamon, nutmeg and cloves, and to French-speaking people, who call it allspice too (*toute épice*), the same three plus pepper—to which some French sniffers add ginger. Elizabeth David writes (dare we say, sniffily?): "I cannot myself see where the nutmeg or cinnamon come in. A hint of clove is certainly there, and more than a hint of pepper." As I was inditing this opinion, it occurred to me to step into the kitchen and take a whiff of allspice myself. I detect the odor of cloves and cinnamon—nothing more.

ALLSPICE. *Drawing from L. A. Bailey:* Cyclopedea of American Horticulture, *New York, 1906*

French has more trouble with "allspice" than English. *Toute épice* has two different meanings, the other covering the seeds of a plant called nigella, whose various species collect picturesque names—capuchin's-herb, Venus's-hair, love-in-a-mist, devil-in-the-bush—tempting us to look further into this variant. But another name for the spice derived from nigella is *quatre épices* (four spices) and this means *three* different things.

Better stop.

ALMOND. There is a pretty Portuguese legend which tells how a Moorish prince of the Algarve (Portugal's Deep South) married a Scandinavian princess who pined away in that winterless land for lack of the sight of snow. Her prince relieved her homesickness by planting the whole coast thickly with almond trees, whose white blossoms covered the land each spring with a snow-white blanket: thus the almond came to Portugal. You are not required to believe this story, nor that the prince and princess were patient enough to wait the necessary three or four years for the first bloom, but at least it situates the almond in its chosen land, the basin of the Mediterranean, and indicates the direction in which it progressed, from east to west.

The almond (*Prunus amygdalus*, or the tonsil plum) was probably a native of Asia Minor, where we hear of it early, from Anatolia, from Babylon, from Hittite chronicles and from the Bible, in which it is one of the only two nuts mentioned (the other is the pistachio). It started its westward march before historic times, for it has been

Almond. *Woodcut from Pierandrea Mattioli:* Commentaries on the Six Books of Dioscorides, *folio edition, Prague, 1563*

found at the Neolithic level under the palace of Knossos in Crete and in Bronze Age storerooms at Hagia Triada, on the same island. The Romans, who were fond of it, indicated the direction from which it had come to them by calling it the "Greek nut." It bypassed Egypt, according to one authority, who says there were no almonds in ancient Egypt, but another says Egyptians used almond oil (it could of course have been imported) as a cosmetic, a purpose it still serves today.

A third authority tells us that almond trees were not planted in southern France until 1548, but Charlemagne ordered them grown on his domains and the first French cookbook, written about 1300, gives much attention to almond milk, one of the two basic sauce elements (with verjuice) in medieval cooking—even in England, where they *must* have been imported; almonds grow ornamentally along England's southern coast today, but rarely reach maturity. The almond is as hardy as the peach, but blossoms about a month earlier, making it more vulnerable to spring frosts. In the United States, certain varieties grow as far north as Illinois, Ohio and Pennsylvania, but their nuts, when they produce any, are of poor quality and commercially uninteresting. The American almond country is California, which produces 99.9 percent of the American almond crop—150 million shelled pounds in 1970. This means half of all the almonds grown in the world (nearly twice as much as are produced by either of the two runners-up, Italy and Spain), and half of that half is exported, supplying 30 percent of the demand even in rival Europe.

Almonds when sold are frequently accompanied by the adjective "sweet" or "bitter," for the highly practical reason that the bitter almond contains prussic acid, which it is not advisable to consume in quantity. Some countries forbid groceries to sell bitter almonds at all, but the precaution is perhaps excessive. Bitter almonds are tastier, and some cooks mix a few with sweet almonds on purpose, for flavor—Swedes, for instance, when they make the rich cheesecake called *ostkaka.*

No one need be reminded of the many luscious uses made of almonds—in marzipan, in nougat and in the French tart *amandine,* possibly the only piece of pastry ever to have had its recipe transmuted into verse and proclaimed from the stage in a play of worldwide renown—Edmond Rostand's *Cyrano de Bergerac.*

Almond oil is so fine that it is used to lubricate watches.

AM
stands for

Amanita, a genus of mushrooms which includes one of the most delicious, A. *caesarea,* Caesar's mushroom, and one of the most deadly, A. *phalloides,* the poison amanita; for the **amaranth,** an edible symbol of immortality; for **amber,** which the ancient Romans used as a seasoning, and **ambergris,** which Marshal de Richelieu used as an aphrodisiac; for **ambrosia,** "nine times as sweet as honey," and for **ammonium bicarbonate,** which no one would so describe.

AN
stands for

the **anemone,** a flowerlike marine animal which tastes like shrimp; for **aneth,** which provided power for Roman gladiators at a period when nobody frowned upon doping; for the **angelfish,** called a bat in Africa and a bream elsewhere; for the **angel shark,** really a ray, which a perfectly serious ichthyologist admitted did look, from below, like an angel provided it were an angel which had been drawn by James Thurber; for the **angel**

wing, a clam one of whose varieties is known as the fallen angel, and the **anglerfish,** a devilish design of nature for trapping other fish; for **annatto,** with which red Americans colored their bodies and white Americans color their butter; for **ants,** relished when chocolate-coated; for the **antelope,** hunted in Africa by cheaters with cheetahs, and **antelope grass,** eaten by these animals but also by natives of Africa; for **antimony,** said to mean "anti-monk" since so many members of religious orders died after taking it to counteract the effects of fasting; for **antlers,** sold powdered in Hong Kong as a sexual stimulant under the name *lu kung*; for the **anvalli,** an Indian nut, and for the **anvlas,** an Indian fruit.

And **AN** also stands for

ANCHOVY. Unless you have been in anchovy country, your only knowledge of this fish is probably in the form of tiny fillets preserved in brine, oil or some other liquid—salty, tangy tidbits which align you with your cultural ancestors, for in some of their forms, preserved anchovies approximate the ancient Roman all-purpose seasoning *garum*, especially in what England calls anchovy essence. The ancients doted on anchovies; the fish oftenest mentioned in old Greek writings, the *aphye*, though not fully identified, is believed to have been the anchovy.

If you ever find yourself in the right place, don't miss the chance to taste fresh anchovies. The flesh is fragile, a little difficult to handle, but it is worth the trouble; the flavor is at once more delicate and more pronounced than that of sardines.

What is the right place? Although anchovies are found in the Atlantic as far north as southern Norway, and in the Pacific off the western coasts of North and South America (the American anchovy is slightly coarser than the European species), they are, or were, at their best in the Mediterranean, where those of the French port of Collioure were reputed to be the best in the world. Fishermen of Provence liked to make breakfast of a fresh anchovy or two crushed by the thumb against a slice of bread, accompanied by generous drafts of wine. This was called *quicha l'anchoio*, and when the Provençal poet Frédéric Mistral wanted to offer his friends a special treat, he invited them to *"faren l'aiolo e quicharen l'anchoio"*—aioli being the garlic-flavored mayonnaise which has been called "the butter of Provence."

Alas, there are no more anchovies in the Mediterranean. Pollution.

ANGELICA. You probably know angelica only as the sweet, bright-green, candied, cylindrical beads which lend color and zest to fruitcake—sometimes counterfeited (angelica is expensive) by bits of other foods (even turnips!) dyed green. If you are suspicious, break open your cake at one of its green tidbits; if the dough is green, it isn't angelica, it is something else whose dye has come off. Angelica, green to its soul, does not run.

I will not rush in where Madame de Sévigné feared to tread by attempting to describe the flavor of angelica, which she described as indescribable. "Its good taste," she wrote, "recalls nothing else I can remember and resembles no other savor than its own."

Most of the incisive seasonings which make food sparkle were born in warm climates, but angelica is a child of the far north, unknown to the Mediterranean ancients or even to central Europe before the Vikings brought it there in the tenth century. It acquired its name when the Archangel Raphael revealed to a pious hermit that it was a remedy against the plague.

To most of us, angelica may seem no more than a grace note of gastronomy, but it is eaten as a serious vegetable in Iceland, the Faeroe Islands, Norway, Siberia and especially by those

ANCHOVY. *Drawing by Angel from Louis Roule:* Les poissons et le monde vivant des eaux, *10 volumes, Paris, 1926–1937*

ANGELICA. *Woodcut from John Gerard:* Herball or General Historie of Plantes, *London, 1597*

Lapps who still live most of the time beyond the reach of modern civilization and its packaged products and have no other vegetable except the inner bark of pines.

French newspapers in 1974 reported the case of Annibal Camoux of Marseilles, who chewed angelica root daily and died at the age of 121 years and 3 months. Marseilles is the city where they tell you about a sardine so large that it blocked the entrance to the port.

ANISE. To arrive at the licoricelike taste and smell of anise, the conjugated efforts of a trinity of essences are required: anethole, also called anise camphor; estragole, also called methyl chanicol; and anisoyl, also called anisic acid. In putting this combination together once, nature had already amply demonstrated her chemical skill; it was sheer showing off to perform the feat twice in two totally unrelated plants. European anise (or green anise), *Pimpinella anisum,* is a bush of the parsley family; Chinese anise (or badian or star anise, from the shape of its decoratively designed fruit), *Illicium verum,* is a tree of the magnolia family.

European anise may really be African anise, a native of Egypt, the only place in the world where it still grows wild. Native or not, the ancient Egyptians knew it; so did the ancient Greeks (Pythagoras, about 550 B.C., called aniseed bread a great delicacy); and the ancient Romans used to end their more elaborate meals with anise-flavored cakes as an aid to digestion, in the days before Romans ceased to care about the state in which they left the table. No Roman wedding banquet was complete without anise cake for dessert, a fact in which some scholars see the origin of the spicy wedding cakes of today. In any case, the persistence of gastronomic tradition is exemplified by the *dragati,* hard, anise-flavored candies, which Quintus Fabius Cunctator distributed to the plebs to celebrate his military victories. The *dragati* of ancient Rome are the *dragées* of modern France, which we call Jordan almonds, handed out at such celebrations as baptisms and weddings. Their hard sugar coatings are often flavored delicately with anise.

In more modern times, anise has aroused mixed feelings among famous French chefs. Taillevent (fourteenth century) was enamored of it and included it in many of his recipes for pastry, fish, game, salads and desserts. Carême (nineteenth century) called it "a medicinal drug."

Illicium, the genus of Chinese star anise or

ANISE. *Woodcut from Pierandrea Mattioli:* Commentaires, *Lyons, 1579*

badian, means "bait" or "lure," a reference to the attractive scent of the tree's wood (the leaves smell more like laurel than licorice). Badian is one of the Five Spices, the standard mixture used in Chinese cooking under the name *heung new fun*, the others being anise, fennel, cinnamon and cloves. Chinese anise was first seen in Europe in medieval Russia at the fair of Nishni-Novgorod, thus offering history a chance to reverse itself a few centuries later. France, which depended on the Asian anise to flavor its anisette, discovered in the 1970s that its price had risen 2000 percent in two years, for political reasons: one of its two sources was North Vietnam, whose trade relations with the West had become a casualty of war, and the other source was southern China, which had been shipping it to the West across Russia; when Sino-Soviet relations soured, Russia, which had first brought star anise to the West, cut it off again.

I. verum, the genuine star anise, has a poor cousin, *I. anisatum*, bitter and toxic, sometimes called instead *I. religiosum* because it plays a role in sacred ceremonies in China and Japan. It is used in the latter to drug the desperate into relative insensibility before they commit hara-kiri.

AO
stands for

aonoriku, powdered green seaweed, a taste treat in Japan; and for the **aoudad,** a wild sheep eaten in the mountains of the Sahara, from which it is fast disappearing.

AP
stands for

the **apio**, a starchy Caribbean root; for the **Aports**, a crunchy red apple from the Alma-Ata region of the Soviet Union; and for the **apple of paradise,** which Marco Polo admired in the Nicobar Islands, but neglected to identify.

And **AP** also stands for

APPLE. If the vegetable kingdom has a royal family, it is certainly the *Rosaceae*, which includes the queen of all flowers, the rose, and the king of all fruits, the apple. The rose has often served to symbolize all flowers, the apple to symbolize all fruits. Whenever a new fruit or vegetable has turned up, provided it was approximately round and in size somewhere between a cherry and a pumpkin, it was likely to be called an apple until it could be fitted with a name of its own. The list of foods which have been, or are, called apples includes such disparate edibles as the akee, the avocado, the bael fruit, the American Indian breadroot, the cashew, the cherimoya, the colocynth, the date, the eggplant, the horse mint, the ivory nut, the lemon, the melon, the orange, the peach, the pineapple, the pine nut, the pomegranate, the pomerac, the potato, the quince, the sweetsop and the tomato—not to mention such non-edibles as the oak gall and the baseball.

The reference books will tell you that the apple originated in southeastern Europe or southwestern Asia—sometimes, with admirable precision, just south of the Caucasus Mountains—and some of them add that it was the Romans who introduced it into more northerly Europe. This second statement is known to be untrue: apples have been found in prehistoric Swiss lake settlements and the imprint of an apple seed appears on a fossil from a Neolithic site in England. The first I believe to be untrue also; it is my belief that the first apples grew not very far from the Baltic. Space does not permit setting forth here the etymological evidence for this thesis, so let me point out simply that the idea that this fruit arose in southeastern Europe or southwestern Asia or south anywhere is denied by the nature of the apple itself. It is so decidedly a northern fruit that the tree requires a dormant period of at least two months (winter) to restore its strength after one year's crop in order to be able to produce

APPLE *by Gabriel Metsu (1615–1667).* The Peeler of Apples, *oil on canvas*

the next: hibernation is not a phenomenon of warm countries. Once started, however, the apple showed itself adaptable to a wide gamut of climates. It even grows in Madagascar; but its heart's in the highlands.

Who cultivated the apple first? Nobody knows. Carbonized apples dated at 6500 B.C. have been found in Anatolia, but whether they were cultivated or wild has not been determined. When Ramses II had apple trees planted in the delta of the Nile, in the thirteenth century B.C., they were of course cultivated apples. We even know how the Egyptians handled the transplanting. Young trees were dug up together with the earth surrounding their roots, and the trees were placed in holes dug in the ground with their roots still undisturbed in the soil in which they had originally grown. Depressions were then scooped out around the bases of their trunks to hold water, a necessary precaution in the climate of Egypt, which was not quite propitious to apples.

APPLE *by Jerome B. Thompson (1814–1886).* Apple Gathering, *oil on canvas*

The Greeks were cultivating apples in Attica at least by the seventh century B.C., but they were rare and expensive; appalled at their price (and also at the increasing extravagance of Athenian weddings), Solon decreed that at marriages the bridal couple might eat only one apple between them, before going to bed. The Romans were growing at least seven different varieties in the time of Cato the Elder (234–149 B.C.), who described that number in his *De re rustica;* two centuries later Pliny, also the Elder (A.D. 23- or 24–79), was able to enumerate thirty-six different kinds of apples in his *Historia naturalis,* distinguishing between perishable kinds and winter apples which would keep in storage.

The apple with the longest history dates from this period or earlier—the Api, named for the Etruscan horticulturist who developed it (the Etruscans were the great farmers of the ancient world, but the Romans collected the credit for their skill). The Api remained in high esteem through the centuries. Grown in the gardens of Louis XIII at Orléans in 1628, it was one of only seven varieties of apples deemed worthy to

Apple *by Paul Cézanne (1839–1906).* Still Life: Apples and a Pot of Primroses, *oil on canvas*

be served to Louis XIV. It can still be bought in France under its original name, as the *pomme d'Api,* and in the United States, if you hunt for it, as the Lady Apple. Small, somewhat flattened, ranging in color from a creamy yellow to a deep crimson, according to its exposure to the sun, delicately perfumed and juicy, the Lady was held in high esteem in Colonial days, when it was sought out at Christmas as a special treat. It should not be peeled, since the skin is particularly flavorful.

The apple has played a part in religion, magic, superstition, folklore, history and medicine as far back as we can go, but it did not figure in the first example which is likely to pop into everybody's mind, the story of Adam and Eve. You could probably make a little money by betting that there is no mention of the apple in Genesis (it is cited in other parts of the Bible, but not in connection with Adam and Eve). What they ate, in the words of the Bible, was the fruit of the tree of the knowledge of good and evil, otherwise unidentified. We may assume that the ancient Hebrews purposely refrained from representing it as any specific known fruit, lest the mystery of the image be dissipated by attaching it to a commonplace object. This was all very well in literature, but when painters and sculptors began to treat the story, they had to give concrete form to the symbol; they chose, naturally, the fruit which stood for all fruits, the apple. Biblical scholars have suggested that if the Hebrews had desired to name a specific fruit they would have been likelier to choose the pomegranate; when Christianity came to India, the forbidden fruit was understood to have been the banana.

Greek mythology is rich in references to apples —at least to what were called apples. The golden apples of the Hesperides were given to Hera as a wedding present when she married Zeus. It was three apples of the Hesperides which Hippomenes dropped in the path of Atalanta during the foot-race which she lost because she paused to pick them up. The Trojan War resulted from the Judgment of Paris, when he presented to Aphrodite the apple of discord, which Eris, angered at not having been invited to the wedding of Thetis and Peleus, had thrown into the midst of the guests, inscribed "for the fairest." This was a golden apple too, and therefore not an apple at all, for, if modern scholars are to be believed, what the ancient Greeks meant when they talked about the golden apples of the Hesperides was oranges or lemons. If so, this makes hash of the legend recounted by Bernardin de Saint-Pierre, an eighteenth-century Norman writer unacquainted with the conclusions of modern scholarship, according to which Thetis, a sea goddess, commissioned a Triton to steal the apple from Aphrodite when the goddess of love came to the sea to gather pearls. Her jealous object was to convert this rare treasure into a common thing, so she planted the seeds in Normandy. Normandy is great apple country, but it produces no citrus fruits.

It was an apple tree which bent its branches low so that the Virgin Mary, too heavy with Jesus to reach the fruit, could pick it; that is why, the story goes, many apple trees still droop their branches almost to the ground. The arrival of the apple in England is dated several centuries too late by a legend of St. Joseph of Arimathea (the follower of Jesus who placed his body in the sepulchre). He traveled to Britain to preach Christianity there, and, standing on Glastonbury Tor, spat the seeds of an apple he was eating to the plain below. Wherever the pips fell, cider-apple trees sprang up, and from them were born the vast cider-apple orchards which today blanket Somerset, Hereford and Devon.

No legend, for Isaac Newton told the story himself, was the circumstance that the fall of an apple from a tree in his orchard at Woolsthorpe in 1666 started the chain of thought which led him to propound the theory of gravitation; but his admirers treated the event with the reverence proper to a legend. The particular tree which was supposed to have let fall the fruit so adventitiously was regarded with veneration and coddled to a ripe old age; when it finally collapsed, its vestiges were piously preserved. Veneration apparently did not go so far as to retain with certainty the name of the species responsible for this discovery, but it was probably a costard.

The apple has sometimes been credited with possessing magical qualities, occasionally compounded with erotic ones. In ancient Greece tossing an apple to a girl was a proposal and catching it an acceptance. In medieval Germany it was believed that eating an apple steeped in the perspiration of a woman one loved would ensure success with her, though one might think that anyone in a position to secure an apple thus imbibed would have to be pretty close to the goal already. The role of the apple as a fertility symbol is still preserved in some remote villages in England in the "apple wassailing" of Twelfth Night, which some superstitious persons continue to believe is necessary to ensure a good crop. The villagers gather around their largest apple tree, from whose branches are hung pieces of toast soaked in cider to attract the robins considered to be the good spirits of the tree. To drive away its evil spirits, villagers stationed in different parts of the orchard blast away with shotguns. Cider is poured over the tree's roots—and also down the throats of the celebrants, who link hands and dance around the tree chanting an ancient charm whose meaning they have forgotten. No longer known either is the origin of the custom of Cumberland, where apples are suspended on strings before the hearth and roasted until they fall into a bowl of spiced or mulled wine placed underneath. In the United States, the apple is prominent at Halloween, which is believed by some to echo ancient Druid rites and by others to hark back to the Roman harvest festival of Pomona, the goddess of fruit and gardens.

When the first English settlers came to North America, they brought with them, an eventual aid against homesickness, the familiar beloved apple. The Pilgrims had in their baggage both seeds and cuttings. They were planted and prospered. A document dated 1649 relates the purchase by John Endecott, governor of the Plymouth Colony, of 200 acres of land from one William Trask for the consideration of 500 three-year-old apple trees. As early as 1741, New England was exporting apples to the West Indies. In the more southern colonies, Virginia, which may have received its original stock either from New England or Old England, turned the tables on the mother country by selling Albemarle Pippins to Britain at least as early as 1859.

The spread of apple territory in the United States was dramatized by the picturesque figure of the folk hero known as Johnny Appleseed. His real name was John Chapman; he was born in Leominster, Massachusetts, on September 26, 1774, and he did not prowl the countryside scattering seeds at random from a bag slung over his shoulder, as artists like to depict him. He knew too much about apples for that, for instance that they do not grow true from seed. Rather, he established nurseries of apple seedlings, a more practical, if less romantic, procedure. He was first noticed in pursuit of this activity in western Pennsylvania in 1800, and by the end of the following year he had established a chain of apple nurseries from the Allegheny River to central Ohio. At the time of his death, in March 1845, he had pushed as far west as Indiana, where he died at Fort Wayne. His favorite apple was the Rambo, and it seems fitting that Indianapolis, at the time of writing at least, was one of the few places where Rambos could still be found on the market. The origin of the Rambo is said to be unknown, but there is a hint of it in the name of one of its varieties, the Rambo Franc. This is probably a corruption of "France," for this particular variety is known to have been imported to the United States from St. Cloud, near Paris, in 1817; but *all* Rambos should be French, from the old-fashioned fruit called *rambour*, itself a deformation of Rambures, the name of the French town celebrated for growing these apples.

Johnny Appleseed fell a long way short of bringing the apple to what is now America's greatest apple-growing country, the Pacific Northwest, pretty much terra incognita in his day; indeed the first apple ever grown there came from the same source as East Coast apples, directly from England, more or less by accident. To please a pretty girl, one Captain Aemilius Simpson kept the seeds of an apple he had eaten in London at a farewell party before he left for America, and planted them in 1824 at Fort Vancouver, now in the state of Washington. Only one of the seeds sprouted, and the first year when the tree it produced bore, it achieved only one apple; but it had progeny thereafter and might be honored today as the ancestor of all the Pacific Northwest's apples if anyone had happened to record its variety.

APPLE *by Lucas Cranach the Elder (1472–1553).* Virgin and Child Under the Apple Tree, *oil on canvas, transferred from a panel*

Serious commercial apple growing in the Pacific Northwest was started by Henderson Luelling and William Meek, both of whom hit on the same idea for the same place at the same time independently (they were both Iowans, but didn't know each other), and joined forces when they met on the spot. Luelling deserves special credit for courage, for he started west in 1847 in a covered wagon filled with earth in which his apple seedlings were growing. This made it too heavy and too slow to keep up with wagon trains, so he had to take his chances as a lone navigator across plains teeming with hostile Indians. Fortunately the Indians were not interested in apples, so he arrived in the Northwest at a propitious time to go into business, just before the Gold Rush. The prospectors who set out to make their fortunes (living largely, as they crossed the plains, on pies made from dried apples, easily transportable and non-perishable) did not all strike it rich, but everybody did who supplied them with food at gold-rush prices. It is on record that a single shipment of four bushels of Washington apples sold in California in 1852 for $500. When the California demand eased, the Northern Pacific Railroad arrived, in 1883, and Washington apples could reach markets everywhere in the country; later they would reach markets everywhere in the world. Today Washington, producing up to 35 million bushels of apples per year, is the top producer in the United States, which, with 100 million bushels annually, is the top producer in the world.

Nobody knows how many different varieties of apples exist in the world today, except that the number runs into the tens of thousands. A quarter of a century ago, 7000 were recorded in the United States alone, and they have since multiplied faster than the recorders can keep up with them. Yet, paradoxically, you can find only half a dozen of the favorites on the national market. This is not a gastronomic phenomenon, but an economic one; you are offered the apples which the supermarkets have found it most profitable to carry. In the United States (and in the world, for that matter) the biggest-selling apple is the Delicious, which accounts for one-fifth of the U.S. crop. The McIntosh comes second, with one-tenth, and the Winesap, the Jonathan, the Rome Beauty and the Stayman account for most of the rest. Best seller or not, the Delicious twice narrowly escaped never reaching the market at all. It first appeared, no doubt a mutant (sown accidentally from seed!), in the late 1860s, in the orchard of an Iowa farmer named Hesse Hiatt; self-planted, it was out of alignment, and in 1870, when it had become big enough to be in the way, Hiatt cut it down. New shoots appeared from the stump the following year, so it was allowed to grow, and when its first apples appeared, Hiatt found them so superior in taste that he entered them in a contest held by a canning company. The judges agreed to award it a prize—and discovered that the basket in which the apples had arrived had lost its identifying label. Fortunately Hiatt resubmitted the Delicious the following year, and its career began. It is sad to be obliged to report that its taste has since been reduced to the lowest common denominator, which has been discovered to be productive of the largest number of sales (neutral taste offends no one), and its yellow variety has become even worse. People who don't like food, A. J. Liebling wrote, "have made a triumph of the Delicious apple because it doesn't taste like an apple, and of the Golden Delicious because it doesn't taste like anything."

There seems to be a sort of Gresham's Law for apples (and perhaps for all foods today): "Minimum taste drives out maximum taste." One of the finest French apples, the Calville (it has been called the "empress of desserts"), with a hint of raspberry in its taste, was defended against uniformization by its French growers, with the result that it was transplanted in California, reduced to dependable mediocrity—and exported as the "California apple" to France, where it has nearly driven the Calville off the market. "You cannot sell a blemished apple in the supermarket," Elspeth Huxley wrote, "but you can sell a tasteless one, provided it is shiny, smooth, even, uniform and bright."

Space prevents us from considering several other remarkable apples: the English Blenheim Orange, an accident like the Delicious, and Cox's Orange Pippin, "the greatest apple of this age"; the French *court-pendu* (low-hung), even tastier than the Calville; and America's own fast-disappearing Rhode Island Greening, once the favorite green apple of the United States, whose name may come from its color or from the fact that it was developed near Newport in 1748 by a man named Green.

Whatever variety of apple you eat, to get the best make sure to buy only those picked by the light of the waning moon. This advice comes from Horace.

APRICOT. The apricot grows wild in the mountains around Peking, marking the country where it originated, and is known to have been cultivated at least as early as 2200 B.C. Throughout its long history it has been slow to spread, perhaps because it exists on the brink of viability. It must have a temperate climate, for it requires the dormant period provided by a cool winter, but it blooms early and is extremely susceptible to frost, which temperate climates have a habit of producing too late in the spring.

The tree took perhaps less time in getting from China to Mesopotamia than it did in progressing farther; it was grown in the hanging gardens of Babylon. The ancient Greeks apparently did not know it, but the Romans did. Some scholars argue that apricots were first planted in Italy about the time of Nero, in the first century A.D.; others think it must have been after Pompey's campaign in Armenia, in the first century B.C., basing this theory on the supposition that the Romans thought the apricot came from Armenia, an assumption echoed in its modern scientific name, *Prunus armeniaca*. But did they? They may simply have been adapting to their own language the Babylonian-Assyrian name for the fruit, *armanu*; indeed, they seem first to have called it *persica praecocia*, which could mean "the early-ripening Persian fruit" (Persia, which at that time called apricots "eggs of the sun," grew them then, and still does). Perhaps the ancient Romans never cultivated apricots at all, but imported them, which would have accounted for their excessively high cost. In any case, they disappeared from Europe when the communications of the disintegrating empire broke down, not to return again until the Crusaders re-imported them, except for Spain, where the Moors raised them on the plains of Granada.

The apricot seems to have been familiar to the French in the fifteenth century, but did not arrive in England until 1562. It has been stated that it reached America as early as the sixteenth century, but it is more probable that it was introduced early in the eighteenth by the Mission Fathers

Apricot *by Jean-Baptiste Chardin (1699–1779).* A Jar of Apricots, *oil on canvas*

of California—which today produces the best apricots in the world for eating fresh (unfortunately only 5 percent of the crop is sold fresh); equaled only by those of Turkey for eating dried (70 percent of the California crop); and the third best in the world for canning in syrup (after Spain and Greece), 25 percent of the crop.

The chief consumers of apricots after man are dormice, who dote on them.

AR
stands for

the **argentine,** when it is not a country but a small silvery deep-water fish of the Mediterranean, and for **Aristotle's lantern,** when it is not a lantern but a sea urchin; for the **arbutus,** the strawberry tree, and the **arctic bramble,** the honeyberry; for the **armadillo,** which according to Darwin tastes like duck; for the **armed gurnard,** a grotesque Mediterranean fish whose aggressively protuberant forked muzzle looks like a slightly opened pair of scissors; for **arracacha,** the Peruvian carrot, which is neither Peruvian nor a carrot; for **arrow arum,** possibly the only reputedly edible plant which wild-food enthusiast Euell Gibbons could not choke down, for it "prickled my throat and burned my mouth"; for **arrowhead,** a plant once eaten in Oregon by Chinook Indians and now eaten in California by Chinese-American farmers; for **arrowroot,** whose starch is among the easiest to digest except when it happens to be poisonous, and **arum,** a plant with varieties named lily of the Nile, Solomon's lily, dragon arum, wake-robin and lords-and-ladies, whose bulbs are edible except when they happen to be poisonous; for **arsenic,** which always happens to be poisonous, except for some Styrians, who swallow it with impunity; and for **artemisia,** the absinthe plant, which is not named for the goddess Artemis, as the reference books will tell you, but for the queen of Caria who built one of the seven wonders of the ancient world, the celebrated sepulchre of her husband, King Mausolus, and was also a botanist.

And **AR** also stands for

ARTICHOKE. "Is this my artichoke or yours?" Columbine asks Pierrot as the curtain rises on Edna St. Vincent Millay's *Aria da Capo.* This invocation of the artichoke, in 1920 at least, established immediately the atmosphere of the heedless, precious, privileged, pampered society Miss Millay was satirizing. The artichoke in those days was a rare, almost unknown luxury in the United States. Possibly it was more familiar in the New Orleans area, where the French had put it on the bill of fare when they held Louisiana.

Artichoke *by Hochst. German ceramic, c. 1750*

If so, the tidings had not percolated into Miss Millay's Northeast. The artichoke had also been introduced into California by the Spaniards when they arrived there, but seems to have departed with them, to return in significant quantities only about a quarter of a century ago. Even so, it can hardly be said that the artichoke has taken the United States by storm. California produces the country's entire commercial crop of artichokes, 70 million pounds a year, or about three-quarters of an artichoke per person. The average Frenchman or Italian eats more than two hundred times as much; but in France and Italy the artichoke has usually been inexpensive, a humble when not a downright humdrum vegetable.

In matters of food, for some reason, the incidence of error is high in even the most respected and reliable encyclopedias and dictionaries. What do the reference books tell us about the artichoke?

1. "It is an improved cultivated development of the thistle." This might be described as evading the issue, unless we can be told what a thistle is. "Thistle" exists in the English language, meaning a prickly plant, but it does not exist in botany. Under "Thistle," the *Encyclopaedia Britannica* lists seven plants called by that name (there are more), of which no two belong to the same genus, and none to the genus of the artichoke, *Cynara*.

2. "The artichoke was first introduced into Europe in the fifteenth century." In all probability, the artichoke was a native of Europe—to be precise, of Sicily. A possible alternative is that it was a native of Carthage which was transplanted on Carthaginian territory in Sicily well before our era.

3. "The artichoke was unknown to the ancients." There are frequent references to it in Roman literature and at least one in Greek, but these are explained away as meaning not the globe artichoke, *C. scolymus*, but its close relative, the cardoon (*C. cardunculus*)—possibly because the Romans ate the leaves of the plant they called *carduus* (thistle) and today we eat, if not quite the leaves, at least the leaf stalks of the cardoon. However, *The Oxford Book of Food Plants* says flatly that "the globe artichoke . . . was known to the ancient Greeks and Romans," and Geoffrey Grigson's *A Dictionary of English Plant Names* suggests that the cardoon "may have been derived in cultivation" from the artichoke—in which case the artichoke would have been the older and hence the likelier to have been known to the ancients, if they knew but one.

The reference books are perhaps on sounder ground when they credit Catherine de' Medici with having introduced the artichoke to France (or re-introduced it, for Charlemagne had ordered its cultivation, but the word he used was ambiguous and could have referred to the cardoon). In any case there was a period during the Middle Ages when Europe does not seem to have been eating artichokes, except in Sicily, where they were grown by Saracens, and around Granada, where they were cultivated by Moors. The artichoke returned to the rest of Europe via Naples, at a time when Naples and Sicily were under the same government, and progressed to Florence, where it began to be cultivated extensively in Catherine's native Tuscany about fifty years before her birth in 1519.

If Catherine did not actually introduce, or restore, the artichoke to France (very possibly she did), she at least gave it notoriety by her scandalous fondness for it—scandalous because in the Renaissance it was not considered seemly for a woman, especially a maiden or a young woman (Catherine was fourteen when she married Henry II), to eat a vegetable reputed to be aphrodisiac. Catherine ate them nevertheless, preferring them, the reference books tell us in a characteristic if minor lapse, as prepared in the recipes contained in the cookbook of Bartolomeo Scappi —which was published in Venice twenty-one years after her death. On one occasion, Catherine ate so many artichokes that a contemporary chronicler recorded, with a certain lack of medical precision, that she "liked to burst." A shocked elderly woman of the period wrote primly, "If one of us had eaten artichokes, we would have been pointed out in the street. Today young women are more froward than pages at the court."

The most familiar artichoke today is the large globe variety, which accounts for virtually the total production in California and in France's Breton peninsula. There are many others. French Provence prefers the small, purplish-russet artichokes drawn out into a spindle shape, or the *verts de Florence*, of Italian origin, both of which can be eaten in their entirety when young. Italy has a wealth of varieties, including medium-sized artichokes with purplish leaves, which in color recall those of Provence, and extremely small ones which, preserved in oil, are exported and can be found in Italian grocery shops all over the world.

The flowers of the artichoke curdle milk.

AS
stands for

asarum, erroneously called wild ginger, and by the French "man's ear," which should not be taken literally either; for **ashes,** mixed with Navaho cornmeal, which may explain the low incidence of cancer among Navahos; for the **ash pumpkin,** a gourd eaten in Madagascar and the Congo; for the **asparagus bean,** called, because of its length, the Yard-Long Bean, and the **asparagus pea,** which is frequently confused with the Goa bean; for the **asphodel,** the flower of the dead, whose starchy roots give flour for your bread; for **astragalus,** a protean pea, which you may encounter as a coffee substitute, as the milk vetch, as gum tragacanth or as locoweed; and for the **ass,** whose meat is the most succulent of the equine family and whose milk restored the Empress Poppaea's skin and François Premier's health.

And **AS** also stands for

ASPARAGUS. Of all familiar vegetables, few have histories less well documented than asparagus. Its place of origin is unknown. We meet it early in the ancient world, or think we do, for the name given it is ambiguous, but where did it come from? We notice its presence in France in the seventeenth century but don't know how long it had been there. It is said to have been introduced into England a century earlier, but from where? Widely naturalized in the United States, it must have been brought there by someone, no doubt deliberately, for it seems to be agreed that it is a plant of the Old World, not the New, but when, and by whom? By Thomas Jefferson, who did grow it from imported seed? Probably not, for it is already mentioned in an American garden book in 1775, and Jefferson did most of his experimental planting later.

The eastern Mediterranean area and Africa

ASPARAGUS. *Print from Artemas Ward:* The Grocer's Encyclopedia, *New York, 1911*

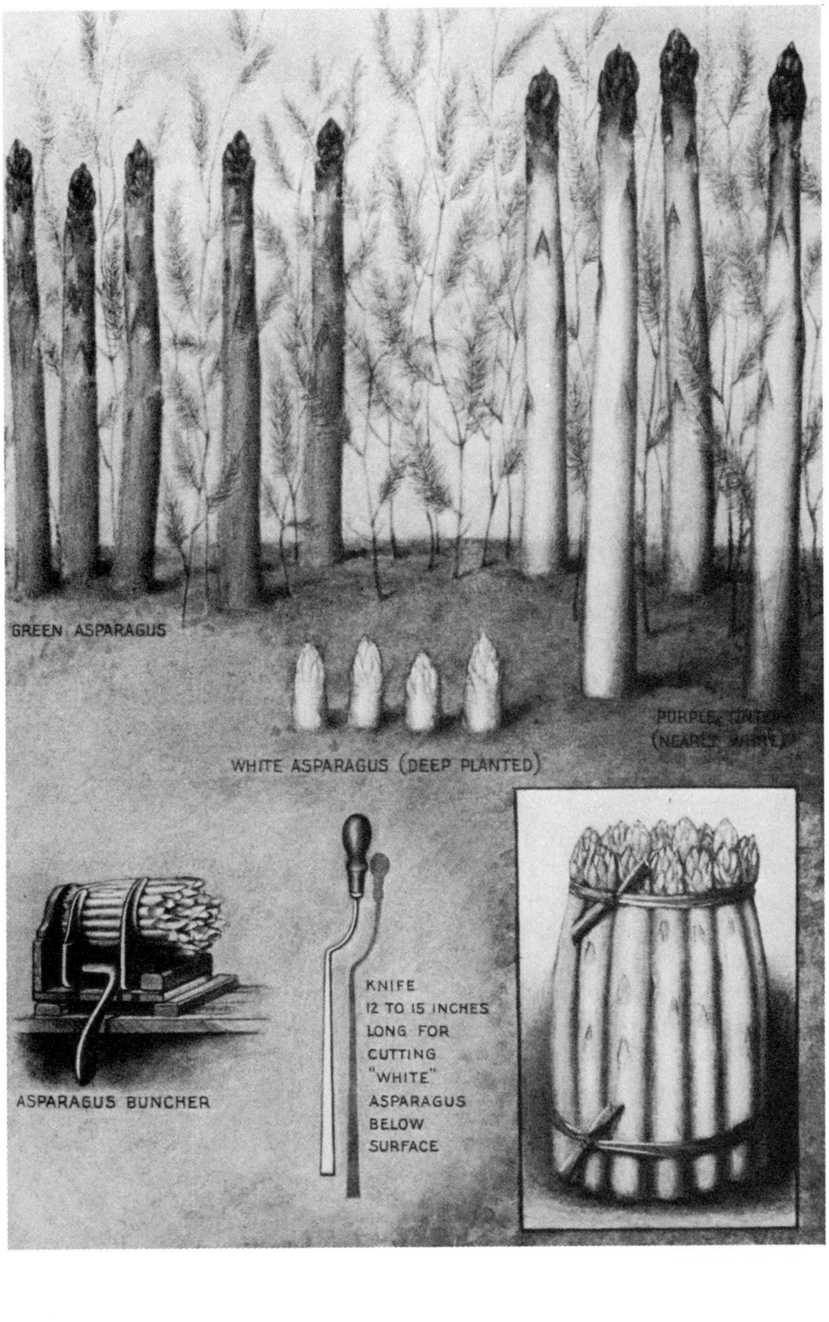

(where at least fourteen species of edible asparagus grow today) have both been suggested as the birthplace of asparagus but seem ruled out by the fact that asparagus thrives best in regions where the ground freezes in winter to a depth of a few inches or more. It is my own guess that today's garden asparagus, *Asparagus officinalis*, developed from an ancestor, now probably extinct or nearly so, which ran along sandy coasts from the Baltic to the Atlantic and the British Isles, perhaps still represented by *A. prostratus*, a rare subspecies which grows wild on grassy sea cliffs in the British Isles. How did it reach the Mediterranean? Birds, no doubt; they were responsible for spreading it throughout the United States.

Cultivated asparagus has been a luxury vegetable throughout its history; but it escapes cultivation so easily (thanks to the birds) that it is found wild, free for the gathering, wherever it is cultivated. Many persons find the wild variety tastier and prefer it—for instance, Juvenal, in the first century A.D., and John Gerard, the English herbalist, in the sixteenth. The ancient Egyptians cultivated asparagus and considered it a worthy offering for their gods. Julius Caesar seems to have eaten it first in Lombardy, where he expressed a preference for it with melted butter, which is how it is served in Lombardy today. The Emperor Augustus evidently knew how asparagus should be cooked to bring out the full flavor—briefly, so it remains a trifle crunchy under the teeth—for he is credited with having invented the ancient Roman equivalent of our "faster than you can say Jack Robinson": *Velocius quam asparagi coquantur,* faster than you can cook asparagus.

Pliny, who liked asparagus, recorded with surprise that he had come upon spears so fat that three of them weighed a pound; this was far from a record, for Ravenna was producing stalks which weighed ten ounces each. Ravenna asparagus, Martial wrote, was the best in the world: *Mollis in aequora crevit spina Ravenna non erit incultis gratior asparagis.* Ravenna still produces the best in Italy. Jean de la Quintinie seems to have been the first to grow asparagus in hotbeds, to assure Louis XIV of a year-round supply. As late as the Gay Nineties in the United States, when ostentatiously costly dinners at establishments like Delmonico's, Sherry's and the Waldorf-Astoria were in fashion, a Tammany Hall banquet at the Waldorf which included fresh asparagus in February evoked the comment that it was "an extravagant rarity."

One of its devotees was the French encyclopedist Bernard de Fontenelle, who, surprised by an unexpected visit from the Abbé Terrasson, who asked if he might stay to dinner, assented grudgingly, grumbling that the abbé was depriving him of half of his favorite asparagus. He ordered that the abbé's half should be served with the white sauce the churchman liked and his own with the oil dressing he preferred. Just before dinner, the abbé suddenly rolled to the floor, stricken by apoplexy. Fontenelle rushed to the kitchen. "All the asparagus with oil!" he shouted.

Despite this, *asperges à la Fontenelle* today means with melted butter and soft-boiled eggs, for asparagus provokes chefs into mislabeling. *Asperges à la Monselet* is named for the poet-gourmet Charles Monselet, who wrote of asparagus tips in scrambled eggs, but the dish does not involve scrambled eggs; and *asperges à la Pompadour* does include egg yolks, which Madame Pompadour combined with them to maintain sexual vigor, and also cornmeal, which is unlikely to have been at her disposal at that period.

It was inevitable that asparagus should be treated as an aphrodisiac given its shape, which, an Elizabethan writer remarked, "manifestly provoketh Venus." In considering the effect of asparagus on humans, writers have neglected the sex life of asparagus itself, thus missing a few titillating revelations—for instance, that while asparagus normally produces male flowers on some plants and female flowers on others, it occasionally puts forth hermaphroditic blossoms, of which both pistils and stamens are functional. I admit I had not delved deeply into the sex life of the asparagi until I published a newspaper article on this food, and received the following information from a reader who had worked on an asparagus farm:

> Americans, practitioners of Women's Lib (and Europeans who prefer wild asparagus), eat heterosexual asparagus. The other Europeans eat boy-soprano asparagus. You, and your readers, may well ask, "How do you tell a male seed from a female?" You don't really. In Europe, you sow the seed twice as thick. The young plants are spindly . . . in the fall you go through the seedling beds, and, literally, eradicate those plants that show berries. . . . The Ravenna variety are undoubtedly bulls, or castrati.

And the rest of the **A's** stand for

the **auk,** which lays pointed eggs which cannot roll off the sea-cliff ledges on which she roosts; for the **aurochs,** rendered extinct by hunters and resuscitated by atavistic back-breeding; for the **axolotl,** which strives to look unappetizing by never leaving the larval stage, discouraging neither ancient Aztecs nor modern Mexicans from eating it; for the **Ayrshire,** the cow which supplies one-fifth of all the milk in Scotland and provides

Avocado *by Paul Cézanne (1839–1906).* Vessels, Basket and Fruit, *oil on canvas*

first-rate beef as well; for the Japanese **ayu,** called with reason the sweetfish in English, and the Japanese **azuki,** a red bean considered to bring good luck to those who eat it (its name means "good health").

AV stands for

AVOCADO. The proof that we live in a franker world today than we did half a century ago is provided by the changed attitude of avocado growers towards what they regard, no doubt correctly, as the greatest asset of their merchandise. Irritated by an inability to publicize it in the 1920s, given the then state of public decorum, they finally followed the advice of an astute public relations man and denied, publicly and indignantly, the insidious, slanderous rumors that avocados were aphrodisiac. Sales immediately mounted.

But when I wrote of this incident in 1972, suggesting that there was no particular reason for believing that the fruit was aphrodisiac, I received a letter from the California Avocado Advisory Board which stated, unblushingly, "Since we so fondly think of our avocado as an aphrodisiac, and have such experts as Mae West [*sic*] explaining its proof positive in this area . . . we certainly do wonder, how do you know it isn't?" Well, I don't, though I have eaten innumerable avocados without remarking any particular effect in this domain one way or the other, but I assume that the avocado's reputation, like that of many other foods—asparagus, for instance—arises from the medieval "doctrine of signatures," the theory that the shape of a plant is a sort of divine revelation of its virtues or vices. The word "avocado" comes from the Nahuatl *ahuacatl,* itself an Axtec shortening of *ahuacacuahatl,* which means "testicle tree." Reference books attribute this name to the supposed invigorating virtues of the fruit, but I suspect that an innocent avocado acquired this reputation from the name of the tree, and the tree its name from the fact that its pear-shaped or round fruits grow in pairs.

The avocado suffers a good deal of mistreatment in the reference books. We are told that its alternative name "alligator pear" results either from the fact that it grows in Florida, alligator country (it didn't until fairly recently), or because its rough exterior suggests alligator hide (some species are rough, some are smooth). Actually this term was applied to the avocado before it ever reached Florida, in English-speaking Jamaica, where "alligator pear" (it is called simply "pear" there now) was the product of folk etymology (substitution of a familiar word for an unfamiliar one) combined with sound etymology (replacement of a word difficult to pronounce or understand by a common one).

We are also told that the avocado is a native of Peru (it is a native of Mexico and adjoining territory), while those authorities who have discovered that this is an error explain that it was caused because it was in Peru that the Spaniards found it first. But Pizarro entered Peru only in 1527, while the avocado had already been described in 1519 in the *Suma de geografía* of Martín Fernández de Enciso, who discovered it near what is now Santa Marta, Colombia. We are told too that avocados were first cultivated in Peru during what is called the Formative Period of Peruvian agriculture, which runs from about 650 B.C. to the beginning of our era; however, Garcilaco de la Vega, son of a Spanish conquistador and an Inca princess, wrote more plausibly that it was brought from Ecuador into the warm valleys near Cuzco by the Inca Tupac Yupanqui, who reigned in the fifteenth century A.D., not long before the Spaniards arrived themselves.

I have no reason for doubting the report that a horticulturist named Henry Perrine first planted avocados in Florida in 1833, but avocado culture did not get under way on a commercial scale in the United States until about 1900, when Florida fruit growers became interested in its possibilities.

Of the three main groups of avocados, the West Indian type is the most determinedly tropical and is the one chiefly planted in Florida, which is the only place in the United States where it can be grown. Mexican avocados, the hardiest, are the specialty of California. In between are the Guatemalan avocados, which can be grown in either state.

One may assume that the avocado first became known to the British when it was taken aboard sailing ships as food for the crews, or at least for petty officers, since the name by which it used to be called in England was midshipman's (or subaltern's) butter.

B

BAGHDADI, CHAMSEDDINE MOHAMED EL HASSAN EL, *in the* Kitabe el-tabih, *1226: The joys of the table are superior to all other pleasures, notably those of personal adornment, of drinking and of love, and those procured by perfumes and by music.*

BONNIER, HENRI: *Cooking is an element of civilization.*

BA
stands for

babirusa, a wild pig of the Celebes which Alexandre Dumas compared to a remarried widower because it has four horns; for the **babisou,** a small tasty mushroom of Languedoc; for the **baboon,** eaten in its extinct giant form by prehistoric Africans and in its scaled-down existing form by tropical Africans today; for the **baboon root,** eaten by South African whites, and the **baboon ixia,** a plant eaten by African bushmen; for the **bachelor perch,** which hides its identity under the name "black crappie"; for the **badger,** eaten by eighteenth-century English peasants hard up for more enticing nourishment; for India's **bael fruit,** fragrant but perishable, also called the Bengal quince; for **baku,** which is another name for the delicious but poisonous globefish of Japan, except when it is **baku butter,** a cooking fat derived from the seeds of a West African tree; for Madagascar's **baladi bean,** which is not a bean, but a tuber of the Egyptian lotus; for the **baldpate,** a duck whose wings whistle when it flies; and for the **Baldwin apple,** first grown in Massachusetts under the name "woodpecker apple" (because of the type of birds which frequented it) until it was rebaptized for its developer, Lieutenant Colonel Loammi Baldwin, an officer of the Continental Army who crossed the Delaware with George Washington at Christmas, 1776.

BA stands for

balm, a gummy resinous substance secreted by some plants, and **balsam,** a subdivision of balm when both words are correctly used, as they seldom are; for the **balsam pear,** an Asiatic fruit also known as the bitter melon; for the African **Bambara pea,** which grows underground, like the peanut, and has lost most of its consumers to the peanut since peanut cultivation became important in Africa; for **bamboo,** an edible plant which commits suicide, and the **bamboo vine,** whose thorns are designed to commit murder; for the **bamboo fish** of North Africa, so called for reasons unknown to me, and the **banner fish,** whose alternative name "poor man's Moorish idol" is a mystery to me also; for **bambuk butter,** a common cooking fat of West Africa obtained from nuts; for the **bantam,** a dwarf chicken too decorative to eat but too good to neglect; for the **baobab,** a tree which is almost 100 percent edible (and drinkable) if you are hungry (or thirsty) enough; for the **barbardine,** which is what the giant granadilla is called in Equatorial Africa; for the **Barbary duck,** which doesn't come from Barbary but from South America, the **Barbary fig,** which doesn't come from Barbary but from North and South America, the **Barbary nut,** which is not a nut but a bulb, and the **Barbary sheep,** which, surprisingly, is a wild sheep from Barbary.

BA stands for

the **barbe-de-Capucin,** a form of endive invented in Belgium, whose name means "Capuchin's whiskers," but is not, so far as I know, ever so called in English; for the **barbel,** a fish popular in the thirteenth century but described in the twentieth as "good neither for roasting nor for boiling"; for the **barberry,** which hides under the alias "Oregon grape" to become that state's official flower; for **bark,** on record as having been eaten by the Vikings, the Chinese, the Russians and the French, but only in times of famine; for the **barnacle,** which Thomas Huxley described as "a crustacean fixed by its head and kicking the food into its mouth with its legs," and the **barnacle goose,** named perhaps from the barnacle, perhaps from its description in Celtic as *bairneach,* "bare neck"; for the **barracuda,** more dangerous than the shark, fished for sport by anglers unaware that it is good to eat, and the **barramundi,** a delicious tropical perch known only to Australians; for the **Bartlett pear,** which is simply the American name for Europe's renowned Williams pear; for the **basket cockle,** a tough but tasty clam of the West Coast; for the **basswood,** whose flowers yield exceptionally fine honey; for the **bat,** said to taste like chicken by Magellan's men but by modern Malays to taste like hare, and for the **batfish** of South Africa and Madagascar, which tastes like neither; for **bauhinia,** a sort of pulse, of which Africans eat the seeds of one species and the pods of another; and for the **bayberry,** usable not only for making scented candles and soap, but also as a seasoning in the form of spice or herb.

And **BA** also stands for

BANANA. The first European since antiquity to set eyes on a banana took it for a giant fig; he was not a naturalist, but an Italian nobleman named Antonio Pigafetta, who had joined Magellan's globe-girdling expedition for the fun of it. What it really is may sound no less strange to non-botanists: the banana is an herb—the world's largest herb, but an herb all the same.

Alphonse de Candolle listed the banana among the plants cultivated more than four thousand years ago, but though it seems to have been eaten in the Indus valley as early as that, whether it was cultivated or wild is an unresolved question. There was every incentive to cultivate it, for wild bananas, which have been described as jungle weeds, are hard, unappetizing and disagreeably full of seeds; nevertheless some wild species are eaten in Africa today, including *Musa acuminata* and *M. balbisiana,* the two which were crossed to give us the cultivated bananas of today. Man improved the flavor immeasurably and got rid of the seeds—thereby rendering all cultivated bananas sterile, unable to reproduce without human help.

BANANA *by David Hockney.* Banana, *crayon drawing, 1970*

Perishable and difficult to transport, the banana was excruciatingly slow in making its way around the world. At least two Assyrian carvings depict what look like bananas, but as both are of royal banquets, it may be that, even if they were bananas, they were in the picture only as examples of rare and luxurious fruits available to no one less exalted than kings. We know that Alexander and his soldiers saw bananas when they invaded India, for Pliny, who described the fruit, gave them as his source of information. Apparently Pliny never saw a banana himself: they do not seem to have reached ancient Greece and Rome. Arabs, often the first importers of foods from the Far East, are thought to have cultivated bananas in the Near East and northern Egypt in the seventh century A.D.—the century of the Koran, which identifies the forbidden fruit of the Old Testament as the banana, not the apple (so did early Hindu Christians, who envisioned Adam and Eve as covering their nudity not with fig leaves but with banana leaves, much more efficient for the purpose, since they run to twelve feet in length and two in width). Probably the banana had already entered Africa to the south before the Arabs imported it farther north, brought to Madagascar by Indonesian invaders early in the Christian era.

The first bananas of America were planted on the island of Hispaniola by Friar Tomás de Berlanga in 1516, but neither in North America nor in Europe, astonishingly, was the banana, so commonplace to us now, available on a really general scale until after World War I. Nevertheless, commercial organization of the banana trade had begun in the United States as early as 1885, when the Boston Fruit Company was organized, which later would become United Fruit and then be absorbed by United Brands. In Europe, the first person to taste a banana may have been the Emperor Napoleon, if the bananas Josephine asked her mother to ship from Martinique arrived in edible condition; otherwise he did not get to taste them until he reached St. Helena, where he was impressed by a new dish served him, banana fritters moistened with rum.

The spread of the banana had to await the development of refrigeration and transportation, for instance of the boats specially designed to transport bananas (accompanied by small boas and large spiders until the technique of flooding the holds with gases not appreciated by those stowaways was developed). Even so, few persons outside banana country ever get a chance to taste two of the most delectable species known (out of 150), the red banana and the perfumed dwarf banana of the Canary Islands. The bananas we eat oftenest belong to *M. sapientum*, "the banana of the wise," so called because, de Candolle wrote, "sages reposed beneath its shade and ate of its fruit." It is not quite clear whether he was suggesting that a diet of bananas imparts wisdom, but it is an arguable thesis, since the banana contains a good deal of phosphorus, "the salt of the intelligence." Another species, *M. paradisiaca*, is the one selected to replace the apple as the fruit of the Garden of Eden.

The banana is an exception to the rule that almost all of the staple foods of the world are either cereals or root crops. Bananas are a staple food, sometimes *the* staple food, of many tropical or subtropical areas, both the sweet dessert fruits we know, and the starchier, vegetable-like "bananas" called plantains.

Used for many other purposes besides food, the banana may have been first cultivated for some other reason. Its leaves, for instance, have served as thatching for houses, as envelopes in which to wrap food (including bananas) for cooking and in India as table mats. *M. textilis* is the source of Manila hemp.

Outside of banana country, the world's largest consumers of this fruit are Americans. The only European country which grows bananas commercially is Iceland (on soil heated by geysers).

BARLEY. The cultivation of food plants began in Neolithic times, when barley was one of the first to be thus raised deliberately; but we know that it was eaten even earlier, by prehistoric men who gathered the seeds of the wild grass which was the ancestor of our modern varieties and, before they had learned how to make flour, scattered them over meat or other foods to add a nutty seasoning. Barley was probably a native of the Ethiopian highlands, a theory borne out by the timetable of its spread from this putative starting point, recorded by civilizations more literate than that of ancient Ethiopia at progressively increasing distances from it. Barley is named in Egyptian hieroglyphics dating from 5000 B.C. and on Sumerian cuneiform tablets of around 3500 B.C. Moving in one direction, it is known to have been growing in northwestern Europe at least by 3000 B.C., and in the other, in the Indus valley, probably quite as early. Barley and rice are the "two immortal sons of heaven" of Vedic literature, while the books of the Emperor Shen Nung, dated at 2800 B.C., speak of it as one of the five sacred cultivated plants of China (the others were rice, soybeans, wheat and millet). By the time Marco Polo wrote of meeting barley in the Far East, we were already into what, for barley, is modern history.

Barley was the chief grain from which the

BARLEY. *Illuminated page from* Old Testament, *France, 13th century*

ancient Hebrews made bread. Among the plagues of Egypt was a bombardment of hailstones, by which "the barley was smitten" (Exodus 1). The penitential diet God imposed upon Ezekiel included barley bread, certainly not severely penitential, since this was what Abraham offered to three angels who visited him. When Boaz first set eyes on Ruth, she was gleaning barley. Absalom ordered his servants to set fire to the grain in Joab's fields; the crop that was burned was barley. The story of the miracle of the loaves and fishes specifies that the five loaves of bread on which Christ fed five thousand people were of barley.

Barley was the chief grain of the Greeks in the most distant times of which we have knowledge, and was apparently then endowed with a religious significance. The secret "orgies" of Demeter reached their climax with the adoration of a suddenly unveiled and brilliantly illuminated spike of grain, which at that period was most likely to have been barley (in French, *orge*). Barley was the grain of Homeric times.

The Romans found the Etruscans making *puls,* a sort of gruel which could harden into a forerunner of bread, from either millet or barley, and chose barley for their own *pulmentum.* Barley bread was important in the diet of the early Romans: Plautus mentions a porridge made of barley flavored with coriander, and Pliny gives a recipe for a sort of oily, highly seasoned barley dough—again almost a modern development, since two and a half centuries earlier Scipio Africanus had already demanded 300,000 bushels of barley in tribute from Carthage. The Carthaginians continued its cultivation following the example of their Phoenician ancestors who had colonized North Africa and had been cultivating barley for many centuries before Carthaginians existed.

Barley was the chief bread grain of continental Europe until the sixteenth century, as important in the European economy then as is rice in many Asian countries today. It was first brought to America in 1543 by the second Spanish governor of Colombia. The Pilgrims planted it in New England without much success, but a little later Pennsylvania proved more receptive to it (and combined it with its limestone water to make whiskey).

Barley lost much of its importance for breadmaking when leavened bread became common, for its low gluten content makes it refractory to the action of yeast. It is nonetheless a valuable food for man, halfway between wheat and rye for nutritive value, and with a higher protein content than rice. Though it is true that more than half the world's barley today goes to feed cattle (and a large part of the rest to make beer), there are still many parts of the world where barley remains an important human food, especially in regions where wheat is not easy to grow. Barley is more resistant to a number of circumstances, such as salinity in the soil, which, together with its close-to-the-surface root system, accounted for its being one of the first crops successfully raised on the salty land reclaimed from Holland's Zuyder Zee. It is much eaten today in Tibet, in northern Germany, in Finland, in the Italian Alps, in Israel, in the Sahara and, fittingly, in the land of its birth, Ethiopia.

BASIL. According to an ancient legend, St. Helena, mother of the Emperor Constantine, was told in a vision that she would find the True Cross in a place where the air was sweet with perfume: she discovered it under a patch of basil. Christian tradition thus fell into line behind the many pagan cults which attributed a religious character to an herb whose very name, from the Greek *basilikón,* means "kingly." In many places and times, indeed, custom demanded that the king himself cut the first basil of the season with a golden sickle; iron, too base a metal, was specifically ruled out.

Sweet basil is a native of India, where it was a sacred plant consecrated to Vishnu; it played a part in religious observances and at funerals. The Egyptians combined it with myrrh and incense in offerings to their gods and included it among the substances used to embalm the dead. For the ancient Greeks and Romans, basil had a curious double association with love and death, echoed in the Boccaccio story which inspired Keats's poem about Isabella, who preserved her murdered lover's head in a pot of basil, and Ingres' painting of the same subject. The association with death was uppermost for the Greeks, for whom basil was a sign of mourning, that with love uppermost for the Romans, who classed basil with the jasmine and the rose as lovers' emblems. It is an attribute of Erzulie, the Haitian voodoo Venus.

Basil, a pungent herb related to mint, has been used in the kitchen since at least 400 B.C., when the Greek physician-botanist Chrysippos described it as one of his favorite seasonings. The Romans included it in bouquets garnis and the Byzantines used it to flavor sauces. In the Middle Ages it worked its way northward through France, where it must have been welcome, for until then the common seasonings ran to such insipid growths as mallow and mosses. Although Paris today seems content to leave basil to southern France, it held onto it for some time; among the street cries

BASIL. *Woodcut from* Gart der Gesundheit, *Ulm, 1487*

which could still be heard there in the nineteenth century was, "Fine green basil, I have handsome basil!"

Basil reached England in the sixteenth century and for a time seemed solidly established there; all the herbalists listed it. Then its favor waned and basil nearly disappeared from English cooking, leaving behind a single reminder of its former popularity: English turtle soup is still traditionally flavored with basil, and no substitute will do. This is also true of the Yugoslav national chicken soup, *tchorba*, and the *pesto* of Genoa, which became the *pistou* of Provence.

In Morocco basil is planted around doors and windows because it is believed to keep mosquitoes out.

BASS. This is a term of infinite confusion. A great many quite unrelated fish, both fresh- and saltwater, have been hailed as bass—almost all of them, by what can only be coincidence, both good game and good food fishes.

The sea bass of the Mediterranean comes first by right of seniority, for we know about it from ancient times, and perhaps also because it is the tastiest of them all. Saltwater fish or not, it ventures into lagoons where the water is only brackish, and even for a considerable distance up rivers. The ancient Romans thought that those caught in fresh water had a finer flavor: "*At in lupis in amne capti praeferuntur,*" Pliny wrote, but few would agree with him today. You will notice that Pliny's word for this fish was *lupus*, "wolf"; it is indeed voracious, ready to eat anything that gets in its way. It is still the sea wolf today in several languages, including French (*loup de mer*), Italian (*lupo di mare*) and German (*Wolfbarsch*). This is the firm, white-fleshed fish you

BASS *by Winslow Homer (1836–1910).* Channel Bass, *watercolor on paper*

see grilling fragrantly over little fires of fennel twigs on the tables of Mediterranean seaside restaurants, where you will be told that what is called *loup* in the Mediterranean is the same fish called *bar* along France's Atlantic coast. This is almost right, but not quite. The *loup*, which is a little better eating, is the common sea bass; the *bar* is the striped sea bass, all the easier to confuse since about 10 percent of the *loup* served on the Mediterranean is really *bar*, taken off La Rochelle on the Atlantic coast; the Mediterranean demand is greater than that sea can supply.

Other saltwater fish referred to as bass, sometimes with justification and sometimes with none, include some sea perches; the groupers; the Atlantic rockfish, an important food for our Colonial ancestors of the East Coast, subsequently transferred to the Pacific coast also; the American sea bass, not the same as the European one, whose many names include, confusingly, black bass and blackfish, not very good eating; the Channel bass, alias the red drum, only good when young; the weakfish (sometimes); and on the Pacific side, the white sea bass, excellent eating; the priestfish (unrelated to the Mediterranean animal of the same name); the sand bass; and, best of all, the again confusedly named black sea bass, which has worked its way across the Pacific for serving at Chinese banquets, where it is so placed on the table that its nose points towards the guest of honor.

The most important freshwater bass are American, as one might suspect from the fact that the French term for "black bass" is *black bass*. Some gourmets maintain that this fish is better eating than the sea bass, which is a matter of individual taste; no one could deny, at least, that the smallmouth black bass is a culinary treat, usually restricted to fishermen who take it for themselves, since the only freshwater bass normally found on the market is white bass. American freshwater bass have been stocked in European waters (where the Germans compliment them by calling them *Forellenbarschen*, trout perch) and also in Africa. The only European freshwater bass is disguised by the name "river perch."

Noble though they are, American black bass have to put up with the indignity of being called by Southern fishermen "hawgs" or "lunkers," which adds insult to the injury done them when they are taken on plastic worms.

BAY LEAF. The bay leaf, alias laurel, is a familiar occupant of our kitchens, always ready to spring to the rescue of a feeble soup, stew, casserole or stock pot and shock it into vigor; but it is so authoritative that a single leaf is all most dishes

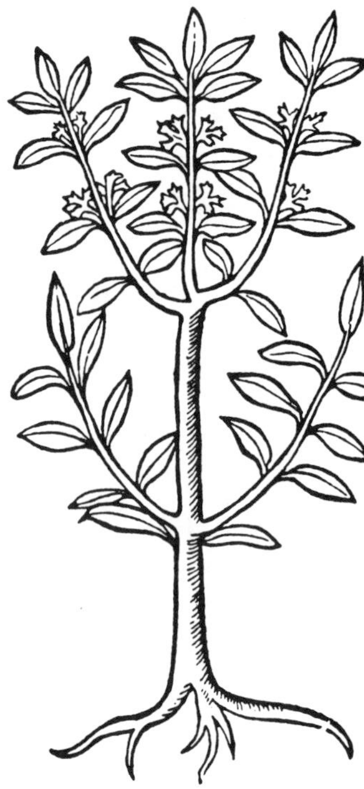

BAY LEAF. *Woodcut from Steffen Arndes:* Hortus Sanitatis, *Lübeck, 1492*

can stand. It is used often in bouquets garnis; a common combination is one bay leaf, a twig of thyme and a sprig of fresh parsley, to which some cooks add rosemary. Unless you live in the right place (preferably the Mediterranean basin, which is where the bay tree—really a shrub—probably started), you will have to make do with dried bay leaf; but bay is one seasoning which retains much of its strength even dried. If you find yours faded in flavor, listen to the advice of Elizabeth David: "To extract a stronger flavor from dry bay leaves, mince them up very fine before putting them in a soup." As for the fresh variety, she writes: "A freshly picked bay leaf gives out a strange scent, bitter and aromatic, with something of both vanilla and nutmeg, and can be boiled in milk for a béchamel sauce or a sweet cream with good results."

After the Greek athletes, who were crowned with bay leaves when they won in the games, the Roman military annexed the laurel. A victorious general did not pin medals on his toga, he wore a crown of bay leaves and carried a branch of laurel in his hand. Julius Caesar was criticized by his enemies for overdoing the wearing of such wreaths and excused for it by his friends, who said that it was only to hide his baldness.

The Romans believed that laurel was the only plant never struck by lightning; the Emperor

Tiberius, a cautious man, always wore a wreath of it during thunderstorms. "Neither witch nor devil, thunder nor lightning," Nicholas Culpeper testified in the seventeenth century, "will hurt a man where a bay tree is." If a plant so beneficient became sick itself, that was obviously a warning of catastrophe. Holinshed chronicled in 1399: "Throughout all the realm of England, old baie trees withered, and afterwards, contrarie to all men's thinking, grew greene againe; a strange sight, and supposed to import some unknown event." That was the year of Richard II's downfall, and Shakespeare, Holinshed's faithful echo, wrote in *Richard II*: "The bay trees in our country all are withered." In 1629, John Evelyn noted that all the bays of the University of Padua had died; this ominous portent was followed by an outbreak of the plague.

Frederick the Great, who liked good food and drink, regarded bay leaves from a purely culinary point of view. He once interrupted Voltaire in the middle of a sentence to compliment his French chef, Noël, on a Mainz ham which he had marinated in a bath of thyme, juniper, savory and bay leaves. This inspired Voltaire to produce a poem in which he depicted Frederick as promising to transfer the laurel of the ham to his chef's toque:

Et je prétends, dans ma reconnaissance
Dérobant les lauriers d'un jambon de Mayence
D'une couronne, un jour, décorer ton bonnet.

This was of course *Laura nobilis*, the genuine article. Other "laurels" (which are not of the genus *Laura*) are bitter or even dangerous. The cherry laurel, *Prunus laurocerasus*, a member of the rose family, contains appreciable amounts of poisonous prussic acid. Both the leaves and the wood of the rose laurel or oleander are toxic; it has happened that picnickers, spitting meat on a branch of oleander to cook it over an outdoor fire, have become ill as a result. The mountain laurel (*Kalmia latifolia*) can poison wild or domestic animals, as some zoos have discovered to their cost; having planted this laurel or its relatives (one particularly decorative member of the group is the rhododendron), they have lost animals because visitors pulled off handfuls of leaves to feed them. Tea made with two ounces of mountain laurel leaves can kill a man. The Delaware Indians used it for suicide.

BE
stands for

the wild **beach pea**, a close relative of the garden pea, which tastes like it, and the wild **beach plum**, which is too tart to eat but makes exquisite jelly; for the **bean clam**, tiny but delicious, which exists in many parts of the world, including both coasts of the United States; for **bear**, which I am informed makes the best hamburgers in the world in the proportion of one part bear meat to two parts deer meat; for **bearberries**, a name applied loosely to a number of wild American bays once eaten extensively by American Indians and, presumably, American bears; for **bear grass**, abandoned as a food since American Indians stopped roasting its roots; for **beaver**, whose tails were once eaten in Poland during Lent, with the ingenious explanation that since they were almost always submerged, they were classifiable as fish; for the **bêche-de-mer**, a two-dimensional aquatic animal lost in a three-dimensional world; for **bee balm**, from which our Colonial ancestors brewed their cherished Oswego tea; for the **beechnut**, edible for man, who usually leaves it to animals; for **beefans**, an obsolescent word for the sort of apples raised for drying; for the **beetle**, whose larvae are or were eaten by Africans, Australians, American Indians and, if we may believe Charles Monselet, a French gastronomic writer of the last century, by some of the more adventurous of his countrymen; for **beggar's blanket**, our third name for the mullein; for **Belle Isle cress**, which is winter CRESS bedecked with a fancy name for merchandising purposes; and for the **Belon**, a superior French oyster of which 600 to 700 pounds are raised annually, and 16,000 sold.

BE stands for

Beluga, the largest, and hence the most expensive, form of caviar; for the **Ben Davis apple**, the variety most widely grown in the South and Midwest in the nineteenth century, and I would tell you who Ben Davis was if I knew; for the **Bengal bean**, eaten only in time of shortage by East Africans, who may be prejudiced against it because it is poisonous; for **benne seeds**, which are sesame seeds; and for **bent-nosed clams**, of which there are two genera, one of which has to lie on its left side because the tip of its shell is twisted to the right, while the other has to lie on its right side because the tip of its shell is twisted to the left, and **bent mussels**, of which Euell Gibbons, a man ordinarily hard to discourage, wrote that "they will stave off the pangs of hunger, but . . . I found them barely edible."

BE stands for

the **benwort**, of which, Henry David Thoreau

dixit, the stem tastes like asparagus; for **benzoin,** or gum benjamin, which the ancient Romans, a brave people, used in sauces; for **berdi,** a reed of which the Tuaregs eat the young shoots in time of famine; for **bergamot,** a citrus fruit which virtually no one has ever tasted because it is more valuable for perfume than for food; for **berries,** a popular conception at loggerheads with botanical reality, for the most specific scientific definition of the word "berry" includes the tomato and excludes the strawberry; for the **betel nut**, whose taste has been described as "a combination of cloves, citronella and carbolic acid," which does not discourage one-tenth of the world's population from chewing it; and for **betony**, a mint so abhorred by serpents that they cannot cross a barrier made of its twigs, Gaius Plinius Secundus *dixit*.

And **BE** also stands for

BEAN. The bean is a protean vegetable, whose forms are so many and so numerous that one of the few things which can be said that applies to all of them is that they go back to prehistoric times. The Asian soybean is on Alphonse de Candolle's list of foods cultivated more than four thousand years ago. The American haricot bean, already in cultivated form, has been found in excavations dating back to 7000 B.C. The European broad bean has been discovered in the kitchen middens of prehistoric Swiss lake settlements.

These are the world's three most important beans, in that order. The soybean comes first. It is associated for most of us with China, but today the biggest grower of soybeans is the United States, which also grows more soybeans than any other kind. If we are less conscious of them, it is because they are used in America as animal food more commonly than as human food, and also because a large proportion of them is shipped abroad, for the United States, the first exporter of soybeans, is the supplier for all the world, including China. Other Asian beans include the Japanese azuki, which has recently attracted attention in the United States because health-food faddists have fallen enthusiastically upon it; the Chinese mung bean; and a number of natives of India—the asparagus pea or Goa bean; the cowpea, a bean despite its name; the tropical climber called the bonavist, whose large, dark seeds become inedible when mature, and the related horse gram; and for good measure, the so-called long bean or "drumstick," which hardly qualifies as a real bean, since its fibrous pod is filled not with seeds but with a marrowlike cream of delicate flavor.

The broad bean of Europe was relegated to third place after the American bean was discovered and supplanted it to a considerable extent; but it possesses distinctive desirable characteristics, so it has by no means been driven out by the New World haricot. Instead, there has been a curious shift in its center of production. Beginning about 1950, at the same period when the United States was displacing China as the world's leading producer of soybeans, China displaced Europe as the world's leading producer of broad beans. This bean is frequently called the fava bean in the United States, which has thus borrowed its Italian name, reproduced in French as the *fève*; in German it is the *grosse Bohnen.* The most important of the broad beans is the one the French call the large marsh fava (*grosse fève des marais*), from which most of the favas eaten today seem to be derived, including the *julienne* or small Portuguese fava, the long-podded Seville fava and the dwarf fava, grown in winter under glass. The English call the fava the Windsor bean or round bean, while the variety called the small field bean or Tuck bean is also the horse bean, used chiefly as animal fodder—the one Shakespeare probably had in mind when he had Puck report:

When I a fat and bean-fed horse beguile,
Neighing in likeness of a filly foal.

The antiquity of the fava bean is so great that it had already split into two main types before the dawn of history, a large-seeded form ascribed by one authority to North Africa and by another more generally to the Mediterranean basin, and a small-seeded form attributed by the first to Persia and by the second to an area extending from the Middle East to west of the Himalayas. Favas have been found in Stone Age sites and in the ruins of Troy.

Herodotus wrote that Egyptian priests were forbidden to eat favas. "They cannot even bear to look at them," he said, "because they imagine they are unclean." He added that the Egyptians never sowed beans and would not eat them if they came upon them growing wild. Herodotus was wrong. The Egyptians did cultivate beans; an important item in the diet of their common people was a bean cake called *tamia*, which is the *tamiya* of Egypt today. The broad bean has never lost its popularity in this region. *Fool*, sold from outdoor stands in the streets of Cairo, is boiled beans; *fool midammis* is baked beans. In Algeria, favas are often served on the side with couscous, while *bissar*, an Algerian mountaineer's dish, is dried beans cooked in water and oil until they coalesce into a sort of gruel, eaten hot or cold. In Turkey these beans, after having been cooked in a piquant sauce called *pilaki*, are served cold as appetizers. In Nigeria, broad beans are mashed with coconut milk, a combination echoed, curiously, on the other side of the world in the Caribbean, though the bean used there is the haricot.

The ancient Chaldeans, who believed in the transmigration of souls, did not limit their metamorphoses to the animal realm; they believed they could be reborn as fava beans. The Hebrew word *pôl* probably meant the fava, in which case it was this bean that was given as a gift to Daniel and was converted into flour to make bread for Ezekiel. In Homeric times, aside from the ubiquitous onions and garlic, favas, chick-peas and lentils were the three principal vegetables. Pythagoras enjoined a vegetable diet on his disciples, but proscribed the bean. A non-culinary use of the bean by the Greeks was its employment as a voting token for the election of magistrates; when Plutarch wrote "Abstain from beans," he was not referring to a diet, but was advising his readers to keep out of politics. Similarly in Rome, at the time of the Saturnalia, the master of the revels was chosen by drawing beans, transformed in Christian times into a rite of Twelfth Night, when the person who received the slice of a holiday cake containing the *fève* baked into it became the king of the festivities, a custom which persists to this day. In England this evolved into the beanfeast, originally an annual dinner offered by an employer to his employees somewhere around the Christmas–New Year's holidays. The broad bean was for centuries a basic dish of the English worker, in combination with bacon, which inspired G. K. Chesterton to write:

But since he stood for England
And knows what England means,
Unless you give him bacon
You must not give him beans.

Christopher Columbus may very well have been the first European to see the American haricot bean, which he encountered near Huevitas, Cuba. It is reasonable to suppose that he sent some home, as he did with all the new foods he encountered, but we may guess that they made no impression until the conquistadors who entered Mexico in 1519 did the same, for the word for this bean is Aztec—"haricot" comes from *ayacotl.* It was discovered again in Florida by Cabeza de Vaca in 1528, and once more by Jacques Cartier shortly afterward, at the mouth of the St. Lawrence. This confirms its great antiquity, for it had

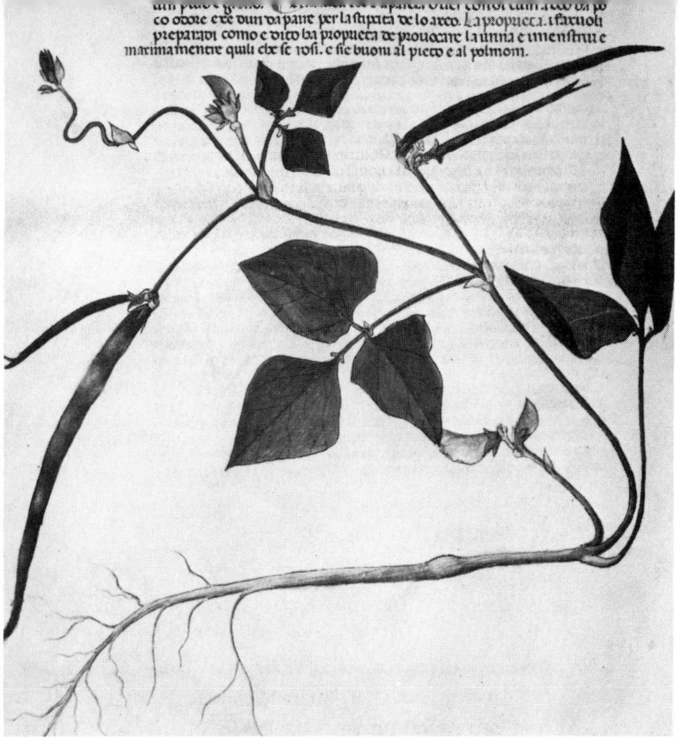

BEAN. *Illuminated page from Serapion the Younger:* Herbolario volgare, *Padua, 1390–1400*

already had time to develop varieties capable of surviving in a number of very different climates. It was, for instance, not only an important food of the American Indians of the cold, damp Northeast, one of two chief ingredients of their succotash (the other being Indian corn), but also of the Pueblo Indians in the hot, dry Southwest.

The haricot is the most versatile of all beans. It comprises tall climbing plants and low bush types. There are beans meant to be eaten young, pods and all, and beans which, though also eaten entire, can be so consumed even in maturity. There are round beans, oval beans, fat beans, flat beans, long beans and kidney-shaped beans. There are white beans, yellow beans, tan beans, green beans, pink beans, red beans, purple beans, black beans and mottled beans. Their pods are flat or round, smooth or irregular, straight or curved, short (three inches) or long (eight inches), and may be green, yellow, red, purple or splashed in different colors. There are the black beans of Central and South America, which make Cuba's famous black bean soup and, when combined with rice, the dish called "Moors and Christians," because of the two contrasting colors; the lima bean, mildly and agreeably poisonous; the pigeon pea, which is not quite a pea but not quite a bean either; the black-eyed pea, which *is* a bean; the reddish pinto bean which the cowboys call "Mexican strawberries"; and, of course, the string bean, today usually stringless.

Although the haricot was destined eventually to become more important in Europe than its former fava bean (one advantage of the haricot was that heavy consumption of it did not bring on the deficiency disease provoked by heavy consumption of the broad bean, for that reason called favism), it was slow to do so. Some New World beans were sent to Pope Clement VII in 1528, which he passed on to Canon Pietro Valeriano in Florence. Valeriano potted them, and when he tasted his first crop, he approved, and gave some to Alessandro de' Medici, who approved too. Thus the Tuscans became *mangafagioli*, "bean eaters," which is what other Italians call them today; it had to be the haricot bean which gave them this epithet, for *fagioli* refers specifically to the New World bean.

Alessandro put a few bags of the new beans in the luggage of Catherine de' Medici when she left for France in 1533 to marry Henry II, but it took something like two centuries for the haricot to work its way into the French kitchen. The first French planting of haricots in any quantity occurred in 1749, near Soissons, with so much success that the particular type of beans planted there are still known in France as *soissons*. Even so, they were looked at askance at first. A slang term for them was *bourre-coquins*, "rascal stuffers," and Brillat-Savarin pronounced anathema upon them—an opinion which was shared in our own times by Don Marquis, who wrote, "There will be no beans in the Almost Perfect State." But Napoleon liked them.

BEEF. "Beef," wrote Marie Antoine Carême, the great nineteenth-century French chef, "is the soul of cooking." "Without the ox," said the eighteenth-century naturalist Georges Buffon, "it would be difficult to live."

More beef is eaten than any other kind of meat throughout the world, even taking into account those areas where religion forbids it (India), where it is too expensive (Japan), or where it runs counter to firmly fixed eating habits (Hawaii, where beef cattle were introduced in fairly recent times and have never succeeded in wooing the natives away from their favorite pork). The roast beef of Old England is proverbial and England is symbolized, significantly, by John Bull, but the English today are not the world's greatest consumers of beef. Americans eat more per capita, and the English are not even the first in Europe: that place is occupied by the French. In Argentina, beef is the daily dish even for the poor. In New Zealand and Australia, though mutton is the most important meat for producers and exporters, beef is the most popular among consumers, who eat it chiefly in the form of steaks and roasts. There are over a billion cows, bulls and steers in the world.

By the time we first encounter beef cattle in history, they are already improved strains developed from the primordial ancestor, of which, from the purely zoological viewpoint, there is only one species. All the domestic cattle of today are descendants of *Bos primigenius*, the aurochs, which is the animal depicted in prehistoric cave paintings: it was still in existence up to the middle of the seventeenth century. The bull was a symbol of strength and fertility in Sumerian and Semitic religions. For the Syrians it was the attribute of the god of storms, later introduced into the Roman pantheon as Jupiter Dolichenus. Zeus himself took the form of a bull to kidnap Europa. Crete had its Minotaur, and it was on that island also that a wild bull, emerging from the sea, wreaked havoc until it was captured by Hercules.

There were domesticated cattle in Egypt at least by 3500 B.C., and perhaps earlier. There are innumerable references to them in the Bible, even in the Ten Commandments, which order "Thou shall not covet thy neighbor's ox," on the same plane as his wife. The possession of cattle was in ancient times equivalent to the possession of wealth. The word "cattle" itself has given us "chattel." The impecunious man was one without cattle (*pecus*). Cattle may not quite have served as money, though they were important in barter, but they could, like money, be used to measure the value of other merchandise. Thus in Homeric Greece a slave was worth four oxen (a concubine cost twenty). The cost of living had doubled by Anglo-Saxon times, when a slave cost eight oxen in England.

Cattle were expensive in Homeric times, which is why the great feasts of Homeric heroes consisted chiefly of beef. The host could have regaled his guests on game, free to anyone who owned a spear, but to do them real honor he slaughtered an ox, thus presenting them with an appreciable part of his wealth. The beast was killed by the host himself, or by one of his sons or sons-in-law, and roasted by the males over an open fire. Beef was a meat too noble to be entrusted to women, or to be boiled.

The archetype of meat in medieval times was beef. The butchers' guild of Paris had its own church, which antedated the tenth century, St. Pierre des Boeufs; on its façade were two sculptured oxen. A fourteenth-century list of French cuts of beef names thirty different kinds, starting with sirloin, which seems to have been one of the most popular. In the eighteenth century Marshal de Richelieu composed a gala repast made up solely of beef, except for a few accompanying trifles, which included four hors d'oeuvres (one was made from the animal's eyelids, while an-

Beef. Pottery Cow, *Delft, 18th century*

other included nasturtiums), four main dishes and six desserts. He seemed to have included everything the animal possessed down to its marrow, but a later critic pointed out that he had omitted the feet, edible if not palatable.

The French monarchy stuck to beef up to the steps of the guillotine: when Louis XVI was arrested at Varennes in his attempt to escape, he had in his coach a supply of short ribs on which to munch during his journey.

In spite of the reputation of the English as beefeaters, it is doubtful whether beef was eaten more extensively across the Channel than in France in medieval times. This was the epoch of the cruel sport of bull baiting in England, when a tethered bull was set upon by dogs. It had at least the gastronomic excuse that butchers were forbidden to slaughter bulls which had not been baited, since this was supposed to make the meat tenderer (it must also have made it bitter). Beef may have been more widely available in the lush Tudor times, when, Thomas Fuller reported in his *Worthies*, the English yeomen of the period ate their principal meal at noon, which often included beef; but yeomen were a privileged group.

By the nineteenth century, Englishmen had been outdone as beefeaters by Americans. Visiting the United States in 1861, Anthony Trollope was astonished at the mammoth consumption of beef—twice as much, he wrote, as was eaten in England. As early as 1854, *Harper's Weekly* had noted that the commonest meal in America, from coast to coast, was steak. In the East, this must then have meant beef from the South, Georgia and the Carolinas, the main source for it at the time, for it was only in this same year that the first Texas Longhorns reached New York, where they were received less as a source of food than as a curiosity, a status to which they have now returned. Today beef is the most popular meat in America. Despite the competition of veal, pork, lamb and mutton, when the American housewife buys meat, she selects beef four times out of seven.

Some connoisseurs maintain that Japan, a newcomer in the field, produces the best beef in the world today. This is a remarkable about-face, for ever since Buddhism swept over Japan in the tenth century, meat had been considered unfit for human consumption, and the Japanese professed to be able to recognize meat eaters by their disagreeable odor. It was only in the nineteenth century that young Japanese intellectuals, making contact for the first time with Americans and Europeans, dared maintain that red meat was a worthy food. The emperor started to eat it in 1872 and the Japanese population immediately followed suit. Eating beef, a Japanese historian proclaimed, was "a sign of an advanced state of civilization," and Japanese breeders set to work to make up for lost time. Their best cattle are massaged daily with Japanese gin to spread the fat throughout the meat. Grazing on rich pasture is supplemented by rations of rice, rice bran and beans. Shortly before the age of three years, the steers are given daily tots of beer as part of their final fattening; they are slaughtered at about forty months.

Beefeaters devoted to favorite cuts run into difficulties when they enter foreign countries, of which no two divide the carcass in the same fashion. The United States, Great Britain, Germany and France all have theoretically standardized fashions of cutting up the animal, no two of them alike, but within these general frameworks there are innumerable local variations. One French food expert has written that in Paris and the north of France the butchering is the "most refined"; that in the southwest it is "coarse"; and that "abroad the cuts often seem to have been hacked out by lumberjacks." In Italy complete chaos prevails, with almost every community cutting up the animal after its own bent. Florence and Siena do use the same system, and these are the only two cities in Europe where you can get the equivalent of the American T-bone steak (usually, however, with the bone removed), though some English loin cuts make a stab at it. The American sirloin steak is rumpsteak in England, while what the English call the sirloin is what in the United States is the tenderloin. The story that the sirloin got its name because some usually unidentified English king was served so superlative a piece of meat that he knighted it on the spot is a fable. The "sir" of sirloin is a misspelling for the original "sur," the prefix meaning "above," locating the position of the cut as above the loin.

BEET. *Beta vulgaris,* an unspectacular but widespread vegetable, has given rise to a large number of varieties which for practical purposes may be classified in four categories: the table beet, eaten chiefly for its root; the leaf beet or CHARD; the sugar beet; and the mangel-wurzel.

A native of the Mediterranean region—probably of Italy, though it is difficult to place it exactly, since it was already being cultivated in prehistoric times—the beet in its original form was closer to chard than is today's table beet. The earliest Romans ate only the leaves. It is believed that the Romans did not develop the root of the beet for food until about the beginning of the Christian era, after which we know they were eating both leaves and roots. The root beet was one of the plants Charlemagne included on the list of those he wanted cultivated in his domains,

BEET. *Drawing by Marilena Pistoia from F. Bianchini and F. Corbetta:* I Frutti della Terra, *Rome, 1975*

but his wishes do not seem to have been followed, for the vegetable had to be reintroduced into France at the time of the Renaissance.

The beet has a relatively high tolerance for salt and has therefore been a favorite for planting on land reclaimed from the sea—the polders which replaced Holland's Zuyder Zee, the fields produced by filling in eel-breeding lagoons in Comacchio, Italy, the silt carried down to the Adriatic in the Polesine region of the same country. It is a biennial, producing its large edible root the first year and seed the second. It grows best in temperate to cool regions; if you encounter red beets which look as if they had faded, it is probably because they were subjected to unusually high temperatures while growing. Though some beets are almost white, they are oftener red, purplish to quite dark. The coloring element is persistent; the Pennsylvania Dutch use a fluid based on beet juice to tint and flavor hard-boiled eggs. It is also capable of coloring the urine, which may become scarlet after eating beets; there is no need to be alarmed about this.

Although the table beet is grown for its root, the leaves are edible also, especially when the plant is young; a particularly delicious salad can be made of the new leaves with tiny beets attached which are obtained when thinning the plants, which, as everyone who has grown them knows, must necessarily be done early, for what is ordinarily called a beet seed is actually a number of seeds stuck together, so that several plants start to grow in the same place.

The sugar beet is a triumph of guided evolution, though perhaps one not as great as some writers, carried away by enthusiasm, have represented it to be. One widely read work described it as unique, the only example in existence of the creation of a new species; even if it had not forgotten about maize, the statement would still be erroneous, since the sugar beet is not a new species at all, but simply a greatly improved variety of *B. vulgaris*. This fairly long, tapering beet, with white flesh and nearly white skin, existed before its value as a sugar producer was discovered, and was then used chiefly to feed animals, though it was also eaten sometimes as a vegetable.

The rise of the sugar beet began, though slowly, when the German chemist A. S. Marggraf discovered that sugar could be extracted from beets; but it was half a century before this evoked any great interest, and it took Napoleon Bonaparte to start the sugar beet on its way. True, a disciple of Marggraf's, Franz Karl Achard, had set up a factory in 1796 to produce sugar from beets, but it was quick to fail. Then the English blockaded France, cutting it off from its sources of cane sugar. Napoleon, who had heard about the possibility that sugar could be obtained from beets, ordered that 70,000 acres be planted to sugar beets, and in 1812 a French financier named Benjamin Delessert opened a refinery to process the beets in the Passy section of Paris. He supplied the palace, as well as ordinary consumers, with the new sugar, and was rewarded by being made a baron of the empire. The Boulevard Delessert now runs in Paris from the Place du Trocadéro to the Place de Passy, in the direction of the site where Delessert's refinery once stood, but few Parisians could tell you whom it honors.

The development of the sugar beet was continued in Germany under the lead of Moritz von Koppy, resulting in the White Silesian beet, from which all the present varieties have evolved. By 1880, beet sugar was being more widely consumed than cane sugar in Europe, but after World War I it dropped back again and the proportion became about one-third beet sugar to two-thirds cane sugar—still enough to make the sugar beet more important commercially than all other varieties of this vegetable put together.

The mangel-wurzel, a large, coarse beet, yellow to reddish orange in color, known also as the forage beet or field beet, is widely grown as food for cattle. It can be eaten by man, but rarely is, except in dire extremity.

BI
stands for

the **bigarade,** or bitter orange, probably the ancestor of all the others, but in any case, the best for making marmalade; for the **big crab,** or Dungeness, big in size and big in taste; for the **bigney,** a fruit of Nepal and the East Indies which is being raised experimentally in Florida; for the **bighorn,** a wild Rocky Mountain sheep so succulent that a century and a half of hunting reduced its numbers from 2 million to 7000; for the **bilberry,** which in England is often confused with the American blueberry, a sweeter fruit; for **billy-buttons,** as Pennsylvanians call the wild mallow; for the **Bing cherry,** named for the Chinese horticulturist who produced it in Oregon; for the **birch,** whose buds have served as famine food; for **bird's nest,** which is probably not what you will be served in Chinese bird's nest soup, because it is too expensive; for **birds' tongues,** eaten only by the Chinese and the ancient Romans, who reasoned that since birdsong is sweet, birds' tongues should be sweet too; for **birthwort,** believed by ancient Romans to be aphrodisiac and by modern Virginians to cure snakebite; for **biscuit root,** of which American Indians made celery-flavored flour; for **bishop's-weed,** used as an herb in Ethiopia, and nowadays almost nowhere else; for the **bitter melon,** which we have already met as the balsam pear; for **bittern,** a marsh bird spurned by modern gourmets though it was featured at the elaborate banquet given in 1399 to celebrate the first marriage of King Henry IV; and for **bitterroot,** first collected by Meriwether Lewis of the Lewis and Clark expedition when he found American Indians making bread from its roots.

And **BI** also stands for

BISON. The largest mammal in Europe, *Bison bonasus,* and the largest mammal in North America, *B. americanus,* both escaped extinction by a hair. The European animal has never regained its place as a provider of meat. The American bison is perhaps now doing so, but in domesticated form.

The bison was an important food animal for prehistoric Europeans, depicted frequently in Stone Age cave paintings. Aristotle recorded its existence in what is now Bulgaria when its range covered the greater part of temperate Europe. It held out in Switzerland until the eleventh century, in France until the fifteenth, in Germany until the sixteenth and in Transylvania until the eighteenth. It was the spread of civilization which

Bison *by Mark Catesby (c. 1679–1749). "Bison by Acacia Tree" from* The Natural History of Carolina, Florida and the Bahama Islands, *London, 1731*

denied the bison the abundant supply of food its bulk demanded, by diminishing the size of forests, for the European bison, unlike its American cousin, is solely a woods animal, living on acorns, the shoots of young trees, bushes, bark, leaves, marsh plants and only incidentally on the grass of forest clearings.

By the twentieth century there remained only two islands of bison in Europe—about 400 head in the Caucasus and 737 in the Polish forest of Bialowieza, according to a count made in 1914. The last survivor in the Caucasus was shot by a poacher in 1919, and the Bialowieza herd was destroyed twice, in the two world wars, and reconstituted twice from animals in zoos. A new population of 400 head was achieved after World War II, and the herd is developing satisfactorily; but there seems no prospect in the foreseeable future of the return of bison meat to European tables.

The first European ever to see an American bison was Cortez, when he visited Montezuma's zoo in 1521. Coronado encountered these animals in great numbers in Texas twenty years later and described them as "hunchbacked cows," while the French, meeting them in Canada, called them, simply, "oxen." It was the English who fixed upon them the name "buffaloes," which they are not, but it stuck. The first bison seen by English colonists were glimpsed near what is now Washington, D.C., in 1612. The animal's range at that time was from Oregon to New York, and from well north in Canada to Monterrey in Mexico. By 1810 almost no bison were left east of the Mississippi, though some old forests in the East are still marked by the trails the great beasts butted through them.

When the white man reached North America, its bison population was the greatest which any large animal has ever attained anywhere at any time, an estimated 60 million head. The chronicler of Coronado's expedition told how a herd was stampeded toward a canyon: "So many animals fell in that they filled it up and the rest passed over their bodies." Their numbers were no guarantee against the white man's rifle and his wastefulness; vast numbers of bison were killed for their tongues, and the rest of their bodies left for the coyotes; a little later it was the hides which were in demand. But there were still enough when the pioneers began crossing the plains to provide them with their most abundant source of fresh meat—"humpbacked beef" they called it. Some of it they dried and took along with them, making "jerky," after the manner of the Indians ("jerky" comes, via Spanish, from an American Indian word, *charqui*). Jerky could also be pounded into pemmican, a concentrated, long-keeping, portable high-energy food; a pound may contain 3500 calories, more than a pound of butter (3200) and very much more than a pound of beef (750).

Then the railroads came, and the bison were no respecters of rights of way. Professional hunters were hired to kill them off, including Buffalo Bill Cody, who shot 4280 in seventeen months. What finally spelled the doom of the bison was the desire to get rid of the Indians. Many of the Plains Indians were totally dependent upon the bison for everything—food, shelter, clothes, weapons, utensils, fuel, thread, grease and even children's toys. The whites reasoned that if they got rid of the bison, they would get rid of the Indians. They did not quite exterminate the Indians, but they did exterminate the bison. The twentieth century opened with no wild bison left on the entire North American continent outside of zoos, except twenty-one in Yellowstone Park and a small herd near Lake Athabaska in Canada, which had been placed under the protection of the Northwest Mounted Police in 1890.

Today the American bison is making a comeback, even as food. The United States government maintains a herd of wild bison of about 12,000 head. This is all the available grazing ground will support, so the herd has to be held down to this figure. When it is thinned, the meat is available; but since it is the older animals which are killed, after they have passed their prime, it is apt to be tough, coarse in texture and strong in taste. Most of the bison meat available today comes from domesticated animals, now being raised in the West; it compares favorably with prime beef, is richer and more tender, and distinguishable from it by a slightly sweeter taste. There is no gaminess, as there can be with wild animals; Alexandre Dumas, writing in the last century, said that bison had "a little sharp wild taste, recalling that of stag"; but all he had to taste was salted jerky.

BL (mostly black and blue) stands for

the **black,** a curt form of address employed in the northeastern United States to designate the tautog; for the **black abalone,** which likes more surf than the green abalone, the red abalone or the pink abalone; for the **black flounder,** which is greener than the yellowtail flounder; for the **black bass,** one of the tastiest fishes of its family; for the **black bean,** a favorite of Cuba and Brazil; for the **black birch,** whose sap makes a refreshing drink; for the **blackbird,** which, whether or not it makes a dainty dish to set before a king, was indeed once baked in pies in England and is eaten with gusto today in Corsica and North Africa; for the **black bream,** a monogamous fish, one of which fought to defend its mate in classical times but attracted very little attention because a combat between Menelaus and Paris was going on at the same time; for **black bryony,** a wild plant which no one has dared use for human food since Apicius; for the **black buck,** an antelope which is astute enough to live in India, a country of vegetarians, where game enjoys a reasonable chance of survival; for **blackcaps,** a wild raspberry particularly appreciated by Pacific Amerindians, and the **black chiton,** a sea cradle particularly appreciated by ditto; for the **black clam,** which is yellow; for the **blackcock,** whose female is the greyhen; for the **black cod,** which is not a cod, but the sablefish; for the **black crappie,** whose other aliases include "calicofish" and "papermouth"; for the **black currant,** which, unlike the white currant and the red currant, is too bitter to eat fresh; for the **black deer,** whose tails are sold in Hong Kong to cure impotence in men; for the **black-eyed pea,** brought to America by black slaves; for **blackfellows' bread,** a fungus eaten by Australian aborigines; for the **blackfish,** which is a sea bass; for the **black gilliflower,** which, unlikely as that sounds, is the sheepnose apple; for the **black haw,** "sweetest of all wild fruits," in whose taste some aficionados detect an echo of the date; for the **black honey** of Brazil and the **black locust honey** of Italy; for the **black Spanish hen,** which would rather lay eggs than raise chicks; for the **black turban,** a tiny California mollusk so called from the shape of its shell; and for the **black walnut,** a species less valued for its fruit than for its wood.

BL stands for

the **bladder,** which gets itself eaten only in the form of sausage casings, and the **bladder cherry,** which is the ground cherry; for the **blaeberry,** which is the Scottish name for the whortleberry; for the **blanket leaf,** our fourth synonym for the mullein; for the **blaspheme-vine,** whose name you will illustrate if, while trying to steal its tender young shoots, you rake yourself on its tough old thorns; for the **bleak,** a small freshwater fish more popular in the Middle Ages than it is now, and the **blenny,** a small saltwater fish which tries to pass itself off as an undersized eel; for the **blesbok,** a large South African antelope whose meat is so tasty that there are no more of them outside of animal reserves; for **blewits,** alias *Tricholoma personatum,* a diffident mushroom of a pleasing lilac color when young; for **blood,** an often unsuspected ingredient in a number of dishes, including one of the oldest of all, black pudding, said to have been invented in Tyre; for the Japanese **blowfish,** famous for its tastiness, but if an inexpert cook fails to remove the deadly poisonous liver, you won't have time to appreciate the taste; for **blubber,** whale or seal, eaten especially, but not only, by Eskimos; for the **blue crab,** a favorite for she-crab soup and soft-shelled crabs; for the **blue-eyed scallop,** which may sound like a joke, but the Buzzard's Bay scallop of Massachusetts does have eyes, they are blue, and there may be as many as fifty of them—placed, unfortunately, on the wrong side to permit it to see where it is going; for the **bluefin tuna,** which used to be an important food fish but which has been all but exterminated because of "gross human mismanagement" according to ichthyologist Frank Mather; for the **bluefish,** "the bulldog of the ocean," the gamest fish in the world for its size; for the **bluegill,** which you may know, and disdain, as the sunny, the sunfish, the sun perch, the gilly or the pumpkinseed, but it isn't bad eating; for the **blueback,** which fishermen call the glut herring in disabused comment on the price it usually fetches; for the **blue marlin,** the fastest fish in the sea, which can swim at fifty miles per hour, famous as game, but it is good eating too; for the **bluemouth,** the famous rascasse of the Mediterranean which is essential in bouillabaisse and has been shown by A. J. Liebling to be more or less identical with the American sculpin; for the **blue mussel,** a tasty but neglected shellfish of the Atlantic coast of northern North America; for the **Bluepoint,** a famous Long Island oyster which is losing its taste, or I am; for **blue sailors,** which is chicory, a name you will understand if you have ever seen it in flower; for the **blue sunfish,** another name for the bluegill; and for the **blue whiting,** which sounds like a contradiction in terms, but anyway gets us out of the blues.

And **BL** also stands for

BLACKBERRY. The most intrepid blackberry fancier in literature was the man who "jumped into a bramble bush and scratched out both his eyes." He was undoubtedly after blackberries, for in England and Scotland the blackberry is called the bramble, the fruit being called either blackberry or brambleberry. This name highlights the most impressive characteristic of the blackberry, the ferocity with which its fruit is defended by its thorns. Similarly the honeyberry of Scandinavia, a variety of blackberry, is known as the arctic bramble, while in France, where the mulberry and the blackberry are confounded under the same name, *mûre,* the latter is distinguished from the former by being called the wild mulberry or hedge mulberry, but more correctly the *ronce,* "thorn" or "bramble."

If the blackberry evokes in all minds the image of its prickliness, it may be largely because, of all the widely known berries, it is the one of which the largest proportion is eaten wild, rather than in the cultivated form; often it is the ultimate consumer who does the gathering, and has thus an opportunity to become acquainted with the vicious nature of the plant. Improved varieties have been developed by cultivation, including thornless ones, but the wild fruit still holds its own.

BLACKBERRY *by Raphaelle Peale (1774–1825).* Blackberries, *oil on canvas*

The blackberry might almost be described as an Anglo-Saxon specialty; it is particularly in English-speaking countries that it is eaten alone, fresh, raw and sugared, instead of being converted into preserves, or occasionally into tarts. The United States leads in cultivating the blackberry. England, though it cherishes a sentimental preference for picking its berries wild or semiwild from hedgerows, is nevertheless second in cultivating this fruit, devoting to it about one-tenth as much acreage as America. The blackberry is not much cultivated on the continent of Europe, where the Germans, who call it *Brombeere,* are probably more addicted to it than the French, who find it too acid to eat uncooked and therefore know it almost exclusively in jams, jellies and alcoholic drinks.

The blackberry grows most plentifully in the eastern United States, on the Pacific coast of North America, in the British Isles and in western Europe, in the last especially as a hedge or woods plant (it often springs up in thick brakes in cut-over or burned-out areas in the latter).

The extra-large blackberries of upper New York State are referred to as "sheep's tits."

BLUEBERRY. The American blueberry is the second among common fruits (after the blackberry) in being consumed chiefly in its wild rather than in its cultivated form. About twice as much acreage as for the blackberry is devoted to blueberry raising in the United States, producing a cultivated fruit larger and sweeter than the wild variety. This is just what persons gifted, or cursed, with a subtle sense of taste hold against the cultivated berry. Sweetness, they argue, is an uncomplicated taste sensation which smothers all others. What they prefer in the wild berry is a tartness which takes the edge off its sweetness and makes it more interesting, like a beauty spot on the face of a plain woman. Everybody seems to agree that wild berries make better pies.

The blueberry, properly speaking, is entirely American. Though blueberries are found in Europe now, they were imported from America because grouped berries are easier to pick than the single ones of Europe's closest relative of the blueberry, the bilberry. One American species, the mountain blueberry, *Vaccinium membranaceum,* is sometimes called a bilberry, but as it

BLUEBERRY. *Postal stamp, 1979, Poland*

grows mostly in British Columbia and Oregon, it is probable that Canadians transferred to it the name of the similar British fruit.

In Australia the name "blueberry" is given to the edible fruits of two trees, the blueberry ash and *Myoporum serratum*, a plant of many aliases: it is also called cockatoo bush, native juniper or native myrtle, and the fruit, besides blueberry, is called native currant or palberry. Neither of them is related to the American blueberry.

Alaskan red-backed voles are so partial to this fruit that most of them have blue teeth during the berry season.

BO
stands for

the **bobolink,** an engaging small bird eaten by the French and the Italians to the horror of the British and the Americans; for the **bobwhite,** or American quail, which is not quite the same as the European quail; for **bog butter,** food residues found in Neolithic sites about whose exact nature scientists are in dispute, and the **bog myrtle,** alias sweet gale, alias the buckbean, also used by Neolithic man, apparently for seasoning; for the **bogue,** a fish whose flavor varies greatly with its food, and one suspects that it eats well nowhere except off Malta, the only place where anybody bothers to fish for it; for the **bogong moth,** a dainty once appreciated by Australian aborigines; for the **boletus,** the most widely eaten wild mushroom in the world; for the **bonavist bean,** an important food in arid tropical regions where not much else will grow; for the **boncretien** (his spelling) **pear,** which Thomas Jefferson, who imported it from France, described as "really delicious and rare"; for **bones,** which Saharan nomads grind and mix with their food; for the **bone-dog,** which is also the dogfish, which does turn up in kitchens but oftener in college laboratories for dissection in Zoology I; for the **bonefish,** also called the banana fish because of its presence in the Caribbean; for the **bongo,** a large African antelope, which also turns up in kitchens but prefers to hide from hunters in dense forests; for the **bonito,** a name which covers a multitude of fins, and the **boops,** an only mildly palatable fish whose saucy-sounding name is actually Greek, meaning "ox-eyed"; for **borage,** an herb whose name is Arabic, from *abu rach*, "father of sweat"; for **boring clams,** tasty if you can get to them in the holes they are capable of drilling in cement piles or hard rocks; for the **Bosc pear,** named for a French botanist who took an unplanned crash course in living on wild fruits and vegetables when he had to hide in the forest of Montmorency during the Terror; for **Boston lettuce,** a variety which belongs to the butterheads, in other words a tastier, tenderer kind than the iceberg lettuce which is all the supermarkets want to sell us today; for **bottarga,** the roe of the Mediterranean gray mullet, a Sardinian specialty; for the **bo tree,** which, since it is a wild fig, ought to provide food to be eaten, but, since it is sacred to Buddhists (and even botanists call it *Ficus religiosa*), ought not, for fear of sacrilege, so Indian hill tribes compromise by eating the young leaf buds; for the **bowfin,** a living fossil which is all that remains of a family which flourished 130 million years ago, but is eaten all the same in the southeastern United States by persons with no respect for antiquity; and for the **bounce-berry,** otherwise the cranberry, the **boxberry,** otherwise the wintergreen, and the **boysenberry,** created in California in 1923 when Rudolph Boysen crossed raspberries with blackberries and got something else.

BR
stands for

bracken, or pasture brake, North America's commonest fern, which is eaten at the fiddlehead stage; for the **Brahma,** the largest domestic hen, and the **Brahman,** an Indian race of cattle imported to the United States to cope with the climate of the Gulf States and there crossed with local stock to produce two of America's top steers; for **brains,** sometimes incisive in function but neutral in taste, except when heightened by exotic seasoning, like that provided by the Emperor Heliogabalus, who served ostrich brains studded with small gold nuggets; for the **brambleberry,** or blackberry; for **bran,** a health-promoting constituent of wheat, which nature puts in and man takes out; for the **Brangus,** an American beef critter, produced by crossing the Indian Brahman with the Scotch Aberdeen Angus; for the **brant,** a small wild goose which rarely reaches the table; for the **Brazil nut,** so uncompromisingly tropical that it has refused to grow in Florida; for the **breadnut** (not to be confused with the breadfruit), the tree oftenest cultivated by the ancient

Mayans; for the **bream,** not tasty enough, in most opinions, to justify the trouble of the technique advocated by Alexandre Dumas, who wrote that "it is possible, by covering it with snow and putting in its mouth a piece of bread soaked in eau-de-vie, to transport it alive for great distances"; for the **Bresse chicken,** the best flavored in the world, which it took breeders three centuries to develop and merchandisers twenty-five years to destroy; for **brill,** a fish of which they say in Romagna, "Baked brill will make you miss a political meeting," which takes some doing in Italy; for the **broad bean,** which was the only kind the Old World knew before the discovery of the New World revealed the haricot; for the **broadbill,** another name for the swordfish; for the **bronze bream,** which, contrary to the adjectiveless bream which Dumas advises us to pack in snow, is held to be improved if it is laid in the sun for a while before eating; for **brood,** which in the vocabulary of the industry means an oyster a year old; and for **broom,** a sort of heather no longer used as food since the English stopped pickling its buds a couple of centuries ago.

And **BR** also stands for

BREADFRUIT. This South Seas plant was the cause of the saga of the sea known to everybody, and bestowed on its hero the nickname Breadfruit Bligh. This would have given him a good reputation had he not also been the villain of the mutiny on the *Bounty*.

The first European to report on breadfruit was William Dampier, who alternated between piracy and legitimate service, as the political winds blew, and navigated extensively in Oceania and Australasia, where an archipelago is named for him. He wrote about breadfruit in his *New Voyage Around the World* in 1697. This was by coincidence the birth year of Baron Admiral George Anson, the second European to notice breadfruit, who between 1740 and 1744 circumnavigated the world more or less by accident, since what he was really engaged in doing was fighting the Spanish. When his flagship, the *Centurion,* found itself becalmed without provisions in the Marianas, his crew, foraging for food, picked up some fifty breadfruit which had fallen from their trees and found them sufficient to sustain strength until the ship's stores could be replenished.

Thirty years later Captain Cook, under whom Bligh was then serving, rediscovered the breadfruit in Tahiti, but was not favorably impressed. He said its taste was "as disagreeable as that of a pickled olive generally is the first time it is eaten." The botanist who accompanied him was of a different opinion, and Cook's sailors, who ate it for several months during the voyage home, agreed with him, or at least he said they did. "No one of the whole ship's Company," he wrote, "complained when served with breadfruit in lieu of biscuit, and from the health and strength of whole nations, whose principal food it is, I do not scruple to call it one of the most useful vegetables in the world." He maintained that a breadfruit diet had cured sick sailors and advocated that it be grown in other areas of the world where food was scarce.

This advice was heeded by British planters in the West Indies who were growing sugarcane with slave labor and were interested in cheap foods which would nourish their workers with a minimum diversion of land from the more profitable function of nourishing sugarcane. The breadfruit tree is a prolific producer of food; a single tree yields in one season enough fruit to last a good-sized family for a full year. "Give me a good working woman and a breadfruit tree," the natives of St. Vincent say, "and I need never work again." The planters petitioned George III to dower them with breadfruit trees, and as a result Bligh was dispatched to the South Seas in 1787 to pick up young breadfruit trees and deliver them to the West Indies.

It was breadfruit rather than brutality which

BREADFRUIT *by Paul Gauguin (1848–1903).* Where Are You Going? *oil on canvas*

ultimately triggered the mutiny on the *Bounty*. Bligh's devotion to his mission provoked discontent in a crew anxious to get back to England when he lingered in the South Seas too long for their taste in order to select a thousand of the sturdiest saplings to bring back. The same concentration on what, after all, was the *raison d'être* of the voyage produced the final explosion when he reduced the crew's rations of drinking water to keep the trees alive. Mutiny broke out, Bligh was set adrift in an open boat and the precious trees were thrown overboard. A few years later Bligh made a second breadfruit voyage, this time successfully. In 1793 what looked like a floating forest sailed into Jamaica's Port Royal Harbor—Bligh's new ship, almost invisible under the plants, which had flourished during the trip (a full-grown breadfruit tree may reach a height of 60 feet). The transplanted breadfruit failed to measure up to the planters' hopes. Their slaves already had a starchy staple in the plantain, the vegetable banana, and preferred it to the import. Nevertheless, breadfruit eventually became an important food in the Caribbean and is grown today on virtually all its islands, and also on the mainland from Mexico to Brazil.

Opinions differ considerably on its taste, beginning with those of Captain Cook and his botanist. "I ate it boiled, which is the way it is frequently served," one sampler reported (the worst way, one might add, though it is the easiest). "It seemed to me completely flavorless." "The fruit boiled or baked is rather tasteless by itself," wrote W. W. Stafford in *Useful Plants of Guam*, "but with salt and butter or gravy it is a palatable as well as a nutritious article of diet." It was Alexandre Dumas who took the most trouble to situate the taste of the breadfruit exactly. He wrote that it tasted like the crustless part of fresh bread with a slight suggestion of artichoke plus Jerusalem artichoke. "The description by Alexandre Dumas is, in my opinion, quite correct," wrote one of my own correspondents, who knew it from the Pacific. "Breadfruit is among the best farinaceous foods of the tropics, with the taro and the sweet potato. I never tasted it when ripe." (It is normally picked slightly before maturity, with the flesh still white and firm; it goes off very quickly after ripening.) Another correspondent, from the other side of the world, wrote me: "Breadfruit is delicious! When we are in residence in our home on the island of Grenada in the Caribbean we eat breadfruit in preference to the potato."

It is possible that the persons who reported breadfruit to be tasteless confused it with its close relative, the jack tree, whose fruits are much larger, but insipid. This is easy to do. The feat has been achieved by the two most important encyclopedias in my possession, one French, the other American.

BROCCOLI. A celebrated cartoon in *The New Yorker*, which depicted a harassed mother trying to persuade a recalcitrant youngster to down his dinner, carried the caption (anonymous, but it was E. B. White who wrote it):

"It's broccoli, dear."
"I say it's spinach, and I say the hell with it."

This bit of folklore is worth recounting for two reasons: it exemplifies the lack of enthusiasm aroused by broccoli, which no doubt accounts for the fuzziness in writings about its history or its nature, since no one was very much interested in setting down precise details about it; and it is a witness to the eclipses which this worthy vegetable has suffered from time to time because, one supposes, of that lack of enthusiasm. The cartoon appeared when it did because it was the period at which the United States was discovering broccoli, beginning around 1925 or 1930, when many Americans seemed to think it was a newly developed plant. Actually John Randolph of Williamsburg wrote about it in 1775, in *A Treatise on Gardening by a Citizen of Virginia.* "The stems will eat like Asparagus," he explained, "and the heads like Cauliflower." But broccoli then succumbed to general indifference and disappeared from American tables, not to be rediscovered until the twentieth century. Its rediscovery for Boston came in a rather curious fashion, according to one of my correspondents, to whom I leave the responsibility for the story. She wrote that when Suffolk Downs racetrack opened in that city the lawn had not yet been seeded on

BROCCOLI. *Engraving from Theodore Francis Garrett:* The Encyclopaedia of Practical Cookery, *London, 1898*

opening day and the track gardener, an Italian, was instructed to plant it with something that would grow fast. He chose broccoli. "Result:" wrote my correspondent, "luscious green from the grandstand, hopeless for pedestrians. The vegetable markets were suddenly flooded with the unknown broccoli (and Oh, Lord, how our Irish cook made it taste like cabbage)!"

John Randolph's description suggests that he was talking about what most of us think of today when broccoli is mentioned, green sprouting or Italian broccoli, *Brassica oleracea italica*, whose tightly closed flower buds, dark green or purplish, and fleshy stems are the parts eaten. The public in general has abandoned another meaning of the word, designating a slow-growing type of cauliflower, *B. oleracea botrytis*. There was also once a third meaning, still current in France, according to which "broccoli" can mean the flower stalk which pushes upward from the center of the ordinary cabbage at the end of its life (it is edible).

The name of this plant informs us that the modern world received broccoli from Italy, for it is obviously an Italian word, adopted almost unchanged in other countries—the same in English, *brocoli* in French, *Brokkoli* in German. It is in Italy that we first hear of it, for the ancient Romans knew it. Apicius was noted for his skill in handling it, and Drusus, the son of Tiberius, was so fond of it that the emperor was obliged to warn him that he was overdoing. It would seem that this was already the sprouting broccoli of today, but where did the Romans get it? Some reference books describe it as a native of Asia Minor and the eastern Mediterranean, which does not accord with the fact that it grows best in moderate to cool climates. Broccoli is a form of CABBAGE, a remarkable plant which has branched out in a number of edible directions—kale, collards, kohlrabi, Brussels sprouts, cauliflower; cabbage is not Mediterranean either, though it became naturalized there early. It may be that the Romans themselves created broccoli from its ancestor, the cabbage, unless the Etruscans, who were better gardeners than they were, did it for them.

Broccoli was introduced into France by Catherine de' Medici. She married Henry II in 1533, and the first known use of the word *brocoli* in French is dated 1560. If this meant the sort of broccoli Catherine brought with her, it should have been sprouting broccoli, which was much improved in her native Tuscany during the Renaissance; but since many speakers of French today still understand this word as meaning the cabbage stalk, precision demands that one say broccoli cabbage or Calabrian broccoli for the sprouting variety. Similarly in England, where broccoli arrived about 1720, this word, or "white broccoli," often still designates winter cabbage.

Broccoli is one of the Western vegetables adopted by the Chinese, who have mastered the art of cooking it so that it comes out crisp and flavorful, which only Italians seem able to do in the West. Its taste has been described as more pronounced than that of cauliflower, less so than that of cabbage. Broccoli is packed with vitamins.

BRUSSELS SPROUTS. The name of this vegetable (also Brussels cabbage in French, but *Rosenkohl*, "rose cabbage," in Germany, obviously from its shape) would seem to point straight to its place of origin, but actually it is a mystery. This variety of the cabbage was developed somewhere in Europe, but whether it was really in Brussels is not on record. There is a tradition that Brussels sprouts were grown as early as 1200 in "Belgium"—there was no Belgium then, though there were Belgians—but the first description of them appeared only in 1587, and not until a century after that did they attract the attention of anybody but botanists.

Scientifically identified as *Brassica oleracea gemmifera*, Brussels sprouts are a winter vegetable, so hardy that I picked them on my Vermont farm long after freezing weather had set in, when everything else was inedible; but they cannot

BRUSSELS SPROUTS. *Engraving from Theodore Francis Garrett:* The Encyclopaedia of Practical Cookery, *London, 1898*

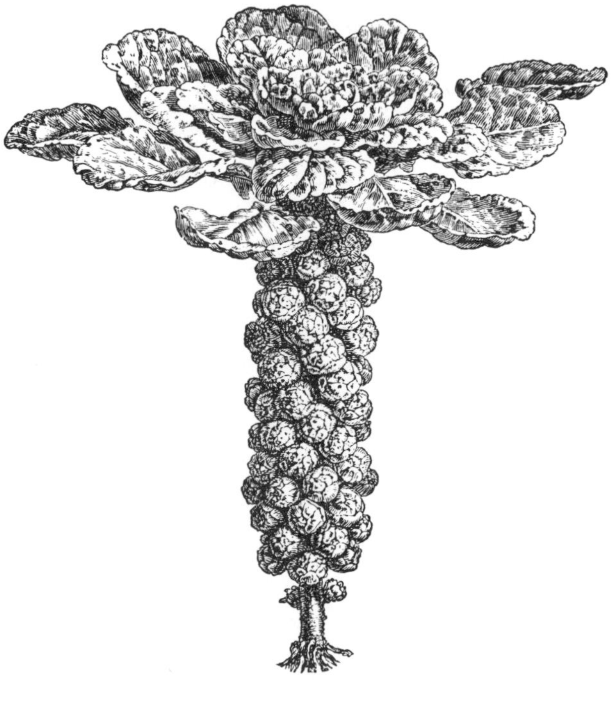

stand heat. The little tightly rolled balls, one and a half inches across at the most, which look like miniature heads of cabbage, grow on the stem between the leaves, and as you pick those above which have ripened first, others develop below them, making picking a continuous process which can continue for a month or two.

The Brussels sprout did not limp into England until the middle of the nineteenth century, but quickly became popular there; the British today are the largest consumers of Brussels sprouts. They devote to this crop, raised especially in Bedfordshire, six to seven times the acreage given to it in the United States, where California and New York grow most of it. Brussels sprouts are among the Western vegetables adopted in China.

BU
stands for

the **buah lye,** which is a Chinese pear; for the **buckthorn,** whose red berries appealed to Papago Indians for enlivening pemmican; for the **buffalo** (which is *not* the same animal as the bison), a potential source of food in Asia and Africa where there are often shortages, but which nevertheless is rarely eaten, and for the **buffalo berry,** a "harem plant," whose male shrubs grow surrounded by four to six females each; for the **bufflehead,** a duck whose flavor is sometimes tainted by the taste of the fish it eats; for the **buff Orpington,** a double-threat hen desirable both for its meat and its eggs; for the **bugleweed,** a MINT of which one eats not the leaves but the tubers; for the **bugloss,** a plant which, according to Robert Burton in his *Anatomy of Melancholy,* is one of only three foods which can be consumed without plunging the eater into deep depression, the other two being whey and lettuce; for **bulgur,** or **bulghur,** Middle Eastern cracked wheat also eaten by ancient Persians and modern health-food addicts; for the **bullace,** which one of our most respected encyclopedias thinks, erroneously, is the same thing as the damson plum; for the **bullfrog,** much sought for the table, since its meat is as good as that of other frogs and there is more of it; for the **bullhead,** the proof that a catfish by any other name would taste as sweet; for the **bull trout,** usually called the Dolly Varden trout; for **bullock's lungwort,** a fifth alias of the mullein; for the **bummalo,** a fish which has only to be salted to turn into Bombay duck; for the **bunchberry,** appreciated by wild-food enthusiasts; for the **bunting,** a small, defenseless bird eaten hard-heartedly by European gourmets; for the **burbot,** often described inaccurately as the only fresh-water member of the cod family; for the **burdock,** which may mean to you only the bothersome weed which affixes its burs to your clothing but is cultivated by the Japanese for its edible roots, stalks and leaves; for **burnet,** an herb little respected today, but in Pliny's time it was good form to apologize to it before pulling it up; for the **burro,** whose meat was once described by Euell Gibbons as delicious; for the **bush pig,** eaten in eastern and southern Africa; for the **buster,** a crab with a pressing desire to become soft-shelled; for the **butcher's-broom,** a plant the ancient Romans thought worth pickling but which has more recently been turned over to folk medicine; for the **Butley oyster,** found only at the mouth of a small stream of that name in Suffolk, England; for **butt,** a name used indiscriminately in the sixteenth century for several different flatfish; for the **butter bean,** an undersized lima; for the delicious **butter clam** of the Pacific coast, oftener called the Washington clam but sometimes the money clam because northwestern Indians are believed to have used its shells for money, as northeastern Indians did with quahog shells; for the **butterfly shell,** which is the coquina of Florida, given this name because of its beautiful variable colors; and for the **buzzard,** eaten by Prince Achille Murat, who will go down in history as an adventurous eater rather than as a dainty one.

And **BU** also stands for

BUCKWHEAT. A grain native to Central Asia, buckwheat was, in my opinion, introduced to Europe (which passed it on to North America) via the Saracens, though there are other theories. For instance, some French dictionaries explain its name, *sarrasin* (*sarraceno* in Spanish, *saracena* in Italian), not as an indication of its origin but as a reference to its dark color, recalling the swarthy complexions of the Moors (it is also called "black wheat" in French). However, Alexandre Dumas reported that "buckwheat was transported into Africa and introduced into Europe by the Moors of Spain"; and though Dumas is not the surest authority in the world, there are reasons for agreeing with him—or, alternatively, holding that Crusaders brought the plant back from Saracen country (it could have been both).

The ancients apparently did not know buckwheat; nearly all new additions to the European larder between classical times and the discovery of America came through the Saracens. Buckwheat is Asian; Asian foods almost without exception reached Europe through the Arabs, particularly those not too far removed from Asia

Buckwheat *by Pablo Picasso (1881–1973).* The Gourmet, *oil on canvas*

Minor, which would have been the case for a cereal sometimes called "tartar buckwheat." The countries which call buckwheat "Saracen wheat" are precisely those which suffered Saracen invasions and were in a position to know if it was the Saracens who brought in this food. It is perhaps significant that the first appearance of the word *sarrasin* for buckwheat in France is dated 1554, which, allowing for the time lag before new foods establish themselves, is about right for a Saracen donation of buckwheat to Europe whether it came from the Moors of Spain or returning Crusaders.

The species of buckwheat most widely cultivated throughout the world is *Fagopyrum esculentum*, with *F. tataricum* second. Human consumption of buckwheat is spotty (animals eat more of it), but there are buckwheat belts here and there, wherever damp, windy or cold climates encourage eating grain coarser and more rib-sticking than wheat, wherever robust eating is a habit, or wherever the soil is better suited to buckwheat than to more refined grains. A fast grower, often sowed on the same land after some other crop has been harvested, buckwheat can produce two crops in one season on good soil when conditions are favorable; but it is rarely planted on good soil, for when such land is available it is more likely to be preempted by wheat, barley or other grains which give heavier yields. However, on poor, rocky soils, buckwheat thrives where most cereals would fail abjectly.

Buckwheat is therefore an important element in the diet of lower Brittany (damp, windy, granitic soil); of Finland (cold); of northern China (cold); of the Pennsylvania Dutch country (robust eaters); of Styria in Austria (robust eaters, plus cold winters and the mountainous terrain buckwheat likes); and, for the same last two reasons, the central plateau of France and the Italian Alps of the South Tyrol and northern Lombardy, where northern Italy's ubiquitous polenta, usually made with cornmeal, is of buckwheat flour.

Buckwheat is impossible for bread, producing a dry, crumbly, tasteless loaf; in buckwheat country the grain is often eaten as porridge, but its most successful avatar is the pancake. Everywhere in the world buckwheat is considered better than barley as poultry food. It is used extensively to fatten livestock. Britain today grows almost no buckwheat except as a grazing crop for sheep or to feed pheasants, for which buckwheat is deemed particularly desirable. It is also grown not for its own sake but as a smother crop to get rid of weeds or for plowing under as green manure. When so planted, farmers often set out beehives among the handsome, nodding, white-flowered heads of buckwheat: buckwheat honey is richly flavorful.

BUSTARD. The largest land bird of Europe, which sometimes exceeds twenty-five pounds in weight, the bustard has a range which also includes all of the temperate and warm regions of Asia and Africa (excluding the Sahara) and even Australia. It may have originated in Africa, where it reaches its greatest size—*Choriotis kori* attains a height of nearly five feet as compared with not much more than three and a half for *Otis tarda*, the European great or bearded bustard—and where it is most widespread, with its principal habitat in Senegal, where it is called *korossobounti*.

"Bustard" comes from the French *outarde*, which comes from the Gallic *austarda*, which comes from the Latin *avis tarda*, "slow bird." The bustard's flight is heavy and it needs a long take-off run with wings outspread to work up sufficient momentum to get off the ground; hunting dogs have been known to reach it before it could rise.

BUSTARD. *Drawing by Ad Cameron from* Birds, *New York, 1976*

The bird makes up for this disadvantage by frequenting open fields or dry, even desert, terrain, where it can spot enemies from a long distance. Thus it had to be hunted in Europe from movable blinds, sometimes built ingeniously in the shape of cows.

Increase in the range and accuracy of firearms reduced the bustard's advantage of distance, at the same time that urban encroachment diminished the expanses of open land able to support so large a bird. As a result the great bustard has disappeared from England, France and some other western European countries, from which it migrated annually to Spain or North Africa, but it is still occasionally found in Spain, Greece, Italy and Sardinia, where it does not migrate, since the climate is tolerable for it all year round. France still has the smaller little bustard, O. *tetrax*, whose official name is *canepetière*, pronounced unblushingly and unhesitatingly even by provincial spinsters, without a thought for the meaning of the word—"farting duck," from the noise it makes in flight.

Choriotis nigripes is the bustard of northwest India, C. *arabs* that of North Africa and the region just south of the Sahara. In South Africa the bustard is called the pauuw, the largest being the great pauuw. C. *australis* is known to Australians as the plains turkey; it is becoming extremely rare because it has been overhunted, both for sport and for the table. All the bustards belong to the Otides, of the same zoological order as cranes, and all of them are good eating.

It is agreed that the breast meat of the African bustard tastes like the white meat of domestic poultry, but there is a difference of opinion about the legs, variously described as recalling golden plover or hare. The European great bustard has a high reputation for delicacy of flesh, like the pheasant, but its meat is a little solid and heavy, so gourmets prefer the finer, lighter meat of the little bustard. Their favorite morsel is the drumstick.

BUTTERNUT. A member of the same genus as the walnut, the butternut is also called the North American white walnut or long walnut. Its habitat is northeastern America, but it pushes a little south, to Georgia, and a little west, to North Dakota, from the region where it is most abundant. An outer light-green husk encloses a hard, rough, walnutlike shell; the kernel is oily, which accounts for its name, and has an agreeable rich and sometimes slightly spicy flavor.

This description does not quite accord with what was called a butternut in central Vermont, of which I gathered more than I could eat from trees possibly wild. The husk was indeed light green, but gave under pressure from the fingers, for there was no hard inner shell; it had very little taste. I have been unable to identify it, and wonder if it may not have been a local sport. The consistency of the meat was that of hard soap, which would justify the name "butternut," whether it was related to the official species or not. For a similar reason, the Brazil nut and souari nut, both South American, are also sometimes called butternuts.

BUTTERNUT. *Drawing from Charles Sprague Sargent:* The Silva of North America, *Boston, 1895*

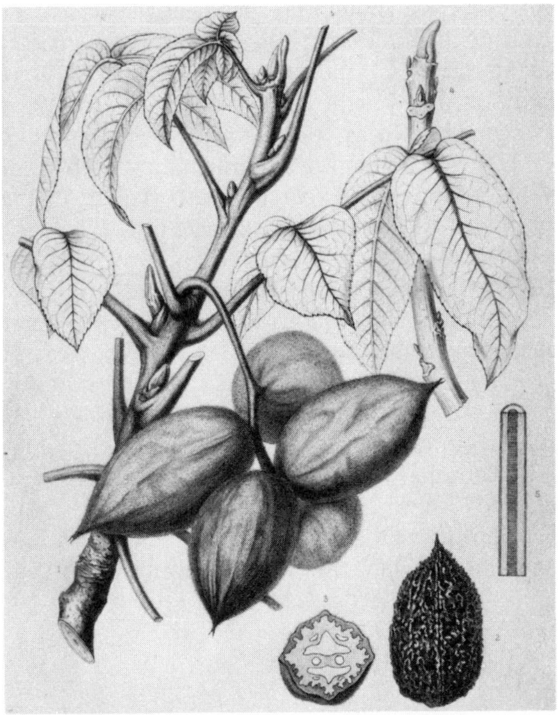

C

CASTRO, JOSUÉ DE: *The history of man from the beginning has been the history of his struggle for his daily bread.*

CAB
stands for

the **cabbage palm,** whose whole tree has to be sacrificed to provide the expensive dish known as "millionaire's salad"; and, of course,

CAB also stands for

CABBAGE. It is often difficult to determine the origin of man's oldest foods, but in the case of the cabbage we are fortunate enough to have been provided with detailed documentation. According to the ancient Greeks, Lycurgus, king of the Thracian Edonians, was caught by Dionysos in the act of pulling up grapevines. The god of wine tied him to a grape stalk to await punishment, in anticipation of which Lycurgus wept profusely, and with reason, for Dionysos, who was not known as "the raging god" for nothing, had him first blinded and then torn limb from limb. Meanwhile, Lycurgus's tears, falling to the ground, had engendered cabbages.

Modern botanists have for some reason been disinclined to accept this explanation and have sought clues elsewhere in the attempt to find out where the cabbage came from. We first hear of it in the Mediterranean basin, but it is obviously not a plant of that warm region, for it grows best in cool, moist climates. It has been suggested that the cabbage originated in cool northern and central Europe, particularly along the coasts, where it benefited from damp air—the area where it is most widely grown and consumed today, in the British Isles, Scandinavia, northern coastal and mountainous (hence cooler) France, central Europe from the Baltic to the southern slopes of the Alps, and the Slavic countries.

The probability that the original home of the cabbage was along the coasts of temperate northern Europe provides ammunition for those who maintain that the ancestor of the cabbage still exists in sea kale (*Crambe maritima*), which does indeed grow in a native state in this area. It resembles certain forms of loose-leaved cabbage and is popularly called "wild cabbage" in some places and "sea cabbage" by the French.

The theory that the cabbage originated in northern Europe is borne out by the direction in which it seems to have spread, apparently southward and eastward into the Mediterranean basin. If it had arrived through the Middle East, as some authorities have suggested, it should have been known to the Hebrews; but it is not mentioned in the Bible. This might also explain the fact that the ancient Greeks, farthest from its home base, accepted it with more reluctance than the Romans, one step closer. The Greeks ate a good deal of it, because it was filling and easy to come by, but they regarded it more as nourishment than as a treat, though Pythagoras, exceptionally, recommended it strongly to his disciples; but Pythagoras was a food faddist, almost a complete vegetarian. The cabbage certainly did not appear to be a symbol of luxurious eating in the exchange between Diogenes and a young courtier, to whom the philosopher remarked, "If you lived on cabbage, you would not be obliged to flatter the

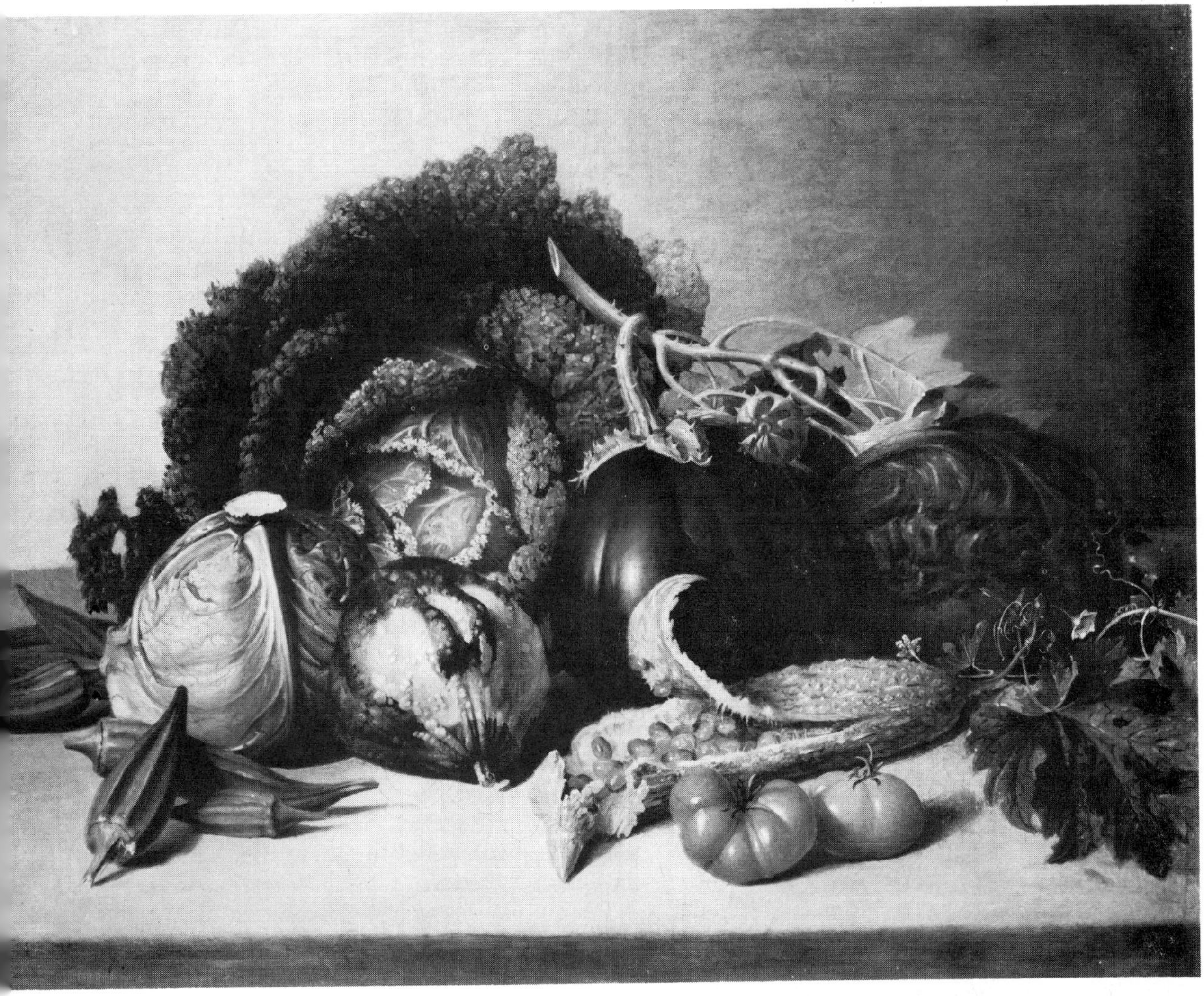

CABBAGE *by James Peale (1749–1831).* Balsam Apple and Vegetables, *oil on canvas*

powerful." "If you flattered the powerful," the young man retorted, "you would not be obliged to live on cabbage."

For the Romans, however, the cabbage was in such demand that it was at first too expensive for any but the well-to-do. It was thus a profitable vegetable for farmers, who gave it special attention. They succeeded in producing cabbages weighing as much as twenty pounds and seem to have developed most of the many variations on the theme of cabbage which we know today. Cato and Pliny were complimentary to the cabbage, and so were the Emperors Tiberius and Claudius. The latter (a glutton and a drunkard, but, it is true, not a gourmet) once convoked the Senate to vote on the question of whether any dish was better than corned beef and cabbage; the Senate, which knew what was expected of it, dutifully decided that none was.

The Middle Ages were not much given to eating vegetables until a breakthrough was achieved in the fourteenth century by Taillevent, chef to Charles VI of France, who served a banquet in which he dared insert a vegetable in the first course; the one he chose was cabbage. At a guess, it would have been the most esteemed variety of the time, Senlis cabbage, which has disappeared, but which, it was said, gave off, when cut open, an odor more agreeable than that of musk or amber. The loss of Senlis cabbage was compensated for by the introduction into France of new tasty types of Italian cabbage by the cooks of Catherine and Marie de' Medici.

Besides being one of the oldest cultivated vegetables, cabbage is also one of the most versatile. In addition to those plants which the layman recognizes as cabbage—head cabbage, Milan cabbage, red cabbage—there are others which in appearance and taste are so different that it does not occur to most persons to call them cabbages—yet they are. BROCCOLI, BRUSSELS SPROUTS, CAULIFLOWER, COLLARDS, KALE and KOHLRABI are not only all cabbages, they even belong to the same species, *Brassica oleracea.* These different plants were not developed by hybridization or by mutation, but simply by encouraging the development of one element or another already present in the original plant. Any leaves with curling veins, like those of the cabbage, can be persuaded to form heads, so from what was probably a collard-like plant, the encouragement of this tendency produced head cabbage—Milan, Savoy, bell and similar varieties. Cabbage contains anthocyanin, which tends to turn plants blue, red or shades in between; development of this element produced red cabbage. By emphasizing the ability of cabbage to form budding heads at the junction of stem and leaves, Brussels sprouts were created. Concentration on the flower resulted in both cauliflower (centripetal inflorescence) and broccoli (centrifugal inflorescence). Swelling pith gave rise to kohlrabi.

We escape from *B. oleracea* with Chinese cabbage, of which the principal varieties are pe-tsai (*B. pekinensis*), a heading cabbage whose tightly closed leaves rise to a point (it has now become important in tropical Africa and Madagascar); celery cabbage, which looks a little like Romaine lettuce, grows like celery and has a thick, yellowish-white stalk about fifteen inches long (the best comes from the region of Shantung); and the latter's close relative, bok choy, which also grows like celery and has a thick white stalk and drooping, dark-green leaves which make it look like kale.

Though unromantic botanists explain the color of red cabbage (blue cabbage, *Blaukraut,* in German) by its chemical composition, the French have a prettier story to account for it. In the days when unmarried mothers were considered to have disgraced themselves, an obviously pregnant young woman of Périgueux returned from the fields balancing an enormous cabbage on her swollen stomach, a spectacle which obliged her to run the gauntlet of the sort of pleasantries you can easily imagine. The charitable bishop of Périgueux happened to pass by. Taking the cabbage from her, he wrapped it in a fold of his mantle and, taking her hand, escorted her to her door. There he handed back the cabbage; it had taken on the color of his episcopal robes.

CAC
stands for

the **cacao,** whose beans were used as money by Mexicans and Central Americans before they became worth more money when converted into chocolate; and for the **cactus,** which the Indians were eating when the conquistadors arrived, but when the Spaniards tried to follow suit "they all fell ill, with headaches and fever."

CAE to CAJ
stand for

Caesar's mushroom, *Amanita caesarea,* one of the most delicious of all mushrooms, which belongs to the same genus as *A. phalloides,* the most poisonous of all mushrooms; for the **cahow,** a small edible sea bird, rendered extinct, it was believed, about 1600 when it was eaten avidly in a time of famine, but which reappeared in 1951, in the Bermudas, was again rendered nearly extinct in 1962 from food polluted by DDT, but has begun to increase again since DDT was banned; and for the **cajan pea,** one of the most valuable of tropical food plants and among the first to be cultivated, as is attested by its presence in Egyptian tombs dating from 2400 B.C.

CAL
stands for

the **calabar bean,** eaten only by tropical Africans accused of serious crimes who, if they die from its poison, are deemed to have been guilty; for **calabash,** a word given to various gourds eaten in antiquity whose identification is hazy, so we had better not use this word to translate **calabaza,** the West Indian green pumpkin, which is more exactly a squash; for **calamondin,** the name given in Australia to a citrus fruit believed there to be the kumquat, but it isn't; for the **calico clam,** which is the coquina, the **calico crab,** which is the lady crab, and the **calico fish,** which is the black crappie; for the **California mussel,** which makes no attempt to distinguish itself from other mussels except by wearing a light-brown shell; for **calipash** and **calipee,** respectively the fat which comes from the upper shell and the lower shell of the turtle; for the **callaloo,** a spinach-like vegetable said to have been brought to the West Indies by slaves from Africa; for **calves' feet,** from which housewives in more strenuous days made excellent jelly, and **calves' heads,** confronted bravely in those times by women who would quail before them nowadays; and for the **Calville,** one of the world's great apples.

CAM
stands for

the **camaron,** an African prawn which, according to some writers, gave its name to the Cameroons, unless it was the other way around; for **camas,** a starchy root from which American Indians made flour; for the **campanula,** which, according to Gerard, "is not used in Physicke, but only for a sallet root boiled and eaten, with oile, vinegar, and pepper"; and for **camphor,** used for food in China and India, and for mothballs in the West.

And **CAM** also stands for

CAMEL. Arthur Weigall, the British Egyptologist, remarked that "the fact that a camel has yellow teeth, a harelip, a hump, and corns, and suffers from halitosis, places the poor creature beyond the range of ordinary sympathy." The *Encyclopaedia Britannica* quotes Sir Francis Palgrave as writing of the camel: "He is from first to last an undomesticated animal, rendered serviceable by stupidity alone, without much skill on his master's part or any cooperation on his own, save that of extreme passiveness. Neither attachment nor even habit impress him; never tame, though not wide-awake enough to be exactly wild." The *Britannica* adds a note of dissent to this. It thinks the camel *is* tame, but finds that "the tameness of the camel is essentially the tameness of stupidity," raising the nice question of just how much intellect is required for the task of being a camel.

These are all Occidental opinions. The Egyptians, who are well acquainted with the animal, explain that the camel's supercilious expression is justified by an undeniable superiority. Of the hundred names of God, they say, the wisest human being knows only ninety-nine; the camel knows the hundredth. The first men to eat camel were probably American Indians. Bones of camels, ancestors of the present animal, have been found in kitchen middens in Nevada; according to carbon-14 dating they are approximately 25,000 years old. There do not seem to have been any earlier similar finds in Central Asia, of which many respected reference books suggest that the camel, or at least the two-humped Bactrian camel, is a native. It is my own guess, based on the distribution of the animal and the dates at which its arrival has been reported in different parts of the world, that it started in North America and migrated to Asia, dying out in America; this would have been toward the end of the Pliocene epoch, about a million years ago, allowing the camel plenty of time to pass itself off as an Asian animal.

If the first consumers of camel meat were American Indians, the second were the ancient Chinese, who are known to have eaten camel, and the third, those who eat it today, the Arabs of the Middle East and North Africa. When it reached this part of the world, the Hebrews passed it up. "These ye shall not eat," says Leviticus 11:4, "of them that chew the cud, or of them that divide the hoof; as the camel, because he cheweth the cud, but divideth not the hoof; he is unclean unto you." Herodotus reports that the Persians thought camel a festive dish. They liked to celebrate birthdays "with a dinner of special magnificence," of which the *pièce de résistance* would be "an ox or a horse or a camel or a donkey baked whole." In Greece, camel was sufficiently esteemed to be served on royal tables, according to Aristophanes, and Aristotle praised it highly. The Roman Emperor Heliogabalus thought the heel the tastiest part. The famous gourmet Marcus Gavius Apicius offered at one of his banquets a dish compounded of camels' heels and flamingos' tongues. In the time of Galen, camel meat was much prized as excellent for the health.

The Arabs, so far as is possible, eat camel only when it is young and its flesh tender. A young

CAMEL *by Nancy Graves.* Camels, *wood, steel, burlap, polyurethane, animal skin, wax, oil paint, 1968–69*

camel, roasted whole on a spit over a fire built in a hole in the ground, can provide the meat for that gala feast known as a *méchoui,* which for most implies mutton; actually the Arab word means simply "roast," without specifying any particular kind of meat.

With the development of modern communications and modern agricultural machinery, the camel has declined in importance as a pack animal and gained relatively as a source of food. There is a greater incentive to breed camels for eating, and it is therefore easier to obtain good-quality meat for the kitchen than it is to find animals of great endurance for desert caravans. In Cairo's Imbaba market, most of the 35,000 camels sold yearly are meat animals; they are the ones which bring the best prices. At a time when working animals could be bought for $320, a good eating animal would fetch $460.

As for the taste of camel meat, here is a report from one of my correspondents, Dr. Lloyd Cabot Briggs, an anthropologist who has spent a good deal of time in the Sahara: "Camel meat [has] a distinctive taste which shows up in a peculiar way. While you're eating it, it tastes just like rather ordinary beef or relatively tasty veal (depending on age), but when you've finished and run your tongue around your mouth, you suddenly discover a slightly sweetish after-taste, like horse but not quite so much so, very faint, but definite."

CAN
stands for

the **Canada goose,** the largest (and perhaps the handsomest) of all geese, and the **Canadian potato,** which is the Jerusalem artichoke; for the **Cancale,** one of the finest oysters of France; for the **candleberry,** or bayberry, the **candlefish,** or eulachon, and the **candlenut,** or lumbang, kemiri or kukui; for the **candleplant** or **candlewick,** our sixth and seventh synonyms for the mullein; for the **canna,** today prized as a flower, but in ancient times and by South American Indians for the nourishing quality of its rhizomes; for the **cantaloupe,** which the president of France, Vincent Auriol, described as "the king of melons"; and for the **canvasback duck,** "certainly worthy of its reputation," wrote Captain Frederick Marryat, a man difficult to please, about 1840, when it was plentiful.

CAP
stands for

capelin, a relative of the smelt, which in happier days piled up along the beaches of Newfoundland so thickly that they were taken by driving a farm cart into the water and shoveling the fish into it; and for the **capon,** a domestic fowl with a villainous temper, out of resentment, one supposes, against the outrage practiced upon it to give it such tender, luxurious flesh.

And **CAP** also stands for

CAPERCAILLIE. Love can be fatal to animals other than man; one of its victims is the capercaillie, the second-largest game bird of Europe, of which the male may reach a length of 34 inches and a weight of 12 pounds (15 has been recorded). It is a member of the grouse family.

During the seasons when the capercaillie has his wits about him, he is one of the most invulnerable of game birds. His sharp eyes can spy a moving hunter before he gets into shooting range, and he is off with strokes of the strong wings which make him a remarkably swift flyer. But in April and May, love plays its baneful tricks. During the courting season the capercaillie, high-perched on a lofty limb, gives voice to his mating call, stretching his neck to its full limit and, unwarily, closing his eyes. Stalkers move up foot by foot during his blind moments until they are within range; then they wait for him to close his eyes once more, and fire.

These tactics are Teutonic, used in Germany and Austria, where the bird is called the *Auerhahn.* They are disdained in Scotland, where beaters frighten the birds from the woods into the moors, where it takes a swift gun to bring

CAPERCAILLIE. *Steel engraving from John Wood:* Our Living World, *New York, 1885*

down a capercaillie bursting suddenly from the shelter of the trees. Scots get fewer birds, but they get tastier ones. They hunt in the late summer and fall, when the animal is succulent from its spring and summer fare of wild fruit, bilberries and aromatic vegetation. The Teutonic hunters bring down birds which since the first heavy snowfalls of the preceding winter have fed exclusively on pines—needles, cones, seeds—giving the flesh an odor of turpentine, which can be weakened but not quite eradicated by soaking the bird in milk for several hours before cooking.

Killed according to the Scottish rite, the capercaillie is one of the most delicious game birds of Europe; some would say unhesitatingly *the* most delicious. Its delicate meat tastes like pheasant, but is finer and whiter.

CAPERS. The piquant, elegant, tasty little beads known as capers are the pickled unopened flower buds of a trailing shrub which since antiquity has been giving a lift to foods otherwise insipid. Alexandre Dumas wrote that the caper came originally from Asia, which may not have been far off if he meant Asia Minor. Another authority says it originated "in the Orient," which covers, cautiously, a little too much ground; and still another states that its homeland is Italy. I suggest that it was none of these, but that unlikeliest of areas for the birth of vegetation, the Sahara Desert. *Capparis spinosa* is clearly designed for desert existence and is indeed known popularly in North Africa as the Sahara caper tree. It remains green, its stems and leaves juicy with sap, even when the soil around its roots is completely dried up; it is believed that the leaves absorb moisture from the humidity of the night air, which contains enough water vapor for its needs even in the driest desert. The plant requires strong sunlight. Olivier de Serres found that out in the sixteenth century; in his *Theatre of Agriculture and the Family of the Fields* he told how he set out his caper plants "outside the orchard, desiring that they should be exposed to full sunlight, since they would be in danger of stifling [in the shade] of the trees." A great many of the 170 species of capers grow in the Sahara and adjoining regions.

Capers are first heard of in ancient Greece, where they were a little slow to arrive. They are not listed among the first spices the Greeks knew, but since they were introduced into France by Greeks about 600 B.C., they were by then presumably known in Greece itself (but not necessarily, for the Greeks in question came from colonies in Asia Minor). The Romans, however, were acquainted with capers as far back as their

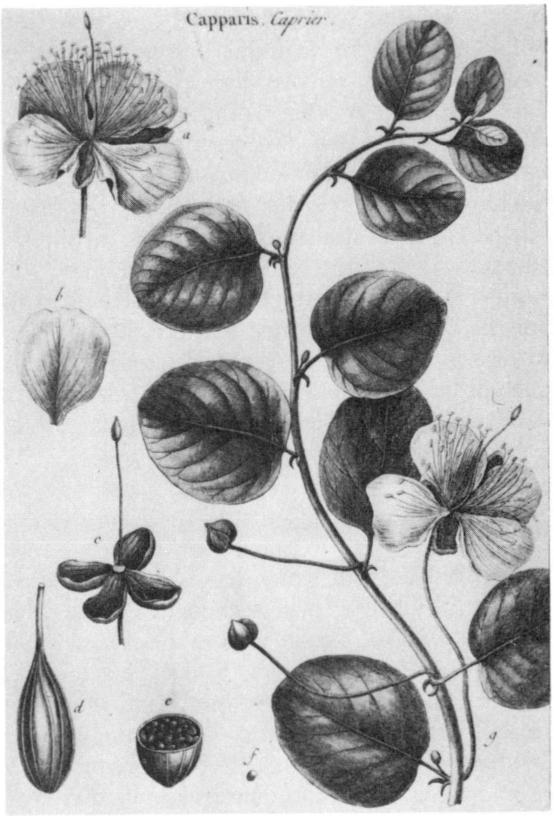

CAPERS. *Drawing from Jean-Baptiste Lamarck:* Encyclopédie méthodique botanique, *Paris, 1823*

written records reach.

"Capers should be gathered before they have fully developed," Brillat-Savarin ruled, and contemporary practice agrees with him; the most prized capers are those which are least developed. The world's best are probably those grown in the French department of the Var, where the plants are set out in terraces fully exposed to the sun; they are picked over every two days to catch the buds at their earliest edible stage. This hand labor is necessarily expensive, so there is a tendency to replace capers by substitutes whenever price is a factor, as it usually is.

CAR
stands for

the **carambola,** or star apple, an agreeable tropical fruit which has to be eaten where it grows, for it is too perishable to travel; for **cardamom,** a ginger-like seasoning which is the world's second most expensive spice, after saffron; for the **cardon cactus,** which may reach a height of 200 feet, and produces golden fruit whose seeds used to be toasted and eaten by the Indians of Baja California; for the **cardoon,** a close relative of the artichoke, eaten in the Middle Ages especially by women who wished to make sure that their children would be boys; for the **caribou,** which enabled man to survive the Ice Ages; for the **carnation,** seldom eaten nowadays except in mustard, but used often two centuries ago; for the **carob,** possibly the "locusts and wild honey" which comprised the diet of John the Baptist in the desert, the flat, leathery pods representing the locusts and the sugary pulp they contain the wild honey; for the **carpenter's weed,** alias the yarrow; for the **carpet shell,** which is the very tasty clam known in France as the *palourde,* apparently not present on the American side of the Atlantic; and for **carrageen,** also known as Irish moss, which is not moss but a seaweed.

And **CAR** also stands for

CARAWAY (with which let us couple **cumin**). All my life I had known, or thought I knew, what caraway was—a small, almost black, crescent-shaped seed whose taste I disliked, encountered in the United States in rye bread and in France in Munster cheese. Scored longitudinally with lighter-colored stripes, its pattern reminded me of a potato bug. It was an object without mystery—without mystery, that is, until I attempted to pin it down for this dictionary. I discovered then that it is almost inextricably entangled with the similar spice known as cumin; and to make it worse, the French *carvi,* which it seems to me ought to be caraway, is referred to by the French themselves as field cumin or mountain cumin and seems in practice to be tossed about cheerily between caraway and cumin with little regard for fine botanical or gastronomic distinctions. German is no better. *Kümmel* means caraway; it also means cumin. Take your choice.

CARAWAY. *Photograph from* Squibb's Atlas of the Official Drugs, *Squibb and Sons, 1919*

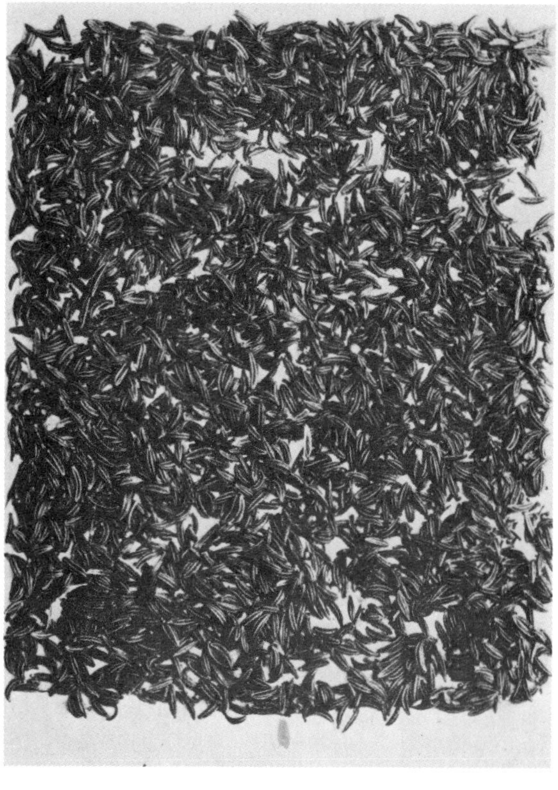

This confusion goes all the way back to classical times, when the ancients made no very exact distinction between caraway and cumin, both of which they knew. In the face of this long-standing mingling of identities, I will state diffidently that the evidence seems to me to point to caraway as *Carum carvi* and to cumin as *Cuminum cyminum,* which is indeed what most botanists will tell you. This does not solve all the problems, for there are about twenty species of *Carum,* and though the reference books say there is only one of *Cuminum,* I have had on my desk at one time three types of seeds which to the naked eye were recognizably different, all of which had been presented to me as cumin. No doubt they were subspecies or varieties.

Caraway, we are sometimes told, originated in warm countries of the Orient. This seems unlikely, and may be the result of its confusion with cumin, which did come from there—Central Asia and Turkestan, according to some authorities, Syria and Egypt according to others. Caraway has characteristics attuned to cool climates; the oldest caraway seeds found were discovered in Neolithic lake settlements in Switzerland. In France it grows in mountains high enough up to permit it to enjoy cool weather, in the Vosges and the Alps. Indeed, the ancient Romans may first have received caraway from Gaul, where it was used to season sausages, which the Romans imported. The spice they brought in from Galicia, in Spain, where it also grew in the mountains, was probably caraway also. It is a fair guess that when the Romans spoke of chewing the seeds of *careum* to banish bad breath, they meant caraway, better adapted for this purpose; and it was probably also caraway of which they ate the roots. Caraway roots are still eaten in some countries, but as far as I know, cumin roots never.

On the other hand, the spice the Romans imported from Egypt was probably cumin, long established in the eastern Mediterranean. Mycenae was using cumin seeds for seasoning two thousand years before the Christian era, and seeds of cultivated cumin are said to have been found in even earlier tombs of the Pharaohs. Both Egyptians and Hebrews sold the whole plant in herb markets, and the Bible informs us that cumin was used in soups, stews and bread. If you happen to have come across, in *The Reapers* of Theocritus, the line "Thou'lt cut thy finger, niggard, a-splitting cumin," it reflects a Greek saying which stems from the small size of the seed. For the ancient Greeks, an avaricious man was one who "divides everything, even cumin seeds."

While caraway had been known to more northerly parts of Europe since the beginning of history, cumin does not seem to have left the Mediterranean area until shortly after the beginning of the Christian era. Charlemagne urged its planting in the imperial domains, and St. Hildegarde, for once thinking gastronomically rather than medically, advised that cheese would taste better if dusted with pepper and cumin seeds. In 1393, the anonymous author of *Le Ménagier de Paris* gave a recipe for chicken flavored with cumin. But it was probably caraway which in central Europe was put in bread served at wakes, presumably because its black color was appropriate for mourning, giving rise to the very old German expression *Kümmel Brot, unser Tod,* "Caraway bread, our death."

In comparing the two spices, some connoisseurs describe cumin as more subtle. A commoner estimate is that cumin has a more pronounced savor, with a strong odor resembling fennel and a taste which is heavily aromatic, hot, spicy, piquant, sharp and bitter. The least complimentary description which I have come across says that the taste of cumin approaches that of coriander and resembles that of the bedbug—without specifying in what circumstances this particular gourmet sampled bedbugs.

CARP. The carp possesses two peculiar properties: whereas most fish swallow their food whole, the carp chews what it eats; and when the water in which it lives becomes poor in oxygen or, in hot weather, dries up, it gulps in a bubble of air, holds it in its mouth next to the gills and, as long as the gills remain moist, can abstract oxygen from the air as well as from water. It is also perhaps the most important freshwater food fish in the world.

There is only one species of carp, *Cyprinus carpio,* but it covers some 1500 varieties. There are green carp, rosy carp, blue carp, white carp, brown carp, yellow carp, golden carp, lake carp, pond carp, river carp, and the man-bred leather carp and mirror carp, respectively the second tastiest and the tastiest of all these varieties.

The carp is a native of eastern Asia, probably of China. A freshwater fish incapable of traversing the barrier of saltwater oceans, it was introduced deliberately into the other areas where it is found today—Europe, Africa (not including Madagascar), North America, and some parts of Indonesia, though not in the Celebes. There are no carp in South America or Australia.

CARP. *Illuminated page from the* Belles heures *of Jean, Duke of Berry, France, 15th century*

Nobody knows when the carp reached the West. It was unknown to the ancient Greeks and Romans. *Larousse Gastronomique* says that it was imported into England about 1614, but it must already have been familiar there in 1603 or 1604, when Shakespeare wrote in *Hamlet,* "Your bait of falsehood takes this carp of truth." There is a record of the existence of carp in Augsburg, Germany, dating from 1558, when its price was four times that of beef. France is often reported to have received the carp thanks to the cooks of Catherine de' Medici, but nearly a century and a half before her arrival the menu of a dinner given by the Abbé de Lagny for the bishop of Paris listed among its dishes "carp from the Marne." The carp could hardly have reached America earlier than the seventeenth century; it was not universally welcomed there, for it was accused of destroying water plants and crowding out fish considered more valuable. It never gained much favor in America, but perhaps it may some day if its capacity for surviving by swallowing air enables it to outlive other fish killed by pollution—assuming that when water runs out of oxygen there will still be some left in the air.

Unlike America, Europe received the carp as a welcome gift which supplied an easily accessible source of food. Tourists shown the carp ponds of old monasteries and châteaux today may look upon them as adornments of the grounds, but their original function was alimentary, not decorative. Fish farming provided one of the major food resources of abbeys and manor houses. Carp, basically vegetarian in their native state, are omnivorous when the opportunity is afforded them, and in older days they were carefully fed to ready them for the table. "Raspins and Chippins of Bread, or almost any scraps from the table," says an old manual, "placed under a cask of strong Beer and Ale, in such a manner that the droppings of the Liquor may fall among them, is excellent Food for Carp. Two quarts of this is sufficient for thirty and if they are fed Morning and Evening it will be better than once a day only."

The cultivation of carp is still being actively pursued. In addition to their native China, carp are raised intensively on flooded pastureland in Taiwan, where they are called grass carp. In the Piedmont region of Italy, carp are a by-product of rice production, released in the same fields which are flooded for that crop. They are raised in France, which does not much care for them, to be shipped alive in cistern cars or boats to Hamburg, where they are made into that city's famous carp pâté. Carp ponds are a feature of many Israeli kibbutzim.

Carp grow rapidly and to a considerable size. One hundred pounds has occasionally been reached in Europe, but the giant carp of India and Burma regularly outdo this; the mahseer of the great Indian rivers reach 120 pounds. According to Alexandre Dumas, the largest carp in history was one caught in the Ukraine in 1711 which weighed 154 pounds. The size reached by carp probably accounts for exaggerated stories of their longevity. I once heard a guide at Fontainebleau inform tourists that the carp they were feeding had been alive in the time of François I, more than four centuries ago, while at the Château de Chantilly it is maintained more modestly that the carp seen there were fed by the Grand Condé himself, a mere 300 years ago. The fact is that all the monastery and château carp ponds were drained regularly for cleaning, all the fish were harvested and the ponds restocked when they were filled again. However, it is believed that carp can live as long as 150 years.

The carp is a symbol of strength in Poland, a symbol of perseverance in China and a symbol of virility, strength and endurance in Japan. Ever since the Middle Ages it has been a traditional Christmas Eve dish in many European countries.

"*La carpe se plaît dans la vase,*" says the *Petit Larousse,* in a delightfully lapidary sentence: "The carp is happy in the mud." It does indeed often inhabit sluggish waters—lakes, ponds, slowly moving rivers and canals—often preferring areas of tangled vegetation and muddy bottoms. Austrian housewives rid them of any muddy taste by buying them alive and keeping them in the bathtub for several days before cooking them. Alexandre Dumas proposed a different method: "Make the fish which has just been taken from the water drink a glass of strong vinegar and at the very instant you will see a sort of thick perspiration spread itself over its whole body, which you will remove by scaling it. When it is dead, its flesh will become firm and have as good a taste as if it had been caught in running water." He gives no instructions for persuading a reluctant carp to accept a swig of vinegar.

CARROT. Edible roots must have been one of the very first foods of man; we can easily imagine prehistoric men, even before they learned to fish or hunt, grubbing up roots from the ground. One of them was the carrot.

A native of Afghanistan, the carrot was already being cultivated in the Mediterranean region long before the Christian era. Greek writers mention it as early as 500 B.C., but neither the Greeks nor the Romans thought highly of it; the Romans preferred the turnip.

In more recent times, according to the *Encyclopaedia Britannica,* "carrots were cultivated . . . in Germany, France and China by the thirteenth century; and by about 1600 were grown in fields and gardens in England." I can offer no date for China, but the others are several centuries too late. Specific information about Germany is sparse before the second half of the sixteenth century, when the first books on agriculture appeared in that country, revealing that the carrot was already among the established and cultivated vegetables there; and large parts of Germany, as well as of France, were included in the domains of Charlemagne, who listed the carrot as one of the foods he wished to have cultivated there. This pushes it back to the beginning of the ninth century, and even this is a thousand years behind the times if French historian Alain Decaux is

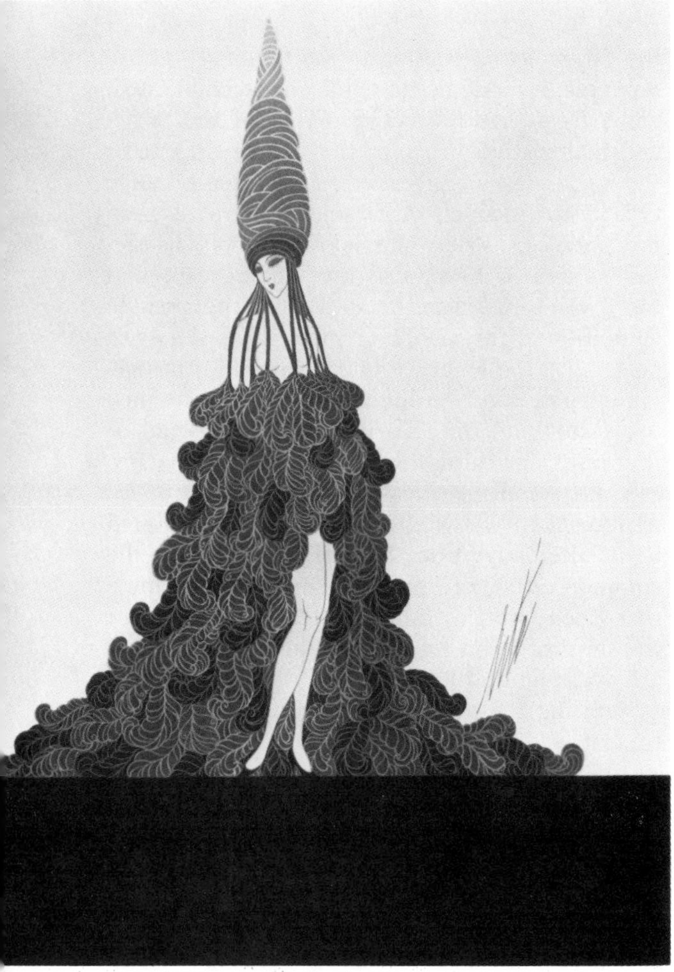

CARROT. *Costume design by Erté for "The Vegetable Ballet,"* George White's Scandals, *1926*

right in asserting that the carrot was cultivated in ancient Gaul before the Christian era. In England it is on record that in the Middle Ages, apparently about the twelfth century, the seeds of wild carrots were being sown in gardens by persons who preferred them to the cultivated kind—so cultivated carrots already existed.

Since the carrot is not a native of Europe, it may well be that it was already a cultivated carrot which first reached northern Europe and that the wild carrots found there now are simply escapees from the vegetable gardens which have reverted to type. This must be what happened in America, for there were no wild carrots in the New World before the English colonists brought in the seeds of the cultivated plant. Today the wild carrot is a common roadside weed in North America, which you certainly know, though you may not realize what it is—Queen Anne's lace, a name which should date from the early eighteenth century, since the Queen Anne referred to is Queen Anne of England, who reigned from 1702 to 1714.

Cultivated carrots are of many shapes and sizes —globular, short and stubby, long and thin, with blunted ends or pointed ones, and of every possible variation in between. In the United States only carrots which are frankly orange are well received, though there is some tolerance of greenish shoulders or slight reddish or purplish tinges in the skin. In Europe, though most carrots offered on the market are orange, the white, yellow, red and purple varieties are also commonly grown; but most of these go to feed animals.

Carrots contain more sugar than any other vegetable except beets, which might seem to qualify them for an important independent gastronomic role, but in practice they seldom rise above the status of supporting players. Carrot dishes barely exist in their own right, aside from soups and hors d'oeuvres, except in a category which seems strange for a vegetable: desserts. The idea of making puddings from carrots has occurred to a few very different people: the Irish, whose writers have been known to refer to carrots poetically as "underground honey"; the Hindus, with their festive *gajar halva,* gay with edible silverleaf; and the Jews, with *tzimmes,* a Sabbath or holiday dish, in which the carrots are further sweetened with honey.

England and the United States make jam from carrots, rarely, and also produce carrot "wine" (even more rarely, thank God).

CAS
stands for

the **cashew**, one of the many poisonous foods relished by man, and **cassareep,** a seasoning which is the juice of the cassava, another poisonous food relished by man; for **cassia,** poor man's cinnamon; and for **cassowary,** unrecommended by those who have tried it.

And **CAS** also stands for the above-mentioned

CASSAVA. The chief staple of the subtropical and tropical American Indians with whom Europeans first made contact, cassava bread never appealed to the white man. It is possible that cassava could be grown in Florida, but so far as I know, no one has ever wanted it to. When Columbus first reached the West Indies, the Arawak Indians fed him bread made from cassava-root flour, and the Spaniards continued to eat it, having no alternative until wheat was imported into the New World; but they did not like it. Bernal Díaz, chronicler of the Cortez expedition,

CASSAVA. *Drawing from Charles Morren:* La Belgique horticole, *Liège, 1856*

called it "poor stuff," and Antonio Pigafetta, chronicler of the Magellan circumnavigation of the globe, who encountered it in Brazil, reported that "it is not very good."

However, there is one form in which cassava has been largely accepted, particularly in the United States: tapioca. Tapioca is made from the residue of the cassava root after its poisonous prussic acid has been pressed out, by one or another of several methods, of which the oldest consists simply of forcing the residue through small holes in a colander to form the familiar small, white, gelatinous, semi-translucent balls of tapioca. A common modern method is to precipitate the residue onto metal plates heated to 300° F.

What the French sometimes call white sago (*sagou blanc*) is really cassava-root tapioca; but the starch sometimes sold as "native tapioca" in the United States is not. "Native" is an artifice of the publicity man, who does not inform us of what country he is speaking. What he means is "native" to the United States, which has no cassava; it is made from potatoes. This replaces cassava tapioca adequately enough in its role as a thickener, but not as a nutrient; the energy value of tapioca, derived from its sugar, is absent from the potato substitute.

CAT
stands for

the **cat,** which, according to the *Larousse Gastronomique,* is a "domestic feline whose edible flesh has a flavor halfway between that of the rabbit and that of the hare"; for the **caterpillar,** one of the world's least appreciated foods, eaten by some Caribbean islanders and southwestern African Bushmen but, so far as I know, by nobody else; for the **catjang bean,** alias the dagarti bean, alias the dolique riz, alias the soso, alias the voehme chinois, alias the niebbe or njébé, alias the agwa ocha, alias the loubia, a lot of names for a vegetable whose most enthusiastic public is confined to western and tropical Africa and the island of Mauritius; for **catnip,** which imparts friskiness to cats, lions and men; for **cat's whiskers,** a tropical African plant whose character is better suggested by its alternative title "bastard mustard"; for the common **cattail,** of which so many parts are edible that Euell Gibbons called it "the supermarket of the swamps"; and for the **cattalo,** a meat animal achieved about the middle of the last century by crossing the polled Angus with the American bison.

And **CAT** also stands for

CATFISH. The catfish is versatile except for the table. It is omnivorous, a scavenger, and is credited with acute hearing. It may be very large (the European catfish, *Siluris glanis,* known to the Germans as *Wels,* but rarely eaten by them, can reach 400 pounds) or very small (*Trichmycterius stegophilus* and *T. vandellia* of tropical America live as parasites in the gills of other fish and are said to enter the urethra of bathers, where they spread their spines and cause infection or death). The Andean prenadillas have suckers with which they climb perpendicular walls to escape from drying waterholes. The American bullhead can survive out of water for many hours, and African catfish live buried in the mud to wait out rainless periods, while others, having internal air sacs which permit them to breathe air, travel from one pond to another in search of water. The African *Malopterurus electricus* delivers electric shocks. Most catfish are dark-colored above, light-colored below, but Nile catfish reverse this—though it makes no protective difference since they swim belly up. In *Aspredo batrachus,* the female carries her eggs on her abdomen, where little cups develop around each of them. Others place their eggs in grass nests in holes scooped out on the banks, guarded by both parents. In other species, the male carries the eggs in his

CATFISH. *Engraving by Nodder, London, 1799*

mouth. The American lake catfish, *Amiurus lacustris*, digs a hole on the bottom for its nest; the male alone guards the eggs and, when they hatch, the young fish.

The *Amiurus* genus, of which there are about twenty-five species, is strictly North American, and, out of the twenty-three different genera with 2000 species of catfish, almost the only one that is generally eaten. About 1855, fingerlings of *A. nebulosus* were imported from the United States into France to be bred for the table on fish farms; but the French never developed a taste for the fish and lived to regret their importation, for the catfish escaped into open waters in 1871 and all but wiped out several valued native fish.

Even in the United States the catfish is appreciated only in the South, and to a lesser degree in the Midwest, its capital being Little Rock, Arkansas, headquarters of the Association of Catfish Farmers of America. It may be suspected that a sort of catfish cult which leads Southerners to speak sentimentally of this fish and class it with "soul food" comes under the head local pride. True, catfish flesh is fine-grained, there are not many bones, and it has a sweet taste, but it lacks character. Sometimes a certain muddiness is discernible in the flavor, especially in the case of the common bullhead, usually taken at about one and a half to two pounds, which likes muddy bottoms—and catfish are bottom feeders. In the Great Lakes, *A. lacustris* may reach 150 pounds, or did when their waters were cleaner, and there is less likelihood of a muddy taste, since this fish feeds on varied bottoms. The best of all is the channel catfish, which likes clean, preferably moving, water, or lakes and ponds with gravel bottoms.

CAU
stands for

CAULIFLOWER. When Mark Twain wrote, "Cauliflower is nothing but cabbage with a college education," he obviously intended a pleasantry; actually this is a reasonably apt description. Cabbage is *Brassica oleracea,* and so is cauliflower, with the addition of the precise "form *botrytis.*" There is only one species of CABBAGE, and all the other plants of its family are simply variations of it, "educated" to allow one part of the plant to develop at the expense of the others. Oddly enough, BROCCOLI is *B. oleracea,* form *botrytis,* too. Different as they look and taste, they are the same thing, a type of cabbage in which it is the flowers that have been developed for eating; there are stages of both when they cannot be told apart. Basically what happened was that the cauliflower was developed as a precocious annual, which, instead of opening its flowers like broccoli if left unpicked, forms them into a head, a modified compact mass of undeveloped flowers technically called the curd. Broccoli is cultivated as a biennial; it would head in the spring of the year following its planting if it were allowed to continue growing that long; but it is literally cut off in the bud during its first year, when its flowers are eaten before they have opened.

This does not mean that if you plant broccoli and wait a year you will get cauliflower, for a large number of subvarieties which breed true have been developed from both types. Thus you have white cauliflower in Milan, green cauliflower in Rome, purple cauliflower in Catania and giant cauliflower in Naples. In France the cauliflowers of the Paris region differ from those of the south.

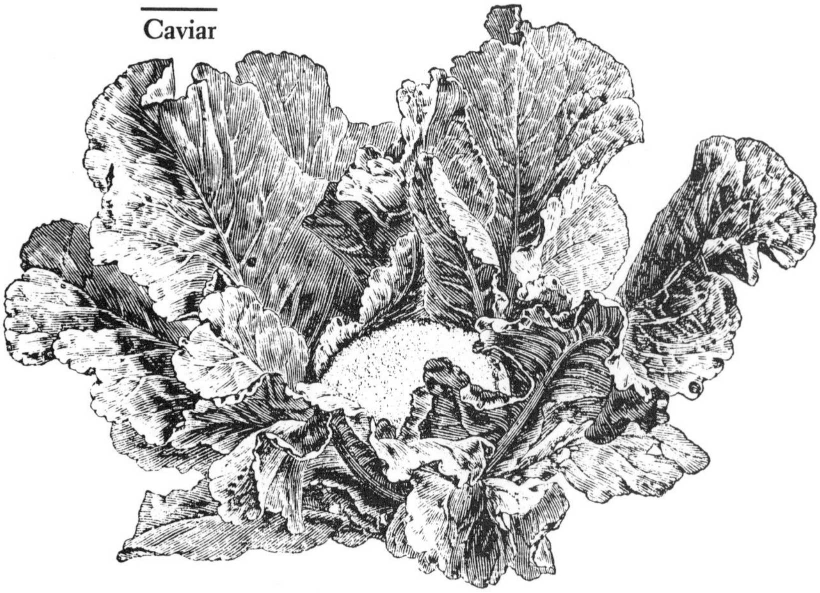

CAULIFLOWER. *Engraving from Theodore Francis Garrett:* The Encyclopaedia of Practical Cookery, *London, 1898*

Holland grows special types of its own, and so does Algeria. So far as I know, America does not grow at all a form occasionally found in Europe, *B. oleracea botrytis cymosa,* spear cauliflower, of which the part primarily eaten is the stalk which bears the curd.

Almost everywhere it is only the curd which is eaten, through unthinking habit, for while the leaves are edible also, being, after all, cabbage, it does not usually occur to the housewife to eat them; if she had wanted to eat cabbage leaves, she would have purchased a cabbage. Besides the curd and the leaves, the flower stalk and the midveins of the big leaves make first-rate eating too, though they are usually neglected, except in countries which like cauliflower soup.

The ancient Romans grew the cauliflower, whether they invented it themselves or imported it ready-made from Asia Minor, which is where most reference books say it originated. It is possible that Italy forgot the art of growing cauliflower during the Dark Ages and that, untended, it reverted to the original cabbage, only to be re-invented or re-imported later; in any case, it does not seem to have been grown north of the Alps before the Renaissance. It is included in a list of new vegetables published in Württemberg in the latter part of the sixteenth century, and the word *chou-fleur* is not known to have entered the French language before 1611—not much ahead of America, for cauliflower has been grown on Long Island since the seventeenth century.

Cauliflower enjoyed a season of high favor after its advent in central and northern Europe, especially as a Lenten food, since it provided filling dishes which broke none of the fasting rules. It was much eaten in France under Louis XIV (seventeenth century) and Louis XV (eighteenth century), when a cauliflower dish was named for the king's mistress, Madame du Barry.

This early enthusiasm has since subsided, and cauliflower today is looked upon in most countries as a rather neutral and uninspiring food, with a few exceptions: Norway and Finland (where it is particularly tasty because of the long hours of northern summer sunlight), Germany, England, Sardinia and even India, where it is made more interesting with curry.

CAV
stands for

the **cavy,** a guinea pig considered a delicacy by South American Indians.

And **CAV** also stands for

CAVIAR. "Caviar," a French expert wrote recently, "is the most expensive food in the world. It could be sold by the karat." Caviar has been called "the pearls of the Caspian," perhaps because of its quality, perhaps because of its price.

Yet caviar was once so inexpensive in the United States that it could be had on the free-lunch counters of saloons (its saltiness provokes thirst) by anyone able to pay for a five-cent beer. It is on record that in 1899, French caviar cost twenty centimes a kilogram (2.2 pounds), but the price rose until just before World War I it had reached forty centimes, a trifle more expensive, weight for weight, than bread. At that period, since Russian caviar had long held the most enviable reputation, canny French caviar makers shipped kegs of their product to Russia, whence it returned bedecked with Russian labels, permitting French gourmets to eat French caviar at the price of the imported article. Russian caviar had already become a luxury item, ever since the Gay Nineties, which coupled caviar, champagne and the famous women known as *les grandes horizontales,* all three expensive.

Today caviar has priced itself beyond the reach of most of us, and it is getting more expensive all the time. Its price is partly a rarity price, and it is becoming increasingly rare. The sturgeon which provides it is a fish which goes back unchanged to prehistoric times and has never adapted itself to cope with modern pollution. In the last century, sturgeon still teemed in the Atlantic, the Mediterranean, the North Sea, the great inland lakes and all the large rivers of the world, including the Hudson, where these fish were so plentiful that sturgeon was called "Albany beef," and children in the streets of New York kicked sturgeon muzzles about for footballs.

There used to be British caviar, but there is none now, for there are no longer any sturgeon in or off Great Britain. The United States still had a flourishing caviar industry at the beginning of this century; it has disappeared. France produces a limited amount of caviar, 90 percent less than ten years ago. Italy still gathers a small amount from sturgeon taken near the mouth of the Po, but their numbers are dwindling as industrialization in that area increases. Black Sea sturgeon are resisting better, but the amount of caviar gathered by Soviet Georgia, Rumania, Bulgaria and Turkey together is no more than one-tenth of what is obtained from the Caspian alone, the sole remaining important source of caviar (the Aral and Azov seas are nearly out of business).

Even in the Caspian, the world's largest saltwater lake, and the Volga and Ural rivers, which flow into it, the take is decreasing fast. In the year 1967 alone, oil and other industrial wastes discharged into the Caspian killed more than half a million sturgeon in the northern (Russian) part of the lake, and in the spring of 1970 there was a caviar shortage in Russia. At that time the Iranian part of the lake was holding out better, but in 1975 it was reported that industrialization in Iran was beginning to kill off the sturgeon in the southern waters of the sea as well.

The ancients do not seem to have known caviar. Athens sent ships into the Black Sea to bring back salt fish, but if there is any record of the importing of caviar I am unaware of it. The Romans ate the Po fish they called the *adana*, a true sturgeon, but apparently did not discover that its eggs were edible. Caviar appeared in Italy in the Middle Ages, when the Christians of Ferrara discovered that the Jews of their ghetto were flocking to the Po in May and June, when the sturgeon were running, to net them for their eggs; following their example, they discovered a new delicacy. (Sturgeon is not kosher, but the medieval Italian Jews must have had some skillful Talmudists among them able to argue that the prohibition did not extend to the eggs; strictly orthodox Jews today do not eat caviar.)

French caviar production was officially organized by no less a personage than Louis XIV's eminent and efficient minister Jean Baptiste Colbert, who established its headquarters on the Gironde, the one place in France where caviar is still gathered. It is a small business today, until recently, and perhaps still, the virtual monopoly of a single Paris restaurant, which in 1922 set up there, in the utmost secrecy, a caviar factory which processes almost all the sturgeon roe in France.

In Russia, the czars were so fond of caviar that Nicholas II imposed on Cossack sturgeon fishers a tax in kind which worked out in practice to about eleven tons of top-grade caviar every year: the Cossacks called it ironically "the fish present." The czars benefited also from the best and rarest of all caviar, the so-called golden caviar, which comes from a species of the fish called sterlet, of

CAVIAR. *Panorama by William B. Benkert,* Development of Fish from the Egg, *1932*

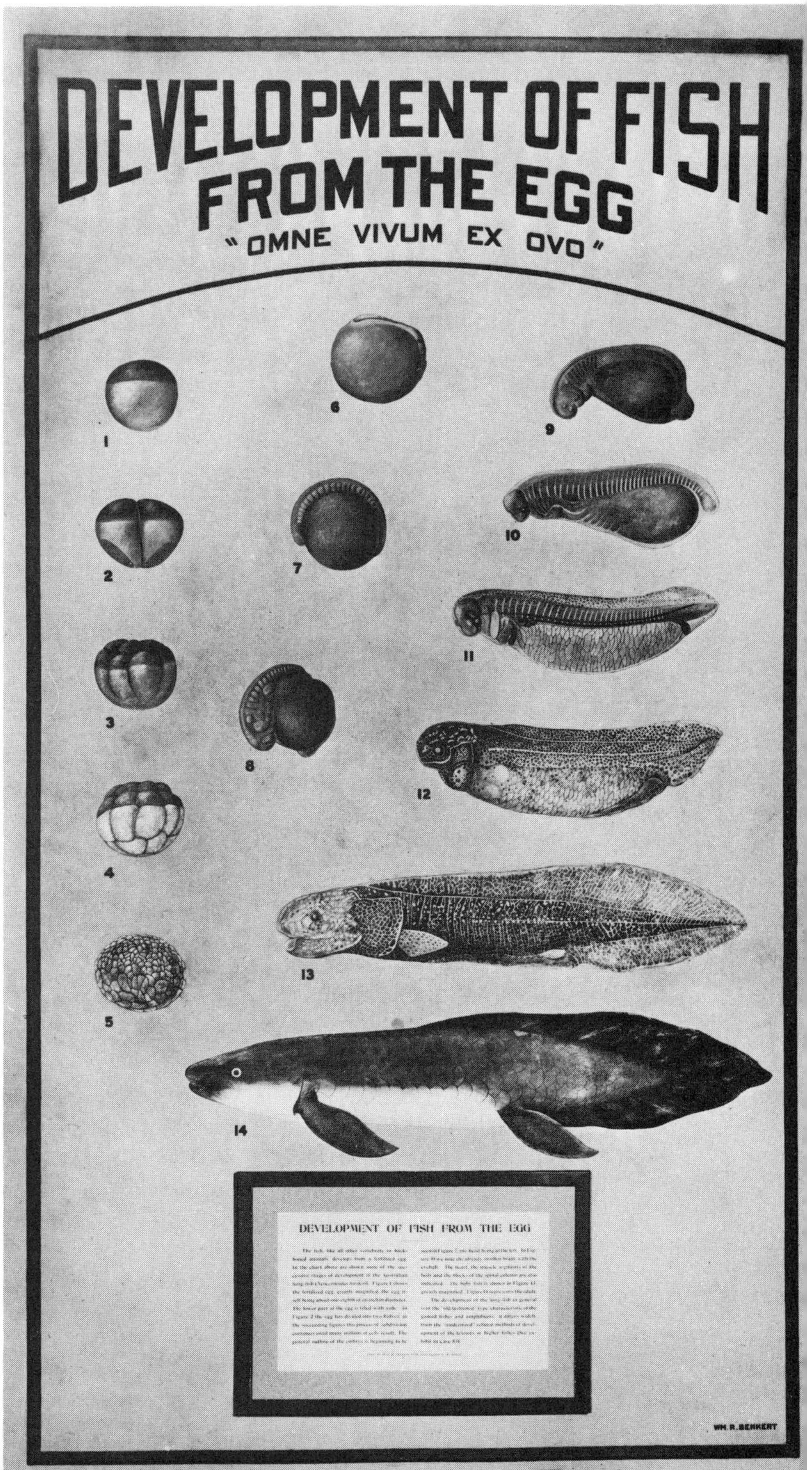

which the annual take nowadays is only about forty-four pounds. In imperial days, all golden caviar taken on the czar's territories went to him. In Stalin's time, he received two-fifths of all the golden caviar fished, the shah of Persia received two-fifths, and the remaining one-fifth was the appanage of the chairman of the Russo-Persian fisheries company, a coveted job. I have no idea who gets the golden caviar now.

The high price of caviar is not solely the result of rarity. Its preparation and handling are painstaking, which means costly. There are problems all along the line, beginning as soon as the female sturgeon is taken from the water. A thrashing fish weighing, sometimes, hundreds of pounds is difficult to handle, yet the eggs must be removed as quickly as possible or they will lose freshness. The fish is immediately bled from an incision made under the last caudal fin to sap her strength. Thus weakened, she is ripped open alive to get the eggs out, with that unconcern about the feelings of fish which man has consistently shown. Later processes involve not merely much handwork, but fingertip work, for instance when the eggs are rolled carefully over a fine-mesh screen to separate them from undesirable fat, bits of ovary and fibrous matter. Salt is worked in at the same time, usually 4 percent to 6 percent, another delicate problem: the more salt used, the less danger of spoilage, the less salt used, the better the taste—and, consequently, the higher the price. Indeed the name for premium caviar, Malassol, is Russian for "lightly salted." Iranians seem to give priority to quality, Russians to safety; hence Russian caviar is likely to be saltier than Iranian caviar. The Iranians also mix borax with the salt, which brings out the flavor; but this caviar never reaches the United States, whose laws prohibit the use of borax.

The different types of caviar are named for the species of sturgeon which produce them. Beluga is the largest and the most expensive. Oestrova is second in size, rarity and price. Sevruga has the smallest eggs, is most plentiful and cheapest, if one dares use the word "cheap" in connection with caviar. There is also pressed caviar, which costs about one-fourth as much as Oestrova, heavily salted bricks made from a mixture of Oestrova and Sevruga eggs discarded for various reasons, for instance because they have been broken in handling. The commercial order of desirability, oddly enough, is not the caviar gourmet's order, especially in the Caspian area itself, where sturgeon fishermen and caviar processors prefer Oestrova to Beluga on grounds of taste, and some even plump for Sevruga, on the theory that the others are too subtle in flavor and they want their caviar lusty. Indeed, among the Russians, who ought to know, and the Greeks, in caviar country too, it is often the lowly pressed caviar which is preferred.

If you are offered caviar at lower than market prices, the chances are that it never knew a sturgeon. Whitefish roe, which is not bad at all, is frequently dyed with cuttlefish ink and passed off as caviar; Iceland makes a specialty of performing this transformation with both whitefish and lumpfish eggs. What is called "German caviar" on the market is made of any available roe which lends itself to dyeing. The product sold under the Russian-sounding name "Maviar" is smoked cod eggs. There is no bargain-rate caviar.

CAY
stands for

cayenne pepper, possibly the hottest food in the world, and for the **cayor apple** of Senegal, also known as the gingerbread plum.

CE
stands for

the **cedar**, which supplies the ashes Navahos add to their cornmeal; for **celandine**, grown in medieval English hedgerows more as medicine than as food; for **celeriac**, developed in Renaissance times by gardeners who persuaded celery to become a turnip; for the **celosia**, an African plant called the silk-cotton tree whose leaves are eaten like spinach; for the **centaury**, an herb so named because its medicinal properties were discovered by Chiron the Centaur; for the **century plant**, an indifferent mathematician, which belies its name by achieving its only flowering at ages varying from five to sixty years; for **cereals**, the basis of finance in medieval France and of economic policy in twelfth- to nineteenth-century England; and for the **ceriman**, a tropical American fruit so strange that its scientific name means "delicious monster."

And **CE** also stands for

CELERY. Celery, *Apium graveolens dulce*, is the cultivated form of the wild *A. graveolens*, otherwise ache, usually described as a native of the eastern end of the Mediterranean. It was at the beginning a lover of seaside soils impregnated with brackish water, growing in the company of rushes and willows. The wild plant still is.

Celery seems to have impinged on human consciousness first in the time of the ancient Greeks and Romans. Ache was a funeral plant,

CELERY. *Woodcut from Jules Gouffe:* Le Livre de cuisine, *1867*

used to decorate tombs; nevertheless Horace wrote, "Fill the cups with Massic wine, which makes us forget all our ills; imbibe the flowers of these mighty springs, and make in haste crowns of ache and myrtle"—because the Romans believed that wreaths of celery would protect them from hangovers.

The Greeks, no great vegetable eaters, apparently restricted celery to the subordinate role of a seasoning; but both Pliny and Dioscorides speak of it not merely as a condiment but as a vegetable eaten for its own sake; and I myself once ate, at a dinner given by a society devoted to reproducing ancient Roman dishes, a dessert of celery cooked with honey and pepper which my hosts assured me was an authentic ancient Roman concoction.

Pliny deals with celery in a fashion which implies that in his time it was already a cultivated plant. Apparently the Romans ate more wild than cultivated celery, but it was not because they did not have cultivated varieties, it was because they preferred the wild plant. It had a stronger odor and a sharper taste than the kind we know now, and Romans enjoyed strong sensations, in food as in everything else. Italians today still prefer wild to cultivated celery when it is to be cooked, especially for soups; I have known foreigners to complain of the quality of Italian celery which they had bought to eat raw, not realizing that they had purchased "cooking celery" when they wanted "eating celery," probably available at the same market.

It may be that with the collapse of the Roman Empire the art of cultivating celery was lost and the Middle Ages knew only the wild plant. It is on record that celery was cultivated "officially" for the first time in France in 1641, in the royal garden which is the Paris Jardin des Plantes today; yet a stylized celery leaf was a common decorative motif for the stone carvers who adorned the Gothic cathedrals. (It also appeared on the coronets of dukes and marquis, perhaps to protect them from hangovers?) I am not sure what constitutes "official" cultivation, but celery had been cultivated in France at least in the century preceding this recognition, for Bruyerin-Champier wrote unambiguously in his sixteenth-century *De re cibaria* about cultivated celery.

The rest of Europe seems to have acquired celery from Italy. "The first I ever saw," Turner wrote in his *Herbal* in 1538, "was in the Venetian Ambassador's garden in the spittle yard, near Bishop's Gate Streete." England has since taken celery to its bosom, or stomach, and even crunches it, raw and salted, with afternoon tea. In France, celery seems in the sixteenth century to have been considered exclusively as a seasoning; this was how Bruyerin-Champier described it, and so did Charles Estienne and Olivier de Serres. They called it "garden ache," reserving the name *sellery* for wide-stalked varieties which were being imported from Italy.

The following century enlarged the role of the plant. In 1651 the *Cuisinier Français* recognized celery as a full-fledged vegetable, recommending especially the "heart" (that is, the base of the stalks and the point at which they join each other), eaten salted and peppered, as a valuable Lenten food. Eight years later, *Le Maître d'Hotel* gave it another promotion, with a recipe for cooked celery combined with lemon, pomegranates and beets. Under Louis XIV, Jean de la Quintinie, a lawyer who had abandoned that profession for the more congenial art of agronomy, greatly improved celery in the royal vegetable gardens at Versailles, where he seems to have been the first to blanch it by heaping earth up about its stalks. By 1904 the French Vilmorin catalogue was able to list more than thirty kinds of celery, including some whose names sounded like those of flowers—the rosy-stalked, or the violet of Touraine. In Italy, the best celery was the produce of Trevi, where it was, and is, cooked in tomato sauce.

Medieval magicians put celery seeds in their shoes in order to fly, but this practice seems to have been abandoned since the invention of the airplane.

CHA
stands for

chalk, consumed unsuspectingly in milk, flour or even wine; for **chamois,** one of the most subtle forms of venison, driven from our tables by the devastating inventions of the high-powered rifle and the telescopic sight; for the **chanterelle,** a delicious MUSHROOM recommended to amateur gatherers by a French authority on the grounds of safety because "it is impossible to make a mistake about it," an underestimate of the human capacity for error; for the **Charolais,** the finest beef critter in France, with the possible exception of the Limousin; and for **chayote,** a tropical American gourd so indecisive in flavor that it is being eaten increasingly in the British Isles, where tastelessness is a virtue.

And **CHA** also stands for

CHAR. If you have ever done any serious eating near the Alpine lakes of France or Switzerland, you have certainly tasted one of the most praised food fishes of the world, honored by the noble name *omble-chevalier*—the knightly *omble.* It is "the finest and most delicate of freshwater fish," says *Larousse Gastronomique,* an opinion I will gladly second if it is amended to read "the finest and most delicate of fish found in fresh water"—for, despite appearances, it is not basically a freshwater fish.

They will tell you with equal conviction at all of the lakes where this fish is caught that it is a local species which exists nowhere else, but it is found also, though not under the same name, in deep, cold-water lakes in Italy, Scandinavia, the British Isles and even North America. It is actually a land-locked Arctic char. What, you may ask, is a circumpolar fish doing in the Alps, and, conversely—this is really the same question worded differently—how does it happen that a fish of the Arctic Ocean is known as *Salvelinus alpinus*? The answer to both questions is found in the curious, complicated history of the char, a history dominated by temperature.

The char is one of those saltwater fishes which swim up rivers to spawn. It likes cold water; during the Ice Ages, following its optimum temperature southward, it ascended rivers far beyond its normal range; some of them led it into Alpine lakes. When temperatures rose again, some of the char were trapped in deep mountain lakes slower to warm up again than the rivers which led out of them, which thus became temperature barriers and prevented the fish from returning to the ocean. They remained in the depths of the lakes, which the sun's heat did not penetrate. Bottom swimmers, they survive only in lakes profound enough to provide cold water—in Lake Geneva, whose mean depth is 500 feet and the deepest point more than 1000 feet down; in Lake Constance, whose floor is at 817 feet; and in others similarly hospitable. The shallowest lake known to me in which the *omble-chevalier* lives is Lake Pavin in the French Auvergne, only 300 feet deep; but this lake was stocked artificially, and its altitude of 6000 feet keeps its waters cold. As for its scientific name, this is explained by the fact that the fish was first identified and named in the Alps, and when it was discovered to be the same as the Arctic char, the name had to be applied to the ocean fish too. A detail which corroborates the dependence of the char on low temperatures is that where they appear in British lakes they do not exceed a weight of one and a half pounds, but in the colder Scandinavian lakes, where they are more in their element, they reach five pounds and up.

Clearing up the history of the char does not quite tell us what it is. It is sometimes called a kind of salmon, sometimes a kind of trout and sometimes, slyly, a salmon-trout; several fish commonly called trout are really chars. The simplest way for a layman to distinguish a trout from a char is to examine the scales; the char's are much smaller, sometimes almost imperceptible. The orthodox view of the *Salmonidae* holds that they are divided into three principal branches, salmon,

CHAR *by Winslow Homer (1836–1910).* Jumping Trout, *watercolor*

trout and char; without getting deeper into the tangle of taxonomy, we may say that any fish whose genus is given as *Salvelinus* is a char. According to this definition, the fish which, if you happen to have been brought up on the Atlantic seaboard of the United States, as I was, you have probably always considered as the very archetype of the trout is not a trout at all, but a char. The scientific name of the Eastern brook trout is *Salvelinus fontinalis.* It is also a char by the temperature test. Most brook trout prefer the higher, colder waters of the streams in which they live; but some individuals break away and swim downstream until they end up atavistically in the sea. This never happens south of Cape Cod, though there are Eastern brook trout as far south as Georgia. In other words, the American brook trout returns to the sea only where it can enter the cold water of the Labrador Current.

Most chars (and trout and salmon too) are both excellent food and game fishes. An exception is another misnamed char, the Dolly Varden trout, *S. malma,* found off the northern Pacific coast of North America; off Russia, particularly the Kamchatka Peninsula; and off northern Japan. It is only mediocre eating, it is not prized as a game fish, and it is highly unpopular because, a persistent predator, it destroys large quantities of salmon eggs and young salmon.

CHARD. Chard is simply a BEET (*Beta vulgaris* var. *cicla*) of which the stalks and leaves have been developed instead of the root. It is also called the leaf beet, Swiss chard (why, I do not know; it is not peculiar to Switzerland) and, especially in England, the sea-kale beet, a complete misnomer since it is related neither to sea kale nor to kale, a kind of cabbage.

Some reference books report that the leaf beet was already being cultivated in prehistoric times, while the root or garden beet did not appear until the beginning of the Christian era. This would imply that the leafy chard was the original type,

CHARD. *Engraving from Vilmorin-Andrieux:* Les plantes potagères, *Paris, 1904*

from which root beets later developed (presumably as the result of cultivation) from a common ancestor; the ancient Romans seem to have had an intermediary form of which both root and leaves were eaten. However, Plautus spoke of both white beets and chard as entering into the same mixture, so there must have been at least two distinct varieties by the second century B.C., and the prized chard of Pompeii seems definitely to have been the leaf beet. The Greeks knew chard too, but failed to describe it for us.

Chard was being eaten in France at least by the fifteenth century, for it is cited in Taillevent's *Le Vivandier*, and France is still the country which probably eats it more regularly than any other. The stalks are cooked either like asparagus or like celery, the leaves like spinach. The French never serve stalks and leaves together and, indeed, cultivate separate subvarieties of each.

CHE
stands for

the **checkerberry,** otherwise the wintergreen; for the **cherimoya,** a luscious tropical American fruit which Mark Twain described as "deliciousness itself"; for the **cherrystone clam,** which is actually only one stage in the development of the QUAHOG; for the **cherry tomato,** smallest but perhaps tastiest of its tribe; for the **Chesapeake Bay oyster,** which industrialization is rapidly rendering extinct; for the **chewing stick,** which is sassafras, and the **chewstick,** of which Africans chew not the stem but the seeds.

And **CHE** also stands for

CHERRY. No one who writes about the cherry seems able to refrain from informing us that it was introduced into Italy from Asia Minor by that ancient Roman general and gourmet, Lucullus. After reading this a score of times, one ends by thinking that it must be true, since it has been confirmed by so many different "authorities." Actually this constitutes a perfect example of how an error, once it has entered into our store of information, or misinformation, cannot be eradicated from it. This statement has not been confirmed independently by the twenty, or fifty or one hundred different authors who have repeated it; they have simply all echoed unthinkingly the mistake of one man. The man happened to be Pliny, a venerated source; but Pliny was wrong. Cherries were already being cultivated in Italy by the Etruscans before Lucullus' time.

What Lucullus may have done was to bring back a special variety of cherry from Asia Minor, and if so, we might even hazard a guess, on the vaguest of premises, as to which variety it was, for: (a) Pompeii was noted for a certain type of cherry; (b) Lucullus had a villa at Naples, near Pompeii; and (c) if it was Lucullus who endowed Pompeii with its cherries, that might well have impressed Pliny, so familiar with Pompeii that he got himself killed there in the famous eruption of Vesuvius.

The cherry may very well have reached Italy originally via Asia Minor, without the help of Lucullus, for it seems likeliest that it originated in northeastern Asia, but it had already occupied its complete range of today—temperate Asia, Europe and North America—in prehistoric times. When the ancient Greeks first wrote of the wild

CHERRY. *Quilt, in the style associated with Baltimore, Maryland. Album (detail): "Cherry Tree with Birds," 1845–1850*

cherry, which they did not like—and with reason, for it was small, hard and bitter—it was already growing in Gaul.

In America, cherries were present early enough so that they had developed distinct species by the time the first colonists arrived; thus the United States today possesses four distinct ancestral types of cherries, in two sets, wild and cultivated, of both American and European kinds, which developed from opposite directions: the first white men found American wild cherries on the spot and developed American cultivated varieties from them, and they also brought European cultivated cherries with them which escaped from orchards and reverted to European wild cherries. Cherries can also be sorted into categories on other bases—for instance, those with colored juice and those with colorless juice, or, more pertinent for the eater, into sweet and sour cherries (which are not necessarily sour, for what the word means in this case is really "acid").

The cherry, despite its long presence in America, does not enter largely into its history. The famous story of George Washington cutting down his father's cherry tree was an invention of Parson Weems, in his *The Life of George Washington; With Curious Anecdotes, Equally Honorable to Himself and Exemplary to His Young Countrymen.* Otherwise, the only example that comes to mind is that of the Japanese trees, a variety developed solely for its blossoms which rarely bears fruit (and when it does, the result is inedible), presented by the mayor of Tokyo for planting in Washington, D.C., in 1910. They were so badly infested with insect pests that they had to be burned. The superintendent of public grounds replaced them with a second shipment in 1912, which was cleaner, but not clean enough. It introduced into the United States the Oriental fruit moth, which dotes on peaches. The American peach crop is still paying heavy tribute every year for the beautification of Washington's Tidal Basin.

Sweet cherries are the relatives of *Prunus avium*, "bird's cherry," a reminder that one of the chief difficulties of the cherry grower is to harvest his fruit before birds do it for him. "I value my garden more for being full of blackbirds than of cherries," Addison wrote in *The Spectator*, but it is probable that it would not have been full of blackbirds if it had not already been full of cherries. Among sweet cherries, those with colored juice are called heart cherries in English and those with colorless juice white heart cherries: the latter is the most popular for eating fresh.

Sour cherries (*P. cerasus*) usually grow on smaller trees than sweet cherries—15 feet high compared to 35 for the others. Some people prefer their acid bite even for eating fresh, while almost everyone concedes that they are superior for cooking. Those with colored juice are morellos, those with colorless juice amarelles. Dukes are crosses between sweet and sour cherries; the Germans call them *Bastardkirschen*.

There are about a hundred natural species of cherries, only ten to twelve of them in Europe and America, but from them cultivation has produced a bewildering choice of varieties and subvarieties. One might expect that wild cherries would have been abandoned entirely, but they still have their admirers. Helmut Schiller, of the New York Museum of Natural History, once told a reporter: "The [wild] black cherry is one of my favorites, and I'm partial also to the pin cherry, which is a little *more* sour; the combination makes an acceptable macédoine."

The black cherry Mr. Schiller mentioned was presumably the common American wild cherry, *P. virginiana*, or chokecherry, which grows on a low tree or even bush and produces very small fruit, usually too acid to be eaten raw, but it is not bad for jelly. (What New Mexico calls the chokecherry is a different species, *P. melanocarpa*; it is less sour than the others.) Mr. Schiller's pin cherry is *P. pennsylvanica*, usually considered edible only in jelly, though occasionally one finds an individual plant whose fruit is sweeter than normal. Another native American cherry is *P. serotina*, the sweet black cherry or rum cherry, so called because in early New England it was used to convert raw West Indian rum into a suave cherry liqueur. The sour cherry or pie cherry is *P. cerasus* gone wild, the degenerate descendant of a European cultivated cherry, and Europe's sweet cherry, *P. avium*, has also gone wild, and is known in America as the mazzard (it has also escaped from cultivation in England, which calls it a gean).

The leading cherry-producing country of the world is the United States, which grows more than one-third as much as all the western European countries put together. Traverse City, Michigan, claims to be the cherry capital of the world; so does Vignola, Italy, which has been growing them for at least 2000 years. If Vignola has perhaps a slight edge on quality, Traverse City is ahead in quantity, with the densest population of cherry trees anywhere, 22,600 per square mile. Its supremacy is attributed to the climate created by Lake Michigan; similarly, the best cherries in Germany are supposed to be those grown near Lake Constance. In France the leading cherry town is Montmorency—but Ceret, famous for its modern art, produces the earliest, about May 15. As for England, Alfred Jingle in *The Pickwick Papers* has told us where its cherries are grown: "Kent, sir—everybody knows Kent—apples, cherries, hops and women."

CHERVIL. This is the "herb of joy" according to its Greek name, *chairéphyllon*. It is a native of southwestern Russia and western Asia. It reached the Mediterranean via Asia Minor well before the Christian era. The Greeks used it, as we do today, to flavor other foods, but the Romans also cooked it by itself, as a vegetable in its own right. It was probably not quite the same plant which was treated in these two different fashions: Pliny and Dioscorides made a distinction between *cerefolium*, eaten alone, probably the chervil we know today, and myrrh, the seasoner, possibly sweet cicely.

Chervil was already being cultivated in French vegetable gardens during the Gallo-Roman period. In the sixteenth and seventeenth centuries it was widely grown in England, but then lost a certain amount of favor there. Today France uses chervil more freely than any other country, leading even that prime utilizer of aromatic plants, Italy. It goes into bouquets garnis, whose other ingredients vary with a legerity which would have displeased d'Aigrefeuille, who wrote that the composition of a bouquet garni was a matter so grave that "its different constituents should be weighed on jewelers' scales and counted out in karats, like diamonds."

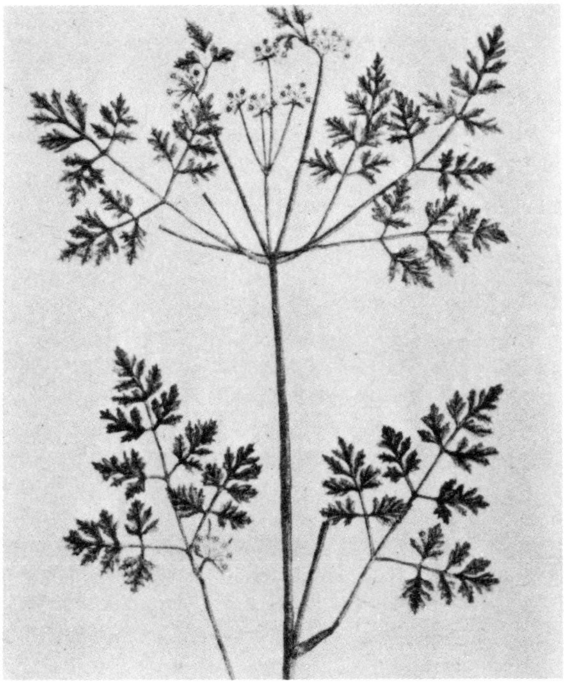

CHERVIL. *Print from Elizabeth Blackwell:* A Curious Herbal, *London, 1737*

Introduced into the United States, chervil is less generously used there than in France; perhaps the American climate is less propitious to it. Comparing writings on chervil from French and American sources, one might wonder if the same plant is being discussed. An American expert has called chervil "the problem child of plants, because of its unpredictable behavior"; all French writers describe it as exceedingly easy to grow. An American authority writes that chervil is used "*sometimes* in the fresh state," implying that it is ordinarily used dried; a French gourmet states flatly that "only the fresh plant is used," but another admits that "it is possible to dry chervil for winter use, though it loses more or less of its taste along with its freshness."

Chervil is a cousin of parsley, which it much resembles. Its odor and flavor manage to be simultaneously both more subtle, sweetened by a suggestion of fennel overlaying the parsley taste, and more assertive—which may account for its lack of favor among Anglo-Saxons, easily frightened by tastiness. All parts of the plant are aromatic, but it is the leaves which are most used today; in sixteenth-century England the favorite part was the seeds, which, English botanist John Gerard wrote in his 1597 *Herball*, "eaten in salad when they are green, with oil and vinegar, by the agreeableness of their taste, are better than other salads through the sweetness of their aroma, and nothing is healthier for weak stomachs."

Chervil loses flavor when cooked, so it is usually chopped at the last moment and sprinkled fresh over the food it seasons. If it *has* to be cooked (in sauces, or in an *omelette aux fines herbes*), it goes in at the very end of the cooking. The chief exception to the rule of minimum cooking for chervil was provided by Ninon de Lenclos, who boiled it lengthily in water, but she was not concerned about its taste; she washed her face with it twice a day to prevent the formation of wrinkles. It must have worked. She was still a beauty at the age of eighty.

CHESTNUT. "Under the spreading chestnut tree / The village smithy stands," wrote Longfellow, who could not have suspected that fifty years after his death not only would the village smithy have disappeared, but the chestnuts too. In Longfellow's lifetime vast forests of chestnuts —the "boundless chestnut woods," wrote Thoreau —covered the eastern United States, from southern Maine to southwestern Florida in one direction and to eastern Arkansas in another. Especially plentiful on the slopes of the Appalachians up to 3000 feet, they were magnificent trees, 100 feet tall, with a girth of 42 inches or more.

Then, in 1904, chestnut saplings imported from the Far East were planted on Long Island. With them came *Endothia parasitica,* a fungus which eats into the bark of chestnut trees, girdling and killing them. Endemic in Asia, the chestnut blight is not particularly destructive there; it proved fatal to species which had never previously been exposed to it. It was remarked in 1908 that the disease had spread to other parts of New York State, but no one dreamed how deadly it would prove to be. When the danger was finally realized, it was too late. By 1940 there were no longer any American chestnuts.

Today the world's leading chestnut is *Castanea sativa,* the European chestnut, oftener called the Spanish chestnut. Its nuts, the largest and sweetest of all species, are eaten, raw or cooked, everywhere. It was introduced into the United States in the nineteenth century, both in the East and along the Pacific coast. Curiously, the blight which spared European chestnuts in Europe killed European chestnuts in America, except for some groves in California and the Pacific Northwest which escaped the general destruction.

The European chestnut, which begins producing nuts in the fifth year after grafting and reaches maximum production at the age of sixty, attains tremendous size. Until a few years ago the French chestnut-producing region of Privas boasted a tree nearly 25 feet around, believed to be six hundred years old. This record is dwarfed

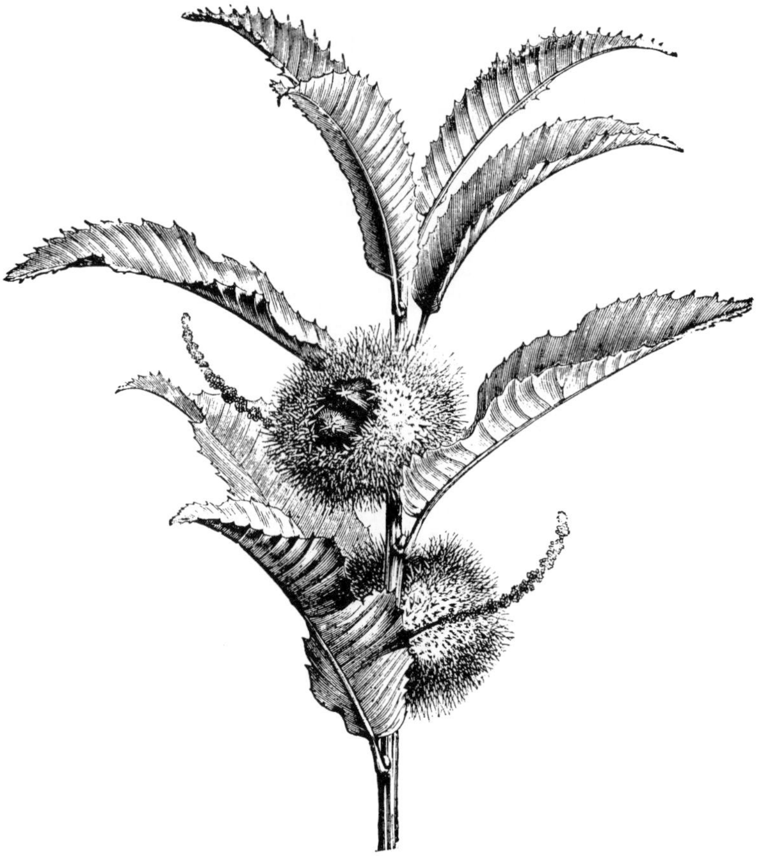

CHESTNUT. *Engraving from Theodore Francis Garrett:* The Encyclopaedia of Practical Cookery, *London, 1898*

by that of a chestnut which until 1850 existed near Acireale in Sicily, at the foot of Mount Etna, which then had a girth of 204 feet and, for reasons unknown to me, was called "the chestnut of a hundred horses." It was said to have been planted by the ancient Romans, two thousand years earlier, before the start of the empire; it was still bearing nuts when it was destroyed by a volcanic eruption.

Latin languages distinguish between two forms of the European chestnut, one called *châtaigne* in French, the other *marron.* The châtaigne has two or three nuts in its bur, the marron only one. Châtaignes are often left to grow wild, when they are described as *châtaignes des bois,* "woods chestnuts"; the nuts are small, comparatively tasteless, and do not keep well. Whether wild or cultivated, they are usually fed to livestock or, after drying, ground into flour for soups, bread or desserts. Alexandre Dumas did not think highly of chestnut flour, from which, he wrote, "bread is even made in places where wheat is rare, but the bread is always of bad quality, heavy and difficult to digest." He had probably encountered only meal ground by primitive methods which left small red points in the otherwise white flour, representing the debris of the husks or inner seed coatings. More carefully milled chestnuts give a finer flour, fragrant to the smell and sweet to the taste, which form a firm, unyielding dough.

Marrons are eaten raw, roasted or boiled, and are the basis for such delectable confections as chestnut stuffings for goose or turkey; *purée de marrons,* an appreciated side dish with game; sweet fritters, cakes and creams; and above all, the famous candied chestnuts known throughout the world by their French name, *marrons glacés.*

Man has been eating chestnuts since prehistoric times, for no food is easier to gather; the nuts when ripe drop to the ground and need only to be picked up. (American Indians, in *their* prehistoric times, made bread of chestnut flour.) There are at least two references to chestnuts in the Bible, one of which describes rather shabby conduct on the part of Jacob, who assured strong offspring for his livestock by putting peeled chestnut twigs in their water trough, neglecting to do the same for the cattle of Laban.

Legendarily, the chestnut passed into western Europe via Castan, a town of eastern Thessaly; hence its generic name *Castanea.* The ancient Romans were fond of chestnuts; their poor counteracted the rank taste of some of the wild greens they ate by boiling chestnuts with them, and the Roman legions are credited with having spread the chestnut (and the WALNUT) through Europe. We hear of them in France in the thirteenth century when St. Louis extended the category of "foods fit for cooking"—called *aigrun*, which rather curiously meant chiefly citrus fruits and a few other acid ones—to include nuts, among them the chestnut. At this period France was eating chestnuts from Lombardy, which were hawked in the streets of Paris; but by the sixteenth century native chestnuts from the central plateau and the region of Lyons had gained favor, and were being served on the royal table. That they were popular in England too may be deduced from the passage in *Macbeth* where one of the witches complains:

A sailor's wife had chestnuts in her lap,
And munch'd, and munch'd, and munch'd. "Give me," quoth I;
"Aroint thee, witch," the rump-fed ronyon cries.

The sorceress was so incensed at being denied a treat of chestnuts that she arranged with her sisters to stir up tempests in the path of the sailor's ship.

In its long history as a human food, the chestnut has been an aliment of extremes: it has produced luxurious dishes for the rich, but more often has provided the basic nutriment of the poor. As a festive food, the chestnut appears on the New Year's menu in Japan (a country where connoisseurs do not hesitate to send to distant cities for the exact type of chestnut they prefer), but this may be less a tribute to the lusciousness of the nut than adherence to the custom of composing this meal of foods which symbolize the virtues it is hoped will be exercised during the coming year: part of the character which means "mastery" suggests the sign for "chestnut"—a pun in ideograms. It is presumably the quality of the chestnut which makes it a holiday food in Modena, Italy, where it is served on St. Martin's Day, soaked in wine must before being roasted. The *marron glacé* is in France the traditional harbinger of the Christmas–New Year's holiday season. This complicated confection, whose preparation involves sixteen separate operations, is claimed by the French, who say they invented it in the time of Louis XIV; but Aretino had praised the candied chestnuts of Chiusa Pesio in the Piedmont 150 years earlier.

In the three countries which today make the largest use of chestnuts—Japan, Italy and France—it has often been the principal food of the poor. It was so described in Italy as early as the third century B.C., and after the collapse of the Roman Empire many Italian populations were reduced largely to a diet of chestnuts eaten boiled or roasted. In English we talk of a diet of bread and water where the French would speak of fasting on water and chestnuts (*jeuner à l'eau et à la châtaigne*—not *marron*, which would carry too rich a connotation). Before the potato entered the French pantry, chestnuts provided the basic food of the poor; in Corsica, always and still one of the poorest parts of France, chestnuts until very recently held the place ceded elsewhere to the potato, long after the latter had become common on the mainland. They were also a cheap substitute for bread; the chestnut was referred to sarcastically as the "Corsican bread tree." Napoleon wrote in his memoirs that to repress the Corsican revolt which broke out in 1774 (when he was five), "Somebody proposed the singular plan of cutting down or burning all the chestnut trees, whose fruit was the food of the mountaineers: 'You'll force them to come to the plains to beg for peace and bread.'" Corsicans still say of persons who eat cheaply, "They eat out of the drawer," a reminder of the days when wild chestnuts gathered in the woods were spread out to dry in bureau drawers, to which one had recourse on the not infrequent occasions when there was nothing else to eat.

CHI
stands for

chia, an edible seed which subjected tribes paid to the Aztecs as tribute; for the **Chianina**, the best beef animals of Italy, identical with the *boves vastos et albos* which the ancient Romans sacrificed to such of their gods as were worthy of it; for **chiarcarc**, the name given by Antonio Pigafetta, chronicler of the Magellan expedition, to a fruit encountered in the Moluccas which he described as having "knots on the outside and inside"; for the **Chickasaw bean**, a coarser variety of the lima; for the **chicken mushroom**, whose sulfurous yellow color frightens amateur gatherers away, though it is good enough eating if picked while still unripe; for the **chickling vetch**, a pulse eaten in Asia, southern Europe and South America, which, consumed in too great quantities, provokes a disease all its own; for **chickus**, an Indian fruit whose taste has been described as midway between that of a fig and a russet apple, wherever that is; for **chickweed**, which, according to an old-time writer, "comforteth, digesteth, defendeth and suppurateth very notably"; for **chicle**, the latex of the tropical American sapodilla tree, whose entire supply is preempted for American chewing gum; for **chicory**, universally confused with ENDIVE; for **chih'**, a variety of artemisia used by the Saharan Tuaregs as a substitute for mint; for the **chiletepin,** a fiery berry gathered wild in Texas; for the **chimpanzee,** *Pan troglodytes,* a brother of man nevertheless eaten in tropical Africa; for the **China root,** which once nourished American Indians and Captain John Smith; for the **chinchard,** a mackerel-like fish consumed in Africa; and for the salty **Chincoteague oysters** found at the ocean end of Chesapeake Bay.

CHI also stands for

Chinese cabbage, including pak-choi, which does not form a head, pe-tsai, which does, albeit a straggly one, wong bok and chihli, the last two being improvements on pe-tsai; **Chinese chives,** important for seasoning from Mongolia to the Philippines; the **Chinese fuzzy gourd,** a sweet subtle squash; the **Chinese gooseberry,** or kiwi; the **Chinese lantern plant,** or ground cherry; **Chinese mustard greens,** pickled to add zest to soup or meat; **Chinese okra,** which despite its name is a squash; **Chinese parsley,** which means the leaves of coriander; **Chinese spinach,** which isn't spinach, but serves the same purpose; the **Chinese water chestnut,** which is not a chestnut but the tuber of a sedge; and the **Chinese yam,** which seems to be eaten nowhere except in Burundi.

CHI stands for

the **chinook,** or king salmon, largest of the five species of the Pacific Northwest; for the **chinquapin,** the poor man's chestnut; for the dark-brick-red **chipotle,** one of the hottest of the chilies; for **chironji,** a green Indian seed which looks like a pea but tastes like a nut; for the **chiton,** an edible if neglected mollusk also known as the sea cradle; and for **chitterlings,** strictly speaking the small intestine of the pig, called "rubbery" and "tasteless" by Reay Tannahill, and in any case little appreciated outside the southeastern United States.

And **CHI** also stands for

CHICKEN. When Plato proposed to the Academy that man be defined as "a two-legged animal without feathers," Diogenes plucked a cock and held it up for the inspection of the Greek sages. "This," he said, "according to Plato's definition, is a man." Plato accordingly altered his definition to: "Man: a two-legged animal without feathers and with broad flat nails."

It is possible that in the light of modern scientific knowledge one might be able to come up with a more comprehensive formula for distinguishing a man from a chicken. This would not alter the historical facts that the two have lived in close association since about 2000 B.C. and that today chicken is probably the most universally eaten of all meats, including beef. The chicken, despite a tropical origin, has become acclimated almost everywhere in the world except in the very coldest regions; among domestic animals only the dog has a wider range. Chicken is easily and inexpensively raised and thus available in areas where other meats are too rare or too dear, such as Africa, where chicken is an important food.

Chicken is singularly versatile, good broiled, roasted, baked, steamed, fried, boiled, fricasseed, barbecued or made into chicken pie or chicken soup. It appears in such national or regional dishes as Arabian couscous, Austrian *Backhuhn,* Chinese beggar's chicken, Flemish *waterzooi,* Florentine *pollo alla diavola,* Georgian *chakhokhbili,* Hungarian chicken paprika, Indian *tandoori,* Indonesian *sambal hati-hati,* Japanese *oyako donburi,* Malayan *satay,* Moroccan *bastelah,* Pakistani *murghi biryani,* Russian *kurnik,* Scottish cock-a-leekie, Spanish *olla podrida* and West Indian Creole chicken; but if in the German Rhineland you order *halve Hahn* (half a chicken) do not be surprised if you are served a slice of aged Dutch cheese smeared with Düsseldorf mustard inserted in a rye-bread roll, and if you hear in New York a bellowed call for Coney Island chicken, it will mean frankfurters.

Chicken has been flavored, stuffed, basted or garnished with almost every other food you can think of, notably anise, apples, bacon, beans, cinnamon, cornmeal, crabs, crayfish, eels, fennel, ginger, grape jelly, herbs, hickory nuts, lemons, lime juice, maple syrup, marmalade, mushrooms, nutmeg, oranges, oysters, peanut butter, pineapple, sake, sesame seeds, soya sauce, truffles and vinegar. Fermented chicken is one of the ingredients of a certain type of soya sauce, and in central France *sanguines* are pancakes made with chicken blood. Chicken dishes have been named for an opera singer (chicken Tetrazzini), an opera composer (*poularde à la Rossini*), a Roman dictator (*poulet César*)—whose recipe is attributed to Julius Caesar himself, improbably, since one of its ingredients, brandy, was unknown to the ancient Romans—and a queen of France (*poulet à la Reine* is supposed to have been created for Marie Leczinska, wife of Louis XV, for whom *bouchées à la Reine* was also invented). A Napoleonic victory is celebrated by one chicken dish (*poulet Marengo*) and a Napoleonic defeat by another (*salade Bagration*).

Chicken *by Huang Chüan, Early Ming Dynasty (1368–1644).* Hen, Cock and Chickens, *hand scroll, colors on silk*

Chicken has so often been considered a luxury that sumptuary legislation has from time to time attempted to curb over-indulgence in it. In 817 the Council of Aachen ruled that it was a dish too sumptuous for fast days and forbade monks to eat it except during four days at Easter and four more at Christmas. The chicken had its fast-day status restored temporarily in the thirteenth century when St. Thomas Aquinas held that it was of aquatic origin and thus edible on the same terms as fish; the Church later decided that St. Thomas had underestimated the chicken and ruled it definitely too good for fasting. Henry IV of France no doubt felt so too when he dangled before his subjects the prospect of a chicken in every pot, which also became the slogan of the Republican Party in the 1932 presidential election (it lost). On the other side of the world, the eighteenth-century Chinese poet Yuan Mei was listing chicken among "the four heroes of the table." William Blake marveled: "More wondrous, wondrous still, the cock and hen"; and Charles Edward Carryl (1842–1920) was certainly not denigrating this fowl when, in "The Plaint of the Camel," he let his ill-fed protagonist moan:

And as for the poodles, they tell me the noodles
Have chicken and cream for their lunch.

A high opinion of the chicken is implied today by the citizens of Rome, who make roast capon their festive dish on Christmas, and by the citizens of Brussels, who have won for themselves the nickname *kiekefretter*, "chicken guzzlers."

Man's association with the chicken began about 2000 B.C. in India, where the wild red jungle fowl was first domesticated, initially as a sacred bird which appeared in religious ceremonies and was consulted by augurs in search of omens. Priests of many times and climes have customarily made alimentary use of the remains of sacrificial animals after offering their less edible parts to the gods, so it is safe to assume that the chicken was not slow in finding its way to the table. Spreading northward and eastward, it made its way through China and on to the Pacific islands; we do not know when it arrived there, but it preceded the white man. The chronicler of the Magellan expedition reported that the natives of the Philippine Islands possessed "large cocks," but didn't eat them; they were raised for cockfighting.

In the other direction, westward, the place of the chicken's advent in Europe is unusual. Most Asiatic foods reached Europe via the Mediterranean, but the chicken is said to have arrived first in central Europe, about 1500 B.C., and not to have appeared in the Near East until at least a century later. Even 1400 B.C. seems a little too early. Before this date Egypt possessed ducks and geese, but apparently no chickens. The earliest representation of a chicken in Egyptian art known to me was a painting found in the tomb of Tutankhamun, hence about 1350 B.C., and the first in Asia Minor about the eighth century B.C., on Assyrian seals. The Hebrews of Old Testament times apparently had no chickens; at least there is no reference to them, not even in Deuteronomy or Leviticus, which give lengthy lists of the birds which it was permitted to eat and of those which it was forbidden to eat: the chicken appears in neither category.

The bird first appears in Western history in Greece, but diffidently. The Greek colonists who founded Sybaris on the sole of Italy in 720 B.C. passed a law barring roosters from the city so that their crowing would not wake them up too early; but though it was a food-conscious city, Sybaris left no other references to the chicken. The Greeks showed little interest in the bird at least up to the fifth century B.C.; chickens were kept for their eggs, not their meat. The Romans likewise showed no haste about introducing the chicken to the kitchen. In the fifth century B.C. we find references to hens' eggs, but the meat does not seem to have been appreciated; probably the birds were given no food except what they could scratch up for themselves and were consequently too scrawny to be appetizing. This neglect continued for at least another two centuries, and then a change set in, though it has not been accurately dated. Chicken was certainly being widely eaten in Rome after 185 B.C., the year when the Asian Army returned from the East, bringing with it new foods and new culinary ideas. It may have been then that the Romans learned how to raise and feed chickens from the Greeks of the island of Cos, who by then had mastered the art of fattening poultry for the table, the first in the Western world to do so. A century later, chicken is found holding a place of honor on the menus of Pompeii, a city accustomed to good eating. Apicius left recipes for preparing it in many different and ingenious fashions; and by the time of Trajan, under whom the food resources of Rome reached their zenith, chicken in all its forms was firmly established in the kitchen.

In more northerly parts of Europe, chickens enjoyed great favor during the Middle Ages, especially in the form of capon. The very first medieval cookbook after the imperial Roman era, which appeared in Italy at some undetermined date between 1260 and 1290, contained recipes for stuffed chickens and capons, while German cookbooks shortly thereafter gave directions for making chicken stew. In 1261 St. Louis took the trouble to issue a decree concerning henhouses; the king's own poultry yard in the rue St. Antoine was one of the most famous in France.

A non-gastronomic note concerning medieval chickens was provided by the Swiss city of Basle, where a court condemned a rooster to be burned alive for laying an egg.

All the chickens in the world, billions of them (chickens outnumber the human race), are descendants of *Gallus gallus*, the wild red jungle fowl domesticated in India four thousand years ago. The modern bird which most resembles this venerable ancestor is the black-breasted fighting cock.

"In Turkey," Alexandre Dumas wrote of the chicken, "its plumage is nearly as rich as that of the pheasant; in China, it has wool instead of feathers; in Persia, there is a whole species which has no tails; in India, they have black flesh and bones, which does not prevent them from being very good to eat." Modern breeders, less picturesquely, divide the chickens of the world into five races—in probable order of antiquity, Asiatic, Continental European, Mediterranean, English and American.

The Brahma is probably the best known of the Asian chickens in the Western world. Among Continental varieties, the most reputed for the table is the famous Bresse chicken of France, whose white flesh is partly the result of a diet in which rice and white Indian corn predominate, while the also famous yellow chicken of the Landes region owes its color to the high-quality yellow field corn of that region. A chicken of the Mediterranean race which is known all over the world is the Italian Leghorn, a better egg producer than a meat bird, which is in general true of the Mediterranean varieties and may help explain why the ancient Romans for so long concentrated on the eggs. The Jersey should be English from its name, and perhaps was originally; but it seems to be American now: the Jersey White Giant is the heaviest American bird, raised almost exclusively for meat, since it is not a good layer. Everyone knows the various kinds of New Hampshires, double-threat birds which give both eggs and meat; the Wyandottes, ditto; the Rhode Islands, better for eggs; and the Plymouth Rocks, of which the white variety is particularly popular for broilers.

It is on record that somebody once counted a Plymouth Rock's feathers on a bet and announced a total of 8325. So far as I know the experiment has never been repeated, either on a Plymouth Rock or any other breed.

CHICK-PEA. Man began cultivating the chick-pea so long ago that its original wild ancestor no longer exists anywhere in the world, not even in its supposed native region, south of the Caucasus and north of Persia. Chick-peas were probably a food of pre-Neolithic Sicily and certainly of Neolithic Switzerland, where they have been found in prehistoric lacustrine ruins. They

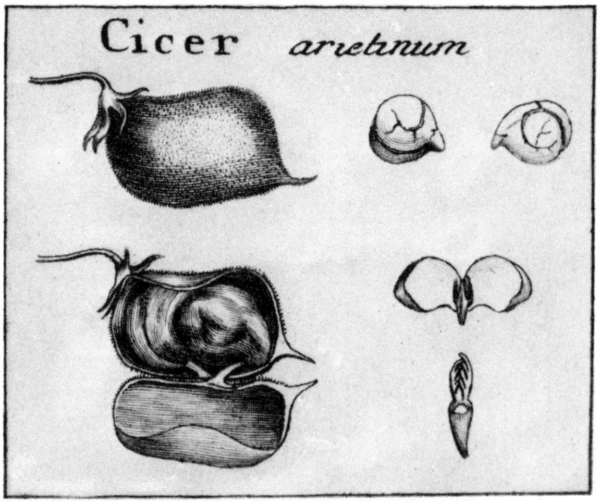

CHICK-PEA. *Drawing from J. Gaertner:* De Fructibus et Seminibus Plantarum, *Paris, 1791*

were grown in the hanging gardens of Babylon, and vast fields of chick-peas were common in ancient Egypt. In Homeric times not much else was available in the way of vegetables except peas, broad beans, lentils and the ubiquitous onion and garlic. The pork and beans of the ancient world were chick-peas and bacon, canned (in amphorae) in Pompeii and exported to the rest of Roman territory.

Gastronomic writers repeat endlessly that Cicero was so called because he had a wart on his nose the size of a chick-pea (*cicer,* in Latin); but this can hardly be so unless it was a hereditary defect, for Cicero was not his nickname, it was his family name, which antedated his wart by countless generations. After the time of Cicero, the chick-pea does not again emerge from its vegetable seclusion until the Sicilian Vespers of March 31, 1282, when Sicilians rebelling against Charles I of Anjou massacred everybody convicted of being French by their inability to pronounce correctly the Italian word for chick-pea—*cece* (pronounced *tchay-tchay*) in the singular, and *ceci* (pronounced *tchay-tchee*) in the plural.

The large, almost round, yellow chick-pea is not a pea, though it does belong to the same family, the *Leguminosae,* but so do 13,000 other species, most of which are not peas. It is also a member of the same subfamily as the pea, the *Papilionoideae,* but even this does not bring it within kissing-cousin range. It is, however, like the common pea in that it grows in a pod, two grains to each.

If you were to draw a map of the world showing the density of chick-pea consumption you would be close to a map of poverty; since this vegetable provides a maximum of nourishment for a minimum of expenditure, whether in the form of money or of labor, it is most eagerly eaten in the poorest parts of the globe. The country where the chick-pea enters most importantly into the normal diet is India, where famine is endemic. Africa, a land of frequent food shortages, ranks second in dependence on the chick-pea. It is neglected in the prosperous United States, but since its acclimatation in the New World it has become a significant item in the diet of Brazil, Venezuela, El Salvador and Mexico, and to a lesser extent in other poor regions of South and Central America. In Europe, where chick-peas appear frequently in soups, stews and salads, from choice oftener than from necessity, they are nevertheless most consumed in one of the poorest European countries, Spain.

CHILI. Paprika, Hungarian? The small, twisted, bright-red hot peppers which are ground into curry powders, Indian? Pili-pili, tropical African? Not at all. None of these were known in Europe, Asia or Africa before the discovery of America, where Columbus found the chili, of which all these are varieties, under the name *ají.* The earliest detailed description of the plant came

CHILI. *Drawing by Avey from* Arizona Highways, *Arizona Highways Department, 1946*

from Valerius Cordus, followed by others who had met it in Brazil and Peru. But curiously enough, it was a German botanist who had never been in the New World, Leonhard Fuchs, who led in calling attention to what he called Calcutta pepper, undoubtedly under the illusion that Columbus had reached India, for actually the chili did not arrive in that country, imported by the Portuguese, until 1611, forty-five years after Fuchs's death. Fuchs probably saw it in Spain, where it had been introduced as early as 1514.

South American Indians in Brazil and Peru began eating wild chilies somewhere between 6500 and 5000 B.C. The first conquistadors found them still growing wild there, but by then they had long been cultivated and had become the principal seasoning first of the Incas and then of the Aztecs. Tenochtitlán, now Mexico City, received chilies as tribute from conquered peoples. From Mexico the chili pushed north to what is now the southwestern United States, where it was adopted enthusiastically by the Pueblo Indians, one of whose favorite dishes today is still green chili stew served with adobe bread and a salad of marinated cucumbers—the last not available in pre-Columbian times, since the cucumber, a native of India, did not exist in America.

The burning sensation produced in the mouth by chilies is not subjective, as you might be inclined to think because of the difference in effect they produce on those habituated to them and those who are not—some very hot chilies developed in India are eaten with impunity by persons brought up on them, but literally blister the lips and palates of unhardened foreigners. The heating effect of chili is objectively measurable: growers, dealers and producers rate it on a scale of 1 to 120. Since the jalapeño, which numbs the mouths of those unaccustomed to it, is rated at 15, it is difficult to imagine what might happen to the unwary consumer of a 120-proof chili.

CHIVES. John Randolph, circa 1770, gentleman of Virginia, may be presumed never to have met Marcus Valerius Martialis, circa 100, poet of Rome, who would hardly have been described as a gentleman by the targets of his pitiless satiric verses. It is just as well; they are in head-on disagreement. Randolph wrote, in *A Treatise on Gardening by a Citizen of Virginia,* that he recommended chives to his friends because, unlike onions or garlic, they left no trace on the breath. But Martial's eighteenth epigram, translated with a certain freedom, asserts that

He who bears chives on his breath
Is safe from being kissed to death.

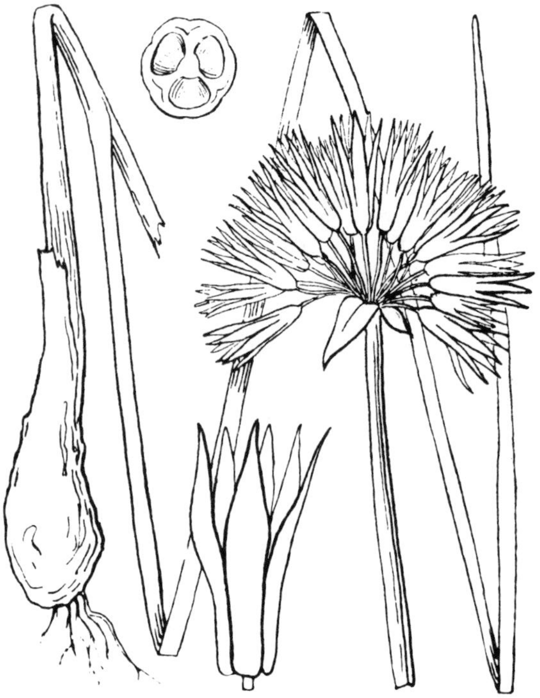

CHIVES. *Drawing from Britton and Brown:* Illustrated Flora of the Northern States and Canada, *New York, 1896*

A reference to chives in Martial is disconcerting for that majority of accepted authorities who are of the opinion that the ancient world did not know chives. This is difficult to believe, for the chive was common in the wild state in both Greece and Italy; it could hardly have been missed. Perhaps the ancients did not bother to cultivate it; it was quite satisfactory wild.

It is possible that North America had chives before Europe. They originated in Siberia, and the theory that they spread from there directly across the top of the world into America is supported by the zone occupied by the American wild chive, *Allium sibiricum,* also called the rush garlic—Alaska to Maine.

The taste of the chive has been described as intermediary between onion and garlic, two flavors sufficiently distinct so that it is a little hard to imagine a midway savor. The chive has a definite taste all its own, simultaneously more delicate and more incisive than that of the onion; you can hardly call it stronger, but it is more arresting. Suppose, in the symphony of tastes, you described the onion as the cornet: the chive would be the oboe.

Few plants are easier to raise. Outside my kitchen window is a long shallow box in which I grow chives, harvesting them pretty continuously from spring to fall. I cut off the upper halves and what is left continues to grow; in fact, chives grow better if they are cropped from time to time. It is this, no doubt, which accounts for their German name—*Schnittlauch,* the cuttable leek.

CHO
stands for

the **chogare**, a delicious Central Asian melon; and for the **chokecherry**, *Prunus virginiana,* a native American wild cherry usually too tart to eat raw, but first-rate for jelly.

And **CHO** also stands for

CHOCOLATE. "It flatters you for a while," Madame de Sévigné wrote to her daughter; "it warms you for an instant; then, all of a sudden, it kindles a mortal fever in you." She was talking of chocolate, yet this opinion did not dissuade a French candymaker from giving her name to a brand of chocolates. Perhaps he had never read this particular tribute to his product, for "the epistolary Marquise," as French gastronomic writer R. J. Courtine put it, reserved the right to change her mind, "praising or accusing chocolate from one breath to the next." In a kinder moment she wrote: "Day before yesterday I took some chocolate to digest my dinner, in order to sup well, and I took some yesterday to be well fed so I could fast until evening; this is what I find agreeable about it, that it acts as you intend it to do."

Mme. de Sévigné was thinking of chocolate primarily as a drink, which takes it a little outside of our framework, but it has wide uses also in solider form: chocolate bars and chocolate candy are the most obvious, but there are also the chocolate doughnuts of New England, the chocolate macaroons of Venice, chocolate cakes, chocolate puddings, chocolate creams, chocolate soufflés, chocolate mousse and, of course, chocolate ice cream, the most popular flavor in the United States after vanilla. The Mexicans combine two ancient Aztec specialties which would seem destined to go very badly together, chocolate and chilies, in their hot *molé* sauce, so unexpectedly wonderful on chicken; the Spaniards follow their example by using on game birds a chocolate sauce containing glazed white onions. In Sicily, Syracusans add a little chocolate sauce to the island's famous dish of stewed vegetables, *caponata.* The Germans were slow to adopt chocolate when it began spreading through Europe, but they have taken to it now with a vengeance, doting on such dishes as chocolate soup, chocolate potato tart and chocolate pretzels.

CHOCOLATE. *Photograph from the Brazilian presentation:* Travel in Brazil, *New York World Fair, 1939–1940*

CHOCOLATE. *Bette Davis as Margo Channing in* All About Eve, *directed and written by Joseph Mankiewicz, Twentieth Century Fox, 1950*

The cocoa (or cacao) tree from whose seeds, called beans, chocolate is made, is a native of tropical America—of Central America and the Caribbean islands, according to some authorities, and according to others, of Mexico. A presumption in favor of the former theory might be seen in the fact that chocolate does not seem to have been important for the Aztecs until they began to receive it as tribute from conquered neighbors.

It was on his fourth voyage, in 1502, that

Columbus discovered cacao beans in what is today Nicaragua and sent some back to Spain, to general indifference; probably no one knew how to rid them of their forbidding bitterness. But in 1519, Hernando Cortez tasted chocolate as the Aztecs prepared it—not only as a drink, but as a sort of paste (the equivalent of the modern chocolate bar?) and in what was referred to as a soup (the ancestor of *molé* sauce?). He not only brought back more beans, but also the knowledge of how the Aztecs treated them. They were given to a monastery, where the roasted ground beans, dampened into a paste, were mixed with cane sugar, another novelty in Europe at that time, producing a food so much appreciated that Spain attempted to keep secret its origin and the fashion of preparing it: a monopoly in chocolate was maintained for nearly a century, shared during part of this time with the Portuguese, who had found the cacao tree in Brazil.

France acquired chocolate when Jews expelled from Spain settled in the region of Bayonne and began to process chocolate there. France regarded it askance as at best a barbarous product and at worst a noxious drug, and Bayonne forbade making chocolate within the city limits, so its manufacturers set up shop in the suburbs. (Later Bayonne would become proud of this product and would celebrate "Bayonne chocolate" along with its other most famous manufacture, the bayonet.) The French queens from Spain helped end the disgrace of chocolate. Anne of Austria, Spanish despite her epithet, married Louis XIII in 1615, and made chocolate a drink of the French court, a missionary effort which was completed when Louis XIV found another "Austrian" bride in Spain, the Infanta Marie Thérèse, who was such an avid consumer of chocolate that she lost her teeth from over-indulgence.

In 1657 a Frenchman opened in London a shop called the Coffee Mill and Tobacco Roll, whose greatest novelty was neither of these two specialties, but chocolate, sold in bars which could be melted either for making a drink or for use in food. It was expensive—ten to fifteen shillings a pound, in those days one-half to three-quarters of the value of its weight in gold—largely because of the high duty imposed on it, so that English and Dutch smugglers quickly worked up a profitable business bringing chocolate into their countries illegally from Venezuela. Fashionable chocolate-consuming establishments appeared in England and Holland, some of which developed into private clubs. About 1700, England improved chocolate by adding milk to it; it remained a luxury, with milk or without, until the excessive duties were eliminated in 1853.

North America's first chocolate factory was opened in Dorchester, Massachusetts, in 1765, financed by James Baker; Baker's chocolate became part of American folklore. The Swiss, great chocolate makers today, were late starters; they began making chocolate bars only toward the middle of the nineteenth century. Switzerland was short on chocolate and sugar, but it had plenty of milk, so in 1876 M. D. Peter, who may have known about the English example, introduced milk chocolate to the world on a commercial scale for the first time.

The process of converting a forbiddingly bitter bean into a luscious confection is arduous and complicated; we have no space to go into it here. Paradoxically, one of its essential elements is the removal by man of the greater part of the nourishment packed into the cocoa bean by nature; but some of it is put back later. Cacao is too rich to be absorbed at its full strength. Most of the bean's fats (cocoa butter), which constitute 50 percent or more of its volume, are extracted, but when eating chocolate reaches the end of the manufacturing process, enough of the cocoa butter is returned to it to bring its proportion up to 15 to 30 percent, or even 35 percent. The more cocoa butter is added, the richer the chocolate, but above this limit it becomes cloying.

"Unsweetened chocolate is inedible," a French authority has written, and indeed in the European definition, chocolate is cacao plus sugar. I have been told that in the United States cooking chocolate exists which contains no sugar at all, but in Europe this ingredient is just as essential as the cacao. What Europe calls bitter chocolate may contain as much as 40 percent sugar. Almost invariably, chocolate also contains some flavoring, oftenest the one the Aztecs used—vanilla. Many others have been tried—cloves, popular in the seventeenth century, anise, ginger, pepper and chilies—but we have retained only a few which marry well with chocolate, such as honey, coffee, almond extract and, in Spain, cinnamon, almost never omitted in that country. Different types of chocolate have been developed for special purposes—bittersweet, for instance, and coating chocolate to cover candy or cookies, which was invented about the middle of the nineteenth century.

Chocolate confections have always and everywhere assumed a festive character. Chocolates are a traditional gift during the Christmas–New Year's holiday season, which was also, in medieval times, a period when the Church could impose a temporary laying down of arms by constantly warring factions. By association of ideas, this respite from fighting at a time when chocolate was much in evidence became known as the *Trêve des Confiseurs,* "the Candymakers' Truce."

CHR
stands for

christophene, a form of the tropical American chayote which looks like a pale avocado but is really a squash; for **Christ's-thorn,** a pulpy fruit related to the jujube, eaten in Africa, whose Moslems prefer to call it the Koran lotus; for **chrysanthemum,** whose petals flavor fritters in Japan and tea in China, and which has preserved from merited oblivion Alexandre Dumas's play *Francillon,* whose chief merit is that it gives a recipe for chrysanthemum salad; for **chrysobalanus,** a fruit highly popular in equatorial Africa which seems to have no name in any European languages; and for **chrysophrys,** an edible saltwater fish known to Ovid but not to me, so called because it wears a golden patch over each eye.

CHU
stands for

the **chub,** a European freshwater fish which, Webster says sniffishly, "is little valued as food"; for the **chuckwalla,** a foot-long lizard eaten by Papago Indians; for **chufa,** a rhizome which tastes something like an almond, first cultivated in ancient Egypt and today exclusively in Africa, especially Ethiopia, since a nineteenth-century attempt to exploit it in the southern United States failed for want of buyers; for the **chum,** the dog salmon of Alaska; for the **chukar,** an Indian rock partridge introduced into the western United States as a game bird with marked success; and for the **"Churchill,"** a freshwater fish important in tropical African diets, known only as *ras al hajar* until it acquired this nickname during World War II in apparent analogy with the British statesman, though no one knows if it is because this fish, of the genus *Petrocephalus,* rock-head, is considered to be of the bulldog breed, or because it is of solid, chunky build, or because it belongs to the family of *Mormyridae,* distinguished by exceptionally large brains, some of whose members are capable of delivering electric shocks.

CI
stands for

cicada, a sort of locust which struck the ancient Romans as a dainty tidbit, perhaps because Virgil maintained that it fed on dew; for the **cichlids,** perchlike fish which may have been the very first ever to have been raised artificially, in Egypt circa 2000 B.C.; for **cilando,** which is what coriander is called when it is the fresh leaves (also known as Chinese parsley) that are used in cooking instead of the seeds, as they are in India and in the Caribbean islands; for **cinnamonwood,** which is sassafras; for **citrange,** a cross between two types of oranges whose offspring is too bitter to eat; for **citronella,** a grass used in the Far East to flavor soya bean sauce and in Africa to make tea; for **ciubritza,** a Roumanian herb resembling tarragon; and for **civet cat,** an over-scented animal no longer eaten in China, though it was featured in a publicity stunt "imperial banquet" in Hong Kong in 1971, but which is still sampled gingerly in equatorial Africa.

And **CI** also stands for

CICELY (or **sweet cicely**). Cicely has fallen victim to modern merchandising, which has eliminated many delicately differentiated old-fashioned herbs from our pantries because supermarkets cannot be bothered handling items in minor demand. Cicely is a European herb, probably native to central and southern Europe, whose leaves are reminiscent of chervil in flavor and

CICELY. *Drawing from Dr. August Garcke:* Illustrierte Flora von Deutschland, *Berlin, 1895*

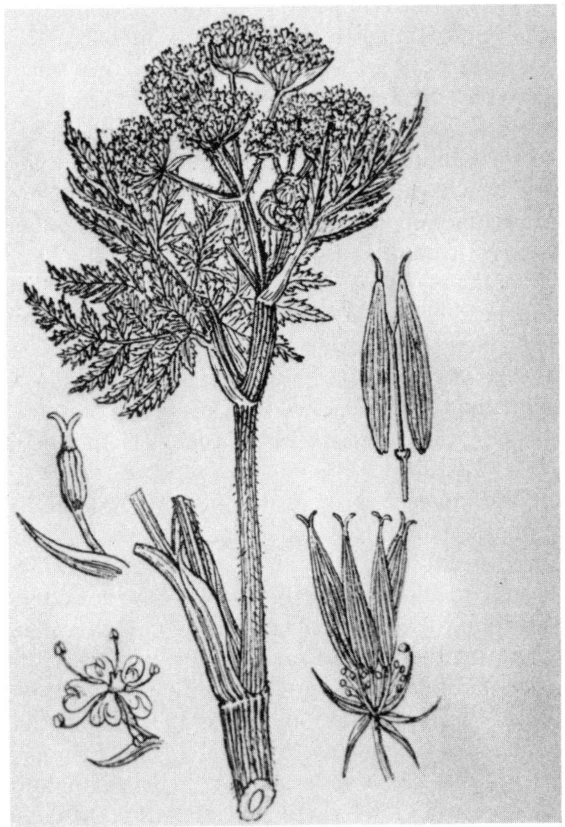

whose aromatic root is also edible. It was widely cultivated in France and England in the sixteenth and seventeenth centuries, and until fairly recently was a common potherb in England, but its use there now is much reduced; it seems to be employed oftenest on fish. Its decline is perhaps accounted for by its taste, which is much more assertive than that of chervil (the French call it musky chervil), and which is not always appreciated by persons unaccustomed to the wide gamut of herbal flavors familiar to our fathers and grandfathers. It still grows abundantly in Scottish and English pastures, and should be encouraged to do so, since cows like it mixed with other pasturage, and it encourages lactation.

What is called cicely in America is not the same plant as that of Europe. The name is applied to a number of different herbs of the genus *Osmorhiza,* distinguished by thick, fleshy roots, especially to *O. longistylas,* known popularly as sweet chervil. The root is sweet-flavored, and it is widely distributed in eastern and central North America, but not, alas, in American pantries.

CINNAMON. About 2700 B.C. the Emperor Shen Nung, to whom Chinese tradition attributes the introduction of agricultural implements for the tilling of the soil and the discovery of the medicinal properties of plants, made in a treaty the first known reference to cinnamon. He called it *kwei,* which in later documents became *tien chu kwei,* Indian cinnamon. It is probable that in those days no very fine distinction was made between the Indian mainland and the island of Ceylon, which lies just east of its southern tip, so the Chinese description of cinnamon as Indian, for which we may read Ceylonese, supports the contention of gourmets that the real cinnamon (it is certainly the best) is *Cinnamomum zeylanicum,* native to the island of Ceylon and nowhere else. The only other species to which they grant the name, somewhat grudgingly, is *C. cassia,* otherwise known as cassia or Chinese cinnamon, which grows in many parts of southeastern Asia, especially in the islands of Indonesia and Malaysia.

The ancient peoples of the Mediterranean, when cinnamon reached them, knew both kinds and possibly also a third, in malabathron, which seems to have been cassia leaves, chewed to sweeten the breath. They distinguished among them on the basis of quality, not geography, for they had no idea where any of them came from. Pliny, Theophrastus and Ptolemy thought that cinnamon originated in Arabia or Ethiopia; Herodotus had a more complicated explanation. "Cinnamon grows where Bacchus was nourished," he wrote, a trifle vaguely, in inaccessible mountains, but "certain large birds transport the twigs, which we call *ledabon,* having learned that word from the Phoenicians," to more attainable regions to make nests from them. "To obtain these bits of cinnamon, the natives have recourse to a ruse. They place under the nests large quarters of meat, of which the birds are fond; they carry them to their nests, which break under the weight and fall to the ground. The natives then only have to pick up the cinnamon."

Cinnamon was almost unobtainable in ancient Greece; what little arrived there, about the fifth century B.C., was used to flavor wine. The Romans put it in wine too (and passed the habit on to the ancient Gauls), but it was very little used in Roman cooking; it cost too much, for it was at times worth more than its weight in gold. Only emperors could afford to keep a supply on hand for their own use. When the Empress Poppaea died because Nero had kicked her in the stomach, he made amends by burning her body with more cinnamon than the spice merchants of Arabia could furnish in a whole year, possibly the most expensive funeral pyre in history.

Most of the spices ancient Rome received from the East disappeared from Europe when the empire collapsed. They began to return in the ninth and tenth centuries when the Saracens moved into Sicily, bringing Oriental foods with them. In the eleventh century, when the Normans took over Sicily from the Saracens, they began to use cinnamon, expensive though it was, to disguise the taste of tainted beef. In the twelfth century, access to cinnamon was increased when the Crusaders returned from the East, bringing its spoils with them. Marco Polo came back from China at the end of the thirteenth century, and the overland spice route was established. Medieval Europeans "liked what the Romans liked," wrote Georges and Germaine Blond in their *Histoire pittoresque de notre alimentation,* "cinnamon and the cinnamon flower." The spice went into sauces whose pungent nature was betrayed by their names —treason sauce, hell's sauce. The French *caneline* sauce took its name from the spice which dominated it (cinnamon is *cannelle* in French); it was a variant of the standard black sauce of the times in which cinnamon replaced the customary pepper. It was probably this sauce which, in the fourteenth century, Taillevent served with capon for Charles VI. But cinnamon was still so rare and dear toward the end of the fifteenth century that eunuchs and white female slaves from Europe were traded to the Arabs for cinnamon and one or two other precious spices. It took the age of exploration and the discovery of the Spice Islands by the Magellan expedition to make cinnamon possibly the most widely used spice of Europe.

The Renaissance took it to its bosom; by the early 1500s, cinnamon was turning up in Italy in almost every dish which could reasonably admit it, as well as some which could not. It became one of the most important seasonings in English cooking, and by the seventeenth century Robert May included it in many of the recipes of the chapter entitled "Kickshaws . . . and à la Mode Curiosities" in his *The Accomplisht Cook*. ("Kickshaws" had come to mean fancy dishes, but it could have stood for almost anything; it is an English corruption of the French *quelque chose*, "something.")

Despite strong Portuguese competition, it was the Dutch who gained mastery over the cinnamon trade, not only in their own Indonesian area, but also in the native land of the genuine cinnamon, Ceylon. The Dutch East India Company grew rich on spices, and its most profitable spice was cinnamon. It was the Dutch who inaugurated the cultivation of cinnamon in the eighteenth century —before then, wild trees had supplied the demand —and the "cinnamon gardens" they established are still displayed proudly to tourists, who, if they arrive by sea, can smell their fragrance several miles before they make their landfall. Later in the century a Frenchman, Pierre Poivre, smuggled some slips out of Dutch-controlled territory and planted them in French tropical colonies. Holland's monopoly was broken.

Cinnamon is no longer as ubiquitous as it was in medieval and Renaissance times. The two Western countries which remain most devoted to it are England and Spain; the latter not only puts it into chocolate and cocoa, but into an almost limitless number of other dishes. Elsewhere also the rich, velvety flavor of cinnamon continues to assure it an important place among the world's seasonings, in such familiar dishes as English apple pie, American cinnamon buns, Danish pastry and Italian vinegar, and in more exotic ones like South African milk soup, Indian curries, Chinese five-spice powder and the fiery *berberé* seasoning which goes on or into every dish to which Ethiopia can possibly apply it.

Cinnamon proper is the inner bark of *C. zeylanicum*, peeled from the tree's shoots in the rainy season, when it is juicy with sap. On drying, the bark rolls up into quills, the form in which it is safest to buy cinnamon if you want to make sure that you are getting the genuine article instead of its numerous cheaper substitutes. It is not impossible to produce counterfeit quills, but it is hardly worth the trouble, given the ease with

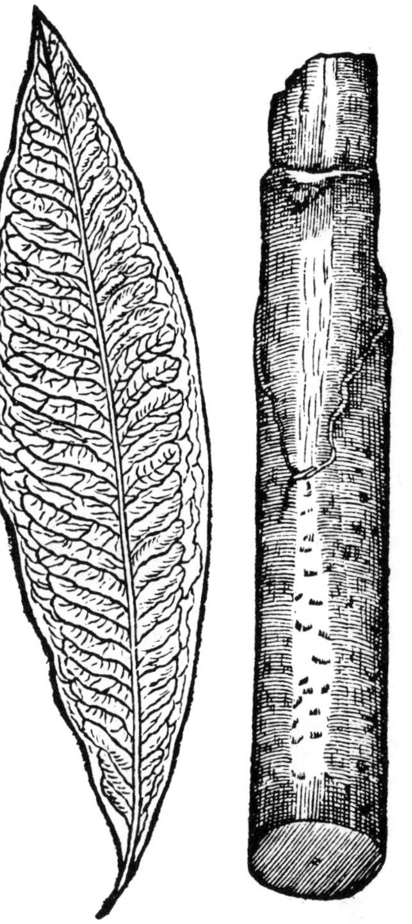

CINNAMON. *Woodcut from Garcia da Orta:* Exotic Plants, Spices and Drugs of the Far East, *Antwerp, 1567*

which cinnamon can be adulterated or replaced when it is sold in powdered form, as it commonly is.

The second most esteemed cinnamon, *C. cassia*, grows wild especially in the Chinese province of Kwangsi and in Tonkin and Annam in Indochina, where it once played a major role in politics and economics. The kings maintained a monopoly of cassia, which was exploited in primitive fashion by Moi mountaineers, who cultivated small groves of trees around their huts or stripped bark from wild trees. Alexandre Dumas wrote impolitely that the cinnamon of Tonkin "would be an important article of trade for a more intelligent nation; the forests are full of it, but it is cultivated only in the woods of the king and in the temples." The trade eventually escaped the monarchs and passed into the hands of the most astute merchants of the Far East, the Chinese.

The taste of cassia has been described by a French authority as "warm and very spicy," but "its odor recalls that of the bedbug." Cassia bark is thinner, smoother and redder, and its taste less pronounced, yet coarser, than that of Ceylon cinnamon, and unless you buy it in powdered form you cannot confuse it with Ceylon cinnamon, for the bark is flattened and attached to wooden bases so that it dries flat instead of forming quills. Almost all the "cinnamon" sold in the United States is really cassia from Sumatra or Indochina. Europeans sometimes refer to it disdainfully as "poor man's cinnamon," and in French it is called false cinnamon or bastard cinnamon. Americans may console themselves for being deprived of the finest cinnamon by reflecting that southern Europeans *prefer* cassia to cinnamon.

CITRON. If you have eaten, for instance in fruitcake, what you took to be lemon peel, you were in all probability really tasting citron. The citron (*Citrus medica*) is a close relative of the lemon (*C. limon*) and looks a good deal like it, but it is larger, shaped rather like a quince, and has a rough skin thicker than that of the lemon. This skin, cut into small pieces, is first preserved in brine or sea water, then cooked, and finally candied. It may be crystallized to be eaten for its own sake, like other candied fruits, or the firm pulp may be used to make jellies or preserves. Bayonne, France, makes a specialty of a sort of jellied citron paste called *pâte de cédrat*. In India the raw flesh of the fruit is pickled in a liquid spiced with curry powders, or, alternatively, cooked, combined with similar powders, and preserved in oil pressed from wild mustard seeds.

CITRON. *Engraving from Theodore Francis Garrett:* The Encyclopaedia of Practical Cookery, *London, 1898*

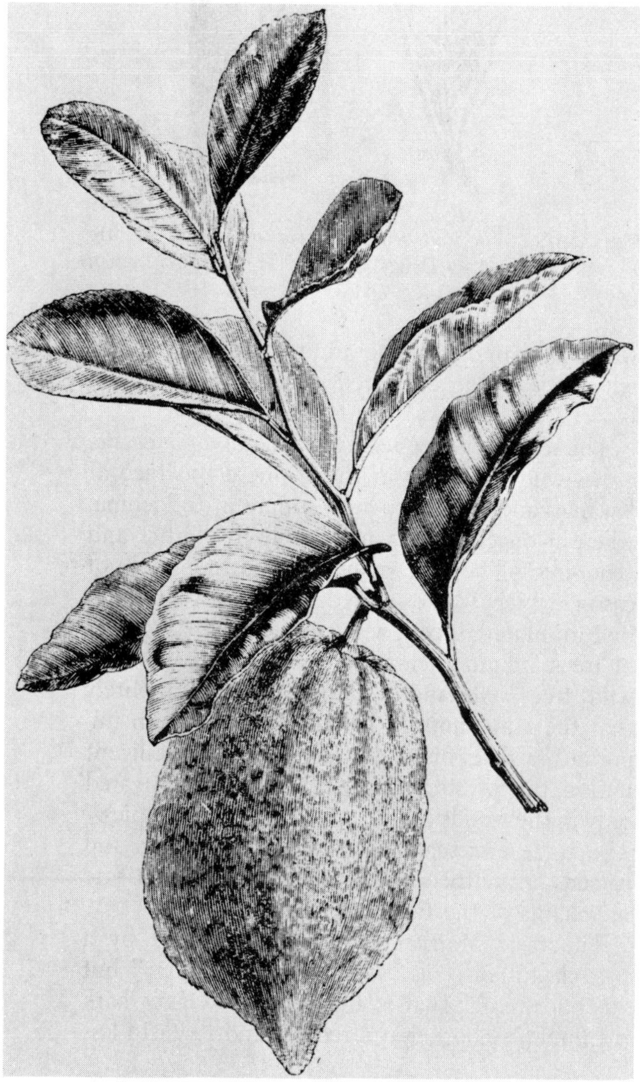

The citron is the same fruit as the Israeli etrog, grown in that country to be put on sale shortly after Yom Kippur, for a season which lasts only seven days. It is one of the four species which appear at the celebration of Succoth, and popular legend identifies it as the forbidden fruit eaten by Adam and Eve; marks which sometimes appear on its upper end are called "Adam's bites."

Reference books are almost unanimous in reporting that the citron is used only to provide candied peel because it is too bitter to eat, but there are many varieties of citron, and in Corsica, which is reputed to produce the best, there are some which can be eaten as a fruit. But its greatest popularity is for fruit juice, in which form it is extensively consumed throughout Africa and in Madagascar. In the New World, to which it has been transported, the citron flourishes on many Caribbean islands, and is a particular specialty of Puerto Rico.

Linnaeus thought the lemon was only a variety of the citron, and we may wonder whether the fruit the ancient Romans knew, translated today as "lemon," was not really the citron. Virgil called it the "Median apple," and it may be significant that French dictionaries of the nineteenth century gave *citronnier médique*, the Median lemon, as a synonym for "citron tree." In any case, the citron is supposed to have originated in Media and Persia; it is not certain where the lemon started.

CL
stands for

clary, an all-but-abandoned herb of the sage family, of which both leaves and seeds were used formerly in French and English cooking, and **cleavers,** an all-but-abandoned herb of the bedstraw family, of which both leaves and seeds are used, the first boiled like spinach, the second roasted and ground to provide a passable substitute for coffee; for **clay,** a substance which does not loom large in the history of food, but of which the Emperor Augustus took the trouble to corner the market for the best variety, that of Naples, to mix with grain in the Roman dish called *alica*; for the **clementine,** a cross between the orange and the mandarin, named for the French missionary who is credited with creating it in Algeria; for the **climber,** a versatile vine of which at least sixteen species offer their fruits to Africa, and the **climbing pea,** an African pulse related to the Florida velvet bean, probably brought to America by slaves; for the **clingfish,** a type of sucker eaten in Morocco; for the **cloudberry,** a masochistic fruit which revels in cold and delights in hardship; for the **cloud-ear mushroom,** delicious, refreshing and slippery, which can be eaten fresh only in China; for **clover,** seldom consumed by man except indirectly, in the form of milk, meat or honey, though it has been eaten in times of famine; for the **clovisse,** a Mediterranean clam which seems to be related to the American carpet shell; for **clown's lungwort,** our eighth alias for the mullein; for the **clubtop mushroom,** whose top actually looks more like a cauliflower and seems to be eaten almost nowhere except in Gabon, and sparingly even there, probably because even its most edible varieties are short on flavor, while several of them are strong laxatives; for the **clusterbean,** of which the leaves are eaten in Chad and the immature beans, pods and all, in southeastern Asia and Africa; and for the **cluster yam,** widely consumed in southern and tropical Africa despite the disadvantage that the wild varieties have to be thoroughly pounded and carefully washed because they are poisonous.

And **CL** also stands for

CLAM. What is a clam?

According to Webster, "any of various equivalve edible marine mollusks that live wholly or partly buried in sand or mud." Equivalve? One of the valves of the common steamer clam is bigger than the other. Edible? In the Puget Sound area *Schizothaerus nuttallii* is called the horse clam and declared uneatable (true, this is an error). Marine? The bent-nose clam survives far back from the sea in brackish water. Buried in sand or mud? The boring clam embeds itself in wood, cement or even rock.

What is a clam?

If we are to believe its etymology, a clam is a shellfish which shuts itself up tightly. "Clam," like "clamp," comes from the Old English *clamm*, "bond" or "fetter," which itself comes from the Old High German *klamma*, "constriction"—echoed in a British dialect verb, to clam, meaning to grasp tightly in the hand. (German itself has dropped this word, but includes the clam along with other bivalves in the category of *Muscheln*, "muscles," which preserves the same idea.) Yet the razor clam cannot close its shell completely. The horse clam is too big for its shell and bulges out at the neck end, which therefore has to remain open. The geoduck bulges out all the way around and cannot close at all; its two valves are held together precariously by the hinge alone.

What is a clam?

For the Scot, usually a scallop. For the Englishman, probably only a member of the genus *Mya* (especially *M. truncata*, which he calls the gaper, meaning what America has named the horse clam) or of the genus *Mactra* (especially *M. stultorum*, since it lives close to him, on the Dogger Bank). For the American, almost any bivalve for which no other name is handy. For the Frenchman, the American hard clam or quahog, to which the name *le clam* was attached exclusively when this shellfish was brought into French waters. And for our own present purposes, any bivalve mollusk which men have taken it into their heads to call a clam unless it is indisputably something else, like what Americans call freshwater clams, in reality freshwater mussels.

Clams exist in every part of the world. The first primitive clams appeared in the Ordovician period of the Paleozoic era, 400 million to 500 million years ago. They range in size from the tiniest clams of Japan, probably the only country which would go to the trouble of harvesting shellfish so minute that it is almost impossible to taste them, to the giant clam of the Indian Ocean which sometimes weighs nearly 500 pounds. They may be round, triangular, heart-shaped, wedge-shaped, conical or so bizarre in form as to suggest fanciful names, like another Indian Ocean shellfish which its eaters call the bear's paw and scientists the horse's-foot clam—*Hippopus maculatus* (*maculatus*, "spotted," because its handsome white ridged shell is adorned with purplish-red splotches).

Most clams show growth ridges on their shells, from which we learn that as a rule they live from one to ten years; but there is on record a Pismo clam which, according to its ridges, survived for twenty-six. The clam's heartbeat is slow, as is normal for sluggish creatures—two to twenty beats per minute, depending on the species, as compared to forty to eighty for squids, which are mollusks too, but livelier ones. Most clams have a "foot" at one end of their body and what the layman calls a "neck" at the other, actually siphons which take care of the clam's respiratory and digestive needs. There are two siphons, the

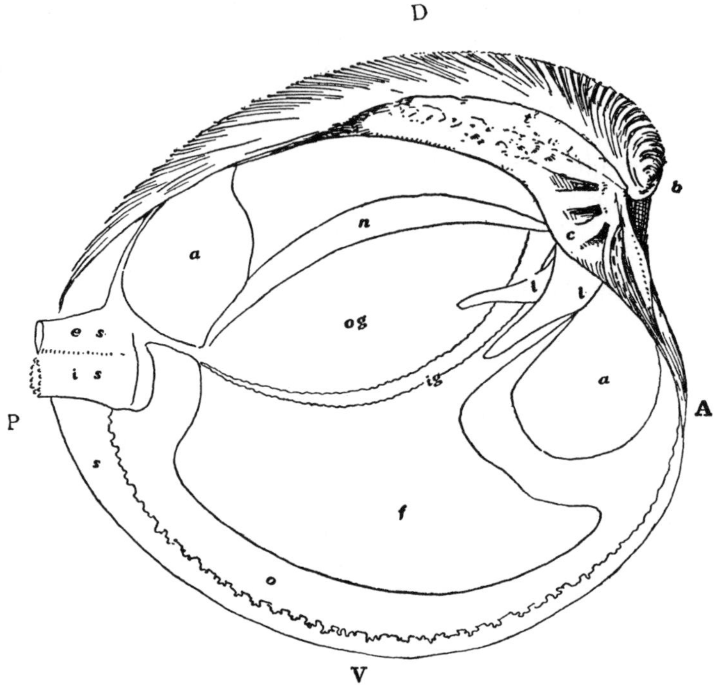

PARTS OF HARD SHELL CLAM (*Venus Mercenaria*)

A,	anterior end	*a, a,*	adductor muscle scar
P,	posterior end	*b*,	beak or umbo
D,	dorsal side	*c*,	hinge teeth
V,	ventral side	*t*,	hinge ligament
es,	excurrent siphon	*l, l,*	labial palpi
is,	incurrent siphon	*f*,	foot
ig,	inner gill	*o*,	border of mantle
og,	outer gill	*s*,	shell border
n,	gill chamber	*Ab*,	lunule

CLAM. *Drawing from Julia Ellen Rogers:* The Shell Book, *New York, 1908*

intake, through which the clam sucks in water, bringing oxygen to the gills and minute food particles to the stomach, and the exhaust, which carries off wastes. Usually these are bound together in a single tube, but they are sometimes separate, for example in the bent-nosed clams.

Shellfish must have been one of the easiest foods for prehistoric man to obtain, and the clam the easiest of all, since it is so often found on beaches uncovered twice daily by the tide. Veritable mountains of clamshells have been found in kitchen middens all over the world, in Scandinavia, in France, in Portugal, in Japan, in Brazil, in the United States—everywhere that prehistoric man has lived on the shores of the sea. It is on record that clams were eaten extensively by most ancient peoples except the Hebrews, whose dietary laws admitted as kosher nothing from the sea which did not have fins and scales. Today clams are eaten enthusiastically all over the world, but warily by Americans, oddly, since the United States is exceptionally well endowed with shellfish—five hundred species on the Pacific coast alone. True, most of the country's area lies inland (though this has been no great obstacle to the consumption of seafood since the advent of the airplane), but it may be that the official statistics are deceptive. Presumably they are gathered from the marketplace, and therefore cover only clams exploited commercially—the QUAHOG, the STEAMER, and not many others. Thousands of devoted clam hunters dig their own, and these may not be accounted for in the statistics.

It may be that there is some distrust about clams, dating from less hygienic times, when spoiled shellfish, which can indeed cause serious trouble for those who eat them, were encountered more frequently than they are now. Clams are perishable and go bad quickly, though they are less vulnerable than mussels, which sometimes attach themselves to toxic supports, while the burrowing habits of clams surround them with a natural filter against pollution from the adjacent water. When clams are eaten raw, the lemon juice or vinegar sauce frequently used on them has mildly bactericidal properties, while the practice of drinking white wine with clams is also held to provide a certain amount of protection; some authorities think white wine kills the Eberth bacillus which causes typhoid, a theory on which it is perhaps advisable not to rely too confidently.

The menus of Japanese wedding banquets customarily include *hamaguri*, clam broth; its role is not stimulant but symbolic—the tight closing together of the two halves of the clamshell provides a model for the union of the newly wedded couple.

CLOVE. In the second century B.C., etiquette of the Han court in China demanded that a person received by the emperor should hold a clove in his mouth to perfume his breath. The Chinese, who called the clove *ki she kiang*, the bird's-tongue spice, imported it for their own use and re-exported the surplus to India. If they knew where cloves came from, they didn't tell.

Half a millennium later, cloves made their first appearance in the West, delivered to the Emperor Constantine in Constantinople in A.D. 335 by Arab importers of the products of Asia. If they knew where they came from, they didn't tell.

It would indeed be another millennium and a half before Europe would discover the provenance of the clove. With the collapse of the Roman Empire and the trade routes which it supported, cloves disappeared from Europe, to be brought back either by the Saracens who conquered Sicily or the Crusaders who, in the Holy Land, failed to conquer the Saracens. In 1228, they were listed among the imports subject to duty in Marseilles and Barcelona; customs authorities can be counted upon to notice quickly the appearance of a new taxable commodity. By this time, the Venetians were importing cloves and other precious spices which they purchased from Arab traders in the Near East. If the Arabs knew where they came from, they didn't tell.

Another illustrious Venetian, Marco Polo, encountered the clove in 1229, and must have seen the plant itself, for he gave an excellent description of it. But he attributed it to central China, where it could not possibly have grown. Perhaps he knew where it really came from, but if so he didn't tell.

Not until 1511 was the clove finally spotted, by Francisco Serrano, serving under Magellan, who discovered Ternate, one of the five small islands of the Molucca archipelago, in the Spice Islands, which were the only places in the world where cloves grew. The Portuguese strove to keep the secret, by publishing for the use of foreigners falsified nautical charts designed to expose competitors to shipwreck. The Dutch arrived all the same, drove the Portuguese out of the Spice Islands in 1605, destroyed all the trees except those on the two most easily defendable islands and decreed pain of death for anyone who tried to export seeds or seedlings. A Frenchman, prophetically named Pierre Poivre (Peter Pepper), contrived to lay his hands on some and planted them on Réunion and Mauritius, in the Indian Ocean, but was foiled by the intrigues of Louis XV's court: his political opponents did not want him to gain the credit for presenting France with a source of riches. His trees were sabotaged, but one escaped; it is the ancestor of virtually all the cloves eaten in the world today, for the production of the Moluccas, as a result of the short-sighted destruction by the Dutch, has dwindled to insignificance. Today the center of clove production has shifted to Madagascar, second-largest supplier of this spice to the world, and Zanzibar, number one by far, for it meets 80 percent of the world demand. In tune with the centuries-old battle for a monopoly on cloves, Zanzibar made it a capital offense in 1972 to smuggle cloves out of the country, and later in the same year fifteen persons were actually sentenced to death for this crime.

The ferocity with which nations have fought for possession, preferably exclusive, of the clove results from the fact that it has always been extremely expensive, and is likely to remain so by its very nature, which requires a tremendous amount of costly hand labor. Cloves are buds picked just before opening, and this means that

CLOVE. *Woodcut from* Gart der Gesundheit, *Ulm, 1487*

the same trees have to be picked over and over day after day to catch the individual buds at exactly the right moment. After the picking comes another handwork process, drying. The buds are first dried in the sun for forty-eight hours, when they turn from rose to brown. They are then separated from their husks and dried for several days more. (Artificial drying results in a diminution of flavor.) Cloves lose 60 percent of their weight in drying; yet the yield from a single adult tree, even after this loss, may still reach seventy-five pounds.

The high price of cloves naturally encourages adulteration or substitution. The pedicles in which the buds lodge, much less flavorful, are often ground and sold as cloves with no mention of the fact that the resulting powder did not come from the tastier buds. The same treatment is also applied to its small fruits, ovoid bays which ripen to dark purplish-brown, each containing one or two seeds. Worst of all, clove buds which have been soaked in alcohol to extract their flavor, fragrance or color, for use in liqueurs, perfumes or dyes, are recuperated and sold as seasonings; they make pretty wan ones, having already been drained of most of their substance.

CO
stands for

coalfish, a word rather than a fish, since it is applied to a number of unrelated though swarthy species, and for **cobia,** one of the fishes thus designated; for **coca,** a South American bush whose leaves are chewed as a stimulant; for **cochineal,** a food colorant made from crushed insects which Bernal Díaz, chronicler of Cortez's conquest, first encountered in the markets of Mexico; for the **cockroach,** eaten by gourmets in China and aborigines in Australia and tropical South America; for **cockscombs,** which Alexandre Dumas described as "a family dish, hardly appropriate for important dinners," but which appealed nevertheless to the highly placed Catherine de' Medici, who was made ill by overindulgence in them; for the **coconut crab,** which shinnies up trees to pick the food for which it is named; for the **coco plum,** a highly popular fruit of tropical Africa, and the **coco yam,** ditto.

And **COC** also stands for

COCKLE. When sweet Molly Malone, in Dublin's fair city (where girls are so pretty), wheeled her wheelbarrow through the streets broad and narrow, calling, "Cockles and mussels, alive, alive, oh!" the merchandise she was offering was *Cardium edule.* In her time this was the only shellfish entitled to the name, but the word "cockle" became attached later not only to all the other species of *Cardium,* of which there are about a hundred, but then to the whole family of *Cardiidae* (made up, as its name indicates, of heart-shaped mollusks); by extension to almost any heart-shaped bivalve; and finally to some clams which seem to be called cockles only for lack of another name. Mary, Mary was so contrary as to have described the ornamental border of her garden as including cockleshells all in a row, when in all probability they were the more symmetrical shells of the scallop; but the dictionary now exonerates her by admitting that any shell which resembles the cockle in having fan-shaped radiating ribs, as the scallop has, may justifiably be called a cockleshell.

C. edule, the original cockle, has a range considerably larger than that often attributed to it, the British Isles. It exists also on the Atlantic coast of France, where it prefers river-mouth habitats, and is what you get when you buy *coques* in Paris, though its correct name is *buccarde.* It is found in the Mediterranean: the Adriatic shellfish called *cuore di mare* or *noce di mare* (sea heart or sea walnut) is *Cardium edule.* This true cockle has even ventured far beyond the Mediterranean, for paleontologists tell us that it reached the Caspian from the Black Sea in the late Quaternary epoch; the prehistoric area of the Caspian, much larger then than it covers now, has been mapped by locating the fossil shells of *C. edule* found on what is now dry land.

In America, the different clams called cockles with dubious justification are more numerous on the Pacific coast than on the Atlantic; and on the latter, contrary to the general rule that shellfish from cold waters are tastier than shellfish from warmer waters, the most interesting species are found to the south. Particularly abundant in Florida, though present elsewhere from Cape Hatteras to Mexico, is the giant Atlantic cockle, *Dinocardium robustum,* which exceeds five inches by four in size. It is tasty, even a little too much so for some fanciers, who find it on the strong side, but is excellent in chowder or cooked stuffed.

Also found in Florida and along the coast of the Gulf of Mexico is the smaller (three inches by two) prickly cockle, *Trachycardium egmontiamum,* also at its best in chowder or stuffed.

On the Pacific coast, the basket cockle, *Clinocardium nuttalii,* offers itself to the clam hunter with suicidal generosity all the way from Alaska to Lower California; it is best in the Puget Sound area. Basket cockles lie temptingly half-buried in the sand or even completely out of

COCKLE. *Drawing from Nicolaus Gaulterius:* Index Testarum Conchyliorium, *1742*

it; all you have to do is pick them up. Their flavor is good, but they tend to be tough, so they had better be chopped or ground for cooking. The bigger giant Pacific (or spiny) cockle, *Trachycardium quadragenarium*, found from Santa Barbara to northernmost Lower California, until recently little eaten because it lies in relatively deep water, has now become available to scuba divers. This is also true of an even bigger clam (seven inches across), the Pacific egg cockle, *Laevicardium elatum*.

There are other Pacific clams popularly called cockles, but they are so far from the real thing that we may justifiably ignore them.

COCONUT. To the American or European nibbling a coconut candy bar or savoring a cake with shredded coconut in its frosting or eating a slice of coconut custard pie, the coconut may seem no more than an airy trifle, agreeably exotic but easily dispensable; yet for one-third of the population of this planet, the coconut is regarded as one of the most important foods in the world. The coconut is even more important for humid tropical countries than the date for arid tropical countries. Its presence dominates a vast Asian-Malaysian-Oceanic-Pacific region stretching from Thailand to Hawaii; it is an essential food in West Africa; and though less prominent in the diet of tropical America, where there are more competing foods, it plays a considerable role in the kitchen even there.

In Bali, women are forbidden to touch coconut palms lest the fertility of the tree be drained off into the fertility of the woman, apparently considered less important. In Thailand, the first solid or semi-solid food a Brahmin baby is permitted to eat is three spoonfuls of the soft, custardy meat of an immature coconut, fed to the infant by a priest. In the Philippines, rival bands no longer fight each other for coconut oil (*latik*) as they used to do, but they commemorate those ancient battles in a dance called *magla-latik*. If you happen to find yourself in Samoa and spy an abandoned coconut lying by the roadside, do not pick it up unless you are looking for trouble; someone knows it is there and has proprietary rights to it. If the law doesn't get a coconut thief, the *tapui* will—the *tapui* being the magical force which protects a fruit that is taboo to everyone but its owner, and punishes the offender by striking him down with lightning or afflicting him with an agonizing, painful and incurable malady.

"He who plants a coconut tree," they say in the South Seas, "plants food and drink, vessels and clothing, a habitation for himself and a heritage for his children."

The coconut does not seem to have been known to the Western world before the sixth century A.D., when it was eaten in Egypt, imported by Egyptian or Arab merchants from the more distant shores of the Indian Ocean. It made little impression, and nothing more is heard of it until Marco Polo encountered it in India, Sumatra and the Nicobar Islands; he seems to have been aware of its Egyptian past, for he called it "Pharaoh's nut." Another two and a half centuries rolled by without news of the coconut until Magellan in his turn came upon it, on an island in the neighborhood of Guam. Coconuts seem to have taken until the sixteenth century to reach France, a country still unreceptive to them, while England waited for William Dampier, half-explorer, half-buccaneer, to convert it to the merits of the coconut, with which he had become acquainted during his voyage to Australia, New Britain and New Guinea between 1686 and 1701.

The origin of the coconut has never been established. Coconuts float, taking root wherever they happen to be washed up, which makes it difficult to determine where they started. The best guess would seem to be that its native land is somewhere in the Indo-Malaysian region, with the second guess reserved for the Pacific islands. Neither Columbus nor the explorers who followed him into the Caribbean reported the existence there of coconuts, though they gave us accounts of almost everything that grew there. However, there were coconut palms in the New World before Columbus, but he did not know it: they were on the far side of South America. Coconuts are represented in pre-Columbian Peruvian pottery, and in northern Chile the Indians were found sweetening their food with boiled-down coconut sap. This seems to support the theory that the coconut reached America from the Pacific islands.

Cocos nucifera will grow anywhere in the tropics where conditions are right—temperatures which never fall below 20° C. (68° F.), rainfall between 50 and 70 inches a year and ample circulating ground water. The chief producing areas lie within 22 degrees of the equator. Coconut trees begin bearing from five to seven years after their nuts sprout. The individual coconuts are slow ripeners—they require a year to reach full maturity from the time when they first begin to take shape—but they make up for this by staging a continuous performance. Ten to thirteen times a year a new flower spike emerges from the crown of the tree, developing into a cluster of six to twelve nuts; the fortunate possessor of a coconut palm is thus assured of food all year round from a tree which knows no seasons.

The ordinary coconut is the same species the world over, but there is another coconut, called in French the *coco de mer*, "sea coconut," and in English the Maldive coconut. For a century or two it was a mystery. Single enormous nuts were picked up from time to time at sea or on beaches where they had washed up, but nobody knew

COCONUT *by Winslow Homer (1836–1910).* Palm Tree, Nassau, *watercolor*

Coconut

Coconut

where they came from. Then, in 1609, the Seychelles Islands, about a thousand miles east of Africa, were sighted and in 1777 settled, by the French, and there *Lodoicea maldivia* or *L. sechellarum,* the sea coconut, was finally located. Of the ninety-three islands in the group, it seems to have existed only on the island of Praslin, and there only in the Vallée de Mer, sometimes referred to romantically as the Garden of Eden.

The Maldive coconut is believed to be the largest and heaviest fruit in the world; it may weigh forty-five pounds, compared to a record six and a half for the ordinary coconut, and it takes ten years to ripen. It is sometimes called the double coconut, for it is two-lobed, as though a pair of coconuts had fused together (there is just one tree in the Vallée de Mer which produces four-lobed coconuts). The French, in carefree moments, refer to the *coco de mer* as the *coco-fesse,* "buttocks coconut."

Marco Polo seems to have been the first Westerner to pay much attention to the coconut as food. "One of these nuts," he wrote, "is a meal for a man, both meat and drink. . . . Under the husk is a food that provides a full meal for a man. It is very tasty, as sweet as sugar and as white as milk, and it is in the form of a cup like the surrounding husk. Inside this fruit is enough juice to fill a phial. The juice is clear and cool and admirably flavored. When a man has eaten the kernel, he drinks the juice. And so from one nut a man can have his fill of meat and drink."

The coconut's first dividends are reserved for those who live where it is grown, for the young immature coconuts are too perishable to ship; they are already a gourmet's delight from the age of six months, which is when their pulp begins to develop. At this stage the nut is still green and is known as the "spoon coconut," for its meat, gelatinous and no harder than that of the muskmelon, is eaten from the shell with a spoon. It has a fresh, fruity flavor, livelier than that of the dried nuts which are all we can obtain in temperate climates.

Even after the nut has ripened, fresh coconut is ordinarily available only where it is grown; the form in which its use is most general is that of coconut milk, which does not mean the liquid found in the nut when you open it, but the juice squeezed from grated coconut meat. Fatty and sweetish, it looks like milk, can be used like milk, and shares some of milk's characteristics. Like milk, it has to be stirred when it is boiled, and its fat is chemically closer to butter fat than to any vegetable fat. Coconut milk is the basic cooking liquid of the eastern tropics.

"The backyard coconut palm must take the place of the family cow," Rafael Steinberg wrote. "Coconut milk plays a more important role in every South Asian kitchen than cow's milk does in America."

If all the diverse cuisines of the vast Asia-Pacific region seem, in spite of local peculiarities, to belong to the same general culinary family, it is in large part because of the unifying effect of a common cooking liquid; and the coconut in any form is the common denominator of this territory, for it is the chief food found in all of its separate parts.

The rarest coconut product known to me is honey made by bees which divide their time between coconut and banana groves. Coconut-banana honey is available in Parisian luxury food stores at the time of writing to anyone willing to pay $90 for a fourteen-ounce jar of it.

COD
stands for

COD. "It has been calculated," wrote Alexandre Dumas, "that if no accident prevented the hatching of the eggs and if each egg reached maturity, it would take only three years to fill the sea so that you could walk across the Atlantic dry-shod on the backs of cod." A normal output for a mature cod in a single breeding season is, indeed, 4.5 million eggs; but the carnage is frightful. Cod eggs float, offered helplessly to an ocean full of hungry fanciers of roe. Those which survive hatch almost equally helpless fry. Young cod grow slowly and require several years to arrive at a size and a strength which permit them to hold their own in the savage world of the sea. Despite these weaknesses, the great prolificacy of the cod ensured the perpetuation, and even the increase, of the species until as recently as perhaps twenty years ago; but today cod are being destroyed wholesale by the animal which has become their most devastating predator—man.

This is a new development. Although man has been fishing for cod since prehistoric times, it is probable that he was the least destructive of all the cod's enemies until he invented the giant trawler and the fish-processing factory ship. Cod today are swept up in fine-mesh nets which leave no young fish behind to provide new generations. The latest ships, especially the Soviet draggers, scrape the sea bottom clean, leaving behind them deserts covered by water. The Japanese and the Russians in particular sail all the seas of the world with unrestrained ruthlessness in search of cod; even the Bering Sea is dragged for it. Today the supposedly inexhaustible cod seems to be on the verge of extinction. The Newfoundland Banks,

COD. *Die of the 1776 New Hampshire State Seal*

once the greatest center of cod fishing in the world, have lately been described, perhaps prematurely, as "deserted" by this fish; and Georges Bank, off the state of Massachusetts, larger than the state itself, has been seriously depleted. There seem to be only two foreseeable ends to the situation—international agreement to save the cod or the disappearance from the waters of the globe of a fish which has played an important role in its history.

The cod may reasonably be described as the world's most important saltwater fish, with a possible reservation in favor of the herring; but the cod seems to have caught the fancy of man first. Few herring remains have been reported in prehistoric kitchen middens, but cod turn up abundantly as early as the Upper Paleolithic. The cod was almost certainly the first saltwater fish to be commercialized in the Western world after the Dark Ages, though it is not certain whether it was the Norsemen or the medieval French who led in curing cod in quantities greater than were required for their own needs and thus had a surplus to sell to their neighbors. The cod lent itself better to this purpose than the herring; no other fish can be salted more successfully or holds out longer once it has been so cured—indeed, it even keeps well without salting, simply dried. Salt cod can be transported by ship without becoming moldy or spoiling otherwise; on land it will last for several years. Smoked or pickled herring keep well too, but these processes are a trifle more complicated than drying or even salting, and may therefore be presumed to have been developed later. Preserved cod was widely established before preserved herring began to travel, and has maintained its head start ever since; herring has never expanded its range of popularity as far as the cod.

In the days before refrigeration, cured cod was in many parts of the world the only fish obtainable at any distance from the coast. To cite an example relatively near to us, the sole saltwater fish which appears in traditional Vermont cooking is salt cod, which could be delivered inland during Colonial times unspoiled despite the deliberateness of transport by horse cart.

Salt cod has almost forced fresh cod off the market. Few people any longer have an opportunity to enjoy the fresh fish unless they live on the coasts where it is taken, and even there they may be frustrated by the modern practice of salting fish aboard factory ships so that it is landed already preserved. Fresh cod is agreeable eating, neither subtle nor of great finesse, but forthright and tasty; the flesh is white, flaky in texture and not at all oily.

Even rarer than fresh cod these days are the dainty morsels which are some cod fanciers' delight; for these it is indeed necessary to be on hand when fresh fish are landed. Newfoundlanders consider the tongue the most exquisite part of the cod, but it is only about an inch long, a size which does not lend itself readily to commercial exploitation. In any case, Newfoundlanders insist that it must be eaten the day the fish is caught, for it quickly becomes hard and sometimes slimy. Newfoundland fries cod tongues, Boston (when it can get them) sautés them, Norwegians sauté or boil them. Boston also goes in for codfish cheeks, or used to, and even eats the entire head, which the uninitiated are apt to throw away. Norwegians insist that the head is the best part of the cod, especially the little lump of meat sunk into a small depression on the top of the skull. Cod's head and shoulders, sometimes stuffed, was an old English dish, to which Mrs. Isabelle Beeton, the most popular nineteenth-century cookbook writer, paid her respects.

The strong odor of cod liver oil may discourage some eaters from attacking the fish's liver, but it is luscious eating nevertheless, which does not recall the oil extracted from it. The roe, which is pink, is a delicacy also; it is sometimes smoked. Those who keep score on such matters have put it down as aphrodisiac, but in Iceland, which has a surplus of it, the only thing they can find to do with it is to sell it to France, which uses it as ground bait to attract sardines.

The period from the end of the eighth to the beginning of the eleventh century has been called "the Age of the Vikings," for it was marked by the spectacular expansion of the Northmen; it might with equal justification be called "the Age of the Cod," for cod provisioned and financed the Viking voyages and made their conquests possible. Cured cod ("the beefsteak of the sea") gave them unspoilable provisions which permitted them to make lengthy sea passages without being obliged to land to take on food, and wherever they stopped, gave them, in their surplus provisions, merchandise which everywhere found eager buyers. The Vikings were at times waterborne warriors, but they were at others waterborne fishmongers. As early as the ninth century there was a fish-processing industry in Norway and Iceland, which supplied not only the domestic market but also foreign trade.

The demand was great in medieval Europe, which ate proportionately much more fish than we do today, for fast days were then strictly observed and there were a great many of them. Cod was particularly welcome to the poor during the long Lenten fast of the Middle Ages: the rich, if they were not too far from the sea, could pay to have fresh fish brought to them by fast relays of force-fed horses, or to vary their menus with foods which, though far from frugal, were by some quirk of ecclesiastical reasoning not on the banned list, like lobster or teal. Those without exceptional means were restricted to pickled herring, salted sardines, tuna preserved in oil (rarely), but above all, salted or dried cod, the easiest to come by and, most important, the cheapest.

The Nordic countries prospered from cod, but as a natural result of popularizing it throughout Europe they inspired competitors and lost their monopoly. Among the competitors were the medieval French, following the tracks of the ancient Gauls, who had probably begun to cure cod before the Norsemen. Norman cod at first was ordinarily dried, not salted; French cod was salted, kept better, and was therefore preferred. Yet it was only in the fifteenth century that salt cod became a commonplace food in France itself, because it was being delivered in great quantities by Basque fishermen, who were not telling where they got it.

When Bretons who had followed the Basques did tell, the cod, which had already made a major impact on history by furthering the Norman conquests, registered a second by leading to the discovery of America.

The Basques were whalers; following whales had led them to the Grand Banks of Newfoundland, where they found tremendous quantities of cod, an easier and more profitable prey. They must have been aware that an unknown continent lay beyond the fishing grounds, and rumors about it may have reached Columbus. You will be told on the Breton island of Bréhat today that some of their fishermen, who had followed the Basques to the Grand Banks, did talk to Columbus and informed him of the existence of the New World. Cod continued to make history after John Cabot told the world in 1497 of their plenitude off the coasts of northern North America. Spain and Portugal, blithely disregarding the existence of other nations, signed a treaty designating which of them could fish where. France and England became involved in a cod "war" which ended only in 1904.

The history of Newfoundland has been the history of cod to this day; and cod was also a determining factor in the history of New England for something like two and a half centuries, after the Pilgrims, following one unsuccessful attempt, established a prosperous cod fishing and curing industry in Gloucester, Massachusetts. By 1640 Massachusetts was already doing so well in the fishing business that it sent in that year alone 300,000 dried codfish to market.

Cod inspired the building of New England's

merchant marine and contributed to the outbreak of the American Revolution. The treaty which ended it won rights for America to fish in British waters, since John Adams, who was not a Massachusetts man for nothing, held firm to his line of "fisheries or no peace." (Henry Clay, a Virginian, lost much of what Adams had gained when he negotiated the treaty which ended the War of 1812.) Cod played an important role in the slave trade. In Africa, slaves were paid for in one of three currencies—Spanish coins, rum or salt cod. The sugar plantations of the West Indies were the best market for New England salt cod, which they used to feed slaves, and paid for in molasses, which made New England rum.

The New England cod industry survived slavery, but not the advent of foreign trawlers; Gloucester today buys its cod from Polish ships which take their fish not much more than fifty miles away and sell it for less than it costs American fishermen to bring them in.

COF to **COL**
stand for

the chest-shaped **coffer fish** of the Caribbean, and the **coffrey**, or obese tuna, of West Africa; for the **coho**, or silver salmon, one of the five species of the Pacific Northwest; for the stimulant **cola nut**, also called, among other names, the ombene, the temperance nut, the guru nut and the bissy-bissy; for the **Colchester**, a British oyster, which as early as 50 B.C. aroused the admiration of Sallust; for the **coley**, a fish whose unappetizing gray flesh, once considered inedible in Britain, is now being eaten there because of the scarcity of more desirable species; for the **colocynth**, possibly the bitterest of all edible fruits, which has been abandoned everywhere except in the Sahara, whose inhabitants eat anything they can get; and for **colza**, a form of rape, which supplies a cooking oil which some nutritionists assert does violence to human health.

And **COL** also stands for

COLLARDS. Cabbage was a well-known vegetable in antiquity, but the plant the Greeks knew and did not particularly like and the one the Romans knew and doted on was not the one we think of today when cabbage is mentioned. Its leaves rose around a long stalk and it formed no head. It is still with us, the favorite form of cabbage in the southeastern United States—the collard, oftenest written in the plural, collards, otherwise called collard greens or, affectionately, collie greens.

COLLARDS. *Woodcut from* Harris Rural Annual, *1893*

Collards are on the list of soul foods, a hazy category difficult to define except as whatever among edibles causes a Southerner far from home to grow misty-eyed. Soul food is more or less identical with the cooking of the people who ruled the kitchens in the Old South—the black slaves who may have saved their white masters from developing deficiency diseases by adding green vegetables to what otherwise might have been an unrelieved hog-and-hominy diet. It may have been black slaves who introduced collards to the South in the first place. Cabbages, Old World plants, were transferred to the New by whites in the North in such developed forms as head cabbage, cauliflower and broccoli, but in the South, where we know that slaves brought many African plants to America with them, it would seem probable that collards were among them. This is, indeed, a form of cabbage popular in Africa; one of the national dishes of Ethiopia, *yegomen kitfo*, is composed of buttermilk curds and collard greens.

COM
stands for

the **comber**, a sort of sea perch eaten on the shores of the Mediterranean and in Africa, usually in soup, because of its generous supply of bones; for the **comb fringe**, a cereal which would be more widely eaten in tropical Africa if it were not in short supply; for the **Comice**, possibly the world's most luscious pear, now disappearing, except in Tasmania, because it is too fragile to be handled by supermarkets; and for the **compass plant**, a species of wild lettuce so called because it turns its leaves as the day wears on to keep them edge-on to the sun.

CON
stands for

the **conch** (pronounced conk), which tastes like a slightly exotic clam, eaten in Florida and the Caribbean islands; for the **Concord,** the most widely grown native American grape, created in that Massachusetts city about 1850 by Ephraim Bull, who crossed several varieties of New World grapes; for the **conger,** frequently called the conger eel, though it is not an eel, and it is not a steer either, in spite of having once been known as "Belle-Ile beef" when it was eaten more enthusiastically on that French island than it is today; for the **Congo acacia,** whose seeds are used as a condiment throughout tropical Africa, for **Congo oil,** used only in the territory which gave it its name, and for the **Congo pea,** probably brought to the New World by black slaves, whose descendants on the island of Jamaica consume it heavily under the name "goongo pea"; and for the **conophor,** of which the leaves are eaten in Sierra Leone and the nuts in Nigeria, the Congo and the Cameroons.

COO to COQ
stand for

coon oysters, which cling to the roots of mangroves along the coast of the southeastern United States and, though they are good eating, are usually collected by raccoons rather than man, since they are too small to tempt most shellfish hunters; for the **coot,** a not particularly palatable water bird, which according to legend dives deep when wounded and clings to weeds at the bottom of the water to keep itself from surfacing prematurely; and for the **copper belly,** the beautifully and variably colored calico clam or butterfly shell, which gives Florida one of its most esteemed regional dishes, coquina broth.

COR
stands for

coralline pepper, a variant of cayenne; for the **coral plant,** whose tuberous roots are eaten in tropical Africa; for the **corb,** a Mediterranean fish whose various local names mean "crow," but which seems to possess no popular name in English, and the **corkwing,** another Mediterranean fish, equivalent to the wrasse; for the **corkwood,** about which you had better keep your definitions straight, for while the corkwood, or umbrella tree, of the Congo provides a succulent fruit and the corkwood, or hissing tree, of equatorial and South Africa an acceptable one, the corkwood, or alligator apple, of the Florida Everglades, though it is related to such luscious foods as the cherimoya and the custard apple, is reputed to be poisonous; for **cormorants,** which according to a respected authority "as squabs . . . are highly esteemed for food by the northern islanders of Europe," but the English royal household no longer has a Master of the Cormorants along with a Master of the Hounds, as it once had; for **corncobs,** usually reserved for hogs, but Indians make excellent jelly from them; for the **cornel,** or cornelian cherry, one of the goodies Circe fed to the companions of Ulysses after she turned them into swine; for the **Cornish game hen,** which John and Karen Hess described as "Victor Borge's funniest joke on the American public" (Borge raised them), and the **Cornish jack,** the tastiest of the rather oily African fish of the *Moryridae* family, which the ancient Egyptians held to be sacred; for **corn salad,** alias lamb's lettuce; and for the **Cortinarius** genus of mushrooms rife in the Pacific Northwest, of which some are delicious, most are edible and one is deadly.

And **COR** also stands for

CORIANDER. "Coriander," an unidentified phrase-maker once wrote, "is essentially a cultivated weed," a formula which has been repeated by almost everybody who has written about this spice since, though if you stop to think about it, you will realize that all our food plants are cultivated weeds, except those which we harvest wild, which are uncultivated weeds. Perhaps coriander was singled out for this accusation because of its basic cantankerousness, which is expressed by differing perversely with its own group of plants, and even with itself. "It is a plant full of contrasts," wrote Louis Lagriffe, "double and opposed in its odor as in its action."

Double in its morphology to begin with, the same plant bears two opposed kinds of leaves and two opposed kinds of flowers. It belongs to the carrot family, of which one characteristic is that its seeds are perishable; those of coriander, on the contrary, are more durable and will grow and thrive even when planted five years after they have been gathered. Coriander is also one of the very few plants of this family which produce fruits with a concave face, and it differs from its relatives again in greater slenderness of stem.

As for its odor, opinions could not be more diverse. "Coriander" is derived from the Greek *koris,* "bedbug," because the ancients were of the opinion that both leaves and seeds smelled like that insect. In more modern times the smell of coriander has been likened to that of rubber.

CORIANDER. *Print from Elizabeth Blackwell:* A Curious Herbal, *London, 1737*

The French eighteenth-century naturalist Louis Augustin Guillaume Bosc d'Antic, who agreed with the bedbug description, wrote that "especially in rainy weather and when storms are threatening, it causes headaches and nausea in those who pause in fields where it grows." Louis Lagriffe wrote that "fresh coriander is endowed with a very agreeable penetrating odor, so strong that it makes you sleepy, at the same time that it recalls the smell of the bedbug." Olivier de Serres, the sixteenth-century agronomist, praised coriander because it smelled so bad that it made other plants smell better. Yet coriander is employed in medicine to counteract the disagreeable smells or tastes of certain drugs, and in the south of France it is chewed to sweeten the breath after eating garlic. It is used in perfumes and soaps, imparting to them the fragrance of lilies of the valley. Elizabeth David, no mean authority, writes that it has an orange-peel scent; others have likened it to lemon peel; some have defined its taste as that of a mixture of cumin and caraway; the Bible compared it to honey.

Coriander was one of the first spices to be utilized by man. Its seeds have been found in Bronze Age ruins on the Aegean islands of Thera and Therasia and in the tombs of the Pharaohs; it is mentioned in the Ebers Papyrus and is known to have been grown in Assyria and Babylon. The Egyptians put it in wine to increase its intoxicating power, while the ancient Hindus employed it in magic and religious ceremonies. The Hebrews called it *gad*, and approved of it. It was used in that oldest of Greek cities, Mycenae, to enliven what was otherwise monotonous fare. The Romans thought Egyptian coriander was the best; they used it in bread, in stews and in an ancient version of the bouquet garni. Plautus recorded the fact that it flavored barley porridge or mixed boiled greens, a dispiriting dish which could use a spot of uplift. Varro wrote that a mixture of lightly crushed coriander and caraway seeds in vinegar would preserve meat throughout the summer, and there was a Roman seasoning mixture composed of rue, savory, mint, wild celery, onion, thyme, pennyroyal and coriander (Virgil added garlic). Apicius created a coriander-flavored dip for oysters or other shellfish.

In medieval times, coriander was grown along the Mediterranean and exported to more northerly Europe; it was one of the plants Charlemagne ordered planted in his domains. It seems to have dropped temporarily out of favor on the continent of Europe, but in the fourteenth century, when almost all vegetable foods were insipid, it made a much-needed comeback, at the same time as a number of other seasoners. For a time it was cultivated in southern England, and was thus relatively cheap when most spices were dear; an account book dated 1265 shows that coriander cost fourpence a pound at a time when pepper and ginger were varying between tenpence and two shillings fourpence, and saffron and cloves between ten and fourteen shillings. It was apparently still being grown in Sussex as recently as the eighteenth century, for Elizabeth David tells us that it was probably obtained locally by William Verral of the White Hart Inn in Lewes for his specialty of ham cooked in milk flavored with coriander.

Coriander was introduced into Latin America by the Spaniards shortly after they discovered the New World, and won instant favor with the Indians. Cultivated by the Mexicans, it was passed on by them to the Indians of what is today the southwestern United States. It is still grown widely by the Zuñi Indians, who use its leaves for salad and flavor meat and chili with its seeds.

American housewives, if they use coriander at

all, are likeliest to know it as a powder, its least desirable form. It is better to buy seeds and crush them oneself, as needed, which can be done easily, in a table pepper mill for instance. Anglo-Saxons are sometimes puzzled when they learn that coriander is also called Chinese parsley; but while many Westerners know it only as a spice, there are many countries which use the leaves as a salad: China, of course; the Middle East, North Africa and Madagascar; Latin America; Spain and Portugal; and Cyprus, where it has been grown since antiquity.

The seeds of the plant have a taste which, like everything else connected with coriander, is contradictory: it is at the same time sharply pungent and lightly sugary. For so egoistic a spice it is surprisingly versatile; it goes with almost everything, no doubt because of its contradictory nature, which permits it to be assertive and arrogant with game, pork or in sausage; subtly caressing with lamb, chicken or fish; unobtrusive in curry powders, from which it is almost never omitted; exotic in blood pudding, cheese or omelets; peppery with rice, mashed potatoes, Chinese noodles or Oriental soup; fiery in Ethiopian *berberé* sauce; and pungent in bread, cakes, puddings or confectionery.

A nonculinary use, suggested no doubt by its odor, is that of keeping bedbugs away by distributing coriander seeds throughout the house. For this purpose, Louis Lagriffe remarks, coriander is probably "totally ineffective"; in any case, he adds, the remedy is worse than the disease. It is hard to follow him on this point. Coriander seeds don't bite.

CORN. *Wall-relief in the tomb of Paheri at El Kab. Dynasty XVIII (c. 1500* BC*), line drawing copy*

CORN. Corn is very possibly not what you think it is: it depends on where you live. If you are American, corn is maize. If you are English, it is likely to mean wheat for you, or oats if you live in Scotland or Ireland. In northern Germany, *Korn* is rye, in southern Germany, wheat: where *Vollkornbrot* ("whole corn bread") means black bread made from the whole kernel of rye, northern influence is dominant; where it means simply bread made from any coarsely ground unpolished grain, usually wheat, southern influence is dominant. In South Africa, Bantu corn is millet. Actually all that corn basically means is "grain"; each locality interprets it as standing for its own most familiar cereal.

COS
stands for

Cos lettuce, named for the Greek island on which it supposedly originated; and for **costmary,** one of those charmingly named, delicate, old-fashioned herbs now, alas, practically forgotten, which tastes rather like tansy, not exactly common nowadays either.

COT
stands for

cotton, which provides not only cottonseed oil but also cottonseed meal for dieting humans who require starchless flour; and for the red-flowered **cotton tree,** whose dried seeds are relished on the Ivory Coast.

COU
stands for

couch grass, eaten by medieval Britons but prob-

A

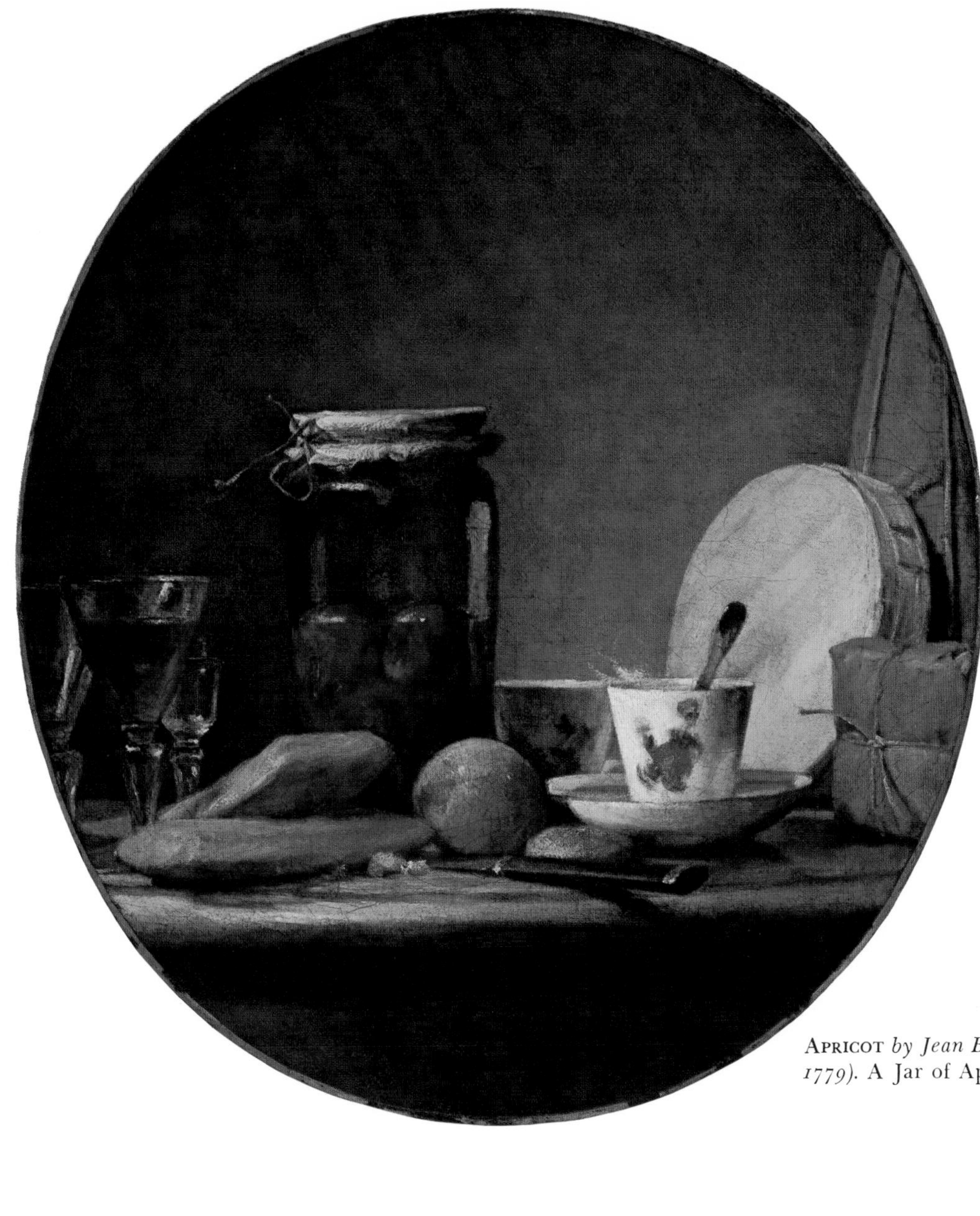

Apricot *by Jean Baptiste Chardin (1699–1779).* A Jar of Apricots, *oil on canvas*

B

Beef. *Pottery cow, Delft, 18th century*

C

CHERRY. *Quilt, in the style associated with Baltimore, Maryland.* Album, *1845–1850*

CUCUMBER *by Carlo Crivelli (active by 1457–died after 1475).* Madonna and Child, *tempera on wood*

D

Duck. *Marble Mosaic, 1st century BC–1st century* AD, *Rome*

E

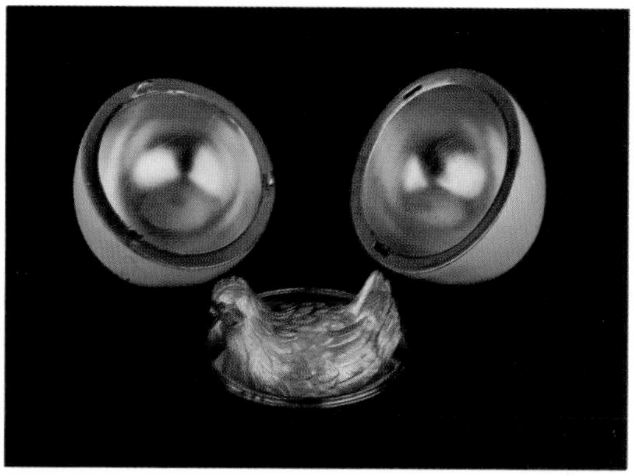

Egg *by Fabergé.* The First Imperial Egg, *Russia, Easter 1886*

F

FIG. *Photograph by Jarry Lang, 1979*

G

GOOSE. *Wall painting in the tomb of Ra-hotpe at Meidum. Reign of Snefru (c. 2900 BC), facsimile*

H

HORSE. *Bronze statuette, Greece, 8th century* BC

J

JERUSALEM ARTICHOKE. *Print from* Curtis's Botanical Magazine, *vol. 53, July 1897, London*

K

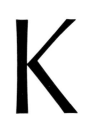

KIWI FRUIT. *Photograph by Ralf Manstein, 1980*

L

LEEK *by David Hockney,* Leeks, *crayon drawing, 1970*

M

MAPLE *by Georgia O'Keeffe*. Pattern of Leaves, *oil on canvas, 1924*

MILLET *by Kano Sanraku (1559–1635)*. Autumn Millet, *Japanese screen*

MUTTON *by Thomas Sidney Cooper (1803–1902).* Reposing on God's Acre, *oil on canvas*

N

NUTMEG. *Print from C. L. Blume:* Rumphia, *4 vols., Amsterdam 1835–1848*

O

Oyster *by Edouard Manet (1832–1883).* Oysters, *oil on canvas*

P

Peach *by Auguste Renoir (1841–1919).* Still Life, *oil on canvas*

PHEASANT. *Tapestry from* The Hunt of the Unicorn: The Unicorn at the Fountain, *wool and silk with silver and silver-gilt threads from the Château of Verteuil, late 15th century, French or Flemish*

P

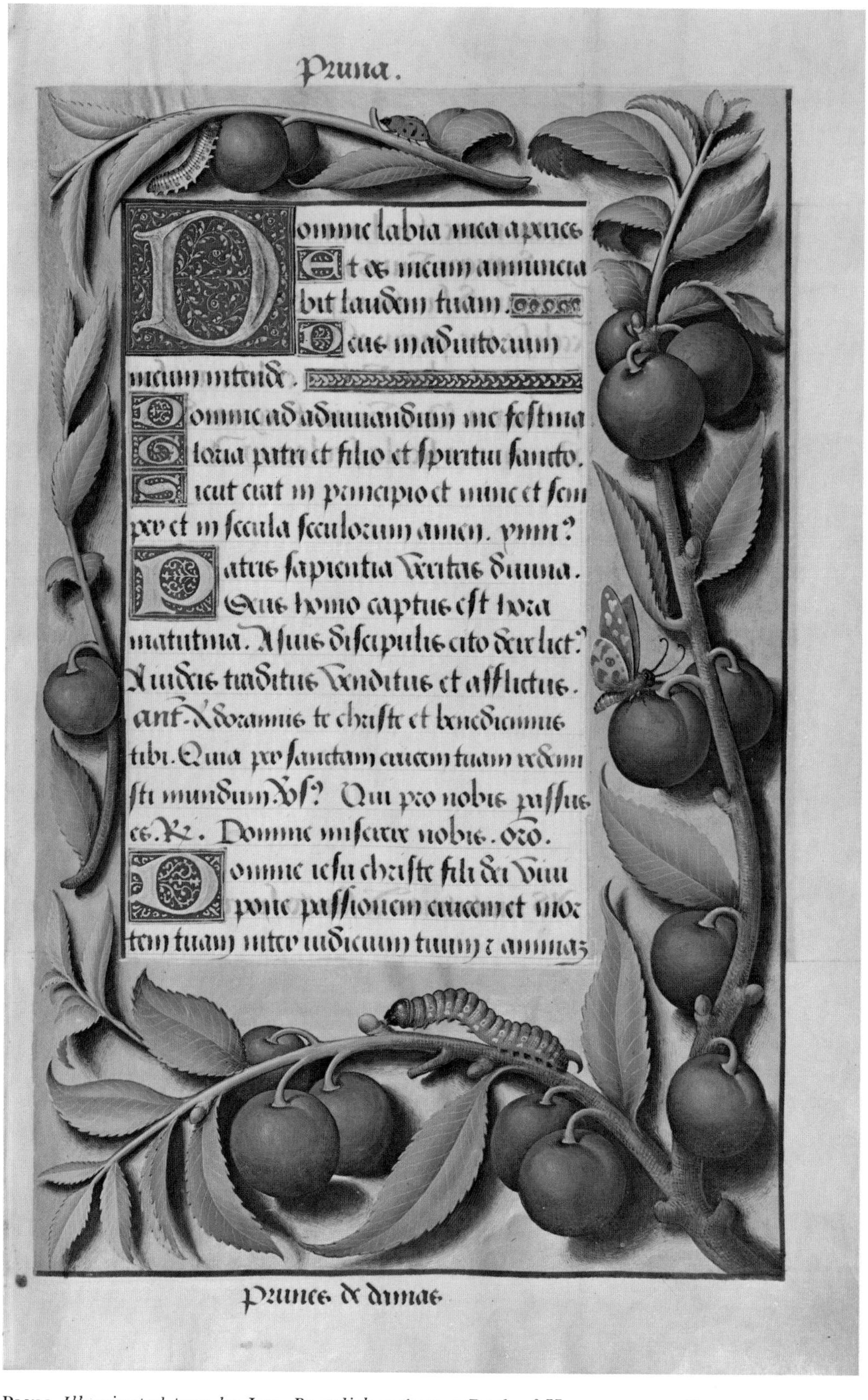

PLUM. *Illuminated page by Jean Bourdichon from a* Book of Hours, *c. 1510, France*

Q

QUAHOG. *Photograph by Emerick Bronson, 1979*

QUINCE. *First-state plate by P. J. Redoute for Jean Jacques Rousseau:* La Botanique, *folio edition, Paris, 1805*

R

Rabbit. Three Rabbits, *colors on silk, Ming Dynasty (1368–1644) in the style of Kung Chi of Northern Sung Dynasty (960–1280)*

S

Salt *by Ralph Goings.* White Tower, *oil on canvas, 1976*

Squash *by Rev. Jonathan Fisher (1768–1847).* The Latter Harvest, *oil on canvas*

T

Turkey *by Norman Rockwell (1894–1978). World War II propaganda poster, U.S. Government*

V

VENISON *by Deruta. Italian dish, lustered maiolica, c. 1515–1520*

W

WHEAT *by Pieter Bruegel, the Elder (active by 1551–1569).* The Harvesters, *oil on wood*

ably not, as has been reported, by the Aztecs; for **couch sea bream,** not a particularly delicate fish, but palatable enough all the same; for **country pepper,** one of the many chilies popular in the Caribbean, and the **country potato,** one of the many tubers popular in Central Africa; and for the **courbina,** which is a weakfish in West Africa and a meagre in North Africa.

COW
stands for

of course the **cow,** which might be considered adequately covered by the entry on BEEF, but one delicacy a steer cannot furnish is cows' udders, a dish so little outdated that it was served in 1974 at a celebrated dinner at the three-star Moulin de Mougins in France; for **cowas,** the Indian biscuit root, which Lewis and Clark compared in taste to celery; for (a) **cowage,** (b) the **cowberry,** (c) **cow parsley,** (d) the **cow parsnip,** (e) the **cowslip,** (f) the **cow tree,** (g) **cow wheat** and (h) the **cow-nosed fish,** which are, respectively, (a) a vine which produces itching powder and also a beanlike seed eaten in India, Indonesia and Africa in blithe disregard of the fact that it is toxic; (b) the lingonberry; (c) any one of three plants, described collectively as "inferior parsley, fit only for cows"; (d) hogweed, to which Turner gave its other name in 1548 when he wrote, "It may be called in englishe Cowpersnepe"; (e) what the English call the primrose, of which one of Disraeli's characters observed, "They say primroses make a capital salad"; (f) a name given to several different trees which exude a milky juice and to one which doesn't; (g) a grass eaten so far as I know by no one except the ancient Romans, who thought it an aphrodisiac; and (h) a far from beautiful fish which seems to be eaten nowhere except in Nigeria.

And **COW** also stands for

COWPEA. The cowpea, says Webster, is "cultivated in the southern U.S. for forage and green manure." One is tempted to cry "Shame, shame!" and ask if Webster has never heard of soul food; but it covers itself hastily by adding a second definition of cowpea: "the seed of this plant used for food esp. in the southern U.S." Actually it is used for food esp. in Africa, and after Africa, Asia, but isolationism is not peculiar to Webster, so this example of it may be overlooked.

The cowpea may not always have been as firmly established in the South as it is today; it was perhaps in danger of dying out when Jefferson instructed his overseer at Monticello to have a certain plot on the estate planted urgently "with cow-pea, of which there is a patch at Mr. Freeman's, to save which, great attention must be paid, as they are the last of the neighborhood."

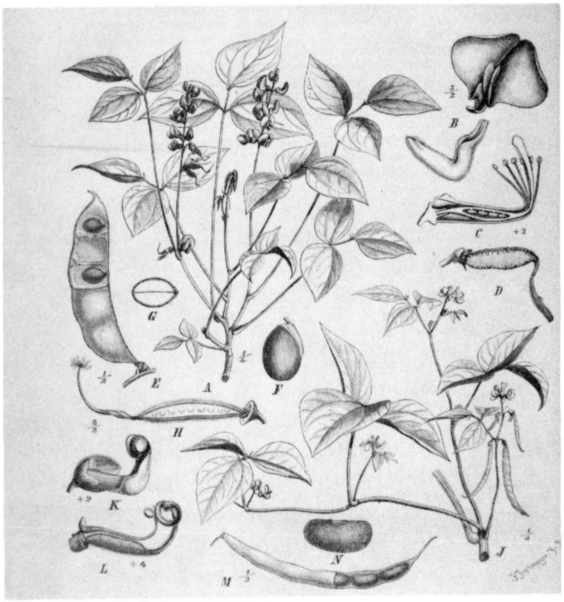

COWPEA. *Drawing from A. Engler:* Die natürlichen Pflanzenfamilien, *Leipzig, 1894*

The cowpea is today an important item on the soul-food menu, which has become the subject of what looks dangerously like a cult. Soul foods include a good many which were brought to the New World from Africa by slaves, which seems to have been the case for the cowpea. It reached the West Indies before the mainland, probably in Jamaica, about 1674. When it arrived in the southern United States, it became known oftener as the black-eyed pea, from the black spot on one end; it is also sometimes called the blackeye bean, or simply the blackeye. Despite its name, it is not a pea, nor a bean either for that matter.

There is one other place where the cowpea is the subject of a sort of cult, in a limited area of southwestern France, including the department of the Charente and part of the Périgord. A gastronomic order created in the city of Saint-Gaudens is called the Taostos Moungetos, dialect for "cowpea tasters," thus elevating this vegetable to the status of a gastronomic symbol of the region.

COX
stands for

Cox's Orange Pippin, developed in 1830 by a retired brewer named Richard Cox; the British boast that it is the finest dessert apple in the world.

CRA
stands for

the **crabapple,** which offers two gifts to mankind, fruit too sour for his palate and wood too hard for his skull—which is why Lord Rochester had the poet John Dryden beaten up by "bravos and crab-tree cudgels"; for **crab grass,** a bane to lawns and a boon to Africans, who eat its seeds, and **crabwood,** whose seeds are eaten in Africa also; for the **crackleberry,** a ground-hugging creeping raspberry gathered wild in the Pacific Northwest; for **cram-cram,** a milletlike grain which Saharan termites steal for its thorns and which Tuaregs steal from the termites; for **cramp bark,** otherwise the highbush cranberry (which is not a cranberry), a nickname given it for reputed healing qualities cited by Chaucer; for the **cranberry bean,** which looks like a paler version of the fruit for which it is named, particularly appreciated in northern New England; for the **crane,** eaten by the ancient Chinese, ancient Romans, Pope Clement V, King Richard II and Captain John Smith, but today only by Africans presumably in disagreement with Alexandre Dumas's opinion that it is "tough, leathery, insipid and difficult to digest"; for the **crapaud,** a large frog eaten on some Caribbean islands, where it is known as "mountain chicken"; and for the **crappie,** a fish whose white variety provides flesh of such smooth texture that the Cajuns of the Louisiana bayous call it *sac-à-lait*, "bag of milk."

And **CRA** also stands for

CRAB. "There are three species of creatures who when they seem coming are going; when they seem going are coming," wrote American statesman John Hay: "Diplomats, women and crabs." He was not 100 percent right about crabs. Most of those with whom we come into contact do scuttle sideways, but that is not because they are crabs, it is because their bodies are so wide that they would get in the way of their legs if they tried to walk forward. Those crabs in which long legs successfully clear a central body—spider crabs, for instance—walk forward in a straight line; but since almost all such crabs are deep-water animals which we do not come upon strolling on the beach, our image of the crab is of an animal which moves sideways.

There are 4400 species of crabs, immensely variable, but one thing they have in common is that all true crabs are edible. They range in size from pea crabs, which live inside the shells of mollusks, to one or the other of the two giants. The biggest, if you go by reach, is the Japanese giant crab, which has provided a specimen spanning twelve and a half feet, or if you go by weight, the Tasmanian giant crab, which can weigh as much as thirty pounds. There are deep-water crabs, shallow-water or beach crabs, brackish-water crabs, freshwater crabs, amphibious crabs, land crabs and, only on the island of Borneo, two particularly individualistic species, of which one lives in caves and the other in the mountains, to an altitude of 8500 feet. Despite dissidents, the sea is the mother of all crabs, in which even land crabs are born and to which the females make periodic visits to release their eggs in the water.

CRAB. *Red-figured calyx krater by Euxitheos and Euphronios, Greece, c. 515* BC

Crabs have very different eating habits. Some of them are hunters, pursuing live prey; others, like lobsters, are scavengers. Many crabs are omnivorous, others prefer a vegetable diet, like the robber crab, which climbs tall palms to pick coconuts for its dinner. Some crabs adopt a ferocious attitude toward shellfish, according to Oppian of Coryncus, member of a crab-eating community, some two thousand years ago:

When we observe the crab in its mossy banks, we can only praise and admire it for all its art. For it is from the Heavens that it has received . . . the power to nourish itself on oysters, a food so fine and so easy to obtain. Oysters are avid for water, and often install themselves among the rocks, their shells wide open, licking the mud. The crab . . . seizes a stone on the beach and, edging up to it, pinches it between its tight claws and carries it away. He sidles up furtively to the oyster and thrusts the stone inside it. Then, installed beside it, he feasts. The oyster, thus hospitable because it cannot close its shell, remains gaping open until its death, while its ravisher eats its fill.

Avenging the oyster, people the world over eat crab. In the United States, crab is second in popularity among crustaceans, outdistancing even that symbol of luxury, the lobster (shrimp is number one). Many West Coast dwellers would not hesitate to put the Dungeness crab at the very top of crabhood; second choice would probably be the Alaska king crab. Renowned in the East are the blue crab. Chesapeake Bay and the Gulf Coast are the chief providers of that remarkable American specialty, soft-shelled crab. Also notable is the stone crab, native to Florida and the Gulf.

The Caribbean islands seem to be the only place where land crabs are widely eaten, except on the West Coast of Africa, precisely the area which supplied the slaves transported to the Caribbean to work the sugar plantations, who may be presumed to have imported their eating habits and perhaps even this type of crab. South America has the centolla, southern counterpart of the Alaska king crab, found in Chile and the Straits of Magellan.

Europe is thickly populated with crabs, of which the most widely eaten are the redundantly named edible crab, the not so redundantly named swimming crab (not all crabs swim), the spider crab, rock crab and green crab. Passing the British Isles and its red zodiac crab, we reach Scandinavia, which thinks highly of its cold-water crabs, but praises them in a somewhat oblique manner: "Very good with aquavit."

The Chinese regale themselves on freshwater crabs, so succulent that they have been exported to Europe and naturalized there. Northern Japan shares with Siberia and the United States the Alaska king crab from Bering Strait and the Dungeness, and is now beginning to show interest in the snow crab, which up to now has been thrown back into the sea when brought up with king crabs in the absence of any clause covering this species in the treaty regulating Japanese fishing in American waters. Southern Japan eats that deep-water giant, but its most prized variety is the Hokkaido, bought alive and eaten raw. In India, crustacean fisheries are more important than any other kind, and there, as in the United States, crab ranks second only to shrimp. Malaysia, Indonesia, Oceania, the Philippines, Hawaii and all the other Pacific islands are heavy crab consumers. Australia finds the Tasmanian giant crab good eating but, despite its unappetizing name, prefers the Queensland mud crab, whose unadorned flavor is so subtle that connoisseurs will regard you with horror if you season it with anything stronger than a few drops of lemon juice or wine vinegar.

CRANBERRY. Cranberry sauce was invented by American Indians. Cranberries were an important food for them long before the first Europeans arrived, and they ate them raw as well as cooked, despite an acidity which discourages us from following their example. When they cooked the berries they sweetened them with maple sugar or honey; and when sugarcane plantations were established in the West Indies, the Europeans

CRANBERRY. *Magazine cover by Will H. Bradley:* The Chapbook, *Thanksgiving Number, 1895*

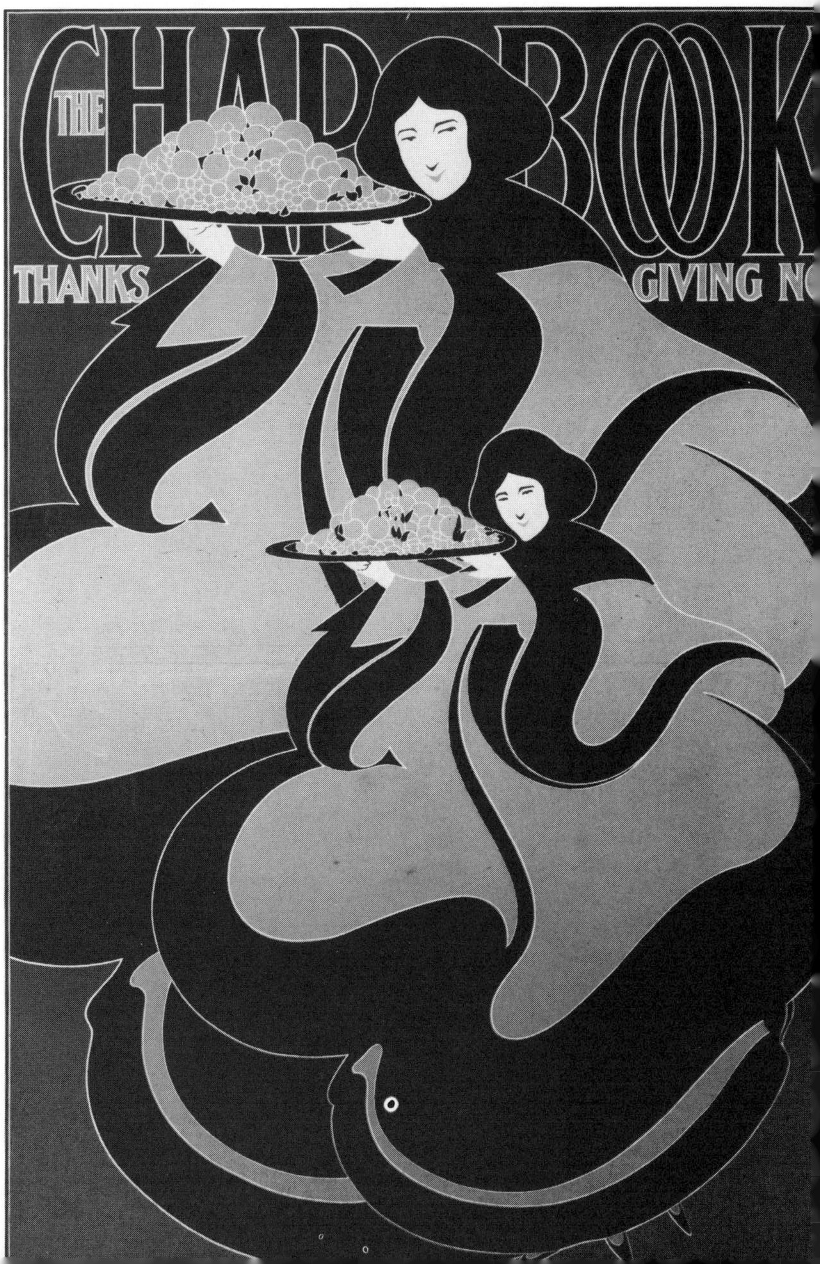

contributed to the dish and appreciated it as much as the Indians did. John Josselyn, who visited New England in 1639, reported on cranberries probably more accurately than when he told of seeing a sea serpent at Cape Ann and a merman in Maine's Casco Bay: "The Indians and English use them much, boyling them with Sugar for Sauce to eat with their Meat, and it is a delicious Sauce."

The Indians of the Northeast also used cranberries in a concoction which we usually associate with Indians farther west—pemmican. Instead of the buffalo berries used by Plains Indians, New England Indians used cranberries, pounded together with dried meat and melted animal fat to produce their version of this iron ration, which would keep almost indefinitely. Cranberries all by themselves will keep almost indefinitely also, protected by their high acidity, and for this reason were perhaps the very first native American fruits to be shipped to Europe commercially. Early in the eighteenth century "Cape Cod bell cranberries" were being hawked on the Strand in London at what must have been a fancy price in those days, four shillings a jar. From England, the cranberry spread to the Continent. It never gained much favor in France, but it was appreciated in Germany.

A large number of small red acid fruits are called cranberries, some of which definitely are not, some are arguable, but one which is indisputably the real thing is the American cranberry, *Vaccinium macrocarpon*. It can claim to be the archetype of this fruit on the brutal principle of might makes right, if on no other, for it is the biggest of cranberries (one-half inch in diameter). It also seems to be the only cranberry cultivated in commercially significant quantity. Other countries send cranberries to the market, but they have been gathered wild. The difference in taste between wild and cultivated cranberries is negligible, but the advantage of cultivation is that it increases the yield.

Also an authentic cranberry is the Finnish fruit which everybody calls a cranberry except the Finns themselves, who name it the *karpolo* (Finnish) or *tranbär* (Swedish). Its taste has been described as "fresh and dry," and so far as I know, it is not cultivated, but a good supply is available from pickers who gather the wild berries, often in the spring after the already ripe berries have spent the winter under the snow, for they are then softer and less acid. At a guess, this is a variety of *V. oxycoccus*, for it grows in marshy ground, which this species likes, while farther south in Europe *V. oxycoccus palestris* is now called *canneberge* by the French and *Moosebeere* by the Germans. It is not cultivated and, so far as I know, not even marketed on a commercial basis.

V. vitis-idaea is probably an authentic cranberry too, although the inhabitants of the several countries where it grows seem unsure of it; it differs from the other two in that it prefers dry ground. It is often called the cowberry (*Vaccinium*, of course, comes from the Latin *vacca*, "cow") or the foxberry in England, and in various parts of the United States, the red whortleberry, the partridge berry, the whimberry, the mountainberry, the rock berry or, by homesick Swedish immigrants, the lingonberry; but it is a different fruit from the one they knew in Scandinavia.

When we leave the *Vaccinium* genus, we are no longer dealing with cranberries, whatever popular usage may say. Thus neither the cranberry tree, alias the highbush cranberry, nor the cranberry bush, alias the lowbush cranberry, is a cranberry, since they belong to the *Viburnum* genus. We are even farther from the mark in Africa, where what is called the cranberry and its cousin, the Cape cranberry, are both members of *Dovyalis*, while the cranberry gourd is a South African vine, *Abobra tenuifolis*. Australia gives the name "cranberry" to two different plants, neither of them even remotely related to the real thing.

CRAWFISH (or **crayfish**). The earliest known definition of the crawfish in French is of sweeping simplicity: "A red fish which walks backward." This underrates the crawfish. It *swims* backward, at least from the human point of view, but it can walk forward just as easily as backward.

The crawfish, or crayfish (there is no difference in meaning between the two forms of the word), is exclusively a freshwater crustacean, if this classification may be extended to cover these animals even when they prefer holes in the ground to water; but in this case their burrows are always in surroundings dampened by fresh water, not salt. The record has been confused by some obstinate peoples, who persist in using the same names they apply to crawfish to denote some saltwater crustaceans, but such names are erroneous.

Crawfish range from an inch in length (the smallest Louisiana species), through three to five inches (Scandinavia, and southern, midwestern and eastern United States), to six inches or more (Australia, New Zealand) to a maximum of six-

CRAWFISH. *Photograph by Arthur Rothstein:* Conch Shells and Crawfish, *Key West, Florida, January 1938*

Crawfish
Crawfish

teen inches and a weight of eight pounds (*Astacopsis gouldi* of Tasmania, the world's largest crawfish); but the largest Australian crawfish, popularly misnamed the Murray River lobster, has more flavor than its giant Tasmanian relative.

The United States is rich in crawfish and also rich in names for them, though they lack scientific precision—crawdads, bay crabs, freshwater crabs, freshwater lobsters and, in Louisiana, creekcrabs, yabbies or, irreverently, mudbugs. American crawfish include some species which belong to that rare category of animals committed neither to nocturnal nor diurnal habits—in zoological parlance they are aperiodic, meaning they don't give a damn what time it is. This lack of interest in the difference between night and day is explained by the fact that they are blind: *Cambarus pellucidus* lives in Mammoth Cave in Kentucky and *Troglo-cambarus maclanei* in several other caves, including Gum Cave and Squirrel Chimney in Florida. Mississippi and Alabama harbor a terrestrial crawfish, *Cambarus hagenianus*, about six inches long, which avoids ponds and streams, living instead in burrows which it digs with its claws, throwing up the evacuated earth into chimneys sometimes a foot high.

Crawfish are eaten wherever they are found, but more widely in the Old World than in the New. They seem to have been the only crustaceans widely consumed in Europe in the Middle Ages, probably because they were easy to collect close at hand wherever one lived, whereas such saltwater animals as crabs or lobsters could not be transported far from the coasts without spoiling. Apparently Paris did not even try to procure saltwater crustaceans, for crawfish could be had locally; as late as the sixteenth century Rabelais dispatched Gargantua to fish for them in Parisian waters, where he would find none today and would not dare eat them if he did.

In France, the great heyday of the crawfish occurred in the eighteenth century. At its beginning they were cheap; in the 1830s Paris was eating about 150,000 crawfish a year and paying three francs a hundred for them. Then a vogue set in, and by the 1850s, though prices had risen to between six and eight francs the hundred, more than 5 million crawfish a year were being sold in the Paris markets. In the 1880s the price was from fifteen to twenty francs, and at the turn of the century, forty. Consumption dropped as prices rose, and it looked as though crawfish would be priced off Paris tables. But this was the Belle Epoque, when the ostentatious display of wealth was the delight of those who had it and the envy of those who hadn't. The expensiveness of the crawfish became an asset: it was a symbol of luxury in a luxury-loving society. It was a symbol of seduction too; an invitation to sample crawfish was equivalent to a formula which would come into vogue some time later: "Come up and see my etchings." A young lady invited to dine out, if she was ushered into one of those private restaurant dining rooms so popular at the period, remarkable for the tact and discretion of their staffs, to find a bucket of champagne and a bowl of crawfish on the table, knew what she had to expect, even assuming that she had had no inkling beforehand.

Why did the ladies expose themselves to the frightful dangers involved in partaking of crawfish in gallant company? Because, French gastronomic writer Robert J. Courtine explained, it gave them an opportunity to display the beauty of their hands: "That is what explains the pleasure a woman takes in eating crawfish; she knows that she is graceful." Mere males engaged in sucking crawfish are only messy.

Crawfish country in the United States is pretty much confined to Louisiana and that part of Texas contiguous to it, though crawfish occur everywhere, abundantly, available to anyone who wants them. Louisiana, a watery state of bayous and marshes which might have been designed expressly as a paradise for crawfish, makes a cult of them, and also a business: it collects more crawfish than any other area of equal size in the world and consumes four-fifths of them itself. The Louisiana legislature has seen fit to institutionalize what had hitherto been the informal and even haphazard pursuit of crawfish, and has designated the town of Breaux Bridge, population 5000, as the Crawfish Capital of the World, a description which will surprise Nantua, France, if it ever hears about it, since the world over a dish described as "Nantua" means one garnished with crawfish, for which that city has long been famous (but it has been virtually fished out of them now). Every second year Breaux Bridge holds a crawfish festival, featuring, naturally, a crawfish-eating contest. Record at the time of writing: thirty-three pounds of crawfish tails dispatched in two hours.

Crawfish are a festive food in Scandinavia also, especially in Finland and Sweden. Gaiety varies with the house rules. Some hosts hold that a glass of *akvavit* should be swallowed after every six crawfish; but others (those who give the merriest parties) insist that each crawfish be honored with a swig of this deceptively innocent-looking *eau de vie*. As the average consumption per guest at such parties runs to about twenty crawfish, it is advisable in such circumstances to limit each intake to a brief sip.

CRE
stands for

CRESS. This plant was widely known in very ancient times; we meet it in history as soon as there is any history to provide a meeting place. But when we meet it, in ancient or medieval writings, we are rarely sure what sort of cress it is. To simplify a somewhat tangled situation, we may divide cresses between those which grow on dry soils, called simply "cress," and those which grow in or at the edge of water ("watercress"). Our first difficulty when we attempt to match the cresses of history to those we know now is that our terminology is vague; the second is that ancient and medieval terminology was even vaguer. The ancient Greeks and Romans used several words to designate cresses, but we do not know which ones stood for which plants, or even if they used them consistently themselves; probably they did not. We are no less in the dark about what precisely a Chinese minister named I Yin had in mind, about 1500 B.C., when he drew up a list of his country's best foods, among them "the cress of Yun-seng."

It has been true throughout history that watercress (*Nasturtium officinale*) has been more generally eaten than all the other multitudinous cresses, true and false, put together. Watercress is also, so far as I know, the only salad plant ever to have been awarded space on a coat of arms, a heraldic distinction which dates from the thirteenth century. Hunting on a hot summer day, Louis IX (St. Louis) was overcome by thirst and called for drink. No liquid was within reach; he was handed a bunch of watercress instead. Louis crunched its peppery leaves and found himself so surprisingly refreshed that he decided on the spot to honor both the plant and the place which had provided it for him. To this day the arms of the city of Vernon, now in the French department of the Eure, bear three fleurs-de-lis, the royal symbol, on one side and three bunches of watercress on the other.

This anecdote underlines the ambiguous character of watercress. So peppery are its taste and odor that one would expect it to provoke a heating effect, yet it is discovered by all who eat it to have, incongruously, a cooling one instead. This phenomenon was noted on the very first appearance of watercress on a menu, in the fourteenth century, when Charles VI's famous chef, Taillevent, determined to outdo himself for a banquet which his royal master was giving in honor of the Comte de la Marche. He was so well pleased with the result that he wrote down the menu for posterity. After the fourth course he inserted: "Watercress, served alone, to refresh the mouth."

Despite the difficulties of translation, we are relatively sure that the ancient Romans had watercress, and were fond of it. But there is no sure record of watercress cultivation, and it seems probable that they simply gathered it wild, which has, indeed, been common practice ever since. We do not know whether the *sisymbrium* which Charlemagne ordered planted on his lands was cress or watercress, but we do know that it was liquid pressed from watercress which sometimes went into verjuice, for a sauce used on roast meats, and that it was replaced in this role when the Crusaders returned from the Near East bringing lemons with them, which could have been as early as the thirteenth century. There was at least one place in France where watercress was being cultivated in that century: in monastery gardens, possibly the very first time that it had been deliberately raised. Otherwise it seems more likely that it was gathered wild; the literature of the Middle Ages refers frequently to the collecting of watercress from the banks of streams.

Cultivated watercress is of little importance in the United States today, but a good many country dwellers, or even picnicking urbanites, gather it wild. Originally, of course, since watercress is a Eurasian plant, it was cultivated watercress which was brought to America, but it was not farmed very diligently and soon escaped to freedom. It grows wild today in every state, including Alaska and Hawaii, and in southern Canada. It grows

CRESS. *Engraving from Theodore Francis Garrett:* The Encyclopaedia of Practical Cookery, *London, 1898*

in damp places, often at fairly high altitudes, and in clear running streams, provided the current is not so impetuous as to tear its roots loose and carry it pell-mell downstream without affording it a chance to cast anchor again. Its normal season is described as spring and summer, but except in extreme climates it is an herb which can be had nearly all year round. It has perhaps the longest season of any salad plant; in the United States south of Pennsylvania it can usually be gathered every month of the year.

Among dry-land cresses, winter cress (*Barbarea vulgaris*) is a food unjustly neglected; there are not many plants which can be picked during the winter. Whenever there are spells of mild weather, even in midwinter, winter cress resumes growing for as long as the thaw lasts, and can be cut and eaten; but it is at its best in late February and early March, when it will be found growing thickly long before any other green plant has volunteered for service.

The only other dry-land cress which is commonly eaten today is garden cress, *Lepidium sativum.* It has a pleasantly peppery taste, though one French dictionary describes it unkindly as having "a piquant flavor and a fetid odor." It has a natural affinity for mustard (as an herb), whose young seedlings are indeed sometimes called "mustard cress." They are often eaten together; "small salad" in England usually means a mixture of the young plants of garden cress and white mustard.

L. sativum is cultivated widely nowadays, in western Asia (especially India), Europe, North America and North Africa. It is eaten in other parts of Africa too, but is generally gathered wild. Tropical Africa consumes the leaves and young shoots, but it is the seeds which are eaten in the northern Sahara and in Nigeria, where the plant is called *algarabbum.*

Alexandre Dumas wrote of garden cress that it was "the healthiest of the *fines herbes.* It is rarely found on the markets of large cities, since it begins to wilt as soon as it is picked, and also because in cultivation it goes to seed too quickly. Children and old maids amuse themselves by growing this decorative cress on dampened cotton." This seems to be a vanished sport. Possibly *L. sativum* refuses to grow on synthetic fabrics. Besides, we have television.

And the rest of the **CRs** stand for

the **cricket,** whose two most luscious varieties are found in Thailand and the southern Mexican state of Oaxaca; for the **croaker,** a noisy fish almost as good eating as the sea bass; for the **crocodile,** which tastes like lobster; for the **crocus,** producer of saffron; for the **crosne,** a rhizome whose seeds are eaten in Asia and used for a coffee substitute in Indonesia; for **crow,** which Alexandre Dumas said "worked wonders" in pot-au-feu, and no doubt it did; for **crowberry,** so named by persons who deemed it food more fit for crows than for humans but which is eaten by humans in Alaska all the same; for **crow's-foot,** another name for the comb fringe grass of Africa; and for **crustaceans,** the noblest foodstuffs of the sea.

CU
stands for

cubeb, an obscure member of the pepper family, known chiefly to persons of my generation from one of Owen Johnson's Stover books, in which a prep-school character smoked it, ostensibly for asthma, but actually to throw disarray into the faculty of an institution where cigarettes were strictly forbidden; for the **cuckoo,** of which a French writer of the Middle Ages said that "of all birds used for the table none could be compared to the cuckoo taken just as it was full fledged"; for the **cucumber tree,** whose fruit is eaten in West Africa; for **cuddy's lungs,** our ninth name for the mullein; and for **cudweed,** an herb related to tarragon, of which John Gerard wrote in 1597: "Those floures which appeare first . . . are overtopt by other floures, which come on younger branches, and grow higher as children seeking to overgrow and overtop their parents (as many wicked children do), for which cause it hath been called 'Herbe impious.' "

CU
stands for

cuisses de nymphe ("nymph's thighs") and **cuisse-madame** ("madam's thigh"), which in the gallant French language denote respectively frogs' legs and a species of pear; for **cumin,** frequently confused with caraway; for the **cunner,** a fish of the wrasse family, moderately good eating, plentiful from Labrador to New Jersey; for the **curassow,** named for the Caribbean island of Curaçao, probably the finest game bird of South America; for **Curcuma,** a genus of tropical herbs of the ginger family which includes turmeric, and occasionally lends its name to that spice; for the **curled octopus,** so called because it seems most at ease with its tentacles bent into the shape of the letter C; for the **curlew,** of which the Eskimo variety, now extinct, was once a common food in New England, where it was called the "dough bird"; for **curry,** not a spice, as many persons believe, but a mixture of spices of infinite variability; for the **curry bean** of Africa, which is the lima of America; for **curry leaves,** which grow on an aromatic Indian tree and are indeed used in curries; for the **cusk,** a fish familiarly evoked in Colonial New England writings about whose identity we are unsure today, except that we know it is not the cusk-eel; for the **custard apple,** or bullock's heart, a fruit served to Columbus, who had never seen it before, on his first landing in the New World; for the **cutlass fish,** which has become so much thinner than its ancestors that ichthyologists call it the terminal member of the mackerel family; for the **cutthroat trout** of the American West, which tolerates both salt and fresh water; and for the **cuttlefish,** which, it appears, is monogamous, at least (like man?) in captivity.

And **CU** also stands for

CUCUMBER. "A cucumber," said Dr. Johnson, "should be well sliced, and dressed with pepper and vinegar, and then thrown out, as good for nothing." One might also cite the Apocrypha (Baruch 6:70): "A scarecrow in a garden of cucumbers keeps nothing."

This is ungrateful treatment for one of man's most venerable vegetables, whose tenure as a cultivated plant grows longer with each successive discovery. Once described as having been grown more than three thousand years ago in India, it has now been pushed back to 7750 B.C., according to carbon dating of seeds from an obviously cultivated plant turned up by a research team from the University of Hawaii near the Burma-Thailand border, which should be not far from the cucumber's place of origin.

The Assyrian Herbal lists a plant whose name has been translated as "desert cucumber" and

CUCUMBER *by Jean-Baptiste Chardin (1699–1779).* Still Life with Plums, *oil on canvas*

another rendered as "squirting cucumber." The first seems to have been a watermelon, the second we have still with us under the same name. Neither of them is a cucumber, but both do belong to the same group, the gourd family. Translation is a trap when we attempt to identify individual plants of this category in antiquity. Some ancient peoples do not seem to have made much distinction among cucumbers, squashes, melons and gourds. Even as late as Roman times, we are not at all sure that when Virgil or Pliny wrote *cucumis* they always meant cucumber.

Assuming that we translate correctly, the ancient Romans were fond of cucumbers. Virgil praised them in the *Georgics* and Apicius provided recipes for them, recommending that they be prepared with honey to counteract what he considered their sharpness. Roman gardeners tried to provide the sort of cucumbers Apicius desired by soaking the seeds in honeyed wine before planting them, on the theory that they would thus obtain sweet cucumbers; we have no report concerning their success.

The cucumber was slow to penetrate into northern Europe, where, after all, the climate was not kindly disposed towards it. It seems to have appeared in France and England about the same time, in the fourteenth century, but it may not have been known in Germany until the sixteenth, if a document of that period which chronicles its appearance in Württemberg was really reporting a novelty.

By then it was probably already known in America, carried there by the Spaniards and adopted so enthusiastically by the Pueblo Indians that some authors have listed it as a native Indian food in ignorance of the fact that it did not exist in America before Europeans brought it there. The most recent progress of the cucumber has been into the Sahara Desert, where it is now extensively grown; it appeared there first at some unrecorded date in the nineteenth century.

While refreshing, and an appetite stimulator when eaten at the beginning of a meal, the cucumber is otherwise about as close to neutrality as a vegetable can get without ceasing to exist. It contains virtually no nutritive elements, and though we are often told that it is rich in vitamins, especially A and C, they are not superabundant, and if you peel a cucumber you cut away most of its vitamin A. Dr. Johnson was not completely wrong.

CURRANT. When I was a boy in New England, a row of tall bushes—five to six feet—grew against our back fence next to the raspberries. They bore small (a quarter-inch across) round red or white berries, through whose shiny skins you could see the juicy pulp, like that of some grapes. We ate them with sugar and cream, delighting in their tart acidity during their season, which was long, for after ripening they did not begin to degenerate at once, but could be left on the shrubs until we wanted them, ready at any time to be eaten garden-fresh. Currants were a common fruit then, but they are almost unfindable now.

The chief reason for the decline of the currant in the United States is that it serves as a host to *Cronartium ribicola,* a parasitic fungus which causes white-pine blister rust. In one of those improbable arrangements of nature which makes one think of the exigencies of Lewis Carroll's *Through the Looking-Glass* insects, it has been decreed that *Cronartium ribicola* must spend part of its life on plants of the genus *Ribes* (currants and gooseberries), to which it does no particular good but no irreparable harm either, and the rest on the white pine, which it girdles and kills. As white pine is a valuable wood, the growing of currants and gooseberries has been discouraged and in some areas is even flatly forbidden by law. This has probably caused no pain to the supermarkets, which determine what we may eat nowadays, for currants are precisely the kind of food they would rather not stock—fussy to handle, perishable in transit and storage and not very profitable anyway.

The currant is a widespread plant of approximately the middle third of the Northern Hemisphere, possibly native to Scandinavia: the oldest known currant seeds were found in a Danish Mesolithic site. The theory has been advanced (though perhaps by persons unaware of the fact that the climate was milder in the year 1000 than it is now) that when the Vikings gave the name Vinland to what was probably today's Newfoundland, too far north for grapes, they were not referring to grapes, but to currants (*vinbär,* "wine berry," in Swedish).

The currant was probably first cultivated, a little before 1600, in Denmark, the Netherlands and perhaps a few points along the Baltic. It seems to have first appeared in England in Elizabethan times and at about the same time in France, shortly after the Dutch began cultivating them. European currants were brought to America early in the seventeenth century by colonists probably unaware that America had some already.

There are more than a hundred species of currants, of which red currants are the most used for food. The white currant, botanically, is a red currant which has lost its pigmentation and, along with it, some of its acidity, making it the sweetest, as well as the rarest, of all currants. Almost every-

CURRANT *by Jean-Baptiste Chardin (1699–1779).* Plums, *oil on canvas*

body agrees that black currants are too bitter to eat fresh, but they are excellent for jams and jellies, which is why the British raise ten times as many black currants as red, more than any other country, even France, which goes in for them heavily, but for drinks (*cassis*). The capital of *cassis* drinks is Dijon, which is also the capital of Burgundy and the department of the Côte d'Or, which produces more black currants than any other department. Burgundy owes a considerable debt to black currants. They used to be grown there between rows of grapevines (they like shade, and in intensive cultivation can be planted with other crops and even under trees); and when in the last century phylloxera destroyed the vines, the winegrowers had another crop to fall back on.

The French do not care much for the currant as food. The chief currant eaters of the world are the British, the Scandinavians, the Germans and the Russians.

CY
stands for

cyclamates, slimming sweeteners now banned in many countries, including the United States, because they are suspected of being carcinogenic; for **cymbium**, a summer squash with a scalloped edge; for **Cyperus esculentus**, which, promising as it sounds, is nothing other than chufa; and for nothing else worthy of our attention.

D

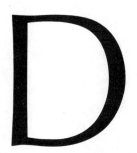

DANTE: *You shall find out how salt is the taste of another's bread.*

DE LA MARE, WALTER: *It's a very odd thing—*
As odd as can be—
That whatever Miss T. eats
Turns into Miss T.

DICKENS: *What a world of gammon and spinach it is, though, ain't it?*

DA
stands for

dab, a right-eyed flatfish, and **dabberlocks,** an edible seaweed; for the **dace,** a carplike fish more appreciated in medieval France than it is today; for the **daffodil,** whose bulbs were served roasted in seventeenth-century England; for the African **dagarti bean,** which is simply the COWPEA; for the **dahlia,** whose petals sometimes decorate salads though they have no taste; for the **daikon,** the white radish of Japan; for the **daing,** the salt-dried fish the Filipinos fed to Magellan; for **daisies,** frequently candied in England a century ago, of which even the young green leaves are edible; for the **Dall sheep,** whose meat is described as "exquisite," but which you are never likely to taste unless you go for that purpose to Alaska, which has a population of 40,000 of them; and for the **dame tombée,** or "fallen woman," which turns out to be nothing more exciting than a sort of wrasse eaten on the island of Mauritius.

DA
stands for

the **damselfish** of Africa, which does not seem to be related to the blue damsel fish of the Mediterranean; for the **damson plum,** of which the English make a paste they call cheese; for **darkie Charlie,** a fish eaten in Algeria which if it were encountered in the Gulf of Mexico would probably be called a pompano; for **darnel,** whose seeds, ground together with wheat, produce bread which can make you drunk; for **dasheen,** another name for taro; for the **dassie,** a sort of rat eaten in tropical Africa; for the **date-shell,** a mussel so called from its shape, once demanded in tribute by the emperor Frederick Barbarossa; for the **dattock,** or tallow tree, whose pods yield a pulp popular in West Africa; and for the **day lily,** a highly decorative flower whose buds and young roots are both recommendable foods.

And **DA** also stands for

DANDELION. Whoever first called the dandelion "a tramp with a golden head" captured nicely the humble rustic nature of this eminently edible plant, which probably accounts for the fact that very little attention has been paid to it in literature. The dandelion is not, I believe, mentioned in the Old Testament by name, though it is supposed that when the phrase "bitter herbs" is used there, the dandelion is included. The ancient peoples of the Mediterranean area ate dandelions, but found little to say about them, except as medicine, and this continued to be true in the Middle Ages. There were references to the dandelion in Renaissance writings—but as an aid to the female complexion. It is true that the eating of green leafy vegetables was comparatively rare until modern times; John Evelyn was an innovator when, at the end of the seventeenth century, he wrote lengthily on salads, including dandelion greens in most of his recipes. They turn up among the mixed greens in Southern soul food in the United States, and in the North the Pennsylvania Dutch pour a dressing of hot cider vinegar and sugar enlivened with bits of bacon over dandelion salad, a traditional dish among them for Maundy Thursday. Perhaps the most unexpected use of dandelion leaves today is in a sweet dessert—the Algerian honey cake called *yubba*.

In the United States dandelions are usually available only to those who gather them; you are not likely to find them in a supermarket. France is probably the country most given to cultivating them; earth is heaped up around the plants to blanch them, as for asparagus, and to make them tenderer. This gives the leaves a pale golden color, and the taste tends to be pale too. Wild dandelions have more flavor than cultivated ones because they are richer in vitamins and mineral salts, and among wild dandelions the best are those which grow naturally in fields of untended and untrammeled grass, not those which, undesirably, bespeckle mowed lawns. The spring treat provided by dandelion leaves does not last long, for the maturing leaves quickly become tough and bitter; the dandelion has been called the "spring tonic" precisely because its season is so short.

Most of us take it for granted that the leaves are the only edible part of the dandelion, a serious underestimate. When the flower buds first begin to form, you can pick them unopened and fry them in butter; they taste like mushrooms. Early in spring, when the first reddish leaves appear, hugging the ground, dig up the crowns from which the leaves start their upward journey; you will find them good eating, and so is the long taproot, which, according to Euell Gibbons, the wild-food expert, is "better than either parsnips or salsify." It is peeled and boiled like a potato—in two or three changes of water if it is beginning to become bitter. It will certainly be bitter during the summer, and so will the crown, so forget about both once spring has passed; but the first frosts of autumn restore mildness to them and they become edible again.

Dandelion honey, thicker in texture than that from most flowers, is worth attention; Colorado makes a specialty of it. The plant also contributes beverages: there is dandelion tea and dandelion wine, and the roots, roasted and ground, make a coffee substitute which many persons cannot distinguish from the real thing.

Dandelion leaves have been used to feed silkworms when their preferred mulberry foliage was not to be had. Dandelion roots contain a milky fluid comparable to latex; in Russia, where a native species has a particularly thick root, it has been used to make synthetic rubber.

DANDELION. *Botanical photograph by E. M. Kuttredge of Carolina Dwarf Dandelion, 1917*

DATE. "Dates are to the people of the Sahara what wheat is to the French and rice to the Chinese," a French author has written, and it is indeed true that in such hot desert areas the date is the indispensable staple food, which flourishes in regions where no other highly nourishing food plants can grow. The date has been described as living "with its feet in the water and its head in the sun," which makes it the oasis plant par excellence, an oasis being by definition a place in a desert—that is, an arid region where no rain falls—at which the desert's infertility is counteracted by the presence of underground water. During its ripening season, the date palm tolerates no moisture in the air (even night dew is harmful to it), but it must have water for its roots or it will withhold its fruit.

The range of the date palm is wider than the range of the fruit it bears. The area within which dates are produced commercially in the Old World extends from the Canary Islands through northern Africa and southwestern Asia to India and Pakistan. The trees, however, will grow in other tropical or subtropical areas up to 4500 feet altitude wherever the temperature never drops below 20° F. for any prolonged period, but it will ripen fruit only in dry climates where the temperature stays between 70° and 92° from April through September. The palms you have so often seen, in person or in pictures, lining the Promenade des Anglais in Nice are date palms, which even produce great clusters of dates—but they never ripen. The only place in Europe where they do is in a small area around Alicante in Spain, planted there probably by the ancient Carthaginians who once ruled this territory and were, in their native Africa, great raisers of dates.

One might expect that a fruit like the date would simply have been gathered wild until a fairly high stage of agricultural development had been reached; on the contrary, it was one of the first fruits to be cultivated deliberately. This is a result of the nature of the plant: date palms are either male or female, so the pollen from male trees must reach female trees to fertilize them; but nature neglected to make the flowers attractive to pollen-carrying insects. It has to be distributed by the wind, which is good enough for nature when a grove of date palms contains an equal number of male and female trees; every female tree has a male partner near enough to be useful. But it is not good enough for man, who cannot afford to give up half of the restricted area of fertile soil provided by an oasis to trees which produce no fruit. In the Sahara, only one male tree is allowed to grow for each fifty female trees, enough to pollinate them all; but this means that the pollen has to be distributed by hand. In Arabia, pollen from especially vigorous trees is bottled and sold at fancy prices to plantation owners, who sprinkle it sparingly by hand over the flowers of their finest female trees.

"The date palm is of African origin," says Volume 17 of the *Encyclopaedia Britannica*. "The . . . date palm is native to the oases of the Persian Gulf" reports Volume 9 of the same work. Volume 9 seems to have the better case. Dates probably originated where they are still most important—in or near Iraq, which is by a considerable margin the world's heaviest producer and largest exporter of dates. The oldest date stones ever found were discovered in the Shanidar Cave of northern Iraq, where they go back to the Middle Paleolithic and Upper Paleolithic, say 50,000 years ago. They were wild dates, but the fruit was already being cultivated in the Sahara in Neolithic times. Records of date cultivation in the Middle East exist since 3000 B.C., and we know that about 2250 B.C. Mesopotamia prized particularly the dates of Bahrein, which still grows them. Herodotus wrote that while Assyria was the richest grain-growing country in the world, it made no attempt to grow any fruit except dates (an error: there were other fruits). Date palms grew everywhere in Mesopotamia, he said, providing the people with all their needs. Honey was known, but date syrup was the commonest sweetener. The ancient Egyptians ate the fruit fresh, dried, or pressed into bricks for preservation.

When did the date first grow in India? Date stones have been found at the archeological site at Mohenjo-Daro, which antedates the Aryan invasion—2000 B.C. perhaps? Dates were in any case eaten in the Indus valley from very early times; the Indians were then in contact with Mesopotamia and may have acquired the date from there.

In the other direction from the Middle East, Carthage was a great date center. The date palm appears on Carthaginian coins, and stelae have been preserved depicting scenes of date harvesting or pollination. Jewish money sometimes pictured date palms too, so it seems curious that the Old Testament mentions this fruit only indirectly, when Jericho is described as "the city of palm trees." Jericho was noted in the ancient world for the quality of its dates; Pliny referred to a particular variety which came from Judaea, especially from the region of Jericho, and bore abundantly.

Xenophon wrote of the dates the Greeks encountered in the Middle East: "Their color was just like amber and the Babylonian villagers dried them and kept them as sweets." He also reported that the Babylonians ate the "cabbage," the terminal buds of the tree, what we call "hearts of palm" today; they had, he said, "a peculiarly pleasant taste," but were apt to cause headaches. Pliny wrote that some of Alexander's soldiers died from eating unripe dates in excessive quantity. These accounts imply that for the Greeks the date was a foreign fruit, and indeed Theophrastus tells us that an attempt was made to grow dates in Greece but some of the trees bore no fruits, while on those which did, the dates did not ripen. The Greeks therefore imported dates from Egypt, and so did the Romans.

Mohammed legendarily exhorted Moslems to "cherish your father's sister, the palm tree," meaning the date palm, which is why the fasts of

DATE. *Print from Artemas Ward:* The Grocer's Encyclopedia, *New York, 1911*

Ramadan are always broken on a date. Arabic names for the many varieties of dates tend to be picturesque, ranging from the romantic (Bride's Fingers for a fine delicate fruit) to the coarse (Mule's Testicles for a thick pear-shaped type).

We hear from China that about the beginning of our era one of the classic Eight Delicacies of that country was suckling pig stuffed with dates. This is probably an error of translation. The stuffing is more likely to have been jujubes, still called Chinese dates in Africa today; Herodotus remarked on the similarity of taste between the jujube and the date.

In the thirteenth century Marco Polo encountered dates in several places where they grew. "In the groves around Baskra," he wrote, "grow the best dates in the world," and he recorded their presence also in the plain of Hormuz, in Aden, and in southern India, where he was impressed particularly by date wine: "And a very good drink it is, and makes a man drunk sooner than grape wine." Dates (then called "finger apples") were well known in Europe in medieval times. We are not sure when they reached England, but the word entered the language in the thirteenth century, which may be when the fruit arrived also. By Elizabethan times all the great households had dates in their pantries, used mostly for sweet puddings. In the fourteenth century, dates were among the desserts served at most formal dinners in France, and in the fifteenth they could be had in Paris by anyone able to pay for them: they were expensive. Not until after the 1830 conquest of Algeria and the subsequent colonization of Africa would dates come within the reach of the average Frenchman.

The California date industry began only in the twentieth century, in 1902 according to some authorities. By 1958, 5000 acres were devoted to commercial date production. There seems to be only one place in the United States propitious to the date, part of California's Coachella valley, which lies in a depression twenty feet below sea level, with air which is dry and hot all summer, while the trees' feet are kept in water by irrigation from the Colorado River. California produces 99.3 percent of all dates grown commercially in the United States, almost all of them in the Coachella valley.

Indio, in that valley, is the capital of California date growing. It holds a yearly ten-day festival in celebration of the fruit, featuring on each day the enactment of a different tale from the *Arabian Nights*, presided over by a pretty girl crowned for the occasion as Queen Scheherazade, which would no doubt astonish the Iraqis if they ever heard about it. In the Sahara, the Teda of the Tibesti Mountains celebrate the date too, at harvest time, but in a slightly different manner—with marriages, with circumcisions and by getting as drunk as possible on the powerful brew made from the pulp of the date-palm heart.

DE
stands for

the **death trumpet**, an unjustly libeled mushroom, since despite its name it is both edible and tasty; for **deer's-tongue**, or mountain lettuce, used as a food and as a perfume; for the **deleb palm** of tropical Africa and Madagascar, of which many parts are edible, including even the bark of its young roots; for the **Delicious apple**, which has been promoted to the position of the world's best seller by being bred to a mediocrity so devoid of character that nothing remains to which anyone could object; for **dendé oil**, used in cooking in eastern Brazil, derived from a palm imported by slaves from West Africa; for the **dentex**, a tasty Mediterranean fish which belongs to the family of breams; for the **detar**, or tallow tree, widely consumed in West Africa; for the **devil's nettle** or **devil's plaything**, which is the yarrow, and the **devil's thorn**, known to the French as the Maltese cross, of which both leaves and seeds are eaten in Africa; and for the **dewberry**, a backboneless black berry *couchant* in growth but *rampant* in pies.

And **DE** also stands for

DEER. The word "parasite" suggests an indolent creature, living lazily on its host; yet the fastest animal in the world is a parasite. The record for rapidity is held by the deer botfly, which has to be speedy to keep up with the animal on whose hide it proposes to deposit its eggs. Deer reach 30 miles an hour in spurts and can keep up 25 over a distance of several miles. They can also make leaps of nearly 30 feet and clear obstacles 8 feet high. They may also hold another mammalian record, for defecation, but this is difficult to document in the absence of sufficient data. The deer's average, it seems, is thirteen piles per deer per day.

Man has been eating deer since prehistoric times; there have been periods when it was the principal human food. Deer were present before men were, in the species we know today, at least by the Quaternary epoch, waiting to enter the human larder as soon as humans arrived themselves toward the end of that epoch. Prehistoric men hunted the stag in China and Borneo 500,000 years ago. Excavations in that cradle of early man, France's Dordogne, have revealed that 110,000 years ago deer was their third most important food (the aurochs was second, the horse first), and that by 23,000 years ago it had become number one.

Deer were eaten widely in Persia 50,000 years ago; in Germany, including some territory now covered by the Baltic, 8000 years ago; in China, during the Chang dynasty, 3700 years ago; and in the Neolithic Swiss lake settlements. White-tailed deer were eaten by prehistoric American Indians in what is now New England, sambar deer and barking deer in what is now Borneo, and red deer in what is now the Soviet Union. The Mesopotamia deer was common in prehistoric Palestine and Mesopotamia in the seventh century B.C., the date of a bas-relief from Nineveh which shows deer being taken in nets. The ancient Hebrews ate deer with the permission of Deuteronomy 14:4–5: "These are the beasts which ye shall eat . . . the hart, and the roebuck, and the fallow deer." Ancient Greek literature frequently mentions deer, and we are told that the Romans imported them from Numidia, though we are also told that there are no indigenous deer in Africa; the explanation seems to be that some red deer strayed from Spain into North Africa in the remote times before the Strait of Gibraltar had opened. Africa is not propitious to deer, so they did not flourish, but there are still a few there, most of them in the neighborhood of Tunis.

The ancient Gauls of the pre-Roman period rode to hounds in pursuit of deer, accompanying their hunts with a sacrificial ceremony which, after they adopted Roman gods, was dedicated to Diana. This looked backward to the magical charms which prehistoric man employed to assure

Deer *by Deruta. Italian dish, lustered maiolica, c. 1515–1520*

success in hunting, and forward to the ritualized stag hunt which, beginning at this period, would endure for the next two thousand years. It was during the Middle Ages that the cult of the deer reached its greatest heights, for hunters and for trenchermen. No important repast was complete without venison. The anonymous *Ménagier de Paris* reports the menu of a fourteenth-century banquet as including "a quarter of roebuck," while the Count of Anjou was host at a feast in 1455 at which the first course included "a quarter of stag which had been a night in salt"; each of the following three courses offered, among other trifles, red deer; and during the whole repast two enormous pies, at either end of the table, within reach of anyone who might feel peckish, held each a whole roebuck as only one of its generous list of ingredients.

When venison lovers reached America they described it as "the home of deer," a trifle cavalierly, since this animal's origin was undoubtedly Eurasia. However, the white-tailed deer has been in America for several million years, enough time to have developed some twenty native species; deer reached their most distant point in the New World in South America in the Pleistocene period. They were found "in wild abundance" by the early colonists, but hunters managed nevertheless to take their customary toll in jig time despite the limited deadliness of the blunderbuss and the small population of whites (about 300,000 in 1700) pitted against the large population of deer. Massachusetts was already obliged to impose restrictions on deer hunting in 1696, and all the colonies except Georgia had followed suit by the time of the Revolution.

Towards the end of the nineteenth century the United States awoke to the danger that it might lose all its deer. Reforestation, winter feeding and the establishment of closed seasons improved the situation, and today deer are probably the most plentiful large game animals in the country. Their population is estimated at six million, of which hunters kill about a million a year; but this is a rate of loss with which these prolific animals can cope. Nevertheless, it remains true that if you want to taste deer in the United States you usually have to hunt it yourself or know somebody who does. There is no commercial hunting, and in most states individual sportsmen are forbidden to sell their kill. Most large cities have butchers who make a specialty of game, but they import their deer, sometimes from Europe, but lately even oftener from Australia or New Zealand, both countries which had no deer at all, until, fairly recently, their woods were stocked with deer introduced from abroad, some from America.

Which of the world's deer (nineteen genera, and I have no idea how many species) makes the best eating? The order is in dispute, but the European roebuck seems to have headed the list since medieval times, when the French physician Bruyerin-Champier wrote that it provided "cuts worthy of kings and rich men." Second would be the fallow deer of Europe: "The most prized parts," wrote Alexandre Dumas, "are the rump and the hind legs, which are the fleshiest. The brain is a most delicious morsel." Next come three American species, first the white-tailed deer (of which the liver is particularly prized), then the black-tailed deer and finally the mule deer. We then return to Europe for the red deer, of which Bruyerin-Champier wrote: "Fried slices of the young horn of the stag are the daintiest of foods." Bringing up the rear is the wapiti, often miscalled the American elk, though it is not an elk; it is almost identical with the European red deer. Even young, its flesh is apt to be tough, and it is rather coarse in flavor.

A word of warning: if you should ever find yourself in China, in a place old-fashioned enough still to be serving a dish more common in medieval times, household deer, you should know that this term is a euphemism for rat.

DI
stands for

Dian's bud, a plant used to wake Titania in *A Midsummer Night's Dream,* which anyone but Shakespeare would have called wormwood; for the large **Digby scallop** of Canada's Atlantic coast and the small **digger wedge** clam of the U.S. Atlantic coast; for the **dika nut** of tropical Africa, a versatile plant whose kernel is eaten as a nut, ground into meal or made into butter, while its fruit pulp is eaten in various countries but not in Angola, where it somehow becomes inedible; for the **dik-dik**, an antelope standing not much higher than a foot at the shoulder, whose endearing tininess does not deter equatorial Africans from devouring it; for **Dingaan's apple**, called thus by those who want to remember the African chief of that name who gained power by murdering his half-brother, lost it by being murdered himself, and was described by a Norwegian missionary as "simply a beast on two legs" (known as the unkokolo by those who prefer to forget Dingaan); and for **dittany**, an herb reputed capable of expelling arrows from your body if you happen to have any in it.

And **DI** also stands for

DILL. Joseph Wechsberg once wrote that dill is the "most frequently used herb in Polish cooking —in the soup, with the boiled potatoes, mixed in with the vegetables. Sometimes I [think] the Poles [overdo] the dill business." Dill does indeed invite extremism: it is used lavishly in regions addicted to it and not at all elsewhere. In Europe, the Poles are joined by the other inhabitants of the colder central and eastern countries in their adoration of dill. Russians are fond of it; Hungary is the Continent's chief producer of dill-seed oil; Scandinavians dote on it; but in the Latin countries it is so little known that certain French dictionaries think it is the same thing as fennel or anise. Northern France seems not to know that it exists, southern France has heard of it but seldom uses it, and while I have been told that in Italy its leaves sometimes go into salads, I have never encountered dill there myself. In Asia it is cultivated oftenest in India.

The United States has adopted it to preserve cucumbers and gherkins so generally that it is the seasoning, not the main ingredient, which has given its name to the dill pickle. This is a common commercial product, but it is so inferior to the homemade version that it hardly seems the same food. However, to produce it, you need to raise your own cucumbers and dill—a plant easy

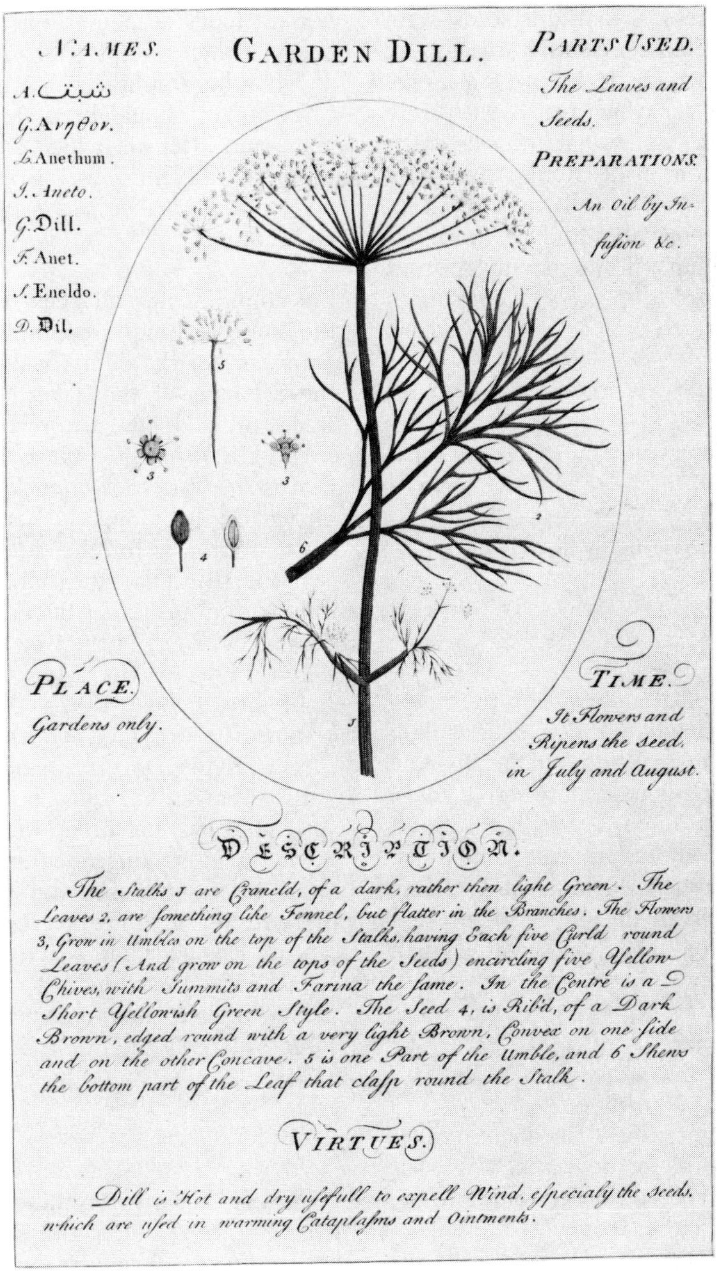

DILL. *Drawing from Timothy Sheldrake:* Botanicum Medicinale, *London, c. 1759*

to grow, which offers itself all summer long, especially if you take the precaution of making successive plantings. All parts of the herb are aromatic.

In addition to being used for pickles, dill often goes into potato salad and sauerkraut, replacing the caraway sometimes used in these dishes for those who find its flavor too strong (dill has been described as like mild caraway, though actually it is difficult to compare its special flavor to anything else). It is also used to give a special taste to vinegar (through its leaves) or to spice bread (usually through its seeds, though James Beard has written that he prefers the leaves for this purpose). It also goes with cabbage (to which it is supposed to contribute digestibility), with vegetables (especially those which are boiled in a minimum of water), with fish, stews, soups, fish and vegetable sauces, veal, pork, kidneys, apple pie (!) and even chutney.

Of venerable age, dill is probably, though not certainly, identical with the aneth of antiquity, a symbol of pleasure for the ancient Romans, who wove wreaths of it to wear at their feasts (dill is called aneth today in some countries). The Romans mixed aneth oil in their gladiators' food in the belief that it was tonic, and it may have been for the same reason that dill seeds were given to American children a century or two back to chew in church, perhaps to keep them awake during long sermons, for which reason they were called "meetin' seeds." Somewhat inconsistently, dill water, a decoction made from these same seeds, was given to babies to lull them to sleep. A soporific effect seems also to have been attributed to dill for adults, if one may judge from an entry in *The Ladies Indispensable Companion,* published in 1854, which provides this useful bit of advice:

To procure sleep.
Wash the head in a decoction of dill seed, and smell of it frequently.

This must have required a highly flexible neck.

DJ
stands for

djamur kuping, the Sumatran version of the cloud-ear mushroom; for **djave butter,** derived in Gabon from the nuts of a tropical tree; for the **djankol,** an acid spicy fruit of Indonesia; for **djeruk-manis,** small, sweet Sumatran oranges; for **djerek purut,** the dried leaves of Far Eastern wild lime trees; for **dji,** currantlike berries which are pressed into round loaves for preservation in the Tibesti region of the Sahara; and for **djon djon,** small Haitian mushrooms.

DO
stands for

dock, a neglected plant which can double either for spinach or rhubarb; for **dog,** which is what you get if you order "special beef" in Hong Kong; for the **dog-cockle,** a rather tough Mediterranean shellfish called in several Latin languages the sea almond, because it is shaped like one; for the **dogfish,** a surly creature not much esteemed by gourmets, though Herbert Hoover coaxed Americans into eating it during World War I on the grounds that it was "nutritious if not attractive"; for the **dog rose,** whose hips were eaten by Egyptian Pharaohs and Chinese emperors; for the **dog whelk,** an American version of the shellfish which furnished imperial purple to dye the togas of Roman emperors; for the **dogwood,** thus named, not quite logically, because its berries are not even fit food for dogs, yet Jamaican bees make honey from its flowers; for **Dolichos,** a genus of pulse plants difficult to identify in the West, where they are so little known that English has no popular name for them, though they are important foods in many tropical countries; for **doll cheese,** which is not cheese, but dwarf mallow; and for the **dolphin,** whose brain structure indicates that it should be at least as intelligent as man—and after all, which of the two has fewer unsolved problems?

DO stands for

the **dolphin fish,** still being caught off Malta by the same technique described by Oppian 2000 years ago; for the **dom** (or **dum**) **palm,** to which the Saharans of the Tibesti have recourse only when other foods are scarce, since only the sweetish rind of its fruit is edible; for **donduri,** a Russian variety of purslane popular among Georgians; for **dong,** a Vietnamese herb with ritual overtones; for the **donkey,** little eaten except in Africa; for the **dood,** a sort of shrimp found, of all places, in the Sahara Desert; for the **dorab,** a food fish of the Red Sea, and the **dorade,** a food fish of the Mediterranean, sacred to Aphrodite, known also as the golden eyebrow because it wears gold-colored splotches on each cheek; for the **Dorking,** a hen rendered so awkward by having five toes on each foot that she is apt to kill half her brood during the first month by motherly mauling; for the **dormouse,** carefully raised for the table by the ancient Romans; for the **dotterel,** a shore bird eaten in seventeenth-century England, but, so far as I know, nowhere now; for the **dove,** dedicated to Astarte; and for the **dowitcher,** an unpursued game bird found along America's Atlantic coast.

DU
stands for

DUCK. There are, Alexandre Dumas wrote, forty-two varieties of ducks; this seems to be a serious underestimate. When, in preparation for writing this entry, I started to list the different ducks deserving of consideration, I quickly passed seventy, and gave up. It was evident that space would not permit even naming all of them, much less attempting to situate them on a scale of taste which ranges, for this bird, from the exquisite to the execrable.

Duck at its best represents one of the most delectable forms of poultry; yet nowhere, during its long history, have men been in any hurry to domesticate it. For one thing, it was unnecessary: wild duck until fairly recent times had been plentiful and easy to take; many duck fanciers prefer wild duck to domesticated duck anyway.

The ancient Egyptians, before they knew the chicken, ate duck, but we may suppose that the

Duck. *Marble mosaic, 1st century* BC—*1st century* AD, *Rome*

rush-bordered banks of the Nile attracted all the wild birds they needed. We know from Martial that the Romans were fond of duck and from Columella that they kept them in net enclosures; but the probability that these were wild birds, taken alive and held captive only until they were wanted for the table, seems indicated by the fact that they were luxuries (domesticated ducks should have been relatively cheap) and that the Romans ate only the breast meat (and the brains); the rest of the wild duck is scarcely worth bothering about.

It is a reasonable guess that the first domesticators of ducks were the Chinese, who seem in any case to have been the first to incubate duck eggs artificially. If the Chinese were not the first, then the initiators may just possibly have been American Indians. The guess has been hazarded that the Incas domesticated ducks, while the Spanish friar Bernardino de Sahagún reported that the Aztecs ate duck; in both cases, however, it seems likelier that the birds were wild. In medieval and Renaissance Europe, though duck was popular, it seems still to have been wild duck: if Europeans had domesticated them they could hardly have continued to believe, as they did, that ducks were born from the decomposition of leaves. Had ducks been domesticated in England by Elizabethan times? They were cheap enough to make that seem likely—six pence for a large bird.

When Europeans reached America, they found

great numbers of wild ducks there; Captain John Smith reported on their abundance in Virginia in 1608. Ducks were still so plentiful in the first half of the nineteenth century that Charles Dickens told of crossing two wide streams on his way from Philadelphia to Washington: "The water in both was blackened with flights of canvas-backed ducks, which . . . abound hereabouts." The canvasback was America's tastiest duck, whose flavor was explained by a diet composed largely of tape grass, alias wild celery. Alessandro Filippini, chef of the most famous restaurant in American history, Delmonico's, called it "the king of birds," and wrote that "no game is more highly praised or more eagerly sought after in Europe than our American canvasback ducks."

Nevertheless, it was not the canvasback, nor any other of the many species of duck available in America, which became the most widely eaten domesticated bird in the United States, but the Peking duck, sturdy, tender, tasty, juicy and with flesh comparatively light in color. This is the fowl eaten throughout the country under the name "Long Island duckling." Long Island produces more than half of all ducks consumed in the United States, plus some for export, a $3-million-a-year industry in 1970. It dates from 1873, when a Yankee Clipper brought from China just nine Peking ducks, from which all the millions of ducks of this species in America today are descended.

Asked to name the tastiest duck of France, most people would probably pick the Rouen duck, which owes much of its fame to the fact that this is the one used for the spectacularly served pressed duck. Its juiciness when squeezed ceremoniously at the table in a silver press, as well as its red flesh and its gamy flavor, result from the manner of its death—it is strangled, not decapitated, so all the blood remains in the body. The most knowing Frenchmen, however, think their country's finest duck is the Nantais, which owes its exceptional flavor to a yearly crossing of domestic ducks with wild drakes.

England might be credited with a favorite duck of its own in the gadwall, which is not confined to the British Isles, but has of late years experienced a boom there, where it is being raised increasingly for the table.

Most of the other widely eaten ducks are international, like the teal, fancied in America as well as in Europe, where it is known in English as the garganey and in French as the *sarcelle*. The mallard, large and flavorful (credited, not quite accurately, with being the ancestor of all European and American domesticated ducks), is a favorite on the two continents, and the pintail duck is appreciated on three, North America, Europe and Asia. Also tasty is the widgeon, which will eat grass rather than defile its flavor with coarser food; the noise made by its wings in flight has caused it to be called the "whew duck" in some localities of England, while one of the two American species is known for the same reason as the "whistler."

The shoveler duck has a broad, flat beak lined with a sort of fringe which lets water run out while holding food particles in, a peculiarity also seen in whalebone whales. Scaups belong to the same family as the canvasback, but are far inferior to it in flavor because of a diet composed fifty-fifty of vegetable and animal matter. The most marine of all ducks are the scoters, which, because they live largely on fish, are apt to have a fishy taste themselves, little appreciated except by the Catholic Church, which lists them with fish among foods which can be eaten in Lent.

The duck which is the most forbidding in flavor of all those raised for food is no doubt the American (Mexico to Brazil) Muscovy duck, whose name is a corruption of "musk duck"; glands in its rump give its flesh a disagreeable musky taste, sometimes so strong as to make it downright inedible. It has been domesticated in southern France under the name "Barbary duck," not to be eaten directly itself, but in a second generation. It is crossed with the Rouen or the Nantes duck, and the offspring are eaten. They are characterized by richly flavored breast meat from which the parental muskiness has disappeared, and are particularly prized for the production of duck foie gras, which seems to me to have more character than the commoner goose foie gras. The Muscovy-Barbary duck is an exception to the rule that domesticated ducks are descended from the mallard, displaying its divergence by such signs as not quacking and by laying eggs which take thirty-five days to hatch instead of the mallard's twenty-eight. Its most unmistakable sign of difference is provided by the fact that the offspring are sterile—like that typical example of incompatibility of different though related species, the mule; hence the French call these birds *canetons mulards*.

I do not know what sort of ducks Brillat-Savarin preferred, but he seems to have been fussy about them. He worked up a great deal of steam in denouncing certain sauces applied to duck as "monstrous, degrading and dishonorable." He wrote also that duck is "slightly exciting" and provokes dreaming.

And DU also stands for

duck potatoes, a form of arrowhead so called

because ducks dig for their tubers; for **duckweed,** which is eaten in China; for the **dugong,** an aquatic mammal whose blubber is eaten in the Far East in callous disregard of the fact that it has on occasion been taken for a mermaid; for the **duiker,** a small antelope eaten in tropical Africa; for **dulse,** an edible seaweed, tough but not tasty, which is nevertheless ingurgitated even in so conservative a region as New England; for **dung,** the spread for bread at the circumcision rites of the Saharan Chaamba; for the delicious **Dungeness crab,** named parochially for a town on Washington's Olympic Peninsula, though it is found all the way from Alaska to Mexico; for the **dunlin,** an edible shore bird of the Atlantic coast of the United States seldom eaten nowadays; for the **durello,** a tasty, hard-fleshed apple which is a specialty of the ministate of San Marino; for the **Durham,** a heavy beef animal developed in England and introduced into the United States, where it was rebaptized the Shorthorn; for the **Dutch Belted** milch cow, brought into the United States, believe it or not, by P. T. Barnum; and for **Dutch nightingales,** a joking name for frogs in Alabama.

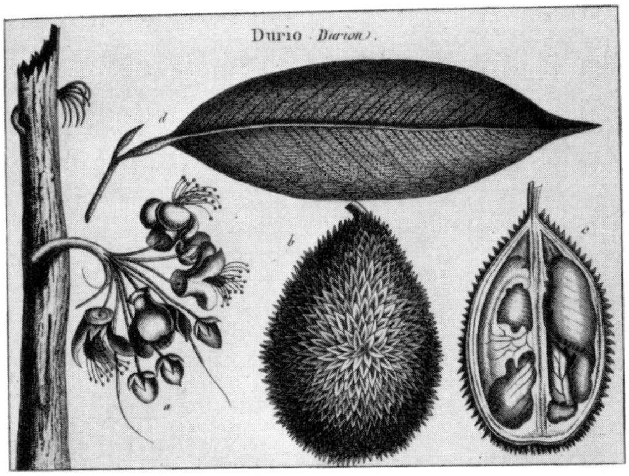

DURIAN. *Drawing from Jean-Baptiste Lamarck:* Encyclopédie méthodique botanique, *Paris, 1823*

DURIAN. A taste and smell like sewage, the description given by an ordinarily reliable English reference book, hardly seems compatible with the often reiterated statement that the durian is one of the most delicious of tropical fruits. The English authority seems to be in a minority of one about the taste, but it has support about the smell. Despite it, the fruit is appreciated not only by the natives of the regions where it grows (primarily Malaysia) but even by Westerners hardy enough to have crossed the smell barrier. Novices desirous of exploring the over-protected exquisiteness of the durian might try standing under a durian tree and falling upon a fruit the moment it is picked, which is when the odor is faintest.

The combination of putrid odor and subtle flavor is found in some cheeses, which is probably why the French call the *Bombacaceae,* the family of trees to which the durian belongs, *fromagers,* "cheese-mongers"; in English the durian has been called the cheese that grows on trees. The tree looks unexotically something like an elm, but its fruit is strange enough to compensate for this commonplace appearance. Universally described as round despite the observable fact that it is ovoid, it is covered with short, stubby, extremely hard, pyramid-shaped spikes set closely together over its whole surface. When ripe it ranges in color from brown to a dull yellow and is variously described as the size of (a) a small melon, (b) a large coconut, (c) a soccer ball; these divergences presumably result from the fact that there are about a dozen species, the one oftenest eaten being *Durio zibethinus,* six to eight inches in diameter, six to eight pounds in weight. Opened, the fruit reveals a sticky cream-to-yellow pulp, with seeds the size of small chestnuts embedded in the pulp of each of the five compartments into which the fruit is divided. Both are edible. It is the pulp about which aficionados rave, but the seeds can be roasted like chestnuts and, indeed, taste like them.

The penetrating odor of the durian is so offensive to non-addicts that some Asian airlines forbid passengers to bring them aboard, while certain hotels, especially those with air-conditioning systems which distribute smells equitably throughout the building, prohibit taking them into the rooms. Durian, like garlic, imparts its fragrance to the breath of those who indulge in it. The only way to protect yourself from a durian eater is to eat durian yourself.

DW
stands for

the **dwarf bean** of Africa, which despite its name has the normal dimensions of any other common haricot bean, which is what it is; for **dwarf lavender,** whose unopened flower buds give fragrance to food; and for the **dwarf mallow,** which gives fragrance to nothing, for even so enthusiastic an eater of wild foods as Euell Gibbons had to admit that its fruits "taste very much like nothing at all."

E

ESCOFFIER: *The culinary art depends on the psychological state of society . . . wherever life is easy and comfortable, where the future is assured, it always experiences a considerable development. On the contrary, wherever life and its cares preoccupy the mind of man he cannot give to good cheer more than a limited place. Oftener than not, the necessity of nourishing themselves appears to persons swept up in the hurly-burly of business not as a pleasure but as a chore. They consider lost the time spent at table and demand only one thing: to be served quickly.*

EA
stands for

eagles, spitting fire, served to Charles V of France by Taillevent in the fourteenth century; for the **ear shell,** which is the abalone; for the **earth almond,** which is the chufa; for the **earth nut,** which English children eat, and the **earth pea,** which tropical Africans eat; and for the **earthpear,** which is what the Scandinavians called the potato in the eighteenth century.

EB
stands for

ebony, a name given, inexplicably, to at least four quite different fruits of Africa.

ED
stands for

eddo, another name for the taro; for the **edible crab,** a title which, though all crabs are edible, has been usurped by *Cancer pagurus* in Europe and by *C. magister* in America; for **edible kelp,** a seaweed of which the midrib is the tastiest part; and for the **edible periwinkle,** which migrated without help from England to America about two centuries after men did.

EE
stands for

EEL. "Most people like Eel from the first taste, if it has been skillfully prepared," wrote Euell Gibbons in *Stalking the Blue-Eyed Scallop*. "The adult has firm white flesh with a delicious flavor." "Here, without doubt," added the French gourmets Henri Gault and Christian Millau, "is the fish which can boast of having inspired the longest and most extravagant list of gastronomic recipes. Nevertheless, except for a few rare regions in France, little interest is shown in it. In Paris, it is almost completely unknown." It is known all the same, on paper at least, for the *Nouveau Larousse Gastronomique* gives forty-nine recipes for eel. But it is very true that it is rarely found on French restaurant menus, or at home either, for handling eel presents problems in our urbanized society. Eels must be kept alive up to the very minute of cooking, or the flesh will soften into an unappetizing gooiness. The greatest obstacle to wider acceptance of the eel, however, is its unfortunate resemblance to the snake, a beast little loved by man. Yet it is unrelated to reptiles, being simply what the crossword puzzles say it is: "an elongated fish."

The first eel eaters we know about were Scandinavians, who left the spines of these animals in their kitchen middens between the Upper Paleolithic and the Iron Age. Even before the Vikings began harassing their neighbors, there was a Guild of the Eel in southern Sweden, whose members met in the first darkening days of autumn to feast on the eels descending the rivers on their way to their rendezvous with love and death. (Or so we are told; it is my personal opinion that the accepted account of the eel's migrations and

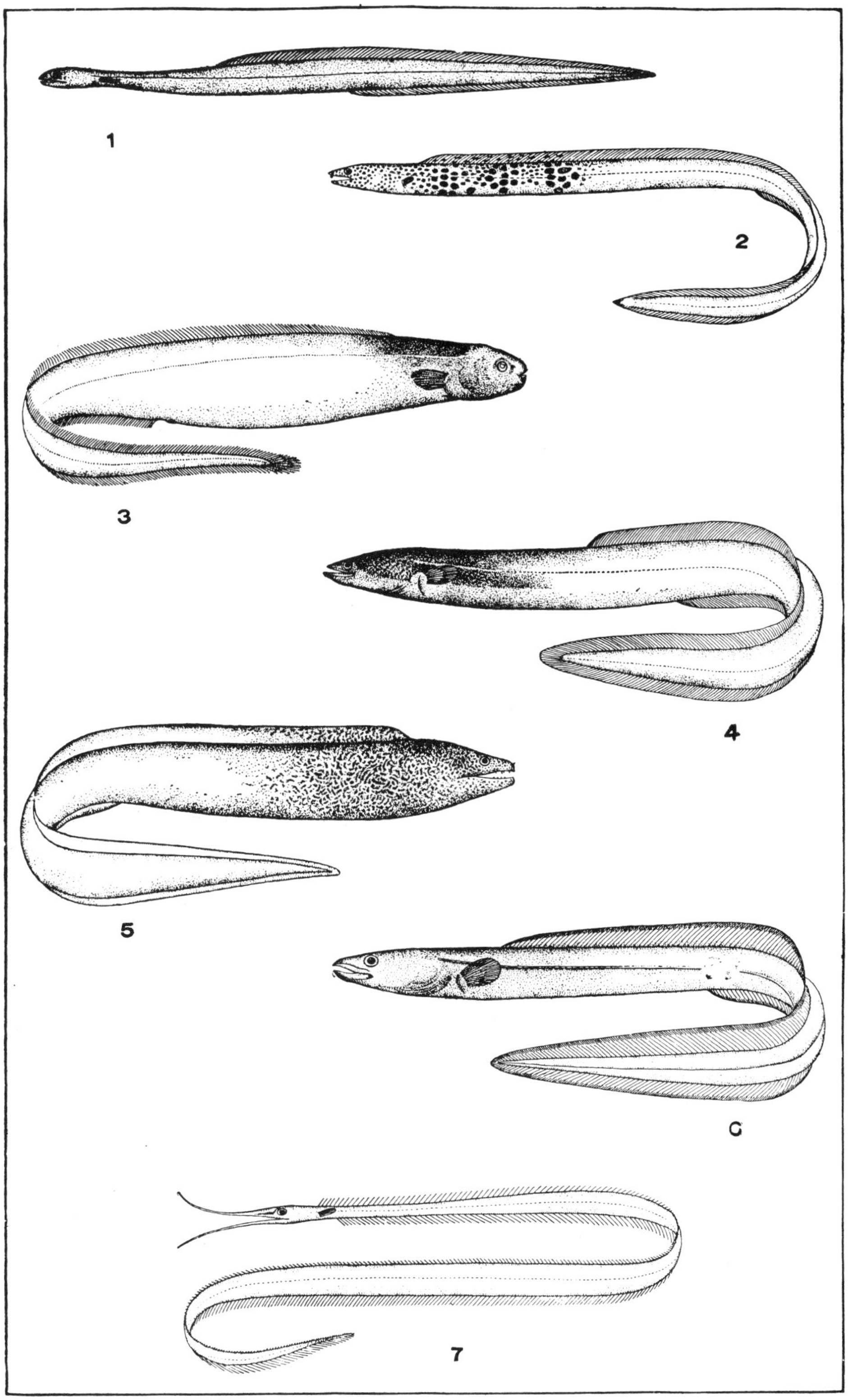

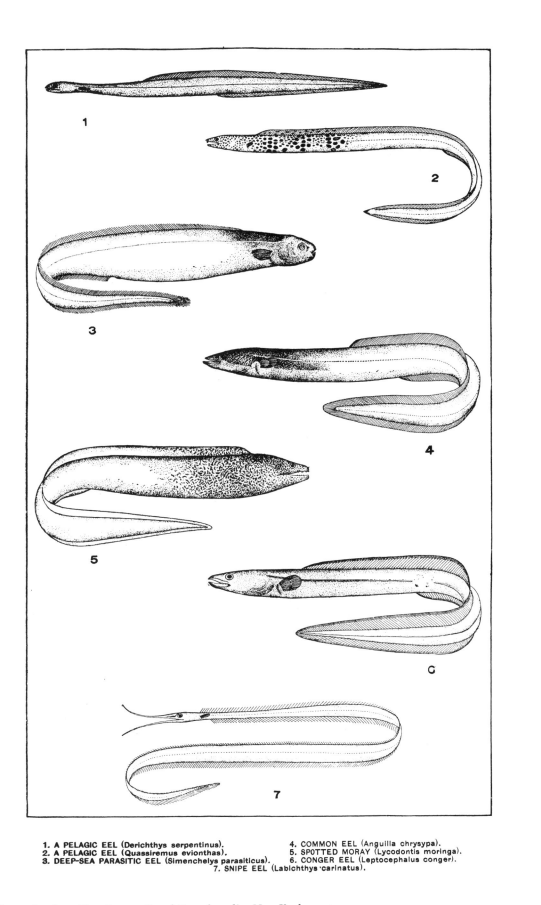

1. A PELAGIC EEL (Derichthys serpentinus).
2. A PELAGIC EEL (Quassiremus evionthas).
3. DEEP-SEA PARASITIC EEL (Simenchelys parasiticus).
4. COMMON EEL (Anguilla chrysypa).
5. SPOTTED MORAY (Lycodontis moringa).
6. CONGER EEL (Leptocephalus conger).
7. SNIPE EEL (Labichthys carinatus).

EEL. *Engraving from* New International Encyclopedia, *New York, 1904* spawnings is completely erroneous, but space does not permit going into it here.) Modern Swedes still call this period of the year "the time of eel darkness."

Most of the ancient Mediterranean peoples seem to have eaten eel, with the exception of the Hebrews, put off by Leviticus: "All that hath not . . . scales in the seas, and in the rivers . . . shall be abomination unto you." Eels do have scales, but they are so small and so deeply embedded as to have been imperceptible to the Hebrews. The Egyptians may have passed up eels as too holy to eat, if we may believe Alexandre Dumas, an author more picturesque than accurate, who wrote: "The Egyptians placed eels on a par with the gods; they made them the object of a religious cult, and raised them in aquariums, whose priests were charged with feeding them daily with cheese and the entrails of animals."

In 334 B.C. the Greek colony of Syracuse, Sicily, was saved from assault when Carthaginian soldiers who had come to capture the city found themselves, before the anticipated battle, fishing for eels in the same marshes about the city as the Syracusian soldiers; fraternization among the fishermen induced the Carthaginians to go home without fighting. Athenaeus tells us that both Greeks and Romans indulged in eel. The Romans probably picked up the eel-eating habit from the Greeks, and Italians have been diligent at it ever since. Dante consigned Pope Martin IV to purgatory for wolfing down the eels of Lake Bolsena, though he was ascetic in comparison with Holy Roman Emperor Charles V, who is supposed to have died from eating too many eel pies. In the sixteenth century the great eel-fattening basins of Comacchio, worked by the serfs of Prince Torlonia, attracted the attention of Torquato Tasso, who put them into poetry, while at Orbetello, then under Spanish rule, the Spaniards taught Italians to prepare eel as they themselves had learned to do in Flanders, great eel country. Today Rome and Naples still eat eel on Christmas Eve; in Rome the mayor himself opens, at 2 A.M. on December 24, the sale of live eels to the public, admitted for that day only to the wholesale market.

In England, the city of Ely is named for the fish of its surrounding marshes, according to the Honorable Bede. Eel Pie Island in the Thames just above London is situated in a stretch of the river once famous for its eels. The industrial revolution of the eighteenth century created a demand for cheap, nourishing, quickly eatable food. The eel supplied it, and the first fish-and-chips shops appeared.

When Europeans reached America they found an abundance of eels and an abundance of Indians eating them. Eel was about the only fish the Pilgrims liked, but they were poor fishermen, so an Indian named Squanto had to teach them how to scoop the eels out of the streams in their hands. Jesuit missionaries were enthusiastic at the skill of the New York Iroquois in cooking eels; the Algonquins dried them for long keeping. Eel eating has fallen off in the northeastern United States except around Narragansett Bay, which remains faithful to an old tradition which provoked the Colonial saying that all it took to make a Rhode Islander happy was a jug of rum and a mess of eels.

Today northern Europe is particularly given to the eel. In Germany, Hamburg makes as much of a cult of its eel soup as Marseilles does of bouillabaisse, and in Pomerania fishermen smoke their eels in the family fireplace over smoldering peat. The taste for eel has spread to the south, where the diamond eels of the Bodensee are especially prized for their large livers, which, fried, are considered a great delicacy; Lindau, on the lake, boasts that it prepares eel in 67 different ways.

In London, eel pies (called "green pies") seasoned with Worcestershire sauce (called "Worcester") are sold in the streets of the East End, and so are jellied eel, accompanied by a thick slab of bread (called a "doorstep").

The Japanese, on what is supposed to be the hottest day of the year, Doyo no Ushi no Hi (the Midsummer Day of the Cow), eat *kabayaki*, grilled eel basted with a sweet but pungent soy sauce (*tare*), with such avidity that the proper greeting on that day is "Have you had your eel yet?" Politicians have themselves photographed tucking it in; this single day's consumption of eels averages 865 tons each year.

"Heliogabalus," wrote James Trager, "maintained a fleet of fishing boats to catch eels, whose roe was prized as modern emperors have prized caviar from Russia's sturgeon." Heliogabalus never saw eel roe, and neither has anybody else since. His boats were probably after conger, moray or lamprey, not eels, which were taken from lakes, streams and shallow waters close to shore, and though he could not possibly have eaten eel eggs he might have sampled elvers, the tiny, often transparent, still-blind baby eels metamorphosed from eel larvae just before they mount the rivers.

Elvers afford possibly the most delicate of all eel dishes, of which Belgium's *anguille au vert* (known to the Flemish, who invented it, as *paling in 't groen*) is probably the most famous incarnation. Several American cookbooks in my library give recipes for it, but none of them know what it is. All of them begin by directing the cook to cut the eel into chunks, a difficult task, since the elvers which should be the basis of this dish run from two and a half to three inches long and are half as thick as a match. They are also a specialty of Pisa and of Torre del Lago (Puccini's home) in Italy; of the Basque country in Spain; of Bordeaux, La Rochelle, the Aunis and southern Brittany in France; and formerly of Trier in Germany, but pollution seems to have banished them from there.

In England they mount the Severn in season by the billion and are scooped up in buckets, which frequently contain more fish than water. They are best simply boiled in the water in which they are taken, when they compare favorably with the delicious whitebait, and worst when inexpert English cooks deep-fry them in batter with an overdose of flour, which makes them taste like library paste.

EG
stands for

the **egg mushroom,** *Amanita caesarea,* the Caesar in question being the Emperor Claudius, so fond of them that he failed to notice it when his wife Agrippina added another variety of *Amanita* to the mess of egg mushrooms he was enjoying shortly before his death; for **eggfruit,** or ti-es, a tropical American fruit related to the sapodilla; for the **eglantine,** or sweetbrier, of which John Gerard wrote in the sixteenth century: "The fruit when it is ripe maketh most pleasant meats and banquetting dishes, as tarts and such like; the making whereof I commit to the cunning cooks, and teeth to eate them in the rich man's mouth"; for the **egret,** served at banquets in fifteenth-century England; for the **egusi,** a melonlike fruit cultivated in West and equatorial Africa; and for the **Egyptian kidney bean,** which is not Egyptian, is not a bean and is of course not a kidney.

And **EG** also stands for

EGG. "The egg," wrote a French gourmet of this century, "is to the cuisine what the article is to speech." This has a nice philosophic ring, though it is not quite evident that it means anything, but the intent was evidently to compliment the egg—which another French gourmet, of the last century, Charles Monselet, called "the Proteus of the kitchen." Walt Whitman described the egg of the wren as perfect, and Brancusi called the egg "the most perfect form of creation," though one may harbor doubts about the story that he gave up sculpture because he could create nothing more successful.

On an earthier level, the *Encyclopaedia Britannica* sums up the place of the egg thus: "Considering all factors, eggs rank next after milk in importance and efficiency among foods of animal origin."

There are many eggs from which hungry humanity may choose. "Almost all animals," wrote Sir John Martin Harvey, "even those which bring forth their young alive, and man himself, are produced from eggs," and to this botanists might add that there is such a thing as plant eggs. But wide as is the choice, man has narrowed it down to almost one: the hen's egg. It is almost without competition, even from the second most important commercially produced egg, that of the duck, hardly eaten at all in the United States. Duck eggs are frequently eaten in England, Holland and Belgium, and commonly in the Orient, where the famous Chinese "hundred-year eggs" (actually closer to one hundred days old) are usually duck. Ducks bred for egg production (the Indian Runner, the Rhaki-Campbell) lay as well as hens or better, but the timid eaters of the United States are put off by the stronger taste and slight oiliness, qualities shared by goose eggs, almost never found on the market. Geese have not been developed as egg layers; all that is demanded of them is that they produce enough eggs to maintain the species. This is true of other domestic poultry as well, though their eggs are palatable enough—those of turkeys, guinea hens and, in the West, pigeons; but the Chinese are fond of pigeon eggs.

Peacock eggs were eaten by the ancient Romans, who, we are regularly told, thought them the best of all eggs; I suspect this is a misunderstanding. The source of this statement is a description of a cooking pan for eggs, provided with three concentric oval-shaped indentations to hold three kinds of eggs; the outermost ring was designed for peacock eggs, and was referred to by the author who gave us this information as *áristos,* translated "best." *Aristos* does indeed mean "best" (consider the English "aristocracy"), but originally only "first." I wonder if the ancient author did not mean simply to tell us that the peacock eggs, which occupied the outermost ring, were first in order in the cooking pan. This would be analogous to the Greek word of the same period for "breakfast," *ariston;* breakfast was certainly not the best meal of the day, but it was the first.

If you were asked to name the third most commercially important egg, after those of the hen and the duck, would it occur to you to cite the ostrich? Ostrich eggs have been eaten at least since Phoenician times; the ancient Egyptians are believed to have consumed them too, and possibly pelican eggs as well. Today they are produced in South Africa, notably at Oudtshoorn, where there is an ostrich farm which is less interested in feathers, once prized but now out of fashion, than in eggs, which are more profitable. There is little likelihood that the ostrich egg will spread beyond its particular perimeter, for it comes in a package a little too large to be easily absorbed by small modern families. An average egg weighs three pounds; a single one suffices to make an omelet for ten to twelve persons. If you are tempted to keep an ostrich for eggs, be warned that its clutch contains about fifteen of them—forty-five pounds of egg—which, curiously enough, is the same number laid by the original Indian jungle fowl from which all our domestic hens are descended.

Gourmets speak with awe of plovers' eggs, which I have tasted only in Holland, where something of a cult is made of them; the first eggs of spring are presented ceremoniously to the queen. I am afraid I found them less good than hens' eggs. I hesitate to pronounce any judgment on an experience so slender, but I note that the Larousse gastronomic encyclopedia observes: "They are much sought after by certain gourmets, not for their taste, which is no better than that of hens' eggs, but because they are rare." They are also expensive.

Among those who profited by the much-touted plovers' eggs were American Indians, who gathered the eggs of plovers, partridges, quails and wild ducks. The Japanese and English appreciate quail eggs; the latter also consider gull eggs a delicacy, though they sometimes have a fishy taste. They have nevertheless seemed attractive enough to Americans so that conservation measures had to be adopted to protect them in at least three of their favorite North American nesting places—Destruction Island, off the coast of Washington; Assateague Island, off the coast of Virginia and Maryland; and Raza Island in the Gulf of California, where tern eggs were gathered too.

I am unable to identify the eggs Magellan's men ate in the Philippines, according to chronicler Antonio Pigafetta: "There are . . . certain large black birds like chickens, having long horns [a different translation makes it "long tails"], and they lay eggs as large as those of geese, and they put them an arm's length deep in the sand. And by the great heat of the sun, the sand hatches them, and when they are hatched they leave the sand, and they live outside. The eggs are good to eat."

After birds, fish are the most important furnishers of eggs for man. At the top of the list is of course the sturgeon, which gives CAVIAR; followed by the SALMON, for the so-called red caviar; the MULLET, provider of the eggs which make the well-known Greek spread *taramosalata*; America's SHAD, famed for its roe; and even HERRING, whose eggs have a delicate flavor and are eaten either fresh or salted. A number of fish (burbot, lumpfish, etc.) lay tasty eggs which are dyed and passed off as caviar.

The turtle is the only reptile whose eggs are at all largely eaten, chiefly in the neighborhood of its nesting places, but they are also relished in England. The Imraguen tribe of the Atlantic coast of the Sahara is also addicted to turtle eggs. When turtle eggs are evoked, it is usually those of the sea turtle which are meant, but American Plains Indians ate the eggs of land turtles. Crocodile eggs are favored by Arabs and East Indians (who eat caiman eggs). Collecting crocodile eggs poses its problems since this animal buries them two feet deep and lurks near the spot, on guard, until they hatch, sometimes sleeping over them. The python, which rolls itself around its eggs until they open, would be even more difficult to deal with, but so far as I know, nobody eats snake eggs, while the only example of the consumption of lizard eggs known to me is provided by the Volta region of Africa, where gray-lizard eggs are eaten, but only by children.

Many animals eat ant or termite eggs—some live almost exclusively on them—but they do not seem ever to have appealed to humans. Nevertheless, foresighted French lawmakers, alert to every possibility, however remote, have taken the trouble to forbid gathering ants' eggs in state forests and private preserves. The idea is not to protect them from omnivorous humans, but to save them for pheasants and partridges, which dote on them.

Nobody knows how many hen's eggs are eaten throughout the world, since reliable statistics are lacking for some of the most populous countries (China, India and Russia, for instance), but 250 billion a year would probably be a conservative estimate. This is enough to give every person alive two eggs a week, but the majority of them do not get their share. Americans get much more, four eggs per day per person. Canada is probably second, Belgium third, England a close fourth and France fifth.

The popularity of the hen's egg is justified by the fact that it comes very close to being a complete food. Its animal proteins, which in the egg appear in their most assimilable form, are accompanied by all the amino acids needed for growth and, being rated as having the highest biological value of all common foods (96 on a scale of 100), are frequently used as the standard against which others are measured. Hens' eggs contain both

EGG *by Fabergé.* Renaissance Egg, *1875*

saturated and unsaturated fats, but a minimum of carbohydrates, demanding of the human system that it cope with no more than 80 to 100 calories per medium-sized egg. The hen's egg supplies all the essential vitamins except vitamin C, and most of the essential minerals in quantities great enough to affect metabolism (its iron is in particularly assimilable form). Eat two eggs for breakfast and you have already taken in half of your total daily requirements in proteins and vitamins. Drink orange juice with it, for the missing vitamin C, and down a slice of buttered bread—additional vitamin D and starch—and you have had a meal which is nearly perfect.

Hens' eggs furnish a rich culture medium for misconceptions. One often hears that eggs are indigestible; not so, eggs are easy to digest. Take them soft-boiled, hard-boiled or poached, and you will have no trouble. Other fashions of cooking them involve fat: it is the fats which are indigestible, especially in combination with a food already so rich. Some people will tell you that brown-shelled eggs are tastier and healthier, others that it is white-shelled eggs which have these merits; and both are willing to pay more to indulge their preferences. The non-partisan verdict is that there is no significant difference. Health-food addicts can become highly exercised over the relative merits of fertilized and unfertilized eggs (so can other people; fertilized eggs are not kosher, and some Indian castes will eat only unfertilized eggs). You will be told that one or the other tastes better or is more nourishing; there is no evidence to support their theories. Bright yolk color is sometimes taken as a sign of quality; it may be a sign only that the hen has been fed marigold petals.

What does make a difference in the nutritive value and especially in the taste of eggs is the feed given to laying hens. The best results are achieved with hens on grain (wheat, maize, oats), left at liberty to pick up in addition their natural foods (grasses, small worms, insects). Too heavy a proportion of insects in the hen's diet can give an undesirable taste to the eggs, but so can too much fish flour or bone flour, sometimes fed in excess to battery-raised hens. It might seem reasonable to believe that caged hens scientifically fed could produce richer and tastier eggs than those left largely to their own devices, and perhaps they would if the primary objective of mass producers of eggs was to achieve a more nourishing or tastier product. Unfortunately, their primary objective is to achieve a more profitable product.

Indisputable is the fact that the freshest eggs are the tastiest and the healthiest. As an Italian saying puts it: "Eggs of an hour, bread of a day, wine of a year, a friend of thirty years."

Hens' eggs, a food today universal and of the first importance, were slow to enter the human larder, particularly the Western larder. It is extremely unlikely that the Egyptians knew the chicken and, consequently, its eggs, in the early centuries of their existence, though many authors tell us so. Neither chicken nor their eggs are mentioned in the Old Testament (the Jewish prohibition against fertilized eggs does not come from any specific reference to them in the Bible, but from application to the fertilized egg of the general ban on eating blood). The probability is that hens' eggs were first eaten in India, with the domestication there of the wild jungle fowl, perhaps as early as 2000 B.C. The Chinese may have been eating hens' eggs a few centuries later; they are in any case credited with having been first to incubate eggs artificially, about 1400 B.C., but these may have been duck eggs. Not until the late sixteenth or early seventeenth century would eggs be incubated in the Western world, by Olivier de Serres in France (unless you count Olivia, wife of the Emperor Augustus, who hatched an egg between her breasts). Artificial hatching of eggs only became general with the advent of electrical heating.

The first chickens in the West seem to have appeared in central Europe about 1500 B.C. They probably reached the Mediterranean area in Greece sometime between 1100 B.C. (for Homer did not mention them) and 720 B.C., when we know that Sybaris banished roosters from the city so that their crowing would not wake late-sleeping citizens. The ancient Greeks and Romans were both more interested in eggs than in the chickens which laid them, probably because the poultry was too scrawny for good eating. Later they learned how to produce plumper birds (which presumably gave them better eggs); but after the collapse of the Roman Empire, the Dark Ages seem to have lost the art of producing tasty chickens, for once again eaters concentrated on the eggs, not the bird. During the Renaissance, eggs were the chief food (and in some places almost the only one) eaten in addition to meat. The historian Benedetto Varchi produced a treatise on boiled eggs early in the sixteenth century, and in the seventeenth the renowned French cook Pierre François de la Varenne wrote a cookbook containing sixty different recipes for eggs.

The New World acquired hens' eggs when Columbus landed chickens in the West Indies in 1493, but there were probably none on the mainland of North America until the settlers of Jamestown and Plymouth imported them more than a century later. In the meantime there was no lack of eggs of other kinds, for Leif Ericsson reported in the year 1000 that he had come upon a land where "there were so many birds that it was scarcely possible to step between their eggs."

EGGPLANT. The humble eggplant has been introduced into at least two countries under illustrious auspices, into northern France by Louis XIV and into the United States by Thomas Jefferson. Louis XIV liked to see rare and unknown foods on his table, and Jean de la Quintinie, in charge of the royal kitchen gardens, gratified him by being the first to grow eggplant in northern France. Jefferson, a tireless searcher for new foods, had seeds and cuttings of plants unknown in the New World sent to him regularly from abroad; among those with which he experimented at Monticello was the eggplant.

The eggplant is a native of southeastern Asia, probably specifically India, where it is believed to have been cultivated more than four thousand years ago. It took its time getting to the West. Almost certainly unknown to the ancients of the Mediterranean region, it seems to have been cultivated first in Spain by the Moors of Andalusia, for it was Arabs who imported it originally from the distant East. It has been cultivated in Italy since the fifteenth century, reached England late in the sixteenth and became generally known in northern France, following the lead of Louis XIV, in the seventeenth. It cannot be said that it was received with wild enthusiasm anywhere. Though in Italy it appeared on the menu of a banquet given by Pope Pius V in 1570, it has never attained in that country the gastronomic peaks it has reached in the Middle East. When it turned up in England, John Gerard advised the readers of his 1597 *Herball* "rather . . . to content themselves with the meate and sauce of our owne country than with fruit and sauce eaten with such perill; for doubtless these apples have a mischievous quality; the use thereof is utterly forsaken."

In France, the eggplant was described as having "fruit as large as pears, but with bad qualities." It was rumored that it provoked fever and induced epilepsy. But under the Directory (1795) it suddenly became a fad with the *incroyables* (hippies?) and the *merveilleuses* (the beautiful people?), who wolfed down slices of grilled eggplant in their disorderly gathering place, the garden of the Palais Royal.

EGGPLANT *by Charles Demuth (1883–1935).* Eggplant and Tomatoes, *watercolor and pencil*

Fear of epilepsy did not account for the slow acceptance of the eggplant in the United States. Many authors report that it was first introduced late in the nineteenth century by the country's most prestigious restaurant, Delmonico's, but American cookbooks published early in the century give recipes for it. Eggplant has never played an important role in the American diet, though it has been gaining a little ground lately.

The greatest devotees of the eggplant are the southern Italians and the Arabs of the Middle East, especially the Syrians and Turks, who claim to know a thousand ways of preparing it.

EI stands for

the **eider duck,** prized more for its down than its meat, which tastes fishy; for **einkorn,** meaning "one-kernel," a type of wheat grown by Neolithic man; and for **e'ia ota,** Tahitian raw fish.

EL stands for

the **eland,** a half-ton African antelope, eaten by prehistoric hunters and by modern ones; for the **Elberta peach,** which, introduced into the United States in 1870, became its leading freestone peach; for the **elder,** whose flowers provided food for Henry V of England and, at about the same period, for the as yet undiscovered American Indians; for the **Eldorado pear,** developed in California in recent years, dear to fruit dealers because it resists spoilage; for **elecampane,** eaten by Pliny in the first century and English schoolboys in the eighteenth; for the **elephant,** the world's largest land animal, hunted and eaten by the world's smallest men, the Pygmies of Africa, of which ancient Greeks preferred to eat the trunk and modern Africans the feet; for **elephant grass,** which Africans eat today and we will all eat tomorrow if the synthetic food wizards have their way; for **elephant's-foot,** a plant whose starchy tuber is known as Hottentot bread; for **elft,** a fish eaten in Africa which somehow sounds more appetizing when it is referred to instead as a bluefish; for the **elm,** of which one species has edible bark; and for the **Elton Heart,** a British cherry developed at Elton, Herefordshire.

EM
stands for

emmer, meaning "starch-grain," a type of wheat

grown by Neolithic man; and for the **emperor-fish** of the Indian Ocean, beautiful to the eye and tasty to the palate.

EN
stands for

entrails, which, when the Lord Mayor of London decreed in 1541 that meals must be restricted to a limited number of courses, were not counted as a course; and for **enokitake,** a richly perfumed, ivory-colored Japanese fungus.

And **EN** also stands for

ENDIVE. What is endive? Or, more precisely, which of the two families in the genus *Cichorium* is chicory and which is endive? In England and Germany it is *C. endivia* which is endive and *C. intybus* which is chicory. In France it is just the opposite, and in the United States popular usage follows the French example and scientific usage that of England and Germany. Since there is no World Court to rule on which nation is entitled to decide the issue between chicory and endive, I am obliged to choose between them arbitrarily for the purposes of this entry. Or not quite arbitrarily: I refer to the nation which leads in the production of both—Belgium. For Belgium, *C. intybus* is chicory, *C. endivia* is endive. So be it.

Endive, then—*C. endivia*—means for us here not the tightly wrapped, spindle-shaped bundle of leaves popularly called endive in France and the United States, but a rather straggly-leaved plant whose several varieties are divided into two main groups: *C. endivia* var. *crispa,* with narrow, finely divided, curly leaves, and *C. endivia* var. *latifolium,* with broad, fleshy, less curly leaves, which is called escarole in several languages and also *batavia* in French.

Endive is a native of Egypt, which makes it reasonable to suggest that it was one of the plants the Jews were enjoined to eat at Passover: "And they shall eat the flesh in that night; and with bitter herbs shall they eat it" (Exodus 12:8), and "The fourteenth day of the second month at even they shall keep it, and eat it with unleavened bread and bitter herbs" (Numbers 9:11). It is probably also the endive which the ancients appreciated for its beneficial effect on the liver; the endive which Charlemagne had sowed in the model vegetable gardens of his domains; the endive of which St. Hildegarde said "the use relieves difficult digestion," adding prudently, "unless God judges otherwise"; but less certainly the endive which Madame de Sévigné used instead of basil to season the old-fashioned stew called *oille,* which would explain why she could never produce a good one.

C. endivia has been cultivated in France since the end of the thirteenth century, in England since the sixteenth, and is also grown in America. The broad-leaved Batavian types are used not only in salads but also for cooking, braised, sautéed in butter, au gratin, or in various other fashions. The narrow-leaved, curly varieties serve almost exclusively for salads. Both are particularly welcome for this purpose, for they continue to be available until late in the year, long after most other salad greens are out of season.

Chicory—*C. intybus*—might be described as resembling a small ear of corn still snugly wrapped in its husk, but it is all husk and no cob. The leaves, however, are glossier and sleeker than corn husks. If this is what you want in France, ask for endive, but England, Germany and Belgium will call it chicory.

C. intybus is extremely rare in America, except wild. If you see it on a menu at all, it will probably be listed as endive. Coming from the Old World—probably from central Europe, for it does not seem to have been known to the ancients of the Mediterranean basin—it reached America as a weed only towards the end of the nineteenth century, but then spread quickly along the Atlantic coast from Canada to Florida and pushed westward as far as the plains, which were apparently not propitious to it. It appears only spottily until the Pacific coast is reached, where it again flourishes.

Americans are usually dismayed to find European coffee mixed with chicory and are inclined to attribute this habit to economy. Not at all; it is a question of taste, and the trouble taken to raise special varieties of chicory for this use makes it about as costly as coffee itself. This mixture seems to have occurred first to the Dutch, but it is now a specialty of Germany: two of the principal varieties of chicory used for this purpose are named for German cities, Magdeburg and Brunswick. Since it is the powdered root which goes into coffee, these types have been developed to produce large, fleshy roots, which can also be used for food, like salsify, though they are not much of a taste treat. For some reason, grubbing up chicory roots has often been attended by superstitious or magical ceremony. In the nineteenth century they were uprooted with a gold or silver coin; in Bohemia it was recommended to gather them barefoot; and the ancient Druids are said to have disinterred them only while fasting. With

ENDIVE. *Drawing by Marilena Pistoia from F. Bianchini and F. Corbetta:* I Frutti della Terra, *Rome, 1975*

Belgian endive
Catalonia chicory

or without magic, the recommended time for collecting chicory roots is after the plant has flowered.

And **E** also stands for

the **ermine,** perhaps not worn in Neolithic times but certainly eaten then; for the **eucalyptus,** whose sap was used by Australian aborigines as a sweetener and whose blossoms provide honey today; for the **eulachon,** a smelt of the Pacific Northwest so fatty that it can be fitted with a wick and used as a candle; for the **ewe,** whose milk makes such distinctive cheeses as, among others, Roquefort; for the **eyed fish** of the Mediterranean and West Africa, whose name denotes what would hardly seem a noteworthy anomaly, but is at least as informative as its alternative name "Spanish dog"; and for the **eyes** of various animals, eaten in the Sahara but, in certain tribes, taboo for the blind.

F

FLETCHER, HORACE: *Nature will castigate those who don't masticate.*

FRANKLIN, BENJAMIN: *Eat not to dullness. Drink not to elevation.*

FORD, GERALD: *Eating and sleeping are a waste of time.*

FA
stands for

fagara, the delayed-action Szechwan pepper which lets itself be swallowed innocently and then smites you with a heat wave when you are off your guard; for **fairy cheese,** which is *Malva rotundifolia,* dwarf mallow; for **fairy spuds,** which are the roots of *Claytonia virginica,* the pretty pink flowers known as spring beauties; for **fairy ring mushrooms,** which might have remained imprisoned in the name *Marasmius oreades* if Shakespeare had not addressed "you demy-puppets,/ That by Moone-shine in the green sowre Ringlets make . . . and you, / Whose pastime is to make midnight-mushrooms"; for **fallen angels,** which turn out to be nothing but boring clams; for the **false banana** of Ethiopia, which is pith, not a fruit; for the **false chewstick** of West Africa, masticated not as a twig but as a seed, the **false cramp bark,** which is the black haw, and the **false Paraguay tea shrub,** which is the North American withe rod; for the **false-teeth shell,** a West Coast mollusk entirely devoid of teeth, real or artificial; for the **fan mussel** of the Mediterranean, whose shape has seemed to namers in other languages less like that of a fan than like that of a ham; for the **far-far tree** of South Africa, which bears bitter but edible berries; for **fatback,** which when it is not pork is the menhaden, a fish American Indians prized less for feeding themselves than for fertilizing corn; for **fat-hen,** which when it is not chicken is a greasy spinachlike vegetable, the hen in its name being a shortening from Good King Henry, a monarch unknown to history; and for **fats,** an essential part of the human diet, whose most important function, perhaps, is to serve as a storage battery for energy, so Julius Caesar was mistaken when he said, "Let me have men about me who are fat," since they would have been no less dangerous than Cassius with his lean and hungry look.

FE
stands for

feet, eaten in modern times when supplied by calves, cows, sheep or pigs (except by lame residents of the Sahara, for whom they are taboo) and in ancient times when supplied by elephants or camels; for the **feijoa,** the South American tree which produces the pineapple guava; for **feltwort,** our tenth name for the mullein, and **felwort,** a species of gentian, inevitably confused with the feltwort; for the **fennec fox,** a creature too appealing to be eaten, but it is, in the Sahara; for **ferns,** considered as a famine food in Europe, but in America Euell Gibbons called fern fiddleheads "one of the greatest delicacies among wild vegetables"; and for **fersig,** a sort of tamarisk which exudes a sticky substance used as a sweetener by the Tuaregs of the Sahara.

And **FE** also stands for

FENNEL. Fennel is a great encourager of arithmetic. Ignoring its inclusion among the forty plants which Thomas Tusser decided in 1557 were indispensable to a complete herb garden, we find that fennel is: (1) one of the ingredients of Chinese five-spice powder; (2) one of the medieval four hot seeds; (3) one of the (relatively) modern five appetite-encouraging roots; and (4), at about the time when Chaucer was writing

Downe by a little path I fond
Of mintes full and fennell greene,

one of the nine holy herbs of the Anglo-Saxons.

The other four Chinese spices were anise seed, Szechwan pepper, cloves and cinnamon. The other three medieval hot seeds were anise, caraway and coriander. The other four appetizing roots were wild celery, asparagus, parsley and knee holly, also known as butcher's-broom because its dried stems served as straws in the small whisks which butchers used to clean off their chopping blocks. If you want to know what the other eight holy Anglo-Saxon herbs were, I fear you will have to ask Chaucer.

Despite a history measurable in millennia, fennel does not occupy a particularly prominent place in the hierarchy of foods. It is little eaten in the United States, though it is grown commercially in California. Its land of predilection is Italy, which some persons think is also its land of origin; it seems in any case to have started in the Mediterranean basin. No single country utilizes the full possibilities of fennel, but France and Italy between them cover most of the ground. Italy considers fennel primarily as a vegetable, concentrating on the bulbous bases of its stalks and neglecting the leaves, while France looks upon it as an herb. Actually all parts of fennel are edible—not only the bulbs and the leaves, but also the stems, seeds and even the flowers.

The respective preferences of France and Italy are a function of the kinds of fennel they grow. Of its four species, the only one which is particularly interesting from the gastronomic point of view is *Foeniculum vulgare*, often picked wild, most prized for its leaves, but the seeds are also employed as a spice. The French put fresh leaves in salads, to which they impart a pleasantly subdued licorice flavor, less blatantly assertive than that of anise, and use dried leaves as wrappers for fish meant to be grilled, or as seasoning in a *court-bouillon* for cooking fish. The Italians use the tender young stalks of *F. vulgare* var. *piperitum* raw as hors d'oeuvres under the name *carosella*; the French dry the stems and use them for a small fire over which they cook the white-fleshed sea bass. The use of fennel as a fish flavorer had found favor in England at least by Elizabethan times, for Shakespeare speaks of eating conger with fennel.

The most versatile variety is Florence fennel, *F. vulgare* var. *dulce*, the only one which has the stalks with swollen bases frequently mistaken by the layman for bulbs. It is eaten like celery, raw or cooked. Florence fennel can also supply, quite as well as the other varieties, tasty stems, leaves, seeds and flowers. The last are used especially in Provence to refine the taste of pickled olives, cucumbers and capers, or to season boiled chestnuts. Fed to rabbits, they add an extra dimension to the ordinarily faint flavor of their flesh.

The ancient Greeks used the young stalks and leaves of fennel (Florence fennel, with its bulbous base, probably did not then exist). The Greek word for fennel was *marathon*; the place where the famous battle was fought was so called because the soil there was overgrown with fennel. The Romans used both the seeds, which they sprinkled on bread (Apicius wrote that fennel seeds should be in every kitchen), and the leaves, which Plautus lists as appearing in a mess of greens of which he did not approve. Columella told how to preserve fennel stems in brine and vinegar. The plant reached the Orient early, where its seeds are a frequent ingredient of curries. They appear also in various versions of Ethiopia's fiery universal seasoning, *berberé* sauce.

Fennel was a common food in Gaul before the Romans entered that territory, at least in the south. It may have been slower to reach the north, where, according to one author, it was introduced by the Benedictines. If so, they did it early, for Charlemagne included fennel in the list of foods which were to be raised in his domains. Later it appears on the menu of a dinner prepared in 1455 by Taillevent when his royal employer, Charles VI, entertained the Count of Anjou. In England fennel was in general use at least by the reign of Edward I, in the thirteenth century.

Fennel, says the Larousse encyclopedia, "little appreciated in France, is consumed in Italy." Yet a century earlier Alexandre Dumas had written that in the streets of France "it is not rare to meet common people with a bundle of fennel tucked under the arm, making of it, with a little bread, their lunch or dinner." And in our own century Colette, the much admired French novelist, showed her familiarity with fennel by writing that female plants are tastier than male plants and can be distinguished from the latter by their flatter roots.

FENNEL. *Drawing by Marilena Pistoia from F. Bianchini and F. Corbetta:* I Frutti della Terra, *Rome, 1975*

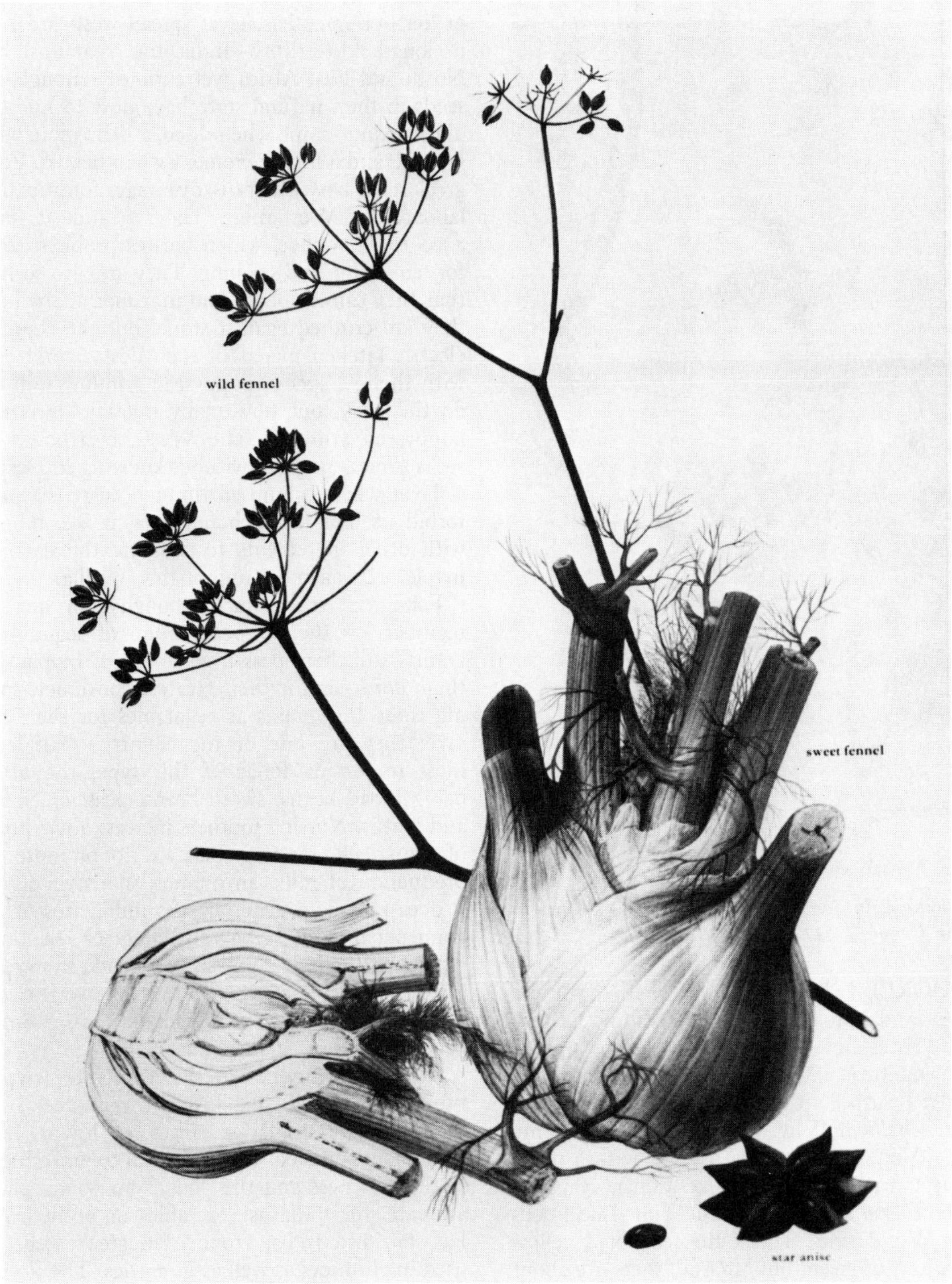
wild fennel
sweet fennel
star anise

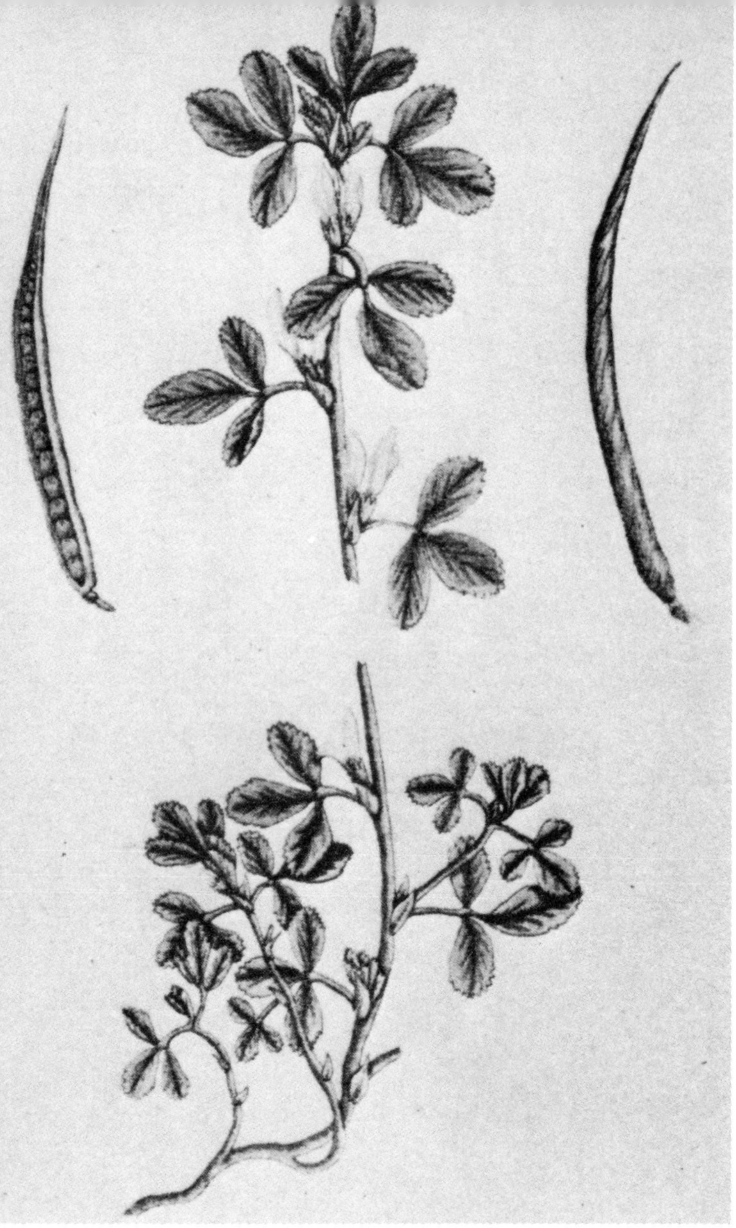

FENUGREEK. *Print from Elizabeth Blackwell:* A Curious Herbal, *London, 1737*

FENUGREEK. I do not know whether you are likely nowadays to be greeted in a Middle Eastern street (necessarily in Arabic) with the phrase, "May you tread in peace the soil where *helbeh* grows!" I suspect it has become old-fashioned. What is *helbeh*? Why, fenugreek. What is fenugreek? "Very small red-brown seeds with a pleasant bitter flavor and a currylike aroma," explains *Middle Eastern Cooking,* of the Time-Life Foods of the World series. To me the seeds look yellow with a hint of green, but after all, there are about fifty-five species of fenugreek and we may have been looking at different kinds. I would also be inclined to turn this description around and say that curry has a fenugreek-like aroma. That strong, dusty, acrid smell of curry powder, which is sometimes displeasing to Western nostrils, and its taste, rather coarse by European standards, are accounted for often by fenugreek, almost never omitted from curries.

The extravagantly exotic flavor of fenugreek is no doubt one of the reasons why this vegetable or herb or spice has never spread westward from its long-held territory—India, the Near East, and North and East Africa; yet curiously enough, the seeds in their natural state have next to no odor. They acquire some when dried, a little more when ground, and a final increment when heated. Fenugreek seeds have other disadvantages for impatient labor-saving Westerners. They are indeed small, 2500 to the ounce, which creates problems both for harvesting and cooking. They are also so hard that they cannot be ground in a mortar. In India they are crushed against stone, but the standard electric kitchen mixers of the West cannot cope with them; a special poppyseed grinding mill will do the trick, but how many households possess poppyseed grinders? The West nevertheless absorbs some fenugreek without knowing it. Despite a flavor which, glimpsed through curry, seems to forbid its uses for such purposes, it is combined with other ingredients to simulate the flavor of maple or, even more improbably, vanilla.

Fenugreek seeds, small though they are, are members of the pea-bean group of leguminous grains—call them peas if you want. Ethiopia calls them *abish,* and is their greatest consumer, cooking these tiny grains as vegetables for their own sake; they are one of the country's half-dozen most important foods of this type, the others being broad beans, sword beans, peas, chick-peas and lentils. Nursing mothers increase their intake of fenugreek, for it is believed to promote the production of milk, an opinion shared in Egypt; it does provide a generous 180 milligrams of calcium per hundred grams of fenugreek. In North Africa, particularly Tunisia, flour made from fenugreek seeds is used for putting on weight: 100 grams give 335 calories and include 129 grams of proteins, plus 5.2 grams of fats.

In this century, when the Yemenite Jews returned to Israel they brought fenugreek with them, using it to flavor sauces. In Egypt, fenugreek flour is mixed with cornmeal to make bread. Both the leaves and the pods from young plants are eaten in India as vegetables or potherbs. In Pakistan and India, ground fenugreek seeds are used in chutneys as well as in curries. The normal use of the seeds is as a condiment, employed sparingly.

FI
stands for

the **ficaria,** a relative of the buttercup whose roots

are relished nowhere except in Algeria; for the **fiddler crab,** perfectly edible if you don't mind doing a lot of work for not much meat; for the **field bean,** which is a dolichos if you are in Asia or Africa, but a horse bean if you are in England; for the **field clam** or **fingernail clam,** not a clam, but a freshwater mussel; for the **field mushroom,** otherwise the agaric, which you have eaten if you have eaten MUSHROOMS at all; for the **field pea,** described as "a poor but robust cousin" of the pea we grow in our vegetable gardens; for the **figwort,** which pulls rank as *Ficaria major* over the ficaria cited above, which is only *Ficaria minor*; for the **filefish,** whose origin you would be well advised to check before sitting down to a dish of it, since there are Hawaiian varieties which are poisonous; for the **finch,** eaten with avidity in countries which know no pity for tiny birds; for **finger grass,** whose seeds are eaten in West Africa; for **fins,** which the shark contributes, involuntarily, to the table; for **fireweed,** which produces honey without the intervention of bees; and for the **Five Flavors,** the **Five Perfumes** and the **Five Spices** of mathematically minded China (after all, who first used the abacus?).

And **FI** also stands for

FIG. William Shakespeare, an inconsistent dramatist, had Iago exclaim contemptuously, "Virtue! A fig!" but let Cleopatra's attendant Charmian sigh, "I love life better than figs." Webster agrees with Iago when it defines "fig" as "the least bit; the merest trifle"; French author Georges Blond sides with Charmian when he describes the fig as "the manna of the Mediterranean countries."

The fig deserves at least the respect owed to seniority. It has been delighting man for a long time. Figs were popular everywhere in the Near East at least as early as 3000 B.C. Assyria used fig syrup as a sweetener, figs were grown in the hanging gardens of Babylon and they were dried for preservation by burying them in hot desert sands. They were important to the Phoenician economy, which implies that they were cultivated, and we know that they were cultivated in Egypt, for we have a description of a walled garden with figs "climbing" (espaliered?) the wall which faced south; baskets of figs have been found in Egyptian tombs. There are numerous references to figs in the Bible.

Figs were a favorite fruit for the ancient Greeks, whose meager soil was ill fitted for grain, but could nourish figs to succulence. They maintained that the fruit was a special gift of Ceres to Athens, and planted a grove of fig trees in that city's agora, dedicated, a trifle illogically, not to Ceres but to Athens. Attic figs attained a quality which caused them to be demanded everywhere in Asia Minor; laws had to be passed to restrict their exportation.

Legend has it that the fig was first brought to Italy by the Greeks, but it could have been the Etruscans. The Romans tended to rate foreign figs above the domestic varieties. They imported them from the Greek island of Chios and from Carthage, while Pliny, listing twenty-nine different kinds, said that the best came from Ebusus (Ibiza). Apicius fed expensive imported Syrian figs to his hogs to improve the flavor of their meat. Less exalted breeders used dried domestic figs and honey to give their pigs hypertrophied livers, from which they made pork foie gras. The final step to what we call foie gras today was taken when geese were force-fed with figs.

The fig spread from the eastern Mediterranean in other directions whenever trade routes opened. As early as the third century B.C. an Indian ruler asked the Greeks to send him figs, grape syrup and a philosopher. They filled the first two items of the order, but explained that philosophers were not an article of commerce. The Romans are credited with having introduced the fig to southern Gaul, and the Arabs extended its range westward from Egypt in the eighth and ninth centuries. Dried figs appeared in Paris in the fourteenth century, as hors d'oeuvres or desserts. The fig tree was introduced into England in the sixteenth century, and by the time of Elizabeth I

FIG. *Wall panel painting:* Loaf of Bread and Two Figs, *Fourth Style (c. 62 AD), Herculaneum*

every important English household kept dried figs on hand to make sweet puddings. Germany started eating figs about the same time. Northern France acquired fig trees when they were planted in the royal gardens of Louis XIV, who delighted in new and exotic foods.

Curiously enough, America knew the fig, then a European fruit, as early as did England. Spanish colonizers introduced it to the New World, as one might guess from the name of one important American variety, the mission fig of California, the state which produces 99 percent of all the commercially grown figs in the United States.

"I call a fig a fig, a spade a spade," wrote the ancient Greek playwright Menander. It sounds like a simple program, but if Menander had applied himself seriously to the task of naming figs, he would have had his work cut out for him. The genus *Ficus* includes more than 600 species according to the *Encyclopaedia Britannica* or 750 according to the *Grand Larousse Encyclopédique*. There are figs which ripen underground, and others which grow high in the air, on plants dangling from other trees. Some figs are villains which strangle and kill their hosts, others are sacred. Some figs grow on low trailing shrubs in the desert, others on tall trees in tropical forests. Some figs are gathered from wild trees, but most from cultivated trees. There are large figs and small figs, round figs and ovoid figs, spring figs, summer figs and winter figs, and figs colored black, brown, red, purple, violet, green, yellow-green, yellow and white. All cultivated figs are sweet when ripe (figs in general have the highest sugar content of any common fruit), but some varieties are sweeter than others. Figs almost certainly originated in Asia Minor, specifically perhaps in western Turkey, home of the Smyrna fig, probably the most famous of all.

According to Matthew 21:19, reporting the entry of Jesus into Jerusalem, "When he saw a fig tree in the way, he came to it, and found nothing thereon, but leaves only, and said unto it, Let no fruit grow on thee henceforward forever. And presently the fig tree withered away." This incident impressed some Britons so vividly that they call Palm Sunday "Fig Sunday," and celebrate it by eating fig pudding. St. Matthew's tree was presumably a male fig, otherwise known as a goat fig or caprifig. The fig-bearing female tree is fertilized by the fig wasp, which carries pollen from the flowers of the male fig to those of the female fig. At least as long ago as the time of Aristotle it was known that male figs had to be grown near female figs to fertilize them, and to promote the process, flowering branches were cut from the male trees and placed in the crowns of female ones. When Smyrna figs were introduced into California at the end of the nineteenth century, male fig trees and fig wasps had to be imported too.

The most revered fig tree in the world grows in the ruined city of Anuradhapura, eighty miles north of Kandy in Ceylon. It is said to have come from a cutting of the very bo tree, *Ficus religiosa*, under which Buddha sat, meditating his way to perfect knowledge; it was sent to Ceylon in 288 B.C., a present from the Indian emperor Asoka. Its Western counterpart is the tree under which Romulus and Remus were suckled by the she-wolf, which survived into historical times in the Roman Forum, where it was honored by annual sacrifices.

One of the oldest identified figs is the sycamore fig, so firmly associated with Egypt in ancient times that Pliny called it the "Egyptian fig." The Hebrew prophet Amos "was a herdsman and a gatherer of sycamore fruit" (Amos 7:14).

The sea fig is in English the beach apple and in French the sea squirt, a wineskin-shaped creature which glues itself to rocks on the bottom of the Mediterranean. The only thing it has in common with land-based figs is edibility.

FILBERT. The filbert is an amiable aliment, unpretentious and unassertive, perhaps the sweetest of all nuts (raw, it outdoes even the chestnut). It manages nonetheless to offer a flavor so individual that it cannot be described by reference to any other. On the contrary, its own very special taste is often evoked to suggest subtle overtones in other edibles—unsalted Charente butter; the aftertaste of certain wines; the elusive aroma of some mushrooms; and even an element sometimes discernible in the complex flavor of Brie. Agreeable when eaten alone, it enhances its own bland flavor and that of its host in chocolate bars and nougat, and supplies a delicate sweetness to cakes, cookies and ice cream.

It is my guess that more Americans say hazelnuts than filberts, while Englishmen are likely to call them cobnuts or cobs. Is there any difference? "In general," says the *Encyclopaedia Britannica*, "filberts [are] long nuts, cobnuts of medium length and hazels . . . short and roundish."

But in England the very same tree is called in one breath the Kentish cob and in the next Lambert's filbert. The proliferation of natural and artificial hybrids has blurred distinctions: the Mildred filbert, much grown in the United States, is a cross between *Corylus americana* (a filbert?) and *C. avellana* (a hazelnut?). But nature, disconcertingly, sometimes produces long nuts this year on a tree which produced short nuts last

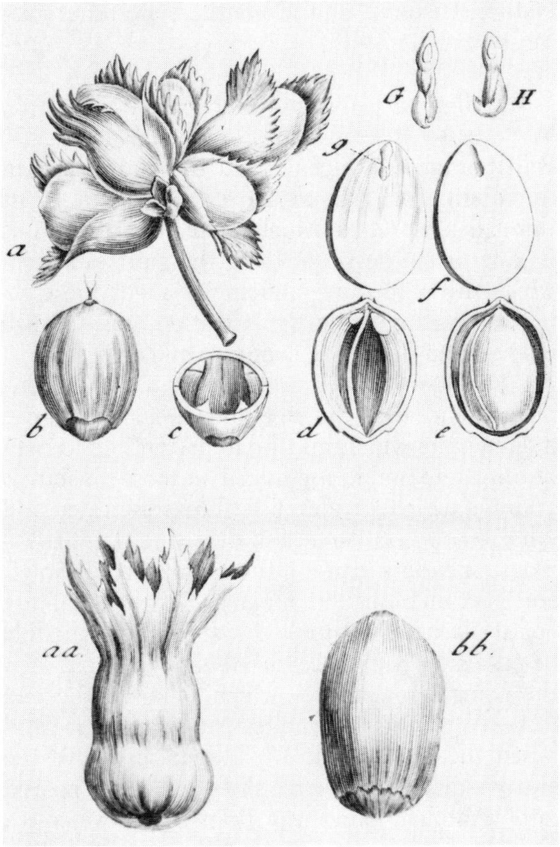

FILBERT. *Drawing from J. Gaertner:* De Fructibus et Seminibus Plantarum, *Paris, 1791*

year, or even worse, produces, on the same tree in the same year, long nuts on some branches and short nuts on others. In 1942 the American Joint Committee on Horticultural Nomenclature decided to call all members of the genus *Corylus* filberts, and to hell with it.

"The filbert came to Western Europe from the Hellespont," wrote Paul Lacroix in *France in the Middle Ages*, and indeed Pliny called it the Pontic nut. The original home of the nut is difficult to localize, for *Corylus* existed before *Homo* throughout its present range, which includes all the land masses of the north temperate zone. (Filberts grow in South Africa today, but they were transplanted from the north.) The first traces of the filbert were found in Central Asia, dating from the Eocene epoch. Filberts were probably being eaten by man in Paleolithic times, and certainly by the Mesolithic, the period of some Swiss lake dwellings where they have been found. They appeared in large quantities in the Neolithic site at Alvastra in Sweden. The filbert was the second most widely eaten nut during the Stone Age, the first being the acorn. This does not necessarily mean that prehistoric man preferred acorns. Probably there were more of them.

Jacob put peeled hazel and chestnut twigs into his watering troughs to encourage his cattle to conceive, an attention he neglected to give the animals of Laban, also under his care. The Greeks and Romans cultivated the trees, but the people of the Middle Ages, at least those farther north, didn't bother: collecting wild nuts in the woods had been good enough for their pre-Roman Gallic ancestors and it was good enough for them, although they made considerable use of filberts for desserts and even as the basis for a drink. On the other side of the Atlantic, meanwhile, pre-Columbian Indians were making crisp cakes of cornmeal flavored with pounded filberts.

American species are inferior in quality to those of the Old World; and when *C. maxima*, widely grown in Europe for its nuts, was transplanted to the eastern United States, the best ground for native filberts, it did not do well. It succeeds best in Washington and Oregon, which account for almost all the commercial filberts produced in the United States. Not enough is harvested to supply the demand, so large quantities have to be imported from Turkey, Armenia, France, Spain and Italy.

Filberts yield a fine oil which improves the tone of violins when used in their varnish.

FISH. Fish, in all probability, constitute the world's second most important category of foodstuffs, the first being, of course, cereals. The second, logically, should be meat, but meat is priced out of the reach of many peoples. "Whole populations," writes the *Dictionnaire de l'Académie des Gastronomes*, "do not know meat. On the banks of the Niger and along the Yellow River, millions of persons live on fish which they mix with cereals, the basis of their diet." We do not know for certain how much fish is eaten in the world, for reliable statistics are lacking concerning the consumption in many countries, including the three most populous ones, China, India and the Soviet Union. A recent estimate of the worldwide commercial take of seafood put it at 70 million tons a year, but this includes shellfish; fish proper—excluding shellfish, crustaceans, housepisciform mammals (like dolphins and whales) and such whimsically named creatures as cuttlefish, jellyfish and starfish— account for somewhere between 35 million and 50 million tons. Americans are not big fish eaters, though they have been eating more fish every year since 1967. A recent count credited them with consuming 11 pounds of fish per person per year, against 13 for the French, 19 for the British, 50 for the Danes and 65 for the Japanese, the world's champion fish eaters.

Fish *by Haronobu (1725–1770). "The Sumida River,"* From the Eight Views of Edo, *woodblock print*

There are more than 20,000 kinds of fish, as many as of amphibians, reptiles, birds and mammals added together; most of them are edible. They are found wherever there is permanent water and even, on occasion, where the appearance of water is intermittent—in the Sahara Desert and other regions where pools and streams dry up during the summer. They live in high mountain streams and ponds, and in lakes below sea level; in streams so swift that they require special organs to hold on, and in waters so stagnant that their flesh tastes of mud. In the oceans, fish are found in the shallows, on the continental shelves (which account for most of the food fish of the world, though they occupy only one-tenth of the ocean area), in relatively deep water (the most important commercial fishing is done above 250 fathoms) and in the abyssal depths (where they are useless for food). "Where there is water there are fishes," wrote Dr. Gareth Nelson of the Department of Ichthyology at the American Museum of Natural History, "and where there are fishes they can be caught."

"No human being, however great or powerful, was ever so free as a fish," opined Ruskin, and Brillat-Savarin must have had the same belief in the ability of fish to move without restraint through a world of which more than two-thirds is water when he wrote that "the great cataclysm which drowned our grand-uncles about the eighteenth century after the Creation was for fish only a time of joy, of conquest and of festivity." Neither Ruskin nor Brillat-Savarin was an ichthyologist, and they did not know that the waters hide barriers which may be imperceptible to man but are impassable for fish. The most obvious is salinity, which divides fish into freshwater and saltwater species. Some fish, it is true, are anadromous, spending part of their time in salt water and part in fresh, but for many of them salinity (or its lack) constitutes a wall which can only be passed on pain of death. About 8500 B.C., when the rising temperatures which followed the end of the Würm ice age melted the northern ice and raised the level of the Mediterranean above the altitude of the Bosphorus shelf, salt water poured into what had previously been a freshwater sea and killed so many fish that the decomposition of their bodies poisoned it permanently; the Black Sea today is virtually without life below 250 feet.

Temperature builds other walls. Though some migratory fish are able to cross temperature barriers (for instance, the tuna, a deep-sea fish capable of finding the temperature it prefers by swimming at the right depth), most of them frequent either cold or warm water, but not both. Consequently, tropical species are apt to be similar everywhere in the world, since they can swim through the nearly continuous girdle of warm water which straddles the equator, but since this belt cannot ordinarily be crossed by fish of the temperate zones, the marine fauna of the Northern and Southern Hemispheres are quite different.

Fish are also limited in their movements by the need for specific foods or by the flow of currents, the first sometimes a function of the second; Peru, for instance, suffers fish shortages whenever the Humboldt Current fails to float in enough food for the fish (and also when it varies in temperature or in salinity). Inherited collective memory may account for some fish inhibitions: those which migrate from the Bay of Biscay to the North Sea by swimming all the way around the British Isles, as they have been doing since England was attached to the mainland, may simply not have been informed that the English Channel now provides a shortcut.

Many of the factors which confine fish to their most hospitable habitats are associated with tastiness. Saltwater fish are in general tastier than freshwater fish. Fish from swiftly moving streams are ordinarily finer in flavor than those from sluggish waters (the black bass versus the catfish), and those from clear water superior in taste to those from muddy water (the trout versus the carp). Fish from cold water are likely to be more flavorful than the same species in warm water.

The oldest living vertebrates, fish may also be the oldest animal food which man dared pursue in sizes larger than individual portions. It is easy to believe that our prehistoric ancestors were capable of dealing with large fish before they discovered how to master large mammals or even large birds; and the fact that their first tackle (after bare hands) seems to have been a bludgeon used to stun basking fish suggests that the victims must have been of substantial size. In Upper Paleolithic times fish were already being killed with spears (which would later be specialized into harpoons), supplemented in the Mesolithic period by the bow and arrow. It was still in Paleolithic times that the hook and line were first used, the line a tendril from a vine, the hook what should more properly be called a gorge—a splinter of stone which lodged crosswise in the fish's throat when the line was drawn taut, after which it had to be hauled in quickly before the fish could shake the gorge out. Later, real hooks were made from thorns (and in at least one case from an insect's leg), and then from bone or horn; barbs were added in the Mesolithic. The fisherman must have learned early how to extend his reach over the water by tying his line to a long twig, thus inventing the fishing rod; but he was still bound to the banks of rivers and the beaches of the sea until, in the Neolithic, the invention of oars permitted him to pursue his prey into its home element. By this time nets existed, and fish were also being trapped by damming streams.

The ancient Assyrians, who had identified fifty different kinds of fish before 2300 B.C., kept fish in vivaria, the ancient Egyptians raised them in irrigation reservoirs, the ancient Chinese in flooded rice fields. Aristotle listed 110 species of saltwater fish, only forty less than would be known a thousand years later, though by then Atlantic as well as Mediterranean fish had entered the catalog. The ancient Greeks used, in basic form at least, every fishing technique known to us today, and probably taught fish eating to the Romans, who had shown little interest in seafood before the Asian Army returned to Italy from Greece and Asia Minor in 185 B.C. They made up

FISH *by Thomas Eakins (1844–1916).* Taking Up the Net, *watercolor*

for lost time with a vengeance. Choice fish sold for such outrageously fancy prices that Cato the Elder wondered if there could be any future for a country where a fish cost more than an ox.

Enormous quantities of fish were eaten in the Middle Ages, largely because the rigorously enforced dietary restrictions of the Church added so many other fasts to the forty days of Lent that nearly half the days of the year were meatless. The Norsemen ruled a substantial section of the world from Scandinavia to Sicily not solely because of the quality of Viking ships and the valor of Viking warriors, but also because in their salt cod they possessed imperishable rations permitting long voyages, whose surplus, at the end of their travels, constituted valuable merchandise. In the thirteenth century, a shift in tides swept the herring of the North Sea into the Baltic, and the Hanseatic League was born, its power founded first on fisheries. When the currents shifted again after the fifteenth century and the fish moved south, Holland developed a fishing fleet and consequently naval power. The English, presented with the same opportunity, were sluggish about seizing it, which is why the Dutch reached the Spice Islands before they did. They had been preceded by the Portuguese, who had circumnavigated Africa as a result of their search for new fishing grounds. Later Elizabeth I recognized the importance of a large fishing fleet as a basis for a navy; she multiplied official fast days and enforced them strictly to encourage fishing (and also to conserve meat, which was scarce and expensive).

Because of their perishability in days before refrigeration, most of the fish eaten in medieval and Renaissance times was dried, smoked, salted or pickled. Fresh fish was available only to those able to pay for such expensive services as the relays from Dieppe and Boulogne to Paris, served by carts whose horses were changed every few miles, to deliver fish to the capital the day after it had been caught. The fastest was organized to supply Louis XIV; as a result Versailles today still enjoys more, fresher and cheaper fish than Paris (freshwater fish were unavailable to the general population, for streams and lakes belonged to the lords of the land or the monasteries, and poaching was punished ferociously).

American Indians were taking fish by sophisticated methods at least as early as 2000 B.C., the date attributed to an elaborately woven weir excavated near Boston. In the Pacific Northwest, fish made up three-quarters of the diet of pre-Columbian Indians. Cortez found the Aztecs raising fish in the lake which surrounded Tenochtitlán (Mexico City), while in Peru the Inca ruler used runners to relay fish from the Pacific to Cuzco, 130 miles inland and 11,830 feet up. The history of Colonial Massachusetts was that of its cod fisheries, which reached their peak ten years before the Revolution and have never since regained comparable importance in the economy of New England.

Today the world's second most important category of food is in danger. Rivers, lakes, seas and even the oceans are losing their fish to pollution. Fleets of modern trawlers scrape fishing grounds bare, leaving no young fish behind to repopulate the devastated areas. Changes made in the environment for the sake of one self-endangered species, *Homo sapiens*, are endangering others which want to make use of the same *Lebensraum*. When New Jersey drains its marshes it prides itself on cleaning up the coast, but the fish which start their lives in their protection disappear. When Egypt builds a high dam and suppresses the flooding with which the Nile used to flush itself clear every year, weeds noxious to fish clog the river and its mineral salts cease to flow into the Mediterranean, diminishing the fish catch of Egypt to one-fourth of its former importance.

The Food and Agricultural Organization of the United Nations has predicted an annual increase in the world fish take of 4.7 percent. If this estimate turns out to be exact, fish will become extinct by 1985.

FL
stands for

the **flags**, marsh plants of different types, some of them medicinal rather than gastronomic; for the **flageolet**, which, when it is not a musical instrument, is a small tasty bean invariably found in France in the company of mutton; for the **flame tree**, or Gabon tulip tree, whose seeds are eaten in East Africa; for the **flamingo**, a bird appreciated by the ancient Romans, who paid special attention to its tongue; for **flannelleaf**, our eleventh name for the mullein; for the **flasher**, a fish also known in English as the triple-fin and in French as the triple-tail, eaten in Madagascar and the Cameroons; and for various inhabitants of water which share a common prefix, such as the **flat garfish**, which is less flat than needle-shaped, the **flathead**, a food fish of tropical Africa and Madagascar, and the **flat lobster** of the Mediterranean, which has endeared itself to underwater hunters by its suicidal habit of clacking its stubby claws together, making a clatter which leads to the platter.

FL stands for

flax, which enters the modern diet chiefly in the

form of linseed oil, but the ancient Greeks put its seeds in bread; for the **flea**, uneaten so far as I know except by monkeys, but the ancient Romans ate both the **flea-plant**, a mintlike herb believed deadly for fleas, and **fleawort**, reputed to be an aphrodisiac whose virtues included the ability to produce male infants when both parents drank its sap; for Africa's **flint bark**, which bears a persimmon-like fruit, and America's **floating spatterdock**, which has an edible root; for the **flor de San Miguel** of Lower California, whose seeds are munched by the local Indians; for the **flounder**, sometimes a specific fish, and sometimes a generic name for all the FLATFISH; for the **flour tree**, whose beanlike fruit is fermented and used as a condiment throughout West Africa; and for **flowers**, of which Raymond Oliver, the famous cicerone of the three-star Grand Véfour restaurant of Paris, wrote, "The purslane and the nasturtium probably bear the only flowers known to be edible," and in the same breath proceeded to deal with ten others which are used in cooking.

FL stands for

the **fluke**, or rather flukes, for this name is applied to several FLATFISH, but oftenest to the summer flounder; for the **flutemouth**, a fish which looks as if it had been designed by nature to perform on this instrument but which is discouraged from pursuing a musical career by the equatorial Africans who consign it to the cooking pot before it has had time to become acquainted with its scales; for the **fly**, disdained as food almost everywhere except in tropical Africa; and for several reputed sharers of a common skill: the **flying fish**, which on several occasions has saved the lives of shipwrecked sailors by landing, badly piloted, on the foodless lifeboats or rafts in which they were adrift; the **flying fox**, really a bat, which lives on fruit and is consequently good eating, whose taste suggests hare; the **flying gurnard**, an evil-tempered fish which is not a gurnard and probably doesn't even fly, much taken for food in the Indian Ocean; the **flying squid**, which doesn't fly either, eaten in the Mediterranean area; and the **flying squirrel**, which should theoretically be as tasty as its non-airborne cousins, but I can offer no firsthand testimony, having severed diplomatic and gastronomic relations with this beast ever since one of them dive-bombed into my face from the tree on my farm in which it was guarding its young.

And **FL** also stands for

FLATFISH. The twin sisters of the sea, wrote the anonymous author of *Le Ménagier de Paris* (1393), are the sole and the pole, and "the only way to tell them apart is to lay them down flat and look down on them from above, and in this position the mouth of the sole will be at the left and that of the pole at the right." The word *pole* seems to have disappeared from the French language, in the piscatorial sense at least, and nobody knows which fish it represented, except that it must have been another flatfish. In this category *pole* comes closest, in the modern French flatfish vocabulary, to *plie*, which is the plaice, but the plaice wears its mouth on the same side as the sole.

Flatfish, described by Proust, who had the turbot in mind, as "all profile," share a common ontogeny. Their larvae start out as though they intended to develop into common vertically constructed fish, but quickly launch themselves into a metamorphosis dedicated to horizontality, thus fitting them for their destiny as the throw rugs of the ocean, doomed to spend their lives lying supinely on the bottom. One eye migrates over the top of the head to join the other on what will become the upper side of the fish, but sometimes not quite far enough. In *Bothus podas*, which has no popular English name known to me, the wandering eye becomes stalled in the neighborhood of the backbone, where it would not seem to be particularly useful. In the halibut the migrating eye does better, but still fails to travel as far as it should to join its fellow, so that its two eyes are more widely spaced than in other flatfish; but as both protrude and turn separately in their sockets, independently of each other, the fish has a wide field of vision.

The displacement of the eye in flatfish, in order to put both of them on the upper side of the head, is matched by a distortion of the mouth in order to get as much of it as possible on the underside, for flatfish feed on bottom-dwelling organisms which lie beneath them—worms, small crustaceans and mollusks, brittle stars, sand eels, gobies. Some flatfish have no teeth at all in that part of the mouth which has not succeeded in reaching the fish's lower side; the halibut has teeth in both sides of its mouth, but the part of its jaw which lies under it is stronger than the part which is on top. The modification in the position of eyes and mouth is completed so early that the young sole, for instance, is only three-quarters of an inch long when it has restructured itself. Losing its original plumpness, it becomes characteristically flat and sinks to the bottom, where it will remain, more or less passively, for the rest of its life.

Flatfish are either dextral (eyes on the right side, so that they lie on the left with the right

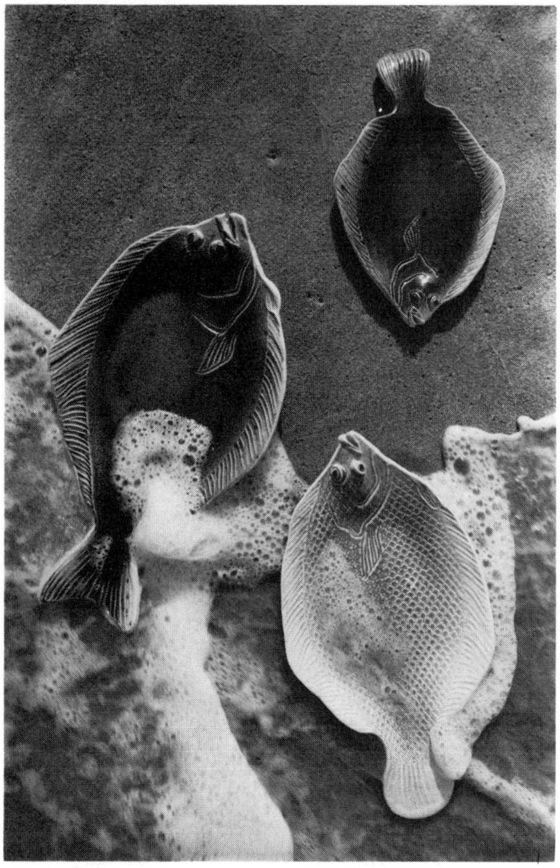

FLATFISH *by Rosalie Stambler Nadeau. Pottery platters,* Flounder, *1979*

side up) or sinistral, which is of course the opposite. In general, flatfish belonging to the families *Solidae* and *Pleuronectidae* (soles, plaices, flounders, turbots) have eyes on the right side, those belonging to *Bothidae* and *Cynoglossidae* on the left, but there are exceptions—among species and also among individuals. A halibut with its eyes on the left side is the counterpart of a left-handed person, but halibut are more conformist than human beings: in man, one individual in 25 is left-handed; in halibut, only one in 5000 is left-eyed.

The usefulness of having the mouth on the underside of flatfish is demonstrated with particular clarity by the sole, which might be described as the archetype of this group of fish. During the day the sole remains half-buried in the sand or mud of the bottom, bestirring itself only at night (or sometimes on cloudy days) to glide over the bottom seeking its food not by sight, in which it is deficient, but by smell and touch. Brushing over its prey, it seems able to identify what is edible by signals transmitted from a cluster of white tags on the underside of its head, which are believed to be tactile organs. When the sole swallows mollusks, it is apparently capable of dissolving their shells, which have been found, half-digested, in the stomachs of these fish.

The undersides of flatfish are white, the upper sides colored. They change color, like chameleons, to match the bottom on which they lie. A flatfish with its contours blurred by the sand or mud which has drifted over its sides, colored like its background, is all but invisible to enemies or to prey. When a flatfish lies across an area where sand gives way to mud, the part of its body which covers sand will be sand-colored, the part which lies on mud, mud-colored. This adaptation of the coloration of the fish to its surroundings is triggered by the eyes; a blind flatfish always remains the same color, no matter what its background.

The sole seems to have the best press among flatfish. Many writers put it first, and one book in my library even asserts that it is the best flavored of *all* fish, flat or not—with the reservation, however, that this is true only when it has been kept two or three days before eating, so that the onset of decomposition can heighten its flavor. This strikes me as a giveaway: it is not the taste of sole which is being admired, but the taste of putrefaction. I am personally not enchanted by the flavor of decay, as in game, for instance, and if it is necessary to wait for a sole to begin to spoil for its savor to be perceptible, it would seem to me that its basic individual flavor must be rather faint. Likewise, when the Larousse gastronomic encyclopedia reports that the sole is considered the best of the flatfish, and then goes on to give forty-six recipes for cooking sole whole, seventy-five for preparing fillets of sole and thirty-one for other concoctions, I am inclined to suspect that sole is one of those foods which can enter into an endless number of combinations because, being neutral in flavor itself, it serves admirably to carry the tastes of other foods without interjecting any pronounced savor of its own.

Foods may be classified, like genetic elements, as dominant or recessive. When they are dominant, there are not dozens of ways of preparing them, there are only a few, for the simplest possible treatments are the best, to preserve undisguised their basic individual flavors. Grimod de la Reynière in the last century called sole the "chameleon of the kitchen," not because he was aware of its ability to change color in the depths of the sea, but because of its protean transformations in cooking. He added that though some of the elaborate preparations of sole might be excellent, the sole itself became in them "little more than a pretext." The late A. J. Liebling once

Flatfish

wrote, I have forgotten where, that sole is the favorite fish of those who do not much like fish, because it does not really have a fishy flavor. This much said in rebuttal of the opinion that sole is the best of the flatfish, it should be added that a good sole is nevertheless a delicate and subtle fish, but it lacks the rich, full, assertive flavor of the turbot.

Robert J. Courtine, gastronomic editor of *Le Monde* of Paris, has written that for centuries the turbot has remained "Number One, *the* aristocrat." The French have paid it an unconscious tribute by designing a special pan in which it can be both cooked and served, the *turbotière*, for turbots come large, often about twenty-five pounds; but it is a shame to cut up in the kitchen, either for cooking or for serving, a fish which presents so magnificent a spectacle when brought to the table whole.

It was its impressive appearance which created a dilemma for Talleyrand when he was preparing a dinner for twelve to be given at a restaurant in the gardens of the Palais Royal in Paris, which had just received two magnificent large turbots, so equal in size and beauty that he was unable to choose between them. He was tempted by the desire to overwhelm his guests by showing them that it was possible to find two such exceptional specimens at the same place and the same time, yet he could hardly serve both, when one more than sufficed to feed twelve guests. That would have been ostentatious, a gesture permissible to a parvenu but unworthy of a great nobleman. Talleyrand, however, was a diplomat noted for his ingenuity: he found a way out. At the fish course, a waiter brought in a turbot in its great pan and presented it ceremoniously to the guests, who saluted it with a hum of admiration; just as he prepared to set it on the table he slipped, and the whole thing went crashing to the floor. There was a cry of horror, but Talleyrand remained unperturbed. "Bring us another turbot," he ordered calmly, and the second appeared, as splendid as the first. Talleyrand's reputation as host and gourmet has caused many such stories to be circulated about him, many of them certainly untrue, but perhaps this one is authentic. If it had been invented, its creator could hardly have resisted the temptation to make the waiter with the second turbot drop it too, in an unrehearsed accident.

FLATFISH *by Jean-Baptiste Chardin (1699–1779).* The Provisioner, *engraving*

Flatfish

It is usually the turbot which is named in the anecdote which we have been told and retold about the Emperor Domitian, who, when he received a magnificent fish as a present, convoked the Senate to vote on the best sauce with which to serve it. Some writers even go so far as to give us the result of the debate—piquant sauce, unanimously. This story comes from one of Juvenal's *Satires*, to which I do not have access at the moment, but I seem to remember that Juvenal did not recount it as a fact, but wrote that it was the sort of thing he could well imagine happening if fish continued to rise in price and in rarity, as they were doing in his time.

The ancient Romans called the turbot the "pheasant of the sea," *Phasianus aquatilis*, and for modern Italians it is still *il fagiano del mare*. Grimod de la Reynière called it the "king of Lent," and seems to have considered the most important event of the French Revolution the circumstance that "during the disastrous year of the Revolution, not a single decent turbot was received at the Paris market." Brillat-Savarin used to eat turbot once a week at a renowned Paris restaurant of his time, the Rocher de Cancale in the rue Montorgueil. The turbot seems to have been considered of high rank on the other side of the English Channel as well, if we may judge from a comparison contained in a letter written on January 28, 1843, by Sydney Smith to a certain Miss Berry: "I have seen nobody since I saw you, but persons in orders. My only varieties are vicars, rectors, curates, and every now and then (by way of turbot) an archdeacon."

In shape a parallelogram studded with bony protuberances which look like nailheads, the turbot in its pan presents a massive metallic appearance, causing the Turks (who are also great appreciators of its roe) to call it *kalkan*, "shield." Its scientific name is *Rhombus maximus*. *R. laevis*, a little smaller, is hard to distinguish from it except by its lack of protuberances. Hence for the Turks it is the nailless turbot, and for the French, who sometimes call *R. maximus* the spiny turbot, it is the smooth turbot, though its normal name is the *barbue*. In English it is the brill. Its flesh is less firm than that of the turbot, and by most people is rated one cut below it in flavor, but in the upper Adriatic, where it is known affectionately in the dialect of Romagna as the *suàso*, it is rated *above* the turbot. "Baked *suàso*," goes a local saying, "can make you miss a political meaning," which, it seems, is the highest praise possible in Italy.

The sole, choice of the majority or not, occupies only third place in the gourmets' hierarchy, after turbot and brill. This means the common European sole, *Solea solea* (or, with equal redundancy, *S. vulgaris vulgaris*), which is famous the world over as Dover sole, but not because it is peculiar to Dover. Its range runs from Norway to the eastern end of the Mediterranean. It acquired this name because it was one of the commonest fish transported by an enterprising nineteenth-century dealer who established a fast express service to rush fresh fish from Dover to London. There are a good many other species of sole—thirty-three off the English coast, according to a British authority, eight in the Adriatic, according to an Italian authority. There are also any number of "soles" which have no right to that name. If you suspect misrepresentation and have a whole fish on your plate, you can easily tell whether or not you are being served the real thing. The sole has a rounded snout, describing a smooth, squat, unbroken curve from back to belly; false soles have pointed snouts.

One of the barriers which inhibits the free movement of fish is temperature. The warm water of the Gulf Stream, cutting diagonally through the colder Atlantic, prevents the three finest flatfish of Europe from reaching America. There are no turbot in American waters. There are no brill either, if by "brill" we mean *Rhombus laevis*, though there is a less luscious fish called a brill in America, *Eupsetta jordani*, more properly the petrale. There are no Dover sole and, we are usually told, no soles at all, but as a matter of fact there are several species of sole off the coast of the United States, such as the tongue sole and the hogchoker, but, being small and inferior, none of them are fished commercially.

Americans may console themselves for the absence of these European flatfish by reflecting that they do share the halibut, which gets by the barrier of the Gulf Stream by skirting it to the north. Alan Davidson, the English gourmet who is knowledgeable both about fish in the water and fish on the plate, would not agree that consolation is required, for he calls halibut the "king of flatfish." For once I am unable to agree with him, but he does have the support of the Pacific Northwest Indians, who have always esteemed the halibut even above the plentiful salmon of their region, though perhaps in part because it possesses the charm of inaccessibility: mature halibut on that coast settle on the sea bottom at a depth of 1200 feet, which must have created difficulties for Indians unequipped with modern trawlers.

Halibut *ought* to be the tastiest of flatfish, for they frequent the coldest waters, in the northernmost Atlantic, the northern Pacific and the Arctic Ocean; it seems to be the rule that marine animals from cold water are tastier than their closest relatives in warm water; but in the category of flatfish, the halibut seems to be an exception.

Perhaps the halibut should not be compared solely with other flatfish, for it is the one which resisted most strenuously nature's decision to convert it from a more normally shaped creature into a flatfish. Not only did it accept only half-heartedly the changing position of the eye and mouth, the latter almost undistorted in the halibut, it is also the least typical of flatfish in other respects. Halibut are the biggest of all flatfish, running to twelve feet in length and seven hundred pounds in weight, or at least the females do; the males stop modestly at five hundred pounds or so. Plumper in form and proportionately longer in body than such of its cousins as the sole, the plaice and the flounder, the halibut also rejects their passive search for food by gliding effortlessly over the bottom, rising instead to attack other fish: fishermen assert that halibut club smaller fish to death with their tails, giving it a reputation for ferocity which perhaps inspired the U.S. Navy when, in the 1950s, it named its first submarine equipped to fire missiles other than torpedoes as its main armament the USS *Halibut*.

For the fisherman, halibuts are "chickens" up to a weight of ten pounds, and "whales" from 125 pounds up. Captain John Smith reported from Virginia that "the large sized Halibut" were so big "that the fisher men only eat the head & fins, and throw away the bodies," a curious procedure if true. It was probably because of its large size that halibut used to be known as "workhouse fish": buy one, and you had dinner for the whole institution.

The typical halibut is *Hippoglossus hippoglossus*, the Atlantic or great halibut, once plentiful on the Grand Banks and off New England, not to mention John Smith's Virginia, but they are beginning to be fished out now. They are still relatively abundant in the Arctic Ocean, but become progressively rarer as one moves south down the coasts of Europe, so by the time France is reached very few are found. This no doubt accounts for the considerable ignorance of the French in regard to halibut, which they tend to confuse with flounder, an error encouraged by the French language, which calls the halibut *flétan* and the flounder *flet*; the two words are often used as if they were interchangeable, which of course they are not.

English does not do much better for the cause of clarity. In America, where it is the flatfish par excellence, "flounder" has two meanings: it can be applied to specific fish, or it can be used generically to cover all flatfish with reckless generosity—dabs, flukes (also abusively called "soles"), but I think not plaice, which seems to be chiefly a European fish, and is confused enough in meaning all by itself, without requiring any help from the flounder. It is *plie* in French, which ought to mean *Pleuronectes platessa*, but the French often use this word also for the brill, which should be of the same shape if we judge by another name given the plaice, *carrelet*, from the word for "square," and even for the lemon sole. Whatever it is, France is not wildly enthusiastic about it. "Of average quality," says the Larousse gastronomic encyclopedia, "not without value on condition that it is eaten perfectly fresh." "Rather fleshy," adds the *Dictionnaire de l'Académie des Gastronomes*, "easy to eat and digest, agreeable to the palate, but don't expect more from it."

Flounders are abundant in Europe as well as in America; the common flounder, *Platichthys flesus*, has been eaten there since Upper Paleolithic times, and ranges all the way from Scandinavia to the Mediterranean, which some authorities think it does not enter. It does, though, and penetrates all the way to its eastern end, where it is the fish known to Turkey as *dere pisisi*. There is some confusion in Europe, though perhaps less than in America, about identifying flounders, but there is one pragmatic criterion which on certain occasions will help you if you happen to know where a fish which baffles you was caught: if in fresh water, it is a flounder; flounders are the only flatfish which mount rivers. They always lay their eggs in salt water, but they show nevertheless a preference for estuaries and river mouths where salinity is low. When a flounder decides to swim up a river, it often goes beyond the reach of the tide, into definitely fresh water, and may even stay there. But flounders which linger in fresh water do not grow as large as in the sea: a good-sized catch for a river flounder is a one-pounder, the minimum at which saltwater flounders are taken.

American flounders as a whole are firm-fleshed and of delicate flavor, and some American writers have expressed the opinion that American flounders are tastier than European flounders—nature's way, perhaps, of compensating for the absence of the most aristocratic flatfish from the Western Hemisphere. There is little difference in flavor among the various fish known as flounders, which are best cooked in the simplest fashion possible, to preserve their taste intact—poached or grilled, with no sauce other than melted butter or lemon juice. Treating all flounders alike has the subsidiary advantage of freeing you from the necessity of worrying about which flounders they are, which is frequently difficult to determine.

It might be reasonable to assume that the winter flounder and the summer flounder are the same fish caught at different seasons, but they are not, though their names do reflect the experience of fishermen. The summer flounder, or fluke, a mottled greenish-brown white-spotted fish found from Cape Cod to the Carolinas, bites enthusiastically in Chesapeake Bay, for instance, during the warm weather, but drops out of sight there as soon as the chill autumn winds begin to blow. It is *Paralichthys dentatus,* whereas the winter flounder, or blackback, rusty brown and often red-spotted, an important food fish of northeastern North America all winter long, is *Pseudopleuronectes americanus.* The yellowtail flounder, or rusty dab, common off the coast of New England, is *Limanda ferruginea,* a cousin of the European lemon sole, but the fish called the lemon sole on the same coast does not belong to the *Limanda* genus, but is *Pseudopleuronectes dignabilis.* Among other fish deceptively called soles, the gray sole, *Glytocephalus cynoglossus,* is probably the most flavorful American flatfish. Other widely eaten East Coast flounders include the dab or sand dab, *Hippoglossoides platessoides;* the dusky olive southern flounder, *Paralichthys lethostigmus,* of the southern Atlantic coast and the Gulf of Mexico; the Gulf flounder, *Platichthys albiguttus;* and the picturesquely marked naked sole, *Gymnarchirus williamsoni,* which wears a zebralike pattern.

The fish of the Pacific coast are named with even less regard for what they really are. There is a sand dab there also, which seems not to be the same fish as the Atlantic sand dab, and also a sand sole, *Pegusa lascaris,* called alternatively the rex sole, the rex, the petrale, the flounder and even, unblushingly, the turbot. There is the so-called California halibut, which is not a genuine halibut, with a range too far south for this cold-water fish, from San Francisco southward into Mexico. North of this, in normal halibut waters, is the arrow-toothed halibut, or American flatfish, but this is not a halibut either, being *Atheresthes stomias.* However, the Pacific coast does have a genuine halibut, *Hippoglossus stenolepis,* which supplies the second most important fishing industry of Pacific Canada (salmon is first); the fish is important also for Washington, Oregon and northern California, not to mention Japan, which takes it in considerable quantities from Bering Strait.

It is the sole whose name is used most abusively on the Pacific coast, which, having no genuine soles, feels free to attach this name to dabs, flounders or any other fish of similar shape. This opened an opportunity for some quick-thinking restaurant owners on the Atlantic coast, who listed two fish on their menus as "Dover sole" and "English sole"—the latter less frequently, since in this case the word "English" is less glamorous than the word "Dover." Sometimes they embellished these listings with the additional information: "imported by air" or "delivered by air." Was it the honest restaurateur's fault if ignorant customers assumed that these fish had been flown across the Atlantic? He had told the exact truth: the fish had indeed been delivered by air—from the Pacific coast. "Dover sole" was *Microstomus pacificus,* the short-finned sole, which is not a sole, but is so called in the West, and, alternatively, with even less justification, the Dover sole. "English sole" was *Parophrys vetulus,* called on the Pacific coast the California sole, the lemon sole or the English sole. No doubt some East coast customers assumed they were being offered *Solea solea,* the European Dover sole, and were accordingly willing to pay for it a price which made it worthwhile flying it across the continent in place of a cheaper but equally palatable flatfish from Atlantic waters. The error was that of the customers. No fraud had been committed—not legally, at least—for the fish had been presented under the names by which they were indeed known in their place of origin. Nothing obliges restaurant operators to give their customers lessons in ichthyology—except, possibly, the agenbite of inwit.

FO
stands for

fogas, a Hungarian fish described as a pike-perch, which has the great merit of being almost devoid of bones; for **folle avoine,** "crazy oats," the name given by seventeenth-century French explorers to wild rice when they encountered it for the first time near the Great Lakes; for the **forest snail,** an outsize gastropod eaten in Ghana; for the **fork-beard,** a small delicate Mediterranean fish, best served fried; for **fowl,** a term used most commonly to designate a chicken too ancient to be edible except after lengthy boiling; for **fox,** a food of prehistoric man shunned today everywhere except in Africa; for **foxgloves,** a family of herbs of which one species may be used for seasoning and another for poisoning; and for **fox grapes,** the species native to the eastern United States, probably so called by the first white settlers not because of a certain muskiness of taste, the common explanation, but because "fox" in this case was simply a synonym for "wild."

FR
stands for

the **fra-fra potato,** a relative of the real thing, eaten in tropical Africa, Madagascar and Mauritius almost as commonly as the Irish potato is eaten in America and Europe; for the **francolin,** a sort of partridge which caught Marco Polo's eye in Asia Minor; for **frankincense,** fed to criminals in ancient Jerusalem just before execution, possibly in the hope that its bitter taste would reconcile them to death; for **French beans,** which are South American, and **French sole,** which would be English if it didn't live in the Mediterranean; for the **frigate mackerel,** which has red flesh; for the **frijole,** a bean dear to American cowboys; for the **frog,** "one of the finest meats known to man," Euell Gibbons *dixit*; for the **frogfish,** too ugly to taste as good as it does; for the **frog-plant,** or live-forever, of which the leaves can be used for salads and the tubers for pickles; for the American **frost grape,** alias the chicken grape or the river-bank grape, for that is where it grows; for the **fruit bat,** which is the flying fox we met a few pages back; and for the **fruta bomba** of Cuba, which is nothing other than the papaya.

G

GERARD, JOHN: *How hard and uncertaine it is to describe in words the true proportion of Plants . . . they best do know who have deepliest waded in this sea of Simples.*

GA
stands for

the **gadwall,** a duck "always esteemed for the table," in the words of the *Encyclopaedia Britannica;* for **galbanum,** a gum resin bitter in taste to man but pleasing in the eyes of the Lord, according to Exodus 30:34, which calls it a sweet spice; for **galingale,** a root of the ginger family, more popular in the Middle Ages than it is now; for the **galinules,** partial to fresh if murky water, which include the European moor hen, the American water hen and, most inescapably, the Florida galinule, an uncomfortably noisy bird; for **Galloway cattle,** close relatives of the noted Angus-Aberdeens, from which they differ by producing better beef in crosses with other races than they are able to achieve on their own; for the **galls** of a number of trees, which ooze a sweetish liquid which deceives bees into thinking it can be made into honey; for the **gannet,** a sea bird nobody thinks of eating nowadays, though it was good enough for Henry VIII; for the **gaper,** or horse clam; for the **gar,** referred to by an English expert as "healthy and delicious" and by an American expert as a "trash fish," and the **gar pike,** which may have been the one the American really had in mind; for the **garden huckleberry,** an African fruit which differs from the unrelated American huckleberry in having virtually no taste; for the **gardenia,** equally happy in the buttonhole or in a fritter; for the **garefowl,** which is none other than the late great auk; for the **garganey,** a small duck otherwise known as the summer teal; for the **garget,** a name given in some localities to pokeweed; for the **garland chrysanthemum,** grown for ornament in the Western world but in China and Japan, under the name shungiku, a green leafy vegetable which, though it looks like salad greens, is served cooked like spinach; for **garlic mustard,** alias jack-by-the-hedge, alias saucealone, the last because it was deemed in former times, when it was used on salt fish or boiled mutton, to be so pungent that no other seasoning was needed; for the **gaur,** the magnificent wild cattle of India, Burma, Malaysia and adjoining territories, and the slightly smaller **gayal,** which some natives of the region maintain is a cross between the gaur and domestic cattle; and for the slender-snouted **gavial,** which we may assume is edible, for other crocodiles are.

And **GA** also stands for

GARLIC. "Gar-licks," wrote Lucy Emerson in *New England Cookery* (1808), "though used by the French, are better adapted to medicine than cookery." This opinion was shared until half a century ago by a majority of her countrymen, who sided not with such garlic appreciators as Aristophanes, Hippocrates and Dioscorides; Pliny, Virgil and the anti-Christian Celsus; Mohammed, Gandhi and Eleanor Roosevelt; Charlemagne and Henry IV; La Fontaine the poet and Pasteur the scientist; Chaucer's Summoner and dogs (who, as all pet-food manufacturers know, dote on it), but rather with decriers of garlic, like Plautus, Horace and Sidonius Apollinaris; Tobias Smollett and the effete John Evelyn; Louis XV, who preferred musk; and vampires, who cannot escape from their graves if their mouths are stuffed with garlic and garlic cloves are scattered about their coffins.

Shakespeare's position on garlic is not clear. He is usually claimed by the anti-garlic faction because of the words he put in Hotspur's mouth:

Oh, he is as tedious
As a tired horse, a railing wife,
Worse than a smoky house. I had rather live
With cheese and garlic in a windmill, far,
Than feed on cates and have him talk to me
In any summer house in Christendom.

"Who wouldn't?" one is tempted to say; certainly the stomach should stand up better to a diet of cheese and garlic than to one composed exclusively of cates—a word which usually gets printed as "cakes," in the belief that a typographical error has been committed. "Cates," now obsolete, but still extant in Shakespeare's time, meant "delicacies" or "dainties." But let us confine ourselves to remarking that no one yet has used this passage to assert that Shakespeare disapproved of cheese. True, he had Bottom say, when he was preparing his play in *A Midsummer Night's Dream*; "And, most dear actors, eat no onions nor garlic, for we are to utter sweet breath." This may be put down as a professional joke; Shakespeare was an actor, and actors are obliged continually to talk into one another's faces, and even shout into them. But the Lunts used to tell their companies: "We don't mind garlic or onions on the breath—but we do object to the smell of liquor."

Garlic has been the vehicle in the United States of a self-reversing snobbery. Before I left America to live in Europe in 1927, you were looked down upon if you ate garlic, a food fit only for ditchdiggers; when I returned in 1940, you were looked down upon if you *didn't* eat it. It had become the hallmark of gastronomic sophistication, and I was overwhelmed by meals offered by thoughtful friends, who catered to my supposedly acquired dashing Gallic tastes by including garlic in every dish except ice cream; their intentions were good, but their premise was faulty.

"Garlic is a necessary presence in many of the most celebrated dishes in every course of both *haute cuisine* and *cuisine bourgeoise*," one of our best magazine writers has explained. The fact is that garlic is regarded almost with horror by the *haute cuisine* and looked on askance by the *cuisine bourgeoise*. In France, garlic is an attribute of neither of the two classic forms of professional cooking; it is a *regional* phenomenon. Garlic reigns almost everywhere south of the Loire, most decisively, perhaps, in the Catalan country. In all of Languedoc the name of the classic garlic soup, translated from one or another of the various forms of Occitan, comes out as "boiled water"—garlic is taken so much for granted that it doesn't even have to be mentioned. To the east it is called "the truffle of Provence," and *aioli*, garlic mayonnaise, is called "the butter of Provence." Garlic is a regional phenomenon in Italy too, where, except for a few special dishes like the Piedmont's *bagna cauda*, it is confined mostly to the south. Southern France and southern Italy were both subjected at the beginning of their histories to Greek influence, which may be why they like garlic today. If so, it seems curious that so many of our food writers insist that the ancient Greeks detested garlic; but much of what has been written in the United States about garlic since Americans discovered it comes under the head of mythology.

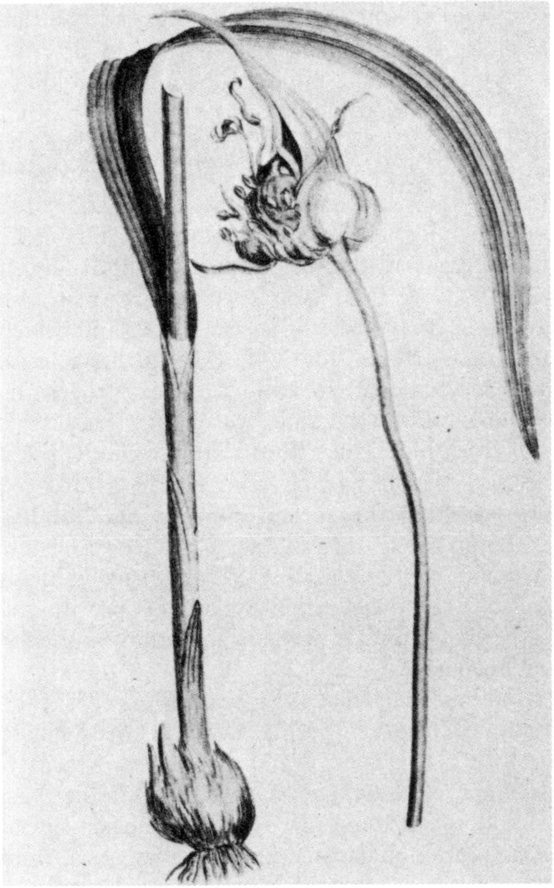

GARLIC. *Print from William Woodville:* Medical Botany, *London, 1832*

We are told that the ancient Greeks disliked garlic because Alexandre Dumas said so, but Dumas was wrong: garlic was one of the most important vegetables in Greece and was eaten there as a real vegetable, in its own right, not simply as seasoning for something else. We are told also that garlic was an important food of the Egyptian pyramid builders, because Herodotus said so (the word he used may have referred not to garlic, but to leeks). We are told that the Egyptians swore by garlic and virtually worshiped it, because Pliny, reporting these facts about the onion, thought it would improve the story if he threw garlic in too; his embellishment has been repeated ever since as if it were Holy Writ. We are told that moly, the magical plant which protected Ulysses from Circe, was garlic, because Linnaeus decided to call one species of garlic *Allium moly* (the one we usually eat is *A. sativum*); but Homer's description of moly, possibly an imaginary plant, does not fit garlic. We are told that the ancient Romans did not like garlic by those who have read Horace's probably half-joking sallies against it, and have perhaps missed the stories which explain his private reasons for showing towards it a hostility unechoed by his fellow Romans.

We are not much better informed on the botanical history of garlic than on its gastronomic history. Garlic is of Asian origin, says a McGraw-Hill encyclopedia; it is a native of Middle Asia, according to the United States Department of Agriculture; of the steppes of Central Asia, from which it was probably brought to Europe by Mongol hordes at a prudently undated period, in the opinion of Louis Lagriffe, author of *Le Livre des épices, des condiments et des aromates*; of Middle Asia west of the Himalayas, says the *Encyclopaedia Britannica*; probably of southern Asia, says the *Encyclopedia Americana*; of western Asia and the Mediterranean basin, says a vegetable dealers' association; of the Middle East, from which it was introduced into Europe after the Crusades by Godefroy de Bouillon, it says in the late Rosie Maurel's *Dictionnaire des Aliments*, which is at odds with Georges Blond's report that "the Moslems who encountered the first Crusaders were more terrified by their strong smell of garlic than by their armor"; of southern Europe, say three American encyclopedias, probably copying one another; of Sicily, according to Linnaeus; and I will put my money on Alphonse de Candolle, who in his *Origines des plantes cultivées* agrees on Central Asia, but remarks that there is a considerable diversity of names for garlic in Celtic, Slav, Greek and Latin languages (the Old English *garleac* was in current use by the year 1000, antedating Godefroy de Bouillon) and adds: "To explain this diversity we must suppose that its original habitat extended farther west than that known at the present time."

Garlic has indeed been reported early in areas included in none of the regions cited above. Magellan found it in the neighborhood of the Philippines. It is usual to assert that garlic was brought to America from Europe, but an unruly member of the Cortez foray into Mexico was nearly half a millennium ahead of the scientists in postulating its existence in the Western Hemisphere. Put into stocks freshly made to order by natives, he complained that the wood smelled of garlic—communicated to it, one may suppose, by well-fed carpenters. He had a keen nose. America does possess wild garlic, notably *A. canadense*, eaten not as a seasoning but as a full-fledged vegetable by pre-Columbian Indians—like the ancient Greeks.

GE
stands for

the **gean**, a plum for the birds according to the taxonomists who dubbed it *Prunus avium*, but it is actually a wild sweet cherry; for the **gemsbok** of southwestern Africa, a game animal becoming ever rarer, on the plains and on the table; for the **genet**, a chiefly African feline, sufficiently less odorous than its close relative, the civet cat, so that natives of southern Africa have been choking it down since prehistoric times; for the **genip**, a Caribbean fruit which looks like green grapes and has flesh resembling pink cantaloupes; for **genitalia**, which various animals contribute to our larder, especially bulls in Spain, and which illustrious personages have deigned to eat, including La Pompadour; for the **geoduck**, a clam of the American Pacific coast so fat that it cannot close its shell, which American Indians gather at the exceptionally low tides provoked by what they call "mad moons"; for **Gerard's pine**, a Himalayan tree whose seeds are edible; for the **gerenuk**, an East African antelope which can stand on its hind legs; for the **germon**, a fish of the albacore family; and for **gesho**, Ethiopian hops.

And **GE** also stands for

GELATIN. "Boil a set of [calves'] feet in four quarts of water," Eliza Leslie advised early nineteenth-century housewives in her *Directions for Cookery* (a set of feet in the kitchen, as on the calf, is four). "They should boil slowly till the liquid is reduced to two quarts or one half the original quantity, and the meat has dropped in rags from the bone. Then strain the liquid; measure and set it away in a large earthern pan to get cold; and let it rest till next morning. Then if you do not find it a firm cake of jelly, boil it over again with an ounce of isinglass, and again

GELATIN *by Edward Hicks (1780–1849).* Noah's Ark, *oil on canvas*

set away until cool and congealed. Remove the sediment from the bottom of the cake of jelly, and carefully scrape off all the fat. The smallest bit of fat will eventually render it dull and cloudy. Press some clean blotting paper all over it to absorb what little grease may yet remain."

For the American housewife today, this would seem like a great deal of travail for arriving at gelatin, or for the housewife almost anywhere for that matter, since gelatin has been more successful than the United Nations in achieving international harmony, and is sold almost everywhere in the world in standardized form and quality—six sheets are universally the correct amount to dissolve in a pint (or half-liter) of water, while the equivalent in powdered form is one-half ounce (a tablespoon) or fifteen grams, the amount contained in one of the small envelopes in which powdered gelatin is packaged in the United States. Calves' feet have been forgotten. All the housewife has to do nowadays is add water to the prepared product; and ever since the passage of the Pure Food and Drugs Act in 1906, she has not been obliged to worry about getting a little lead or arsenic along with her gelatin.

This is a development of our century, but it need not have been. Powdered gelatin existed in the 1840s, even in combination with sugar and artificial flavors, the ready-prepared gelatin dessert of today (whose flavoring seems to have been synthetic from the very beginning), but nobody knew about it. Half a century later, packaging and merchandising of gelatin got under way, but it was still slow to gain public favor until refrigeration became more general—or so we are told. There was perhaps another potent factor, the lack of a trademark to run trippingly off the tongue, which in the realm of foodstuffs has often been decisive for success—for example, in the case of Kellogg's Toasted Cornflakes, Coca-Cola and, in this case, Jell-O.

The commonest food use of gelatin is for desserts, in which case it is usually bought in the form of the already sugared and flavored package which demands of the purchaser only that he or she add water. Unflavored gelatin remains in some demand, however, for soups, gelatin salads (which personally I can do without) or aspic.

Gelatin is not obtainable, as many persons believe (perhaps among them, in her time, Eliza Leslie), from hoofs or horns. When Miss Leslie boiled calves' feet, she derived the gelatin not from the hoofs but from the scraps of white connective tissue which still clung to them—cartilage, sinews, skin and ossein (the protein matrix of bone). Commercial gelatin is made 10 percent from ossein, 90 percent from hides. Of the total commercial output, 60 to 65 percent goes into foods, and the rest into various other uses: it provides the outer covering for medicines delivered in soft capsules, it gives us emulsions for photography, it is used in the printing of fabrics, it is involved in some types of duplicating equipment, like the hectograph, and it serves for clarifying wine and beer—which, via industrial uses, gets us back to the food category again, as does its addition to ice cream as a stabilizer (it prevents the formation of ice crystals).

Gelatin, strictly speaking, is animal jelly (fish jelly, obtained especially from sturgeons, is called isinglass). However, by analogy the name has been extended to vegetable products of similar properties, which can be obtained from a number of sources ranging from Irish moss to oat gum, but especially from seaweed (Irish moss, despite its name, is a seaweed, and agar-agar, sometimes offered under that name in the United States, is derived from seaweed too). Agar-agar is pretty much a specialty of the Japanese, the world's greatest exploiters of seaweed, whose own favorite seems to be a type of algae called *tengusa*, alias "heavenly grass." This produces a liquid which has the advantage over animal products that it sets without refrigeration. In this form it is called *tokoroten*, but further processing reduces it to little stiff sticks, the equivalent of our brittle gelatin sheets, called *kanten*, or "cool heaven."

Gelatin is largely protein, 85.6 grams of it for each 100 grams of dry gelatin, which generate only 59 calories—so weight-watchers might consider it an ideal means for taking in protein without being besieged by calories. But there is a catch: dry gelatin may have 85.6 grams of protein per 100, but the commercial gelatin you buy has only 9.4 grams, and by the time this has been dissolved in the necessary amount of water, you have 1.5 grams of protein per 100 grams of intake. Moreover, much of this minute residue cannot be utilized, for gelatin has a low amino-acid content, which makes it one of the few foods with a negative protein efficiency ratio—which means, to oversimplify a little, that laboratory rats fed on it would lose weight instead of gaining it. Gelatin has no fats, but it has no mineral salts or vitamins either. It is, indeed, about as close to being no food at all as any food can possibly get.

As for weight-watchers, since gelatin is usually eaten in the form of a dessert, accompanied by milk and sugar, not to mention, horror of horrors, whipped cream, it is hardly to be recommended, unless you are resigned to munching or drinking pure tasteless gelatin or chewing isinglass.

GH
stands for

ghee, the clarified butter which, the Hindus tell us, accounts, in liquid form, for the fourth of the seven concentric oceans which surround the world; for the **gherkin,** considered a weed in England, perhaps because its very name means "unripe," but used with excellent results in the United States for pickling; and for the phantom-colored **ghost crabs,** so called because as soon as you spot them they aren't there anymore.

GI
stands for

the **giant Atlantic cockle**, a cockle larger than most other cockles, plentiful in Florida; for the **giant crabs,** crabs larger than any other crabs, of which there are two: the Japanese deep-sea spider crab, the widest, and the Australian sea crab, the heaviest; for the **giant macoma,** or white sand clam, a macoma larger than other macomas, otherwise known as the bent-nose clam, a lover of mud; for the **giant Pacific cockle,** a cockle larger than most other cockles except the giant Atlantic cockle; for the **giant puffball,** a mushroom decidedly larger than most other mushrooms, since it can reach a diameter of five feet; for the **giant sea cradle,** a chiton of America's Pacific coast, larger than any other chiton; for the **giant urchin,** also of America's Pacific coast, larger than other sea urchins; and the **giant whelk,** a whelk larger than any other Atlantic coast whelk, or than any other mollusk found north of Cape Hatteras, for that matter.

GI stands for

the **gibbon,** an endearing ape which was eaten in Borneo in prehistoric times but has, unless I am ill-informed, since been removed from the category of the edible; for the **giganturid,** a fish which can swallow other fish nearly twice its own length by doubling them up, whose own edibility remains in doubt because its habit of remaining between 1500 and 6000 feet down allows us scant opportunity for tasting it; for **gill-over-the-ground,** or ground ivy, which the sixteenth-century English herbalist John Gerard recommended for "ache in the hucklebone"; for the **gilthead bream,** which, probably because it wears a gold spot on each cheek and a golden crescent between the eyes, is dedicated to Aphrodite, no doubt in one of her shadier aspects; for **gingelly oil,** which the Japanese prefer for deep frying, and the **gingko nut,** which they eat roasted; for **ginseng,** of which a man who makes his living raising it remarked candidly: "There ain't a thing in the world it's good for except to make money"; and for the **giraffe,** whose bone marrow is one of Africa's greatest delicacies.

And **GI** also stands for

GINGER. Since a main object of this book is to be useful, let us open this entry with two items of practical information: ginger root, according to a French Dr. Fallet so obscure that I have been unable to discover either his first name or his dates, "confers on those who use it absolute power over any tigers they may happen to meet; they become so gentle that a man can ride them like a horse." In case surly tigers do not happen to be your problem, here is another helpful household hint: ginger will dispel incubi.

It is not surprising that a spice to which such portentous powers were attributed should have been considered synonymous with force. Ginger is an ingredient of chutneys, a word which comes from the Hindi *chatni,* designating strong, spicy condiments; and in the Basilicata region of southern Italy, when a dish is called "strong" it means that it is dominated by ginger, a flavor there so common, probably because the Saracens once ruled this area, that it is unnecessary to name it specifically.

Ginger is the root (botanically the rhizome) of *Zingiber officinale,* "prob. native to the Pacific islands," says Webster, to which one can only answer, "Prob. not." The Pacific islands were still uninhabited at the period when old records tell us that ginger was already being cultivated in India; but the incidence of error on the origin of ginger is high. One can excuse John Gerard for writing, in his sixteenth-century *Herball,* that "ginger groweth in Spain, Barbary, in the Canarie islands, and the Azores. Our men who sacked Domingo in the Indies, digged it up there in sundry places wilde." But how explain that a contemporary, André Castelot, who enjoys, among French television watchers, a reputation as a reliable historian, can write that ginger "comes from the West Indies"? There was no ginger in the New World until Europeans brought it there; what is called wild ginger in the United States is the same thing the ancient Romans called wild ginger when they obtained it from Egypt or Illyria, asarabacca, whose taste and odor recall ginger, but which does not even belong to the same family of plants.

Ginger is a native of tropical Asia, where it has been cultivated for so long that its wild forebear no longer exists, probably of India and Malaysia.

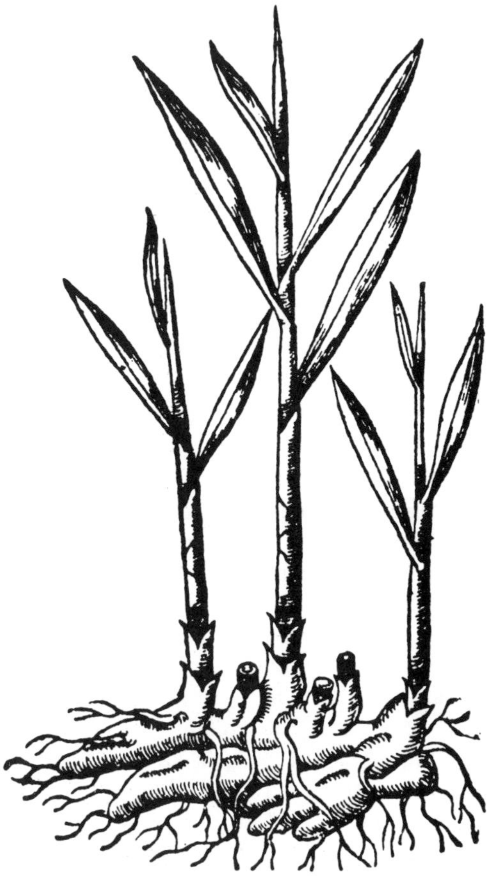

GINGER. *Woodcut from John Gerard:* Herball or General Historie of Plantes, *London, 1597*

Its name comes from the Sanskrit *sringavera,* which means "horn-root," from the fancied resemblance of its misshapen flattened rhizome to the horns of some animal or other; today the roots are spoken of as "hands," which appears to be a little more accurate, and in the trade as "races," which may seem a baffling term unless you happen to know that *raices* is the Portuguese-Spanish word for "roots." *Sringavera* has proved to be a word susceptible of infinite variation, remaining recognizable in all the languages through which it has passed—ancient Greek, *dziggiberi;* Latin, *zingiber;* Italian, *zenzero;* Spanish, *gengibre;* French, *gingembre;* German, *Ingwerd;* Dutch, *gember*—and, of course, English, ginger.

The ancient Romans had all the ginger they wanted, perhaps, indeed, too much, which was why it cost fifteen times as much as black pepper. Most Oriental spices were expensive in those times because they were scarce; ginger was expensive because it was plentiful (and in demand). The volume in which it was imported made it worthwhile to tax it heavily. To maintain the fiction that Roman citizens did not pay taxes, what might be called a transshipment tax was imposed on it before it entered Roman territory proper, at Alexandria, where it was put aboard ships bound for Rome's port of Ostia. Pliny, who was not duped by this device, complained about the artificially high price of ginger (six denarii a pound), whose cost, like that of tobacco, alcoholic liquors and gasoline in many countries today, did not depend on its own value, but on the levy the government imposed on it.

The Romans did not know where their ginger came from, except that it arrived via the Red Sea, so they attributed it vaguely to southern Arabia. It must actually have come from India. The sea route between that distant country and the eastern coast of Egypt antedated the overland caravan route—the Silk Road—which would not be opened until the second century A.D. Ginger made this long trip in greater abundance than other spices because it was shipped in root form, and thus was less perishable than most others.

We are usually told that ginger disappeared from Europe after the collapse of the Roman Empire until Marco Polo rediscovered it in China and India; it seems, however, that some trickled through all the same. One British authority says that ginger reached England only in the thirteenth century, but another maintains that it was known there "before the Conquest"—that is, before 1066. There was enormous incentive to import it, for all the early travelers who met it in the Far East marveled at its cheapness, but it brought fancy prices in Europe. Marco Polo reported from the first point where he came across it in China that "one Venetian groat will buy forty pounds of fresh ginger of excellent quality," and from the second that the same groat would buy eighty pounds there. Ginger had deteriorated in value by the fourteenth century, or the groat had mounted, for Friar Odoric de Pendenone wrote then, also from China: "Here you can buy three hundred pounds of fresh ginger for less than a groat." At this rate Venetian spice importers could well afford to bribe the Master of the Treasury yearly with a standardized list of gifts, including one pound each of pepper, cinnamon and ginger, to induce him to let their merchandise enter Europe at a reasonable customs rate. In Europe a pound of ginger would buy a sheep. In thirteenth-century England, the household accounts of Eleanor, Countess of Leicester, showed that she paid from ten pence to two shillings four pence for a pound of ginger. The significance of these figures will be apparent to all those familiar with the fluctuations of the Venetian groat in the thirteenth and fourteenth centuries and the purchasing power of the shilling in the thirteenth.

If most of medieval Europe reveled in ginger for a century or two after it became readily available, its favor declined in those areas where delicacy of taste achieved the ascendant over shocking flavors, for instance France; but England remained wedded to ginger, "hot i' the mouth," as Shakespeare's clown remarked in *Twelfth Night*. Queen Elizabeth herself is said to have invented the gingerbread man by ordering that little cakes flavored with this spice be baked in the form of portraits of her familiars, whose likenesses must necessarily have been approximate. The conquest of India helped maintain the British appetite for hot spices; as late as 1954 Sir Robert Perkins made a speech in the House of Commons attacking the kitchen committee which ran its restaurant, complaining that it was three hundred years since the menu had listed maupygernon (chicken smothered in ginger and cloves).

The English carried their taste for ginger to America, which was avid for ginger from the very beginning of its history. Ginger cookies were among the goodies passed out to the incorruptible voters of Virginia to induce them to choose the correct candidates for the House of Burgesses. Ginger was included in the standard rations of American soldiers during the Revolution, and after it the consumption of this and other seasoners was hardly discouraged by the fact that the number one spice port of the world during the first half of the nineteenth century was Salem, Massachusetts, because of the speed of the Yankee Clippers. Perhaps this accounts for the fact that ginger ice cream can still be found in New England, though hardly anywhere else. Until fairly recently it was a common practice, on the Atlantic coast at least, to pass candied ginger around after a meal, to aid digestion and curb flatulence.

From its original Asiatic homes, ginger has now spread to many other tropical areas. It is grown today in Australia; in South America; in Indochina, whose ginger is particularly hot; in tropical West Africa, where it tends to be harsh and peppery; and in Jamaica, where its pale color and delicate, distinguished aroma have given it a reputation which has encouraged other Caribbean islands to borrow its name for their own products: the ginger sold in most American Chinatowns and in Oriental grocery stores is usually described as Jamaican, but most of it comes from Puerto Rico. Jamaica supplies most of the world exports of peeled (white) ginger, India much of the unpeeled (gray) ginger, West Africa a little of both in the form of fresh or dried roots, and China specializes in ginger preserved by being boiled and packed in syrup. Britons, Germans and the Dutch are its biggest eaters.

Let us end, as we began, on a practical note. Horse traders are accustomed to apply a piece of ginger root as a suppository to their merchandise, encouraging the animals to hold their tails up, which is, it appears, a sign of vigor in horses. This information will remain useful only as long as the horse stays with us; ginger has no known effect on internal combustion engines.

GL
stands for

the **gladiola,** from whose corm the ancient Romans made bread; for **glassfish,** which, being transparent, do not look as if they were capable of providing solid nourishment, yet some species do; for the **globe artichoke,** grown not only as a food but also for ornament; for **gluten,** which, to keep things simple, will be defined here in the words of the *Encyclopaedia Britannica* as "a mixture of glutencasein (Liebig's vegetable fibrin), gluten-fibrin, gliadin (Pflanzenleim), glutin or vegetable gelatin and mucedin"; and for **glycol,** which provides emulsifiers to make ice cream smoother than it has any right to be.

GN
stands for

the **gnu,** an ungainly African antelope, whose excellence as game has caused the species, also known as the black wildebeest, to disappear as a truly wild animal; but the brindled gnu, or blue wildebeest, is still fairly plentiful in central Africa.

GO
stands for

the **Goa bean,** a double-threat vegetable of which both pods and root are edible; for the **goat,** which the late A. J. Liebling advised eating in its youth, because "in later life [it grows] muscular through overactivity"; for the **goat nut** of Baja California, which has edible seeds; for the **goatsbeard,** a salsify-like root which was on one occasion the only ration Julius Caesar had for his army; for **gobo,** the root of the great burdock, common in the United States, but which only finds buyers there when it is sold under this Japanese name in Oriental food stores; for the **goby,** one of whose 500 species, believed to be the smallest vertebrate in the world (½ inch long), is too tiny to eat, but of which larger varieties are valuable food fishes, especially those of Indo-Australian waters; for the **godwit,** a tasty wading bird of widespread distribution; for **gold,** inedible for Midas, but eaten in India; for the **golden carpet-shell,** a yellowish clam; for the **Golden Delicious,** a sweet yellow apple which started its career by accident and worked its way up to third place among best-selling American apples; for the **goldeneye,** a duck which makes a whistling noise in flight and a sizzling noise in the oven; for the **golden gray mullet,** the fish which provides the smoked *likorinos* dear to Turks; for **golden needles,** which are dried tiger-lily buds, used as seasoning in Chinese cooking; for the **golden plover,** already an appreciated game bird in ancient Roman times; for the **goldeye,** a fish which, first pickled and then smoked, provides one of northwestern Canada's greatest delicacies; for the **goldfish,** no longer required eating at Harvard; and for **gold of pleasure,** the name given by the sixteenth-century herbalist John Gerard to a variety of marigold, in tribute to the flavorful oil pressed from its yellow seeds.

GO
stands for

Good-King-Henry, a now neglected potherb whose name is a corruption of Güter Heinrich, given it in Germany to distinguish it from Böser Heinrich, Bad Henry, an undesirable weed; for **goma,** sesame seed, a popular spice in Japanese cooking, and **goma-abura,** the oil made from it; for the **goongoo pea,** popular Jamaican for "Congo pea," a pulse supposed to have been brought to the New World from Africa by black slaves; for the **goosefoot,** a wild potherb unpromisingly called pigweed in the United States, though it is a close relative of the more respectfully named Good King Henry; for **goose grass,** so called because geese eat it, but humans have done so under the name "Lenten pottage," in which it is cooked like spinach, whose taste it approximates; for the **goosetongue,** a seashore relative of the inland plantain, usable either raw in salads or as a cooked vegetable; for the **goral,** a sort of Asian chamois relished by the natives of the Himalayas; for the **gorilla,** eaten in tropical Africa; for the **gourami,** a freshwater fish of India which can live for a short time out of water if there are no hungry Hindus about; for **gourds,** grown often for ornamental purposes, though many of them are edible, like the bitter gourd, the snake gourd, the bottle gourd, the wax gourd and the Egusi melon of West Africa, which despite its name is cultivated not for its flesh but its seeds; and for the **governor's beans** of South Africa, named for the anonymous official who first planted them there so that the spice ships of the Dutch East India Company could pick them up en route to or from India as protection against scurvy.

And **GO** also stands for

GOOSE. Open any book dealing with the history of food, look up what it has to say about geese, and fifty to one you will come upon the information that the ancient Romans were so fond of the geese of Picardy, in what is now northwestern France, that great flocks of these Gallic geese were herded cross-country from Picardy to Rome, on foot, to make a Roman holiday. Apparently none of the numerous writers who copied this detail parrot-like from their predecessors ever paused to ask themselves how long it would have taken to drive geese 1200 miles to market over a route which included crossing the Alps. The original author of this improbable account seems to have been Alexandre Dumas, a slipshod writer, who had misread Pliny. After reporting on Rome's preference for Gallic geese, Pliny continued: "Wonderful to relate, the bird comes all the way from Morino to Rome on its own feet—the weary geese go before, and those following by natural pressure urge them on." "Wonderful to relate" and "all the way" were phrases which impressed Dumas, a man with a nineteenth-century perception of distances, and caused him to assume that Morino was in Picardy. It is in fact near Naples, so the distance the geese covered was only 150 miles—still quite a stroll from the point of view of Pliny, who had a first-century perception of distances, and, no doubt, also from the point of view of the geese.

Dumas' slapdash approach to history cropped up a second time on this same subject when he dealt with the most famous episode in which geese are alleged to have figured, the occasion when they raised a ruckus which roused the Roman guardians of the Capitol in time to save it from invading Gauls. Dumas suggests that this made the goose a sacred bird; but the fact is that the geese of the Capitol were sacred birds already, and that is why they were there: they were attached to the temple of Juno. It is true that the Romans did not eat goose for some three and a half centuries after the date of this manifestation, 390 B.C., but it was not out of gratitude, it was because the species of goose employed by Juno did not make good eating. Three and a half centuries from 390 B.C. brings us to the period when a conquered Gaul was sending its best foods to Rome, including plump, tasty geese.

We know that the ancient Egyptians ate geese, but were they domesticated, in which case the chances would have been good that they belonged to the same species which failed to enthrall the Romans, or were they tastier wild birds of other species, trapped during their migrations when they paused to feed in the tempting marshes of the Nile? Archeologists tell us that geese were "probably" domesticated from Neolithic times, "probably" (again) as "a follow-up from the fattening of captured fledglings," but the record is a trifle hazy. The ancient Greeks must have domesticated geese, for they are known to have fattened them for the table on moistened grain; perhaps it was this which made them fit fare: after all, the Romans, who do not seem to have had a happy hand with poultry, had no palatable chickens until the Greeks showed them how to fatten them. There is, however, no doubt about the Gauls. Long before the Romans moved in, they were feeding geese on gruel made from barley or millet; indeed, they were doing so even before the Germanic tribes invaded Gaul, and the Germans were sufficiently impressed by their example to abandon conquest and settle down on farms where they too started raising chickens and geese. Goose was still highly popular in France in the sixth century, perhaps even too popular in the opinion of Venantius Fortunatus, bishop of Poitiers, who addressed to a nobleman who set a good table a poem in which this passage occurs:

Nectar and wine and food and scholar's wit:
Such is the fashion, Gogo, of thy house.
Cicero art thou, and Apicius too,
But now I cry you mercy: no more goose!

Three centuries later Charlemagne ordered that his domains be kept well stocked with geese, which in his time were more prized than any other kind of poultry. Geese still enjoyed so much esteem in the later Middle Ages that when a conquered city was delivered to pillage, its geese were reserved for the Grand Master of the Crossbowmen.

Goose was popular in the Middle Ages in central Europe, and still is. The current German practice of stuffing it with apples existed at least by the sixteenth century. Great flocks of geese were a common sight in the German countryside in the seventeenth and eighteenth centuries; the king of meats there was pork, but goose came second.

In England, goose was the second most popular fowl. "The English inhabitants," wrote Fynes Moryson (1566–1630), "eat almost no flesh commoner than hens, and for geese they eat them in two seasons, when they are fattened upon the

Goose. *Wall painting in the tomb of Ra-hotpe at Meidum. Reign of Snefru (c. 2900* BC*), facsimile*

stubble after harvest and when they are green about Whitsuntide." Queen Elizabeth, who was fond of roast goose (with the sage and onion stuffing which New England puts into turkey today), was eating this dish when the news was brought to her at table that the English had won a victory over a Spanish fleet; she ordered that the day should be celebrated thereafter with a feast of roast goose, so September 29, St. Michael's Day, became associated in England with goose as Thanksgiving in the United States is associated with turkey. In central Europe and Scandinavia, goose is eaten on St. Martin's Day (November 11) or its eve, but I have been unable to find out why; it also appears frequently at Christmas in these countries, and in England too. In France, it used to be eaten on Christmas Eve and New Year's Eve, particularly the latter, but has now given way largely to turkey—a pity, for French turkey has less character than American turkey—or at least than American turkey used to have.

On the other side of the world, the importance of goose was recorded by Marco Polo, who reported from Fuchow that "this . . . country produces geese of such a size that a single one weighs 24 pounds. They have a big swelling under the throat and a sort of protuberance on top of the bill next to the nostrils, like that found on a swan only much bigger." In the fourteenth century Friar Odoric de Pordenone, writing from Canton, added that the geese there were "bigger and finer and cheaper than anywhere in the world. For one of them is as big as two of ours, and 'tis all white as milk. . . . And these geese are as fat as fat can be, yet one of them well dressed and seasoned you shall have there for less than a groat."

"In poor country," I wrote in 1958 in *The Food of France*, "poultry means geese—for while it takes four pounds of grain to put one pound of meat on a turkey and three pounds of grain to put one pound of meat on a chicken, it takes only two-thirds of a pound of grain to raise a pound of goose." The producers of battery-raised chickens have since crossed me up by reducing the chicken's intake per pound of meat to less than two pounds of feed, and it isn't even grain, it's fish flour and chemicals, which is why chicken today tastes like moist cardboard. It still remains true, however, that goose is poor-country food, for the bird is a grazer capable of fending for itself. Turn geese into a meadow and they will operate very much like sheep (and require almost as much pasture). Web-footed they may be, but geese are nevertheless the most terrestrial of water birds. They need some water about, but can make do with much less than ducks.

The ability of geese to feed themselves on whatever greenery happens to be handy, with a minimum of expensive fattening before they are killed, maintains their favor in poorly endowed regions, where they are raised on a small scale for the farmer's family and perhaps a few of his neighbors, but this is in fact what goose rearing almost always means nowadays even on richer territory, in the Western world at least. "Commercial goose production does not exist," a French weekly asserted flatly in 1975. "The goose is an animal raised only on small farms." The writer forgot Germany, Austria, Scandinavia and even certain local exceptions in France itself, but in general it is true that geese are not raised for mass markets. Modern dietitians did a great deal to banish the goose from our tables by stigmatizing it as too rich and too fat. It does indeed contain a greater proportion of fat than any other familiar type of poultry, but a good cook should be able to deal with that. It is sad that goose fat has been allowed to drive goose flavor off the market, for goose is one of the tastiest of birds (and its fat is excellent for cooking).

The nineteenth-century gastronomic writer Grimod de la Reynière, whom no one has accused of consistency, wrote on one occasion that goose was "common, even dry, tough, and forbidding," and on another that "it is a snappy brunette, with whom we get along very well, especially in the absence of our dear blonde"—which, I suppose, means the chicken. Balzac called goose "the pheasant of coopers," a slightly sibylline statement, which perhaps reconciles the two contradictory aspects of this bird: although it is a poor-country dish, food for the humble, it also plays the glamorous role of the gastronomic treat, suitable for times of rejoicing. Thus it would perhaps not be quite exact to translate Balzac's phrase as meaning "the poor man's pheasant." Goose has often been as welcome as pheasant on the tables of the great, of kings and lords, which accounts for an old French saying, "He who eats the king's goose will cough up feathers for a hundred hours," a phrase which permits a multiplicity of interpretations.

From the point of view of the gourmet, wild goose and domesticated goose are almost two different meats. What is considered today the disadvantage of the domesticated goose, its plentiful supply of fat, does not appear in the wild goose, which works off its fat in flight. This exercise also guarantees that the wild goose will become tough early, so that its rich flavor can only be fully appreciated when it is eaten young. However, this is true also for domesticated geese, which are best at a weight of six to eight pounds, corresponding to an age of seven or eight months—just right for Christmas eating, since geese normally lay their eggs (five or six to a clutch) in the spring.

Geese nest over a wide range of the Northern Hemisphere, from Lapland to Spain and from Scotland to China. The domestic geese of the West are believed to have been developed from the wild graylag goose, which, since it is considered the archetype of its genus, has been gratified with the scientific tag *Anser anser*. Oriental domestic geese are probably descended from *Cygnopsis cygnoid*, the Chinese goose, which when domesticated is referred to disconcertingly as the Guinea goose. The Chinese bird, as Marco Polo correctly observed, is the largest living wild goose, dwarfing even that giant of the West, the Canada goose, which can reach a weight of fourteen pounds and a wingspread of six feet.

The chief geese raised for the table are the German Embden goose, a favorite in England, and the French Toulouse goose, which, though it bears the same name, is not the one used to produce foie gras. There are two varieties of the Toulouse species, known to their breeders as the industrial type and the agricultural type. The industrial goose carries under its belly a large fold of skin which can make room for the fat produced by the force-feeding necessary to arrive at the swollen livers of foie gras; after the liver has been removed, the rest of the bird is nearly inedible, except in the form of *confit d'oie*, preserved goose, which has thus become automatically the second specialty of the foie-gras country of southwestern France. The agricultural goose is not equipped with the belly fold, except in rudimentary form, and therefore packs no more than a reasonable quota of fat—just enough to deliver to the table a sizzling steaming bird with crisp crusty crackling skin and richly flavorsome flesh—when, of course, it has been roasted by a cook who knows his business. A dish fit for a king!

If you happen to find yourself in New Zealand and on a restaurant menu come across a dish described as "colonial goose," don't order it unless you want lamb.

GOOSEBERRY. William Robbins, in *The American Food Scandal,* lists gooseberries among the foods which it is difficult to find in American supermarkets; but while it is true that this is the kind of hard-to-handle fruit which supermarkets prefer not to offer, they cannot be accused in this case of depriving the American consumer of something which he would dearly like to have. Americans have never been great gooseberry fanciers, an exception to the rule that American eating habits are a prolongation of British eating habits. My family is British Isles on both sides, which probably explains why, when I was a child, gooseberries grew in our backyard and we ate them with delight—fresh, with sugar and milk. Our neighbors gave us little help in maintaining that tradition.

The English are the world's most fervent gooseberry eaters, with some help from the Scandinavians and the Teutons (gooseberry pie was a favorite dish of Adolf Hitler). Even in Britain, however, the gooseberry can hardly be classed as a major fruit, and its place on the tables of the world is negligible. It is grown in the British Isles perhaps oftener by private persons for their own pleasure, in hedgerows or under the trees of orchards (the gooseberry dotes on shade), than by professional providers for the market. Commercial plantings of gooseberries in Britain occupy only about 7000 acres, commercial production is around 15,000 tons annually (divide by 20 for the American figures). Something like a thousand varieties of gooseberries have been offered to British gardeners; the United States and Canada together grow only about a dozen.

One of the reasons why the gooseberry is so much less important in America than in Britain (or even in northern Europe in general) may well be that it is a less attractive fruit in the United States. A plant of the Northern Hemisphere, the gooseberry is represented by native species on both sides of the Atlantic, but the European fruit and the American one seem to have developed from different wild ancestors. The British gooseberry is considerably larger; by giving special care to its most popular variety, the Lev-

GOOSEBERRY. *Photograph by Murray Alcosser.* Gooseberries, *1979*

eller, British horticulturists have obtained fruits weighing an ounce each; but the all-time champion, from the point of view of the time during which it held the lead, was the London, of the last century, which for thirty-seven seasons without a break (1829 to 1867) sent the largest gooseberries to agricultural exhibits.

Another reason for British supremacy is that while gooseberries grow readily almost everywhere in the United Kingdom, in the United States they are confined to the northwest and northeast coasts (reference books say not south of Massachusetts, which was where we grew them, but they must have gotten as far south as the Carolinas, for the Cherokees ate them); the shores of the Great Lakes; and Alaska, where they are gathered wild. Gooseberries cannot tolerate hot sun, which they meet in the United States; this accounts for the fact that we do not hear of them in antiquity, since for us antiquity is located in the sun-drenched Mediterranean basin.

The gooseberry has also been deliberately discouraged in the United States; like its very close relative, the CURRANT, it transmits blister rust, which kills the native American white pine, a tree of great commercial value and majestic beauty. The gooseberry besides does some discouraging itself. The currant has smooth stems, but those of the gooseberry bristle with often vicious spikes. America's best-known hybrid is named the Pixwell (get it?), because its fruit has been induced to hang from long stems, well below the protective thorns: it can be gathered without losing blood.

The cultivated gooseberry is a fairly recent addition to the human larder. The Normans are supposed to have brought it into France, but probably in a wild variety, which should mean about the tenth century or a little later; but not until the sixteenth century did it begin to spread from its original foothold into the rest of the country. It enjoyed a certain favor in the seventeenth and eighteenth centuries, but by the end of the nineteenth it had worn out its welcome in France, where very few gooseberries are cultivated today. England may have been the first to take the gooseberry seriously, and develop it deliberately, instead of putting up with the wild fruit: it was being grown in English gardens as early as 1600.

The Chinese gooseberry is not a gooseberry, but the kiwi. South Africa's Cape gooseberry is not a gooseberry, but a ground cherry. The Otaheite gooseberry tree of Hawaii does not produce gooseberries, but bears edible though acid fruits which recall them. The gooseberry garnet is of course not a gooseberry, but a semiprecious stone whose often rounded shape and pale greenish color make it look like one.

GRA
stands for

grains of paradise, otherwise known as Melegueta pepper, and the **gram,** otherwise known as the chick-pea; for the **grampus,** a dolphin which has been accused of eating men, but in any case men have eaten grampus, in Elizabethan times at least; for the **granadilla,** otherwise the passion flower; for **grass,** seldom eaten by man except after its metamorphosis into flesh by more gifted animals; for **grasshoppers,** once eaten in China under the name of "brushwood shrimp"; for **grass-of-Parnassus,** which secretes honey; for the **grass pea,** a famine food of which over-consumption can lead to paralysis; for the **Gravenstein,** an apple too weak to pollinate itself; for the **grayfish,** otherwise known as the dogfish; for the **gray gurnard,** a sea robin tasty in the mouth, which does its own tasting with its fins; for the **grayling,** an excellent troutlike game and food fish which is having a hard time holding its own against pollution in the contiguous forty-eight states, but is still flourishing in Alaska, *oleoducto volente*; for the **gray mullet,** a fish much appreciated by the ancient Romans, which does not bear even kissing-cousin relationship to the red mullet; and for the **gray sole,** a flatfish caught off the coast of New England.

And **GRA** also stands for

GRAPE. "A drinker at table," Brillat-Savarin wrote, "was offered grapes for dessert. 'Thank you,' he said, pushing the plate away. 'I am not accustomed to taking my wine in pills.' " Besides being rude, Brillat-Savarin's spokesman was ignorant about grapes. Although some wine grapes can be eaten as table grapes, and some table grapes can be converted successfully into wine, grape growers had been developing separate varieties for each purpose centuries before Brillat-Savarin's time. It is not on record when a distinction between wine grapes and dessert grapes was first made, but we could deduce from the fact that Pliny described ninety-one varieties of grapes but only fifty wines made from them that certain grapes in his time were reserved for eating; as a matter of fact we know from other sources that the ancient Romans grew special kinds for the table. They also differentiated between grapes meant to be eaten fresh and those designed for conversion into raisins, which, Columella explained, were made from the largest and sweetest white grapes.

Man has been eating grapes since prehistoric times, probably already cultivated then. Grape seeds have been found in the ruins of Swiss lake settlements dating from the Neolithic and Bronze ages, and in the New World in American Indian

GRAPE. *Greta Garbo's* Queen Christina, *directed by Rouben Mamoulian, M-G-M, 1933*

sites going back to 1800 B.C.—both at some distance from this fruit's place of origin. Though its birthplace is not known for certain, if you put it somewhere in the neighborhood of the Caspian and its first cultivation on the Persian side of that sea, you ought not to be far off. From this starting point grapes spread first south and west throughout Asia Minor, where they are already heard from in the oldest known written language, the cuneiform Sumerian, in which, under the name *gestin,* they are included in the diet of Enkidu, a friend of Gilgamesh in the epic of that name. This could not have been later than 3000 B.C., but we have evidence of the existence of apparently cultivated grapes a thousand years earlier than this, not written, but painted on Egyptian tombs. We know that grapes were being cultivated in ancient Egypt some time later (and in the hanging gardens of Babylon too); the tomb of Tutankhamun (about 1350 B.C.) contained a jar marked "unfermented grape juice," unfortunately too far gone to be sampled. The Bible, as everyone knows, is full of references to grapes.

Grape seeds have been found in Bronze Age excavations in Greece, where the vine was being cultivated at least by 1700 B.C. if archeologists are right in reporting that it was at this time that it was introduced into Argos via Mycenae. Special varieties were being cultivated for the table in Greece at least by the first century B.C., and the Romans, who may have obtained their first grapes from Sicily, where the Greeks had planted them, followed their example. Dessert grapes were extremely popular in Rome, and were even stored for the winter, most easily in the form of raisins. The Romans also imported grapes primarily for eating, notably from Málaga. They are credited with having introduced grapes into northern Europe, which may well be true for England, but the claim is more dubious for France, where they are supposed to have planted vines in the Burgundy and Bordeaux regions and along the Rhine. It is reported contradictorily that it was the Phoenicians or the Greeks, both of whom preceded the Romans, who gave France the grape, while another account says that grapevines were brought back from Italy by the Gauls themselves, after the invasion during which, according to legend, they would have captured Rome itself if it had not been for the Capitoline geese.

Grapes, however they got there, were highly appreciated in France, where Richard the Lion-Hearted, not yet King of England but only a French noble, the Duke of Guienne, ordered that the theft of a bunch of grapes should be punished by a fine of five sous or the loss of an ear, whichever, one supposes, the thief could best afford to lose. It is not certain whether Richard thought of the grape primarily as a food or as the basis for wine, but the story goes that a later notable of France, Francis I, had his interest in the fruit kindled when he first tasted one and discovered that it was good for something other than drink. Guides may tell you that the famous trellis at the Château of Fontainebleau was planted by Francis himself, but actually it dates from two centuries later.

What Francis may have done was to introduce into this region the grape grown at Fontainebleau, the Chasselas Doré, still one of the finest table grapes of the world. The Chasselas is sometimes described as Burgundian, because there is a town of that name (which grows no Chasselas grapes) in Burgundy; it seems likelier that the grapes came from Cahors. Thoméry, about five miles from Fontainebleau, is the capital of the Chasselas, whose cultivation occupies a quarter of the town's population, which grows them on espaliers covering two hundred miles of walls and ripens them in chambers of controlled temperature and humidity, their cut stalks immersed in tanks of frequently changed water to which charcoal has been added. Within the memory of persons still living, there was, in Samoreau, two or three miles from Thoméry, a trellis which *was* perhaps planted at the order of Francis I, between 1531 and 1533, but it bore a different variety of grape; all trace of it has now disappeared. The oldest existing French vine is probably at Moissac, and dates from the first half of the eighteenth century; it is of the Chasselas Doré variety too.

The oldest and also the most famous grapevine in England is the Great Vine of Hampton Court, planted in 1768 by "Capability" Brown, landscape gardener to George III. Its main bole, measured in 1957, was then 81 inches around, and the main branch 114 feet long. It used to bear 2000 bunches of Black Hambro (no doubt a shortening of Black Hamburgh, a much-grown variety) dessert grapes, but it was decided to trim away all except 650 bunches every year to maintain the plant's vigor. But 2000 bunches a year were allowed to grow on a vine at Kippen, Stirlingshire, which, it is claimed, is not only the largest in England, but in the world. I do not have its measurements.

The most expensive commercially grown grapes are no doubt the hothouse product of Belgium, which developed this culture through the accident that it was the only country with enough surplus coal to heat the thousands of greenhouses which you will encounter if you do any exploring in the regions around Brussels. The green to dark purple spherical or tear-shaped grapes are nursed along by cutting all slow-developing or defective grapes from the bunches, permitting the others to grow larger. They are picked and handled with the greatest care in order not to dislodge the fine silvery dust which powders their skins, are packed delicately in cotton batting, and are sold at staggering prices in luxury food shops. No country has surplus coal now, nor any other fuel to spare, while the land labor required to produce the grapes has become prohibitively dear. As a result, these aristocratic grapes are being priced out of the market and are gradually disappearing.

Of the approximately 8000 varieties of grapes, natural and cultivars, as artificially created varieties are called, all those of the Old World have developed from a single species, *Vitis vinifera*. This is the wine grape par excellence, but it has been developed to produce many fine table grapes. When America was discovered, about forty new species were added. The colonists of the Northeast called them "fox grapes," which is usually explained by a certain muskiness in their taste (which accounted for the richness of pre-war grape juice, seldom encountered now, since most grape juice is made in California from V. *vinifera* grapes), but which in the minds of our ancestors seems simply to have been another way of saying "wild grapes." These native American grapes refuse to flourish west of the Rockies, while V. *vinifera*, imported from Europe, the basis of the California grape industry, will not grow east of them. (Thomas Jefferson was among the persons who tried to raise V. *vinifera* in the East and failed.) The native American grapes differ between the North, where V. *labrusca*, a slip-skin variety, is perhaps the most important, and the South, which produces muscadines, like V. *rotundifolia*, which has given us the scuppernong. The

GRAPE by Severin Roesen (1815/20–c.1872). *Still Life with Watermelon*, oil on canvas

Northern grapes have often been crossed with types of *V. vinifera,* producing such well-known varieties as the Catawba, the Concord and the Delaware. The Eastern grapes are primarily eating grapes, and are usually available only locally; 92 percent of all the table grapes consumed in the United States come from California and are varieties of *V. vinifera.*

The use of grapes for beverages—juice, wine, brandy—does not concern us here; but the vine provides foods other than the dessert grape. The most obvious is the raisin, the dried grape sometimes called the currant because the best of the ancient world came from Corinth. Raisins were probably first produced deliberately in Asia Minor by the simple process of burying fresh grapes in hot desert sand. Raisins might be described as concentrated grapes, for drying removes only the water, leaving the other constituents of the fruit practically intact, particularly the sugar.

Grape sugar was of great importance in ancient times; it was the only practical and easily obtainable sweetener the Romans possessed, except honey. The situation remained the same for Europe during the Dark Ages, until the Crusaders opened up the Near East and cane sugar became an article of commerce. (In India during the Middle Ages grape sugar was considered a kind of honey, which was defined as "that made by bees and the juice of grapes.")

A common by-product in the Middle Ages was verjuice, the juice of unripe grapes, used, for instance, to lend tartness to sauces—hardly an innovation, for the ancient Egyptians served verjuice sauce with fish. Verjuice is still called for in some recipes, but, except in the Near East, the prescription is seldom filled; it is easier to substitute lemon juice, as Europeans have been doing ever since the Crusaders restored to that continent the lemon which had disappeared from it with the collapse of the Roman Empire.

Grape leaves are eminently edible, but only when they are young and still tender. Even then they are too tough to be used raw in salads, but vine leaves stuffed with various fillings, mostly based on rice, and then cooked to succulence are met with everywhere in a crescent running from Greece and Rumania through Asia Minor and on into North Africa. In the West, small birds—quail, for instance—are sometimes wrapped in grape leaves for cooking, giving them added flavor.

Even grape seeds may be used for food. When French cheese is studded thickly with a protective armor of grape seeds, it is probable that they are meant for decoration rather than for eating; but oil is sometimes pressed from the seeds and used in cooking.

The grape nowadays is grown everywhere throughout the world in all but the coldest stretches of both north and south temperate zones. It is classified as one of the five most important fruits eaten by man in Volume 11 of the *Encyclopaedia Britannica* and as one of the four most important in Volume 9 of the same work. It is thus precious in one sense, but not sufficiently precious in another (unless it comes from a Belgian hothouse) to justify the line pronounced by Mae West in *She Done Him Wrong*: "Beulah, peel me a grape."

GRAPEFRUIT. The grapefruit is perhaps unique in being a new species—not simply a new variety or a hybrid, but a full-fledged species—which appeared in America after its colonization by Europeans. To make it all the more surprising, it belongs to a group of fruits, the citruses, which was not represented in the New World at all until settlers from the Old World brought them there. The grapefruit is not yet two hundred years old, an infant in a world where most commonly eaten foods count their ages in millennia. In spite of the fact that the birth of the grapefruit took place under the eyes of a society already well versed in botany, its origin is a mystery; and most of those who have written about it have failed to throw much light on the subject because they have become lost among three names which appear in it—pummelo (or pomelo), shaddock and grapefruit itself.

The first intimation the world received of the existence of the grapefruit was provided by John Lunan, in his *Hortus Jamaicensis*, in which he reported that there was a new fruit in Jamaica which tasted like a grape. This is probably the origin of the name "grapefruit." Grapefruit does not taste like grapes, so subsequent authors produced an alternative explanation: that the name comes from the circumstance that grapefruit grow in clusters like grapes, a theory which has worked its way into most dictionaries. It happens that grapefruit do not grow in grapelike bunches, except in the minds of persons endowed with flexible imaginations or obsessed by a need to introduce human logic into nature; if individual fruits sometimes grow very close together, producing in this case a clusterlike effect, it is because the tree bears heavily, ripening up to thirty or forty fruits on a single branch.

After some hesitation the grapefruit was accepted in 1830 as a genuine species and gratified with the name *Citrus paradisi*. Its place of birth seems to have been Jamaica, certainly not any of the regions where the other citrus fruits originated—China, Malaysia, Indonesia, perhaps even the Pacific islands—where diligent research has failed to find grapefruit. How did it happen that this fruit first appeared in Jamaica?

There are two theories: one, that it was created on this island by a natural cross between two other citrus species which had been brought to the New World; the other (which seems to me the more probable), that it arose by mutation. In the first case one of its parents, and in the second its only parent, was most probably a fruit believed native to Malaysia or Indonesia, though it was first mentioned in China by I Yin about 1500 B.C. It is known by various forms of the word "pummelo" (which in the spelling "pomelo" is used in some places today, including, occasionally, England, to mean the grapefruit), a name supposed to have come from the Dutch *pompelmoes* (transmuted to *pamplemousse* in today's French and *Pampelmuse* in German), usually translated as "big lemon," though what strikes me as a sounder authority makes it "melon-lemon." Pummelo seeds, according to Sir Hans Sloane, writing in 1707, were brought to Barbados in 1696 by an East Indian trader, Captain Shaddock, about whom nothing else is known, and for this reason was there called the shaddock. A link is missing in the story here, for the grapefruit did not appear in Barbados but in Jamaica; possibly birds carried seeds from one island to the other.

Some writers seem to assume that the pummelo and the shaddock are two different fruits; in all probability, these are simply two different names for *C. grandis* or *C. maxima*, depending on which system of taxonomy you patronize. The pummelo-shaddock is, in fact, as these tags suggest, the largest of citrus fruits. This was no doubt the fruit Richard Osborn Cummings misnamed in *The American and His Food* (1940) when he wrote: "The grapefruit . . . was 'not much admired' and called by some 'forbidden fruit,' the shaddock or pomelo." The pummelo, though it has a pungent, slightly acid but rather agreeable flavor, cannot compete with the grapefruit: it is rather coarse in comparison, too bitter to be eaten fresh without heavy dosing with sugar and therefore found oftenest in jam and other preserves, and, according to one overcritical American gardening encyclopedia, "thick-skinned and worthless."

Nature unaided endowed the grapefruit with qualities which human horticulturists would no doubt have tried to give it if they had been its creators. It comes into bearing early, producing commercially profitable crops four to six years after planting; it gives heavy yields (1300 to 1500 pounds per tree); it requires comparatively little care (in the matter of pruning, for instance); it can survive a moderate, if brief, amount of frost

GRAPEFRUIT *by Joanne Klein.* Still Life: Grapefruit and Two Oranges, *oil on masonite, 1979*

(indeed, trees growing where there is some seasonal variation in temperature give better-tasting fruit than those in less variable climates); it is more resistant to wind than most other citruses; it shows wider adaptation to different types of soil, succeeding better than its fellows in the tropics and in deserts (one of the tastiest varieties of grapefruit in the world is grown at El Golea, in the Sahara Desert, but is unfortunately too thin-skinned to be shipped elsewhere). These qualities more than offset the fact that the grapefruit is sensitive to alkali and requires somewhat more water than, for instance, the orange, since the tree which bears it is larger, twenty to forty feet high.

The superior taste of the grapefruit tends to drive out the pummelo wherever the former has been transplanted on the territory of its ancestor. Africa grows both the pummelo, there called either the pomelo or the shaddock, and the grapefruit, given either that name or, confusingly, pomelo also. The pummelo, probably there first, is now less popular, while grapefruit is consumed widely and has spread to Madagascar, where the pummelo seems to be unknown. Grapefruit is now grown in the Mediterranean basin, but does not attain the same quality there as in its native Western Hemisphere, so 90 percent of the world's grapefruit is produced in the United States, in California, Florida, Texas and Arizona. The chief variety is the Marsh Seedless, which has some seeds; but no citrus fruits are entirely seedless: in the trade "seedless" means not more than five seeds per fruit. Texas grows pink grapefruit, for instance the Thompson Seedless, whose juice is yellow, like that of all pink grapefruit except the Florida Burgundy. Some people profess to find the pink variety sweeter, but personally its taste seems to me to be only more pallid. I suspect that pink grapefruit was developed solely to satisfy the somewhat infantile predilection of Americans for color, preferably unsubtle, in their foods, a peculiarity which accounts for the production in France of pink champagne, for the Anglo-Saxon trade only, by vintners who are likely to deny all knowledge of such a product if taxed on their home grounds with making it. Half of the American grapefruit crop is processed, to be marketed as juice or canned fruit segments. As is the case for the orange, Florida grapefruit (like the Florida Duncan) is better for juice, California grapefruit for eating fresh; this probably is a result of the relative rainfall.

The grapefruit was slow in gaining popular acceptance. Commercial cultivation began in Florida only in 1890, sixty years after the species had been recognized. Grapefruit today is the second most important citrus fruit in the world, after the orange, but it did not become common in Europe until after the Second World War, and even in the United States not until after the First. It gained familiarity during the depression which followed the stock market crash of 1929, because citrus fruits, including grapefruit, could be had free for orange food stamps (their color and the name of the chief citrus fruit was only a coincidence). This brought the fruit into families which had previously been so ignorant of it that welfare boards received the same complaint from a number of housewives: they had boiled grapefruit for hours and it still remained tough.

GRE
stands for

the **great auk**, sufficiently good to eat so that pothunters went to the trouble of exterminating it; for the **greater weever**, an edible fish found in the Mediterranean called "weever," derived from "viper," because of its unamiable habit of burying itself in the sand, sharp back fin up, waiting for a bare foot to tread upon it; for the **great skua**, an athletic shore bird which is better as a flyer than a fryer; for the **great Washington clam**, an outsize mollusk also referred to as the big-neck, gaper, horse clam, ottershell, rubberneck or summer clam; for the **green abalone**, which is reddish brown, and the **green amaranth**, which is called the redroot; for the **greenbrier**, edible enough to tempt wild-food enthusiasts to gather it despite prickles so vicious that it has been nicknamed the blaspheme vine; and for the bellicose **green crab**, which uses its claws as fiercely as the greenbrier uses its spines; for the **green fleabane**, whose name suggests danger, but the ancient Romans used it in salads; for the **green gram**, or mung bean, from which the Chinese produce bean sprouts; for the **Greenland turbot**, whose superior flavor is attributed to the coldness of the waters in which it lives; for the **green mango**, which, disdaining the example of the green abalone and the green amaranth, is unblushingly green; for the **green monkey**, eaten without a qualm in tropical West Africa; for **green pepper**, which is, as you might expect, unripe black PEPPER, possessed of the endearing charms of youth, though it escaped notice until a famous Paris food shop exploited it, when it suddenly began to appear on everything except ice cream; for the **greenshank**, one of the largest of the sandpipers, along with its close relative, the redshank; for the **green turtle**, once so plentiful in the Gulf of Mexico that it was known as "the buffalo of the Caribbean"; and for the **green urchin**, a sea creature referred to by its intimates as *Strongylocentrotus drobachiensis* for short.

GRI
stands for

the **griffin**, which, being mythical, should make fabulous eating; for **grilse**, young salmon returning to fresh waters from the sea for the first time; for the **Grimes Golden**, a Virginia yellow apple with a tart, spicy flavor, much liked in the South, now apparently on its way out because it does not keep well enough to please supermarkets; for the **grive**, whose delicacy is so highly praised in France that it is referred to by its French name everywhere in the world, including Anglo-Saxon countries, which perhaps prefer not to think about eating thrush; for the **grivet**, so closely related to the green monkey that it too is no doubt eaten by Africans who make no fine distinction between *Cercopithecus aethiopa* and *C. aethiopa sabacus*; and for the **grizzly bear**, which can be eaten by man and vice versa.

GRO
stands for

groats, cracked wheat, one of the few foods cherished both in Scotland and the Near East; for **gromwell**, a seed which disappeared from the spice cupboard after the thirteenth century; for the **Gros Michel**, a banana which dominated the world market for many years, but is now giving way, in the United States at least, to a variety more resistant to the stresses of commerce; for the **ground bean,** eaten by tropical Africans if they are quick enough to get to it before the weevils; for the **ground cherry,** of which one variety may be familiar to you as the Chinese lantern, often found in dried flower arrangements and, though it doesn't look it, is good to eat; for the **groundhog,** good to eat too, but seldom included in dried flower arrangements; for the **ground holly,** which is wintergreen, and the **ground ivy,** which is Lizzie-run-in-the-hedge; for the **groundnut,** which is not sure what it is, but offers itself helpfully for human consumption whether in the guise of the Bambara nut, the Indian potato or the peanut; for **groundsel,** which in 1976 nipped in the bud the career of a new London food columnist who unfortunately introduced into her third newspaper article a suggestion that groundsel be added to salads, bringing down upon her head a flood of letters from botanists who informed her that groundsel is poisonous; for the **ground squirrel,** an agoraphobic animal which prefers to hide itself underground in burrows, or under liquid, in Brunswick stew; and for the **grouper,** a fish appreciated throughout the world, but nowhere more enthusiastically than in Valencia, where the opinion that lamb is the best food of the mountains and grouper the best of the sea is expressed in the saying: *De la mar el mero y del mont el cordero.*

And **GRO** also stands for

GROUSE. When in 1773 that ardent Scot James Boswell showed Dr. Johnson the sights of Edinburgh, he felt that the day should be ended with a meal worthy of the occasion. "We gave him," Boswell wrote, "as good a dinner as we could. Our Scotch muir-fowl, or grouse, were then abundant and quite in season." So Dr. Johnson ate moorfowl, alias red grouse, *Lagopus scoticus,* which all Britons, and especially all Scots, will tell you is the finest flavored of all grouse, or, for that matter, of all game birds. "Much prized in England," writes the Larousse gastronomic encyclopedia of the red grouse, "but less so in France." It goes against the grain to rate British judgment in gastronomic matters above that of France, but in this case I fear there is no alternative. One of my fondest memories of game is of a dinner in Paris featuring freshly killed *Lagopus scoticus,* with which my host had just flown over from London. When I discovered among the half-dozen guests the man whom I considered the greatest chef in Paris at the time, the late Georges Garin, I gave the host and hostess high marks for

GROUSE *by J.M.W. Turner (1775–1851).* Grouse Shooting, *watercolor*

courage. It was not every amateur who would have dared invite one of the greatest culinary artists among professionals to dinner. It turned out to be a case less of courage than of foresight. At the proper moment Garin disappeared into the kitchen and it was he who roasted the grouse, a whole bird for each guest. If there is any such thing as perfect meat, this was it, and there had been no nonsense about hanging it, a form of snobbishness particularly lamentable in the case of young birds, whose flavor is not improved by inviting them to rot, and which are already tender enough as nature has molded them. As for older birds, Scots in Boswell's time, and I hope still, did not even consider roasting them, but used them in soups called skinks.

The flavor of the various kinds of grouse, and of the red grouse in particular, is a happy balance between the suavity of domestic fowl and the rich tang of wild birds. Grouse do indeed resemble hens, with which they share many peculiarities of behavior: a matronly silhouette and, most important for their taste, the circumstance that they have become relatively ground-bound. Their terrestrial habits account for the fact that their meat is lighter in color than that of most game birds, in which the breast meat is dark because a rich blood supply is required by strong flyers. Grouse can fly fast, as every hunter knows, but only for short distances. They nest on the ground and find their food close to it, in seeds, berries and young plant shoots. Feed is a great shaper of flavor, so the groundling birds take on tastiness, especially on the Scottish moors, with their pungent herbs and spicy bays.

Some grouse, however, particularly those which spend more time in trees, acquire a hardly desirable resinous tinge from the pines they are apt to favor, particularly in central Europe, where snow may come early and lie deep, covering all food except the pine seeds, cones and needles on the trees. This taste occurs especially in wood grouse, *Tetrao urogallus,* hazel grouse, *Tetrastes bonasia,* and Canada spruce grouse, *Canachites canadensis.* But sometimes it is the hunter who is at fault: he has stalked his game so late in the season that the bird's diet for the last month or two has been the winter's fare of pine. In Scotland this is less likely to happen. The grouse season opens on August 12 —the "Glorious Twelfth," British hunters are apt to put it, pronouncing the words with capital letters and an exclamation point—and closes on December 10, a period when the birds have profited from varied feeding, especially as the climate there is insular rather than continental. Nevertheless, even in Scotland old birds living in or near pine woods may by accretion finally acquire a more or less permanent savor of resin. If you have to eat such old birds, or younger ones which taste of pine rather than heather, you can get rid of the resin, or most of it, by soaking them lengthily in milk before cooking.

"Grouse" is a term which covers a considerable number of birds characterized by the heavy bodies which recall the domestic hen, by feathered legs, by a fidelity to polygamy, by that habit of hugging the ground and, of course, by their perfumed flesh. They are all birds of the Northern Hemisphere, of which six genera are found in North America and four in Eurasia, while only one appears in both—the ptarmigan, since its habitat is a large circle with the North Pole for its center. Ptarmigan are birds of the *Lagopus* genus; hence Scotland's red grouse, *L. scoticus,* is a ptarmigan. This is presumably the bird which author-diplomat Harold Nicolson had in mind when he discoursed on the substantial character of English Sunday breakfasts in the reign of Edward VII:

> On a table to the right between the windows [he wrote, describing one of them] were grouped Hams, Tongues, Galantines, Cold Grouse, ditto Pheasant, ditto Partridge, ditto Ptarmigan. No Edwardian meal was complete without Ptarmigan. Hot or cold. Just Ptarmigan.

After the red grouse, the best-tasting ptarmigan is probably the willow ptarmigan, *L. lagopus,* plentiful in Alaska and found in the Old World too—the only bird of its genus of which the cock is reputed to help rear the chicks and even to take them in charge completely if the hen dies. The circumpolar ptarmigan is naturally the extreme example among grouse of adaptation to cold and snow. The white-tailed ptarmigan of western North America, *L. leucurus,* also called the snow grouse, shares this nickname with the rock ptarmigan (*L. mutus*), which Norway presents proudly as one of its finest foods; the two are much alike. The rock ptarmigan and the willow ptarmigan undergo three moults a year, which provide them with a camouflage always in harmony with the seasonally changing background, with all-white plumage in winter to render them almost invisible against snow. The scales of their feet develop lateral projections in winter, which act as snowshoes (this phenomenon occurs also in the eastern American ruffed grouse).

All grouse prefer cool climates, sticking either to the higher latitudes or to higher altitudes in lower latitudes, which, climatically, comes to much the same thing. This is why grouse were so rare in ancient Rome that they had to be imported in cages, as Varro tells us, fed on the way with wild fruit, birch catkins and juniper berries. The grouse the Romans ate was probably the hazel grouse, *Tetrastes bonasia,* which would explain why Hungarians called it "Caesar's bird." This seems to be the bird Alexandre Dumas had in mind when he wrote that it was the only game the feudal lords of Germany dared put before their guests for several meals in a row. This seems dubious, for the hazel grouse, though common, is rather weak in flavor. It seems likelier that the bird in question was the largest of the grouse tribe, the CAPERCAILLIE, alias the wood grouse, *Tetrao urogallus,* which is the one the French put ahead of the red grouse, giving to it the name *coq de bruyère,* "heather cock."

Another flavorful European grouse is the blackcock, *Lyrurus tetrix,* also called the black grouse or the black game, while the drabber female is the greyhen. A European grouse worthy of mention is the pin-tailed grouse, *Ganga cata,* which develops a delicate flavor when it feeds on the herbs and berries of southern France.

The tastiest American grouse is probably *Bonasa umbellus,* which the Northeast calls a partridge but which is more properly called the ruffed grouse (Louisiana calls quail "partridge"). One of the most famous American grouses owes its notoriety to the fact that it is extinct—the heath hen, *Tympanuchus cupido cupido,* of which the last sur-

GROUSE *by Louis Agassiz Fuertes (1874–1927), for American Wildlife Institute*

vivor died on Martha's Vineyard in 1923. The heath hen was an Eastern species, whose Western counterpart is *T. cupido americanus,* the prairie chicken or prairie hen, in some danger of following its relative into oblivion. A few prairie chickens are still clinging precariously to life, mostly in Texas, but there is justification for considering them an endangered species.

Diminishing in numbers also is the largest upland game bird of America (with the exception of the turkey), the sage grouse, *Centrocercus urophaesianus,* first seen by Lewis and Clark, who called it "cock of the plains." The bird and the sagebrush for which it is named live in a state of symbiosis: sagebrush is the principal food of the grouse, which pays for its nourishment during the spring courtship parade when it scratches up the soil around the plants so energetically as to till it, at the season when cultivation is most called for. The sage grouse's territory is now being diminished by cattle raisers who are trying to replace sagebrush with grass, probably unwisely, for land that grows sagebrush is ill-suited for pasturage.

Other American grouse include the Canada spruce grouse, which may be suspected of having reached its present territory from northeastern China, whose sharp-winged grouse, *Falcipennis falcipennis,* much resembles it, and its smaller relative, Franklin's grouse, *Canachites franklini,* also called the fool hen because of its nonchalant unwariness; the Sierra grouse is just the contrary, a bird difficult to approach (and another one which is apt to pick up a resinous flavor in winter). The blue grouse is the one known to hunters as the sooty grouse.

The reputation of the grouse, of whatever species, as one of the finest foods of its type has so impressed Australians that they use the word "grouse" slangily to signify anything that is great, excellent or wonderful.

GRU
stands for

grubs, which according to Pliny were fattened on flour for the tables of ancient Roman gourmets; for the **grunion,** a worthy food fish which leaves the water to lay its eggs in the sand; and for the **grunt,** a worthy food fish so little disposed to leave the water that when removed from it, it makes the protesting noise which accounts for its name.

GU
stands for

guaiacum, also known as lignum vitae, "wood of life," whose gum when chewed lights a small fire in the throat, but is added to lard all the same; for **guajillo,** a shrub found in the southwestern United States which is an important source of honey; for the **guan,** a bird of tropical South America which so much suggests chicken that several attempts have been made to domesticate it, all unsuccessful; for the **guanabana,** better known as the soursop; for the **guanaco,** eaten wild by the Incas and by Charles Darwin; for the **gudgeon,** a small fish which is, depending on whose opinion you solicit, either (a) "sweet, tender, delicate, delightfully tasty, wholesome" or (b) "fit only for bait to catch better fishes"; for the **guelder-rose,** which is the highbush cranberry; for the **guenon,** a long-tailed African monkey relished by the Africans who share its habitat, and the **guereza,** a long-tailed Ethiopian monkey which does not seem to enjoy the same popularity; for the **Guernsey,** a breed of cattle developed on the island of the same name, whose milk contains so much butterfat that it is yellow; for the **guero,** a mild yellowish-green chili much used in Californian-Mexican cooking; for the **guillemot,** a member of the auk family which, unlike the great auk, has not appealed to the palate sufficiently to have been rendered extinct; for **Guinea corn,** a somewhat disdainful name for sorghum; for **Guinea pepper,** made from the seeds of a plant related to cardamom; for **guinea-hen weed,** served with mutton in Jamaica despite the arbitrary dictum of a critic who wrote, "Avoid this altogether" because of its "detestable taste"; for the **guitarfish,** which the French and Italians, not to be outdone, call the violin fish; for the **Gulf blue crab,** the only crab of edible size in the Gulf of California; for the **gull,** served on the best tables in the time of Henry VIII; for **gum,** of which several kinds enter into food, though tangentially; for **gumbo,** a synonym of African origin for okra; for the **gum boot,** or giant sea cradle, the largest mollusk of the group known as chitons, once eaten by West Coast Indians and the Russians who first settled Alaska; for **gum-jum** ("golden needles") and **gum-tsoy** ("golden vegetable"), dried day-lily flowers which in the Far East are added to soups; for the **gurnard,** or sea robin, of which some varieties have a better reputation for food nowadays than that given them by Falstaff when he said, "If I be not ashamed of my soldiers, I am a soused [pickled] gurnet"; and for **gutta percha,** used in golf balls and chewing gum.

And **GU** also stands for

GUAVA. On the Molucca Islands, reported Antonio Pigafetta, chronicler of the Magellan expedition, the explorers found a fruit "resembling the peach and called *guau* (guava)." The anonymous translator who inserted the word "guava" parenthetically in this passage was presumably not a botanist. The guava, a fruit native to tropical America, had been seen by nobody except American Indians before the time when the Arawaks served some to Christopher Columbus in the Caribbean. Guavas are quick spreaders, but not quick enough so that a fruit first seen by Columbus (on his landfall in the West Indies, 1492) would have been likely to arrive before Magellan (departure on the world's first globe-girdling voyage, 1519) in the Moluccas, pretty much unknown themselves at the time. Even the name of the fruit did not reach Europe until the middle of the sixteenth century.

There are approximately 150 species of guava, all of which originated in tropical America. They belong to the genus *Psidium,* Greek for "pomegranate," probably so named because the many small hard seeds enclosed by the pulp recall the pomegranate. The French Academy of Gastronomes compares the guava instead to the quince, since both have forbidding aspects: the quince is too acid to eat fresh; the guava, while its flesh is sweet, gives off a musky, sometimes pungent odor which is not relished by everybody. The guava's seeds are also disconcerting, rasping the throat like sand. As a result, guavas are often eaten stewed, a process which detaches the seeds and makes them more manageable, or in the form of preserves, jam, jelly and especially the semi-solid guava paste, of gelatin-like consistency, but nevertheless firm enough to be cut with a knife. Guava paste is exported throughout the world from several Caribbean islands.

On its home grounds, the guava is an important and popular fruit, often eaten fresh from the hand, sometimes together with hard dry goat cheese, which may distract attention from the seeds; or sliced and served as a dessert with sugar and milk; or, when eaten as preserves, accompanied by cream cheese.

Improved modern varieties have been developed which have banished most of the seeds, making it necessary to reproduce the small trees or large shrubs of the guava by grafting, instead

GUAVA. Plate from Manuel Blanco: *La Flora de Filipinas, Manila,* 1877–83

of planting the seeds, which is nature's sometimes too successful way: the wild plant is prolific and in some regions spreads so abundantly as to become a pest. When the guava was introduced into the Hawaiian Islands it went berserk and choked out several native Hawaiian plants. In southern India, where it was also transplanted, it was kept under better control, and is a much appreciated fruit there today, used especially in chutneys.

Guavas were probably already being cultivated in what archeologists call the Formative Period of Peruvian agriculture—the last seven and a half centuries before our era. The common guava, *P. guajava,* produces round to pear-shaped fruits, sometimes reaching three inches in diameter, but this is exceptional. It is sensitive to frost, and can be grown commercially in the United States only in southern Florida. *P. cattleianum,* the strawberry guava, so called because some people detect in it a taste similar to that of the strawberry, bears smaller round fruit and is a trifle hardier. Though this one is also raised for the market only in southern Florida, it is sometimes planted in private gardens in southern California; it has no commercial importance there. Another variety of this guava, instead of its customary reddish fruits, produces bright yellow ones, which has impelled some botanists to recognize it as a separate species, to which they have given the name of *P. lucidum.*

No other guavas are of more than local importance, including the Brazilian guava, *P. guineense,* so named in the mistaken belief that it was a native of Africa. As several species of guava, especially the strawberry guava, are grown in Africa today, we may suspect that it was the Portuguese who transferred them in the sixteenth century from their Brazilian territories to their African territories, thus mixing up the nomenclature, as they did with a number of other foods—for instance, the South American musk duck, which thus acquired the misleading name "Barbary duck." Two other species eaten on their home grounds strike most outsiders as too faint of flavor to justify putting up with their excessive acidity, *P. friedrichsthalianum,* called the *cás* in Costa Rica, and *P. molle,* the *guisaro.*

Guavas are rich in minerals, while some species boast a higher vitamin C content even than citrus fruits. They are healthful for those who eat them, and healthy themselves, for they are all but immune to insect pests and plant diseases. They are less well armed against birds, if we accept the theory that Gandhi was usefully employed when, as a child, he wrapped a cloth around each of the fruits on the family guava tree, explaining that he was protecting them from the birds. Possibly this story should be ascribed less to history than to hagiography.

GUINEA FOWL. Ever since our poultry raisers succeeded in taking the taste out of turkey, the most flavorful bird of the barnyard has been the guinea fowl. This is perhaps because the guinea, though it lives on farms, has not resigned itself to being domesticated, and has consequently not completely lost the dark flesh of wild birds and their gamey taste; it is frequently compared with pheasant.

As everyone who has raised guineas (I have) knows, they are virtually wild animals. They like to roost on the topmost branches of the tallest trees, and display no interest in coming down to be killed for dinner or for the market. They descend when grain is offered, but remain so wary that it is difficult to approach them; one suspicious movement from the farmer, and the whole flock is off. They can get along without his grain, for guineas are perfectly capable of foraging for themselves. Their acceptance of foods is wide, ranging from ants' eggs, for which they will tear anthills open, to carrion. A French nature writer has reported seeing several guineas devouring, vulture-like, a large dead fox; and indeed guineas, with their bare unfeathered heads, do seem at times to resemble vultures; there is even an East African species called *Acryllium vulturinum.*

Guinea fowl. *Print from Brehm:* Tierleben, *Leipzig, 1911*

One way of dealing with the difficulty of killing guineas is that which is sometimes utilized in southwestern France, shooting them down from their trees, but this is hardly practical for anyone handling guineas on a large scale; you bag one, and that is the last you see of the others for several days. Another solution is to keep them caged (in a cage the size of a small aviary, for they require space); but they will not lay in confinement, though they do so prolifically when free. Unlike many wild birds, which produce only one clutch a year, guinea hens lay continuously from May until cold weather sets in; but they do not lay in a fashion favorable to farmers. They hide their nests in hollows scratched out of the ground under bushes or other shelter where they are practically unfindable.

As though this were not enough to discourage the raising of guinea fowl, they are also irascible and noisy. They cow other barnyard birds, even turkeys, though turkeys are much larger, and keep up an incessant nerve-wracking screeching, which has been described as sounding like the noise made by a rusty windmill. This racket is said to have the advantage of making it possible to distinguish the cocks from the hens (their plumage is identical), for while one sex cries *pot-rack, pot-rack, pot-rack,* the other repeats *rack-pot, rack-pot, rack-pot*; but this means of identification has never worked for me.

One result of the guinea's self-serving savagery seems to be its freedom from disease, in striking contrast to poultry which has benefited from the tinkering of man, like chickens and turkeys, which are subject to an interminable list of diseases and sometimes seem to take positive pleasure in succumbing to them. Despite this lone advantage, the difficulties have discouraged most poultry raisers (among whom was Thomas Jefferson, who was fond of them), so that, except in France, almost nobody attempts to produce guineas for a mass market. They appear as luxuries in high-priced restaurants which buy them directly from small-scale producers who aim exclusively at such outlets. This accounts for the fact that very few new varieties have been developed by breeders, the most important being white guineas, which, like white turkeys, seem to have been created to cater to a popular delusion that whiteness, a symbol of purity, guarantees finer flavor.

In the days when Europeans were bestowing names on unfamiliar foods, any exotic product was apt to be ascribed more or less at random to any exotic locality, of which only a few, vaguely localized, were recognizable to the general public. The guinea fowl was an exception, identified correctly from the beginning as an African bird. Its origin is usually given as West Africa, which is, of course, where Guinea is located. The area is very probably the birthplace of *Numida meleagris galatea,* from which the imperfectly domesticated modern bird is supposed to have descended. Either this bird had acquired a wider range in classical times than is attributed to it now, or it was some other of the score of African species which the ancients, not given to fine nomenclatural distinctions, consumed. They had not adventured as far as Guinea, but they imported birds from North Africa. Greece, which knew them by 500 B.C., presumably received them from Egypt, the source of many of her foreign foods. Significantly, this bird is known in Italian today as *gallina faraona*, Pharaoh's hen; but the Romans, when the guinea hen became an appreciated item on upper-class menus, apparently preferred to bring them in from nearer regions of North Africa, for they called them Numidian hens or Carthaginian hens—except when the host was putting on the dog, for a wedding banquet, say, when they might appear under such fancy names as Phrygian chicken (used on one Pompeiian menu which has come down to us) or Bohemian chicken, even more impressive, since Bohemia in those days was exquisitely exotic, a place of which Romans had heard but had never seen.

The guinea fowl never got down to a common level in the ancient world, unlike the chicken, so when the Roman Empire disappeared, the guinea went with it. It does not seem to have reappeared until the sixteenth century, when merchants from Portugal, by then in control of Guinea, started selling them to France, where they were first called, *gyunettes* or *poules de Guinée* and then, incorrectly, *poules de Turquie* or *poules d'Inde*, a name transferred shortly thereafter, with equal inexactitude, to the American turkey. The French naturalist Pierre Belon wrote in 1555 that guinea fowls "had already so multiplied in the houses of the nobles that they had become quite common." This disposes of the often repeated assertion, by which, in the past, I have been taken in myself, that it was Catherine de' Medici who introduced the guinea hen to France; actually the bird reached there before the marrying Medicis did. That it was indeed the Portuguese who brought the bird to France is attested to by its name in French today, *pintade*, from the Portuguese *pintada*, "painted," or, in this case, "splotched," referring to the round spots which speckle the guinea's plumage. A Greek legend explained that the sisters of Meleager, son of the king of Calydon, were so grief-stricken when their brother died that they broke into uncontrollable weeping, which ended only when they were changed into guinea hens; the spots are their tears. Hence the ancient name *meleagris* for this bird, preserved by modern taxonomists in the scientific names given to many of its species.

The guinea hen was also appreciated in Italy in Renaissance times; from Africa and Europe it has now spread all over the world. The first to reach the Far East may have been those which Pierre Poivre took to Cochin-China when, in 1749, he was negotiating for the right to open a French trading counter there. Among the presents he gave the king of Cochin-China were some guinea fowl, which according to his account were at that time unknown there. In the New World, they seem to have appeared first in Haiti, probably imported along with slaves bought in Guinea. Live poultry was often taken aboard ships, to provide fresh food during long voyages; Africa could not have provided chickens in those days, but it could offer guineas. We may suppose that the surplus birds of the ship's stores, still alive at the end of the trip, were taken ashore.

I notice with a certain surprise that many writers describe the guinea fowl as ugly. Despite its vulturelike head, it has always struck me as a notably decorative bird. Some of its varieties are so handsomely patterned that I can imagine their having been designed by Van Gogh.

GUINEA PIG. If the guinea fowl provides a rare example of a geographically named food whose geography is correct, the guinea pig exemplifies a much commoner phenomenon—an exotic food decked out with an exotic place name which makes no sense. The guinea pig bears no relation to Guinea, in Africa, being a strictly American rodent, but when the exploring Spaniards encountered it they called it the Guinea pig because Guinea was shadowy, foreign and distant, and so was America. The French called it *cochon de Guinée* too, but quickly shifted to what is still its name today, *cochon d'Inde*, "pig of India," pretty far off the mark as well, unless they were still harboring the idea that the Spaniards had landed in Asia.

When the Spaniards reached the Andes, they found the Incas eating guinea pig, but it had already been domesticated in pre-Inca times in

GUINEA PIG. *Type shot:* cavia, *specimen prepared by David Schwendeman, 1960*

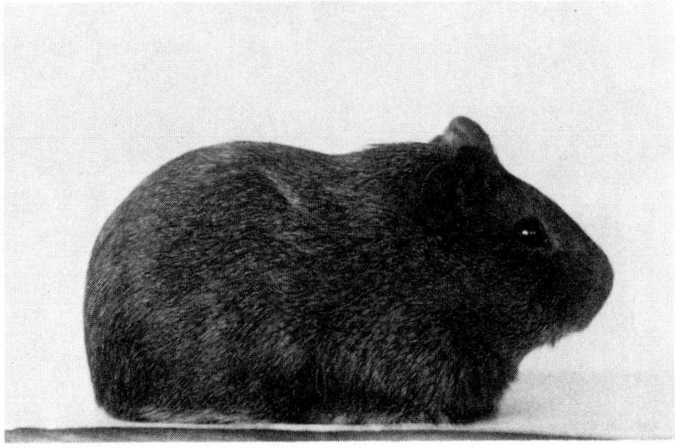

what are now Peru, Ecuador and Colombia. There was a shortage of animal protein in the Andes, so the guinea pig was appreciated there; but it is perhaps jumping to conclusions, as two American authors have done recently, to assert that the guinea pig was the main source of meat for the Incas (actually only one author made this assertion and the second copied him, giving himself away by reading the original so carelessly that he made a telltale mistake in repeating it). After all, the Incas, at the time when the Spaniards found them, had already domesticated the llama and the alpaca, rather larger bundles of meat than the guinea pig, and though the first was too valuable as a pack animal and the second as a provider of wool to be sacrificed young, they could still provide some rather tough chewing toward the end of their lives. In the meantime, communal hunts took their wild cousins, the guanaco and the vicuña, along with several other kinds of game, including another native rodent, larger than the guinea pig, the viscacha. The Incas are also believed to have domesticated ducks, but if not, they at least ate wild ones.

The guinea pig is a domesticated cavy. The progenitor of the tame species seems to have been the Peruvian *Cavia cutleri,* and the one which subsequently became most important for the table, *C. porcellus.* Encouraged by hungry Incas, the domesticated guinea pig learned how to produce two or three litters a year, with two to eight young in each litter, whereas the wild cavy had been able to give birth only once a year, and then to no more than one or two offspring.

Far from being revolted at the idea of eating guinea pigs, the Spaniards introduced them into Europe early in the sixteenth century, where they were at first considered a delicacy. Then the novelty palled, and Europe abandoned the new meat to go back to more familiar fare.

Guinea pig, under the name *cui* or *cuy,* is still an important food in Peru and Ecuador, where it is sometimes broiled and sometimes made into a rich ragout which has been compared with Germany's *Hasenpfeffer,* hare stew. It is apparently no longer eaten anywhere else, serving only as a pet or as a laboratory animal for medical and biological research, for which it provides a useful parallel to man because it shares with him (and with the Indian bulbul) a rare defect: unlike almost all other animals, it is incapable of converting sugars into vitamin C.

GY
stands for

gypsum, of which the correct proportion to be used in adulterating wheat flour is one-quarter gypsum to three-quarters flour, said Pliny the Elder.

H

HORACE: *Persian luxury, boy, I hate.*

HERRICK, ROBERT: *A little meat best fits a little belly.*

HAN FEI-TSE (third century): *The richness of a nation does not depend on the number of its inhabitants but on the quantity of food at their disposition.*

HA
stands for

Habañeros, Havanas, not cigars, but tiny bell-shaped red chilies which may strike inhabitants of temperate regions as almost unbearably hot, but are only run-of-the-mill in chili country; for **haberdin,** a word which may give you pause if you encounter it on a sixteenth-century menu, but it means nothing more exotic than dried salted codfish; for the **hackberry,** the very first fruit of its kind man is known to have picked; for **hag's taper,** our twelfth synonym for the mullein, and **hare's beard,** the thirteenth; for **hakusai,** a Japanese name for a Chinese cabbage; for the luscious **halawy date** of Persia and Iraq, where the first dates in the world probably grew; for the **halfbeak,** so called because its lower jaw is longer than the upper, a fish agreeably edible, but only in Africa is much advantage taken of this opportunity; for the **half-ware,** a three-year-old oyster; for **hamburgh parsley,** grown not for its leaves but its root; for the **hami melon,** an exceptionally sweet fruit of China; for the **hammerhead shark,** whose fine-grained flesh is most widely appreciated in Japan, but it has also been fished in Florida for the sake of the rich shark-liver oil; for the **hamster,** eaten occasionally in various parts of the world ever since prehistoric man started the practice in what is now Russia; for the **hapaku,** a grouper-like fish much fancied in New Zealand; for **harbinger-of-spring,** a prettily named relative of parsley; for the East Coast **hard clam,** more familiarly known to most of us as the QUAHOG, and the **hard cockle,** the West Coast's answer to the quahog; for the **harder,** a name given in Africa and Madagascar to certain fish of the mullet family; and for the **harpfish,** for which Archestratus gave us a recipe in what was probably the world's first cookbook, of little use today since nobody knows what a harpfish was (could it have been updated into the guitar-fish?).

HA stands for

the **hartebeeste,** a large ungainly antelope, eaten since prehistoric times and still on the menu in southern and tropical Africa wherever there are enough hartebeeste left; for **hartshorn,** powdered deer antlers, the medieval precursor of baking powder, which some German and Scandinavian cooks think they are still using, but the modern version is a counterfeit, ammonium carbonate; for **hart's-tongue,** a fern recommended as an aphrodisiac in 1542 in A *Dyetary of Helth* by Andrew Boorde, who had been a monk until he thought better of it; for the **hatchet clam** of the Gulf of California, of which only the muscle is eaten; for the **hatchetfish** of South American fresh waters, not the deep-sea hatchetfish, which is too remote from the dinner table; for the **Hausa groundnut,** or **Hausa potato,** of West Africa; for the **hautbois,** a wood strawberry which brandishes its fruit above its leaves instead of hiding them coyly beneath them, designated by the French word which means "oboe," since both, in somewhat different ways, are "high woods"; for the

Hawaiian duck, a fine-flavored descendant of the mallard, and the **Hawaiian goose,** a probable descendant of the Canada goose, which has become so terrestrial that it has lost some of the webbing from its feet and dislikes to swim; for the **hawfinch,** large for its kind, which dotes on green peas, making it unpopular with the gardener and popular with the gourmet; for the **hawksbill turtle,** whose meat is too strong for most tastes but whose eggs are much appreciated; for the **hawthorn,** whose wood, according to experts in such matters, is ideal for transfixing the hearts of vampires to discourage them from leaving their graves; for **haymaids,** which are, or is, ground ivy; and for **hazelwort,** a not very useful form of wild ginger which Charlemagne nevertheless ordered planted in his dominions.

And **HA** also stands for

HADDOCK. Alexandre Dumas, never reputed for understatement, seems to have outdone himself when he reported that the haddock reaches a length of 22 to 23 feet and a weight of over 150 pounds; the maximum figures I find anywhere else give a length of under 4 feet (even 3 feet is exceptional, says the *Encyclopaedia Britannica*) and a weight of 36 pounds. Even for Dumas, multiplication by five is a little over par, but he may have been closer to the mark when he asserted that in his time a boat manned by three fishermen could be filled with haddock twice a day within a mile of the English coast. This would be hard to do today. Haddock used to account for half the weight of fish taken by trawlers in the North Atlantic, but their numbers are rapidly diminishing. Nevertheless, this fish is holding out better than the cod, for which it is being substituted in English fish-and-chips shops, which prefer cod but can't get it. On the American side of the Atlantic, overfishing has taken a greater toll of haddock. Francis Higginson was amazed, in 1630, by the abundance of haddock off the Massachusetts coast, and until well into this century it was the favorite fish of New England, but what is served there as haddock now is more likely to be pollack. Off the New Jersey coast, once an important fish-breeding territory, haddock is now considered an endangered species.

Haddock has been an important food fish in northern Europe for longer than human memory holds; its bones have been found in kitchen middens dating from the Upper Paleolithic to the Iron Age. It was already being salted, dried or smoked in medieval times, when its unassertive flavor was intensified for the palates of an age which liked its foods exciting by some rather strange mixtures—for instance, dried haddock was made into a paste together with almonds, figs boiled in ale, dates and pears, which was then wrapped in dough and fried in oil. By the time of the Tudors, hucksters were filling their barrows with haddock at Billingsgate, the oldest market in England, and pushing them painfully up Fish Street Hill to hawk them through the streets of

HADDOCK. *Print from* Annual Report, *New York State Forest, Fish and Game Commission, 1907*

London. When England became conscious of Indian cuisine, it imported a dish of spiced rice and lentils called *khichri* in Hindi, and, wreaking mayhem on both the dish and its name, added to it, among other things, smoked haddock and hard-boiled eggs, called it kedgeree, and installed it on the British breakfast menu.

The range of the haddock, a fish which likes cold water, starts around Iceland, with one important breeding ground off that island and another in the North Sea, from which it branches down both coasts: on the west, along Newfoundland and New England, it once got as far as Cape Hatteras, but seems to be petering out now before it gets there; on the east, from the important fisheries off the Skagerrak, the Faeroe Islands, northwest Scotland and Ireland, it moves southward through the English Channel, diminishing in numbers as it advances towards the Bay of Biscay. It does not get into the Mediterranean; the fish called the Jerusalem haddock in Africa is not a haddock, but the opah, the sunfish or the kingfish (the last two names are shared with several others), *Lampris regius*. The haddock is *Melanogrammus aeglefinus*, a member of the *Gadidae*, the cod family. It is much like the cod, but can easily be distinguished from it by the dark patch on either side, behind the gills and below the backbone—St. Peter's thumbprints. St. Peter got around. A number of different fish bear similar marks, all explained by one version or another of a legend according to which St. Peter caught a fish and then tossed it back into the water, branded for all posterity with his signature.

Haddock are excellent fresh, and are so eaten wherever they are taken. New England used to bake the fish, or cut it into chunks for fish chowder. Straight off the boat, haddock is eaten in England with the simplest of sauces; in Norway it goes into fish pudding, ground and shaped into a loaf and served under a rosy shrimp sauce. It was presumably fresh haddock which provided a proud success for the express industry when this new business succeeded in 1852 in shipping haddock on ice from Boston by rail to Buffalo and by lake steamer to Chicago, to be sold there a few days after being landed in New England.

However, the great majority of haddock is eaten smoked, a process which changes not only its nature, but its name. In France, where fresh haddock is *aiglefin*, sometimes spelled *églefin* (or even, by mistake, *aigrefin*, which means a sharp dealer), it is called haddock when smoked. One assumes it acquires the British name with the British (or more exactly, Scottish) process, in part because the French don't really know what fresh *aiglefin* is; at least their reference books don't. In English, smoked haddock is likely to be called finnan haddie, a name eroded from "Findon haddock," Findon being the place where, according to a story which may or may not be true, the virtues of smoking haddock were discovered accidentally when a warehouse full of salted haddock caught fire. Some food writers, and at least one respected American dictionary, give the name of the birthplace of finnan haddie as Findhorn, which I judge to be an error. There *is* a Findhorn in Scottish haddock territory, on the north coast, but it is the east side of northern Scotland which could really be called the Haddock Coast. Here Findon, too small to get on the maps, lies in Kincardine County, bounded on the north by Aberdeen County, containing Aberdeen, reputed to provide the best haddock in the world, and on the south by Angus County, containing Arbroath, reputed to produce the most delicious smokies in the world. Smokies, which Aberdeen makes also, are hot-smoked haddock—already cooked by their intensive smoking, so you can eat them as you buy them, though of course you can warm them up if you so prefer. Most other kinds are cold-smoked (but Germany makes hot-smoked haddock only), and the acme of the art of cold-smoking is to smoke the fish as lightly as possible. This leaves them with a fresher flavor (tinged in Aberdeen with the memory of the ocean when the smoking is done over seaweed), but they do not keep long and must be eaten soon after they are bought. They generally receive further cooking, though perhaps this is not necessary; haddock can be eaten raw if you like, so no doubt smoked haddock could be too.

To make sure of getting the real thing when you buy smoked haddock, don't let yourself be led astray by color. The genuine article has a dull surface, rather pale; but the markets nowadays bewilder one with "golden cutlets," which might be haddock but are likelier to be dyed whiting; the smoky taste is added with chemicals.

The male haddock, a romantic creature, hums gently to the female as they mate.

HAKE. "What have we here?" asked Trinculo in *The Tempest* when he came upon Caliban cowering on the beach. "A man? or a fish? dead or alive? A fish! He smells like a fish—a very ancient and fish-like smell—a kind of, not of the newest, poor-john."

To the nostrils of Trinculo—a gourmet, no doubt—Caliban did not smell like just any aging fish, but like a specific aging fish—the hake. "Poor-john" was the name given in Shakespeare's time to dried salted hake because it was the cheapest of all fish. It might be called poor in

HAKE. *Print from* Annual Report, *New York State Forest, Fish and Game Commission, 1907*

another sense also, but a sense in which poverty can be a virtue: it has the least fat of all commonly eaten fish, along with the sole, so digestible that it can be given to infants from the age of fifteen months. The flesh is tender, white and flaky; but it does not keep well, which explains why it has not been more energetically exploited. The part that spoils first is a long transparent, gelatinous segment of the throat, which is therefore usually cut out immediately after the fish is taken, before it is sent to market. It is often thrown away, but not on the Spanish Basque coast, where this morsel is considered the choicest part of the fish. Called *kokotxas* in Basque, it is sold separately in the early-morning fish markets when the boats come in from overnight fishing (hake feed only at night); and if cash is short, fishermen may sometimes be paid off in *kokotxas*, which can be swiftly sold.

One of the codlike fishes, the hake, genus *Merluccius*, is exceptional in being the only important member of this group found in both the Northern and Southern Hemispheres, and also in the Mediterranean, where it is an important food fish, especially popular in Spain, Italy and Yugoslavia. Temperature sets up some of the most difficult barriers for fish to cross; no other member of this family, which inhabits cool waters, is capable of crossing the equator, or even of getting into the Mediterranean. (Some Mediterranean fish are misnamed there, as though they belonged to the cod group, but they are impostors.) There is misnaming in the United States too, where the small (two to five pounds) silver hake is genuine (it is *M. bilinearis*), but the so-called white hake and squirrel hake are not. Both belong to the *Phycis* genus, whose fish the English call forkbeards because the first ventral fin, which starts just under the chin, has been reduced to two long, trailing filaments. The name "hake" is also sometimes given in the United States to the northern whiting, *Menticirrhus sexatilis*. Erring in the other direction, Americans sometimes apply the name "codling," which should mean a young cod, to hake, probably because hake are smaller than cods.

There are also genuine hakes on the Pacific coast of North America and of South America from Chile to Patagonia; off New Zealand; and in the waters of South Africa, the country where the hake is most intensively exploited. Here it is called the stockfish, confusingly, for everywhere else this means dried unsalted cod; but it is a genuine hake, *M. capensis*. Hake as well as cod are often preserved in stockfish fashion too, so the South African adoption of this name may be taken as an anticipation of the hake's destiny, so treated to ready it for export; the hake is the most valuable commercial fish in this area. The South African species is probably the largest of the hakes, for it reaches a length of four feet, about a third more than the limit for most others.

The second most important hake fisheries in the world are those of Europe, which take the typical member of the genus, *M. merluccius*, the European hake. It is now showing signs of having been overfished.

Hake are voracious beasts, well armed for their business: their large mouths contain unusually sharp teeth, hinged to bend backward to let prey in, after which they snap back to an erect position, preventing escape. Cannibalistic fish are not uncommon, but the hake rather overdoes it; 21 percent of its food intake is composed of smaller hake. Though they are deep-water fish, hake are sometimes seen pursuing other fish into the shoals, for instance herring; hence the English saying: "What we gain in hake, we lose in herring."

HARE. Charles Lamb, in his essay in the series *Popular Fallacies, That the Worst Puns Are the Best,* offers this example: "An Oxford scholar, meeting a porter who was carrying a hare through the streets, accosts him with this extraordinary question: 'Prithee, friend, is that thy own hare, or a wig?' "

One might suspect zoologists of aiming, on the same subject, at an even lower level of humor, that of the schoolboy question-and-answer conundrum: "When is a hare not a hare?" "When it's a rabbit." Pointless as this may sound, it is hardly an unfair rephrasing of a definition given by a standard encyclopedia when it informs us that the word "hare" covers "all the numerous allied species which do not come under the designation of rabbits." There are, as a matter of fact, many more positive indications which permit telling the hares from the rabbits: Hares are in general larger than rabbits; they build nests on the ground, while rabbits dig burrows; young hares are born with their eyes open and a full coat of fur, able to fend for themselves after a single month's suckling, while rabbits come into the world blind, naked and helpless; and, if you push your research to the point of taking pulses, you will find that in normal circumstances the rabbit's heart beats 200 times a minute, but the hare's only 64.

There are, however, baffling intermediate species which refuse annoyingly to conform with the definitions; one sometimes feels that taxonomists decide such borderline cases by flipping a coin. Thus the same encyclopedia quoted above insists in Volume 19 that what Americans refer to erroneously as the cottontail "rabbit" is really a hare; in Volume 6 it calls the cottontail a rabbit with no reservations; and in Volume 11, while classifying this species among the hares, it admits that though American usage is wrong, "the cottontail is called a rabbit with [some] reason; it resembles the true rabbit, often lives in holes and its young are helpless, nearly naked at birth." This difficulty has been side-stepped by not classifying the cottontail with the hare genus, *Lepus,* but giving it one of its own, *Sylvilagus,* to which some other southern American species have been assigned for good measure. The counterweight to the cottontail, a hare which acts like a rabbit, is the Belgian *lapin-lièvre,* a rabbit which looks like a hare.

The archetype of the genus is *L. europaeus,* the European hare, found in England, southern and central Europe and the Caucasus. North of this patriarch lives the smaller blue hare, called, from a characteristic of the family which particularly impressed its observers, *L. timidus*: habitat Scotland, Scandinavia, northern Europe and northern Asia, the Kamchatka Peninsula and Japan. Each country seems also to have developed its own private species—*L. hibernicus,* often russet-colored, in Ireland; *L. granatensis* in Spain; a white hare in Italy's Valle d'Aosta and a special type of hare in Sardinia; Swiss hares called in French Mayence hares, though Mayence (Mainz) is in Germany; German hares larger than those found elsewhere, except for the Austrian variety called the Vienna hare, which seems to be the largest in the world; the Tolai hare in Tibet; an indigenous species in Egypt; and the Cape jumping hare, or springhaas, of the African veld, supposedly a hare too, though it has been given a separate genus, *Pedetes capensis.* There are, in short, native hares everywhere in the world except in Madagascar, Australia (those there now were imported) and South America, where nature's neglect has been remedied by giving the name "Patagonian hare" or "pampas hare" to an animal which is neither a hare nor a rabbit, but an agouti.

In North America, hares start far to the north with the Arctic hare, *L. arcticus,* and the Greenland hare, *L. groenlandicus.* The Arctic hare is also called the varying hare, and so is the blue hare of Europe, because both change the color of their fur to provide effective camouflage through the changing seasons—white against snow, darker shades against foliage. Farther south, both *L. californicus* and *L. townsendii,* though they are hares, are called jackrabbits, which seems to suggest to many people that this means males; actually "jackrabbit" is a shortening of the animal's original name, the jackass rabbit, given it because of its exceptionally long ears. (Another misunderstood word in haredom is "greyhound," for which dictionaries unsuspectingly give the separate derivations of the two components of its name, "grey" and "hound," undeterred by the detail that greyhounds are not usually gray. This is the dog which was used to hunt hares not by scent, but by sight. They were accordingly called "gaze-hounds"; when this began to sound archaic, it was modified in popular usage to what by then sounded like a more probable, if less accurate, form.) The snowshoe "rabbit," *L. americanus,* plentiful in Alaska, where its hollow hairs help it survive temperatures of 70 degrees below zero, is a hare too.

The American habit of calling hares "rabbits" has been extended even to what Europe calls the Easter hare, which in the United States has become the Easter rabbit.

The curious connection between the hare (or rabbit) and Easter antedates Easter. In ancient Egypt, the hare was associated with the moon, because it feeds at night and is born with its eyes open; like the moon, the hare is "the open-eyed watcher of the skies." Easter is, as everyone knows, a date on the lunar calendar, and was marked everywhere, long before Christianity, by observances appropriate to the springtime rebirth of vegetation. In ancient Egyptian, the word for hare was *un*; it also meant "periodicity" and "opening," thus becoming a fertility symbol referring to the opening of new life and the beginning of its periodicity. The egg is the fertility symbol par excellence; hence the pretence that the Easter hare laid the Easter eggs. On the other side of the world, some Algonquin Indian tribes worshiped "a mighty great hare," who welcomed them to heaven when they died.

Hare bones have been found in prehistoric kitchen middens in sites as far apart as New England (the snowshoe "rabbit"), Russia (the blue hare and the tailless hare) and Africa (the jumping hare). The ancient Hebrews did not eat this animal, for Leviticus 11:4 proscribed it: "He cheweth the cud, but divideth not the hoof; he is unclean unto you." But the ancient Romans did, with all the more avidity because they believed that eating hare for seven days in a row would banish ugliness; they kept hares in their game parks, no doubt as aids to beauty. The ancient Greeks thought that eating hare caused insomnia; and indeed Brillat-Savarin two thousand years later said that eating hare provoked dreaming, but added that dreaming was good for the health, a theory concerning which modern medicine has only recently caught up with him. In England, Fynes Moryson wrote in the early seventeenth century that "hares are thought to nourish melancholy, yet they are eaten as venison both roast and boiled."

The ancient Gauls disliked rabbit, whose flesh they considered insipid, but they were fond of hare, provided it was young enough. "An old hare and an old goose are foods for the devil," one of their proverbs put it, and French recognition of the relationship of age to palatability is implicit in the series of names applied successively to the hare. In general, hare is *lièvre* and specifically this means the male; the female is a *hase*, and the young, a *levraut*. The *levraut* is a *financier*, a banker, for the first few months of his life. He then becomes a *trois-quarts*, a term also used, literally translated, in English (a "three-quarter"), and in the Berry region a *conseiller*, an adviser—a term which is good until he reaches mating age, at about one year and five pounds weight. This is the ideal age for a roast hare; the animal has attained full growth, but has not yet dissipated any of its energy, or flavor, in amatory exertion. After mating, the male becomes a *bouquin* (buck), a reproducer, and is better for stews than for roasting, though the female remains tender to the age of two. A three-year-old hare, weighing seven or eight pounds, is a *capucin* (Capuchin) and had better be reserved for pâtés and terrines.

Hares which live in hills or mountains are usually tastier than those which live on plains. The best part of the hare is the saddle, a cut from the back running from the first ribs to the thighs. It used to be customary to end this piece not at the thighs but far enough along to include the tail; and it is thus still served in French families which respect old traditions, even if they don't know what they represent. This practice is a holdover from the eighteenth century, when the tail and the flesh around it was considered the choicest tidbit; it was called "the hunter's morsel," and was offered to the guest of honor.

Hanging hare is a relatively recent aberration to which our ancestors did not subscribe. In France, for instance, it was the custom at large hunts for the person who killed the first hare to hasten with it back to the château or manor, where it was put to simmer in a corner of the fireplace, to be eaten the same night. In less formal circumstances it was customary to eat hare *au bout de fusil*, "from the end of the rifle," meaning in practice within two or three days. "Hare should never be allowed to become gamey," says the *Larousse Encyclopédie Gastronomique* firmly. Nature has given this richly flavored, dark-fleshed animal all the gaminess it needs.

In the French department of the Aveyron, stress is laid on the importance of not overcooking hare. The local formula calls for the animal to be grilled in the heat provided by burning a single newspaper (and French newspapers are much less voluminous than American ones). It is grudgingly admitted that people who like their meat overdone may be permitted to burn two newspapers, but that is the limit. Anyone who wants more is looked upon as peculiar.

Treating hare as naturally as possible goes all the way back to what is probably the world's first cookbook, that of Archestratus, whose spirit was modern:

HARE *by Albrecht Dürer (1471–1528).* The Hare, *water and body colors*

1502

Many are the ways and many the recipes for dressing hares [he wrote about 330 B.C.], but this is the best of all, to place before a group of hungry guests a slice of roasted meat fresh from the spit, hot, seasoned only with plain simple salt. . . . All other ways are quite superfluous, as when cooks pour a lot of sticky gooey sauce upon it.

The French administration charged with the protection and proliferation of game estimates that one-half of all the hares it releases in the open each year are killed by automobiles.

HE
stands for

the **heart**, a tough but edible organ contributed to the diet of various animals, including man, by various animals, including man; for the **heartnut**, or Japanese walnut; for **heartsease**, grown in Illinois for honey, and **heartseed**, grown in tropical Africa as a vegetable; for the **heart urchin**, alias the sea porcupine; for **heather**, whose honey was considered inferior by ancient Romans but superior by modern beekeepers; for the **heath hen**, gone but not forgotten; for the **hedgehog**, esteemed as a delicacy by fifth-century Romans, fifteenth-century Englishmen and twentieth-century Africans; for **heglik oil**, pressed from the nuts of an African hardwood, much used in the cooking of the Ivory Coast, Chad and East Africa; for the **heifer**, whose slaughter was forbidden by the Emperor Alexander Severus; for **helianthus**, valuable for its oil when it is the sunflower and for its tubers when it is the Jerusalem artichoke; for the **hemlock** (the tree, not the plant which caused the death of Socrates), whose wood is not recommended for fireplace cooking because of its explosive propensities; for **hemp**, whose leaves produce hashish and whose seeds produce soup; for the **hen clam**, or surf clam, the largest bivalve of North America's Atlantic coast; for the **Hereford**, an excellent English beef critter introduced into the United States by Henry Clay; for the **hermit crab**, which has the sea snail for its landlord and the sea anemone for its umbrella; for the **heron**, a bird palatable enough to have been eaten by Henry VIII; and for the **hévi**, described at the time of Louis XV as the best fruit of Tahiti, but what it may be today deponent knoweth not.

And **HE** also stands for

HERRING. "The herring," wrote Bernard Germain Etienne de la Ville, Comte de Lacépède, "is one of those products whose use decides the destiny of empires. The coffee bean, the tea leaf, the spices of the torrid zones, the worm which spins silk, had less influence on the wealth of nations than the northern ocean." By writing "the northern ocean" instead of repeating "the herring," Lacépède deftly sidestepped all arguments over whether the herring or the COD has been the most important food fish in the history of the world. Both inhabit the northern ocean.

Cod and herring alike owed their importance, before the days of refrigeration and rapid transport, in large part to the same circumstance: they could be cured for delivery to the consumer far from the source of supply; neither of them was much eaten fresh, except in fishing ports. The cod enjoyed a head start in this respect because it lent itself, better than the herring, to the simplest, and hence the earliest, methods of preservation. The simplest of all is drying fish, otherwise untreated, in the air. This suffices for cod, but not for herring, which is too oily: fats account for 6 percent of its weight. Hung up to dry, it would probably spoil first. It did not come into its own until a somewhat more sophisticated method of curing was developed: smoking. Cod can be smoked too, but it is the herring which responds most appetizingly to this process.

Smoking, though less primitive than drying, nevertheless began very early. By the twelfth century herring had become a staple in the European diet, in peaceful coexistence with cod, then usually salted. In Paris in 1170 Louis VII granted letters patent to a guild of dealers in saltwater fish, thus reviving a corporation which had existed under the Emperor Tiberius but had petered out along with the Roman Empire. By this act, fish dealers became divided into two groups—dealers in freshwater fish, who retained the general name *poissoniers*, "fishmongers," and handlers of saltwater fish, who became *harengères*, "herring sellers," a term which implied the ascendance of the herring over all other saltwater fish, including cod. The streets of Paris resounded with the cry of vendors: *Sor et blanc harenc frès pouldré* ("Herring, smoked or newly salted"). The *harengères* were the aristocrats of fish dealers, and the herring itself, in the twelfth century, was considered a luxury; but a century later its very abundance had caused it to be demoted in popular esteem to the status of a cheap food for the poor, though it remained an enriching one for its sellers. The snob value of the herring was not improved either when, because of its relative cheapness, it acquired the reputation of being suitable for those living on charity, a reputation to which St. Louis contributed in the thirteenth century by donating 70,000 herrings a year to monasteries, hospitals and plague-houses.

Herring

HERRING. *Illuminated page from the* Album of the Prague New Town Herring Market, *1619*

Infra dig or not, the herring trade brought prosperity successively to a number of nations, depending on where herring were most numerous at various times. The first were the Danes. "Once dressed like simple sailors," an envious twelfth-century chronicler wrote, "the Danes today wear scarlet and purple." Such ostentation was of course intolerable to other nations, so English, French and Dutch fishermen set out to win scarlet and purple, via the herring, for themselves. The English suffered a setback in 1238 when the Mongols—"pouring forth like devils from Tartarus, so that they are rightly called Tartars," as Matthew Paris wrote from the sanctuary of his monastery of St. Albans—frightened from the seas the Scandinavian and Frisian ships which had formerly delivered English herring to the Baltic and elsewhere, picking up the fish at Yarmouth, which had become the great herring center of England. Faced by a glut, Yarmouth was obliged in desperation to invent new methods of preserving herring to keep them until the Mongols went away. This may have caused the invention of the bloater: Yarmouth bloaters are considered the best in the world today.

Among the many influences which the herring exerted on, in Lacépède's words, "the wealth of nations," one of the most important was its contribution, in the thirteenth century, to the development of the Hanseatic League. Acquiring a monopoly on the transport and sale of herring, the Hansa cities grew rich on this lucrative trade, among others, during a heyday which lasted for two centuries.

The sixteenth century saw the apotheosis of the herring, in good times a staple food for armies and such institutions as schools, hospitals and prisons, and in bad times the aliment which saved whole populations from famine. It saw also the apotheosis of the Dutch herring fisheries, which had been taking the bulk of the world catch since 1450, thanks to bigger and better boats and improved methods of curing the catches; Amsterdam, it was said jocularly, was built on herring bones. The Dutch were quicker than the English to realize that a large fishing fleet can provide the basis for a large merchant marine, and a training school for the navy to protect it, which is why they reached the Spice Islands before the British did. "We are daily scorned by these Hollands," wrote a disgruntled Englishman in 1614, "for being so negligent of our profite, and careless of our fishing, and they do daily floute . . . us at sea." Waking tardily, the English under Charles I proceeded to build up what was to remain for three centuries the world's most powerful navy. It is not too great an exaggeration to say that the herring played an important role in creating, each in its turn, Dutch seapower and English seapower, as the cod had earlier played an important role in creating Norman seapower.

Today it is Great Britain which dominates the herring fisheries of Europe, taking more of these fish than all the other European countries put together; and today too it is definitely the herring which dominates the cod. The much higher consumption of herring is not, however, a question of preference, it is a question of necessity. There are not enough cod left to supply the demand. The cod has been overfished to such an extent that this one of the world's two most important food fishes may well be considered an endangered species; and there is a possibility that the other may soon go the same way. It was no doubt premature when the Paris daily *France-Soir* printed a scare headline on January 14, 1975: "If we fish one more herring, the species will become extinct." Premature, but perhaps not much.

"Ah, Tam! ah, Tam! thou'll get thy fairin' / In hell they'll roast thee like a herrin'!" wrote Robert Burns, but failed to specify whether he thought Tam o' Shanter deserved cool smoking or hot smoking, the two methods used to cure herring in this fashion. Probably more herring are eaten smoked than in any other form; in any case, only a small percentage are eaten fresh.

The most enthusiastic devourers of fresh herring are the Dutch, who maintain that "a herring a day keeps the doctor away." Each year when the herring boats return from their first fishing forays in the spring, the streets of Holland blossom with little white carts like those which in the United States would be purveying ice cream. In Holland they are selling fresh raw herring. Each vendor is surrounded by a knot of intense Dutchmen (and women), practicing a skill which must be innate, for few aliens ever master it. Head bent back as far as it will go, mouth strained open, each herring fancier hoists a small fish deftly by the tail, suspends it for a split second over the gaping gullet and lowers it into the expectant orifice without losing a single one of the little chips of onion sprinkled over it. More dangerous still are herring which are dunked into a drippy creamy sauce in preparation for this act of levitation. Having lived two and a half years in Holland, I am convinced that no foreigner should attempt this feat except when wearing his oldest clothes. (I left Holland twenty-five years ago. A Dutch correspondent writes me that, alas, the herring carts are now becoming rare; he reminds me also that the first keg of herring landed each year is painted orange and presented to the head of the House of Orange, the queen of the Netherlands.)

Lack of space has banished consideration of processed foods from this book, but we may allow ourselves a swift look at the meaning of some widely used herring terms. Rollmops are raw herring fillets, rolled around chopped shallots, capers and sliced gherkins, secured with a wooden skewer and packed, immersed in wine vinegar seasoned with mustard seeds and peppercorns, in glass jars. Matjes herring (*matjes* means "little girls") are fish which have not yet reached the reproductive age, which for herring is four to five years. Red herring are the original and least subtle incarnations of smoked herring, left ungutted, salted heavily and cool-smoked (a process which flavors but does not cook it) for several weeks over smoldering sawdust. The bloater might be described as a special case of the red herring, for it also is cured whole and ungutted. Nowadays it is only lightly cool-smoked and only lightly salted, just enough to give it a smoky taste without drying it to an extent which would make it tough; bloaters are therefore perishable and are not meant to be kept long before eating. Bückling, in turn, is a special case of the bloater, for it is preserved whole, unsplit and hence ungutted too, but since it is a German invention it is hot-smoked (and consequently cooked), the favorite process in Germany (and in Scandinavia too). The kipper, the most subtle of smoked herrings, is not, as most of us think, the venerable product of a long tradition, but a form of herring which did not exist before about 1850. It is split open according to a prescribed method, cool-smoked as lightly as possible, and therefore will not keep more than a short time—unless refrigerated, which I would not recommend. It requires cooking. In England it is the king of the breakfast table.

The typical herring is the Atlantic herring,

Clupea harengus, whose Pacific counterpart is *C. pallasi*. They are both circumpolar and have been accused by some marine biologists of being the same fish; but the differences in their egg-laying habits, among other things, seem too fundamental for fish of the same species. The Pacific fish, also taken in Siberia and Japan, gets down the American coast farther than its Atlantic counterpart, for the cold-water California Current permits this northern fish to reach the Mexican border. The Atlantic herring, the same one Europeans take on the other side of the ocean, is described by the reference books as having its southern limit at Long Island, but what Chesapeake Bay fishermen call the Labrador herring seems to be the same fish. There are important herring fisheries on both coasts of the United States: capital Alaska, on the Pacific side; capital Maine, on the Atlantic. Maine concentrates on young herring, which it cans as "sardines." However, the herring has also been canned honestly under its real name far enough back so that it has entered American folklore, through the medium of a well-known song:

Light she was and like a fairy,
And her shoes were number nine;
Herring boxes without topses,
Sandals were for Clementine.

Herring sneeze when removed from the water.

HI
stands for

the **hibiscus**, which you undoubtedly know as a handsome flower, but change a gene here and a gene there and you have *Hibiscus esculentus*, edible hibiscus, which, lo and behold! is nothing but okra; for the **hickory nut**, which supplied American Indians with milk before they met cows; for **hides**, not a gourmet item, but they kept Magellan's men alive in the Pacific long enough for them to reach more luscious food; for the **highbush cranberry**, an American fruit-bearing shrub which is not a cranberry but the almost identical twin of the European guelder-rose, which is not a rose; for **hijiki**, one of the six principal varieties of algae eaten by the Japanese; for **hips**, bitter but healthy when they grow on roses; for **hippomanes**, a growth on the forehead of newborn foals which, it was held in antiquity, "will make men mad with love"; for the **hippopotamus**, so tempting a tidbit for East Africans that it had to shift from diurnal to nocturnal feeding habits a thousand years ago to elude hunters.

HO
stands for

the **hobblebush**, or American wayfaring tree, whose fruit Thoreau described as "rather insipid and seedy"; for the **hog**, an animal Homer considered worthy to be served to Odysseus by Achilles; for the **hog apple**, which is the May apple; for the **hog banana**, a large, coarse, red-skinned fruit which I suspect of being really a plantain; for the **hogchoker**, a small flatfish so called in Chesapeake Bay because its rough scales inhibit swallowing it; for the **hog cranberry**, which is (a) the crowberry or (b) the bearberry; for **hog corn**, maize of a quality which encourages leaving it to the pigs, and **hog fennel**, or sulphurwort, held in similar esteem; for the **hog deer** of southeastern Asia; for the **hogget**, a lamb which has just been promoted from the suckling category; for the **hognut**, which is the earthnut, the pignut or the Jamaica cobnut; for the **hog peanut**, which American Indians used to appreciate; for the **hog plum**, a relative of the mango; for the **hog potato**, or man-of-the-earth; for **hogweed**, also referred to in a swift mammalian metamorphosis as cow parsley; for **holly**, which you had better pass up as food unless it happens to be ground holly, which is wintergreen, or, in a pinch, sea holly, which is eryngo; for **hollyhocks**, whose pickled leaves were eaten by the ancient Egyptians; and for the **Holstein**, a cow which produces large quantities of milk with small quantities of butterfat.

And **HO** also stands for

HONEY. "The principal things necessary for the life of man," according to the Bible, "are: water, fire and iron, salt, milk, and bread of flour, and honey, and the clusters of the grape, and oil and clothing." In Biblical times honey was more of a necessity than it is now: it was the principal sweetener, and sometimes the only sweetener, almost until our day. The ancient world had a few alternatives, but rather unsatisfactory ones: grape sugar in the western Mediterranean, carob pods in the south, date or fig syrup in Asia Minor and Africa. Even in the Orient, where sugarcane grew, it could not always compete with honey, which is easier to extract and to use; in India cane sugar did not displace honey as the principal sweetener until the third century, when cane sugar was already ancient history there. Cane sugar reached Europe about the thirteenth century, but it was too rare and too dear to oust honey until the eighteenth.

The earliest known representation of honey

gathering is a Stone Age painting in Spain's Araña cave, near Valencia, which shows a climber plundering a nest of wild bees hidden in the cleft of a cliff. Bees in that region still construct their nests in such sites and honey is still gathered there in the same fashion. This is also true in Ceylon, where cliff-climbing Veddas, honored as practitioners of an ancient art, take the prized honey of the bambara bees which nest high in the crevices of the rocks, while in South Africa Hottentots smoke them out from similar refuges. The amount of honey which could be reft from wild bees sufficed for a long time in history; the Bible, for instance, is full of references to honey, obviously an important food (at Emmaus the resurrected Christ was fed with "a piece of a broiled fish, and of an honeycomb"), but it does not mention beekeeping, although bees had been domesticated in other areas since the Bronze Age. (The ancient Hebrews were for a long time largely nomadic, a state incompatible with such sedentary occupations as raising bees.)

In Egypt, bas-reliefs in the temple of Niweser-re at Abusir, dated at 2600 B.C., picture a series of beekeeping operations little different from those practiced today. The hives shown are cylindrical, suggesting the hollow tree trunks which were probably prehistoric man's first hives; hives of the same shape can still be found in Egypt today. The Greeks no doubt learned about domesticating bees from the Egyptians, but apparently preferred wild honey, especially when it was what they considered their best, that from Mount Hymettus, not far from Athens, where the bees feasted on thyme. The worst in their history was encountered by the army of Alexander the Great, whose soldiers, after eating it, were incapacitated by vomiting, diarrhea and loss of muscular coordination. It was probably Black Sea honey, notorious for its toxicity; the bees of that region took nectar from a species of rhododendron whose bitter honey was digestible by bees but not by men. The Romans made beekeeping a science and an art, but were stronger in practice than in theory: they had not pierced the mysteries of sex in the case of bees, and referred to the queen as the king. (So did Shakespeare.)

Charlemagne ordered that the larders on his estates should always be kept stocked with beeswax and honey, which continued to be the principal sweetener throughout the Middle Ages. All manor houses maintained hives, which were often destroyed in the frequent wars, causing local shortages of sweets. (I am somewhat skeptical about the story that hives containing live and, under the circumstances, justifiably angered bees were used in medieval warfare as projectiles, a form of artillery which would seem all too likely to backfire.) In the sixteenth century some German principalities obliged all peasants by law to keep bees. An important source of honey was the monasteries; their primary purpose in maintaining apiaries was to provide wax for liturgical candles, but honey was the inevitable by-product. When Henry VIII abolished the monasteries, England suffered a shortage of honey. Fortunately, this was just about the time when cane sugar became plentiful enough and cheap enough to take its place.

It is often asserted that America had no bees before Europeans imported them, or alternatively, that it had bees but they did not make honey. Neither statement is true. American bees are indeed poor producers of honey in comparison with the Eurasian *Apis mellifica*; but when the first Spaniards arrived in the New World they found both the Aztecs and the Mayas eating honey from a domesticated bee, *Melipona beecheii*, using hollow logs for hives. The Pilgrims nevertheless found it advantageous to import the more efficient European honeybee (immediately named "white man's fly" by the Indians), thus giving them, in their phrase, both "tree sweetenin' and bee sweetenin' "—maple sugar and honey. It is often taken for granted that the European bees the Pilgrims had by 1634 were Italian, the most widespread variety in the United States today, but they were in fact probably Dutch, either brought along by the Pilgrims themselves from exile in Holland or purchased from the Dutch of New Amsterdam, who may have imported them without attracting the attention of historians. Swarming honeybees of course escaped into the woods, went wild, and undertook a slow but sure progress across the continent. They had crossed the Mississippi at least by 1800, and in 1821 Stephen F. Austin reported from Texas that he had taken a gallon and a half of honey from a bee tree inhabited by descendants of *A. mellifica*.

Honey may be the only food nature presents to man predigested; at least I am unable at the moment to think of another, with the possible exception of Asian birds' nests. The process of converting flower nectar into honey begins immediately the bee has taken possession of it, on its way back to the hive. The nectar is carried in the honey stomach, where the bee's digestive juices provoke transformations in its sugars. Arrived at the hive, the gatherer discharges his booty into the mouths of the youngest bees, who roll it over their tongues, breathing across it to evaporate some of its water content and concentrate it; meanwhile their glandular secretions cause further changes in the liquid. It is then transferred to the storage cells of the honeycomb, where the high temperature maintained inside the hive concentrates it further. (If it thickens too much, the bees dilute it with water, to return it to optimum consistency.) When the combs are removed from the hive, they no longer contain nectar, they contain honey, a manufactured product, but not one manufactured by man.

Honey as extracted from the comb is liquid; when it crystallizes many people think it is beginning to spoil. Not at all: crystallization is natural for honey (the most important exception is acacia honey, which remains liquid); it can be returned to liquid form by plunging its container into hot (not boiling) water. Indeed, the granulation of honey is a guarantee that it has not been tampered with (as, for example, by pasteurization). Personally I regret the days of my boyhood when I used to bite directly into the crunchy comb and munch honey and wax together. I do not suppose that honey eaten in this fashion actually tasted better, but its crusty texture made you think it did. It is hard to find honey in the comb nowadays. The suspicious may, if they are so minded, attribute this in part to the great difficulty of adulterating honey in the comb. Once extracted, it can be persuaded to yield a little extra profit by replacement of some of the expensive pure honey with glucose, gums, starches or sugar, or by simply giving it more bulk with chalk or plaster.

Honey carries the distinctive flavors of the flowers from which it is made. The beekeeper who wishes to offer special types of honey must make sure that his insects do not pay attention to a mixed bag of flowers. I have read that a given hive of bees, on its own initiative, will collect honey from only one species of flower, but I am not convinced. It seems likelier that when unmixed honey is produced without the deliberate intent of the beekeeper, it is for one of two reasons: either the hive is placed where a single species of flower is dominant (as in an apple orchard), or the illusion of selectivity on the part of the bees is the result of the fact that a certain type of flower will produce nectar at one period, and a different flower at another, thus automatically sorting themselves out. Beekeepers, disinclined to trust to the choosiness of bees, often move their hives to positions where they will necessarily visit a certain kind of flower, and when they think the bees have exhausted the trove offered by a species about to go out of season, they remove the filled or partly filled combs and replace them with empty ones, so that there will be no mixture of honey from different sources.

If you pass in review the opinions of all times and all places, you will probably conclude that honey made from thyme has been the world's favorite; but others which have been rated ahead of it from time to time include acacia, apple blossom, orange blossom, heather, rosemary, clover, chaparral and sage-blossom. Some bees which live near pine woods produce honey with a pronounced taste of resin, which many people find disagreeable.

HONEY. *Bas-relief in the tomb of Pa-bu-sa*

Color too is affected by the nature of the nectar. Buckwheat honey is dark (and its flavor strong) because of its tannin, while the darkest of all, almost brown, is perhaps that made from the rank growth of the Corsican *maquis*. Thyme honey is clear and golden. Clover produces a pale color and a bland flavor. The famous French Gâtinais and Narbonne rosemary honeys are almost pure white. The number of different kinds of honey is almost unlimited; I have heard of one store which offers its customers a choice of 110 flavors. In general, other things being equal, honey gathered in the spring is finer than honey gathered in the fall. As an English jingle puts it:

A swarm of bees in May is worth a load of hay.
A swarm of bees in June is worth a silver spoon.
A swarm of bees in July is not worth a fly.

Bees are not the only insects which produce honey; certain ants secrete it too, notably the sugar ant, *Melophorus inflatus*; some primitive peoples collect it by the simple process of biting off the distended honey-filled abdomen of the ant and swallowing half-ant and honey together. The sweet white coating on Australian eucalyptus leaves is a secretion of the larvae of certain insects. Honeydew is not honey but the sweet sap which oozes from the leaves of some trees if they produce an excessive amount of it (when it results from the puncturing of leaves by insects, honeydew may be considered a product of disease). In Alaska, where bees cannot survive the long winters, "squaw honey" is made without the intervention of insects; nectar-filled flowers are boiled in sugar syrup until all their fragrance has been transmitted to the liquid and it has been reduced to the consistency of honey, when the flowers are strained out and it is bottled. The result looks like honey and tastes like honey—not the best, perhaps, but acceptable.

As we have all known for the last quarter-century, bees have a language in which they communicate with one another, not by word of mouth, but, like Sherlock Holmes's dancing men, through a sort of *pas seul* performed by a bee which has struck it rich and returns to the hive to report to his comrades on the direction, distance, quantity and quality of his find. All bees of the same species can "talk" to each other and be understood; but bees of different speeches communicate with each other only with difficulty or not at all: they dance different dialects.

HO stands for

the **honeyberry**, called in its native Finland *mesimarja*, the fruit of the Arctic bramble; for the **honeydew melon**, unknown in the United States before this century; for **honey fungus**, a mushroom which owes its name to its color, not its taste, and is only edible if it has been cooked lengthily until it has excreted all its toxic juices, which must then be thrown away; for the **honey locust**, which bears pulp-filled pods eaten by the Indians of tropical America; for **honey pot**, a South African grape whose English name is a corruption of the Afrikaans *Hanepoot*, "cock's foot"; and for **honeysuckle**, whose roots have been eaten in times of famine.

HO
stands for

hontaka, a very hot red chili which has somehow become a favorite of Japan; for the **hooked mussel**, "barely edible" in the estimate of Euell Gibbons, a hard man to discourage; for the **hopa crabapple**, which many people grow as an ornamental, unaware that its fruit makes superb jelly; for **horenso**, a sort of Japanese spinach; for **horns**, usually those of stags, which, converted into jelly, are reputed to preserve women against sterility and men against impotence; for the **hornpout**, of zoologically confused nomenclature, called the bullhead in the eastern United States and the Sacramento cat in the West; and for the **hornshell**, a cone-shaped mollusk used to make soup in Italy.

HOPS. For most of us, no doubt, hops represent a product whose only use is to flavor beer; but they have been, and are, used as a food. I do not know whether hops were used in beverages in 789 (probably they were) when a donation of Pepin the Short included *humularia*, hop gardens, but they were so employed when the earliest references to hops appeared in English, and were also then recognized as food. It was in 1574 that Reynolde Scot brought out the very first English work on this vegetable under the hardly succinct title *A Perfite Platforme of a Hoppe Garden, and necessarie instructions for the making and mayntenance thereof, with notes and rules for reformation of all abuses, commonly practised therein, very necessarie and expedient for all men to have, which in any wise have to do with hops.*

There will some smell out the profitable savour of this herb [the *Perfite Platforme* explained], some wyll gather the fruit thereof, and will make a sallet therewith (which is good in one respect for the bellye, and in another for the Purse), and when the grace and sweetenesse hereof conceived, some will dippe their fingers therein up to the knuckles, and some will be glad to licke the Dish, and they that disdayne to be partaken hereof, commonly prove to be such as have montaynes in fantasie, and beggary in possession.

John Gerard in his *Herball* chimed in with:

The Hop doth live and flourish by embracing and

HOPS. *Woodcut from Scot:* A Perfite Platforme, *London, 1576*

taking hold of poles, pearches, and other things upon which it climeth. . . . The Hop joyeth in a fat and fruitfull ground. . . . The buds or first sprouts which come forth in the spring are used to be eaten in sallads; yet are they, as Pliny saith, more toothsome than nourishing, for they yeeld but very small nourishment. . . . The floures make bread light, and the lumpe to be sooner and easilier leavened, if the meals be tempered with liquor wherein they have been boiled.

Although these early writers granted a certain versatility to hops, the only parts of the plant eaten nowadays, so far as I know, are the young sprouts, collected in the spring before they have had time to become woody, like asparagus. They can indeed be cooked in any manner appropriate to asparagus, and Alexandre Dumas maintained that they tasted like asparagus; the current *Dictionnaire de l'Académie des Gastronomes* comments more guardedly that they resemble asparagus by their tenderness. A work of the last century reported that "the poorer classes in some parts of Europe still eat the young hops as vegetables," but those were rustic times when almost everyone was within reach of land on which hops could be grown. If you want to eat hops today, you must compete with the beverage makers, who are accustomed to buying up commercial crops in their totality. Hops have become a rarity, even a luxury, for those who want to bring them to the table, except in a few countries which have not forgotten their excellence for this purpose. The most fervent admirers of hops are the Belgians, who are likely to serve *jets de houblon*, creamed hop shoots, during their short season, as a side dish with almost every meal, or even to make a main dish of them, in which case they are likely to be gifted with added importance by an accompaniment of poached eggs. The Lake Constance region of Germany, the only part of that country which does not overcook vegetables, is partial to hop sprouts, served with melted butter or with light unsweetened whipped cream flavored with a touch of lemon juice. England seems to have lost interest in hops as a food, and America, I believe, never developed any.

The most widespread species of hops is *Humulus lupulus*. The relation between hops and wolves may seem obscure, but Linnaeus went back to the ancient Romans for this name. They called the hop plant *lupus salictarius*, because it had on the willows among which it usually grows wild much the same effect as a band of wolves in a flock of sheep, a comparison which can be appreciated by modern farmers, who know what happens when wild hops intrude as weeds among crops where they aren't wanted. There appears to be only one other species, the Asian *H. japonicus*, though some botanists have given distinctive names to two other varieties which they claim are native to America; the majority opinion seems to be that they are only variants of *H. lupulus* which developed after European hops were brought to the New World, in 1629 to the New Netherlands (from which New England acquired them and found that they did not grow well there, though they did in Pennsylvania) and in 1648 to Virginia.

The hop plant is almost certainly a native of temperate Europe and western Asia. It extended its original range during the fifteenth century, powerfully aided by the Dutch, who had become the hop merchants for all of northern Europe. It was first grown commercially in England about 1520, while Olivier de Serres is credited with having introduced it into France late in the same century, some authors say from England, others from Flanders; in either case, it must have been a return engagement, on the evidence of Pepin the Short.

Cultivated hops can be a precarious crop. They are sensitive to weather, frost, mildew and insects, but when they fend off these perils they are so profitable that, in tithe-paying days, land sown to hops was taxed more heavily than that devoted to other crops. They grow fast—six inches a day when they are young if conditions are right, pushing their roots down as far as fifteen feet and shooting up aboveground to as much as twenty-five. They hang on to their necessary supports by means of hooked hairs, and the climbing vines wind around them in a clockwise direction (in the Northern Hemisphere at least). Male and female flowers are borne on separate plants and are fertilized by wind-blown pollen. A hop acre is two-thirds of an ordinary acre; it is the space occupied by one thousand plants set out in rows six or seven feet apart.

The hop plant is useful for other things besides food and drink. Its leaves make good animal fodder, which is reputed to enable cows to give more milk. The stems can be persuaded to give up a vegetable wax, while the sap is convertible into a fast reddish-brown dye. The fine quality of Bohemian glass results partly from the use of hop ashes in its manufacture. Paper of excellent quality, resistant rope (the hop belongs to the hemp family), and tough if coarse fabrics can also be manufactured from it. Before the development of modern film, photographic plates were coated with a solution containing hop juice, while glucose and tannin can be derived from its roots. Among its many alleged medical virtues is the ability to cure insomnia; whenever George III entered one of his demented periods, his doctors had him sleep on a pillow stuffed with hop leaves.

The most peripheral use of hops must be their service as a mnemonic device to fix in the mind the name of one of the twelve cranial nerves, by dint of its presence in a jingle, which I must have partly forgotten, since it doesn't correspond with the terminology of today, unless some of the nerves have changed names since my school days:

On old Olympus' piny tops
A fair-armed girl is picking hops.

Hops? Hypoglossal!

HORSE. When prehistoric man first encountered the horse, he looked upon it as a wild animal like any other, interesting only as food. We may even go so far as to assume that it was his favorite big game on the evidence of Stone Age cave paintings, widely believed to have been meant as a magical means of inducing edible animals to present themselves handily before the hunters' spears and arrows. The horse appears more frequently in European Upper Paleolithic cave paintings than any other animal, with an 18 percent lead over the bison, the runner-up, and a 65 percent lead over deer and reindeer combined, which hold third place. It is of course possible that prehistoric painters favored the horse because it is such a magnificent model for the artist; or perhaps it held first place because it was easiest to kill. The wild horse must have been a less redoubtable prey than the aurochs or the cave bear, and there was a short and simple way of dispatching it—by turning against it its chief defense, speed. It was only necessary to stampede a herd towards a cliff, and the deed was done. At Solutré, in Burgundy, which gave its name to the Solutrean epoch, archeologists in 1866 excavated a site beneath a cliff conveniently located for this purpose and uncovered some 100,000 horse skeletons—a carpet of bones three feet deep which covered two and a half acres.

Prehistoric man had none of the reasons which developed later for abstaining from horseflesh. The animal was not less useful for food than for agricultural labor at a time when agriculture did not yet exist. Probably no Stone Age man ever dared try to ride a horse, much less harness one. Horse racing was not yet in vogue either. In the ancient Western world the first systematic breeding of horses was probably that undertaken by the Romans for chariot racing. Later the most powerful deterrent to eating horse would be the sentimental relationship developed by man for his "most noble conquest." Curiously enough, the French, considered today the principal consumers of horsemeat, were the slowest to accept it, once the ancient Gauls had given it up. One hears little about eating horsemeat in France except in times of famine, though it was once a common food for Britons, Germans and Scandinavians (Swedes still eat paper-thin slices of smoked horseflesh and call them "hamburgers").

Horsemeat was not eaten by the ancients, who did not have enough horses to cede them to the kitchen. In Greece there was a dearth of suitable pasturage; the few horses available were not thought of as food but as a means for moving farm carts—not plows, which were drawn by oxen. The Romans were short of horses too, except for the chariot-race steeds, too valuable to eat when young and too tough when their careers were finished. They did not even use them much in war, except by proxy. Their cavalry was made up of peoples from the steppes, who had always been, and still are in some areas, members of a society based on the horse: first the Scythians and then the inheritors of their territory, the Sarmatians, "who nourish themselves on the blood of their horses," Martial wrote. Herodotus reported that the principal food of the Scythians—whom the Greeks referred to scornfully as "mare-milkers," which they were—was horse, though they had cattle too. Marco Polo noted that later inhabitants of the steppes, the Tartars, ate horse also, while the Mongols, when on forced marches, carried no provisions but lived, like Martial's Sarmatians, on horses' blood. Each warrior traveled with a string of eighteen horses, enough so that he could open a vein and drink blood from each horse in turn, at ten-day intervals, in amounts sufficient to maintain his own vitality without impairing that of his horses. When a rich Mongol died, he was buried with a horse, a mare, her foal and a jar of her milk, and a fat horse was eaten at his wake.

At this period (about 1200) horse had almost ceased to be eaten in Europe. England gave it up in 732 when Pope Gregory III ruled that horse was unfit meat for Christians (Moses had already declared that it was unfit for Jews). This hurt horse eating in Germany too, though a voluminous cookbook written by Max Rumpolt in 1604 included directions for cooking horse, but it was specified that it was for *wild* horse, which may have transferred it to the unforbidden category of "game." In addition, horse eating fell into disrepute during the age of chivalry (the very word comes from *cheval*, "horse"), when this animal became a social symbol. Nobles rode, commoners walked, particularly in the armies, but in civilian life too. The nobility of the rider seems to have been transmitted to the mount by osmosis, however thick the saddle, making it disrespectful to eat horse.

In the seventeenth century a group of British horse lovers (in one sense) tried to revive an old-time dish by organizing the Parisian Hippophagic Society, which died a swift, unlamented and indeed even unnoticed death. Its name, however, suggests that horse eating was not then unknown across the Channel, though the historians seem not to have noticed it. One may suppose that the fact that it was eaten is confirmed by the circumstance that it seemed necessary to prohibit it; in the seventeenth century it was forbidden to eat horse in France "to prevent the diseases which the use of such meats cannot fail to induce." This prohibition went by the board during the famines of the Revolution, but in 1802 the consumption of horsemeat was forbidden again. Five years later an event occurred which put the prohibition in question.

This was the Battle of Eylau, in 1807, after which the army found that it had lost track of its commissary department. The sound and the quick were able to set out in search of it, but the sick and wounded had no food, to the great distress of Napoleon's surgeon-in-chief, Baron Dominique Jean Larrey, whose resourcefulness under adverse circumstances had won him the nickname "*la Providence du soldat*." It occurred to the baron that the battlefield was rich with meat in the form of dead horses. Using cavalry breastplates for cooking pans, he grilled chunks of horsemeat seasoned with gunpowder and was amazed at the exceptional speed with which his charges recuperated on this diet. The baron even ventured to serve a portion of breastplate horsemeat to Marshal Masséna, though in deference to the latter's rank he replaced the gunpowder with a little genuine salt which he had cannily held back for his personal use. A horsemeat enthusiast as a result of this experience, Baron Larrey campaigned in its favor, and was joined by such eminent food authorities as Parmentier, better known for having helped induce the French to eat potatoes.

HORSE. *Bronze statuette, Greece, 8th century* BC

By the 1860s horsemeat had become the object of a cult. One Geoffroy Saint-Hilaire sponsored a spectacular all-horsemeat banquet at the Grand Hotel in Paris on February 6, 1865; the menu was: horse consommé with vermicelli; horse sausages; boiled horse; horse *à la mode*; horse stew; fillet of horse with mushrooms; potatoes sautéed in horse fat; salad with horse oil (sic); and, just to show that even dessert daunted no one, rum cake with horse marrow. The wine? That excellent *cru* of St. Emilion—what else?—Cheval Blanc, "White Horse."

Alexandre Dumas did not approve:

> Eating horsemeat means eating meat which is superlatively tough: horsemeat is in fact of a tighter texture than beef. [True; the muscular fibers of the horse are packed more closely together than those of the steer.] It is red and oily . . . it is very doubtful that it will ever become an article of daily consumption. . . . As long as the horse is not raised, fed and fattened like beef, with the sole view of eating it, it should never appear on the table.

Raising, feeding and fattening horse for the table was exactly what the French set out to do, and it became an article of daily consumption in Dumas' own time, spurred by the belief that horsemeat was a remedy for tuberculosis, the great killer of those times. Dumas, never deterred by inconsistency, took up his pen again and wrote that horse's blood and horse's meat were "highly tonic and highly nutritive." In this he was right. Horsemeat is richer in glycogens, the principal form in which carbohydrates are stored in animal tissues, than other meats. For certain disorders, patients are advised to eat uncooked meat. Horsemeat is not always specifically prescribed, but if you are going to eat raw meat at all, horsemeat is the safest. The horse, unlike the steer, is resistant to tuberculosis, and it is not afflicted by the taenia tapeworm, which may be found in beef and pork. What puts me off it personally is a lingering sweetness in its taste, which is not disagreeable, but is disconcerting in meat. It is tolerable once in a while, for a change, but for regular consumption beef, in my opinion, is much superior.

Most French horsemeat eaters do not indulge in horsemeat for its flavor, nor, as many foreigners assume, because it is cheap. The contrary is the case; at the time of writing, horsemeat cost about one-third more than beef. Almost the sole motive for which Frenchmen eat horse is because of its reputation for healthiness; many French physicians prescribe it as a fortifier. It was therefore particularly vulnerable to an incident which occurred in 1967 and impaired that reputation. An outbreak of salmonella, a form of food poisoning, occurred at a girls' school; one of the students died, and it was established that the collective intoxication had been caused by chopped horsemeat. This was no fault of the horse, but of the butcher who had tried to augment his profits by chopping scraps of condemned meat together with good meat, no doubt with the idea that the good meat would hide the taste of the bad. Perhaps it did, but it was unable to neutralize salmonella. He went to jail and the horsemeat industry into near bankruptcy. Bad beef would have produced the same dire result, but it happened that the tainted food had been horsemeat, and this was what the public remembered. Horsemeat sales dropped—by as much as 80 percent according to the maximum estimate.

In an attempt to save the horse butchers (who had no other string to their bow, since by law they could handle no other meat, as horsemeat restaurants could serve no other also), raw chopped horsemeat, roast horse and sausages of horse tripe were eaten valiantly on television by Information Minister Georges Gorse—a gourmet who once confided to me that his secret dream was to get out of politics and open a restaurant devoted to such specialties of his native southwest as hot white-wine sausages with cold oysters—but to no avail. Horsemeat consumption eventually recovered slightly, but will probably never again return to the 3.52 pounds per person per year which France consumed before that accident. The magnificent butcher shops with a gilded horsehead over the door and splendid fat carcasses displayed within, artificial roses running like buttons down their spines and bright ribbons fluttering along their flanks, have become rare sights today.

In America, the history of horse eating is intermittent. Prehistoric Indians ate horse, but the climate changed about 7000 B.C. and the horse became extinct in the Western Hemisphere. When the Spaniards brought horses back, the Indians stole them with great skill, at first for food; but they quickly discovered that they were more valuable as mounts. Some white Americans in earlier times, like prehistoric men, made little distinction between horses which had reverted to a wild state and other types of game. In 1832 Nestor Clay led a party seven hundred miles up the Colorado River and down the Brazos, reporting that they had lived for two months on "different kinds of wild flesh: Buffalo, Mustang, horse, wild Cow, antelope, Panther, Bear, wildcat, mountain cat, Polecat, Leopard cat" and various birds. But neither Americans nor Englishmen took much advantage of the opportunity to buy unrationed horsemeat during World Wars I and II (more Americans tried horse when beef prices skyrocketed in the early 1970s, but the publicity was better then).

One convert made by horsemeat during World War II was Carleton S. Coon, who found he liked it so much that he continued with it even after the meat shortages were over, and became a proselyte for it in the respected club of which he was then the secretary. That is why the Harvard Faculty Club today serves horsemeat, or at least lists it on its menu.

HO
stands for

a long series of foods whose names begin with "horse," thus maligning a worthy animal, for its commonest significance as a prefix is coarseness of one kind or another: the **horse bean**, which is nothing other than the broad bean largely displaced in Europe by the American haricot; the **horse chestnut**, which only American Indians have eaten with success; the **horse clam**, whose large shell is usually inhabited not only by this mollusk, but also by tiny pea crabs, edible too; the **horse-eye bean** of eastern Nigeria; the **horse-fish,** which in Italian designates a sort of mackerel plentiful in the Adriatic; the **horse gram,** a pulse eaten by the poor in India and Ceylon; **horseheal,** which is elecampane; the **horse mackerel,** which in English designates the sort of mackerel known also as scad; **horsemint,** much like peppermint, perhaps so named because the plant is covered with tiny white hairs; the **horse mushroom,** larger than its close relative, the common field mushroom or agaric, and like it agreeable in flavor; **horse parsley,** from which the ancient cookbook writer Apicius concocted purée; the **horse tamarind,** a pulse native to tropical America, accused of causing baldness; and **horseweed,** which is wild lettuce and probably owes its name to its rank growth (up to nine feet high)—but it also happens that horses dote on it.

HO
stands for

the **Hottentot**, a fish of South Africa, for the **Hottentot cherry**, a fruit (but not a cherry) of South Africa, and for the **Hottentot fig** (or horse fig to Afrikaaners); for the **Houdan**, a chicken which sports an extravagant bonnet of feathers on its head; for **hound's-tongue**, a sort of borage; and for the **houseleek**, known also as St. Patrick's cabbage and as (take a deep breath) welcome-home-husband-however-drunk-and-late-you-may-be, a useful plant to possess, for it protects the house against lightning.

HORSERADISH. The radish is worth its weight in lead, the beet its weight in silver, the horseradish its weight in gold. We have this assessment from no less an authority than Apollo, who himself received it from the Delphic oracle, which seems on this occasion to have expressed itself with unaccustomed clarity. Unfortunately, clarity is not characteristic of the ancient nomenclature of the horseradish and the plants closely related to it, so our translations of their names in modern times, even if the plants themselves have remained unchanged, are largely a matter of guesswork—especially when the persons who attempt to do the translating not only are not sure what the ancient words meant, but are not sure what the modern words mean either. Thus a French writer who informs us that the horseradish is pictured on Egyptian tombs of the XII dynasty is unconvincing, since it is evident that she has succumbed to an error common in France, that of using the word *raifort* correctly to mean the horseradish, *Armoracia lapathifolia,* but also incorrectly to designate the black winter radish, *Raphanus sativus* var. *niger,* in the belief that the two are identical. The depictions referred to in this particular case are, I imagine, those which deal with the diet of the pyramid builders, in which case it is probably the ordinary radish which is involved. We must assume nevertheless that the Egyptians knew the horseradish at least by the XIX dynasty, about 1500 B.C., the presumable date of the Exodus, if it is true that the horseradish (probably its leaves, which when young and tender are usable in salads) was, as we are often told, one of the five bitter herbs which the Jews were enjoined to eat at Passover. (The others included coriander, lettuce, horehound and nettles.)

HORSE RADISH *pot and spoon by Edward Aldridge. Silver with dark blue glass lining, London, 1771–1772*

The imprecision with which the ancients themselves referred to several closely related plants (they seem to have made no clear distinction between the radish and the horseradish until Rutilius Palladius did so in the fourth century A.D.), plus our own doubts as to what their various terms really meant, have made it possible for some writers to assert that the horseradish was known in the ancient world only as a food and for others to say that it was known only as a medicine; for some to say that it was only gathered wild and for others to say that it was cultivated expressly for the table. Under the circumstances I can only resort to quoting a work which sums up the position of the horseradish in the

Horseradish

ancient world as follows:

Radishes were esteemed largely for their medical qualities, but horse-radish was cited not only for this, but also on gastronomic grounds. Of the former Dioscorides maintained that they improved the eyesight and favored menstruation, while Pliny believed they dissolved gallstones. Of horse-radish, Pliny wrote that "persons who have overeaten should take it as sharp as possible, and asthmatics should eat its seeds, roasted, or crushed with honey." As a food, opinions on it were divided. Cato, in his earliest of Roman agricultural treatises, thought it worthwhile to give directions for its cultivation, and it is granted pride of place in a wall painting which may still be seen at Pompeii today. Some held it in low esteem because it provoked belching, while others consumed it copiously in winter for its warming qualities. Apicius thought it too bland, and proposed accompanying it with peppered wine, or that strongly flavored condiment, *garum*. Its juice was much used for cooking, the best for the purpose being considered that of Mount Algidus, in the Alban hills, whose volcanic soil seems to have been just right for horse-radish.

There seems little point in giving you the source of this quotation, which you will not be able to verify anyway, but for your information, and because I like to give credit where credit is due, I will identify it as a passage from *The Food of Ancient Greece and Rome,* by Waverley Root, a book which no publisher at the time of writing had been foolhardy enough to bring out.

The uncertainty about the place of horseradish in the ancient world is paralleled by a similar uncertainty about the place of its origin, difficult to determine now, since it has become naturalized all over the world. It has been attributed to the Mediterranean area (*Encyclopaedia Britannica*); southeastern Europe and western Asia (*The Oxford Book of Food Plants*); western and southeastern Asia (*A Dictionary of English Plant Names*); the Orient (*Larousse Gastronomique*); southeastern Europe and Siberia (*Le Livre des Bonnes Herbes*); and no doubt other regions as well. It would be my own guess that horseradish originated not far from the area where it is most consumed and most appreciated today, Germany. Georges and Germaine Blond, in their *Histoire pittoresque de notre alimentation,* place it among "specifically Gallic vegetables," an ethnic adjective which can include those Gauls who migrated originally from Germany, and describe it as "the great horse-radish of Germany, which grew to the size of a small infant." Some of the first intimations that horseradish was being cultivated, not simply gathered wild, in Europe (Cato's example had apparently been forgotten) came from Germany, and it seems to have spread from central Europe northward to Scandinavia and westward to England in Renaissance times. The first mention of it in England as a food (it had been known there as a medicine since the thirteenth century) seems to have been made by a sixteenth-century herbalist who wrote that in Germany it was used to make "a sauce to eate fish with and such like meates as we do mustarde." Not until 1640 was it admitted that it was resorted to in Britain by "country people and strong laboring men . . . it is too strong for tender and gentle stomachs." But shortly afterward horseradish sauce had become in England the standard accompaniment for beef even on the tables of those with tender and gentle stomachs. Horseradish is called "German mustard" by the French today.

"Woe to the cook whose sauce had no sting," wrote Chaucer. He could not have complained when it was made from horseradish, which has been described as the most pungent of cultivated edible roots. All the cookbooks in my library refer to horseradish as eaten only in sauces, which involves grating or crushing it, or simply grated and used as a garnish for meat or fish, otherwise untreated, except at times with the addition of a little salt and distilled vinegar (ordinary vinegars discolor it). Euell Gibbons, indeed, says that it *must* be grated to bring out its flavor:

Strangely, the hot, biting taste and pungent aroma do not exist in the unbroken root, but are developed during the grating by a chemical reaction between constituents that are found in separate cells in the growing plant. Therefore, horseradish has to be grated fine before it has much flavor.

I hesitate to disagree with a man who almost never errs, but my experience with horseradish as it is often eaten in France—unnoticed, apparently, by food writers—does not bear this out. In France horseradish is consumed as an hors d'oeuvre and promoter of the appetite; the root is brought whole to the table and the diner cuts off a slice, salts it, eats it without further ado, and continues to repeat the process until the vegetable has vanquished him. I have yet to hear anyone complain that horseradish eaten in this fashion was not hot enough. Is chewing perhaps equivalent to grating? Or is there a difference between wild horseradish, *A. lapathifolia,* which Mr. Gibbons was talking about, and cultivated horseradish, *A. rusticana,* which is the variety served at my table?

The worst gastronomic use to which this worthy seasoning has been put must have been that invented by the devoted researchers of Ohio State University's Department of Dairy Technology, who perfected, if that is the *mot juste*, brassicaceous beer ice cream, flavored with root beer and horseradish.

HU
stands for

the **Huchen**, a tasty Danube salmon which runs up to a weight of thirty-five pounds; for the **hurtleberry**, a mispronounced whortleberry; for the **hummingbird**, whose roasted heart is reputed to be aphrodisiac; for **hungry rice**, a cereal widely used in West Africa for making couscous; and for the **husk tomato**, which is nothing other than the ground cherry.

And **HU** also stands for

HUCKLEBERRY. When he "had a surfeit of human society," Henry David Thoreau wrote, he deserted his habitual haunts for "fresh woods and pastures new," and "made my supper of huckleberries and blueberries on Fair Haven Hill, and laid up a store for several days."

The fruits do not yield their true flavor to the purchaser of them, nor to him who raises them for the market. There is but one way to obtain it, yet few take that way. If you would know the flavor of huckleberries, ask the cow-boy or the partridge. It is a vulgar error to suppose that you have tasted huckleberries who never plucked them. A huckleberry never reaches Boston; they have not been known there since they grew on her three hills. The ambrosial and essential part of the fruit is lost with the bloom which is rubbed off in the market cart, and they become mere provender. As long as Eternal Justice reigns, not one innocent huckleberry can be transported thither from the country's hills.

It was fitting that an author so thoroughly American should sing the praises of the huckleberry, which, though a member of the heath family, is a thoroughly American plant, unknown to the Old World—especially an author who, like the huckleberry, was untamable. Did the nature of the huckleberry account also for its selection as a name for one of his best-known heroes by Mark Twain, relatively untamable too? Huckleberry Finn was not only a thoroughly American character, he was also a wild one, refractory to the idea of being transplanted from his free if savage background, to have his bloom rubbed off in the market cart and his asperities absorbed in a society of bland and bourgeois blueberries.

Huckleberries cannot be reft from their cherished woods and pastures; they are gathered wild,

HUCKLEBERRY. *Etching from* The Natural History of New York, *6 parts, Natural History Survey, Albany, 1842–1879*

for they do not repay cultivation. They show refractoriness too, by producing ten large hard seeds each, which take delight in lodging uncomfortably between the teeth; blueberry seeds are more numerous but smaller, and can be ignored. This difference provides the layman with his surest clue for telling the blueberries from the huckleberries, though many of them are guided rather by the belief that the huckleberry appears on low-growing, spreading bushes and is darker and smaller than the blueberry. This is true in most cases, but not in all.

The botanist proceeds otherwise, by identifying an ambiguous plant as a member either of the genus *Vaccinium* (blueberries), which also has species in Europe, or of *Gaylussacia* (huckleberries), which has not. When I was a boy in New England and went a-berrying with a retired lard can for equipment, I do not remember making any distinction between huckleberries and blueberries; but it appears that Americans who live east of the Appalachians are better at telling them apart than natives of parts farther west. What many people on the Pacific coast between central California and British Columbia call the mountain huckleberry is actually the evergreen blueberry, *V. ovatum.* I have heard from the same quarter of a red huckleberry, of which I find no trace in any botanical work, so I suspect it is some variety of *Vaccinium* also, unless it is even farther removed from the genuine article. Conscientious huckleberries should be blue or black.

In the East, it appears that berry pickers usually identify correctly the common huckleberry, G. *baccata* (or G. *resinosa*), also called the black huckleberry or the highbush huckleberry, whose dark shiny fruit is tarter than that of the blueberry and is accordingly preferred for pies. Blueberries are rated first for cake (or blueberry bread, as it is also called), but a mixture of the two does no harm in either case. G. *frondosa*, the blue huckleberry, called also the dangleberry or tangleberry, is less tasty, but nevertheless the best after G. *baccata*. G. *dumosa*, the bush huckleberry or gopherberry, bears rather insipid black fruit. G. *brachycera*, the box huckleberry or juniper berry (no relation to genuine juniper), is not worth the trouble of picking.

HY
stands for

the **hyacinth,** whose bulbs were torn up from the gardens of England's Radley College and eaten by half-starved students; for the **hyacinth bean,** or lablab niger; for **hydragyrum cum creta,** a handy seventeenth-century antidote against misfortune in love; for the **hyena,** which was fattened for the table in ancient Egypt; for the **hygrophorus,** an obstinate mushroom of which one variety persists in growing under snow; and for the **Hyracoidea** or **hyraxes,** ambiguous African mammals which are frequently mistaken for rabbits, whether in the field or in the skillet.

And **HY** also stands for

HYSSOP. "Hyssop," says a modern herbal, "is hardly used at all in modern cooking," and so finds it unnecessary to give any information about it. An ancient herbal offers exactly the opposite reason for acting in exactly the same fashion: hyssop is so widely used that it needs no attention. John Gerard, at the end of the sixteenth century, while remarking that "all kinds of Hyssope do grow in my Garden," explained:

> Dioscorides that gave us so many rules for the knowledge of simples, hath left Hyssope altogether without description, as being a plant so well known that it needed none: whose example I follow not onely in this plant, but in many others which be common, to avoid Tediousnesse to the Reader.

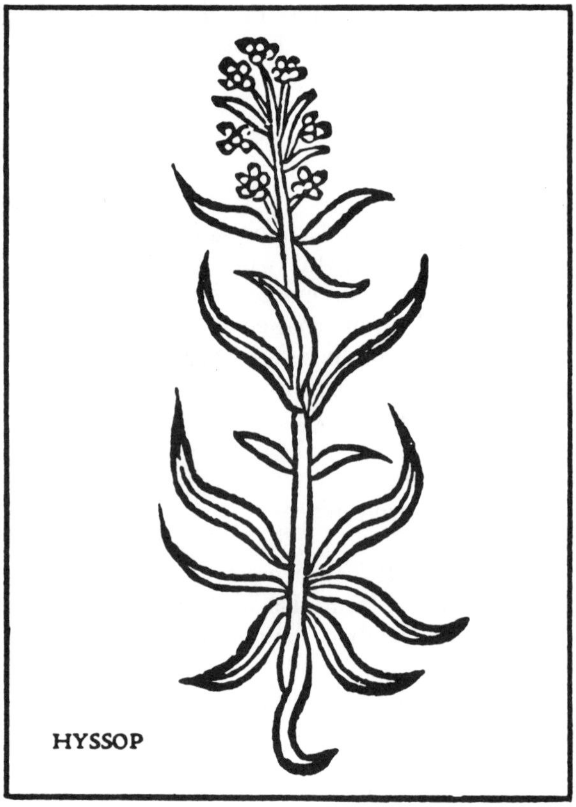

Hyssop. *Woodcut from Peter Schoeffer:* Herbarius, *Mainz, 1484*

It was perhaps the very abundance of hyssop which led the translators of the King James Bible to fall unsuspectingly into an error which has persisted to this day. They construed the Hebrew word *ēsōb* or *ēzōbh* as hyssop, a mistake all the easier to make since this word is indeed the ancestor of the English "hyssop"; but *ēsōb* and hyssop are not the same plant. What we call hyssop today did not grow in Palestine. The Biblical hyssop was a plant propitious for sprinkling, a service we find it performing in a number of scriptural passages, most notably in Exodus 20:12, when it was prescribed to mark the doors of Jewish houses so that the angel of death, striking down the first-born of Egyptian families, would pass over the dwellings of the Hebrews: "Ye shall take a bunch of hyssop, and dip it in the blood [of a sacrificed lamb] . . . and strike the lintel and the two side posts with the blood." The hyssop of the Hebrews, which was one of the ingredients of their holy oil, was granted a sacred or magical role, perhaps because it was believed to have great medical virtues. We find it in Leviticus curing a leper, while Psalms 51:7 prays: "Purge me with hyssop, and I shall be clean." Other peoples of the eastern Mediterranean seem to have shared a belief in the mystical powers of this herb: but what was it? Among the plants which have been suggested are capers, marjoram, mint, rosemary, origanum and savory, the last particularly common in Syria and Palestine; but actually nobody knows.

The hyssop of the Bible was probably also the hyssop of Dioscorides which Gerard cited, but probably not the hyssop of Gerard himself, which is apparently the herb we have today. Our hyssop was probably that of the Middle Ages, which liked strong seasoning, but its highly pungent, mint-like flavor has proved too pronounced for contemporary tastes; yet only forty years ago an authoritative gardening manual was able to write that hyssop was "widely grown for ornament and as an herb for flavoring." The fact that it has not yet disappeared altogether in the United States may be the result of this first factor. A low-growing shrub, twelve to eighteen inches high, with blue, rose or white flowers, it makes an attractive edging for an herb garden and is also a recommendable rock-garden plant, with a positive aversion to water: "*Ne veut estre arrousée,*" wrote Olivier de Serres in his charmingly outmoded French, "*qu'en temps sec et aride, en tout autre hayssant l'humidité.*" ("It doesn't like being watered except in dry and arid weather, in all others hating dampness.") It has been saved in France, where it is cultivated to a small extent, by its inclusion in a number of liqueurs. It can also be used to make herb tea; its flowers give a delicious, highly perfumed honey; and its oil goes into eau de Cologne.

The hedge hyssop is not hyssop, since it belongs to the genus *Gratiola,* and is even dangerous; where it grows abundantly, as in some parts of Switzerland, cows have to be kept away from it, since it is toxic for them. When its name is borrowed by other plants, usually to indicate that they are aromatic, the result is sometimes picturesque, as in hyssop loosestrife and hyssop skullcap.

In Switzerland and Bavaria, old women slip hyssop leaves between the pages of their missals in the hope that its strong odor will prevent them from falling asleep during boring sermons.

I

IRWIN, WILLIAM WALLACE: *Statistics show that of those who contract the habit of eating, very few ever survive.*

IRWIN, WILLIAM WALLACE: [*Gastronomic literature*] *is the product of well intentioned ignorance, and is written in the thrilling and captivating style of an employee of the Civil Service reporting on the tonnage of gramagrass seed imported during the decade 1925–1935.*

I
stands for

the **ibex,** a wild Eurasian mountain goat which would taste like gamy mutton if it had not become too scarce for anyone to taste; for **iburu,** a cereal eaten in West Africa, where its French name means "black manna"; for **icaqueira,** a fruit eaten in equatorial Africa which is related to the coco plum; for **Iceland moss,** used in northern Europe to produce slightly bitter gelatin; for the **ice plant,** of which one species bears edible fruit; for the **iguana,** a lizard of which a large South American variety is served in French Guiana, nostalgically, as "iguana in the style of Provence," a region which has no iguanas; for **ihii,** the red squirrelfish of Tahiti; for the **impala,** an antelope which provides some of the most relished venison of Africa; for the **Imperatore,** an Italian apple noted for producing heavy yields; and for the **incense tree,** whose nuts are eaten in tropical Africa, and so is its pulp, but only after a precautionary scalding.

I
stands for

a long list of foods identified as Indian, sometimes East Indian, sometimes West: for instance, in the East, the **Indian almond,** which is the Hawaiian kamani nut; the **Indian butter bean,** of which some varieties are eaten pods and all; **Indian mustard,** of tropical Africa and Madagascar; the **Indian nut,** which was Europe's first name for the nutmeg, and **Indian salt,** which was Europe's first name for sugar; the **Indian pea,** which, consumed in great quantities, can induce paralysis; and **Indian shot,** a sort of canna whose root is eaten in tropical Africa despite its scarcity; and, in the West, **Indian corn,** which of course is MAIZE; **Indian cress,** which is nasturtium leaves; the **Indian cucumber,** whose scientific name, *Medeola virginiana,* refers to Medea the sorceress; the **Indian fig,** or prickly pear; **Indian ginger,** or Canadian snakeroot; the **Indian potato,** or groundnut (but sometimes it means a yam); **Indian rice,** or American wild rice, which is not rice; the **Indian runner bean,** which *is* a bean; and the **Indian turnip,** alias jack-in-the-pulpit.

I
stands for

the **inga,** whose beanlike pods contain a pulp eaten in South America and Pacific islands; for the **inkberry,** in some localities the pokeberry and in others various bays which, so far as I know, are not eaten; for the **inkfish,** a type of cuttlefish which confuses its enemies by squirting clouds of dark liquid into the water; for **innards,** a coy word employed by those who shudder at the thought of eating the internal organs of animals, with the possible exception of the liver; for **inoy,** a seed eaten sparingly in West Africa; for **insects,** of which man has been eating since antiquity, and still eats, more kinds than you would be likely to expect, including those which Aristophanes called "four-winged fowl"; and for **intestines,** cooked by the Tuaregs in the Sahara Desert according to an ingenious technique which requires no use of precious water.

And finally **I** stands for

the **Ipswich clam,** by which inhabitants of Massachusetts' North Shore mean the mollusk known elsewhere as the steamer; for the **iris,** which flavored Louis XIV's custard; for **Irish moss,** a seaweed used in making blancmange; for the **iroko,** an African plant whose young leaves are occasionally eaten in the Congo basin; for **ironwood,** a name given to several different trees of which one, *Lophira alata,* provides edible seeds for tropical Africans, while another, *Olneya tesota,* does the same for Mexican Indians in Lower California; for the **isard,** or izard, the chamois of the Pyrenees, smaller and, in some opinions, tastier than its Alpine counterpart; for **isinglass,** a gelatin obtained from the air bladders of fish, notably the sturgeon; and for **ivory,** which the ancient Romans thought they were eating when they munched elephant trunk, but it was only cartilage.

J

JAMES, WILLIAM: *Few of us are adventurous in the matter of food; in fact, most of us think there is something disgusting in a bill of fare to which we are unused.*

JOHNSON, DR. SAMUEL: *The great source of pleasure is variety.*

JOHNSON, DR. SAMUEL: *To make dictionaries is hard work.*

JA
stands for

the **jaboticaba**, a purple fruit of the myrtle family, highly popular in Brazil, but little known elsewhere except in Hawaii; for the **jaçana**, a wading bird which builds a floating nest; for the **jack**, one of the two most valuable food fishes in the Philippines; for the **jackal**, considered a game animal in the Sahara since at least A.D. 900; for the **jack bean**, widely eaten in Latin America despite its reputation, fortunately exaggerated, for being poisonous; for the **Jack Dempsey**, an Amazonian fish described as "very aggressive [but] the fighting between males . . . is ritualized"; for the **jackfruit**, the poor man's breadfruit; for the **jack-in-the-pulpit**, or Indian turnip, which you had better not eat unless you are as skillful as American Indians were about getting rid of the irritant raphides on its starchy corms; for the **jackrabbit**, which is not a rabbit but a HARE; for the **jackknife clam** of California, not much eaten because, according to Euell Gibbons, "these clams are smarter than most clam diggers"; and for **Jacob's staff**, our fourteenth synonym for the mullein.

JA
stands for

the **jaguar**, hunted for food by American Indians in what is now the southwestern United States about 8000 years ago; for the **jalapeño**, a chili which, being grass-green, looks cool, but don't trust it; for the **jaliscote chapas**, a tree bearing beanlike pods, known only in Mexico, where both the pods and the beans inside them are eaten, without its being necessary to go to the trouble of shelling them; for **Jamaica dogwood**, once and perhaps still an ingredient of Lydia Pinkham's Vegetable Compound for Female Troubles; for **Jamaica pepper**, which is allspice; for **Jamaica sorrel**, alias red sorrel or roselle, used to make acid jellies; for the **jamberry**, so called because it is too flavorless to be worth eating in any other form; for the **jambolan plum**, or **Java plum**, a fruit of the West Indies and Burma closely related to the wild **jambos** of South Africa and the **jambu** of India and Malaya, this last also called the rose apple (whose native species in Hawaii is the *'ohia ha*), linking all these fruits (are you still with me?) with the **jamrose** of Africa, the fruit of the rose apple tree, making them all descendants of the mythical Hindu jambu, or gambu, which bore (*phew!*) the golden fruit of immortality: "Done!" as James Joyce puts it triumphantly in the musical chapter of *Ulysses*.

JA
stands for

Japanese knotweed, whose young shoots look like asparagus but don't taste like it; for the **Japanese medlar**, which is the loquat; for **Japanese millet**, which is eaten, though it is scarce, in West Africa; for **Japan pepper**, a condiment indeed resembling pepper, used in China and Japan; for the **Japan**

plum, another term for the loquat; for the **japonica,** closely related to the quince but even sourer; for the **jargenelle,** a pear highly popular in Europe in the seventeenth century; for the **Java almond,** eaten in East Africa, and the **Java olive,** a nut too in spite of its name, eaten in Senegal; and for the **javelina,** the only native wild pig of the United States (into which it oozed from Mexico), which doubtless started out as a peccary in South America.

JE
stands for

the **Jefferson plum,** named in honor of a devoted developer of foods who found time also to preside over the destiny of the United States, a task less complicated in his time, it is true, than it is now; for the **jeheb,** a sort of desert pulse eaten in Somalia and Eritrea; for the **jellyfish,** which appears in a recipe left us by Apicius, who, unfortunately, neglected to explain how you go about handling a jellyfish in the kitchen; for the **jelly melon,** or spiny melon, of Africa; for the **Jennetting** (or Jeaneting or Juneting), a charming old-fashioned name for a charming old-fashioned apple particularly popular in the days of Good Queen Bess; for **jerboas,** or jumping mice, unknown south of the Sahara according to the reference books, which does not prevent tropical Africans, who do not consult reference books, from eating them in great numbers; for **Jarden's courser,** a shore bird on the verge of extinction; for the **Jersey,** a cow developed on the island of that name, whose milk is exceptionally rich in butterfat; for **Jerusalem corn,** a type of sorghum popular in East Africa; for the **Jerusalem haddock,** a fish eaten all the way down the Atlantic coast of Africa, which may be an opah but isn't a haddock; for the **Jerusalem oak pazote,** a name bestowed by California food packagers on the epazote, or goosefoot, a strongly flavored Mexican herb used to season beans and tortillas; for the **Jesuit's nut,** also called the water caltrop or, when encountered in Chinese cooking, the water chestnut; for the **jewelfish,** a freshwater creature eaten in tropical Africa despite its small size (four inches); for **jewelweed,** known to many of us as the flower-bearing impatiens, whose young sprouts are reported to be excellent eating by wild-food enthusiasts and poisonous by non-enthusiasts; for the **Jew's apple,** which is the eggplant; for the **Jew's ear,** a corruption of "Judas's ear," since this edible jelly fungus grows on the elder, a tree on which, according to legend, Judas hanged himself; and for **Jew's mallow,** a name mistakenly applied to coriander leaves in the Middle East, though it should be restricted to a type of jute whose foliage, fresh or dried, is widely eaten in tropical Africa and Madagascar.

And **JE** also stands for

JERUSALEM ARTICHOKE. Of all the hitherto unknown foods which a newly discovered America bestowed bountifully upon Europe, the only vegetable of any consequence contributed by North America was the Jerusalem artichoke; all the others, including the "Virginia" POTATO, originated in South America. It was not an overwhelmingly generous contribution. The Jerusalem artichoke is of less interest to the gourmet than to the etymologist; but for reasons of space, the etymological aspect of foods has been arbitrarily ruled out of this volume. We are thus even barred from, among other things, examining the etymological evidence which contradicts Gerard's *Herball*, the first widely circulated work of its kind in English, in its statement concerning the Jerusalem artichoke that "al these that have written and mentioned it bring it from America, but from far different places, as from Peru, Brasill, and Canada." Actually the place of origin of the Jerusalem artichoke, which is the tuber of a sunflower, *Helianthus tuberosus*, is the central United States and Canada. A fast spreader, it had reached the Atlantic coast, where it grows wild from Nova Scotia to Georgia, before the white man did, and was there diligently cultivated by American Indians. It was in an Indian vegetable garden on Cape Cod that Samuel de Champlain

JERUSALEM ARTICHOKE. *Engraving from Vilmorin-Andrieux:* Les plantes potagères, *Paris, 1904*

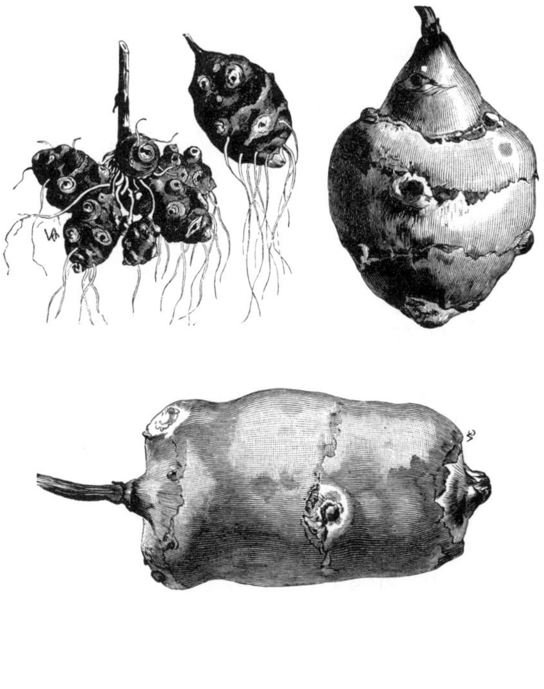

first saw it, and so reported in 1605. In 1616 he rediscovered it in Canada and sent some of the edible tubers to France. Whether or not he had done so the first time I do not know, but somebody did, for Marc Lescarbot's *Histoire de la Nouvelle France,* whose first edition appeared in 1609 and its last in 1618, said that they were then being sold in Paris, where street merchants had been instructed to hawk them under the name *topinambours,* which is what they are still called in France today.

Meanwhile in Italy, Fabio Colonna had seen the plant in the gardens of Cardinal Farnese, but at what date I am unable to say, except that it had to be earlier than 1633, when this fact was reported in the amended edition of Gerard's *Herball,* which described Colonna as "one of the first setters of it forth"—as he must have been if the *Herball* took this information from the book Colonna published in Naples in 1592. At that date, the Farnese tubers could only have been supplied by the Spaniards, and indeed Colonna testified that they had come from the "West Indies." This should have been too far south, but as the Spaniards ranged up and down the coast, sometimes as far as New England, they might easily have picked up some tubers to the north and then shipped them to Europe from the Caribbean. It was their habit to present samples of new plants to the Pope, and the Pope's habit to pass them on to some current favorite (this was how the American haricot BEAN got its start in Italy), so this could explain how they reached the garden of Cardinal Farnese, who had, precisely, been elevated to this rank personally by the Pope.

The first Jerusalem artichokes on record as having reached England were a pair of roots given in 1617 to one John Goodyer by a Flemish merchant (and amateur gardener) named Franqueville, who may have received them from one of the persons with whom he traded. Goodyer planted one with great success and reported that fact in 1621, in a passage usually cited as the first reference in English to this vegetable. However, a year earlier a physician and health fanatic of Bath, Tobias Venner, in his *Via recta ad vitam longam* (*The Straight Way to Long Life*) had already described the "Vertues" of the Jerusalem artichoke, so it must have been available before Goodyer wrote it up. For that matter, the *Oxford English Dictionary* had listed "Artichocks of Jerusalem" in 1620.

England and France, in direct contact with North America, began eating Jerusalem artichokes early in the seventeenth century, and we hear of their being grown in Germany in 1632. It was perhaps the reassuring familiarity of the word "artichoke" which won them this swift acceptance, while the potato, offered at about the same time, was shunned as strange and therefore suspect. When the potato was finally accepted, the Jerusalem artichoke was dropped—partly, perhaps, because a superstition had developed that it caused leprosy, based on the resemblance of its irregularly shaped roots to fingers deformed by that disease. From that time forward, the Jerusalem artichoke was considered more or less famine food, commonly eaten only by underprivileged peoples, as it is today in Egypt, eastern Africa and South Africa. Otherwise it is resorted to only when other aliments are lacking, particularly the potato, the two playing complementary roles. Thus in 1722, when food shortages caused a prize to be offered for the proposal and promotion of new food sources, the French pharmacist Antoine Parmentier won the prize by suggesting the potato, for which he is remembered, and also the Jerusalem artichoke, for which he is not. During World War II, the Jerusalem artichoke regained favor in several countries as an aliment which could be had without a ration card. A Marcel Aymé story of this period notes: "They were served . . . in exchange for a 100-gram bread ticket with a Jerusalem artichoke sandwich." The emergency over, the Jerusalem artichoke returned to what is today its usual role, that of providing fodder for livestock, especially pigs.

The fact is that Jerusalem artichokes are not particularly satisfying from any point of view. Euell Gibbons says "they have as much food value as potatoes," but I fear that this is one case where he has allowed his enthusiasm for wild food to lead him astray. James Trager writes that "the rather sweet starch in the roots of the Jerusalem artichoke . . . made the plant popular with the early settlers"—though a peculiarity of this vegetable is that, unlike most edible roots, it contains no starch. The late Rosie Maurel, though she held a degree in medicine, made the same error in her *Dictionnaire des Aliments.* What both mistook for starches were inulides, in which Jerusalem artichoke tubers are particularly rich; they might be described a little freely as a form of sugar which can be tolerated by diabetics, no doubt because they have little value as food.

The taste of the Jerusalem artichoke can hardly be described as fine, delicate or subtle; and even those who like it admit that satiety comes quickly. To many its flavor does not even suggest artichokes, though it did to Champlain, who seems to have been the first to give it that name. Nicolas de Bonnefons, gentleman-in-waiting to Louis XIV and a gourmet of parts, wrote of

Jerusalem artichokes that "in salad, they have the taste of artichoke hearts, a little less firm, however; fried in fritter dough, they evoke salsify; boiled, they resemble, but from afar, potatoes"—by which he probably meant sweet potatoes. An unidentified French traveler is quoted by Rosie Maurel as describing the "roots as large as turnips [an exaggeration] or truffles, very good to eat, with a taste reminiscent of cardoons [a relative of the artichoke] and even more agreeable." Lewis and Clark were happy indeed to come upon wild Jerusalem artichokes during a starvation period of their expedition, for, of the many roots the local Indians ate, it was the only one they recognized or found palatable. John McPhee, in a *New Yorker* article on a trip he made with Euell Gibbons, during which they lived on wild food alone, included this passage:

For dinner, we had boiled Jerusalem artichokes. . . . They look like small sweet potatoes, since they are bumpy and elongated and are covered with red jackets. The flesh inside, however, is delicate and white. Boiled, it has the consistency of boiled young turnips or summer squash, and the taste suggests the taste of hearts of artichokes. . . . Gibbons . . . said he was sorry that Jerusalem artichokes and a number of other wild foods . . . had been named for more familiar foods. "These things are not substitutes for tame foods," he went on. "They have flavors of their own, and it is not fair to them to call them by the name of something else. These are not artichokes. They're sunflower tubers." With a knife and fork, he laid one open and then scooped up a mound of the white flesh. "Boy!" he said. "That goes down very gratefully. Just eating greens, you can get awfully damn hungry." . . . For a while we ate without speaking, because the artichokes were so good.

As for that pioneer planter of Jerusalem artichokes, John Goodyer, he rendered his verdict in 1621 as follows:

These roots are dressed divers wayes, some boile them in water, and after stew them with sacke [sherry] and butter, adding a little ginger. Others bake them in pies, putting Marrow, Dates, Ginger, Raisons of the sun, Sacke, etc. Others some other way as they are led by their skill in Cookerie. But in my judgement, which way soever they be drest and eaten they stir up and cause a filthie loathesome stinking winde within the bodie, thereby causing the belly to bee much pained and tormented, and are a meat more fit for swine, than men.

JO
stands for

the **job jaune,** or "yellow job" in French, a selachian fish which seems to have no name in English, but makes up for it by being called the holy white dog in Creole, and is eaten avidly under any name in what used to be called Mozambique; for **Job's tears,** which might be classed as millet if its seeds were not so large, eaten in parts of southeastern Asia, the Philippines and the Congo; for the **Jonah crab,** which seems to be the one I used to cook over a bonfire on the shores of the Providence River when I was seven; and for the **Jonathan,** an American apple a little younger than the country in which it was born, since that happy event dates from circa 1820.

And **JO** also stands for

JOHN DORY. When Pliny reported that the John Dory was the favorite fish of Cádiz, he apparently meant to imply that it was appreciated nowhere else; but when Elizabeth David tells us that it is a favorite fish of Venice, she clearly does not want us to think that Venice is alone in liking it. The John Dory is indeed one of the most esteemed food fishes in Mediterranean countries, with firm white flesh whose taste has been compared to that of the turbot, high praise indeed. It is also found along the eastern coasts of the Atlantic, southward as far as South Africa, northward normally to the southern coast of England, but is occasionally encountered even off Norway. The maximum length reported is 22½ inches, the maximum weight 18 pounds; but 12 pounds is a good size for this fish.

The John Dory was prized during the Middle Ages, when it was a fish for the rich, too dear for most people. It is indeed relatively expensive today, for the same reason as in earlier times, its

JOHN DORY. *Drawings from Mrs. Isabella Beeton:* The Book of Household Management, *London, 1861*

high proportion of waste: two-thirds of its weight is accounted for by its large head and its viscera. For this reason also, while it can be cooked whole, the John Dory is usually presented in fillets.

The John Dory is to most of our familiar fish as a nineteenth-century automobile is to one of the mid-twentieth century, Alan Davidson has remarked. It is indeed a primitive fish, not sufficiently limber to weave or dart at its prey, so to snap up smaller fish it has been fitted with an extensible jaw which can be thrust suddenly forward from the body, which remains attentively motionless behind it, waiting to learn the result of this unexpected lunge. The result is usually good, for the victim is apparently unaware that it is within range of danger; it does not know that its enemy is equipped with a trick mouthpiece. The curious construction of the John Dory's head pulls the corners of its mouth lugubriously down, so that it seems perpetually on the verge of bursting into tears.

The John Dory is peculiarly built in other respects also, all height and no width, showing considerable bulk if you come upon it broadside, but resembling a knife edge when encountered head-on: it has been described as plate-shaped. Its most conspicuous marking is a large yellow-rimmed black spot behind the gills on both sides, which is why it is called the *saint-pierre* in French, the *San Pietro* in Italian and the *Peterfisch* in German. The legend goes that these are the marks of the thumb and forefinger of St. Peter, who, after having caught one of these fish, took pity on it when it gave vent to plaintive cries of despair, and threw it back into the sea. A slightly different version of the story says that the fisherman saint caught a John Dory on the instructions of Christ, who told him that he would find in its mouth an obol to pay the temple tax; Peter took the piece of money and threw the fish back, marked with his fingerprints as, we may imagine, a sort of receipt. There is even a third story, ascribing the marks to St. Christopher, who is supposed to have plucked the fish from the water while carrying the infant Christ across a river on his shoulders. Sticklers may tell you that the first story should be reserved for the John Dory, the second for the halibut and the third for a freshwater tilapia. Pooh.

JU
stands for

the **jubaea**, a Chilean palm known as the monkey-coconut, which yields to primates slightly higher on the evolutionary scale a sort of sugar or honey obtained from its seeds; for **Judas's ear**, a mushroom which grows on the trunks of trees too old to prevent it; for the **Judas tree**, one of many to which has been attributed the honor of having been selected by Judas for his hanging, whose flowers are eaten in salads or fritters; for **jueyes**, the land crabs which routed Sir Francis Drake in the Caribbean; for the **jugo bean**, which you may also call, as fancy dictates, the Bambara groundnut, the Congo goober, the earth pea, the Kaffir pea, the ground bean, or the Madagascar or stone groundnut; for the **jumlums**, a small purple fruit of southern India; for the **jumpy bean** of tropical America, eaten at the risk of losing the hair; for the **Juneberry**, of which various species are known alternatively as the serviceberry, the sugarberry or the shadbush, all of them somewhat neglected since American Indians and pioneers stopped eating them; for the **June drop**, an immature orange; for the **jungle fowl**, the wild ancestor of all the world's domestic hens; for **jungle rice**, which in defiance of its adjective is cultivated, in West Africa; for the **juniper**, whose berries were a favorite seasoning of American Indians in the Pacific Northwest; for **junsai**, the "slippery vegetable" or water shield, a wild-plant delicacy of Japan; and for **jute**, widely cultivated for its fibers, but one of the species grown for this purpose, *Corchorus olitorius*, is intercepted by tropical Africans, who eat its leaves.

And **JU** also stands for

JUJUBE. When Ulysses reached the Land of the Lotus Eaters (now identified with the Tunisian island of Djerba), Homer tells us, his companions abandoned themselves to the local diet, forgetting home and families and desiring nothing except to remain in the country of the lotus, in perpetual idleness, forever. The Lotophagoi, according to ancient writers, lived on the lotus exclusively and also made a drink from it. Was it lotus eating or lotus drinking that deprived Ulysses' men of energy? One of the alternative names given to the plant which Homer had in mind associated it with a fruit from which an alcoholic drink is made, strong enough to provoke at least temporary oblivion: the date. The lotus of Homer was not the lotus of Buddha nor of the Nile, but *Zizyphus lotus*, alias the Chinese date, alias the jujube; date spirits have a reputation for headiness. True, not only is the jujube not a lotus, it is not a date either, but it does share other characteristics with the date besides the similar taste, which was remarked by Herodotus. The jujube resembles the date also in size, shape, sweetness, outer color (but the inner flesh is white) and in containing a single elongated

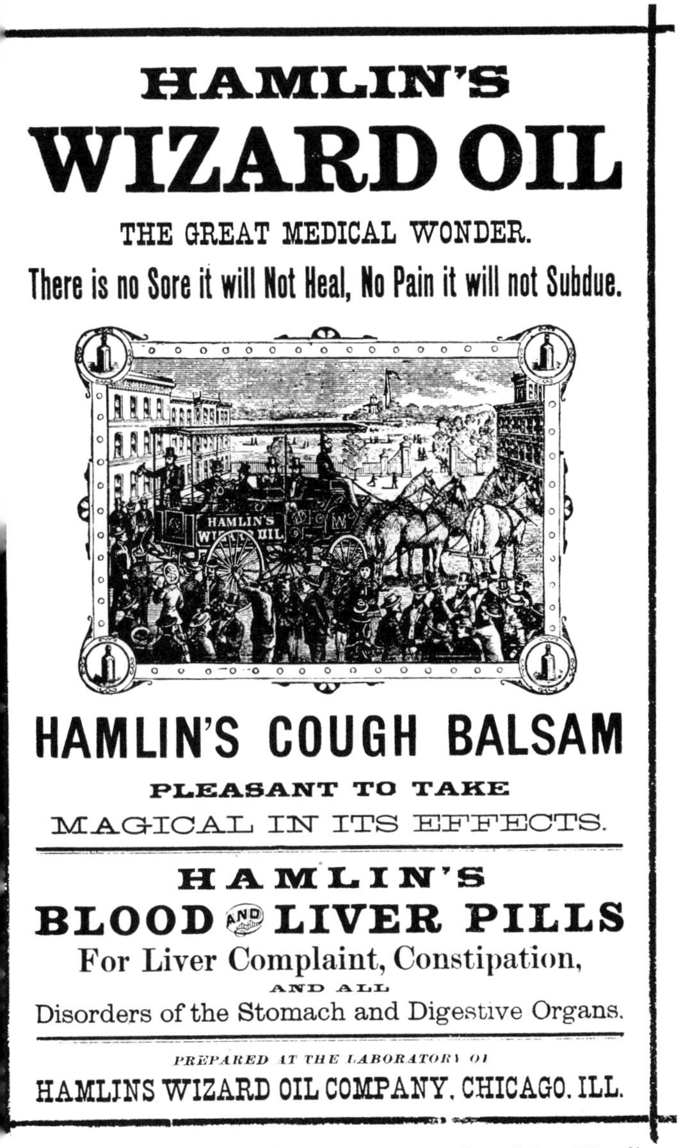

HAMLIN'S
WIZARD OIL
THE GREAT MEDICAL WONDER.
There is no Sore it will Not Heal, No Pain it will not Subdue.
HAMLIN'S COUGH BALSAM
PLEASANT TO TAKE
MAGICAL IN ITS EFFECTS.
HAMLIN'S
BLOOD AND LIVER PILLS
For Liver Complaint, Constipation,
AND ALL
Disorders of the Stomach and Digestive Organs.
PREPARED AT THE LABORATORY OF
HAMLINS WIZARD OIL COMPANY, CHICAGO, ILL.

JUJUBE. *Advertisement from early 1860s. Hamlins Wizard Oil Company, Chicago*

kernel. It still grows wild in Tunisia.

The jujube is attributed without dispute to Asia, but there is a difference of opinion about whether it started at the western or eastern end of its Asian range. Some believe it originated in Syria, others that China was its birthplace. The latter seems likelier for several reasons: (1) China is the home of the typical species of jujube, Z. *jujuba*; (2) it is the place where the most luscious varieties are found; (3) it seems to be the country which has cultivated jujubes longest, for at least four thousand years; and (4) it is firmly anchored in Chinese gastronomic tradition. In the Middle Ages one of China's "Eight Delicacies" was suckling pig stuffed with what European translators called dates, but which were in all probability jujubes; Marco Polo reported seeing jujubes "twice the size of dates . . . used by the natives for making bread" (meal is made from jujubes in tropical Africa today); and the jujube remains one of the five principal fruits of China.

It is believed that this fruit was grown in Assyria, where, according to some historians, it did not appear before the first millennium B.C. This would have been a little late for Homer; but even if we push the Assyrian date back a few centuries, it is still a good deal later than the time of the first cultivation in China, and even after the time when several varieties were already being grown in India. (The main Indian jujube, Z. *mauritiana*, called the cottony jujube because the undersides of its leaves are woolly, bears smaller fruit than the Chinese jujube, of inferior flavor.) Pliny dated the importation of the jujube tree into Italy as having occurred only during the reign of Augustus. A spiny shrub or tree, which sometimes reaches a height of thirty feet, it was, according to one legend, the plant which provided the Crown of Thorns.

The jujube is little known in America, except as a cough lozenge or occasionally as a confection, made by processing the fruit in syrup. Yet there is a native American species, Z. *obtusifolia*, the Texas jujube or buckthorn; however, its fruit is inferior even to that of the Indian species. Chinese jujubes were introduced into the United States in 1837 and grew well enough in southernmost Florida, but no serious effort was made to exploit them. (France, where jujubes are acclimated in the south, has also shown little interest in them.) Improved Chinese varieties were brought into the United States in 1906, and have since been grown in the Southwest, especially in California, but without excessive zeal.

The jujube, with the aid of its resident insects, offers two non-edible items to international commerce. The tussah (or tussur) silkworm disdains the mulberry leaves which are the usual food of its kind, but will feed on those of the jujube. The other useful inhabitant of the jujube tree is *Coccus lacca*, an insect from which is obtained one of the oldest colorants in the world, lac dye. In former times, shellac was a by-product of the dye; nowadays, when the dye has been almost driven off the market by modern chemical colors, it would probably have disappeared completely if the situation had not been reversed: today lac dye is a by-product of shellac.

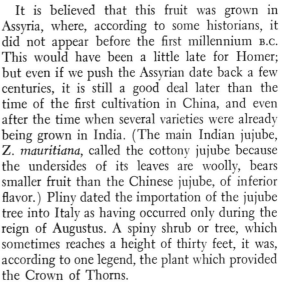

K

KING, BENJAMIN FRANKLIN: *Nothing to eat but food.*

KIPLING: *Anything green that grew out of the mould / Was an excellent herb to our fathers of old.*

KEATS: *Who, of men, can tell
That flowers would bloom, or
that green fruit would swell
To melting pulp, that
flesh would have bright mail.*

KEATS: *Four seasons fill the measure of the year.*

KA
stands for

kabeljaauw, the Dutch word for cod, which in Africa has become attached mysteriously to a species of meagre, an unrelated fish; for the **Kabuli gram,** an overgrown chick-pea found in India; for **kachai,** the name Thailand gives to a pungent root resembling ginger; and for the **kadota fig,** one of the three principal varieties of this fruit cultivated in California.

KA
stands for

a considerable number of foods designated as "kaffir," which in the minds of the white men who named them probably indicated no great esteem either for the foods or their eaters, including: the **kaffir bean,** which is nothing more nor less than the familiar cowpea of the southern United States, and should not be confused with the **kaffir bean tree,** actually closer to the pea, despite its alternative names "Boer bean" and "African walnut"; **kaffir bread,** which is sago, eaten in Africa though it is scarce there; the **kaffir cherry,** which, believe it or not, is a gardenia, but its fruit is eaten in South Africa all the same; **kaffir corn,** or Guinea corn, which is simply SORGHUM; the **kaffir melon,** popular all over Africa and Madagascar, and why shouldn't watermelon be popular?; the **kaffir orange,** a name applied to several species of *Strychnos,* some of which are also dubbed monkey apples; the **kaffir pea,** which is the jugo bean we met under the letter J; **kaffir millet,** which might just as well be called millet with no adjective; the **kaffir plum,** a name applied to two entirely distinct fruits, one of which, *Harpephyllum barteri,* is eaten only in the form of jelly, in South and West Africa, while the other, *Solerocarya caffra,* is eaten fresh, in East Africa; and the **kaffir potato,** which again needs no adjective, for it is the same potato we all eat.

KA
stands for

kagné butter, pressed from the seeds of a tropical African plant; for the **Kaido crab apple,** a Japanese species of that widespread fruit; for the **kaki,** the Japanese persimmon; for **kaku oil,** pressed from the nuts of a tropical African plant; for **kalkoentjies,** an edible South African root whose name means "little turkeys"; for the **kamani nut** of Hawaii, alias the mastwood or poon tree; for **Kamerun grass,** an African variety of sorghum; for the **kamias** of the Philippine Islands, there called a fruit, though it is cucumber-like and sour; for **kanga butter,** which like kagné butter is pressed from the seeds of a tropical African plant, but not from the same kind of seeds; for the **Kandils,** an esteemed light-green apple of Alma-Ata, in the Kasakh Republic of the Soviet Union; and for the **kangaroo,** whose tail makes a soup which Australians consider a luxury—and it is getting to be more so every day as the dog-food furnishers continue to finish off the kangaroos.

KA
stands for

kangkalaga, whose leaves are eaten in West Africa, so it might as well be called African spinach, and **kang kung,** whose leaves are eaten in China, so it is called Chinese spinach; for **kangra buckwheat,** a species grown in India; for **kanpyo,** which, improbable though this may seem, means shavings from dried gourds, used in Japan as a garnish; for **kaolin,** which if you are determined to eat clay at all is probably the best kind to grapple with; for **kapok,** cultivated in most places for its fiber, but in West Africa for its seeds, which are ground into meal; for **kari leaves,** India's answer to the bay leaf; and for the **kayan,** a tree whose leguminous grains resemble chestnuts and are important in the diets of Samoa and Tahiti.

And **KA** also stands for

KALE. Kale may well have been the first form of CABBAGE to be cultivated. It was almost certainly one of the varieties of the versatile cabbage family known to the ancients, though it is not always easy to match their names for plants to the ones we use today. Cato was a champion of cabbage, but he lacked precision. He lumped all the kinds he mentioned under one word, *brassica,* unless it was a case of wild cabbage, when it became *brassica erratica.* When Theophrastus wrote about curly-leaved cabbage, it was probably kale, and certainly cultivated, since he made a distinction between it and wild cabbage. What Pliny named *halmyridia,* specifying that it grew on the sea coast, was probably sea kale.

The ancients had not gotten around to making the distinction we draw today between plants of the genus *Brassica,* which groups cabbages of all kinds, including true kale, and the genus *Crambe,* which includes "kales" whose legitimacy we contest—sea kale is *C. maritima*; Abyssinian kale, whose leaves are eaten in Ethiopia, is *C. abyssinica.* Neither one is kale to our way of thinking. What we mean by kale is *B. oleracea* var. *acephala,* which means non-heading cabbage. This scientific tag covers COLLARDS too, but collards and kale are not the same thing. Collards in general have straighter, smoother leaves than kale, whose foliage is curled or crimped like some varieties of parsley (kale in French is *chou frisé,* "curly cabbage"): the rule seems to be that the curlier it is the better it is, for human consumption at least. More kale is fed to livestock than to people, which is why it is sometimes called cow cabbage (it is also known as boricole).

KALE. *Seed packet of the Portland Seed Company, Portland, Oregon, 1908*

Kale is a healthy food which should be welcome to weight-watchers; 100 grams of cooked kale leaves produce only 28 to 31 calories. It is particularly rich in vitamin C, and contains a plentiful dosage of calcium, 121 to 134 milligrams per 100 grams; calcium deficiency is one of the weak points in the average American diet. Many persons avoid kale nevertheless, as too strongly flavored for their taste uncooked and insufficiently succulent cooked. In that case, they have perhaps not found the right kind; there is a wide range of flavors among the different cultivated varieties. There is also an alternative to eating the leaves. Many kales branch out freely, and in the spring their young shoots may be gathered. They are more delicate in flavor than the leaves, with a taste which suggests hazelnuts.

The Scots seem to be the world's champion kale eaters. The popularity of kale in Scotland is accounted for by the fact that it flourishes in the Scotch climate and therefore presumably reaches in it the summit of its somewhat limited possibilities. Kale grows well near the sea, never far away in Scotland, and it likes cool climates. Scotch kale shows Scotch stubbornness in being the least adaptable of all its many varieties to summer heat.

The other principal kale-eating countries of

Europe are, like Scotland, in the north, as is appropriate for a hardy winter plant which in home gardens continues to provide a leafy vegetable even after the other cabbages, though they are relatively hardy too, have succumbed to the cold; kale sometimes holds out all winter. England eats kale, though perhaps less enthusiastically than Scotland. Danish housewives use it as the standard accompaniment for cured loin of pork or ham. It is highly popular in Germany, which serves it chopped and boiled. On the other hand, Italy and France pay little attention to it, though in the latter country it was being cultivated in the royal kitchen gardens of Versailles in 1620. An exception to the north-south rule is Portugal, where the *caldo verde* ("green broth") of the north has become something of a national dish. It is built around a special Portuguese variety which is more strongly flavored than the kale of most other European countries; indeed, it is possible to wonder whether it is not less closely related to kale than to sea kale, also called wild kale, which, unlike true kale, is not a member of the cabbage family, although some botanists think it may have been the ancestor of the cabbages.

In America, kale is eaten mostly in the South, where it appears among the mixed cooked greens so popular there. The greens most frequently associated with this use are the collards, but kale and collards may be found together in the same pot, together perhaps with other greens, such as turnip tops. In the rest of the country, kale, once described as "an old regular" in food stores, is disappearing from the supermarkets: it is not the kind of food which it is profitable to handle on a large scale, and as a result the northern United States is being deprived of it.

KE
stands for

keck, otherwise known as hogweed or cow parsley, which had better be left to those animals; for the **kedondong,** or hog plum, a miniature Malayan mango; for the **keladi,** a tuber which looks like a yam, relished in Malaysia in defiance of the fact that it tastes like soap; for the **kelt,** a salmon which has somehow survived spawning; for the **keluak,** a bitter black nut of Indonesia whose taste has been described as "single-minded and masculine," and **kenari,** a bland blond nut of Indonesia, related to the almond, which I will resist describing as scatter-brained and feminine; for the **kembong,** a mackerel which takes the whole Indian Ocean for its province; for the **keng,** a vegetable of the Ivory Coast, where its flowers are eaten delicately as soon as the buds begin to burst; for **kentjur,** a pungent Javanese root vaguely akin to ginger; for the **Kerguelen's Land cabbage,** a true cabbage astray in the Antarctic, where it is one of only eighteen flowering plants found in that region; for the **keta,** a salmon known also as the chum or dog salmon; and for the **key apple,** or Digaan's apple, which is not an apple but the umkokolo for the South Africans who eat it; and the **Key lime,** of the Florida Keys, which perversely reverses the color scheme of more conservative limes by hiding green flesh under a yellow rind.

And **KE** also stands for

KELP. Everybody knows that the Japanese are the world's greatest eaters of seaweed, notably kelp, but perhaps everybody does not know that the United States harvests on the order of 170,000 tons of kelp a year, 90 percent of it off the coast of California. It is probably a safe guess that the greater part of the kelp which gets into American mouths never gets into American stomachs: kelp is an important component of the substance used to take dental impressions.

Nevertheless, virtually all Americans have eaten kelp without knowing it. It provides jellylike alginates, which go into ice cream, prepared desserts and salad dressings, sometimes as a substitute for Irish moss, which is often used in blancmange, or for agar-agar, which gives us gelatin. Pacific Northwest Indians used to eat a good deal of kelp, a welcome food which was available all year round; they also used its large median ribs as containers for seal or fish oil. It is still in the Pacific Northwest that Americans eat kelp knowingly. Its hollow midriff ribs are peeled, cut into slices and pickled in a sweet-and-sour liquid containing vinegar, sugar and whatever spices the maker favors. The honey-colored rounds look rather like miniature gelatinous pineapple slices and taste like watermelon-rind preserves which have acquired a disconcerting but not unpleasant whiff of the sea. Alaska also makes relishes from kelp.

"Kelp" is a somewhat fuzzy term, which covers a considerable number of species, most of which belong to the genera *Laminaria* or *Fucus*; the simplest way to bring them all together under one head is to describe them as brown seaweeds (Irish moss and agar-agar are red seaweeds). The kelps are the largest of all seaweeds, and the largest of the kelps is *Macrocystis pyrifera,* the giant Pacific kelp, which may grow fronds up to 100 feet long, though 20 to 30 feet is more usual. This is the kelp eaten in Japan and also the

KELP. *Print from William Henry Harvey:* Phycologia Britannica *or* A History of British Seaweeds, *London, 1846*

species harvested off California, the only kind which goes into American foods.

Of the six principal algae eaten in Japan, which among them account for 10 percent of the Japanese food intake, kelp is apparently considered the best; at least, it costs the most. It is processed by a complicated series of dryings, boilings and compressions, emerging from the operation under the name *kombu. Kombu* is obtainable in powdered form, for seasoning, or in sheets, for cooking. In the latter form it goes into *tsukudani,* dishes which combine fish and kelp; or makes instant soup (*dashi*); or is cut up into small strips which are woven into little baskets no more than an inch high, deep-fried, and filled with minute cubes of cooked vegetables; you eat both the vegetables and their container. On the coast kelp is sometimes eaten fresh, with ordinary salad dressing.

The Japanese go in for culinary punning: names of foods are often matched to the occasions on which they are eaten. For Japanese, the word *kombu* evokes another word, *yorokobu,* which means "happiness." Hence *kombu* is considered a suitable food for celebratory or ceremonious meals. Kelp broth turns up at the collations served in connection with the elaborate tea ceremony; or a kelp dish will appear on the New Year's menu; and kelp cannot be omitted from a marriage banquet, for *kombu* also means a pregnant woman, so its appearance at weddings symbolizes a wish that the young couple will not only be happy but will be blessed with children. Japanese department stores sell gift-wrapped boxes of assorted kinds of *kombu,* suitable for presenting to one's hostess, like a box of chocolates in the West.

In Europe, kelp is gathered on the west coasts of Scotland and Ireland; in the latter country it is boiled lengthily until it has been reduced to a sort of thick green gruel, which is then served with mutton, boiled also. Brittany used to gather kelp, but today goes in to a greater extent for a red seaweed, known inaccurately as red lichen; but except when hidden in processed foods, kelp is in any case not eaten in France, where it is used instead for fertilizer. Nevertheless, a growing demand for it for industrial uses caused a processor in 1971 to advertise for amateur kelp gatherers, who were offered an opportunity to pick up a little pocket money while vacationing in Brittany. The Bretons immediately pointed out that in 1681 Louis XIV had granted them a monopoly on harvesting kelp off their coast, and that the Fourth Republic had confirmed this privilege in 1953. The kelp processor desisted.

In recent years food faddists have been looking to kelp as a healthy form of nourishment. Actually, kelp does not seem to merit unlimited praise. True, it is a better source of potassium and iodine than almost any other vegetable food, and it contains considerable quantities of vitamins A and D. But it offers little protein, and its carbohydrates are of a type not readily digestible by humans.

Marine biologists and ecologists are not happy about the boom of kelp as a health food. They fear it may lead to overcropping of the kelp beds in which so many useful fish and shellfish have their habitat and find their food—the kelp bass, the kelp crab, the kelp greenling and kelpfish, the last a sweeping term which covers a number of different species which live among these seaweeds. The ecologists also feared that the kelp beds might suffer because of the predictions, which were being freely made by some scientists a few years ago, that vast quantities of human food would be derived from seaweed. Today the ecologists have decided, with relief, that seaweed is not likely to become a significant source of nutrition. Some of them have even been unkind enough to suggest that the hullabaloo raised about the potential importance of seaweed as food came from marine researchers who wanted to call attention to their work and thus woo funds for further research from donors who could be tempted by the promise of tangible progress. The monetary angle does not seem to be absent either from the advocacy of seaweed by the suppliers of food faddists, if we may judge from this passage in *Health Foods* by Sidney Margolius:

"From the sea came life," one vitamin manufacturer advertises, and from kelp comes [sic] large profit margins. Since many health foodists insist, or have been led to insist, on getting their minute daily needs of iodine from "natural" kelp tablets rather than free with iodized salt, they pay at retail up to three times the factory cost.

KI
stands for

kibeto-beto, a leafy green plant eaten in the Congo; for the **kid-glove orange,** which is the tangerine, thus nicknamed because its segments come apart so easily you can eat it without wetting your hands; for the **kidney** BEAN, which, though of American origin, is called the French bean by the English because it was first brought to northern Europe from Canada by French explorers; for the **kigelia,** the tropical African sausage tree, whose fruits do indeed look like long sausages dangling on cords from the branches; for the **kikondji,** another plant whose young leaves are eaten in the Congo; for the **killdeer,** an American plover which has never lifted a beak in anger against any member of the *Cervidae*, but which utters a cry which has been interpreted as advocating this action; for the **kingfish,** a denizen of the Indian Ocean otherwise known as the Spanish mackerel; for the **king klip,** a fish which lavishes its lusciousness on South Africa; for the **king mackerel,** alias the black salmon, the cero or the silver cero; for the **king orange** of what used to be called Cochin-China; for the **king oyster** of America's Pacific coast; for the **king salmon,** alias the chinook, the quinard, the spring or the tyee; for **king's clover,** or melilot, whose leaves season a certain Swiss cheese and whose honey is appreciated everywhere; for the **Kingston Black,** an English apple which in Devonshire is called the Sheep's Nose; for the **kinni-kinnick,** which is nothing but the bearberry brandishing its Indian name; for **kiskh,** an exotic spice on sale in unexotic Oakland, California; and for the **kissing gourami,** an ostentatiously affectionate fish which in spite of its endearing behavior is eaten in Southeast Asia, where it is possible that kissing is held in low esteem.

And **KI** also stands for

KID. In fourteenth-century France an author whose identity is unknown to us except by his own self-portrait—"a man of ripe age who has just married a young girl fifteen years old"—wrote for the guidance of his bride *Le Ménagier de Paris* (*The Parisian House-Keeper*). His laudable purpose was to guide her in fulfilling the whole duty of a wife, which was, of course, to bend all her efforts toward assuring "the salvation of the soul and the peace of her husband." In the development of his text, the author occasionally lost sight of the salvation of the soul in favor of the delectation of the stomach. The household he envisaged seemed to consist mostly of dining room, pantry and kitchen, so his book continues to be cited today as a repository of gastronomic wisdom. Among the pearls which were the fruit of experience and of the satisfaction of concupiscence, enshrined appropriately in a menu for a wedding breakfast one of whose numerous courses consisted of a quarter of a kid for each guest, was the dictum: "A quarter of kid is better than a lamb."

Six centuries later an authority of our own times, Elizabeth David, wrote: "Kid is just as good as, and very often better, than lamb." Twenty-three centuries earlier a Chinese poem, "The Summons of the Soul," had intoned a sort of litany of fine foods, among them "roast kid served with yam sauce." In the Old Testament we find kid gracing the feasts of patriarchs and kings, and figuring also from time to time as a handsome present, though not always (Genesis 38:20) in the most creditable circumstances; and it was kid which provided the example for the kosher prohibition against eating milk and meat at the same meal: "Thou shalt not seethe a kid in his mother's milk" (Exodus 23:19). In the first century A.D., Juvenal baited a dinner invitation by promising to serve "a plump kid, tenderest of the flock." In the tenth century, the Arab poet Mahmud ibn al-Husain al-Kushajim, describing a Bagdad banquet, wrote:

First a roasted kid, a yearling,
With its innards firmly strung.
And upon it, well to season,
Tarragon and mint are hung . . .
Lemons too, with nadd *besprinkled,*
Scented well with ambergris,

KID. *Illuminated page, "Joseph Tending Flocks" from* Jami: Yusuf Zuliakha, *Bokara school, c. 1540, Persia*

And, for garnishing the slices,
Shreds of appetizing cheese.

Westerners would, perhaps, have preferred to ambergris and *nadd* (which is a mixture of perfumes), the "herbs of strong taste, old wine of Spain, fine honey, and good unguents from overseas" with which Jean Leclercq, cook to Francis I, basted a roast kid for his royal master. "Enough, enough!" the king cried in delight. "Master Jean, do you want to make us burst with your good cheer?"

In the Middle Ages, kid was so much more popular than lamb in France that unscrupulous merchants used to attach a kid's tail to a lamb's carcass to sell it at the higher price commanded by kid, giving rise to a popular description of cheats as "sellers of half-goats." In the reign of Louis XV, kid was still sufficiently familiar to Pierre Poivre, the man who procured cloves and nutmegs for the French islands in the Indian Ocean, so that he could complain, when he reached the French trading counter at Pondicherry: "Kids are found here, but their flesh is tasteless. This comes from the great aridity of the country and the poor quality of the soil, which gives livestock only burned-up pasturage, in very small quantity." Kid is still eaten in France today, though less commonly than a century or two ago, except in some of the provinces, notably Corsica, which stuffs it with rosemary and garlic. Popular in Italy in Renaissance times, it is still very much on the menu there today, though one no longer finds *capretto incaporchiato*, "trapped kid," for which the newborn animal was strapped under its mother's belly in a wicker basket, so that it could reach the udder but not the grass, thus ensuring authentic milk-fed kid for the table. Roast kid is considered a worthy dish for a formal dinner in Portugal, while in Greece a whole suckling kid is the traditional *pièce de résistance* for the Easter dinner. Kid remains a gala dish in Arab countries, and perhaps still graces betrothal banquets in Burma and Cambodia.

How does it happen, then, that kid is shunned in the British Isles and the United States, where a familiar phrase which represented the soul of wit in my adolescent days, "I love my wife, but oh, you kid!" was not, unless I am greatly mistaken, a gastronomic pronouncement? Things were not always thus. Boswell recorded that he and Dr. Johnson had regaled themselves on roast kid at Inverness on August 29, 1733; kid was often the meat which went into Irish stew in the nineteenth century; and Eliza Leslie, in her *Directions for Cookery*, published in the United States in that century, gave a recipe for roast kid. Yet nowadays kid is in bad odor in the United States —probably because of the popular impression that goats themselves are, quite literally, in bad odor, which is true only of the adult male. You have probably eaten kid, but it has been passed off on you, reversing the practice of the Middle Ages, as lamb. If kid has acquired a certain local acceptance in Tex-Mex cooking, where it appears chiefly at barbecues, it has not become completely naturalized even there; at big barbecues, where the food is often set out in two sections, American style and Mexican style, *cabrito asado*, ideally from animals a year old, weighing between ten and fifteen pounds, appears on the Mexican tables.

Otherwise, if you want to eat kid knowingly in the United States—for instance, by ordering it for Easter (a week in advance) in San Francisco, where this can be done—you will have to pay a premium price for it (perversely, it would seem, since its rarity results from the contempt in which it is held; but nonconformism of any kind has to be paid for).

KIDNEY. "Leopold Bloom," James Joyce informed us at the beginning of the second section of *Ulysses*, "ate with relish the inner organs of beasts and fowls. He liked thick giblet soup, nutty gizzards, a stuffed roast heart, liver slices fried with crustcrumbs, fried hencod's roe. Most of all he liked grilled mutton kidneys which gave to his palate a fine tang of faintly scented urine." This would seem to justify Alexandre Dumas' statement that "the flavor of urine which characterizes [kidneys] is what appreciators of this sort of food seek." The tone of Dumas' comment seems to indicate disapproval, but he followed it with twelve recipes for kidneys all the same.

If Mr. Bloom was not deliberately seeking this less than unanimously desired flavor, his butcher was taking advantage of him. We are specifically told that he doted on mutton kidneys, not lamb kidneys, and they must have come from an animal which had ceased to be a lamb a considerable time back. The kidneys of aged sheep and old steers may indeed develop a *soupçon* of urine in their odor, more than in their taste, but the more desirable kidneys do not. This means calves' kidneys, usually the easiest to find on the market, and lamb kidneys, the kind most favored for mixed grills. Both are delightfully delicate in flavor, and tender under the teeth provided they are not cooked too long: kidneys, curiously, become tougher with cooking, so veal or lamb kidneys should be taken from the stove while they are still rosy. Beef kidneys, which are stronger in taste, are already so tough that long cooking can make them no tougher; it is con-

KIDNEY *by Jean-Baptiste Chardin (1699–1779).* Meat-Day Meal, *oil on canvas*

sidered preferable to cook them thoroughly. Pork kidneys, often granular in texture, are stronger in taste than veal or lamb, but they are almost as tender; nevertheless, they should be well cooked, almost as much as beef kidneys. The ancient Romans preferred pork kidneys, which were for them, indeed, one of the most esteemed parts of the pig. Petronius introduced them in his description of Trimalchio's banquet, in which certain of the courses symbolized the twelve signs of the zodiac. Pork kidneys, which of course come in pairs, appeared on the platter dedicated to Gemini, the Twins.

Early nineteenth-century American cookbooks include recipes for preparing kidneys and other internal organs now looked at askance by most Americans, more timid eaters than their forebears. Rather than recognize the true nature of what they hesitate to envisage as food, Americans refer gingerly to these dubious substances as "variety meats" or "utility meats," or, seeking escape in the opposite direction, call them with brutal and defiant rusticity, "innards." The limit of edibility in this domain is reached for many Americans with liver; a few daring souls progress to kidneys. These are likeliest not to be risked at home, but in a restaurant, preferably French, which permits listing them on the menu not as kidneys but as *rognons*, a veil as disarming as a sauce. (The French use *rognons* as a euphemism too, but they go a little farther down the line: what they call *rognons blancs*, "white kidneys," are testicles.)

Widespread American distrust of the esoteric kidney makes it difficult to find a butcher who will cut for you what in England is called a lamb loin chop with kidney. The adjacent meat is cut from the carcass with the kidney still attached to it, the meat is rolled around the kidney, and it is cooked with the kidney inside. The same cut exists in France and Germany, usually with veal kidneys, called in France a *rognonnade* and in Germany *Kalbsnierenbraten.*

A gastronomic book of the coffee-table school informs me that "prehistoric warriors believed that kidneys imparted courage," which leads me to wonder how anyone found out what prehistoric man believed. However, Falstaff seems to have felt that it represented something of the sort, for in *The Merry Wives of Windsor* he railed at the indignity which thrust "a man of my kidney" into a hamper of dirty laundry.

Balzac must have been fond of kidneys, for he mentions them often; but in his time they were considered a home dish, suitable for serving only within the family circle; if eaten in restaurants at all, it had to be at lunch, an easygoing meal. They were not considered suitable for the more formal repast of dinner. Among the many anecdotes connected with the Café Anglais, a famous eating place of the early nineteenth century, is one which tells how Napoléon d'Abrantès (son of Napoleon's General Junot, the Duke of Abrantès) took umbrage when a diner at the table next to his presumed to order spitted kidneys. With offensive ostentation he ordered his table moved to the farthest spot in the room from the scene of this desecration. The kidney eater finished his meal and crossed the room to Abrantès's table. "Sir," he said, "you object to kidneys in the evening. Do you object to duels in the morning?" Abrantès did not, so dawn found him spitted on his opponent's sword as neatly as any kidney. He spent the next three months in bed.

At an Algerian *méchoui*, the kidneys of the animal which, roasted whole, provides the main element in the feast are presented to the most honored guest as the choicest morsels. The animal which provides them is ordinarily a sheep, but it can be almost anything else, from a moufflon to a camel. Charles Monselet, a nineteenth-century French gastronomic writer, once published the menu of a sumptuous Algerian dinner of which one course was porcupine garnished with antelope kidneys. Africans eat the kidneys of a number of animals unfamiliar to Western tables, and Eskimos eat those of seals.

The French naturalist Buffon informed mankind in the eighteenth century that in mammals the left kidney is fatter than the right. So far as I know, there has been no attempt since to confirm this assertion, or to disprove it either.

KING CRAB. The Alaska king crab (*Paralithodes camschatica*) may or may not be the best of all crabs, as its addicts maintain, but it is certainly the best publicized. Its fame has led to the creation of a consort, apparently by spontaneous generation, for the somewhat similar but smaller crab taken in the Gulf of St. Lawrence and dubbed in recent times the "queen crab" is unknown by this name to science, making it difficult to avoid the suspicion that it was thus baptized in the hope that it would benefit, remuneratively, from the reflected glory of *P. camschatica.*

The Alaska king crab is unaware of the existence of the St. Lawrence. It is a creature of the Pacific, a lover of extremely cold waters, found therefore in the Bering Sea and the *northern* Northern Pacific. As it moves south its quality diminishes, until it finally disappears from the waters altogether, to reappear in an only slightly different reincarnation in the cold *southern* Southern Pacific waters, off Chile to the east and off southern Australia to the west.

The king crab is the darling of seafood processors, partly because its large size makes it easy to handle. It is not the largest of edible crabs, as Webster thinks; the Japanese giant crab and the Tasmanian giant crab are both bigger and both edible. However, it is large enough, with a leg span of four to five feet and a weight of fifteen pounds, while the waters off Kodiak occasionally yield monsters with a span of six feet and a weight of twenty-five pounds.

Most of its meat is in the long, large legs and is easily pressed out of them, yielding flesh in attractive chunks for packaging. Some writers maintain that this constitutes *all* the meat of the king crab, but they are wrong. There is also body meat, harder to extract, and sold, when the labeling is honest, as bits or shreds of king crab. The meat lends itself admirably to freezing as well as to canning, which has encouraged producers to work at its exploitation so diligently that they have nearly succeeded in depleting waters once deemed inexhaustible, while the crabs now being taken are diminishing in average size. In the meantime the king crab has been marketed extensively beyond its natural hinterland, notably in Europe, where it is sold under its English name, since there are apparently no popular names for it in western European languages. Americans seem to have been the pioneers in opening this market, but their competitors now include Russians, Japanese, Canadians and Chileans.

If "king crab" for an American means automatically the Alaska king crab, for a European it is more likely to evoke his native spider crab, *Maia squinado.* The name is also applied to the horseshoe crab, inedible except for its eggs, which

Kiwi Fruit

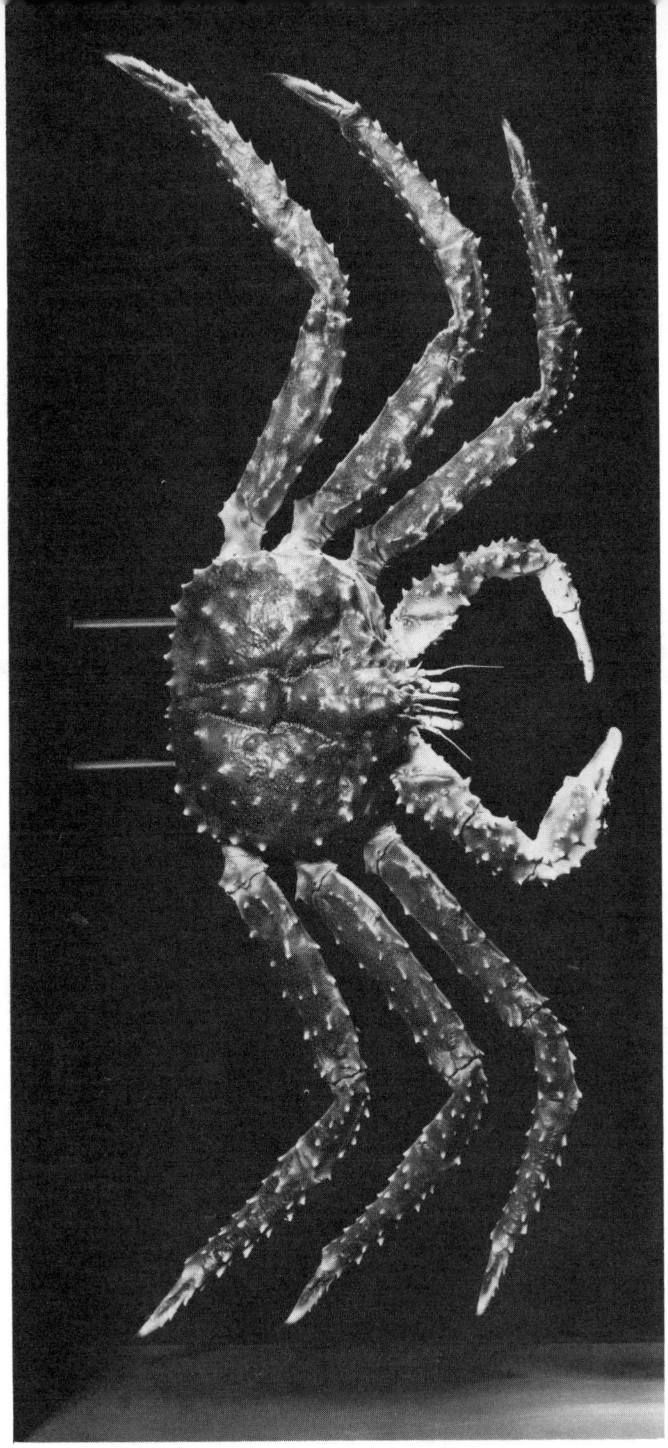

KING CRAB. *Diorama, Seafood Exhibit, 1959, Hall of Ocean Life, American Museum of Natural History*

are sometimes eaten in Asia. The horseshoe crab is not even a crab. It is a limulus, a living fossil which has been around for 200 million years and forgot to exit with the dinosaurs.

KIWI FRUIT. The long arm of coincidence has reached out and tapped me gently on the shoulder with a kiwi fruit. Let me explain:

On October 10, 1979, as I was making final corrections to the manuscript of this book, I reached the entry on the kiwi fruit, which dealt with the mystery of its name. Why was it so called, I wondered; nobody seemed to know. Well, somebody did know, and it was just one day later, on October 11, that I received enlightenment; and just to stretch the long arm a little longer, it came, not from New Zealand, of which the kiwi fruit is a native, but from, of all places, Bangladesh.

I had written originally:

The kiwi fruit is known popularly as the Chinese gooseberry and scientifically as *Actinidia chinensis*, but I can find in no reliable reference book at my disposal any record of its existence in China or anywhere else except New Zealand—whose flora and fauna, as everybody knows, are largely peculiar to its own two islands and are rarely found outside them, except for those species which have been deliberately exported. [I might have added that none of my reference books even used the name "kiwi."]

The name "kiwi fruit" refers to the flightless bird likewise known as the kiwi, which is so much the symbol of New Zealand that New Zealanders sometimes call themselves Kiwis (and have so baptized their national football team). Did they give this name to a foreign fruit, from China or elsewhere, to naturalize it, or was it an assertion that it was their very own? Nobody seems to know. In any case, New Zealand appears to be the only country in the world where the kiwi fruit is cultivated on a genuinely commercial basis, though it is also grown on a small scale in California—which imported its plants not from China, but from New Zealand.

The day after I had checked this passage, a worker for CARE stationed in Bangladesh, whose functions had no doubt carried him also to other far-flung regions of the world, wrote me apropos of an article I had contributed to the *International Herald Tribune* in which I had written that at one time ducks imported into the United States

KIWI FRUIT. *Detail of photograph by Ralf Manstein, 1980*

from the East had to be accompanied by a certificate of origin to prove that they had not been raised in a Communist country, in which case they could not be admitted to the United States under one of those quaint laws which Congress passes from time to time as comic relief, one supposes, after the strain of such more taxing labors as dissecting the budget. My correspondent thought I might be interested in a vaguely analogous case, and he was right:

> It seems that in the early '50's [he wrote], when New Zealand was looking to expand its agricultural exports to the United States, the Chinese gooseberry was selected as a natural. It grew well in that part of the Antipodes but was unknown as a commercial crop in the States. The suspect name passed U.S. Customs inspection but the people did not buy. Market researchers of the day discovered that McCarthyite ill will extended as far as the gourmet fruit counter. And so was born the name Kiwi Fruit. . . .
>
> The Kiwis generally still refer to the fruit as the Chinese gooseberry.

This clears up the mystery of the name "kiwi" and only leaves to be explained the mystery of how it came to be called the Chinese gooseberry in the first place, since it was almost certainly never Chinese.

Kiwi fruit, né (illegitimately) the Chinese gooseberry, dangles from its shrub like potato croquettes suspended from the branches—cylindrical, light brown, fuzzy, and two or three inches long. Though the plant is not large, it produces about three hundred pounds of fruit a year. Served sliced, the cross section shows a pleasing pattern—pale green flesh, with a rather large whitish center surrounded by dark brown stippling, which is the seeds. The taste and texture approach those of the honeydew melon. Kiwi fruit enters into a creamy dessert which has become something of a national dish, but has a foreign name too—Pavlova, allegedly because it is as light on the stomach as Pavlova was light on her feet.

KL
stands for

Klein's sole, a fish which perpetuates the memory of an eighteenth-century German naturalist; for **klippfisk,** salted cod air-dried on the cliffs of Norway; for the **klipspringer,** a small tasty African antelope which has the arduous habit of always taking off uphill when startled; and for **kliukvy,** tiny Russian fruits which recall cranberries.

KN
stands for

knight's milfoil, an Old World herb which has been stanching the wounds of battle since the siege of Troy, and **knitbone,** an Old World herb which has been persuading broken bones to grow together since the time of the ancient Romans; for the **knobbed whelk,** the largest shellfish on America's Atlantic coast north of Cape Hatteras; for **knob celery,** which is celeriac; for the **knot,** a flavorful shore bird which at the end of the nineteenth century was being sold in game-loving Boston for ten cents the dozen; for the **knotted wrack,** an edible seaweed which, being brown, is classifiable with KELPS; and for the **knotweed,** whose stalk can serve with equal grace as a vegetable or as a fruit, depending on how you cook it.

KO
stands for

the **Kobe cattle** of Japan, the world's most pampered beef animals, which are gratified with a ration of beer and a daily massage; for the **koko,** whose young leaves are eaten in equatorial Africa; for **kokotxas,** a gelatinous substance found in the throat of the HAKE, avoided by some people, but Spanish Basques pay premium prices for it; for the **kola,** whose caffeine-rich nuts are chewed by Africans when they want to develop quick energy; for the esteemed **Kona crab** of Hawaii; for **kona sausho,** the prickly-ash pepper of Japan; for the **koompassia,** or tropical Asian honey tree, which supplies this sweetener to man via wild bees; for the **kopior,** an almost too sweet offbeat variety of the coconut found in Indonesia and the Philippine Islands; and for **kouma-kouma,** which in spite of belonging to the frequently fatal dogbane family (but so does the Natal plum) is one of the most popular fruits of tropical Africa and Madagascar.

And **KO** also stands for

KOHLRABI. According to the *Encyclopaedia Britannica,* kohlrabi is a cabbage "of recent European origin." I do not know what the *Britannica,* possibly misled by the fact that the word "kohlrabi" only entered the English language in the nineteenth century, considers to be recent, but Charlemagne ordered that kohlrabi be grown in his domains twelve centuries ago, while I suspect that the ancient Romans knew it, though their names for the various members of the cabbage family have never been satisfactorily translated. The reason for suspecting its early presence in Italy, given the obstinacy with which peoples cling to their eating habits, is its continued presence in that country (which gave this vegetable its name, via German), although this is a heavier sort of vegetable than Italians are accustomed to eating today. It could, however, be a later Austrian influence which accounts for its present popularity in Venezia, for kohlrabi is most eaten by humans (it is also a favored livestock food) in Austria, Germany and the countries of eastern Europe; that is to say, by peoples living in a continental climate, receptive to bulky, filling foods with scant regard for coarse or insipid flavor. In the United States, kohlrabi is encountered oftenest in the South as one element of that region's boiled mixed greens. It is also eaten, to a moderate extent, throughout Africa and in Madagascar.

Kohlrabi is "a most underrated vegetable that more people should grow and eat," Richard Gehman wrote in *The Haphazard Gourmet,* and the fact that he wrote "should grow" gives away one detail connected with it: it is not often found in stores, so if you want to eat it you usually have to grow it yourself, which is what I did. The scant acquaintance Americans and Britons have with this vegetable accounts for the widespread misinformation regularly printed about it. Some writers describe it as a hybrid between the cabbage and the turnip (which ought to be impossible, since they are not members of the same species, though they do belong to the same family, *Brassiceae*), and others describe it flatly as a turnip, apparently unaware that it is a member in good standing of the cabbage group. All the cabbages, despite their very diverse developments, belong to the same species, *Brassica oleracea.* Kohlrabi is *B. oleracea* var. *gongylodes* sub-var. *caulorapa,* as filling a mouthful as the food it represents. Writers ill acquainted with the vegetable itself may have been led astray by the fact that it is sometimes called the "turnip cabbage," but this is meant only as a description of its appearance, better indicated by the alternative "turnip-rooted cabbage," while the best name of all is probably "stem cabbage." The edible bulb of kohlrabi is in fact not a root, like the turnip, but a swelling of the stem just above ground level; in German when it seems necessary to be precise the vegetable is called *Kohlrabi über der Erde,* "aboveground kohlrabi," to distinguish it from the turnip-like swede, which is called *Kohlrabi unter der Erde,* "underground kohlrabi."

It is perhaps its verbal association with the turnip which persuades some people that it tastes like one. It certainly does not have the bite of the turnip (perceptible especially when it is eaten raw; cooking tames it), but is blander and sweeter. Kohlrabi is difficult to place in terms of other tastes, partly because it is rather faint and unassertive, though of its two varieties purple kohlrabi has more flavor than green. Both are easily forgettable, though pleasant enough provided they are eaten young, when the globes are two to two and a half inches in diameter. If allowed to grow larger they become woody, like asparagus, and disagreeably bitter.

KOHLRABI. *Engraving from Vilmorin-Andrieux:* Les plantes potagères, *Paris, 1904*

KR
stands for

the Finnish **kräftor,** which are described in the official tourist guides as small lobsters, but which manage to get themselves confused with crayfish; for the **kramuli,** a finely flavored white-fleshed fish found only in the lakes of the Caucasus; for **krebs,** a word Africans apply to so many different edible seeds that its meaning seems as all-encompassing as "grain"; for the **krill,** a small Antarctic crustacean which has become so plentiful since the whales which used to eat them have been hunted to near extinction that they occasionally transform vast areas of the southern ocean into a thick seafood soup; and for the **krul-uintje,** or curl bulb, a wild root eaten in South Africa.

KU
stands for

the **kudampili,** a South Indian fruit too tart to eat raw, but it is used in cooking; for the **kudu,** a large antelope which has been on the African menu continuously since prehistoric times; for the **kukui,** or candlenut, a Hawaiian seasoning; for the **kumara,** a New Zealand yam which was the staple food of the Maoris before the white man came; for the **kunzea,** an Australian fruit edible only when cooked; for **kurper,** the name South African fishermen give to the *Tilapia* when they do not call it the freshwater bream; for the **kurrat,** a close relative of the leek, eaten most avidly in Egypt; for the **kurum oil tree** of Southeast Asia; for the **kussaie lime,** which, though sour, is really a mandarin; and for the **kutzu,** the tuber of a leguminous plant eaten in Southeast Asia and the Pacific islands.

And **KU** also stands for

KUMQUAT. "East of Mount Ch'i," I Yin wrote prettily about 1500 B.C., "where the bluebird lives, sweet kumquats grow." It would take another three thousand years for Europeans to become acquainted with the kumquat. A native of eastern Asia, it was known to exist at least by the seventeenth century, when its name entered the English language in the form "cam-quit," but the fruit was not introduced into Europe until 1846, when it appeared thanks to Robert Fortune, a collector of plants for the London Horticultural Society. He was rewarded by having the kumquat genus named *Fortunella,* displacing the tag *Citrus japonica* by which it was previously known to the few specialists then aware of it. This change of name was welcome to those botanists who hold that the kumquat is not a true citrus fruit, which is not a unanimous opinion. It certainly looks like an orange—in miniature, for it is not much larger than an olive. Whether the kumquat is or is not a genuine citrus fruit, it is so close as makes no matter. A kumquat by any other name would taste as sweet.

KUMQUAT. *Drawing from Tomitaro Makino:* An Illustrated Flora of Nippon, *Tokyo, 1917*

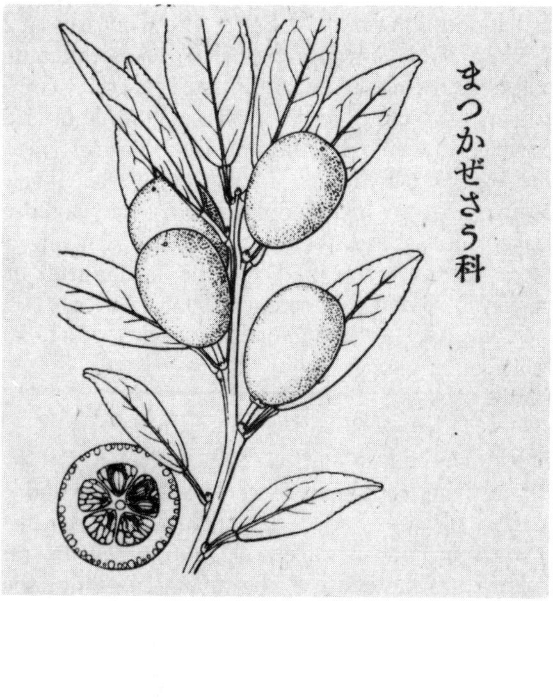

There are some who contest even its sweetness. It has been described as too acid to be eaten except in the preserved forms in which it is oftenest purchased, either in sweet syrup or, conversely, in vinegar, pickled. Others describe it as reversing the usual order of things by having a rind sweeter than its pulp; the spongy rind in any case is eaten along with the rest. The kumquat's flavor resembles that of the orange; the differences in the reports about it probably result from the fact that there are several species of kumquats. The commonest, *F. margarita,* to go along with the latest terminology, also known as the oval or nagami kumquat, presents a contrast of tartness and sweetness in the same fruit. *F. japonica,* the round or Marumi kumquat, known only in cultivated forms, tends to be acid. Both pulp and rind are sweet in *F. crassifolia,* the Meiwa kumquat, which seems to be a natural hybrid derived from two other members of the genus.

A good deal of deliberate hybridization has been imposed upon the kumquat, either to make it less acid, or to make other citrus fruits hardier; the kumquat can stand more cold and grow farther north than any other plant of this sort. It has even entered into a triple hybridization, crossed with citranges, themselves hybrids obtained from the combination of any sweet orange (*Citrus sinensis*) and the hardy trifoliate orange (*Poncirus trifoliata*). The result is known by the barbarously artificial name of citrangequat; there is also a limequat.

The kumquat has remained pretty much of an exotic fruit, little eaten outside of China and Japan. It now exists in North, South and East Africa, and is grown in commercial quantities in Florida, where it is usually grafted on orange trees or on *P. trifoliata*; but it is of minor importance compared to the state's other citrus fruits. Florida kumquats are usually marketed preserved, but occasionally fresh fruit is available, to lend a revivifying note to fruit salads or to garnish meat dishes, for instance duck.

What Australians call kumquats are not the genuine article, but they are not far from it. The name seems to be applied indifferently to both *Eremocitrus glauca,* which belongs to the same family as the kumquats, the *Rutaceae,* and to the calamondin, a little known but genuine member of the citrus group, classified as *C. mitis.*

Kumquat means "golden orange"—*kam kwat* in Cantonese, *kyem kywit* in Middle Chinese.

LEONARDO DA VINCI: *The body of anything whatever that takes nourishment constantly dies and is constantly renewed; because nourishment can enter only into places where the former nourishment has expired, and if it has expired, it no longer has life. And if you do not supply nourishment equal to the nourishment which is gone, life will fail in vigor.*

L

LADELL, W. S. S.: *Provided men are well fed they can remain fit and well in any climate.*

LINCOLN, MARY: *All civilized nations cook their food, to improve its taste and digestibility. The degree of civilization is often measured by the cuisine.*

LA
stands for

labba, a jungle rodent of Guyana, whose inhabitants assure visiting foreigners that if they eat it they will be sure to return; for the **lablab,** which with a little latitude can be called a bean, widely eaten in northeastern Africa and southeastern Asia, preferably cooked, as it can be poisonous raw; for the **laburnum,** whose leaves are eaten only when it is African, which is to say when it is not really a laburnum; for **Lactarius deliciosus,** probably the first mushroom to have had its portrait painted, in a Pompeiian fresco; for **la cuite,** the name Louisiana Acadians give to maple syrup at the end of a run, when it becomes so thick as to be almost solid; and for **lad's love,** an aromatic herb with a rakish reputation.

LA
stands for

the **lady apple,** which under the name of Api was cultivated by the ancient Etruscans; for the **lady crab,** a brightly colored crustacean which nips bathers' toes from Cape Cod to Florida; for the **lady fern,** consumed at the eater's risk, for it can become toxic; for the **lady pea,** alias the cowpea; for **lady's-bedstraw,** which curdles milk; for the **lady's-finger,** alias okra; for the **lady's-nightcap,** whose root was described as edible in Gerard's *Herball* in the sixteenth century, though it is possible that nobody has tried it since; for the **lady's-purse,** a relative of the cabbage; for the **lady's-slipper,** alias balsam; for the **lady's-smock,** which is wood sorrel, and **lady's-sorrel,** which is yellow wood sorrel; for the **lady's-thistle,** whose juice is supposed to increase the flow of milk in nursing mothers; for the **lady's-thumb,** used in salads in Vietnam; and for **lady's-tresses,** whose name comes from the braidlike arrangement of its flowers, but whose gastronomic interest, not quite overpowering, comes from its tubers.

LA
stands for

the **lake herring,** an important commercial food fish of Lake Superior and points north, and the **lake trout,** a native of Europe; for **lambi,** a Caribbean name for the conch; for **lamb's lettuce,** or corn salad, which does indeed go into salads, especially in winter when more desirable leafy plants are lacking, and **lamb's-quarters,** which can be used in salads too, but is oftener employed as a potherb; for the **lamprey,** the Dracula of fishes, considered a great delicacy in France and inedible in the United States; for **lamy butter,** pressed from the seeds of an African tree, widely used in the tropical regions of that continent; for **lana,** a shrub which normally provides fodder for camels, but becomes human food in India in times of famine; for the **lancelet,** a marine animal halfway between a fish and a worm, much relished by the Chinese; for **land cress,** otherwise known as winter CRESS; and for **landlady's wig,** a seaweed so called for its disheveled appearance when washed up on the beach, which I am not sure is edible, but I couldn't resist the name.

LA

stands for

the **lane snapper,** a fish plentiful from Florida to Brazil; for **lantana weed,** or wild sage, which despite this name is a fruit, eaten in West Africa; for **laos,** a pungent ginger-like root much used as a seasoning in southeastern Asia; for the **lapwing,** an Old World plover which occasionally visits the New; for the **large-eyed dentex,** a Mediterranean food fish, for the **large-mouth black bass,** an American freshwater food fish, and for the **large-spotted dogfish,** a western Atlantic and Mediterranean food fish if you aren't too fussy about your food; for the **lark,** which can be cooked without being cleaned because, a medieval writer explained, larks "eat only small pebbles and sand"; for **larvae,** of which, the United Nations Food and Agricultural Organization informs us, there is a "fairly high consumption" in Africa; for the **latchet,** which is the yellow gurnard; for the **lathyrus,** a pea-like legume which for centuries has served as a famine food in India despite the discouraging detail that eating too much of it provokes a spastic paralysis of the legs called lathyrism; for the **lattice-leaf plant** of Madagascar, whose leaves have become reduced to a network of veins, which has an edible root; for the **laurel,** which gives us the BAY LEAF; for the **lavaret,** an excellent European food fish related to the salmon, though devoid of the salmon's fighting spirit; for **lavender,** which Perdita in *The Winter's Tale* suspects of being an aphrodisiac ("Hot lavender, mints, savory, marjoram / . . . these are flowers/ of middle summer, and I think they are given / To men of middle age"); for **laver,** a red seaweed eaten in Ireland, Wales, Brittany, China and Japan; and for the **lawyer's wig,** or shaggy-mane mushroom, *Coprinus comatus,* edible and of pleasant flavor when young, but it must be cooked immediately on gathering, for it is quick to spoil.

And **LA** also stands for

LAMB. Isabella Beeton, whose *Book of Household Management,* published in 1861, enjoyed almost scriptural authority in the English-speaking world for half a century, wrote that lamb was "of all wild or domesticated animals . . . without exception, the most useful to man as food." This may seem somewhat sweeping (and astonishing from a subject of a kingdom traditionally associated with beef), but she would not be contradicted by, for instance, Arabs, who, when they speak of meat without specifying the kind, may safely be assumed to be thinking either of lamb or mutton.

The Arabs' Middle East, with its gastronomic extensions into North Africa and southeastern Europe, is indeed the world's most concentrated area of sheep eating. "Towards the end of Ramadan, the Moslem feast," Donald Aspinwall Allan wrote in "Flavors of Lebanon" (*Gourmet,* August 1974), "live sheep may even be seen on the balconies of Beirut apartments. Families with traditions rooted in the desert fatten and slaughter at home . . . forget all you've heard about the honored guest being offered an eye: The honored guest wants the tenderest pieces of leg, like everyone else."

The dominance of lamb in the Middle East started early. The oldest find of domesticated sheeps' bones, which dates from 9000 B.C., was made in Iraq, where the majority of them came from sheep which had been killed before reaching the age of one year: prehistoric man, gross creature though we imagine him to be, was eating lamb rather than mutton. Similar finds have been made in Libya, where they are dated at 4800 B.C.; domesticated sheep are pictured in Egyptian tombs of 2500 B.C.; and they were present in Mesopotamia by 2000 B.C. at the latest, and probably much earlier. Sheep were also raised in prehistoric Greece, where lamb is still the favorite meat and suckling lamb (or kid), roasted whole, is the traditional dish of Easter. (Outside of the Middle Eastern area, in Italy, the Latins, even before they had become Romans, were shepherds living largely on sheep, and their taste for lamb lasted throughout the lifetime of the Roman Empire.)

The Middle East has been working for centuries on the development of tasty breeds of sheep, with results which unfailingly attract the attention of American visitors comparing the taste of lamb there with the taste of what they have eaten at home. Iranian lamb is sweeter than American lamb, Harry G. Nickles reported in *Middle Eastern Cooking,* while George Papashvily, sampling the flesh of the famous fat-tailed sheep (already known to the Sumerians) at a little distance from their native ground, in Uzbek, wrote in *Russian Cooking,* "I had never before tasted such delicious meat . . . super-lamb . . . as much superior to a well-finished Southdown as that aristocrat of sheep is to a middle-aged billy goat."

The admiration Westerners feel for Middle Eastern lamb seems undiminished by the fact that it is cooked through, though the Western taste is for less well done lamb which comes rosy-tinted to the table; but Middle Easterners have culinary tricks of their own to preserve the tenderness and tastiness of their favorite meat.

In India, lamb is important too, especially in

Moslem areas, where beef and veal are ruled out by the climate and pork by religion; but it is also favored by those Hindus who have not gone vegetarian. The Hindus of Kashmir, for instance, have been eating lamb since early Vedic times and still do, largely because they were isolated from their co-religionists behind their high mountains at a time when many Hindus gave up meat, and therefore failed to fall in with this new tendency. For the Kashmiri Hindus the traditional meal for occasions of rejoicing, like weddings, is "the Seven Dishes"—all of lamb.

In China, the *Book of Songs*, 600 B.C., contains a description of the propitiatory spring sacrifice of a lamb, so carefully seasoned that we may suspect that the priests participated in enjoying the sacrifice, as they so often did in many countries: "God on high is much pleased: / 'What smell is this, so strong and good?' "

In France, lamb has had its ups and downs. In the Middle Ages, the French did not care for the meat of young animals, which they thought insipid, but they made an exception for lamb. It declined in relative popularity when veal was accepted and suckling pig began to replace suckling lamb, but the custom of blessing a lamb at Easter kept alive the tradition of serving a whole lamb on this holiday into the time of Louis XV, who then gave a new fillip to the consumption of lamb by importing Merinos from Spain, on the hoof, and carrying out what seems to have been the first hybridization of sheep in France. The Merinos, valuable first of all for wool, were converted into Rambouillets, valuable first of all for meat. Encouraged by the example of his royal master, the poet J. Lebas not only wrote a recipe for braised leg of lamb in verse, but even set it to music. The ever-hungry Louis XVI followed up by referring to lambs as "walking cutlets."

The monarchistic associations of lamb may have made it suspect for the Republic, and it seems still to have been in bad odor under Napoleon, for a minor scandal was provoked when the Comte de Bausset, a high palace official, served a leg of lamb at a formal dinner—"a menu so vulgar," wrote a disapproving critic, "that the reputation of the imperial family suffered greatly in public opinion." Today lamb is held in high esteem in France, particularly in the classic form of the *gigot*, a leg of lamb usually flavored with garlic and accompanied with white beans, especially if it comes from an animal with built-in seasoning, either because it has grazed on the salt meadows which lie under the shadow of Mont-Saint-Michel or along the estuary of the Gironde at Pauillac, or alternatively on the plateaus or mountains of the lower Alps or Provence, where the animals feed on pungent wild herbs.

LAMB. *The back part of a Morse, or reliquary. Paschal Lamb with eagle of St. John and ox of St. Luke. Walrus ivory, English, 11th century* AD

A Spanish opinion that lamb is the best of all meats is enshrined in the Valencian saying *De la mar el mero y del monte el cordero*: "The sea gives cod and the mountain gives lamb." Suckling lamb, preferably spit-roasted out of doors, is the traditional Easter dish of Rome, and this animal, represented sometimes by its humblest morsels, is enjoyed everywhere throughout Italy. Central Europe is standoffish about lamb. Austria pays scant attention to it, but in Germany, where it was little eaten until very recently, lamb has lately acquired a certain popularity; nevertheless, it is still found only in the larger butcher shops. Holland is proud of its Texel lamb, another grazer in salt meadows, in this case those of the Frisian Islands. In Scandinavia it is Norway which eats the most lamb (imported), but Finland has a specialty of sauna-cured lamb, which from the outside looks shriveled and dry but, from the moist heat in which it was cured, remains tender and juicy inside. Greenland maintains that it produces the finest lambs in the world (a claim which the Mideast would probably dispute) because they browse on Arctic willow and juniper. The pampas of Latin America are beef country, but Uruguay raises, and consequently eats, more lamb than her neighbors. Finally, New Zealand is the world's number one sheep-raising country—3 million people, 60 million sheep; the best is exported and the New Zealanders themselves eat the second best.

The United States is sulky towards lamb. Americans eat only four pounds per person per year, half as much as they did at the beginning of the century, and their consumption continues to decline. The French eat over 50 percent more lamb than Americans, the British five times as much (counting lamb and mutton together, for that is what the statistics do). Lamb is a bad fourth in the United States, after beef, pork and veal, in that order.

Part of the American distaste for lamb seems to represent a survival of the contempt for it which was, illogically, a by-product of the Western conflict between cattle raisers and sheepherders, diffused throughout a country where beef became king. Texans refer to lamb chops as "wool on a stick," and Westerners eat very little lamb, which they call disdainfully "sheep" or even "goat." The West raises some excellent lamb, but it is shipped to the markets of the East, and in lesser degree to certain emancipated cities of the Pacific coast or the Great Lakes region. American coldness toward lamb may also be attributed to the diminishing quality of this meat in the United States, which has given rise to the opinion that lamb is uninteresting by its intrinsic nature. "It doesn't taste good unless considerable work is done on it," Richard Gehman wrote in *The Haphazard Gourmet*, an opinion which I fear I cannot share; and after expatiating for two pages on this theme, he gives the show away by ending, "Maybe I just don't like lamb much."

It is probable that a majority of Americans don't like lamb much, but it is because they seldom have a chance to taste it—what is customarily foisted off on them as lamb is mutton, or very close to it. A lamb is, by American dictionary definition, a sheep not more than a year old, a description with which most countries would agree, for a natural taste-changing development occurs at this age in sheep, signaled by the appearance of the first two teeth.

In the Western world, the French and the Italians eat the youngest lamb, along with some fortunate Britons, but English practice is so eccentric that it is difficult to generalize about it. In Italy, *abbacchio* should designate true suckling lamb, meaning an animal which has never tasted grass, whose sole food has been milk. The equivalent French term is *agneau de lait*, but in French there is a series of gradations. French lambs are not slaughtered until their weight has reached 15½ pounds, before which the meat is held to be insipid, and they continue to be *agneaux de lait* up to 22 pounds—in other words, between the age of five and seven weeks. If the lamb is called instead *agneau blanc*, it has not been weaned, but it may possibly have eaten grass as well as milk (if it is certain that it has, it is a *broutard*, a grazer, but ordinarily a lamb so described would be three months old). This is where Germany begins: *Milchlamm*, suckling lamb, is that old in Germany, and even at that is a name rather than a reality for most Germans; it is hard to find lamb this young on the market, and when you do find it, it has been slaughtered between three and five months, at a weight of 25 to 30 pounds.

In France, suckling lamb is followed by butchers' lamb (*agneau de boucherie*), so called because it has graduated to the butcher shops from the poultry shops, the traditional sellers of suckling lamb. At this stage a lamb weighs between 26½ and 44 pounds, and is succeeded by an animal of five months or more weighing 45 pounds and up, known as a *laiton*, somewhat speciously, since this suggests milk (*lait*) feeding, but the animal is by now on pasturage. The meat has taken on an assertive flavor, so, for the benefit of those who, inexplicably, demand lamb that doesn't taste like lamb, France produces *agneau d'écurie*, "stable lamb," raised indoors on mash; the flavor is bland, not to say non-existent. Meanwhile Germany, after the first five months, calls everything *Lamm* until the age of a year, while in New Zealand suckling lamb is followed by "hogget," which remains the correct term until it is succeeded by "two-toother," lamb a year old or a trifle more.

In principle, French lamb becomes mutton at the age of one year, but recognition of its adult hood is sometimes staved off by calling animals which have developed only their first two teeth *antenais* until the first middle teeth appear, when they become irrevocably providers of mutton. Germany also postpones the evil day by referring to "yearling lamb" up to the age of eighteen months. From that time on, everywhere in the

LAND CRAB. *Drawing by Kate Greenaway:* Almanack for 1884, *London*

world, the flesh of the sheep is indisputably mutton.

In the United States, it would be almost correct to assert that what France, Italy, England and even Germany call suckling lamb is not to be had; but there is one exception. Pennsylvania and New Jersey slaughter lamb just under two months—the upper limit for what the French call suckling lamb—and sell it to New York, almost its only market, for no other city contains enough gourmets to pay the nearly prohibitive price it commands. Otherwise Americans get nothing younger than what the United States Department of Agriculture has dubbed officially Genuine Spring Lamb, three to six months old, past the age at which European interest in lamb begins to decrease. There is also year-round lamb, which runs up to eleven months, nearly mutton by European standards. It quickly becomes mutton by American definition too, and is therefore abandoned, for Americans by then find its taste too strong.

LAND CRAB. In 1585 Sir Francis Drake, whose purpose was to harass Spaniards wherever he could find them, was lying in ambush with a detachment of harassers on the island then called Santo Domingo, and now, in the official parlance of the United States, Hispaniola. Hoofbeats resounded from the strand, emanating, Sir Francis estimated, from a body of cavalry, which could only be Spanish, too large to be affronted. He ordered quick retreat to his boats before the enemy could cut him off from them, and must have felt a little foolish when his men emerged onto the beach to discover that they had been routed by a company of noisily scampering land crabs.

Land crabs exist on most of the warm shores of the world, especially on the west coast of Africa and in the Caribbean, which is the area where they are most prized for food. Elsewhere cooks seem to hold that the place of the crab is in the sea or in the pot, and if it is abnormal enough to leave the first, it must be a *lusus naturae* which had better not be popped into the second; so far as we know, land crabs have filed no dissenting opinion to this theory. The low esteem in which they are held in some circles (and it is true that their flesh is less firm than that of sea crabs and, being slightly rubbery, demands diligent chewing) accounts for the refusal of Floridians to eat them, though they are plentiful in Florida. Yet as close to the mainland as Puerto Rico they are considered a great delicacy. It helps, no doubt, that they are treated there with particular care. Shut up in wire pens when caught, they are simultaneously purged and fattened for three days before being delivered to the kitchen. Their first day's diet consists of coconut meat, the second's is corn and water, and the third day they eat dry corn alone. On the fourth day they are ready for the table.

Puerto Rico, which is partial to stuffed land crabs, calls them *jueyes*, but in Martinique, where land-crab omelets are a specialty, the word for this animal is *courlourou*.

Despite its name, the land crab is at heart a sea crab; the place of all crabs *is* in the sea. True land crabs have alienated themselves from their original medium to the extent of developing enlarged body cavities which can breathe air like lungs, though as a rule crabs breathe by means of gills; nevertheless, they return to the sea when it is time to lay and fertilize their eggs. Having done so, the adults go back to land, while the eggs they have left behind hatch into larvae and pass through all the first stages of the animal's development in the water, which they leave for dry land only after they have become full-fledged adults.

The crustacean called a land crab in Australia is not a crab, but a crawfish, *Eugaeus fossor*, which lives in holes it digs in the ground, like the Louisiana CRAWFISH, *Cambarus hagenianus*.

LE
stands for

the **lead tree**, whose beanlike seeds are eaten in tropical America, and the **leaf tree**, whose leaves and young shoots are eaten in tropical Africa; for **leather-breeches beans**, which are simply air-dried green beans; for the **leather CARP**, rated the second best of its kind for the table; for the **leatherskin**, an edible fish of eastern and southern Africa and Madagascar; for the **leatherwood**, a Tasmanian gum tree whose flowers yield fine honey; for **leaves**, of which many kinds are eaten normally, but others which are not are being fed experimentally to children in India to find out if their protein content can be made compatible with the human digestive system; for the **lechosa**, or fruta bomba of the Spanish-speaking islands of the Caribbean, which is the papaya of the English-speaking islands of the Caribbean; for the **leerfish**, whose firm reddish flesh is much appreciated everywhere around the Mediterranean except in Turkey; for the **left-handed whelk**, whose non-conformism in the spiraling of its shell has so infuriated taxonomists that they have named it *Busycon contrarium*; for **legs**, a part of animals which Saharan Jews from families afflicted with hereditary lameness are forbidden to eat; for the **Leghorn**, a chicken adept at laying eggs but not at putting on meat; for **legumes**, which in English covers the large family of plants whose fruit is borne in pods, like peas and beans, and in French *all* vegetables; and for the **lemming**, edible but little eaten, credited with suicidal intent when in its mass migrations it plunges into the sea, but which is more probably the victim of a lack of information about the distance which has to be covered to reach the opposite shore.

LE
stands for

the **lemon balm**, a delightfully flavored form of mint; the **lemon cucumber**, which though yellow and oval is a real cucumber, used for pickling in the Pacific Northwest; the fragrant-leaved **lemon geranium**, a seasoning which is a native of Peru; **lemon grass**, used freely in Vietnamese cooking; the **lemon sole**, which is not a sole but a dab; **lemon thyme**, excellent for flavoring soups; **lemon verbena**, more properly called melissa; and **lemonwood**, an African evergreen whose fruit is eaten in Malawi.

LE
stands for

the **lemur**, the world's oldest primate, which was eaten by the oldest of the world's youngest primates; for the **lentisk**, or mastic tree, whose gum is eaten in Africa; for the **leopard**, whose marrow, on toast, has been recommended by Graham Greene; for the **leopard-spotted goby**, too small to be fished deliberately for food, but it sometimes gets accidentally into whitebait; for the **lerenes**, a crunchy Caribbean tuber whose English name, if it has one, is unknown to me; for the **lesser-spotted dogfish**, or rough hound, which is not as good eating as the smooth hound, and the **lesser weever**, which is not as good eating as the greater weever; for the **lettered perch**, so called because its flanks appear to be marked with inscriptions in an unknown alphabet; for the **lettuce-saxifrage**, which lends itself to the confection of boiled greens or steeped perfumes; for **Leucaena esculenta**, whose beanlike fruit can be eaten pods and all, here presented under its scientific name since the one by which it is known in Mexico, the only country where it grows, is jaliscote chapas, no nomenclatural improvement; for the **leveret**, a hare not older than a year; and for the **Lewis moon shell**, a large mollusk found on the Pacific coast from British Columbia to Mexico.

And **LE** also stands for

LEEK. Almost everybody who has written about leeks has given us two bits of information: (a) the cultivated vegetable is so ancient that no wild variety from which it may have been developed still exists today; (b) it is native to the eastern Mediterranean. Both of these assertions are open to doubt.

The leek has indeed been cultivated for as far back as our knowledge goes. Its scientific name is *Allium porrum*, a shortening of *Allium ampeloprasum* var. *porrum*. *A. ampeloprasum* is the wild leek, which grows all about us; and the very same people who tell us that the ancestor of the cultivated leek is unknown add innocently that the wild leek shows a "distinct affinity" with the cultivated variety.

As for the Mediterranean origin of the leek, this seems to be belied by the very nature of the plant. It is one of our hardiest vegetables, which, wherever temperatures do not drop below 10° F., can be left in the ground all winter long, and will provide edible shoots and bulbs whenever they are wanted. In colder climates, seeds can nevertheless be planted in autumn or early winter; they will survive the cold and grow in the spring; or plants can be set out in the open as early as two months before the normal date of the last spring frost. They are less resistant to heat. Leeks are often planted in shallow trenches, like asparagus, and earth is heaped up around them to blanch the long root, really a bulb, its most luscious part—but if they are too warmly buried, they rot. This is not the sort of behavior normally developed by plants native to mild climates.

But if not the Mediterranean, where does the leek come from?

There is an Irish legend about its origin. St. Patrick was consoling a dying woman. She told him that in a vision she had seen an herb floating in the air, and that it had been revealed to her that unless she ate it she would die. "What kind of herb?" the saint asked. "It looks like rushes," she answered. St. Patrick transformed some rushes into leeks, she ate them, and was cured.

You are not required to believe that this is the authentic version of the birth of the leek, but it might be held to indicate that the Irish looked upon this vegetable as their very own; however they have rivals on the opposite shore of the Irish Sea. The leek is the national emblem of Wales. On St. David's Day, Welshmen wear bits of leek in their buttonholes in memory of the victory of King Cadwallader over the Saxons in A.D. 640, in a battle in which the Welsh avoided smiting the wrong fighters by wearing leeks in their caps as

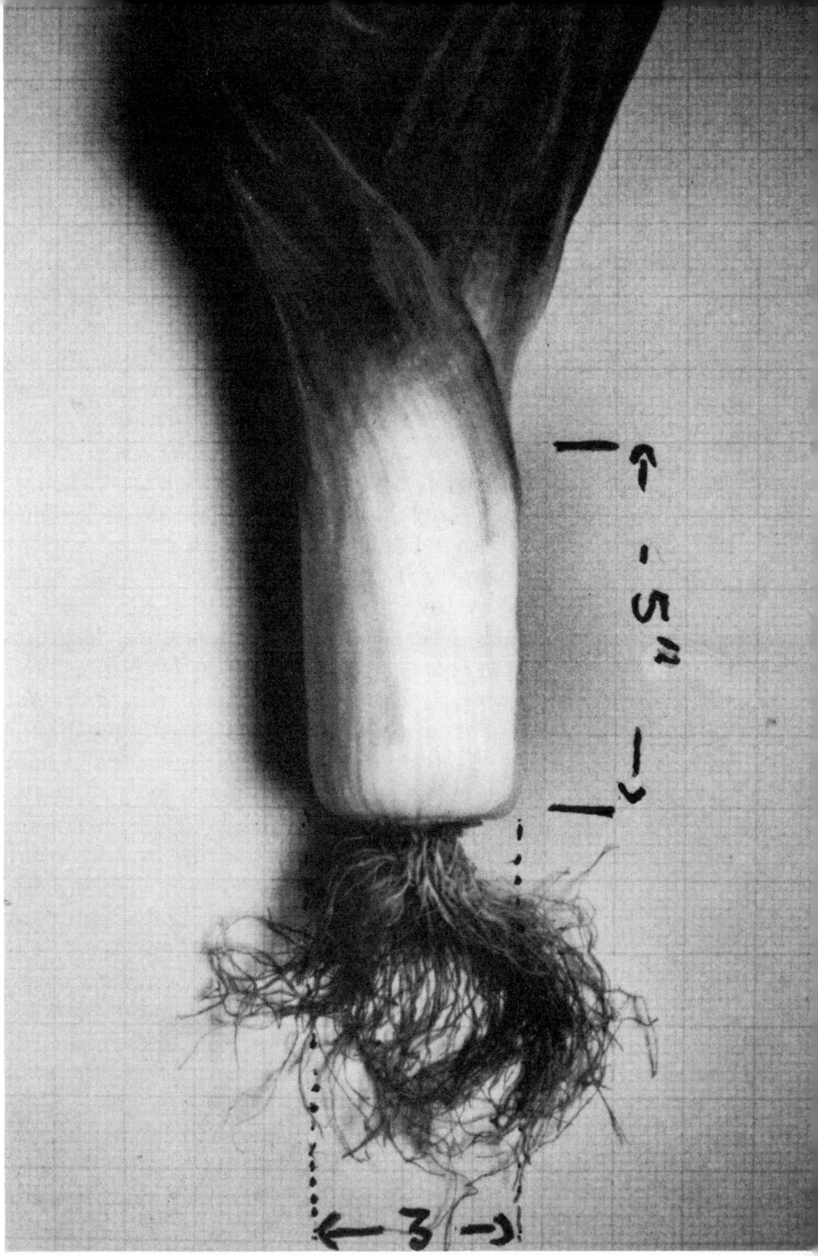

LEEK. *Prize-winning leek grown by Mr. Millar of Ashington, England, 1971*

an identifying badge. The cult of the leek in Wales probably goes even farther back than this, to whenever the annual spring plowing festival, the *cymmortha*, had its origin; on this occasion each participant contributes a leek to the communal stew which is served after it. The association of the leek with Wales is reflected in *King Henry V*, when Shakespeare's comic Welshman, Fluellen, enters to be greeted insultingly by Pistol: "Hence! I am qualmish at the smell of leek."

In the third Celtic area of the British Isles, we find Scotland addicted to cock-a-leekie soup, of which an old recipe says that the leeks in it "must be boiled down into the soup until it becomes a lubricious compound."

Wild leeks grow freely in this region, especially on the offshore islands of Wales. Dictionaries disclaim knowledge of the origin of the word "leek," but its Old English form, *lēac*, has a decidedly Celtic look. All this does not add up to proof that the leek is a native of Celtic Britain, but it would be a likelier place of origin than the Mediterranean for a plant so disdainful of cold; alternatively, Celts from northern Europe may have brought it to Britain from the mainland, and also, during the southern surge of their many migrations, to the eastern Mediterranean.

Wherever they came from, leeks were being cultivated in ancient Egypt from the time when its history begins: another story about the leek which has been repeated endlessly is that the ancient Egyptians worshiped it. The source of this statement is Juvenal, who wrote that Egypt was a country where "onions are adored and leeks are gods." This sentence appears in his *Satires*, and it seems clear that he meant it as a joke; but humorless dissectors of the past have presented it to us as historical truth. In a more serious vein, Herodotus reported that leeks were among the rations of the workers who built the pyramids, and Cheops is on record as having paid his court magician a fee of 1000 pears, 100 pitchers of beer, an ox and 100 bunches of leeks. Pliny wrote that the finest leeks of his time came from Egypt, and the Israelites, fleeing that country, regretted bitterly in the desert "the cucumbers, and the melons, and the leeks" they had left behind them.

The leek seems to have antedated Egypt in this part of the world. "Linguistic evidence suggests that leeks . . . go back to at least the Early Bronze Age," Don and Patricia Brothwell wrote, but the earliest more or less certain date we have is 2100 B.C., when Ur-Nammu of Ur grew them in his garden. An Assyrian herbal recommends leeks to keep the hair from turning gray. In China, the first reference to leeks which has come down to us appeared in a guide to good eating by I Yin, which would be about 1500 B.C.

Democritus advised soaking the seeds of other vegetables in leek juice to protect them from blight and mildew. Hippocrates taught that leeks stopped epistaxis, an impressive word for nosebleed. Nero may not have been entirely wrong when he earned the nickname Porrophagus by eating leek soup daily to improve the sonority of the voice with which he declaimed or sang his own verses—after all, Aristotle attributed the piercing cry of partridges to their fondness for leeks, and in our own time folk medicine has used leek syrup to calm coughing, and even whooping cough. Apicius has given us a recipe, little used nowadays, for stuffed womb (sow's, probably, though he does not say), in which ground meat and leeks are the two principal ingredients.

Leeks were on Charlemagne's list of the foods to be cultivated in his domains, and they were a favorite vegetable during the Middle Ages, when so many more delicate and subtle foods had disappeared from the markets. In Elizabethan times an author who was also a farmer wrote that "peas and leeks make porridge for Lent," a period during which leeks, in the absence of more exciting foods, seem to have been particularly prized.

It was poor fare in some opinions. "I holde a mouses herte nat worth a leek," Chaucer wrote, and in Italian today there is a saying, *ne valer una fronda di porri*, "not worth a leek leaf," that is to say, not worth a tinker's damn. A supercilious Frenchman, Alphonse Kerr, wrote of the *flamiche*, the leek tart of northern France and Belgium, that "it would be very bad if it were possible to eat it." Yet the Italian Easter tart, *torta Pasqualina*, is, in keeping with its festive function, distinguished from other Italian vegetable tarts by being made with a richer dough and a richer filling, the latter based on leeks. Leeks have been described as having a flavor less fine but more robust than asparagus, and they are indeed often called "the poor man's asparagus." They are "one of the mainstays of the French kitchen," Joan M. Jungfleisch wrote in *For Innocents Abroad*, and it should indeed be a recommendation for this vegetable that the country in which it is most eaten, as a seasoning in soups and stews or as a vegetable in its own right, is the one which is reputed to eat best, France. "Leeks . . . are delicious as a braised vegetable," Mrs. Jungfleisch continued, "not to mention cream of leek soup." The French gastronomic writer James de Coquet called the leek "this marvelous vegetable."

There exists in one region of England a curious cult of the leek about which I was informed by a reader from Ashington, apparently its capital, who wrote:

> In Northumberland and Durham—the North East of England next E. Scotland now known as Northumbria—there are working men's clubs, of immense importance to the social life and tradition of the miners and shipbuilders. They hold leek shows every year in late September. The leeks are seeded, nurtured and guarded by the miners till they are ready—at least 3½″ to 4″ in diameter—to win first prize. . . . They are washed, shampooed, combed, polished in oil and/or milk, and displayed and judged. A grower must display two or three leeks together, of equal splendour, to hope for a prize. And the prizes furnish their houses.
>
> It is the hobby of the miners grown out of the depression. It is secret, no man will ever say exactly what he feeds his prize leeks on—brown sugar is the most palatable food, wine, etc., the least. Leeks

are marked weeks before a show to prevent cheating. Leeks are also troubled by other leek growers—gardens vandalized by a Northeastern leek Mafia protection racket. They are nursed and loved and guarded night and day. The seeds are treasured, exchanged among friends but never sold. It is a unique strain. . . .

In Ashington . . . the leek show ends with a great boil-up of the prize-winning vegetables into a soup for all. . . . Women are not usually allowed in the clubs but make it at leek show time simply to slave over the soup.

Despite its long history in Europe, the leek has not been much eaten in America, where it was even difficult to find it listed in seed catalogs a few years ago, though earlier in the century many varieties were offered. It is now appearing in the catalogs again, but if you want leeks, you will probably have to grow them yourself: they are not usually available in markets. Even in France, though the leek has never been abandoned, if only for lending fragrance to pot-au-feu, it suffered a decline during the postwar years; but then it staged a comeback, with the aid of a new generation of young chefs who found original uses for it, inspiring Robert J. Courtine, the food editor of the Paris daily *Le Monde*, to refer to "the leek, that hardly explored vegetable . . . which reserves for cooks of imagination some dazzling discoveries."

Even Chaucer made amends for his slighting estimate of the leek by saying of his Summoner, approvingly it would seem:

Wel loved he garleek, oynons, and eek lekes,
And for to drinken strong wyn, reed as blood.

LEMON. "The lemon," says the *Encyclopaedia Britannica*, "seems to have been unknown to the ancient Greeks and Romans and to have been introduced into Spain and the north African countries some time between the years A.D. 1000 and 1200." Neither Aristophanes nor Virgil had the privilege of consulting the *Britannica*, and so were not protected against exposing their ignorance, the first by writing about the lemon under the name *axioma persicum* and the second under "Median apple." Theophrastus and Antiphanes also did not know that they did not know the lemon, and were therefore undeterred from writing about it. A painter of walls and a maker of mosaics in Pompeii took the liberty of depicting the unknown lemon, and by the fourth century A.D., with the Roman Empire still holding out, not only the fruit but even the tree appeared in mural paintings, perhaps because of the exploit of the Roman agricultural writer Palladius, who is credited with having planted the first lemon tree in Italy in that century. A hundred years earlier Athenaeus had illustrated the Roman belief that the lemon was an antidote for all poisons by telling of two criminals who were thrown to venomous snakes, one of whom had eaten a lemon beforehand and thus survived, while the other succumbed to snakebite. By this time the Hebrews were supposed already to have planted lemon groves in Palestine, and lemons were perhaps also being cultivated in Greece. In the time of Trajan (first–second century A.D.) they were being imported from Libya. However, lemons, though present in ancient Rome, were always rare and expensive, and it may be that their sporadic cultivation in the Mediterranean basin was abandoned when the empire collapsed, removing the market for them.

If so, the return of the lemon also occurred earlier than the date given by the *Encyclopaedia Britannica*. It was during the eighth and ninth centuries that lemons were planted in the Sahara by Arab invaders. The Moors are credited with having established the lemon orchards of Andalusia; they had taken over most of Spain in the eighth century. We may suppose that it was also they who introduced the fruit into Sicily, which they conquered in the same century. Northern Europe, however, probably did wait until the Crusaders returned from the Near East to become acquainted with the lemon, not quite at the *Britannica*'s earliest date, A.D. 1000, but conceivably by its second, 1200 (though the word "lemon" did not enter the English language until the fourteenth century).

The confusions of the *Britannica* may be explained by the ambiguous nature of the lemon itself and the mystery which clouds its origin. It appeared unwitnessed some time during the evolution of the citrus fruits; it was already being cultivated more than two thousand years ago, Alphonse de Candolle wrote in 1833, but where? Malaysia, says one authority, but only one. China, say several, but the lemon seems to have been a relatively recent arrival there, unchronicled before the tenth century, when the first known written reference to this fruit told how two bottles of lemon juice had been presented to the emperor, which justifies us in assuming that it was a rarity. Persia, says a third school, but if the lemon started there it should have been present in the Middle East early enough to be grown in the hanging gardens of Babylon; food historian Georges Blond says it was not. No definite date for its presence in Asia Minor is known before 185 B.C., when the Asian Army returned to Italy, bringing with it what were apparently the first lemons Romans had ever seen. It is the majority opinion today that the lemon originated in the Indus valley, though so far no identifiable seeds have been found there; but an earring in the form of a lemon was discovered at the site of Mohenjo-Daro, which goes back to 2500 B.C.

In the absence of other data, the conditions under which a plant grows best often offer a clue to the region where it originated and developed its habits; the lemon, perversely, thrives today in circumstances which coincide with none of its suggested places of origin. A tender subtropical evergreen tree which also does well in tropical climates provided the conditions are right, it is fussy about those conditions. It likes plenty of water but not plenty of rain (hardly compatible with the theory that it comes from monsoon country), for it is a fertile developer of diseases when drenched. It also responds badly to sudden fluctuations of temperature, and subtropical or not, it is vulnerable, like humans, to sunburn. Hence its favorite habitat is on more or less rainless coasts, where the sea holds the temperature even and the air provides humidity, but not in the form of rain. Such coasts exist in Sicily, which produces 90 percent of the total Italian lemon crop, and southern California, which produces 80 percent of the total American lemon crop (Florida is too damp to offer serious competition). The lemon needs less total heat than the orange during the year (which is synonymous with its growing season, for it sets fruit all year round), yet it is more sensitive than the orange to cold—more sensitive, indeed, than any citrus fruit except the lime.

The very nature of the lemon is mysterious. Is it even a full-fledged distinct species? Linnaeus thought not, and described it as a variety of the CITRON, *Citrus medica* var. *limonum*; it has since been promoted to full membership in the hierarchy under the name *C. limon* (formerly *C. limonia*). Yet its cultivated varieties do not breed true from seed, so to make sure that a lemon tree will produce the same sort of fruit as its parent it is propagated not from seed, but by budding on a rootstock, often that of the sour orange tree. Some botanists suggest that it is a hybrid.

Lemons fall into three categories: common or acid lemons, which are the commercial varieties we all know, of which the most popular are the Eureka, which the *Britannica* says was developed in California and other authorities say was imported from Sicily about 1870, and the Lisbon, which, despite its name, reached America from Australia; rough lemons, used chiefly as rootstock for other citrus fruits (except other lemons); and sweet lemons, which are horticultural curiosities. They seem less sweet than insipid, and in fact they do not contain more sugar than other lemons, only less acid. These seem to have been the kind into which the ladies of Louis XIV's court bit from time to time to keep their lips seductively red.

That detail informs us that by then lemons were generally available in France, at least to those whose means permitted them to live at Versailles. Lemons had been obtainable before the Crusaders returned, from the Moorish plantations in Spain, but only the very rich could afford them. After the Crusaders came upon lemons in Palestine, they were retailed in Paris in the thirteenth century by the *marchands d'aigrun*, who had a monopoly on citrus fruits (*aigrun* came from *aigre*, "acid"). Verjuice, sour-grape juice, was replaced by lemon juice in sauces requiring an acid touch, while in Italy the first post-Roman cookbook, published in 1474, advocated substituting lemon juice wherever feasible for the spices which were then being used to an excessive extent. We hear from the Azores in 1494 that lemons were being cultivated there for sale to England. The same year gives us another tidbit of information: it was also in 1494 that Cesare Borgia sent to his wife, Carlotta d'Albret, who was being detained in France by Louis XII, a sumptuous selection of presents, among which were oranges and lemons, from which we may deduce that they were highly esteemed at the time. Another dated item is the record of the planting in 1559 in Stuttgart, at the same time as oranges and citrons, of the first lemon trees in Germany; considering the climate of that country, they may also have been the last.

In America a similar misconception of the proper terrain for the lemon occurred early in her history: in 1733, *A New and Accurate Account of the Provinces of South Carolina and Georgia* described those colonies as terrestrial paradises where "all things will undoubtedly thrive," and went on to assert specifically that their lemons were "so delicious that whoever tastes them will despise the insipid watery taste of those we have in England." This was a trifle daring in view of the fact that no lemons were growing in those territories, but for that matter, none were growing in England either. England seems to have been adequately supplied with imported lemons, however, or was at least by the time of Sydney Smith (1771–1845), otherwise that distinguished churchman could not have described the remoteness of

LEMON *by Jan van de Velde III (1620–1662).* Glass of Wine and a Lemon, *oil on canvas*

his parish by writing, "My living in Yorkshire was so far out of the way, that it was actually twelve miles from a lemon."

The lemon is something of an anomaly in being an important food which is nevertheless almost never eaten *in toto* by itself. India does preserve green or very young lemons in mustard oil heightened with exotic spices, Morocco has a specialty of provocatively aromatic salted lemons; the Middle East dries lemons until they become black, as hard as stone, and almost weightless; and even in staid England, after the conquest of India gave Britons a liking for pungent dishes, lemons were pickled, "hotted up," Elizabeth David wrote, "with horseradish and mustard flour." But ordinarily lemons enter into cooking only through their juice (it was one of the first flavorings of soda water about 1840, it is the fourth most popular kind of sherbet in the United States after orange, pineapple and lime, and it is at its most subtle in desserts like soufflés); their peel (but housewives began to distrust lemon rind when they learned that its bright golden color was produced by ethylene gas, while it was preserved by diphenyl); and even their flowers (whose worst use is perhaps that of being scattered over onion soup).

There is a belief among musicians that if you suck a lemon within sight of a trumpeter, his lips will pucker up to such an extent that he will be unable to play. I do not know if this theory has ever been scientifically verified.

LENTIL. It was during World War I that my father returned home one day clasping in his embrace a large paper bag whose contents, turned out on the kitchen table, looked like a heap of gravel. "What in the world is that?" my mother asked. "Lentils," he replied. They were one of the foods patriotic Americans were being urged to eat in the interests of wartime economy. My father, a man of civic spirit and gastronomic adventurousness, had heeded the call of duty. I think it was the first time I had thought of lentils as a food suitable for human beings.

Yet man had been eating lentils for more than eight thousand years; they were one of the first vegetables to be brought under cultivation. Their place of origin is unknown, but it seems reasonable to place it not far from the earliest localities where they have been found: Qalat Jarmo, in what is now northeastern Iraq, which according to carbon dating goes back to about 6750 B.C.; Halicar, Turkey, about 5500 B.C.; and Anatolia, where ancient containers of lentils bear markings identifying them as having been grown in Sumeria. It is on record that lentils were cultivated in the gardens of King Merodach-Baladan in Babylon in 800 B.C., but they must have been grown there much earlier, for this was on the route of their penetration into Egypt, where a sort of lentil purée was discovered in a Twelfth dynasty (1750 B.C.?) tomb at Thebes, while other Egyptian finds suggest that there were lentils in Egypt even in pre-dynastic times, which would mean 3000 B.C. at the latest. On the European side of the Mediterranean, Herodotus tells us that lentils were an important food of the Graeco-Scythian Callipidae, who cultivated them. They seem to have moved up the Danube valley, entering the Balkans and southern Germany in Neolithic times, and they have been found on St. Peter's Island in the Lake of Bienne, in Swiss lacustrine settlements, then in their Bronze Age. We may be justified in assuming that they reached India early simply from the fact that this is the greatest lentil-consuming country in the world, which grows fifty varieties of this pulse and uses them so subtly that the Parsee dish called *dahnsak* requires a mixture of three to nine different kinds of lentils to achieve a balance which satisfies the cook. The Middle East, where this vegetable presumably originated, is still the world's second greatest area of lentil eating.

Throughout the ages, lentils have been consistently cheap in comparison with most other available foods, which has earned them the contempt of the snobbish and the pretentious, though they have simultaneously received praise from those capable of judging foods by other criteria than that of price. The ancient Greeks, we are told, thought lentils a food for the poor, and consequently disdained them; some of their philosophers ate them ostentatiously to demonstrate that they were above worldly pleasures and self-indulgence. Yet whether they affected to despise them or not, Greeks of all classes ate lentils—in Homeric times, when the vegetables eaten oftenest were chick-peas, broad beans and lentils; in fifth-century Attica, when they were cabbages, onions, garlic, peas and lentils; and in the Periclean Age, when vegetables were not much eaten at all because they were too dear, but broad beans and lentils, usually served mashed, were the exceptions. When Athens was in full flower, lentils were a staple, and Hippocrates prescribed them for liver ailments (accompanied, startlingly, with slices of boiled dog; but they were small slices). When Aristophanes had one of the characters in his play *Plutus* say of a man who had just acquired wealth, "He doesn't like lentils any more," was he expressing disdain for an unworthy food (which is usually the assumption of those who quote this passage), or was he expressing disdain for the pretentiousness of the newly rich?

In Rome, when the simple foods of the early Latins gave way to more refined dishes borrowed from Greece, lentils, according to some writers, were left to the plebeians; Martial apologized when he put them before his guests. Yet both Virgil and Pliny approved of them, and credited them with producing in men a temper of moderation and mildness. Though Apicius was a snob, he included in his cookbook a recipe for lentils with chestnuts, a second for lentils with mussels and a third for barley soup enriched with lentils, peas and chick-peas. Heliogabalus, whom it is hardly possible to confuse with the common people, offered at one of his banquets a dish of lentils mixed with topazes, opening the possibility of simultaneously winning a fortune and losing a tooth. The excavation of Pompeii brought to light in the market a quantity of lentils, rather overdone, and the Roman demand for them was heavy enough to keep a constant stream of lentil-carrying vessels plying between Alexandria (for the small red Egyptian lentils were the best) and Ostia. Pliny tells us that a special ship was built to bring to Rome the obelisk which stands today in front of St. Peter's and that it made the voyage buried under the rest of the cargo, 2,880,000 Roman pounds of lentils.

The Old Testament reported that the penitential bread Ezekiel was required to eat contained lentils, but "penitential" seems an unnecessarily severe term for the bread which he did indeed eat during a period of penitence, for it sounds rather rich for the times: "Take thou also unto thee wheat, and barleys, and beans, and lentiles, and millet, and fitches [vetches] and make thee bread thereof" (Ezekiel 4:9). As for the "mess of pottage" with which Jacob purchased Esau's birthright, it may well be that it was described as composed of lentils because they were considered a poor food and thus emphasized the insufficiency of the consideration Esau accepted in exchange for his inheritance; but less publicized Hebrews ate lentils in great numbers. In Lebanon today *miqeddrab*, a dish of lentils, rice and onions, eaten hot or cold, is also called "Esau's dish of lentils."

In the Middle Ages, the lentil was not only looked down upon as a food unworthy of the solvent, it was also accused of being difficult to digest and prone to inflame the stomach, weaken eyesight and engender nightmares. In Paris, where peas, broad beans and lentils comprised about all there was to eat in the way of vegetables over the winter, lentils were resorted to chiefly when the others were lacking. In Italy, Platina wrote in 1475 that lentils were "the worst of all vegetables."

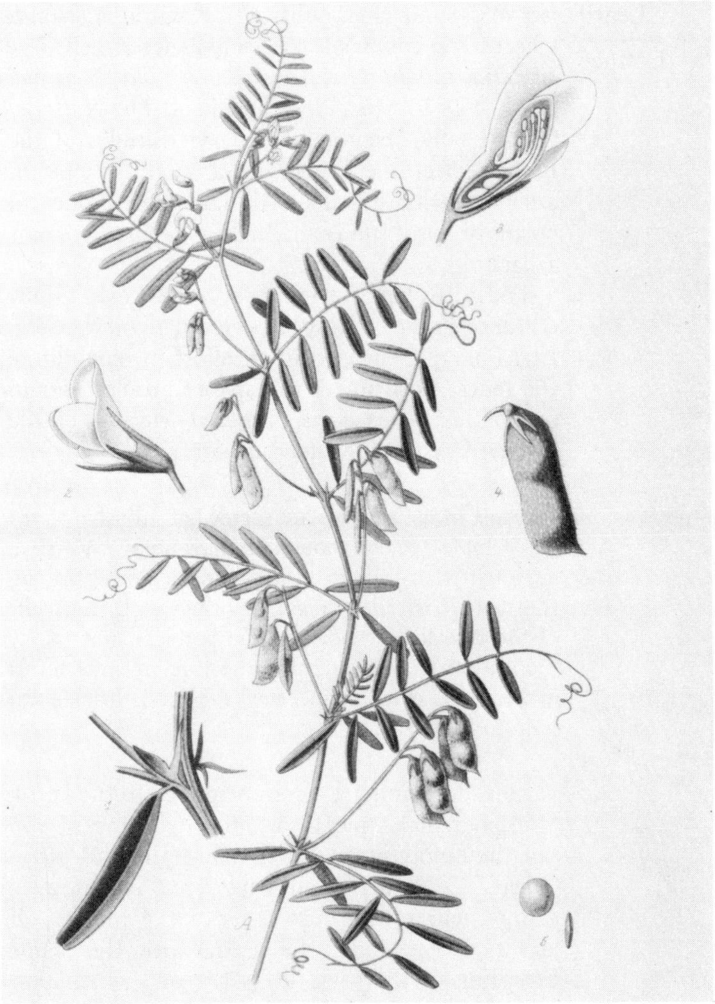

LENTIL. *Print from Amadée Masclef:* Atlas des plantes de France, *Paris, 1889–1891*

In Germany, Sebastian Munster provided in 1588 a description of the miserable life of peasants who subsisted on black bread, oatmeal and boiled peas or lentils. The asceticism of Trappist monks was expressed in a diet "of which the most delicate foods were lentils, broad beans, carrots and other coarse vegetables."

Yet lentils were among the plants Charlemagne ordered planted in his domains. In the sixteenth century the French physician Ambroise Paré used lentils against smallpox. In the reign of Louis XIV, Mme. de Sévigné wrote ecstatically of a soup of *nantilles,* so called I do not know why (the French word is *lentilles*), unless they were grown near Nantes. One king later, the tiny green lentils of France, which were, and are, considered the country's best, were rebaptized *lentilles à la reine,* the queen in question being Marie Leszczynska, wife of Louis XV, who is credited with having made fashionable in the highest circles the humble vegetable esteemed in her native Poland. The politically versatile A. Viard, whose 1806 cookbook was called successively *The Imperial Cook, The Royal Cook, The National Cook, The Imperial Cook* again and *The National Cook* finally, according to the vicissitudes of the French government, provided a notable recipe for duck with lentil purée. Ali-Bab offered one for cream of lentil soup, of which one ingredient was a partridge.

Today Robert J. Courtine, the gastronomic editor of France's most respected daily newspaper, *Le Monde*, is engaged in an effort to rehabilitate the lentil, both in his newspaper articles and in one of his books, *One Hundred Marvels of the French Cuisine*, in which he wrote:

> It seems to me that we are somewhat unjust towards a vegetable which, though it may not be worth a birthright . . . merits the consideration of the gourmet. It is called vulgar. It brings with it a whiff of the boarding school and the barracks, not to say the prison. . . . Nevertheless the true gourmet revels in it . . . at every moment of the meal, from lentil soup to lentil salad.

Indeed, the phrase so often applied to the lentil, "the poor man's meat," is only derogatory if you put the emphasis on "poor man's" instead of on "meat." This may well have been meant as a compliment by the first users of the phrase. Of all dried vegetables, the lentil, with the single exception of the soybean, is the one which best substitutes for meat because it contains the most proteins; you have to eat 134 grams of beef to absorb the number of grams of protein (almost 25) which you get from 100 grams of lentils. However it may have been regarded the rest of the year, the lentil was welcomed in Catholic countries during Lent as the best fast-day food for those who could not afford fish, which until rather recently meant most of the population.

The citizens of the United States, however, have never taken the lentil to their bosoms. The first Americans to make acquaintance with lentils were probably Iroquois Indians, introduced to them by Jesuit missionaries. Father St. John, working among the Indians along the St. Lawrence, wrote home to France early in the seventeenth century: "We began to work and dig the earth, to sow purslane and turnips and to plant lentils." They do not seem to have taken very deep root. The only place where they are grown now is the Pacific Northwest, and even there only to a limited extent, though the United States imports considerable quantities of them.

It must be admitted that, left to their own devices, lentils are a trifle monotonous in flavor; you would not want to eat them as often as you could put up with, for instance, beans. But their very neutrality opens large possibilities for the application of subtle seasonings and the creation of harmonious combinations which can result in memorable dishes. As Richard Gehman wrote in *The Haphazard Gourmet*: "God, how my mouth waters when I think of lentil soup!"

LETTUCE. "Lettuce," wrote John Gerard in his *Herball* (1597), "is a cold and moist pot-herbe, yet not in the extream degree of cold or moisture, but altogether moderatly; for otherwise it were not to be eaten." We would be more likely to describe it as refreshing today, when it is indeed widely eaten, more than any other salad plant. It has been on the human menu at least since 800 B.C., when an Assyrian herbal listed it among the 250 plants growing in the gardens of King Merodach-Baladan in Babylon. Herodotus wrote that the kings of Persia had lettuce on their tables about 550 B.C., and it was also being grown in Egypt. Lettuce seeds have been found in Egyptian tombs, and we have a description of its stalks rising from the checkerboard squares into which ancient Egyptian gardens were divided by their irrigation ditches, but we do not know precisely when the plant appeared there first.

The lettuce of those times did not form heads, but put out leaves from a tall central stalk, which our cultivated varieties remember only when they go to seed and send up their seedstalks. For this reason the ancient Greeks called lettuce "asparagus," a word then applied generally to all spike-like plants. Hippocrates said a good word for lettuce, and Theophrastus recorded the presence of four varieties—flat-stalked, round-stalked, Laconian and white; the last was the sweetest and tenderest, and was the first to reach Italy, at least by 500 B.C., when it is on record that the favorite Roman vegetables of the period were artichokes, cabbage and lettuce. It remained the only variety in Italy for a considerable time, according to Pliny. It was the Romans who taught it to form heads, but they took their time about it. The education of lettuce had apparently not yet occurred in the first century A.D., when Columella mentioned a number of kinds of lettuce, but gave no indication of acquaintance with any which formed heads.

Apicius provided a recipe for a purée of lettuce leaves and onion, and Columella gave directions for pickling lettuce, but as a rule the ancient Romans treated it as we do, serving it as a salad with dressing. In the time of Augustus it ended the meal, but under Domitian it was shifted to the beginning, causing Martial to inquire (in the

LETTUCE. *Photograph by Dorothea Lange:* Filipinos Cutting Lettuce, *Salinas, California, January 1935*

translation offered by Gerard): "Telle me why Lettuce, which our Grandsires last did eate, / Is now of late become, to be the first of meat?" The answer seems to be that the Romans had come to realize that lettuce arouses the appetite. Of all the Roman emperors, Diocletian, whose only admirable characteristic was that he loved gardening, seems to have been the one who most appreciated lettuce; no doubt it had been taught to head by his time. When he abdicated in A.D. 305 in favor of his co-emperor Maximian, the latter, alarmed at being left alone on a throne whose mounting constituted an incitement to murder, pleaded with Diocletian to change his mind. "If you saw what beautiful lettuces I am raising," Diocletian said, "you would not urge me to take up that burden again." Thanks to lettuce, Diocletian was one of the rare post-Antonine emperors to die in his bed, but Maximian was not assassinated, at least not officially: it was called suicide.

Lettuce seems to have been slow to reach the Far East; only in the fifth century A.D. do we hear of its cultivation in China. In Europe meanwhile it was spreading north and west from the Mediterranean area. The Anglo-Saxons gathered the wild plant, but did not cultivate it. Charlemagne, however, included it in the list of plants to be grown in his domains. Lettuce became a common enough plant in French home gardens, but it was not easy to find it on the market; watercress seems to have been preferred there during the Middle Ages. Lettuce must have enjoyed luxury status, for at all the great medieval banquets, the season permitting, three or four different kinds might be served—which exhausted the possibilities, for according to Liébault, writing in 1574, only four kinds of lettuce were then being cultivated in France: the small, the common, the curled and the Roman (our Romaine).

There are two explanations for the name of Romaine lettuce, which seems to have been first applied to this crisp upright variety in France (causing it to be called Paris lettuce in some other localities). One of them credits Rabelais with having brought from Rome in 1534 seeds given him by the Pope, who grew the plant in his private garden. However, it seems fairly well established that Romaine lettuce had reached France some two centuries earlier, having been brought by the Popes when they abandoned Rome for Avignon.

The name "Romaine" has caused some contemporary writers to suppose that this type of lettuce originated in Rome; but its alternative name, Cos lettuce, tells us where the Romans got it. It is still an important crop on the Greek island of Cos, a place which gets a good deal of sun; Romaine, accordingly, is the only lettuce able to resist heat.

England perhaps graduated to cultivated lettuce in the fifteenth century; it was in 1440 that it was listed among vegetables which could be grown in that country and presumably it was, for a little later the favorite vegetables of England were given as lettuce, cabbage, spinach and radishes. In France the popularity of lettuce skyrocketed in the seventeenth century because Louis XIV was fond of it, preferably seasoned with tarragon, pimpernel, sweet basil or, if possible, violets. The Republicans who overthrew the monarchy were no less esoteric in their treatment of lettuce. At the time of the French Revolution, not only in France but also in England it was fashionable to eat "sharpened" salads, in which lettuce was combined with anchovies, herring, or other dried or marinated fishes, while such bold seasonings as capers and mustard completed the task of smothering completely the modest, unassertive flavor of the lettuce.

Columbus himself is supposed to have introduced lettuce to the New World, where it was eaten chiefly in the following centuries by those who grew it themselves, among them Thomas Jefferson. Otherwise a nation of meat eaters proved able to resist the charms of lettuce, and not until after World War I did Americans pay much attention to it; but today they are so devoted to lettuce that it is one of the few foods whose consumption does not fall off when its price rises. California produces 70 percent of all the nation's lettuce, and Arizona another 15 percent, figured on a year-round basis; but during the six months when lettuce is out of season elsewhere, these two states together supply from 90 to 98 percent of the demand.

Nobody knows where lettuce originated, except that it is a plant of the Northern Hemisphere, and almost certainly of Eurasia. A good guess might be that it is a native of the Caucasus, for history shows it to us first in Asia Minor or not far from it, but its intolerance of heat suggests growing habits formed in a cool climate, which in that part of the world implies altitude.

The ancestor of our cultivated lettuce is believed to be the wild *Lactuca scariola*, widespread in Eurasia, and also in the United States, where it is an immigrant from the Old World. There is a native wild lettuce too, *L. canadensis*, alias tall lettuce or horseweed.

Cultivated lettuce is *L. sativa*, of which there are innumerable varieties. They may be classified in four groups, of which one is almost unknown to the public—*L. sativa* var. *angustana*, asparagus lettuce, which represents the survival into our times of the plant known to the ancients, for it produces a fat, tasty central stalk. There are two spherically heading lettuces, *L. sativa* var. *capitata*, cabbage lettuce, with a tightly folded head, and *L. sativa* var. *crispa*, leaf or curled lettuce, with a looser head. The familiar Romaine, *L. sativa* var. *longifolia*, may be said to form a head too, a long cylindrical one, though it sometimes has to be cajoled into doing so by tying a band around the tips of its leaves.

Head lettuces are subdivided into two groups: butterhead lettuces, tender and pleasing to the taste, but soft and hence difficult to pack, ship and store; and the crisp, hard-headed types, inferior from the gourmet's point of view, but they mean less waste for sellers, so that is what we get. The commonest lettuce in the United States is the hard-headed iceberg variety—which, unfortunately, offers only one-ninth as much vitamin A as Romaine, one-third as much calcium as Romaine, and one-fourth as much iron as butterhead. Butterheads include the popular Boston lettuce, and Bibb lettuce, developed by an amateur horticulturist, John B. Bibb, in Frankfort, Kentucky, excuse enough for serving it at Kentucky Derby breakfasts.

Lettuce has engendered offspring of the highest order, as we learn from Thoreau, who in *Walden* hails "Hebe, cup-bearer to Jupiter, who was the daughter of Juno and wild lettuce, and who had the power of restoring gods and men to the vigor of youth. She was probably the only thoroughly sound-conditioned, healthy, and robust young lady that ever walked the globe, and wherever she came it was spring."

LI
stands for

liberation salt, which for French Revolutionists

meant the saltpeter used for making gunpowder, and **liberty cap,** an edible mushroom so named for its resemblance to the Phrygian bonnet, adopted by the same revolutionists as a symbol of the new Republic; for **lichen,** which some authorities maintain was the manna eaten in the desert by the Hebrews during their exodus from Egypt; for **licorice,** whose name is a corruption of a Greek word meaning "sweet root"; for the **lightning whelk,** a left-handed shellfish; for **lights,** or lungs, called numbles in medieval times, at least if they came from venison; for the **lilac,** a commercially exploited food in France, where its flowers are candied and exported; for the **lily,** from whose bulbs Thoreau made a soup which was "palatable enough, but it reminded me of the Irishman's limestone broth."

LI
stands for

the **Lima bean,** luscious even though it is a trifle poisonous around the edges; for the **lime,** whose juice British sailors of the nineteenth century put in their grog to stave off scurvy and which New Caledonians of the twentieth century rub into their hair to stave off lice; for the **limpet,** or Chinaman's hat; for **limu,** a fleshy, sharp-tasting seaweed eaten on several Pacific islands; for the **limulus,** or horseshoe crab; for the **linden,** whose leaves served as famine food in Poland during World War I and whose flowers are used in cooking in France today; for the **lined periwinkle,** a pedestrian shellfish which within the last two centuries has promenaded from its original northern limit in Florida all the way to Cape Cod; for the codlike **ling** of the Atlantic and the **lingcod** of the Pacific, neither of which is a cod; for the **lingaro,** an exotic fruit being grown experimentally in Florida; for the **lingonberry,** beloved of Scandinavia, whose resemblance to the cranberry has caused it to be misnamed the lowbush cranberry in the United States; for **linseed,** already being cultivated for its oil by Swiss lake dwellers in the Bronze Age; for the **lion,** which provided more meat than the wild boar in Upper Paleolithic Europe; and for the **lionhead goldfish,** whose head looks more like a raspberry than a lion.

LI
stands for

liquidambar, a sweet gum native to North America; for the **litchi** (or litchee, or lichee, or lichi, or lychee), a plum-sized Chinese fruit with jelly-like pulp and an acid-sweet flavor; for the **little cuttlefish,** whose ink pouch poses fiendish problems for the amateur cook; for the **littleneck,** which on the Atlantic coast of North America is a clam trying to make up its mind to become a quahog, but on the Pacific coast or in Japan is something else again; for the **little tunny,** a small tuna whose back looks as if it had been written upon in an unknown alphabet; for the **live-forever,** a wild plant with eminently edible leaves, stems and tubers, and the **livelong,** which is its close relative except in Africa, where it is a wild grape; for the **liverwort,** an herb once believed to be beneficial to the organ for which it is named; for **lizards,** of which many kinds have been eaten at many times in many places; for the deep-swimming **lizardfish,** whose flesh is eaten oftenest deeply embedded in fritters; and for **Lizzie-run-in-the-hedge,** which is ground ivy.

And **LI** also stands for

LIVER. When I was a boy, charged with picking up the family meat order, the butcher, before wrapping up the parcel, would pause to ask, "Some liver for the cat?" and if the answer was affirmative, would lop off a generous portion and throw it in, free. This was not only a measure of the easy-going economy of the period, but also of the slight esteem in which liver was then held.

There is no danger of this sort of butcherial bounty today, though organ meats are still looked upon with distrust in America, liver being the only one many Americans will eat. The Chinese, less standoffish about the hidden assets of animals, often pay more for liver than for muscle meats, which gives them a better deal in the nutrition-money ratio, aside from the fact that many Chinese like liver better. The nutritive virtues of this meat are lost on the Mahadena clan of the Tibesti Teda of the Sahara, who refuse to eat liver because, in their opinion, it looks like clotted blood, while Saharan Jews, whenever an unusual number of stillbirths occurs in a family, enjoin all the members of that family, for reasons difficult to discern, from eating liver. It might have been either because they esteemed it little or much that in several ancient countries, when an animal burnt offering was sacrificed to the gods, all that was actually burned was the liver, kidneys and fat, while the priests helped themselves to the rest.

We are inclined today, in unimaginative fashion, to attribute the value of liver to its high content of calcium, iron, vitamins A, D, E and K, and above all to the B vitamins, in which it is especially rich, notably in B_1, B_2, B_6 and B_{12}. Earlier ages, more picturesquely, prized liver on a mystical basis, holding that it is the repository of courage, a theory which led Dakota Indians, not so very long ago as historical time runs, and some African tribes, even more recently, though neither were otherwise cannibalistic, to eat human liver in order to ingest its heroic virtues. The Africans held that it had to be eaten raw, as cooking would destroy its magic, and this seems to have been a sage precaution, for whether or not cooking destroys magic, it does destroy vitamins, and it would have been a waste to cook human liver, which contains 95 percent of all the vitamin A in the body. Liver is also the largest human gland, so quantity as well as quality was granted to Jeremiah Johnson, a "mountain man" of the Far West who, early in the nineteenth century, consumed, according to his own count, the livers of 247 Crow Indians.

The association of the liver with courage has persisted into our times in such terms as "lily-livered." Shakespeare, consistently impressed by this aspect of the liver, "white and pale, which is the badge of pusillanimity and cowardice," wrote also, "If he were opened, and you find as much blood in his liver as will clot the foot of a flea, I'll eat the rest of the anatomy." The liver from this point of view appears as a surrogate symbol for the heart. While Iago spoke of wearing (or in his case, not wearing) his heart upon his sleeve, the South African poet Roy Campbell writes:

We had no time for make-believe
  So early each began
To wear his liver on his sleeve
  To snarl and be an angry man.

LIVER. "Pain de fois-gras à la Renaissance," *engraving from Urbain Dubois and Emile Bernard:* La Cuisine Classique, *Paris, 1888*

Eaters of the orthodox mammalian livers agree more or less on the hierarchy of palatability. Most in demand is calves' liver, the finest and tenderest, better in Europe than in the United States, for in Europe the animal is slaughtered younger. Lambs' liver is a close runner-up; in the Middle East it is preferred, and in England more lambs' liver than calves' liver is being eaten at the time of writing because it is cheaper, and the cost differential is greater than the quality differential. Adult sheeps' liver, a little stronger in flavor and a little tougher, seems tied for third place with pigs' liver, which is tenderer but also the strongest in taste, which does not please everybody. Beef liver is not quite as strong but is the toughest of all (better braise it), so it brings up the rear on the scale of palatability; but if the criterion were vitamin content, it would have to be promoted to top rank (however, it doesn't rate quite as high in mineral salts).

Calves' liver and its mammalian fellows are what we are apt to think of first when liver is mentioned, but we would be quick to recall that most of us eat other kinds of liver as well, from poultry or fish; there are also some less than common treats among mammalian livers. In second-century China, dog liver was one of the Eight Delicacies. Eskimos eat seal liver, and in the United States there are aficionados who extol the delicacy of porcupine liver. Among barnyard fowl, chickens yield their livers for many purposes, ducks and geese provide them either for ordinary uses or for the great luxury which is foie gras, and turkey livers are sometimes eaten also, especially in the stuffing when the bird is roasted. American Indians appreciated the tomalley, the green liver

of the crab, and with reason: it is delicious. The Roman Emperor Vitellius dedicated to Minerva a dish containing pike livers, and Francis I ate burbot liver stewed in Spanish wine. Cod liver (which does not taste at all like cod-liver oil) is familiar enough, and in Baja California fishermen value the liver of the hammerhead shark and its brownish cousin, the *sardinero*, in which this organ is exceptionally large. So far as I know, the upper Adriatic is the only region which dotes on the liver of the torpedo ray, a malevolent fish capable of delivering a strong electric shock to anyone seeking to deprive it of this or any other organ.

For those not enamored of liver as a food, it presents another field of usefulness, though admittedly one to which little recourse is had nowadays. It has been reputed to be a producer of auguries since at least the time of the Etruscans, who left us the Liver of Piacenza, a large bronze model of this organ, carefully marked off, for the guidance of soothsayers, into compartments, each labeled with the name of the god or the house of the zodiac responsible for that particular section, recalling the charts of half a century ago on which phrenologists mapped the specialties of the various areas of the brain. It was of course only fiction, or myth, when Euripides in *Electra* showed us Aegisthus discovering in the presence of Orestes that a lobe was missing from the liver of a sacrificial animal, a dire portent duly followed by the murder of the former by the latter. But we reach the realm of history when we read of the same omen being found by haruspices examining viscera in the interests of Alexander the Great, who thought it appropriate to fulfill this prophecy of doom by his death (after an orgy of eating and drinking, possibly, though he was only 33) from cirrhosis of the liver.

LL
stands for

the **llama**, which would make excellent eating if it were not so useful as a work animal that it never reaches the table until it is too tough to chew.

LO
stands for

the **loach**, a small Old World food fish with nearly two hundred species, the **Loch Leven trout**, a single variety among nobody knows how many TROUTS, and the **Lochmaben vendace**, a kind of small whitefish which is one of only two species; for **locusts**, of which one is an insect whose proteins are alleged to have provided nourishment for St. John the Baptist and the other a tree whose flowers provided fritters for Euell Gibbons; for the **locust shrimp**, which is really a squill; for the **Lodi**, a yellow cooking apple produced in New York State in 1924, and the **loganberry**, a cross between the blackberry and the raspberry produced in California in 1881; for the **loir**, which is the European dormouse, eaten in antiquity; for **London pride**, alias St. Patrick's cabbage, **London rocket**, alias hedge mustard, and **London alderman's turtle**, alias (unimaginatively) the green turtle; for the **longan**, a subtropical fruit which looks something like a loose cluster of yellowish grapes, called in China "dragon's eyes"; for the **long-billed spearfish**, an Atlantic marlin, the **long-eared sunfish**, which lives in fresh water, and the **longfin tunny**, which in the United States is the only member of its tribe which may legally be canned under the name White Meat Tuna; for the **Longhorn**, a vanishing Texas steer described as "all belly and no beef," and the **longhorn sculpin** of the Atlantic coast of North America; for the **Long Island duck**, which comes from Peking; for the **long-neck clam**, which is the familiar steamer, the **long-nosed butterflyfish**, which gave the archerfishes a bad name, and the **long-nose gar**, which inhabits the Great Lakes and points south; for **long pig**, a euphemism used by cannibals; for the **longspur**, a game bird which rarely sings except on the wing; for the **longtail tuna**, whose tail to my inexperienced eye seems no longer than that of other tunas; and for the **longtom**, which is the garfish.

LO
stands for

loofah, an African approach to vegetable marrow which seems to have originated in the valley of the Nile; for the **lookdown**, a scad whose eyes are not low-slung, as one might expect, but perched on top of its head; for the **loon**, tough and not tasty; for the **loquat**, or Japanese medlar; for **lords-and-ladies**, otherwise bulls-and-cows, or men-and-women, or stallions-and-mares, or priest's-pintle, or cuckoo-pint, or, more familiarly as a food, Portland arrowroot; for the **Loricariid catfish**, whose suckerlike mouth permits it to hang on to the bottom when streams flow swiftly; for the **loris**, a type of lemur eaten by prehistoric men in Borneo; for the **lote**, which is the burbot; for the **lotus**, which was not eaten by Homer's lotus eaters, but whose rhizome and seeds are eaten today, notably in China; for the **Louise-Bonne**, a delicious French pear developed, legendarily, in Avranches, Normandy, by a certain Louise, surname unknown; for the **louse**, which seems to have been eaten by prehistoric men in the Ozark Mountains; for **louvana,** a leguminous herb cultivated in the Mediterranean area as an animal food which is sometimes preempted by man; for **lovage,** an herb which has fallen out of fashion, though in earlier times it was eaten as a vegetable, like celery, while its stem was candied, like angelica; and for **love apple,** which is of course the tomato, **love grass,** which turns out disappointingly to be nothing more than Ethiopian millet, **love-in-a-mist,** whose seeds can serve as seasoners, and **love-lies-bleeding,** of which the leaves are widely eaten in tropical Africa, with no discernible effects on love.

And **LO** also stands for

LOBSTER. Marie-Thérèse Louise de Savoie-Carignan, Princesse de Lamballe, whose nerves lay only skin-deep (which was why she did not last very long as director of the household of her friend Marie-Antoinette), fainted away when she saw a lobster. "She closed her eyes and remained motionless half an hour," a historian tells us. (Fortunately, this sensitive flower was spared foreknowledge of her end, when her head was promenaded on a pike in the midst of a howling mob.) It is understandable that she was impressed by a creature of somewhat nightmarish aspect which might have been designed by Albrecht Dürer or Vincent Van Gogh. It comes naturally to mind when one thinks of the fantastic, even to a mind as earthy as that of Finley Peter Dunne, who chose the lobster for an absurd image when he wrote:

A man that'd expict to thrain lobsters to fly in a year is called a loonytik; but a man that thinks men can be tu-urned into angels be an iliction is called a rayformer an' remains at large.

Mr. Dunne was presumably not aware that lobsters do fly, as we know from John Hookham Frère, a contemporary of the Princesse de Lamballe, who wrote in 1799 in his *Poetry of the Anti-Jacobin*:

Ah! who has seen the mailèd lobster rise,
Clap her broad wings, and soaring claim the skies?

Scientists, however, have not classified any species of lobster as *Homarus volitans*, and indeed it may be asked whether there is more than one species even of seaborne, not airborne, lobsters. The books give us two, the European *H. gammarus* (*H. vulgaris* is the same thing in another taxonomic system) and the American *H. americanus*; but some biologists think that both are only varieties of the same species. The only significant difference between them seems to be that the American lobster is larger, and this might be the result of habitat, food or the circumstance that commercial lobster fishing got under way in Europe a millennium and a half before it began in America, giving Europeans more time than Americans to kill off their bigger (that is, older) lobsters. The size of American lobsters has been dwindling since five- to six-footers were reported in New York waters in the early seventeenth century, so we may well arrive eventually at the dimensions of European lobsters, whose top today, barring an occasional exception, is about ten pounds.

Webster's dictionary reports another species, which it calls *H. capensis*, described as a very small lobster found off the Cape of Good Hope, of which I can find no trace in any other source. In principle it should not exist. The lobster is a crustacean of the Northern Hemisphere (and of the Atlantic Ocean) and it has no business to be frequenting these waters. I suspect confusion with one of the many other crustaceans which are called lobsters although they are not (that is, they are not members of the genus *Homarus*), possibly with the second most important shellfish of the kind, the spiny lobster or rock lobster, *Palinurus vulgaris*, which does indeed exist in the waters of the Cape of Good Hope and provides us with the familiar South African frozen lobster tails. This is the same crustacean, says the *Dictionnaire de l'Académie Gastronomique*, as the Norway lobster, which it is not. The Norway lobster is *Nephrops norvegicus*, and is a deep-water animal smaller than the lobster, found from Norway to the Mediterranean.

Other spurious lobsters include the squat lobster, which according to the *Encyclopaedia Britannica* is *Munida evermanii*, found only in deep water off Puerto Rico, and according to John Teal of the Woods Hole Oceanographic Institute is the galatheid, which I take to be *Galathea squamosa*, which he reports seeing in the Sargasso Sea. What is called the *red* squat lobster in the Mediterranean and West Africa is the squill, a name which covers a number of species of the genus *Squilla*, while the flat lobster of the Mediterranean is *Scyllarides latus*. The Murray lobster is a name given indifferently in Australia to at least two large crawfish, *Euastachus armatura* and the freshwater *Astacopsis serratus*. What the Finnish tourist bureau touts in its literature as a "miniature lobster" (*rapula* in Finnish, *kräftor* in Swedish) is, I am pretty sure, though I have not been able to procure its scientific calling card, a crawfish too.

Lobsters or not, all of these creatures are tasty in their own right, but there seems to be little dissent from the opinion that the true lobster—the cardinal of the seas, French writer Jules Janin called it—is the most flavorsome crustacean of the ocean. It is tastiest in cold waters, as off the coasts of Maine or of Brittany. Lobsters exist in the Mediterranean, but they are not abundant there and they are inferior in flavor. When you read about Mediterranean lobsters, it is generally the spiny lobster which is meant, though I have eaten excellent true lobsters in Corsica, and friends tell me that small but excellent ones are found in the Bosphorus.

The fine flavor of the lobster seems paradoxical in view of the sort of food *it* eats. The scavenger of the seas, it is attracted by decaying flesh, to which it finds its way chiefly by its sense of smell. "Rank bait for lobsters, fresh bait for crabs," its fishers say, and that is what they put in their lobster pots. Dim-sighted, despite eyes mounted on long stalks which permit it to see in all directions, and no doubt dim-witted as well, the lobster probably finds the pot by bumping against it as he pursues the pungent odor of the bait. It then blunders its way in and feeds, but the nature of its nourishment does no harm to its own flavor when it becomes nourishment in its turn.

To savor lobster at its best you must be able to get it fresh from the sea. Few foods lose their fine edge more quickly, as I discovered when I occupied, in Rockport, Massachusetts, a house on the shore from which I could see my lobsterman hauling in his pots. Whenever he appeared I filled a huge kettle with sea water and put it on the stove, where it was already boiling when he rowed to shore and dropped two or three lobsters, still dripping from the sea, into the pot. *That* was lobster, and for some years after I left Rockport I was unable to bring myself to eat lobster in the lamentable condition in which most people consume it and find it superb. It was in Rockport also that I tasted what I remember as the best of all lobsters—chicken lobsters, by which we then meant those taken below the legal limit, which were unbelievably sweet and perfumed. However much I may deplore this crime, now legally forgiven under the statute of limitations, I do not seem able to regret it. ("Chicken lobster" today, I understand, has become the trade name for the smallest legally salable lobster, which weighs about a pound; but a pound and a half seems to be the optimum weight among permissible lobsters.)

The Larousse gastronomic encyclopedia records an opinion that the best lobster is the *paquette*, which means the female lobster at the time when she is carrying a packet of eggs under her tail (in English, she is described as "berried" at this period). I suspect that this is a theory influenced by the charm of the unattainable, for it is forbidden to take lobsters in this condition. I have never eaten a berried lobster (which indicates, I suppose, that I am less of an ogre for women than for children), but my experience with other crustaceans is that they are at their poorest during reproductive periods, which, indeed, seems to be a general law of the sea, where many fish exhaust themselves in spawning, and some, like the salmon and the eel, find it fatal. However, the female, egg-bearing or not, does possess in the head a band of delicious flesh which is absent in the male; and she is, of course, the sole possessor of the coral. The coral seems to frighten off many American eaters, either because of its bright-red color or because it is the material from which the eggs will be fashioned. It is rich and delightfully tasty, while another element common to lobsters

LOBSTER. *Original drawing by Sir John Tenniel for Lewis Carroll:* Alice's Adventures in Wonderland, *1865*

of both sexes, the greenish tomalley, the liver, is also of exquisite flavor, and also regarded with distrust by many Americans—in this case perhaps with a certain justification by those who are put off by yielding textures.

To get lobsters as fresh as possible you must buy them alive—alive and lively. Pick up a lobster (whose claws we will assume are securely pegged) and turn it over; if it fails to agitate its legs and flap its tail, reject it. Even live lobsters are not necessarily fresh in flavor; lobsters start dying as soon as they are taken from the sea, and refuse to be fooled by being kept in tanks awaiting sale. Your chances of getting fresh lobster are, oddly enough, better if you buy lobster wrapped in seaweed or even kept on ice than if you take it from a tank (unless it is a lobster pound set in the sea). When a lobster remains more than five days in a tank, its flavor deteriorates seriously. If too many lobsters are crowded together in a tank they are apt to fight and you may get one which has lost a leg. If you boil a lobster thus mutilated, the flesh can drain out through the hole into the water; cork it with a pellet of bread before cooking it.

The lobster was mobilized by the British during World War II as cover for a reconnaissance activity carried out by small boats operating in the Channel disguised as lobster boats. To deceive any possible German observers, the men assigned to watch for signs of an impending invasion spent a good deal of their time in spurious activity, hauling up lobster pots and removing from them rubber lobsters which after dark were lowered back into the water to be pulled up again the next day. We have no report from the German side about the success of this deception, but if it fooled any Germans they must have been as ignorant of the dark blue-brown-green-black color of live lobsters as the British manufacturers of their rubber facsimiles, which they had taken care to paint in the bright scarlet of the cooked crustacean.

LU
stands for

the **lucky bean,** of which, oddly, it is not the grain but the leaves which are eaten in Malawi; for the **lucuma,** or star apple, cultivated in Peru since 750 B.C.; for the **luk-lug-u-nuk,** a game bird known to non-Eskimos as the black brant; for the **lumbush,** of which both leaves and fruit are widely eaten in tropical Africa and Madagascar with cheerful disregard for the detail that some of its varieties are poisonous; for the **lumpfish,** whose eggs, artfully dyed, are frequently passed off as caviar; for the **lungfish,** which breathes air and feeds Africans; for **lungs,** eaten with impunity in many countries, but banned in the United States by the Department of Agriculture; for **lung yen,** the native name of the longan; for the **lupine,** cultivated for its nutritious seeds since at least the Bronze Age; for **luzerne,** which ordinarily provides fodder for livestock but whose tender shoots occasionally serve as human food in Africa; and for the **Luzon goby,** a fish of the Philippines believed to be the world's smallest vertebrate, which despite its impractical size (half an inch the long way) sometimes gets into whitebait, though, it is true, accidentally.

LY
stands for

the **lycopodium,** whose root is no longer eaten as an aphrodisiac; for **lyme grass,** a rather tormented attempt to Anglicize the word "elymus," a kind of millet; for the **Lynnhaven oyster,** of which Maryland is justly proud; and for the **lynx,** which an Alaskan couple told the Associated Press in 1972 was their favorite form of meat.

M

MONSELET, CHARLES: A *gourmet is a being pleasing to heaven.*

MONSELET, CHARLES: A *true gastronome should always be ready to eat, just as a soldier should always be ready to fight.*

MUMFORD, LEWIS: *The present . . . takes pride in its ability to produce ever larger quantities of food—pasteurized, homogenized, sterilized, frozen, or otherwise reduced to an infant's standard of tastelessness.*

MAC
stands for

the **macadamia,** a nut which is a native of Australia but a specialty of Hawaii; for **mace,** which is either the fleshy network which envelops nutmeg but has its own distinctive aroma, or an herb named for it because it has a somewhat similar scent; for **Macedonian parsley,** of which both leaves and root are eaten; for the **mackerel scad,** eaten on the west coast of tropical Africa, the **mackerel shark,** eaten by man and vice versa, and the **mackerel tuna,** eaten on the east coast of Africa; for the **Mackinaw trout,** which lives in deep lakes in North America; and for the **Macoun apple,** developed in New York State and presented to the public in 1923, which is considered by fruit fanciers to be the finest dessert apple of the northeastern United States, a sort of superior McIntosh.

And **MAC** also stands for

MACKEREL. The mackerel is a Turkish fish, at least in Italy, where *pesce turchino* means a fatty fish, particularly if it is blue or dark in color, a category unknown to ichthyology. It is found in the neighborhood of Turkey, but everywhere else in the Northern Hemisphere too, which faults the Italian language on this point; however, it is definitely fatty. Technically, a fat fish is one which contains more than 1 percent fats; mackerels run from 6 to 13 percent, depending on variety, habitat, feeding habits and the time of year. Its high proportion of fat is what causes it to spoil so quickly. "Mackerel cannot be eaten in perfection except at the seaside, where it can be had immediately out of the water," Eliza Leslie wrote in her early nineteenth-century cookbook. "It loses its flavor in a very few hours, and spoils sooner than any other fish." In France, mackerel guaranteed to have reached the fishmonger less than twenty-four hours earlier used to be sold at a premium price under the name "hunting horn mackerel," a reminder of the times when the arrival of fresh fish from the coast was announced by a raucous blast on a horn.

You should indeed wait to buy mackerel until the day you intend to eat it. Its swift decline has had the unfortunate effect, for its good reputation, of bringing it to the minds of writers seeking an image of corruption—Shakespeare, when he had Falstaff say, "You may buy land now as cheap as stinking mackerel," or John Randolph when he wrote of Edward Livingston, "He is a man of splendid abilities, but utterly corrupt. He shines and stinks like rotten mackerel by moonlight."

Yet cooked fresh, and especially young, mackerel, "often overlooked and under-rated in the United States," presents, as the magazine *Gourmet* wrote in April 1976, a "combination of flavor, versatility and economy hard to match." The last factor has perhaps militated against this fish in America, so conscious of status symbols. Mackerel is such a good buy that it is disdained.

Yet fresh mackerel, cheap or not, has been praised for centuries. We may ignore the circumstance that Stone Age man, presumably no gourmet, left piles of mackerel bones in the kitchen

MACKEREL. *Photograph by Frank Puza:* Mackerel on Beach

middens of northern Europe, or that the ancient Romans thought mackerel the best of all fish for making their universal seasoning, *garum,* a liquid derived from decomposed fish. ("When a white liquid surrounds the saffron-colored yolks," wrote Martial in a poetic look at fried eggs, "let the sauce of Spanish mackerel season the eggs.") Skip to the twelfth-century *Roman du Comte d'Anjou* and we find mackerel included in a list of "the best fishes." In fourteenth-century Paris a banquet given for the bishop of Paris, a feast so splendid that its menu has come down to us, made place for a dish of mackerel.

The nineteenth-century French poet Charles Monselet wrote that "the month of May is as dear to gourmets as to lovers," because it brought with it the best mackerel, and especially its particularly flavorful milt. "Great schools of little mackerel . . . seem to break up in summer and come up the beaches and into tidal inlets," wrote Jonathan Norton Leonard in *American Cooking: New England.* "They are searching for smaller prey and will take any shiny, fishlike bait even though it is nothing but a strip of bright tin. . . . Tinker mackerel weighing half a pound or so are divinely delicious eating. They are seldom offered in markets, apparently because the public does not know about them and so the demand is too large to encourage commercial fishermen to go after them." The public knows about them in Norway, where it is explained that mackerel are best in spring and early summer because it is then that they are fattest—and so they are, for this is just before the spawning period, after which the fish are temporarily spent, and less nutritious.

The changes in the quality of mackerel at different seasons are a function of their annual cycle, about which not much was known until quite recently, for the major part of their lives is spent in deep water, where observation is difficult. Alexandre Dumas, always too much entranced by the picturesque to allow sober fact to get in his way, wrote that mackerel "pass the winter in the Glacial Sea [if he meant the Arctic Ocean, its waters are too cold to please mackerel], their heads buried in the slime and seaweed." He failed to tell us what nineteenth-century witness observed this sea-bottom behavior, nor does he substantiate his anecdote about a sailor who fell overboard and was devoured instanter by these fish. Mackerel are indeed voracious, but it is not on record anywhere else that they are dangerous to living human beings.

What mackerel are now believed to do in winter might be described as the equivalent of hibernation among land animals.

> At the end of October they quit the surface [according to a British encyclopedia of fish], go to the bottom and lie densely packed in the troughs and trenches [ceasing to feed, apparently]. Towards the end of December they spread outwards over the surrounding seabed. At the end of January they move up to the surface [which seems to be a slow process, during which they feed at mid-depths on the tiny plankton, a sort of hors d'oeuvre for the savage

gluttony which follows as they stuff themselves to prepare for the ordeal of spawning].

In May, with ravenous appetites, they move toward the coast in great schools, often signaled to fishermen by the clouds of equally ravenous sea gulls flying overhead in the hope of mackerel for dinner. In the Adriatic, they devour everything in their way, leaving the sea as empty as locusts leave the land; Italian makes from the word *sgombero*, "mackerel," the verb *sgombare*, "to sweep clean." The fishermen of Malta take tremendous hauls of the swarming mackerel in the Mediterranean, and in the Atlantic the half-square-mile Portuguese island of Berlenga, eight miles off the coast, is besieged by millions of mackerel, from which the fishermen haul in great numbers of two-pound fish as fast as their arms can work, with the aid only of lures, not bait, as for New England's tinker mackerel. Off the coast of Brittany, stale fish blood is poured into the water to call the mackerel, which, having bad eyesight, hunt mainly by smell; they flock to the spot in such numbers that they are simply scooped out of the water. Other French fishermen, putting out lines from an anchored boat, throw flour into the water to attract the fish. The French, with their acute sense of taste, call fish so taken "flour mackerel," and claim that they can recognize their inferiority in taste to "lead mackerel," which means those taken on lines trailed behind a moving boat, and even to those caught by the large trawlers, which sometimes spread flour on the water too.

Prepared by heavy feeding for their task, mackerel spawn in the summer and, as soon as they have recovered from the effort, begin to leave the coasts for deeper water in September and October, feeding on the way to take in enough nourishment to carry them over the winter before they sink to the depths again.

Mackerel are second in importance as food only to herring among pelagic fish. There are about ten species of true mackerel, and many more which are called mackerels but are not—for instance, the horse mackerel, which is a scad; the frigate mackerel, which is closer to the tunas; and the snake mackerel, which usually hides some 3000 feet down, but came to the attention of the public when one of them, slumming near the surface, jumped aboard the *Kon Tiki* and had its picture taken.

I can assert with some degree of confidence that there is no flying mackerel, since the authority on this point is the poet John Hookham Frere (1769–1846), whose obsession with flying animals was revealed when he called attention to the flight of the lobster. He if anyone would be ready to celebrate a flying mackerel if there were one, but he informs us that there is not:

The feather'd race with pinions skims the air—
Not so the mackerel, and still less the bear.

We live and learn.

MAD
stands for

the **Madagascar bean** of Peru, the **Madagascar potato** of central Africa, and the **Madagascar yam** of India; for **madder,** a tint for Titian but an edible root for the ancients; for the **Madras gram,** also called the horse gram because in India and Ceylon that animal shares it with humans; and for the **madtom,** a catfish you might as well forget about, since its five-inch length does not produce enough flesh to be an adequate reward for dodging its possibly poisonous spines.

MAG
stands for

the **Magdalena chiton,** a large shellfish of America's Pacific coast found from Alaska to Catalina; for the **magose,** a bitter bean grown on the shores of the Indian Ocean, where Westerners are content to leave it; for the **maguey,** whose root is eaten by modern Mexicans, and the **maguey slug,** whose flesh was eaten by ancient Mexicans.

MAI
stands for

the **maiden,** a salmon of either sex returning from the sea to its spawning grounds; for the **maidenberry,** a species of myrtle found on the Caribbean island of Anguilla; for the **maiden blush,** an early-ripening apple; for the **maidenhair fern,** edible in its fiddlehead state without increasing the ferocity of man as it is supposed to increase the ferocity of fighting cocks; for the **maiden pink,** neither more nor less edible than other pinks; and for the **mailed catfish** of South Africa, which is capable of emerging from the water and going for a stroll.

And **MAI** also stands for

MAIZE. On November 5, 1492, two Spaniards whom Christopher Columbus had sent to explore the interior of Cuba returned to report to the Admiral of the Ocean Sea that they had come upon "a sort of grain they called maize, which was well tasted, bak'd, dry'd and made into flour." Columbus confided to his journal: "There are large cultivated areas which produce roots [cassava], a sort of bean [the haricot] and a sort of grain called maize." It was thus that Europe became aware of the existence in America of its only native cereal, "the most valuable food plant contributed by the New World to the Old," according to *The Practical Encyclopedia of Gardening.* (Leif Ericsson had reported half a millennium earlier that he had found "self-sown wheat" growing in Vinland, which could not have been wheat, since there was none in America until Europeans imported it, but no one had realized from this description that he had come upon something new.)

Maize (*Zea mays*), or, if you prefer, Indian corn, or simply corn, is a plant of immense versatility. Some types are only two feet tall; others rise to twenty. The size of the ears varies from the length of a man's thumbnail (a type of popcorn) to two feet (the giant maize of Mexico's Jala valley). The number of kernels may be sixteen or five hundred, or any number in between, provided they can be arranged in an even number of rows. They are usually white or yellow, but may also be rose, red, purple, blue, brown, near-black or of different colors on the same cob. The stalks, leaves and shucks are in the majority of types green, but some are red, purple, brown, golden or striped, and the silks are green, yellow, salmon, brown or one of several different shades of red.

Somewhere in the world a crop of corn is reaching maturity during every month of the year. Fast-ripening varieties mature in sixty days (Canadian Gaspé Peninsula flint corn), leisurely ones may take eleven months (Colombian tropical corn). Maize is cultivated below sea level (the Caspian basin) and above 12,000 feet (the Peruvian Andes). It grows from 58 degrees north latitude in Canada and Russia to 40 degrees south latitude in South America and Africa, wherever its requirements are met: a growing season with temperatures reaching 70° to 80° F. with plenty of hot sun, and 15 inches of rain during the year (a single corn plant sweats off 440 pounds of water, enough to fill a barrel, during its short life).

Maize is the world's second most plentiful cereal, measured by the bulk of grain produced, behind rice but ahead of wheat. More acreage is planted to wheat, but corn gives heavier yields: it can exceed 300 bushels per acre; 100 bushels is close to the record for wheat, and 40 to 50 is good. More maize is eaten by animals than by man, but man eventually eats it all the same in the form of pork, poultry, veal, beef, eggs or milk.

Maize is certainly the only cereal, probably the only food plant and possibly the only living producer of food, animal or vegetable, which cannot reproduce itself without the aid of man. Its seeds (the kernels we eat) are prevented from making contact with the soil by the tough, impermeable shuck wrapped tightly around the ear; if men did not open the ear and sow the seeds, maize would become extinct from one year to the next. How a wild plant so constituted could have survived to give us domesticated corn is a mystery, and indeed no wild maize has ever been found, though there are several theories about the nature of the ancestor of corn. It seems probable that wild maize never existed; the plant we have now could have been developed, either deliberately or by accidental mutation, from a forebear already domesticated and already being eaten.

Maize is described by the *Encyclopaedia Britannica* as "the grain that built a hemisphere." "Its domestication," wrote John Collier in *Indians of the Americas*, "brought about the change from wandering to settled life and the possibility of such populations as those estimated for the Inca Empire at its height—ten to sixteen million. . . . Without it [the Aztec, Mayan and Inca] cultures and civilizations could not have come into existence."

When Cortez reached Mexico, he found Montezuma eating the maize tortillas and tamales which are still staple foods in Mexico today. Corn was so plentiful that it was planted along the roadsides so that those in want might help themselves; nobody in Mexico could die of hunger at a time when Europeans could and did. In Peru the Spaniards found an Inca Empire whose prosperity was built on maize. Everyone between the ages of twenty-five and sixty was obliged to work in the fields, which were fertilized with guano brought from the offshore islands where sea birds nested; it was forbidden on pain of death to set foot on them during the nesting season. The Spaniards reversed the Inca priorities, which put corn first and gold second, and gave Peru the gift of malnutrition. In 1781 the Indians revolted and attempted to impress upon the *corregidor* Don Antonio Arriaga the relative importance of precious food and precious metal by pouring molten gold down his throat. The rebels were, inevitably, put to death in turn, with appropriate cruelty but with no further waste of gold, molten or otherwise.

Maize crossed the Rio Grande from its probable place of origin, Honduras, Guatemala and the adjoining area of Mexico, at a leisurely pace. Kernels dated at 6600 B.C. have been found in caves of old Mexico, but at only 4500 B.C. in caves of New Mexico; and the seeds had not yet turned up in the Ohio mounds of the Adena culture a mere two thousand years ago. But everywhere, as soon as it did arrive, maize became the staple food of the Indians, with the exception of those nomadic tribes which followed and lived on the buffalo, and even some of them were captured by corn, when they planted the crop, remained in the neighborhood to harvest it and thus developed sedentary habits.

Maize saved the first white Virginians from starvation in their very first winter when Indians gave Captain John Smith five hundred bushels of corn, which tided the Cavaliers over until spring, and the first white New Englanders from the same fate on their very first day, when, according to one version of the story, Miles Standish found an Indian cache of maize and beans immediately after they landed, in winter, with the *Mayflower*'s stores exhausted after the long Atlantic crossing. A few grains of corn "were thought as good as a feast," said Governor William Bradford of Plymouth, but all the same the Pilgrims would have preferred their familiar wheat. When they imported it, it was destroyed in the fields by a smut called "the blast"; and even after it had become acclimated, it remained so much more expensive than maize that Americans continued to depend chiefly on corn for two centuries, by which time they had come to like it.

This was more than Europeans did. Maize first began to be raised in quantity in Andalusia, Spain, about 1525, and from there was distributed around the shores of the Mediterranean. It was planted early in the Middle East, whence it doubled back to central and northern Europe, which is why it was there called Turkey wheat or Turkey corn. It first reached England in 1562, where John Gerard wrote of it in his *Herball*:

> Turky wheat doth nourish far lesse than either wheat, rice, barly or otes. The bread which is made thereof is meanely white, without bran; it is hard and dry as Bisket is, and hath in it no clamminesse at all; for which cause it is of hard digestion, and yeeldeth to the body little or no nourishment. Wee have as yet no certaine proofe or experience concerning the vertues of this kinde of Corne; although the barbarous Indians, which know no better, are con-

MAIZE. *Photograph by John Vachon:* Nebraska Farmer Shucking Corn, *October 1938*

strained to make a vertue of necessitie, and thinke it a good food; whereas we may easily judge, that it nourisheth but little, and is of hard and evill digestion, a more convenient food for swine than for men.

That was still the English opinion in 1765, when an attack on Indian corn by an anonymous letter writer to a London newspaper nettled Benjamin Franklin into replying:

Pray, let me, an American, inform the gentleman, who seems ignorant of the matter, that Indian corn, take it for all in all, is one of the most agreeable and wholesome grains in the world; that its green leaves [ears] roasted are a delicacy beyond expression; that samp, hominy, succotash, and nokehock, made of it, are so many pleasing varieties; and that johny or hoecake, hot from the fire, is better than a Yorkshire muffin.

Europe as a whole was not of Franklin's opinion and resisted this new strange grain except where it borrowed familiarity by resembling foods already known, as in Italy, where it became the chief cereal from which polenta is made, the last in a series dating from Etruscan times, for this dish was made successively of millet, spelt, barley, wheat and finally maize; or where it was accepted because there was nothing else to eat, as in Russia, today the second most important maize producer of the world, where, however, Indian corn became a major crop only after Herbert Hoover sent large quantities of it to starvation areas there in 1921. Even famine was not always enough to make maize welcome. When Sir Robert Peel imported maize for an Ireland starving as a result of the potato blight of 1846, it was called, because of its yellow color, "Peel's brimstone"; stories were circulated about its having poisoned those who ate it, and poorhouse inmates rioted when they were given it.

Maize was first introduced into Africa in the Portuguese-held territories on its west coast, early in the sixteenth century, from Brazil, which was also Portuguese thanks to the expert navigation of Pedro Alvares Cabral, who bumped into it by accident while trying to round the Cape of Good Hope into the Indian Ocean. The Portuguese planted Brazilian maize in Africa to provide food for the slaves being shipped to America; the grain was so welcome to a region poor in cereals, and for that matter in cultivatable crops in general, that it quickly blanketed the whole continent and improved its diet. "Among history's many ironies," wrote Reay Tannahill in *Food in History*, "is that a food introduced to fuel the slaving ships should have led to a general population increase in tropical Africa which ensured that these same ships would never sail empty of human cargo." Maize became in Africa the "kaffir corn" or "mealie" which fed the black laborers on the white man's plantations and in his gold and diamond mines.

Maize had reached China at least by 1550, the date of a document which records that it had been received at court in tribute, which might indicate that it was a rare curiosity, but five years later it is cited in a regional history of the province of Honan, so it had already penetrated into the interior. The first Chinese picture of it appeared in 1578.

In the United States, Indian corn has always been an element of the national history. Encroachment by whites on Indian cornfields was the cause of the 1622 massacre in Virginia of one-third of the total population, and two hundred years later of the Black Hawk War, in which served two young officers named Abraham Lincoln and Jefferson Davis. During the American Revolution, Lafayette wrote to George Washington to commend the valor of the mountaineers under his command "living on cornmeal," while in France Parisians steeled themselves for the first and last time in their history to eat cornmeal mush and molasses as a symbol of sympathy with the newborn United States. During the War of 1812 the British overran Monticello and plundered Thomas Jefferson's corn cribs to feed their horses. The Duke of Liancourt, on a visit to America, testified that Indian corn was "the national crop. Indian corn was eaten three times a day in another form as salt pork." A formidable tourist from England who intimidated the natives by the size of her ear trumpet, Harriet Martineau, wrote in 1837 that "a man who has corn may have everything. He can sow the land with it; and, for the rest, everything eats corn, from slave to chick." During the Civil War, Great Britain, tempted to intervene on the side of the South, was perhaps deterred by the fact that England needed the corn of the North more than the cotton of the South.

Corn gave rural America the husking bee, at which finding a colored ear entitled the finder to kiss the person of his choice, "apparently a modification of a much less decorous Iroquois custom," wrote J. C. Furnas. It appears in art forms as various as musical comedy ("The corn grows as high as an elephant's eye," from *Oklahoma!*) to the short story (Stephen Vincent Benét's "The Devil and Daniel Webster," in which the unfortunate Jabez Stone loses his crop to the corn borer, a truly remarkable demonstration of the power of diabolic magic, since Daniel Webster died in 1852 and the European corn borer did not appear in the United States until 1916).

Corn is important to the economy of the United

States, which produces more than half of all the corn harvested in the world; it is grown in every state of the Union and on three-quarters of all its farms.

There is only one species of maize, but there are innumerable varieties, sub-varieties and sub-sub-varieties, even in nature; maize hybridizes freely, not only with other kinds of corn but also with other wild grasses, such as teosinte and tripsacum, both of which have been suspected of being its ancestor. Not content with nature's efforts, man has produced thousands of hybrids of his own; the first book on hybridization was written in 1716 by a rather surprising authority—Cotton Mather, whose fame has been won in other fields. Not until more than two centuries later, in the 1920s, did the real frenzy of hybridization of maize set in, with such profitable results as to prove that Ralph Waldo Emerson had chosen a good example when he wrote in his *Journal* in February 1855:

> If a man has good corn, or wood, or boards, or pigs to sell, or can make better chairs or knives, crucibles or church organs, than anybody else, you will find a broad hard-beaten road to his house, though it be in the woods.

There is no mention in this passage of the mousetrap, which hybridizes much less easily than corn.

Since 1920 the number of different kinds of corn which have been developed has become uncountable, but botanists have been trying to count them all the same in an effort to bring order out of chaos. They have grouped the various types into races, on the basis of the characteristics they share, and have cataloged about two hundred different races throughout the world. In doing so, they made the discovery that the different races of corn correspond to different breeds of livestock; it would seem that man has been the unwitting instrument of nature in the creation of a series of new ecological niches within each of which soil, climate, feed and animals have evolved together into a consistent, balanced system.

The multiplication of strains of corn designed to meet exact specifications has made it possible for a farmer to select what might be described as tailor-made corn which fits precisely the conditions of his land—including such factors as average amount of sun, average amount of rain, the seasons of precipitation, the drainage of the soil, its exposure and its chemical composition.

The hybridization of maize has been called one of the agricultural triumphs of the twentieth century, but it may be a triumph limited in its applications. One of the reasons why maize has spread so rapidly in certain areas, like Africa, has been its uncomplicated rustic sturdiness, which has given large yields under primitive conditions for the undernourished and usually overpopulated poorer regions of the world. But some of the new strains are being priced out of the reach of poor countries because their cultivation demands modern techniques and modern chemicals which the poor countries cannot afford.

Of the many families of maize, the one which is now the favorite for human consumption, sweet corn, was not found by the first colonists who reached the Atlantic seaboard of North America, and when it was found it was not at first appreciated. It was being grown by the Indians at least by the beginning of the seventeenth century, but on the far side of the Appalachians, where the Iroquois were raising it along the headwaters of the Susquehanna in central New York. It was discovered there in 1799 and planted along the coast, but evoked no particular interest. It only began to be widely cultivated after the Civil War. Today canned sweet corn is America's favorite preserved vegetable, which has been outselling all the others since World War I.

Sweet corn should be eaten while its kernels are still tender and milky; it is then botanically green, but it is gastronomically ripe. It should also be eaten as soon as possible after it has been picked, for perhaps no other vegetable deteriorates as quickly as corn, whose sugar begins to turn to starch as soon as it is separated from the stalk. Mark Twain recommended putting a kettle of water in the middle of the cornfield, building a fire under it and, when the water begins to boil, picking the ears within reach and shucking them directly into the kettle. I almost managed this when I owned a farm in Vermont. I put water to boil on the stove while I went out to pick corn from a patch planted just outside the door to put minimum distance between corn and kitchen. The ears were cooking within minutes of picking. I have never tasted better corn in my life.

MAK
stands for

the **mako shark**, a restless creature which never stops swimming, for it has to swim to breathe.

MAL
stands for

the **Malabar nightshade**, which is not related to the deadly nightshade, fortunately for the Asians and Africans who eat it under the name "Ceylon spinach"; for **malabathrum**, or cassia leaf, a seasoning more used in ancient times than today; for **malagkit**, a variety of rice particularly rich in gluten, grown in the Philippines; for **malagueta pepper,** a hot spice difficult to identify, for it is described variously as (a) the seeds of a plant related to cardamom, (b) a small chili, (c) the berry of the bay-rum tree—and no doubt I could have found other definitions if I had kept on looking; for **malanga,** a mealy root of delicate flavor which recalls the taro of the Pacific islands, but is found in the West Indies; for the **Malay apple,** which comes from where its name says it does, though many Hawaiians, who call it the mountain apple or 'ohi'a 'ai, think it a native fruit; for the **male fern,** which has suffered from sexual misattribution ever since the sixteenth century; for the **mallard,** a duck respected by sportsmen and trenchermen; for the **mallow,** praised by a twentieth-century French writer as "a sage flower which wears the delicate hues of half-mourning," but abandoned by sixteenth-century French eaters as an insipid food; for the **Malpeque,** a fat yellowish oyster of Prince Edward Island, reputed to be the fastest grower of its race; and for **malukang butter,** which is more exactly an edible oil extracted from the seeds of a West African plant.

MAM
stands for

the **mammee** apple of tropical America, which is not an apple so it is called instead the tropical apricot, though it is not an apricot, or the marmalade plum, though it is not a plum; and for the **mammoth,** which has not been eaten since the Ice Ages because of a shortage of the basic material.

MAN
stands for

man, a domesticated animal still extensively raised, one wonders why, since it is rarely eaten nowadays, and the **manatee,** which despite its name is not related to the former, from which it may be distinguished by the fact that it is an aquatic mammal rather than a terrestrial one, that it has no hind limbs (which has caused it to be confused with the mermaid) and that it is more frequently eaten for its agreeable porklike flavor; for the **manchineel** of the West Indies, whose fruit is sweet-smelling and its juice poisonous; for the **mandarin orange,** so called because in color, shape and size it recalls the button which topped the hats of imperial Chinese officials, and the **mandarin duck,** so called because its colorful plumage recalls the robes of the same imperial Chinese officials; for **mandioca,** another name for manioc; for the **mandragora,** a plant reported to provoke dreaming, and the **mandrake,** which differs from it only by its disconcerting habit of shrieking when pulled up; for the **man-eater shark,** with which human beings have a reciprocal gastronomic relationship; for the **mangel-wurzel,** a type of beet so highly regarded by the French that they call it *disette,* "famine," and the **mange-tout,** French also but just the opposite, since it means "eat all," which is just what one does with this broad flat pea and its pods; for the **mangle boton,** a black mangrove eaten in West Africa only in the form of the first tiny shoots which appear aboveground; for the **mangosteen,** a Malaysian fruit whose deliciousness is denied by nobody, but which is little grown because it is of difficult cultivation, is slow to mature and is perishable in transport; for the **mangrove,** a tropical fruit found in both Old and New Worlds which is sweet and healthy if you catch it before it starts putting out roots, which it does while still on the tree; for the **mangrove-tree oyster,** which caused Sir Walter Raleigh to be ridiculed when he reported its existence, for everybody knows oysters do not grow on trees; and for **manioc,** which is cassava by another name.

MAN
stands for

manna, which fed the ancient Hebrews in the desert and has been identified as or with: a sweetish liquid which oozes from the bark of the flowering ash, *Fraxinus ornus* (*Encyclopaedia Britannica,* Volume 2, page 505); a product of the Iranian *Astragalus florulentus,* a member of the pea family (*Encyclopaedia Britannica,* Volume 2, page 573); one or the other of the lichen *Lecanora esculenta,* the resin of the camel's thorn, *Alhagi maurorum,* the sap of the tamarisk *Tamarix gallica,* a secretion of an insect which lives on it, the sap of the flowering ash, or "a dozen other arid land species" (*Encyclopaedia Britannica,* Volume 14, page 815); an edible lichen or excretions of the tamarisk, the ash or the willow (Georges and Germaine Blond, *Histoire pittoresque de notre alimentation*); a spice resembling coriander (Mary S. Atwood, *A Taste of India,* and Rosemary Hemphill, *Fragrance and Flavour,* both echoing the Bible); a glutinous secretion of the larvae of insects which feed on the eucalyptus (Don and Patricia Brothwell, *Food in Antiquity,* page 68); the secretion of a small insect which lives on the tamarisk (the same, page 81); an excretion of the Mediterranean manna ash (the same, page 82); the sugary sweat of certain unnamed vegetables (Claude Manceron, *Les vingt ans du roi*); the seeds of a species of tamarisk which grows in the

Sinai Desert (A. P. Stanley, *Lectures on the History of the Jewish Church*); a sweet juice manufactured by insects gnawing the leaves of plants (W. H. Roscher, *Nektar und Ambrosia*); and a carbohydrate precipitate created by a near collision of Venus and Earth (Immanuel Velikovsky, *Worlds in Collision*): anyone courageous enough is invited to choose the right one.

MAN
stands for

the **mantis shrimp**, which is not a shrimp but a squill whose forelegs are part of its mouth; for the **manzanillo olive**, a popular California variety; and for **manzanita** (Spanish for "little apple"), evergreen shrubs of the heath family common in western North America, whose flowers provide tasty honey.

And **MAN** also stands for

MANGO. The food which has been called "the king of fruits" has probably never been tasted by the great majority of the inhabitants of the world's temperate zones. The mango is also sometimes called "the apple of the tropics," since it is the most widely eaten and the best liked of all tropical fruits.

I consider the mango . . . one of the most delectable fruits with which God graced an already bountiful world [Euell Gibbons wrote in *Stalking the Wild Asparagus*]. Yet, when I was in the tropics, I saw tourists from temperate regions refuse mangoes because they didn't taste like peaches. . . . Such people have my pity, but hardly my respect.

This high opinion of the mango reaches well back into the past. In 1727 a traveler reported that "the Goa mango is reckoned the largest and most delicious to the taste of any in the world, and I may add, the wholesomest and best tasted of any fruit in the world"; and even earlier, in 1673, another expressed the opinion that "for Taste, the Nectarine, Peach and Apricot fall short [of the mango]."

In contrast to this praise, many Westerners who taste a mango for the first time dislike it. In some cases the reason for this reaction is that the experimenter has been offered an inferior fruit which misrepresents the mango as everyone in the tropics knows it. There are only about thirty species of mangoes, and of these almost none reach the market except derivatives of just one of them, *Mangifera indica,* whose ungrafted, inexpensively produced fruits can indeed be fibrous and consequently rather disagreeable eating, while often, underlying the characteristic luscious mango flavor, there is a perceptible, or even assertive, taste of turpentine. Both of these disadvantages have been eliminated from the better grafted varieties, which thus offer the pure magnificence of the mango at its best. There remain two other disadvantages: the flesh clings to the single large, flat stone of the fruit, and the mango is so juicy that no matter how you handle it you are likely to need a finger bowl afterwards.

The mango was already under cultivation before history began, so there is no record of where it came from; it is believed to be a native of the area running from eastern India through Burma (but the best Indian mangoes are supposed to be those of the Bombay region, all the way across the subcontinent). The fruit was slow to spread beyond its native territory. Not only is it extremely perishable and averse to travel, but even the seeds lose their vitality quickly.

The ancient Greeks and Romans did not know the mango, despite a Pompeiian wall painting in which some observers have professed to recognize this fruit. It is probably a badly painted peach,

MANGO *by Paul Gauguin (1848–1903).* Two Tahitian Women, *oil on canvas*

unless some veteran of the army of Alexander the Great, which invaded India, brought back a description of it, or even a specimen, which would necessarily have been in sorry condition by the time it reached the Mediterranean. The first known reference to the mango from outside its territory was by a Chinese traveler, Hwen T'sang, who mentioned it in the first half of the seventh century A.D. The first Westerner to report it seems to have been a certain Friar Jordanus in 1328, followed by John de Marignolli in 1349. Marco Polo missed it. Mangoes are believed to have reached Africa in about 1000, brought there by travelers from Persia. Their first implantation in the Western Hemisphere took place in Brazil in 1700, and about forty years later they were transferred to the West Indies (tropical Australasia received them about the same time).

The only area in the continental United States where mangoes can be grown with any assurance of success is in southern Florida; they have fruited in California, but cannot provide a dependable crop there, being extremely sensitive to even a small amount of frost. Mangoes were growing in Florida about 1825, but they are usually dated there from 1889, when the United States Department of Agriculture had improved grafted varieties planted—the beginning of a modest mango-growing industry capable of supplying the not very heavy domestic demand, mostly for preserves like chutneys, into which mangoes enter as an ingredient, rather than for whole mangoes. Originally Florida grew only the Indian *mulgoba,* the most widespread variety in the parent country, which is superb in flavor but grants only moderate yields. Starting with this mango, Florida developed the Haden, which, without too much sacrifice of quality, is more productive, with fruit of attractive appearance and large size. The Haden is now the chief kind grown commercially. It has been described as "rich, sweet and spicy, with flesh of melting texture and free of objectionable fibers."

India, naturally, is the world's most important producer of mangoes, with 2.2 million acres planted to them, producing between 5 million and 7.5 million tons of fruit a year, between 75 and 80 percent of the world total. Indian mangoes range in size from that of a small plum, weight about six ounces, to fruits of four or even five pounds, but those found on the markets are usually the size of a large pear and weigh no more than a pound and a half. They may be round, oval, pear-shaped, peach-shaped, heart-shaped, kidney-shaped or long and thin. They are of many colors, but the commonest are red, yellow or dull green; the flesh is orange.

The mango tree is tall (fifty to sixty feet), begins bearing five to seven years after planting and continues to yield abundantly until about the age of forty, when its productivity starts to decline. It is a handsome tree, welcome to dwellers in the sweltering tropics for its shade as well as for its fruit. Its dense foliage also provides a haven for mosquitoes.

MAP
stands for

MAPLE. Sap is extracted from maple trees by two species of animals, *Homo sapiens* and *Sciurus carolinensis.* Others partake of it, like the insects which settle on the bark wherever sap oozes from the trees, but without tapping them deliberately. Attracted by the sticky sweetness of young maple twigs during the sap season, moose nibble them with sufficient regularity so that the striped maple, *Acer pennsylvanicum* (otherwise called the goosefoot maple, from the shape of its leaves), is also known as moosewood, while every farmer with both cows and sugar maples knows better than to let the former graze among the latter, or they will destroy the young saplings and get drunk on their fermenting sap into the bargain. Insects, moose and cows only find the sap; *Sciurus carolinensis,* the North American squirrel, like man, provokes its running. Squirrels bite off twigs at their bases or gnaw holes in the bark to let the sap out and feast on it; when the emerging liquid freezes overnight they eat the icicles in the morning.

Maple syrup and maple sugar are perhaps the only foods which are produced nowhere except in North America. The New World has given the Old many others—Indian corn, the potato, the tomato, the turkey—but they are now raised in the Eastern Hemisphere too. Attempts have been made to produce maple sugar in Europe, by transplanting the American sugar maple, *A. saccharum,* to that continent, but without success, for it isn't the tree which produces the sugar (the European Norway maple, *A. platanoides,* and the plane-tree maple, *A. pseudoplatanus,* have been used to make sugar too—in the United States—though they are less rich in it), it is the climate. Only in the northeastern United States and the adjacent areas of Canada is the weather just right to cause the sap to run in sufficient quantity to make tapping the trees worthwhile. This requires a long, cool period during which the temperature falls below freezing during the night and rises above freezing the following day. The alternation acts as a sort of thermal pump which forces the sap to circulate.

Maple sugar and maple syrup, luxuries today, were in Colonial times the commonest sweeteners,

Maple

MAPLE *by Georgia O'Keeffe.* Pattern of Leaves, *oil on canvas, 1924*

and for the Indians before Colonial times, the only sweeteners—indeed, almost the only *seasoner*—they had. The northeastern Indians, precisely those who lived in sugar maple territory, never learned to make salt from sea water, and in its absence used maple sugar as their general seasoning. Early European explorers marveled at this Indian food. The Jesuit Father Nouvel reported with surprise the existence of "a liquor that runs from the trees toward the end of Winter, and which is known as Maple-water." The sugar maple was still able to astonish Europeans as late as 1751, when the Swedish botanist Peter Kalm wrote:

When we reached the villages of the savages we received more than anything else gifts of large pieces of sugar which stood us well in hand on our trip into the wilderness. When the savages cooked gruel or mush for us from corn meal they added large lumps of sugar to make up for the lack of milk, for the savages have no livestock, if you except dogs and fleas.

It is possible that those gifts did not in the eyes of the Indians represent so much a food to give their guests nourishment, but a present of money, for cakes of maple sugar sometimes served the Indians as a medium of exchange.

The first colonists had a slightly larger choice of sweeteners than the Indians. In 1630 they imported Italian honeybees, giving them both "tree sweetenin' and bee sweetenin'," "tree sweetenin' " meaning, of course, maple sugar; but for a long time honey was rare. Molasses soon began to arrive from West Indian sugarcane plantations (the sugar of which it was a by-product was too expensive), but maple sugar nevertheless retained its importance, for to begin with, it was free. In those rustic times virtually everybody had access to a maple or two from which he could draw enough sap for his own needs. For anyone who lived a little way back from the sea—for instance, in the hills of Vermont, sugar maple country *par excellence* and still the number one maple sugar state, producing 20 million gallons of sap per year—even molasses was too costly, since it had to be brought up from the coast by pack horse or sledge. Besides, both molasses and cane sugar were disapproved of in the Northeast, for they were produced by slave labor. "Make your own sugar," advised the *Farmer's Almanac* in 1803, "and send not to the Indies for it. Feast not on the toil, pain and misery of the wretched." Maple sugar remained the major sweetener, at least in the Northeast, until nearly the end of the nineteenth century; two hundred years ago the American consumption of maple syrup was four times what it is today.

"In contemplating the present opening prospects in human affairs," Benjamin Rush ("the Hippocrates of Pennsylvania") wrote to Thomas Jefferson in 1791, "I am led to expect that a material part of the general happiness which heaven seems to have prepared for mankind, will be derived from the manufacture and general use of Maple Sugar." If he had survived into our times, he might have clung to his view about heaven's intentions in regard to mankind, but he would certainly have been obliged to admit disappointment about the importance of the role played by maple sugar. Jefferson too was impressed by the sugar maple and made several attempts to produce sugar, but finally had to confide to his Garden Book that he had met with no success in transplanting Vermont trees to Virginia. Like the Europeans, he did not realize that the secret lay less in the trees than in the climate.

Where the climate is propitious, the maple sugar season begins anywhere from mid-February to mid-April, depending on locality (country folk eliminate the factor of locality by explaining that the sap begins to flow "when the first crow flies"). The length of the season, and consequently the amount and quality of the crop, varies greatly from year to year, from as little as five days to as much as six weeks. One season long remembered in New England was that of 1816, when there had been not only a drought, but also frost every month of the year, with snow in both July and August. The sap was thinner than anyone could remember its ever having been before, and for years afterward nobody spoke of that year as "eighteen sixteen," but as "eighteen hundred and froze-to-death."

The sap drawn from the maple for sugar is not the normal circulatory liquid of its growing period, but a special seasonal secretion whose origin and function is something of a mystery; one theory holds that it is a natural anti-freeze solution which protects the tree over the winter and can be dispensed with, to the benefit of men and squirrels, once the cold weather is over. In any case, the levy they make upon it is far from exhausting; normal tapping takes only about 8 percent of the tree's sugar, an amount it can easily replace before the following year. Maple sap, often to the surprise of the non-initiated, is colorless and nearly tasteless, giving to man, if not to the moose, no hint of its sugary content, even during the first run of the season, which produces the best syrup. "The first run, like first love," wrote John Burroughs, "is always the best, always the fullest, always the sweetest; while there is a purity and delicacy of flavor about the sugar that far surpasses any subsequent yield."

The mathematics of maple sugar making is complicated. A sugar maple tree requires from thirty-five to sixty years to reach tappable size, which is 10 to 12 inches. One 15-quart pail can be hung on a tree of this size, and another added for each 5 inches of increased girth. Profitable commercial exploitation requires a minimum of 500 trees, the number which under ordinary circumstances one man can handle, but 1000 is better. The yield of individual trees is as variable as the yield of individual cows, but most of them would probably fill between 6 and 12 quarts of sap per pail at the height of the run, or 12 gallons per season—which would boil down to 1¼ quarts of maple syrup or 3 pounds of sugar. On a good day during a good run from a good tree, 120 to

150 drops a minute may fall into the pails, or on a very good day 400; but the rate of drip varies enormously during the day. At an average rate, a tree 10 inches around would have to drip for five and a half days to produce 35 gallons of sap, which when boiled down by a twentieth of a cord of wood would produce one gallon of syrup. (But at the height of a good season, 20 gallons of sap sometimes suffices to make one gallon of syrup, while at the nadir of a bad one it can take 80.) It is on record that a single maple, hung with ten buckets, once produced 50 pounds of sugar, seventeen times normal, in a single season. It then died.

There is probably no food of which a larger proportion is sold directly to the consumer by the producer than maple syrup, from roadside stands or by mail. If you buy it otherwise, you risk acquiring a product which is 80 to 90 percent corn or sugar syrup or even, under the label "pure Vermont maple syrup," one which has in it no maple syrup at all, but only synthetic maple flavor fabricated in a chemical factory. The demand for genuine syrup absorbs the total production each year, and there is little likelihood that acquiring maple syrup will ever become easier, for the number of trees is decreasing and so is the number of maple sugar producers: the work is heavy and the profit margin slight. The maple syrup business might have died out already if it were not for the circumstance that the considerable labor it involves occurs at a time of year when most other farm activity is at a standstill.

Maple syrup is tested and graded by each producing state, a common formula running from Fancy Grade through Grade A and Grade B to Grade C, which is used only for cooking; the best are the lightest in color. Other maple products include the familiar maple sugar usually packed as candy, but sometimes cast into bricks so hard that pieces can be broken off only with the help of a hammer or a chisel; maple butter or maple honey, of about the consistency of peanut butter, which can be spread on bread; granulated "Indian sugar," usually made only to order; maple vinegar; and maple beer, produced either from sap or syrup, mercifully rare, for the Reverend Nathan Perkins seems to have pronounced the definitive judgment in 1789 when he said, "Maple cyder is horrible stuff."

Possibly the best maple product is maple wax, or "sugar-on-snow," which is never tasted except by those present among the maples at sugaring-offs, when sap is boiled beyond the syrup point until it reaches the thickness of molasses, then is poured on fresh snow, hardening immediately into ice-cold chewy ribbons of deliciously delicate flavor. When I lived in Chelsea, Vermont (where I made my own maple syrup), there was an annual sugar-on-snow party in *August,* using snow preserved in an icehouse since the preceding winter.

In Europe, at the period when young European maple leaves were eaten pickled, medieval magic recommended maple as an ideal wood for skewering the hearts of vampires to induce them to remain harmlessly in their graves.

MAR
stands for

the **maracujá**, a type of passion fruit grown in Brazil; for the **marasmius**, a mushroom partial to beech woods, which can be used as a substitute for garlic; for the **mare,** valued not for her meat but for her milk, which has been relished by consumers as diverse as Homer's Greeks and Genghis Khan's Tartars; for **Marennes,** tasty French oysters whose merits were sung in ancient times by the Roman poet Ausonius and are celebrated in our times by a confraternity called the Gallants of the Green Marennes; for the **margosa,** whose leaves are eaten as greens in East Africa when nothing better presents itself; for the **marigold,** sometimes described as "the poor man's saffron"; for **marine angelfishes,** eaten by the locals wherever they appear, despite their tough skin; for the **markhor,** a Himalayan wild goat which, being a slave to fashion, wears its horns at a different slant to accord with the taste of each of its habitats; for the **marlin,** famous as a game fish, but good to eat too; for the **marmalade plum,** which is the same thing as the mammee apple; for the **marmot,** a member of a numerous family of rodents which includes the woodchuck, many of them with white flesh resembling rabbit, but often tough; and for **marrow,** which is either the rather mucilaginous matter which fills bones and is considered a particular delicacy by cannibals, or a sort of squash most appreciated in England, though it is suspected of being a native of America.

MAR
stands for

the **marsh hare,** which is the muskrat, and the **marsh hen,** which is the coot; for the **marshmallow,** a plant no longer used in the confection to which it gave its name; for the **marsh marigold,** which is the cowslip; for the **marsh periwinkle,** which has taken it into its head to migrate from Florida to Massachusetts; and for the **marsh rabbit,** which gets us back to the muskrat again.

MAR
stands for

the **marten,** a sort of weasel eaten in France in Neolithic times but probably not since; and for the **marvola plum,** a drupe about which I know nothing except that it is consumed with enthusiasm in East and South Africa.

And **MAR** also stands for

MARJORAM. Shakespeare called marjoram "the herb of grace," but it is not certain whether the plant he had in mind was really marjoram; it might have been OREGANO. The two have been thoroughly confused since the beginning of their histories, and for once the major part of the blame cannot be attributed to popular whimsy. It was no less an authority than Linnaeus who decided to call marjoram *Origanum majorana,* thus mixing things up completely. Marjoram is, properly, a plant of the genus *Majorana,* oregano a plant of the genus *Origanum.* By wrapping them both together in the same parcel, Linnaeus licensed popular fantasy to exercise full freedom in the nomenclature of these two seasonings, and popular fancy has not failed to take advantage of the opportunity.

To begin with the relatively sure, marjoram, Linnaeus to the contrary notwithstanding, is a plant of the genus *Majorana,* of which the only commonly cultivated species is *M. hortensis,* garden marjoram, also called sweet marjoram, precisely because its flavor is less sharp than that of oregano; or annual marjoram, because, though it is a perennial, it is so vulnerable to frost and hence so unlikely to weather a severe winter that it is often treated as an annual; or knotted marjoram, because its small purplish or whitish flowers crowd closely together in dense whorls which at first glance look like large, complicated knots.

Marjoram originated somewhere close to the Mediterranean—in Europe, says one writer, which covers a little too much ground; in Asia Minor, says another; in North Africa, says a third; and at least one Italian-French dictionary gives us as the French equivalent for *maggiorana* not only *marjolaine,* but also *persa,* as though it wanted to suggest that the plant is Persian. This word appears in no French dictionary known to me, so I fear our lexicographer may have become lost in a sea of parsley (*persil*).

Sweet marjoram grows as high as two feet, about medium for herbs. A member of the mint family closely related to thyme, it does not perfume the air where it grows, as do several other herbs of the same kind, notably basil, which releases its pungent odor at the slightest touch of the hand or under the spray from a hose. You must pick a stalk of marjoram and perhaps even crush it a little before it consents to release its soft, sweet, spicy scent. As is the case for many herbs, marjoram is more pungent dried than fresh, which does not necessarily mean that it is better; freshness and pungency are different qualities, each with its own kind of charm.

Trouble in keeping marjoram and oregano apart intensifies as soon as we get into the kitchen. The average housewife, if she uses the charming but old-fashioned marjoram at all, probably does not know whether it is the real thing she is using or oregano, especially since the people who write her cookbooks frequently do not know the difference between them either, or for that matter, even realize that there is one. Often, besides, the home cook has no choice between marjoram and oregano; she has to buy whichever is available where she lives. It is more likely to be marjoram in temperate regions, which as a rule prefer flavors more restrained than do warmer areas.

Thus Greece, Italy and North Africa prefer oregano (which, however, is a Spanish word), while France and England choose marjoram; but this is a rule with so many exceptions that it has almost ceased to be a rule. One large exception has to be made for the periods one may be talking about. When France first started eating these herbs, probably in the fourteenth century, it was to seek relief in seasoning from an insipid diet whose vegetable constituent had been represented largely by such characterless foods as mallows and mosses, so oregano was preferred (but it was sweet marjoram which went into medieval puddings and cakes). Similarly England liked stronger flavors in Elizabethan times than it does now, while later taste buds which had become addicted to the sharp spices of India kept English food lively until the nineteenth century; so we may suspect that earlier British recipes calling for marjoram were really made with oregano.

The delicate but spicy fragrance of marjoram recommends it for potpourris and scent bags; in earlier times it was strewn on floors to make houses smell sweet. The yellow essential oil of marjoram goes into cosmetics, like perfumed soaps. In Renaissance times, fine ladies grew marjoram in pots for the sachets which perfumed their linen, and the ancient Greeks made from it a pomade with which they anointed their hair and eyebrows.

The task of keeping marjoram and oregano separate becomes hopeless when we reach the realm of legend. The stories told about them are attributed with cheerful carelessness now to one of them, now to the other, and often to both.

MARJORAM. *Woodcut from Peter Schoeffer:* Hortus Sanitatis, *Mainz, 1485*

Marjoram, whatever was meant by that name, has been well treated in myth and folklore, except by St. Hildegarde, who warned against touching it because she thought it transmitted leprosy. In antiquity it symbolized love and honor, and was reputed to bestow peace and happiness on those who used it. In both ancient Greece and Rome, bridal wreaths were made of marjoram to ensure happy marriages, and it was planted on graves to ensure happy after-lives. Marjoram, mythology tells us, was odorless when Aphrodite first began cultivating it on Mount Ida; it gained its sweet perfume from her handling of it. Whether this was marjoram or oregano hardly matters: there is little point today in trying to ascribe a precise identity to the herb Venus used to cure the wounds of her son Aeneas.

MAS
stands for

the **masgoof**, a carp-like fish of goodly size which has been described as "Iraq's premier delicacy"; for **mastic**, a licorice-flavored gum popular in Arab cooking; for the **masu**, a Japanese salmon; and for the **mastodon**, a favorite American game animal up to about 7000 B.C.

MAT
stands for

matjes, virgin herring, and for **matsutake**, richly flavored Japanese mushrooms which grow in the shade of pines.

MAU
stands for

the **Maui onion** of Hawaii, which can be sliced without weeping; for the **ma-uk**, a Southeast Asian plant whose bitter-sweet berries are relished in Thailand; for the **Mauritius bean**, toxic, but eaten in East Africa all the same; and for the **Mauritius papeda**, a rare type of sour orange found on two islands, Madagascar and the one for which it is named.

MAW
stands for

the **maw** of fish, eaten only in China and not often there.

MAY
stands for

the **mayanga**, a freshwater fish widely eaten in tropical Africa; for the **May apple**, or American mandrake, of whose flavor Euell Gibbons wrote, "I am reminded of several tropical fruits, the guava, the passion fruit and the soursop, but I can't honestly say that it tastes like any of them," and for the **maypop**, which does taste like the passion fruit, for that is what it is.

MAZ
stands for

the **mazóla**, upper Adriatic dialect for a fish which on close examination appears likely to be a gurnard; for **mazzancolle**, *scampi* in the wrong waters, off Lazio instead of off Veneto; and for the **mazzard**, which is Europe's cultivated sweet cherry run wild in the intoxicating air of America.

Mc
stands for

the **McIntosh**, an apple which turned up as a sport in Ontario, Canada, in 1810 and has since become the third-best-selling variety in the eastern United States.

MEA
stands for

meadow garlic, a wild American variety of this potent seasoning, whose chief disadvantage is the ease with which it can become confused with field garlic, a *too*-wild American variety; and for the **meagre**, a tuneful fish whose music was mistaken by Ulysses for the song of the sirens.

And **MEA** also stands for

MEAT. "Alice B. Toklas," composer Virgil Thomson told the Paris *Herald Tribune* in 1962 (when Miss Toklas was eighty-five), "eats only fresh fish and game. She is not interested in butchered animals." In the fifteenth century William Nelson wrote, "I have no delyte in beffe and motyn and such daily metes. I would onys have a partridge set before us, or sum other such." "No meat is pleasant in itself," wrote Petronius. "It is adulterated in some way and made acceptable to the reluctant stomach."

These eminent personages appear to have disdained meat for gastronomic reasons; there are also those who eschew it for moral motives. "I rather wonder," wrote Plutarch, "both by what accident and in what state of soul or mind the first man . . . touched his mouth to gore and brought his lips to the flesh of a dead creature, he who set forth tables of dead, stale bodies and ventured to call food and nourishment the parts that had a little before bellowed and cried, moved and lived." "That meat is unnatural is substantiated by the indifference of children towards flesh food," wrote Jean-Jacques Rousseau, who of course did not know that the taste buds do not develop early in children and who had perhaps failed to appreciate the wisdom of nature in not giving children an appetite for meat before they developed the incisors designed to deal with it. "Great eaters of meat," Rousseau continued, "are in general more cruel and ferocious than other men"; and the American naturalist Henry Fairfield Osborn added that "the explosive, dominant groups, which appear to have made the strongest impact on the course of human civilization . . . resorted in the earliest times to hunting, combat and killing." Janet Barkas, a vegetarian writer, goes so far as to assert that among chimpanzees "a consequence of meat-eating is an increase in aggressive behavior."

Since meat eaters are thus represented as cruel, ferocious, aggressive and dominating, one may wonder why the world is not ruled today by the race whose diet is composed almost exclusively of meat—the Eskimos, a relatively gentle people. (The name "Eskimo" dates from 1611, when a Jesuit missionary thus shortened the word *eskimantsik*, by which American Indians designated the Eskimos; it meant "eaters of raw meat.")

Despite all the denigrators of meat eating, the consumption of animal flesh continues to increase throughout the world, rising everywhere as affluence increases. It is the universal experience that peoples everywhere, unless there are religious or cultural inhibitions, tend to eat as much meat as they can afford. The brake on meat consumption is not that it is a disliked food or a morally unjustifiable food, but that it is an expensive food. If everybody could pay for it, it would no doubt quickly become the world's second most important category of food, after cereals, if indeed not the first; it is at the expense of bread that meat gains ground as countries become more prosperous. This tendency cannot continue indefinitely, for the world's capacity to produce meat is limited.

If everybody on a planet already populated by a billion more individuals than it can comfortably support were equally able to pay for meat, nobody would be able to eat meat at all. It takes two acres of land per person to provide the amount of meat eaten by Americans; since the world contains only one acre of arable land per person, it is already impossible for everybody to eat as much meat as Americans—who are nevertheless not the world's biggest meat eaters. Argentinians and New Zealanders both eat more meat than Americans, and perhaps a few others as well. The French, not the British, as most persons would guess, eat the most meat among Europeans, the Italians and the

MEAT. *Engraving from Urbain Dubois and Emile Bernard:* La Cuisine Classique, *Paris, 1888*

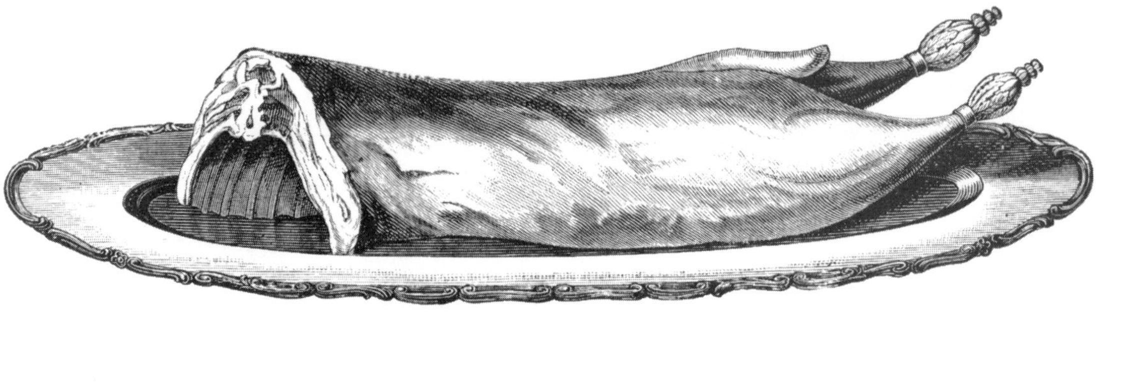

Pet. vander Borcht inuenit.
Ioan. Baptiſta Vrints excud.
Om een lecker beetken int vleeſchuys te cryghen, ſietmen deſe vroukens neerſtelyck ſpoyen.
Want het maeckt goet ſop, ende verblyt den gheeſt, ſoo elck can beuroyen.
Pour du chair les frians morceaux auoir, font ces damoiſelles grand debuoir
Car ceſt de la qui vient le bon potage, qui faict reſiouir tout le meſnage.

MEAT. *Engraving by Pieter van der Borcht (17th Century).* The Meat Market

Greeks the least; the latter are on the same level as the Egyptians, whose low consumption is the result of poverty. But the peoples who bring up the very bottom of the list, eating only one-fifth as much as the Egyptians, are deterred by other factors—cultural in the case of the Japanese, religious in the case of the Hindus.

Increasing populations, and the consequent burying of ever more cultivatable land beneath the high-rise buildings necessary to house them, bring us daily nearer to the solution recently proposed by Dr. Magnus Pyke, who advised English butchers to prepare to switch from the real thing to synthetic meats—analogues, as they are unappetizingly called. In the meantime those of us who are still able to afford meat can only intone the Selkirk Grace, which may or may not have been written by Robert Burns:

Some hae meat, and canna eat,
And some wad eat that want it;
But we hae meat and we can eat,
And so the Lord be thankit.

Meat is a highly concentrated food in the sense that it packs its nutrients into a small volume; Brillat-Savarin remarked that meat is a natural nourishment of man because his stomach is too small to deal with the bulk of food he would have to take in if his diet were restricted to fruit and vegetables (he neglected fish, as the Hindus and

Japanese do not). Because we are apt to feel a certain heaviness in the stomach longer after eating meat than after other foods, we tend to think that meat is difficult to digest; the truth is just the opposite. Meat does stay in the stomach longer than carbohydrates, but it is digested slowly because it is digested more completely; there is a minimum of waste in meat of good quality.

Meat is often maligned also on a purely mathematical basis—a given quantity of meat providing so much protein, so many vitamins or so many mineral salts is compared with some other food which provides more. Such comparisons are usually over-simplified. Two different foods which contain the same proportion of protein, from the point of view of chemical analysis, may not contain the same proportion of protein from the point of view of the quantity the human body is able to assimilate. On the scale of what nutritionists call the biological value of proteins, with 100 representing the optimum, muscular meats are rated at 80, while the richest cereal, rice, stands only at 70. The most important elements which would be missing in an all-meat diet would be calcium among mineral salts and vitamin C among the vitamins. Meat, while an excellent food, is not a complete food; but what is?

Among the disadvantages of meat, one of the most important was described by a representative of the United States Department of Agriculture: "In meat, we've got a product not only subject to easy contamination but extremely amenable to adulteration and to concealment of adulteration. Partially spoiled meat can be subjected to cooking and curing operations and chemicals that make it look fine." This is an art which was learned early in America, for Jonas Green, in his *Almanack for the Year 1760*, gave directions "by which Meat, ever so stinking, may be made as sweet and wholesome, in a few Minutes, as any Meat at all." The example may have come from the mother country, if we may trust G. K. Chesterton, who wrote in his "Song Against Grocers":

He crams with cans of poisoned meat
The subjects of the King,
And when they die by thousands
Why, he laughs like anything.

Space is lacking here to discuss the dangers to human health which may result from the use of antibiotics or hormones to hasten the growth of meat animals and bring them to marketable size more quickly; many governments have prohibited some of the products so used. But whether modern miracle fodders are harmful or harmless to health, they reduce the quality of our meat. Unimpressed by chemicals, nature refuses to modify its growth rhythms to cooperate with them. Bone tissue and nervous tissue grow most quickly in young animals; the more nourishing and tastier muscular tissue takes over later. Regardless of its weight, an animal slaughtered before it is adult will in general provide only gristly or characterless meat. Another characteristic of animal growth is that the proportion of water in the flesh diminishes and that of fats increases as the animal matures; in a pig, the proportion of water is 82 percent at birth, but 75 percent when it becomes adult. Slaughter it in adolescence and, whatever its weight, you get waterlogged meat.

A final menace to meat was pointed out in the eighteenth century by David Garrick when he wrote: "Heaven sends us good meat, but the Devil sends cooks." There is at least one occasion on which the skill of the cook is of minor importance; indeed, cooking meat at all would seem superfluous for the use which is to be made of it. In Hawaii, the superstitious roast meat before throwing it into streams of lava flowing from Mauna Loa or Kilauea; but no doubt it is worth the trouble if this rite achieves its purpose of appeasing Pele, the goddess of volcanoes, and staving off eruptions.

MED
stands for

the **Median apple**, which was Virgil's name for the lemon; for the **Mediterranean ling**, which resembles the whiting, and the **Mediterranean scad**, which resembles the horse mackerel; and for the **medjhool date** of Morocco, which grows as long as a hen's egg.

And **MED** also stands for

MEDLAR. A small fruit about the size of a crab-apple, the medlar is dowered with a curious anatomy. Its five dark-brown hemispherical pits, instead of being decently contained within the flesh as is the case for most pulpy fruits, are grouped in a cup at its tip, behind the five lobes of the calyx, which do not quite succeed in wrapping themselves around the fruit to give it a complete covering of skin. The seeds may thus be glimpsed from without, hiding coyly behind the calyx network like a Spanish belle of earlier times listening to a serenade from the shadow of her latticed window. The curious disposition of the medlar's seeds suggested a less romantic image to our uncouth ancestors, whose original name for this fruit was the openarse. In the fourteenth century decorum set in, and the old word was replaced gradually by "medlar," borrowed from the Old French *medlier*, a term which the French themselves have abandoned in favor of *nèfle*.

Brillat-Savarin listed the medlar as a fruit which cannot be eaten until it has begun to rot, and all the authorities I have consulted agree with him; but their sources were all northern French or English. In Italy the medlar (there called the *nespola*) can be eaten ripe off the tree. This is impossible farther north because the medlar, though it grows wild throughout temperate Europe as far north as Holland, is there far from its native clime. It originated in southeastern Europe or southwestern Asia, probably in Persia, and, being hardier than the quince, which comes from about the same area, has spread widely northward; but it never really ripens in alien climates.

If left on the tree for some time after the first killing frost, the medlar, like the persimmon, will become edible by itself, but the usual process in England, France and central Europe is to pick the fruits, spread them out on shelves or straw ("Man, like medlars," Balzac wrote cynically, "ripen on straw.") and give them two or three weeks to become well "bletted"—from a French word borrowed by English because it sounds better than "rotten." In England the advice is to harvest the fruit on a dry day in November, a little late for the variety some connoisseurs consider the best, the Saint Lucas medlar, so called because tradition calls for picking it on St. Luke's Day, October 18. After bletting it becomes, in the words of *The Oxford Book of Food Plants*, "soft, brown and more palatable than might be expected," a wording which does not sound as if the writer was wildly enthusiastic about the medlar's flavor. The Larousse gastronomic encyclopedia calls it "astringent and tart, not edible until it has rotted completely, when it possesses a rather agreeable wine-like flavor." Its acidity is usually submerged in sugar before it gets to the eater, for except in the countries where it ripens on the tree, it is rarely eaten as a fruit on its own, but only in the form of preserves, compotes, jams and jellies.

Although a few varieties are cultivated (medlars were already being cultivated on Charlemagne's domains), they are more often gathered wild, at one's risk and peril, for wild medlars have thorns, which the cultivated varieties have not. In the Middle Ages, when the fruit was more widely eaten than it is now (in fourteenth-century France it appeared frequently among the desserts), peasants prowled the woods regularly at the right season to pick wild medlars for the table. The medlar seems to have been first cultivated by the Assyrians, from whom the Greeks had it. Theophrastus mentioned three varieties, and Pliny listed it as one of the "apples" known in antiquity; but since

MEDLAR. *Woodcut from Pierandrea Mattioli:* Commentaries on the Six Books of Dioscorides, *folio edition, Prague, 1563*

we hear little more about it in classical times, we may assume that it made no great impression on the ancients.

The scientific name of the medlar is *Mespilus germanica*, a curious tag for a plant probably Persian, but we must suppose that Germany is where the taxonomists first encountered it. It is the only species of its genus. Using up a whole generic name for a single fruit seems to have struck some classifiers as wasteful, so they proposed doing away with *Mespilus* and putting the medlar in the genus *Pyrus*—the category of pears, to which medlars are indeed closely related. Popular usage tackled the problem in the opposite fashion, by giving the under-employed name "medlar" to a number of fruits which are not medlars, but look or taste more or less like them. There are a considerable number of plants available for this accolade, which grow with abandon on one another's wood. The usual method of propagating the medlar is to graft it onto thorn, quince or pear stock, and English gardeners sometimes amuse themselves by producing thorn trees which appear to have gone crazy, for they bear simultaneously boughs of pear, rowan, whitebeam, medlar and azarole. Medlars grafted on hawthorn have produced chimeras, which in biology means living matter containing tissue from elements of different genetic constitutions. At the point where a medlar graft is inserted in hawthorn, a shoot often develops between the graft and the host plant in which are combined characteristics of both, an abomination of nature.

What English calls the Japanese medlar and French the *nèfle du Japon* is *Eriobotyra japonica.* Purists are discouraging these inexact popular names in both languages, with some success, for they are becoming rarer, being replaced in English by "loquat" and in French by *bibacier* or *bibassier*, from the Japanese name for this fruit, *biwa.* The loquat looks like a small apricot, and like the medlar proper has five pits, but wears them orthodoxly inside, sheltered from public view. The editors of the big Larousse encyclopedia describe this fruit unkindly as "sharp and disagreeable, but when they are bletted" (could there be a confusion here with the true medlar?) "they then have a slightly sweet flavor and a smell of ether." The Larousse *gastronomic* encyclopedia, a little out of step with its parent, says that the "white flesh" of the *nèfle du Japon* is "acid and sweet," while an American authority writes that "its yellow flesh is agreeably acid." This fruit is grown not only in the Orient, but also in southern Europe and Algeria. The wood of its tree is prized by violin makers.

I do not know whether the wood of the Neapolitan medlar, alias the Spanish thorn, has any special uses, but perhaps it should have. The plant's scientific name is *Crataegus azarolus,* and *Crataegus,* derived from Greek, means "hard wood"; however, *Crataegus,* in contrast to *Mespilus,* is an overcrowded genus, with more than a thousand species, and this epithet does not necessarily apply to all of them. The other half of its label gives us its more accurate popular name, the azarole. A sort of hawthorn, the azarole is a little larger than a cherry and, though acid, is delicious fresh, a fact to which I can attest personally, for when I lived in Villefranche-sur-Mer, on the French Riviera, I had an azarole in my backyard (the neighbors persisted in calling it a *nèfle du Japon*). The azarole is grown in Algeria, Spain, Italy and southern France, where there are at least three cultivated varieties—the scarlet azarole with, as its name suggests, red flesh, sweet and only slightly acid; the pear azarole, tarter, but still agreeable; and the hedgerow azarole (*Azerole tanaise*), whose taste has been compared to that of the Api apple, the famous variety which, developed by the ancient Etruscans, has maintained its favor ever since, and is represented today in the modern Lady apple. The azarole goes into preserves, marmalade, jelly and even a liqueur.

Africa has a genus of fruits which are called wild medlars for want of any popular name—in Western languages at least, for *Vangueria infausta,* which may be the prototype, is known as *matugongo* in equatorial and southern Africa. Its fruits are spherical, brown when ripe, and sweet but acid; the pits are sometimes eaten as well as the pulp. It is called the small wild medlar in English, though its cousin, V. *madagascariensis,* of Mozambique, Madagascar and the Indian Ocean islands of Mauritius and Réunion, is known as the Spanish tamarind. The name "wild medlar," not otherwise described, is given indiscriminately to V. *tomentosa,* V. *venosa* and a fruit of a related genus, V. *lanciflora,* which is reported to be the tastiest of them all.

If World War II general Anthony McAuliffe had been French instead of American, he would not have answered the German demand for surrender at Bastogne with the comment "Nuts!" but would have replied, "*Des nèfles*!"

MEG
stands for

the **megapodes** of Australasia, which include the Australian brush turkey and the Australian native pheasant, or mallee-bird.

MEL
stands for

the **melancholy thistle,** which inconsistently, according to Nicholas Culpeper, makes a man "as merry as a Cricket"; for **melde,** a type of tasty green which grows wild throughout central and northern Europe and may or may not be the plant referred to in English as Good-King-Henry; for **melilot,** a sort of clover sometimes eaten second-hand, or second-mouth, by feeding it to domestic rabbits to make them taste like wild ones; and for the **melon tree,** which is what they call the papaya in tropical Africa.

And **MEL** also stands for

MELON. "There are only two good things in the world," wrote the French poet Malherbe, who was not nicknamed "Father Lust" for nothing, "women and roses; and two choice tidbits, women

MELON. *Photograph by Walker Evans:* Mrs. Frank Tengle and Laura Minnie Lee Tengle, *Hale County, Alabama, Summer 1936*

and melons." He lived in the heyday of the melon in France:

It invaded France at the end of the fifteenth century [wrote Georges and Germaine Blond]. It was often called the *pompon*. Ronsard celebrated it many times under this name; a gardener proud of his produce, he offered some to Charles IX, a great lover of melons; Henri IV appreciated them no less: "I am going to sit down at table to eat my melons and swallow a draft of muscat." And Montaigne: "I am not excessively fond of salads nor of fruits, except melons." Melon was all the rage. 1583 even saw the appearance of a *Succinct Treatise on Melons* by the very serious Professor Jacques Pons, dean of the College of Doctors of Lyons, which listed fifty ways of eating this fruit, as hors d'oeuvre, chilled, with sugar, salt or pepper, cooked, in soups, in fritters and in compotes. Even the rind was used for compotes. Renaissance France smelled of melon.

The spirit of the times was expressed, just short of swooning, by Marc Antoine de Gérard Saint-Amant, who wrote:

O manger précieux! Délice de la bouche!
Oh! beaucoup mieux que l'or, chef-d'oeuvre d'Apollon!
O fleur de tous les fruits! O ravissant melon!

("O precious food! Delight of the mouth! Oh, much better than gold, masterpiece of Apollo! O flower of all the fruits! O ravishing melon!")

Sickened either by such effusiveness or by the Renaissance smell of melon, an anonymous author rebelled in the 1674 *Art of Fine Catering, a Curious and Very Gallant Work Useful to All Persons of All Conditions* (anonymous, except that it must have been written by one or the other of two Officers of the King's Mouth):

[The melon] is today the object of universal zeal. . . . The stomach is stuffed with this pernicious food which hides beneath the honey of its sugared flesh an agreeable poison. . . . You cannot eat a single meal into which it does not enter. It is served in pyramids and mountains, as if it were necessary to eat it to the point of suffocation. . . . [It] refreshes too subtly, moistens too much, turns bad too easily in the stomach.

And he added, with an obvious undertone of "serves them right," the information that in 1459 the Germanic emperor Albert of Austria and in 1471 both Pope Paul II and "the great poet and great philosopher" Antoine Goneau died from eating melons, assertions which I have not been able to verify.

The melon originated somewhere in the Middle East, probably Persia. We first hear of it in the Sumerian epic of Gilgamesh, whose hero ate what has been translated as "cassia melons," which parallels the modern name "nutmeg melon," indicating the spicy aromatic character of the fruit, for cassia is a form of cinnamon. Assyrian bas-reliefs show on festive tables what appear to be slices of melon, and we are told that Ur-Nammu of Ur grew melons in his garden about 2100 B.C.; the garden of King Merodach-Baladan also contained them, and the Assyrian Herbal lists melons. Pictures of a fruit which some authorities identify as melons are included in Egyptian paintings dated at 2400 B.C., despite Brillat-Savarin, who maintained that melons were not known in antiquity and that what translators have so named were really cucumbers eaten with highly seasoned sauces. This seems unlikely, for Egypt at least; a famous passage in the Bible names both as different foods, when the Hebrews wandering in the desert lament "the fish, which we did eat in Egypt freely; the cucumbers, and the melons" (Numbers 11:5).

The Greeks had melons at least by the third century B.C. Pliny wrote in the first century A.D. of a plant grown in the Campania called the *melopepo* whose fruit did not hang suspended from the vine, as did cucumbers, but rested on the ground; it was spherical and yellow, and when ripe detached itself from the stem—a detail characteristic of most melons. A wall painting in Herculaneum shows what seems to be a melon, cut in half so that its interior structure is visible. The Greek physician Galen described the medical virtues of melons in the second century A.D., and in the third, Roman manuals gave directions for growing them. In general, however, the Romans preferred to import them, from Armenia; they were at that time only about the size of our oranges today.

There is a somewhat dubious theory that melons were eaten in the Indus valley in prehistoric times, but the earliest reliable report we have, from the Far East, tells us that melon seeds were much relished in China about 200 B.C. In 1973 the body of a Chinese noblewoman was exhumed in the province of Hunan, so perfectly preserved, by dint of having been buried sixty feet deep in a nested series of six airtight coffins, that it was possible to perform an autopsy. Melon seeds were found in the esophagus, stomach and intestines. The coffin was identified as that of the wife of the Han dynasty Marquis of Tai, of the principality of Changsha, which fixes the date of those melon seeds at about 125 B.C.

On the road to China, we have a report from Marco Polo, who tells of reaching the city of Shibarghan,

plentifully stocked with everything needful. Here are found the best melons in the world in very great quantity, which they dry in this manner: they cut them all around in slices like strips of leather, then put them in the sun to dry, when they become sweeter than honey. And you must know that they are an article of commerce and find a ready sale through all the country around.

Shibarghan is in Afghanistan, Persia's neighbor, which may have been in the original melon country, and is in any case in today's secondary center of melon growing, along with northern Pakistan and Kashmir.

With the collapse of the Roman Empire, the flow of melons from Asia Minor to Italy dried up and the fruit disappeared from Europe. It is reported to have returned to Italy only in the fourteenth century, still in the orange-sized version of ancient Roman times, which would soon be developed to more generous proportions. However, the melon is listed among the fruits Charlemagne ordered grown on his domains, which would mean about A.D. 800; he could have encountered them not in Italy but in Spain, where his armies campaigned. Andalusia seems indeed to have been the first European territory re-conquered by the melon, planted there by the Moors, which could have meant early in the eighth century. Despite Charlemagne's orders, the melon does not seem to have taken hold in France. Its effective introduction into that country is attributed by some to the Popes, when they abandoned Rome for Avignon, which would have brought the melon to France in the early fourteenth century; but melons were not being eaten commonly even in Italy until the end of that century, and it may be that this story was born simply because the Popes and the melon were associated for another reason: melon seeds brought from Armenia were planted in the Papal domain of Cantalupo, near Tivoli (hence the cantaloupe); but this was not until the sixteenth century. The likeliest theory seems to be that melons were brought to France in 1495 by the soldiers of Charles VIII returning from Italy.

Bruyerin-Champier, physician to François I, wrote that only in Languedoc did they know how to grow melons, then known as *sucrins* (from *sucre*, "sugar") because, Charles Estienne explained, "gardeners watered them with honeyed or sweetened water." The fact was that only in southern France did the climate permit growing melons in the open. Jean de la Quintinie grew seven varieties for Louis XIV at Versailles, but under glass.

In America, Hernando de Alvarado informed Coronado that the Southwest was rich in maize, haricot beans and melons. He was right about the first two but necessarily wrong about the third, since there were no melons in the New World until Europeans brought them there. Perhaps what he took for melons were squashes. The Navahos seem to have begun to grow melons about the middle of the nineteenth century; they were probably Spanish, delivered via Latin America. In our century, the British novelist Michael Arlen, visiting Armenia, was told that Armenians had introduced into California the casaba melon, whose name comes from Kasaba, in Turkey. The first officially recorded import, however, seems to have been the Netted Gem variety, imported from France in 1881. This started commercial melon cultivation in the United States, though not until 1895 did they develop reliable quality in this country, starting in Colorado. About 1900 the French White Antibes winter melon was planted in the United States, where it became known as the honeydew.

There are three things which cannot support mediocrity, a French poet once said—poetry, wine and melons. Claude Mermet, writing about 1600, apparently felt that mediocrity in melons was to be expected; of melons as of friends, he wrote, fifty had to be tried to find a single good one. This figure was doubled in the English translation:

Friends are like melons. Shall I tell you why?
To find one good, you must a hundred try.

The translation of "fifty" by "one hundred" is an example of poetic license: scansion over accuracy.

Brillat-Savarin objected to that jingle, maintaining that in his time the melon had already been developed to a point at which good ones were the rule and bad ones the exception; but he did add that melons were a fruit which had to be eaten at the exact moment when they had attained "the perfection which is their destiny." Melons cannot be picked before they are completely ripe, to finish their ripening on the way to the table. Some fruits will continue to manufacture sugar after picking, under favorable circumstances—for instance, if placed in the sun—but not melons. Their sugar content begins to decrease as soon as they are picked; they may soften, but they will not ripen. So important is optimum ripeness for the melon that it has its own cut-off system to end its development at the right moment. When its sugar content reaches saturation, a separation layer develops in the stem at the point where it joins the fruit, a shield which prevents further nutrients from entering the melon, which may then be lifted away from the vine with only the slightest pressure (as Pliny had observed). A melon thus picked shows no scar where the stem breaks; if you buy a melon which shows damaged tissue at the end of the stem—or which has been cut from it—it is a sign that the melon was unripe when picked.

Given the sweetness of the perfectly ripe melon, it may seem surprising that its sugar content accounts for only 5 percent of its weight, only half as much as for an apple or a pear; but as 94 percent is water, this still gives sugar a five-to-one advantage over all the other taste-producing elements.

Melons are the despair of gardeners and taxonomists. All of them belong to the same species, *Cucumis melo*, and they interbreed and overlap so readily that seed growers must plant different varieties at least a quarter of a mile apart to prevent insects from cross-pollinating them and producing results very different from those desired. This exaggerated friendliness of melons also makes it difficult for taxonomists to arrange them in categories with any degree of fixity, but they have bravely tried all the same, though sometimes a new variety has to be assigned to one category or the other more or less by guess and by golly.

The classifiers recognize three principal groups, muskmelons, cantaloupes and winter melons. The first, C. *melo* var. *reticulatus*, also called the nutmeg melon or the netted melon (or, by the French, the embroidered melon), usually carries a raised network on its rind, usually lighter in color than the green or yellowish background color of the fruit. It is marked by an aromatic odor and a similar flavor in its light-green to salmon-orange flesh. This is the melon we often eat in America under the name "cantaloupe," thus usurped because what the Old World calls cantaloupes are not grown commercially in the United States.

These come under the head C. *melo* var. *cantalupensis*, usually with a hard, rough, warty or scaly rind, but not a netted one. Cantaloupes are often deeply grooved into segments, and the flesh, fragrant like that of the muskmelon, is usually orange, but on rare occasions green. This is the variety most grown in Europe.

C. *melo* var. *inodorus* includes the winter melons, which, as their scientific name suggests, lack the spicy odor of other melons and differ from them also in not forming a separation layer in the stem when ripe—an unnecessary device, for they are late-season plants whose growth, if they are not picked earlier, is going to be cut off by frost, with no aid from the melon. There is a good deal of variety among winter melons, whose hard rinds may be smooth, ridged or corrugated, and may have whitish, light-green or orange flesh; casaba and honeydew melons both belong to this group. They are popular with growers who ship to distant markets, for they keep best of all melons (muskmelons are the most perishable), may be stored for a month or more, and are not easily damaged in transit from grower to retailer.

Flaubert raised the question of whether the melon is a vegetable or a fruit. A fruit, most of us would say, judging by its sweetness; but the mango melon (also called the vegetable orange or the vine peach), *C. melo* var. *chito*, has white, nonfragrant flesh and suggests a cucumber rather than a melon; it is used largely for pickling. *C. melo* var. *flexuosus*, the snake melon, which is long, slender, smooth and crooked, and *C. melo* var. *dudaim*, the pomegranate melon or Queen Anne's pocket melon, which is small, round and fragrant, are both inedible, but are sometimes grown in the United States as ornamental plants. The *egusi* melons of West Africa, of which the pulp is not eaten, but which are cultivated for their seeds, eaten roasted, or pressed to extract their edible oil, are not quite true melons, for they do not belong to the *Cucumis* genus, but to *Cucumeropsis*. This is also true of the watermelon, *Citrullus vulgaris*, which cannot be cross-pollinated with other melons. Farthest of all from the real thing is the melon pear or melon shrub, alias the pepino, a native of Peru now grown for its fruit in many warm countries; it is *Solanum muricatum*, a relative of the potato and the tomato.

MEN
stands for

mended kelts, salmon which have indecently refused to die after spawning, as all right-thinking salmon should, but have returned to the sea relatively intact; for the **menhaden,** a fish which breathes too fast for its own good; and for **meni oil,** which, pressed from nuts, is one of the most important culinary oils of West Africa.

MER
stands for

mercury, otherwise known as Good-King-Henry, an herb which it is preferable not to confuse with mercury the metal; for the **merganser,** a fish-eating duck, which frequently tastes like a duck which has eaten fish; for the **Merino,** a sheep devoted to the production of wool which Louis XV converted into a sheep devoted to the production of meat; and for the **merle,** in French either a blackbird which is sometimes white or an edible fish found only in the Mediterranean which seems to have no name in English.

MES
stands for

the **mesquite,** a legume whose pods were eaten regularly by the ancient Incas and Aztecs.

MEX
stands for

the **Mexican apple,** or white sapote, native to tropical America but appreciated nowadays in eastern and northern Africa; for the **Mexican black bean,** which has yellow pods, black seeds and a flavor like that of mushrooms; for the **Mexican cavefish,** whose turbulent behavior at mating time causes currents which permit males and females to find each other, for they are blind; for the **Mexican nut pine,** whose seeds are eaten not only in Mexico but also in the southwestern United States; for the **Mexican persimmon,** which produces black fruit; and for the **Mexican strawberry,** a cowboy name for the common red bean.

MIG
stands for

mignonette, which nowadays usually means coarsely ground pepper, but two centuries ago meant a mixture of pepper, pimento, coriander and cinnamon.

MIK
stands for

the **mikan,** a Japanese orange which resembles the tangerine.

MIL
stands for

the **milkfish,** which spawns nobody knows where, except when it is raised for food in brackish enclosures in Southeast Asia, but, wherever it comes from, is taken on the African shores of the Indian Ocean and in the Red Sea; for the **milk**

thistle, whose juice is supposed to increase the flow of milk in nursing mothers; for the **milk tree**, or cow tree, a name which may indicate either the Venezuelan *Brosimum utile*, with agreeably sweet sap, or the Brazilian *Mumusops huberi*, whose edible latex is as thick as cream; for the **milk vetch**, whose seeds are eaten in the Near East and North Africa; for **milkweed**, a recommendable wild food provided you know how to boil the bitterness out of it; for **milkwort**, another plant credited with the ability to increase the flow of milk in mothers, and, for that matter, in cows too; for the **miller's-thumb**, an edible freshwater fish, if you are willing to settle for a maximum length of five inches, and the **millions fish**, even smaller (one inch), originally so named because it appears in schools of such great numbers, but now usually called the guppy; and for **milt**, fish sperm, a rare delicacy which is described prudishly in the culinary vocabulary as soft roe.

And **MIL** also stands for

MILK. "In spite of its liquid state," says the *Nouveau Larousse Gastronomique*, "milk must always be considered as a food and not as a beverage." This is indeed what it is for all of us at the beginning of our lives, and not simply a food, but *the* food, the only one we have. Yet after babyhood milk is not, as many people believe, beneficial to everybody. Milk-tolerant adults are in a minority in the world. Most Africans, many Asians and some American Indians cannot digest milk—80 percent of the world's non-white population. Nettled at the idea that this inability represents an inferiority, a Nigerian health official exclaimed: "Adults are not supposed to drink milk." He was right.

Nature designed milk to nourish babies and designed babies to digest milk. Milk contains 4.8 percent of a rich sugar called lactose, which can only be digested with the aid of an enzyme confusingly called lactase which is produced in the intestine, by babies in much greater profusion than by adults. The lactase level decreases as the child grows older. When nature programed babies, there was only one kind of milk—breast milk; when that dried up, lactase was no longer required. Nature had not foreseen that one species—our own—was going to call on other species to contribute more milk when the mother's supply was exhausted. To simplify the reason why white adults are more likely to maintain some lactase in their systems than non-whites, we might say that it depends in large part on the ancestral history of different races. Some American Indians still consider milk disgusting; they belong to a people which drank no milk before Columbus because they had no milk animals. Seventy percent of American blacks cannot digest milk; their ancestors were brought from West Africa (where an even higher proportion of the population cannot drink milk); at the time of the slave trade there were no cattle in West Africa because the tsetse fly had killed them off.

What kind of milk should babies drink? Human milk. The milk of each species of mammal constitutes a complete food for that species and for no other. Human beings are no exception. One might add, its own mother's milk. Mothers have many advantages over wet nurses, such as identical chemical constitutions and identical timing, counting from the act of birth, with their children, quite independent of the moral duty which many philosophers, mostly male, have ascribed to breast feeding by the mother. "If Nature gave you enough strength to give birth to a child, she gave you enough to nurse it," wrote the fifteenth–sixteenth-century humanist Desiderius Erasmus. "A mother ought to nurse her child. . . . The duty of women on this point is not to be doubted," said the eighteenth-century moralist Jean-Jacques Rousseau. Erasmus does not seem to have made much impression on his readers, but Rousseau, a romantic figure, did. Frenchwomen who had been accustomed to confiding their babies to wet nurses began bringing them back home in droves, to the great dismay of the wet nurses. Mme. Roland bewailed publicly that she had too little milk to feed her child. Either she managed to conquer this affliction later, or she was a great actress under trying circumstances; as she mounted the steps to the guillotine she cried dramatically, "Goodby, dear child, whom I nourished with my milk!"

It was Mme. Roland who put her finger on a disadvantage in substituting a wet nurse for the mother three centuries before the child psychologists caught up to her. When she realized her deficiency as a milk producer, she said, "There's no use trying to hide it from myself, the nurse will have the child more than I." An infant does, indeed, tend to identify itself with the woman whose breast it takes. This made the choice of a wet nurse, in the days when they were a more familiar phenomenon than they are now, a problem even graver than it always had been. The first requirement was that the foster mother be in good health and clean in her habits: the scrofula and the defective eyesight from which Dr. Johnson suffered all his life have been attributed to a prejudice against washing on the part of his nurse. "Bull's *Rules for Choice of Wet Nurses*," Philippa Pullar tells us in her *Consum-*

ing Passions, "recommended that all candidates be perused like cows: the soundness of their teeth and gums, the clarity of their tongues and complexions, the firmness of their breasts and above all the goodness of their characters were each to be carefully examined."

Character was important, for the belief that it is sucked in with the milk goes back at least as far as to the ancient Hindu Upanishads. In Renaissance Florence, where many families had Saracen servants, they refused to employ them as wet nurses for fear that the children might develop Oriental characteristics or even embrace Islam. As late as the beginning of this century a manual for English girls going to India or other colonies warned that "the milk of a native woman should contaminate an English child's character when that of the beasts . . . is held to have no such power." Our own Old South was exceptionally broad-minded when it permitted black servants to nurse white children.

Even adults could not resist the insidious influence of woman's milk. The man who founded and gave his name to Caius College of Cambridge University survived on nothing but milk—human milk—for the last few years of his life. According to Dr. Thomas Muffet, "What made Dr. *Cajus* in his last sickness so peevish and so full of frets at Cambridge when he suckt one woman (whom I spare to name) froward of condition and of bad diet; and contrariwise so quiet and well, when he suckt another of contrary disposition? verily the diversity of their milks and conditions, which being contrary one to the other, wrought also in him that sucked them contrary effects."

For somewhat different reasons, the effect of human milk on its receiver has of late years caused a considerable diminution in the number of advocates of breast feeding—because the majority of nursing mothers tested in the United States have proved to have traces of antibiotics, pesticides or other pollutants in their milk, up to four times as much as is permitted for marketable cow's milk. "If it were packaged in any other container," conservationist David Brower told a committee of the House of Representatives, "we wouldn't allow it to cross state lines."

If the infant does not drink human milk, what does it drink? Cow's milk, probably. Of all the milk provided by other animals utilized by the human race, 89 percent comes from cows; it is perfect for calves but less so for babies. The favor enjoyed by the product of the cow depends less on the quality of the milk than on the character of the animal, docile in domesticity and responsive to improvement through breeding. The best substitute for human milk would be one not found on the market—ass's milk, the closest approach to human milk. Its greatest disparity is in fats, in which human milk is nearly three times as rich (which is why it has a caloric superiority of 50 percent over ass's milk), but as this is the least digestible constituent of milk, it is the category in which a deficiency does the least harm.

The second most important milch animal in the world is the goat, "the poor man's cow." Americans are prejudiced against goat's milk, because it is reputed to have a rank taste. It is in fact sweeter than cow's milk, but the male, which has musk glands not present in the female (among goats, not exceptionally, only females give milk), is smelly and should be kept away from the milk; or, preferably, one should not keep a male at all: a billy goat's services can always be rented when needed. A goat will eat anything, and if it grazes on the wrong sort of pasture, its milk will taste bad, but so will a cow's in the same circumstances. Goat's milk might be described as naturally homogenized, for its fat globules are smaller than those of cow's milk; as a result, while goat's milk is richer than cow's milk (4.3 percent butterfat as compared with 3.9 percent), it is easier to digest. Hospitals pay a premium price for it.

I do not know of any region where sheep's milk is drunk directly, except the Sahara, where food is often so scarce that anything available is taken advantage of at once. But it is often used for making cheese, including one of the great cheeses of the world, Roquefort. The existence of Roquefort probably accounts also for the existence of the Manech sheep of the Basque country, which has been bred not with an eye to wool or mutton, but to milk. This is rare, but not unique; there are other milch sheep in the world.

In the Middle Ages children were sometimes put to suckle a sow, and vice versa; I have seen an old engraving showing a woman giving one breast to her child and the other to a piglet. I do not believe any humans nowadays use pig's milk.

About half the milk consumed in India comes from buffaloes, which also contribute significant amounts of it to the diets of Africa, China, the Philippines and other parts of Asia. Southern Italy uses buffalo milk to make cheese. Reay Tannahill writes of buffalo milk that at the time when eating habits were being formed in ancient India "the higher castes, then as now, probably had an aversion to the rich, greenish liquid with its highly distinctive flavor." Writing in *The New*

MILK *by Jan Vermeer (1632–1675).* Maid Servant Pouring Milk, *oil on canvas*

Yorker, Suzy Eban said in "A Cairo Childhood," "Buffalo milk, which was commonly used, was rich and heavy, and we disliked it."

"Milk is a fairly important by-product of camel breeding," according to the American anthropologist Lloyd Cabot Briggs in *The Tribes of the Sahara*, "for camel's milk is a highly prized luxury throughout the desert but, even under the most favorable conditions, a milk camel gives only some six to ten quarts a day. Personally I find camel's milk unpleasantly heavy and sweet [Pliny remarked on its sweetness too]; it is a good deal like what is known commercially as 'evaporated milk.'"

Of all the domesticated animals regularly milked, the reindeer probably gives the richest milk. It has 22.5 percent butterfat but only 2.5 percent sugar, which may account partly for the healthiness of Laplanders. Reindeer milk also contains 10.3 percent protein, nearly three times as much as is produced by cows. Unfortunately, they give only about a cup a day at the height of the season.

The yak is milked today in Tibet; in ancient times it seems to have been domesticated over a much wider area of Central Asia than it is now. Its milk is nourishing and plentiful.

All of these milks of today have eclipsed what was the commonest milk of all in the days when milk drinking began—mare's milk. The nomads of the Eurasian steppes were the first great consumers of milk. The Mongols, wrote Marco Polo, "are accustomed to drink every kind of milk," but though they had flocks of sheep and goats, it was mare's milk which they preferred. (They used sheep's milk, disdainfully, to caulk their tents.) "These Tartars are of low stature and rather thin," Marco Polo said, "owing to their diet of mare's milk, which makes a man slim, and their strenuous life."

Some other milks lead us into the realm of fantasy. I have read that Australians—aborigines, I suppose—drink kangaroo milk, but until someone explains the *modus operandi* to me, I shall permit myself to disbelieve it. A kangaroo cannot be milked: it has no nipples. Its milk is sweated out of the skin and the babies in its pouch lick it off the fur. Another story which I regard with skepticism is that the blue whale squirts its milk onto the surface of the sea in enormous pools, from which the baby laps it up, like a kitten from a saucer. If so, the blue whale is a backward creature in comparison with the gray whale, whose calf makes a waterproof seal around the mother's nipple with tongue and palate, whereupon the mother pumps her milk, a gallon or two at a spurt, by pressure of her abdominal muscles, into the baby's mouth. The milk is rich, with about eight times as much butterfat as is found in human milk, but without sugar. All the mammals of the sea, whether fish-shaped or seals, have rich milk. If you want the richest of all, try that of the killer whale, 35 percent butterfat, if you can find it in your supermarket.

Man began practicing the art of milking in the enlightened Neolithic era, and it was normal that it should begin among nomads, for they traveled with herds of milk-giving animals which provided most of their food. The Aryans who entered India about 1750 B.C. came from the steppes and brought their herds with them, bestowing upon the subcontinent eating habits which depended so heavily on milk and milk products that the cow became there a sacred animal. Among the peoples who stayed on the Eurasian steppes, Homer wrote of the *hippemolgoi* (literally "mare milkers"), Herodotus of the Scythians, and Pliny of the Sarmatians. Marco Polo reported in the thirteenth century that the Tartars "live on meat and milk and game and on Pharaoh's rats [a sort of mongoose], which are abundant everywhere in the steppes. . . . When they are going on a long expedition, they carry no baggage with them. They each carry two leather flasks to hold the milk they drink. . . . [They] have their dried milk, which is solid like paste"—the first condensed milk.

In the ancient Mediterranean regions, milk seems to have been rare. The first record of its presence is a milking scene on a frieze at Ur dated 2900 B.C. Georges and Germaine Blond think that milk was "a rare treat" for the Egyptians. The Greeks had only goat's and sheep's milk, and preferred the former, but used it mainly to make cheese. The Romans, whose Latin ancestors were shepherds, showed the opposite preference, but also used the milk for cheese; it was seldom drunk, except mixed with wine. The Hebrews may have used more milk, for there are many references to it in the Bible, but the possibility that it was something of a luxury might be deduced from the circumstance that it seemed to be synonymous with riches, as when Canaan was described as "a land flowing with milk and honey." This seems to have been the case in China, where milking began about 2000 B.C.; the literary references to milk seem confined to the wealthy, as when we are told that it was an emperor who ate milk and rice in a frozen dish (an ancestor of ice cream, almost the only form in which the average Chinese consumes milk today?).

Another milk-supported society grew up in another nomadic territory, the Sahara, where

MILK *by Mary Cassat (1845–1926).* La visite. *Dry-point and aquatint in color.*

Sallust expressed surprise in the first century B.C. because the Numidians got along without salt; they imbibed it with milk, just as nowadays the desert nomads escape scurvy thanks to the vitamin C in milk. The medieval world used little milk, partly because medieval cows did well to produce enough of it in a week to make a pound of butter. England had more milk than most other countries, and referred to it as "white meat." Milk drinking was not popular from the seventeenth to the nineteenth century either, because the sanitary conditions in which milk was produced and sold were appalling. In the United States until about 1825, children often drank beer because neither the milk nor the water was safe.

Alas, every "improvement" which has been effected in the handling of milk has been paid for by a deterioration of its taste—even in the case of pasteurization, where concern for health is an overriding factor. Nevertheless, no one who is acquainted with the full richness of unpasteurized milk is likely to resort willingly to the pasteurized variety. Gail Borden called milk a "living fluid," but pasteurized milk is dead, all its beneficial bacteria killed along with the harmful ones, and its vitamin C destroyed. Sterilized milk, which is heated above the boiling point, is dead and buried. One may ask oneself wistfully whether, if the tuberculin test had come in twenty years before pasteurization instead of the other way around, we would not be drinking tastier milk today.

Our economic system, based on mass marketing and large-scale operations, has condemned us to the acceptance, in the case of milk, of what might be called a dependable standard of mediocrity. The dairy cooperative was inevitable, and a boon for farmers, but when it dumps all the milk of the region it serves into one big vat, the best with the worst, it destroys the incentive, and even the possibility, in a competitive system, of producing superior grades of milk. In the United States, as a result, the Holstein, "a giant machine that gives twice as much milk, with less cream," as John and Karen Hess describe it, now outnumbers all other breeds of cattle, including the Jersey, which probably gives the best cow's milk in the world. The number of cows in the United States has been cut in half in the last thirty years; and in the last ten, the demand for milk has dropped by 10 percent, and for cream by 50 percent.

MILLET. "Millets are a motley crowd, from *Setaria* to *Sorghum* and *Eleusine*, and even the French distinction between *mil* and *millet* is not very helpful," Mr. J. O. Grandjouan, a knowledgeable correspondent, once wrote me. Mr. Grandjouan's misgivings about the difficulty of sorting out false millets and real millets could have been documented immediately in the case of sorghum, which he has here placed among millets. "Sorghum is erroneously called millet," says the *Encyclopaedia Britannica*, 1962 printing, Volume 15, page 49. Nevertheless, Volume 1, page 430, writes about a "group of food grains including sorghum and collectively known as millets," and on page 426 of the same volume, the *E.B.* lists among the millets of India a species called *jowar*—which is *Sorghum vulgare*. My curiosity aroused by this intramural conflict, I turned to Volume 21, entry SORGHUM, to find out whether the *Britannica* really thinks sorghum is a millet or not. It didn't say.

Most Americans have never tasted millet, nor most western Europeans either. In the United States it is grown for pasturage, silage or hay, and in Britain for birdseed, which is why you occasionally find a clump of millet sprouting valiantly from an English dump: somebody has cleaned the birdcage. In France the delicious small birds called ortolans are trapped, caged and fattened on millet for a few days before being delivered to the chef. In the United States browntop millet, *Panicum ramosum*, is sown where game birds feed. Millet does enter the American diet, but only through the good offices of an intermediary species, wild or domestic.

Elsewhere millet is an important food for at least half a billion people, and a basic food for many of them—Indians, Africans, Chinese and even some Russians. It stands not far below wheat in protein content, in which all but its poorer varieties are superior to rice and maize. Several of the tropical millets contain a high proportion of minerals in comparison with other cereals. Millet is a good third among the world's cereal crops. Wheat takes up about 25 percent of all the acreage planted to cereals, rice 20 percent and millet over 19 percent. In tonnage, however, it accounts for only about 10 percent of the whole, for its yields are smaller; this is largely because it is planted only on poor soils where other grains would not grow at all. In Africa it is often the first crop planted when ground has been cleared by burning off the brush and the last crop yielded by marginal land which is being swallowed by the desert. It is the role of millet to give grain to peoples who otherwise would have none.

Millet was probably the first cereal to be cultivated, during the Neolithic era. Barley and a primitive variety of wheat soon joined it in the fields, but for centuries it remained by far the leading grain. Reference books guess that it originated in Africa or Asia; a significant peculiarity of the plant points to Asia. In the absence of water, millet goes into a dormant state; with the return of moisture it awakes with a start and begins growing excitedly, to take advantage of the water while it is still there. The Moors of the Sahara, great millet eaters, plant it wherever a rare heavy rain has temporarily filled hollows with water; it ripens forty-five days after planting. This suggests that millet developed in monsoon country, where hot, dry periods alternate with sudden rains: the monsoon belt runs from the Arabian Sea across India to China.

The first written record concerning millet is in the Fan Shên-Chih Shu, dated at 2800 B.C., which tells us that the five sacred crops of China were soybeans, rice, wheat, barley and millet, and gives directions for growing and storing millet; and we know that millet was also being cultivated in India in prehistoric times. We first recognize it in Europe in the Swiss lake settlements, at the same period as that of the Chinese record (but its use in Europe did not become common until the first millennium B.C.). It seems to have come overland across the Eurasian steppes, north of the usual route through the Mediterranean basin taken by foods moving from Asia to Europe, and then turned southward to the Mediterranean. It was probably also from Asia that it reached the Middle East, where its presence is noted in the Old Testament, and we know that it was grown in the hanging gardens of Babylon. Herodotus, who called Assyria the richest grain-producing country in the world, wrote that millet grew so tall there that he would not give its height, for he would not be believed. But it remained a minor crop, which skipped Egypt entirely. The fertile Nile valley could grow wheat and barley, so millet was left to the regions south of the Sahara which couldn't.

Millet was being cultivated in Gaul before the Romans got there, and also in Cisalpine Gaul, Lombardy today, by those great cereal farmers, the Etruscans. They made *puls* from it, a gruel or porridge, which is the form in which most millet is eaten today. It reached Rome from the north, exported from Milan, capital of Lombardy, which has been millet country ever since. In Rome, where the staple food of the poor was grain, largely millet at first, it was made into *pulmentum*, a copy of the Etruscan *puls*. The Romans were not overfond of millet and shifted to barley as soon as they could get it, or at least mixed barley and millet flours together.

Charlemagne ordered that millet be stocked in his domains as a Lenten food. Marco Polo reported that under the Great Khan "they have no shortage, because they mostly use rice, panic or millet [panic is millet too], especially the Tartars and the people of Cathay and Manzi . . . they do not use bread, but simply boil these three sorts of grain with milk or flesh"—the classic millet gruel again. In Europe during the Middle Ages, more millet was grown than wheat.

The characteristics which once made millet an appropriate food for primitive times have kept it in our day an appropriate food for primitive places. It is one of the hardiest of cereals, capable of fending for itself in the wild state; but when it is cultivated it responds gratifyingly to even the most rudimentary care. Its very small seeds facilitate its spread, with the aid of birds, for instance, or even of the wind. It keeps well in storage; finger millet, the longest-lasting, has been held for as long as five years in the form of unthreshed heads before being eaten. Thus millet is often stocked as a reserve food in case of famine. On the other hand, the very small seeds are hard to handle, and, having no gluten, millet flour does not rise and can be made only into flatbread. But the greatest objection to its wider use is that, as

MILLET *by Kano Sanraku (1559–1635).* Autumn Millet, *Japanese screen, detail*

the *Encyclopaedia Britannica* puts it, millets "are the least palatable of cereals and are eaten from necessity rather than choice." The Tuaregs and the Haratins of the Sahara, who prefer it to wheat, would not agree, but most other millet eaters would. It is therefore doomed to be grown only on inhospitable soil where tastier cereals will not flourish.

The many genera of millets can be divided into tropical millets and temperate millets; the latter will grow in hot, dry tropical climates as well as in the warmer regions of the temperate zones. The most important temperate millet genera are *Panicum*, *Setaria* and *Echinochloa*. *P. miliaceum*, often called broomcorn millet because the shape of its ear suggests an old-fashioned twig broom, is widely eaten in China, Japan, Africa, Arabia, Russia and sparingly in southern Europe. *S. italica*, or foxtail millet, is so old that no wild form is now known to exist; despite its name it is in all probability a native of Asia, believed to have been the species which was the most important food crop of China in the third millennium B.C. *E. frumentacea*, called Japanese millet, is eaten less in Japan than in West Africa.

The leading tropical millets are *Eleusine* and *Pennisetum*. *E. coracana* is called finger millet because grain-bearing spikes radiate from the ear like fingers from the hand, in India long and slender, like César Franck's, in Africa short and stubby, like Wolfgang Amadeus Mozart's. If you have trouble with crab grass on your lawn, you might try forgetting the lawn, cultivating the crab grass and, when and if it produces seed, eating the grain: Africans do. It is *E. indica*. *P. glaucum*, pearl millet, popular in India and Africa, may grow as high as ten feet, giving good yields even with little moisture and inferior soil. *P. spicatum* has an ear which is a long, thin cylinder surrounding the tip of its stalk, and is therefore called the bulrush millet in English and candle millet by the French—and also sometimes, by taxonomists, *P. americanum*, one wonders why, for though its origin is unknown it is almost certainly not American.

A specialty of millets is producing what might be called tailor-made varieties to fit the very exigent peculiar specifications of small areas. *Panicum miliaire*, little millet, is grown almost exclusively straddling the Tropic of Cancer in India, where it is without importance on the national scale but is the absolutely indispensable staple food of the states of Madhya Pradesh and Uttar Pradesh. *Digitaria exilis* is confined to a few particularly dry areas in West Africa and Nigeria, where it is called "hungry rice," possibly because it is the sole recourse against famine, possibly because it is itself so voracious in extracting nourishment from a grudging soil. "Native millet," meaning various species of *Paspalum*, is grown here and there in limited areas of Africa, even *P. scrobiculatum*, which is suspected of being toxic, but the natives eat it all the same. Peculiar to the Philippines and a few other localities in southern Asia is the picturesquely named *Coix lachryma-jobi*, "Job's tears," which some botanists refuse to classify with millets because of the size of the large grains which give it its name, which is also one of the objections raised in the case of sorghum.

The outstanding example of a millet of vital importance in one area and of none at all elsewhere is the Ethiopian *Eragrostis abyssinica*, popularly called *tef*. Instead of being used for gruel, it goes into flatbread, which looks very much like Mexican tortillas and is used in the same way, to convey to the mouth other foods ladled onto it.

"I would not say *tef* is really a millet [it is, though]," Mr. Grandjouan wrote me. "It is, as far as I can remember, a biggish grass (looking a little like blue grass) which is virtually the only food grain crop of Ethiopia. It bears a multitude of very tiny seeds, pinhead size. . . . During two months or three in Addis Ababa, my wife and I had, once or twice a week, the product of Ethiopian bread-making. It is called *injera* in Amharic, is usually (at least every Sunday) eaten with a fierce stew called *watt*, made of meat and very hot chillies, and looks, to all intents and purposes, like a towel soaked in mud."

MIN
stands for

mink, a nasty-tempered animal which is likely nowadays to get in the first bite itself, but was eaten in prehistoric times by the Indians of New England; and for **minnows**, fish too small to interest most eaters except Africans just south of the tropical zone and Finns just north of the temperate one.

MINT. *Woodcut from John Gerard:* Herball or General Historie of Plantes, *London, 1597*

And **MIN** also stands for

MINT. A good many years ago, exploring the ruins of Ostia Antica, the chief port of ancient Rome, I sensed that I was crushing plants beneath my feet and backed off hastily as a sweet, pungent fragrance rose around me. I had been walking on mint—mint planted there two thousand years earlier and still alive. It is the destiny of mint to be crushed. Its name comes from the myth of the nymph Minthe, who was surprised by Persephone in the arms of her husband, Pluto; Persephone threw her to the ground and trampled on her. But, Ovid assures us, she lives on as mint. Planting paths with sweet-smelling herbs in order to walk on them and enjoy the protesting perfume of the bruised plants was a refined pleasure practiced by the Elizabethans. "Those which perfume the air most delightfully," wrote Sir Francis Bacon, "being trodden upon and crushed, are three—that is burnet, wild thyme and watermints: therefore you are to set whole alleys of them to have the pleasure when you walk or tread."

The species I trod upon at Ostia was in all probability *Mentha pulegium*, excellent for providing ground cover and for allowing itself to be walked over, for it is a creeping variety only about two inches high. We call it pennyroyal, a pretty name which, unfortunately, means "flea plant." It was believed to attract and kill fleas; it was thus one of the most favored mints for strewing on dining-room floors to sweeten the room in a period which was accustomed to throw its leftovers under the table to feed the dogs. Albertus Magnus reported, for the benefit of anyone faced with this problem, "that drowning bees and flies may be revived if placed in warm ashes thereof: they shall recover their lyfe after a little tyme." However, it was water mint which John Gerard held "to be good against the stinging of bees and wasps, if the place be rubbed therewith." It may or may not have been pennyroyal which went into the herb brush used in the nineteenth century to swab the interior of a new hive with brown sugar or honey to persuade swarming bees to accept it as a residence, but it was balsam mint which in the seventeenth was rubbed on the landing shelves of dovecotes to persuade pigeons, who were supposed to dote on it, to remain faithful to the home roost.

Pennyroyal is supposed to have been an ingredient of the sacred drink, *kykeōn*, probably unpleasant, which ancient Greeks seeking initiation into the Eleusinian mysteries were required to gag down; was it also the mint among the bitter herbs which the Hebrews were enjoined to eat at Passover? It was in any case the species which disciples of Bacchus wore as wreaths upon their heads to dispel drunkenness. ("A Garland of Pennie-Royal," John Gerard wrote many centuries later, "made and worne about the head is of great force against the swimming in the head, and the paines and giddiness thereof.") Greek girls wove pennyroyal into wreaths too, for brides, but there seem to have been for this custom no reasons more exotic than that the long, flexible stems of pennyroyal are easy to braid, that its flowers are abundant and that its odor is festive. Gerard instructs us on another use for pennyroyal: "If you have when you are at the Sea Penny Royal in great quantities dry, and cast it into corrupt water, it helpeth it much, neither will it hurt them that drinke thereof." In his time pennyroyal seems to have been used commonly in food, for he also calls it pudding-grass.

There are so many different kinds of mint that Walafrid Strabon, the medieval abbot of Reichenau whose nickname was Geoffroy the Cross-Eyed, wrote that anyone who wanted to enumerate them needed to be capable of counting all the fish in the Red Sea or the number of sparks thrown out by Etna in eruption. This is a considerable exaggeration, for though the mint family, *Labiatae*, contains over 2000 species, divided among 150 genera, only one genus, *Mentha*, is allotted to true mints, with somewhere between 25 and 40 species. It is true that mint hybridizes easily, and has produced any number of subspecies, varieties and subvarieties, often difficult to tell apart.

All mints are relatively pungent because of their volatile oil, containing menthol, carried in resinous dots on the stems and leaves. "The smell of mint stirs up the mind and appetite to a greedy desire for food," wrote Pliny, and Gerard added that "the savor or smell of the water mint rejoyceth the heart of man." Perhaps it rejoyceth not the hearts of fleas and their fellows; mints are very little bothered by insect pests.

"Mintes put into milke," says a cookbook of 1588, "it neyther suffereth the same to curde, nor to become thick, insomuch that layed in curded milke, this would bring the same thinne againe." A modern French authority asserts that cheese cannot be made from the milk of cows which have grazed on mint.

Only two mints are of much commercial importance nowadays, spearmint and peppermint. Neither of them is native to the United States, but they were planted in New England very early and have become so thoroughly naturalized that both are now found growing wild throughout the country. Spearmint, *M. spicata*, is believed to be the oldest of all mints, perhaps the one mentioned in the Bible, probably the one called by the ancient Romans *menta* when cultivated and *mentastratum* when wild.

Peppermint, *M. piperita*, also called brandy mint because it is the kind used oftenest in alcoholic drinks, is a newcomer, which seems to have been first discovered in Hertfordshire in 1696. It is cultivated in England most assiduously in Mitcham, Surrey, and is accordingly called Mitcham mint. Almost all French peppermint comes from Milly-la-Forêt, where Jean Cocteau lived and is buried, but it would no doubt be farfetched to attribute to the influence of peppermint the *enfant terrible* character of Cocteau's writings.

Peppermint has a strong taste of menthol, not noticeable in spearmint; the high menthol content accounts for a characteristic sensation of coolness which invades the mouth after the original pungency has died away. There are many varieties of peppermint, but for trade purposes they are all grouped under two heads, the purple-stemmed black peppermints and the white peppermints. Black peppermint is the kind most grown in the United States because it yields more oil, of which the United States is the world's biggest producer, supplying nearly three-quarters of the total demand. White peppermint is less hardy and less productive, but its oil has a more delicate flavor and commands a higher price.

Many of the wild mints, plus some still cultivated in home herb gardens but not for sale in markets, have delicate and subtle flavors whose natures are often indicated by their popular names—apple mint, bergamot mint, pineapple mint, citrus mint, orange mint. Many herb fanciers regret that these and other varieties have been driven off the market by the brasher spearmint and peppermint; if I were better acquainted with them myself I would perhaps have been more appreciative of mint, which I had ranked rather low and was surprised when I discovered that it is the most widely used of all aromatic herbs; recipes for mint outnumber by far those for all the others. As it is, I still feel that mint is too strong for most of the uses to which it is put; but at least I do not side with the *Dictionnaire de l'Académie des Gastronomes,* which writes loftily: "To go so far as to discuss rare roast beef with mint sauce, which is the delight of certain foreign [sneer!] tables, would be beneath us, for we are concerned with honesty and reason, not barbarity."

MIR
stands for

mirabelle, a small European plum which the chronicler of the Magellan expedition is reported to have encountered on the island of Borneo, but perhaps he was betrayed by his translator; for the **miraculous berry** of Africa, so called because it sweetens acid fruits and even vinegar; for the **mirliton,** or vegetable pear, which is not a pear but a squash; and for the **mirror carp,** a species created accidentally by breeders, who thus achieved the tastiest of all CARP by mistake.

MIS
stands for

mispel, which is not a mispelling of mispell, but a South African version of the prickly pear; for the **mission** FIG, introduced into California in the seventeenth century by Spanish friars and still going strong in the twentieth, and the **mission grape,** ditto; for **misticanza,** a salad plant regarded with mystical veneration in Rome, but not elsewhere, since it is nothing other than the lowly vegetable known in English as rockets; and for **mites,** which seem to have been appreciated as food only by prehistoric Indians in what are now Arkansas, Missouri and Mexico.

MOL
stands for

molasses, of which Thoreau wrote improbably that "I found I could make a very good molasses either of pumpkins or beets"; for **mollusks,** a versatile family of sea animals, including a few which have moved to land, exemplified by such tasty members as CLAMS, MUSSELS, OYSTERS, SCALLOPS, snails and squid; and for **moly,** the magic plant which prevented Circe from turning Ulysses into a pig but which in its present incarnation, as a sort of onion, is incapable of preventing men from making pigs of themselves with no help from Circe.

MOM
stands for

mombin, a tropical African fruit which suggests a plum and has, I believe, been grown experimentally in southern Florida, but my filing system, if it is privy to this fact, refuses to disgorge it.

MON
stands for

the **monarch,** a pear named anonymously, if one dares put it that way, for William IV, who ascended the throne the year before it was developed; for the **money clam,** which is not, as you might expect, the eastern quahog which Atlantic coast Indians cut up into wampum, but a western clam which Pacific coast Indians used intact for money; for the **mongongo nut,** unknown to my dictionaries, which if you believe vegetarian writer Janet Barkas constitutes 50 percent by weight of all the food eaten by the Kung bushmen of African Botswana; for the **mongoose,** eaten in Borneo by prehistoric man and in South Africa and Chad by contemporary man; and for the **monitor,** a large lizard relished, so far as I know, by no one except tropical Africans.

MON
stands for

the **monkey,** which caused strained relations between Zaïre and Egypt when hotel cooks in Alexandria refused to cook for the Zaïre soccer team the monkeys it had foresightedly brought along with it to provide proper provender for their athletes in a country which they had correctly expected might be deficient in it; for the **monkey apple,** a tropical African fruit sometimes compared to a plum, and the **monkey ball,** a tropical African fruit sometimes compared to an orange;

for **monkey bread**, an African fruit so full of starch that it can be converted into meal; for the **monkey guava**, another African fruit which the French call the bush persimmon; for the **monkey nut**, which is simply the peanut; for the **monkey puzzle**, or Chile pine, with edible seeds, thus named because its branches intertwine in a fashion so inextricable that they constitute a maze for monkeys; and for the **monkey star apple**, which was simply the star apple in its native tropical America but expanded its name when, transplanted to Africa, it appealed not only to human but also to non-human primates.

MON
stands for

monkfish, a form of anglerfish; for **monosodium glutamate**, known chummily as MSG, a taste enhancer derived from seaweed, which has been accused of causing the allergic reaction known as the Chinese Restaurant Syndrome, an ailment unknown in China; and for the **monstera deliciosa** ("delicious monster"), otherwise the ceriman, a tropical American fruit which looks like a pale-green banana covered with lizardlike plates.

MOO
stands for

moonfish, or perhaps one should say moonfishes, for the name is bestowed generously on at least four unrelated edible fish, of which one is consumed in the Caribbean, while the three others are eaten extensively in Africa, including one which, because of the resolute shape of its jaw, is also called Mussolini; for the **moonflower**, whose leaves seem to be eaten nowhere except in Sierra Leone; for **moon shells**, found on both Atlantic and Pacific coasts of the United States, which do not particularly recall the moon but may have been so named to disguise from timid eaters that they are really seagoing snails; for the **moorhen**, which the Middle Ages tried to domesticate, but the moorhen refused; for the **Moorish idol**, a highly decorative fish with an original name whose meaning is mysterious, but as it has gone out of style, if you want to buy it on the markets of Hawaii today you had better ask for *kihikihi*; for **moose**, of which Thoreau said that the nose was the choicest morsel and the tongue came second; and for **mooseberries**, eaten of course by the moose, but also by Thoreau.

MOR
stands for

the **moray**, an edible eel-like fish, which, we are told by no less an authority than the ancient Greek writer Oppian of Corycus, leaves the sea from time to time to mate with serpents; for the **morel**, a hollow, convoluted black mushroom which is called in Scandinavia "the truffle of the north"; for the **morello**, a sour cherry whose name announces that it is black, though some perverse persons persist in calling amarelles "red morellos"; for the **Moreton Bay bug** of Queensland, Australia, a libelous name for a delicious crustacean somewhere between a crab and a crawfish, and the **Moreton Bay chestnut**, an over-complimentary name for a nut which, if you fail to soak and roast it as the aborigines do, may make you ill; and for the **moringa**, an African tree from whose seeds the ancient Egyptians pressed an important cooking oil.

MOS
stands for

moscardini, tiny Italian cuttlefish also known as sea strawberries; for **mosquitoes**, eaten by ancient Aztecs and modern tropical Africans; and for **moss**, in the Middle Ages a monotonous but not uncommon food, and in ours an ingredient for jelly, blancmange and ice cream (but it is true that we cheat, for our Irish moss comes from seaweed).

MOT
stands for

moths, notably bugong and ghost moths, eaten by Australian aborigines, whose gourmets prefer them in caterpillar form; for the **moth bean**, a specialty of India; and for **moth mullein**, our fifteenth name for this plant.

MOU
stands for

mouflon, a wild sheep which Homeric Greeks hunted under the impression that it was a wild goat; for the **mountain apple**, a native of India and Malaysia, which bears crimson fruit a little smaller than a tennis ball, filled with slightly sweetish white pulp which offers little nourishment but is pleasantly refreshing for the thirsty hiker in hot countries; for the **mountain ash**, which produces clusters of small bright-red fruit, edible if it is the sort called the sorb apple, but if you happen on the wrong kind of mountain ash don't blame me; for the **mountain goat**, which has been described as tasting like pastrami, but only after having been soaked in milk to reduce its gaminess; for **mountain lettuce**, a sort of saxifrage which grows from Pennsylvania to Georgia and provides tasty cooked greens while its leaves are still young and tender; for **mountain mint**, a not very successful imitation of the real thing by another genus of the mint family than the one patronized by real mint; for **mountain misery**, a heavily scented herb of California's High Sierra called *kit-kit-dizze* by the Miwok Indians, who look upon the tea made from its leaves as a panacea; for the **mountain pawpaw**, a pawpaw which differs from the ordinary variety in that it has to be cooked before eating and, of course, in that it grows higher; and for the **mountain plover**, a shore bird rarely found on a shore.

MOU
stands for

the **mourning dove**, found in all of the forty-eight contiguous states and eaten with delight wherever game laws permit; and for **mouse**, of which the going price varied between a ducat and half a ducat on Magellan's ships when they ran out of food after rounding the tip of South America.

MUD
stands for

mudbug, a disrespectful way of referring to the crawfish; for the **mud crab**, an inhabitant of salt marshes on America's Atlantic coast; for the **mudfish**, which is either the air-breathing living fossil eaten in the southern United States or a much more ordinary animal using the same name, appreciated in southern and tropical Africa; for the **mud hen**, the unappetizing name given to the rail in Louisiana, where it is eaten all the same; for the **mud minnow**, which is not a minnow, but does live in the mud; for the **mudskipper**, a goby large enough to be eaten, so it is, in West Africa; and for the **mudsucker**, rather inaccurately known as the African carp.

MUK
stands for

muktuk, a delicacy which it should be safe to describe as restricted to Eskimos, as there seem to be no other connoisseurs of narwhal skin.

MUL
stands for

the **mulato**, a large, dark, relatively pungent chili popular in Latin America; for the **mule**, which anthropologist Lloyd Cabot Briggs wrote me he was offered in Spain "as a rather special delicacy [which] I found to be the best equine meat of all"; and for the **mullein**, which John Gerard told us "is called in shops, *Tapsus Barbatus*: of divers, *Candela Regia, Candelaria*, and *Lanaria*: in French, *Bouillon*; in English, Mullein, or rather Woolen, Higtaper, Torches, Longwort, and Bullocks Longwort; and of some, Hares beard."

And **MUL** also stands for

MULBERRY. "A tedious brief scene," Shakespeare called the play-within-a-play acted in *A Midsummer Night's Dream* by Bottom and his company of "hard-handed men, that work in Athens." Bottom's play, the story of Pyramus and Thisby, was cribbed from Ovid's *Metamorphoses*, and, possibly tedious, is at any rate not brief enough to be recounted here, except for its ending, when both of the two lovers commit suicide, shedding so much blood as to soak the roots of the tree under whose branches this double death took place, causing its white fruit to turn red forever. The tree was a mulberry.

Ovid, when he produced this explanation for the color of a blackberry-like fruit, which is actually more closely related to the fig, drew upon his imagination when he conceived of a mulberry originally white. There *is* a white mulberry, *Morus alba*, but the ancient Romans did not know it. They had the black mulberry, *Morus nigra*, probably a native of Persia, which was not quite the color of blood but more of a dark purple. Ovid could not have convinced modern botanists that any amount of drenching with blood would explain the mulberry's color, nor would Pliny have gotten along with them any better when he asserted that blood-red apples were produced by grafting apple branches onto mulberry trees: apple wood will not develop on mulberry stock, and even if it did, that would not affect the color of the fruit.

The ancients held the mulberry in more esteem than we do. For us it is a home-grown fruit, restricted to those people fortunate enough to have space to raise mulberries, or a wild one, destined to be picked and eaten immediately. You will not find mulberries on the market, for they are perishable, easily bruised in handling and difficult to keep or store.

The black mulberry was being cultivated at least four thousand years ago. We know it was grown in Mesopotamia, where its seeds have been excavated from ancient ruins, and in early Egypt, where they have been found in tombs. II Samuel and I Chronicles both report the same military action in which David surprised the Philistines by slipping behind them under cover of a grove of mulberry trees. Mulberries were eaten early in Greece, though the fruit mentioned by Homer was probably not the mulberry but the blackberry. Virgil depicted a naiad smearing the face of a drunken slumbering Silenus with mulberry juice, and Horace told us that mulberries constituted a healthy ending for meals taken during the heat of summer, to which Pliny rejoined that this was precisely not the right occasion for eating them. Pliny also informed us that the mulberry was the wisest of all trees, for it refrained from budding until all danger of frost was over, when it burst into full flower overnight, making a great noise as it did so.

The progress of the black mulberry northward from Italy during the Middle Ages seems to have been spotty and intermittent. We have no solidly documented information about it between Charlemagne and Henry IV. Charlemagne ordered mulberries planted on his domains, which does not necessarily mean that anyone actually carried out his instructions. The Duc de Sully, minister to Henry IV, commissioned the sixteenth-century agricultural expert Olivier de Serres to import eight thousand mulberry trees from Italy, which were planted on the grounds of the Sully château at Rosny-sur-Seine; Henry IV subsequently had others planted for ornament in the Tuileries Gardens and along the banks of the Seine. It was also in the sixteenth century that mulberries were planted, apparently for the first time, in Württemberg, Germany, but it seems to have been to feed silkworms rather than people. The fruit probably reached England during the same century, in time to get into *A Midsummer Night's Dream,* written about 1595, and to give a name to a London establishment which John Evelyn, the diarist, referred to in 1654 as "Mulberry Garden, now the only place of refreshment about the town for persons of the best quality to be exceedingly cheated at."

The black mulberry is the tastiest of the twelve species of this fruit, which grow in the temperate zone of the Northern Hemisphere, most opulently in the warmer areas, or at moderately high altitudes in the tropics; they are all Asian in origin except one, which is American. Many people would agree with Joan M. Jungfleisch that "mulberries tend on the whole to be rather sweet but tasteless"; however, their flavor can be greatly improved by growing them in greenhouses, while you can also find superior fruit by shopping, so to speak, among wild mulberries—one tree will bear mediocre fruit, while that of the tree next to it may be superb.

The white mulberry, *Morus alba,* is the most insipid of the three chief mulberries of the world, sugary to excess, devoid of any relieving acidity,

MULBERRY. *Woodcut by David Kandel from Hieronymus Bosch:* De Stirpium, *Strassburg, 1552*

and with no other flavor than an empty sweetness. Alexandre Dumas said it was suitable for feeding to barnyard poultry. Nevertheless, this is the species which is a staple food in Afghanistan, where it replaces bread during certain months of the year, while Syrians also sun-dry mulberries and grind them up for flour.

Elsewhere the white mulberry is valued chiefly as food for silkworms, which is what it was used for in China, where it probably originated. It was introduced into Italy for this purpose in 1596, where it was later supplanted by one of its offspring, *M. alba* var. *multicaulis,* the highly esteemed Philippine mulberry, now considered the best for raising silkworms. This was the variety introduced into Georgia in Colonial times, on the optimistic theory that a Georgia silk-producing industry would give employment to twenty thousand people in America and as many more in England. The failure of this enterprise did not result from using the wrong mulberry or the wrong silkworm, but from having the wrong climate. (But Virginia kept silkworms alive on mulberry trees long enough to provide the material for the coronation robe worn by Charles II in 1660.)

The only American species, the red mulberry, *M. rubra*, is much tastier than the white mulberry, but less so than the black. Its original range extended along the East Coast from New England to Florida and thence west to Texas; but it has since been introduced into all parts of the country, and wherever it finds favorable conditions produces abundantly, though never better than in the South. There it was already so important in pre-Columbian times that the Natchez Indians of Louisiana named one of their thirteen months for it.

MULLET. The name of the fish known to the ancient Romans as *mugil* entered the English language, through the devious processes of etymology, as "mullet." Unfortunately, the name of the fish known to the ancient Romans as *mullus* also emigrated into English as "mullet." This confusion has bedeviled us ever since, and though we have tried to keep them separate by referring to the first as the gray mullet and to the second as the red mullet, most people, I imagine, think of them as different varieties of the same fish. They are in fact quite distinct. The gray mullet belongs to the family *Mugildae* and the genus *Mugil*; the red mullet belongs to the family *Mullidae* and the genus *Mullus* (known less formally as goatfish). There are between seventy and one hundred species of *Mugil*, found in most of the tropical and temperate waters of the world (and off both the Atlantic and Pacific coasts of the United States), of which seven or eight are of considerable importance as food fish, and about forty species of *Mullus*, most of them in the tropical and subtropical zones of the Indo-Pacific ocean; but the two which demand our attention inhabit the Mediterranean. One of the two, *M. surmuletus*, the striped mullet, ventures out of this sea and swims north along the Atlantic coast of Europe as far as England and Normandy, which permitted Balzac to write of "the honor of Norman tables, the red mullet," in which he was echoing Brillat-Savarin, who had called it an "exquisite fish."

Of the two mullets, the red mullet is by far the tastiest. Grilled, its flesh is dry, firm and flaky, and with a strange richness which suggests, oddly for a fish, the redolence of game. This might account for the description of the red mullet, attributed to Brillat-Savarin, as "the woodcock of the sea." As a matter of fact I believe that it was not Brillat-Savarin who first produced this nickname but Grimod de la Reynière, and he was not thinking of the fish's flavor. He compared it to the woodcock, which is cooked without having been cleaned, because the red mullet, which secretes no bile, can also be cooked without cleaning. An alternative method, in the days when cooks went to more trouble than they ordinarily do nowadays, was to remove the mullet's internal organs through the gills, so that the fish could be presented intact and appear to full advantage in its unusual pink color.

The ancient Greeks thought the red mullet one of their finest fish and dedicated it to Hecate, but they never lost their heads over it as the Romans did. The latter abandoned themselves to a red mullet craze which can only be compared to the tulipomania which seized Holland in 1637, when a single tulip bulb was sold for 2600 guilders. I have no idea how this sum in seventeenth-century Holland compares in purchasing power with the sixty gold pieces the knight Crispinus paid for a single red mullet in second-century Rome, but I imagine that they represent about the same level of madness.

When the Emperor Tiberius heard that three red mullets had been sold on the market for 3000 sesterces, he was so shocked that he imposed a price ceiling on them, but apparently it didn't take, for in the following reign, that of Caligula, a three-and-a-half-pound mullet (about the top weight for this fish) was sold for 6000 sesterces. One modern calculator has estimated that the three mullets whose cost appalled Tiberius brought a price equivalent to $400 per fish today, and a second calculator put the 6000-sesterce fish at $1000. The wide spread between these two figures makes it evident that comparisons in terms of money are meaningless; it is more significant to know that when Asinio Celer bought a large red mullet for 8000 sesterces he could have had, for the same amount, four yoke of oxen. The demand for red mullet was such that Juvenal wrote: "My lord will have his mullet, imported from Corsica or from / The rocks below Taormina: home waters are all fished out." Rome also imported red mullets from Marseilles; the small fish, hardly larger than sardines, found along the coast from Marseilles to San Remo, were considered the most flavorful of all red mullets, and they are still.

MULLET. *Drawing by Norman Weaver from Edward Migdalski:* The Fresh and Salt Water Fishes of the World, *New York, 1976*

You have probably read that ancient Roman banqueters took pleasure in watching the changing colors of fish boiled alive in glass bowls placed on dinner tables; the fish so treated was the red mullet. The practice so impressed writers that they repeated the story again and again (it seems to have started with Varro in the first century B.C.), but it would be my guess that this was an exceptional act, staged by some host who wanted to astound his guests by this refinement, if that is the right word for it, which may have been repeated by one or two others; I doubt if it ever became common. The many writers who tell us about this spectacle refrain from asserting that they were ever themselves eyewitnesses to it, and Pliny makes it plain that he was not.

If the gray mullet, a larger fish than the red mullet, up to twelve pounds, cannot match the red mullet in flavor, it is nevertheless a fish tasty enough so that it was named as a luxury food, in the same breath with the red mullet, in the medieval *Roman du Comte d'Anjou.* The *Dictionnaire de l'Académie des Gastronomes* describes its flesh as "very white and very light . . . as good as that of the sea perch." The Roman emperors appreciated this fish too, and it is now thought that the once mysterious tanks at Orbetello were gray mullet traps, to take the fish in this fashion because the ancients believed that touching its scales injured it and netting it killed it. Modern experience does not bear this out, but it is true that British fishermen, who like to go after this prize because it is difficult to hook, difficult to land, and a good fighter, often lose gray mullet which have taken the bait because the hook tears itself out of the fish's tender mouth.

Gray mullet offer the closest approach of any ocean fish to freshwater fishing (some anglers even use a float), and it takes a most terrestrial bait—boiled macaroni. This is consistent with the character of a fish which can shift more or less instantaneously from salt to fresh water or vice versa without showing any signs of inconvenience; there is a theory that some rapid chemical adjustment occurs in its body with a change in the salinity of the water, but no one yet knows how it works. Although it is a migratory schooling fish of the high seas, the gray mullet is partial to brackish waters and often runs far up rivers with the tide; if it doesn't get back, it doesn't seem to mind. The classic example of the gray mullet's versatile nature you can witness for yourself if you visit Syracuse, Sicily. The Fountain of Arethusa there was described by Cicero as "an incredibly large spring, teeming with fish, and so placed that it would be swamped by the waves of the sea were it not for the protection of a massive stone wall." I do not know what species of fish Cicero saw there, but today the spring, with its massive flow of the freshest of fresh water, is full of ocean mullet. Some centuries ago an earthquake breached the wall, letting in the sea and the mullet with it. When the wall was repaired, the mullet stayed, and they flourish still.

MUN
stands for

the **mung bean,** which provides the bean sprouts

used in Chinese restaurants and can be grown in your own home if you so desire.

MUR
stands for

murex, an edible Mediterranean shellfish whose chief claim to fame is that it produced the imperial purple dye for the togas of Roman emperors; for the **murgentina,** a grape transplanted in ancient times from the volcanic soil of Sicily to the volcanic soil of Pompeii, where it flourished until A.D. 79; for **murlin,** the edible seaweed otherwise known as dabberlocks; for the **murre,** an auk-like bird of the North American Atlantic coast which lays pyriform eggs on cliff ledges so that if disturbed they roll in a circle instead of over the edge, and the **murrelet,** an auk-like bird of the North American Pacific coast of which the marbled variety provides "the greatest unsolved mystery in American field ornithology" because nobody knows where it lays its eggs; and for the **murrel,** or snakehead, an air-breathing fish capable of surviving for several months buried in mud unless in the meantime it has the misfortune to be disinterred in Africa or South Asia, where it is an important food.

MUS
stands for

muscari, the grape hyacinth, whose bulbs were eaten in antiquity; for the **muscat grape,** the sire of particularly luscious raisins; for the **Muscovy duck,** which has nothing to do with Moscow, its name being simply an error for "musk duck"; for **musk,** a much misused and abused word, which will be taken here to mean the plant whose leaves were used in salads in medieval times; for the **muskellunge,** a Great Lakes PIKE which is the largest species of this family; for the **musk mallow,** which is the abelmosk, used to clarify sugar in northern India; for **muskmelon,** whose secrets are revealed in the entry MELON; for the **musk ox,** whose meat is excellent, and the **muskrat,** whose meat is less excellent but is eaten in Louisiana all the same under the euphemism "marsh hare"; for the **mussel crab,** which lives inside the shellfish for which it is named and should not be evicted, for, cooked with the mussel, it constitutes a natural seasoning; and for the **mustard tree,** unrelated to mustard, whose leaves are eaten in East and West Africa.

And **MUS** also stands for

 MUSHROOM. "Fungi ben mussherons," says the *Grete Herball*, published in 1526. "There be two manners of them; one manner is deedly and sleeth them that eateth of them and be called tode stooles, and the other dooth not. They that be not deedly have a grosse gleymy [slimy] moysture that is dysobedyent to nature and dygestyon, and be peryllous and dredful to eate & therefor it is good to eschew them."

Well, mussherons ben fungi, but fungi ben not mussherons, at least not all of them. There are believed to be about 100,000 species of fungi, but less than half of them are mushrooms, or at least what you and I call mushrooms. The botanist is more broad-minded, and has no objection to referring to all fungi—yeasts, lichens, penicillin, etc.—as mushrooms, but on the other hand he might shy away from calling mushrooms "mushrooms"; he is more likely to speak of them as "fruiting bodies," a comparatively rare phenomenon produced by the main body of the mushroom, which remains underground. The botanist is more accurate, but let us stick here to the popular terminology. Scientists and laymen can meet on the proposition that there is no biological justification for distinguishing between "tode stooles" and "mussherons" on grounds of edibility; most botanists avoid the word "toadstools" altogether.

How many mushrooms are good to eat? If you believe the *Grete Herball*, none. Non-believers are numerous enough so that some two thousand species are eaten throughout the world, the kinds varying according to the eating habits and, of course, the available species of each area. About eighty species are eaten in France, but only twenty are found on the market. Finnish markets can produce fifty. Great Britain and the United States are underprivileged when it comes to mushrooms. In both countries only one mushroom is offered in markets and restaurants, and even that one, *Agaricus bisporus*, in cultivated form only, is characterless in comparison with its wild cousins, like the common meadow mushroom, *A. campestris*. In both countries, the rich and varied flavors of wild mushrooms are known only to those who gather their own.

How many mushrooms are dangerous? Fewer, probably, than you think. Eliminating those which are simply hard to digest, as many foods are hard to digest, one expert counts thirty-two species (out of perhaps 40,000) which are known to be definitely toxic; different authorities name from five to nine which can be "deadly"; and there is one which provokes almost certain death —*Amanita phalloides*, the deadly amanita or death cup, which accounts for between 90 and 95 percent of all deaths from mushroom poisoning.

Statistically, the danger of dying from eating

MUSHROOM *by John Ruhlander. Glass paperweight, Millville, New Jersey, 1890–1910*

the wrong mushroom is not great; but nobody wants to become a statistic (and nothing else) despite the honor of being a *rare* statistic. Hence, no doubt, the bad press which has afflicted the mushroom for two millennia. Hippocrates, it is true, used mushrooms both as a food and a medicine, but he did not forget to warn us of their potential toxicity. Euripides stressed their dangerous character, as well he might if it is true that he lost his wife, two sons and a daughter to mushroom poisoning. Seneca said that mushrooms "are not really food, but are relished to bully the sated stomach into further eating." Athenaeus informed us that "few of them are good and most produce a choking sensation" (but forgetfully wrote in another passage of the same work that mushrooms are "good for the stomach and pass easily through the bowels and are very nutritious"). Diderot said in the *Encyclopédie* that "whatever dressing one gives to them, to whatever sauce our Apiciuses put them, they are not really good but to be sent back to the dung heap where they are born." This was also the opinion of Edmund Gayton, who told us in the seventeenth century that:

Pepper and oyl and salt, nay all cook's art,
Can no way wholesomeness to them impart.

Spenser, who was in on the very beginning of mushroom eating in England, called the mushroom a "grislie Todestool." Keats, Shelley and Tennyson all took swipes at it, and in our own time, D. H. Lawrence compared "the beastly bourgeois," for whom one gathers he had little sympathy, to "an old mushroom, all wormy inside, and hollow." Emily Dickinson likened the mushroom to Judas Iscariot.

To the frequent charge that the mushroom is not nutritive, one can oppose the observation of Charles Darwin, in the *Voyage of the Beagle*, apropos of a Patagonian mushroom:

> In Tierra del Fuego the fungus in its tough and native state is collected in large quantities by the women and children and is eaten uncooked. . . . With the exception of a few berries, chiefly of a dwarf arbutus, the natives eat no vegetable food besides this fungus.

It is also significant that for the aborigines of Australia mushrooms were "blackfellows' bread." Mushrooms have no sugars (and are therefore a good food for diabetics), not much carbohydrate, and that mostly in the form of indigestible cellulose (and are therefore a good food for weight-watchers), many minerals and vitamins (varying with the species of mushroom) and above all a good deal of protein (not all of it assimilable), which has caused them to be described as closer to meat than any other vegetable.

The most widely eaten wild mushroom in the world is probably the boletus, of which *Boletus edulis*, the most admired species, which tastes vaguely of raw chestnuts, is the celebrated *cèpe* of France. In Germany it is the *Steinpilz*, "stone mushroom," but it is also called the *Herrenpilz*, which might be translated "the master mushroom." The name "Caesar's mushroom," given to the one which many connoisseurs consider the tastiest in the world, may have been conceived in the same spirit, in tribute to its imperial quality, rather than to the fact that the Emperor Claudius was eating them when his wife Agrippina added a few *Amanita phalloides* to the dish, thus succeeding in her objective of putting her son, Nero, on the throne. It is perhaps because of the ease with which *A. caesarea* can be confused with *A. phalloides* that it is not as widely eaten as the boletus. The Italian term for the boletus is *fungo porcino*, "pig mushroom," which sounds less than complimentary, but it refers simply to the fondness shown for this mushroom by pigs turned into the woods to fatten on acorns. The opinion of the pig is not to be disdained in this domain; it is, after all, the animal which roots up truffles.

B. edulis is common in the United States, and

so are many other delicious mushrooms ignored at home, about which Americans traveling abroad sometimes wax ecstatic in their ignorance. It is rather funny to read an American account of the Japanese *matsutake* "which may very well be the world's most delicious mushroom. Certainly no other mushroom I have eaten ever tasted like steak." The writer thus betrayed his ignorance of such American mushrooms as *Fistulina hepatica*, the beefsteak mushroom, so named precisely because that is what it tastes like; the oyster mushroom, *Pleurotus ostreatus*, which must have been named for its appearance, since it also tastes like meat; the morel, which has been compared variously to sweetbreads, buttery eggplant and country-style steak; the milky cup ("like lamb kidneys done up in crumbs"); the shaggy-mane ("a slightly meaty taste combined with something like the perfume of burning leaves"); and several others which suggest meat. As for the *matsutake*, it is *Armilleria ponderosa*, known in the Pacific Northwest, where it grows abundantly, as the pine mushroom. The United States also offers the puffball, an enormous sphere of which some species grow to the size of a football, from which one-foot slices can be cut off and fried in butter, to delicious effect; the chanterelle, which, according to Tom Robbins, writing in the *Seattle Magazine*, "looks like a ruffled yellow trumpet, smells like apricots, has the consistency of chicken and tastes like eggs scrambled in wood smoke and wine"; and *Craterellus cornucopioides*, which the French must have named the death trumpet to scare others off and keep for themselves a mushroom which is eminently edible and tastes like truffles.

The most widely eaten cultivated mushroom, the agaric—touted by Tennyson as the "foul-fleshed agaric . . . carrion of some woodland thing"—is the only one generally eaten in America; it accounts for 70 percent of the more than one million tons of artificially grown mushrooms eaten throughout the world.

The first cultivators of mushrooms were ants, which were so good at it that the entomologist Peter Farb has written that "thanks to the numerical superiority which they owe to their prosperity," the mushroom-raising species are the lords of antdom, who measure their gross national product in terms of mushrooms, not money. The first human mushroom cultivators were probably the Japanese, who have been raising the *shii-take* for at least two thousand years. The ancient Greeks and Romans did not really cultivate mushrooms, they simply encouraged wild ones to grow. Mushroom cultivation in the Western world may be said to have really gotten under way when Olivier

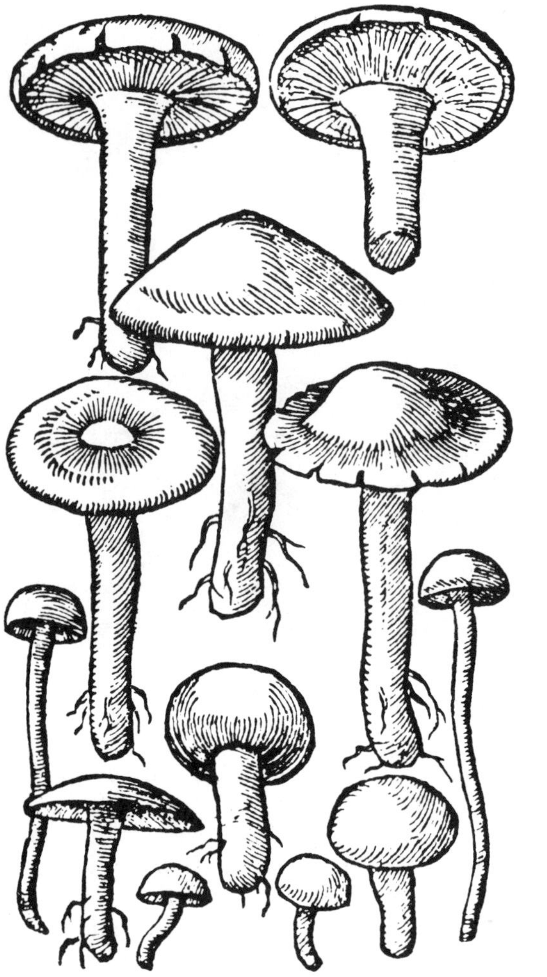

MUSHROOM. *Woodcut from John Gerard:* Herball or General Historie of Plantes, *London, 1597*

de Serres, agronomist to Louis XIV, began experimenting with mushrooms, using the same agaric we are still growing today.

Some mushroom fanciers think Olivier de Serres should have left well enough alone, for the cultivated mushroom provides only a faint echo of the flavor of wild varieties (and the agaric even in the wild state is far from aggressive in the matter of taste). It is possible that generations of inbreeding have caused the flavor of mushrooms to deteriorate. In the last century Balzac wrote ecstatically about the *champignon de Paris*, again the familiar agaric. Commenting sourly on Balzac's enthusiasm, Robert J. Courtine, gastronomic editor of the Paris *Le Monde*, wrote that today these mushrooms are "pure mold, mere toys for chefs," and the novelist Colette declared:

I am in revolt against the mushroom of Paris, an

insipid creature born in the dark and incubated by humidity. I have had enough of it, bathing chopped in all the sauces it thickens. I forbid it to usurp the place of the chanterelle or the truffle; and I command it, together with its fitting companion, canned cocks' combs, never to cross the threshold of my kitchen.

MUSSEL. When I was a boy in New England, the beaches I frequented were usually littered with long, narrow black shells, invariably empty, which I suppose I must have known belonged to mussels, but the idea that this was an edible shellfish never entered my head, nor did anyone I knew ever refer to mussels as food. The mussel occurs on both sides of the Atlantic and it is the same mussel, *Mytilus edulis*, but Europeans eat it and Americans don't. There is a reciprocal prejudice: our soft-shell clam or steamer, *Mya arenaria*, also exists on both sides of the Atlantic, but Americans eat it and Europeans don't. These eating habits go back a long way: prehistoric kitchen middens on the Atlantic coast of Europe are full of mussel shells but contain none of soft-shell clams; on the Atlantic coast of America, they are full of clam shells, but contain few mussel shells.

Why didn't the first Europeans to reach America continue to eat there the familiar shellfish they knew at home? They were all mussel eaters—the French, who settled in Canada; the Dutch, in New Amsterdam; the English, in New England. (We can ignore settlements farther south. *M. edulis* prefers cold water; its range on America's Atlantic coast is from the Arctic to Cape Hatteras.) The usual explanation is that the newcomers stopped eating mussels because the Indians told them American mussels were poisonous, and the Europeans took their word for it.

In 1974 I wrote a newspaper article on clams with a passing reference to the mussel, which brought from Mr. Owen Lattimore an informative letter on the subject.

In the 1940s, the first time my wife and I spent a few weeks on Cape Cod, George Boas, then Professor of Philosophy at the Johns Hopkins . . . told us of a tidal creek where we could find all the mussels we wanted. His wife told us to steam them only in their own moisture content with no added water. Just a cup of white wine for aroma.

Boas told us we'd find plenty of mussels because most of the summer visitors didn't know about them, and the "natives" never touched them. He explained (he comes from Providence, R.I.) [so do I] that all along the New England coast the pre-White Indians were divided between those who ate shellfish and those for whom all shellfish were tabu. Not just one long coastal strip of tabu and one of non-tabu, but sectors of tabu wedged among sectors of non-tabu. Usually, when the white men came, they observed the local rule, and on many bits of coast the old rule still holds, he said.

One would have to know more than I do about the pre-White coastal Indians to venture an explanation, but your statement that mussels "sometimes attach themselves to toxic supports" interests me. It would be striking if pre-White Indian tabu sectors could be identified with pre-White existence of such "toxic supports."

Mussels are indeed the Typhoid Marys of the sea. Not poisonous in themselves, they can pick up toxins from their environment and pass them on to those who eat them. But it is difficult to imagine what toxic elements East Coast mussels could have found to pass on to the Indians before the whites came. One of the chief villains accused

MUSSEL. *Illuminated page "Saint Ambrose" from* The Hours of Catherine of Cleves, *c. 1440, Utrecht, Netherlands*

today of providing poison for the mussel is copper; but the Indians were living in their Stone Age and there was no copper to which mussels could attach themselves. The Indians were not numerous enough or modern enough to pollute the sea with sewage or industrial wastes. They had no problems with oil spills from passing tankers or from chemical pesticides or from radioactivity. What made them think mussels were poisonous?

The Atlantic coast Indians had non-poisonous mussels and were afraid to eat them; the Pacific coast Indians had poisonous mussels and ate them all the same. Nearly half the flesh food consumed by prehistoric Pacific coast Indians was provided by shellfish; and among shellfish, in a kitchen midden found on Catalina Island dated at 4000 to 3500 B.C., two kinds dominated all the others—the abalone and the mussel. Mussels are not edible along the Pacific coast from May through October, but it is not the fault of the mussel (here principally *M. californianus*), it is the fault of its food. When the water warms in spring, the plankton of the Pacific proliferates in great quantity, especially a genus of dinoflagellates, *Gonyaulax*, which contains a powerful poison, saxitoxin. Mussels eat the dinoflagellates, and the saxitoxin becomes concentrated in their livers, often building up to levels dangerous to humans. This is an annual phenomenon, so the Indians had learned to live with it. The proliferation of plankton produces the phenomenon of phosphorescence in the sea. When the water began to glow, the Indians stopped eating mussels; when it returned to normal, the Indians returned to mussels.

The Atlantic coast has its dinoflagellate too, *Gymnopodium brevis*, which when it multiplies in great numbers produces the toxic "red tides," one of which frightened Gloucester fishermen a few years ago when the fish of the area began to die. This is a rare phenomenon, probably because New England waters are too cold to encourage a disproportionate growth of *Gymnopodium*; but precisely because it was rare, strange, unexplained and therefore terrifying, it may have created panic among Indians who were its victims. At a guess, Professor Boas's tabu areas were places where red tides had occurred before the white man came.

Among European mussel eaters, the French claim to have possessed the first mussel farm, in 1235, their national pride no whit diminished by the fact that it was an Irishman who established it, and his achievement, if it can be called that, was the result of a series of mistakes. His first error was to become so unpopular with the police that it seemed advisable to leave Ireland in a hurry. His second was to do so in a boat unequal to its task. His third was to become wrecked on the coast of France. His fourth was to try to feed himself by trapping sea birds. To this end he drove a few stakes into the water at the edge of the beach, in the form of a W, his initial (his name was Patrick Walton), and stretched nets among them. The sea birds declined to fly into the nets, but after a time he noticed that mussels had attached themselves to the stakes and were growing famously there; he shifted from game to seafood. He is also credited with having invented a flat-bottomed boat, named an *acon*, capable of navigating on a heavy dew, to harvest his mussels from their shallow-water habitat.

The stakes are called *bouchots*, and in France today the most prized mussels are *moules de bouchots*, smaller, tenderer, paler and tastier than other kinds, and twice as expensive. Assuming that the tale is true, it does not make Patrick Walton Europe's first mussel cultivator, even if it is not exact, as some writers allege, that the ancients were raising mussels at Taranto about 500 B.C., lowering bundles of branches or ropes into the water for the mussels to cling to. The ancient Gauls seem to have been cultivating mussels before the Romans came; when the Romans arrived they did the same (but in beds, not on stakes); Patrick Walton's *acon* is mentioned in the capitularies of Charlemagne only about A.D. 800.

France today has planted more than 600 miles of *bouchots* along its Atlantic coast, producing about 45,000 tons of mussels a year, which is only half of what the country consumes. The rest is imported, chiefly from Spain. France cannot look north for them, for Belgians are heavy mussel eaters too, consuming not only all of their own but Holland's surplus as well, which is not of *moules de bouchots*, but deepwater mussels, harvested by dredging.

Moules et frites (or *mosselen met friten*) [Jan Sjöby wrote in the *International Herald Tribune* in 1974] are to a Belgian what a hot dog or a hamburger is to an American. Street stands with mussels, French fries, and boiled sea snails are found all over this small kingdom, with a heavy concentration in the more popular quarters of Brussels. Sidewalk mussels are eaten raw at the stand or carried to the nearest corner café to be washed down with a glass of beer.

Earlier in the century, Mr. Sjöby would have found Belgians eating "mussels by the cough." It was once a common practice to charge a fixed price for as many mussels as you could eat until you coughed (there is something about mussels from the North Sea which provokes coughing). If you deemed yourself cut off too abruptly, you could put up the same ante again and continue until the second cough, and so on, as long as your appetite, your throat or your pocketbook could stand it.

Mediterranean mussels are of different species from Atlantic mussels. Along the southern coast of France one finds *Mytilus galloprovincialis* and *Modiolus barbatus*, the bearded or hairy mussel. They are larger than the Atlantic *bouchots*, darker in color (deep orange, sometimes verging on red), fleshier and coarser in flavor, with a perceptible hint of iodine. Meridional Frenchmen eat them raw, with a splash of vinegar and a little chopped shallots, thus helping the Belgians make hash of the comforting and often repeated assurance that mussels are the safest of shellfish because they are never eaten raw. (Even American Indians, when they ate mussels at all, always cooked them.)

The waters around La Spezia in Italy are noted for a species called *Lithodomus lithophagus* (rock-dwelling, rock-eating), an apt name, for this is a boring mussel, which digs into the rock formations of the coast and looks as if it had grown out of them. Sometimes a group of them emerging together from a rock look like fingers sculptured by an underwater Rodin, so they are called, in a different taxonomic system, *Lithodomus dactilus*, rock-dwelling finger mussels. Otherwise they are known as date mussels, for they resemble dates in shape and color. The emperor Frederick Barbarossa thought so highly of these mussels that he issued in 1154 a decree commanding his Ligurian vassals, whenever they had occasion to send a delegation to him in Rome, to assure its welcome by bringing along a shield heaped high with mussels.

The Atlantic *M. edulis* can also produce historic evidence of its excellence. When Citizen Garat, Minister of Justice during the French Revolution, convoked some of his colleagues to hear his proposed draft for the decree sentencing Louis XVI to the guillotine, his cook was so enraged at hearing the document that she tore it from his hands and trampled on it. Given the temper of the Terror, this might easily have sent her to the guillotine too, but Garat insisted to his guests that she was too good a cook to be lost to the Republic. She then served them a mussel dish of her own creation and it was unanimously agreed to remember the mussels and forget the outburst.

There exist in the United States shellfish described as "freshwater clams," but they are not clams, they are mussels, of the family *Unionadae*, found also in Asia and Europe. In Europe they have mounted so high above the level of the sea, which it would seem ought to be their normal habitat, that at least one of them, *Pisidium cazertunum*, is popularly called the "mountain-climbing mussel"; it is found in Alpine waters at altitudes as great as 7200 feet. The tiny American fingernail "clam," not much over a quarter-inch long—which you may have come across on the ground along banks of streams, for which reason it is also called the "field clam"—belongs to this category. When found thus out of water, it can be assumed that receding spring floods have left it stranded, but a foresighted nature seems to have provided it with a means of getting back into the water again. If the ground is wet enough, you may see a mussel open its valves slightly, thrust out a fleshy foot and drag itself painfully over the grass.

Freshwater mussels are good eating. The Osage Indians of the Ozarks used to hold them in high honor, and in a recent contemporary account of boating on the Allagash River in Maine I came across the opinion that the mussels of that stream, though tough and chewy when they reach full growth, are when young "crisp, succulent, tender and delicious." The author of this description, an out-of-stater, added that the natives of Maine were afraid to eat them.

Freshwater mussels have been exploited commercially in the United States, but as the raw material for making buttons, not as food. The interior of the shell is lined with mother-of-pearl, and indeed in Europe a beginning had been made in inducing freshwater mussels to form pearls, but then the "Oriental pearl" was developed in Ceylon and the freshwater mussel was abandoned as hopelessly out-distanced.

Along the Pacific coast, the mussel's chief enemy is the black oystercatcher, which belies its name by preferring mussels. If you examine the demolished mussel shells an oystercatcher leaves behind it on the beach (it is capable of prying open and swallowing two hundred in an hour), you may be surprised to notice that it is always the *left* valve which is broken, never the right. The black oystercatcher is left-handed, if one may apply such a term to a bird; but the slang "southpaw" would be even worse.

MUSTARD. It is no wonder that the ancient Romans called their military baggage trains *impedimenta* if the legions really carried from Italy into the rest of Europe as many foods as they are credited with having distributed on that continent. One of them is mustard, which might very well have been carried by the Romans, who were fond of it, but it is far from certain that this plant, which spreads itself far and wide with great efficiency and has no need of Johnny Mustard-

MUSTARD. *Woodcut from Pierandrea Mattioli:* Commentaires, *Lyons, 1579*

seeds, Roman or otherwise, bothered to wait for the good offices of Julius Caesar to invade Europe. According to Georges and Germaine Blond, mustard was being cultivated in much of Europe in the Stone Age; according to Don and Patricia Brothwell, in the Glastonbury lake villages of England in the Iron Age; and according to Alain Decaux, in prehistoric Gaul before the Roman era.

Mustard growing presents no difficulties with which prehistoric man would have been unable to cope. "Cultivation" in its case might have consisted simply in strewing the seeds broadcast and waiting for them to grow. Perhaps the Romans themselves did not always do much more. Pliny remarked that mustard grew in Italy without being sown; the Romans had only to gather it wild. In the absence of deliberate sowing, mustard fends for itself first by producing seed with such profligacy that for the ancient Hindus it was a symbol of fecundity. Three-quarters of a pound of black mustard seed or two pounds of white mustard seed will produce on one acre 110 million second-generation white-mustard seeds in a bad year to 500 million black-mustard seeds in a good one. They are of minute size, which facilitates their distribution by birds, small animals or the wind. Self-sown mustard was already widespread in Asia, Europe and North Africa in prehistoric times.

Mustard is often presented as the typical plant of the *Cruciferae* (so called because they bear flowers whose four petals are arranged in the form of a cross), a large family (over 200 genera and perhaps 2000 species) and a virtuous one (it includes no poisonous members). A common characteristic of the family is that its seeds contain a good deal of oil—30 to 35 percent in the case of mustard—and the oil is often endowed with elements which produce a peppery effect in such diverse *Cruciferae* as cress, radishes, horse-radish, turnips and, of course, mustard itself. Among seasonings, mustard is second only to pepper in world trade.

The seeds, from which commercial processed mustard is made, are the most important edible part of the plant. They were also the simplest to prepare for the first users of mustard, or more exactly, did not need to be prepared at all. Ancient Egyptians usually, ancient Romans frequently, and ancient Hindus probably popped a few seeds into their mouths while chewing meat, which was thus seasoned automatically. With or without meat in the mouth, mustard seeds do not sear the palate, as you might expect; they are on the contrary pleasantly nutty to chew, with only a delicate tang of the sometimes fiery flavor of commercial mustard.

Mustard leaves are also edible, as the ancient Greeks and Romans knew. Plautus did not appreciate the mixed greens of his time:

> They are masses of silage, grass made edible by other kinds of grass, mixed with coriander, fennel, garlic and Macedonian parsley, to which are added sorrel, cabbage, white beets and chard, diluted with a pound of silphium, the whole mixed with ground mustard, a frightful poison which does not allow itself to be crushed without making the eyes water.

Though Plautus was discussing greens, this passage sounds as though he were thinking of the mustard as added in the form of ground seeds; but the Romans did eat the leaves as a vegetable, raw or cooked, and Pliny remarked on their ability to improve the taste of other plants with which they shared the pot.

It may have been African slaves who brought to our Southern states the habit of eating greens and the kind of mustard which provides one of their most popular varieties. In Africa then, and in Africa now, a favorite species was and is *Sinapis juncea*, sometimes called Indian mustard;

but many people think Africa may have been its original home. It is sometimes known as leaf mustard in the United States, and is the species from which special varieties have been developed for their leaves, notably Southern Curled Mustard. Mustard greens will probably persist in the South, where there is great demand for them, but they are disappearing elsewhere in the United States. They are not profitably exploitable in supermarkets.

Mustard-seed oil is widely used as human food in Asia. Vast plantings of it are made in India specifically for the oil. In Bangladesh, where they like it very hot, it is perhaps the most widely used of all cooking oils; it is particularly prized for cooking fish.

Mustard is everywhere indispensable, or was so in the mind of the anonymous author of a jingle obviously outdated today, here translated approximately from its original French:

From three things may the Lord preserve us:
From valets much too proud to serve us;
From women smeared with heavy fard, good grief!
From lack of mustard when we eat corned beef.

MUT
stands for

the **muttonbird,** a sort of petrel which has difficulty reaching adulthood because in its youth it is temptingly fat, fit fare for the frying pan; and for the **mutton snapper** of the West Indies, good eating if it hasn't itself been feeding on a poisonous blue-green alga of the Caribbean, which doesn't bother the mutton snapper, but will bother you if you eat snapper after snapper has eaten alga.

And, as will certainly be no surprise to you,

MUT also stands for

MUTTON. Meat, like the clarinet, has a series of characterless notes in its middle register. This is most noticeable in steers, where the period between true veal and true beef is bridged by a tasteless product which processors have tried to convince us is palatable by calling it baby beef, but the educated palate refuses to be deceived. The same phenomenon, a little less marked, occurs with sheep, where we start with tender white lamb and finish with rich red mutton, but between the two is a time of compromise when, in the words of George du Maurier in *Trilby,* you don't know whether it is lamb "or mutton—flesh, fowl, or good red herring." "Flavor is mainly a matter of age," Elspeth Huxley wrote. "Youth is insipid; maturity equals flavor; ripeness is all." Brillat-Savarin would have agreed in the case of sheep at least, for he said that its flesh should be eaten only at the moment when it has "attained the full perfection to which it is destined."

"To my taste," wrote Jay Jacobs in the *Gourmet,* "there is no meat this side of paradise as supremely satisfying as a good, hefty mutton chop properly prepared, but it's literally as easy to come by hippopotamus steaks as mutton chops almost anywhere in New York City these days." On the rare occasions when you do find a mutton chop of quality, he advises ordering it rare, "when it is a deep burgundy red beneath a scorched exterior, steams with its own sealed-in juices at the touch of a fork, and has a full-bodied flavor with which that of no red meat, the finest steaks included, can compare."

As early as 1737 William Byrd wrote that American mutton was "always as good as the best European can be, since the pastures in this country are very fine," and as late as 1889 Alessandro Filippini, a chef at Delmonico's, said that American mutton, "if not superior to, stands at least fully on a par with, the English rival." Yet Americans have never eaten much mutton, even during the blissful period bounded by Byrd and Filippini. Harriet Martineau, an English visitor to the United States, noted of mutton in 1837 that "so far from being despised, as we have been told, it was much desired but not to be had." Yet she was visiting Kentucky, where it was most prized; indeed Calvin Trillin in 1977 tracked down a region in western Kentucky which is still doing honor to its traditional local specialty, barbecued mutton.

Despite the early tributes to American mutton, it is very little eaten in the United States, and has never enjoyed the popularity of pork or beef. Perhaps Mrs. Martineau had trouble finding it because it spoils quickly, which in the days before refrigeration may have reduced it to a seasonal and regional role. It could have been preserved by salting, as pork regularly was (preserved mutton is extremely popular in Norway, and mutton ham is delicious), but early Americans may have been deterred from eating it by the Hundred Years War. This deceptively named conflict had ended, it is true, nearly half a century before America was discovered, but its influence lingered on. One of its results was that in England salt became too expensive to be squandered on mutton, a meat then stringy and tough, for it was obtained from sheep better adapted to producing wool than meat, and even then from animals slaughtered only after they had done their full duty as wool bearers. Later the quality of mutton improved and the relative cost of salt diminished,

MUTTON *by Thomas Sidney Cooper (1803–1902).* Reposing on Gods' Acre, *oil on canvas*

but the English had simply gotten out of the habit of curing mutton. The first colonists to settle America from the British Isles followed unthinkingly the customs of the mother country.

The days of Byrd and Filippini have passed, so the very low consumption of mutton in America today is understandable because the quality of mutton on the market is not high—and it is not high because there is so little demand for it, a vicious circle if ever there was one. Lambs are often fattened for the table before butchering, but older sheep usually go straight from pasture to processor on no other food than grass. Mutton is graded as prime, choice, good, commercial, utility and cull; the best grade you are likely to find on the open market is "good." The two top grades are tailor-made meat, raised on order for luxury restaurants and food shops. Much of our mutton, whether so graded or not, is cull in the ordinary sense: it comes from ewes which have passed breeding age, by which time they have also passed the age for producing good mutton. When sheep are slaughtered at a less advanced age, the meat of ewes is considered the best, that of castrated males second best, and that of uncastrated rams comes last. If you want to know what you have on your plate, you can tell from the color of the fat: white for ewes, yellowish for rams. If you eat mutton from sheep of a race not developed primarily for meat, your chances of getting good mutton are better with a breed raised for milk than with one raised for wool.

The greatest mutton eaters of the world are the Moslems of the Middle East and North Africa, and the very best mutton in the world may very well be that of their fat-tailed sheep. Their existence was first reported to the Western world by Herodotus, but nobody believed him: a sheep whose tail accounted for one-sixth of the total weight of the carcass had to be a figment of the imagination. Marco Polo came across the same sheep in Rudbar, southern Afghanistan, where there were "sheep as big as asses, with tails so thick and plump that they weigh a good thirty pounds. Fine, fat beasts they are, and good eating." Captain Edmund Bacon, Thomas Jefferson's overseer, must have been speaking of this breed when he wrote that his employer "imported from Barbary I think four large broad-tailed sheep. . . . Made very fine mutton, but were not popular—did not disseminate [propagate?] and ran out in a few years."

The fat-tailed sheep is older than the Moslem religion, but its development was given a great fillip by the advent of Islam, for the size of its tail, often so heavy that it has to be supported on a little cart which the animal draws behind it, is accounted for by the heavy concentration of fat it contains. Because Moslem dietary laws forbid cooking meat in lard or butter, and the olive was scarce or non-existent on much of the territory of the Near East and North Africa, mutton-tail fat became the chief cooking oil of this region, and still is.

The second-best mutton of the world may well be that of the *pré-salé* ("saltwater meadow") sheep of France, which absorb built-in seasoning from seashore pasturage periodically covered by flood tides. Strictly speaking, this term is legally applicable only to sheep which graze in the Mont-Saint-Michel area, but the public often bestows it also on other sheep raised in the same circumstances, notably those of Pauillac, in the Bordeaux region. France also derives superior mutton from the southern sheep which on the high plateaus eat the aromatic herbs of Provence, for instance those which in the Basses-Alpes feed in fields of lavender.

In Britain and the United States, the Downs breeds give perhaps the best mutton, particularly the Southdown (the kind I once raised myself in Vermont). Alas, the Southdown is disappearing even from its native Britain in the absence of an educated public to demand it. "There are not many farmers who are prepared to support flocks of Southdown sheep when they can increase production with the Dorset Horn, which produces lambs twice a year," Adrian Bailey wrote in *The Cooking of the British Isles*. One more example, alas, of the prevailing gastronomic tendency of our times: we are trading quality for quantity.

MY
stands for

the **myrobalan,** an astringent Asian fruit which was allowed, briefly, to pucker the lips of Parisians when it became a fad in France toward the end of the eighteenth century, but was quickly forgotten on the arrival of the even more astringent French Revolution; for the **myrtle,** a berry sometimes chewed by airplane pilots in the belief that it sharpens eyesight; and for the **myrtle sedge,** which is none other than *Acorus calamus*, called Venus's plant by the ancient Romans, who considered it a powerful aphrodisiac.

N

NEEDHAM, JOSEPH (quoting an eleventh-century Chinese physician): *Experts at curing diseases are inferior to specialists who warn against diseases. Experts in the use of medicine are inferior to those who recommend proper diet.*

NA
stands for

naartje, a South African tangerine with a thin skin; for **nabk,** an ancient Egyptian berry which, judging from its remains found in a Second Dynasty tomb, was not unlike a cherry; for the **nagoonberry,** or wineberry, plentiful in Alaska; for the **naked catfish,** a European variety which to the naked eye seems no more naked than any other catfish, and the **naked sole,** an American Atlantic variety, which to the naked eye seems no more naked than any other sole, and indeed less so, since it wears its zebra markings like a garment; for the **nameko,** a slippery Japanese mushroom golden-orange in color, small in size and large in flavor; for the **nannyberry,** alias the sheepberry, wild raisin, highbush cranberry, black haw or sweet viburnum, oval, bluish-black and sweet, and the **nannynose,** alias the long clam or soft-shelled clam, oval, chalky white and sweet in a fashion foreign to the nannyberry; for the **Nantes chicken,** which made the nineteenth-century poet-gourmet Charles Monselet "quiver with contentment"; and for the **naras,** an African fruit relished by Hottentots but labeled by an unappreciative taxonomist as *Acanthosicyos horrida.*

NA
stands for

nard, an Indian root less valued today than in ancient times, when the Romans used it for seasoning and also to cure rabies, with little success in the latter case; for the **narwhal,** whose fat is prized by Eskimos; for the **naseberry,** which is the sapodilla; and for the **Nassau grouper,** a species of fish of which most members are born female, but, discovering at about the age of five that this does not work out very well, enough of them change into males to enrich their social lives.

NA
stands for

the **nasturtium,** whose leaves and flowers can be used in salads and whose seeds and buds may substitute for capers; for **Natal grass,** which plays in some parts of Africa the role of spinach, and for the **Natal plum,** which plays in East Africa the role of (what else?) the plum; for **native mint,** the only member of its family which originated in America, and the **native oyster,** which is the Olympia oyster of North America's Pacific coast; for the **nautilus,** which gave Oliver Wendell Holmes a poem and Magellan's chronicler Antonio Pigafetta a tasty dish; for the **navew,** which up to the sixteenth century was the turnip; and for the humble familiar **navy bean,** so called, the *Random House Dictionary dixit,* because of its relentless use by the U.S. Navy.

NE
stands for

the **Neapolitan medlar,** which is not a medlar but an azarole, which is almost a hawthorn; for the

nectarine, a small, richly flavored peach so confused that if you plant its pits you may get nectarines or you may not; for the **needlefish,** an executioner rather than a dinner which has been known to leap from the water, stab a fisherman in the jugular vein and return unscathed to the sea; for the **neem tree,** whose leaves are eaten by Africans and whose twigs are used for toothbrushes by Hindus; for **negro coffee,** a type of senna whose leaves are eaten in Africa but which gets its name from the fact that a drink is made from its roasted seeds; and for the **nene,** pronounced *nay-nay,* the state bird of Hawaii, a goose which by dint of spending all its time 5000 to 7000 feet up in the mountains has practically forgotten how to swim.

NE
stands for

Nepal pepper, so named in defiance of the fact that it is a variety of cayenne pepper, a native of South America; for the **nettle,** which can be eaten with impunity and even with relish in the form of soup, preferably in May, since, as John Gerard pointed out, "if it be withered or boiled it stingeth not at all, by reason that the stiffenesse of the down is fallen away," and the **nettle tree,** whose sweet fruit, eaten in Africa, was confused by the ancients with the lotus; for the **Newark Pippin,** an apple of excellent quality which you are not likely to find on the market today, and the **Newton Pippin,** another fine apple which you are also not likely to find today, though its quality was so high that after being developed in Newton (now Flushing, in Queens, New York), it was the first American apple to be exported to England, in 1759; and for the **New Zealand wrasse,** otherwise known as the butterfish.

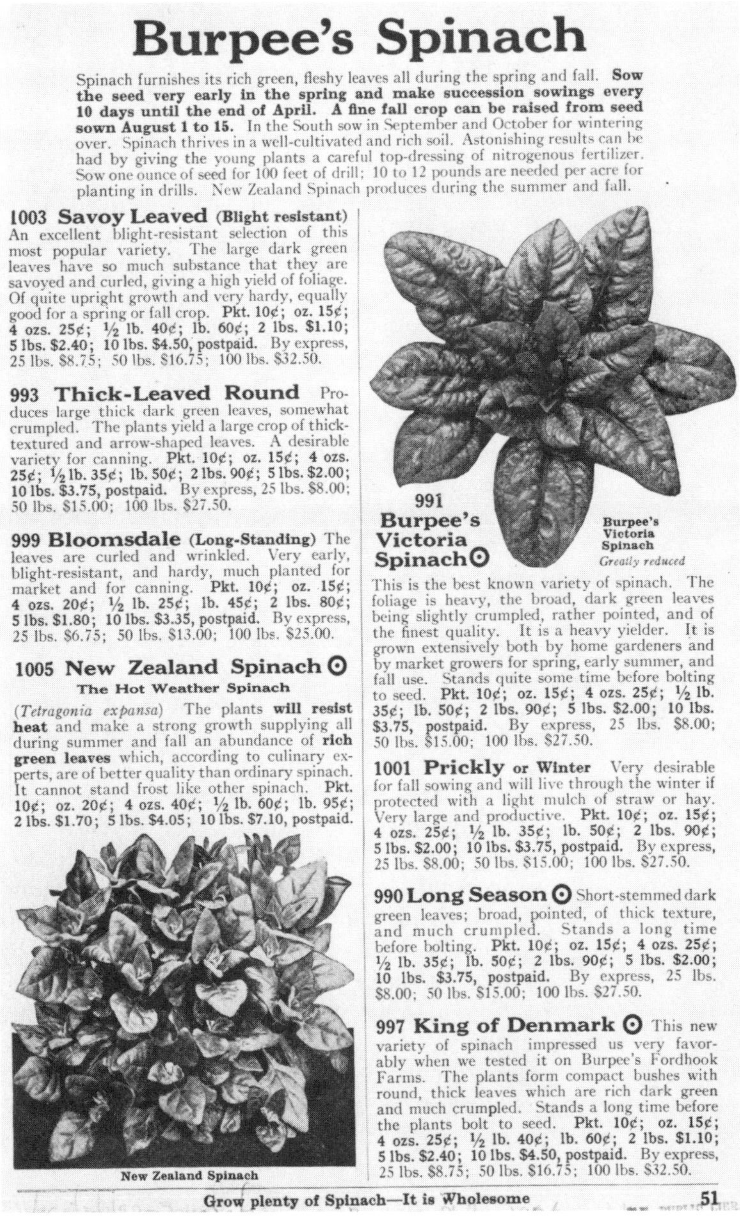

Burpee's Spinach

Spinach furnishes its rich green, fleshy leaves all during the spring and fall. **Sow the seed very early in the spring and make succession sowings every 10 days until the end of April. A fine fall crop can be raised from seed sown August 1 to 15.** In the South sow in September and October for wintering over. Spinach thrives in a well-cultivated and rich soil. Astonishing results can be had by giving the young plants a careful top-dressing of nitrogenous fertilizer. Sow one ounce of seed for 100 feet of drill; 10 to 12 pounds are needed per acre for planting in drills. New Zealand Spinach produces during the summer and fall.

1003 Savoy Leaved (Blight resistant) An excellent blight-resistant selection of this most popular variety. The large dark green leaves have so much substance that they are savoyed and curled, giving a high yield of foliage. Of quite upright growth and very hardy, equally good for a spring or fall crop. **Pkt. 10¢; oz. 15¢; 4 ozs. 25¢; ½ lb. 40¢; lb. 60¢; 2 lbs. $1.10; 5 lbs. $2.40; 10 lbs. $4.50, postpaid.** By express, 25 lbs. $8.75; 50 lbs. $16.75; 100 lbs. $32.50.

993 Thick-Leaved Round Produces large thick dark green leaves, somewhat crumpled. The plants yield a large crop of thick-textured and arrow-shaped leaves. A desirable variety for canning. **Pkt. 10¢; oz. 15¢; 4 ozs. 25¢; ½ lb. 35¢; lb. 50¢; 2 lbs. 90¢; 5 lbs. $2.00; 10 lbs. $3.75, postpaid.** By express, 25 lbs. $8.00; 50 lbs. $15.00; 100 lbs. $27.50.

999 Bloomsdale (Long-Standing) The leaves are curled and wrinkled. Very early, blight-resistant, and hardy, much planted for market and for canning. **Pkt. 10¢; oz. 15¢; 4 ozs. 20¢; ½ lb. 25¢; lb. 45¢; 2 lbs. 80¢; 5 lbs. $1.80; 10 lbs. $3.35, postpaid.** By express, 25 lbs. $6.75; 50 lbs. $13.00; 100 lbs. $25.00.

1005 New Zealand Spinach ⊙
The Hot Weather Spinach

(*Tetragonia expansa*) The plants **will resist heat** and make a strong growth supplying all during summer and fall an abundance of **rich green leaves** which, according to culinary experts, are of better quality than ordinary spinach. It cannot stand frost like other spinach. **Pkt. 10¢; oz. 20¢; 4 ozs. 40¢; ½ lb. 60¢; lb. 95¢; 2 lbs. $1.70; 5 lbs. $4.05; 10 lbs. $7.10, postpaid.**

New Zealand Spinach

991 Burpee's Victoria Spinach ⊙

Burpee's Victoria Spinach
Greatly reduced

This is the best known variety of spinach. The foliage is heavy, the broad, dark green leaves being slightly crumpled, rather pointed, and of the finest quality. It is a heavy yielder. It is grown extensively both by home gardeners and by market growers for spring, early summer, and fall use. Stands quite some time before bolting to seed. **Pkt. 10¢; oz. 15¢; 4 ozs. 25¢; ½ lb. 35¢; lb. 50¢; 2 lbs. 90¢; 5 lbs. $2.00; 10 lbs. $3.75, postpaid.** By express, 25 lbs. $8.00; 50 lbs. $15.00; 100 lbs. $27.50.

1001 Prickly or Winter Very desirable for fall sowing and will live through the winter if protected with a light mulch of straw or hay. Very large and productive. **Pkt. 10¢; oz. 15¢; 4 ozs. 25¢; ½ lb. 35¢; lb. 50¢; 2 lbs. 90¢; 5 lbs. $2.00; 10 lbs. $3.75, postpaid.** By express, 25 lbs. $8.00; 50 lbs. $15.00; 100 lbs. $27.50.

990 Long Season ⊙ Short-stemmed dark green leaves; broad, pointed, of thick texture, and much crumpled. Stands a long time before bolting. **Pkt. 10¢; oz. 15¢; 4 ozs. 25¢; ½ lb. 35¢; lb. 50¢; 2 lbs. 90¢; 5 lbs. $2.00; 10 lbs. $3.75, postpaid.** By express, 25 lbs. $8.00; 50 lbs. $15.00; 100 lbs. $27.50.

997 King of Denmark ⊙ This new variety of spinach impressed us very favorably when we tested it on Burpee's Fordhook Farms. The plants form compact bushes with round, thick leaves which are rich dark green and much crumpled. Stands a long time before the plants bolt to seed. **Pkt. 10¢; oz. 15¢; 4 ozs. 25¢; ½ lb. 40¢; lb. 60¢; 2 lbs. $1.10; 5 lbs. $2.40; 10 lbs. $4.50, postpaid.** By express, 25 lbs. $8.75; 50 lbs. $16.75; 100 lbs. $32.50.

Grow plenty of Spinach—It is Wholesome 51

NEW ZEALAND SPINACH. *Burpee's Seed Catalog, 1926*

And **NE** also stands for

NEW ZEALAND SPINACH. With the heat of summer, leafy green plants, from lettuce to spinach, express their disapproval of the temperature by lying down limply on the ground, by turning brown, or by becoming uninteresting in taste and texture. The remedy for this, the seed catalogs say, is to go in for New Zealand spinach, less hardy than such other spinach substitutes as chard or orach, and vulnerable to frost, but which makes up for this by thriving in heat and resisting drought. New Zealand spinach can be grown, according to Norman Taylor's *Practical Encyclopedia of Gardening,* whenever or wherever the heat is too great for genuine spinach.

With my mouth made up for a leafy green vegetable even in summer, I took the plunge, in the days when I raised my own food, and bought New Zealand spinach seed, presented in packages brave with tempting pictures in full color of a vigorous bush which looked as if it should fairly sprawl over the ground—and indeed in nature, I am told, this is just what it does, but for me it never came up, belying its scientific name of *Tetragonia expansa,* whose second word suggests willingness to spread widely. (Its first word means "four-angled," and refers to the shape of its seed; when, in the past, it was called *T. cornuta,* this referred to the horns which crown the hard, nut-like fruit, inside which are found, stingily, only one or two seeds.) I have since learned that its seed germinates very slowly and that it is advisable, before planting it, to soak it for several hours in very hot water.

New Zealand spinach, according to Georges Gibault's *Histoire des légumes*, is "the only potherb which Europeans have derived from Australasia." It is not even certain that it is an exclusivity of this part of the world, for while it is native to Australia, New Zealand, New Caledonia and other large Pacific islands, it is also found wild in China, Japan and even Chile; but it is possible that seeds from Australasia were carried to these countries by birds, winds or ocean currents and became naturalized there. However, it was man who took it to Africa, where it is eaten more extensively in Morocco, tropical Africa and Madagascar than it is in either Europe or the United States.

The man who was chiefly responsible for the transfer of New Zealand spinach to Europe was Captain James Cook. On his first circumnavigation of the world he took along Sir Joseph Banks, a botanist who discovered the plant in New Zealand in 1770 and brought back seeds, which were planted in Kew Gardens in 1772 and promptly forgotten; apparently it occurred to nobody that it might be edible. On Cook's second voyage, a botanist named Foster again found New Zealand spinach growing abundantly near Queen Charlotte's Strait, and was reminded by its thick, fleshy leaves of the spinach substitute orach. He took it aboard ship as a possible remedy for scurvy, which had been giving Cook's crew a good deal of trouble, and discovered that it was indeed a protection against that malady; it contains much the same health-giving elements as true spinach, though with considerably less iron.

Foster found it again on the island of Tongatabu, whose Polynesian natives had not realized it was edible. They had tried it raw, but New Zealand spinach has to be cooked to be palatable. Thus treated, it becomes a pulpy mass, more unctuous than spinach in consistency, which some persons think makes it more agreeable eating, while others think not. Differing individual opinions on this point may have been influenced by the fashion in which the New Zealand spinach was picked. Young tender leaves are much superior to older ones, which tend to develop a taste too assertive to please everyone. One system for picking this plant is to take only the leafy tips of branches where new growth is developing.

It can hardly be said that Europe pounced on its new plant with avidity. It was cultivated almost exclusively as a curiosity in botanical gardens. England, though it had been the first to receive the plant, had apparently forgotten all about it, and planted it in Kensington Gardens in 1820 as a novelty received from France. By 1828, however, it had gained acceptance in England and also in the United States. In Belgium, a country much given to raising plants of this kind, it began to be eaten about 1830.

The first seed merchant to offer New Zealand spinach in France, a certain Tollar, reported in 1805 that there were few takers. Nevertheless, the royal botanical garden in Paris began to distribute the seed, and in 1819 Comte d'Ourches, who took a lively interest in promoting new food plants, tried to popularize it. It was grown in almost all château and manorial gardens, and in many modest home gardens as well, but it did not reach the big markets. It is still being eaten in southwestern France, and is findable in local markets there, the produce of small-scale market gardeners, but one would be hard put to find it in Paris. This is the situation almost everywhere in Europe and the United States, where those who want to eat New Zealand spinach usually have to grow it themselves. Its small importance as a commercial plant no doubt accounts for the fact that it has been little developed in cultivation and as grown today is essentially unaltered from its wild form.

NI
stands for

niam fat, an important West African cooking oil extracted from a nut locally known as the *mémé*, which we reach by deftly sidestepping the alphabetically inconvenient **n'ghat oil**, a tropical African fat used for the same purpose; for the **nightingale**, whose tongues were served by the Roman emperor Heliogabalus on the theory that a songbird's tongue should be sweet; for the **Nile fish**, which swims either forward or backward, and generates an electric current to locate smaller edible fish by radar, the **Nile perch**, which the ancient Egyptians appreciated enough to mummify, and the **Nile wedge shell**, the favorite shellfish at the mouth of the river for which it is named; for the **nilgai**, or blue bull, the largest antelope of India; for the **nine-eyes**, or butterfish, of the North Atlantic, called nine-eyes because of the row of prominent black splotches which run along its backbone; and for **nipples**, which the ancient Romans considered one of the most succulent parts of the sow.

NO
stands for

Noah's ark, a shellfish eaten in the Mediterranean,

so called I don't know why; for **nongus,** an Indian palmyra fruit; for **nook abessin,** whose seeds are chewed in Abyssinia; for **nopalitos,** the fleshy fat paddles of the prickly-pear cactus, a delight for Latin Americans; for **nori,** vitamin-rich Japanese seaweed which is not simply gathered as nature provides it, but carefully cultivated for the table; for the **Norman cow,** the most successful race in France, which accounts for one-quarter of all the cattle of that country; and for the **North American bluefish,** the largest of its family, which can reach a weight of forty-five pounds.

NO
stands for

the **northern barracuda,** alias the sennet, of the western North Atlantic, a medium-sized fish which reaches a length of eighteen inches, not much as barracudas go; for the **northern lobster,** which is simply the familiar crustacean we find from Labrador to Virginia, and the **northern moon shell,** which occupies much the same range and is the tastiest of its kind; for the **northern pike,** a fierce hunter in the heavyweight category (the record catch weighed fifty-three pounds); for the **northern scallop,** which, from the Bering Strait to San Diego, lies only on its right side; for the **Northern Spy,** born toward the end of the eighteenth century, which in some opinions is the tastiest American apple ever developed, yet it is no longer grown commercially; for the **northern swellfish,** which is the one sometimes offered on the market under the name "sea squab"; for the **northern haddock,** which is really a scorpionfish, but fish dealers know better than to offer it for sale under such a name; and for the **Norway lobster,** which may or may not be the Dublin Bay prawn, which may or may not be the French *langoustine,* which may or may not be the Venetian *scampi,* which may or may not be the Gulf of Gaeta *mazzancolle*: there are several hundred species, which is too many to disentangle here.

NU
stands for

nug oil, derived from the seeds of an Ethiopian plant; for **numbles,** which meant venison lungs in the fifteenth century, when people ate venison lungs; for the **nurse hound,** which is the greater-spotted dogfish; for **nut grass,** which is chufa, an edible sedge whose rhizomes taste like a cross between coconut and almonds; for the **nutria,** a large South American rodent described as good eating by those who have been courageous enough to eat it; and for the **nut tree,** which sounds to Americans like a vague term, but in England means specifically the European filbert.

And **NU** also stands for

NUT. A nut, according to the botanists, is a one-celled indehiscent fruit with a hardened endocarp, but for everyday use I imagine most of us would prefer to stick with the popular conception, put into words by *The Oxford Book of Food Plants* as "any seed or fruit containing an edible and usually rather hard and oily kernel within a hard or brittle shell." This brings together a number of fruits, indehiscent or otherwise, which share several common characteristics, even though they arrived at them from different directions, which prevents scientists from approving of grouping them into a single category. They tell us that the Brazil nut is not a nut, it is a seed; that the peanut is not a nut, it is a legume; and that even the walnut, structurally speaking, is not a nut, nor is the almond. A great many other foods which we call nuts are really seeds, rhizomes, tubers, or something else non-nutty, but the popular word has a justification in nature all the same, for the fruits it groups constitute a coherent category not only because of superficial resemblances, but also by being gastronomically and nutritionally very much alike.

Although the demand for nuts has been rising steadily during this century, particularly in the United States, where it has created a flourishing industry, it is probable that nuts played a much more important role proportionally in the diets of prehistoric and primitive peoples than in that of our contemporaries. They possess two great advantages for such societies: they are easy to gather and easy to store. Nuts keep indefinitely without salting, pickling, smoking or other manipulations, which was a tremendous virtue in times when many foods could only be kept from spoiling by eating them as soon as they were acquired. Primitive peoples often lived to a rhythm of alternate feasting and fasting, stuffing themselves with all the food they could hold when it was available, and tightening their belts, if they had belts, when it was not. The periods of privation were often bridged by having recourse to stored nuts, for nuts, of one kind or another, have almost always been present in every part of the world where men were present too.

Nuts have been found in many Stone Age middens, even as far back as the Middle Paleolithic, which is the period of the cave dwellers of Shanidar (northern Iraq), who ate chestnuts, walnuts, pine nuts and acorns. The last seems strange to us today, but the acorn, which has three hundred species, was originally the most widely eaten nut of all, even in Europe, where it remained important into medieval times. This was still the case in the Mesolithic period, about 8500 B.C., when nuts were an important element in the European diet, and acorns were still leading in the fifth millennium B.C., according to the evidence of the Jarmo site in Iraq, and for that matter, even in Neolithic Greece, at Sesklo. In Neolithic times, however, forests were razed to clear land for agriculture, and as a result the hazelnut took first place. The hazel had already been important in the Mesolithic lake settlements of Switzerland and, on the evidence of the Alvastra site, in Neolithic Sweden. Walnuts have also been found in quantity in Mesolithic remains, while beechnuts were plentiful not only in Swiss but also in English lake dwellings, at Glastonbury, which brings us to the Iron Age. Meanwhile, climatic changes were accounting for other alterations in the types of nuts eaten. In Iraq and the Near East oaks and walnuts died out, but chestnuts and pines remained (pine seeds, however, seem to have been little eaten before classical times). A further shift in this region made its two leading nuts the almond and the pistachio, the only ones mentioned in the Bible.

For an example of the wide use of nuts in a society living under primitive conditions, we need look no further than to American Indians. Their importance for the Natchez Indians of the South was indicated by the naming of the next to the last of their thirteen months for the chestnut, and the last for nuts in general. In this part of the country pecans were frequently ground into meal, and so were hickory nuts, the ones Thomas Hariot, an early English colonist of Virginia, probably had in mind when he wrote of the Powhatan Indians that "besides their eating of them after our ordinary manner, they breake them with stones and pound them in mortars with water to make a milk which they use to put into some sorts of their spoonemeat, also among their sodden wheat [hominy], peaze, beanes and pompions [pumpkins] which maketh them have a farre more pleasant taste." (A parallel to this example of the ability of nuts to fill in for foods missing in a certain area can be found in the Pacific islands, where the absence of cereals and legumes like peas and beans promoted nuts to a more important role in the diet.) South American Indians used nut meal for thickening soups and stews or to make bread, including acorn bread, but the real masters of the acorn were the Yosemite Indians of California, who not only succeeded in making that bitter species palatable, but also treated the even more refractory horse chestnut so that it became edible. Just to their north, the Pacific Northwest Indians used acorns, chinquapins, walnuts, hickory nuts and hazelnuts. In the Great Lakes region, sites dated at 2000 B.C. have yielded acorns, walnuts, hickory nuts and butternuts. The Narragansett Indians of the Northeast used butternuts too, extracting their oil by boiling, and employing it as a seasoning for vegetables and to make "butter" to spread on bread; like their cousins to the south, they also made hickory "milk." The Algonquins ate beechnuts and acorns, which were pounded into a sort of flour, mixed with cornmeal and shaped into cakes which were fried in fat.

Less primitive societies made considerable use of nuts too, and seemed to consider them too commonplace to develop cults around them, as they did for some other foods. Certain ancient rites have been interpreted as signifying that nuts were a fertility symbol for the Greeks and Romans, but alternative interpretations are possible. In Athens, when a bride entered her husband's home for the first time nuts and dried figs were poured over her head, a custom in which some commenters have seen an allusion to fertility. But the same ceremony marked the entrance into the household of a new slave, so it may have symbolized nothing more than admission to the family table. At Roman weddings, nuts were thrown to children (who might represent the results of fertility) not only by the bride, which might seem more appropriate if this was the meaning of the rite, but also by the groom. ("Fling nuts in the air, as bridegrooms do," Virgil wrote in one of his pastoral poems.) Nuts were used in many children's games (jackstones, for instance), so this may have been simply a gesture of renunciation of childhood.

In classical times, nuts and seeds provided cooking and seasoning oils, even in regions where the olive was present. The ancient Persians made meal of powdered almonds, pistachios and walnuts to thicken and flavor dishes, the Arabs adopted the custom, and the Crusaders, picking it up from the Arabs, transferred it to Europe. The favorite nut was undoubtedly the almond, which, in the form of sauces based on almond flour or oil, seems to have gotten into a majority of the most esteemed dishes of the fourteenth century.

Nut oils were recommended as cooking fats in Villanova's *Rules for Health*, written about 1300, but there has been a recession since. Today Europe and the United States, when they depart

NUT *by Albrecht Dürer (1471–1528).* Squirrels, *water and body colors*

from olive oil, do not venture into exoticism. Linseed oil, peanut oil or sunflower oil may be used in cooking, but the most daring flight we allow ourselves today is putting walnut oil into salad dressing. It is the less privileged regions which still make important use of nut oils, sauces and flours—Russian Georgia; Indonesia, which uses local nuts unknown elsewhere; and Latin America, where nuts enter especially into luxurious dishes.

Nuts also occupied the luxury position in ancient times, as part of the dessert, which was when the ancient Romans served nuts—all kinds except the lowly acorn, deemed suitable only for the poor. For a long time nuts continued to appear with the dessert or after it, hence our common saying "From soup to nuts."

NUTMEG. The eighteenth-century botanist Nicolas Céré, who should have known, since he was an accessory to the breaking of the Dutch nutmeg monopoly on behalf of France, called the nutmeg "this inconceivable tree." It is indeed a plant of many wonders, of which not the least is its fruit; but the tree which bears it has noteworthy qualities too—its sexuality, for instance. Nutmegs are male or female; Rosie Maurel wrote that botanists have nicknamed it "the pasha of tropical flora," because one male tree suffices to fertilize from ten up to twenty females. It is rather difficult to imagine botanists employing this ponderous phrase in laboratory chitchat, or even on field trips; it smells of the writer striving laboriously for an image. Besides, botanists already have a term for this phenomenon, which is not restricted to nutmegs. The nutmeg is a "harem tree."

Nutmeg producers feel that ten female trees to one male is about the right proportion, which they achieve by planting the right kind of seeds. Nutmeg exploiters who find themselves dealing with self-sown nutmeg trees have to cull most of the males, since nature, which has no objection to monogamy in nutmegs, produces both sexes in more or less equal quantity. This method has the inconvenience of imposing a wait of seven or eight years until the first flowers appear, to permit recognizing the sex of the plants, by which time the trees which must be eliminated are fairly sizable, though nothing like the sixty-foot monsters they can become. On the average, it takes about eight years for nutmegs to flower and propagate, and twenty-five to reach maximum bearing, which for good trees means 1500 to 2000 nuts per tree. Nutmegs produce fruit for sixty years or more.

"When ripe," according to Mary S. Atwood in *A Taste of India*, "[the nutmeg] is one of the most beautiful fruits in nature." This must also have been the opinion of Sultan Husain, shah of Persia, if we may trust Joseph Addison, who wrote in the *Spectator* in 1711: "The present Emperor of Persia denominates himself 'the sun of glory and the nutmeg of delight.' " Nature was indeed at her artistic best when she created the nutmeg, a delight to the eye in all its avatars, from the completely garbed to nudity. On the tree it is a smooth fruit, oftenest of a pale greenish-yellow color, about the size of an apricot, with a groove running down one side along which, when it is ripe, the fruit splits open in almost equal halves to let the seed drop out. Its appearance leads one to expect a plumlike interior, and indeed there is a small amount of soft, fleshy pulp, which is ignored by commerce; the Indonesians make candy of it.

Opening the fruit exposes its most spectacular aspect: the central kernel is wrapped in a bright scarlet net, which botanists call the aril and spice merchants call mace. Mace is the secondary spice of the nutmeg, purchasable in the United States nowadays only in powdered form, which probably represents a loss in flavor since the days when recipes in old cookbooks called for "a blade of mace." (Blade mace is still findable in Europe, however.) Beneath the mace is the nutmeg proper, the seed of the plant, enclosed in a thin, hard, glittering inner shell. When this is removed, we come at last to the essential nutmeg, as decorative, though in more austere fashion, as when wrapped in its aril, with a ridged pattern obscured when we buy it by a dusting of limewash powder, a protection against worms, and perhaps also against its sometimes irritant quality for the skin: in Indonesia, workers who prepare nutmegs for the market powder their faces with sago-palm flour for protection.

Nutmeg was the last of the major spices (the Middle Ages would have said the "noble spices") to reach Europe. The first undisputed report of its appearance dates from 1190, when the Emperor Henry VI visited Rome and the streets were fumigated in honor of the occasion with, among other spices, "India nuts." This was still more than three centuries before the first Europeans saw nutmegs growing, when the Magellan expedition discovered in 1521 the only place in the world where nutmegs (and CLOVES) then grew, the Moluccas, which were accordingly baptized the Spice Islands. Friar Odoric de Pordenone had already reported seeing nutmegs in Java early in the fourteenth century, but the fruit only, not the trees, which did not grow there. Marco Polo was apparently unaware of the nutmeg's existence.

The ancients almost certainly did not know the nutmeg, despite a few dubious reports which might conceivably refer to it. A French source asserts that nutmegs have been found in the tombs of the Pharaohs, but without corroborative detail; even if true, the presence of a few nutmegs, which might have been placed there precisely because they were rare and precious, does not permit us to assume that Egyptians below the Pharaonic level ever used nutmegs, and there is no evidence for the supposition. Theophrastus mentioned a spice from India which he called *comacum*, but since he neglected to describe it, its occasional identification with the nutmeg is pure speculation. Plautus spoke of *macis*, the word the French use today to designate mace, but does not give details about it either. If the nutmeg had really existed in ancient Rome, Pliny would certainly have listed it. He did not.

The occasional assertion that the nutmeg entered Europe in the fifth century A.D. is apparently based on the fact that Aetius of Amida, a Byzantine physician of that century or the next, concocted a medicine which he called *suffimis gum moschatum*, but we are not sure it contained nutmeg, and besides, Byzantium was not quite Europe. The Persian physician Avicenna mentioned nutmeg about A.D. 1000, by which time the Arabs, who seem to have been the first to carry nutmegs westward, had probably already begun importing them in their dhows, hugging the coast from the East Indies to the Persian Gulf. It may have been the Arabs themselves who first began to deliver nutmegs regularly to Europe, or it may have been Italian traders who, at the time of the Crusades, ignored the Pope's ban against trading with the infidels *ad majorem mercati gloriam*.

The new hot spices of the East were received enthusiastically by a medieval Europe which up to that time had been eating, with the exception of game, relatively tasteless foods, especially when they were vegetables. It had suddenly become possible to add interest to these dishes, and of course the cooks at first overdid it. In fifteenth-century England this excess was manifest in the fact that mace, which is hotter and less subtle than nutmeg proper, almost crowded out notemygge, as it was then spelled, except by Chaucer, who wrote of "nutemuge put in ale."

The spice craze lasted through the seventeenth century and well into the eighteenth. Spices, of which cinnamon and nutmeg were the most popular, were used to an extent which revolted the French poet Nicolas Boileau, who wrote in "The Ridiculous Repast": "Do you like nutmeg? It's in everything." In England the vogue for nutmeg gave rise to a new article of personal adornment—the nutmeg grater. Whole nutmegs were brought to the table to permit guests to sprinkle foods, many of which already had nutmeg cooked into them, with more nutmeg, freshly grated by the diners' personal pocket nutmeg graters. English silversmiths turned out little marvels in the form of this utensil, some of which are found in museums today.

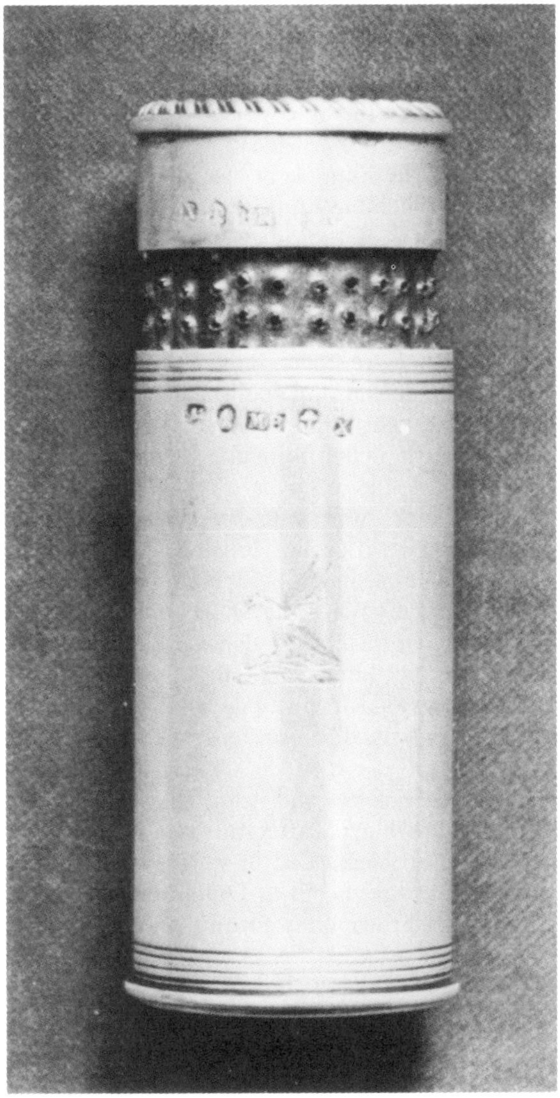

NUTMEG. *Silver grater, England, 1795*

The recipes of the seventeenth, eighteenth and even the nineteenth century are heavy with spices, half a dozen or more to a single dish; it is impossible to avoid the conclusion that our ancestors made abusive use of them. But it is only fair to point out that these were natural spices. They were less powerful than their modern versions, which have been subjected to processes which concentrate and enhance their flavors.

Nutmeg

With spices in such demand, the trade in them became a way to riches; nations fought undeclared wars to control their sources. After Magellan's men discovered the Spice Islands, the Portuguese (oddly enough, for Magellan was in the service of Spain at the time) kept everybody else out of the area by such ingenious devices as distributing falsified charts of the adjacent seas designed to lead any rivals to shipwreck rather than to nutmegs. The Dutch dislodged the Portuguese in the seventeenth century, destroyed three-quarters of the trees to leave them only on islands which were easy to defend, and applied the death penalty to anyone caught trying to smuggle out nutmegs. Their yearly profit from the spice trade was estimated at the time as 500 million French pounds, which sufficed to keep between 80,000 and 90,000 employees in Holland's Asian trading posts without cutting noticeably into the revenues which were the basis of the whole Dutch economy. In 1770, when there was a danger that the supply might outstrip the demand, an amount of cloves and nutmegs said to be equal to an entire year's harvest was burned in Amsterdam to keep prices up.

A French explorer and, later, colonial administrator, Pierre Poivre, after thirteen years of unflagging effort, succeeded in spiriting young nutmeg trees and seeds out of Dutch territory about 1773, planted them on Mauritius, and in 1780 the first French nutmegs reached Paris. The Dutch monopoly had been broken.

French nutmegs were planted in Guiana, but failed to flourish there, as was the experience in several other tropical localities (Brazil, for instance). Nutmegs require very special conditions to grow well, and it turned out that only one other place in the world besides the Moluccas could provide them—the West Indian island of Grenada. Today, despite plantings in several other areas, including Mauritius, the nutmeg trade is divided almost exclusively between the Moluccas, supplying 70 percent of the total world demand, and Grenada, which produces the rest. Most of the Grenada nutmegs, coarser and oilier, go to the United States, but the better-educated palates of Europe demand the choicest Indonesian grades, and since Europe is readier to pay a premium for quality, Europe gets the best.

The flavor of nutmeg is aromatic, warm, sweet, piquant, full, rich, strong and smooth. Many writers maintain that female nutmegs are preferable to male ones; either this is literary fancy, or they have subtler taste buds than I have. One person with notoriously developed taste buds was the famous French gourmet Curnonsky, who once wrote that "anyone who has tasted this spice no longer desires others, just as anyone who has made love with a Chinese woman no longer desires to make love with other women." I am not quite sure that I know what he meant by that.

O

OPPIAN: *What suffering results from over-eating! Let man, then, drive from his heart and from his hand the idleness which finds its delights in blamable pleasures and cleave to moderation when he eats . . . for there are many among men who fail to hold the reins taut, but let them drop loosely upon their bellies.*

OVID: *How little you know about the age you live in if you fancy that honey is sweeter than cash in hand.*

OA
stands for

the **oak,** which produces the acorn, a seed more edible than you may think, and the **oak apple,** a gall less edible than you might think; for the **oarfish,** which probably nobody has tried to eat, not to be confused with the paddlefish, which has been tried, but not particularly appreciated; and for the **oarweed,** an alga eaten by people in Scotland, Ireland, China and Japan and by cattle in Scandinavia, a phrase which sounds suspiciously like a partial plagiarism of what Dr. Johnson said about

OATS, when he defined them in his *Dictionary of the English Language* as "a grain which in England is generally given to horses, but in Scotland supports the people." Inconsistently, the opinionated doctor, while at Tobermory on the island of Mull in the year 1773, ate immoderately of sowans, the soured fermented inner shellings of this cereal. Oats in this form were not sufficiently ingratiating to mollify Johnson about the grain, but he seems to have thought better about the Scots, for he wrote later to Boswell, who had lured him into the visit to Scotland during which this gastronomic experience occurred: "I will not send compliments to our friends by name. . . . Tell them, as you see them, how well I speak of Scotch politeness and Scotch hospitality and Scotch beauty, and of everything Scotch, but Scotch oatcakes."

Oats have suffered from a bad press for centuries. Pliny, writing of the Germans, dedicated oat eaters, asked disdainfully, "How can one eat the same food as animals?" In medieval times, when classifying everything was a passion, oats were listed among coarse foods, and coarse foods, it was assumed, coarsened the characters of those who ate them. "Cheese, milk and oatcakes," Paracelsus wrote, "cannot give one a subtle disposition." As late as the time of Sydney Smith (1771–1845), who had perhaps not enjoyed his five years in Edinburgh, where he had settled more or less by accident when war turned him back from a trip to Germany, we find this prelate referring to Scotland as "that knuckle-end of England—that land of Calvin, oat-cakes, and sulphur."

Contempt for the oat may have been born at the time when it was less of a food than a nuisance, for the oat is the Horatio Alger hero of cereals, which progressed, if not from rags to riches, at least from weed to health food. Wild oats first forced themselves upon the attention of farmers by invading fields of wheat or barley, from which they were pulled up and burned. The story is told that cattle were observed one day eating oats stacked up for burning, which gave their proprietor the idea of feeding the weeds to livestock, from which they graduated later to feeding men. The story is a little too pat to be true. I find more plausible the explanation offered by Reay Tannahill in *Food in History,* which is that while wheat was capable of holding its own against oats in the warm lowlands, at higher, cooler altitudes the oats tended to choke out the wheat, driving farmers to harvest the weeds instead of the wheat.

The preference of oats for cool climates makes hash of the theory that they originated somewhere in the Mediterranean area, a place to which many writers ascribe their beginnings. One book which I will not pillory by naming it here, for it is reliable on most points, asserts flatly that the oat of western Europe is indigenous to the region from Armenia along the Mediterranean to the Iberian Peninsula. The fact is that in 1000 B.C. oats were being grown in Germany, Denmark and Switzerland, but were unknown in the Near East. I suspect they originated in, or not far from, northern Germany. They had time to spread to the Mediterranean before classical times, for they were being eaten in northern Europe, perhaps still from wild plants, in Neolithic times; were being cultivated in central Europe in the Bronze Age; and reached Britain in the Iron Age—the epoch of the expanding La Tène culture, which could also have carried oats towards the Mediterranean.

The ancient Romans disdained oats, but the Greeks had a dessert called *plakous*, a cake of oat flour, cheese and honey; and I suspect that oatmeal porridge was a constituent of the sacred drink, *kykeōn*, which initiates to the Eleusinian mysteries were required to swallow, with the apparent intention that the experience should be memorable rather than agreeable. Even today, oats are not important in the Mediterranean basin as a whole. North Africa, and to a certain extent East Africa, make considerable use of this grain (in warm-climate species which may have been relatively late to develop), but one suspects that this is because oats are able to extract nutrients from soil on which wheat or barley would starve. They constitute therefore a suitable crop for comparatively barren regions of Africa. On the European shores of the Mediterranean the cultivation of oats is negligible.

Despised or not, oats have played an important role in human nutrition for as far back as our records reach. It is true that their primary role is to feed animals, especially horses, who take to them with particular avidity. In the United States, 93 percent of the oat crop is used for fodder (but its use as human food has been increasing since early in the century, with a recent jump caused by its adoption by health-food faddists, while the demand from horses is decreasing, for so are the horses). In other parts of the world oats, though still primarily animal food, have played a relatively more important role in the human diet, particularly in poor countries, and in times of dearth. A basic food of the poor, and even of the not so poor, has always been porridge—mush, if you prefer—made of one grain or another; the grain was oats especially in the grimmer periods of history—partly because oats have usually been the cheapest grain and partly because oats are often the last to hold out against unfavorable growing conditions which fell other cereals first.

Certain peoples have always preferred oats even when other grains were equally available. The ancient Germans sowed oats for their mounts and for themselves, and when the barbarian invasions which put an end to the Roman Empire rolled over the west and the south from Germanic central Europe, the form of porridge eaten in the occupied territories, for instance Gaul, shifted from whatever grains had been used formerly to oats. Oatmeal remained popular, or at least useful, through medieval times because a great deal of the food then eaten was heavily salted to preserve it. The cook's problem was to get rid of enough of the salt to make dishes palatable. When it was discovered that oatmeal absorbs salt, it became common practice to hang a muslin bag full of oatmeal in the kettle in which salted foods were boiling; when the bag was removed, a good deal of the salt left with it.

The peoples who felt the greatest affinity for oats were mostly Celts, first of all the Scots. An old Scottish cookbook calls the oat "one of the sweetest grains to cook with," an opinion which may not be universal. Scots have their own ritual fashion of eating oatmeal. In 1786 Bartolomé Faujas de St. Fond, a French visitor to the Isle of Ulva, described this national dish as "a sort of pap of oatmeal and water; in eating this thick pap, each spoonful is plunged alternately into cream, which is always alongside." This remains the traditional fashion for eating oatmeal in Scotland. Scots look upon those who sugar it or pour milk over it as effete. They put cream or milk in a separate bowl and dip each spoonful of oatmeal into it as they go along. The Welsh take their oats in the form of brewis, oatmeal broth, or siot, oatcakes soaked in buttermilk. The Irish are confirmed oats eaters also, but if they have any special formula for dealing with them, I am not aware of it. In France, where the Bretons are Celts too, oatmeal is sometimes called "Breton gruel," because of the importance of oats in the diet of Brittany.

In non-Celtic France, oats do not normally enter to any great extent into the diet, but there is one curious usage—that of employing roasted oats as a substitute for vanilla, whose taste they closely resemble in the opinion of the Larousse gastronomic encyclopedia, but not in that of Honoré de Balzac. In *La Rambouilleuse*, Balzac

OATS. *Drawing by George Cruikshank for Charles Dickens:* Oliver Twist, *London, 1838*

placed some of his characters "in face of little pots of cream in which the vanilla had been replaced by burned oats, which resembled vanilla as much as chicory coffee resembles Mocha."

OC
stands for

the **oca,** a South American tuber too acid to eat fresh which nevertheless, if dried for weeks on end, develops a taste reminiscent of another dried fruit, the fig; for the **ocarina,** which in spite of being called the sweet potato is not edible; for the **oceanic bonito,** a wide-ranging fish particularly appreciated by the Japanese, who eat it under the name katsuwo; for the **ocean catfish,** of which the male hatches the eggs in its mouth; for the **ocean perch,** one of the important food fishes of the northeastern United States; for the **ocean quahog,** which the U.S. Coast Guard has now decided is the continental shelf quahog; for the **ocean sunfish,** whose brain is smaller than its kidney; for the **ochrous pea,** cultivated in the Mediterranean basin primarily for cattle, but eaten by humans when times get tough; and for the **octopus,** whose reputation among the ancient Romans for being aphrodisiac was milked for laughs by Plautus, not the most subtle of classical playwrights, in his *Casina.*

OH
stands for

the **ohelo,** a Hawaiian berry which contributed tellingly to the Christianization of its islands; for the **'ohi'a apple,** also attributed to Hawaii, which was probably brought there by colonizing Polynesians; and for the **Ohio shad,** which is not a shad.

OI
stands for

oil, fat in its most liquid form, prized by some for frying fish and by others for seasoning salad, but by the Greeks of Homeric times for clothing, since, long underwear not yet having been invented, they coated their bodies with it in winter to keep warm; for the **oil bean,** which contains a toxic substance, but Nigerians eat it anyway, after exorcising the poison by soaking the beans in water and then boiling them for twelve hours; for the **oilbird,** or guacharo, which arouses itself for the day at the beginning of the night and then arouses everybody else by making a noise like a flourish of castanets, for which it is rewarded by having its young eaten on the island of Trinidad, where they are esteemed a great delicacy; for the **oil palm,** which yields more oil per acre than can be obtained from any other source, vegetable or animal; and for the **oil tree,** alias the African oak, alias the red ironwood, whose seeds are relished in tropical Africa.

OK
stands for

the **okaokao,** a Saharan marmot which the Tuareg think tastes like rabbit; for the **okapi,** nowadays a rare treat for the natives of the Congo, for it has become a rare animal for which they could demand a rare price if they only knew how much more it is worth in a zoo than in a kettle; and for **okazu,** a Japanese category of foods of enormous vagueness, since what the word means is anything which can be eaten with rice.

And **OK** also stands for

OKRA. A vegetable is not without honor, save in its own country. The tomato and the potato are natives of the New World, but the United States did not accept them until, having traveled abroad, the tomato was returned to America from Italy and the potato from Ireland. A similar phenomenon occurred in the reverse direction when okra (which admittedly provides less incentive for gourmets than either the tomato or the potato), a native of the Eastern Hemisphere which might easily have been imported from the Middle East or from Africa, did not attract the attention of Europe until it returned to the Old World after having been transported to the New.

OKRA. *Woodcut from* Harris Rural Annual, *1893*

Okra was introduced into the Western Hemisphere by black slaves from Africa, probably its place of origin, though some votes have been cast for Asia. I have read that it was eaten in Africa in prehistoric times, but this information was not accompanied by any details which would permit confirming or confuting it. The *Horizon Cookbook* reproduced an ancient Egyptian painting which was alleged to depict slaves harvesting okra from trellises, but if the fruits shown were supposed to be okra, the Egyptians were very inaccurate painters. I have yet to come across any convincing evidence that okra was known to any literate society before our era, a point in favor of an African rather than an Asian origin, for Asia became literate before Africa did.

A significant testimonial to the close association between okra and Africa is provided in Brazil, where a sect known as the Candomblé has transferred its customs from one continent to another and maintained them intact for four centuries on alien soil. Among the consecrated dishes which are prepared by its priestesses for their ritual observances is one based on okra, which has to be made according to a rigid formula from which deviation would be a sacrilege. It not only calls for cutting the okra pods into minute pieces (even the small seeds have to be cut into two or more parts), but it also prescribes the order in which the cuts must be made. To prepare the dish in accordance with the sacred rules takes several hours.

Okra is also tied to Africa by its very name. It comes from *nkruman* or *nkrumun*, from the Twi language spoken on the Gold Coast. Slaves from Angola brought in okra too, but called it, in Umbundu, *ochinggombo* or *ngombo*. This became "gumbo," but has changed its meaning. "Gumbo" originally meant the vegetable, but is now applied to almost the only dish in which okra is used in the United States, a catch-all stew adopted from the Indians (one of the meats it caught in their time was owl), which was thickened with filé powder made from dried sassafras leaves. When okra appeared on the scene, it displaced filé powder as the thickener and gave its other name to the stew. However, there are traditionalists (who do not know they are traditionalists) in the South who still prefer filé powder to okra as the thickener, so today there are gumbos which have no gumbo (i.e., okra) in them at all. I am told that using both in the same dish would be inadvisable unless you like stew with the consistency of glue.

Okra is always harvested unripe, about ten weeks after planting, when the pods which are its edible part are no longer than nine inches at the most; if allowed to ripen, okra becomes fibrous and indigestible. In America, where it appears almost exclusively in stews and soups, it is usually seen in cross section, cut into disks which look like little wheels, with a seed nestled between each pair of spokes. The taste is pleasing, a little tart, clean, and the disks feel crisp under the teeth—curiously, since the outstanding characteristic of okra is that it is mucilaginous, which is what makes it a good thickener. It is seldom cooked in the United States as a separate vegetable for its own sake, though there are exceptions —an okra and tomato dish in Texas, for instance, or Charleston's okra pilau, otherwise known as Limping Susan. Fresh okra used to be a fixture in American vegetable markets, but is disappearing now, for it is the sort of food which supermarkets would rather not handle; we get it instead canned, frozen or dried, which may be why interest in it is dying. In a 1974 survey made by the United States Department of Agriculture, adults named okra as one of the three vegetables they liked least, and children rated it with four which they liked second-least.

In Europe, there is no problem of a decline of interest in okra, for there has never been any, exception made for the extreme southeast corner, which is in the Middle East gastronomic belt, and Spain, where the Moors introduced it. I read with some surprise in a guide for Americans abroad that okra (which, incidentally, is described as a sort of squash, proof enough that its author is not a Southerner) is "very common . . . in France; in England and Germany less so." It happens that I have lived in France for more than forty years and I have yet to see okra there; my maid, who is French, didn't know what it was when I asked her, and my wife, French also, has seen it in exotic food shops but never tasted it. The only Frenchman who to my knowledge has ever shown interest in this vegetable was Pierre Paul François Camille Savorgnan de Brazza, who said that he had planted okra, a fast-growing plant, wherever, in his travels, he stopped for a few months, because it was "wholesome and nutritious." But de Brazza had exceptional opportunities to know about okra, for he was an explorer of Africa, a country where okra is found elsewhere than in luxury food shops.

Okra, indeed, is the very opposite of a luxury food. Now grown almost everywhere in tropical, subtropical and warm temperate regions, it is a food of the Third World, where it is much more than a thickener. In India, where a slightly different variety from the American one is known as *bendi-kai*, it is eaten fresh, prepared like asparagus, or is pickled. In the Middle East, including Greece and Egypt, where it is called by its Arabic name *bamyah* or *bamieh*, the tender young pods enter into various combinations, a favorite being a dish of okra and chopped meat. In North Africa, tropical Africa and Madagascar the pods, fresh or dried, and the leaves, also fresh or dried, are widely eaten; the young shoots get around a little less; and even the calyxes are eaten, though rarely. It is Africa which has bestowed its okra dishes on the region of the New World which eats okra most enthusiastically, the Caribbean, as we know by their names. The celebrated callaloo, a rich stew or soup, takes its name from a spinach-like vegetable which is one of its ingredients; coo-coo is an okra dish whose name is a corruption of an African word meaning meal or mush; and foo-foo comes from another African word which refers to the pale color of foods which have been pounded. Foo-foo is belovéd of Fidel Castro, who has described it as a "great delicacy" and explained that it was "our beefsteak" in the days when he and his guerrillas were operating from their hideouts in the hills.

OL
stands for

the **olachen**, or candlefish, so fatty that it can be equipped with a wick and used as a lamp; for old man, which is southernwood, and **old man's pepper,** which is yarrow; for the **old squaw,** which is a duck whose down is as fine as the eider's, the **old wife,** which is the black bream for North Africans, and the **old woman,** which is sea wormwood; for the **oleaster,** whose edible fruit masquerades as the Trebizond date or the Russian olive; and for the **Olympia oyster** of the Pacific Northwest, tiny, but one of the most luscious in the world.

And **OL** also stands for

OLIVE. "No fruit tree," wrote an anonymous author in *Gourmet* in November 1969, "has exerted so profound an influence on the growth of civilization as the olive. It has provided the sustenance, the means for survival, in all the countries of the desert fringe in which it grows. The rich, oily fruits have shaped the whole character of the Mediterranean, the distinctive flavor of its food." "Except the vine," said Pliny, "there is no plant which bears a fruit of as great importance as the olive." Plato, because he had a delicate stomach, was a light eater but a discriminating one: he came to the conclusion that the olive was his favorite food.

These tributes to the importance of the olive may seem exaggerated in the case of a fruit of which we are conscious chiefly as an appetizer, or a garnisher of a limited number of dishes, or an ingredient for salad dressing along with a number of other oils which are frequently substituted for it, or a diver in the depths of a martini—in short, or so we think, a fruit whose disappearance we would hardly notice. But in ancient times, when our civilization was being shaped, the olive was not simply a preface or a decorative touch to the more important dishes of the meal, it was often the most important dish itself. (It still is in the Middle East.) Its oil is not merely one member of a family of indifferently interchangeable vegetable fats, but is almost unique among them in possessing a decided character irreplaceable by others. The function of most oils is mechanical rather than gastronomic. They moisten salads to make them easier to swallow or they provide a cooking fat to keep foods from sticking to the pan, but they do not alter dishes by adding flavors of their own. Olive oil, on the contrary, contributes both flavor and nutrition to any dish anointed by it or cooked in it, and becomes a full-fledged ingredient on its own. It has thus, over a period of five thousand years or more, shaped the cuisines of the Middle East, Greece, Italy, Spain and southern France as we know them today and as they are likely to remain, immutable, as long as the olive, a tree nearly immortal, continues to exist.

The versatility of the olive made it indispensable to the ancient world in other roles besides that of food. "There are two liquids especially agreeable to the human body, wine inside and oil outside," said Pliny, for his countrymen in his time anointed their bodies with scented oil as a perfume (we have cosmetic uses for olive oil too), while Homer's countrymen in his time did the same thing in winter for warmth—especially the women, who led a relatively inactive life indoors: olive oil was the Homeric equivalent of mink.

Olive oil was also a cleanser, for the ancients had no soap. It was a medicine too, which Homeric Greeks, biblical Hebrews and ancient Romans believed capable of penetrating the skin and bestowing health and longevity on the body (we know today that the olive tree contains salicylic acid, the active element in aspirin). Burned in earthenware lamps, olive oil provided the most convenient source of light. In ancient Egypt, it is believed to have been used as a lubricant to help move obelisks and the great blocks of stone which built the pyramids. It was, and is, used to preserve many other foods—tuna, sardines, and anchovy fillets, for instance. The pulp which remained after the oil had been pressed from olives was fed to animals or used for fertilizer; the liquid residue served the ancient Romans as a weed killer and a discourager of insect pests when sprayed on cabbages. The olive tree provides hardwood, close-grained and whorled, beautiful and strong. The Bible tells us it was employed in constructing the tabernacle of Solomon's temple. It was used to make spear shafts in those days and adze handles in ours.

When Cecrops founded a capital city in Attica, the always practical Greeks offered to name it for the god who gave them the most valuable gift. Poseidon produced the horse; Athena struck the ground with her spear and an olive tree arose. The city was called Athens. Since we are also told that it was Cecrops who introduced the olive to Attica from Argos, we might consider this one of the cases in which historical truth lies behind a myth—except that Cecrops was a myth too, half man and half serpent. But it is probably true that Attica received the olive from Argos, where the first olive trees of Greece, obtained from Crete, are believed to have been planted about 1700 B.C. in Mycenae, which got them from Crete, which at that period exercised a strong influence over Mycenae.

Crete may have been the birthplace of the olive; it was at least somewhere at the eastern end

Olive *by Vincent van Gogh (1853–1890).* The Olive Orchard, *oil on canvas*

of the Mediterranean, where the olive seems to have been cultivated as far back as Neolithic times. One theory is that Egypt cultivated it first, because Egyptian art depicts olive picking; but this does not prove that the olives were cultivated rather than wild, or, indeed, even that they were eaten: they might have been gathered for lubrication or lighting. The majority opinion seems to be that the olive was first cultivated in Syria and Palestine, as early as the fourth millennium B.C.; but it seems to have been cultivated in Crete also about 3500 B.C., and when we discover olive oil in international commerce, probably no later than 2500 B.C., it seems to be Crete which is shipping it to Egypt and Asia Minor, not the other way around.

Wherever it came from, the olive found in Greece conditions ideal for its development. The soil was not good enough for many crops, and not even very good for pasturage, so that there was a dearth of animal fats, leaving a niche wide open for olive oil. The olive could thrive on Attica's meager ground, for which its affinity was so pronounced that the oil of Athens was considered the best in the ancient world. Drawing the logical conclusion from this fact, the Athenians adopted the policy of devoting themselves to raising olives and buying their indispensable grain from other countries with the profits of the olive trade. This obliged Athens to build up a navy capable of defending its supply lines to the granaries, and for a time it was the world's greatest sea power. Realizing where Athens was economically vulnerable, the Spartans took every opportunity to cut down the olive groves of Attica. This may have led to the unseating of Pericles, for the Athenians resented his strategy of defending the city and leaving its outlying olive plantations (which included some of his own) at the mercy of the enemy. (History repeated itself in 1815 when Joachim Murat, king of Naples, was shot after he had courted unpopularity by having the olive trees cut down because he felt that they gave the peasants too easy a life and he wanted them to work harder.)

The western Mediterranean received the olive from the eastern Mediterranean in illogical order—not from Greece to her nearest neighbor, Italy, and thence through France to Spain, but just the other way around. Spain probably acquired its first olives in the fourth century B.C., when Carthage controlled a considerable part of the Iberian Peninsula; by that time Carthage was well launched in olive cultivation, as we know from the works of the fourth-century Carthaginian agricultural writer Mago, who devoted a good deal of space to this fruit. France received olives sometime between 680 and 600 B.C. from the Phocaean Greeks from Asia Minor who founded Marseilles. There seem to have been no olives on Roman-ruled territory as late as the reign of Tarquin the Elder, about 550 B.C.; but shortly afterward they were planted in Latium, the territory of which the city of Rome was the capital.

The Romans, heavy consumers of olives, ate them at the beginning of the meal as appetizers, as we do, and often also at its end, to freshen the mouth; in between, the meal might include dishes of which olives were the principal ingredient. Cato the Elder wrote that olives and bread were the staple foods of Roman peasants and workers. He gave his own laborers and slaves rations of these two foods plus salt and wine, but cannily fed them on windfall olives and inferior ones deficient in oil, saving the best to sell to the wealthy for the table and the second best to make oil.

Outside of olive-growing areas, the fruit and its oil were all but ignored in medieval and Renaissance times. The chief cooking fat then was lard, and even in the Mediterranean basin olive oil enjoyed no monopoly. Italy used not only olive oil but also lard, while Greece and the Middle East also employed mutton fat. Spain was the exception, because the Moors ruled there and prohibited pork products. Consequently Spain cooked exclusively with olive oil and achieved a head start in its use which has kept her to this day the world's foremost producer of olives.

It seems incredible that olive oil was virtually unknown in Paris until the Revolution, when it was introduced by a Provençal restaurant opened there then; but apparently Thomas Jefferson could not find it in Paris when he was Minister to France, for in 1786 he wrote to the United States consul in Bordeaux to order "12 pint bottles of best Provence oil." One of Jefferson's greatest disappointments as an impassioned farmer was his failure to induce olives to bear fruit in the southeastern United States. He wrote of the olive that "of all the gifts of heaven to man, it is next to the most precious. Perhaps it may claim a preference even to bread, because there is such an infinitude of vegetables, which it renders a proper and comfortable nourishment." He planted olive cuttings at Monticello in 1774, but many of them did not take root, and those which did were killed when Virginia was visited by a cold spell. On the theory that the olive was "the worthiest plant to be introduced into America" he sent about five hundred olive tree pieces from Aix-en-Provence to South Carolina in 1791, but wrote sadly twenty-five years later, "If any of them still exist, it is merely as a curiosity in . . . gardens, not a single orchard of them has been planted." He wrote a friend in North Carolina in 1817 that he hoped that state might become "a country abounding in wine and oil," and urged it to "go forward in this culture, the olive, the Sesamus, the Cane & Coffee." Nothing came of this either, nor of many other attempts to raise olives in the Southeast, made both before and after his time.

What Jefferson did not know was that while he was trying despairingly to grow olives in Virginia and the Carolinas, they were already being produced elsewhere in America. The Franciscans who moved into California from Mexico planted the first olive trees there, at the latest by 1769; some of the original trees are still alive. Less impressed by the virtues of the olive than was Jefferson, Californians paid little attention to it for something like a hundred years, and only in this century did they begin to develop the olive with real intensity, with a success which we all know.

The Spaniards gave olives to South America too, where they planted three saplings in Lima, Peru, in 1560. One of them was subsequently stolen and transplanted in Chile. These three trees seem to have been the sole ancestors of all the olives now grown on that continent, including the not inconsiderable quantities produced in Argentina.

Olives are believed to have been first planted in China during the sixth century A.D., but are little used there; the Chinese cuisine is incompatible with a cooking oil which intrudes its own distinctive flavor into every dish cooked in it. China never uses it for deep frying, for instance, though in Japan, where tempura cooks have a habit of devising their individual blends of cooking oils, it goes into some formulas, but always in a minority role, to add to the dish a little authority but not too much. India, which tolerates almost all other vegetable oils, never uses olive oil; it is too rich for the Indian cuisine.

Commercial olive growing is feasible everywhere between 30 and 45 degrees of latitude, north or south, where its growing requirements are met; but these, formed over the millennia in the very special climate of the Mediterranean, are narrow, and are not found in many places. Though the olive shows no discomfort when five or six months pass without a drop of rain and other plants dry up, this does not mean that it can get along without water. It needs eight to ten inches a year, but it doesn't matter when it falls or how, whether in the slow, ground-drenching rains most plants prefer or in the sudden short downpours which run off quickly without benefiting them: the olive will send down its long taproot all the way to the water table to pick up moisture when it needs it. It loses virtually no moisture by evaporation, for its leaves, a leathery, waxy green above, a hairy, silvery gray below, are water-tight. Consequently it is not happy with *more* water than it needs, for it can't get rid of the excess. Thus the tree grows well on the coast of the Gulf of Mexico but does not set fruit because there is too much humidity in the air.

The olive needs full sunlight and does not tolerate shade. Its heat requirements are high: flowers or fruit are injured when the temperature falls to 28° F., the tree itself is injured below 15° and is killed at 10°. Thus it grows lushly in the tropics but again does not produce fruit; it requires a winter resting period, like trees of the temperate zone. It also has an altitude restriction: it rarely grows above 2000 feet. These requirements mean that olive growing in the United States is restricted to the interior valleys of California and the warmer parts of Arizona; California in fact produces 99.9 percent of all the olives grown commercially in the United States.

The olive's rhythm is unruffled wherever it grows. Picking times are the same everywhere in the Northern Hemisphere: for green olives, which are green not only in color but also in the sense of being unripe, September (the best come from Andalusia, Spain); for black olives, which are the same ones left to ripen on the tree ("The more black olives ben wythout," wrote John of Trevisa in the fourteenth century, "the more ripe they ben within"), November (the best come from California); for oil olives, still the same ones, left on the tree beyond ripening, January (the best oil comes from Lucca, Italy, the second best from Provence, France).

The olive's schedule for bearing and its yield are more responsive to local conditions. It has a habit of bearing abundantly only every other year, which may be associated with the fact that it produces fruit only on the new wood of the previous year's growth. Its normal timetable might be set at ten years to the first fruit, thirty years to the first profitable crop. Some Mediterranean peoples believe that the olive's natural production and calendar cannot be improved with care, and indeed that it does better untended: "Pamper an olive tree and spoil the fruit," say the Spaniards. But in California careful care has produced yields five to ten times that of Mediterranean countries, and fruit has been encouraged to start forming at three or four years on nursery stock.

Slowness in beginning to bear is usually associated in the plant world with longevity, and the olive is no exception. Botanists describe the tree's normal life span as from 300 to 600 years, but admit that individual trees may exceed this. The oldest trees for which we have unassailable records are 700 years old. This makes it extremely unlikely that the tree which may be pointed out to you in the Vatican gardens in Rome was really bearing fruit in the time of Charlemagne, which would make it 1200 years old, much less that certain Italian trees which will be shown you in various parts of Italy were really growing in the days of the Roman Republic. When I was living near Nice in 1952 a tree in that vicinity was presented as the oldest olive in the world, reputedly 2000 years old; in 1973, when I was last there, it seemed to be unknown: either it died or human credulity did. Guides in Jerusalem will show you trees on the Mount of Olives which, they claim, witnessed the betrayal of Christ; you can believe them if you are so minded. Other guides, in Athens, point out the very tree under which Plato sat to think deep thoughts; they do not all select the same tree, but that is hardly important, since it is almost certainly untrue for any of them. It is not always the same tree either which is shown you on the Greek island of Skyros as the one under which Rupert Brooke sat daily to write his poems; this is even less important, for, although Rupert Brooke is indubitably buried there, in an olive grove, he never set foot on Skyros while he was alive. Ah, well! It is the function of historians, not of guides, to seek out the truth. The function of guides is to fascinate tourists.

ON
stands for

the **onager,** or wild ass, which ancient Romans ate in imitation of ancient Persians and tropical

Africans eat in imitation of nobody; and for the **once-spawned-sea-fish,** or mended kelt, a salmon which has survived spawning and returned to the sea, from which it may return to spawn a second time and even (rarely, rarely!) a third.

And **ON** also stands for

ONION. The onion is a lily, but so are the asparagus, the tulip, the asphodel, the yucca and the red-hot poker. Break down the *Liliaceae* family into its various tribes, and one of them turns out to be the *Allioideae,* whose largest genus is *Allium,* with about 325 species of which some 70 are natives of North America. Here we are on familiar ground, odorously surrounded by a group of plants well known in the kitchen, whose most conspicuous shared characteristic is strength in smell and taste—leeks, shallots, scallions, garlic and, of course, onions.

"Garlic," says the French writer Raymond Dumay, "is peasant, rustic; the onion is urban. The onion brings to the kitchens of the cities a little of the countryside . . . the onion offers always, and especially in winter, a little of the springtime of the soil, preserved in its bulb." "The onion," wrote French gourmet Robert J. Courtine, "is the truffle of the poor." And Dean Swift added:

There is in every cook's opinion,
No savoury dish without an onion:
But lest your kissing should be spoiled
The onion must be thoroughly boiled.

Cooking does indeed render harmless the raw onion, which draws tears from the eyes, creates difficulties for those of weak digestion, and offends many by its sulphurous smell. These qualities stem from the diabolic origin of the onion, of which we are informed by an ancient Turkish legend which explains that when Satan was cast out of heaven, garlic sprouted where he first placed his left foot and onions where he placed the right.

Skeptics who boggle at accepting this simple account have no good substitute to offer: for them the origin of the onion remains a mystery. It was already being cultivated by prehistoric men when they were still in the collecting stage which preceded the pastoral and agricultural stages, when roots and bulbs were easy to gather, and the onion perhaps easier than most, since it gave itself away by its smell. Where was it sniffed out first? Most authorities put it somewhere in Asia, either in the southwest corner or the center of that continent. One way to check this theory might be to identify the world's oldest onion, the ancestor of all the others, and try to find out where *it* comes from. Some authorities think this is A. *fistulosum,* so primitive that it has not learned how to form a bulb; the bottom part of its stem thickens, like that of the scallion, but it stops there. If this is indeed the first onion, our problem would seem to be solved, for its popular name is the Welsh onion, but the Welsh onion is not Welsh. It was not introduced into the British Isles until 1629, and has never been much cultivated in Wales. Its name is a corruption of a German word meaning "foreign," given it when it first turned up in central Europe at the end of the Middle Ages. Turned up from where? Eastern Asia, many experts say; but this is in conflict with the assertion that the onion was unknown in China before the sixth century A.D.; and besides, A. *fistulosum* is unknown in Asia in the wild state, usually the sign of an immigrant rather than a native.

So far as I know, the seekers of the earliest onion have not turned their attention to the tree onion, which like other onions develops when it is ripe a globe at the summit of its central stalk, which in the others is composed of tiny flowers which give rise to seeds, but in the tree onion is composed of bulbils, miniature bulbs; the tree onion has not even learned how to form seeds, relatively sophisticated mechanisms for reproduction. Or, rather, since it is not consistent in this —sometimes its globe contains bulbils, sometimes seeds—it seems to be a beginner in the seed business. This should make it older than the Welsh onion, which has solved the seed-producing problem. If this is the world's oldest onion, once again one of its popular names should point out to us the origin of the onion, for it is also called the Egyptian onion. This name seems as misleading as "Welsh onion" (does it come, perhaps, from confusion with the gipsy onion, A. *ursinum?*), for the tree onion was unknown in Egypt, and for that matter in the Old World in general, until a Frenchman, Jacques Dalechamp, was astonished to see a specimen of this species in 1587. Where did it come from? Its scientific name is A. *canadense,* given it when it was officially introduced into Great Britain in 1820, coming from Canada. It grows wild in North America, and so does the Welsh onion. Can it be that the place of origin of this vegetable is where no one has thought to look for it, in America?

Wherever the onion originated, its written history seems to begin in Mesopotamia, and on its first appearance it is already in bad odor, though the onion itself was innocent, unless you admit guilt by association. A cuneiform inscription in

Onion *by Paul Cézanne (1839–1906).* Still Life with Onions, *oil on canvas*

the oldest written language we know, Sumerian, tells us that about 2400 B.C. the municipal authorities of the city which may not yet have been called Babylon were caught misusing the property of the temple: "The oxen of the gods plowed the city governor's onion patches. The onion and cucumber patches of the city governor were located in the gods' best fields."

The onion was one of the most familiar vegetables of ancient Mesopotamia. The oldest known body of law, the Code of Hammurabi, stipulates that the needy shall receive a monthly ration of bread and onions. Onions seem to have been regarded primarily as a food for the poor, who ate it raw on bread, a combination which formed their staple diet. But it was grown also in the gardens of kings, from that of Ur-Nammu of Ur (2100 B.C.) to that of Merodach-Baladan of Babylon (716 B.C.).

The ancient Egyptians were great onion eaters too, but it is probably untrue that they were also onion worshipers, as Pliny and Juvenal alleged. They may have been led astray by the fact that there was a small sect whose members refused to eat onions for religious reasons (whether because they worshiped them or not, we do not know) in Pelusium, a city at the eastern edge of the Nile delta which happened to be particularly well known to Romans; but this does not justify calling all Egyptians onion worshipers, any more than we would be justified in calling all Frenchmen onion worshipers because there exists today in France a sect with about four thousand adepts who consider the onion immortal and hence divine. The onion is the plant shown oftenest in Egyptian art, which was hardly surprising in a country where the staple diet of the humble was bread, onions and beer. If it was sometimes depicted on altars, that was not because it was a divinity, but because it was a sacrifice; in the Old Kingdom, baskets of onions were considered the second-best funerary offerings, the best being bread.

We do not know exactly when the onion reached Greece. It was present at least by 500 B.C., when we find that Attica, though it was not much given to growing vegetables, did produce considerable quantities of onions (the only other important vegetables were garlic, cabbage, peas and lentils). By the time of Pericles the market of Athens offered a much wider choice, but the consumption of most vegetables remained limited, for they were expensive. This was not the case for the onion, which was still being eaten widely, especially by the poor.

We do not know either when the onion reached Rome, where it was also a food of the poor, for the first mention of it which I have come across is by Horace, who included it in his "economical diet." Later Apicius, whose cookbook is clearly designed for the wealthy, did use onion in his sauces or as an accompaniment for other dishes, but he avoided recommending it as a vegetable in its own right, or admitting that it might be eaten whole or, *horribile dictu*, raw; yet we know that ordinary Romans had long been addicted to such reprehensible practices as starting the day with a breakfast of raw onion on bread. We are probably, Don and Patricia Brothwell suggested in *Food in Antiquity*, "faced with class differences in taste, as onions were in fact very widely grown in Italy." Class differences in means too, one might add: the onion was still a poor man's food.

Columella, the first agricultural writer of the Christian era, praised the onions of Pompeii. As it happens, one of the items found in the ruins of Pompeii was a basket of badly overcooked onions, discovered, not as one might expect, in the market, but in one of the city's better equipped brothels, from which we may deduce that Pompeian onions were not so strong as to discourage this establishment's *raison d'être*. The onion seems nevertheless to have been held in low repute in Pompeii, where the guild of fruit and vegetable vendors refused to admit onionmongers, who were therefore obliged to form a separate association, considered the lowliest of all. But by the time Trajan built his market, about A.D. 110, onions were respectable enough in Rome so that they hung in tressed strings, like a forest of stalactites, from the ceiling of the market's first floor.

The barbarians arrived, but needed no lessons about onions: the ancient Germans were accustomed to seasoning roasts and stews heavily with onions and garlic. During the Middle Ages, we are told, onions were a favorite food of the common people, but they were appreciated also by persons not quite so common, beginning with Charlemagne, who ordered them planted in his domains. Onions appear in French feudal deeds more frequently than any other vegetable except garlic. They were often listed as one of the crops in which rent had to be paid to the lord of the land, or even as one of those symbolic payments so dear to feudal times as token acknowledgments of sovereignty: we find a string of tressed onions, for instance, as the sole tribute demanded annually for the use of land.

Marco Polo reported from the Persian island of Hormuz that its inhabitants ate dates, salt tuna and onions, "and on this diet they thrive." Farther east, the onion was less welcome. When the ancient Aryans invaded India, they allowed their conquered inferiors to eat onions if they felt like it, but forbade members of their own more refined race to indulge in them; a Chinese traveler reported that some of them did all the same, but only outside the city limits. Indians as a rule dislike onions, and garlic too, to this day. The Chinese were more broad-minded, and Peking cooking is still characterized by use of "the three strong-flavored seasoners," onions, garlic and ginger.

Meanwhile in England onions had been popular since at least the thirteenth century, when Alexander Neckam, abbot of Cirencester, listed them among vegetables worthy to be planted in noble gardens, and set the example by growing them in his own. In Elizabethan times, onions and leeks were the favorite vegetables of England; salads were made chiefly of onions and herbs.

In America, Cortez saw onions on his way to Tenochtitlán, while farther to the north, and a century later, Père Marquette told of being saved from starvation by eating nodding onions and tree onions, native wild American varieties. This was in 1624, when his explorations took him from Green Bay to a point on the southern shore of Lake Michigan which still commemorates its abundance in onions by having taken for its name the Indian word for their odor: *chicago*.

Despite the variety of native American onions —at least one species in each of the forty-eight contiguous states, and often several—the onions eaten in the United States today are almost always descendants of the Eurasian A. *cepa*, first known to have been planted in Massachusetts in 1648. Pre-Columbian Indians, however, had eaten many of the native varieties, not only, like Marquette, the tree onion, A. *canadense*, and the nodding onion, A. *cernuum*, but also the prairie onion, A. *stellatum*, and A. *reticulatum*, whose popular name, if it has one, I do not know. It is possible that it was a native onion which American cowboys used to put into son-of-a-bitch stew, of which they considered it an indispensable ingredient, even though they had endowed it with a disrespectful name: skunk egg.

OP
stands for

the **opah**, alias the sunfish, kingfish or Jerusalem haddock, large and brilliantly colored, eaten especially in West Africa, the closest land to its preferred deep-ocean waters; for the **openarse**, or MEDLAR, whose name is explained by its morphology; for the **ophthis**, a small limpet without which old-timers consider no Hawaiian luau complete; and for the **opossum**, whose succulence is most appreciated in the southeastern United States, where it is perhaps not widely known that it has no objection to eating worms.

OR
stands for

orach, sometimes used as a substitute for spinach, which explains why it is also known as mountain spinach; for the **orange scorpionfish**, which like scorpionfish of whatever color makes use of poisonous spines to protect its edible flesh; for the **orang-utan**, which means "man of the woods," unclannishly eaten by a cousin which inhabits the same area, the man of Borneo; for the **orchid**, whose root was eaten by ancient Romans, and the **orchis**, whose root is eaten by modern invalids; for the **Oregon grape**, which is not a grape, and **Oregon honey**, from bees which prey on fireweed; for **organ meats**, a straightforward description of such foods as kidneys, liver and sweetbreads, often referred to in Nice Nelly fashion as variety meats or utility meats; for the **oribi**, a pygmy antelope of South Africa, described in one reference book as having been eaten in prehistoric Africa, but it is eaten in contemporary Africa too; for the **Orkney sea trout**, which, unoriginally, frequents the Orkney Islands; for the **ormer**, the name given in the Channel Islands to the abalone; for **orpine**, also called stonecrop, live-forever, Aaron's rod or frog-plant, a wild constituent of salads; and for the **ortolan**, a European bunting so highly thought of by French gourmets that *ortolans sauce blanche* is a synonym for luxury.

And **OR** also stands for

ORANGE. The orange is a 20-million-year-old (say paleobiologists) berry (say botanists) which is one of the five or six most important fruits in the world (say economists) and certainly among the most delicious (say gastronomists). It is presumed to be a native of southern China on the positive evidence of the large number of wild varieties present there and the prevalence of pests and diseases which it has pleased nature to provide to prey upon it, and to have remained a Chinese monopoly for centuries on the negative evidence of the failure of Alexander the Great's eagle-eyed companion Nearchus to report its existence (though he did not miss the banana and the sugarcane) in 325 B.C. in the valley of the Indus —where it would nevertheless be signaled, for the first time outside of China, in the first century A.D.—also the century when Rome would become acquainted with it. This would have been at least a couple of millennia after China had begun to cultivate oranges, which we know from old texts to have been probably as early as 2400 B.C., but certainly not later than about 1500 B.C., when I Yin, minister of the Emperor Ch'eng T'ang, recommended "the bitter oranges of Chiang-p'u."

There were no oranges in the hanging gardens of Babylon, they are not mentioned in the Bible, and it is questionable whether the ancient Greeks knew them. The usual route by which foods from the East reached the Mediterranean, through Asia Minor, was bypassed by the orange in its voyage to Rome by coast-hugging Arab dhows from India to the Red Sea coast of Egypt, by camel caravan to the Nile, by Nile boat to Alexandria and by Mediterranean ships to Ostia, the port of Rome. This meant three to four months en route, a long time for oranges to hold out in transit, but saplings were probably planted early in North Africa. That they did get to Rome we know from Martial's directions for protecting the trees from cold, but they were always rare and expensive there, and cease to be heard from after the collapse of the empire.

The Moors revived the history of the orange in Europe when they conquered Spain, where they arrived in the eighth century, probably at first too busy fighting to concern themselves with planting, but by the twelfth they had converted the region from Granada to Seville into one vast citrus orchard. The Saracens of Sicily were likewise responsible for the fact that oranges were being cultivated there in the eleventh century, and with great abundance by the thirteenth, when Italy seems to have acquired them as well: St. Dominic is said to have planted orange trees in the garden of Rome's Santa Sabina convent in or about 1200, while the five golden balls on the coat of arms of the Medici family, which dates from the fourteenth century, may represent oranges.

Mediterranean France was and is orange-growing country, so it is not surprising that the first reference to this fruit from France is a customs list which shows that they were being exported from Nice by 1332; but we find them farther north only a year later, for the household accounts of Humbert, dauphin of the Viennois, list an expenditure for transplanting orange trees. Did he already have an orangerie, that status symbol for sovereigns, destined to enhance royal glory by demonstrating an ability to finance the production of a rare, exotic and expensive fruit in a climate to which it was not accustomed? Returning from an ill-conceived campaign in Italy, where he had seen oranges for perhaps the first time, Charles VIII added an orangerie to his château d'Amboise about 1495, whereupon his wife, Anne de Bretagne, not to be outdone by her simple-minded husband, did likewise at her château de Blois. Early in the 1500s the constable of Bourbon established an orangerie at Chantilly, one of whose trees is reputed to have lived 436 years. Henry II made a present to his mistress, Diane de Poitiers, of an orangerie for her château d'Anet and Henry IV to his mother-in-law, Catherine de' Medici, for the Tuileries Palace, which she had built on a whim and then never occupied because an astrologer told her the place was unlucky. Oranges did not much occupy the orangerie either, which Henry IV gave over mostly to mulberries, in a vain attempt to make silkworms happy in Paris. The most famous orangerie, of course, was the one built at Versailles for Louis XIV by Mansart, considered a more splendid example of architecture than the château of Versailles itself; it held 1200 orange trees in silver tubs plus 300 other exotic trees. That it was built for show rather than for food was evident when Louis, away at the wars as it neared completion, wrote to his principal minister, Colbert, in May 1674, "Let me know what effect the orange trees at Versailles are making." He didn't ask how they tasted and indeed didn't eat them; oranges for the royal table were imported from Portugal. After Louis XIV, every king, prince and princeling of Europe had to have his orangerie; the record for orange housing seems to have been held by Frederick Augustus I, elector of Saxony, who started to build a new palace with the orangerie and spent so much money on the orangerie that he could never afford to construct the palace.

So far as I know, the first record of oranges reaching England dates from 1290, when a Spanish ship loaded with them arrived at Southampton and the queen, Eleanor of Castille, who seems not to have been a reckless spender, bought seven. They were rare in early Tudor England but a trifle more familiar by Elizabeth's time. Shakespeare refers to them several times, once, in *Much Ado About Nothing,* rather cryptically: "The Count is neither sad, nor sick, nor merry, nor well; but civil Count, civil as an orange, and something of that jealous complexion." By the time of Charles II the fruit was so common that "orange girls" sold it in theaters, and, at a slightly higher price, themselves. Among them was Nell Gwynn; "The darling strumpet of the crowd," Lord Rochester called her. "Anybody may know she has been an orange wench by her swearing," said Louise de Kéroualle, Duchess of Portsmouth. Nell was "false, foolish, old, ill-natur'd and ill-bred," according to Dryden. It is to be suspected that the duchess objected less to Nell's swearing (Charles did not) than to the fact that Nell shared the king's bed, and so did her ladyship.

The first importer of oranges to the New World was Christopher Columbus, who picked up seeds or saplings in the Canary Islands on his second voyage and planted them on the island of Hispaniola in 1493. The climate of the West Indies pleased the orange, and by the 1520s many of the islands were covered with orange groves. The first point on the mainland where they took root was probably Panama, where they are known to have been growing at Caribana in 1516. Bernal Díaz del Castillo tells of sowing them in Mexico in 1518: "The trees came up very well, for when the *papas* [Aztec priests] saw that these were different plants from any they knew, they protected them and watered them and kept them free from weeds. All the oranges in the province are descendants of these trees." Pizarro is supposed to have planted the first oranges in Peru, which would have had to be before 1541, when the Incas, who were not of the opinion that the gift of oranges compensated for some of his other actions, took the liberty of assassinating him. Oranges are known to have been growing in Brazil by 1587, where they must have been planted by the Portuguese.

The first introduction of oranges into what is now the territory of the United States may not have been the work of Hernando de Soto, who planted some in Florida in 1539, but it is the first on record. Oranges were no doubt planted in

ORANGE *by Henri Fantin-Latour (1836–1904).* Still Life, *oil on canvas*

St. Augustine not long after it was founded in 1565; they were growing there abundantly in 1586 when Sir Francis Drake sacked the city and maliciously ordered the orange trees cut down. Orange trees are hard to destroy: new shoots sprouted from the severed trunks, and a few years later St. Augustine was eating home-grown oranges again.

One appreciator of the new fruit was the Seminole Indian. When naturalist William Bartram visited the Seminoles in 1791, they served him red snapper steamed with fresh oranges; dessert was sliced oranges which had been marinated in honey for several days.

The first oranges of the West, imported from Mexico, were planted in the missions established in Arizona between 1707 and 1710, and in California when the San Diego mission was founded in 1769; but the California orange industry did not really get under way until a pair of navel orange trees from Bahia, Brazil (via Washington, D.C., which is why this variety is called the Washington Navel today), was planted in the state in 1873. All the navel oranges of California are supposed to have descended from them.

Oranges are not full-fledged tropical fruits, but characteristically subtropical plants. Though they resist frost better than lemons and much better than limes, they prefer fairly equable temperatures; too much heat in spring or early summer causes the loss of young fruit in a phenomenon called "June drop." The orange does not demand a dormant resting season in winter, like trees of the temperate zone, but it is grateful for a few months of cool weather (though temperatures below 28° F. injure the fruit and below 20° may kill the tree) and signals its appreciation by acquiring its characteristic color. This is not an indication of ripeness, but simply a reaction to low temperatures. Oranges grown in the tropics remain green though fully ripe (they have less flavor than the same species in the subtropics). Fruit which has turned orange with cool weather may become green again if there is a late warm spell before it is picked. Oranges, unlike many other fruits, do not continue to ripen after being picked. Alluring advertisements promising "tree-ripened" oranges mean nothing at all; oranges are tree-ripened or not ripened at all.

Orange trees grown from seed bear fruit in about ten years, those grafted or budded onto already existent rootstock in about five years; they will then continue to set fruit abundantly for fifty to eighty years. In the United States, the average tree may be expected to yield 1500 oranges a year (in France, the figure would be about 500). Individual trees have been known to yield as many as 12,000 pieces of fruit at one harvest.

The important oranges of the world can be divided into three groups. The bitter or sour orange, *Citrus aurantium*, also called the bigarade, is in all probability the ancestor of all the others: it is the hardiest and it usually grows true from seed, as the others usually do not. Represented today by the Seville orange, it is better for cooking than the sweet orange, and is the soul of the best English marmalade. This is the one which reached the West temporarily in the first century A.D. and permanently in, probably, the ninth or the tenth.

The sweet orange, *C. sinensis*, is probably a mutant of the bitter orange which appeared in China at least by the beginning of our era, and probably before. It reached the West in the sixteenth century, imported by the Portuguese, which caused the Elizabethans to call it the "portyngale." Its most ubiquitous representative is the Valencia orange, the most widely grown everywhere in the world except Valencia; of all the oranges grown in Spain, only 2 percent are Valencias, and Valencia itself grows only half of those. The navel orange is probably a mutant of a more orthodox type of sweet orange, a Johnny-come-lately as evolutionary time goes, which appeared in Brazil in the seventeenth century.

The mandarin, *C. reticulata*, is also probably a mutant of the sweet orange, which occurred perhaps in Cochin China, nobody knows when, except that it may have been not long after the development of the sweet orange itself; it reached the West nobody knows when either, having perhaps slipped in surreptitiously via North Africa —picking up in the city of Tangiers the alternative name "tangerine," which does not seem to correspond to any botanical differentiation. The clementine, however, does appear to be a distinct variety. First discovered in 1902 in the Algerian garden of the French missionary Father Clément, it is thought by some to be a special kind of mandarin, by others to be a cross between an orange and a mandarin, and by still others to be a mutant.

I have no information on the extremely sweet blood orange, except that Luigi Barzini says it is the favorite of Italians and John McPhee says it frightens American women.

OREGANO. Few people today, except specialists, can tell the difference between oregano and MARJORAM, including the housewife, who, not knowing one from the other, asks for either more or less at random and takes whichever is given her by the grocer, who doesn't know one from the other either. Though each of these delightful spicy herbs does have its own personality, you will make no serious error in substituting one for the other.

There should be no problem distinguishing oregano from marjoram for those who use their scientific names, for the species identified generically as *Origanum* is of course oregano; marjoram is *Majorana*, or should be. Unfortunately, no less an authority than Linnaeus himself mixed things up two hundred years ago by baptizing marjoram *Origanum majorana*, but by now order has been restored, or nearly so. Popular usage ordinarily identifies oregano (alias origanum, origan or, if you are old-fashioned, organy) by adding some qualifying adjective to the word "marjoram"—bastard marjoram, wild marjoram (usually equated with *O. vulgare*, disconcertingly the only species which is cultivated) or dwarf marjoram (oregano does not grow as high as marjoram, though its leaves are thicker and bushier). Country folk call oregano "shepherd's thyme," a percipient name, since oregano is indeed very close to thyme in chemical constituents.

"Pot marjoram," which some writers use as a synonym for oregano, is a complete misnomer.

OREGANO. *Illuminated page by Philippe de Mazerolles for Petrus Crescentius:* The Book of Rural Profit, *c. 1470, Bruges*

Par intencion de
parler des jar
dins et de lart
de leur labourai
ge et de toutes les herbes qui
y sont semees pour nourre
ture de corps humain et
auec ce je diray ensemble
de celles qui viennent sans
labourer ailleurs par leur
nature et vertu du soleil
selon lordre des a.b.c. selon
le latin et en diray la vertu
qui puet aidier et nuire
au corps. Car ce vault moult
especial a ceulx qui demeu
rent aux champs qui ne
peuent avoir medicines
compousees a leurs desirs
et plaisirs.

Des vertus des herbes en com
mun.

Marjoram can be grown in window boxes or indoors in pots, but not oregano, which has a spreading root system and tends to sprawl over the ground. Marjoram stays put, oregano demands *Lebensraum.*

Oregano is hardier than marjoram and consequently enjoys a wider distribution. Marjoram sticks close to the Mediterranean basin, where it was born. Oregano penetrates even into quite cool areas of the temperate zone; it grows wild in England, for instance. When it first appeared there, in 1597, John Gerard called it in his *Herball,* "Bastard Marjerome of Candy," that is, of Ceylon. We may guess that it was oregano, the globetrotter, which was the herb sacred to Shiva and Vishnu, though it may have been marjoram which was dedicated to Osiris.

Oregano will grow on arid soils which would discourage marjoram. In southern and western France it is particularly flavorsome when it comes from barren hillsides exposed to the sun.

Oregano and marjoram are exceptions to the rule that foods are most widely eaten in the territories to which they are native. On this basis, marjoram should be favored around the Mediterranean, oregano elsewhere; but in fact, it is just the other way around. Mediterranean peoples prefer oregano.

The explanation lies in their tastes. Mediterraneans like spicier and hotter foods than peoples in cooler regions: oregano smells and tastes stronger than the delicate sweet marjoram. Neapolitans insist that oregano, not marjoram, should flavor pizza, the Bolognese make the same stipulation for their *ragú,* the Near East uses it freely on dishes of tomato and eggplant, and the Greeks, for their mutton kebab, not only demand oregano, but a special local species, *O. dubium,* which is much more pungent than *O. vulgare.*

Considering the relative strengths of oregano and marjoram, one might wonder whether Erasmus (or his translator) did not get the wrong plant by the stem when he wrote: "Thus . . . speaks the marjoram: 'Keep away from me, swine: my scent is not for you,' for although this plant has a sweet smell, swine cannot endure its scent."

OS
stands for

the **osprey,** which preys on fish and used to be preyed upon by American Indians; for the **ostrich,** whose meat, according to the Italian Renaissance chef Antonio Frugoli, is "of the worst possible quality . . . because it digests iron"; and for **Osetrova,** a middle-of-the-road CAVIAR with eggs smaller than Beluga and larger than Sevruga.

OT
stands for

the **Otaheite apple,** which comes from Tahiti but is now found in Sierra Leone, where it is eaten under the improbable alias "Inglish plom"; and for the **otter,** which was eaten by prehistoric Asians and pre-Columbian Indians of the Pacific Northwest, but probably not more recently except by the post-Columbian Indian of the Atlantic Northeast who, Thoreau tells us, created a gourmet soup of yellow-lily roots and otter fat.

OW
stands for

the **owala oil tree,** whose seeds are eaten in Nigeria, after twelve hours of cooking, a precaution which gets most of the poison out of them; and for the **owl,** a type of poultry which Prince Achille Murat preferred boiled.

OX
stands for

(what else?) the **ox,** an animal whose value serves as a useful measure of inflation, since a slave cost four oxen in Homeric times but commanded eight in pre-Roman Britain.

OY
stands for

oyster crabs, the tiny crustaceans which live inside oysters and are apparently eaten by no one except oyster shuckers, who consider them a delicacy; for the **oyster mushroom,** so called for its look rather than its taste, of which it doesn't have much; for the **oyster nut,** which does have enough taste so that tropical Africans have shifted from gathering it wild to cultivating it; and for the **oyster plant,** alias the vegetable oyster, alias salsify.

And **OY** also stands for, of course,

OYSTER. The largest heap of seashells in the world may well be the one in Denmark which measures 984 feet long, 200 feet wide and 10 feet deep. It dates from Neolithic times, and the most common shellfish represented in it is the oyster. All the oysters are of the species *Ostrea edulis,* the European flat oyster, of which in prehistoric times and, indeed, well into historic ones, a great barrier reef lay off the coasts of Europe. It started in Scandinavia, ran all the way down the Atlantic coast, turned into the Mediterranean, followed

OYSTER *by Edouard Manet (1832–1883).* Oysters, *oil on canvas*

the southern coast of France and the western coast of Italy, passed under the sole of that peninsula and, losing hardly any oysters to the Adriatic, jumped to Greece and ran around its shores to the spot where Leander failed and Lord Byron succeeded in swimming the Hellespont. There it stopped so abruptly that the ancient Assyrians and Babylonians never heard about the oyster. It is not mentioned in the Bible, probably not because it was, according to the definition of Leviticus, unclean, but because it was unknown. When Shakespeare wrote in *Antony and Cleopatra,* "The firm Roman to great Egypt sends / His treasure of an oyster," he was for once not committing an anachronism. Italy had oysters, Egypt had none.

At the northern end of this 4000-mile-long bank of oysters (of which there remain now only five meager islands, three in the Atlantic, two in the Mediterranean) nobody bothered to cultivate them until the ninth century, when the Vikings were in full vitality, but the rest of Europe, sunk into the lethargy of the Dark Ages, had virtually abandoned them. At its southern end the ancient Greeks, who had been eating wild oysters as far back as the records go, made the first timid gestures toward farming them in the fourth century B.C. Aristotle reported that fishermen at Rhodes, noticing that young oysters attached themselves to pieces of broken pottery which had fallen into the water and thrived on them, threw more shards into the sea to encourage their growth. He also wrote of oyster raising "as now practiced," telling us that "fishermen on the island of Chios took some oysters at Pyrrha, on the island of Lesbos, and moved them to another place in the sea nearby, where the waters formed a current; the oysters fattened greatly, but did not reproduce at all, although they remained there a long time." Aristotle had thus already observed what we have confirmed since, that the places where oysters grow well are not necessarily those where they reproduce.

Throwing them supports to cling to, or even moving them to waters whose currents bring them food, may not qualify as full-fledged cultivation, but at least we have here the basis for one of the two principal processes still used for growing oysters today, the horizontal method, which consists in giving them something solid to which to attach themselves on the sea bottom. The Greeks used pottery shards, we use plastic tiles. We have perfected the details since, but the essence of the system is the same.

The other technique, the vertical method, was used where most historians locate the first genuine deliberate oyster farming, at Taranto, on the sole of Italy. Here the oysters attached themselves to branches suspended in the water from overhead frames. Once again, this is essentially the same method used today in the same place to produce Taranto's 3 million oysters per year, except that hempen ropes have replaced the branches.

The ancient Romans were great oyster fanciers. Pliny called this shellfish "the palm and pleasure of the table"; and even Seneca, who wrote that oysters "are not really food, but are relished to bully the sated stomach into further eating," nevertheless consumed one hundred dozen per week.

The Romans were bullied out of the opinion that the oysters of Taranto were the best by an aggressive promoter, Sergius Orata, who would probably have been the president of a conglomerate today, since in the first century B.C. he busied himself with such diverse interests as the heating system for the baths of Pompeii and the cultivation of oysters in Lake Lucrine, near Naples. He persuaded the customers that Lucrine oysters were superior to those of Taranto, but Romans were always ready to fall for the latest fashion, and decided, each time they discovered a new oyster, that it was better than any they had known before. They occupied southern Gaul and told themselves that the finest oysters were those fished between the eastern end of the Pyrenees and Narbonne. They pushed north and promptly promoted the oysters of Bordeaux to first place: Germanicus, brother of the Emperor Tiberius, tossed down a few hundred before dinner, and the poet Ausonius, perhaps not impartial, since he was a native of the place, composed a poem in which he praised their "fair white flesh" and "sweet and delicate juice," but admitted grudgingly that "there are also admirers of the oysters of Breton waters." There were indeed, and when the Romans reached them, they set up an express service which carried the shellfish overland in winter in carts packed with ice or snow, replenished regularly from icehouses established along the route (a method of transport used in France up to the middle of the nineteenth century). In warmer weather they were carried in cistern carts full of sea water. Pliny said they improved in transit, and he may have been right. Then Britain was reached, and English oysters became the new passion of the Romans. The Gulf of Baia was seeded with oysters from Camulodunum (now Colchester, where an annual oyster festival has been celebrated each October 8 since 1318). "Poor Britons!" said Sallust. "There is some good in them after all. They have produced an oyster."

Nero claimed that he could recognize an oyster from anywhere in the world at the first taste, and if he could, he had a palate comparable to that of the modern sommelier who can distinguish among different wines all from the same region, for in Nero's world there was only one kind of oyster, *O. edulis*. It remains today the only species of flat oyster in Europe. All the continent's famous oysters—English Colchesters and Whitstables, Dutch Zeelands, Belgian Ostends, French Belons and Marennes—and those of all sizes, from the tiny *boudeuse* ("sulker") of Arcachon to the huge *pied de cheval* ("horse's hoof") of Normandy, are the same oyster. Nowadays, when wild oysters are virtually nonexistent and all of them are cultivated, the chances are good that any flat oyster you eat anywhere along the Atlantic coast will have been grown from a seed oyster which came from within ten miles of the La Trinité bridge on an estuary of southern Brittany, which supplies them to everywhere else.

Oysters are like wine: it isn't the parent which determines its character, it's the environment in which it was brought to maturity. Take cuttings from the same Traminer vine, plant them in, respectively, Alsace, the Jura and Italy's Alto Adige, and you will reap three completely distinctive types of wine. Take seedling oysters from the same bed in Brittany, plant them in Whitstable,

Belon and Marennes, and you will harvest three completely different types of oysters. Even the Marennes, which certainly looks like a separate species, since it is greenish where the others are white (Mme. de Maintenon thought them poisonous, and tried, without success, to keep Louis XIV from eating them), is *O. edulis* like all the others, but puts on its new dress in three or four months of feeding in waters full of a diatom called *Navicula ostrearia,* which changes its color.

It is almost the unanimous opinion that *Ostrea* is the best-flavored oyster in the world (it sometimes recalls hazelnuts). The only other species of *Ostrea* I know about, the tiny Olympia oyster of America's Pacific coast, is also considered the tastiest available in its region. Gourmets sometimes pay as much as three times the price of ordinary oysters for the Olympia, *O. lurida,* a price which reflects the labor required to handle such tiny shellfish: two of them (shucked, of course) can be fitted into a thimble and it takes 1400 to make a gallon.

Europe acquired a second genus of oysters in 1868, when the *Morlaisien,* Captain Patoiseau master, carrying a cargo of oysters from Lisbon to, I think, England, was slowed by stormy weather. The oysters developed an unbearable stench and the captain dumped them off the Bordelais coast. They were not all dead. Oystermen there began bringing up a new type of oyster, with a rugged shell instead of a smooth one and cup-shaped instead of flat; they were promptly named *portugaises.* The newcomer was *Crassostrea angulata,* an Asian genus, as the Pacific Northwest of the United States learned in 1902, when the large *C. gigas* was transplanted there from Japan. (Some authorities think *gigas* and *angulata* are the same species.) But where did Portugal get an Asian oyster? A theory is that it arrived clinging to the hulls of the ships of Vasco da Gama and other Portuguese explorers.

Crassostrea has another habitat—the Atlantic coast of America, where the species is *C. virginica,* probably so called because that is where the oyster classifiers first came across it. It was a great favorite with American Indians, as we know from the heaps of shells they piled up, such as one in Maine which is estimated to contain seven million bushels. On both Pacific and Atlantic coasts, pre-Columbian Indians seem never to have eaten oysters raw, only cooked, which is one of the reasons why they are often credited with having invented American oyster stew.

As is the case for *O. edulis* in Europe, *C. virginica* on America's Atlantic side seems to be the only species, with one minor exception. When Sir Walter Raleigh returned from a voyage to Trinidad he was nearly laughed out of Queen Elizabeth's court because he insisted he had there seen oysters growing on trees. This was of course ridiculous, but as it happened, Sir Walter was right. He had encountered *C. frons,* which attaches itself to the stiltlike roots of mangrove trees, which grow on muddy shores from the Carolinas southward. They are called coon oysters in the southeastern United States because when they are exposed at low tide, raccoons scamper across the mud flats to feast on them.

There is a third genus of oyster, to which some experts refuse that name because it lies on its right side, whereas any legitimately born oyster is expected to lie on its left, though I am not quite sure how you determine which is the left side of an oyster. This nonconformist genus is *Pinctada,* which is supposed to be native to Australasia. It appears to be divided into more species than the other two, but I do not think many of them are eaten. In the case of one, edibility is not the point: it is fished for another reason. This is *P. margaritifera,* the pearl oyster.

Both Europe and America experienced oyster manias which lasted for a couple of centuries each. Europe had more or less abandoned the oyster after classical times: the barbarians who ended them were not afraid of the Roman legions, but they seem to have been frightened by the oyster. Resuscitated by the Renaissance, along with classical philosophy and architecture, the oyster appeared again, but not until the middle of the seventeenth century did oyster eating become a craze. The quantities consumed were incredible. A little ahead of the times, probably because he lived on the coast of Normandy, was St. Evremond, who, in the eighth century, at the age of eighty-eight, consumed several dozen daily for breakfast. Henry IV often worked up an appetite for dinner by swallowing three hundred oysters. Montaigne told of a doctor whose ration was thirty to forty dozen. Louis XIV ate them by dozens too, making a piker of Casanova, who took only fifty a day with his evening punch. Louis XIV's oysters came from his own private park, tended by a man who rejoiced in the name (in translation) Hyacinth Ox, while Louis XVI's also came from private beds, managed at Etretat by the Baron de Bellevert, an adventurer whose title was self-bestowed, and who let it get around that he was producing oysters at the personal request of Marie Antoinette, who had probably never heard of him. Brillat-Savarin promised a surfeit of oysters to a friend who had complained that never in his life had he had his fill, but called it off at the thirty-second dozen because, after having quit at the end of three dozen himself, he was getting tired of waiting for the rest of the dinner. In the mid-nineteenth century the French gastronomic author Charles Monselet wrote to a friend: "Oysters seem to be losing ground this year. It can't be more than a breathing spell, a bad joke of fortune." It could, though. Europe was running short of oysters.

The United States followed the same pattern. The first Europeans to report from there—the Spanish in the Caribbean, Captain John Smith in Virginia, Francis Higginson in Massachusetts, the Dutch in New Amsterdam (where they bought from the Indians not only Manhattan but also Oyster Island, now renamed Ellis Island) —were all struck by the abundance of American oysters and by their size—a foot long in New York Bay. This was a little much for Thackeray, who said that eating an American oyster was like swallowing a baby. Captain Frederick Marryat, brought up on *O. edulis,* was sniffish about *C. virginica.* "Oysters," he wrote, "are very plentiful, very large, and, to an English palate, rather insipid. As the Americans assert that the English and French oysters taste of copper, and that therefore they cannot eat them, I presume they do, and that's the reason we do not like American oysters, copper being better than no flavour at all." Dickens was less critical, noting the ubiquity in New York of "oyster-cellars—pleasant retreats, say I!" Oyster houses existed in all the coastal cities and offered their wares at a standardized price: "All the oysters you can eat for six cents." (They were $20 a plate in San Francisco, but that was because of the Gold Rush, and even that price was not high enough to prevent Washington's Shoalwater Bay from being scraped bare of oysters.)

Beginning in 1842 express wagons carrying oysters packed in damp straw or ice were thundering across the Alleghenies non-stop, except for the brief intervals necessary to change horses and drivers, permitting Abraham Lincoln in Springfield, Illinois, to give oyster parties at which the shellfish were devoured in great quantities, but all the same not as gluttonously as in Europe. Peddlers hawked oysters on every corner; the oyster supper became a favorite community rite.

Towards the end of the nineteenth century the United States found itself faced with the same disaster as Europe: it was running out of oysters. In Delaware Bay, fifteen times as many oysters were taken in 1880 as we are getting today; its waters support fifty oyster boats instead of five hundred. In Chesapeake Bay, America's largest oyster fishery, Maryland's lion's share of the catch is one-tenth of what it was in 1886; Virginia's has been cut in half since 1960. Our experts are working desperately to return the oyster to its former productivity, but largely in vain.

"Not that our scientists . . . aren't as informed and dedicated as any," wrote Eleanor Clark in *The Oysters of Locmariaquer.* "The question is only whether their hard work and knowledge has any serious relation to the survival of mollusks . . . and the answer to date is no. Every year . . . we know more and have fewer oysters, and most that we do have have less taste."

P

PEPYS, SAMUEL: *Strange to see how a good dinner and feasting reconciles everybody.*

PITT, WILLIAM (last words): *I think I could eat one of Bellamy's veal pies.*

PAB
stands for

pa beuk, probably related to the catfish, but, related or not, the world's second-largest freshwater fish as its name indicates ("huge fish," in case your Laotian is rusty).

PAC
stands for

pacae, a fruit cultivated in Peru about 750 B.C. for its sweet, white, fleshy seeds; for the **pachira,** a starchy nut eaten in West Africa and Zaïre, né the Congo; for the **Pacific egg cockle,** a bivalve which runs up to seven tasty inches across; for the **Pacific goose barnacle,** which tastes a little (a *little*) like lobster; for the **Pacific mackerel,** whose wide range runs from Alaska to the Gulf of California; for the **Pacific perch,** which isn't a perch, it's a rockfish; for the **Pacific purple urchin,** a small sea urchin which digs itself a nest in solid rock, nobody knows how; and for two fish which show effete Easterners where they get off: the **Pacific salmon,** which boasts six species to the Atlantic salmon's one, and the **Pacific swordfish,** which outweighs and outreaches the Atlantic swordfish by 50 percent.

PAD
stands for

the **paddlefish,** a prehistoric leftover hanging onto existence nowhere except in the United States and China; and the **paddy straw mushroom,** which you can taste nowhere except in tropical Africa.

PAK
stands for

pak-choi, "white vegetable," because the ribs and stems of this Chinese cabbage are white.

PAL
stands for

palms, the princes of the plant kingdom according to Linnaeus, which give us oil, vinegar, salt, sugar, syrup, honey and two kinds of flour, not to mention wax and vegetable ivory; for the **palmetto,** whose heart tastes just the same whether you call it millionaire's salad or swamp cabbage; for the **palolo,** nicknamed "Samoan caviar," which a squeamish writer for a gourmet magazine described as "a marine creature," thus avoiding admission that it is a worm; for the **palometa,** an African moonfish otherwise known as the pompano; for the **Palomino,** or Golden Chasselas, used to make sherry, which is one of the very few great wine grapes which is also delicious to eat; and for the **paloverde,** whose edible seeds help nourish the Indians of Mexico's Baja California.

PAM
stands for

the **pampano** (or pompano), an African moonfish otherwise known as the palometa.

PAN
stands for

the **pandanus,** or screw pine, an eccentric fruit-bearing tree which in Malaysia and on islands of the Indian Ocean or the South Pacific often chooses to stand on stilts; for the **pandora,** an aggressively red Mediterranean fish whose taste, even grilled, does not live up to its name; for the **pangolin,** an unappetizing-looking scaly anteater which is consumed by tropical Africans all the same; for **panic grass,** which, if we take Marco Polo's word for it, was an important cereal for the Tartars; for the **panini,** an edible fruit of a Hawaiian cactus; and for the **pansy,** which has been so thoroughly improved as to have lost the original sweetness which nature bestowed upon it, so that its function as food has been reduced to decorating cake frostings or jellies.

PAP
stands for

the **papeda,** a citrus fruit found, so far as I know, only on the islands of Mauritius and Madagascar; for the **papermouth,** more widely known as the blue crappie, a game fish which in the Pacific Northwest rejoices also in the names of calico fish and bachelor perch; for **papiones,** an unidentified animal given that name by Marco Polo, who said that it resembled a fox and was very good to eat; for **paprika,** a hot chili which tries to pass itself off as Hungarian, but came from tropical America like all other chilies; for **papyrus,** on whose leaves ancient Egyptians wrote and on whose roots they dined; and for the **pawpaw,** or papaw, an odiferous fruit beloved only by the young, which has perversely strayed into North America from the tropics.

And **PAP** also stands for

PAPAYA. Shortly after landing in the West Indies, Christopher Columbus confided to his journal that the natives were "very strong and live largely on a tree melon called 'the fruit of the angels.'" I do not know of any place where this tree melon is attributed to angels today, but it has a number of other names, but the most widespread is "papaya." In the English-speaking islands of the Caribbean it is often called also the pawpaw or papaw, a name I shall avoid, since it is also given to an unrelated fruit of North America, *Asiminia triloba,* while the papaya is *Carica papaya.* It is also the *mando* in Brazil, the *melon zapote* in Mexico, the *lechosa* in Puerto Rico and the *fruta bomba* ("hand-grenade fruit") in Cuba,

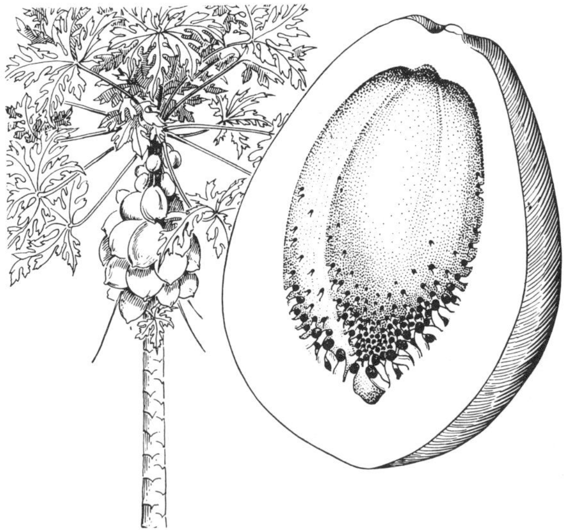

PAPAYA. *Information bulletin, Chicago Natural History Museum, 1927*

where you had better refrain from referring to it as a papaya, there a slang term for the female sex organ.

The papaya leads a disorderly sexual life. Normally some plants bear female flowers and others male flowers, putting it in the category of "harem trees," whose cultivators usually conserve precious soil by culling superfluous males from their plantations. In the case of the papaya, male trees are thinned out as soon as their sex can be determined, to leave one male for each eight to fifteen females, though one authority has so much respect for the value of the soil, or for the virility of the male, that he recommends a ratio of one to fifty. The papaya is not always normal. Hermaphroditic trees appear, bearing both male and female flowers, while others change their minds in mid-career and shift from male to female or vice versa. Miscegenation is rampant too. In Florida, the only place in the continental United States where the fruit can be grown with consistent success (the rest of the country knows the papaya chiefly through its juice), there are thousands of papayas which have escaped from cultivation and degenerated into wild plants, whose pollen invades cultivated plantations and plays havoc with their offspring.

The papaya, a native of the Caribbean area, is a swift traveler which had reached Peru at least by the first millennium of our era, as we know from Chimu and Nazca pottery modeled in its shape. It was planted in other tropical areas of the world not long after Columbus first encountered it; when it was introduced into Nepal in 1626, the seeds did not come from the West Indies but from the East

Indies, where the plant was already so firmly established that it provided seed also for the Philippine Islands. One of the reasons for the rapid spread of the papaya was probably that Holland, France, England and Portugal, colonizers of tropical America shortly after the Spaniards, all had East Indian trading companies as well as West Indian ones, which carried papaya seeds to the Orient. In areas relatively neglected by these powers—China, Japan and some of the islands of the Indian Ocean—the papaya is not reported before the nineteenth century. There seems to be no record of its first appearance in Africa, but it should have been early, if only because of the slave trade. It is only sparingly eaten on that continent, except when it is picked unripe and cooked as a vegetable in the tropical regions, but it is more popular in Asia (especially India) and in several Pacific islands (Hawaii, Fiji). But nowhere is it more important than in its native tropical America, where it is second only to the banana, is universal, and is cheap.

The papaya tree bears from twelve to thirty fruits per year, but only for three or four years, frequently dying by the fifth. Some cultivators allow their trees to bear only two crops, or even one, and then replace them (they ripen fruit a year after planting). One expects greater longevity from a tree, and as a matter of fact it doesn't look like a tree, but what else can you call a plant which may reach twenty-five feet in height? (Fifteen to twenty feet is more usual.) One observer has called it a "herbaceous 'tree' " (but it is not an herb either); another has described it, somewhat helplessly, as "really not a tree, but the woody stalk of a giant plant." One might be tempted to call it an overgrown shrub, except that shrubs are apt to become bushy, while the papaya stalk or trunk normally puts out no branches. It sprays out from its summit a rather ridiculous jet of fernlike leaves which look as though they had been designed by a whimsical Bunthorne for a smaller plant; the large fruit hangs in a bunch from the stalk for all the world like a display of not quite fully inflated Rugby balls suspended from the ceiling of a sport goods store.

Though this shape, which might also be described as that of a somewhat elongated melon, seems to be the commonest, the fruit may vary from spherical to cylindrical. It does indeed suggest a melon, to such an extent that the plant is sometimes called the melon tree. The fruit can be not only melon-shaped but melon-sized, though it is apt to be larger, fifteen pounds in weight (it can reach twenty-five, and a length of twenty inches); a single large papaya can serve a dozen persons. The biggest papayas are not the best; choose those having the dimensions of a very large pear. The worst are the small ones developed for export, but they are not in fact much exported because they are tough and tasteless. Normally the papaya is so perishable that it can be eaten fresh only where it grows.

The unripe fruit has a smooth green rind like that of many melons, but generally turns yellow or orange when ripe. Cut open lengthwise, the papaya is found to have a central cavity in its pinkish, yellow, salmon or orange flesh, filled with seeds as in the case of a melon—rough, wrinkled, pea-sized, shaped like a somewhat flattened egg, and black, so that the fruit seems to be filled with caviar.

Opinions on the taste of the papaya vary. Tourists who encounter it for the first time expect it to taste like a muskmelon, the fruit it most resembles, and when it doesn't they are put off. There is a certain musky flavor to some papayas, of a kind different from that encountered in the muskmelon, which some people don't like; others are dubious at first, but quickly become enthusiastic and wax dithyrambic about the flavor. One of the chief taste defects of the papaya is that sometimes there isn't much of it: the fruit is so unrelievedly sweet (it contains from 7 to 9 percent sugars) that it can be monotonously cloying; but some varieties offer a slight redeeming acidity, which makes all the difference. Because of its tendency to blandness, when a papaya is eaten as a breakfast or after-dinner fruit it is often sprinkled with salt and pepper or enlivened with a few drops of lime juice.

The papaya is a vegetable as well as a fruit. Picked unripe, it is either boiled or, better, split in half and baked in the oven like a squash; the taste is not unlike that of a sweet squash. The leaves are eaten too, boiled like spinach; the flavor has been compared to that of dandelion greens, with only a hint of bitterness. So far as I know, the only place where the young shoots are eaten is Rhodesia.

In 1978 the *International Herald Tribune* printed an article of mine giving essentially the information set down above, but at this point I added that I had heard that the seeds were also eaten as a sort of spice, but had found no confirmation of it. This elicited a letter from a woman in Singapore, who wrote:

> It is true that the fruit has very little flavor, but it slides down easily and is wonderfully cool on muggy humid tropical mornings. For zest, bite into one of those shiny black seeds—"a stomachic"—it will give more zing than the commercial for peppermint candy on TV. "Full of pepsin," said the British, "and very good for the digestion." In the old British

hotels and clubs, the slice of papaya was served for breakfast, chilled and sprinkled with lime juice, with a scattering of seeds left on it.

My correspondent added that when she was living in southern India, "where papaya grows like a weed," it was not eaten by the natives—a great pity according to her doctor, who said that papaya was rich in vitamin A, and that vitamin A deficiency was the cause of about half the blindness in newborn babies in India. Why was papaya not eaten on its home grounds? My correspondent remarked that, after all, "papaya, picked from the tree, unchilled and not flavored with fresh lime, tastes quite insipid," a negative explanation, but then she suggested a positive one for avoiding it, at least by women:

In Madras, the servants forbade me to eat papaya once they discovered that I was pregnant. Papaya caused abortion, they claimed. I checked this one with an American missionary doctor, and she said she had never heard it from any medical authorities or read it in any medical books, but she did know one Indian lady doctor who ate great quantities of papaya if ever her menstrual cycle was delayed—and she didn't have any surprise babies.

So far as I know, this is, outside of the area affected, new information. No reference book consulted by me reports this belief, even as a local superstition. It is worth recording from this point of view, and I put it down here for that reason; I have no opinion on its possible validity. But is it unreasonable to wonder whether the papaya may not have on living flesh effects comparable to that which we know it has on dead flesh? The most remarkable property of the papaya is, in fact, its ability to make tough meat tender. Its juice and latex contain an enzyme called papain, which acts like pepsin, the element in gastric juices which breaks down animal tissues and permits digestion of their proteins. This tenderizing capability was known to, and utilized by, pre-Columbian Indians, and our commercial tenderizers today are based on papain. Put a papaya leaf or two into a pot in which you are boiling tough meat and in a matter of minutes it will become so tender that it falls away from the bone. Wrapping tough meat in the leaves, or moistening it with a few drops of papaya juice, produces the same magical effect. I am a little skeptical about the ability of the papaya tree to breathe its enzymes out into the air, yet it appears that in China and India tough chickens and cuts of meat are suspended in the foliage to tenderize them.

I doubt even more if it makes much difference to Pele, goddess of fire and of volcanoes, whether the roast meat which natives of Hawaii toss into lava flows to propitiate her is tender or not, but in any case they throw in a few papayas too just to make sure.

PAR
stands for

the **parakeet**, apparently eaten today only in Madagascar, and even there with diminishing enthusiasm; for the **paraná pine,** whose seeds are chewed chiefly in Brazil; for the **parasol mushroom,** which lifts a sort of nipple from the center of its cap, and is excellent breaded like a veal cutlet; for **parkia,** the African locust bean, whose seeds are made into an odorous condiment called *soumbara,* appreciated exclusively by East Africans; for the **parr,** a salmon which has managed to survive all the perils of the sea up to the age of one year; for the **parrot,** which the nineteenth-century French gourmet Charles Monselet said he had eaten and found "very good, I suppose a chicken parrot would have been more delicate, but I didn't have one handy"; for **parrotfish,** which have been called "the cattle of the sea," not for gastronomic reasons but for their herding habits, which does not prevent them from being good eating; and for the **partridgeberry,** which is also called the winterberry because it tastes better after a frost, to men and partridges alike.

And **PAR** also stands for

PARSLEY. "To take parsley away from the cook," wrote Louis Augustin Guillaume Bosc d'Antic about the end of the eighteenth century, "would make it almost impossible for him to exercise his art." Yet parsley takes up little space in the literature of food, probably because it is so ubiquitous that it has become commonplace. Its presence is so much taken for granted that nobody remarks on it, and it does not even have the ability to call attention to itself possessed by another ingredient also taken for granted, salt, which, if I dare put it that way, makes its presence felt in its absence.

Although parsley is an almost universal seasoning (Pliny said that sauces and salads should never be without it), it hardly ever composes a dish in its own right. Alexandre Dumas did go so far as to say that it was indispensable in "Watter-Fisch," by which I suspect he meant Flemish *waterzooie*, and in "parsley Dutch style," by which he meant I don't know what, unless it was Hollandaise sauce, which, in defiance of Pliny, doesn't include parsley. Bartolomeo Scappi in 1570 gave a recipe for "parsley broth" (also called "apostles' stew"), but though it was abundantly seasoned with this universal herb, it was really mutton stew; a similar misnomer exists today in Cornish "parsley pies." Offhand, the only food I can think of in which parsley is the dominating ingredient is a parsley herb sandwich, for which it may or may not be combined with cream cheese. This is a descendant of a common breakfast of the ancient Romans, a piece of bread made more interesting by the light, peppery taste of parsley—or the stronger, sharper taste of Macedonian parsley, which, precisely because of its strength, was considered by some Romans as the best kind, while others (Plautus, for instance) detested it.

The ancient Romans knew five kinds of parsley and so do we, though they are not necessarily the same five. Rome was well placed to receive parsley if, as we are usually told, it is a native of Sardinia. It could have been, but it would be safer to describe it as having originated in the Mediterranean basin; as far back as history goes, we find it growing wild in southern Europe from Spain to Macedonia, in Lebanon, and in Algeria. I suspect that it has been attributed to Sardinia because it is on record that English gardeners imported Sardinian strains of parsley in 1548, for, says a text of the times, "the seeds help those who are light-headed to resist drink better." This also would account for the often-repeated information that it was only in 1548 that parsley entered England, which is difficult to believe, since that would mean it took at least seven hundred years to cross the English Channel. Its arrival in northern France is sometimes misreported too; since Catherine de' Medici is known to have introduced certain Italian vegetables into France, many writers have gotten into the habit of stuffing her baggage with other foods, apparently at random, including parsley. Yet Charlemagne had ordered it planted in his domains about the year 800, and it was also being grown in French monasteries at this period. The *Journal de Paris* mentioned parsley during the twelfth and thirteenth centuries; the *Ménagier de Paris*, written about 1393, gives directions for planting it; the *Grant Herbier* sings its praises in the fifteenth century; and Jacques Dalechamp, in the sixteenth, speaks of a dish of leeks seasoned with parsley.

The misreporting about the time when parsley arrived in different countries may have worked the other way around in the case of America. Verrazano said that he saw it on the coast of Massachusetts about 1524, but vigilant writers since have insisted that this could not have been true, since parsley is an Old World plant. The rectifiers were perhaps wrong. There were Norsemen not far from Massachusetts, if not actually there, five hundred years before Verrazano, to say nothing of the Basque fishermen who came from parsley country to the Grand Banks off Newfoundland before Columbus and went ashore to cure their cod, where perhaps they let drop a seed or two; parsley could easily have migrated from Newfoundland to Massachusetts in a couple of centuries. However, I know of no written record of the presence of parsley in America before 1806, when both plain and curled varieties were being grown there (by 1828 there were three kinds; by 1881, four).

Our five kinds of parsley today are the plain-leaved, the curly-leaved, the fern-leaved, the celery-leaved and the turnip-rooted. Of these, the plain-leaved is probably the original form; at least plants of this type sometimes appear mysteriously in the middle of fields of curly parsley, apparently throwbacks to their ancestor. It is tastier than the curly-leaved parsley, and is therefore extensively grown in Europe, but has almost disappeared, commercially, from the United States, where prettiness seems to be preferred to tastefulness, except in southern Louisiana, where the Creole cuisine demands it.

PARSLEY. *Print from Eugen Köhler:* Medizinal-Pflanzen, in naturgetreuen, *Gera, Germany, 1898*

Curly parsley has shouldered its way in because of its decorative quality when it is used to garnish dishes, from which it is usually pushed aside uneaten. Most writers put it down as a recent development, but in A.D. 42 Columella gave directions for cultivating curly as well as plain parsley, and Palladius in 210 told how to develop the curly variety from the plain.

About 1912, French seed catalogs offered what was described as a new variety of parsley, which because of its much segmented, very dark green leaves was called fern-leaved parsley. Its novelty was questionable. It had appeared in American seed catalogs in 1878, but that was only a slight advance compared to that of Caspar Bauhin, who had written of it in 1598. It does not seem to be much grown anywhere nowadays.

Celery-leaved parsley might be described as a recent discovery for much of the world, for until the end of the nineteenth century it was called Neapolitan parsley and according to E. L. Sturtevant was "scarcely known outside of Naples." It is now being grown a little more extensively under the name "Italian parsley," which is confusing, for this name is often given also to the ordinary plain-leaved parsley. I am inclined to suspect that today's Neapolitan parsley is the ancients' Macedonian parsley (also called black parsley), not only because of the strength of its flavor but also because Pliny described Macedonian parsley as having thick white stalks which could be eaten, and so has Neapolitan parsley, whose stalks are sometimes blanched in growing, like celery.

Turnip-rooted parsley provides an exception to the rule that parsley seasons other dishes but does not constitute one itself. Turnip-rooted parsley does, but it fails to come to mind when we think of parsley, which we have ticketed firmly as a leafy vegetable. As a matter of fact the leaves of this variety can be eaten, but it is raised not for them, but for its roots, which look like small parsnips and taste like celeriac. It used to be known as Hamburg parsley, suggesting a German origin, but the Germans called it Dutch parsley, and it is probable that it was indeed developed in Holland.

Parsley might well be awarded the title of first among leafy seasonings, for whenever a combination of such herbs is used, others may be omitted but parsley almost never. The constituents of a *bouquet garni* may vary, but it nearly always starts with parsley, and *omelette fines herbes*, whatever others it contains, invariably has parsley, and sometimes parsley alone. Since Plautus, everybody has had a good word to say for parsley except Chaucer, and he was not really criticizing the parsley, he was criticizing Hogge of Ware, a cook who was careless about what else got into the parsley with which he sprinkled his goose:

Of many a pilgrim hastow Cristes curs,
For of thy persly yet they fare the wors,
That they han eaten with thy stubbelgoos;
For in thy shoppe is many a fly loos.

PARSNIP. The parsnip, an unjustly neglected vegetable, lost a formerly proud position in the domain of food through the competition of the potato—an unlikely competitor, since it does not resemble the parsnip either in taste or texture. The area of their competition, however, was not gastronomic, it was nutritive: both are heavy providers of starch.

The heyday of the parsnip was the Middle Ages, when fast days, and especially Lent, were rigorously observed. Obliged to renounce meat, fasters turned to fish or vegetables. When it was vegetables, heavy, filling, starchy ones were preferred: the German botanist Hieronymus Trager wrote in 1552 that parsnips and the European broad bean were the basic foods of Lent. When it was fish, that meant, except for seaside populations, salt cod or smoked herring (freshwater fish were a monopoly of feudal lords or monasteries). Dried fish required an accompanying vegetable for palatability: parsnips and salt cod were a common combination. Turnips and carrots were available too, but parsnips were more nourishing. Nowadays carrots are everywhere eaten much more widely than parsnips, but in medieval times it was the other way around. The supremacy of the parsnip lasted through the eighteenth century, for though the POTATO had been known ever since the discovery of America, it took Europeans nearly three centuries to work up enough courage to eat it. When they did, its neutral taste, which permitted it to be combined with almost any other food, delivered a death blow to the pungent parsnip.

The origin of the parsnip is mysterious. It is usually ascribed, vaguely, to northeastern Europe, but I wonder if this might not be widened to make it, even more vaguely, northern Eurasia. A characteristic distribution for foods originating in northern Asia takes them across the Bering Strait into western North America in one direction and into Europe in the other: this is precisely the distribution of the parsnip. In the eastern United States the parsnip is considered an immigrant from Europe, and so it is in that part of the country; but in the West, the wild parsnip ranges from the north southward as far as the Red River, and even becomes a troublesome weed at some points along the Pacific coast. On the other hand, the earliest finds of parsnip seeds known to me are far into Europe, in the Neolithic lake settle-

PARSNIP. *Portland Seed Company packet by Stecher Lithographic Company, Rochester, N.Y., 1908*

ments of Switzerland and at Glastonbury in England. Georges Blond asserts that the parsnip is "specifically Gallic," but does not claim that it is exclusively so; one wonders why he bothered to try to annex for France a vegetable which, as a dish in its own right, has practically disappeared from the French cuisine, though it does still lend its aromatic blessing to consommé and *pot-au-feu*. The ancient Romans did import parsnips from Gaul, but they thought the best came from Germany; it was to the Rhineland that the Emperor Tiberius sent for parsnips worthy of the imperial table (unless it was skirret; it is sometimes difficult to tell which edible root Latin writers are talking about). However, we seem to have hold of the right one by the first century A.D., when Columella distinguished between wild and cultivated parsnips, though a doubt could intrude, since he wrote that the flower buds of the plant he was discussing were used as herbs: the foliage of the parsnip is indigestible.

Columella's mention seems to be the first uncontested report of cultivated parsnips; it is quite possible that they were not cultivated earlier, for there was little incentive to take the trouble. Wild parsnips could be pulled up whenever they were wanted, even in winter. Parsnips keep in frozen ground, and indeed are better after freezing weather has set in; low temperatures convert their starch into sugar. In those days cultivated parsnips would not have been much of an improvement over wild ones anyway; not until the Middle Ages was a really fleshy parsnip developed, with the hollow-crowned varieties whose foliage springs from a circular depression in the top of the root, as in most of our best parsnips today.

The parsnip does not seem to have been much esteemed in the thirteenth century, if Gauthier de Coinci is typical. When he wanted a vegetable to serve as a symbol for unappetizingness, he chose the parsnip, writing in his *Miracles de la Vierge*:

Car une truie une banaie
Aime assez mielx c'un marc d'argent.

("A sow prefers a parsnip to a silver mark.")

Unimpressed by the opinion of Gauthier de Coinci, the anonymous author of the *Ménagier de Paris* (1393) gave directions for sowing parsnip seed. One circumstance, besides the exigencies of Lent, which kept the parsnip in the kitchen, liked or unliked, was that it was cheap—barring occasional periods of famine when nothing was cheap, as in 1473, when the weather wreaked such havoc among root crops that *"les navets, les pastenées et racines estoient sy chières con vendoit IIII navets II deniers, III pastenées I denier"* ("Turnips, parsnips and roots in general were so expensive that four turnips cost two deniers and three parsnips one denier"—so parsnips all the same were cheaper than turnips). The parsnip was not solely a dish for the poor, however; La Varenne served it to his princely employers in the seventeenth century napped in a rich white sauce. Commoners ate parsnip fritters.

Meanwhile in Germany, where a rash of books on agriculture broke out in the second half of the sixteenth century, parsnips were honored by all their authors. At the same period the Dutch doted on them. No less a personage than Sir Francis Bacon praised them in England, where, even ignoring those prehistoric seeds at Glastonbury, parsnips had been generally available at least five centuries before his time, and were widely eaten despite a belief that old parsnips could cause delirium or even permanent madness. The first colonists brought the vegetable to America, to Latin America first (Venezuela 1564, Peru 1605) and then to North America (Virginia 1608, Massachusetts 1629). The new vegetable appealed to the Indians; parsnips were among the crops destroyed in 1779 by General John Sullivan in the course of a retaliatory raid on the Iroquois of western New York.

In addition to the familiar long funnel-shaped parsnip which looks like a white carrot, a round turnip-shaped parsnip was introduced into the United States in 1834. It never gained popularity there, though in Europe, where it seems to have first appeared in the seventeenth century, it is often preferred, because its less abundant foliage makes cultivation easier, it grows faster, and it obeys the mysterious rule of nature that round roots usually ripen earlier than long roots. American eaters, often timid in the face of assertive tastes, may have disliked it because the already strongly scented flavor of the long parsnip becomes even more robust in the round variety. However, no parsnip is avidly sought out these days, either in America or in Europe, perhaps because it is hard to find really good ones. Parsnips pulled during or just after hot weather are often floury and tasteless; soft parsnips are apt to be pithy; and large ones may have become woody, like asparagus when it has passed its prime.

Yet a perfect parsnip is delicious, sweet, nutty and aromatic. I would like to say a good word for it, but, as Sir Walter Scott reminded us, "Fine words butter no parsnips."

PARTRIDGE. As a New Englander, when I learned that the bird which I had trustingly called a partridge to the end of my adolescence was an impostor whose real name was the "ruffed grouse," the disillusionment was comparable to that of a child when he discovers that there is no Santa Claus. Indeed, the demotion of the partridge was even more devastating, for I got through my accession to the Higher Learning about Santa Claus rather easily. The definitive initiation came when I was permitted to help my parents fill the stockings of the four younger children, so the accolade of adulthood took the sting out of the bitterness of reality—and besides, I had already begun to have doubts, inspired by the similarity between the artifacts allegedly delivered overnight by Santa Claus and those available to all comers at the five-and-ten-cent store.

The misnaming of the ruffed grouse in America (the situation was even worse in the South, where "partridge" meant quail) may be excused because even those in the know seem almost as confused about this bird as the O. Henry character who referred to "Esau, that swapped his copyright for a partridge." The word "partridge" seems to embody a poetical concept rather than a precise scientific definition. Noah Webster, doing the best he could, defined partridge as "any of various typically medium-sized stout-bodied Old World gallinaceous game birds of Perdix, Alectoris and related genera that have variegated but not gaudily colored plumage, short wings and tail, and rather short legs and neck." The Larousse gastronomic encyclopedia says that *perdrix* is "a popular name which covers a large number of wild birds, all edible." Having thus informed us that while there are many partridges, *the* partridge does not exist, it goes on to tell us that *the* partridge was "introduced into France by René, King of Naples, who brought several pairs from the island of Chios to raise them in Provence." This dubious statement was lifted word for word from the *Grand Dictionnaire de Cuisine* of Alexandre Dumas, even including the failure to identify "René, King of Naples" in terms which the average Frenchman might be expected to understand.

I asked several French friends, out of curiosity, who "René, King of Naples" was and they all flunked, leading me to wonder whether the editors of Larousse had failed to explain Dumas because they didn't know either. Yet for once Dumas, usually more picturesque than reliable, was right, though pedantically so. He was referring to the sovereign fondly known to all Frenchmen as Good King René, inseparably associated not with Naples, but with Aix-en-Provence. Provence is not a kingdom, but René was called "king" because it was the highest of his many titles, and it did indeed come from Naples, of which he had been nominally king for a while, though he was not afforded much opportunity to act in consequence. He may have introduced *a* partridge into France, but certainly not *the* partridge. Though Dumas expanded his misinformation by maintaining that partridges were unknown in France before 1440, at least two species are native to that country. There are directions for cooking them in the *Vivandier* of Taillevent, chef to Charles VI, and the anonymous *Ménagier de Paris*, both written before Good King René was born. The latter throws in hints on how to hunt partridges with falcons and explains how to make a chicken look like a partridge, to preserve a host, in that heyday of game, from the ignominy of being caught serving a domestic fowl, on a day, one supposes, when his falcons were sulking.

Those gallinaceous game birds which we may venture to call true partridges are natives of Europe, North Africa and Asia. To put some order into the family, there is probably no better way to start than with the bird whose specific name repeats its generic name, always the sign in taxonomy of a species considered to be typical.

PARTRIDGE. *Drawing by Archibald Thorburn,* Encyclopedia of Sport *(Earl of Suffolk and Berkshire, Hedley Peek, and F. G. Aflalo, Eds.), New York, 1897–1898*

Perdix perdix is indeed called the common partridge, as well as the gray partridge (and hence, sometimes, *P. cinerea*) and the English partridge, naturally enough, since it seems to be the only partridge native to the British Isles, and the first to be called a partridge in English. Birds are mobile, even this one, though it is no long-distance flyer, so we may assume that it managed to flutter across the English Channel early in its history (if it was not there already) to colonize a continent where today it remains the partridge most frequently encountered in western Europe.

This may not last, for the gray partridge, an earth-hugging ground-nesting bird, though thoughtfully protected by nature against the chief peril of an earlier epoch, is ill-equipped to survive in ours. Ground nesters, more or less tied to one spot during the breeding season, are easy prey for sharp-nosed predators like foxes, who catch a whiff of bird and home in on it for dinner. The gray partridge is so constituted that she ceases to emit her characteristic giveaway odor during incubation. This foils foxes, but is little help against hunters, pesticides and mechanical mowing machines, to which the gray partridge is more vulnerable than the second most numerous partridge of western Europe, the red-legged partridge in English, the red partridge to the French, a perching bird which likes woods better than fields, and is consequently better fitted, as long as the woods last, to hold its own against the perils of the modern world.

This gets us into a new genus, for the red partridge is *Caccabis rufa* (or *Alectoris rufa* for those who fail to appreciate the onomatopoetic attempt of *Caccabis* to imitate the cry of the young partridge). The red-legged partridge used to be particularly common in Spain and southern France (it seems not to have reached England, where it is sometimes called the French partridge, before the last quarter of the eighteenth century), but it is now overtaking the common partridge everywhere in France because it is being killed off less rapidly. *Caccabis* (or *Alectoris*) is a restless genus, bent on planting the pennant of the partridge over as much territory as possible. Sardinians are proud of their local partridge, the only game animal on that island which at the time of writing was protected by an all-year-round closed season, and boast that it is found nowhere else in Europe. They are right so far as Europe is concerned, but it seems to be the same species as *C. petrosa*, the Barbary partridge, which has hopped the Mediterranean and is found north of the Atlas Mountains in Morocco, Algeria and Tunisia.

Caccabis–Alectoris lays down a carpet of partridges across Europe and Asia—or indeed two, for there is a series of partridges running through northern Europe to Tibet and Siberia, whose scientific names I do not know, and another paralleling it to the south in a series of relays. *C. rufa* gives way to *C. saxatilis*, which is still, I think, the dominant species in Hungary, though probably not as plentiful as before the war, when even a mediocre marksman could expect to bag thirty birds in three hours in the Hungarian maize fields. The Hungarian partridge was imported into the United States for the pleasure of hunters as early as the eighteenth century, though never, I think, by Thomas Jefferson, who wrote to James Madison in 1785 that he intended to import European partridges. As he wrote from Fontainebleau, he probably had the gray partridge in mind, but so far as I know *P. perdix* has been allowed to remain in Europe.

Farther east, *C. chukar* takes over from *C. saxatilis,* with a range which reaches at least into India; the chukar partridge has also been imported into the United States for hunting. There is even a third European-Asian parade of partridges, again of a different genus—*Ammoperdix heyi,* of North Africa and the Sahara Desert, merges into *A. bonhami,* found in Israel and Iran.

The rarest European partridge is the one which nevertheless covers the most territory, with a range extending from the Alps through China. This is *Caccabis graeca* or *Alectoris graeca,* the bartavelle or Greek partridge. We have now met all four of the partridges which Dumas said were the leaders for delicacy and succulence of flavor, the gray, the red, the bartavelle and the rock partridge or gambra, for this last is the Sardinian–North African bird.

Argument about which partridge tastes the best usually revolves around the gray and the red partridges. In the eighteenth century the gray seemed to be favored, in the nineteenth the red. In this century I find one food writer stating authoritatively, in a tone which brooks no contradiction, that the gray is better, and another, equally qualified, asserting with the same firmness that it is the red. The only common denominator which seems to lie vaguely behind the many conflicting opinions is that at different times and in different places the partridge picked as superior tends to be the one which is most rare: snobbery has always accompanied the eating of game. Brillat-Savarin expressed what was probably the soundest opinion when he said that differences in taste depended less on the species of the bird than on where it had been living and consequently what it had been eating. "The taste of a red partridge from the Périgord," he wrote, "is not the same as that of a red partridge from the Sologne."

Partridges of whatever kind have been appreciated at least since Martial wrote about them in the first century A.D., though one wonders how the ancient Romans knew what partridge tasted like. Apicius cooked them, undressed, feathers and all, and stuffed them afterward with dates—at least he used the best dates, those of Jericho. Lucullus ordered his partridges boiled in a *court-bouillon,* also in their feathers, after which they were plucked, cooled and drenched in verjuice, mint and a mixture of other strong seasonings which must have obliterated every trace of partridge flavor.

Under these conditions, one wonders if the ancients could have been as finicky as modern cooks are, or should be, about the age of the birds they prepare. For the French, masters of fine distinctions in the matter of food, the *perdreau,* meaning a young bird killed in the same year in which it was hatched, is the only one worth eating, at least roasted whole. The adult bird is a *perdrix,* and according to a French jingle:

A la Saint-Rémi
Perdreaux sont perdrix.

You may find *perdrix* in a French restaurant kitchen, but you will never find them on a French restaurant bill of fare; there, however venerable, they are always *perdreaux.* The single exception to this rule is *perdrix aux choux,* partridge with cabbage, and its aristocratic form, the splendid *perdrix en chartreuse* or *chartreuse de perdrix;* the reason for this is that an old bird, because it can be cooked longer, imparts more flavor to the cabbage than a young one, which should not be cooked longer than fifteen minutes. Unfortunately, the cabbage absorbs most of the flavor of the *perdrix,* leaving it relatively dispirited. The remedy for this is to roast a *perdreau* separately from the main dish, substituting it for the *perdrix* during the last five minutes of the cooking. This has become pretty much of a lost art, for it is hard enough nowadays to find a customer wealthy enough to pay for one partridge, let alone two.

St. Rémi's Day, when *perdreaux* become *perdrix,* falls on October 1, and indeed Prosper Montagné, the doyen of French gastronomy during the early years of this century, said that partridge is only at its best in September. Less exigent gourmets admit that it is still pretty good in October and November, and even quite edible in December; but Charles Monselet, a gastronomic writer of the last century, printed the opinion that "after the first snowfall, partridge no longer exists except in a flabby and stringy state." This brings us back to Christmas, and also to disillusionment, disillusionment this time neither with Santa Claus nor the ruffed grouse, but with the quality of true love. Remember the old English folk song:

The first day of Christmas
My true love sent to me
A partridge in a pear tree.

What must we think of a lover who deferred sending his gift until it had reached a state in which he was probably no longer interested in partaking of it himself? Even the pear tree would not have been bearing at that time of year.

PAS
stands for

pasilla, a thin, seven-inch-long, mahogany-colored chili sufficiently good-humored to light only a small fire in the mouth; for **Passacrassana,** a superb pear developed in France but known worldwide under the Italian form of its name, Italy's revenge on France for having converted *piselli* into *petits pois*; for the **passenger pigeon,** a North American game bird so tasty that its numbers were reduced from 9 billion at the beginning of the seventeenth century to 0 by the beginning of the twentieth; for **passion fruit,** so named because its flower is supposed to picture all the instruments of the Crucifixion; and for **pasture brake,** the commonest fern of the United States, which sacrifices itself succulently for the delight of gourmets during its fiddlehead stage.

PEA
stands for

the **pea bean,** an authentically pure-blooded bean striving manfully to live down the stain on its escutcheon inflicted by slanderous rumors that it has been hybridized by the pea; for the **peacock,** an edible bird which you don't just carve, for the correct term, according to the fourteenth-century *Bokes of Kervyne,* is "dysfygure that pecake"; for the **pea crab,** a version of this crustacean so successfully miniaturized that it lives inside the horse clam; for the **pear conch,** which neither looks nor tastes like a pear, and isn't a conch, but a whelk; for **pearlash,** the first chemical baking powder which first appeared in the first American cookbook, written by Amelia Simmons in 1796; for the **pear tomato,** a tomato which would look more like a pear than a pear, if pears were only an inch and a half long; and for **pearmain,** a pear in the fifteenth century, an apple in the sixteenth, and an unknown to Webster's "unabridged" dictionary in the twentieth, and **pearwood,** known to Webster only as wood from a pear tree, but to West Africans as a fruit of the sapodilla family.

And **PEA** also stands for

PEA, of course. Driven out of Europe by the fall of France in 1940, I boarded an American ship at Lisbon, and at my first meal aboard found myself confronted with peas almost as big as marbles, in color an aggressive chemical green, and in flavor easy to confuse with library paste. I was almost home.

The United States could have peas as good as those of Europe if it were not for two delusions which for at least half a century have been playing havoc with American cooking: (1) that bigger is better, and (2) that prettier is tastier. These errors make trouble all along the line, but they are particularly disastrous for peas, for (1) the best peas are the smallest peas, and (2) the sleaziest peas are the best peas. Wrinkled peas (developed, and preferred, in England) contain proportionately less starch and more sugar than the smooth round peas which Americans demand because, I suppose, they look so much neater when photographed in full color for women's magazines.

Americans who know the pea only through the tasteless samples which at charity luncheons accompany the cardboard chicken which follows the watery consommé and precedes the synthetic ice cream must think Europeans off their chump when they hear them drooling over the deliciousness of the pea—unless, of course, they are lucky enough to be able to raise their own, as I did on my farm in Vermont and as Thomas Jefferson did on his in Virginia (he outdid me, in this respect as in so many others, by planting thirty varieties to my five). The pea was his favorite vegetable. He was not too busy as President to write from Washington to his overseer that he was to plant a certain plot "to Ravenscroft peas, which you will find in a canister in my closet."

James de Coquet, a gastronomic writer for the Paris *Figaro,* called a dish of peas "an *allegro*" and added, "*Petits pois* are like children; you have to understand them." Robert J. Courtine, the gastronomic editor of the Paris *Le Monde,* wrote that peas possess "freshness of soul."

"In the vegetable world," William Wallace Irwin said in *The Garrulous Gourmet,* "there is nothing so innocent, so confiding in its expression, as the small green face of the freshly shelled spring pea. Asparagus is pushing and bossy, lettuce is loud and blowsy, radishes are gay and playful, but the little green pea is so helpless and friendly that it makes really sensitive stomachs suffer to see the way he is treated in the average home. Fling him into water and let him boil—and that's that." This is an American tribute to the European pea, for Mr. Irwin's interest in gastronomy began when, as a Chinook-speaking cowboy, he tried to reduce the monotony of chuck-wagon fare. A puckish destiny transferred him, courtesy of the First World War, to Paris, where, when I knew him before the Second

World War, he was secretary of the United States Chamber of Commerce, had two kinds of salt and three of pepper on his table, a small jungle of herbs growing in his window boxes, and a French wife whose maiden name was d'Estrées, like that of the famous mistress of Henry IV, a good eater too.

It seems now to have been decided officially, so far as such matters can become official, that there is really only one species of edible pea, *Pisum sativum*, also called *P. hortensis*, the garden pea; but it has several hundred varieties. The last pea to lose certification as an independent species was *P. arvense*, the field pea, cultivated nowadays chiefly for livestock fodder or for green manure, thought until recently to be the wild ancestor from which *P. sativum* had descended. It is now believed that the field pea was never a genuine wild pea, but one formerly cultivated which escaped from vegetable gardens and reverted to nature, so conscientious botanists now write its name *P. sativum* var. *arvense*. What sixteenth-century botanists used to call *P. majus* and *P. minus*, as though they were separate species, are now considered mere varieties, highbush peas and lowbush peas. As a grower of both, I can testify that the highbush pea, which has longer pods and thus produces more peas per plant, also provides better ones; but it requires some sort of support, which can be a nuisance during cultivation, so lowbush peas are more commonly grown in the United States. Another distinction is between smooth peas, dimpled peas and wrinkled peas.

The "Chinese" snow pea, so tender when young that it can be eaten pod and all, is not Chinese; you can find it in almost any market in Lancaster County, Pennsylvania, where, as a specialty of the Pennsylvania Dutch, it is called the Mennonite pea, as well as the snow pea or the sugar pea. It is not Mennonite either, but a variety grown and eaten throughout Europe, usually under its accurately descriptive French name, *mange-tout*, "eat everything."

The pea is so ancient that its original ancestor seems to have become extinct and its place of origin is unknown. It is usually attributed to a band of territory sweeping from the Near East into Central Asia; those who try to relate it to a narrower area usually allocate it to the Near East. This is belied by the very nature of the pea, which flourishes in cool weather and perishes in heat; it should be incompatible with the climate of the Near East, of which the characteristic pulse has always been not the pea, but the chick-pea, which does not object to warm weather.

It would be my guess that the pea originated at the other end of this band of territory, in India or not far from it, for two reasons: first, the word "pea" is believed to have come from Sanskrit; second, the oldest find of peas so far, carbon-dated at 9750 B.C., was made in what archeologists call the "Spirit Cave," on the border between Burma and Thailand. The oldest find in the Near East was that at Jarmo, in northwestern Iraq, uncertainly ascribed to the sixth or seventh millennium B.C., at least two thousand years after the Burmese discovery. This is north of the usual route taken by foods which reached Europe from Asia, passing through Mesopotamia, Sumer, Assyria, Phoenicia or adjacent territories; but peas are not known to have been grown in the hanging gardens of Babylon. We know that they were grown in Mycenae, one of the most ancient Hellenic cities, while in the time of Pericles hot pea soup was sold in the streets of Athens. How did the pea reach Greece? Possibly it traveled overland from India, not across the hot lowlands of the Near East, but by way of the cooler mountainous country a little farther north, which would be consistent with the other prehistoric finds made of it—at Stone Age sites in Hungary and Switzerland, at Bronze Age sites in northern Greece and France, and at the Iron Age site at Glastonbury, England. It would have entered Greece not from the east, but from the north.

The possible early presence of the pea in the Near East is clouded by uncertainties of translation and identification. On the first score, we are told that the pea is mentioned in Hittite writing. What this really means is that we have been pleased to translate as "pea" a Hittite word which refers to some sort of pulse. We are reminded also that the pea is mentioned at least twice in the Old Testament. So it is, in St. Jerome's Latin version. He used the word *pisum* to translate the Hebrew *qāli*. What did *qāli* mean? According to modern scholars, any sort of seed, toasted—the offering made to King David may have been toasted peas or it may have been toasted grains of wheat.

On the other score, we are told by some archeologists that peas have been found in ancient Egyptian tombs and by others that they have never been found there. I offer timidly a possible explanation for this divergence. The botanists who tell us that the only edible cultivated pea is *P. sativum* have missed one—virtually unknown, it is true, to the West. *P. elatius*, the oasis pea, so called because it grows in the Sahara, is cultivated in Algeria and is believed to be a native of the Nile delta. Perhaps archeologists who encountered it in Egypt, realizing that it was not *P. sativum*, decided therefore that it was not a pea, and told

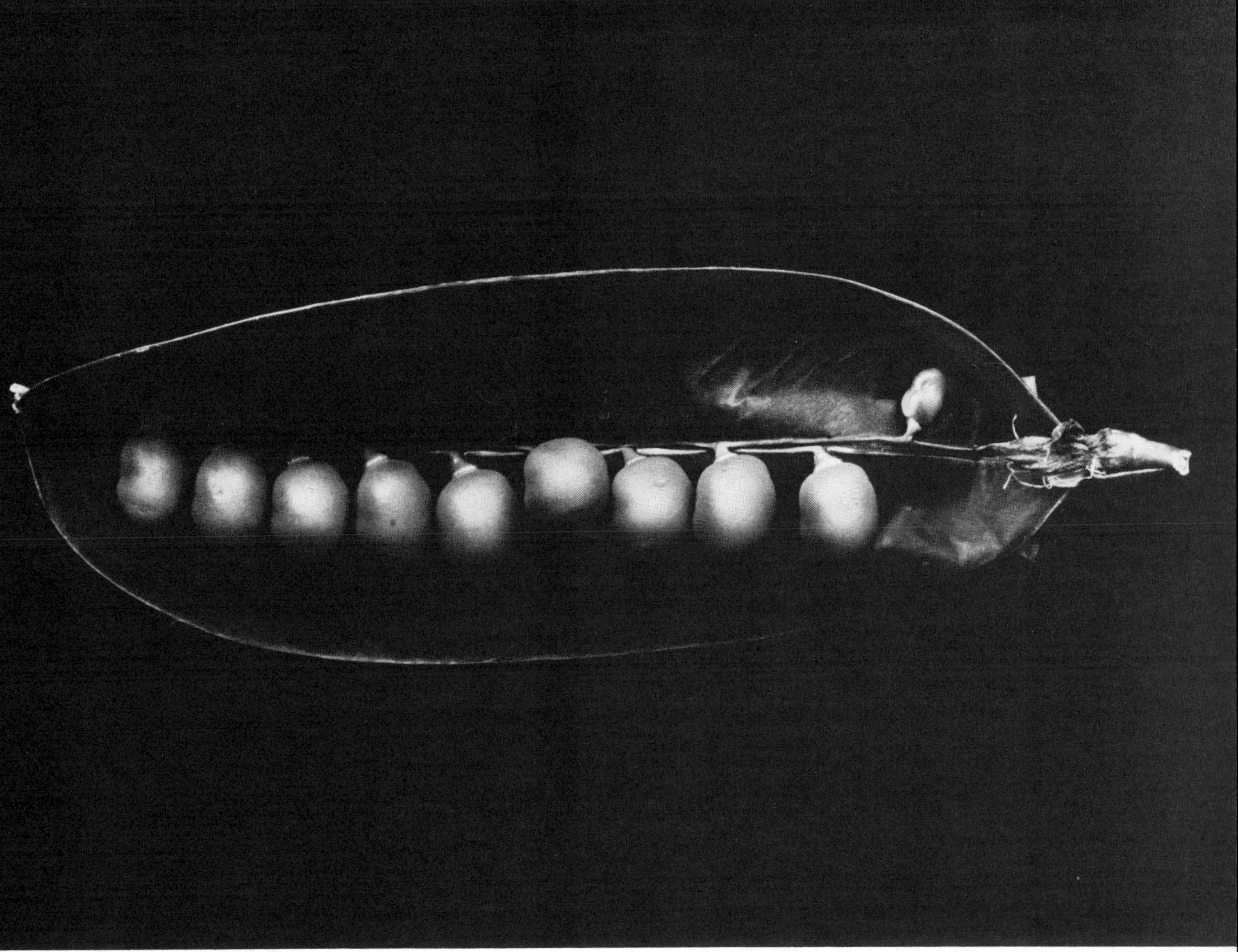

PEA. *Photograph by Murray Alcosser,* Pea Pod, *1977*

us that there were no peas in ancient Egypt. Other archeologists, who recognized it as a pea though it was not *P. sativum,* told us the opposite. It may well be that in antiquity there was *P. elatius* in Egypt, *P. sativum* in Greece, and between them, in the Near East, a void.

Not many vegetables were grown in Attica, but one of them was the pea, which the Greeks usually ate dried, as did the Romans. Peas were a common food in both countries; thirty-seven varieties of peas were sold at one season or another in Trajan's market. Apicius gave a number of recipes for peas in his cookbook, and labeled one of them with his own name. As he was not a man who held himself in low esteem, we may deduce from this that the pea was not held in low esteem either.

The writers who tell us that peas were not eaten in France before (a) Catherine de' Medici or (b) Louis XIV are wrong. Charlemagne ordered them planted in his domains about 800, and in 1393, well before either Catherine or Louis, the *Ménagier de Paris* dealt with them, noting mysteriously that they would not cook properly in well water. What is true is that the tiny peas which are now considered the best did not exist before the Italian Renaissance, when Italy developed the *piselli novelli,* which were eaten unripe and fresh. Before that, Europe ate dried peas mostly, though not, as we are often told, exclusively. One of the thirteenth-century food cries of Paris was *J'ay pois en cosse tous nouviaus* ("I have fresh peas in the pod") and in the seventeenth there was *Les pois verts pour la Caresme / Qui sont aussi doux que la cresme* ("Green peas for Lent, as sweet as cream"). Peas were popular as a Lenten and fast-day dish (in Paris's Hôtel Dieu 150 fast days were observed during the year) not only in France, but also in England ("Peas and leeks are boiled in Lent," an Elizabethan author wrote). Dried peas, which kept well, were also stocked as a reserve against the frequent famines of the time, for which reason Salic law imposed harsh penalties for damaging peas or stealing them from the large fields given over to raising them in Frankish times. Purée or soup made from dried peas was a standard ration for those dependent on public charity. The Paris street on which I have lived for twenty years, the Rue du Cherche-Midi—the Street of the Hunt for Noon—for whose name many fanciful explanations have been given, was actually so called because of the large convent there which distributed pease porridge to the poor every day at noon.

Catherine de' Medici brought *piselli novelli* with her from Florence in 1533 when she married Henry II of France, when they were referred to as a "royal dish" (at a time when boiled peas, but certainly not this variety, were a basic food for poor peasants in Germany), and apparently were not shared with the population in general, for they had been forgotten and were hailed as a novelty when they were brought into France again, this time from Genoa, during the reign of Louis XIV. *Piselli novelli* became so popular at the French court, which at that time set the fashions for all Europe, that they became *petits pois* and have since borne that French name everywhere in the world. Mme. de Maintenoy, in a letter written to Cardinal de Noailles on May 10, 1695, which everybody attributes to Mme. de Sévigné, wrote:

> The subject of peas is being treated at length: impatience to eat them, the pleasure of having eaten them, and the longing to eat them again are the three points about which our princes have been talking for four days. There are some ladies who, after having supped with the King, and well supped too, help themselves to peas at home before going to bed at the risk of indigestion. It is a fad, a fury.

One person who did incur indigestion from overeating of peas was Louis himself, as his doctor, Fagon, related in unedifying detail. However, he got off lightly in comparison with King John of England, whose death has been attributed to a surfeit of peas by some historians (others allege that it was lampreys, unripe peaches or toad's blood in his ale). Peas were not brought to England by the Romans, as some writers have reported, nor were they unknown there before the time of Henry VIII, as others have asserted, in ignorance of those Iron Age peas at Glastonbury. They are heard of oftener after the Norman Conquest of 1066, so it may be that a French example encouraged the English to eat more peas. They imported some varieties from France; for instance, Turner reported in 1557 on the Rouncival pea, named for the Roncevaux of the *Chanson de Roland*. The English have been fond of peas ever since, and took the lead in developing new varieties; in the eighteenth century Thomas Knight seems to have been the first to cross peas artificially, specializing in wrinkled peas.

It may have been the Dutch who developed the *mange-tout*. It is on record that French Ambassador to Holland de Bohy imported some from Holland about 1600, and Nicolas de Bonnefous wrote in *Le Jardinier Français* (1651): "There is a species which can be eaten green [whole?] which is called the Dutch pea and was very rare not long ago." In England in the reign of Elizabeth I, it was reported that peas brought in from Holland were regarded as great treats by women because "they come from so far and cost so much."

If Pierre Martyr is right, the first peas in America were planted by Christopher Columbus in 1493 on Isabella Island. The new vegetable was accepted enthusiastically by the Indians, who were growing them in Florida in 1602; and they must have traveled rapidly from Mexico to New Mexico if it was really peas which the Spaniards found there in 1540. In the north, Jacques Cartier's report that the Hochelagan Indians were raising them in 1535 where Montreal now stands seems dubious; perhaps he took for peas the American string bean, then unknown to Europe. The chances are better that it was really peas which French traders found Indians growing along the Ottawa River in 1613; at any rate Captain John Smith, who had already written in 1608 of feasting on "Virginia pease," reported that New England Indians were growing them in 1614. There is no doubt that it was peas which General John Sullivan destroyed, along with other crops, during his punitive raid against the Iroquois of western New York in 1779.

The first peas in New England were planted in 1602 by that almost forgotten hero of early American exploration, Captain Bartholomew Gosnold, on the island of Cuttyhunk. By 1629 there were in the governor's garden at Plymouth, according to the Reverend Francis Higginson, "a store of green peas . . . as good as ever I eat in England."

PEACH. On November 10, 1977, the British news agency Reuters reported the discovery at Ch'ang-sha, China, of the perfectly preserved body of a woman later identified as the wife of the Marquis of Tai, who had been buried in the second century B.C. Egyptian mummies have held out longer than this, but they are preserved in one of the driest countries in the world, while Ch'ang-sha's province of Hunan enjoys between 50 and 58 inches of rain per year. Egyptian mummies, moreover, had the viscera, always quick to decay, removed before embalming. The Chinese lady was so far from having been eviscerated that the Reuters correspondent reported with awe that "undigested melon seeds" were found in her intestines (melon seeds are not digested, they are passed). The reporter attributed the state of the remains to the fact that the woman had been buried in a series of coffins nested one inside of the other, each hermetically sealed by a coating of charcoal and clay. If he had interviewed a Chinese of the second century B.C. he would have learned that he was barking up the wrong tree when, in his fascination with melon seeds, he ignored the really important food found in the tomb, a bowl containing peaches. Ever since the Ch'in dynasty the Chinese had known that peaches, eaten in time, preserved the body from corruption "until the end of the world." Chinese still serve on birthdays a steamed roll in the shape of a peach, called *shou-tao,* which means "long life peach." (Incidentally, Ch'ang-sha was the place from which Marco Polo reported that he had come upon very large peaches "weighing fully two small pounds apiece.")

The peach was the object of a sort of cult in China, where for poets, sculptors and painters it was a symbol of immortality, despite the fact that it grows on a short-lived tree (some commercial growers replant their orchards every eight to ten years, others wait for twenty). Friends gave each other peaches, real or in porcelain, to attest to their affection. The veneration accorded the peach no doubt arose from its ancient and peculiarly Chinese character, for it is believed to have originated in China, where it is called *tao.* Chinese writings contain references to the peach dating from 2000 B.C. (dubious) and from the fifth century B.C. (trustworthy), including some from the works of Confucius, at least three centuries before we hear of this fruit from anywhere else. Peach trees are found growing wild in China, and I think nowhere else, though the *Encyclopaedia Britannica,* while admitting that the white-fleshed peach started there, goes on to say that "there is little evidence that yellow-fleshed peaches are indigenous to China proper outside of the province of Yunnan . . . and . . . it is found growing wild in parts of the North-West Frontier Province of India." Yunnan is Chinese enough for me, and as it lies along the border of what was the North-West Frontier Province (now part of Pakistan), I am not convinced that we should rescind the identification of the peach as Chinese because some trees straggled across a man-made political frontier concerning whose presence the peach had probably not been properly notified. Chinese wild-peach trees are apt to be gnarled and squat, their fruit is small and the pit large, but the flesh is exquisite in flavor. Chinese peach trees breed true from seed, which is not the case for peach trees anywhere else in the world, justifying the belief that all peaches except those of China are hybrids, and therefore probably alien to the areas in which they are found.

PEACH *by Dante Gabriel Rossetti (1828–1882).* Silence (Mrs. William Morris), crayon drawing

It was long thought that the peach originated in Persia (where it does not grow wild), and indeed its scientific name is *Prunus persica,* because it was from Persia that the ancient Romans imported the fruit, and from the Romans that we first heard about it. They could not have known that Persia had acquired it, across a good deal of intervening territory, from China, a country whose existence they did not suspect. We might even wonder whether the Persians had the peach much earlier than the Romans. Xenophon got to Persia with the ill-fated expedition of Cyrus early in the fourth century B.C., but made no mention of it; it is true that he had other cares on his mind. Alexander's army followed later in the same century, but does not seem to have noticed peaches, unless it was the source for an apparent reference to them by Theophrastus. The Romans could not have known about the peach at the beginning of the second century B.C., for if they had, Cato would certainly have mentioned it; and though the Asian Army brought back many new foods from the East when it returned to Italy in 185 B.C., it is doubtful that the peach was among them. Pliny wrote about it in the first century A.D., called it the Persian apple (*Malum persicum*), and said that the Romans had imported it from Persia for the first time only shortly before —apparently by a very indirect route, for he added that the trees were first planted in Egypt (where we never hear of them again) and then on the island of Rhodes, but bore no fruit in either place. He would not have known why, but we do. The peach is definitely a fruit of the temperate zone. Though it prefers its relatively warmer areas, it can survive temperatures as low as —15° F. if they do not last too long, and most important, it requires a resting period (in other words, winter cold) for at least two months in order to work up strength for the ordeal of producing leaves and flowers in the spring.

The peach seems never to have achieved a foothold in ancient Greece, but in Rome several varieties were developed—from two to five depending on how you translate; the nectarine seems definitely not to have been among them. The peach was not common in Rome either, for Pliny says it was hard to grow in Italy, so the Romans imported it from Persia, which made it expensive.

One might wonder whether ancient Gaul did not know the peach before ancient Rome. Columella, whose *De re rustica* may possibly have been written before Pliny's *Historia naturalis* (Pliny was a little slow getting around to his chief work, having been preoccupied earlier with such subjects as *De re iaculatione equestri unus—The Art of Throwing the Javelin from Horseback*)—said that the peach was cultivated in Gaul, where, indeed, the climate should have been more favorable to it than in much of Italy. Georges Blond wrote that peaches appeared at the banquets of the Franks (before Charlemagne), but were rare; when Charlemagne ordered them grown on his domains they were still rare.

Medieval peaches seem to have been small and not very good. The anonymous author of the fourteenth-century *Le Ménagier de Paris*, who refers to them both as hors d'oeuvre and dessert, is silent about their quality, but we may suspect that they were less than superb, otherwise Rabelais and Henry IV's physician would, in the sixteenth century, have been less ecstatic about the new Corbeil peach, a variety which seems to have been half wild, was no larger than a damson plum, and had "dry and solid flesh, not adhering to the stone."

It was probably from France that the peach reached England, where it fulfilled the warning of William Lawson's *A New Orchard and Garden* (1618): "Meddle not with Apricoekes nor Peaches . . . which will not like our cold parts unless they be helped with some reflex of Sunne." Most of the peaches eaten in England today are imported or grown in hothouses. The records say that peaches were introduced into England in 1562, but four centuries earlier King John was said to have died from eating too many of them (other accounts say that it was peas, not peaches).

One sovereign who did overdo with peaches was Louis XIV, a glutton in respect to every food he liked. When peaches were placed before him, he was so impatient to have at them that he could not wait to peel them, but bit directly into the fruit, ignoring the unpalatability of their fuzzy skin. He once granted a pension to a man who furnished his table with particularly fine peaches from Montreuil, a Paris suburb which once raised some of the best peaches in France and now raises ugly jerry-built housing.

His fondness for peaches was a taste Louis XIV shared with American Indians. The Spaniards brought this fruit to the New World, where the Creeks and Seminoles fell upon it avidly and the Natchez named one of their thirteen months for it. Passed from tribe to tribe, the peach tree spread through Indian America faster than the white man did. It reached, among others, the Susquehanna Indians of Pennsylvania. In a letter dated August 16, 1663, William Penn wrote from Philadelphia: "There are . . . very good peaches, and in great quantities; not an Indian plantation without them . . . not inferior to any peach you have in England, except the Newington." Meanwhile settlers from England had introduced the peach into Virginia and Massachusetts, where the quality of American-grown peaches remained high.

A French peach is juicy [James Fenimore Cooper wrote in *The Travelling Bachelor*] and when you first bring it in contact with your palate, sweet, but it leaves behind it a cold, watery, and almost sour taste. It is for this reason so often eaten with sugar. An American is exceedingly apt to laugh if he sees ripe fruit of any sort eaten with anything sweet. The peaches here leave behind a warm, rich and delicious taste, that I can only liken in its effects to that which you call the *bouquet* of a glass of Romanée.

Thomas Jefferson agreed: "They [the French]

PEACH *by Pierre Auguste Renoir (1841–1919).* Still Life with Peaches, *oil on canvas*

have nothing which deserves the name of a peach," he wrote from Fontainebleau to James Madison, not yet President, on October 28, 1785, "there being not sun enough to ripen their plumbpeach and the best of their soft peaches being like our autumn peaches." Nevertheless, he planted European peach stones at Monticello in 1802; but they had been sent him by his friend and former neighbor in Virginia, Philip Mazzei, who had returned to his native land and dispatched the seeds from Pisa, Italy, a country which does not lack sun.

PEANUT. The peanut was introduced into the White House by President Richard Milhous Nixon, who may not have known it. He had ordered the razing of several disreputable temporary structures near the Washington Monument, whereupon the rats who had been living there, dispossessed of their accustomed lodgings, moved into the White House—which, it was agreed, was no place for rats. They were disposed of by traps baited with peanut butter. President Franklin D. Roosevelt had not been friendly to peanuts; he had placed limits on their planting. If these incidents seem to have given the peanut a Republican rather than a Democratic orientation, the imbalance was corrected with the move into the White House of President Carter, whose association with the peanut is a secret for nobody. Indeed, signs at the Democratic Convention which nominated him urged: "Make the peanut our national tree," which, unless the delegates were jest a' funnin', displayed a lamentable lack of knowledge about peanuts, which do not grow on trees. They are not nuts either, but leguminous plants, related to peas, so that the first syllable of their name is apt, but not the second. The most accurate of the several hundred names which exist for the peanut (among them arachide, cacahuète, earth almond, earth nut, earth pistachio, Erdnuss, gedda, goober, goober pea, grass nut, ground nut, maní, monkey nut, nguba, pindar and turrabele) is ground pea.

The justification for approaching the peanut from the point of view of its incidence on American politics is that it is a food 100 percent American (in the sense that "American" does not apply solely to the United States, as the adjective is so often used, but to both continents of the New World). When George Washington Carver, the great promoter of the peanut, who discovered three hundred different uses for it, was admitted to the Columbia University Hall of Fame in 1977, an article in *The New York Times* explained that the peanut was two thousand years old and that the Chinese pressed oil from it, which seemed to imply that the Chinese so acted in ancient times (they did not); and that the popular name "goober" was of African origin, which seemed to imply that the peanut itself was of African origin (it is not). China acquired the peanut only in the 1600s via the Malay Peninsula, where the Spaniards, who had brought it from America, had introduced it a hundred years before China got it; and though "goober" does come from the Gedda *nguba*, applied to the peanut by black slaves when they met it in America, it did not then mean "peanut" in Africa (it may now), where there were no peanuts at the time, but referred to analogous underground foods, first of all, probably, to *Voandgeia subterranea*, the Bambara groundnut or Congo goober, which has a number of other popular names, several of which it shares with the peanut. Misguided also, the Larousse encyclopedia states that the peanut is native to Africa (the Larousse *gastronomic* encyclopedia, however, gets it right). The peanut actually got to Africa only when Portuguese slavers brought it there from Brazil and planted it on the West African coast to provide cheap and nourishing food for their captives while they were waiting for ships to carry them to the New World.

The peanut is a native of South America, according to some authorities specifically of Brazil, where Europeans first found it growing wild, but more probably of Peru, where it has been found in ancient mummy tombs and where it is pictured on Chimu pottery, antedating the Incas; either the Chimu or the Incas were probably the first to cultivate it. Another error about the peanut is made within the American framework by those who want to situate it on territory today included within the United States. Miles Standish, on the settlement of the Pilgrims at Plymouth, discovered a cache of Indian food, which probably saved the lives of the colonists, containing maize and "groundnuts." It has been written that what were then called "groundnuts" were peanuts (*Arachis hypogaea*); actually they were "Indian potatoes" (*Apios tuberosa*). Even in the Southeast, where we are told (correctly) that Virginia ham was an American Indian invention, one of whose requirements is that it comes from pigs fed on peanuts, it is implied (incorrectly) that it was pre-Columbian Indians who created this food; it could not have been pre-Columbian Indians, for they had no pigs: it was Europeans who imported them. Actually, peanuts were not observed by the incoming Europeans farther north than Mexico, where Cortez saw them, and Haiti, where Columbus saw them. The earliest reference to peanuts in the United States known to me dates from 1791 or 1792, when Thomas Jefferson, who may have been an innovator for this crop as for so many others, is known to have grown them.

The United States is inclined to regard the peanut more as a treat than as a substantial food, suitable for candy bars or as adornment for ice cream sundaes, or to munch at sporting events or nibble with a before-dinner drink, but elsewhere it is treated with more respect; it is, indeed, one of the world's fifteen leading food crops. George Washington Carver once demonstrated the versatility of this food to a group of Alabama businessmen by serving them a meal based solely on peanuts—peanut soup, ersatz "chicken" made from peanuts, peanuts treated as a vegetable, peanut-flour bread, salad with peanut oil dressing, peanut ice cream, peanut cookies, peanut candy and "coffee" made from peanuts (some Americans drank a coffee substitute derived from peanuts during World War II). This failed to popularize the peanut as a solid food, and its most substantial use in the United States continued to be in the form of peanut butter, whose manufacture consumes half of the country's total crop. They make peanut butter in Africa and Indonesia too—pure, with nothing added—but to enrich and thicken sauces and soups; they are surprised in those countries to hear that in America (and in Australia too) it is a spread for bread.

However, peanut butter, though virtually unknown in France, is described by the *Dictionnaire de l'Académie des Gastronomes* as having "a rather agreeable flavor," and it is accordingly recommended that it be spread on—gingerbread! Having thus disqualified itself as a spokesman for the subtle French sense of taste, the *Dictionnaire* adds that peanut oil, the one form in which peanuts are commonly consumed in France (as everywhere in the world), "pleases those who see nothing in oil except a lubricant, of which they demand absolute neutrality in taste, but is despised by gourmets." This presents as a fault what is actually a merit, for there are times when an oil with no marked taste of its own is precisely what is wanted. In my own home we use olive oil for most purposes, but when we eat those large luscious mushrooms which France has made famous the world over under the name of *cèpes* (which is nothing other than the boletus, found also in the United States) we switch to peanut oil, for we want our *cèpes* to taste like mushrooms, not like olives.

If we accept the popular definition of the peanut as a nut, we learn that it is the most important food of this category in international trade, while if we compare it with other legumes, we find a publication of the United Nations Food and Agriculture Organization opining that it is "perhaps of greater importance than all the haricot beans." This is because of its high protein content, 26 percent of its weight, exceeded among generally available food plants only by the soybean (36 percent); but the peanut provides its proteins more cheaply. In Africa it gives the highest protein yield per acre, the runner-up being the chick-pea, only about four-fifths as much. It is also advantageous for countries prone to devastation by locusts, which may destroy the aboveground foliage of the plants, but, provided they do so late enough in the growing season, leave behind the protected buried peanuts. This seems to be the reason why, at the end of an evolutionary period, peanuts decided to take refuge underground, for they are not tubers, as we are often told, nor do they grow from the roots of the plant, as we are often told also, but from the flowers. After they have bloomed, the flower stalks bend down until they touch the ground, whereupon they grow into it and ripen their fruit in safety beneath the surface. In all probability, the ancestors of the peanut produced their nuts in the open air.

Garcilaso de la Vega wrote in 1609 that the peanut was being raised by Indians under the name *ynchic*, and "is very like marrow and has the taste of almonds" (we may deduce that he met the peanut in Peru, since *ynchic* [or *anchic*] is a Peruvian word). After it had reached Africa, the missionary Father Merolla found it in 1682 growing in the Congo under the name *mandois*, and though he did not specify that peanuts *tasted* like almonds, he did write that they grew "three or four together like vetches but underground and are about the bigness of an ordinary olive. From these milk is extracted like to that drawn from almonds." Alexandre Dumas, a writer not noted for accuracy, wrote that peanut roots taste like licorice (so far as I know, nobody eats the roots; did he mean the nuts?); that eating raw peanuts provokes headaches and violently sore throats; and that the Spanish call the peanut *cacohuette* because it tastes like cacao and is used by them to make chocolate for the poor. (The Spanish don't call it *cacohuette*, they call it *maní*; the French call it *cacahuète* because they first received peanuts, not via Spain or Portugal, but direct from Mexico along with its Aztec name—in Nahuatl, *thalcacahuate*.) Another reference to the taste of peanuts is grimmer:

In the southern states [Rachel Carson wrote in *Silent Spring*] peanuts are usually grown in rotation with cotton, on which BHC [benzene hexachloride] is extensively used. Peanuts grown later in this soil pick up considerable amounts of the insecticide . . . only a trace is enough to incorporate the telltale musty odor and taste. The chemical penetrates the

PEANUT. *Print from Artemas Ward:* The Grocer's Encyclopedia, *New York, 1911*

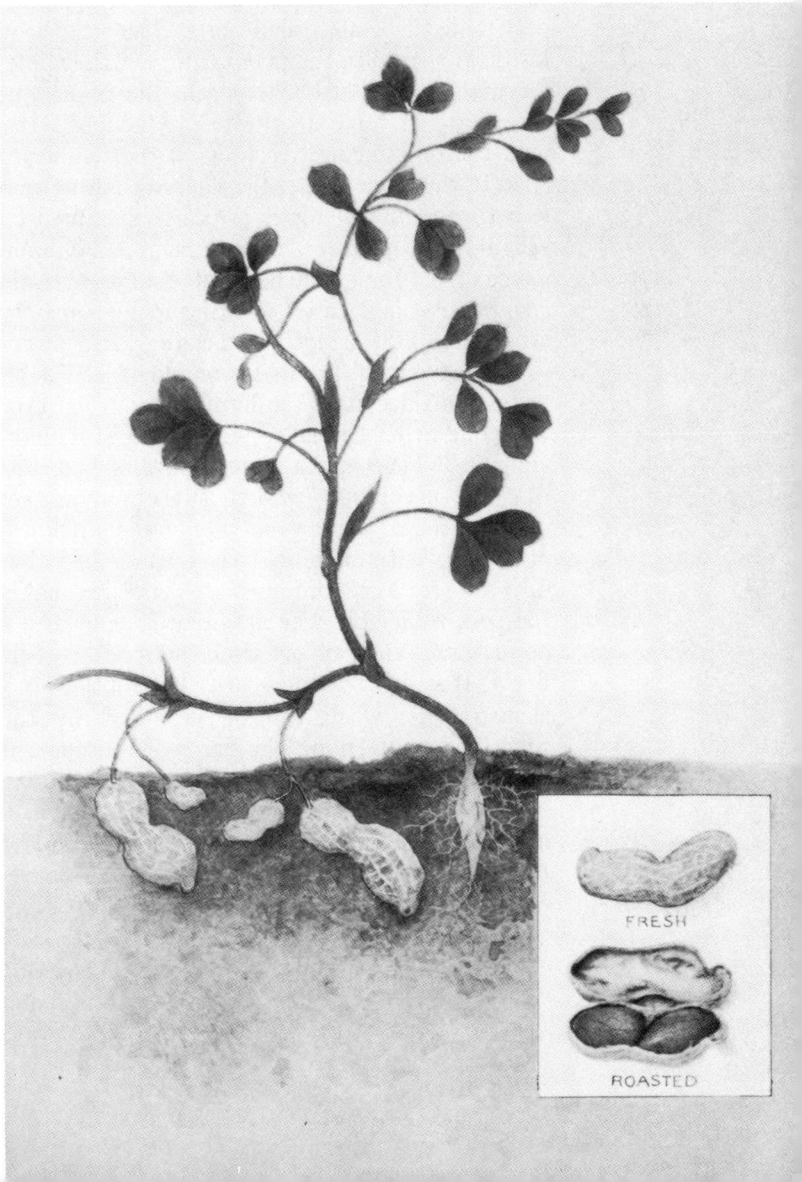

nuts and cannot be removed. Processing, far from removing the mustiness, sometimes accentuates it.

I have occasionally tasted mustiness in peanuts —from less dangerous causes, I hope—but I have never come across peanuts which tasted like pistachio nuts, licorice, cacao, or even almonds. In my opinion, peanuts taste like peanuts.

PEAR. "The pear," wrote François Pierre de la Varenne about 1650, "is the grandfather of the apple, its poor relation, a fallen aristocrat, the man-at-arms of our domains, which once, in our humid land, lived lonely and lordly, preserving the memory of its prestige by its haughty comportment."

Oof and amen! Reducing La Varenne's dithyramb to more prosaic terms, we find that the pear is indeed the grandfather of the apple in the sense that it was cultivated earlier, more than four thousand years ago, but not in the sense of being its direct ancestor. Both are members of the *Rosaceae*, but so are 100 other genera and 2000 other species. They do not belong to the same genus and consequently have never been successfully hybridized; graft pear on apple, or apple on pear, and the graft usually dies. The pear may justifiably be called the poor relation of the apple, for though it exceeds the peach, the plum and the cherry in total worldwide production, it remains second among tree fruits of the temperate zone to the apple alone: the United States grows four times as many apples as pears (measured by weight), Europe three times as many. The dominance of the apple may be ascribed to democratic adaptability; it is easier to bring to high quality everywhere. The aloof, aristocratic pear, harder to grow, fussier about its surroundings, resists efforts to reduce it to uniformity and rob it of what one writer has called "the charm of its individuality." Pears differ more in size, shape, texture and flavor than perhaps any other product of the orchard. Great variability gives us richness of choice, but variability may operate in either direction, for better or for worse. Versatility makes the pear vulnerable. Pay attention as you taste a perfect pear, and you can sense the fragility of its flavor. It is delicate and subtle, but subtlety is a characteristic which can be destroyed by the slightest imperfection. The flavor of the apple is more robust.

Despite the pear's resistance to the blandishments of the gardener, it is cited by Alexandre Dumas as an outstanding example of the improvements which can be achieved through cultivation. "The small size, the hardness and the bitter taste which is offered us by the wild pear," he wrote, "compared to the great volume, the sweetness and the tenderness of so many fine fruits, make us appreciate the influence of cultivation. The wild pear is not edible, it serves only to make a cider of low quality, and so it has been named the pear of anguish [*poire d'angoisse*]."

The wild pear has indeed never been extolled as a taste treat. As long ago as the fourth century B.C., when Alexis of Thurii cited it as one of the principal foods eaten by an impoverished family, it was with the evident intention of emphasizing the hardship of their lot. Both Alexis and Dumas overlooked one characteristic of the wild pear: its bitterness disappears when it is cooked. The fourteenth-century *Ménagier de Paris*, recommending that wild pears be first boiled and then roasted, did not think it necessary to caution cooks about their bitterness, but did remark that if they were pale in color they could be given a more appetizing look by adding hay to the cooking water. To this day a half-wild pear, locally called *botzi*, is eaten in Switzerland, not raw, out of hand, but cooked, caramelized to encourage sweetness.

There were no pears in either the Western Hemisphere or the Southern until they were brought there from Eurasia. As far back as we can go, we find pears occupying a belt extending from central Europe to northeastern Asia, but at exactly what point within this area they originated is anybody's guess. Don and Patricia Brothwell, in their *Food in Antiquity*, suggest northern Persia to Anatolia, which seems a little too far south for a fruit that was slow in reaching the warm Mediterranean basin, that grows well in Himalayan surroundings and that demonstrates its status as a tree of the temperate zone by refusing to flourish except where a marked winter gives it a dormant period. Its climatic limits may always have been what they are today: Norway is too far north, though an occasional bearing pear tree may be found there; southern India is too far south. In respect to time of blooming, and hence of vulnerability to late spring frosts, the pear is not quite as hardy as the apple, since it blooms before it, but is hardier than apricots, peaches or almonds, blooming after them.

I am tempted to wonder whether pears did not originate in China, where they have been found in a tomb dated at 2100 B.C. Seeds of a small-fruited pear have also been found in prehistoric Swiss lake settlements, but not in large quantity. The pear tree may have been a recent arrival then.

Theories vary about the epoch when the pear first appeared in the Near East. One authority tells us there is no evidence that it existed in ancient Assyria, but another asserts that it was

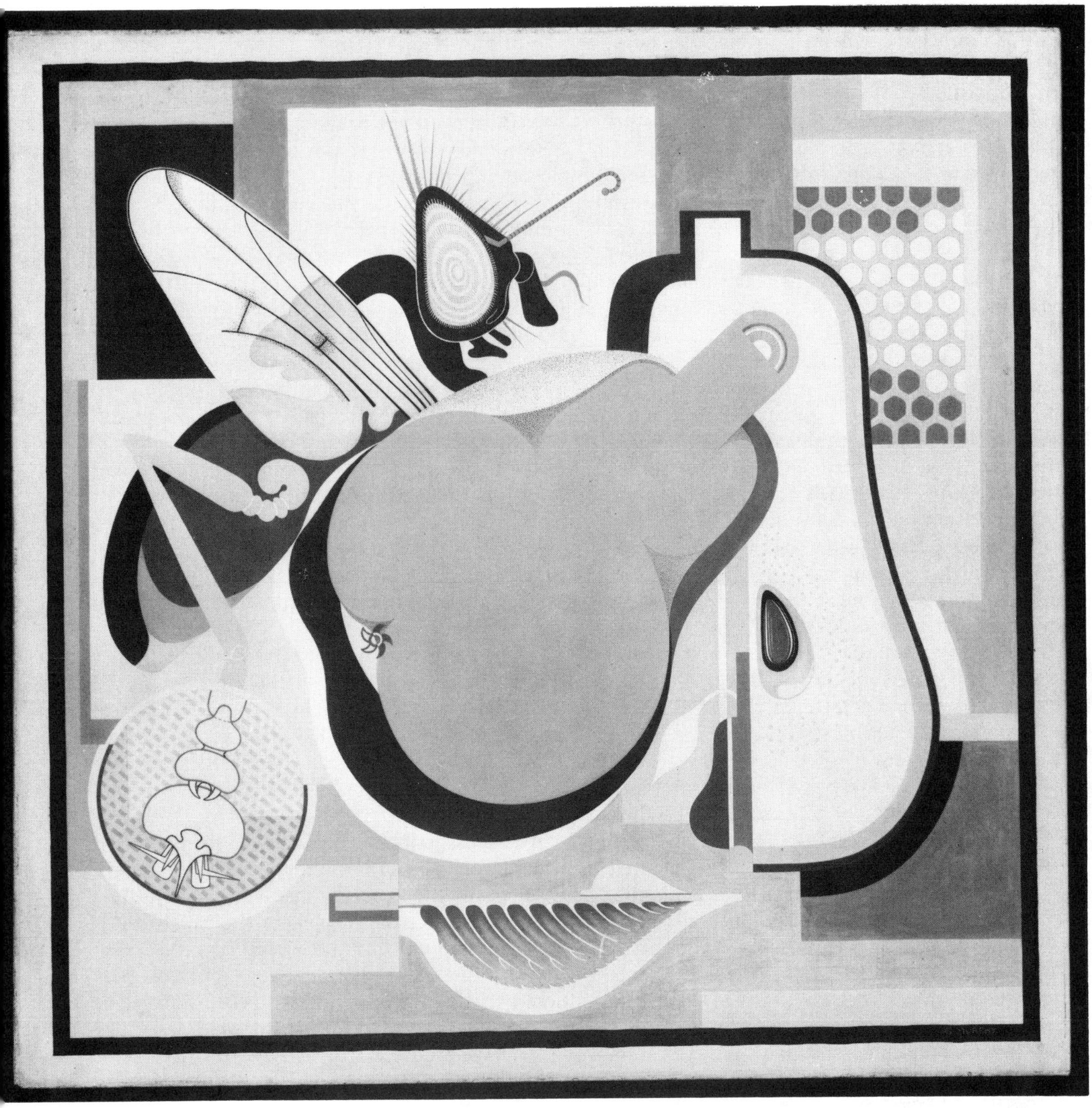

PEAR *by Gerald Murphy (1888–1964).* Wasp and Pear, *oil on canvas*

known to the Sumerians (and thus in pre-Assyrian Assyria), though only as an ingredient in medicines. We should not forget that in that place and in those times errors of identification or translation are always possible. This has to be borne in mind when we read that the Hittites cultivated pears, that they were raised by the Phoenicians, and that the ancient Hebrews possessed a number of greatly improved varieties. We are sure, at least, that the pear was known to the Greeks from very early times, for when Homer writes of it, it is already growing in orchards, evidently under cultivation. It seems to have been the Greeks who passed it on to Egypt, comparatively late, and also to the Romans, perhaps not until after Gaul was already raising pears. The Chinese introduced it into northern India, but far too late to throw any light on its origin—in the first century A.D.

In historic times, one of the most astonishing phenomena we note about the pear is the speed with which it develops fresh varieties. It enters with remarkable versatility into new combinations and metamorphoses and throws off mutants as a burning brand throws off sparks. Theophrastus mentioned three kinds of pears; Cato recorded five, or possibly six; Pliny, depending on how you translate him, thirty-eight to forty-one; Palladius, fifty-six; and Columella said pears were too numerous to list.

In seventeenth-century Italy, one catalog of pears named 209 varieties, another gave 232. Charlemagne grew 168 kinds in his domains. Louis XIV was fond of pears, which explains how Jean de la Quintinie came to be ennobled. A lawyer who tired of the courts, he abandoned his profession to raise pears in Auteuil, giving some to Racine. The poet marveled at their flavor and introduced La Quintinie to Le Notre, the king's landscape gardener, who was impressed also, to the extent of appointing him superintendent of the royal orchards, a post which brought him into frequent fruitful contact with the king. La Quintinie was conservative in his estimate of what constituted a genuine new variety. When Nicolas de Bonnefoũs listed 400 varieties of pears in his *Jardinier Français,* La Quintinie said there were only 300, "of which 25 are unmatchable." The British must have been slow in taking up the pear, for they were cultivating only 64 kinds in 1640; but by 1842 there were more than 700, and a catalog of 1868 listed 850.

The pear penetrated America from several directions. French Jesuit missionaries moving southward from the St. Lawrence valley bestowed pears on the Iroquois, who adopted them enthusiastically. A memorandum of 1629 refers to sending pear seeds to the Massachusetts Bay Colony, and in 1640 it is recorded that a pear tree was planted by Governor Prince at Eastman, Massachusetts, and another at Yarmouth. New Amsterdam acquired a tree from Holland in 1647, while in the following year *A Perfect Description of Virginia* recorded that "Mr. Richard Kinsman hath had for this three or four years forty or fifty Butts of Perry [pear cider] made out of his orchard, pure and good." French settlers planted pears on the shores of the Detroit River in 1705. Thomas Jefferson grew them of course, perhaps varieties obtained in France, for he wrote from there that while French apples and peaches were inferior to American kinds, and strawberries and cherries only fair in quality, the pears were "infinitely beyond anything we possess." In the West, Spanish friars planted pears in the California missions; they grow much better on the Pacific coast, where the equable climate is more propitious to them, than in the East. In 1879 the American Pomological Society listed 115 varieties of pears suitable for cultivation, and since then about 1000 varieties have been cataloged in the United States—and 5000 in Europe, a remarkable number for a fruit which counts only 15 to 20 species in all, of which two alone are responsible for almost all the varieties, the European *Pyrus communis* and the Asian *P. sinensis.*

Desirable though it usually is, variety has perhaps been overdone in the case of the pear. Richness in quantity does not necessarily guarantee richness in quality, and though pears have been greatly improved over the centuries, not all of the innovations have been improvements. "In Belgium and France from 1775 onward a few wealthy and painstaking amateurs produced the excellent varieties we grow today," *The Oxford Book of Food Plants* remarks, adding, with a certain sting for earlier horticulturists: "It seems more difficult to raise good new pears than apples, possibly because there are few good parents to choose from." Just to make sure that justice is applied equally to later growers as well, the same authority notes on another page that despite the large number of new varieties then being developed, "the fruit tree breeders of the eighteenth and nineteenth centuries in England produced only two outstandingly successful pears, namely the 'Williams' Bon Chrétien' and 'Conference.' " The Conference is a long, thin, yellow-green to brownish pear, juicy and refreshing, the variety most widely grown in Great Britain. (In northern Germany the most widely grown pear is the Köstliche von Charneau, also known as the Burgermeister Birne, "mayor's pear.") The Williams' Bon Chrétien we shall come to in a moment.

In the eastern United States, where pears find it hard going, there is usually some crossing with Oriental species, because the Far Eastern trees are more resistant to fire blight, the worst enemy of pears. The disadvantage in such crosses is that they risk increasing the grittiness you may have noted at one time or another in pears. This is due to the presence in their flesh of what are called grit cells or stone cells, which are produced more plentifully as the pear approaches full ripeness. For this reason pears are picked unripe; separated from its source of vigor, the pear ceases to proliferate grit cells and remains soft and mellow. The Chinese pear has a much higher proportion of grit cells from the beginning, which is why it is also called the sand pear. This does not seem to bother the Chinese or the Japanese, nor was it mentioned by Marco Polo when he reported from China that among the items regularly for sale were "above all huge pears, weighing ten pounds apiece, white as dough inside and very fragrant." A contemporary visitor to China has praised the pears of Tientsin as "crunchy and juicy," but most Westerners feel that a little crunchiness goes a long way, and dislike the rough, coarse texture of the Chinese pear.

The pears Westerners eat are varieties of *P. communis*, grouped into families by shape: round or flattened, a group which is made up mostly of old varieties; top-shaped or bergamot (because the typical pears of this group came from Bergamo, Italy); conical, tapered, but without a waist; pyriform, with a waist, a redundant term which informs us that we are faced by a pear-shaped pear; oval; and calebasse, long and straight.

The best pear in the world may well be the Comice, and the most widespread and most successful commercially, the aforementioned Williams' Bon Chrétien. The Comice, often called "the queen of pears," sweetly and subtly perfumed, is so soft that it is best eaten with a spoon, a tenderness more appealing to gourmets than to those who have to pick, ship, handle and store it in constant fear of ruinous spoilage. It is becoming ever more rare, although some conscientious—and obstinate—growers, especially in Oregon's Hood River valley, are still producing it for the luxury market, picking each fragile fruit separately from the tree as though it might explode if jarred, and packing it carefully for the few takers appreciative enough—and wealthy enough—to pay the high cost of giving each pear individual attention during its progress from plant to palate.

The Williams' Bon Chrétien is a late-ripening pear (end of September), very juicy, with a rich muscatel flavor. It is the same pear called the Bartlett in the United States, because it was introduced by Enoch Bartlett of Dorchester, Massachusetts, from England, where it was originally called simply the Williams, suggesting an English origin and a horticulturist of that name, especially as it is called the Williams on the Continent too; but I have no information about him. The French introduced complete confusion into the nomenclature of this pear by calling it also the Bon Chrétien ("Good Christian"), alleging that St. Francis of Paola brought it from Italy as a present to Louis XI. As Louis XI reigned in the fifteenth century and the Williams certainly goes no farther back than the eighteenth, this story must be apocryphal and of relatively recent date (it was probably evolved from a more authentic legend which depicts St. Francis as bringing, not a pear, but four spices to Louis XI). The English have nevertheless been tolerant enough to tack the French addition onto the name of their pear, and so, sometimes, do the Germans, producing an almost ludicrous effect with the name Wilhelm Christ Pear (*Wilhelm Christbirne*).

By whatever name you call it, this pear has been a worldwide success, despite the fact that it doesn't keep well and must be eaten (or preserved) soon after picking. Bartletts are grown on about three-quarters of America's pear-producing acreage and extensively in other parts of the world, including some far from the native territory of the pear, like South Africa and Australia. The United States has also developed the Red Bartlett, little grown though it is hardier, because, it appears, red pigmentation in pears makes them relatively resistant to disease. Another mysterious connection between color and a seemingly unrelated phenomenon may be facing us in regard to green. Since pears are so highly individualized, it is advisable to select a variety specifically adapted to whatever purpose you have in mind—for eating raw as a dessert, for stewing, for roasting, for canning, for pickling, for preserving in spirits, for drying (a treatment of the pear appreciated apparently only in Germany), or for making pear cider or vinegar. Curiously, the best varieties for cooking seem to be found chiefly among pears which remain green when ripe. Some of the best cooking apples are green also. Could there be some natural affinity between greenness and adaptability to cooking?

Space forbids mentioning all the pears of historical, botanical or folkloric interest, many of which have in any case disappeared from the markets. France seems to have lost the Rousselet, a small musk-flavored gray-green pear of Rheims, where it was customary to make gifts of it, along with champagne, to visiting sovereigns; Henry IV, Louis XV, Louis XVI, Charles X and Napoleon are known to have been among those so honored. America is witnessing the gradual decline of two of her historic pears, the Kieffer, which is the archetype of the cross between Occidental and Oriental pears, and the Seckel, a mutant named for the grower who exploited it shortly after the American Revolution, instead of for the man who really discovered it, a trapper named Jacobs.

In France, the Durondeau, still available, and thus one of the oldest pears in circulation, is credited with being the first pear to be called a *beurré* (butter pear), in recognition of its creamy texture. Gone, so far as I know, is the popular medieval English warden pear, "shaped something like acorn squash . . . bright green with black skin bruises . . . they taste like winter pears and quince."

The name of the French medieval pear called *caillou* is explained by attributing its origin to Caillou, in Burgundy; but as it was extremely hard, it may have been a simple description: *caillou* means "pebble." The *cuisse-dame*, "lady's thigh," was presumably tenderer. *Tant-bonne* ("so *good!*") explains itself; *brute bonne* ("good brute") was ugly in appearance but seductive in taste; *Louise-bonne* is supposed to have been so named to immortalize a woman of Les Essarts, in

Poitou, but if so, it was only partly successful, for nothing else is known about her.

One French name, *poire du curé* (parish priest's pear), does not refer to any particular variety, though many Frenchmen will tell you that it does. It stands for any pear of sufficiently good appearance to be offered without shame as a present to the parish priest, but not so tasty that the giver will regret not having kept it for himself.

PEB
stands for

nothing you would care to put into your mouth, though Demosthenes so employed **pebbles**, to nourish his eloquence.

PEC
stands for

peccary, the only member of the pig family native to the Americas, which reaches its farthest north in Texas under the name jabalina or javelina.

And **PEC** also stands for

PECAN. The pecan is a nut originally 100 percent American which has been allowed to remain 95 percent American. Most of the tasty new foods Europeans discovered in America eventually made their way around the world, some quickly, some slowly, but the United States has been left in almost undisputed possession of the pecan. Pecans have been planted, sparingly, in some far-flung areas—New South Wales in Australia, Natal in South Africa—but they are not much eaten even there, nor, indeed, anywhere outside of America, though the nuts can be found in luxury food stores in large cities throughout the world. Even in export, the pecan remains American: the chief foreign buyer of United States nuts is Canada.

The pecan may even be American in the narrowest sense of that term, a product of the United States alone, to the exclusion of the other Americas. Reference books usually say that its native territory is the United States and Mexico, but it is doubtful that it had progressed into Mexico even as far as that country's northern highlands before Texans took it there. Texas may well be where this nut started, despite its scientific name, *Carya illinoensis*, the Illinois hickory. Illinois lies in the northernmost part of the pecan's range, so its origin should be sought nearer the center. It was probably named for Illinois because that is where it was first encountered by explorers given to classifying new finds—presumably French missionaries pushing southward from the St. Lawrence valley. Quite possibly De Soto saw the pecan before them, at Madrid, Alabama, about 1540, but he did not bother to tack a scientific name onto it. This was at the eastern limit of the pecan's range at that time, for though it grows along the Atlantic coast today, it was introduced there only when Thomas Jefferson moved some trees from the Mississippi valley to Monticello. He gave a few to George Washington, who planted them on March 25, 1775—just in time, one might say, for if he had waited a month longer he would probably have had other things on his mind. As it was, the trees were installed at Mount Vernon, and three of them are still there.

Just as we had better look farther south than Illinois for the birthplace of the pecan, so we had better look farther west than Alabama. Texas is not unlikely; it is at least the territory where this nut is most appreciated today. Commenting on the fact that almost all the butter pecan ice cream made in the United States is consumed in Texas, an expert on this subject wrote: "Texans will buy anything with pecans in it." There are an estimated 70 million nut-bearing trees in Texas, most of them wild, and not particularly productive; hence it is Georgia, not Texas, which is the leading pecan-producing state today.

"Pecan" is an American Indian word, which appears in varied, though always recognizable, forms in the languages of all the tribes which shared its habitat. Pre-Columbian Indians used pecans extensively. They pressed oil from the nuts and seasoned cooked fruits with them; they ground them into meal with which to thicken meat stews; they mixed pecans with beans in a vegetable dish; and they roasted them to carry on hunting trips as a fortifying emergency ration, a role for which they were well fitted, for pecans produce 687 calories per 100 grams of nuts and are rich in fats (71.2 grams per 100).

If the pecan has failed to gain popularity outside of America, it is not because it lacks tastiness (it is agreeably sweet and mild) but because it lacks originality: the flavor is a good deal like that of the walnut, and since the walnut was already well established in the Old World before the pecan was found in the New, there was little incentive to bring in a new nut which would add little to the gamut of flavors already available. Removed from its shell, the pecan looks like a walnut too. It is similarly convoluted; one might think it a walnut which had been squeezed between the palms to flatten its roundness into a narrower, longer oval. Hence a more appropriate name for it than the "Illinois hickory" is another of its scientific names, *Carya olivaeformis*, the olive-shaped hickory.

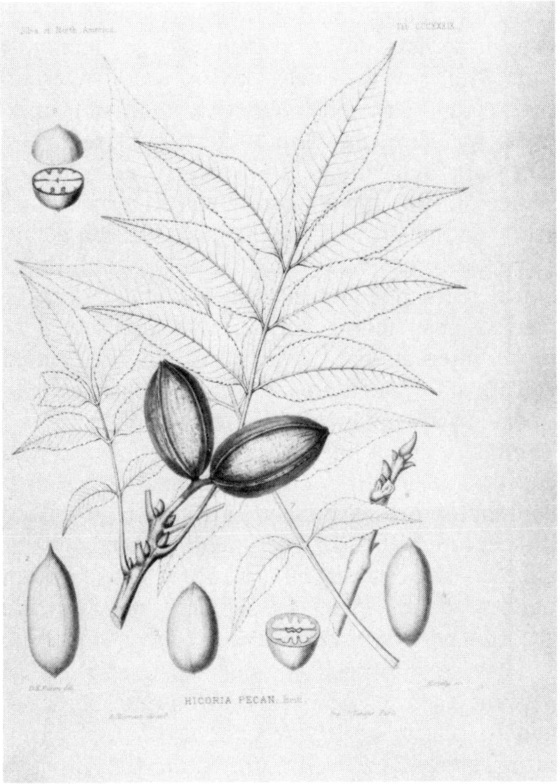

PECAN. *Plate from Charles Sprague Sargent:* The Silva of North America, *Boston, 1895*

Another obstacle to the spread of the pecan is its crotchety character: it is difficult to grow. Wild pecans are highly erratic both in the number and the quality of the nuts they produce, and cultivated trees, though more reliable, are finicky. About one hundred named varieties (which have been more or less standardized quite recently) are available commercially, but only a score of them can be expected to give profitable yields, and even with these the pecan grower must be very careful about the kind he chooses to plant. Each variety demands its own favorite mini-climate and peculiarities of soil, and if it doesn't get them will refuse sulkily to produce many nuts or good nuts. Neither wild nor cultivated varieties grow true from seed, so the type wanted must be budded onto rootstock, a laborious process which most growers leave to plant nurseries.

Pecans will survive quite cold winters, but they require high summer temperatures both day and night to set good fruit. Mature pecan trees can give between 100 and 600 pounds of nuts a year, but they may take a long time reaching productivity. A nursery seedling planted in the orchard may yield no more than 6 to 20 pounds of nuts ten years later; it may need twenty to become fully productive. Another disadvantage of the pecan is that it uses up a good deal of space. The largest tree of its genus, it may exceed 180 feet in height and 8 feet in diameter, and since its roots extend twice as far from the trunk as the branches, pecans must be planted 80 feet apart. The Old World understandably has not jumped at the opportunity to cope with so difficult a tree, in the absence of the stimulus which would have been provided by a novel taste; but in North America the pecan is cultivated in orchards more widely than any other native tree.

Despite its resemblance to the walnut in appearance and taste, the pecan is closer to the hickory. Indeed, one might maintain that it *is* a hickory which has only been honored with a separate name because it produces the best nuts of the genus *Carya,* the hickory genus. Almost all its other members are called hickories—shagbark hickory, small-fruited hickory, broom hickory, white-heart hickory, and so forth. (Both hickories and walnuts belong to the same family, *Juglans,* which is also the generic name of the walnut.) All hickories are nut-bearers, but not all hickory nuts are edible; the pecan intervenes to improve some of them. The hican is a hybrid of pecan and hickory which produces tasty nuts farther north than the pure pecan can provide them. The bitternut hickory is inedible (from an overdose of tannin), but the pecan-bitternut hybrid gives nuts of good flavor, pleasing to the palate—which is perhaps why nurserymen have dubbed it (taking a slight liberty with spelling) the pleas.

PEE
stands for

the **peeler,** a hard-shelled crab on the verge of becoming a soft-shelled crab; for the **peepul,** another name for the bo tree, the sacred wild fig which shaded Buddha; and for the **peewit,** alias the lapwing, the chief provider of plovers' eggs in countries which still allow plovers' eggs to be gathered.

PEL
stands for

pelargonium, a highfalutin name for the pot geranium, whose many varieties can be used (a) in cooking, (b) for seasoning, or (c) for making attar of roses less expensive; for the **pelican,** which Orthodox Jews are forbidden to eat, a prohibition which is accepted with resignation; and for the **pelican's foot,** a cone-shaped mollusk with the disconcerting habit of spreading the edges of its shell into the shape of a webbed foot.

PEN
stands for

the **penguin**, which hunters are forbidden to shoot in France, though it was fishermen, not hunters, whose taste for the king penguin rendered that bird extinct in France in the eighteenth century; for **pennyroyal**, a form of MINT which, Columella *dixit*, you will find useful for fumigating your newly hatched chicks; and for the **pen shell**, which is not only edible but wearable, since its byssus provides the raw material for what the Middle Ages called "cloth of gold," a fabric so fine that a large scarf made from it could be passed through a wedding ring.

PEP
stands for

pepino, an aromatic, pulpy yellow fruit with purple splotches, grown since prehistoric times on the coastal plain of Peru; for **pepper dulse**, a seaweed whose flavor is described by its name; for **peppergrass**, which is the garden CRESS; for **peppermint**, one of the most popular members of the MINT family, though it is a relative newcomer as mints go, discovered only in 1696; for **pepperroot**, an American cousin of the European horseradish; for **peppers**, or sweet peppers, a less aggressive form of chilies; for the **pepper tree**, a native of tropical South America, so called for the fiery taste of its fruit; and for **pepsin**, no longer, I believe, numbered among soda water flavors, a disappearance which does not seem to be much regretted.

And **PEP** also stands for

PEPPER. In November 1973, Prince Charles of England crossed the Tamar River at Launceston, thus entering Cornwall, of which Queen Elizabeth had named him Duke, and received his feudal rent—a load of firewood, a pair of gilt spurs, a hunting bow, two greyhounds and a pound of peppercorns. The last was classic. A "peppercorn rent" is a term still used in legal documents in England to signify a nominal payment which does not represent the real value of the use of the property involved, but constitutes simply a legal acknowledgment by the tenant that the premises he is occupying or exploiting remain the property of the landlord.

When the amount was *one* peppercorn, it was indeed a nominal rent. But a *pound* of peppercorns was another matter. This was a serious rent, though perhaps not an overcharge for the 1356.5 square miles of the duchy of Cornwall. At certain periods during the Middle Ages a pound of peppercorns was the equivalent of two or three weeks' salary for a farmhand in England; at others it sufficed to buy freedom for a serf in France; and often, both in ancient and medieval times, a pound of peppercorns was worth a pound of gold. Rents—real rents, not nominal ones—could indeed be paid in peppercorns. Peppercorns also served to make international payments; they represented a more stable medium of exchange than gold or silver in days when every petty sovereign (and a number of important cities as well) struck his own coins and only an Archimedes could assess their content of precious metal, even without taking into account the common habit of scraping or clipping some of it off as money passed from hand to hand. The gold standard was less sure than the peppercorn standard.

The use of pepper as money spanned a period of some 1500 to 2000 years. From ancient Greek and Roman times it was a means of paying tribute: Rome saved itself from Alaric the Visigoth in A.D. 408, by paying tribute including 3000 pounds of pepper, and from Attila the Hun in 452 by "presents," among which were cinnamon and pepper. In 1143 Archbishop Bertrand and in 1283 Archbishop Rostang de Noves imposed upon the "perfidious Hebrews" of the city of Tyre an annual tribute of two pounds of pepper per head. Peppercorns served not only to pay rent for land but also to buy it, not only to pay tithes and taxes but also to pay customs duties: when St. Bathilde founded the Abbey of Corbie in A.D. 657, Clotaire III, king of Neustria, granted it revenue in kind from customs duties which included thirty pounds of pepper annually. Pepper provided rewards (the Genoese soldiers who participated in the taking of Caesarea Palestinae by Baldwin I in 1101 were given a bounty of two pounds of pepper per man) and also punishments (the bourgeois suspected of having instigated the assassination of Roger, Count of Béziers, in 1107 were fined three pounds of pepper per year per family). Pepper was left as a rich legacy in wills and was bestowed as dowries in marriages: John III of Portugal (which enjoyed a monopoly of pepper at the time) paid part of the dowry of his sister Isabella in that spice when she married Charles I of Spain in 1524. In the Middle Ages pepper was highly acceptable as a bribe, whether to the Masters of the Treasury in Venice, where the big merchants assured themselves of being able to stay in business by making them an annual present of one pound each of pepper, cinnamon and ginger, or to the magistrates

PEPPER *by Ralph Goings.* White Tower, *oil on canvas, 1976*

of Paris, who left in their archives the brief for one case with a marginal note saying that it had not been heard because the plaintiff had neglected to gratify the judges with the customary present of pepper.

In medieval times the habit arose of expressing a man's wealth, no longer in terms of the amount of land in his estate, but of the amount of pepper in his pantry. One way of saying that a man was poor was to say that he lacked pepper. The wealthy kept large stores of pepper in their houses, and let it be known that it was there: it was a guarantee of solvency. A fabliau of the thirteenth or fourteenth century exposes the evident malice of a poet writing of his neighbors:

Ils n'ont ne poivre ne moutarde
Espoir bien lor vient, mais molt tarde.

("They have neither pepper nor mustard; I hope they'll get some of course—but much, much later.")

The aristocracy of Saxony gave the contemptuous nickname "pepper bags" to nobles who married commoners for their money, and it is even reported that some of these traitors to their class were waylaid and forced to swallow such inordinate quantities of pepper that it killed them—an expensive form of murder.

Just how early pepper first appeared in the Mediterranean world is uncertain, but Homer does not mention pepper, and the scholarly Liddell and Scott Greek dictionary does not seem to have found any reference to it before the fourth century B.C., unless we admit the writings dubiously ascribed to Hippocrates, who may just barely have squeezed into the fifth. At first it trickled into the area in small quantities, carried by caravans from market to market, all the way from India to the home grounds of Arab traders, who resold it without knowing where it came from. This ignorance was ended early in the Christian era when the ancients discovered that the monsoon winds blow eastward for half of the year and westward for the other half ("monsoon" means "seasonal"). Ships then began sailing from Egyptian Red Sea ports to India in the summer, coming back with Indian produce in the winter, pepper first of all.

Whenever it reached the Mediterranean world, pepper seems at first to have attracted less attention as food than as medicine; it was so cited by Hippocrates (or whoever was signing for him),

Theophrastus, Dioscorides and Pliny, though Pliny expressed the opinion that it was worthless as medicine. However, its gastronomic merits were quickly recognized, and it began to be added to almost all Roman dishes, even desserts. Horace, addressing his gardener in one of his *Satires*, told him he "would rather see pepper and incense grow in my garden than wine grapes," which we may suspect was not intended as a practical planting instruction. Horace thought the perfect general seasoning was a mixture of black salt with white pepper. White pepper cost nearly twice as much as the black variety, but Horace, after all, was being supported by the richest nabob of his times. Besides black and white pepper, the Romans knew long pepper, and perhaps cubeb pepper also.

The Roman avidity for pepper and also for the other spices which followed it became so great that the Emperor Domitian built a special spice market, the *horrea piperataria*. The street which led to it was the Via Piperatica, Pepper Street, corrupted to Via Biberatica, which has disappeared today, but unless my memory is playing me tricks, it was still there under that name in 1929, when I recall seeing it running from the Forum, a likely location for Domitian's market, past the ruins of Trajan's Market. When Trajan built this imposing edifice, Domitian's spice market was replaced by a whole floor devoted to spices, closed to the general public and heavily guarded because of the precious nature of the merchandise it contained.

Even after the collapse of the Roman Empire had severed the trade routes to the East, some pepper continued to trickle into medieval Europe, where it was in great demand for the same reasons as in ancient Rome—a scarcity of home-grown seasonings and the absence of other uplifters of the soul, which would only appear later—tea, coffee, distilled drinks and tobacco. One of the perquisites of royal emissaries under the Merovingian kings—to give their lives, in the words of an ancient text, "a savor more intense"—was a provision of pepper and other spices to carry on their travels to enliven the food of foreign parts in case it turned out not to be as tasty as that to which they were accustomed at home. St. Boniface, a man who established such strict rules for the monks under his orders that he can hardly be considered a champion of good cheer, nevertheless received from Rome, when, in the eighth century, he was dispatched to evangelize Germany, cases of pepper and cinnamon; but they might have been meant as medicine. In the eleventh century St. Anselm, Archbishop of Canterbury, was obviously not thinking of medicine when he referred to the double pleasure, appealing to the senses of both taste and smell, provided by the eating of "immoderate quantities of chicken spiced with pepper and cumin"—two spices whose names turned up frequently in Anglo-Saxon writings.

When the Crusades began to loosen the Islamic girdle which encircled Europe, Venice rented her ships to carry fighting men to the Holy Land and brought them back loaded with pepper and spices from Alexandria. The monopoly thus acquired was occasionally breached by the Genoese, but in the main Venice throughout the Middle Ages was the European capital of pepper, at a time when Europe was consuming 6.6 million pounds of this spice annually. When the Portuguese reached the Spice Islands, the monopoly passed to them.

Portugal used the great commercial house of Fugger as an agent in selling its pepper to central Europe. That company's newsletter reported complacently in 1580: "The pepper business is profitable indeed; when the Lord God grants by His Mercy that none of the ships take damage either in coming or going, then the merchants wax rich." No wonder, when they were buying pepper at Calicut, India, for three ducats a hundredweight and selling it in Europe for eighty!

Businessmen of other countries could not be expected to allow the Portuguese monopoly to last forever. The Dutch East India Company was formed, wrested the pepper monopoly from the Portuguese, and proved so much more voracious that in London the price of pepper rose in 1599 from three shillings to eight shillings per pound, whereupon eighty London merchants got together to form the British East India Company and compete with the Dutch; and so did the French under the inspiration of a man who seemed to have been destined for this service by his name—Pierre Poivre, Peter Pepper. Competition brought prices down and pepper monopolies were ended, unless we consider as a monopoly a partial one, which covered only the pepper of northwest Sumatra—but Sumatran pepper was the most esteemed.

The city which, in a way, paralleled the position of Venice as the pepper capital of the West resembled Venice in no other respect: it was Salem, Massachusetts. In 1791 the United States had re-exported only 500 pounds of pepper to other parts of the world; in 1805, thanks to Salem, it re-exported 7.5 million pounds, 15,000 times as much. The curious position of Salem, about as far from Sumatra as you can get, as the chief handler for the first half of the nineteenth century of Sumatran pepper was an outcome of American skill in shipbuilding, which was to culminate in the clipper ship, the fastest craft in the world. It is difficult all the same to accept the assertion that the *Eliza* alone, in the year 1806, ferried 1 million pounds of pepper from Sumatra to Salem, unless it was as large as a tanker or as fast as an airplane.

Certain plants embody so completely the essence of their kind that they stand for the whole category to which they belong. The rose, "queen of flowers," represents all flowers, and by reference to it many other flowers have been called roses, though they are not. The apple, "king of fruits," is so typical that many others (and some vegetables too) were, when first discovered, called apples of one kind or another before they acquired names of their own. Pepper, hailed with equal banality as "the king of spices," is the archetype of its race, and, true to the rule, many spices we call pepper are botanically unrelated to the real thing.

Pepper, according to Elizabeth David, is "the world's most valuable although not most expensive spice." It is "the great lord which dominated the whole era of spices," wrote Marthe de Fels. "Pepper," said Plato, "is small in quantity and great in virtue." It was the first Oriental spice to reach Europe and it is today, throughout the world, the most widely used of all spices. Its ability to represent spices as a whole is the result of its innate character. Take pepper into your mouth, and its first report to your palate is that you are dealing with a spice; only after that does it reveal to you which spice it is. Its generic quality overwhelms its individuality, though this is a quality which it does not lack. A certain neutrality of flavor allows it to cover a wider area of sensual perception than more striking, but for that very reason more narrowly limited, spices like cinnamon or saffron. "Let us salute in it," wrote Louis Lagriffe, "the spirit of spice."

One often hears of the pepper tree, but pepper does not grow on a tree, it grows on a vine. The pepper vine is equipped with tendrils, by which means it clings to any convenient tree for the support it must have, and climbs it sometimes to a height of thirty feet or more from the ground. When they enjoy optimum conditions—no more than ten to fifteen degrees from the equator, fairly high temperatures, a long rainy season and partial shade—pepper vines start bearing in two to five years, and may keep it up for forty, or even longer. The small grains, no more than a quarter-inch across when full-grown, are at first green, becoming a yellowish red as they ripen.

Peppercorns destined to reach the market as green pepper are picked youngest and are thus green in both senses, in color and in being unripe. They are sold fresh, soft enough to be mashed into a paste for cooking, but the best way to use them is to strew them whole over your food, to enjoy to the full an aroma so delicious that it is difficult to believe that before World War II green pepper was unknown in the Occident. It is a specialty of Mangalore, on the Malabar coast where pepper originated, the only kind of which India has managed to remain the chief supplier. Otherwise she has been outdistanced in the production of her own native spice by Indonesia, where Java makes a specialty of black pepper and Sumatra of white.

Many people think black and white pepper represent two different species, but they do not: both are *Piper nigrum.* Ancient and medieval peoples often believed that the two came from different plants, but a fourteenth-century friar who realized that they were the same came up with an ingenious explanation for their difference in color. "Pepper," he wrote, "ripens in the heat of the sun and serpents defend the woods where it grows; to pick it, the trees are set on fire [to drive the serpents away] and the pepper becomes black." He must have assumed that white pepper came from areas where some Oriental St. Patrick had driven the snakes away.

For black pepper, the grains are picked at a slightly later stage than those meant to be sold green, just before they begin to redden. They are still unripe. They are then dried, preferably in the sun; in a few days they turn black and are ready for shipping. For white pepper, the berries are allowed to ripen before being picked, and are then soaked in water to loosen the outer skins, which are rubbed off. White peppercorns are dried too, but the core does not darken as does the skin left on the black pepper. White pepper is considerably more expensive than black, both because one more process is involved and because it loses a good deal of salable weight with its skin.

True pepper is the fruit of plants of the genus *Piper,* of which there are, according to the *Encyclopaedia Britannica,* Volume 17, page 497, 600 to 700 species, or, according to the same work, same volume, page 946, "more than 2,000 described species." Of the true peppers, *P. nigrum* might be described as the *true* true pepper: it gives us by far the greatest part of all the pepper we eat, and all three of the commonest forms, green, black and white. The runner-up would probably be *P. longum,* long pepper, sweeter in taste but less aromatic than *P. nigrum.* Long pepper was used much more commonly in ancient and medieval times than it is today, probably because white and black pepper were scarcer. It is gradually disappearing from the markets of the West.

Among other true peppers, the most used are *P. betle,* which provides the leaves wrapped around betel nuts for chewing, and *P. cubeba,* which is of course the producer of cubebs, once used for seasoning, but now only for medicine.

Of the peppers which are not pepper, the largest group was misnamed by Christopher Columbus, who had set out to find Asia, the land of pepper, and when he entered the Caribbean thought he had found it. Accordingly, when the Indians served him with a hot spice on his food, he called it pepper. Actually it was powdered CHILI, of the genus *Capsicum,* unrelated to *Piper;* but the name stuck, so we call many chili powders "pepper" today—for instance, cayenne pepper.

Of the other non-pepper peppers, the most widely used is probably *Aframomum melegueta,* Melegueta pepper, a spice related to cardamom which enjoys a plenitude of alternative names—Guinea pepper, Guinea grains, grains of paradise (a much abused term applied to several other spices), Selim grains, in French *maniguette* and couscous gum, and in Senegalese *m'bep. Xylopia aethiopica* is called African pepper, Negro pepper, Guinea pepper or, of course, Ethiopian pepper. Jamaica pepper is allspice, *Pimenta officinalis.* Australian pepper, *Schinus dependens,* despite its popular name and its new habitat, is a native of tropical America. So is *Clethra tinifolia,* particularly prevalent in Jamaica and southern Brazil, where it is known as sweet pepper, soapwood or, curiously, the wild pear. Poor man's pepper, *Lepidum latifolium,* also called dittander, is not even a spice but a form of cress, so called because it has been used as a pepper substitute when pepper itself was too expensive.

It was undoubtedly *P. nigrum* which Sylvester Graham, the father of the Graham cracker, had in mind when he warned that excessive use of pepper would cause insanity.

PER
stands for

Père David's deer, too rare to eat, which became so bored by life in the imperial park at Peking, where the missionary for whom they are named discovered them in 1865, that they busied themselves by shedding and regrowing their horns not once a year, like busier deer, but twice; for the **peritoneum,** a component of the animal organism which will probably never rival the liver in the human diet, but in the Sahara it is wrapped around the liver to provide fat for its cooking; for the **periwinkle,** less commonly eaten today than in the time of Charles Dickens, when winkle shops were common in London's East End; for the **Persian lime,** which is the common lime we all know, given its full name when it has to be distinguished from the Key lime of Florida; for **perut,** an Indonesian root which has so little taste and so much cellulose that feeding on it has been described as like eating paper; and for the **Peruvian parsnip,** a South American root which when grown in North America was described as worthless, but South America, Africa and India take a kindlier attitude toward it.

And **PER** also stands for

PERCH. When I was a boy in Fall River, Massachusetts, my father and I used to row out to the center of the South Watuppa Lake to fish, with rod or hand line, for black bass; what we usually got was yellow perch. This was hardly a disappointing result, for though bass, whose flavor has been compared to that of brook trout, may be a trifle better eating, yellow perch, whose flesh is delicate, easily digestible and nutritious, is, despite a few too many bones, among the most delectable of freshwater fish. The Latin poet Ausonius, who lived in Burdigala (Bordeaux) in the fourth century A.D., wrote loftily of the fine flavor of perch, worthy of the elite, while shad, pike and tench, he advised, should be left to the riffraff. In the sixteenth century the perch of the Seine was so highly esteemed that it was nicknamed the freshwater partridge. If a perch ventured into the Seine today, unless it was well upstream from Paris, it would probably be poisoned.

When my father and I failed to come upon either bass or yellow perch, we sometimes ran into what was locally called white perch, a very tasty fish too. Those white perch, I have since learned, were not perches at all. "White perch" is a name given to at least four different fish, none of them perches, and perhaps to others I have not heard about. I do not know what we were taking from the Watuppa under the name "white perch," but I suspect that it may have been the white crappie, *Pomoxis annularis,* also known as the bachelor perch or the papermouth—"highly esteemed as a panfish," says Webster, which fits my memory of our catch.

We were always happy when we pulled up a white perch, or white crappie, or whatever it was, for they travel in schools, and if we hooked one we were likely to hook more. Yellow perch travel in schools too, but the older they get the smaller their schools become. Three-year-old perch (the age at which they become adult) are apt to travel in groups of no more than half a dozen, and older fish are prone to hunt alone. This is consistent with their pernicious tactics, which are linked to their decorative appearance. The yellow perch is a handsome fish, whose back is greenish brown, shading into yellowish hues on the flanks, colors duplicated in the water plants among which it lurks. The effectiveness of this camouflage is completed by the five or seven dark vertical bands which run from spine to belly, confounding themselves with the stalks of the plants. Virtually invisible, the perch, a voracious carnivore, springs from hiding when a smaller fish goes by, bites off its tail, thus putting its steering gear out of commission, and then swims around it to eat it head first.

The American yellow perch, *Perca flavescens*, an Eastern species unknown west of the Rocky Mountains before men moved it there, is almost identical with the European *P. fluviatilis*, the river perch, which may be considered the archetype of its family. Both are caught ordinarily at a length of about ten to twelve inches and one pound in weight. A two-pound perch is a very nice catch, while four and a half is, with luck, about the most you can expect. According to the French Syndicat des Pisciculteurs, the record catch is 6.6 pounds.

The Old World river perch, which, despite its name, is just as happy in lakes and even prefers that its moving waters not move too swiftly, has been eaten in Europe since the Stone Ages; its bones are frequently found in prehistoric kitchen middens. The ancient Gauls fished for perch with net or line before the Romans entered their lives. In the Middle Ages the streams and lakes of Europe were rich in perch (the fourteenth-century *Ménagier de Paris* gives recipes for them and for their roe, which was then esteemed), but they were less accessible to the population than in Gallic times, for feudal lords and monasteries owned the fishing rights to most inland waters and were not generous about sharing them.

The most ancient perch about which we have documentary evidence is the giant Nile perch, which can reach six feet in length, known both to the Pharaohs and to us. It is in the wrong place for a perch, a fish of the temperate regions of Eurasia and North America which does not enter the tropics and in theory ought not to exist in this territory, where it is found not only in the Nile, but in the hinterland south of it; indeed, some connoisseurs think the tastiest Nile perches are those of Lake Rudolf in Kenya, which is not far from the equator. Those taxonomists who call the fish *Lates nilotica* may doubt that the Nile perch is really a perch; those who label it *Perca nilotica*

PERCH. *Woodcut frontispiece by Eric Fitch Daglish for* The Compleat Angler, *London, 1928*

obviously do not. All Nile perch are well flavored, and those in the Nile itself are said to be getting bigger and better thanks to the High Aswan Dam. The dam was a disaster for the fish of the Nile delta and the Mediterranean waters adjacent to it, for it held back the silt, rich in fish food, which the river had earlier delivered to the sea. It is backed up behind the dam now, but so are the Nile perch, which are making the most of their modern manna.

It is not only difficult to determine whether the Nile perch deserves that name or not, it is difficult to pin down the authenticity of any perches at all once you stray far from the prototype river perch. For instance, the *Dictionnaire de l'Académie des Gastronomes* tells us that the tastiest of the perches is the *perche-soleil*, which is not a perch but a sunfish. It nominates for second place the *perche noire*, which is not a perch either, but the small-mouth black bass. When it gets to the real river perch, the *Dictionnaire* remarks sniffishly that it is only about half as good as carp. Either the eminent gastronomes have been short-changed on perch, or I have been short-changed on carp.

The difficulty of keeping the perches straight

has not been lightened by the fact that its name has been given to the largest order of fishes, the Perciformes—perch-shaped fish, a definition which offers wide latitude for error. Perches are oftenest confused with bass, a much mixed family too: in fifteenth-century England "bass" meant, quite correctly, the river perch. A distinguishing feature of both fishes is the aggressive dorsal fin, which can puncture your hand painfully if you neglect to slide it along the back, beginning at the head end, to flatten the fin against the spine before removing the fish from the hook. There is a theory that both "bass" and "perch" are derived from the same now obsolete word which meant "bristly," but agreement on this point is far from unanimous.

Among the numerous fish called perches, with varying degrees of justification, two are very strange indeed, their peculiarity being a dislike for water. These are the walking perches, of which several central African species of the genus *Anabas* are also called climbing perches, for they not only leave the water for a stroll, they even climb trees. The snakehead of Africa and southern Asia, where it is an important food fish, surfaces from time to time when it is in the water for a gulp of fresh air, and is said to be able to live out of water for months at a time. If these fishes are not genuine perches, they are at least closely related to them.

Whether what the French call the Madagascar perch deserves that name or not I do not know. But one which does is *Stizostedion vitreum*, since *Stizostedion* is one of the perch genera. This is the American pike perch, also called the yellow pike, the wall-eyed pike or simply the walleye, a fish which may reach a weight of 25 pounds. What Europe calls the pike perch is a different fish, *Sander lucioperca* or *Lucioperca lucioperca* (the sander in English), which has a cousin, *Sander wolgensis*, in Hungary and Russia. This is a big fish too, 25 to 30 pounds. All the pike perches make first-rate eating.

"When a fish looks like a trout," wrote Maurice and Robert Burton in their *Encyclopedia of Fish*, "yet in some ways resembles a perch, the obvious name to give it is troutperch . . . it is related to neither." The Columbia trout perch of the American West and the blunt-nosed trout perch of the East have little importance as food fish, for they are too small (6 inches). Even smaller is the pirate perch (5 inches), which gets its name from its ferocious behavior toward its fellow fish. Among other minute fish sometimes placed with the perches are those of the genus *Ethestoma*, the darters. Small though it is, the snail darter recently made history by blocking the construction of the Tennessee Valley Authority's Tellico Dam, in the interest of saving an endangered species. I am usually on the side of the ecologists, but it may be that in this case they overreached themselves a trifle. There are, after all, a great many endangered species nowadays, including man, and one may wonder if all of them merit preservation at no matter what cost.

All the above are freshwater fish, which in principle is what perch ought to be, but by analogy many saltwater fish are also called perches, and in the sea as in the lakes the greatest confusion is between perches and basses. The fish known in the Mediterranean as the *loup* ("wolf") and in the Atlantic as the *bar* ("bass") is called the sea perch by many Frenchmen, but it is more correctly the sea bass (it is very good eating). "Sea perch" is a name which should be reserved for the serran, as it is by the Italians, who call *Serranis cabrilla* the *perchia* (English avoids the issue by naming it the comber) and usually put it into fish soup because they are dismayed by its oversupply of bones; however, if you have a fish large enough to make it worthwhile to eat only the rear part, which has fewer bones, you will find it can be fried to advantage.

Unfortunately for clarity, the *Serranidae*, the sea perch family, includes the *Morone*, the sea bass genus. Thus *M. americana*, of the Atlantic coast of the United States, is a bass but is frequently called the white perch. (On the Pacific coast, the black perch is the black sea bass, or Pacific surf fish.) The name "sea perch" is bestowed on fish of at least six different genera found off Africa, including the Accra sea perch, the saltwater black perch of the Red Sea and the giant sea perch of the western Pacific and Indian Ocean. All of them are eaten.

The ocean perch of the American Pacific coast is not a perch but a rockfish (a sea perch found off the coasts of Africa and Madagascar seems to be a rockfish too), while the ocean perch of the American Atlantic coast is not a perch but the redfish, also sold on the market as the rockfish, the rosefish, the red perch and, again, the white perch. It is a bright pinkish red, 10 to 24 inches long, and is endowed with particularly vicious spiky back fins. In England it is called the Norway haddock and in Germany *Rotbarsch* or, less often, *Goldbarsch*. I have heard the barramundi of Australia's Great Barrier Reef described as a tropical perch, but I have no idea whether it really is one or not. It has at least one perch-like quality: it is good eating.

Ichthyologists, indulging themselves in a spot of experimentation, once removed a perch's forebrain (the part with which thinking is done, if done at all) and returned the fish, after con-

PERSIMMON. *Japanese two-fold screen by Hoitsu Kishin (1761–1821).* Persimmons, *ink and colors on paper*

valescence, to the water, where it went about its business normally. This seems to prove that a perch doesn't need a brain.

PERSIMMON. In March 1789 a magazine called the *American Museum* published an article entitled "Advice to American Farmers about to Settle in New Countries." "Carry with you, wherever you go, a large kettle, in which you may make maple sugar in summer, and potash in winter" was part of its counsel. "Be careful likewise to preserve all the sugar maple, persimmon and chestnut trees you find on your farm. The two former will afford you excellent sugar and syrup." Some readers may have doubted the competence of a writer who did not know when maple sugar is made and who expected to find maples and persimmons on the same farm (this is not impossible, though one or the other would be likely to give disappointing yields); but what might have seemed even more questionable was the information that sugar could be obtained from the persimmon, a fruit which many Americans consider too bitter to eat. Nevertheless, the anonymous author, on this point at least, was right. There is plenty of sugar in persimmons; you can even derive molasses, of a sort, from them, as Euell Gibbons, the wild-food expert, pointed out in a chapter of his *Stalking the Wild Asparagus* headed, brashly, "The Sugar-Plum Tree." This is hardly an apt name for the persimmon if you pick its fruit before it is fully ripe, as Gibbons once did himself, during an extended wild-food expedition with John McPhee of *The New Yorker.*

> The substance of breakfast [McPhee subsequently reported] was a great mound of hot persimmons, which had been stewed in maple sugar and were now glued together with concentrated maple syrup. We stuffed them eagerly into our mouths, but we found that all the astringency of slightly unripe persimmons seems to be brought out powerfully when they are stewed. They puckered not only our mouths but also our throats. Gibbons observed, without apparent alarm, that he thought his esophagus was going to close. Nevertheless he kept shoving in the styptic persimmons, and I followed his lead. . . . Each mouthful tasted fine on entry, but quickly turned into something like a glut of blotting paper, requiring a half dozen forced swallows to squeeze it down. . . . I excused myself and went for a walk, taking deep breaths.

The accepted story about the persimmon is that when Europeans first encountered it in America they found it too acid to eat and abandoned it until the Indians explained to them that it becomes sweet and palatable after the first frost. Writers ever since, including myself, have been stating confidently that it is frost which tames the persimmon. It isn't. The Indians must have known better, but their calendar was nature, and when they said that persimmons were best after the first frost, they were only dating this phenomenon in terms which for them were equivalent to Euell Gibbons's statement that persimmons are best in October. They did not mean that frost *causes* the persimmon to lose its astringency and reveal its basic sweetness. Actually the appearance of frost slows up the ripening of the persimmon, but it will keep on maturing all the same, even after cold weather has set in, as long as it gets some sun. It is probably the latest ripener of all tree fruits, reaching palatability after the others have given up the ghost. Ripeness, even overripeness, is what makes persimmons edible. The time to gather them is when they have become so ripe that they fall from the tree, or when by shaking it you can bring down a shower of fruit. If left on the tree, persimmons can be picked and eaten in midwinter, even when there is snow on the ground, provided the weather has not become so bitterly cold as to freeze them on the branches, which it seldom does in the favorite territory of the American persimmon, the Southeast and the Gulf States.

The first Europeans to encounter the persimmon, *Diospyros virginiana*, were either the Spanish conquistadors, who fed largely on them during their grueling march, barefoot and hungry, from Florida to New Mexico, or Hernandez de Soto, who reported circa 1540 that he had found Indians along the Mississippi eating bread made of "prunes" (they dried the persimmons before converting them into a sort of dough), which produced loaves "like unto brickes, also plummes of the making and bigness of nuts and have three or four stones in them." Other explorers who came across the persimmon were Lemoyne, in Florida; Hariot, on the Roanoke ("unfit to eat until soft and tender," he reported); Strachey, on the James River in Virginia; and Porcher, who put it on record that the ripe fruit is "very sweet and pleasant to the taste, and yields on distillation, after fermentation, a quantity of spirits."

All of these witnesses referred to the fruit as orange, so it came as a surprise when Timothy Flint's *A Condensed Geography and History of the Western States* spoke in 1828 of a small *blue* persimmon. Flint had come upon *Diospyros texana*, a native of Mexico, where it is called the *sapote-pieto*. It is indeed very sweet—cherry-like, but so soft that it melts in the mouth.

Americans did not become enthusiastic about the persimmon, exception made for some inhabitants of the area in which it grows most profusely, the only place where it could be gathered in optimum condition. The circumstances that the season of palatability is so late and the fruit so small (about the size of a grape) discouraged interest in cultivating the tree, and the wild persimmon was undependably variable in quality, not only from place to place, but even from tree to tree. Stores were not much interested in a fruit which had to be gathered in a state so gooey that it was almost impossible to handle, or else so unripe that it was inedible, obliging the buyer to complete the ripening off the tree, never with results as happy as if it had been left on it.

Interest in the persimmon, to a limited extent, was aroused only when the Japanese persimmon, whose existence had not previously been known to most Americans (though Caroli Petri Thunberg had seen it in Japan in 1776), was introduced into the United States, according to some accounts by Commodore Matthew C. Perry in 1855. If Perry was not actually the first to import them, it is at least established that he brought in some trees, one of which was still growing in Washington, D.C., early in this century, but should be dead by now. America seems to have acquired Asian persimmons before Europe, where the first fruits appeared on the Paris market in 1873.

It would seem probable that the difference between American and Oriental persimmons is to a large extent the result of cultivation. The *Diospyros* genus is divided between America and the Far East; they share many characteristics. Though the Far Eastern persimmons seem never to have been as mouth-puckering as the American species, all of them have a touch of astringency. I have seen a photograph of Japanese children gathering persimmons in October in the midst of a snow-covered landscape, indicating that they have the same seasonal peculiarities on both continents; but the Japanese persimmons we know, after centuries of cultivation, are much larger than the American fruits, about tomato size, and they become sweet earlier. They are grown commercially on a rather limited scale in California, and on an even more limited scale in the Gulf States and Georgia.

"Japanese persimmon" is a misnomer. The Oriental tree is actually a native of China, but was adopted so early by the Japanese that the persimmon has become one of their traditional foods for the New Year. Its scientific name is *D. kaki*, and it is generally called the kaki everywhere in the world, though it has at least two alternative names, the date plum and the keg-fig. There are between 150 and 200 species of *Diospyros*, but only five are regularly eaten, with one other lurking in the background. Besides the American, Japanese and black persimmons, there is *D. lotus*, also called the date plum, found in China and the Himalayan region. It is grown to a certain extent today in the Near East and Italy, and is sometimes used in California as rootstock on which to graft the kaki. *D. mespiliformia* is a popular fruit in tropical Africa, where it is known as the monkey guava, swamp ebony or African ebony in English, the bush kaki in French, and *soun-soun* in Bambara. The persimmon which may or may not become important is the mabolo, scientific name unknown to me, which was imported from the island of Mauritius and is being grown experimentally in Florida.

Opinion is unanimous among those who have tasted persimmons, of whatever variety, that at their best they are delicious, but the nature of their deliciousness is diversely described. I have heard the taste of the persimmon compared with the mango, with the guava, with a flavor midway between the apple and the apricot, wherever that may lie, and with the fresh apricot alone. I would myself class it as closest to the apricot, but I do not recollect ever having tasted an American persimmon. I remember eating only the kaki, on the French Riviera, where it is now grown.

The persimmon could be valuable for another reason than for its fruit, but so far as I know its other potential asset has never been exploited: its wood should be valuable, for it belongs to the ebony family.

PET
stands for

the **petrale sole**, which is a Pacific coast dab, and for **pe-tsai**, which is a Chinese cabbage.

PH
stands for

the **phalanger**, a bird eaten, so far as I know, only by the aborigines of New Guinea, who hunt it with a bow and arrow, and the **phalarope**, a bird eaten, so far as I know, only by Eskimos, who do not object to the taste in its flesh of the phalarope's favorite food, fish; for **pharaoh's nut**, which was Marco Polo's name for the coconut; for the **phenomenal berry**, like the loganberry and the boysenberry as artificial as its name; and for the **phinnock**, a trout of the British Isles which some ichthyologists think is a separate species while other ichthyologists think not.

And **PH** also stands for

PHEASANT. It is possible that the most lavish feast in history was the one given in 1453 in Lille, one of his Flemish fiefdoms, by Philip the Good, Duke of Burgundy, which has gone down in social and gastronomic history as the Banquet of the Vow of the Pheasant. Its high point occurred when a long file of servitors appeared, each carrying a salver on which a live pheasant was tethered, and stationed themselves before the knights present, each of whom swore solemnly by the pheasant and before God to abstain from whatever action his imagination could conjure up—not to sleep in a bed, not to change his clothes—until Constantinople had been taken back from the Saracens who had just conquered it. This well-fed Christian mobilization was the sensation of western Europe, momentarily, but after the fevered emotions of the moment, fed by much good food and wine, had faded away, sober second thought prevailed, and in the end neither the Good Duke himself nor any of the knights who had taken the oath judged it expedient to do anything which might annoy the Saracens. Thus the Banquet of the Vow of the Pheasant must be set down as a failure, unless, of course, Philip's real aim, as malicious gossipers insinuated at the time, had been only to demonstrate that the Duke of Burgundy was richer and more powerful than the king of France—then Charles VII, whose control over his dominions had dwindled to such an extent that he was being referred to, sarcastically, as "the king of Bourges."

But why the pheasant? Swearing by a pheasant had become ritualized in the Middle Ages, according to some because the pheasant was a bird so noble ("the king of feathered game," according to the nineteenth-century French gastronomic writer Robert Robert) that it was a fit witness to the pledges of similarly noble specimens of the human race. This seems to have been more or less the point of view of the anonymous author of *Le Ménagier de Paris* (1393), who composed a menu for a formal dinner including "pheasant for the nobles." This restriction does not seem to have been accounted for by a shortage of pheasants or a correspondingly high price (there were plenty of pheasants available at the time), but only by the lofty character of the bird: it was too good for commoners.

A second possible reason why swearing by a pheasant may have been considered appropriate when it was a case of taking a vow to fight for the Holy Land was that this sacred territory lay to the east, symbolized by the pheasant, a bird of the East, as nobody was allowed to forget by the paraphrase adopted in speaking of it by the poets. "The bird of the Phasis is a dish for the gods," Voltaire wrote in the *Henriade*. The word "pheasant" comes from Phasis, the river which for the ancients was the boundary between Europe and Asia. We do not think it so today, for, under its modern name Rion, it runs into the eastern end of the Black Sea from Soviet Georgia, the ancient Colchis, which is why the scientific name for the typical pheasant species is *Phasianus colchicus*. According to legend, Jason and his Argonauts, after capturing the Golden Fleece, sailed for home down the Phasis River, where they discovered pheasants and brought some birds home to Greece. The Romans then imported pheasants from Greece and subsequently introduced them into the countries of their European conquests, including England.

"The pheasant, it seems," Elizabeth David wrote, "is a bird which inspires fantasies in the kitchen." The Romans were certainly not ones to pass up an opportunity for culinary fantasy. Their most humdrum treatment of the pheasant was to skin the bird carefully, cook it, and then tuck it back into its feathers for serving—worth the trouble, they thought, because the pheasant's plumage is so brilliant. An ancient story told how King Croesus, seated on a jewel-encrusted throne, a diamond-studded crown on his head, dressed in robes of the richest stuffs spangled with gold, received Solon in state and asked him if he had ever seen such sumptuous attire before. "Yes," said Solon, "I have seen pheasants and peacocks."

The Roman fondness for making a display of pheasant at the table was imitated during the Middle Ages, when pheasants were served occupying a dais in the center of the table, beaks and legs gilded. During the minority of Louis XIV, pheasants were presented with their identifying feathers left on the head, neck and one wing. But other eaters of the pheasant, including Charlemagne, who was fond of this bird, were less inclined to follow the Romans in their culinary fantasies. The gourmet Apicius had served pheasants' brains to his guests, and this was also an ingredient of a dish dedicated curiously to the goddess of wisdom, Minerva, by the Emperor Vitellius, who invented a concoction which besides pheasant brains included peacock brains, pike liver, flamingo tongues and lamprey roe. Later ages showed less respect for pheasant brains, gastronomically or otherwise. The French writer Emile-Louis Blanchet remarked of the pheasant that "God neglected to screw its brains down tight." He was thinking probably of the way in which a startled pheasant will often try to escape danger by running rather than by flying, a poor choice in the case of a bird whose erratic flight patterns frequently confuse hunters.

The pre-Jason range of the pheasant is usually given as from the Caucasus to Japan, but as there are birds closely related to it in West Africa (notably the guinea hen) there is a theory, supported by fossil remains, that in Miocene times the *Phasianidae* also thrived in the territory between these two extremes, but for some reason, presumably climatic, became extinct in the center.

Within this wide area the likeliest place of origin for the pheasant would seem to be rather far to the east. Could it have been China, where, Marco Polo reported, "There are pheasants here twice as large as those of our country," where "a Venetian groat of silver will buy three pheasants"? Perhaps likelier is India, rich in representatives of

PHEASANT. *Tapestry, detail from* The Hunt of the Unicorn: The Unicorn at the Fountain, *wool and silk with silver and silver-gilt threads from the Château of Verteuil, French or Flemish, late 15th century*

the twenty genera and forty-eight species of this family, including the peacock, almost a pheasant, and the Indian jungle fowl, ancestor of all our domestic chickens. So closely related is the splendid pheasant to the humble hen that they can be crossed; their offspring is called in English pero and in French, less politely, *faisan bâtard*, "bastard pheasant." The French also have a special term to recognize another phenomenal pheasant, *faisan coquard*, "cocklike pheasant," a female which has passed the egg-laying age and has begun to take on the plumage of the male. This seems to confirm a theory that the reason why the male is so often brilliant and the female drab among nesting birds, especially those particularly vulnerable ones which, like the pheasants, build their nests on the ground, is that the hen's inconspicuous coloring is protective during the period of incubation when maternal duty rivets her more or less to the same spot.

This Asian bird did not exist in pre-Columbian America. It does now, in thirty-four states, where the pheasant has adapted itself to the American habitat more successfully than any other imported game bird: but who was the first to acclimate it? Thomas Jefferson wrote to James Madison from France in 1785 that "I propose . . . to endeavor to colonize their [i.e., the French] . . . pheasants of different kinds," but if he actually brought in any birds they do not seem to have prospered. Richard Bache, an Englishman who married Benjamin Franklin's only daughter, imported English pheasants and attempted to raise them on his New Jersey estate, apparently without success. The accepted account is that an American consul in Shanghai established Chinese ring-necked pheasants on his farm in Oregon in 1881, and that a little later hybrid pheasants were introduced into New England; thus the pheasant would not have become American before the 1880s. Yet Eliza Leslie's *Directions for Cookery in Its Various Branches* (1848 edition) gives two recipes for roast pheasant with no intimation that there was anything rare or unusual about it, nor has she gotten the wrong bird by the tail, for she distinguishes it from the grouse and the partridge. The pheasant must have become naturalized in America earlier than we thought.

Eliza Leslie did not believe in hanging pheasant. "It is not the custom in America, as in some parts of Europe, to keep game till it begins to taint; all food when inclining to decomposition being regarded by us with disgust." She was then in conflict with the most venerated dictators of European gastronomy, but Europe has since caught up with her.

In the eighteenth century Grimod de la Reynière had said that "pheasant should be waited for like a governmental pension by a writer who has never flattered anybody." He expressed the opinion that a pheasant killed on Mardi Gras would be just right to eat on Easter Sunday and suggested hanging a pheasant by the tail and eating it when the tail rotted through and the bird fell to the floor. No wonder he thought that "a good capon will always be preferred to it by a real gourmet."

At the beginning of the nineteenth century Brillat-Savarin wrote that "every substance has its apogee of excellence, some when they begin to decay, like the pheasant. Eaten within the three days which follow its death, nothing distinguishes it; it is neither as delicate as a pullet nor as tasty as a quail." We may grant him his three days' grace, but I part company with him when he advocates waiting to eat a pheasant until its breast meat turns green. Perhaps those snobbish American food writers who are now insisting authoritatively that game should be hung, in the belief that they are getting on the same train as Grimod de la Reynière and Brillat-Savarin, should be informed that this particular train has stopped and is no longer going anywhere. Today French gourmets oppose the hanging of game, and during its season some of the better Parisian restaurants print on their menus a notice that they do not follow this practice. It has finally been realized that the gaminess of early times, to which diners long remained attached, obstinately, by sheer force of habit, was a flavor imposed originally upon game not because anybody liked it, but because the means were lacking to keep it from spoiling.

Pheasant is the most widely eaten of all feathered game, and is, in the almost unanimous opinion, the finest flavored of game birds, with the possible exception of the grouse. The hen pheasant is suaver in flavor than the cock, but often difficult to find, for many countries forbid shooting it, except in private preserves which are restocked each year, depriving the hen of the immunity she owes elsewhere to her indispensability as the reproducer of the race. Pheasant is the most digestible of game birds because it is the leanest—hence the necessity, when roasting it on the spit or in the oven, for wrapping it in a strip of bacon to supply for its cooking the fat the bird lacks.

Personally I prefer pheasant roasted in the simplest possible manner to elaborate dishes in which the subtle savor of the bird is smothered in other tastes. This is applicable, of course, only to tender young birds, killed no later than December of the year in which they were hatched. Old birds do require more elaborate treatment to counteract the dryness of their flesh. To find out if a bird offered you is really young, press its beak and the area above the breastbone; if it is a first-year bird, they will give under the pressure of your fingers. A young bird is also recognizable by its pointed tip wing feather; in an older bird it becomes rounded, as is the case also for the PARTRIDGE.

A contemporary gastronomic writer has put it on the record that "the cock pheasant, though polygamous, is extremely jealous." That is a *non sequitur* if ever I heard one.

PIC

stands chiefly for Pisces, represented specifically by the **picarel,** a Mediterranean fish which, when salted, is a very *local* local specialty of the island of Hvar off the Dalmatian coast near Dubrovnik; for the **Picasso fish,** a modern name of course, inspired by this animal's modernistic pattern and color scheme, thus hiding from us the realization that it is nothing other than the southern Pacific triggerfish which we had all been accustomed to calling the humahuma-nukanuka-a-puaa; and for the **pickerel,** which in my juvenile innocence I thought I was catching when a boy, but the ichthyologists tell me now that there is no such fish as a pickerel, which is only a name applied abusively as an Americanism to certain species of PIKE.

PIG

stands for

of course, the **pig,** perhaps the world's most generous meat animal, carrying on magnanimously despite the disdain in which it is held by important segments of the population of this planet; for the **pigeon,** which Americans eat less commonly nowadays, perhaps out of unconscious guilt, than in the days when they reduced the number of passenger pigeons in the United States from 9 billion to 0; for the **pigeon pea,** whose praises are sung in a Jamaican folk song under the alias "goongoo pea"; for the **pignut,** which Caliban offered to dig in *The Tempest;* and for **pigweed,** a disrespectful name for lamb's lettuce.

PIK

stands only for

PIKE. The pike is a fish which seems to have been designed by a military artificer. It has been dowered with protective coloration which provides perfect camouflage when it lurks in ambush among water plants, waiting for its prey. Its own version of sonar—the vibrations set up in the water by an approaching fish—warns it that the time for action is near. It locates the position of its intended dinner less by smell, unlike some other predators, than by sight, for which it is admirably equipped. As its hiding place among underwater vegetation keeps it low in the water, it is provided with a periscope (eyes placed high on the head so that its line of vision points forward and upward) and with sights (two grooves running from the eyes to the tip of the snout which permit it to aim itself at its target). It can spot its victim fifty feet away in daylight (it can also see at night), good vision under water, and when it comes into range it fires itself like a torpedo, propelled by anal and dorsal fins set far back on its body which make it the fastest of all freshwater fish. Its initial lunge carries it twenty or thirty feet, usually enough so that on this first spurt it has the unfortunate prey in its mouth, an infernal machine from which there is usually no escape. There are no teeth in the upper jaw, and those in the lower jaw, strong, large and sharp, can be depressed toward the rear (but not toward the front), leaving a large space through which the fish can be dragged, prolonged by a straight intestine which permits pulling it even farther in, so the pike can swallow a fish almost its own size. No matter how violently the victim thrashes, it cannot pull out: the lower-jaw teeth curve backward, making the pike's maw a one-way street—a dead end in more senses than one. Meanwhile seven hundred smaller teeth, deployed in bands across the pike's tongue and palate, rasp the victim to death.

It is to the credit of Maurice and Robert Burton, to whose *Encyclopedia of Fish* I am indebted for many of these details, that after having described the pike as a triumph of weaponry, they resisted the temptation to score an easy point against the military mind by pointing out that all these arms can be operated by a brain which accounts for only $1/1350$ of the pike's total body weight—most of which, moreover, is occupied by the optical lobes which control its sighting apparatus. They content themselves with observing that this fish's minimal brain capacity "reflects the little effort the pike needs to make a living."

The pike uses its terrifying armament with such voracity that it is also called the river wolf or the freshwater shark; in French, the second compliment is turned around in the opposite direction when the barracuda, probably the most ferocious of saltwater fish, which commits many of the crimes for which the shark is blamed, is nicknamed the sea pike. Grimod de la Reynière called

PIKE. *Engraving from Evert Augustus Duyckinck:* History of the World, *New York, 1889*

the pike "the Attila of ponds and rivers."

The pike's normal food is other fish, but it is apparently ready to try anything else which comes within its reach. I do not know if Alexandre Dumas' story of a whole duck having been found in a pike's stomach is true or not, but there are any number of accounts of pike having eaten, besides ducks, frogs, moorhens, coots, water voles, muskrats, foxes and even small dogs. Some of these reports have been authenticated, some not; in the latter case, there is always a tendency to disbelieve the story, for the pike seems fated to attract legends.

I am prepared to believe that Charles IX kept in a fish pool in the Louvre a pike which answered to its name—Lupul—for other fish have been trained to come when called for feeding. I regard with more skepticism the assertion that pike secrete such powerful digestive juices that they dissolve swallowed hooks; on the contrary, the pike would seem to be a slow digester, for when it has swallowed a particularly large fish it sinks to the bottom and remains there, unmoving, slantwise, with its muzzle grazing the ground, until it has assimilated its catch, which may take as long as a week. As for the story of "the Emperor's Pike," that has now been thoroughly discredited—but it still keeps popping up.

This fable was first printed in 1558, not exactly lightning-like reporting of a catch said to have been made in a Württemberg lake in 1497. The fish then taken was described as a pike 19 feet long, weighing 550 pounds, and encircled at the gills by a copper ring inscribed with the information that it had been placed there by Emperor Frederick II in 1230—making the fish about 270 years old. Skeptics immediately pointed out that if the ring had been placed in this position 270 years before on a growing pike (pike continue to grow as long as they live), it would have strangled the fish a couple of centuries earlier. Nevertheless, there was documentary evidence—a painting of the fish in Lautern Castle, Swabia, while its skeleton was said to have been preserved in the cathedral of Mannheim. Nobody bothered to check on this until the nineteenth century, when a group of scientists visited the cathedral and found that there was indeed a fish skeleton there (though no ring). Their first observation was that it had too many vertebrae to be a pike; it was either some other fish or, more probably, an artificial construction produced by a joker with time to spare—a piscine parallel to Piltdown Man, the forged skeleton which in our century fooled the scientific world for forty years.

There is only one species of pike in Europe, *Esox lucius.* It lives normally about seven years, though individual instances are known in which pike have exceeded ten years. At the age of one year, a European pike is about 20 inches long, at the age of five about 30 inches. The biggest pike ever taken (on a rod; I do not know if figures exist for netted fish) was about 4½ feet long and weighed 53 pounds. This pike was caught in Lake Conn, Ireland, in 1920, and the record has stood ever since. It is not likely ever to be bettered, since under modern conditions fish no longer reach the sizes or ages they attained in earlier times.

E. lucius is called the northern pike, though there is no southern pike; the name seems meant to stamp it as a fish of the Northern Hemisphere, or perhaps to remind us that the farther north it is found, the bigger, the tastier and the more numerous it becomes. It is found in the lakes, ponds and rivers (preferably wide, slow-moving ones) of northern Europe, northern Asia and northern North America, where its range is from Alaska to British Columbia and eastward to New York, with stops at the Great Lakes and in the Ohio River on the way. In Europe it is found from Lapland to the Po (fed by cold water from Alpine streams), on whose bank lies the town of Luzzara, said to have been named for this fish (*luccio* in Italian). Normally, except for a few freak instances, there are no pike in significant numbers farther south in Italy, nor in Greece, Spain or Portugal.

Asia has at least one more pike than Europe, the black-spotted pike, *E. reicherii*, but it is America which is richest in pikes, though, in a sense, it doesn't know it, for the only one it calls a pike is *E. lucius*. There are several smaller members of the genus, but America persists in calling them pickerel, to the horror of purists and Britons ("an *Americanism!*"). America also has a giant pike, *E. masquinongy*, which is the muskellunge of the Great Lakes and farther north. It can reach a length of 8 feet and a weight of 110 pounds.

Pike are disappearing progressively from the dinner tables of the world, chiefly because of pollution, a phenomenon which will presumably afflict you in proportion to the extent of your enthusiasm for this fish. In France it vies with the trout for first place among freshwater fish, in Great Britain it is considered tops in this category more because it is a good game fish than for its popularity as food, and in Germany it appears to be well liked. I am not myself bowled over by the flavor of pike, which seems to me to provide a minimum of sensation, exception made for those I caught myself, during my boyhood, which were cooked within an hour or two of being taken from the water, which makes a good deal of difference in any fish.

The Middle Ages ate a great deal more pike than we do today, partly because more fish of every kind were eaten then, as a result of the large number of fast days and the seriousness with which they were observed. However, the pike seems to have been particularly esteemed. It is listed among luxury foods in the medieval *Roman du Comte d'Anjou*, and in England there was even a special phrase to describe cutting it up—"to slat a pike." We are told that at Saint-Ay in the Loire valley, noted for its pike, the longest recipe ever concocted (this would seem to be the sort of record easy to beat) was devised for cooking a three- or four-pound pike; its preparation demanded several days and such additional ingredients as a lobster (female), scallops and truffles. It was from this same village that Rabelais wrote to an illustrious personage who was considering visiting it that he could offer the inducement of some fine carp for his dinner. He failed to mention pike. Did he feel, like me, that pike lacks character?

Pike presents two disadvantages peculiar to its nature. One is that when it lives in still waters, it sometimes acquires a muddy taste (and its flavor coarsens during the two or three months of its spawning season). The other is that its flesh is threaded with a multitude of long, fine, forked bones which make it difficult to deal with. This circumstance is credited with having inspired a certain Bontemps, chef of Marshal Moncey about the beginning of the nineteenth century, to invent *quenelles*, pike patties or dumplings, to present the flavor of pike without the bones. Escoffier believed, prematurely, that the *quenelle* had banished the fish itself from the menu. Pike, he wrote, was "used only in the preparation of forcemeat and *quenelles*." It has always seemed to me that this reduction of pike to a sort of dough produced the most tasteless version of a fish which in my opinion was not particularly flavorsome to begin with, so I was gratified to find Robert J. Courtine, gastronomic editor of the most serious of Paris dailies, *Le Monde*, writing that *quenelles* are "gastronomically overestimated." Elsewhere he has said that "without *beurre-blanc*, pike is nothing." This reminded me that the only time since my youth that pike had impressed me was precisely when I ate it with *beurre-blanc* at the Paris restaurant of la Mère Michel, reputed to be the world's best concocter of *beurre-blanc* (as she made it, butter, shallots, vinegar and an educated wrist which sensed the exact moment to stop beating the mixture). Pike is cited by everybody as the best food to display the quality of *beurre-blanc*, and I suspect that this is precisely because it has not sufficient character of its own to get in the way of the superb simple richness of the sauce. It is true of *quenelles* also that the point of serving them is not to permit you to taste the *quenelles*, but to appreciate whatever sauce is poured over them.

Following this line of thought back through the centuries, I realized that in the medieval heyday of pike it was almost never served plain, grilled or baked, for its own sake, but was consistently modified by a complicated sauce or a hot seasoning. The canons of Basle, at the end of the twelfth century, enjoyed pike with pepper sauce. Other old recipes doused it with egg sauce, herb sauce, horseradish sauce, mustard sauce or, very commonly, with saffron. In our own times, a British gourmet has remarked that "pike may need to be stuffed." This would seem to provide the clue for reconciling my own feeling that pike is a fish without much flavor and the fondness felt for it in earlier times, as well as by some pike fanciers today: pike is a delicious fish provided it is made to taste like something else.

PIL–PIM
stand for

pilchard, a name adopted by certain European fish when they decide they have become too old to put up with being called sardines, and **pilgrim scallop,** a name adopted by certain European shellfish when the pilgrims headed for Santiago de Compostela decided to make it their symbol; for **pili-pili,** a name given to powdered chilies in certain countries of Africa, and **piment, pimento** or **pimiento,** names given to powdered chilies in certain countries of Europe; for **pillepesara,** a bean of India which has become a bean of Africa; for the **pilotfish,** which since the time of the ancient Greeks has been credited (erroneously) with guiding sharks, whales and ships to their destinations; and for **pimpernel,** an herb sadly neglected nowadays despite the Italian saying, "A salad without pimpernel is like love without a girl."

PIN
stands for

the **pincherry,** a wild mouth-puckering libel on the real thing; for the **pine,** which offers more edible foods than you think, from nuts to needles; for the **pineapple guava** relished in Africa, the **pineapple sage** relished in herb gardens, the **pineapple strawberry** relished in the mouth, and the **pineapple weed** relished only in the pharmacopoeia; for the **pinecone fish,** which hardly seems worth the trouble of catching, since it is only a few inches long, but the Japanese eat it all the same; for the **pink,** a flower which can double as a food; for the **pink abalone,** appropriately a bit smaller in size as well as paler in color than the red abalone, the **pink jackknife clam,** a bit smaller than the yellow jackknife clam, the **pink salmon,** a bit smaller than other salmon, and the **pink seaperch,** a bit more resourceful than most fish, since it produces fully formed young instead of eggs; for the **pintail duck,** which can fly away from the hungry hunter at a speed of 65 miles an hour; and for **pinto beans,** referred to by American cowboys as Mexican strawberries.

And **PIN** also stands for

PINEAPPLE. After something like a decade of research on food, I thought I had become hardened to the enormity of the errors one finds on this subject in even the most reputable of reference books, but I was staggered all the same when I opened the *Grand Larousse Encyclopédique* to the entry "Ananas" to read: "Pineapple: Variety of large cultivated strawberry . . . discovered in Brazil by Jean de Léry in 1555."

The pineapple was not discovered in Brazil, but in Guadeloupe; it was not discovered in 1555, but in 1493; and it was not discovered by Jean de Léry, but by the companions of Christopher Columbus. These are not negligible errors, but they are insignificant in comparison with the incomprehensible identification of the pineapple as a strawberry. The pineapple is a member of the bromelia family, which includes 45 genera and over 1600 species, none of which are strawberries: strawberries belong to the rose family.

The Spaniards who first reached the New World in the islands of the Caribbean found the pineapple ubiquitous there, and later, on the mainland of Central and South America too. Carib Indians hung pineapples or pineapple crowns at the entrances to their huts as a promise of welcome and refreshment to all comers, but planted thick hedges of pineapple plants around their villages to keep strangers out—effective protective barriers, for the sharp, spiky edges of pineapple leaves can inflict nasty cuts; Carib boys at initiation were made to run at full speed between two closely planted rows of pineapples to prove their courage. (Modern horticulturists have now produced smooth-leaved varieties to spare pickers' hands.)

The pineapple had already been cultivated by American Indians for a very long time when Europeans first encountered it. Archeologists tell us, on the evidence of its appearance as a decorative motif on ancient Peruvian pottery, that its cultivation dates at the latest from the first millennium of our era, but botanists think it much older than that, for the cultivated pineapple does not normally produce seeds, the sign of a plant which has been dependent on man for its repro-

PINEAPPLE *by Edward Hopper (1882–1967).* Tables for Ladies, *oil on canvas*

duction for a time so long that it has abandoned this function itself.

As a native of America, the pineapple should have no history in classical antiquity, that of the Mediterranean basin. "We do not know what to make of Wilkinson's statement of one instance of the pineapple in glazed pottery being among the remains from ancient Egypt," Edward Sturtevant wrote towards the end of the last century. (Other Egyptologists have referred to this representation as a tomb painting.) We are also told that a carving found at Nineveh is believed to represent a pineapple, while there is also a Pompeiian mural depicting a number of fruits, one of which resembles a pineapple. I have seen no representation of the alleged Egyptian pineapple, which contemporary archeologists seem willing to forget, so I suspect it was an error. I *have* seen a drawing of the Nineveh sculpture, which requires a livelier imagination than mine to see in it any resemblance to this fruit. I have also seen the Pompeiian mural, which does indeed look like a pineapple. Yet it seems to me that one botanist who tried to explain its presence there only dug himself in deeper when he suggested that Roman traders brought a pineapple back from Micronesia, "with which they were probably acquainted." They weren't, and for that matter, Micronesia was not then acquainted with the pineapple.

If the Pompeiian picture doesn't represent a

pineapple, what does it represent? It has apparently occurred to nobody in this connection to remind himself why the pineapple was called the pineapple: it was because it looked to the first Europeans who saw it like a large pine cone. The pine cone is an object which was familiar to the painters of Pompeii, and for that matter also to the artists of Egypt and the sculptors of Nineveh.

When Europeans discovered the pineapple, it was a case of love at first sight. According to Peter Martyr, when Columbus's men found it on the West Indian island of Guadeloupe during his second voyage, its "flavor and fragrance . . . astonished and delighted them." It was first accurately described in 1535 by Gonzalo de Oviedo y Valdés, who reported that it had a delicious taste which combined the flavors of melons, strawberries, raspberries and pippins, and that although pineapples grew on plants like thistles they were "in taste, one of the best fruits in the world. . . . For those who are surfeited and do not want to eat, it is an excellent arouser of appetite."

In 1519 Magellan's ships paused in Brazil and encountered "sweet pineapples, a very delectable fruit." Benzoni, who lived in Mexico from 1541 to 1555, said that no fruit on God's earth could be more agreeable. De Soto sampled "great pineapples" in the West Indies and found them "of a very good smell and exceeding good taste." José de Acosta, the Jesuit missionary whose translation of the catechism into the Quichara and Aymara languages was the first book published in Peru, wrote in 1578 in his *De natura novi orbis* that the pineapple was of "an excellent smell, and is very pleasant and delightful in taste, it is full of juice and of a sweet and sharp taste," while Jean de Léry, the man who did not discover the pineapple except in the Larousse encyclopedia, described it as being of such excellence "that the gods might luxuriate upon it and that it should only be gathered by the hand of a Venus." In 1595, Sir Walter Raleigh reported on "the great abundance of *pinas*, the princesse of fruits, that grow under the Sun, especially those of Guiana," while Père du Tertre changed the sex and elevated the rank of this regal fruit by writing:

> The flesh of the pineapple melts into water and it is so flavorful that one finds in it the aroma of the peach, the apple, the quince and the muscat grape. I can with justice call it the king of fruits because it is the most beautiful and the best of all those of the earth. It is doubtless for this reason that the King of Kings has put a crown upon its head, which is like the essential mark of its royalty.

The only sour note in this paean of praise came from Charles V, who, as king of Spain as well as Holy Roman Emperor, had an early opportunity to taste the pineapple and refused for fear that it might poison him.

Of all the new fruits which tropical and subtropical America offered the world, the most successful was the pineapple. It is the only fruit of this origin which has won for itself a permanent place in the markets of Europe (only recently has the avocado begun to join it, but it is still far from rivaling the popularity of the pineapple). As a rule, any new food is slow to enter foreign diets; often two or three centuries pass before those unfamiliar with it dare eat it. The success of the pineapple was immediate; in little more than half a century after its first discovery by Europeans, it was being grown—and eaten—in tropical areas throughout the world.

Its transfer to other countries may at first have been partly accidental. Ships leaving America took pineapples aboard to provide fresh food for their crews during the voyage—an excellent idea, for pineapples are rich in vitamin C, the anti-scurvy vitamin—and the crowns, cut off when the fruit was to be eaten, were planted wherever the ship touched land to see if they would grow there. When the climate was propitious, they did. One of the first countries to benefit by this vitality of the pineapple crown was India, where an early traveler's report stated that pineapples were already common in 1549. This came from an anonymous source and therefore should perhaps be disregarded; but it seems established that the Portuguese carried pineapples to India during the reign of the Mogul emperor Akbar, who mounted the throne in 1556. We have written records of its cultivation in India, apparently already well established there, in 1583. It should have been about the same time that pineapples began to be grown in the East Indies. We do not know when they were first planted on Java, but by 1599 they had already been there long enough to have escaped from cultivation and to have naturalized themselves as wild plants in the jungle—where they learned to produce seeds again!

One theory holds that China received the pineapple from Peru, across the Pacific, about 1592, another that it came from America, around Africa to the Philippines, and thence to China. In any case, pineapples were being cultivated there at least by 1594 and were thoroughly at home by the time the Jesuit missionary Father Boymins wrote of them in his *Flora sinensis*, published in 1636.

Nobody knows when the pineapple reached Africa, but it seems to have appeared first on the west coast, where Portuguese ships shuttled back and forth between their country's territories in America and Africa, perhaps as early as 1550. The Pacific islands do not seem to have had pineapples until Captain Cook planted the fruit on some of them in 1777.

Meanwhile pineapples were being imported into Europe, on a small scale, for those who could afford them. According to one authority, the first pineapples imported into England, in 1555, came from Brazil; later England's principal source for this fruit became its own possession, Barbados. John Evelyn's diary, which began in the year 1640, records his introduction to the pineapple thus:

> Standing by his Majesty at dinner in the presence, there was of that rare fruit called the King-pine, growing in Barbadoes [the spelling of the times] and the East Indies, the first of these that ever I had seen. His Majesty having cut it up, was pleased to give me a piece off his own plate to taste of; but, in my opinion, it falls short of those ravishing varieties of deliciousness described in Captain Ligon's History, and others, but possibly it might be, or certainly was, much impaired in coming so far; it has yet a graceful acidity, but tastes more like the quince and melon than of any other.

Italians seem to have made the first attempt to grow the pineapple in European hothouses, in 1616, but did not succeed. Shortly afterward, but we do not have the exact date, pineapples were persuaded to ripen in Leyden, Holland. In 1672 the first English-grown pineapple was presented to Charles II. There is a stilted painting of this momentous event, by Thomas Danckerts, in which Charles is shown gazing out of the canvas with an annoyed expression on his face, ignoring the pineapple, which is being held out to him by the royal gardener, whose name, appropriately for his profession, was Rose. Mr. Rose is on his knees, either in homage to the king or in apology to posterity for misleading it about the author of this exploit. The first English pineapple had not been produced in the royal gardens by Mr. Rose, but by the gardener of the Duchess of Cleveland, who had sent her firstborn to the king.

In France also the first home-grown pineapple was offered to the king, but this time it had really been produced on the royal premises, in the hothouse at Choisy-le-Roi. The king at the time was Louis XIV, but the idea of raising pineapples may have come from Mme. de Maintenon, who, when she was still a young woman named Françoise d'Aubigny, had visited the West Indies and been impressed there by this fruit. The regal tasting cannot be described as an unmitigated success. When the pineapple was shown him, Louis, with characteristic greed and impatience, bit into the fruit without giving anybody time to peel it for him, and cut the royal lips severely on the pineapple's sharp eyes. This ended pineapple growing in France until Louis XV mounted the throne and handed two unpromising half-dried pineapple eyes to the Versailles gardeners, asking if they could be coaxed into growth. They could be and were, "the heart being good," as was explained by the Abbé Pluche, whose name fitted his activity as a writer on botany, for *pluches* are fruit or vegetable parings. Enchanted, Louis XV ordered a special hothouse constructed for pineapples alone, and when he was informed that this would entail adding to the gardening budget an extra 1000 francs a year, a large sum in those days, for wood to heat it, he pooh-poohed this niggardly objection, unworthy of being taken into account by a sovereign who is alleged to have said, "After me, the deluge!"

After him, at any rate, the pineapple, which gained favor in France. Grimod de la Reynière called it "the most distinguished of the fruits seen on our tables." Alexandre Dumas, a keen observer, wrote that it became bluish when ripe; that its juice tasted like Malmsey wine; that its leaves were hollow and filled with clear water excellent for quenching the thirst, for it was always cool no matter how hot the weather; and that the way to prepare it was to cut it into slices, soak them in water to banish acidity, and then eat it in sugared wine. Balzac was fond of pineapple fritters and conceived the idea of getting rich quick by raising pineapples on his property at Jardies, near Paris; but as he lacked Louis XV's resources and could not afford a hothouse, he discovered that no fortune could be made trying to raise pineapples outdoors in the climate of Paris.

The United States was slow to benefit by its proximity to pineapple-growing country, for pineapples have to be fully ripened on the plant to reach optimum flavor, and when so ripened are sadly subject to spoilage in transport. The country was near, but not near enough. Americans were nevertheless not ignorant of the existence of the pineapple, including the first among them. In 1751 George Washington, accompanying his brother Lawrence to the warm climate of Barbados, where he went to recuperate from an illness, confided to his diary that of all the unknown fruits he had tasted there, "none pleases my taste as do's the pine." This was also the opinion of an English traveler in the West Indies at about the same time, Lady Jane Schaw, who wrote that she had tried thirty-two tropical fruits new to her and had been most pleased by the pineapple.

Yet the pineapple remained a foreign fruit for most Americans until the development of fast coastwise shipping in the middle of the nineteenth century. (Florida could grow pineapples, but Florida was about as far as the West Indies from most of America before the institution of fast railroad service; after that, the state did enjoy, briefly, a considerable pineapple industry, but it declined for various reasons, and the United States today eats mostly Hawaiian and Puerto Rican pineapples.) Even during the second half of the nineteenth century pineapples remained rare, a curiosity for many Americans. Not until this century did they become widely accessible and widely appreciated. America's second most popular sherbet flavor, after orange, is pineapple; its third most popular canned fruit is pineapple, after applesauce and peaches.

Hawaiian pineapples have dominated the world market so thoroughly that many people would probably be surprised to be told that this fruit was not planted in the islands until almost three centuries after its discovery by Europeans, in 1790. It began to be cultivated there on an important scale only in the 1880s, and not until this century did Hawaii assume the leading place in pineapple production, whose peak was reached in 1951, when three-quarters of the world crop came from Hawaii. Then union successes backfired. When the unions secured for workers on the Hawaiian plantations the highest agricultural wages in the world, $2.85 an hour, the big fruit companies began moving part of their operations elsewhere—to the Philippines (where wages for field workers sometimes fell to as little as 15 cents an hour), Kenya, Thailand and some other areas. Hawaii remains the largest pineapple producer, but its share of the market has been seriously diminished.

It was on the Hawaiian plantations that the pineapple became the most ruthlessly regimented of all cultivated fruits, living out its life in an artificial atmosphere of man-made chemicals and subjected completely to the manipulations of machines. Its chemical baths begin with fumigators of the soil and fertilizers, continue with weed killers and pesticides to defeat the nematodes which are the pineapple's worst enemy, and reach an apex with plant hormones designed to make all the fruits ripen to exactly the same size at exactly the same time. The plants are not even permitted contact with Mother Earth, with the unavoidable exception of their roots, which pass through the dead centers of squares of asphalted mulch paper, all cut to the same size, so that when they are laid out in a vast checkerboard over the soil they hold 15,000 or 20,000 plants per acre in a rigid alignment which permits their mechanical overseers to locate each plant with a minimum of groping. If an occasional rebellious pineapple dares differ from its fellows by ending up too large or too small for the robots which are to carry them automatically through all subsequent processes until their cans are sealed, the picking machines leave them to rot in the fields. Uniformity is perfection for the pineapple.

PIP
stands for

the **pipefish**, which has already achieved women's liberation; for the **piper**, a fish which looks as if it had been designed by a modernist artist; for the **piping plover**, whose popular name, the feeble, does not refer, as some persons think, to its mental capacity, but to its cry; and for the **pippin**, an apple grown from a seed, or pip.

PIR
stands for

fish, fish, freshwater fish: the **piranha**, eaten by man and vice versa; the **pirarucu**, which Brazilian Indians used to hunt with bow and arrow; and the **pirate perch**, edible, but hardly worth taking, since it is only three inches long.

PIS
stands for

the **pismo clam** of California, which Euell Gibbons described as "a clam refined to the absolute ultimate," and for the **pissabed**, or DANDELION, whose popular name is explained solemnly by a manual which fears somebody might miss the point by the reminder that "*Taraxacum officinale* has genuine diuretic powers."

And **PIS** also stands for

PISTACHIO. If it were not for its color, the pistachio nut might have remained virtually unknown outside its home territory. It is agreeably flavored, sweet and mildly exotic, suggesting a spice rather than a nut, but its taste is not sufficiently striking to explain its success over the years in surmounting the principal obstacle to its wide dissemination, its high cost—if it had not possessed a color needed in cooking. The appearance of food is important. It can please the palate without pleasing the eye, but if it also pleases the eye it will please the palate even more. Taste is a mysterious phenomenon, to which psychological factors contribute largely; one

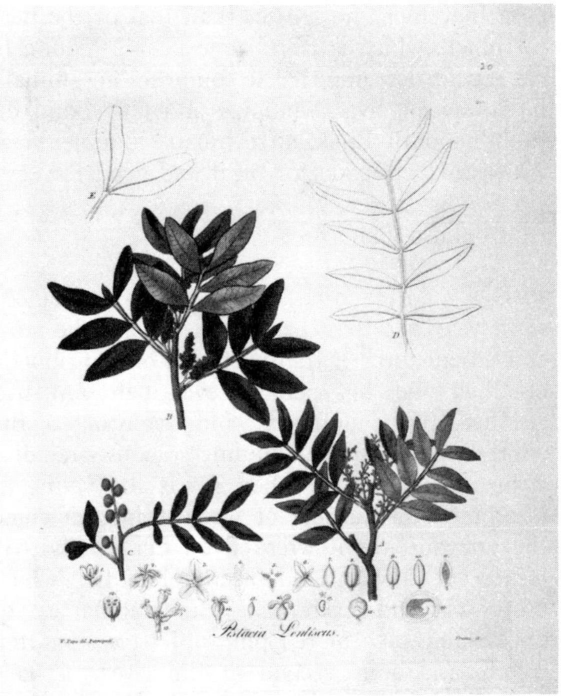

PISTACHIO. *Print from Dr. Friedrich Gottlob Hayne:* Getreue Darstellung und Beschreibung der in der Arzneykunde Gebräuchlichen Gewachse, *Berlin, 1837*

of those factors is color. It is probably most potent at the beginning of a meal and at its end. Color in hors d'oeuvres stimulates the appetite, color in desserts harmonizes with their gay, festive nature. One light-hearted color is lacking for desserts: green. It is a color easy to find for other departments of the meal, but there are not many green ingredients consistent with the character of cakes, cookies, puddings, and the like. Angelica? Its range is limited. Fortunately, pistachio is there.

The pistachio nut is only a pale green, pleasing all the same when bits of it peep up at you shyly from the sausages and galantines in which they are often embedded. But its combination with the other ingredients of pastry and confectionery seems to confer heightened brilliance upon it: what other food tolerable in ice cream could give us that pronounced but not over-assertive appetizing green it derives from pistachio?

The pistachio tree (*Pistacia vera,* the true pistachio, otherwise known as the green almond) is probably a native of Persia and the territories contiguous to it. It is still grown chiefly in this area, in a belt stretching from Afghanistan to the eastern end of the Mediterranean. Only two species of the genus *Pistacia* are cultivated to any extent elsewhere. One, the Chinese pistachio, *P. chinensis,* is grown almost exclusively as an ornamental tree because of its brilliant autumnal foliage. It bears nuts, but I do not know if anyone eats them. The other out-of-place pistachio is the only member of the genus native to America, *P. mexicana,* which provides Mexicans with edible nuts, a trifle less enticing than those of *P. vera.*

Pistachio was eaten so long ago that its nuts have been found at the archeological site at Jarmo, dated at 6750 B.C., in what is now northeastern Iraq. However, the modest, retiring nature of pistachio seems to have caused it to be more or less neglected until about 2000 B.C., when, according to Reay Tannahill's *Food in History,* an increase in population was probably what obliged the peoples of the Near East to exploit marginal foods which until then had been drawn upon only at times of shortage; among them was pistachio.

From that time forward the nut was never abandoned in its native region. It was grown in the hanging gardens of Babylon at the time of King Merodach-baladan, about 700 B.C. It is one of only two nuts mentioned in the Old Testament (the other is the almond). Tradition says that the pistachio was brought to ancient Rome by the Emperor Vitellius, circa A.D. 50.

The Persians used large quantities of ground almonds and pistachios to give body to desserts and sauces, the Arabs apparently learned this art from them, and medieval Europe perhaps from the Arabs, who exercised a considerable influence over European cooking during the centuries when they ruled in Spain and Sicily. The Middle Ages went in heavily for sauces based on almonds, but they were more sparing of pistachio because of its cost, although medieval merchants in France were prepared to supply the nuts to anyone who could afford them. They seem to have been first imported into England in the sixteenth century.

The *Anacardiaceae,* the cashew family, to which the pistachio belongs, is composed largely of tropical plants. The pistachio, however, is a plant of the temperate zone, though of its warmer parts. The only place where it can be grown successfully in the continental United States is California. Florida is warm enough, but too damp; the pistachio likes arid countries. California does indeed grow a limited number of pistachios, but most of the nuts consumed in the United States are imported, notably from Turkey.

Pistachios are still more expensive than most other common nuts, a circumstance which encourages substitutions. This is not easy, for pistachio possesses a flavor which is almost unique.

The closest approach to it is not, as you might expect, in its own genus, but in a different one. It is what the French call the false pistachio (and also, I don't know why, the *nez-coupé,* "cut nose"), more formally the European bladdernut, *Staphylea pinnata.* In Europe the bladdernut, seems to be eaten almost exclusively by German children, but the American bladdernut, *S. trifolia,* distinguished by the sweetness of its oil, is consumed by people of all ages, probably in the belief that they are pistachios.

In French the *pistache de terre,* "earth pistachio," means the peanut—which, says the *Dictionnaire de l'Académie des Gastronomes,* "is really insulting for the pistachio."

PIT
stands for

the **pitanga,** a tropical American fruit which Edward Sturtevant says snobbishly "is about the size of a button and is considered agreeable by the natives"; for the **pitch apple,** which is the strangler's fig; for **Pithecolobium lobatum,** a southeastern Asian fruit which seems to have no popular name and should have no popular following, but Indonesians are obstinate enough to eat it although it has a disagreeable smell, is toxic, and irritates the genitourinary tract; for the **pitomba,** a Brazilian fruit of the myrtle family which may become a Floridian fruit if horticulturists there succeed in their efforts to improve and naturalize it; and for **pi-tsi,** which is not a Greek-letter fraternity, but the Chinese water chestnut.

PL
stands for

the **plaice,** economically but not gastronomically the most important of the FLATFISH; for **plankton,** which we usually eat in the form of fish as we eat grass in the form of meat, but a French investigator tried consuming it directly, only to report: "It's nothing to write home about, and you wouldn't believe how much seasoning it takes to make it palatable"; for the **plantain,** *Musa sapientum,* which would be a BANANA if it were a fruit instead of a vegetable, and the **plantain,** *Plantago coronopus,* which the Indians called "white man's foot," for it appeared in American colonial times wherever Europeans did; for the **plough fish,** so called in English in western and equatorial Africa, but in French "the Mussolini"; for the **plover,** much eaten roasted but not drawn in the Middle Ages, and for **plover eggs,** considered a great delicacy for centuries, but the only time I tasted them, in Holland, they seemed an achievement no greater than that of the hen; for **pluck,** which is what some people require to eat it after learning that it comprises an animal's heart, spleen, liver, windpipe and lungs; and for the **Plymouth Rock,** an estimable double-threat American hen, good for meat and good for eggs.

And **PL** also stands for

PLUM. Old fogy that I am, I became convinced some years ago that the automobile was the most convenient form of transportation only if nobody else had one; but perhaps even before it had scarified the countryside and asphyxiated the cities, I had acquired an unconscious prejudice against it, at an age when I was too young to interpret as a warning of worse things to come the grievous loss it wreaked on our family. My father cut down a magnificent plum tree which every year had given us a bountiful harvest of sweet juicy blue or red plums, I have forgotten which, and every second or third year, I have forgotten which again, a bumper crop, in order to make room for a backyard garage. The car it contained was only a Maxwell. A whole fleet of Rolls-Royces would not have compensated for the home-made fresh plum ice cream which disappeared with our tree.

The plum is one of the world's most luscious fruits. I imagine that if you asked anyone to list the leading fruits of the world he would not get far beyond half a dozen before naming the plum. Among stone fruits (in botanical parlance, drupes), the plum is second only to the peach in commercial production, and surpasses the peach in wideness of distribution: plums grow on every continent except Antarctica. The plum also displays the greatest diversity among stone fruits: there are more species, subspecies, varieties and subvarieties of plums than of any other drupe, not to mention the many non-plums (that is, fruits which do not belong to the genus *Prunus*) which are called plums because they look like, taste like, smell like or are used like genuine plums. The proliferation of plums is a recent phenomenon, which has occurred only in the last century or century and a half. The ancients seem to have known no more than three or four species of plums. In 1539, according to one authority, Europe still knew only seven kinds, and in 1623, according to another, sixteen; but in between these two dates, we find Olivier de Serres naming eighteen. In the nineteenth century, 150 varieties were being offered in American nursery catalogs; I

PLUM. *First state plate by P. J. Redouté for Jean-Jacques Rousseau:* La Botanique, *folio edition, Paris, 1805*

Peint par P. J. Redouté.
de l'Imprimerie, de Langlois,
Bouquet, Sculp

have no idea how many plums there may be now.

Despite the great number of plums, only four species are commercially important in the United States: *Prunus domestica*, the European plum; *P. salicina*, the Japanese plum; *P. americana*, the American plum; and *P. insititia*, a label which in the United States seems to have been affixed to the damson, though in Europe I find the damson plum described as *P. damascena*, while *P. insititia* is the bullace. Of this quartet, only two wield worldwide importance, the European plum and the Japanese plum, which between them account for almost all the canned plums of commerce; and of this duo, the European plum dominates by far, being more widely grown throughout our planet than any other type of plum—perhaps even more widely than all the others put together. (The Japanese plum replaces the European plum chiefly in climates too warm to please the latter.)

Prunus is an overcrowded genus which also includes the apricot, the peach, the cherry and the almond, but the only one with which the plum can be crossed successfully is the apricot. This is achieved especially with the Japanese plum; the resulting fruit is known as the plumcot.

The listing above of the world's most important plums is based solely on commercial criteria, not on gastronomic ones. It does not include what is in my opinion the best of all plums, the greengage. We might as well look first at this paragon of plums before starting in orderly fashion with Plum Number One, *P. domestica*, since the greengage refuses to lend itself to systemic arrangement; in a sense, we do not know exactly what it is. It has a penchant for adopting the name of anyone concerned with it, as it has done in both French and English, in the process losing its original name, and leaving us in the dark about its antecedents.

The greengage is only the most notable of a group of gages, differing from the others in having a round rather than an oval pit. Botanically the gages are very closely related to damsons, though they do not always look very much like them. Gages tend to remain globular in shape, damsons verge toward the ovoid; the prune damson is even pear-shaped. *The Oxford Book of Food Plants* describes gages as "deliciously scented and sweet flavored"; because of their richer taste and higher sugar content, the small gages are often crossed with larger species to give us more sweetness in a larger package. Many of our best dessert plums have one gage parent.

The English name for this plum comes from Sir Thomas Gage, who introduced it into England from France in 1725, or, more probably, reintroduced it, for it seems to have existed there much earlier but had died out. In French, it was the *reine-claude*. The Queen Claude in question was the first wife of Francis I, one of the most glamorous kings in French history, who had nevertheless accepted a wife with a congenital limp inherited from her mother, and was also, because of what we would recognize today as glandular malfunction, revoltingly obese, and would become progressively more so to the end of her short life. Francis married her because she was Duchess of Brittany, and the kings of France were trying almost desperately to acquire Brittany by marriage. Two of them, one after the other, had married Claude's mother, Anne of Brittany, despite her limp—Charles VIII and Louis XII, the first in a shotgun (or, less anachronistically, a crossbow) wedding: his army had besieged her in Rennes until she consented to the marriage. Anne foiled both her royal husbands by failing to leave them a male heir, which France, governed by the Salic laws, required for the passage of Breton sovereignty to France. Brittany recognized descent through the female line, so Claude inherited the duchy from her mother. The game of conquest by marriage had to be resumed with her. Francis did his duty, and so did Claude, for despite her unpromising physical condition, she gave birth in eight years to seven children, four daughters and three sons, before dying from "a disease of langour" at the age of twenty-five. One of her sons became Henry II, heir to France and to Brittany, which thus ceased to be a separate political entity.

While Claude lived, she presented a problem to diplomats and courtiers. A queen of France, by virtue of her rank, had to be complimented and even flattered, but her unfortunate physical appearance would have made the customary tributes to grace and beauty derisory. One solution, we are told, was to name the most luscious plum of France in her honor. Some writers explain the appropriateness of this action simply because she was supposed to be fond of gardening. Alexandre Dumas carried the idea a little further by reporting that she had a branch of the plum "grafted onto a tree in her garden so that everybody could enjoy them." Another story says that the first plum of this kind was served at her wedding banquet, necessarily untrue, since the greengage was older than she was. André Castelot, a French popular historian, wrote that Queen Claude was particularly fond of these plums, "so it was to her that Pierre Belon, an explorer who came from Blois, dedicated the famous plum which we know by her name." Belon must have been precocious, for he was only seven years old when Claude died.

Certainly more credible than this last explanation is the popular tradition which attributes the name to a ribald popular spirit like that which in our time has caused a certain type of life jacket to be called a Mae West. The greengage is deeply cleft on one side from stem to blossom end, its shape suggesting buttocks, with which the queen was amply endowed. The plum, in consequence, was referred to as a Queen Claude. The humor of the populace is earthy, and not always refined.

The status of *P. domestica,* the European plum, as the archetype of this large family of fruits is implicit in its other popular name, the common plum, and even more convincingly when it is called simply the plum. Other plums may need explanatory adjectives, but not *P. domestica*: it is *the* plum, the embodiment, the essence and the true incarnation of plumhood, to which other plums must refer and defer. This is not because of seniority. The European plum is not the sire of the others: the original wild plum, from which all others sprang, is unknown. Far from being the ancestor of other plums, *P. domestica* is their descendant. It appeared on the scene quite recently, about two thousand years ago, a sort of synthesis of plums, arrived at by combining many into one. The European plum, says *The Oxford Book of Food Plants,* is "a hybrid between the forms *P. spinosa* and *P. cerasifera* [which] grew together in Asia Minor and have interbred for thousands of years." A simple cross between only two species seems insufficient to account for the multitudinous differences in color, shape, size and flavor displayed today by the subspecies and varieties of *P. domestica. The Practical Encyclopedia of Gardening* is probably closer to the truth when it writes that *P. domestica* is the result of the mingling of "many hybrid races." We may safely assume that among them were the two cited by the Oxford book, so let us begin with them.

P. spinosa is the sloe, primitive by nature, and certainly very ancient, for the earliest European finds of plum pits were those of sloes (and their closest cousins, the bullaces) in the ruins of Swiss lacustrine settlements. This may date their presence as far back as Neolithic times, but in any case no later than the Bronze Age. The sloe is the black sheep among plums, associated with boozing and swindling. Nobody has a good word for it. "It has no value except for making wine and sloe gin," says the Oxford publication. It participates in fraud in at least three forms: its juice is one of the ingredients of cheap wines foisted off on the public as port; unripe sloes are sometimes sold in France as olives; and the leaves of the plant are used to adulterate tea. Its tree has a bristly and aggressive character which makes it useful at least as a protective barrier and accounts for its alternative popular name, blackthorn (it is unrelated to what is called the blackthorn in America). Under this alias the unfortunate sloe is blamed in England even for bad weather. When the return of warmth in the spring is interrupted by an unseasonal return of low temperatures after the sloe, an early bloomer, is already in flower, this is referred to as "blackthorn weather." The wood of the sloe is used to make Irish blackthorn shillelaghs.

The fruits of the sloe are small, nearly spherical, and blue with reddish pulp. I do not know of its being cultivated commercially anywhere, except for making gin, but the fruit is often gathered from wild trees, notably in English hedgerows. Combined with much sugar it makes passable preserves, but the fresh fruit is too sour, bitter and astringent to eat. It seems a very unlikely ancestor for the luscious European plum, but most great families conceal a disreputable member in their genealogical trees, usually among the lowest branches. The sloe may be considered to be playing this apparently indispensable role for plums.

The Oxford publication does not name the bullace among the ancestors of the European plum, despite its early association with the sloe in the Swiss lake settlements and elsewhere. Perhaps this is because some botanists class them both as belonging to *P. spinosa,* though others (ignoring American usage) give the bullace the separate species label *P. insititia.* Nevertheless, these two ancient plums are not difficult to tell apart. The stone of the sloe is pointed, that of the bullace rounded off at its end. The bullace is small and spherical, a little larger than the sloe, and softer and sweeter; but it is still sharp enough in taste so that it is not usually picked until after a good frost or two has mellowed its acidity. It is sometimes planted as a shelter tree around orchards, but otherwise is found chiefly in the wild state. The color of the fruit varies, from black through blue-black, purple, green and yellowish green to yellowish white. It makes good preserves.

It is also strange that *The Oxford Book of Food Plants* does not mention a third plum as one of the possible ancestors of *P. domestica,* for it is the only one of which we find much specific mention in ancient writings: the damson. Once again, this may be because it was assumed that the damson was included under *P. spinosa,* for it is so closely related to the sloe and the bullace that some botanists have suggested that the damson is only the cultivated form of the bullace. This is apparently not the case. The damson has a species name of its own, *P. damascena*, which of course means "plum of Damascus," which is the place from which the ancient Romans imported it. They probably did not do so before the time of Cato the Elder, who died in 149 B.C., for he does not mention it in his exhaustive agricultural work, but when we come to Pliny (first century A.D.), we find him writing that the *prunus Damascena* migrated from Syria to Greece and thence to Italy. He may have been mistaken. The Greeks before his time seem to have been eating only a small, acid, hard wild plum, perhaps a bullace. First-century Romans, or at the very latest, second-century Romans, were bringing their Damascus plums into the port of Ostia direct from Asia Minor, bypassing Greece. They seem to have been of a quality which implied long cultivation, and we know that they had been cultivated in Mesopotamia for as far back as the records go. Plum trees grew in the hanging gardens of Babylon, and the Assyrian Herbal recommends eating them with honey and—butter! Petronius specified that it was Syrian plums which Trimalchio served at his spectacular banquet, where everything was of the best, or at least the costliest. Apicius always specified in his recipes that the plums used should be those of Damascus; yet he employed them not for their own sake, but chiefly as ingredients of sauces. The Romans seem mostly to have eaten them fresh, in season, though they did preserve them in vinegar for winter use, as well as in *sapa* (a woman's drink) or in *defrutum*, both made by boiling down grape juice.

When *The Oxford Book of Food Plants* named *P. spinosa* as one of the European plum's two ancestors, it perhaps meant to include the sloe, the bullace and the damson under this single name. Its other candidate is *P. cerasifera*, the cherry plum, which comes by its name logically, for it looks like a cherry—the same size (or a trifle larger), same shape, same color (or colors). The cherry plum grown in England (sparingly, for it is not particularly hardy, and sulks in the English climate) is bright red. France has a yellow variety called the mirabelle, which I have seen gratified with a separate species tag, *P. myrobalan*. Perhaps there are two distinct species of cherry-sized plums. Magellan's chronicler reported seeing mirabelles in Borneo, where it would have been surprising to find them if they were offshoots of the European or Asia Minor *P. cerasifera*; some botanists think the mirabelle originated not in Asia Minor, like the cherry plum, but in Southeast Asia. However and whenever it arrived in Europe, the mirabelle is today a specialty of the French provinces of Alsace and Lorraine, one of the most delicious of all plums, in my opinion, when cooked. I have never eaten fresh mirabelles, but I am told that they have little taste; apparently cooking is necessary to bring out their flavor. They are wonderfully sweet and juicy in tarts, are among the best kinds for canning, and are renowned for making jams and jellies. The tree of *P. cerasifera* is reputed to provide the best rootstock on which to grow other types of plums.

We know when the various plums which fused to produce *P. domestica* were put together—about two thousand years ago—but we do not know where. It has been speculated that it first saw the light where most of its putative ancestors are supposed to have originated—in the region of Anatolia, northern Persia and the Caucasus. This is dry country, where it is difficult to imagine the birth of a fruit which, when transplanted to the United States, proved to prefer the neighborhood of water. It does quite well within smell of the ocean in the northeastern United States and in sheltered localities along the Great Lakes, and best of all along the Pacific coast, particularly in California. We might expect, then, that the birthplace of *P. domestica* was somewhere in Eurasia where the climate and topography resembled that of California. I cannot think of any region in the Old World more like California than Italy. We know that as soon as the ancient Romans acquired the plum tree, they set to work diligently to improve its fruit, concentrating on growing plums from grafts, the approved method of propagating them today. Was it in Italy that the European plum first saw the light? It was there, in any case, that Pliny wrote of it: "No other tree has been so ingeniously crossed."

P. domestica, whether predominantly a product of man or of nature, seems to have been a greater success than *P. americana*. The first European who reported seeing plums in America seems to have been Bernal Díaz, chronicler of the Cortez conquest of Mexico, who wrote that on the eve of Easter Sunday in 1519 the *caciques* brought a supply of food to the conquistadors, including plums "which were then in season." A few days later the Aztec notables turned up again with baskets of plums "which were very plentiful at that season." No details were given which might enable us to identify the type of plums in question, and we are also in the dark about the exact nature of the wild plums whose pits were found by archeologists in Peru, where, we are told, the Incas began to cultivate them in the first or second century B.C.

When we reach North America, we are no

longer in doubt: the dominant species was *P. americana.* It was still wild. New England Indians planted plum stones, but did not cultivate the trees. They were allowed to grow as they would, and the Indians picked what nature was pleased to give them. Even the Cherokees farther south, though they had a gift for agriculture, did the same, and so did the western Indians, who stuffed themselves with the wild fruit in its season and dried for future consumption what they could not eat at once.

Wild plums were among the foods eaten at the first Thanksgiving dinner in 1621, but they do not seem to have been a great success. The Memorandum of March 16, 1629—the shopping list of the Massachusetts Bay Colony—included plum pits, and the Pilgrims did indeed plant European plums despite the presence of American varieties. (To the north, the French were also bringing European plums into Canada.) The first settlers complained about the quality of American plums, naturally enough, for they were comparing wild fruit with a plum which had two thousand years of cultivation behind it. Indeed, although the American plum has been much improved since 1621, and many new varieties have been developed, it has never caught up with the European plum, probably because there was not a great deal of incentive to work on an inferior plum when the already perfected foreign fruit was growing so splendidly in America. There is, so far as I know, only one example of an exchange in the opposite direction: an American variety, the Jefferson plum—developed in 1825 in Albany, New York, by Judge J. Buell, who had so named it, of course, in honor of the third President—was planted in England, where it has become highly popular and is widely grown.

P. americana enjoys a good many other names besides American plum—August plum, goose plum, hog plum, yellow plum, sloe—so many, indeed, that it is often difficult to tell what species is being mentioned, for there are others in addition to the basic *P. americana.* This is a yellow plum, which sometimes passes through various shades of reddish yellow to become, in some varieties, frankly red. It grows from Maine southward to Florida, westward to Utah, and northwestward to Manitoba. We hear from time to time in pioneer literature of providential finds of wild plums, but we rarely know whether the fruits in question were *P. americana,* some other species of plum, or not plums at all. The men who broke the plains were not botanists, and were not only uninterested in the classification of edibles, but often far from fussy about their taste or their condition. As Richard Osborn Cummings informed us in *The American and His Food*:

> Wild fruits, particularly the plum, were gathered along streams and preserved in barrels of spring water over which a scum quickly formed. The plains dwellers were happy to have this sort of preserves even though it was sour and unpalatable.

The plums of the first Thanksgiving may have included a unique American species, *P. maritima,* the beach plum. It grows along the Atlantic coast (and usually refuses to ripen fruit if moved out of range of salt air) from Maine to Virginia, with occasional stragglers appearing as far south as the Gulf of Mexico. It is commercially non-existent, unless you count the jars of beach plum jelly offered at roadside stands at fancy prices by individuals who have made it at home. The beach plum season is an event in New England, whose citizens turn out en masse to pick the fruit from its bushes or small trees, and have been doing so ever since Edward Winslow in 1621 and Francis Higginson in 1629 called attention to it.

The beach plum is globular and small, half an inch to an inch in diameter, ripens from a pinkish hue to purple (in September and October in New England), and has a tough skin; but the flesh is juicy, and its flavor suggests the guava. Most people find it too astringent to eat fresh, but it makes excellent preserves, jams and, above all, jelly (superb as an accompaniment to roasts), like such other astringent fruits as the quince and the crab apple.

Not only do beach plums grow on what seems most unpromising ground, as on sand dunes along the beaches, they seem to prefer difficulty and resent any attempt to coddle them.

> Beach-plum jelly brings handsome prices [wrote Jonathan Norton Leonard], but it is almost always scarce because the recalcitrant bushes have baffled all efforts to grow them commercially. Cultivation seems to offend them. When planted in rich, well-fertilized soil, they grow tall but produce hardly any fruit. Even when planted in the poor sandy soil that they seem to prefer, they sulk in captivity. Apparently they need the stress and adversity that is inseparable from life along the shore.

The New England character.

P. salicina, the Japanese plum, is probably misnamed. It seems to be a native of China; but the Japanese adopted it so early, and were so diligent about cultivating it and improving it, that they have made it their own. It has become so important for them that the six weeks of wet weather which usually occurs in spring at about the time when the plums are ripening is known as the "plum rains."

Like most of the major species of plums, *P. salicina* has developed a bewildering number of subspecies and varieties, but it is basically a plum of attractive appearance, yellow with red blushes; sometimes the pulp is bright red too. It was introduced into the United States about 1870, and became a little too popular a little too quickly. It adapted itself to many kinds of soil and to different regional climates. It was immune to several plant diseases and insect pests, and it usually gave heavy yields. But a certain amount of disillusionment followed the first favorable impression: it was a clingstone plum for one thing, and an earlier bloomer than either the European or American plum, so that the grower risked losing the crop whenever there was a late spring frost. It was soon discovered, however, that American and Japanese plums hybridize well, producing hardier trees and tastier fruits than either of the two parents. Except in California, almost all the descendants of the Japanese plum in the United States today are hybrids.

Of the damson, the fourth and last commercially important plum raised in the United States today, I have little to say because of the rules of the game adopted for this book, whose contents are limited strictly to foods which are raw materials. Once they have undergone processing, even in the slightest degree, they are beyond its scope; and drying is a form of processing. Prunes are therefore excluded from our field of observation; and in the United States the damson, for commercial purposes at least, is almost exclusively a prune plum. Virtually all the prunes of the United States are produced from damsons grown on the Pacific coast, 91 percent of them in California.

PO
stands for

the **pochard,** a diving duck which is good eating on condition that you take it when it is frequenting fresh water, not salt; for **poke,** a potherb which according to Euell Gibbons is the most widely used wild vegetable in America, despite the fact that parts of it are poisonous; for the **polar bear,** a meat treat for those Eskimos who live in the wrong places for hunting caribou; for the **pole bean,** which seems to me to taste better than corresponding varieties in the lowbush form, but it's more work to pick it; and for the **polecat,** whose meat was described by William Byrd of Virginia in the early eighteenth century as "surprisingly sweet."

PO
stands for

the **pollack,** a member of the cod family which obliges fishermen by coming closer to the shore than any other cod, but it is not as good eating; for **pollen,** which health-food fanatics think is food for men, though nature thinks it is food for bees; for **Polynesian arrowroot,** whose tubers have to be soaked lengthily to make them safely edible, and the **Polynesian chestnut,** which isn't a chestnut but tastes like one; for the **pomelo,** a poor cousin of the grapefruit; for the **pomerac,** a Caribbean fruit which looks like a pear and smells like a rose; for the **pomfret,** a fish which has the grace to be almost boneless, the **pompano,** a fish which Mark Twain praised by calling it "as delicious as the less criminal forms of sin"; for the **pompelmous,** which is the shaddock; for the **pond apple,** which isn't an apple; for the **poor cod,** which is rich in bones, the **poor-john,** dried salted HAKE, which was the cheapest food of medieval times, and the **poor man's weather-glass,** which is the scarlet pimpernel; for **popcorn,** which may be the oldest form of MAIZE; and for the **Poppering pear,** named for the Belgian town which developed it, a long time ago (as the poet John Skelton wrote, in his *Speak, Parrot* [1521]: "In poperinge grew peres, when parrot was an eg").

PO
stands for

the **poppy,** of which some species give leaves and flowers of agreeable taste, and **poppyseeds,** often scattered whole on bread and cakes, perhaps because they are too hard to grind; for the **porcupine,** whose liver is considered the choicest tidbit by porcupine fanciers, and the **porcupinefish,** which is not poisonous if you know how to prepare it; for the **porgy,** whose sometimes bitter taste seems to disappear when it is grilled; and for the **porpoise,** whose popularity as a food in fifteenth-century England waned after the country lost faith in the usefulness of having leftover porpoise skin on hand to cure lunatics according to one recipe for treating the "fiend-sick": "Take skin of a mere-swine, work it into a whip, swinge the man therewith, soon he will be well, Amen."

PO
stands for

the **Port Jackson shark,** whose cooked flesh has "a delicate and excellent flavor"; for the **potato bean,** a leguminous plant of the West Indies which wears its beans on its roots, yielding them to man either for his own nourishment or to kill vermin, and the **potato vine** of Latin America, which does not grow potatoes but is cultivated for its edible tubers all the same; for **potherbs**, whose definition sometimes becomes strangely complicated, but they all boil down to "a mess o' greens"; for **pot marjoram,** which is not simply a dwarf version of ordinary marjoram, but a separate species hardier than others; for the **Poulsard,** the oldest grape of France's Jura region, whose juice is excellent for cooking; for **poultry**, which is dealt with in this book under the entries for its numerous avatars; and for the **pout**, a fish which Thoreau said was disdained in Maine and esteemed in Massachusetts.

And **PO** also stands for

POMEGRANATE. Western artists, confronted with the problem of how to represent the fruit of the tree of the knowledge of good and evil, found themselves depicting it in the form of an apple; but if the ancient Hebrews had desired to adulterate the mysticism of their non-figurative description of the dainty which was the downfall of Eve by referring it to a specific fruit, they would have been more likely, it has been suggested, to choose the pomegranate. "Thou art fair, my love," sang Solomon. "Thy temples are like a piece of pomegranate within thy locks." The fruit had been cultivated in Egypt long before the time of Moses: the Jews wandering through the wilderness remembered with longing the pomegranates of Egypt, and were heartened when the scouts they sent into Canaan brought some back from that "land of wheat, and barley, and vines, and fig trees, and pomegranates." They had been there for a long time; carbonized pomegranates found in a tomb at Jericho have been dated from the Bronze Age. King Solomon maintained a grove of pomegranates.

Because of the number and the assertiveness of its seeds, the pomegranate represented fertility and abundance in ancient times, and even today Sephardic Jews set bowls of scented pomegranates on the table at Rosh Hashanah, the Jewish New Year: if they turn out to be rich in seeds, this is taken as a prediction that the appropriate members of the company will be blessed with many children. For the ancient Greeks, the pomegranate had been created by Zeus from the blood of Agdistis, mutilated by Dionysos, a good god to keep away from. Aphrodite, according to Athenaeus, planted the first pomegranates on Cyprus and in Greece. The fruit is most clearly associated with fertility in Greek mythology in the story of

Pomegranate. *Ceramic tile, Dutch, early 17th century*

Persephone, daughter of Demeter, goddess of agriculture, herself goddess of spring; her symbol is the pomegranate. The legend of Persephone is obviously an allegory recounting the stilling of vegetable life with the approach of winter and its rebirth in the spring. As you will remember, Persephone was kidnaped by Hades and carried away to the underworld to share his throne there. Demeter appealed for her return, but was only partly successful because Persephone had made the mistake of eating in the underworld—six pomegranate seeds, condemning her to spend six months of the year in the shades, though during the other six she was permitted to return to the realm of the sun and of life. There are many variations of this story, differing, for instance, on the number of seeds she had eaten and consequently on the length of time she stayed in the underworld, some of which represent her as having even eaten the fruit itself; but whatever form the story takes, the food cited is always the pomegranate.

At the October festival of Demeter, open to all the wives of Athens (men were excluded), the third and final day, the Calligenera ("beautiful generation"), was devoted to the fertility of women. The eating of pomegranate seeds was an important feature of the rites, some of which were much less innocent. At another Demeter festival, women were, on the contrary, *forbidden* to eat pomegranates.

The pomegranate, "if cut down the middle," Robert Browning wrote, "shows a heart within blood-tinctured, of a veined humanity." It is a striking fruit, whose design is tempting to artists and intriguing to botanists for its unique character. It is so special that a separate family had to be created for it, the *Punicaceae*, which contains no other genus than *Punica*, of which *P. granatum*, the pomegranate, is the only species cultivated. It is decorative enough so that even dwarf varieties, useless for fruit, are grown as ornamentals because of their handsome scarlet flowers. Even before Browning's knife has cleft it, the pomegranate is already satisfying to the eye. The size of a fist, attempting with no more than indifferent success to become six-sided, it has, according to an esthetically inspired contributor to the 1870 *Treasury of Botany*, "a tough leathery rind of a beautiful, deep golden color tinged with red and crowned with the remains of the calyx lobes." Other varieties are red, green or white.

Cut in half, the fruit is seen to be divided by pith walls into compartments, in a pattern so decorative that a favorite fabric of Renaissance Italy carried the design of the opened fruit. Each cell contains a considerable number of long, angular seeds embedded in the pink-to-crimson pulp so inextricably as to oblige the eater either to develop skill in sucking the pulp away from the seeds to which it sticks or to swallow seeds and all. In Florida, horticulturists are working on the improvement of the pomegranate, including the diminution or suppression of the seeds, but they are kicking down an open door; the seeds were eliminated long ago in the Middle East. Richard Burton, the famous English traveler who was, I believe, the first non-Moslem to get into Mecca, about the middle of the nineteenth century, wrote that in Arabia he had come across a red, very sweet pomegranate called the *shami*: "It was almost stoneless, delicately perfumed and as large as an infant's head . . . I never saw a finer fruit in the East except at Mecca." The best pomegranates today are reputed to be those with very small seeds and sweet juice which come from Kabul, Afghanistan. A seedless variety grows along the Kabul River; the U.S. Patent Office distributed cuttings from it in 1860, an unpropitious moment, perhaps, for Washington to have set out to develop a fruit which will grow only in the South. The reason why seedless pomegranates, though they exist there, are not widely grown in the Middle East is simple: many pomegranate fanciers like to crunch the seeds; besides, an agreeable juice can be pressed from them.

Afghanistan may well be the place where the pomegranate started, though the fruit is so old that no one knows for certain. Different authorities have also suggested Persia, Armenia, the Caucasus, India and even the Himalayan region. The last two seem unlikely, though the fruit must have been known in India very early, for there is a Sanskrit word for it. We are told that it did not reach China until the Han period, in other words, not before 100 B.C.

It was almost certainly from the Middle East that the pomegranate spread westward around the Mediterranean, particularly on its African shores, and became one of the world's oldest cultivated fruits, a prehistoric one. For the ancient peoples of Asia Minor it was as important as the grape and the fig. The fruit was widely grown in Persia and was common in Hittite orchards. The Assyrian Herbal refers to two kinds of pomegranate, one bitter, the other sweet; representations of it are found in the art of Assyria and of Egypt, which it apparently reached at the time of the New Kingdom as a result of the Syrian campaigns initiated by Thutmose I in the sixteenth century B.C.

The pomegranate is mentioned in the writings of Theophrastus, Herodotus and Homer, who put pomegranates in the orchard of Alcinoüs. It is pictured on plaques found in the Etruscan city of Caere, dated at the sixth century B.C. (the Etruscans may have reached Italy from Asia Minor), but the Romans seem not to have attempted to raise pomegranates, preferring to import them, particularly from Carthage, for which reason they called it the Carthaginian apple, *malum punicum*—which is perhaps why the Larousse gastronomic encyclopedia reports, erroneously, that it is a native of North Africa. Roman importation began early, for the pomegranate is mentioned by Cato the Elder in his agricultural treatise, the first in Latin. Pliny described nine varieties of this fruit, and Columella gave directions for preserving it.

We hear nothing about the pomegranate in Europe for some centuries after the collapse of the Roman Empire; if it had died out there, the Saracens brought it back in the ninth and tenth centuries, probably first in Sicily and then in Spain, where the thirteenth-century Moorish writer Ibn-al-Awam described ten varieties which were then being grown in southern Spain. The fourteenth-century *Ménagier de Paris* gives several recipes using pomegranates, and since the word entered English in the same century, it may well be that the fruit became obtainable in the British Isles at the same period. It was at any rate familiar enough in Elizabethan England to permit Shakespeare to refer to it in the celebrated ornithological debate between Romeo and Juliet:

It was the nightingale, and not the lark,
That pierc'd the fearful hollow of thine ear;

Nightly she sings on yon pomegranate tree:
Believe me, love, it was the nightingale.

The Spanish conquistadors brought the pomegranate to America, where it escaped from cultivation early enough to be found growing wild in the ruins of Frederica, Georgia, by William Bartram in 1773, about ten years after Father Baegert had found it similarly naturalized in California. The pomegranate, no doubt because of the plenitude of its seeds, has a penchant for going wild; it has done so in Europe not only in such propitious areas as Spain, southern France and Greece, but also in southern Switzerland and the South Tyrol.

The enthusiasm felt for the pomegranate in the Middle East has not been echoed everywhere. Alexandre Dumas remarked that it was little eaten outside of the countries where it grows, but recommended that it be used, cut open, to crown baskets of fruit for decorative reasons, not for gastronomic ones. "We must confess," wrote Cohier de Lampier, "that with the exception of this excellent role as a decoration of our tables or buffets, the pomegranate is a fruit which not only cannot match the currant, it is not even any better than the barberry." Pomegranates "can be eaten," writes Joan M. Jungfleisch in our own times, "but we agree with those who think there are easier things to eat and enjoy. However, in fruit and flower arrangements, they make an interesting and attractive addition." The pomegranate, says *The Oxford Book of Food Plants,* "is not to everyone's taste, having large numbers of seeds and a quantity of acid pulp in relation to the comparatively small amount of juicy flesh." The complaint of acidity is often made by Westerners, but that is in part because they are not sampling the right varieties—no wonder, in countries where pomegranates are selected for their appeal to the eye rather than to the taste buds. In the Middle East, varieties can be found which range all the way from outright sour through subacid to almost cloyingly sweet; if you eat the pomegranate in the arid countries of this part of the world, you will appreciate one of the distinctive qualities of this fruit, its ability to refresh—most marked in the pleasantly tart subacid varieties. This has perhaps contributed to making the pomegranate, in the words of Joseph Mitchell, "the autumn fruit of the South," which means especially Georgia, Alabama and Florida.

In France and Italy, it is the juice of the pomegranate which is most used—for jelly or sherbet in France, and in Italy for, among other things, basting spit-roasted turkey.

The ancients believed that pomegranate trees, planted beside other trees, bushes or vines, would protect them from noxious insects, and we have of course been smiling condescendingly at their naïve superstition for centuries; but the contemporary agricultural encyclopedia *Geoponika* now advises us to use an extract from pomegranates as a spray for plants to preserve them from pests. Perhaps the fruit has a similar effect on man: "Eat the pomegranate," said Mahomet, "for it purges the system of envy and hatred."

PORK. In the interests of literature, gastronomes, I feel, should leave to poets the task of celebrating food in forms other than prose. A. E. Housman evoked the cherry in more effective terms than the nineteenth-century chef Rouyer, and did so in a few lines, while Rouyer required ten or twelve stanzas. It was in the same century that Charles Monselet, an otherwise inoffensive gastronomic writer, took it upon himself to apostrophize the pig in poetry, with this result:

For all is good in thee:
Thy flesh, thy lard, thy muscles and thy tripe!
As galantine thou'rt loved, as blood pudding adored.
A saint has, of thy feet, created the best type
Of trotters. And, from the Périgord,
The soil has blessed thee with so sweet a scent
It could have woo'd Xantippe, all her anger spent
To join with Socrates, whom elsewise she abhorred
In worship of this lord
Of animals, dear hog: angelic meat, say we.

(The saint referred to is St. Ménehould; the French town bearing her name is famous for its fashion of stuffing and cooking pigs' feet.)

In China, the pig constituted not one, but *two* of the Eight Marvels of the table: pork and ham were listed separately. Raising the ante slightly, Italy's Abruzzi region calls this versatile animal "the thirteen-flavored pig." Pliny outdid both ancient Chinese and modern Italians when he claimed to be able to distinguish fifty different tastes in pork.

Grimod de la Reynière described the pig as "the encyclopedic animal, a veritable walking repast. One throws no part of it away, even to the feet, one eats it all." Backing up his poetry with his prose, Monselet wrote:

The pig has lived only to eat, he eats only to die. . . . He eats everything his gluttonous snout touches, he will be eaten completely. . . . He eats all the time, he will be eaten all the time. . . . His ignoble gluttony is echoed in terrible fashion. . . . The pig is nothing but an immense dish which walks while waiting to be served. . . . In a sort of photography of his future destiny, everything announces that he will be eaten, but eaten in such a fashion that there will remain of him not the smallest bone, not a hair, not an atom.

"Pygges, specially some pygges," wrote Andrew Boorde in 1542, in his *A Dyetary of Helth,*

is nutrytyve; and made in a gelye it is restoratyve, so be it the pygges be fleed, the skyn taken off and then stewed with restoratyves, as a cocke is stewed to make a gelye. A yonge fatte pygge in physicke is singularly praysed, if it be well ordered in rostynge, the skyn not eaten.

Mrs. Patrick Campbell, the actress, must have agreed with her countryman about the nutrytyve and restoratyve virtues of pork when, during the course of a rehearsal, she screamed at the peppery vegetarian playwright George Bernard Shaw, "Shaw, some day you'll eat a pork-chop and then God help all women!"

The most important butcher's meat in the world is, and always has been, pork. "Of all animals," wrote Georges and Germaine Blond in their history of food, "the pig is the one most widely used in the kitchen." The pig "is the king of unclean animals," wrote Grimod de la Reynière, "the one whose empire is the most universal and whose qualities are the least contested. . . . Without it . . . there is no cuisine."

The pig population of the world is probably on the order of 400 million; it is impossible to give it with precision, for it is capable of wide variation from year to year, and there are areas for which we have no figures, including what is perhaps the leading pork-eating nation of the world, China. The American Central Intelligence Agency estimated that at the beginning of 1978 there were more than 280 million pigs in China, compared with 75 million in the Soviet Union and 60 million in the United States.

Until well after the Civil War, pork was the most important meat of the United States; it has now been passed by beef, but remains in second position. At the time of writing, Americans were eating 180 pounds of meat per year per person (not counting poultry and game), of which about 100 pounds were beef and 70 pounds pork. Austrians are the champion pork eaters of Europe, averaging 84 pounds a year (60 percent of all the meat they buy), West Germans consume nearly 74 pounds, Frenchmen 61, Britons only 25 (but in Ireland, pork is almost the peasants' only meat). The importance of pork in Italy is evident from the rich variety of Italian pork sausages. Hungary is said to be second only to China in the number of fashions in which it utilizes pork. Preserved pork is one of Poland's most valuable exports, and Denmark raises about 11 million pigs annually, considerably outnumbering the 4 million human beings of that country. Pork is the principal meat of the Pacific and Indonesian islands and of Southeast Asia.

Pork became, and has remained, the leading meat of the world because it is the most economical, from every point of view. There is virtually no waste in the pig, not only because almost all of it can be eaten, but also because even its few nonedible parts have value: its skin makes excellent leather, its glands provide essences useful in pharmacy, its stomach produces pepsin, the inedible part of its fat serves for lubrication and its hair goes into upholstery and insulation. Its meat can be kept without spoiling; no other is easier to preserve. Hams can be smoked, salted or air-dried; the flesh, shredded or whole, can be put up in a protective coating of its own lard; sausages and bacon keep for long periods; salt pork was the dominant meat of North America for two centuries.

The pig is the most prolific of all domesticated animals except the rabbit. Vauban calculated that in twelve years a sow could accumulate 6,434,838 descendants, but perhaps he was assuming that most of the piglets would be female—though nature's ratio for pigs is 111.8 male births to 100 female births. The pig returns a large contribution of fertility to the soil on which it feeds. A single pig produces four to five tons of manure a year. "If we could achieve one pig per person," Mao Tse-tung said (in a country which has reportedly increased its pig population fivefold since its revolution), "then our main fertilizer problem would be solved." The pig

as a supplier of meat [writes Marvin Harris in *Cannibals and Kings*] . . . is unrivalled. It is one of the most efficient converters of carbohydrates to proteins and fats in the entire animal kingdom. For every hundred pounds of feed consumed, a pig will produce about 20 pounds of meat, while from the same amount of food, cattle produce only about seven pounds. In terms of calories produced per calorie of food, pigs are over three times more efficient than cattle and about two times more efficient than chickens. (Pound for pound, pork has more calories than beef.)

The pig is capable of finding its own food when man is unable to provide it. One might not expect particularly luscious pork from foraging pigs, but the result is sometimes better than the expectation.

When American wheat-breeder Norman Borlaug heard that China had about 250 million pigs [wrote Frances Moore Lappé and Joseph Collins in *Food First*] . . . he could hardly believe it. What could

PORK. *Engraving by Pieter Brueghel the Elder (c. 1525–1569).* The Gross Cooks

they possibly eat? He went to China and observed, as he put it, "pretty scrawny pigs." Their growth was slow, but he admitted, in awe, that by the time they reached maturity they were decent-looking hogs. And all on cotton leaves, corn stalks, rice husks, water hyacinths, and peanut shells! It *is* hard for us Americans, brought up on corn-fed beef and milk-fed veal, to get the idea that livestock's unique role is to make food fit for humans out of things we *cannot* eat.

For twenty centuries, pork was virtually the only meat of European peasants, mostly from pigs allowed to fend for themselves. Some of them enjoyed relatively palatable pork, when they happened to live near the right kind of woods. "The fatherland of the pig is everywhere that there are acorns," Fénelon wrote about 1700, and acorn-fed pork has been prized from ancient times despite an occasional tendency to bitterness, which can be corrected by changing the animal's food shortly before slaughtering. Beech mast produces pork which is not bitter, but less full-flavored. Chestnuts produce the tastiest pork, but chestnut-fed pigs, instead of giving firm white fat, boil down to a black oil. City dwellers too ate pork from foraging pigs, which were turned out into the streets to feed themselves on urban garbage. Their pork presumably caused no ecstasy among gourmets, but it had considerable nutritional value, and it cost nothing.

Pigs roamed the streets of the city-states of ancient Greece, living on their refuse, and they did the same in Rome. In medieval times they obstructed the thoroughfares of London, though the municipal authorities tried from time to time, ineffectually, to get rid of them. The situation was the same in Paris: pigs thronged the streets, finding their food in the gutters, furnishing the only meat of the poor. Nor was it the poor alone who ate city-refuse pigs; even bourgeois families kept two or three pigs, which were allowed to roam the streets by day and were shut up at night. Sometimes the authorities considered them useful scavengers, sometimes they tried to banish them as a nuisance. In 1131, when a street pig ran between the legs of the horse of Crown Prince Philip, son of Louis the Fat, frightening that animal into throwing the prince, who died from a fractured skull, pigs were ordered off the streets, but they were soon back again.

The roving city pig was a feature of New York life well into the nineteenth century. The poor notched the ears of these urban foragers, hoping that no one else would violate this assertion of proprietary rights before they deemed "their" pigs fit for killing. When the city authorities finally decided to get rid of these animals and sent out hog carts to round them up, the housewives of New York battled the city agents with broomsticks and fingernails in an effort to defend their pork.

Naples was probably the last important city of the West to permit pigs to feed in the city streets because until quite recently it had no other street-cleaning service. The custom there, however, was not to give the animals free run of the streets. Each house had its own pig tethered by a twenty-four-foot rope, the right length to permit it to clean up the street in front of its own premises. It was not considered wise to allow it to stray into foreign territory, from which, especially if it were fat, it might never return.

Pork is the world's most widely eaten meat despite the fact that of the four leading religions —Christianity, Judaism, Buddhism and Islam— two, Judaism and Islam, forbid eating it, while Buddhism has a tendency to turn its adherents toward vegetarianism (but Buddha himself, the vegetarians take pleasure in telling us, is supposed to have died from eating spoiled pork). There are in addition islands of non-pork-eaters scattered haphazardly throughout the world: Navaho Indians in North America and Guiana Indians in South America; Laplanders in northern Europe and Yakuts in Turkey; Borneans in Indonesia and, until very recently, the Japanese. In ancient Greece, worshipers of Cybele, goddess of grain, and Attis, god of fruit, were forbidden to eat pork or fish, probably because these foods were in competition with those of their patrons. In Hawaii, women were forbidden to eat pork until 1819, and even today they are not allowed to prepare and cook the *kalua* (roast pig) which is the main dish of the ceremonial feast, the luau. Sylvester Graham, promoter of graham bread, advised his followers not to eat pork.

"The swine, because it parts the hoof and is cloven-footed but does not chew the cud, is unclean unto you," Leviticus warned sternly. "Of their flesh you shall not eat, and their carcasses you shall not touch."

"Forbidden to you are carrion, blood, the flesh of swine, what has been hallowed to other than God, the beast strangled," the Koran echoed.

The prohibition against pork was not necessarily an invention of the Israelites; they may have picked it up from the Egyptians. Herodotus wrote that swineherds were despised in Egypt, and were not allowed to enter the temples.

> The Egyptians regarded the pig as an unclean animal [Alexandre Dumas wrote]. If someone of any social status touched a pig, he was supposed, to purify himself, to wade into the Nile, clothes and all. Only on one day and in one circumstance was it permitted to eat pork, at the time of the full moon: the animal was being sacrificed to Bacchus and Phoebe. Everybody knows that the Israelites regarded the flesh of the pig as unclean; but everybody knows that this proscription was less religious than hygienic.

"I have never been able to accept the explanation that 'pork is unhealthy in the Near East,'" Owen Lattimore wrote to me in 1974. "In spite of ceremonial washing and purification gestures, the pre-modern Near East . . . was never notable for hygiene." Indeed, the argument that pork spoils quickly in the climate of this part of the world hardly holds water: so does the mutton which replaced it there; and its ancient peoples were skillful in the art of preserving food. Pork was widely eaten in the Near East, including Egypt, from Neolithic times; not until about 1800 B.C. was it frowned upon. The reason does not seem to have been hygienic.

Owen Lattimore continued:

> When the ancient migrating Hebrews approached the coast, they found it held by the Philistines— another Semitic people, but maritime and urban. An English archeologist pointed out long ago, so long ago that I have forgotten his name, that not a single Philistine settlement has ever been excavated that was not rich in pig-bones. . . . When the Hebrews encountered the Philistines, if a Hebrew family began to rely for food on coastal shellfish [also prohibited for Jews] and keeping pigs, that meant settling down, and a loss of manpower to the still nomadic sheep and goat herding tribes. For the chieftains, who needed instantly mobilizable warriors, this meant that "this practice must now be stopped," and in such cases it is usual to find and apply a religious or quasi-religious sanction defining the "unclean." . . .
>
> The Mongols, who have never been under Semitic influence, Hebrew or Arab, still have lingering prejudices against both fish and pork, though the present government is persuading people to eat both. In the case of pork, the traditional prejudice is socially expressed: if you eat pig, you're starting to "go Chinese."

The prohibition against pork, in short, would seem to result from the circumstance that the pig is incompatible with a nomadic society. Pig raising implies settling down, stability, the acceptance of a sedentary existence. For peoples who did not want to settle down, the pig represented a threat to their way of life, all the more dangerous because it was tempting. The nomadic Hebrews and Arabs and the nomadic Mongols protected the way of life they preferred, the first two by religious ukase, the third by social disdain. It may be pointed out that some of the other groups which do not eat pork are nomadic too: the Laplanders still are, and the Navaho Indians were until their wanderings brought them into contact with the sedentary Indians to their south, who converted them to agriculture.

The taboo against pork did not necessarily stem from a single cause. There may also have been causes rooted purely in religion—or in superstition, if you prefer. During the Middle Kingdom, Egyptians began to identify the pig with Set, god of evil. This view of the pig made the Laderene swine appropriate animals into which to drive the devils expelled from a victim possessed by them. Magical powers were attributed to pigs in early times, but was it a case of black magic, which was to be dreaded, or white magic, which was to be welcomed? It is difficult to interpret the feeling the ancient Greeks may have had about this animal when they purified a house in which a death had occurred by sprinkling the blood of a sacrificed pig about the dwelling. On the other side of the world and at least two millennia removed in time, we find Magellan being offered a feast in the Philippines, preceded by an elaborate ceremony which his chronicler, Antonio Pigafetta, described as "a rite for blessing swine"—in his mind, apparently, analogous to the saying of grace; it seems quite as likely to have been a means of propitiating the spirit of an animal capable of wreaking revenge for the injury done it.

The view of the pig as a diabolic animal seems sometimes to have seeped into Christian traditions, for instance in the case of St. Anthony (an Egyptian), whose symbol is the pig. There is a legend which accounts for this by telling how a sow led her litter, born blind, to the saint, who restored their eyesight; the grateful mother became his faithful companion for the rest of her life. This does not explain why the representations of the saint always show him leading the pig by a leash, but there is what seems to be an earlier story which credits the saint with having gained power over the devil by resisting his temptations, so that thereafter he led him about, tethered, in the form of a pig. This story would be more consistent than the other with the fact that St. Anthony is the patron of sausage-makers.

Was it because the pig represented evil, if only vaguely, that eating pork was considered a much more heinous violation of Lenten fasting than consuming other forbidden foods? "He who has eaten pork instead of fish is taken to the torture like a parricide," Erasmus wrote, and indeed one of his contemporaries, the poet Clément Marot, was imprisoned and narrowly escaped being burned alive for having eaten pork in Lent.

The magical powers of the pig have been channeled into innocent directions in our time. On the Balearic island of Formentera, pig-sticking time is, as in country districts throughout the world, a time of high festivity. If, during the merriment, a young man succeeds in attaching the animal's tail to the back of a girl's dress, she is considered formally betrothed to him. One may suspect that the girl is not a passive participant in the process, and is only tagged when she wants to be. In Lorraine, the young woman was officially granted the right of choice. It was customary there until recently for suitors to make their proposals of marriage at the season when the pigs were being slaughtered, thus providing the material for the conventional answers. If the girl was willing, she sent the young man a pig's foot, decorated with laurel—the symbol of victory, in this case victory in love. If she rejected the suit, she sent him the animal's tail, accompanied by a pickle.

The origin of the common pig is mysterious; it seems to have been an invention of man. In the zoological sense of the word (ignoring the literary extension of the name "pig" to cover all types of swine and some animals which are not swine, like the guinea pig), there has apparently never been a wild pig, with the exception of some which escaped from domestication and took to the woods. Man apparently domesticated the presumed ancestor of the pig, the wild boar, and evolved a recognizably different family of animals, distinguished from its ancestor by a number of characteristics, such as the recession of the tusks.

This may have happened as early as the Mesolithic period (which would make the pig man's second domesticated animal, after the dog) and in the Crimea, where what seem to be the oldest pig remains have been found at Tash Air. Pigs were in any case abundant in the Neolithic, which would make them, at the latest, coeval with sheep and goats. The Crimea is a geographically likely place of origin for the wild boar, which we may reasonably assume had a single ancestor somewhere, since it lies between the habitats of the two Eurasian species from which all of today's domestic pigs are believed to have descended, *Sus scrofa*, the Celtic boar of northern Europe, and *S. cristatus*, the Chinese boar found not only in Asia but also in southern Europe. It is not quite clear where African boars (like the warthog) fit into the picture, but they go far back, for today's animals were preceded by giant "bush pigs," extinct today. There are no native swine in Australia, nor in the islands of the Indian and Pacific oceans where pork is the chief meat today (their pigs came from imported members of *S. cristatus*), nor in the Americas, where no fossils have been found. It is assumed that the South American peccaries (of which one type, the Mexican javelina, has penetrated into Texas and Louisiana) crossed what is now the Bering Strait from Asia thousands of years ago, at the same time as the men who became the American Indians.

Evidence of pig raising in writings and in art appears about 5000 B.C. in two widely separated regions, Egypt and China. The popularity of pork has never flagged in China, where it impressed Marco Polo and where Jesuit missionaries attributed the exquisite quality of Chinese pork to a diet of human flesh. (This was untrue, but extraordinary diets will produce extraordinary pork; in the time of Louis XIV the best pork was reputed to be that of Montanchez in central Spain, where the pigs were fed on acorns and vipers.) Today everybody in China eats pork on New Year's Day, and on as many other days as they can afford it. Eastern Asia is where this meat is consumed most avidly.

The story in Egypt is different. Not only was pork eaten there in pre-dynastic times, at least from the fifth millennium B.C., but it was also popular along the coast of Asia Minor. Clay models of pigs found in lower Mesopotamia have been dated back to the fifth or fourth millennia, and 30 percent of the animal bones excavated at Tell Asmar were those of pigs. The consumption of pork began to decline about 2400 B.C., perhaps because of ecological changes which decreased the wooded areas of the region, so propitious to the self-feeding of pigs. The arrival of nomadic pig-hating peoples half a millennium later further reduced the consumption of pork, and the religious taboos followed, virtually ending it.

In ancient Greece, meat was too expensive for most people, except pork, which was more readily available in the country than in the cities, whose populations waited eagerly for religious festivals, usually marked by the distribution of meat from sacrificed animals. In Homeric times, raising livestock was more important than cultivating crops, and we may judge that the most important meat animal was the pig from the fact that it was the swineherd—the divine Eumaeus—whom Ulysses trusted to oversee his domains during his absence. Eumaeus, we are told, presided over twelve pig-houses, each containing fifty sows and their litters (the males stayed outside). Ancient Greek pigs fed on the common land, in woods where they picked up acorns or other fodder; their shelters were built on the edge of the woods, open to the sky, like sheepfolds, and they were herded into them at night, as protection against wild animals. Pigs remained abundant in the age of Pericles; Plato remarked that swineherds were necessary for the state. The Athenians thought the best pork came from animals which had died from overeating. They were expert at preserving pork by salting, smoking or drying.

In Italy, the Etruscans were great pig raisers, and as they were great musicians also, they trained their herds of pigs to march to the sound of the *buccina*, the ancient trumpet. The Latins, originally shepherds, were accordingly eaters of mutton, but they learned to prefer pork by the beginning of the Republic; and by the beginning of the Empire, the pig was held in so much esteem that Virgil deemed it appropriate to depict Aeneas as preparing to sacrifice a sow as a thanks offering for his safe arrival in Italy after the flight from Troy. The animal disrupted the ceremony by giving birth unexpectedly to thirty piglets, which Virgil construed as a happy omen, though it might have seemed otherwise to a swineherd unless the sow had thirty nipples.

Roman armies sometimes brought pigs with them, to provide fresh meat in the field. In the third century B.C. when Pyrrhus invaded Italy with a new weapon—twenty elephants, a dress rehearsal for Hannibal—the elephants were stampeded by the Roman commissary's pigs at Asculum, and though Pyrrhus won the battle, it was so dearly bought that he uttered his famous saying, "Another victory like that, and we are done for"—a tribute to the pig.

Mutton remained a common dish for the Romans, but pork was a festive one, of which, with characteristic extravagance, they professed to dote especially on the udders and vulvas of the sows and the testicles of the boars. They produced what is believed to have been the world's first foie gras by force-feeding pigs on dried figs and honey. By the time of Nero, the most widely eaten meat in Rome was pork, followed by mutton (preferably in the form of lamb) and

PORK. *Engraving by Albrecht Dürer (1471–1528).* The Prodigal Son

goat (preferably in the form of kid). The Romans separated the pork butchers (*suarii*) from the butchers of beef and mutton (*pecurarii*), housing them in separate buildings, a segregation still followed in France today.

"Gaul feeds so many herds and above all so many pigs," Strabo wrote shortly before the beginning of the Christian era, "that it supplies not only all Rome, but all Italy with lard and salt meat." The Germans and the Gauls alike lived in thickly wooded country, often among oak forests, where pigs (which probably looked less like the svelte animals of today than like their ancestors, the wild boars, and behaved as savagely) grew fat on acorns. Strabo wrote that it was dangerous to approach them: "A wolf itself would run a great risk in doing so." The Gauls succeeded nevertheless in reducing them to sausages and smoked ham, exported in great quantity to Roman territory, where they were more highly esteemed than similar homemade products. The second chapter of the Salic law is concerned solely with the penalties for pig stealing, and the laws of the Visigoths devoted four articles to the same vital subject.

Early in the Middle Ages the Vikings were formidable warriors, who should have had no particular reason to fear risking death, for if killed they went to a heaven where they could feast perpetually on boiled pork supplied by the boar Saerimme, which, though eaten completely one day, would reappear intact on the next. For other medieval peoples, the chief fresh meat of the upper classes was game; butcher's meat was despised, but an exception was made for suckling pig. For those who were less well off, pork was the basic meat when meat could be eaten at all. It was usually salt pork, which was just as well, for fresh pork must have been dangerous, given the primitive sanitary measures of the times. In Paris the medieval meat inspectors were called *languayeurs* ("tonguers"), because their work consisted in lifting a pig's tongue to see if there were white ulcers under it. If there were, the animal was condemned as capable of spreading leprosy; if not, it was released for sale. Trichinosis had not yet been recognized.

Occasionally some medieval document gives us a glimpse of the extent of pork eating in those times. Thus in 1345, when Humbert, crown prince of the Viennois, led a Crusade (which subsequently failed), he established the regulations for his wife's household in his absence. It was to be limited to thirty persons, and the rations he considered adequate for this number included one freshly killed pig each week, plus thirty salted pigs a year, nearly three pigs per person per year. As for the less illustrious, every family, rustic or urban, tried to raise a pig or two, and when the family pig—"Monsieur," he was called respectfully in France—was slaughtered, it was a time for feasting and jubilation, to which all the neighbors were invited; in many European country districts it is still.

The first pigs to enter what is now the United States were almost certainly the thirteen animals landed in 1542 near today's Tampa by Hernando de Soto. We hear constantly of salt pork or live pigs being carried on the ships of the conquistadors, and Cortez, who had live animals with him when he invaded Mexico, had already introduced the pig to America at a feast of roast pig offered at Coyoacán, now a suburb of Mexico City, to his Indian allies, who were most impressed by the richness of pig fat, in which their lean peccaries were deficient. Latin-American Indians took enthusiastically to the European pig as a provider of lard to enrich a diet poor in fats. "It would be an exaggeration to say that modern Mexican cooking is Aztec cooking plus pigs," wrote Jonathan Norton Leonard in *Latin American Cooking*, "but the statement is not far out of line."

The Pilgrims in Massachusetts and the Cavaliers in Virginia were not slow to import pigs, and by 1640 Massachusetts was already carrying on a profitable trade in salt pork. Four years later the pig was responsible for an important development in the colony's administration: a neighborhood dispute over a stray sow snowballed to such proportions that it caused the General Court (the colony's governing body) to split into two houses.

In Virginia, with its mild climate, "the Hogs run where they list, and find their own support in the Woods, without any Care of the Owner," Robert Beverley reported in 1705. "Hogs swarm like Vermine upon the Earth, and are often accounted such." Virginians ate so much pork, William Byrd complained, that they were becoming "extremely hoggish in their temper . . . and prone to grunt rather than to speak"; but it was good pork, "always as good as the best European can be, since the pastures in this country are very fine." The safest way to slaughter the half-wild hogs loosed in the woods was to shoot them. Later another technique was developed to catch the pigs alive for a final fattening before killing them, using teams of dogs. "Trail dogs" would run a hog down and bay to give its location to "catch dogs," which would then hold it by the ears until it could be lassoed and penned.

Visiting foreigners were impressed by the abundance of pork in the early United States. Captain

Frederick Marryat, who found himself in New York on a Fourth of July during the 1830s, wrote in astonishment:

> What was more remarkable, Broadway being three miles long, and the booths lining each side of it, in every booth there was a roast pig, large or small, as the center attraction. Six miles of roast pig! and that in New York City alone; and roast pig in every other city, town, hamlet and village in the Union!

Pork was eaten chiefly in salted form:

> Indian corn was the national crop [Henry Adams wrote], and Indian corn was eaten three times a day in another form as salt pork. The rich alone could afford fresh meat. Ice-chests were hardly known. In the country fresh meat could not regularly be got, except in the shape of poultry or game; but the hog cost nothing to keep, and very little to kill and preserve. Thus the early rural American was brought up on salt pork and Indian corn, or rye; and the effects of this diet showed itself in dyspepsia.

In America as elsewhere, the close association of pig and man involved the former from time to time in the history of the latter. There were some difficulties with Pennsylvania during King George's War, the American offshoot of what Europe called the War of the Austrian Succession, because pacifistic Quakers balked at providing pork for the army. Voters electing the members of the Virginia House of Burgesses were helped to make the right decisions by quantities of barbecued pork offered to them by the candidates. Neighborly peace was furthered in Virginia when Sally Fairfax, who had married George Washington's best friend in spite of the fact that she was in love with Washington, who had married Martha Custis instead, became good friends with Martha in mutual admiration of each other's pork pâtés. A minor scandal occurred in the supplying of British troops during the American Revolution when five ships carrying four hundred hogs each were dispatched from London to Boston to feed His Majesty's soldiers, and the London *Public Advertiser* reported: "What from Diseases, and other Accidents, five ships landed only four Hogs, which, after paying every Expense, stood Government in the very moderate sum of Eleven Hundred Pounds per Hog." General Charles Cornwallis referred in more than one of his letters to his preference for staying in New York and feasting on its salt pork rather than taking his army south and becoming involved in distasteful hostilities, which, judging from the result when he moved, he might better have done.

Thomas Jefferson appeared in his best light when he imported fine Calcutta hogs and invited his neighbors to send their sows to mate with his boars to improve the breed, and in his worst when he cornered the pig market and charged the butchers all that the traffic would bear, annoying them to such an extent that they draped the fence around his house with pig entrails and nicknamed him "the hog governor." Abraham Lincoln's two favorite breakfasts were fried apples with salt pork, and ham with cream gravy and biscuits.

The Civil War and the army's need for meat doubled pork production in the North, which opened 25 million hitherto unexploited acres to homesteaders and had enough civilians to work them, while the supplies of the South dwindled because its territory was limited and all its able-bodied whites—and many of the blacks too—were in the army. Lee lost at Appomattox partly because his soldiers were half-starved. At the war's end, shrewd judgment about what was going to happen to pork prices enabled Philip Danford Armour to make the then incredible profit of $2 million and start the modern meat-packing industry.

America was built by pioneers and pigs. The covered wagons which started west even before the Gold Rush usually carried seventy-five pounds of bacon per adult. The Yankee Clippers took aboard both salt pork and live hogs for their crews to eat. Lewis and Clark started out on their expedition with fifty kegs of pork among their provisions. The strongly muscled *voyageurs*, whose canoes provided almost the sole communication with the interior of Canada, were called "pork eaters," since this was the only meat in their energy-building diet. Salt pork was also the only meat of the slaves who worked the Southern plantations, while the universal white diet was "hog and hominy." Immigrants from pork-eating countries brought their techniques for treating the meat along with them, for instance the Pennsylvania Dutch and the Germans who in the 1830s and '40s caused Cincinnati to be nicknamed Porkopolis. The quality of American pork improved after the advent of the railroads; pigs which had formerly been bred to be tough enough to walk to market were now carried there, and could be developed with a view to flesh which would be tenderer and tastier.

The versatility of pork, which in all its parts serves a multitude of gastronomic uses, is matched by the versatility of the pig, underestimated by Marvin Harris when he held that it was of no use for anything other than food: "Pigs can't be milked or ridden, can't herd other animals, pull a plow or carry a cargo, and don't catch mice." Yet he himself remarked elsewhere that the ancient Egyptians used pigs to tread seeds into the mud of the flooding Nile. We have already seen that the pig provides fertilizer and has for centuries played a useful role as a scavenger; indeed, it has been asserted that prehistoric peoples raised pigs as scavengers before they realized they were good to eat, which seems either to underrate prehistoric man's ingenuity in finding food or to overrate his concern for cleanliness. It is with the aid of the pig that men find truffles, and the animal enters the high realm of esthetics when it serves as an entertainer. This it does not only in the passive role of providing the prize for greased-pig catching (not an invention of American country fairs, but an amusement already practiced in the Middle Ages), but also in the more elevated status of a public performer: trained pigs provided entertainment between the courses of ancient Roman banquets, and they were dressed as human beings to perform the same function at the court of Louis XIV.

Pigs are easily trained, for they are among the most intelligent of all animals—more so than the horse, but less so than man, or at least this was what Cuvier thought. "The volume of [the pig's] brain," he wrote, "is . . . much less important [than that of man], which proves that its faculties also are much less important . . . greatly inferior to that of our academicians."

POTATO. The most important intellectual event of the reign of Louis XV (who cannot be accused of having personally done much to further it) was the appearance of the *Encyclopédie*, whose principal editor was Denis Diderot. It spread such enlightenment as the authorities permitted throughout the Western world, but it was not uniformly happy in the accuracy of its information. It defined the potato as "an Egyptian fruit whose cultivation may possibly have some value in the colonies."

It was, as a matter of fact, already having some value in France, but it cannot be said that it enjoyed great esteem. In 1749 the French naturalist Raoul Combes wrote of the potato, in his *L'Ecole du Potager* (*The School of the Kitchen Garden*): "Here is the worst of all vegetables in the general opinion; nevertheless the people, which is the most numerous part of humanity, feed themselves with it." The word "people" must be understood here to be more or less synonymous with "riffraff," and it was used with similarly unflattering intent by Legrand d'Aussy in his 1783 *Histoire de la vie privée des Français* (*History of the Private Life of the French*) when he wrote: "The pasty taste, the natural insipidity, the unhealthy quality of this food, which is flatulent and indigestible, has caused it to be rejected from refined households and returned to the people, whose coarse palates and stronger stomachs are satisfied with anything capable of appeasing hunger."

Brillat-Savarin waved potatoes away: "None for me. I appreciate the potato only as a protection against famine; except for that, I know of nothing more eminently tasteless." In England, William Cobbett called the potato "Ireland's lazy root," and added: "In whatever proportion the cultivation of potatoes prevails . . . in that same proportion the working peoples are wretched." In Germany, Nietzsche wrote: "A diet that consists predominantly of rice leads to the use of opium, just as a diet which consists predominantly of potatoes leads to the use of liquor." For a century and a half almost everybody agreed with Diderot:

> This root, no matter how you prepare it, is tasteless and floury. It cannot pass for an agreeable food; but it supplies a food sufficiently abundant and sufficiently healthy for men who ask only to sustain themselves. The potato is criticized with reason for being windy, but what matters windiness for the vigorous organisms of peasants and laborers?

No matter. Today, "in volume of fresh product, the potato ranks first among the world's most important food crops" (*Encyclopaedia Britannica*). "The world potato crop is second—a very close second—only to the world's wheat crop" (James Trager). It is "the world's fourth largest food crop, after corn, wheat and rice" (the United Nations Food and Agricultural Organization). It is one of only fifteen food products which feed the entire world (Frances Moore Lappé and Joseph Collins in *Food First*). And it is "the staple vegetable crop of the temperate world" (*The Practical Encyclopedia of Gardening*). The potato is undeniably a success.

That success is probably due largely to two factors: comparatively neutral in taste, it provides a palatable background or accompaniment for almost all other foods; bulky and starchy, it satisfies the appetite more quickly—and at less expense—than almost any other vegetable (one might almost say than any other food except bread). Still valid today is the summing up of Georges Gibault, making *amende honorable* for Diderot, in his *Histoire des Légumes*, published in 1912:

> For all the peoples of the white race living in the temperate countries of Europe and America, the

POTATO *by Camille Pissarro (1830–1903).* Potato Gatherers, *oil on canvas*

Potato, with Wheat, is certainly the principal food resource of vegetable origin. It is the most useful gift which the New World has made to us. Cultivated to a feeble extent at the end of the eighteenth century, its expansion was prodigious during the nineteenth century, and in our times the amount of land planted with potatoes is still increasing each year. . . . The entrance of the Potato into our foods has banished forever the spectre of the famines which formerly devastated Europe periodically.

There *was* one other famine in Europe after the potato had become firmly established there, but it was because the potato itself had failed. In the middle of the last century, when the potato blight destroyed utterly what had become almost the sole food crop of Ireland, the extent of the disaster was so great that botanists started hunting, almost desperately, for some other vegetable capable of supplementing or replacing the potato. They all arrived at the same conclusion:

There is no substitute for the potato.

John Gerard was kinder than Denis Diderot when he wrote "Of Potato's of Virginia" in his *Herball* (1597):

The temperature and vertues be referred to the common Potato's [for Gerard the "common potato" was the sweet potato], being likewise a food, as also a meat for pleasure, equall in goodnesse and wholesomnesse to the same, being either rosted in the embers, or boiled and eaten with oile, vineger and pepper, or dressed some other way by the hand of a skilfull Cooke. . . .

It groweth naturally in America, where it was first discovered, as reporteth Clusius, since which time I have received roots hereof from Virginia, otherwise called Norembega, which grow & prosper in my garden as in their owne native country. The Indians call this plant Pappus [right], meaning the roots; by which name also the common Potatoes [wrong] are called in those Indian countries . . . we may call it in English, potatoes of America or Virginia.

Thus, on the redoubtable authority of Gerard, this vegetable was indeed called the Virginia potato, bedeviling food historians who were to find, at this period, no trace of the Virginia potato in Virginia. True, Captain John Smith wrote of the Indians eating roots "much of the greatness and taste of potatoes." But what were they? Not potatoes, or he would not have compared them to potatoes, as a different vegetable (but for him, as for John Gerard, a "potato" at this period meant the sweet potato). The potato recommended as "hygienic and strengthening" by Sir Francis Bacon was the sweet potato. The potato mentioned several times by Shakespeare was the sweet potato. John Smith had probably encountered the Indian potato or groundnut, *Apios tuberosa,* or, less likely, the Jerusalem artichoke. It could not have been the potato; at the time when the first Europeans reached America, the "Virginia" potato not only did not exist in Virginia, it did not exist anywhere in North America.

When Columbus arrived in the West Indies, he was quick to discover the sweet potato, but he never saw a white potato, nor did any other European in Columbus's lifetime. It was not native to the Caribbean region, but only to South America, and a very restricted part of South America at that, the high sierra of the Andes, where it had been developed because the staple food of the South American Indians, maize, would not grow above 11,000 feet. It remained restricted to the Andes, and did not spread even to other parts of Latin America; Mexico, for instance, does not seem to have had potatoes before the eighteenth century.

The first Europeans to see the potato, probably near Quito, Ecuador, not much later than 1530, were Pizzaro's men, one of whom, Pedro de Cieza de Leon, wrote about it in his *Chronicle of Peru,* of which the first part was published in 1553. South American Indians must have been cultivating the potato long before the discovery of America. Reay Tannahill has written that the potato had been domesticated in Peru by 3000 B.C., and archeologists have reported that excavations have established the fact that it was being cultivated at least by the beginning of what they call Peru's Formative Period, which starts at 750 B.C. Peruvian pottery in the shape of potatoes has been found dating from the second century A.D.

How did this exclusively Andean vegetable become known as the Virginia potato (and, incidentally, acquire the reputation of having been imported from Virginia to England by Sir Walter Raleigh)? It was a question of accident and of misunderstanding. In 1586 Sir Richard Grenville, a cousin of Raleigh, sailed to do battle with the Spaniards in the Caribbean (he would get himself killed doing so) and was asked to stop first in Virginia to deliver provisions to premature colonists there who were engaged in starving. Thomas Hariot, one of Raleigh's men, went along as far as Virginia to keep Grenville company. They found that the colonists had had more than enough of America, and despite their new supplies wanted nothing more than to go home. We may suppose it was Sir Richard who relayed this request to Sir Francis Drake, about to sail for England after a successful bout of harassing Spaniards in the Caribbean. Drake took provisions aboard for the return voyage at Cartagena, Colombia, including some potatoes. Making a stop in Virginia, he picked up the discouraged colonists and Hariot, who was intrigued by the potatoes. It was apparently he who gave some to Gerard to plant in his own garden (and no doubt also to Raleigh, who is supposed to have planted them on his property at Youghal, near Cork, Ireland, in 1586). Since the last land Sir Francis's ship had touched was Virginia, Gerard assumed, and told the world, that the potatoes were natives of that area.

If Sir Walter Raleigh was really growing potatoes in Ireland, this lends plausibility to the story that he presented some potatoes to Queen Elizabeth for her delectation, but that the gift was not a success: a bewildered cook served the leaves and threw away the tubers. It seems not to have been an unthinkable error, for while Gerard displayed in his *Herball* the knowledge that it was the tubers which were eaten, he also described "the whole leafe resembling those of the Winter-Cresses, but much larger; in taste at the first like grasse, but afterward sharp and nipping the tongue."

When did the Virginia potato really reach Virginia? "That vagrant vegetable, the potato, took a century and a half and two ocean crossings to get from America, where it was born, to America, where it is eaten," the Associated Press put it in 1962, on the authority of the United Nations Food and Agricultural Organization, a reasonably accurate statement of the present theory, with the reservation that it fails to tell us that "America" in the first instance means South America and in the second, North America, and that it should have allowed the potato nearly half a century more to make the voyage. This brings us to 1719, when Ulstermen settled in Londonderry, New Hampshire, bringing the potato with them—which is why it was called the Irish potato or, slangily, the Murphy. This is believed to have been the first place in North America where potatoes were grown, the only place on that continent where they existed at that time, and the source of the potatoes planted by one of the first farmers to interest himself in them, Thomas Jefferson—who wrote, nevertheless, that what he called "round potatoes . . . were found in Virginia when first visited by the English, but it is not said whether of spontaneous growth, or by cultivation only." Jefferson, of course, was not present when Virginia was first visited by Englishmen, and he believed, like everybody else, what Gerard had reported.

The potato, omnipresent in the United States today, cannot be described as having leapt to instant popularity after 1719. The earliest reference I find to commercial potato growing dates from 1762, when it became a field crop in Salem, Massachusetts. In the following year Connecticut valley potatoes are listed as an article of export, but this was no compliment to their quality: the buyers were West Indian planters, who wanted the cheapest possible food for their slaves. Despite Jefferson's example, most Americans thought of potatoes as food for animals rather than for human beings; as late as the middle of the nineteenth century the *Farmer's Manual* recommended that potatoes "be grown near the hog-pens as a convenience towards feeding the hogs." Nevertheless, Eliza Leslie's *Directions for Cookery* offered four recipes for potatoes in 1848, though she perhaps represented the avant-garde, for as late as 1904 Célestine Eustis, though she did admit one potato recipe to her *Cooking in Old Creole Days*, warned housewives to throw away the water in which the potatoes had been cooked because it was poisonous.

In 1806 the *American Gardener's Calendar* mentioned only one variety of potato; by 1848 nearly one hundred kinds were exhibited at the fair of the Massachusetts Horticultural Society. Only about half a dozen of them were being grown commercially, for instance by the Mormons, who made a good thing out of selling this filling food to the forty-niners passing through Utah on the way to the gold fields. At mid-century, the potato was still held in low esteem, a symbol of the coarse and the ordinary, which was the view Margaret Fuller took of it in a somewhat highfalutin passage which she contributed to the New York *Tribune*:

> When an immortal poet was secure only of a few copyists to circulate his work, there were princes and nobles to patronize literature and the arts. Here is only the public, and the public must learn how to cherish the nobler and rarer plants, and to plant the aloe, able to wait a hundred years for its bloom, or its garden will contain, presently, nothing but potatoes and pot-herbs.

It was, in all probability, Pedro de Cieza de Leon who sent, or took, the first potatoes to Europe. What became of them?

Nobody really knows. There is a tradition which says that they were planted by the monks who administered the Hospital de la Sangre in Seville, and the earliest date I find for cultivation of the potato in Spain is 1539, but it is not verifiable. It is not until 1753 that we have documentary evidence, which comes precisely from that hospital —potatoes appeared on a list of provisions ordered for its inmates. But for the first half of the seventeenth century, potatoes seem to have been eaten by nobody in Spain except the poor and soldiers (it might be a good guess that as a cheap and filling food they were given to prisoners too).

In Spain, potato cultivation became a specialty of Galicia. From there they were shipped to Genoa, and as a result Italy seems to have been the first country after Spain to eat potatoes on an appreciable scale. The potato would not seem to be particularly compatible with either the climate or the cuisine of Italy, but it was a food for the poor, and Italy had plenty of poor. Reports that potatoes were being grown there were heard as early as 1580; the Bauhin brothers of Basle, Switzerland, wrote in 1590 that the potato was being cultivated in Italy; and Clusius added that it was common there in 1601. Clusius, incidentally, had first seen potatoes in 1588, having received some from Philippe de Sivry, papal legate to the Low Countries, and had painted (unless de Sivry was the artist) what was probably the very first representation of the potato ever produced; it is now in the Plantin Museum in Antwerp. The first picture of the potato ever *published* was not given us, as we are usually told, by John Gerard in his *Herball* (1597), nor by Rembert Dodoens, from whose *Stirpium historiae pemptades* (1583) Gerard is often accused of cribbing it, nor even by Teodor Tabernaemontanus, from whose *Icones plantarum* (1590) he is also accused of cribbing it by those who have discovered that it is not in the Dodoens book, but by Jacob Bergzaben, from whose *Neuw Kreuterbuch* (1588) he actually did crib it.

The Bauhin brothers—Jean, the elder, and Gaspard, the more famous (professor of the curious combination of botany and anatomy)—played an important role in the history of the potato. When Gaspard received some plants in 1590, possibly directly from Peru, he was fascinated by them, and the brothers were studying them in their garden in Basle by 1592. Gaspard Bauhin wrote what seems to have been the first really accurate description of the potato in his *Phytopinax*, published in 1596, and gave it the name *solanum tuberosum esculentum*; Linnaeus kept the first two words as the scientific label for the potato when he set up his system of taxonomy. It was in Switzerland also that what is believed to have been the first cookbook written by a woman was published in 1598; it contained a recipe for *Kartoffelnrösti*, still a popular potato dish in Switzerland.

The Bauhins are sometimes credited with having introduced the potato into France; Clusius may have had something to do with introducing it into Germany. Or, as the French food writer Robert J. Courtine thinks, the potato may have progressed on its own from Italy into Germany, where, he says, it was already present in the sixteenth century. Or Germany may have had it from Spain, either indirectly, via the Low Countries, where the governing Spaniards are supposed to have acclimated it about 1588, or directly, in the fashion recounted by Georges Blond:

> Towards 1640, the [Thirty Years] war had lasted for 23 years. In certain parts of the countryside, "you could cover several leagues without seeing a man, an animal, or even a sparrow; in the villages the houses which had remained standing were full of corpses and carrion, men, women, children, farmhands, horses, pigs, cows, side by side or some piled on the others, swarming with worms, gnawed by birds, wolves and dogs, for there was nobody to bury them, pity them or weep for them." A few phantoms haunted these cemeteries, eating grass and earth, cannibals on occasion. Imagine the arrival of the Spanish soldiers in Saxony and Westphalia in the midst of this nightmare! When they gave potatoes to the peasants, these unfortunates began by eating them just as they were, raw, weeping with joy. A little later they planted them.

Germans are among the world's biggest potato eaters today, and they should have acquired the habit early, for both the climate and the heavy cuisine of German-speaking central European peoples were more in harmony with the potato than had been the case in Spain and Italy. This was also true for the Baltic and Slavic states farther north and east; Silesia contains some of the world's best soil for potatoes. Yet trustworthy dates are hard to find before the eighteenth century.

Frederick William I, disturbed by disastrous failures of cereal crops, imposed the planting of potatoes on Prussian peasants about 1720 under pain of draconian punishment; but they seem to have been less than obedient, for in 1750 Frederick the Great was obliged to repeat the decree, which the peasants continued to disobey. Convinced that potatoes caused leprosy, they pulled up the potatoes Frederick had planted, obliging him to post soldiers to guard the fields where they were growing. He finally won over his subjects, the story goes, by eating potatoes publicly himself, on the balcony of his palace; but in 1774, when the citizens of Kolberg were struck by famine and Frederick sent wagonloads of potatoes to the city, its starving inhabitants refused to touch them.

Other German states may have been more receptive to the potato than Prussia was. In Trier this vegetable was sufficiently entrenched in the first half of the eighteenth century so that tithes were being paid on it. In 1778 the War of the Bavarian Succession was nicknamed "the potato war," because its operations were confined chiefly to attacks on the food supplies of the contesting armies, which would seem to indicate that by then the potato was well established. Nevertheless, as late as 1795, when Benjamin Thompson, Count Rumford, the only American peer of the Holy Roman Empire, attempted to feed the poor with barley soup, they would not eat it because it had been thickened with potatoes.

In the British Isles, whether or not one accepts the theory that the potato was planted in Ireland on Sir Walter Raleigh's estate in 1586, this date turns up relentlessly, given by those who think the potato reached Ireland from Flanders as well as by those who assert that the first potatoes planted in Ireland came from a ship of the Spanish Armada wrecked on the Irish coast. Whenever it arrived, it was a godsend, at first, to a country perpetually on the verge of famine. Even on the poor soil of Ireland, the potato would yield up to six times as much nourishment as grain. "A tiny cottage plot," wrote Reay Tannahill, "could produce enough to feed a man and his wife, six children, and perhaps even a cow and a pig." There was also the advantage, for a country ravaged continually by warfare, that this underground food would not be trampled into inedibility by the passage of soldiers. The potato saved Ireland from famine in 1740, but when the potato itself failed in 1845, though the blight struck other European countries as well, it was Ireland which suffered the most disastrous consequences, for Ireland had become a one-crop country.

A minor result of this situation was that the Irish forgot how to cook. "There is scarcely a woman of the peasant class in the West of Ireland whose culinary art exceeds the boiling of a potato," Charles Edward Trevelyan, permanent head of the British Treasury at the time of the famine, wrote in 1846. "Bread is scarcely ever seen, and the oven is unknown." Father Matthew, a contemporary advocate of temperance, said that "the potato deluge during the past twenty years has swept away all other food from our cottagers and sunk into oblivion their knowledge of cookery." In our own time a Dublin nutritionist, Dr. Stephen Boyle, who apparently subscribed to the conspiratorial view of history, wrote that without the potato "the Machiavellian activities of the London government and the absentee landlords could never have come to fruition."

England was more reticent than Ireland about accepting the potato, but it was probably known earlier to low-income country dwellers than to high-income urban writers, who failed to notice its presence until it had been on hand for some time. We are usually told that it was pretty much unknown in England until the middle of the eighteenth century; that there were not enough potatoes to be put on public sale before 1770; that potatoes did not become a field crop until 1780; and that they were so despised during the reign of George III (1760–1820) that Thomas Coke had to carry out seven years of patient experiments with them before it was agreed, grudgingly, that they made a good enough winter food —for cattle.

Yet some Englishmen knew the potato in the seventeenth century. There is a record of its cultivation in Lancashire beginning in 1634, which went unnoticed by botanical writers until 1728. In 1663 the Royal Society of England recommended growing potatoes as a safeguard against possible famine. One year later John Forster published a book entitled *England's Happiness Increased, or a rare and easie Remedy against all succeeding Dear Years; by A Plantation of the Roots called Potatoes.* A French source described the potato as common in England in 1698, and this was confirmed the following year when a Dr. Lister, an English scholar who had accompanied the Duke of Portland on an official mission to France, published an account of his visit in which he expressed his surprise at the difficulty of finding potatoes on the Paris market—"those tubers which are so widely eaten in England."

Nevertheless, hardly a good word was said for potatoes by the country's respected botanists. Worlidge wrote in 1687, "I do not hear that it has yet been essayed whether they may be propagated in great quantities for the use of swine and other cattle." John Mortimer, in his *Gardener's Kalendar* (1708), said, "The root is very near the nature of the Jerusalem artichoke, although not so good

POTATO. *Engraving by Gimbrede of J. B. White's painting* General Marion Inviting a British Officer to Dinner; *also known as* The Potato Dinner. *Historical embellishment from* Godey's Lady's Book, *April 1845*

and wholesome, but it may prove good to swine." In 1719 we have Bradley opining that potatoes "are of less note than horse-radish, radish, scorsoners and skirret; but, as they are not without their admirers, I will not pass them by in silence." Finally Miller tells us, in 1754, that they are "despised by rich and deemed only proper food for the meaner sort of persons."

The meaner sort of persons did indeed know the potato. In 1830, when a workman made anywhere from sixty-two cents to five dollars a week, he could treat himself to what he considered a luxurious meal of tea and boiled potatoes; the tea cost more than the potatoes, which were priced at 12½ cents for twenty pounds. In 1832 the English authorities decided to recognize the wholesomeness of the potato and amended the Bread Acts so that potato flour could appear in that food without forfeiture of its legal right to be called bread. By 1884 we find Friedrich Engels, writing of the poor in northern England manufacturing towns, explaining that "we find the animal food reduced to a small bit of bacon cut up with the potatoes; lower still, even this disappears, and there remain only bread, cheese, porridge and potatoes, until on the lowest round of the ladder, among the Irish, potatoes form the sole food."

In Scotland, potatoes were opposed by Presbyterian ministers who deemed them an ungodly food because they were not mentioned in the Bible. But they were accepted there all the same, in 1683 or 1725 or 1728 or 1739, depending on whom you read; and they are reported to have been first cultivated on a large scale about 1728 by one Thomas Prentice according to Gibault, who is the reporter of the earliest of the dates cited above.

In France, the touchstone for matters gastronomic, all the writers tell us the same thing: the French did not take to the potato and refused to eat it until it was, so to speak, thrust down their throats by the determined championship of Antoine Augustin Parmentier in the early 1770s. "For almost two hundred years," one author tells us, "France would have nothing to do at all" with the potato. "At the beginning of the nineteenth century," writes another, "they were cultivated only for animals." An author a trifle more charitable to the potato of that date says that not before the beginning of the nineteenth century did potatoes finally become a staple food in France, while another turns the same idea from negative to positive by asserting that at the start of that century the potato did become a staple. Georges and Germaine Blond tell us that in the first half of the seventeenth century, "the people of France did not eat potatoes. They were beginning, here and there, to give some to animals, but human beings didn't want them. They did not know how to cook them and they were disgusted by them."

This reluctance of the French to accept the potato is often explained by the belief that it was unhealthy, a theory which, as we have seen, was not restricted to France. We read again and again that in 1630 the parliament of Besançon passed a decree which read: "Whereas the potato is a pernicious substance and its use can cause leprosy, it is forbidden, on pain of a fine, to cultivate it on the territory of Salins." I have been guilty of repeating this myself, overwhelmed by the weight of numbers, before I learned that when one hundred writers assert the same thing it does not necessarily mean that the alleged fact has been confirmed by a hundred different sources, but sometimes only that everybody is rewriting everybody else. I have since discovered that there was no parliament in Besançon in 1630; the regional parliament was at Dole, where a French researcher named Roze, who was writing a history of the potato, tried to find this decree and could discover no trace of it. "It never existed," he concluded.

In France, as in many other European countries, the potato made its first appearance well before the dates usually given, and was being eaten more and more commonly during the period when it is described as having been non-existent in that country. Long before Parmentier launched his campaign in its favor, the potato was already being eaten in every province of France. A number of earlier dates are given, but they are dubious, so until more reliable evidence turns up, we must continue to situate the first plantings of potatoes in France, whether directly inspired by the Bauhin brothers or not, at the time and places where they reported its presence—in 1593, in that part of Burgundy which later became the Franche-Comté, in the region of Lyons and in the Vosges. "This plant," Gaspard Bauhin added, "called *Cartouffe*, bears fruit (tubers) of the same name, like truffles, and by some so called. It came from Switzerland [which explains the German name] into the Dauphiné not long ago."

In 1600 Olivier de Serres (who had been called to Paris by Henry IV in the belief that his agricultural skill would be equal to the task of raising silkworms in Paris) wrote his *Theatre of Agriculture and the Management of Fields*, in which he included a chapter on what he called the *cartoufle* or *truffe*, which he had been raising on his own property. It has been suggested that this plant was the Jerusalem artichoke; but though Olivier de Serres' description lacks clarity, there can be little doubt that he was talking about the potato.

"All eastern France knew the potato 100 to 150 years before the birth of Parmentier [1737]," wrote Georges Gibault, which is certainly an exaggeration, but it is true that Parmentier himself, in his *Examen chymique des Pommes de Terre*, wrote in 1773:

> The employment of this food plant was adopted a century ago. . . . It is so widespread that there are provinces in France where Potatoes have become part of the nourishment of the poor; for several years now we have seen whole fields covered with them in the neighborhood of the capital, where they are so common that all its markets are filled with them and that they are sold at street corners, raw or cooked, as chestnuts have long been sold.

Thus Parmentier himself has given us a date of 1673 at the latest for the French potato, and we know that it was being cultivated on a large scale in Lorraine on the evidence of a decree issued there establishing a tithe on potatoes, which notes that they had been growing in the region for fifty years. Twenty-one years before this decree, in 1693, a priest of Saint-Dié had won a suit obliging the farmers of his parish to pay such a tithe, and it was then pointed out that Saint-Dié had been cultivating potatoes at least since 1675. The Abbey of Remiremont was accepting payments in potatoes "during the reign of Louis XII"—say about

1620—and Saint-Etienne was eating them regularly "during the reign of Louis XIV"—say about 1670.

By the first half of the eighteenth century the potato was already fairly well established in France, as we learn from the *Ecole du Potager* (1749) of Raoul Combes, the same work in which he called the potato "the worst of all vegetables":

Here is a plant of which no author has spoken [he forgot Clusius, Bauhin and Olivier de Serres], and probably it is because of contempt that it has been excluded from the class of culinary plants, for *it is too anciently known* [my italics] to have escaped their knowledge; however there is an injustice in omitting a fruit which serves as nourishment *to a large part of the men of all nations* [my italics]. I do not wish to exalt it more than it merits, for I know all its defects . . . but I deem that it should have its place with the others, since it serves usefully and has its appreciators; it is not only the poor people and the country dwellers who live on it in most of our provinces; there are even the wealthiest persons of the cities . . . many persons have a passion for it: I leave aside the question of whether this is an affectation in high places or a depraved taste; it has its partisans; that is enough for me. . . . It is not unknown in Paris, but it is true that it is left to the humble and that persons of a certain social rank consider it beneath them to let it be seen on their tables; I do not want to inspire in them a taste I do not have myself; but one ought not to condemn those whom it pleases.

It was the famine of 1770 which produced Parmentier. Alarmed by its ravages, the Academy of Besançon sponsored a contest for the best "study of food substances capable of reducing the calamities of famine." Parmentier won the prize.

The tubers of [the potato, he wrote] have the advantage of standing up to the destructive effects of hail, of replacing bread in bulk, of entering into its composition whatever their state, frozen or sprouting, and of economizing flour when an exceptional event makes this last rare and expensive . . . [Let winegrowers], instead of nourishing themselves on rough bread made of barley, buckwheat and screenings in which weeds predominate, plant potatoes at the foot of their vines, and thus supply themselves with a sort of food which supplements all others and can replace them in the most complete fashion in case of famine.

Several other contestants for the Besançon prize mentioned the potato too, but Parmentier offered a larger choice of alternate foods: he also proposed the acorn, the horse chestnut, and the corms of iris and gladioli.

Who was Antoine Augustin Parmentier?

A publicist, not an agronomist [wrote his severest critic, Georges Gibault]. . . . The partisans of the legend of Parmentier support themselves by the influence of his books and articles . . . which are supposed to have triumphed over prejudices against the cultivation of the potato on the part of the peasants, who read so little today, and who did not read at all 130 years ago. It is evident that not a single farmer read his major work, the *Chemical Examination of the Potato.*

Actually, Parmentier was a military pharmacist, who at the age of twenty took part in the Seven Years War, was wounded, held prisoner in Germany, and was there impressed by the importance of the potato, then widely eaten in that country. By the time of his prize-winning thesis, he had become pharmacist-major and director of the military laboratory in the Hôtel des Invalides, a position which was to facilitate contacts with the king. It is somewhat ironic that his fame today rests on his advocacy of the potato, concerning which he was more articulate than effective, for his interests were wide. He wrote ninety-five books and pamphlets on a variety of subjects, and his contributions in other fields were perhaps more important —for instance, his search for substitutes for cane sugar, his improvements in the milling of flour and the baking of bread, his pioneering studies on refrigeration, and above all, his introduction of vaccination against smallpox in the army. His reputation as the chief champion of the potato is posthumous. In his own time he was much contested, and when his friend François de Neufchâteau proposed that the potato be called the *parmentière,* in honor of its "discoverer," he got nowhere. But today his name has been given to a soup, a hash and an omelet, all, of course, containing potatoes.

A last-minute worker [Gibault wrote], Parmentier reaped the benefit of the efforts of those who had preceded him, and who have remained unknown. It is the men of the second generation, those who knew Parmentier only through his writings, who asserted his right to the gratitude of humanity.

The men of the second generation—and of the third, fourth and fifth generations—do seem sometimes to have confused biography with hagiography, and have done their idol no service by circulating stories about him which are manifestly absurd. We may believe, however, the story that Parmentier served, perhaps more than once, a dinner at which all the courses—soup, entrée, entremets, salad, cake, cookies and, of course, the bread—were made of potatoes, though it is more doubtful, as has been alleged, that Benjamin

Franklin was one of the guests. Some of the stories about Louis XVI's support of Parmentier and the potato sound more dubious. Parmentier is represented as having given the king some potato flowers on his birthday (which was August 23, a little late for potatoes to be in bloom). The king, it is said, placed a bouquet on his table and wore a flower in his buttonhole, and Marie Antoinette twined some in her hair. A more romantic version of the last story alleges that Louis was entranced by Marie Antoinette the first time he saw her because she had potato blossoms in her coiffure (the meeting occurred in 1770, before Parmentier had taken up the cudgels for the potato). If Louis XVI really did display potato flowers, it could hardly have been very effective propaganda: nobody at court would have recognized them.

Whoever deserves the credit for it, the potato today is the most widely eaten vegetable in France.

Resistance to a strange new food is a normal phenomenon everywhere. In the case of the potato it was strengthened by a widespread belief that it was poisonous. This was not as absurd as it sounds to us today. The potato *is*—or rather, was—toxic. Some housewives still, when they cut open a potato and find it lightly tinted with green, throw it away instead of cooking it. The green color betrays the presence of solanine, which is indeed a poison, common to plants of the potato's family, the *Solanaceae* (which includes the deadly nightshade). Our modern potatoes do not contain a large enough proportion of solanine to bother anybody; but the potatoes of the sixteenth and seventeenth centuries contained higher dosages of it. Even Renaissance potatoes were not capable of killing anybody, but they did sometimes cause the skin to break out in a rash; this was enough to make the timid fear that they had contracted the most dreaded disease of their times, leprosy.

A second handicap of the potato was unpalatability. The unfavorable opinions of the potato quoted above did not spring from mere prejudice; they had a certain basis in the nature of the potatoes of that period, which could not have competed in quality with those we eat today. They were, in the first place, afflicted by an unfavorable heredity. When modern botanists set out to improve a plant, they select the choicest specimens to reproduce the species: generation by generation the best features are perpetuated, the weaknesses sloughed off. The Andean Indians, unfortunately, ate their biggest and best potatoes and planted the rejects. Their potatoes grew smaller and smaller, and more and more floury, and progressively less tasty. That was the sort of potato which first arrived in Europe. The attractiveness of this vegetable was not improved by the fact that it seldom occurred to anybody to peel it.

How did Europe reproduce its potatoes? As you and I do (but we buy our seed potatoes from breeders), by cutting last year's potatoes into small pieces, with one or more eyes in each, and planting the pieces. This prevents evolution, for better or for worse. The second-generation potato is not really a potato of the second generation; it is last year's potato reduplicated. Potatoes did improve a little, all the same, by their own action: when they found themselves in better soil, or more adequately fertilized than usual, they tended to produce mutants of higher quality. But not until 1760 did breeders start to improve the potato by working, not with its tubers, but with its seeds. Potatoes improved, the demand for them increased, more land was planted to them, and more people ate them—just in time for Parmentier to be credited with bringing about the change.

Most of us do not pay much attention to the taste of the potato, unless we get a bad one. It is a relatively neutral food, usually an accompaniment to something else; it seems to lack individuality, and its variations in flavor, from best to worst, do not strike us as covering a very wide range. Because we think this, we buy potatoes with great casualness, and our lack of discrimination necessarily confirms our opinion that one potato is very much like another. I used to think myself that while freshness is all-important for, say, Indian corn or spring peas, it is a negligible factor in potatoes—until I began to grow my own. The potatoes I pulled up from my own patch just before a meal had a flavor which seemed to have no common denominator with that of the potatoes I had formerly bought from a store, where they had been lying in a bin for a month or so. One would hardly describe the potato as subtle in taste, but it can certainly be better than neutral.

When I took my French wife to the United States for the first time, I asked her, after a month divided among Washington, New York and Boston, which American food she had liked best. She named the Idaho baked potato. This is, indeed, I think, the king of all potatoes; I have come across nothing which can compare with it in Europe, and it would be of no avail to plant the same variety abroad. The Idaho potato is wedded to its native soil and, planted anywhere else, even in the United States, refuses sulkily to give of its best. The potato is one of the rare foods for which France has proved unable to outdo America. In the case of the baked potato, this may be attributed to the superiority of the tuber; but in the case of mashed potatoes, it would seem to be a matter of know-how. To my mind, American mashed potatoes at their best (at their *best*, mind you, for the United States can also produce lamentable libels on this dish) are highly preferable to French mashed potatoes, which are fluid and tasteless. I deduce that the French soul, despite the ubiquity of French fries, does not vibrate to the frequency of the potato.

Unfortunately, there is little opportunity nowadays for most people, in America or elsewhere, to taste the potato at its best, and that opportunity is decreasing steadily. After having improved the potato to what was probably the limit of its possibilities from the point of view of taste, the breeders kept on improving it, and since there was nothing left to do for its taste, they improved it from the point of view of profit. Even Luther Burbank's first major achievement, the Burbank Russet of the past century, welcomed by potato growers and handlers as a solution to some of their problems, represented a slight step backward in taste. Now we are finding that new varieties developed for high yields pay for increase in quantity by a decrease in quality. They also risk becoming highly vulnerable, almost too rarefied to live outside an incubator, figuratively speaking. Professional growers can cope with them, but amateurs had better not try. One determined onslaught on these pampered potatoes by a disease or an insect, and even the professionals may be in trouble.

Is there a danger that we are all going to forget forever the fine flavor of the best potatoes? The decline in quality is being paralleled in the United States by a decline in consumption. In 1900, Americans ate 200 pounds of potatoes per person per year. Today Americans eat 120 pounds—75 pounds of fresh potatoes and 45 of processed potatoes. (They were all fresh in 1900.) Some of this decline can be attributed to a rise in the standard of living: everywhere, as incomes increase, more meat is eaten and, consequently, less potatoes (and bread). But some of it, I suspect, results from disappointment with today's potatoes. Processing potatoes not only processes much of the taste out of those particular potatoes, it also attacks the quality of all fresh potatoes, for growers shift to varieties which they can sell to the processors, which are not the best varieties for eating fresh.

Dehydrated potatoes were first concocted on a large scale for the U.S. Army during World War II. Frozen potatoes came later, starting with tubers which had suffered no greater mayhem than being pre-cut to make French fries, but this was followed by potatoes already fried, with a result reported by *New York Times* columnist Russell Baker as: " 'French fries' say the menus, but they are not French fries any longer. They are a furry-textured substance with the taste of plastic wool."

The potato, John and Karen Hess wrote in a magazine article,

> is one of nature's best-designed products; it is born in a sturdy package, with wonderful shelf life. Yet we haul it from field to factory, peel and slice it by machine, cook it in hot grease, dose it with additives, wrap it in a petroleum or natural-gas derivative, freeze it, store it in a frozen warehouse, haul it across the country in a diesel refrigerated truck, store it in another frozen warehouse, deliver it in a reefer truck to a supermarket freezer, move it to a kitchen freezer, and, eventually, we reheat it.
>
> Then we eat it.

"The more a potato gets processed," wrote Frances Moore Lappé and Joseph Collins in *Food First*, "the more its price goes up and its nutritional value goes down."

PRA
stands for

the **prairie apple**, or breadroot, eaten by Plains Indians and the Lewis and Clark expedition; the **prairie chicken**, once served in the diners of the Chicago and North Western Railroad, but an endangered species today; the **prairie dog**, reputedly edible, but most people seem willing to take this on trust; the **prairie oyster**, which can mean one of two things, the first being a hangover remedy; the **prairie strawberry**, the cowboy's name for the red Mexican bean; and for **prawns**, which once confused an English court called upon to decide if it constitutes cruelty to these crustaceans to fry them to death instead of boiling them to death.

PRI
stands for

the **prickly amaranth**, whose leaves are eaten with relish in tropical Africa, South Africa and Madagascar; the **prickly cockle**, palatable if confided to chowder; **prickly lettuce**, which will not only feed you in the wilds, but will show you how to get out of them, which is why it is called the compass plant; the **prickly pear**, a cactus which the Aztecs tamed before Burbank did; the **prickly pen shell** of the Atlantic coast from the Carolinas to the West Indies, sweet in the plate but nasty on the beaches, where it lies just below the surface, sharp edges up, waiting for barefoot bathers; for the **priestfish,** so called because its eyes are turned upward toward heaven, and the **priest's-pintle,** used to make the pleasantly poisonous Portland arrowroot; for the **primrose,** a potherb once but only a flower now; and for the **prince's-feather,** whose leaves are boiled like spinach in Jamaica and its seeds ground like wheat in India, and the **prince's-plume,** once eaten by Indians in the canyon country of the American Southwest in casual disregard of the detail that it is poisonous.

PRO
stands for

the **prodigal son,** a fish eaten in East Africa and Madagascar; for the **pronghorn,** the only American antelope, unless it is a goat, but however you class it, it is so succulent that hunters almost succeeded in wiping it out despite the fact that it is the fastest land animal on the continent; and for the **prosopis,** or mesquite, of tropical America, whose dried ground pods have been described as perhaps the most nutritious breadstuff used anywhere in the world.

PT
stands only for

the **ptarmigan,** a northern PARTRIDGE whose dark breast meat is held in Norway to be that country's choicest game.

PU
stands for

puddingwife, a brightly colored tropical American fish which looks good enough to eat and, since it is a wrasse, presumably is; for **puffball,** a mushroom you should eat only if its flesh is white; for **puffers,** GLOBEFISH which can blow themselves up into near-spheres for protection, some of them delicious eating if you cut out the organs which secrete tetraodontoxin, one of the most violent poisons of nature, but if you don't, will offer your survivors an object lesson on the reason why Polynesians call it *maki-maki,* "deadly death"; for the **puffin,** which is ingenious enough to moult its bill, and is eaten by those who do not mind in its flesh the flavor of the fish it eats, or if they do, know enough to soak it in milk before cooking; for **pullets,** which are, or are becoming, old enough to lay eggs but are still too young and giddy to be allowed the responsibility of hatching them; for **pulse,** a picturesque word little used outside of scientific writings except to describe the diet of ancient hermits, with the result that few people realize that all it means is beans, peas, lentils and their like; for the **puma,** eaten by the ancient Incas and by Charles Darwin, who said it tasted like veal; for the **pumpkin,** whose very identity is so inextricably intertwined with that of the SQUASH that you will find it under that entry, and the **pumpkinseed,** which is not the seed of the pumpkin but a North American freshwater sunfish which many people think inedible, but is actually quite flavorful for those not afraid to do battle with its bones; for the **puntasso,** a sort of bream eaten in Mediterranean Africa; for the **pupae** of many insects, eaten in South Africa and Madagascar; for the **purple clam,** a tasty but brittle-shelled species of the southern California coast, the **purple mullein,** our sixteenth name for this plant, the **purple shell,** alias the dog whelk, which is armed with a sharp tongue capable of drilling a hole through the shells of its neighbors, and the **purple urchin** of California, which manages mysteriously to dig shelters for itself in solid rock; for the **pursetassel,** whose roots were eaten by the ancient Greeks and Romans; and for **purslane,** which William Cobbett described in 1819 as "a mischievous weed that Frenchmen and pigs eat when they can get nothing else."

PY
stands for

the **pygmy angelfish** of subtropical eastern American waters, the **pygmy devil ray** of Australian waters, the **pygmy** (or blue-spotted) **sunfish** of North American fresh waters, the **pygmy hatchetfish** of deep-sea waters, and the **pygmy mackerel** of Indonesian waters; and for the **python,** which according to a French cookbook called *La Cuisine de Bacchus* should be served with a light muscadel.

Q

QUINCEY, THOMAS DE: *Dyspepsy is the ruin of most things: empires, expeditions, and everything else.*

QA
stands for

qāt, a bush whose leaves are chewed by Arabs in need of stimulation.

QUA
stands for

quack grass, a poverty-stricken relation of barley, and for **quail grass**, highly popular in tropical Africa, but less so in China; for **Quaker rouge**, our seventeenth name for the mullein; for **quamash,** a root which Lewis and Clark ate at the instigation of Pacific Northwest Indians; for the **quandong nut** of Australia, where it is called, misleadingly, the native peach; for the **quarrenden,** a small deep-red apple which dates from the fifteenth century and is still being grown in southwestern England; and for **quarters**, which is fourths everywhere else, but in Africa the snot-apple.

And **QUA** also stands for

QUAHOG. "Mercenary Venus" sounds like a promising, not to say scandalous, name even for a clam, but the quahog has been dubbed *Venus mercenaria* (or, tautologically, *Mercenaria mercenaria*) in all innocence. *Venus* stamps it as one of the 150 to 200 species of this genus of the family *Veneridae*, named for a goddess born of the sea, and *mercenaria* identifies it as the wampum clam. Other seashells have been used for money, but the Indians of what was to become the northeastern corner of the United States preferred the quahog for this purpose because its heavy shell was durable and provided them with two denominations for their currency. A dirty gray outside, the quahog is creamy white within, with purple splotches; usually one edge of the shell is purple too. Strings of polished beads made from the white part (or from whelk shells) served as ordinary money, but those made from the purple parts were worth twice as much. Wampum was not only a medium of exchange among Indians, it was also accepted by Europeans, who may sometimes have found it more dependable than their own coinages. "When an early settler tendered a golden guinea in payment for some low-priced item," Euell Gibbons wrote in *Stalking the Blue-Eyed Scallop*, "he was likely to receive white wampum, purple wampum, English shillings, Dutch guilders, and Spanish pieces-of-eight in his change."

QUAHOG. *Drawing from Nicholaus Gaulterius:* Index Testarum Conchyliorium, *1742*

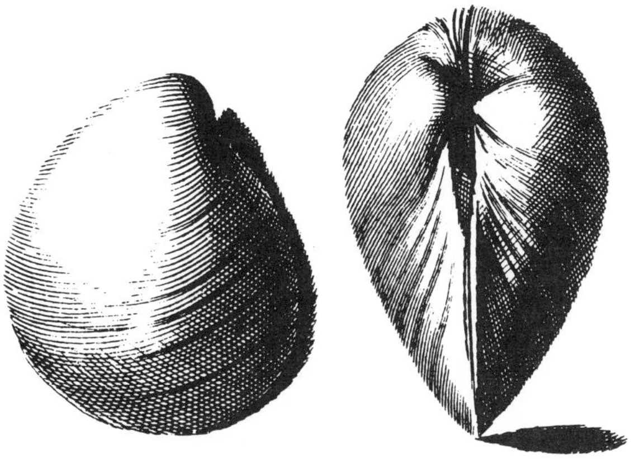

The quahog changes its name confusingly as it gets older and bigger. Professional clam diggers divide quahogs into five grades, called, from youngest to oldest, littlenecks, topnecks, cherrystones, medium clams and chowder clams. Eaters are less precise. The smallest edible quahog is indeed known to them as the littleneck, thus usurping the name of another clam which has no other. Then comes the well-known and much-liked cherrystone, resembling its namesake in shape and size, with an appropriate blush of pink in its color. Thereafter the clam acquires its adult name (quahog in New England, hard clam or round clam farther south) and also a certain toughness. When it reaches three and a half inches, it is advisable to give up eating the quahog raw, but it is still acceptable steamed. Clams much bigger than that had better be chopped up or ground, to go into sauces or chowder.

The quahog shares with the razor clam the widest distribution of all shellfish along the Atlantic seaboard, where it is found from southern Canada to Florida. Since the razor clam is not available commercially, the quahog is the most widely known Atlantic clam (but steamers—soft-shelled clams—are the most consumed). Commercially, the quahog is most important in the stretch of coast between Nova Scotia and Maryland, particularly in the New York area; nearly half of all the quahogs eaten in the United States come from Long Island's Great South Bay, or did in the days before pollution. Always one of the most important food clams of the United States, quahogs were an essential part of the American Indian diet before the first Europeans arrived; it was Indians who taught the Pilgrims how to gather and prepare them. Quahogs are easily collected. Since their siphons are very short, they lie just below the surface; and they prefer sheltered mud and sand beaches in estuaries and inlets, not difficult of access for clam hunters. On open beaches they are found abundantly in the intertidal zone, though they also exist off the coast in as much as twenty or twenty-five feet of water. The heavy, thick shell of this clam, marked with ridges and concentric growth lines, quickly reaches four to five inches in length and nearly as much across (they tend to grow bigger in the southernmost part of their range), making them large enough so that a useful quantity can be gathered with minimum effort.

The southern quahog, *Mercenaria campechiensis*, is also important enough to be dug commercially. So is the black (or mahogany) quahog, *Arctica islandica*, a deep-water species found off the New England coast, for which it is necessary to dredge. If this is not the same clam called in another taxonomic system *Cyprina islandica* (Cypris is a name for Venus too), it is in any case very much like it.

It seems probable that the quahog is a native of Atlantic America, though nowadays it also exists elsewhere. Several French clams, the *palourde*, the *clovisse* and the *praire* (and at least one Italian one, the *vongole*), have been described as the same mollusk, but erroneously. In France, the quahog is *le clam*, a fine example of the phenomenon called *franglais* by French purists, who are enraged by such onslaughts on their language. *Le clam*, now plentiful all along the French Atlantic coast, was imported from America, but there are conflicting opinions about how and when this happened. The Larousse gastronomic encyclopedia says that *le clam* has been acclimated there since the First World War, without further explanation. The *Guide Gourmand de la France*, by Henri Gault and Christian Millau, reports on page 45 that the American clam was introduced into France before the First World War by a famous Parisian seafood restaurant, Prunier, and on page 798 that an oyster cultivator of Chaillevente, a little north of Bordeaux, imported some quahogs in 1902; since they seemed in sad shape after a long transatlantic crossing, he had them thrown overboard into the Seudre River. Healthier than they smelled, the clams prospered there and spread all along the coast, but, according to this authority, are nowhere better than in the Seudre, where they acquired "a very delicate flavor and a pretty green color." The *Dictionnaire de l'Académie des Gastronomes*, with what sounds suspiciously like chauvinism, dismisses these explanations impatiently with the assertion "The clam everybody talks about is nothing more than our good old *lucine*, a sort of large *clovisse*." The definition of *lucine* (when it means a clam; there is also a butterfly of that name) certainly fits the quahog: "A bivalve mollusk with a thick rounded shell marked with concentric lines or plates, with smooth or very finely toothed edges." But is the *lucine* really a good old French shellfish? Its scientific name is *Lucina pennsylvanica*.

QUAIL. One of the sweet simple memories of my idyllic boyhood is of lying on my back in the middle of a field which seemed to be trying to grow more daisies than grass and listening to the clear but plaintive whistle "Bob—bob *white*! Bob *white*!" If the birds were silent I would mock their call and they would answer. I thought I was dialoguing with quail; if anyone had told me that there were no quail in America I would have put him down as ignorant; but he would have been right. If I had been brought up in the Southeast instead of New England, I would have been just as sure that my friendly bird was a partridge (or if among the Louisiana Cajuns, a *perdreau*). There were no partridges in America either.

When the first Europeans came upon a New World bird for which they had no name, they called it after the Old World bird they thought it most resembled. In Virginia this was felt to be the partridge, in New England the quail. The first name remained localized, the second was applied throughout the United States to birds of the same kind; the American quail acquired no distinctive name of its own except the bobwhite, which sounds more like an affectionate nickname. Both Old World and New World quails are *Galliformes*, but of different groups. The Old World quail, which we must consider the real one by right of seniority, is best represented by *Coturnix coturnix*, the New World quail by *Colinus virginianus*. They have in common firm flesh of exquisitely delicate taste, but I have no opinion on which is better, for though I often heard their call in the United States I cannot remember ever having eaten quail there; and though I have eaten quail in France, I do not remember ever having heard their call there. Perhaps I did not recognize it. French quail say, *Paye tes dettes! Paye tes dettes!* "Pay your debts!"—bad advice in inflationary times. The most raucous of all quails is probably the mountain quail of North America's West Coast, alias the plumed partridge, whose *Quee-ark! Quee-ark!* can be heard for three-quarters of a mile. (The West Coast also has a valley quail, the state bird of California, but when a quail farm in Sonoma, in that state, ran out of breeding stock, it could find none nearer than Chile; there are fewer valley quail now than in the nineteenth century, but they cover a much wider range, for they have been exported and acclimated as far away as New Zealand.)

Another characteristic shared by Old World and New World quail is an aversion to flying, though the Old World bird, unlike that of the New World, is migratory. This is not unconnected

QUAIL. *Print by Currier and Ives,* The Cares of a Family

with their flavor. Quail have large, white-fleshed muscles which permit rapid flight, but in brief bursts only. They lack the rich blood supply which feeds strong-flying birds with fuel in the form of oxygen delivered rapidly and in great quantity, necessary for sustained flight. It is this abundant blood supply which gives many game birds dark meat, too strongly flavored for some tastes. The flesh of the quail is more lightly colored than that of strong flyers, and its taste less overpowering and more subtle—at the optimum point, in many opinions, between the blandness of barnyard fowl and the pungency of more athletic wild birds.

Quail, if they have a choice, prefer to flee danger by running rather than by flying, a suicidal habit they share with pheasants. The most pedestrian of these birds must be mountain quail, whose usual habitat lies between 1500 and 10,000 feet of altitude; sometimes obliged to undertake a vertical migration in winter when their food is deeply covered by snow, they descend to lower levels, not by flying, but by walking, often in single file. It is perhaps no coincidence that the mountain quail is reputed to be the most delicious of American species, though a statistic given us to mark its precious nature, its price in San Francisco at the time of the Gold Rush, does not impress us very much today—$2.50 to $4 per dozen.

When startled quail have to resort to flight, they do not do so in a fashion which creates much difficulty for hunters. In Europe the quail flies low but in a straight line, with only a slight wobble. The bobwhite may create a little more difficulty, especially if surprised in its sleeping formation, when the birds settle on the ground in a tight circle, which keeps them warm in fall and winter, but more important is the fact that the tails are in the center and the heads on the rim of the circle, giving the covey as a whole 360-degree vision. If startled, the circle explodes into the air, with the birds shooting out in all directions, like shrapnel, confusing the hunter or the predator. Quickly tired, the covey settles to the ground in a short distance, and if roused one or two times more, the birds become so exhausted that they can then be picked up in the hand.

Old World quail can hold out longer, but they exhaust themselves similarly in their migratory flights. They cross the Mediterranean by island hopping, stopping when they are so worn out that they can also be picked up without resistance, to be caged and fattened for the table. One of their island stops is Capri, whose bishop, a few centuries ago, earned himself the nickname "the Bishop of Quails" because it occurred to him to impose a tithe on the birds taken there. Sicily was another way station for migrating quail, which explains the miracle of Santa Lucia, patroness of Syracuse. The story goes that when Syracuse was stricken by famine, the saint sent great flocks of quail which fell to the ground and were easily captured; hence Syracuse today still eats quail on the saint's secondary feast day, which falls in May, the month of the spring migration.

> The quail [Brillat-Savarin wrote] is of all game . . . the most delicate and the most agreeable. A good fat quail pleases equally by its taste, its shape and its color. You show your ignorance whenever you serve it otherwise than roasted or *en papillote*, for its savor is extremely volatile and every time the animal is put in contact with liquid, it dissolves, evaporates and perishes.

He might have added that it should never be hung, an opinion shared even by those who advocate hanging other types of game.

In Brillat-Savarin's time, gourmets claimed that they could tell by the taste whether a quail had been taken when the wind was blowing north or south. Since the game season was in the fall, quail were shot or netted during their north-south migration. If they had a north wind behind them, helping them along, the reasoning went, they would not stop, and would consequently be lean and tough. If they were battling a south wind, head on, they would stop to rest, and feed on taste-building grapes, ripe at that season.

The sixteenth-century physician Antoine Mizauld recommended quail for a non-gastronomic reason, moved perhaps by the touching devotion of this bird to monogamy, an unusual habit among similar feathered game:

> Husbands who love their wives [he wrote], wives who want to be loved by their husbands, have only to take a pair of quails, from which you will extract the two hearts, to wear them on your persons, the husband that of the male, the wife that of the female, and you can count on getting along well together.

It was in Egypt that the first mass slaughter of quails was recorded. In the words of a contemporary American writer whose name I will be considerate enough not to cite, "These birds saved the people of Israel from famine—the event is told in *Exodus*. In two and a half days, nine million quail were massacred." (I am intrigued by this figure, which I do not find in the Bible; perhaps our author worked it out arithmetically, on the basis of the area the birds covered, or perhaps, knowing that Moses had 600,000 Israelites with him when he crossed the desert, he proceeded on the basis of the number of *omers* [Exodus] or *homers* [Numbers] which each person may be presumed to have consumed: an *omer* is one-tenth of an *ephah.*) It is unfortunate that this writer, before informing us that quails saved the Israelites, did not look up the more detailed account of the same event in Numbers 11:31–34, where we read:

And there went forth a wind from the Lord, and brought quails from the sea, and let them fall by the camp, as if it were a day's journey on this side, and as it were a day's journey on the other side, round about the camp, and as it were two cubits high upon the face of the earth.

And the people stood up all that day, and all that night, and all the next day, and they gathered the quails: he that gathered the least gathered ten homers: and they spread them all abroad for themselves round about the camp.

And while the flesh was yet between their teeth, ere it was chewed, the wrath of the Lord was kindled against the people, and the Lord smote the people with a very great plague.

And he called the name of that place Kibroth-hattaavah: because there they buried the people that lusted.

Modern ornithologists can explain this calamity without blaming it on the wrath of the Lord. It has been discovered that quail dote on the seeds of some poisonous plants, which they eat with an immunity which is not passed on to those who consume the birds while the poison is still in their tissues. One of their favorites is hemlock, a plant well known in the eastern Mediterranean region, where it was fatal to Socrates. It contains conine, a deadly vegetable poison which acts swiftly.

The version of Exodus was perhaps bowdlerized; it preferred to throw the emphasis on the beneficent manna, which appeared at the same time as the quail. Psalms 105:40 prefers this viewpoint too: "The people asked, and he brought quails, and satisfied them with the bread of heaven"—manna. John Dryden was not deceived. Mindful of the penchant of men for provoking their own destruction, he wrote: "We loathe our manna and we long for quails."

QUE
stands for

Queen Anne's lace, a familiar weed which is nothing other than the wild carrot; for the **queen angelfish,** eaten by natives wherever it appears despite a diabolically tough skin, and the **queenfish** of Madagascar and points west, which should be pachydermous too since it is also called the leatherskin; for the **queen triggerfish,** so named for the shape and ingenious locking mechanism of its forward dorsal fin, perhaps poisonous if it itself has just eaten contaminated food; for the **queen crab,** which I suspect is nothing but an addition to the vocabulary of those who feel that if there is a king crab there ought to be a queen crab, and the **Queensland mud crab,** whose delicious sweetness deserves a more tempting name; for the **Queensland grouper,** which is eaten by man—and vice versa, if we can believe the stories that in its largest size (twelve feet long, nearly half a ton in weight) it has swallowed skin divers, and the **Queensland nut,** which is the macadamia; for **quelites,** a "wretched vegetable" eaten by the Aztecs, according to Bernal Díaz, whose English translator could not identify it, and neither can I; and for the **quetsch,** a small acid, purple plum, superb for tarts, which botanists fight shy of classifying, but I suspect that this is only a Teutonic word for the damson.

QUI
stands for

the **quick** or **quickset thorn,** also called the white thorn or the hawthorn, apparently cultivated for its insipid mealy fruit only in India; for the **quickbeam** or **quicken,** also called the mountain ash or rowan tree, whose small, juicy scarlet berry is too sour to be eaten except in jam, though in famine times it has been ground into meal and used in bread; for **quick grass** or **quitch,** also called quack grass, couch or twitch, a form of couch grass, one of the poorest foods known to man; for the **quinnat** or Chinook, also called the king, the spring or the tyee, one of the five principal kinds of Pacific Northwest SALMON; and for **quinoa,** also called petty rice, of which both leaves and seeds are edible, grown by pre-Columbian Andean Indians in conjunction with potatoes because it provides nutritive elements which the potato lacks.

And **QUI** also stands for

QUINCE. The appreciation of taste is, I suspect, an artificial phenomenon acquired by education, like the appreciation of Western music, also an artificial phenomenon acquired by education, so that our ears accept a scale which is out of tune (and do not even perceive it is out of tune) in exchange for the ability to move up or down it without limit and to modulate without difficulty through the entire gamut of our keys. The infant is born with an uninitiated ear and unprejudiced taste buds, which at first transmit to the brain a message about the taste of whatever is being eaten without making any judgment about whether that taste is good or bad. The child learns quickly how to convert the measurable chemical and physical stimuli reaching it from the exterior into an esthetic estimate of quality—the transfiguration of mathematics into emotion. It discovers what it likes and what it does not like within the ecology of which it is a part—the biological ecology (the plants and animals it eats because they occupy the same habitat) and the social ecology (the eating habits of the society in which it lives). Once learned, these judgments harden into prejudices. That is why it takes so long for an unfamiliar food to be accepted in regions uneducated to appreciate it.

The subjective and artificial nature of our responses to the stimuli of taste is beautifully betrayed by the quince.

Almost all of us today would agree that the quince is too sour to eat fresh, and can be tolerated only when it is cooked with great quantities of sugar. The quince, says *The Practical Encyclopedia of Gardening*, almost brutally, is "of a peculiar, almost guava-like flavor when cooked (useless otherwise)." Yet in ancient times the quince was eaten as a fresh fruit, and even today, in some countries, is eaten whole cooked with a minimum of sugar.

Almost all the other venerable fruits (the quince has been cultivated for more than four thousand years) have gained in favor since antiquity; the quince has moved in the opposite direction—and only since medieval times, when, according to Paul Lacroix in his *France in the Middle Ages*, it was "generally cultivated" and "looked upon as the most useful of all fruits," and in the Orléanais "formed the basis of the farmers' dried preserves." The quince does not seem to have changed during that period: it is our gastronomic education which has changed. Since the coming of sugarcane, we have learned to demand sweetness in our food. The ancient countries where the quince was eaten fresh, and Europe in the Middle Ages, were brought up on less efficient or less plentiful sweeteners, like honey or grape sugar. They could appreciate not only foods which were sweet, but also foods which were sour.

Many taxonomists were at first reluctant to believe that the quince was a separate fruit: they thought it a kind of pear, and tagged it *Pyrus cydonia*, the Cydonian pear. It does look, after all, like a pear. It is often pear-shaped (but also sometimes a flattened sphere); it is golden yellow, like many pears; and when it is cut open the cross section resembles that of a pear, but with yellowish flesh which turns a pretty dull-pink when cooked. Since 1870, most pears have been grown on quince rootstock, which holds the height of the pear tree down, making picking easier, and encourages it to bear fruit earlier. But the quince will not hybridize with the pear, which is why it has now been decided that the quince is a quince, not a pear. Its scientific name has accordingly been changed to *Cydonia oblongata* or *C. vulgaris*, the only species of its private genus, though there are several subspecies and numerous varieties.

The quince is a native of at least Persia and Anatolia, where it still grows wild, and perhaps of an even larger area, extending into the Caucasus and Greece. We hear of its cultivation in Mesopotamia first, and next in Greece, where the ordinary mainland quince was improved by grafting onto it scions brought from Cydonia, on the island of Crete, which produced the finest quinces in the ancient world. Rome imported Cydonian quinces too, and Pliny remarked that the variety he called Mulvian was the only one which could be eaten raw, which suggests that the Romans knew fruit no less astringent than ours. Columella wrote that "quinces yield not only pleasure but also health," and distinguished three varieties, which he called the sparrow apple, the golden apple and the must apple.

The ordinary Roman name for the quince was the Cydonian apple, hence its modern scientific label. It was also called the golden apple, and it has been suggested that it was the golden apple of the Hesperides, but it seems likelier that this was the orange, or even the lemon. I do not know whether the quinces Petronius represented Trimalchio as serving at his ridiculously extravagant banquet were raw or cooked, but it would probably have been inadvisable to eat them either way, since Trimalchio had studded them with thorns to make them look, Jupiter knows why, like sea urchins.

At a slightly later period, Athenaeus wrote that Athens was importing from Corinth quinces which were "as delicious in taste as they are beautiful to the eye." For the Greeks the quince was a symbol of fertility, dedicated to the goddess of love. In Athens quinces were tossed into the bridal chariot in which the groom was conducting his bride to her new home, where she would be offered a piece of wedding cake flavored with sesame, honey and, as a charm for fruitfulness, a date or a quince.

In the Middle Ages quinces were so highly esteemed in France that presents of a quince pre-

QUINCE. *First-state plate by P. J. Redouté for Jean-Jacques Rousseau:* La Botanique, *folio edition, Paris, 1805*

serve called *cotignac*, a sort of marmalade which was a specialty of Orléans, were ordinarily made to kings, queens and princes in cities which were honored by their visits; when Joan of Arc arrived to lift the siege of Orléans, the first gift offered her was *cotignac*. The menu of a splendid banquet given by Pope Pius V in 1570 included quince pastries on its menu, with the meticulous specification: "One quince per pastry."

The best quinces of that period were held to be those of Portugal, which is why "marmalade" comes from *marmelo*, the Portuguese word for quince, the fruit originally used to make marmalade. It was not made with oranges until 1790, when orange marmalade was first manufactured in Dundee, Scotland. A British cookbook published several marmalade recipes in 1669, but none of them used oranges: most were based on quinces. The fruit was known to Chaucer, who mentions "coines," a spelling which suggests that the fruit came from France, where its name today is *coing*. Baked quinces appeared on an English banquet menu in 1446.

Quinces enjoyed a period of popularity along America's eastern coast in Colonial times. The Massachusetts Bay Colony's Memorandum of March 16, 1629, listing the seeds it wanted sent to it from England, called for quince seeds, and there are at least two seventeenth-century mentions of the quince in Virginia, in 1648 and 1669, while they were reported in 1720 to be growing there abundantly. An old New England specialty was quince cheese, preserved fruit solidified by all-day boiling, and a small amount of quince was often added to apple butter. In New England especially, the quince was once common in home gardens and was also grown in commercial orchards, but today it has lost favor even there; it is now the least grown of all tree fruits in the United States.

Elsewhere the quince has remained in favor in certain countries whose cuisine contains many fatty foods: the acidity of the quince counteracts greasiness. This is true of Germany and of South Africa, for instance. In the latter the popularity of the quince has been heightened because apples, which grow well at the Cape, do badly in the interior; the quince there replaces the apple. Quince sauce is made exactly like applesauce. Fatty meats like mutton or pork are frequently accompanied by whole baked quinces, cored, and only lightly sugared. Quinces appear fresh in *sambals*, which are mixtures of raw grated, spiced fruits and vegetables, used as condiments.

I do not know whether quinces are still eaten raw in Latin America, but they used to be. When they reached this part of the New World, brought there by the Spanish or the Portuguese or both, either the new climate produced new sweeter varieties or the acidity of the quince did not disturb the natives, who may be presumed to have had a gastronomic education different from the one which shapes our tastes now. One early nineteenth-century explorer in Chile reported large quinces there which were acid and astringent but became "sweet and good" if allowed to ripen completely. From Santa Cruz, Mexico, John Russell Bartlett, who may be presumed to have been of the orthodox American gastronomic school, wrote in 1854:

> There are two varieties of the quince here, one hard and tart like our own, the other sweet and eatable in its raw state, yet preserving the rich flavor of the former. The Mexicans gathered and ate them like apples but I found them too hard for my digestive organs.

R

RABELAIS: *Appetite comes in eating.*

RUSKIN, JOHN: *Thackeray settled like a meat-fly on whatever one had for dinner, and made one sick of it.*

ROSSETTI, DANTE GABRIEL: *Eat thou and drink; tomorrow thou shalt die.*

RAB
stands for

the **rabbit berry,** which, without change of dimensions, is the bearberry; and the **rabbitfish,** which has been colonizing the eastern Mediterranean ever since the Suez Canal was opened.

And, of course, **RAB** also stands for

RABBIT. I do not suppose that this is the primary function of the rabbit, but it can serve as a touchstone to separate food snobs from those earthy characters who really like to eat. HARE is respectable, even distinguished; rabbit is common and vulgar, and it is good form to turn up the nose at it. Almost two hundred years ago, Grimod de la Reynière wrote of it (it is true that he was referring to the domesticated variety): "It should be kept off of tables even only slightly concerned about their good reputation." The gastronomic writer who uses de la Reynière's name today as a *nom de plume* for his articles in the Paris *Le Monde,* Robert J. Courtine, notes that this is still the attitude, but he does not approve of it:

In restaurants you do not find it on the menu. It seems that the chef is ashamed to serve it. In the home it remains an occasional, almost accidental, dish, but care is taken never to cook it for a guest. A hostess would be ashamed also.

But why the devil is that? Is it because rabbit stands, first of all, for *gibelotte?*

Gibelotte, a popular word not found in all French dictionaries, is rabbit stew. It has been referred to disdainfully as a janitor's dish; and indeed, not so very long ago, I can remember that many a Paris courtyard sheltered a rabbit hutch maintained by the concierge, "between the washtub and a discarded mattress," like that of the concierge of Balzac's Cousin Pons, skilled at producing a savory *gibelotte.* Rabbit, not only stewed, but roasted, fried or grilled, appeared frequently in humble workmen's bistros, like the one where I ate almost daily in 1927 (it was cheap), and in the *guingettes,* the light-hearted establishments, all but vanished now, usually found on the banks of the Seine or the Marne, given to outdoor eating and dancing (see Renoir's *Le Moulin de la Galette.*

[Rabbit] is the festive dish of the country dweller as of the workman [wrote Fulbert-Dumonteil, I do not know whether in this century or the last], the game of the humble. . . . It is present at all banquets; it presides over the weddings of the suburbs and the baptisms of the villages. Its robust scent pervades the farms and the *guingettes.*

Forgetting that there are snobs in France too, another food writer tried to turn appreciation of rabbit into a national trait: "In Australia it is abhorred, in America despised, elsewhere ignored. It has to have the air, the grass and the sky of France." It is true that the French are much more given to eating rabbit than, for instance, Americans. The United States consumes 50 million pounds of rabbit meat a year, which sounds like a lot until you compare it with the scale of the country's population. This tots up, if my arithmetic is correct, to about 3½ ounces per person. The Frenchman eats 6.6 pounds, about thirty times as much; more than a quarter of French revenues from barnyard animals, meaning poultry and rabbits, comes from the latter.

The rabbit was once much more popular in America. Among its fanciers was Thomas Jefferson.

Old Master had a great many rabbits [his former slave, Isaac, told an interviewer in 1847]. Made chains for the old buck rabbits to keep them from killin' the young ones. Had a rabbit house—a long rock house. Some of 'em white, some blue; they used to burrow underground.

They may not all have been natives. Jefferson wrote to James Madison from France on March 3, 1817: "I propose also to endeavor to colonize their hare, rabbit," etc., but I do not know whether he did or not.

The rabbit (and the hare) reached America before the Europeans did. The Aztecs had a rabbit god, associated with the moon, who presided also over Mexico's most characteristic alcoholic drink, *pulque*. Pre-Columbian Indians ate a great deal of rabbit; the Shoshone had an elaborate system of communal hunting, brought into action whenever rabbits were plentiful. Nets hundreds of feet long were set up in a tremendous semicircle, in a position chosen by an experienced hunter (whom the whites dubbed "the rabbit boss"), and the women and children of all the tribes in the vicinity drove the animals into the nets, where the men clubbed them to death. At one locality, arriving Europeans found rabbits so plentiful that they named the place for them—Coney Island. (Coney, or cony, is the old name for the rabbit, still used today in the fur industry.)

Americans seem to have an aversion for the word "hare," preferring to call all animals of this sort rabbits, for instance the snowshoe rabbit and the jackrabbit, which are both hares. The hare genus is *Lepus*, the rabbit genus is *Oryctolagus*, but the taxonomists were baffled by America's commonest animal of this type, the cottontail, which exists in every state of the Union, and stands somewhere on the middle ground between rabbit and hare. They swept the problem under the rug by abandoning both *Lepus* and *Oryctolagus* and baptizing the cottontail *Sylvilagus floridanus*. Of *O. cuniculus*, the common rabbit—from which, though it is still abundant wild, all our domestic varieties have been developed—the *Encyclopaedia Britannica* informs us so many different kinds have been bred that there are more variations among rabbits than among any other domesticated animal except the dog. I wonder if the author of this statement did not really mean more than any other mammal, for there is also a bewildering number of varieties among chickens; but I must admit that I have counted neither of them.

The rabbit was one of the last of our familiar farm animals to become domesticated,

probably due to the limited distribution of the wild form in the post-glacial period [Don and Patricia Brothwell speculate in *Food in Antiquity*]. This appears to have been common only in the extreme south-west of Europe, though it had begun to spread by Roman times. . . . Both hares and rabbits . . . were reared in the Roman *leporaria*, this method of enclosure continuing through into medieval times.

It is perhaps not quite certain that the rabbit (and the hare) were sparsely distributed in the post-glacial period. We are usually told of both of them that they are native to southwestern Europe, though some authorities think they originated in northwestern Africa, crossed from there into Spain, and then expanded into France on the way to invading the rest of the world. Since the first Europeans to settle America found rabbits and hares already firmly established there, and since their bones have been found in prehistoric American Indian sites, it would seem that they must have been among the species which crossed the Bering Strait before the post-glacial period; and for that to happen, they must also have reached the Far East in time to migrate. (It is not impossible, since American Indian prehistory does not go back as far as, for example, Middle Eastern prehistory, that they were introduced by the Vikings or by the pre-Columbian fishermen who sought cod on the Grand Banks of Newfoundland.)

This, of course, applies to the wild animal; as for domestication, it seems likely that this did not begin until the Christian era. The rabbits the Romans "reared" were probably not genuinely domesticated; they were wild animals, caged after being netted for fattening before being transferred to the table. There was, indeed, little incentive to domesticate an animal which could be so easily taken wild, especially as wild rabbits are better flavored than domestic ones. One theory is that rabbits were first domesticated in medieval

RABBIT. Three Rabbits, *colors on silk, Ming Dynasty (1368–1644) in the style of Kung Chi of Northern Sung Dynasty (960–1280)*

Rabbit

monasteries of strict disciplines, where meat was seldom or never eaten. The Church had ruled that the flesh of newly born or not-yet-born rabbits (the monks ate their fetuses) was not meat. (From time to time, when a wave of austerity swept over the Church, it would be decreed that even this could not be eaten on fast days.)

It has never proved possible to domesticate hares, though it has been tried, because they refuse to breed in captivity; but rabbits are notorious for their readiness to breed anywhere and everywhere. Because of the frequency and size of their litters, rabbits can increase with frightening rapidity whenever natural checks cease to operate. Pliny and Varro both reported that so many rabbit burrows were hollowed out under the city of Tarragona, Spain, that twenty-five or thirty houses collapsed into the undermined soil. The modern example of the unwonted speed with which rabbits multiply is of course that of Australia, where they were brought into a land where there were no natural predators and rapidly became a scourge of the countryside. However, when Alexandre Dumas tells us that a single wild female can give birth to 800 or 900 young in a year and that domesticated rabbits reach ten times that number, we are not obliged to believe him. The common wild rabbit will have at most seven litters in a year, and at most, eight young per litter—total, 56. Even if we multiply this by his also exaggerated figure for domestic births, we are still far short of the fertility he attributes to the wild animal. It is true that some of the females born at the beginning of a year may be raising families themselves before its end, for they can reproduce at the age of six months, and their gestation period is thirty days. In practice, domestic breeders prefer not to mate their females before the age of eight months, and the males not before one year. When more than six are born in a single litter, those above that number are taken from the mother and placed with other females which have fallen short of six, otherwise some of them will be runts.

The wild rabbit is much superior to the domesticated race in flavor, almost as good as hare. In France it is called the *lapin de garenne*, from the old feudal word *garenne*, which meant a game preserve. The domesticated rabbit is the *lapin de choux*, the cabbage rabbit, from its principal food. Food is all-important in giving zest to rabbit meat. Wild rabbits which in France feed in those areas where thyme, rosemary and similar fragrant herbs grow wild have a superb savor. Domesticated rabbits are as good as their raiser allows them to be. In my own home we have rabbit brought in from country farms, but even so, there is great variation in their taste, depending on how generously they have been nourished. Rabbit flesh is close-textured, and it can be rubbery if the animal has not been fed to plumpness. Rabbit does not have enough natural fat to produce its own gravy; in cooking, it usually requires added fat if the result is to be satisfactory.

Food falsifiers are always with us, and rabbits have not escaped their attention. Since the better-flavored wild rabbits have patches of reddish hair under the tail and on the feet, the fur on these parts of the domestic animal is singed in an attempt to pass it off as its wild cousin. The fraud is easy enough to unveil if you are wary: often this operation leaves the odor of burnt hair behind it, and if it doesn't, washing the suspected parts will make the color come off. This has lost its point nowadays, since nobody any more buys unskinned rabbits, much less live ones, as many cooks did not very long ago. Another form of fraud could only be practiced with cooked animals: cat was substituted for rabbit. This was once so common in Spanish inns that the language still contains, as a synonym for swindling, the phrase *vender gato por liebre*, "to sell a cat for a hare" (or rabbit).

Perhaps this did not always make very much difference. Fynes Moryson, writing of English food in the early seventeenth century, reported on the fondness for hare, and continued: "They have also great plenty of conies the flesh whereof is fat, tender, and more delicate than any I have eaten in other parts. The German conies are more like roasted cats."

RAC
stands for

the **raccoon,** which you might try stuffing with sweet potatoes the next time you roast one, and the **raccoon berry,** which is not a berry, but the May apple, which is not an apple, but the American mandrake, which is not a real mandrake, so you can eat its fruit without danger, but it is perhaps safer to shy away from the root.

RAD
stands for

radicchio, Italian red winter lettuce, *un fiore che si mangia,* "a flower which is eaten," they say of it in Treviso, where it is a specialty.

And **RAD** also stands for

RADISH. Radishes, Georges Gibault tells us in his *Histoire des Légumes,* "are nothing more than appetite-provoking condiments," and Alexandre Dumas starts his entry on this vegetable in his *Grand Dictionnaire de Cuisine*: "The radish offers us more than ten different varieties, and it is unnecessary to say that they are only eaten raw." Unnecessary—and untrue. There are more radishes in heaven and earth, Alexandre, than are dreamt of in your philosophy—or in mine either, for that matter. When I came upon a recipe for pickling radish pods in Mrs. J. Chadwick's *Home Cookery* (New York, 1852), I wondered what vegetable could be meant by "radish pods." Not radishes, certainly. Radishes don't have pods. I knew that because I had grown them myself.

Well, radishes *do* have pods, which look very much like those of peas or beans. I had never seen them because they do not appear until after the radish has passed the pink of perfection, and mine had always been pulled up before they got around even to thinking about pods. Perhaps more than any other vegetable, radishes have to be harvested young, as soon as they become edible. An old radish is a worthless radish—woody, usually wormy and frequently hollow in the center.

Radishes, Dumas to the contrary, *are* cooked. And while he was right about there being more—many more—than ten varieties, he was perhaps not quite right in the way he understood it. All the radishes which are important in the human diet belong to a single species, *Raphanus sativus*, though you would not think it to look at them. From the gastronomic point of view we might divide them into four groups: radishes raised primarily for their roots (including the familiar kind we eat); radishes raised for their pods; radishes raised for their leaves; and radishes raised for their seeds—or more precisely, for the oil which can be pressed from them.

The radish is believed to have been under cultivation in Europe as early as Neolithic times; its origin is uncertain, for it is so old that the original wild ancestor of *R. sativus* has disappeared. Some botanists suggest that *R. raphanistrum*, a wild radish which is a troublesome weed in the Mediterranean area, was the one *R. sativus* came from. Others think not, and propose instead the Spanish radish (a belittling name, for its range runs from the Iberian Peninsula to the Caucasus), *R. maritimus*. But both of these species are native to Europe, and the majority opinion holds that the radish probably originated in the Far East, specifically in China. It is still China (with Japan) which makes the greatest use of the radish as a full-fledged food, not simply as an appetizer, and the oldest documentary reference to the radish known to me comes from China, in the *Rhya*, of 1100 B.C.

RADISH *by Jim Dine.* Radishes, *1972, watercolor and graphite pencil*

It is possible that in ancient Egypt the first cultivated radishes were those grown for radish-seed oil; Egypt used it before it acquired the olive. Presumably there were more substantial eating radishes too, if we believe Herodotus, who tells us that he saw in Egypt an inscription honoring radishes, onions and leeks as the foods which supplied the necessary strength to the workers who built the pyramids. This seems to overestimate the muscle-building merits of the radish, a vegetable dear to weight-watchers because it offers almost no nourishment, its contribution to the human diet being vitamin B, iron and sulfur (the last accounts for its sharp peppery taste and also for the fact that it is not always easy to digest and should therefore be chewed thoroughly). Radish-seed oil was still so important in Pliny's time that he complained about farmers who ceased to grow grain in order to sow radishes because they produced great quantities of profitable high-priced oil. In China a special variety of *R. sativus* is cultivated today for its seeds and their oil. The very pungent seeds of the "wild radish," *R. raphanistrum* (also known as wild mustard, jointed charlock or runch), are used as a substitute for mustard seeds. India uses a good deal of radish-seed oil, but from varieties developed primarily not for their seeds, but for their leaves.

Upper Egypt cultivates a special type of radish exclusively for its leaves; the leaves of *R. raphanistrum* are also sometimes eaten; the poor of Italy make salads from the leaves of landra, the Italian radish, *R. landra*; and in the ancient world Dioscorides reported that Spanish radishes were used as potherbs. For that matter, the young tender leaves of our ordinary radish can be eaten fresh, like cress, or boiled, like greens.

The radish oftenest raised for its pods, especially in India (which eats its leaves too), is *R. sativus* var. *caudatus*, the rat-tailed radish (or snake radish to the French), so called because the long root does not swell into edibility: all the plant's vigor goes into the pods, frequently twisted, which reach a length of eight to twelve inches. They are eaten raw, like the common radish root, and taste about the same, and are also pickled.

The radishes raised for their roots include our own familiar radish ("gay and playful," according to William Wallace Irwin), which is simply *R. sativus* with no modifying varietal name—small, usually red or red and white, which may be a sphere, an oblong or a cone. Today it is usually confined to pre-meal munching or, sliced, to adding spiciness to salads. It covered a little more ground in earlier times. Not so long ago it was served as a salad on its own, with vinaigrette sauce, in some French provinces; or it was cooked, in any fashion suitable for turnips.

It is a little strange that this radish has remained almost alone among root radishes in the West, for another group, intrinsically more interesting as food, seems to have been present in southern Europe during antiquity, and in northern Europe into the Renaissance period; but its members are now eaten chiefly in the Far East. This is the winter-radish family of radishes, which are slower to grow and keep correspondingly longer, well into the winter, for their flesh is solid and firm, and does not, like that of our more familiar radishes, become spongy and tasteless if not eaten within a few days of being pulled up, nor does it become hollow. These radishes include the famous Japanese daikon, *R. sativus* var. *longipinnatus*, a white giant often three feet long; a rose-colored Chinese radish, long and thick; and a number of black radishes. "Black radish," incidentally, is a much-abused term: properly it represents certain varieties, but it is also used as a synonym for the Spanish radish; it often means black salsify; and if you ask in Paris for horseradish (*Cochlearia armoracia*), black radish (*R. sativus* var. *nigra*) is what you get. These radishes can be eaten raw, and frequently are, but they are very often cooked; the effect is turnip-like, with less sweetness. They are also pickled; the Japanese like to finish a meal with a bit of pickled daikon to cleanse the mouth.

It seems that only this type of radish can account for ancient and medieval references to this vegetable which imply that it played a more substantial role in the meal than that of a mere appetizer. It seems to have been known in Europe in prehistoric times. Though the ancient Greek and Roman names for different kinds of radishes are difficult to match to our own, both small and large root radishes seem to have been present. In Greece, where a physician named Moschian wrote a whole book about radishes, Theophrastus listed five kinds, of which he described the Boeotian variety as the sweetest and best. This seems to have been our common radish of today, which is indeed milder than most of the others; but it may have been the large cooking varieties which won so much esteem from the Greeks that when making vegetable sacrifices to the gods they "presented" turnips in lead, beets in silver and radishes in gold—a wording which has inspired some to assert that the offerings were replicas of these foods modeled in metal, but it can be understood that it was only the platters on which they were placed which were so made.

The Greeks thought more highly of the radish than Pliny, who, apart from its usefulness in producing oil, called it "a vulgar article of the diet," and pointed out that radishes "have a remarkable power of causing flatulence and eructation." Cowper nevertheless was not far off when he described "a Roman meal . . . a radish and an egg," except that the egg was a trifle much if he was speaking of breakfast, as should have been the case. "Bread and a relish" was the usual Roman opening of the day, and the relish could be radish.

When an English manuscript dated 1440 suggested that under Henry IV few vegetables were eaten in England except lettuce, cabbage, spinach and radishes, it would seem that the radishes should have been of the large cooking type now eaten almost exclusively in the Far East; and from the descriptions of their size by Albertus Magnus in the thirteenth century and of Rembert Dodoens, who called it the common radish of England, in the sixteenth, this super-radish should have been the one most eaten in northern Europe. However, Gerard, a contemporary of Dodoens, who said that there were four varieties, seemed to be speaking of our small radishes when he explained that they were "eaten raw with bread," but perhaps not when he reported that another kind was "used as a sauce with meates to procure appetite."

I have no idea why Oaxaca, Mexico, celebrates the Night of the Radishes on December 23 by carving giant radishes into fantastic figures of animals and people.

According to the serious authority of one of the world's most scholarly works, the great Liddell and Scott Greek-English dictionary, adultery was punished in ancient Greece by thrusting a radish up the rectum of the offender. The species used is not identified.

RAG
stands for

ragee, a tropical cereal of which Georg Schweinfuth said unenthusiastically in his *The Heart of Africa* (1874) that "it has a disagreeable taste and makes only a wretched sort of pop"; for **ragged sailors,** which is chicory, whose pretty blue flowers have a tattered appearance; and for **rag paper,** our eighteenth name for the mullein.

RAI
stands for

the **rail,** a game bird which lives in marshes and is therefore referred to inelegantly as the mudhen; for the **rainbow trout,** so called because of a reddish band along its flanks, and the **rainbow wrasse,** so called because of an orange band, ditto; and for the **rain tree,** which yields edible pods to Mexicans, and the **raisin tree,** which yields agreeable fruit to Hindus.

RAK
stands for

rakam, a Siamese fruit which resembles a strawberry.

RAM
stands for

the **ram,** which you had better leave to the ewes unless you like your MUTTON strong; for **rambutan** (otherwise **rampostan**), a Malaysian fruit which looks like a chestnut and has a flavor which, according to E. Lewis Sturtevant, "perhaps is more agreeable than any other in the whole vegetable kingdom"; for **ramontchi,** the batoko plum, common in the jungles of India, which isn't a plum; for the **ramoon tree** of the West Indies, whose berries are the size of grapes and as pleasant to eat; for **rampion,** now neglected, of which the leaves were once much eaten, raw in salads or cooked like spinach, while the roots, which taste like walnuts, were also eaten raw or cooked; for **ramsom,** or bear's garlic, as much stronger than man's garlic as bears are stronger than men; and for **ramtil,** an Abyssinian plant whose seeds yield a sweet bland oil.

RAN
stands for

the **Rangoon bean,** a name which makes it sound more exotic than what it is, the familiar lima bean, a doughty traveler now found in most parts of the world; and for the **Ranunculus** genus, to which the buttercup belongs, whose seeds were used by the ancient Egyptians for flavoring cakes, especially those of *Ranunculus edulis,* otherwise known as the egg-yolk.

RAP
stands for

rape, from whose seeds an edible oil is expressed, nowadays usually called colza, perhaps because the older name was felt to be in bad odor, but so is colza now, for some food purists have accused it of being unhealthy.

RAS
stands for

rascasse, the one indispensable fish for a Mediterranean bouillabaisse, to which its venom contributes a needed fillip.

And **RAS** also stands for

RASPBERRY. "There is a harmony among all things and the places where they are found," I wrote twenty years ago in *The Food of France.* "Would you need to know the name of the Pekinese to realize that it was originally from China? The peacock, and for that matter the common hen, are obviously natives of India. Where could the eucalyptus have come from except Australia?"

Similarly the flavor of the raspberry stamps it "Made in Asia." It breathes of the Orient—rich, exotic, spice-laden and with a hint of musk. Botanists, who are not allowed to believe the evidence of the palate and the nose, will not say flatly that the raspberry is a native of Asia, but most of them think it is, and even narrow its area to eastern Asia, where there are more than two hundred known species. (Europe has only one;

North America has three important species and a few minor ones.)

The raspberry is the most perfumed among its sort of fruits; it is hard to understand the disdain with which it was treated for centuries west of Mount Ida—Mount Ida, because it was on the flanks of that mountain (the one in Turkey, not the one on Crete) that the finest raspberries of antiquity were gathered, which is why the European species is called *Rubus idaeus* today. It was perhaps precisely because of its markedly Oriental character that the Occident found it at first incompatible with its tastes. Not until the Crusaders approached Jerusalem did they also begin to approach the raspberry, inspiring one of their poets to observe that

Raspberries grow by the way,
With pleasure you may assay.

Moving in the opposite direction, they would have found little sympathy for the raspberry, especially in the Latin countries, whose spirit was the essence of the Occident and hence the antithesis of the spirit of the East. Pliny mentioned the raspberry, but only as a wild fruit, and the Romans did not bother to cultivate it. Indeed, only a few years ago when I was in Italy, it occurred to me that I could not remember ever having seen raspberries there. I inquired of a *maître d'hôtel* if they were not eaten in Italy; he could not identify the fruit from my description, nor could he suggest a possible name for it. Twenty-four hours and one dictionary later, I asked him about *lampone*, but he still looked blank; several other Italians questioned in the next few days had never heard of it either.

In France, as we know from a chance reference to them by Bruyérin-Champier, physician to Henry II (1519–1559), raspberries were known there only as a wild fruit; not until the next century would they be cultivated. Even today French reference books are vague about the raspberry, although it is not difficult to find it on the market; one gastronomic dictionary defines it as "a cultivatable wild thorn plant." Except as a basis for beverages, the raspberry has only in this century become more or less familiar in France, where it is found in appreciative private homes, and in luxury restaurants rather than humble ones. For that matter, despite no dearth of raspberries, they were still considered a luxury in the United States as late as 1840, when the Whigs attacked Martin Van Buren during his presidential campaign for wallowing lasciviously in raspberries.

In England, raspberry cultivation dates from about 1630. Yet wild raspberries had been eaten in Europe since prehistoric times. They have been found in Mesolithic sites in Denmark, Neolithic sites in Switzerland and Iron Age sites in England. Germany may have been a little quicker about cultivating raspberries (and it consumes more of them today) because there the way to adopting these Eastern fruits was not barred by too large a dosage of anti-Oriental Latin culture.

Another reason for the delay in cultivating the raspberry may have been that it was already good enough wild; it did not call for the expenditure of effort. Individual raspberry plants can differ greatly in quality, and there is of course more variability in wild berries than in cultivated ones, but in general it is fairly safe to assert that in the United States most tasters would not find the wild black raspberry inferior to the cultivated varieties, while the wild red raspberry is considered by some to be superior to the cultivated fruit, in the sense that the peculiarities of the raspberry flavor are in the wild berry more marked, more savage—cultivation has tamed it. Yellow raspberries are mutants of red raspberries and taste like them; black and purple varieties taste quite different. Other factors being equal, raspberries picked from canes which started their growth the previous year have a fuller flavor than those picked in September or October from the current year's canes. (After raspberry canes have fruited, the whole branch dies, and should be cut away to allow new canes to rise from the root.)

The raspberry defends itself ferociously against pickers with vicious thick-set thorns, and it proves thorny to taxonomists too. "Perhaps no genus of plants [*Rubus*], except Crataegus," says *The Practical Encyclopedia of Gardening*, "is in such a chaotic condition as to Latin names and identities as the brambles. While there are supposed to be 400–500 species, some authorities recognize nearly twice this number." (*Crataegus* is a prickly genus too, that of the hawthorns.) One of the first problems in identifying raspberries is to distinguish them from blackberries. Both are compound fruits, with small drupelets clustered tightly together around a central core. Pick one, and if the fruit comes off the core, a small white cylinder which remains attached to the plant, while the fruit shows a corresponding cuplike depression in its top, it is a raspberry. The core of the blackberry is part of the fruit and comes away with it.

In Europe the raspberry situation is simple. The European raspberry, *R. idaeus*, sometimes called in England by its French name, *framboise*, is the only species. It grows almost everywhere throughout Europe, as far north as Scandinavia, and

RASPBERRY. *Drawing from John Lewis Childs:* Seed Catalogue of Specialties and Novelties, *1911*

extends through northern Asia into the Orient (more precisely, it extends from Asia into the Occident). With native American raspberries all around them, the early American colonists preferred to import and grow this one, no doubt because they were used to it, until the Civil War, when there were forty-one cultivated varieties of the single European species on record as against only twenty-three of the several American species. "Wild" European raspberries are still found in Vermont and Connecticut, escapees from gardens, their seeds carried into the woods by birds.

Four chief groups of raspberries are grown in the United States today, in the order of their cultivation the European raspberry, the American red raspberry, the American black raspberry and the purple-cane raspberry, a hybrid between red and black.

The American red raspberry is *R. strigosus,* first heard of in 1607 when the French lawyer, traveler and writer Marc Lescarbot accompanied an expedition to Canada and reported that his fellow explorers "amused themselves by gathering raspberries." Edward Winslow listed it among wild Massachusetts fruits in 1621. There were at least six cultivated varieties at the time of the Civil War, when the United States began to turn from the European raspberry to its own native kinds.

We are usually told that the American black raspberry is *R. occidentalis,* also called the blackcap or thimbleberry, whose rich acid flavor makes it perhaps the best of all raspberries for cooking. It is perverse enough, though "black," to turn up sometimes in the wild state masquerading as red or even yellow. This is an eastern species, and there is also a western black raspberry, *R. leucodermis.* Ignoring some other minor North American raspberries, a scattering of Latin-American species and, certainly, the two hundred kinds of Asia, we may bow briefly to the peculiarly flavored Rocky Mountain or boulder raspberry, R. *deliciosus*; the dwarf raspberry, R. *triflorus*; and the lowbush raspberry, named in derisive Latin R. *trivialis.*

Some writers class the wineberry, R. *phoenicolasius*, among the raspberries, others do not. It seems to be agreed that the salmonberry is no more than a close relative; and those who describe the crackleberry as a trailing raspberry are probably indulging in a spot of poetic license.

The worst insult ever delivered to the raspberry was the fault of Joris Karl Huysmans, who should have forfeited forever his reputation for esthetic sensitiveness when he spread raspberry jelly on buttered gingerbread and actually ate it.

RAT
stands for

the **rat**, which Thoreau said he ate "fried . . . with a good relish"; for **rat's tail grass**, whose seeds are eaten in West Africa, and **rat's vein**, whose leaves were, and perhaps still are, used in American home medicine; and for the **rattlesnake**, whose (I am told) tasty meat is said to cure stomach ulcers, and **rattlesnake root**, which is said to cure rattlesnake bites.

RAV
stands for

the **raven**, of whose meat the Hebrews, no doubt to their deep regret, were deprived by the edict of Leviticus; and for the **ravensara**, a clovelike spice of Madagascar.

RAY
stands for

the **ray**, or skate, a fish which, in contrast to its fellows, is said to be better eating when it is not fresh, and the **ray's bream**, a fish which, in conformity with its fellows, is better eating when it *is* fresh.

RAZ
stands for

the **razorback hog** of the southeastern United States, in which the romantically inclined see a descendant of the imported wild boar and the literally minded only a domestic pig gone wild; and for the **razor clam**, the world's fastest burrower, which, laid on the sand, can disappear from sight in seven seconds and continue downward at the rate of nine inches a minute.

REC
stands for

Recluz's moon shell, an edible mollusk of the California and Mexican coasts which is wrapped bewilderingly around itself like a cornucopia which has lost its way.

RED
(when it is a question of fish)
stands for

the **red bandfish**, called by the French the ribbon or the belt, much eaten on the African side of the Mediterranean, and the **red bream**, much eaten on both sides of the Mediterranean; for the **redeye**, which in the Pacific Northwest is the rock bass, and the **redfish**, which in the same Pacific Northwest seems to mean a specially marked type of salmon, but which on Cape Ann, Massachusetts, when I lived there, meant a white fish with red spots believed by the locals to cause cancer, so instead of eating it themselves they canned it for foreigners west of Boston; for the **red gurnard**, a sort of sea robin, and the **red** **MULLET**, whose name is frequently attached to the red gurnard, but in error; for the **red salmon**, which is not only a color description but also a species description, identifying it as being the sockeye or blueback; for the **red snapper**, a popular name with little scientific precision, which means whatever it does wherever you are, and the **red sea snapper**, which is white with yellow trimmings; for the **red soldierfish** of the Indo-Pacific, which is actually a squirrelfish; and for the exceptionally tasty **red stumpnose** of South Africa, which is also called the Roman, though the Roman nose is far from being a stump.

RED
(when it is a question of shellfish)
stands for

the **red** **ABALONE**, largest of its clan, a slowpoke of which the female takes six years to reach the spawning size of four inches across; for the **red cockle**, alias the prickly cockle, which is less red than pink, and that on the inside of its shell; and for the **red turban** of America's Pacific coast, which is also called the top shell, but so are a good many others.

RED
(when it is a question of crustaceans)
seems to stand only for

the Pacific **red crab**, which like the red salmon

has a name which describes not only its color but also its species.

RED
(when it is a question of birds)
stands for

the **redbreast,** or European robin, a bird too endearing to be eaten, but it is, and the **red-headed woodpecker,** a bird too handsome to be eaten, and it isn't, or so I hope; and for the **redshank,** a shore bird which in 1552 yielded a quota of its members to the pantry of Sir William Petre, Henry VIII's Secretary of State.

RED
(when it is a question of meat animals)
stands for

the **red deer,** excellent eating, but gourmets rank it only third in its class, behind the roe DEER and the fallow deer; and for the **Red Steppes** cattle of the Russian Ukraine.

RED
(when it is a question of trees)
stands for

the **redbud,** or Judas tree, whose flowers are edible; for the **red cedar,** whose seeds are eaten in West Africa; and for the **red elm,** which is the slippery elm, whose inner bark was used by our grandmothers only as medicine, but which American Indians boiled with buffalo, and Euell Gibbons made junket from it.

RED
(when it is a question of seasonings)
stands for

the **red bay** of Florida's Okefenokee Swamp, whose leaves are so aromatic that they evoke the exotic spices of the East; for **red pepper,** which is not pepper, but a CHILI; for **redroot,** which, silly as it sounds, is green amaranth; and for **red salt,** a seasoning used in Polynesia, and if anyone knows its exact nature, I would appreciate being told about it.

RED
(when it is a question of fruit)
stands for

the **Red Astrachan,** an apple introduced into the United States from Russia because it delights in severe winters; for the **red currant,** which sometimes becomes the white CURRANT when pigmentation goes awry; for the **Red Delicious,** the world's best-selling APPLE, of which, A. J. Liebling wrote, "people with . . . apathy toward decided flavor . . . have made a triumph because it doesn't taste like an apple"; for the **red haw,** or hawthorn, of which Euell Gibbons reported the opinion of a friend: "When they are good, they are not very good, and when they are bad, they are horrid"; for the **red** MANGO, as handsome to look at as it is good to eat; and for the **red whortleberry,** which, in Canada at least, is the mountain cranberry.

RED
(when it is a question of vegetables)
stands for

the **red** BEAN, which in China is a type of soybean and in Louisiana is an object for worship; for **red** CABBAGE, so much relished by deer that I was never able to get any to eat myself on my Vermont farm; and for the **red flower,** which in the Ivory Coast, where its seeds are munched, is called the silk-cotton tree, and in Jamaica, where its young leaves and buds are cooked like okra, is called the god-tree.

REE
stands for

reed birds, which was what early nineteenth-century American cookbooks called for in order to avoid confessing that they were catering to an appetite for bobolinks; for the **reed buck,** of which enough still remain alive outside the animal preserves to provide meat for tropical Africans; and for the **reed mace,** so called in England, where its shape recalls the symbol of power of such august institutions as the House of Commons and the Lord Mayoralty of London, but in the United States it evokes the more rustic image of the cattail.

REI
stands for

the **reindeer,** the staff of life for the Lapps, in more ways than one, which for all practical purposes is simply a domesticated caribou; for the **reine-claude,** a luscious PLUM so named for ambiguous reasons; and for the **reinette,** which originally meant an apple propagated by grafting, as opposed to the pippin, an apple raised from seed.

REN
stands for

renkon, or lotus root, a specialty of Japan; and

for **rennet,** which the heroic American housewife of the last century removed personally from the stomachs of calves.

RES
stands for

restharrow, so named because its strong, deep-buried roots could check a plow in its course, of which John Gerard wrote: "The tender sprigs or crops of this shrub before the thornes come forth, are preserved in pickle, and be very pleasant sauce to be eaten with meat as sallad, as Dioscorides teacheth."

RH
stands for

rhinoceros, which is not yet a rare meat in tropical Africa, and **rhino-fish,** the "African carp," even commoner in the same area; for the **Rhode Island Greening,** which is a green apple, as one would expect, but apple history attributes its name to the fact that it was produced in 1748 by a tavernkeeper named Green at Green's End, near Newport, and the **Rhode Island Red,** a hen which is an indefatigable egg layer; and for the **Rhodesian pimpernel,** whose leaves are eaten occasionally as a vegetable in a few parts of Africa, not including Rhodesia, and the **Rhodesian plum,** whose fruit is eaten avidly in many parts of Africa, not excluding Rhodesia.

And **RH** also stands for

RHUBARB. Antonio Pigafetta, chronicler of the Magellan expedition which first circumnavigated the world, seems to have been depending largely on hearsay when he wrote from Siam:

> Rhubarb grows in this place, and it is found thus: Twenty or twenty-five men gather together and they go into the forest, and when night falls, they climb into the trees, as much to catch the scent of the rhubarb as for fear of the lions, elephants and other wild animals. And the wind carries the odor of the rhubarb to them from where it is growing, then when day comes, they go in that direction, and search until they find it. Rhubarb is a large rotted tree. And if it were not rotted, it would not give off such a good odor. This tree has a root, but the wood is the rhubarb and it is called *calama.*

The description of rhubarb as a large rotted tree is somewhat disconcerting; but Lord Henry Stanley provided the explanation in his book on the Magellan voyage: "Pigafetta has confounded rhubarb with the decayed wood of a tree found in Siam, which, when burnt, gives a very sweet perfume, and which sells at a high price."

Pigafetta was at least on the right continent. Nobody knows what the original species is, and there is little point in trying to identify it, since our rhubarb is not likely to have had a single ancestor. It does not breed true from seed, usually the sign of a hybrid, and therefore has to be propagated by cutting the root into pieces with a bud attached to each, and then planting them separately, as we plant potatoes. But if we do not know what the first rhubarb plant was, we are pretty sure we know where it was—in northern Asia, though whether first in Siberia, Mongolia, northern China or Tartary remains uncertain. It is from China that we hear of it first, in the Pen-king herbal, believed to date from 2700 B.C. It was described there as a medicine and would continue to be regarded as that, and not as a food, for four and a half millennia, during which time its root was widely used as a purgative.

Rhubarb reached the Western world about the beginning of the Christian era. Dioscorides and Pliny both mentioned it, but considered it unimportant. How did it get from northeastern Asia to the Mediterranean at a time when the Greeks and Romans did not even suspect the existence of the countries from which it came? The answer is in its name, which is a description of an itinerary. "Rhubarb" comes from the Latin *Rhabarbarum,* "Rha of the barbarians." Rha is the name of the river on whose banks rhubarb was cultivated by the barbarians. The name of the Rha today is the Volga; the barbarians who lived along it were Tartars. The scientific name of our common garden rhubarb, also taken over from antiquity, is even more explicit: *Rheum rhaponticum,* rhubarb which comes from the Rha, which flows into the Pontus. *Pontus* in Latin, *pontos* in Greek, was the sea—on the sea, the Greeks wrote, *epi oinopa ponton,* "the wine-dark sea, the scrotum-tightening sea." But which sea? Not the Mediterranean, which was *mare*; not the Atlantic, which was *oceanus.* When the word *pontus* was used, alone, with no accompanying name to tell which sea it was, it was understood that it was the most important after the Atlantic and the Mediterranean—Pontus Euxinus, the Black Sea, into which the Volga flows.

Rhubarb does not loom large in the history of food, but we catch a glimpse of it from time to time, sometimes from travelers, mostly Venetian, including, of course, Marco Polo, who wrote that from China it was exported "far and wide," and sometimes from writers, like the Arab Ibn-el-Beithar, who in the thirteenth century wrote that rhubarb was by then "very common in Syria and

RHUBARB. *Engraving from Culpeper:* English Physician, *Dr. Ebenezer Sibly quarto edition, London, 1805*

Persia . . . like chard, it has fairly thick stalks." The comparison suggests that he may have realized that it was good to eat, and even which part of the plant should be eaten. In the West, it had not yet occurred to anybody that rhubarb was edible, and when the idea dawned, Westerners began by eating the wrong part. Rhubarb trickled into European apothecaries throughout the Middle Ages, but it arrived in the form of a root already cleaned and prepared for sale. Europe did not know what the plant looked like, not even the not-so-distant variety Ibn-el-Beithar was talking about, *R. ribes*, the currant-fruited rhubarb, which does indeed taste like currants. The sixteenth-century botanist Leonhard Rauwolf saw it in Lebanon sometime between 1573 and 1575, but he does not seem to have brought any back with him, and it would not be imported into France until 1724, when the *Bon Jardinier* was to describe it as the best kind of rhubarb.

Meanwhile the plant was already growing in Europe unnoticed in monastery gardens (imported, probably, by missionaries) to stock abbey pharmacies with its medicinal roots. It emerged into the lay sector when Adolf Occo, a physician of Augsburg, planted it in Germany and reported the fact in the pharmacopoeia he published in 1570. In 1578 Henry Lyte, the English translator and adapter of Rembert Dodoens's *Niewe Herball* [sic], slipped in a reference to rhubarb as "a strange plant cultivated in the gardens of some herborists out of curiosity." He does not seem to have known it himself or to have had any precise information about it. It did not occur to him that it might be useful as food, nor to Prosper Albinus either, though he was growing it in the botanical gardens of Padua, and published a drawing and a description of it. Rhubarb was still a medicine, and its important part was the root.

The idea that rhubarb might serve as food apparently came first to English botanists, though they failed to focus on the stalks. John Gerard (though I do not know whether in his own 1597 edition, the one of which everybody gives the date, or in its enlarged, corrected and improved version brought out in 1636 by Thomas Johnson, the one which everybody quotes) wrote that the leaves could be eaten like leeks or spinach. John Parkinson, who obtained some seeds before publishing his first book on gardening in 1629, said that the leaves had an acid but highly refined flavor. It was excusable to make this error 350 years ago, but in 1962 the French *Dictionnaire de l'Académie des Gastronomes* wrote that rhubarb leaves "are treated like spinach. The taste does not please everybody; but there is at least agreement on finding it refreshing." Agreement among the survivors, one supposes. Rhubarb leaves should never be eaten. They contain oxalic acid: "Eating rhubarb leaves as a vegetable," warns *The Oxford Dictionary of Food Plants*, "has sometimes caused death."

It was perhaps the false start of eating the leaves which delayed the further importation of rhubarb plants into Europe for a century and its acceptance as a food for two. England forgot about rhubarb, outside of the pharmacies, after the early seventeenth century. Neither the 1721 nor the 1731 edition of Miller's important *Dictionary of Gardening* mentions it; but it appeared in the 1768 edition. Those cooks who noticed it put rhubarb leaves in soups—whose other contents diluted the oxalic acid—but soon gave it up as unpalatable. Yet little by little all the most important species of rhubarb were seeping into Europe. Seeds of *R. undulatum*, Bucharian or Moscovy rhubarb, reached the pharmaceutical gardens of Chelsea and of Paris in 1732, and the botanical gardens of Leyden in 1750. (This species has bright red stalks, which have always sold better than green stalks, probably on the grounds of appearance alone, for it would be difficult to distinguish between them in taste since they are commonly encountered, in pies or compotes, heavily sugared.) *R. compactum* arrived from Chinese Tartary in 1758, and *R. palmatum*, Chinese rhubarb or shop rhubarb (pharmacists' shops are meant), about 1773. (Chinese rhubarb is the only kind other than the common garden rhubarb grown commercially in the United States today; its flavor has been improved from its relative tastelessness of the eighteenth century.) *R. emodi* did not appear until 1823; one botanist compared its taste to that of apples, while another said it was good for nothing except to provide leaves with which to cover baskets of fruit or vegetables.

Preceding them all was the one we eat today, *R. rhaponticum*; though we have no date for it, it seems to be the one known to Adolf Occo, Prosper Albinus, John Gerard and John Parkinson. Bunches of it began turning up in London's Covent Garden market about 1815, and by 1830 it had become generally established—at about the same time as in the United States, where its round pouch of unopened flowers was then esteemed a delicacy, though apparently nobody eats the unexpanded flowers any more, except in northern Asia, where *R. tataricum* is raised for that purpose.

The French have never had much use for rhubarb, though it has not lacked champions in France. In 1805 the *Bon Jardinier* called it to the attention of those interested in discovering new food plants, in 1830 the *Revue Horticole* printed several favorable articles about it, and under Louis Philippe (1830–1848) the royal gardener tried to popularize it. In vain: Dumas did not mention it at all in his *Grand Dictionnaire de Cuisine*, understandable in the middle of the nineteenth century, but neither did André Castelot in his *l'Histoire à Table* in 1972. The Larousse encyclopedia tells us that it is grown as an ornamental plant, but concedes that "there exist some species which are cultivated as food plants." Nevertheless, rhubarb can be found in the markets of Paris, but there is not much demand for it. In France it is little eaten except along the northern frontier, in French Flanders, and on the Continent it is consumed chiefly in Holland, Scandinavia and northern Germany. After all, rhubarb's primary use, indicated by its popular name, the pie plant, is in a dish most honored in Anglo-Saxon countries. "Edible rhubarb," Georges Gibault stated firmly, "is an English vegetable." An American one, too.

If you come across references to Spanish rhubarb, wild rhubarb, mountain rhubarb or monk's rhubarb (none of which, so far as I know, are cultivated in the United States), do not be led astray. None of them are rhubarbs. They belong to the genus *Rumex*, and are varieties of sorrel.

Alaskan Eskimos and Afghanistanis eat rhubarb raw.

RI
stands for

the **ribaldo**, a fish which has a certain importance in the diet of the Canary Islands; for the **ribbed pod**, a small clam found from Nova Scotia to North Carolina, but so sparsely that few persons have ever been lucky enough to savor its flavor, which is excellent; for the **ribbonfish**, which can mean the oarfish, long (20 feet), thin, and with a bright red erectile mane, whose extraordinary appearance has given rise to reports of sea serpents, but usually designates the edible creature of the West African coast also known as the hairtail or cutlassfish; for the **Ribston Pippin,** a tasty apple named for Ribston Hall in Yorkshire, where the first one appeared in 1704, a sport from seed imported from Rouen, France; for the **rice bean,** a native of tropical Asia now eaten more commonly in tropical Africa, whose pods are so fragile that a considerable part of the crop is lost in the picking; for the **rice bird,** a name given in the southeastern United States to the bobolink because rice is what it prefers to eat there, making it highly unpopular with rice growers; for the **rice eel,** a species of swamp eel, misnamed, since it isn't an eel though it looks like one, a frequenter of flooded rice fields, where it risks ending up as part of the risotto; for the **rice grass** of the American Southwest, whose grains American Indians used to grind into a sort of flour, but today they can do better at the nearest grocery; for **rieng,** an Indochinese root resembling ginger, but stronger; for the **ring-necked PHEASANT,** a Chinese bird which is now one of the commonest species of this delectable game in the United States; for the **river hog,** an African wild pig much eaten in tropical Africa and Madagascar, the **river shrimp,** a small, delicious, but unfortunately rare variety of this crustacean found only in the Mississippi and other fresh waters in Louisiana and Georgia, the **river trout,** a name applied to one species of this fish in Sweden and another in the British Isles, but many ichthyologists today suspect that all European trout belong to the same very versatile species, and the **river willow** of the Mississippi valley, a dispenser of honey.

And **RI** also stands for

RICE. According to *The Oxford Book of Food Plants,* rice "is one of the world's two most important food crops (the other being wheat)."

Rice is the staple food of more people than wheat. "A third of the population of the world is nourished exclusively on rice," Rosie Maurel wrote conservatively in her *Dictionnaire des Aliments,* adding, "Rice has more importance for human alimentation than wheat and rye put together." Emily Hahn raised the ante, recklessly it might seem, in *Chinese Cooking*: "Half the globe's population is dependent on rice," but Reay Tannahill, a careful researcher, went her one better: "Rice is the main item of diet for six out of every ten people in the world." E. L. Sturtevant put it that "this important grain . . . supplies food for a greater number of human beings than are fed on the produce of any other known plant."

The bare figures on the number of rice eaters, whatever they may be, do not give the whole picture. "Rice often supplies a very high proportion of the total food intake in the countries where it is grown," the Oxford book continues. It is true that in many rice-eating areas, particularly in its native Asia, rice comes very close to being not merely the leading food, but virtually the only food of enormous populations. In wheat territory, it is much oftener true that alternative or supplementary foods are also eaten; rice eaters make rice a larger proportion of their total intake than wheat eaters do of wheat. Wheat eaters, moreover, often consume rice too; rice eaters do not often consume wheat. On boundaries between wheat country and rice country, rice has the slight but not negligible advantage that it can go straight from the paddy into the pot; it does not have to be ground into flour. (It does demand care from the cook, though: "Rice . . . has a very bad disposition," said William Wallace Irwin.)

Asians have become so accustomed to the obligatory presence of rice that however much they stuff themselves with other foods, they still feel hungry if they have had no rice. Emily Hahn was humiliated to learn that students whom she invited to dinner at her Shanghai apartment filled up on rice before arriving; she had thought she was giving them a treat by introducing them to Western food, so she served no rice. ("A meal without rice," according to a Chinese saying, "is like a beautiful girl with only one eye.")

In Japan the word for rice, *gohan,* also means the full meal; *shushoko,* the "main food," also designates rice. "A Japanese doesn't feel he has eaten until he's had his bowl of rice, regardless of how many other good foods may have led up to it," wrote Rafael Steinberg in *The Cooking of Japan.* In the Philippines you can stuff your guests with food, but if there is no rice it is not considered that you have offered them a meal.

In those islands the supremacy of rice dates from the Bronze Age, which is when the natives of Luzon began terracing their hillsides to create basins which would hold water for a plant brought in before the first millennium B.C. from the flatlands of China, where water-filled paddies did not require terracing; from that time forward, rice was the basic food of the islands. In China it was already that by at least 2800 B.C., when the Five Sacred Crops were named as rice, soybeans, wheat, barley and millet; it also appeared in the dish called the Eight Marvels, which combined rice, oil, onions, mushrooms, pork, ham and eggs with soybean sauce. In southern and central China rice is the basic food, to which 28 percent of all the cultivated acreage is devoted—and it gets the best soil. As far back as the time of Marco Polo there were no food shortages, for under the Great Khan, he reported, there was plenty of rice; he noted also that Zanzibar was a rice-eating country and that in Aden "no grain is grown here except rice, and not much of that; but it is imported from abroad at a great profit."

In India, where from one-fourth to one-third of all the arable land is planted to rice, it is the basic food for the majority of the population, and almost the only cereal in the east and south, where it is served straight through the meal, and at the end is often mixed with yogurt to cool the mouth after its bout with highly spiced curries. Here also it has been the staple since very early times; it was shortly after the beginning of agriculture, about 3000 B.C., that barley (in the north) and rice (in the south) were dubbed "the two immortal sons of heaven."

Rice came later to Japan, via China, perhaps not before the first century B.C., and the Japanese still eat less of it than the Chinese, half a pound a day to the Chinese pound—probably more than a Westerner could manage to choke down in a single day. Rice had nevertheless become so important in Japan in feudal times that a man's holdings were ranked not according to their acreage, but according to the amount of rice they produced, and samurai were paid in rice. It was the Japanese who, in 1970, made the most original use of rice. When Japan's first nuclear ship, the *Mutsu,* developed a radioactive leak on its trial voyage, its engineers tried to stop the leakage with a paste made of boiled rice and neutron-absorbing boron crystals. It didn't work.

In Indonesia rice is the main course for every meal. In Vietnam, where the diet is based on rice and fish, with rice the more important, it is one of the five acceptable offerings in the temples, along with incense, flowers, eaglewood and candles.

Rice is one of the most important foods in the Middle East, which has given us the Turkish pilaf; in Italy, Europe's biggest producer and consumer of rice, with its many kinds of risotto, which comes close to displacing pasta in the Piedmont, Lombardy and Venetia; and less so in Spain, though it is the basis for the diverse varieties of paella.

Rice acreage is increasing throughout the world, on commercial plantations in the United States and Australia, and on small farms in Africa and South America. Among countries where, though a comparative newcomer, it has become important, are Costa Rica, where it is one of the most important complementary foods after maize, the staple; some of the West Indian islands, where it is itself the staple; and southern Brazil, where it is the staple also. Even in Hawaii, which does not seem to have known rice before the nineteenth century, it is now the chief, and indeed almost the only cereal.

The importance of rice for two billion human beings has not been noticeably diminished by the disapproval of two nay-sayers—Nietzsche, who was of the opinion that potato eating led to alcoholism and that rice eating drove its victims to opium, and Brillat-Savarin, who wrote:

> It has been observed that food of this kind saps the moral fiber and even courage. Cited as proof of this are the Hindus, who live almost exclusively on rice and have abased themselves before anybody who wanted to subject them.

To guess where rice comes from, you would need only to consider its way of life, which in cultivation imitates the conditions under which it grows best in nature. Started in nurseries for about four weeks, the seedlings are transplanted into paddies covered with shallow water, where they remain for the four months required for their ripening. After the transplanting, the water level is raised during the principal growth period, but drained off a few weeks before the harvest. Only one kind of climate provides these conditions naturally—that of monsoon country, where 60 to 150 inches of rain fall during the rainy season, flooding the fields, followed by a period when no rain falls at all, drying them up.

Monsoon country, then—but which?

Until quite recently, rice was thought to be native either to China or to India, where it had been cultivated since Neolithic times, about as soon as agriculture began. China possesses the earliest written documents, dating the presence of rice at 2800 B.C. (but the documents are dubious); the earliest Indian document dates from 1000 B.C. (it is of unquestioned authenticity). China was also where the earliest actual finds were made—husks mingled with pottery shards, tentatively dated at 2000 B.C.; India's oldest is carbonized grains found at Hasthinaput, Uttar Pradesh, from possibly as far back as 1000 B.C. (but there is an as yet unauthenticated report of a find dating from 3000 B.C.). In favor of the theory of Indian origin is the fact that the word "rice" can be traced back through many metamorphoses in many languages to the Sanskrit *vrihih.* It is also sometimes claimed that rice is descended from a wild Indian grass called *newaree,* of which I have been able to find no trace except this bare assertion.

It is now believed that neither China nor India was the birthplace of rice. In 1970 it was reported that rice grains had been found at an archeological site in northern Thailand dated at 3500 B.C. Rice

Rice. *Woodblock print by Katsushika Hokusai (1760–1849) from* Hokusai Manga or Hokusai's Sketches from Life, *1814–1878*

fanning out normally in both directions from a center somewhere in the Thailand–Malaysia–Indochina–Indonesia area could have reached China to the east and India to the west in time to be present at the earliest dates cited for each, and could have been expected to enter those countries at their nearest areas to the center—in southern China, as it did, and in eastern India, as it seems to have done also, in the Ganges area, despite the usual report that it started in the Indus valley on the west—an error probably made because it was there that Westerners first saw rice, in the persons of the soldiers of Alexander the Great.

"The Greeks began widespread cultivation of rice when Alexander the Great returned with the grain from his campaigns," I read in a magazine article, whose author's name I will omit out of pity. "Egyptian granaries were bursting with rice, and many a Roman legionnaire marched sustained by a rice cake." It would be difficult to be more wrong. No Roman legionnaire ever saw a rice cake. Alexander the Great did not bring rice back, but some of his companions did tell Theophrastus of its existence, and the occasional assertion that Greece began cultivating it after Alexander's return is based on a careless reading of Theophrastus, who actually wrote that there was a plant called rice in India, but did so in terms which implied that the living plant did not exist in the Mediterranean area. (This error appears in the Larousse gastronomic encyclopedia, which may be what led our magazine writer astray.) As for "Egyptian granaries bursting with rice," I suspect that she fell victim to the Demon of the Temptation to Succumb to Picturesque Imagery, for nothing contradicts the assertion of Don and Patricia Brothwell in their *Food in Antiquity* that "there is no evidence of rice in ancient Egypt." A few timid attempts to locate rice in the hanging gardens of Babylon (also propitious to Picturesque Imagery) are not convincing, though we should not rule out the possibility that a few stray plants may have turned up there, to be grown briefly as a curiosity before they died because nobody would have known how to care for them. It seems safe to assert that rice was not grown in the Mediterranean area in antiquity. Celsus, Pliny, Dioscorides and Galen all knew it existed, but none of them spoke of its cultivation in their world. It does not seem to have been eaten in ancient Rome even as an import.

There was probably no rice in Europe until the Moors brought it to Spain and planted it in Andalusia, which could have been in the eighth century, but may have waited until the ninth. From there it passed to Italy, some reports say as early as the tenth century, which is dubious, but it is probably safe to go along with the statement that it was being grown in the Po valley by 1475. The Renaissance took to it; it is supposed to have been in 1574 that what might be considered the most famous single rice dish of Italy was created, *risotto alla milanese,* whose most conspicuous feature is the saffron which colors the rice, inspired perhaps by the Spanish paella.

To the north, specifically in France, we are told that rice was all but unknown in the Middle Ages. Paul Lacroix, in his *France in the Middle Ages*, writes in a passage only hazily dated (but he had just been talking about the sixteenth century): "It was only later that . . . rice came into use . . . useless for bread, [it] was employed . . . for making cakes, which, however, were little appreciated." "The Middle Ages hardly knew it," said historian André Castelot. Georges and Germaine Blond went off the deep end when they asserted that rice arrived in Europe at about the same time as maize. Thus assured that rice was unknown in France in medieval times, I picked up the *Ménagier de Paris* (1393) and found there several recipes for rice, served not only in the form of rice cakes but as a dish in its own right, plus some suggested menus including rice dishes, and even one that had actually been served—at the celebrated banquet given by the Abbé de Lagny for Paris notables in 1379, which included rice with almonds. The anonymous author of this fourteenth-century work mentioned two kinds of rice, one which, I suppose, was the ordinary everyday variety, while the other, *ris engoulé,* I take to be the glutinous or sticky rice dear to the Chinese. Both kinds, we are told, should be washed "in two or three pairs of water," which throws a fresh light on hydrodynamics. One of the recipes given in this book had already appeared in almost identical form in what is believed to be the first cookbook ever written in France, Taillevent's *Le Vivandier,* published some time between 1373 and 1380.

Most of the reference books tell us that rice cultivation in France dates from the Second World War, when rice could no longer be imported. Actually, it began in obedience to a decree issued by the Duke of Sully, Henry IV's principal financial counselor, dated August 23, 1603; he was backed up by Olivier de Serres, agricultural adviser to the king, who expressed the desire that the French "should not refuse to test [the new plant], as has been done in Piedmont." It was planted in the region where it is still grown today, the Camargue, the marshy delta which lies along the Mediterranean between the Rhone and the Little Rhone. The experiment failed, probably because there was too much salt in Camargue water. In this century, the saline water was pumped into the Vaccarès lagoon and was replaced by fresh water from the Rhone. Rice was planted again, and this time flourished; the Camargue now supplies one-third of the needs of France. This was not, however, during the Second World War: it started in 1904.

The French are not great rice eaters, probably because they are great bread eaters. During the eighteenth century, when rice was still only an import, it was not much used except in soups. Since then some classic combinations of rice with other foods have been developed—boiled fowl with rice, for example, or the homely *blanquette de veau,* veal stew, ordinarily accompanied with boiled rice. French consumption of rice is only about 3⅓ pounds a year, about half the American figure, though Americans are not great rice eaters either. Asians eat 265 pounds a year. One explanation for the relative French coolness toward this cereal may be implicit in an observation of Elizabeth David: "The French have never found out how to cook rice."

The British picked up a few new eating habits from India during the period when they ruled it (a liking for chutney, for instance), but addiction to rice was not one of them. The chief reminder of Empire in this domain is kedgeree, which they borrowed from the Indian *kitcherie,* made of curry-spiced rice and lentils, replacing the lentils with leftover fish and making it a breakfast dish. They were not eating much rice when they started to colonize America, but this did not deter them from calling on the new colonies to produce it. Sir William Berkeley sowed half a bushel of seed in Virginia in 1647 and reaped fifteen bushels of grain, but it then petered out because nobody in Virginia knew how to care for it. William Byrd wrote in 1737 that though their bread was ordinarily made from wheat, many Virginians preferred bread made from a mixture of maize and rice; but by then they could have been getting rice from the Carolinas.

South Carolina was rice's real port of entry into North America. The details of the story differ with everyone who tells it, but what seems to be the most trustworthy account says that the first rice of the Carolinas was brought from Madagascar by Captain John Thurber, who gave it to Henry Woodward, described as one of the founders of the Carolinas. Woodward planted it in his own garden, in dry soil, where it died. Carolina is reported to have had its second chance in 1694 when the captain of a Dutch brig, also from Madagascar, gave a peck of rice to "Governor Smith" (no first name specified), who distributed it among his friends for planting, with what success we are not informed. A third story tells us that a 100-pound bag of seed rice was sent to Charleston at an unspecified date by "Ashby"—unidentified, but this time we can locate our man. "Ashby" must have been Lord Ashley, a member of the London proprietary board for the Carolinas, who, according to the *Encyclopaedia Britannica*, "prepared for the province an elaborate feudal system of government that would have been obsolete even in Europe." (The colonial assembly rejected it.) In 1698 sixty tons of rice grown from Ashley's seed were shipped to England.

The success of rice in America dated from the time when it was realized that it needed to be grown in water and that the swamps along the coast of South Carolina could provide the water. It also required a great deal of labor. Slaves could furnish that, so South Carolina became the colony which imported the most slaves. This was at the time when Huguenots driven from France by the revocation of the Edict of Nantes began to arrive in South Carolina, and for some reason acquired an important role in rice growing. (Huguenots must have had a special affinity for rice: the Duke of Sully and Olivier de Serres were both Huguenots.) Leaving the slaves to work the plantations along the malarial coast, the planters, who by the mid-eighteenth century had become rich from rice, indigo and slaves, lived in town houses in Charleston and developed there a charming gracious urban society. Rice was then being referred to as "Carolina gold," and it did indeed serve on occasion as money.

South Carolina exported 42,000 barrels of rice in 1731 and three times that in 1765, much of it to England, where it brought high prices, but some of it to southern Europe, to which South Carolina was permitted to ship rice directly, for its own profit, by a special exception to the Trade and Navigation Acts, which in general stipulated that all commerce to or from the American colonies should pass through England. Came the Revolution, and the British occupation of Charleston. They harvested the entire rice crop and sent it to England, including the grain which should have been saved for seed.

I do not know whether he was the first to help revive the stricken South Carolina rice industry, but in any case Thomas Jefferson in 1787 did provide the Carolinas with new seed, which he smuggled out of Italy while on a diplomatic mission there—an illegal action, for Italy was producing the best rice in Europe and intended to keep it for herself. As President, Jefferson persuaded the French to pay in advance for shipments of Carolina rice, hoping in this field at least to loosen the stranglehold the British still exercised over the American economy. He failed, for the trade channels with Britain were too strongly established and the British were too eager to offer Carolina growers credit terms the French could not meet. It was a good deal for Britain, for there was nowhere else where she could buy rice so cheaply, and a good deal for Carolina too: the rice trade was one of the factors which helped the South to recover from the economic ravages of the Revolution more quickly than the North.

By 1840 Carolina was producing 60 percent of all the rice grown in the United States (North Carolina and Georgia were her chief competitors). After the Civil War, large tracts were planted to rice in Louisiana (where the plant had first been introduced by the Company of the West in 1718) and by 1877 it was one of that state's most important crops. South Carolina eventually lost the lead to Louisiana, which now raises twice as much rice as any other two states put together. Rice had also been brought early into California, where Father Baegert reported that it was flourishing about 1760; but commercial production of rice was undertaken seriously there only in 1912, in the Sacramento valley. California now claims the highest yield per acre in the world (5000 pounds, compared to the world average of 1450), but so does Italy, and also some of the countries now using the new strains of "miracle rice." Today the

United States produces about 10 billion pounds of rice a year on more than 2 million acres of land, and is the world's leading exporter—despite the fact that 90 percent of all the world's rice is grown in Asia. But Asia itself eats all the rice it can produce and buys more: the world's total import-export trade is carried on with only 5 percent of all the rice grown.

America's wild rice is not rice, but it was so called by the early explorers who found American Indians living on it in the Great Lakes region because, like rice, it grows from the water, rising three or four feet above its surface—looking very much like rice in a paddy. French explorers preferred to call it "crazy oats," while the Indians themselves named it *manomin*, "the good berry." It has since acquired other names—Indian rice, Tuscarora rice, Canadian rice, water rice, and water oats. For the botanist it is *Zizania aquatica.*

Wild rice was so important a food for the Indians in its area that it converted them from nomadism; they dared not move far from the cereal which for them was even more essential than maize. "When it is Cleaned, fit four youse," wrote an early trader, in spelling so determinedly picturesque that it is difficult to believe it authentic, "Thay Boile it as we Due Rise and Eat it with Bairs greas and Sugar"—maple sugar, one supposes.

Wild rice is very nearly an Indian monopoly still. Ninety percent of it grows on or near the Chippewa White Earth Reservation, where only Indians are permitted to gather it. They harvest it as they always have, from canoes which glide almost invisibly through the water among the tall plants. They bend the stalks over the canoes, smack them with a stick, and the grain drops into the canoe—or more exactly, about 10 percent of it does. The other 90 percent falls into the water, where it is not quite a dead loss, for it reseeds the stand and feeds fish and wild ducks. The fact that so little of the potential crop is retrieved explains why wild rice is so expensive.

The few white exploiters who work the other one-tenth of the wild rice area with modern machinery (but themselves get no more than 30 percent of the grain, it shatters so easily)· grumble that the "backward Indians" are wasting precious food. But gourmets seem agreed that the rice harvested by the Indians tastes better than that which has enjoyed the blessings of modernization.

Wild rice is not an American monopoly, as we are usually told. It is the *kaw-sun* of China, where the part most appreciated is the solid base of the stem.

ROA
stands for

the **roach**, a freshwater fish related to the carp, more eaten in the Middle Ages than it is today; and for the **roan antelope**, more eaten in prehistoric Africa than it is today, but only because there are no longer so many of them.

ROB
stands for

the **robber crab**, another name for the coconut crab, an indirect indication of the importance of the coconut for the inhabitants of coconut country; and for the **robin**, a sacred bird in ancient Britain, but not sacred enough to keep it out of pies in Colonial America.

ROC
stands for

rocambole, the sand leek or giant garlic, which when used as a substitute for the latter gives more the impression of being small garlic; for the **rock badger**, forbidden food for Jews, who seem to be accepting this deprivation with good grace; for the American **rock bass**, which isn't a bass but a sunfish; for the **rock beauty**, whose brilliant markings, perhaps the most striking among the angelfishes, do not deter the natives of the regions where it is found from eating it, and neither does its tough skin; for the **rock cockle**, a sweet and tender Pacific coast relative of the Atlantic coast quahog; for the **rock cod**, which isn't a cod but a grouper; for the **Rock Cornish hen**, much praised in the United States except by John and Karen Hess, who described it as "a flabby midget"; for the **rock CRAB** of the Pacific coast of the United States, whose enormous claws will give you enough meat to make up for the trouble you will have catching it; for the **rock cranberry**, a name sometimes given in the eastern United States to the cowberry, and the **rock eel**, a name sometimes given by British fishmongers to one of their wares to shield the customers from the knowledge that they are eating dogfish; for **rockets**, "a good salat-herbe" in the opinion of John Gerard but "fetid and offensive" according to a later appraisal—which must be the opinion of Anglo-Saxons, for they have abandoned it to the Romans, who consider it their own special salad plant, under the name *misticanza*; for the **rockfish**, which is Chesapeake Bay's name for the striped bass; for the **rock goby**, whose flighty mother lays her eggs and then goes off on a bender, leaving the conscientious father behind to guard them with all the solicitude of a mother hen; for the **rock lily,** an Australian orchid whose cucumber-sized bulbs are eaten by natives; for the **rockling,** a member of the cod family which has taste buds on its back so it can find out what it is letting itself in for before taking food into its mouth; for the **rock purple,** which is the dog whelk, the **rock oyster,** which is the rock scallop, and the **rock scallop,** which is the rock oyster, the most sedentary species of its clan; and for **rock tripe,** a lichen eaten by natives of the Arctic.

ROE
stands for

roe, or fish eggs, of which man eats, among others, those of the sturgeon (CAVIAR), the SALMON (red), the SHAD, the burbot, the whitefish, the COD, the HERRING, the CARP, the gray MULLET, the red mullet, the TUNA, the lungfish, the lamprey and the sea urchin, but not those of the PIKE, reputedly toxic; for the **roebuck,** considered by many to provide the tastiest venison of all DEER; and for the **roebuck berry** of the far north, acid but agreeable if eaten with plenty of sugar.

ROK
stands for

roka, a strongly flavored Turkish salad plant whose leaves look like those of the dandelion; for **rokam,** a Malaysian approach to the cherry; and for **roker,** which is the thornback ray.

ROM
stands for

Romaine, a crunchy LETTUCE whose name tells us that it comes from Rome, but it doesn't, it comes from Cos; for the **roman,** a South African fish otherwise known as the red stumpnose; and for the **Rome Beauty,** the largest commercially handled red cooking APPLE, which is grown in Italy but takes its name from its place of origin—Rome, Ohio.

ROO
stands for

the **rook,** made into pies in England when young and tender, but not as often as in earlier times; for the **rooster,** which Brillat-Savarin tells us is most flavorful when it is virgin; and for **roots,** which are eaten in many avatars, from SALSIFY to GINGER, except by the Jains of India and the members of certain religious communities forbidden to eat foods which grow underground in the domain of the Devil.

ROS
stands for

rosary pea, "the hardest and most indigestible of all the pea tribe," so it is used chiefly for making chaplets; for the **rose,** whose beauty alone seems sufficient justification for admiration, but I find that there are at least seventeen different culinary uses for its petals, buds, hips and leaves, not to mention the medicinal ones, and for the **rose,** a bivalve eaten in all the countries of the northern shores of the Mediterranean; for the **rose apple** of tropical eastern Asia, whose dry fruit is described as not worth eating fresh by a majority of botanists, but it gets by in preserves; for the **roselle,** a tropical Old World plant whose flowers are used in tarts and jellies in Jamaica, to which it has been transplanted; for the **rosefish,** which seems too enticing a name to give to a scorpionfish, since it is uncertain whether this particular variety is or is not too poisonous to eat, a field in which very little research has been hazarded; for the **rose geranium,** which can be used as a seasoner; for the **rose myrtle,** alias the hill gooseberry or hill guava, made into jellies and preserves in tropical eastern Asia; for the **rose of China,** a sort of hibiscus whose leaves and flowers are sometimes eaten in Malawi and the Congo, and the **rose of Sharon,** whose young leaves are sometimes eaten in China; for **roseroot,** a name which sounds more attractive than "scurvy grass," but that is what it is; and for **rosinweed,** whose tuberous roots were still being eaten by American Indians along the Columbia River at the beginning of this century but have by now probably been superseded by TV dinners.

And **ROS** also stands for

ROSEMARY. Elizabeth David, a cookbook author with whom it is ordinarily difficult to disagree, is nevertheless a little hard on an herb I happen to like myself—rosemary.

> With sage [she wrote of it in *Spices, Salt and Aromatics in the English Kitchen*], this herb figures in my kitchen as a decoration only—with their grey-green and reddish leaves both herbs are beautiful in a jug of country flowers but in cooking I don't want either. Many Italians stuff joints of lamb and pork almost to bursting with rosemary, and the result is perfectly awful. The meat is drowned in the acrid taste of the herb and the spiky little leaves get stuck between your teeth. Once, in an out-of-doors Capri café I saw an old woman basting her fish—with a bunch of rosemary dipped in olive oil. That's about as much of rosemary as, personally, I want.

I find this estimate all the more surprising because Elizabeth David is an expert on Italian cooking, and it seems to be the Italians who are today the greatest devotees of rosemary in the West. One of my more vivid food memories—perhaps because it had so unexpected a setting that I was exceptionally impressed by it—is of stopping at a restaurant on the express highway at Frascati. I never eat at express highway restaurants if I can conveniently get off the highway, but this time I couldn't, so I resigned myself to the prospect of, as Miss David would put it, a perfectly awful meal. I was served a superb *porchetta* (roast pork) seasoned subtly with rosemary, whose fragrance, not at all acrid, had penetrated perfectly the perfumed flesh of the pork. Florence, great *porchetta* country, uses rosemary with it too, but this is an herb perhaps commoner in Rome than in Florence. It is not Rome's characteristic herb (wild mint is), but it is honored there. The classic Easter dish of Rome, *abbacchio*, suckling lamb, is not authentically Roman unless it is flavored with rosemary. Everywhere in Italy, rosemary turns up in rice dishes. I presume that its favor there can be explained by two factors: first, the great skill Italians show in growing such plants; second, the great skill they show in the kitchen, where they manage to deal subtly with strong flavors.

"This spice [*sic*] quickly becomes brutal, difficult to handle," Louis Lagriffe warned in *Le livre des épices, des condiments et des aromates.* "It blankets all other flavors, stifles its cousin, thyme, with its wild incense. Take care!" The word "incense" was well chosen; the fragrance of rosemary does suggest it. It comes from a special type of camphor apparently unique to this plant. Louis Lagriffe says that the ancient Greeks called rosemary *libanotis,* after a young priest named Libanus, who according to legend was assassinated: his blood drenched a clump of rosemary, which acquired the scent of incense in reminder of his sacerdotal role. But as it happens, *libanotis* does not mean rosemary, it means frankincense. A Christian legend attributes the odor of rosemary to a stop made by the Holy Family during the flight into Egypt, when the Virgin Mary spread the clothes of the infant Jesus on a rosemary bush to dry; as a result, in the words of the poet John Oxenham, "that bush forthgives, the faint, rare, sacred sweet of Him." Was it during the same wayside stop that the Virgin flung her scarf over one of the bushes, whose flowers thus acquired their sky-blue hue? It used to be believed that rosemary never grows taller than the stature of Jesus Christ, in which case he must have been seven feet tall; after the age of thirty-three (Christ's age when he was crucified), it is further explained, rosemary never grows taller, only wider.

"There's rosemary, that's for remembrance; pray you love, remember," sang Ophelia. It stood for remembrance long before her time. Perhaps the Egyptians had other reasons for putting bunches of rosemary in their tombs, but we know that in the case of the ancient Romans this was why they placed branches of rosemary in the hands of their dead. In Australia today, a sprig of rosemary is tucked into the buttonhole on Anzac Day, in memory of the dead.

Rosemary had two symbolic roles which might seem incompatible. In Athens and in Rome it stood for love (and so for life), and it stood also for death: maids of honor carried sprigs of rosemary at weddings, and branches of the plant were laid on coffins. Shakespeare succeeded in reconciling both symbolisms in one, when Friar Lawrence, gazing on the body of Juliet, not yet really dead, exhorted those present:

Dry up your tears and stick your rosemary
On this fair corse, and, as the custom is,
And in her best array bear her to church.

This was followed by the stage direction: "They all but the Nurse go forth, casting rosemary on her."

Rosemary is a native of the Mediterranean region, where it likes arid growing conditions along the seashore. This might seem a difficult pair of requirements to fill, but it is provided here, or at least used to be: the climate of the Mediterranean littoral has been changing gradually since the time when I lived on the French Riviera, from 1950 to 1952. In those days it rained in November and then knocked off for the rest of the year, leaving the coast parched, to the delight of rosemary. It seems to prefer watering only by the evanescent humidity which drifts in from the sea. Its name comes from the Latin *ros maris* or *rosmarinus,* "dew of the sea" (its scientific name is *Rosmarinus officinalis;* it is the only species of its genus). Pliny explained that rosemary grew in places where there was a good deal of dew, whose plenty in his part of the world may be attributed to the proximity of the Mediterranean: it is true that rosemary is never so richly flavored as when it grows by the ocean. The name was depaganized, so to speak, during the period when the cult of the Virgin caused the names of many plants which even vaguely suggested her name to be revised in tribute to her. *Ros,* "dew," was thus reborn as "rose," and *maris* or *marinus,* "sea," became "Mary." Rosemary became Mary's rose.

In the Middle Ages, which reveled in stronger

ROSEMARY. *Drawing by Anne Ophelia Dowden from Jessica Kerr:* Shakespeare's Flowers, *1969*

flavorings than we usually care for today, rosemary was grown in many private gardens. It was sometimes called the troubadour's herb, because it was considered a suitable present for minstrels to offer to the patronesses whose charms they chanted.

Rosemary seems to have gained instant favor in England, where, we are usually told, it was imported from southern Europe in the time of herbalist John Gerard (1545–1637); but it had already figured in the eleventh-century Saxon herbal, the *Leech Book of Bald*, which treated it solely from the medicinal point of view. It had begun to move toward the category of foods by the time it came to the attention of Gerard, who described it as a "wooddy shrub," and explained:

> Rosemary groweth in France, Spaine, and in other hot countries; in woods, and in untilled places: there is such a plenty thereof in Languedocke, that the inhabitants burne scarce any other fuell: they make hedges of it in the gardens of Italy and England, being a great ornament unto the same; it groweth neither in the fields nor gardens of the Easterne cold countries; but is carefully and curiously kept in pots, set into the stoves and cellers, against the injuries of their cold Winters.

A recipe for candying rosemary flowers was given as early as 1594 by Sir Hugh Platt in his *Delights for Ladies*. It may have been about at this time that the English West Country saying was born: "Rosemary will not grow well unless where the mistress is master," which is said to have caused some husbands to do secret damage to the plant, not, we may suppose, because they thought this would alter an existing situation, but to deprive the neighbors of a pretext for jocularity. Spenser called it the "cheerful rosemarie," for it was credited with uplifting the spirits; nearly a century later Mme. de Sévigné wrote, "I use it every day, I always have some in my pocket, I find it excellent against sadness."

Rosemary is a useful herb to have at hand for use fresh, it goes so well (used sparingly) with so many foods—in stews, for instance, or with fish and game (remember the Christmas carol which glorifies the boar's head "bedecked with bays and rosemary"). Its pungency counteracts the sometimes woolly taste of mature mutton. A useful rule of thumb is that it goes well with pale meats. "I like it particularly with veal and chicken," wrote Violet Stevenson in *A Modern Herbal*. "I have eaten it with goat and when meat was scarce and we lived off the land I always used it with squirrel."

There are many reasons for which you might want to have rosemary at your beck and call: Carrying a sprig of it wards off evil. It foils black magic and thwarts the evil eye. You can use its wood to make carpenter's rulers and lutes. It repels moths and prevents baldness. A sprig carried to bed with you staves off nightmares. And fairies use its blossoms as cradles, which amuses the children.

ROU
stands for

the **rough hound**, which is a dogfish, the **rough periwinkle**, which is a shellfish trying to become a land animal, the **rough piddock**, which is a boring clam, and the **rough weed**, which is the green amaranth; for the **round clam**, which is the QUAHOG; and for the **Rousselet**, a PEAR which was once the pride of Rheims but has now disappeared.

RO
stands for

the **rowan**, whose small juicy scarlet berries are so bitter that only the Welsh, the Scots, the Swedes, the Latvians and the Kamchatkans are hardy enough to eat them fresh instead of in heavily sweetened jam; and for the **Roxbury Russet**, said to have been developed in Massachusetts early in the seventeenth century, in which case it is probably America's oldest named APPLE.

RU
stands for

the **rubber tree,** which in Africa is a species with a fruit called *abo* or *aboli* relished by the natives, and in India is a species with a fruit which tastes like a medlar relished by natives and Europeans alike; for the **rubber vine,** whose fruit is eaten in various parts of Africa; for the **rubberneck clam,** which despite its name minds its own business (which is being the horse CLAM); for the **rudd,** a Eurasian fish which has been introduced into the United States, no doubt as an illegal wetback, for its identity is disguised there under the alias "pearl roach"; for the **ruddy turnstone,** a shore bird no longer legally pursuable as game, whose name comes from its technique for finding food; for **rue,** which John Gerard called "herbe Grace" and described as having "a very strong and ranke smell, and a biting taste"; for the **ruff,** a European shore bird which in the mating season nearly knocks itself out trying to impress its hen, the reeve, a monster of indifference; for the **ruffe,** a small perch of the British Isles; for the **ruffed grouse,** that tasty North American game bird which in my native New England is called the partridge; for **rumen,** one of the stomachs of cud-chewing animals, which turns up at the table under the name "tripe"; for the **runner,** which sounds like an animal but is actually a fish, of Madagascar and East Africa, where it is also known as the prodigal son, and the **runner bean,** eaten in tropical Africa, where it is also known as the scarlet bean; for **rushes,** which include the scouring rush of the Ozarks, a redoubtable food according to Richard Rhodes, who wrote, "The hill people . . . ate the plant's cones, after carefully boiling and frying them, but since the scouring rush . . . contains a chemical that can act as a nerve poison, the practice is not recommended to casual gourmets"; for **Russian tarragon,** or false tarragon, an inferior substitute for the real thing; for the **Russulae**, a family of mushrooms eaten by prehistoric men and recommended by a historic one, Pliny; and for the **rutabaga,** or swede turnip, a root more admired a century or two ago than it is now.

RY
stands for

RYE. A parvenu which started life as a weed, rye ended rich enough to have weeds of its own. "Rank weeds, that every art and care defy, / Reign o'er the land, and rob the blighted rye," George Crabbe wrote at the end of the eighteenth century. If he had lived five centuries earlier, he would probably have made it something like: "Rank rye, which every art and care defeat, / Reigns o'er the land, and robs the blighted wheat." Rye did indeed first force itself upon the attention of farmers as a pestilential and unwanted growth which invaded wheat fields and contaminated the crop. As it could prosper on unfertile soils which starved wheat, and flourished farther north (to the Arctic Circle) and higher up (14,000 feet above sea level in the Himalayas) than wheat could, it frequently threatened to crowd out the wheat and take over completely on marginal land. "Ultimately," wrote one food historian, "farmers were reduced to harvesting the weeds rather than the wheat." Actually, what seems to have happened is that the farmers adapted their technique to the whims of nature; instead of shifting from wheat to rye, they let the mixed stands grow, harvested the wheat and rye together, threshed them together, made flour of them together, and replanted their fields to the seed mixture they had produced, still wheat and rye together.

This combination is called maslin, French *méteil,* two words which look different enough, although English borrowed it from French. They were more alike in the twelfth century when the borrowing occurred; the French word was then *miscelin,* "mixed." Between the fourteenth and seventeenth centuries, maslin flour was the commonest kind in Europe. The mixed stands occupied vast territories in France during the Middle Ages, and the two grains were still being grown together in that country up to the nineteenth century. The bread the mixture produced was of good quality, and after maslin was no longer being grown, maslin bread was still made, from two-thirds wheat flour to one-third rye flour, which may well have been the proportions reached by natural growths in fields where farmers were trying to grow wheat but were having trouble because they had been invaded by rye.

We are usually told that rye originated in southwestern Asia (Asia Minor or the Caucasus), though one author gives himself a little more leeway by placing it "somewhere between the Austrian Alps and the Caspian Sea." One may wonder whether, in ignorance of the exact provenance of rye, writers did not simply succumb to force of habit and attribute it to the same region which produced its relatives, wheat, oats and barley. So far as I know, only one dissenter has placed rye elsewhere: Charles Pickering, who in 1888 expressed the opinion that rye had originated in northeastern Europe and the adjoining regions of Asia. I suspect that the lone dissenter was right; everybody is out of step but Pickering. Not only is this theory consistent with the nature of a

Rye *by Job Berckheyde (1630–1693).* The Bakery Shop, *oil on canvas*

plant which prefers the far north, but it is also borne out by archeological and linguistic evidence.

The many foods which did indisputably originate in the fecund center of the Caucasus and Asia Minor tended to fan out eastward to the subcontinent of India and southward and westward to Egypt and, via the Mediterranean, to the countries on its northern shores, which it entered from the east or south. Rye, however, was unknown in ancient India or ancient Egypt. However, the ancient Greeks seem to have known it. We are told that they made bread of unsifted rye flour, held to be especially digestible, and that rye had reached them through Thrace and Macedonia—from the north. There could, of course, be an error of translation here. I do not know which Greek word has been rendered as "rye," and although many Latin food words are transliterations from the Greek, I find no Greek word from which the Romans might have derived their word *secale* (which has been adopted as the modern generic term for rye, *Secale cereale*). For that matter, not everyone is agreed that *secale* means "rye"; it is certain that it stood for a grain of some kind, but not necessarily for this one. Nevertheless, it is thus translated when Pliny uses it. He told us that it was cultivated at the foot of the Alps (in Cisalpine Gaul?) and hence it came from the north, and adds that its grain was detestable, fit to be eaten only by persons suffering from extreme hunger. The Romans apparently made no use of it; and though we are sometimes told that they introduced it to northern Europe, it does not bear a Latin name there, as should be the case if it was a Roman import. On the contrary, in all the northern European languages it bears a name akin to its present one—in Old English, *ryge*—and seems to have done so a thousand years before the Romans arrived. The earliest known remains of rye were discovered in Iron Age Britain—another indication that it originated in the north. It may be that the reason why researchers have never succeeded in identifying the wild ancestor of rye is that they were looking in the wrong place. The chief candidates for the honor of being the patriarch of rye are *Secale montanum*, which grows wild in Afghanistan, and what taxonomists have taken the liberty of naming *S. ancestrale*, which grows wild in Afghanistan and Turkey; neither of them quite seems to fill the bill. Perhaps the researchers should turn their attention to northeastern Europe.

Rye is a relative newcomer among human foods. It does not seem to have attracted much attention in civilized communities before 1000 B.C., by which time it was already being cultivated in Britain, Germany and other parts of central Europe, and perhaps even on the infertile interior plateau of Turkey, though if so it had little importance there. In the Middle Ages, rye became the principal cereal over a wide belt extending across north-central Europe into Russia, where its presence was reported by merchants, the only Westerners who, up to the seventeenth century, had access to that vast savage country.

Rye flour is a brownish gray. When used alone it produces the black breads of central Europe, like pumpernickel and its fellows, still popular in Germany. (In northern Germany the continued domination of rye is expressed by calling it *Korn*, the word used in all the Teutonic-Scandinavian–language countries to designate whichever grain is the most important.) Usually rye flour was mixed with something else, automatically when it was maslin, but otherwise with wheat, barley or pea flour, producing a light-brown bread of agreeable taste and texture, which had the disadvantage, in an age accustomed to eating its bread soaked in soup, that it did not absorb liquid as easily as white bread, and the advantage, in an age when bread had to be baked in the ovens of the feudal lord, that it kept much longer, so that enough bread for the next fortnight or month could be cooked at one time.

Medieval and Renaissance authors are in disaccord about the healthiness of rye bread. Some said it was more difficult to digest than white bread. Bruyerin-Champier recommended it to "preserve beauty and freshness among women." Parisian doctors prescribed bread made half and half of wheat flour and rye flour "to preserve the health," but whether wheat was supposed to take the curse off rye or vice versa is not clear. Perhaps it was to meet their prescription that France developed "two-colored bread," in which the flours were not mixed, but the loaf contained alternate layers of wheat and rye bread, like a layer cake; it is stated that it was eaten chiefly by persons of limited means. The respective merits of the various flours available were entertainingly set forth by Henry Best, a Yorkshire squire, in instructions for the feeding of his household which have been passed on to us by Reay Tannahill in *The Fine Art of Food*:

> For brown bread. Rye, pease, barley in equal quantities. In summer less barley.
>
> For the folks' [i.e., the servants'] puddings. Barley . . . Never use any rye for puddings, because it maketh them so soft that they run about the platters.
>
> For our bread and for the folks' piecrusts. Maslin . . . The folks' piecrusts are made of maslin, as our bread is, because paste that is made of barley meal cracketh and splitteth.
>
> For our own pies. Best wheat.

Rye was probably first planted in the New World by the French, at Port Royal, Nova Scotia, in 1606, and Samuel de Champlain had it in his garden at Quebec four years later. Jesuit missionaries introduced it to the Iroquois and were more appreciative of the splendor of their gift than were the Iroquois. "You would be astonished to see the great number of ears of rye," Father Paul Le Jeune wrote home from Canada. "They are longer and more grainy than the most beautiful I have seen in France." The Indians preferred their maize.

Both rye and wheat were planted in Virginia and in New England, on land studded with tree stumps, inexpertly cleared by immigrants unaccustomed to this sort of work, and at first did not do well. Wheat fell victim to the blast, but rye succeeded sooner and better, though a good deal of it was diverted to the manufacture of whiskey. Wheat was dear for another two centuries in New England, so rye, oats, barley or maize were used for bread, sometimes mixed with a little wheat, but oftener in various combinations with each other. A New England favorite was "rye and Injun," bread of mixed rye flour and cornmeal. In the United States, as in Europe, wheat bread was held to be the best, but rye enjoyed its special dominions. In Europe it goes into gingerbread, in the United States into Boston brown bread. To this day rye bread, with an admixture of wheat flour, is, thinly sliced, the traditional accompaniment of oysters in France. In the United States, any large city delicatessen is likely to be asked to make up a considerable proportion of its sandwiches "on rye." Not everybody would agree that rye bread is as characterless as was implied by Margaret Fuller (pen name Ossoli) when she wrote in her diary: "This was one of the rye-bread days, all dull and damp without."

The *Encyclopaedia Britannica* calls rye the least important of cereal crops, from which I deduce that its criteria are exclusively commercial. It is true that rye ranks last of the world's principal cereals—wheat, rye, barley, oats, maize, millet and rice—in volume of production (but there are no figures for the largest rye producer, the Soviet Union, believed to grow 40 percent of all the world's rye). It also ranks last in trade, which should follow naturally from the production figures, but there is also the element that the rye-eating countries are also the rye-growing countries, which raise the grain for their own use and neither export nor import it.

But rye is the second most important cereal measured by the acreage sown to it. If this seems inconsistent with its tail-end position for production, the reason is that its yields are low. But need they be so low? Rye is always planted on the worst soil and in the most unfavorable conditions; when soil or conditions are better, the land is turned over to a cereal deemed more profitable. Nobody knows what yields might be achieved if rye were given a better chance.

Rye is one of the three most important cereals from the point of view of providing human food. Wheat, rice and rye are mostly eaten by people; barley, oats, maize and millet are mostly eaten by animals. Rye is one of the two most important cereals for bread making: only wheat and rye contain the gluten which makes bread rise.

Rye has from time to time made spectacular sorties onto the stage of history because of its greatest weakness—its susceptibility to ergot, which rarely appears in any other cereal. Ergot is the result of the contamination of grain by a parasitic fungus called *Claviceps purpurea*, which provokes uncontrollable muscular contractions in anyone who eats it. The effects are extremely varied, from violent manifestations which lead to death to milder ones which may not even be perceived as having been provoked by any external agent—deafness, dimming eyesight or psychotic disorders including hallucination. Among the more serious afflictions are gangrene, when constriction of the blood vessels cuts off circulation to some part of the body; disturbances of the nervous system, which sometimes cause itching so intolerable as to provoke insanity; or convulsions which may or may not end in death. One of the effects of ergot, even when poisoning by it is not involved, is contraction of the unstriped muscle of the pregnant uterus, causing miscarriage. Medieval women used ergot to provoke abortions, and I have known of its being used for the same purpose in our time. Ergot is one of the substances in the modern pharmacopoeia, and is sometimes called upon in difficult births, but it is employed with extreme caution, for it is extremely dangerous: it contains twenty different poisons.

In the Middle Ages, the outbreak of any mysterious and incomprehensible malady was interpreted automatically as supernatural: it was the work of God or the work of the Devil. If it was the work of God, punishment was evidently being visited upon mortals for some sin; the remedy was repentance and redemption through prayer and pious actions, such as the making of vows or the construction of expiatory chapels. If it was the work of the Devil, his hand was ordinarily easy to identify because of the limited number of tricks he knew how to perform. One of them was throwing his victim into convulsions; this was obviously a case of demonic possession and was dealt with by exorcism. On a lower diabolic level, his underlings, the witches who had sold themselves to the Evil One, favored striking cattle down. In rural areas, the illness or death of cattle which had been in good health a day or two before was always a valid reason for suspecting witchcraft; it still is today, as you will note if you read the papers carefully.

The first identifiable epidemic of ergotism was blamed on God, the second on the Devil. In 857 several thousand persons died in the Rhine valley from what must have been poisoning by contaminated rye, though at that time the peasants had no idea what caused it. It took the form of inflammation of the skin, which caused its victims to feel that they were being burned alive. It was called the Holy Fire or St. Anthony's Fire.

One of the reasons why this epidemic was so widespread was that it occurred in time of famine. Ergot gives no warning of its danger by provoking a putrid or fetid taste in the grain: there is a slight mustiness, but otherwise the flavor is rather sweet. It is manifest to the eye, for the spike of rye fills with purple grains. The peasants did not know what this meant, but in ordinary times they would have refrained from eating a familiar food when it presented an unfamiliar appearance. But these were not ordinary times. They could not afford to be fussy. They were starving.

They were starving again in the French Limousin in 943. At the beginning of autumn (in other words, at the harvest season),

> a strange malady appeared in the region of Limoges [wrote Georges and Germaine Blond]. Passersby fell suddenly in the street, twisting in convulsions. In the middle of a meal men and women would spring up, screaming, "I'm burning!" and thrash about like epileptics, their eyes starting from their heads. All these unfortunates died and almost at once their bodies turned black. The living shunned the corpses, but to the general surprise the disease did not seem to be contagious. Nevertheless some villages lost their entire populations in a single day. The cause of the Mal des Ardents [the Malady of the Burning —it sounds almost frivolous in English] was discovered: it was the bread. It turned black—the color of the devil. . . . When the flail—a plague, it was called—ended at last, it had made more than forty thousand victims.

The same scenario was repeated from time to time during the Middle Ages, and not only in the Middle Ages. The last extensive epidemic occurred in 1816, affecting a wide area from Lorraine through Burgundy, but localized attacks still occur. As a journalist working in France I found myself reporting one of them in, if my memory is correct, the early 1950s. It occurred at the town of Pont-Saint-Esprit (the Bridge of the Holy Ghost, a name ideally suited to give rise to supernatural interpretations), and its cause was not even eating ergot. Sacks which had held contaminated rye, thrown away when its condition was perceived, were not thrown away also; nobody dreamed that the poison was so violent that it could impregnate the sacks and be communicated to anything else which might be placed in them. What was placed in them was flour which was delivered to a local baker. I have forgotten how many people died—perhaps scores, perhaps hundreds; in any case, enough to shock all France. The source of the infected flour was traced down and the unfortunate baker saved with difficulty from lynching: the mob accused him of witchcraft.

Witchcraft!

The most famous witchcraft case in the history of the United States occurred, as everybody knows, in Salem, Massachusetts, in 1692—usually referred to as the Salem witch burnings, though actually nobody was burned. Some historians trying to explain this affair have suggested that vindictive individuals took advantage of an excellent opportunity to avenge personal grudges. Others have suggested mass hysteria. Probably Linda Caporael was investigating this second hypothesis when she began to study the Salem witchcraft trials, for she was a graduate student in psychology at the University of California at Santa Barbara; but she came up with a quite different explanation, which was published in the magazine *Science* in April 1976.

Miss Caporael found that many of the persons who thought themselves bewitched lived among or near fields of rye, and that the conditions under which rye was grown in Salem were ideal for the proliferation of *Claviceps purpurea.* One of the first signs of sorcery was the illness of cattle—that classic symptom—cattle which, as it happened, had been feeding on rye. Some of the bewitched had experienced convulsions—classic again. In an attempt to find out if they were really victims of sorcery, the inhabitants of Salem commissioned a slave from Barbados named Tituba to make a "witch cake," to be fed, as a test, to a dog. Its ingredients were rye (so it must already have been suspected as the vehicle of sorcery) and the urine of afflicted girls. The contemporary chroniclers, poor reporters, neglected to tell us in detail what happened to the dog, but the test seems to have been conclusive. It was only after it that specific accusations against specific persons began to be made. Respected members of the community, suffering from some of the symptoms of the bewitched, testified to "diabolical deeds and distempers" of which they had personally been eyewitnesses. They were obviously sincere, they were known to be trustworthy. At a time when no sensible person doubted the existence of witches, their evidence was held to be conclusive. No conscientious judges could have ruled otherwise.

One of the principal poisons of ergot is ergotamine. When ergotamine gets into flour, and the flour is made into dough, and the dough is baked, it is transformed into lysergic acid diethylamide—LSD. (The Swiss scientist who first isolated and purified LSD started from ergot.) As everyone knows, LSD is a hallucinatory drug. The witnesses at Salem were honestly describing exactly what they had seen: but what they had seen were hallucinations. If Miss Caporael is right —and she presented a convincing case—the nineteen witches who were hanged at Salem, and the one who was pressed to death, were victims of contaminated rye.

S

SMITH, SYDNEY: *I am convinced that character, talents, virtues, and qualities are powerfully affected by beef, mutton, pie crust, and rich soups.*

SMITH, SYDNEY: *Madam, I have been looking for a person who disliked gravy all my life: let us swear eternal friendship.*

SAB
stands for

saba, a sweet cooking banana relished in warm countries as far apart as Africa and the Philippines; for Florida's **sabal palmetto,** which produces a food known confusingly either as millionaire's salad or swamp cabbage; for the **sable antelope,** which appeals to hunters, and the **sablefish,** which appeals to fishermen broadminded enough to overlook the fact that it is often fraudulently called the black cod, and under either name has a delicious flavor, especially when smoked; and for the **sabre pea,** one of the favorite legumes of Ethiopia.

SAC
stands for

the picturesquely named **sacalait,** which means "bag of milk," the Louisiana Creoles' name for the white crappie; for **saccharin,** 425 times as sweet as sugar, whose desirability in the diet remains a matter of dispute; and for the **Sacramento perch,** which is a sunfish, and the **Sacramento salmon,** which is the Columbia salmon.

SAD
stands for

the **saddled bream,** a food fish found in the Mediterranean, so called because it has a black band astride its narrowest girth, between back fin and tail, as though inviting small mermaids to hop aboard for a ride—sidesaddle, of course.

SAF
stands for

the **safflower,** which produces an edible oil, but whose main function is to make believe it is SAFFRON; and for **safrole,** derived from sassafras bark, whose use as a flavoring was abruptly discontinued when it was discovered that it provokes cancer in rats.

And **SAF** also stands for

SAFFRON. "The odor of saffron is extremely penetrating," according to Alexandre Dumas. "It can cause violent headaches and even death." John Gerard, more moderately, said that it was "of a strong smell . . . when dried, which doth stuffe and trouble the head." Nicholas Culpeper, most reasonable of all, described it as a "useful aromatic, of a strong penetrating smell, and a warm pungent bitterish taste." He called it an herb of the sun. "It refreshes the spirit," he continued, "and is good against fainting-fits and the palpitation of the heart." He did warn against over-indulgence in it, but the warning was hardly necessary: Who could afford to over-indulge in what is, and almost always has been, the most expensive spice in the world?

What makes saffron so expensive is the unavoidably large amount of hand labor necessary

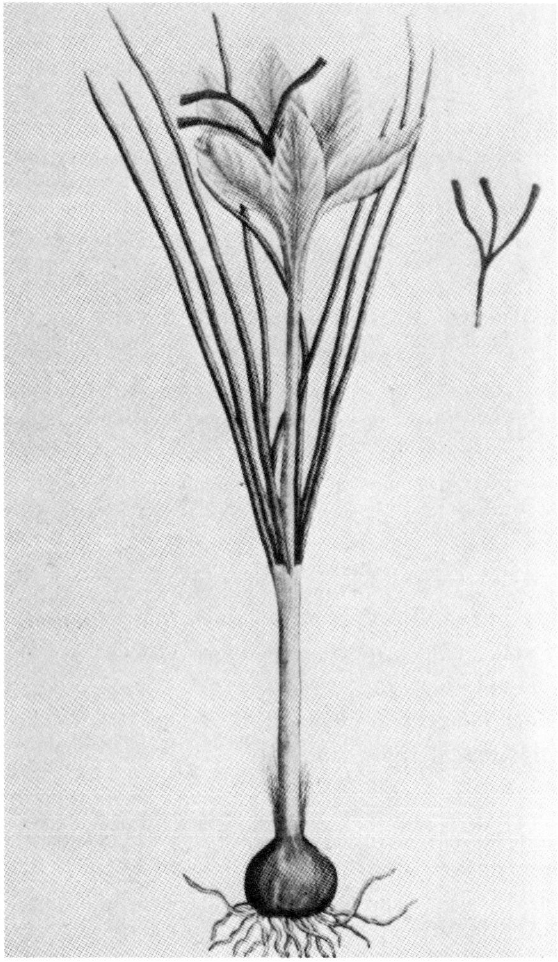

SAFFRON. *Print from Elizabeth Blackwell:* A Curious Herbal, *London, 1737*

to produce a small amount of it. Saffron is the dried stigmas, and usually part of the styles, of the flower of *Crocus sativus*, which have to be picked painstakingly out of each blossom, flower by flower. During the two years of life allowed commercially grown saffron, according to Louis Lagriffe in *Le livre des épices, des condiments et des aromates*, one hectare (2.47 acres) of land can produce 50 kilograms (110 pounds) of flowers. It takes 100,000 fresh flowers to produce 5 kilograms (11 pounds) of fresh stigmas, which dry down to 1 kilogram (2.2 pounds) of saffron. To get 1 pound of saffron you need between 300,000 and 400,000 stigmas (Mary S. Atwood); more than 200,000 stigmas (Rosemary Hemphill); 50,000 stigmas (Joan M. Jungfleisch); 45,000 stigmas (Louis Lagriffe); 85,000 flowers (Elizabeth David); or 75,000 flowers (Santha Rama Rau). The most cowardly commentator of all evades the issue by writing vaguely that it takes "acres of plants to produce a small quantity" (Waverley Root).

Fortunately, we do not need to beggar ourselves to enjoy this pungent, interesting and, regardless of Alexandre Dumas' opinion, inoffensive seasoning, for a little saffron goes a long way.

> One grain [writes Elizabeth David], or one 547th of an avoirdupois ounce, of these tiny fiery-looking orange and red thread-like objects scarcely fills the smallest salt spoon, but provides flavor and coloring for a typical Milanese risotto, Spanish paella, or bouillabaisse, for four to six people.

"Thread-like objects" may puzzle American housewives, who, if they use saffron at all, buy it in powdered form, put up in little envelopes with the greatest of care so that none of it will be inadvertently lost when they are opened, as if the contents were gold dust, and indeed they very nearly are. But saffron can also be had in other forms—in cakes, with stigmas and styles pressed together, or as "hay saffron," the unpulverized individual stigmas, which is the way many Europeans prefer it; some European recipes even give the exact number of the little threads you should pick carefully out of the heap to flavor one dish or another. The stigmas are strong in flavor, too strong to be added directly to any dish. They are put into a cup and covered with hot water. When the liquid has become bright yellow and gives off the characteristic saffron odor, it is added to the dish.

Whole Valencia stigmas (which many cooks consider the best) impart a richer, fuller flavor to food, and cost only half as much as powdered saffron. Saffron in powdered form has the further disadvantage that it lends itself freely to adulteration, which is always to be feared in the case of high-priced foods. Some merchants, though not exactly scrupulous, limit themselves to moistening saffron with oil or water, thus charging you the price of saffron for the added weight of the liquid, but others shamelessly mix saffron with safflower (*Carthamus tinctorius*, false saffron in English, bastard saffron in French), which produces the same color but has virtually no taste; or they may even counterfeit saffron with marigold petals. Turmeric (*Curcuma longa*, called Indian saffron by the French) could easily be used as a saffron adulterant, turning rice, for instance, as yellow as saffron does, but it is oftener used knowingly as a saffron substitute, for it has its own characteristic flavor, as interesting as that of saffron, but different.

Saffron probably originated in Asia Minor and Greece; it was an important item for Phoenician traders. Cilicia was its most abundant area of cultivation ("Cilicians, who perfume themselves with saffron," Juvenal wrote disdainfully), Sicily also produced a good deal of it, but Mount Tobus in Phrygia was, in the general opinion, the site which produced the best saffron of the ancient world. It does not seem to have reached Egypt, though we are often told it did; one coffee-table history of food tried to clinch this point by citing the Ebers Papyrus as describing the gardens of Luxor covered with the golden bells of saffron: saffron flowers are mauve.

Saffron was cultivated from very early times. Murals in the ruins of the palace of Knossos on Crete, which probably antedates the second millennium B.C., depict saffron harvesters at work. Homer said that Zeus slept on a bed of saffron, lotus and hyacinth flowers. Theophrastus wrote lyrically of the saffron-covered hillsides and roadsides of Greece in the fourth century B.C. Aristotle said saffron grew in such plenty on the Sicilian promontory of Pelorus that it was gathered by the wagonload. It grew wild in Canaan, it was mentioned in the Song of Solomon under the Hebrew name *carcom*, and the ancient Israelites, who seem to have had a taste for color, used it when they wanted to dye their robes yellow.

We read of saffron in the writings of Hippocrates, Theocritus, Lucretius, Virgil, Dioscorides, Pliny, Columella and Martial, from which we gain the impression that the Greeks were the greatest appreciators of saffron in ancient times. Its color was considered a symbol of royalty until it was taken over by the most refined prostitutes of history, the hetaerae.

Saffron grew wild in ancient Italy, but the Romans, always willing (after their Stoic period at least) to let other peoples work for them, preferred to buy cultivated (and already prepared) saffron from Greece. The same food "history" which changed the color of saffron flowers asserted unblushingly that the Romans imported saffron from the foothills of the Himalayas, so patent an absurdity that one wonders how it ever got into print, for with saffron so near, the Romans had no need to send to India for it, even if they had known that the Himalayas existed, which they did not, or if the peoples of the Himalayas had known that saffron existed, which they did not. Saffron seems, indeed, to have been late in reaching the Orient. Marco Polo did not report encountering it in his travels, though he knew what it was, for he wrote of Foochow that "there is a [food here] which resembles saffron; though it is actually nothing of the sort, it is quite as good as saffron for practical purposes." (Could it have been turmeric?) Saffron is supposed to have entered China when that country was invaded by the Mongols, who made considerable use of it in their cooking, which would mean early in the thirteenth century, but it does not seem to have been listed in any written document before the second half of the sixteenth century, when it appears in the *Pun tsaou*, a pharmacopoeia.

The Middle Ages were slow about adopting saffron. There was a hiatus of several centuries after the collapse of the Roman Empire during which we hear nothing at all about it. It had not disappeared; it was still growing wild, in Greece and Italy at least. What had disappeared was refinement. The use of saffron is only imaginable in a refined society, and a society which has time and money for the superfluous. It is not really a food in the sense of providing nourishment; it is a decoration for food. Its function is limited to seasoning and, even more, to coloring. The harsh, coarse, belligerent society which succeeded the Roman Empire could not be bothered with decoration. Where were the customers to pay for the fastidious work of picking stigmas out of flowers to prettify unsubtle foods? Refinement had taken refuge in the Arab world; when the Arabs entered Europe they brought refinement back, and they brought saffron back too. They planted it in Spain and gave it a new name. It was no longer crocus, from Greek, it was saffron, from Arabic—*sahafaran* or *zahafaran*, in Persian, *zafran*.

There is a tradition that France gained saffron directly from the Moors when they were stopped at Poitiers in 732 by Charles Martel; it is not impossible, but if so, the Moors gave saffron to the French more than two centuries before they grew it in Spain themselves. Perhaps surer is a second tradition which says that saffron first entered France at Avignon at the end of the fourteenth century. This was during the period when the papacy was taking refuge in France, which suggests that saffron might have come from Italy. It was indeed quite possible that, though the Moors reconverted Europe to saffron, once their missionary work was done northern Europe sought it, not necessarily from Spain, with which exchanges were rare, but directly from the Middle East: this would explain why Venice, the great importer of spices from that area during the time of the Crusades, opened a special Office of Saffron.

England too has a double tradition concerning the first appearance of saffron. It was known there in the tenth century, for a pharmaceutical work of that period describes it; perhaps it was an import from Spain. Four centuries later, Hakluyt wrote that saffron was first brought to England from Tripoli by a pilgrim who had hidden a stolen bulb in his hollow staff.

However and whenever saffron made its comeback, it took medieval Europe, and even more, Renaissance Europe, by storm. There were times and places when a pound of saffron would buy a horse.

By Renaissance times, saffron was growing widely throughout Europe. In Germany it was perhaps being cultivated in the fifteenth century, but certainly by the sixteenth, though apparently chiefly for dyes—a use of saffron which has all but disappeared nowadays, partly because its color is rather unstable, but more importantly because it is too expensive (but in India ceremonial garments and bridal veils are still colored with saffron). The Larousse gastronomic encyclopedia says that saffron began to be cultivated in France in the sixteenth century also, which is probably an error of two centuries; the encyclopedia may have been misled because it was in that century that Olivier de Serres began to cultivate it.

There were a number of saffron-growing areas in England, but one of them captured all the attention by adding the name of the seasoning to its own—Saffron Walden, in Essex, where John Gerard wrote that saffron "groweth plentifully . . . as corne in the fields." Saffron workers there were called "crokers," a harking back to the ancient name for the plant. Started in the fourteenth century, the Saffron Walden industry petered out about 1770, but the municipal arms still bear three saffron flowers enclosed by turreted walls. There is also a street in London called Saffron Hill; the land it covers was once part of the gardens of Ely Palace, where saffron was grown. It was an important seasoner in Elizabethan England. "What made the English people sprightly," said Sir Francis Drake, "was the liberal use of saffron in their broths and sweet-meats." Survivals from their sprightly days include Cornish saffron cakes and the saffron buns of the English tea table, which, wrote Adrian Bailey, "have a yeomanlike solidity that defies any but the strongest teeth and the stoutest hearts."

Paradoxical as it may seem, the most expensive spice in the world plays an important role in the cooking of a people reputed for their simplicity, and little given to luxury or self-indulgence—the Pennsylvania Dutch. Since they grow their saffron themselves and eat it themselves, its price on the world market is a negligible factor. The considerable amount of hand labor involved accords well with their philosophy: they are hostile to machines and prefer to work with their muscles, and they are given to raising large families, which provide an abundant supply of labor. Their addiction to saffron is more or less an accident, to which the clue is provided by a recipe found in almost all Pennsylvania Dutch cookbooks, that for Schwenkfelder cake. The Schwenkfelder family emigrated to the United States in the eighteenth century, bringing with it the materials of the business it had been pursuing in Germany—growing saffron. Saffron flourished in their new home, where the Schwenkfelders and their neighbors acquired such a taste for it that today it is one of the commonest spices in Pennsylvania Dutch country, appearing in almost all chicken dishes, in noodles, in soups and sauces, and in sweet pastries.

"When falcons have worms," wrote the anonymous fourteenth-century author of *Le Ménagier de Paris*, "give them meat with saffron wrapped up in it, and the worms will die." Few persons keep falcons nowadays, but this counsel has been updated, relatively, by Elizabeth David, who quoted *Law's Grocer's Manual*, 1892 edition: "A few threads of saffron put in the water for canaries occasionally makes a good stimulant." I do not guarantee that this treatment will make your canaries as sprightly as Sir Francis Drake's Englishmen, but at least it will give you very expensive canaries.

SAG
stands for

sag, leafy greens eaten in India which resemble spinach, but not very much; for the **sage grouse,** particularly plentiful in Wyoming and particularly tasty wherever it can feast on its favorite food, sagebrush; for **sago,** an edible starch obtained in the Old World from sago palms and in the New World from sago cycads; and for the magnificent but disappearing giant of its family, the **saguaro cactus,** whose fruit tastes like watermelon.

And **SAG** also stands for

SAGE. Garden sage, *Salvia officinalis*, the *Encyclopaedia Britannica* informs us, "has been known for at least three centuries." Indeed it has. Theophrastus wrote of it in the fourth century B.C. under the name *elelesphakos* and Pliny in the first century A.D. under the name *salvia*. The ancient Greeks made an annual offering of its leaves to Cadmus, credited in legend with having discovered its healing properties. In the first century B.C., Strabo ranked it first among the health-giving herbs in his garden. Hippocrates, Dioscorides and Galen used it as a medicine, Apicius used it as a seasoning. The ancient Druids believed it possessed curative powers so magical that it could even resuscitate the dead.

In the ninth century Charlemagne ordered sage planted in his domains, in the thirteenth Albertus Magnus wrote about it, in the fourteenth the anonymous author of *Le Ménagier de Paris* told how to grow, prepare and cook it. During the period of the Crusades it was described rather startlingly as "good for venom or poison," but what the writer meant was that it was good *against* venom or poison. In Elizabethan times it was a favorite seasoning for meat pies. In the seventeenth century the German botanist Paullinia wrote a 400-page book, *The Sacred Herb*, whose subject was sage.

This brings us up to the *Encyclopaedia Britannica*'s "three centuries ago," when sage, far from starting its career, was beginning to lose momentum. It is indeed much less used today than it was in the Middle Ages. "Sage deserves a better fate than its present slide into obscurity and disuse," Euell Gibbons complained, while Violet Stevenson was writing in *A Modern Herbal*: "It certainly is the most popular of all herbs. Literally tons of sage are sold each year, most of it for stuffing." This disparity is accounted for by the fact that Euell Gibbons was writing for Americans and Violet Stevenson for the English, who remain more faithful to sage than Americans, despite the redoubtable disapproval of Elizabeth David.

As for sage [wrote Miss David], Italian cooks, like ourselves, are fond of it, and use it for a number of veal dishes. To me, it deadens the food with its musty, dried-blood scent. Instead of sage it is worth trying dried mint or basil, especially in a sauce or stuffing for duck.

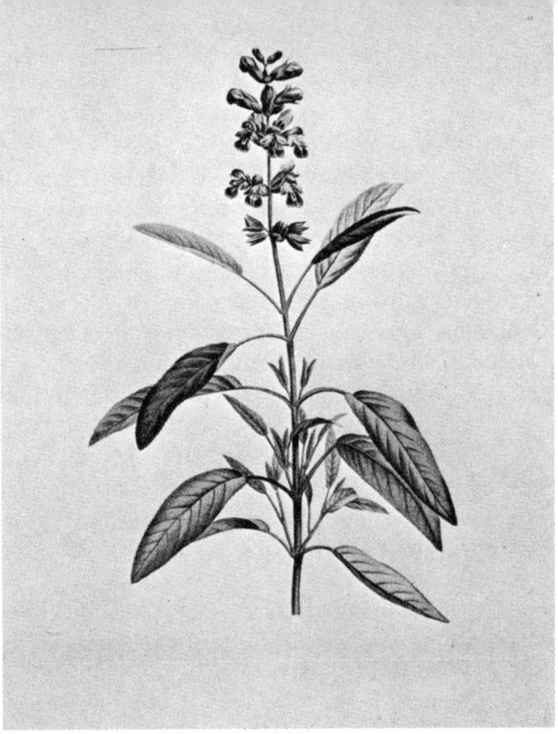

SAGE *by P. J. Redouté from Jean-Jacques Rousseau:* La Botanique, *Paris, 1805*

Duck is almost automatically accompanied by sage and onion stuffing in England, though it seems to me that duck has so marked a flavor of its own that it ought not to be intruded upon by a competing taste as strong as that of sage. I would think it the least suited among the commoner forms of poultry for sage stuffing, which would seem to go better with chicken, still better with goose (which even the French, little given to sage, used with it in the days when they ate goose more commonly than they do today), and best of all with turkey. One of the great taste memories of my childhood is of roast turkey (which had more flavor then than it has now) with sage stuffing. A few years ago, to prove to French friends that an American cuisine exists, I invited fourteen of them to a Thanksgiving dinner in a Paris restaurant, whose *pièce de résistance* was of course turkey with sage stuffing and cranberry sauce, excellently reproduced by a Burgundian chef from a recipe my sister sent me from New England. The guests found this unaccustomed dish delicious; I am not sure that they would have been equally enchanted with English stuffing. My sister's recipe incorporated, besides the sage, parsley, onion, celery, diced toast, milk, beaten egg and the chopped innards of the bird; the English seem to content themselves with bread, onion and sage. This mixture can be bought in the British Isles packaged in a dehydrated state, ready to go into the bird after being reborn by soaking in hot water, a process which ought to help Elizabeth David discourage the use of sage.

The British seem to be hard to discourage on this point. They eat Derbyshire cheese layered with streaks of green, produced with the juice pressed from fresh sage leaves, particularly at Christmas, and they like finely chopped sage leaves mixed with cream cheese or cottage cheese as a sandwich spread. Sage is used to flavor leek tarts, baked tomatoes, sausage meat and bread, and it is boiled with beans. A bouquet garni of sage, thyme and marjoram, a rather powerful combination, is used in English cooking.

In America the use of sage nowadays seems to be restricted chiefly to stuffing, though it had wider application in earlier times. Sage is not native to America, but it was probably planted there long before its first recorded appearance, in 1806. It has in many places escaped from gardens and become naturalized as a wild plant.

Sage is a native of the Mediterranean area, where it prefers the arid soil of hillsides, especially if it is chalky. Its flower represents one of nature's most ingenious arrangements for assuring the reproduction of a plant which requires the ministrations of insects for its cross-pollination. A broad lower petal provides a convenient landing platform for bees, which, indeed, can hardly get at the nectar from any other stance, since an upper petal curves over the entrance to the blossom and prevents access to it from above. The weight of the bee on this landing point causes it to act as a lever against the stamen, which pivots around, powdering the bee's abdomen with pollen. When the messenger visits the next flower, its stigmas, placed at its entrance, rub off some of the pollen, and the next generation is on its way.

Like many other foods, sage got into the pantry

by way of the medicine chest. *Cur morietur homo cui salvia crescit in horto?* asked the School of Salerno: "Why should a man die when sage grows in his garden?" Sage users die all the same, but on a less exigent level sage was held to perform like a panacea. "Originally," wrote Euell Gibbons, "sage was added to sausage, to stuffing for fowls, or to pork dressing, to counteract the tendency of these rich foods to cause indigestion and flatulence. Its health-protecting advantages have been forgotten, but meanwhile, we have learned to like its flavor." This is not true for everybody; the taste of sage is strong and barely veils its bitterness. It should in any case be used discreetly.

Of the five hundred species of *Salvia*, a genus of the mint family, only *S. officinalis*, with a few minor exceptions, is used, or indeed is usable, for seasoning. (It is also the only one which defies the strict definition of an herb, for it has a woody stem.) The leaves are the only parts employed.

Red sage, often grown as an ornamental, can be eaten too, but it is not a separate species, only a variety of *S. officinalis*. Clary sage, *S. sclarea*—to which some botanists deny the title "sage," calling it simply clary—with a flavor described as "harsh and brutal," is almost never eaten nowadays, though in the eighteenth century it was relished in omelets. Pineapple-flavored sage (*S. rutilans*, not very hardy) is sometimes dipped into a hot liquid destined to become jelly to lend it some of its flavor, but is removed before the liquid sets. Lavender sage, not hardy either, is enjoyed, so far as I know, only for its looks and its scent. Black sage (*S. mellifera*) and bigflower sage (*S. grandiflora*) are not used for seasoning, but they give good honey. One of the commonest types of sage, *S. pratensis*, meadow sage, does not seem to be edible.

Bengal sage, *Meriandra benghalensis*, is not sage, but a substitute for it (not a very good one), used in lower Bengal. The wood sage of Europe, *Teucrium scorodonia*, is not sage either, but an extremely bitter plant which smells and tastes like hops. Bethlehem sage, *Pulmonaria saccharata*, is the lungwort or the Jerusalem cowslip, while Jerusalem sage is misnamed too, being *Phlomis fruticosa*. What the American West calls white sage, or sometimes "winter fat," because cattle graze on it after the snow falls, is *Eurotia lanata*, also not sage.

Sage is not hard to grow if you do not mind giving away your financial status: European superstition holds that it will not flourish if your money affairs are in bad order. With your own sage supply at hand, you might experiment with some of its more esoteric uses. It is reported that in northern Europe the young shoots are eaten in salads, which must be rather pungent. The leaves can be pickled, and they also go into sweet dessert fritters. In Provence, sage is boiled with chestnuts; it is sometimes added to the Provençal garlic soup, *aigo boulido*; and it is even used to flavor watermelon preserves. The most unusual food use of sage is probably that of the Ionian Greek island of Zante, where the galls which develop on sage stalks when they are punctured by insects are mixed with honey and made into preserves.

According to old-timers, a mixture of sage and tea will restore youthful color to gray hair, and the teeth will become whiter if they are scrubbed with sage leaves.

SAI
stands for

the **saiga**, a desert antelope which in prehistoric times ranged all the way from Europe to Alaska, but whose habitat today has been reduced, with the help of hunters, to the Kirghiz steppe; for the **sailback scorpionfish**, poisonous if you step on its spines but palatable if, unscratched, you can ease it into a pan; for the **sail-bearer**, *Mollienisia velifera*, and the **sailfin**, *M. latipinna*, which are members of the carp family; and for the **sailfish**, good eating and good angling, for it is probably the fastest animal in the sea, where it has been clocked at seventy miles per hour.

SAINT
stands for

St. George's mushroom, edible and excellent, so called because it makes its first appearance of the year on or about April 23, St. George's Day; for **St. John's bread**, more prosaically known as the carob, which, it is hazarded, was what John the Baptist really ate in the desert instead of the Scriptural locusts and honey; for **St. Patrick's cabbage**, a sort of saxifrage which is both Iberian and Hibernian; for **St. Peter's fish**, an African freshwater species of the genus *Tilapia*, unrelated to the saltwater fish given the same name in several Latin languages, which in English is the John Dory; and for the **St. Thomas bean** of southeastern Asia, which it is prudent to separate from its toxic components before eating it, and the **St. Thomas tree**, whose leaves are chewed by Filipinos when they run out of vinegar.

SAL
stands for

salad burnet, which in the seventeenth century was "a very common and ordinary sallet furniture," according to John Evelyn; for the **salak,** the fruit of a small palm tree appreciated by Malaysians, and the **salal,** a spicy acid berry appreciated by the American Indians of the Northwest; for the **salema,** a Mediterranean fish which Algerians call "the goat," because it grazes on seaweed; for **salep,** a tuber whose bitterness can be neutralized in four or five days if you think it's worth the trouble; for **saligot,** a water plant whose nuts, when boiled, taste like freshly made cheese; for the **Sally Lightfoot,** a crab which owes its name to its mincing gait; for **salmonberries,** eaten especially by American Indians, but also by Laplanders, who preserve them by burying them in the snow; for the **salmon-dace,** which is neither a salmon nor a dace, but a sea BASS; for the **saltbush,** whose flowers are eaten by Indians in desert areas of Baja California and whose leaves are eaten by Tuaregs in desert areas of northern Africa, unless, of course, it is of the species known as toothbrush tea; for **saltpeter,** which has been described as the cosmetic of the preserved-meat industry; for **saltwort,** which may be either Jamaica samphire or marsh samphire, unrelated in spite of their names and of the fact that both are used for pickles; and for **sal volatile,** a very effective leavening agent if you don't mind working in a kitchen which reeks of ammonia.

And **SAL** also stands for

SALMON. In Colonial America indentured servants benefited from a clause in their contracts which stipulated that they were not to be fed salmon more than once a week, echoing an English Thames Valley regulation which protected apprentices from being given salmon oftener than this. Both were twice as well off as British apprentices of a slightly earlier date who objected only when salmon was served more than twice a week. Farm workers in Brittany resigned themselves to eating it three times a week and servants in Norway, five times a week. The record in this matter seems to have been held by the monks of the French Abbey of Lavôute-Chillac, who were patient until they began to find salmon on their plates more than *once a day,* when they rebelled so violently that the prior hastily promised "to restore calm, that thereafter they would eat salmon only once a day and not more than three days a week." Dickens wrote that salmon and poverty went together, so we may assume that in his time it was still a cheap fish. If he could be resurrected today and taken to a fish restaurant, he would be in for a surprise.

It is only in the last quarter-century that salmon has become almost a luxury—particularly in the form of smoked salmon, about which a good deal could be said, but space limitations will not permit us to say it here. Until then there was not only an abundance of salmon, there was a glut of it; but times have changed. The Rhine was the richest salmon river of Europe so recently that I myself once helped eat a magnificent Rhine salmon in Alsace; today the Rhine is the sewer which carries the industrial wastes of four nations to the sea. It is mortal to salmon.

In France, where salmon were taken from the Seine at Paris in the Middle Ages, and dozens of rivers swarmed with salmon until twenty or twenty-five years ago, only the Loire, its tributary the Allier and, in the Pyrenees, the Adour are hosts to any appreciable number of salmon today. In Brittany the annual salmon catch has dwindled from 5000 tons a year to 200; as for Paris, any salmon which lingered in its sullied waters today would be a candidate for early death. The southern limit for European salmon used to be Portugal; there are no salmon in Portugal today nor many left in Spain, where 10,000 fish a day were taken from Galician rivers in the eighteenth century. No unstocked salmon have been seen for 150 years in the Thames, which "fat and sweet salmon" used to mount to a depth of 65 miles upstream from London. Even the famous salmon rivers of Ireland and Scotland are less frequented than they used to be.

In the United States, salmon once swam far up the Hudson to spawn, and along the coast, from the Connecticut to Canada, more than thirty rivers were invaded each year by swarming salmon. Today there are no longer any salmon in the Hudson and "any salmon trying to navigate

SALMON. *Label from can of salmon packed on the Columbia River c.1900*

the lower Connecticut River, which drains the sewage of city after city, would have to make the trip in a space suit," wrote Jonathan Norton Leonard. All the other coastal rivers are devoid of salmon until Maine is reached, a state which in the last century produced 150,000 pounds of salmon annually. Today its commercial salmon industry is dead, and only by dint of much restocking do Maine rivers manage to provide 1000 pounds a year for sportsmen, who number 4000.

One of the first traders to reach America's Pacific Northwest reported that during the spawning season salmon filled the rivers from bank to bank so densely that one could walk across the stream on their backs. In 1805 the boats of the Lewis and Clark expedition had literally to force a passage through the fish. "The number of dead salmon on the Shores & floating in the river [the Columbia] is incredible to say," wrote William Clark, "and at this season [the Indians] have only to collect the fish, split them open, and dry them on their scaffolds." Pacific salmon are holding out better than Atlantic salmon, but all the same the 17 million pounds now being taken annually in the Columbia is a considerable drop from the 49 million of 1911, and the cannery pack has decreased from 4.3 million cases to 3.4 million.

"It has been suggested," write Maurice and Robert Burton in their *Encyclopedia of Fish*, "that the salmon may be doomed to extinction." The causes for the diminution of the salmon population are multiple. Salmon are particularly vulnerable to the menace we tend to think of first—pollution. Probably no fish except its close relatives, trout and char, are more dependent on finding cool, clear, clean oxygenated water over gravel beds in order to be able to spawn; such water is becoming increasingly rare. Pollution is paralleled today by another major threat to the salmon—deep-sea fishing. Until about 1964, the trawlers which scraped the bottom of the ocean clean (and have rendered the continued existence of cod and herring problematical) did not touch salmon, which kept to the upper levels of the water. Besides, nobody knew where they were. Then the well-meant tagging of salmon, and the less well-meant use of radar and aerial observation, revealed the location of their feeding grounds. The Atlantic take of deep-sea salmon rose from zero in 1964 to 910 tons in 1968, and one year later 2000 tons were taken off Greenland alone. Salmon taken in the ocean are fish which have not yet returned to the rivers to spawn; deep-sea fishing is decimating not only the present generation, but future generations as well.

Dams, unequipped with adequate fish ladders to permit salmon to reach their breeding grounds, are another important factor in diminishing the salmon population of the world. In Alaska, nets are sometimes placed so close to river mouths as to prevent mature salmon from mounting the rivers to spawn or young salmon to descend to the sea to achieve maturity. Even individual fishing is getting out of hand—by poachers, who use dynamite in Ireland or electrocution in France, thus killing all the salmon in a given area, leaving none to reproduce, and by sports fishermen, whose inroads are beginning to take on alarming proportions. The annual international salmon-fishing contest at Navarreux in the French Pyrenees, the favorite breeding grounds for the salmon of the Adour, now threatens to end that river's long history as a salmon stream. On America's Pacific coast, salmon might seem too plentiful to be much affected by sports fishing; yet in the state of Washington alone, nearly 850,000 pounds of salmon are caught by anglers each year, a figure which is far from negligible.

The stages at which salmon are most desirable for the table, and are therefore the stages at which they are most fished, are unfortunately those at which they should be spared if the race is to be allowed to propagate itself. Salmon are at their tastiest when they start their homeward journey to their spawning grounds. Their flesh is firm and red, packed with fats and nutrients, for they have been feeding heavily to gain strength for their long trip and the ordeal of breeding which awaits them at its end. The best time to take them, from the gourmet's point of view, is when they move up the rivers to spawn, and this is indeed when most of them have been taken up to now; but caught then, they never get to spawn. They are at their second best in the ocean, where they feed on crustacean-like constituents in the plankton, which give them their distinctive color; taken then, as they have been taken since 1964, they are, once again, prevented from spawning. They are at their third best as young salmon, before they have left fresh water for the sea; if they are caught at this stage, they have not even become mature enough to breed. In short, for the survival of the race, there is no time when salmon can be fished in great quantities without preventing the replenishment of their population except after they have spawned; but nobody would eat them then. Atlantic salmon, after spawning, degenerate visibly. Their flesh becomes unappetizingly white, spongy and tasteless. They are so weakened as to be unable to resist disease, and perhaps as many as 85 percent of them die. The Pacific salmon (which belongs to a different genus) has been described as arriving at its spawning grounds after its long, exhausting swim "a mere bag of bones containing eggs or sperm"; *all* Pacific salmon die after breeding.

Tastiness in salmon depends on other factors in addition to that of the point in their life cycle at which they are taken. For instance, lake salmon, whether naturally land-locked or seeded artificially (like the coho and some Chinook salmon in Lake Michigan), are smaller, species for species, and less tasty than their sea-going twins. The most important influence on taste, however, seems to be the species. Nobody disagrees with the judgment that the Atlantic salmon, *Salmo salar* (there is only one species), is the best of its kind. Its taste varies greatly, nevertheless, with its habitat. Scotch salmon is universally acclaimed as the best (with the reservation that Irish salmon is a worthy rival), after which opinions diverge. The only New World Atlantic salmon spoken of in the same breath as European Atlantic salmon, though the species are the same on both sides of the ocean, is Greenland salmon. Maine and Canadian salmon are rated below the European fish for taste.

Pacific salmon are in general ranked below Atlantic salmon for flavor. Here the pre-Columbian Indians spoke of five "tribes" of salmon, and when German naturalist Georg Wilhelm Steller classified them in 1741, he agreed that there were indeed five species, not counting a sixth which the Indians could not have known about, the Japanese *masu* (*Oncorhynchus masou*), which keeps to its own side of the ocean, and is the least tasty of all salmon.

Tastiness in Pacific salmon correlates with two factors: the length of time the fish spends in the ocean, in its best feeding grounds, and its strength, measurable by the distances it can cover to reach its spawning place. The five American species all bear scientific names based on Russian, a reminder that Russians were the first fishermen of the northern Pacific coast. In the descending order of flavorfulness they are as follows:

1. The Chinook salmon, *O. tshawytscha.* Its tastiness is legitimately won: it spends the longest time in the ocean, eight years, compared to a limit of four or five for other salmon, and it mounts rivers farther than any others, having been found as far as 2250 miles upstream. It is also the largest (record catch, 108 pounds) and the gamest fighter when hooked, for which reasons it is called the king salmon. Its other names are the Sacramento salmon (the Sacramento River is its southernmost territory), the Columbia salmon (the Columbia River is where it is found in the largest numbers), the quinnat (from Lake Quinault in Washington, which it sometimes enters to breed), and the tyee. Purists give it this last name, the Chinook word for "chief," only when it weighs more than 30 pounds.

2. The sockeye salmon, *O. nerka,* stays in the ocean almost as long as the Chinook. It is a favorite of the canneries, because of its dark red flesh, rich in oil. It is also known as the red salmon or the blueback.

3. The coho salmon, *O. kisutch,* spends two or three years at sea and moves only a short way upstream to spawn. It is also called the silver salmon.

4. The pink salmon, *O. gorbuschka,* matures more quickly than any other salmon, at two years, and is the smallest. It is the kind most often canned, for it is the commonest. It is also called the humpback salmon because just before spawning a ridge of cartilage forms along the spine of the male.

5. The chum salmon, *O. keta,* is little valued for its flesh, which is yellowish or an unappetizing pale pink, but is fished especially for its roe (*keta* is Russian for "salmon roe"). It is also called the keta or the dog salmon, the latter a name given it by the Athapaskan Indians of the Yukon, who eat choicer species themselves and give the chum to their dogs—to the great annoyance of the Eskimos of the Arctic Northwest, who have no other kind to eat and have to make do with chum.

A fish of the Northern Hemisphere which dotes on cold water, the Atlantic salmon does not enter the Mediterranean and thus has no classical history, with this one exception: the ancient Romans were the only people of their era ever to have tasted salmon, provided they were rich enough to pay the cost of transporting the fish, alive in lead-lined cistern carts, or dead, packed in ice or snow, across Gaul and down the Italian peninsula all the way from the Rhine or the Loire. Salmon, Atlantic or Pacific, has virtually no Asian history either, except that Marco Polo reported that Lake Baku was well stocked with them.

Salmon may have been a cheap fish, detested by the lower orders when it was forced upon them too often, but this did not prevent the gentry of medieval times, who did not have to eat it except when they wanted to, from appreciating its excellence. "Salmon was the pièce de résistance at banquets given by the kings of Ireland, when it was cooked on a spit, after being rubbed with salt and basted with butter and honey," Theodora FitzGibbon wrote in *A Taste of Ireland,* and indeed why would they have snubbed the food which gave the legendary Fionn mac Cumhail the power to foresee the future? A favorite fast-day dish for the twelfth-century canons of Basle was salmon cooked in oil, accompanied by leeks. It was on a fast day too that the Abbé de Lagny, at the famous banquet he gave in the fourteenth century for the notables of Paris, included salmon among the five saltwater fish on the menu. In the same century it was the custom in England to present to the abbot of Westminster the first salmon taken in the Thames at the beginning of each year's run. The fisherman who delivered the salmon was entitled on that day to sit at the abbot's table and order the cellarer to serve him bread and ale; the cellarer was then permitted to take from the fish's tail as much flesh as he could remove with "four fingers and his thumb erect."

The first fish specifically mentioned in American history is the salmon—by Eric the Red, who reported that the Vikings had encountered there "larger salmon than they had ever seen before." Larger did not necessarily mean better. Captain Frederick Marryat, after visiting the United States in 1837, told his English compatriots: "Their salmon is not equal to ours"; and unless there has been a change in comparative salmon quality since, he was probably right. Nevertheless, New England salmon was still good enough to create a local tradition. Longfellow described John Endicott as

a solid man of Boston.
A comfortable man, with dividends,
And the first salmon, and the first green peas.

But Longfellow missed a point. It was especially on the Fourth of July that New Englanders ate steamed salmon, with a creamy onion-scented egg sauce, flanked with boiled new potatoes and fresh peas—it was the right season for all three of them.

When America's settlers reached the Pacific Northwest, they found themselves in the realm of salmon. Few societies have been so closely wedded to a single food as the Indians of that region were to salmon. Three-quarters of their food was fish and shellfish, and three-quarters of that three-quarters was salmon. Fish—one might as well say salmon, for in several of the Indian languages the word for "salmon" was also the word for "fish"—had shaped Indian society, obviating for the Tlingit, the Salish, the Kwakiutl, the Bella Coola and others the necessity for turning to agriculture. Because different species ran at different times (and some of them might run twice during the year) there were from five to seven major invasions of salmon annually, providing an almost permanent supply. With each run, the tribes exploded into feverish activity, working day and night; the men took the fish in great nets woven from vines, the women opened and cleaned them.

It has been written that the Pacific Indians knew sixty-six ways of cooking salmon, a dubious figure, for recipes fall into the category of things which are by their nature uncountable, but we may at least note that we probably owe to the Indians some of the methods by which we cook salmon today.

Since salmon was the principal food of the Northwest [I read in that recommended work, *Eating in America*, by Waverley Root and Richard de Rochemont], there were many ways of cooking it, but the simplest was considered among the best: the fish, opened and cleaned, was pinched between two small branches cut from any handy tree, and pinioned between them too was a series of lateral twigs, like ribs, to hold the fish spread open before (not over) the fire. By turning or inclining the central branches, the amount of heat reaching various parts of the salmon could be regulated to insure even cooking. A delicate refinement, after the fish had been split open and cleaned, was to rub the interior with sweet ferns, imparting a delicate flavor to the flesh. The Indians had two fashions of cooking what we would call planked salmon today. A king salmon was skewered to a piece of driftwood (which thus provided built-in seasoning) and held over a high flame to sear the fish and prevent its juices from escaping. The fire was then allowed to burn down, and the piece of driftwood with its attached fish placed on the embers to cook slowly and thoroughly. It would be charred on the outside, but succulently juicy inside, with a marked flavor of smoke. The other method consisted in making a sandwich of a salmon split open, flattened and enclosed between two thin slabs of alder wood, which was then laid over a bed of glowing embers. Too many salmon for immediate consumption were always taken during the spawning season, so the surplus was smoked for future use, much more heavily than we smoke salmon today; it was often left in the smokehouse for two weeks, emerging brown rather than salmon-colored. Sometimes smoked salmon was also dried, seasoned and cut into thin strips, ready to be chewed between meals by anyone who felt hungry; this was "squaw candy." The red roe of the salmon was first spread out on the rocks to dry, and then smeared on bread like butter.

There was also another way of preserving salmon: it was dried, smoked and pressed compactly into seal bladders to protect it from deterioration. The whites called it "Siwash cheese."

Some Indian tribes offered yearly prayers for the return of the salmon or performed dances as a charm to lure them to the rivers. Others resorted to more elaborate ceremonials, particularly where it was believed that salmon were not merely fish, but spirit people who lived in the sea, assuming from time to time the form of salmon to feed the peoples in whom they took a benevolent interest, and returning magically to their underwater abode after having been eaten. It was important to treat the first salmon taken with the greatest respect, lest it become offended and order those following it to turn back. Sometimes it was laid with appropriate care on the bank, its head pointing upstream, to show the salmon the direction they should take.

The Chinook Indians believed [wrote Dale Brown] that anyone involved in preparing a corpse for burial could drive the fish away, and to avert this danger they went so far as to bury the infirm alive. They also believed that menstruating women . . . were tainted, and would not permit [them] to partake of the salmon lest the fish retreat from the river or disappear altogether. . . . "Upon catching a fish," an observer wrote, "they immediately take out his heart and conceal it until they have an opportunity to burn it, their great fear being that this sacred portion . . . may be eaten by dogs, which they shudder to think would prevent [the salmon] from coming again to the river."

There may be equivalent superstitions among Eskimos and Alaskan Indians, though I have not come across any record of them; perhaps salmon have always been so plentiful there that it never occurred to anybody that charms or propitiatory rites were necessary to keep them coming.

Salmon is the most important seafood export of Alaska, worth $100 million a year at the time of writing. There are at least nineteen streams there named for this fish—thirteen Salmon Creeks and six Salmon Rivers—but many others attract spawning salmon too, like the Kobuch, where an aerial count one summer showed that 100,000 salmon were mounting this single stream. The Eskimos

use every part of the salmon [John McPhee wrote in *The New Yorker*]. They eat the eggs with bearberries. They roast, smoke, fry, boil, or dry the flesh. They bury the heads in leaf-lined pits and leave them for weeks. The result is a delicacy reminiscent of cheese. Fevers and colds are sometimes treated by placing fermented salmon on the skin of the neck and nose. A family might use as many as a thousand salmon a year. To feed dogs, many salmon are needed. . . . Dog teams have been largely replaced by snowmobiles . . . and, as a result, the salmon harvest at first declined. Snow machines, however . . . break down now and again, and are thus perilous. A stranded traveller cannot eat a snow machine. Dog teams in the regions are increasing in number, and the take of salmon is growing as well.

Eskimos seem in no imminent danger of running out of salmon. In Europe, where this is not true, a solution has been sought by raising the fish in captivity from egg to table size, which is now being done in Brittany, in Denmark and, horror of horrors, even in Scotland. The drawback is that mysterious law of nature which decrees that foods, whether animal or vegetable, develop taste to its full potential only when they have been put to the test of the struggle to survive against the perils of their environment. Artificially raised salmon have little taste. James de Coquet, gastronomic editor of the Paris daily *Le Figaro*, was moved to investigate this matter when he was served what he was assured was Scotch salmon and found it "perfectly insipid." He demanded an explanation.

I was shown two specimens of salmon [he wrote], one manufactured by Nature, the other by man. They wore the same garment of silver spangled with black patches. The giveaway was the tail fin. On the fish which had made prodigious bounds to speed towards its future loves, this appendix is a veritable fan, in which one senses an enormous force. On the fish which idled in the pens, which had not pursued intruders threatening its eggs, which did not hunt its own food, in short this fish living on its dividends in fresh water, the tail fin was atrophied. It was hardly larger than a playing card. [This salmon] was no longer a hard-bellied athlete. You could sink a finger into its flesh as if it were an eiderdown coverlet.

Salmon are like men: too soft a life is not good for them.

SALSIFY. Salsify must taste like oyster to some persons, otherwise it would not have acquired its alternative names "oyster plant" and "vegetable oyster." "When properly cooked," wrote Alex D. Hawkes, in *A World of Vegetable Cookery*, its taste "is indistinguishable from that of the oyster, though the texture is considerably firmer than that marvelous mollusk." All I can say is that salsify doesn't taste like oysters to me, though it is quite possible that I didn't cook it properly. Ordinarily I do not cook, just eat, but I had to cook salsify because nobody else in the family showed any interest in it. It is also possible that my salsify was not of the best to begin with. The only time I ever entered into extensive contact with this vegetable was when I grew it myself, in central Vermont, at the extreme limit of its range. Salsify requires a long growing season, and I was probably lucky to have any at all, flavorless or not.

I have toyed with another theory to account for the resemblance so many people perceive between salsify and the oyster, instigated by Théophile Gautier, who referred to "slimy little salsifies, like marshmallow roots, much esteemed for their digestive qualities." Slimy! Could salsify have been likened to the oyster originally because of its texture, hypnotizing its eaters thereafter into believing that it tasted like oysters too? Taste is a strange sense, susceptible to distortion by psychological influences. However, it is difficult for me to take refuge in this hypothesis, for salsify doesn't seem slimy to me either.

The fact is that salsify, or at least the salsify I grew, does not seem to me to have much taste at all—a sort of faded sweetness, perhaps. I notice that its partisans tend to describe its flavor as "delicate," which may be a giveaway. Certainly nobody would call it aggressive. Salsify does not force itself upon the attention, which may be the reason why it has never, at any time or in any place, occupied a particularly important rank in gastronomy. One gardening book which wants to convert us all to eating salsify puts it that carrots, turnips, beets and their like are the best sellers among root crops, but that salsify, while it cannot pretend to equal eminence, has solid merits all the same. Its lack of marked individuality, nevertheless, provokes nobody into taking the trouble to deal with it. It has to be peeled, or, better, scraped, and its dimensions make it difficult to handle. It looks like a parsnip, but an undernourished parsnip—up to six inches long, but extremely thin. If you want to experiment with salsify, cook it first and scrape it afterwards. Not only is this easier, but it allows you to skip one step in its preparation. It discolors quickly, so if you peel it first it is advisable to drop it at once into a bowl of water containing a little lemon juice or vinegar before you cook it.

Gardening books, when they deal with salsify at all, usually bewail the neglect of so useful a winter vegetable, complaining that it deserves more attention, as though it were particularly meritorious to put up with a food of faint flavor. Salsify does indeed increase the short list of fresh vegetable foods available during cold weather. Ripening in the autumn, it can be left in the ground over the winter, wherever temperatures do not normally fall below 10° F., and can be pulled up whenever you want to eat it during the next five or six months.

In the United States it is difficult to find salsify in the markets. In Europe it is readily available during its season, and turns up in fritters, or serves as the basis for a cream soup, or is even cooked like asparagus. In some places the first tender young shoots are also eaten, sometimes raw in salads.

Salsify is believed to be a native of the Mediterranean basin, possibly first on the African side, but its pale elusiveness did not make much more impression on the ancients than on us. We are told that the Greeks and Romans ate it, sometimes with the added information that they consumed the shoots rather than the roots; but though it is certain that the ancients ate something of this kind, it is far from certain that it was salsify, *Tragopogon porrifolius*, which then as now was confused with a number of similar plants. The one of which we can be surest is goatsbeard, *T. pratensis*, so called because of the silky filament attached to its seed. This plant made itself conspicuous when Julius Caesar's army, surrounded by Pompey's, was cut off from its supplies and lived on goatsbeard, which, providentially, grew thickly on the spot. Another close relative of salsify, *T. crocifolius*, also with an edible root, seems to be the one Pliny mentioned as eaten in Egypt. A Pompeiian painting shows what is usually described as a bundle of asparagus, but it looks more like the salsify we know, prepared for the market. Whichever plants the ancients ate seem to have been gathered wild; nothing is said about their being cultivated.

Salsify excited no great interest in the Middle Ages either. The earliest reference to it seems to have been in the thirteenth century, when Albertus Magnus wrote of a plant he called *Oculus porce* or *flos campi*, now believed to have been salsify. It was a wild plant, and though salsify was mentioned subsequently by many botanists, it was not until 1587 that it was described as cultivated. It was obviously new to Olivier de Serres (1539–1619), for he wrote: "Another valuable root has been brought to our attention very recently, holding an honorable rank in the garden, the Sercifi." This was about the time of John Gerard, who paid more attention in his *Herball* to goatsbeard, also called Joseph's flower, star of Jerusalem, noon tide or go-to-bed-at-noon (because it closes its blossoms under the full sun of midday), than to salsify, which slips in as a sort of afterthought under the name "purple goatsbeard" (the color of its flower; that of goatsbeard is yellow).

The plant oftenest confused with salsify is less closely related to it than those mentioned above, a member of a different genus, *Scorzonera hispanica*, known as black salsify, black oyster plant and even as black radish—and also as viper grass, because its sap was once believed to be an antidote for snakebite (*escorso* is Catalan for "viper"). The root looks like a twin of salsify, except for being black instead of white, and the taste is so similar that French cooks use one or the other interchangeably. Scorzonera is described by some writers as inferior to salsify and by others as superior to it; many Europeans do prefer it to salsify proper. The French southwest has a specialty of unopened scorzonera buds in omelets, in which use they are described as more exquisite than asparagus tips.

An also-ran in the salsify category is *Scolymus hispanicus*, the Spanish oyster plant, or golden thistle. Two other edible plants which could hardly be confused with salsify except in name are a second goatsbeard (in French), which is a mushroom, and a second oyster plant (in Eng-

SALSIFY. *Print from Artemas Ward:* The Grocer's Encyclopedia, *New York, 1911*

lish), also called sea lungwort, sea bugloss or sea gromwell, which is the coastal *Mertensia maritima,* whose leaves taste like oysters.

SALT. I suppose we must class in the category of humor known as the Irish bull the statement that salt makes its presence felt only in its absence. It is not quite exact. Salt also makes its presence felt when it is used to excess, which, given the shortcomings of cooks, occurs only too often. The strongest and the most assertive of all seasoners, salt must be used with discretion. In what seems to have been the world's very first cookbook, the Sicilian Greek Archestratus warned us to "be sparing of salt" in his directions for baking dogfish, and this advice has been repeated ever since, though not always from a strictly gastronomic point of view. Thus Léon de Fos wrote in 1870:

Le sel, pris à l'excès, est aussi malfaisant
Que pris avec raison il est sain et propice,
Car, admirez où va se nicher sa malice:
Il excite la femme et rend l'homme impuissant.

Or, translated with great freedom:

Malicious salt makes human beings alter.
Employed with measure, it leaves all things well
But taken in excess, provokes its private hell:
Makes women hot, but men inclined to falter.

Agreement with M. de Fos on the aphrodisiac powers of salt (for one sex) is not universal. The abundance of salt in medieval Venice (and its effect on both sexes) has been cited in explanation of the parallel abundance of another specialty of that city, but an old piece of doggerel attributes it to a less direct intervention of salt:

In Venice why so many whores abound?
The reason sure is easy to be found,
Because, as learnèd sages all agree,
Fair Venus' birthplace was the salt, salt sea.

I am not quite sure what position Dickens was taking on this question in *Silas Wegg*: "Meaty jelly, too, especially when a little salt, which is the case when there's ham, is mellering to the organ."

The very name of salt breathes of health: it comes from the Roman god of health, Salus, who gave to the English language such words as "salutary" and "salute"—originally a gesture meant to express a wish of good health for the person saluted—not to mention "salvation." Salt is "basic to all the needs of man's life," says the Apocrypha, a judgment apocryphal only in the most literal sense. "What am I, Life?" John Masefield asked, and supplied the answer himself: "A thing of watery salt / Held in cohesion by unresting cells." The description is fair enough. Salt, in proper proportions, is not only beneficial to human life, it is essential for it. To function properly—sometimes simply to survive—the body requires a constant presence of 3½ ounces of salt, and its absence makes itself felt in dire fashion—perhaps by a decrease in arterial tension, perhaps by general debility.

The proportion of salt in the human bloodstream is close to its proportion in sea water; some theorists have gone so far as to suggest that it is identical with that of the ocean at the time when life first emerged onto land from "the unplumb'd, salt, estranging sea," as Matthew Arnold put it, or, in Carl Sandburg's words, "the great naked sea shouldering a load of salt." Some of that salt is lost every day, in urine, sweat and tears; it is daily that we must replace it. Different authorities have different ideas about how much salt is normally lost each day: the lowest figure I find in any reputable source puts the loss at 5 to 6 grams (3½ ounces is the equivalent of 100 grams); the highest is 30. This divergence is perhaps explainable by the tendency of each expert to consider as universal the situation in the climate with which he is personally familiar. The loss or retention of salt in the human body depends to a considerable extent on climate. Europeans in tropical countries are obliged to suck salt tablets to replace the salt they lose in excessive perspiration; the natives of those countries are ordinarily dark-skinned: their pigmentation protects them from the ravages of the sun. However much salt an individual may lose during the day, a normal Western diet will return to his body only about 1 or 1½ grams; the rest must be added in the form of seasoning—seasoning with salt. You can get along without other seasonings—cinnamon, nutmeg, cloves, even pepper—but you cannot get along without salt. What the body needs is sodium chloride—in other words, salt. Persons deprived of it have been known to chew earth, in a desperate instinctive attempt to profit by the minute amount of salt it may contain.

It is dangerous to attempt to lose weight by following a saltless diet, unless you have been instructed to do so by a physician. True, you will probably lose weight, for a function of salt is to retain water in the tissues. Though water accounts for a large proportion of the body's weight, the body needs that water. It is dangerous too to oversalt your food. "Laboratory research suggests," wrote Reay Tannahill in *Food in History*, "that an ounce of salt a day (a not uncommon dose) can shorten a man's life by as much as thirty years."

Since salt is essential to human life (and animal life too, for that matter), how does it happen that some peoples do not use it? "It may well be that some seek not gold," wrote the Visigothic statesman Cassiodorus in the fifth century, "but there lives not a man who does not need salt." Yet down the ages we have reports again and again of areas where salt was shunned. Homer told us that his heroes always ate salt with their meat, so the companions of Ulysses noted in surprise of certain inlanders they encountered in their wanderings: "This people does not eat salt with its food!" Sallust could not understand how the Numidians could get along without it. Not very far from their territory the Hadbramaut Bedouins today do not salt their food, and the *Encyclopaedia Britannica* reports that in parts of central Africa salt is still a luxury, available only to the rich. The pastoral Toda people of India do not seem to have used salt until Europeans introduced them to it.

American Indians puzzled the first Europeans. All along the Atlantic coast, with that great reservoir of salt, the sea, ready to provide all that was wanted, there were alternating stretches where the Indians had learned to extract salt from the sea and where they had not, and consequently did not use it; and this situation extended even to the islands of the Caribbean, completely surrounded by salt water, some of which took advantage of it, while others did not. The usual explanation is that some Indians did not use salt because they possessed other seasonings—like maple sugar in the Northeast or chili pepper in the Caribbean.

In 1859 Johann Georg Kohl, a German visitor to the United States, wrote:

> Sugar serves [the Indians] instead of salt, which even those who live among Europeans use very little or not at all. . . . That great cookery symbol, the salt-box, which is regarded among salt-consuming nations with a species of superstitious reverence, is hence hardly ever found in an Indian lodge. But the large sugar makak may be always seen there, and when the children are impatient, the mother gives them some of the contents, and they will sit at the door and eat sugar by handfuls.

In 1896 W. J. Hoffman added that the Ojibwa Indians showed "an almost abnormal fondness for [sugar]. It virtually forms a substitute for salt"; and that "salt is not used by the Nemonimi during meals, neither does it appear to have a place in the kitchen for cooking or baking." As for the Plains Indians, George Catlin wrote in 1857: "I have, in travelling with the Indians, encamped by such places where they have cooked and eaten their meat, when I have been unable to prevail on them to use salt in any quantity whatever." The Eskimos too had an aversion to salt.

Maple sugar and chili pepper may be gastronomic substitutes for salt: they are not chemical substitutes, for they are incapable of providing the sodium chloride the body must have. The fact is that these peoples who astonished observers by not eating salt *did* eat salt; what they did not eat was *added* salt. They were either great drinkers of milk (the Bedouins), or great consumers of animal proteins (the Eskimos), or both (the Todas, whose society and economy were based on herds of buffalo). Cow's milk contains 1.6 grams of salt per liter (three times as much as human milk), meat on the average contains 0.1 to 0.15 gram of salt per 100 grams of weight. Prehistoric man did not exert himself unduly to find salt. He was a carnivorous animal, living largely on game. Carnivorous animals show little interest in salt; they get it from eating herbivorous animals, who do crave salt, and find it in salt licks. Prehistoric man ate both carnivorous and herbivorous animals, and derived salt from both.

A great change occurred when Neolithic man achieved the second great gastronomic revolution—the invention of seasoning. (The first, of course, was the invention of cooking.) It was forced upon him. He had to discover seasoning, because he changed the nature of his society—from hunting to herding to agriculture. He began eating less game and more vegetables—which demanded salt for reasons of gastronomy (they were comparatively tasteless) and for reasons of health (they did not contain enough salt to meet human requirements). Some was obtained from burning salty plants and extracting salt from the ashes (millennia later west-coast Danes would do the same with dune grass), but this was not enough. To make matters worse, Neolithic man soon found himself deriving his basic foods from cereals, which contain virtually no salt. At the same time, he had produced another momentous invention—cooking pots resistant enough to be placed over a fire. Before that time his meat was roasted, either on a spit or in a hole in the ground lined with heated stones. Now he could boil it, a more convenient method, requiring minimum attention from the cook: but while roasting conserves the salt content of meat, boiling leaches it out. It became necessary to find salt.

Neolithic man, it seems, was already mining what are believed to be the oldest salt mines in Europe, those of Austria's Hallstein and Hallstatt, of which the latter has given its name to a prehistoric culture because the rich community which developed around the salt deposits left behind a treasure of archeologically interesting objects, some of them preserved by the salt, including bodies of the ancient miners. The salt caverns are a tourist attraction today, visited from Salzburg, which means, of course, Salt City. There are twelve other known sites in Europe where salt may have been mined in Neolithic times (plus two each in France and England where it was extracted from sea water), but if they were not quite that early, they were at least being worked in the Bronze Age. Salt mines are widely distributed throughout the world, found in rock of all geological ages, buried deep in damp areas, because of the solubility of salt in water, close to the surface in arid regions, where there was no moisture to dissolve it and wash it away. Land deposits of salt reveal the presence of an absence—the absence of ancient seas which drained away or evaporated or disappeared for some other reason, leaving their salt behind. Traces of this process are visible today where salt lakes, once common in Asia, Africa and America, have dried up, becoming instead salt plains. Salt mines produce rock salt, which is colorless in a pure state, but is rarely pure: the walls of the mine may glisten with gray, yellow, pink, red, blue or green hues, to the delight of the tourists who visit them. In some of the mines which have now been converted into tourist attractions, lights have been placed behind the translucent pillars left to hold up the ceilings, casting prismatic colors in underground rainbows against the walls, roofs and floors.

SALT. *Cruet frame with five cruets, silver and glass, London, 1770*

We do not know if Asian salt mines go back as far as the earliest of Europe. When Alexander the Great invaded India, in 328 B.C., he found vast mines in full exploitation; five kinds of salt were enumerated there: sea salt, rock salt, red salt, black salt and earth salt. A very ancient preoccupation with salt is implicit in the legendary Indian description of the structure of the world: it consisted of a series of concentric continents with Mount Meru at their center, separated one from another by seven seas, each of a different substance: the one nearest to Meru was of salt. We hear of salt in China as early as 2000 B.C. Three and a half millennia later, Marco Polo found it at least on his way to China. Having escaped from the territory of the Assassins, he reached a town which he called Talikhan, where

> the mountains to the south of it are very large and are all made of salt. Men come from all the country round, for thirty days' journey, to fetch this salt, which is the best in the world. It is so hard that it cannot be got out except with a stout iron pick. And I assure you that it is so plentiful that it would suffice for all the world to the end of time.

The notorious salt mines of Siberia, which have given us a household phrase, were probably not exploited until comparatively recent times. The chief reason why they had to be worked by convicts rather than by free labor was presumably the rigorous nature of the climate, which did not attract workers. There may have been a contributing cause too, which is not in harmony with the reputation of salt for healthiness: constant contact with the salt thickened the miners' skin and provoked the opening of ulcers in their legs.

Rock salt is usually what one gets in the United States (except in health food stores), but Europe buys sea salt. "Food cooked with sea salt tastes so much better than that cooked with powdered salt [i.e., ground rock salt] that people who are accustomed to it notice a startling difference when deprived of it," wrote Elizabeth David. It may be derived directly from the sea, but more often it comes from lagoons or salt marshes along the coast.

In France the great majority of sea salt (95 percent) comes from one place: Aigues-Mortes, a name which for most persons will evoke the Crusaders, many of whom sailed from there. In 1418 the salt of Aigues-Mortes rendered a singular service to its city. A band of Burgundians made a surprise attack upon it, but with so little success that they left more dead bodies behind than could be coped with easily. They were dumped into a convenient tower, and the tower was filled with salt. The Aigues-Mortes works today are among the most modern in Europe; its product serves more conventional purposes.

Italy eats sea salt too. Nearly half of it comes from the coastal flats near Cagliari in Sardinia, exploited since 150 B.C., now the largest salt works in Europe; most of the rest comes from similar flats which extend for fifteen miles southward from Trapani, Sicily. The Mediterranean should be able to replenish these deposits indefinitely. It is saltier than the Atlantic, in accordance with the general rule that enclosed seas are always saltier than open oceans (the extreme example is the Dead Sea), and it possesses in addition riches apparently peculiar to this sea, which were discovered as recently as 1970. It was in that year that the American exploratory ship *Glomar Challenger*, making borings in the bottom, discovered that under a thin layer of sediment there lies a thick cushion of salt, laid down an estimated five or six million years ago. In some places it is 3000 feet deep.

The oceans are our greatest potential reservoir of salt. On the average, each gallon of sea water contains .2547 pound of salt. Its total bulk is 14½ times that of all Europe above the high-water mark, and if it could be extracted completely from the water and spread over the land, it would cover the continents and the islands to a depth of 115 feet. We may exhaust our oil, our coal, our iron and our copper, but it looks as if there should be enough salt to last.

If you should find yourself in Rome and whimsy should prompt you to set foot on the very soil which engendered the Roman Empire, do not go to the Palatine Hill, where in 753 B.C. Romulus plowed the furrow which marked the first perimeter of his new city, but drive instead up the Via Veneto—which you will certainly know, for no visitor to Rome can escape it—to the splendid park known as the Villa Borghese, turn right along the Corso d'Italia, and left when you come to its first *piazza*. You will find yourself on a modern automobile road, but beneath its smooth cement lie the rough paving stones of the oldest of the network of roads which Roman engineers spread first over Italy and then over the world, the road whose ancient activity flowered into the power of ancient Rome. It was called the Via Salaria in antiquity and it is called the Via Salaria today; you can follow it, if you are so minded, all the way to the Adriatic. Via Salaria: the Salt Road. It began as a pair of ruts worn by Roman carts carrying surplus salt to Rieti, the capital of the neighboring Sabines. Sabine demand encouraged the increase of Roman production, to a point where Romans and Sabines together could not absorb it, so the carts pushed on beyond Rieti in search of other buyers—across Umbria, across the Marches, and finally to the eastern sea.

Delivering salt from the Tyrrhenian coast to the Adriatic coast may sound, anachronistically, like carrying coals to Newcastle, but it was not quite that: the Tyrrhenian has a higher salt content than the Adriatic, since great quantities of fresh water from Alpine streams pour into the upper reaches of the Adriatic. Carts laden with salt were followed by others carrying mutton, wool and cloth, the products of Latin sheep, and by still others with an increasingly varied selection of merchandise. The flag followed trade: the Roman legions marched along the Salt Road on their way to conquest. The empire expanded from this artery; salt, in a sense, may be said to have founded the empire.

The Romans knew a thing or two about salt. Before Rome existed, their ancestors, the Latins, were humble shepherds living among the salt marshes at the mouth of the Tiber, from which they extracted salt for their sheep and for themselves. When they moved up the river they were still, in Rome, less than twenty miles from their source of salt. Their *salinatores* continued to boil brine in shallow pans until the water evaporated, leaving its salt behind—essentially what we do today. They were conscious of the importance of salt. When Pompey defeated Mithridates and found in his palace an antidote to poison, he was struck by the directions which accompanied it: "to be taken fasting, a grain of salt being added" —hence our modern expression "take with a grain of salt." (It was Petronius, in the *Satyricon*, who gave us another: "not worth his salt.") Salt was one of the rations issued to Roman soldiers. Sometimes, instead of the salt itself, they were given money with which to buy it—salt money, *salarium*, our word "salary."

Salt was then, and possibly still is today, the single most important commodity of world commerce. Rome was not alone in having a Via Salaria. Everywhere in the ancient world, land areas were crisscrossed by salt routes: one of the oldest roads in Languedoc was beaten out by carts carrying salt from the Greek colony at Agde to the towns of the Rhone valley. The Mediterranean and the Aegean were traversed by ships carrying salt, and salt caravans moved even across the deserts. Herodotus described a caravan route which linked all the salt oases of the Libyan Desert, collecting their precious seasoner and delivering it to saltless territory. Even today, the most important commodity carried by the few remaining Saharan caravans is salt. The Tuaregs still supply it to the Sudanese, who have none; in the Middle Ages they paid for it its weight in gold, receiving it from Idjil, in what is today Mauritania, whose salt works have been known since the sixth century. The caravans which carried salt in one direction worked up a sideline in slaves for the return trip. In 1352 the Moroccan traveler Abou Abdallah Mohamed ibn Battuta, traversing a Saharan salt-producing region, came upon "an unattractive village, with the curious feature that its houses and mosques are built of blocks of salt, roofed with camel hides." In the fifteenth century the entire African nation of the Vakarango moved several hundred miles northward when it exhausted its source of salt. It was probably a caravan route along which salt from the Syrian oases was sent from Palmyra to the cities of the Persian Gulf.

In Egypt the salt of the Nile delta was treated in salting tubs in the small fishing village of Rhacotis, where Alexander the Great would later establish the city which still bears his name. Egypt shipped salt overseas, for instance to Homeric Greece; and in A.D. 900 it was still exporting it in the form of fish "sent salted to the horizons," if we may accept the authority of a writer who took nearly six hundred years to report this fact, Ibn Zuhayra, who included it in *The Shining Virtues of the Good Things of Egypt and Cairo*, written in 1483. Despite its sea-indented geography, Greece could not produce enough salt for its own use, and not only imported it from Egypt but also sent ships into the Black Sea to bring it back from the salt pans at the mouth of the Dnieper, either pure or in the form of salt fish. Salt was an important element in the waterborne commerce of China, according to Marco Polo.

In the eleventh century, the Vikings handled the salt trade in the North Sea. In that same century, salt described as "the best in the world" was the principal export of Cognac, where brandy had not yet been invented. In the thirteenth, the Flemish replaced the Vikings in the north, growing rich from transporting the salt of the German Baltic city of Lübeck, used chiefly for the preserving of herring. In the fifteenth, most of the salt of Europe came from deposits at the mouth of the Loire. In the sixteenth, the Flemish merchant fleet, based chiefly on Antwerp, had as "its function . . . to exchange . . . the products of the Baltic—corn, timber, iron—against the salt and wine of Biscay," according to Charles Wilson in *The Divided Netherlands*.

We all know that the glittering wealth of Venice was built on the spice trade, and in our minds we tend to match its Byzantine splendor with the exotic fragrances of cinnamon, nutmeg and cloves, which seem so much in harmony with it. Yet the first seasoner which brought riches to Venice, and the most important of them all, was not one of the romantic products of the East, but the commonplace, though indispensable, salt (which Venice exchanged in Constantinople for the spices of Asia). The Adriatic might not contain as much salt as the Tyrrhenian Sea, but it contained more than the Po. When Venetians learned how to extract salt from their seaside marshes, they established a salt monopoly in the Po valley.

A single food nourishes all alike [Cassiodorus observed in a letter to the Maritime Tribunes of Venice]. All your rivalry is expended in your salt works; in place of ploughs and sickles you turn your drying pans, and hence comes all your gain, and what you have made is your very own.

It was indeed. It is difficult to believe, as we are told, that caravans sent to Venice in the thirteenth century to buy salt for Hungary, Croatia and eastern Germany sometimes required as many as 40,000 horses to carry the load. It was a mighty trade, and Venetians understood so well the importance of their exclusive control of salt in this part of the world that when Comacchio tried to break the monopoly in 854, they razed that city; and when Cervia in its turn tried to provide competition, they annexed it. But Cervia had the last laugh: Venice produces no salt today, but Cervia does.

It is no wonder that a commodity so valuable was sometimes used as money, in places as distant and as different as Abyssinia and Tibet.

Salt was sacred for the ancient Aryans, because, it has been suggested, they used it to preserve the bodies of their dead. (So did the early Egyptians, who did not for that reason grant any particular status to salt, while the ancient Romans, who cremated their dead, nevertheless used salt in their rituals.) The ancient Greeks held that bread and salt were gifts of the gods, and for them and for the Romans it appeared on altars on the same footing as incense. It appeared on Hebrew altars too: Moses ordered that every sacrificial offering of meat should be sprinkled with salt. It was perhaps because solemn occasions were usually marked by sacrifices that we find the Bible speaking of "covenants of salt"; the preservative powers of salt may have made it seem particularly appropriate to durable commitments: "a statute for ever," as Numbers 18:19 put it, "it is a covenant of salt for ever before the Lord unto thee and to thy seed with thee."

A sort of unvoiced covenant was implicit in the reception of strangers and the sharing with them of salt; it constituted a pledge of protection which could not be violated without invoking divine wrath. For all Semitic peoples, an offer of salt was an offer of hospitality, with all its duties; but this obligation could be avoided by strewing salt across the sill of a house or the entrance of a tent to warn strangers that they were not welcome. When the Greeks said, "Trespass not against the salt and the bread," they were echoing the Arab: "There is salt between us," still alive today in the Iranian *namak haran*, "untrue to salt," a synonym for ungratefulness, untrustworthiness or disloyalty.

From the ancients, the Church inherited the doctrine of the sanctity of salt. Salt was the seasoner of Christianity; as such it was taboo at those diabolical gatherings known as witches' sabbats. In 1624 a young girl accused of witchcraft confessed she had participated in sabbats, where she had eaten great quantities of black flesh, black bread which she believed had been made from cinders, and no salt at all. In 1652 Suzanne Gandry, who was subsequently strangled and burned as a witch and apparently felt that the Devil should do things in style, explained that there was "neither salt, nor napkins, nor table cloth" at the unholy feasts at which she had been present. This is why dinners at which no salt appeared were once referred to in France as "diabolic banquets" or "witches' suppers." In Guyenne the occasional appearance of minor demons unprovided with tails was considered to be a sign that someone had succeeded in sprinkling salt on these appendages; this caused so much agony to their possessors that they had gnawed them off—a feat which, indeed, would require devilish flexibility. It had been known also, since the eleventh century, that human beings were always subject to demoniac possession; there were precisely 6,666 demons assigned to this activity, and any number from one to 6,666 might assail a single victim. The way to guard against such an invasion was to listen to a great deal of music or to eat one's food heavily salted.

An institution which disappeared from France not so many years ago (indeed, it is not certain that it does not still exist in remote rural districts) was that of the sin eater. Called to a home where a death had occurred, he found a saucer containing salt and a piece of bread placed on the body; he ate it, and with it the sins of the defunct, who thus benefited by a shortening of his term in purgatory, or perhaps escaped even more dire punishment. Sin eaters were despised, but the survival of the custom was assured by making the function hereditary.

I doubt if the Isle of Man still honors one of its ancient traditions, a rite performed on November 1, All Saints' Day. Each member of the household filled a thimble with salt; they were then upended on a plate and the thimbles carefully withdrawn, leaving a series of little domes in a circle on the plate. If any of them were found to have crumbled the next morning, it was a warning that the person whom it represented would die within a year. Not necessarily death, but some dire disaster, was once thought to await anyone who, on May 1, violated the Irish precept that neither fire, water nor milk should be allowed to leave the house that day. If a traveler passed and asked for a drink, a few grains of salt would be added to it, a defense against the dictates of destiny. Salt is associated with life rather than death, a little ambiguously perhaps, among Arabs who rub a newborn baby with it; neglect to perform this rite means that the infant is deemed unworthy to live.

There are any number of other superstitions connected with salt, of which one of the oldest is that it is unlucky to spill salt, illustrated in Leonardo da Vinci's *Last Supper*, where Judas is shown upsetting the salt. In France's Charente a farmer taking his cow to market for sale places half of a pinch of salt between her horns and puts the other half in his pocket; this assures a good price. In the Armagnac area, salt is thrown into the fire to protect a house from being struck by lightning; some scoffers pooh-pooh this precaution, but it is a fact that very few houses so treated have ever been struck.

Not a superstition, but a symbol of the respect accorded to salt, was the circumstance that in former days salt-cellars were often monumental pieces, veritable works of art (one thinks of Benvenuto Cellini's famous salt-cellar), placed before the host, while at a banquet served at several tables, a large salt-cellar appeared on the main table and smaller ones on the others. As everybody knows, the expression "below the salt" originates from the fact that the places of honor were reckoned by their position in regard to the salt. This custom was transferred to New England, where what used to be called "the standing salt" was usually the most prominent, and often the only, piece of plate on the table; and there too the social standing of the guests was echoed in their placement in respect to the salt.

We use much less salt now than our ancestors, who did not have at their disposition the convenient means of refrigeration which permits us to eat in their fresh state foods which in the past it was necessary to salt. Nevertheless, there are many foods which we still prefer to eat salted because it gives them an added dimension—ham, bacon, sausage, several cured meats, cheese and several kinds of fish. Fish in particular accounted for a heavy proportion of the salted food of medieval times. Fast days were many and were strictly observed; dispensations, even for reasons of health, were hard to obtain; and the principal food during periods of fasting was fish. This could be had fresh only by those who lived along the coasts or on the banks of lakes or streams; fish requires heavy salting for its preservation.

> Today we think of sugar and salt as complementary flavorings for food [wrote Margaret Wade Labarge in *A Baronial Household of the Thirteenth Century*] and our domestic accounts would show a great predominance of sugar. This was not so in the middle ages, and it is easy to underestimate the quantities of salt required in the medieval household. The emphasis in their diet on salted meat and fish, and also on the use of brine or souse for pickling, called for generous amounts of salt in the kitchen. It was a common necessity, so frequently purchased that price records can be kept with almost the same regularity as those for grain.

There was one medieval use of salt for preservation which I think it fairly safe to assert is no longer employed:

> When villains were hanged, drawn and quartered [Reay Tannahill informs us in *Food in History*], their heads—before being exhibited in public to discourage others—were first parboiled "with bay salt and cumin seed—that to keep them from putrefaction, and this to keep off the fowls from seizing on them."

It is interesting to note that bay salt was specified for this purpose: it was the best of the times.

SAM
stands for

samphire, an English plant known also as sea fennel, described long ago as "of a spicie taste with a certaine saltnesse," not to mention the samphire which is the seaside purslane, the prickly samphire which is the sea parsnip, the Jamaica samphire which is saltwort, or the marsh samphire which is saltwort too, but a different kind, known also as chicken claws or glasswort, since it was once used to make glass, a safer use perhaps than eating it, for John Gerard wrote that "a great quantitie taken is mischievous and deadly," but it did have the advantage that "the smel and smoke . . . of this herb being burnt drives away serpents."

SAN
stands for

sand, which sixteenth-century French women swallowed to assure clear complexions and which William the Conqueror swallowed, to the extent of two mouthfuls, from the beach where he landed in England to symbolize, in rather literal (and littoral) fashion, his absorption of that country; for **sandal,** a tropical Asian fruit, and **sandalwood,** an Australian fruit, but it was probably the large red sandalwood tree of eastern Asia which, powdered and renamed "sanders," was used to impart color to medieval foods; for the **sand apple,** which isn't an apple but is eaten instead of it in South Africa where real apples often hesitate to grow; for **sand cherries,** which Thoreau "tasted . . . out of compliment to Nature, though they were scarcely palatable"; for the **sand collar snail,** which is the moon shell, and the **sand crab,** which is the lady crab; for the **sand dab,** one of the sweetish and most satisfying of FLATFISH; for the **sand eel** or **sand lance,** at its delicious best when a score or so of its fragile young are served up on your plate looking (but not tasting) like a jumble of jackstraws; for the **sanderling,** a cosmopolitan sandpiper found on the shores of all seven seas, which thinks nothing of flying eight thousand miles to nest; for the **sand goby,** of which the male is a faithful guardian of the eggs, a virtue for which he is rewarded by being little eaten; for the **sand grouse,** which is less of a grouse than a pigeon, and the **sand leek,** which is less of a leek than an onion; for the Asian **sandpaper tree,** whose leaves are eaten in the Himalayas and whose green fruit is eaten in Burma, and the unrelated African sandpaper tree, whose fruit is eaten in Angola; for the **sandpiper,** a pedagogically minded bird bent on illustrating Bergmann's Rule, Gloger's Rule and Allen's Rule, but a violator of Eave's Principle, which did not prevent it from being a favorite food of King Canute; for the **sandroller,** which is the blunt-nosed trout perch, the **sand shark,** which is the guitarfish, the **sand smelt,** which is the grunion, and the **sandsnake,** which is an eel; for the **sand sole,** which, unlike many fish called soles, is the real thing, but it less fished than a number of false soles; for the **sand stompkop,** a fish whose very name should tell you that it is found off South Africa; for **sanguinary,** which sounds less formidable when it is called yarrow; and for the **Santa Gertrudis** steer, an American breed developed on the famous King Ranch of Texas from Brahman bulls and Shorthorn cows, which produces what may well be the best beef in America, if not in the world.

SAP
stands for

sapistan, the Assyrian plum of West Africa; for the **sapodilla,** or naseberry, which in its native South America is too bitter to be eaten before it is rotten, but when it was transplanted in India, a naturalist wrote that "a more luscious, cool and agreeable fruit is not to be met with in any country in the world"; for **sapota,** a name applied not only to the sapodilla, *Achras zapota,* but also to *Lucuma bifera,* a Chilean fruit which looks like a chestnut, to *Matisia cordata,* a Peruvian fruit which tastes like an apricot, and to *Casimiroa edulis,* the white sapota, all of which share the characteristic of being palatable only in decay; for the **sapphire gurnard,** which is not a separate species of fish but only, confusingly, the young of the yellow gurnard; and for the **sapucaya,** a little-known South American nut which resembles the Brazil nut, but tastes even better.

SAR
stands for

Sarotherodon galilaea, a tilapia so named in the belief that it was the species which provided the miraculous draught of fishes of the Bible; for the **sardine,** a word which, since it covers many fish, covers no fish, and which it would be futile to consider in any case since, as we are informed in the immortal opening lines of Howard Spoerl's *Finlandia*: "The sardine, since it has no head, / Is frequently encountered dead"; for the **sargo,** a sort of bream widely eaten in Africa; and for **sarsaparilla,** of which John Gerard wrote: "Zarza parilla of Peru is a strange plant. . . . The roots . . . be long and slender, like to the lesser roots of common liquorice. . . . They have little taste, and so small a smell that it is not to be perceived."

SAS
stands for

sashimi, Japanese raw fish, to which I was initiated in what was then the only Japanese restaurant in Paris by Kyo Momatsu, the Japanese journalist and translator who was the model for Kyo in André Malraux's *Man's Fate,* and was killed while reporting the war in Vietnam; for **saskatoons,** berries of Saskatchewan; for **sassafras,** whose dried leaves were pounded by American Indians into filé powder for thickening soups, giving them, E. L. Sturtevant wrote cautiously, "a peculiar flavor much relished by those accustomed to it"; and for **sassamanesh,** which is the American Indian word for cranberries.

SAT
stands for

the **satin-flower,** otherwise bolbonac, penny-floure, mony-floure, silver plate, pricksong-wort or honestie, of which the seed, wrote Gerard, "is sharpe of taste, like in force to the seed of Treacle mustard: the roots likewise are somewhat of a biting qualitie, but not much: they are eaten with sallads as certaine other roots are"; for **satinwood,** a tropical tree whose fruit is "sweetish and not unpalatable but it is scarcely worth the trouble of eating, the seed being so large in proportion to the pulp"; for the **Satsuma,** a newly developed type of tangerine, named for the Japanese province where it was first grown; for **satureia,** a wild mint which may or may not be the same thing as savory; and for **satyrion,** which Paracelsus cited as an example of the Doctrine of Signatures, writing: "Behold the *Satyrion* root; is it not formed like the male privy parts? . . . Accordingly magic discovered it and revealed that it can restore a man's vitality and passion."

SAU
stands for

sauce-alone, alias jack-by-the-hedge or garlic mustard, whose flavor is so strong that if you add it to a dish you need no other sauce; for **saunf,** a form of fennel found in India; and for the **saury,** or skipper, a relative of the garfish or needlefish, so thin that it seems to have no flesh, but it makes good eating all the same.

SAV
stands for

savannah bamboo, whose young shoots are eaten in Uganda when there is nothing better at hand; for **savory,** *Micromeria juliana,* a European sixteenth-century herb unused today, or *Thymus capitatis,* headed savory, an American nineteenth-century herb unused today, or *Satureia montana,* winter savory, an ancient Caucasian herb unused today, or *Satureia hortensis,* which may be the satureia of the ancients, still used today; and for the **Savoy cabbage,** said to have been introduced into France by Catherine de Medici from the province of Savoy in Italy, where it is called the cabbage of Milan, which is in Lombardy.

SAW
stands for

sawdust, which was really eaten in bread during the famines of the tenth century but not during the nineteenth at the time of the Paris Commune, though after the troubles were over bread made of clay and sawdust was manufactured for sale to souvenir-hunting English tourists as "siege bread"; for the **sawfish,** a 5000-pound dainty relished in tropical Africa and Madagascar, one supposes by large families, and the **saw shark,** which is a sawfish too but primarily a shark, which the other is not, though it looks it; for the **saw palmetto,** or scrub palmetto, from whose pith Florida Indians once made flour, but it is now reduced to the role of providing foliage for Christmas decorations; and for the **saw-toothed pen shell,** an edible but vicious shellfish which delights in ripping bathers' bare feet from Carolina to Texas.

SAX
stands for

saxifrage, which may be golden saxifrage, *Chrysosplenium alternifolium,* whose leaves are eaten in salads in France's Vosges Mountains; or meadow or pepper saxifrage, *Silaus flavescens,* which Pliny described as a rather acid potherb; or lettuce saxifrage, also called mountain lettuce or deertongue, *Saxifraga micranthidifolia,* which grows on high ground from Pennsylvania to Georgia and offers its tender young leaves to connoisseurs of wild food in the spring.

SCA
stands for

the **scabbardfish,** which despite its fine flavor is not mentioned in the writings of those fervent fish fanciers, the ancient Greeks and Romans, perhaps because its habit of haunting deep water foiled their fishing equipment, or perhaps simply because they failed to differentiate it from the eel; for **scabwort,** forgotten today, but prized by the ancients as an appetizer, digestive and tonic; for the **scad,** or horse mackerel, less good eating than ordinary mackerel, except perhaps in the opinion of the Spanish and the Portuguese, who are alone in fishing for it on a large scale for human consumption, while elsewhere it is ground into fish meal for animals; for the **scaldberry,** or bumblekites, a sort of Old World blackberry, which, according to J. C. Loudon, has been eaten by children in every country where it grows wild since the time of Pliny, and the **scaldfish,** which tries to make us believe that it is a lemon sole; for the **scale-foot,** which is what the scabbardfish is called in some parts of Africa, though it doesn't have scales, nor feet either; for **scampi,** which are not SHRIMP or prawns, as we are usually told, but a sort of small lobster; for **scandix,** which according to ancient scandalmongers who disliked Euripides was, most improbably, sold in the market by his mother, which if true would have stamped her as of lowly birth; for the **Scaphirhyncus,** a fish which ought to be extinct but is still holding out in some of the faster inlets of the Aral Sea; for the **scarlet pimpernel,** a salad plant which is also called the poor man's weatherglass because it closes its flowers at the approach of bad weather; for the **scarlet runner bean,** whose young leaves and mature pods are edible, but whose roots are poisonous; for the **scaup duck,** a diving bird which keeps to the far north and is so called because it lives on scaup (broken shellfish), which gives an unappreciated flavor to its flesh; and for the **scavenger,** a sea bream much eaten in tropical Africa and Madagascar.

And **SCA** also stands for

SCALLION (or **Shallot**). The scallion has no standing with Noah Webster, his heirs and assigns, who define it as "an onion forming a thick basal portion without a normal bulb as a result of disease, attacks of insects or unfavorable conditions"—in other words, a sick onion. The *Random House Dictionary* is more cautious, defining the scallion as "any onion that does not form a large bulb." Such a broad definition manages to sidestep the confusions of popular usage, the hair-splitting of naturalists and the disorderly conduct of Mother Nature, who permits the 325 species of *Allium* to intermarry with disconcerting nonchalance about the nature of their offspring. The greatest confusion in *Allium* terminology occurs in the case of the scallion and the shallot, concerning which different authorities will tell you (a) that they are the same thing; (b) that only one of them exists; (c) that both exist; or (d) that neither of them exists. Most authorities concede, however, that the shallot exists and that it is the species known as A. *ascolonicum.*

It is my feeling, though I advance it with some diffidence, that the scallion, whether Webster recognizes it or not, exists too, not simply as a sick onion but as a plant in its own right, and that its scientific name is A. *fistulosum*—a term which turns up in Webster, but under the definition for Welsh ONION. A. *fistulosum* is also called the ciboul or the two-bladed onion by persons who avoid calling it the scallion, names which do little for clarity. It does not help either that many people use "shallot" and "scallion" interchangeably, or that "scallion" is used popularly not only to mean "shallot," but also either "leek" or "young onion"—one which has not yet formed its bulb. This causes the scallion to be called also the spring onion, and as the shallot is frequently described as the green onion, this presents us with another area of confusion.

When you ask for shallots in a market, you are often given young onions instead. If the substitution strikes you as important, the way to tell what you are being offered is to inspect the base of the plant. If it is an onion, it shades off to a paler green or even becomes white at the bottom; shallots and scallions are dark green along their whole length. As for distinguishing by the eye alone between a shallot and a scallion, assuming that they are different, you have me stumped; by the taste buds, still assuming that they are different, you can distinguish the shallot by its more subtle taste: but this you cannot find out until you have returned home with your ambiguous purchase.

One person who assumed that these two plants were different was Marcus Valerius Martialis, who, accepting the belief of his times that the onion family possessed invigorating powers, wrote:

If envious age relax the nuptial knot,
Thy food be scallions, and thy feast shallot.

This would seem to establish the simultaneous existence of these two different onionlike plants; but I do not have access to the original, so I do not know which Latin words Martial used, and even if I did, the exact meaning of the Latin words applied in his time to the various members of the onion family is hard to pin down: taxonomy had not yet been invented, and plant names were subject to carefree improvisation. We are at the mercy of the translator, and there is indeed one who has substituted the word "mushroom" in this couplet for "scallion." It is difficult to see how the word for mushroom, *fungus,* could have been mistaken for any of the terms Martial might have used to describe any member of the onion family; "mushroom" may represent only a desperate attempt on the part of the translator to reconcile Martial's wording with his own conviction that the scallion and the shallot are the same thing.

Charlemagne, in his capitulary *De villis,* referred to one plant which may have been the shallot and to another which may have been the scallion, but here again we are faced with the uncertainties of translation. Even contemporary authorities do not help us very much. Joan M. Jungfleisch in *For Innocents Abroad* writes, "The word scallion is . . . sometimes applied to shallots and vice versa, but shallots are quite a different onion," without further explanation; and when John and Karen Hess say in *The Taste of America,* "American shallots are the coarse-tasting red ones and are often rancid as well; since the superior gray ones are unobtainable, we frequently use scallions instead—they work, and give us a fresh taste," it is not specified whether they are thinking of a distinct plant or are using the word "scallions" in its perfectly legitimate meaning of young onions.

The history of the shallot has been obscured for us by the prestige of two eminent authorities, both of whom seem to have suffered a lapse at the moment when they were dealing with this plant—Pliny the Elder and Alphonse de Candolle, the Swiss botanist whose *Origine des plantes cultivées,* though published in 1833, remains a frequently consulted classic. Pliny is supposed to have been talking about the shallot when he referred to a plant described by Theophrastus, adding gratuitously that it was a native of Ascalon (the town in Judaea where Herod the Great was born) because the word used by Theophrastus was *askalonion.* But *askalonion* does not appear to have been derived from Ascalon. It could have been the other way around, since Ascalon was noted for growing some sort of onionlike plant, though it is not clear which one it was. Pliny seems to have read Theophrastus carelessly; his description does not fit the shallot: it sounds more like the ordinary onion. Nevertheless, it seems to be accepted today that "shallot" is derived from Ascalon, though "scallion" would be closer. For that matter, "onion" appears *in toto,* letter by letter, in the word *askalonion,* but so far as I know, nobody has suggested that this is where it comes from.

As for de Candolle, he may have been thrown off course by Pliny's assertion that the shallot was a native of the Ascalon region, so when he found no trace of wild shallots there, he jumped to the conclusion that there was no such species and that the shallot was only a variety of onion, thus denying it a specific identity just as Webster denies a specific identity to the scallion. This did not deter taxonomists from giving the shallot the specific name *A. ascolonicum*, influenced perhaps not only by Theophrastus as amended by Pliny, but also by the regularly repeated myth that the shallot was first introduced to Europe by the Crusaders returning from the Holy Land—"a fantastic tradition," Georges Gibault commented in his *Histoire des légumes*. (Its most fantastic form is perhaps that presented in a highly reputed English-language reference book which tells us that the shallot was unknown in Europe until the Crusaders brought it back from Ascalon, and in the same breath names the authority for this origin of the vegetable as Pliny, who I believe antedates the Crusaders.)

The shallot rises from a tight cluster of small bulbs which might be taken at first sight for separate plants growing too closely together if you did not happen to notice that the whole cluster stems from the same root system. It is as if a garlic bulb, whose cloves are all enclosed within the same paperlike wrapping, had split into its component parts, with each clove wrapped separately in its own envelope. There are two main varieties, the red shallot and the one which the French call the white shallot, but which turns up in some other languages as the gray shallot or the green shallot; the latter, as the Hesses pointed out, is of a finer flavor. It is more subtle than the onion, with a tinge of nutty tastefulness. "It perfumes without imposing," wrote the nineteenth-century French gourmet Charles Monselet. Shallots are the soul of that simple but remarkable sauce known as *beurre blanc* (white butter), and they also enter into Béarnaise. It is impossible to make a good piquant sauce without shallots, according to Alexandre Dumas.

When we pass beyond the ordinary shallot, *A. ascolonicum*, we find ourselves in the deep waters characteristic of the onion family. The Canadian catawissa is probably a shallot, producing its characteristic multiple tiny bulbs, though not in their characteristic position (they are where the flowers ought to be); it is especially good for pickling. There are doubts about the Egyptian shallot, which should perhaps be considered a form of garlic (it *is* called Spanish garlic in French and giant garlic in English, but in German is called the rye onion, *Rockenbolle*, while others want to classify it as a leek). It is safest to stick to its scientific name, *A. schorodoprasum*. One sign that a plant is a shallot is that it reproduces from bulbs, as right-minded shallots do; but an

SCALLION *by Julie Metz.* Still Life, *watercolor, 1979*

anarchistic nature has decreed that the Jersey shallot must reproduce from seed.

The scallion harbors a similar rebel in its family. Scallions normally reproduce from seed, but the Saint-James scallion, *A. lusitanicum*, propagates by division (I venture to call it a scallion because it does not produce bulbs like shallots, but simply thickens the lowest part of its stem). Its taste is coarser than that of the shallot, closer to that of a young onion. It is believed to be of Siberian origin, and was probably unknown in the ancient world.

In an attempt to keep the onion family straightened out, the French coined the terms *cive* and *civette* to cover onionlike plants which do not form bulbs, which gave rise to the popular names *ciboule* and *ciboulette*. Unfortunately, usage has made them all more or less synonymous and has attached them almost exclusively to a single form of bulbless onion, the chive, whose scientific name, *A. schoenoprasum*, means the leek-shaped rush, which does not particularly help us to keep our onions straight, but does give us some justification for appropriating the name "scallion" for any *cive/ciboule* which is not a chive. The term *cive* is rarely heard nowadays; *ciboule* still exists, but is not much used either; *civette* and, oftener, *ciboulette* still appear, to stand for the chive. (*Cive* lives on in the word *civet*, meaning a stew, particularly one of game, for originally game stews were flavored with chives. The historic tobacco shop of the Palais Royal was called La Civette because chives were also once used to perfume tobacco.) *Ciboule* too, like other attempts at keeping the species straight, has suffered by the whimsical behavior of nature. *Ciboule commune*, the ordinary chive, is bulbless, which is what the first part of its name means; but it threw off a variety which perversely produced a bulb, enveloped in a copper-red skin, which had therefore to be called *ciboule commune à bulbe*, "the common bulbless bulb."

SCALLOP. At a time conveniently unspecified, an old legend tells us that a nobleman described as the Lord of Maya, about to be married, was riding in the wedding procession on the coast of Spanish Galicia when his horse bolted, plunged into the sea, and swam to an approaching vessel. It proved to be carrying the body of the apostle St. James the Greater. Horse and rider returned to land, escorting the body of the saint, both by then covered with scallop shells. The Lord of Maya, convinced that he had participated in a miracle, became converted to Christianity. The horse, we may assume, was already in a state of grace.

This legend (which, as is the way with legends, is contradicted by others dealing differently with the same subject) is one of the stories recounted to explain why the scallop shell is the symbol of St. James and the symbol also of the devout who made what was for several centuries the major pilgrimage of Europe, to the Galician shrine of Santiago de Compostela, to pray before the body of St. James. American books usually inform us that the scallop was the sign of a pilgrim who had been to the Holy Land, but this is an error. The scallop shell was linked closely with Santiago de Compostela, where a complicated network of pilgrimage routes converged, starting from all the important cities of Europe; for instance, the Rue Saint-Jacques in Paris led, and still leads, all the way to Santiago.

A more matter-of-fact account of the origin of this symbol leaves no doubt about the place to which it refers: it explains that in medieval times Galicia was almost the only place where the scallop was fished. Pilgrims brought shells back from there as proof that they had really made the pilgrimage. An even more matter-of-fact story reminds us that the pilgrims were supposed to beg their way; the scallop shell (those of Galicia run to about five and a half inches long) made convenient begging bowls. It is at least established that returning pilgrims wore scallop shells on their hats, as a sort of badge, which is why, through a slight confusion between two similar shellfish, the scallop and the cockle, hats of the shape favored by the pilgrims came to be known as cocked hats. The scallop is called in English (rarely) the pilgrim scallop, in French (always) the St. James shell, and in the Adriatic, of which it is the largest shellfish, the *cappa marina* (the sea cape, from its shape) by the impious, but *cappa santa* (the holy cape) by the devout. Scientifically, it is *Pecten jacobaeus.*

The scallop suggested not saintliness but sacrilege to me when I learned that in preparing scallops for the American market the "eye" is cut out and the rest thrown away. This would toss into the discard the part which Europeans consider the best, the coral, a pinkish segment attached to one side of the "eye." Some writers berate Americans for being afraid of this colored portion of the scallop (and of being even more afraid of the somewhat startling deep-red coral of the lobster), but I found one who asserted that the scallops of the United States do not have coral. This sounds like a simple fact to confirm or invalidate, but I haven't been able to. Coral or no coral, sacrilege is involved in throwing away a large portion of the scallop, for all of it, European or American, is good to eat; it contains no waste meat.

The "eye" is really the adductor muscle which opens or closes the shell, particularly large, fleshy (and tasty) in the scallop because instead of having two such muscles, like most bivalves, the scallop has a single massive one. It needs a powerful muscle because it is the most mobile of shellfish, hopping about on the sea bottom by opening its shell and clapping it shut again, at the same time squirting two strong jets of water from the two sides of its hinge, so that it soars like a rocket. It likes to live in eel grass. Jonathan Norton Leonard wrote that "one of my pleasantest memories is of swimming along underwater close to a thicket of eel grass and watching scallops fly up like quail from a field of corn stover." The hopping technique of the scallop accounts for its decorative shape. To permit this exercise, the shell has to be light in weight but also strong, so a thin shell is reinforced by the fluting which radiates like the ribs of a fan from hinge to edge. Scallops which live under the heavy pressure of deep water and consequently need heavier shells dispense with the fluting, which is absent, for instance, in the Canadian Digby scallop, the favorite shellfish of the Maritime Provinces, found in the icy water of the Digby Cut, six fathoms down in the Bay of Fundy, and in the sea scallop, *Pseudamussium neooceanicus*, which has been dredged up from more than 2000 fathoms in the Pacific.

When Euell Gibbons wrote a book called *Stalking the Blue-Eyed Scallop*, it is probable that many people took the title for a joke; but the scallop does have eyes, forty to fifty of them, on the edge of the mantle. They are not really blue, rather an iridescent green; they look blue because they are encircled by turquoise-colored rings. They are the closest approach to vertebrates' eyes found in this category of animal, with a cornea, a lens and an optic nerve. They cannot distin-

Scallop *by Simone Martini (c.1284–1344).* Saint James Major, *oil on wood*

guish form, however, only light and movement.

Scallops, besides being decorative in shape, can also be beautiful in color. They may be white, yellow, rose, red, purple, blue, brown or black; all the same color or mottled; marked with concentric circles or spreading rays of one color against the background of another. There are nearly three hundred species of scallops, inhabiting all the salt waters of the world, all of them edible. Scallops are "the most delicious and delicate of all mollusks," wrote Joan M. Jungfleisch. "The flesh of the scallop is a round, almost translucent creamy white morsel with a flavor verging on that of lobster." I will go along with her on the first assertion, but not on the second. A scallop may suggest lobster, but not by its taste, which is unique (so is that of the lobster). Its *texture* gives the illusion of resemblance to the lobster: it is the firmest fleshed of all shellfish, with the possible exception of the abalone.

As is true of many shellfish, and for that matter also of crustaceans and of fish in general, the scallop seems to develop its best flavor in cold water. It is generally agreed that the tastiest scallop of America is the small (2½ to 3 inches) bay scallop, *Aequipecten irradians,* found from New England to Cape Hatteras, but fished mostly in the northern part of its range. This mollusk is frequently shipped to the Pacific coast, though the Pacific area has plenty of scallops of its own. South of Cape Hatteras, the East Coast has the zigzag scallop, somewhat comically referred to in the solemn language of Latin as *Pecten ziczac.* It is too small to be exploited commercially (1½ to 2 inches), but as this scallop is usually found in thickly populated beds a family expedition can quickly scoop up enough for a gala dinner.

If West Coast scallops are sometimes compared unfavorably to East Coast scallops, it may be because the big market for them is in California, whose waters are comparatively warm; but some of the Pacific scallops found on California's shores also extend their range far to the north, and when they mature in the cold currents which come from the Arctic they acquire a flavor richer than that which they develop farther south. The thick scallop, *Aequipecten circularis,* about the same size as the East Coast bay scallop, has a range which runs all the way from Monterey Bay to Peru. In Peru, where they are called *conchitas,* and in Chile, where there are larger scallops, midway between bay scallops and sea scallops, they are often eaten like oysters, raw on the half-shell, and natives of these countries are surprised to learn that they are not so eaten in the United States. In the other direction from California there is the northern scallop, *Chlamys hindsii,* about the same size, which runs from San Diego to the Bering Sea, and is tastiest in the north. The Alaska scallop, which reaches such dimensions that eight of them (minus their shells, of course) weigh a pound, is a deep-sea shellfish. The Pacific coast also has the rock scallop, likewise called the rock oyster—ambiguously, for a number of other bivalves, none of them oysters, are also given this name. It is *Hinnites giganteus,* which may reach a length of six inches, the largest shallow-water scallop, which, so far as I know, is the only one which does not enjoy leaping about. It cements itself to the underside of any half-uncovered rock and remains there for the rest of its life, growing in time into a shape which conforms to the rock, until it becomes unrecognizable as a scallop. Despite the depredations of its worst enemy, the starfish, it is still plentiful in what has always been its favorite habitat, British Columbia.

I have read in American books that the scallop cannot be found on the market in its shell, because the scallop's habit of opening its shell after being caught causes it to lose its liquid and it dries up. This is certainly not true in Europe, where scallops are regularly sold in their shells (although, alas, many fish dealers now carry frozen dispossessed scallops instead of fresh ones). I doubt if it was true in the United States either in the last century, for cookbooks of that time give recipes for scallops cooked in their shells without ever having been removed from them, and they also advise keeping the shells for other uses (indeed, the term "scalloped" applied to certain dishes comes from the fact that they were originally cooked in scallop shells). The Japanese keep the shells for raising oysters, using them as bases for seed oysters as Western breeders use tiles.

On the European side of the Atlantic, besides the pilgrim scallop already mentioned, the species most eaten in Britain is *Pecten opercularis,* of which there are beds in the Firth of Forth and the Irish Sea. France has the large *Aequipecten maximus,* the smaller *Chlamys opercularis* and the even smaller *Chlama varia,* the *vanneau* or *petoncle.* A deep-sea variety is *Placopecten magellanicus,* one of the biggest.

A trick sometimes employed by unscrupulous fishmongers is to buy a slab of inexpensive shark meat, acquire a cookie cutter of the appropriate shape and size, and lo and behold!—expensive scallops!

Not so many years ago it looked as if the world were about to run out of scallops. In New York, where fifteen scallop trawlers each brought in 800 bags of scallops per day in 1965, there remained in 1974 only one, which thought it a good day if it took 200 bags. In France, the scallop beds of Brittany, though they had only begun to be fished intensively at the beginning of this century, were exhausted in 1930 and were abandoned; but after thirty years' neglect, fishermen discovered that the beds had recovered and today, under strict protection, they are yielding 3700 tons of scallops a year, more than half of the total French take. Meanwhile strict conservation measures in New York and New Jersey have restored the beds there, while in New England (where it is considered unlucky to have a woman aboard a scallop dredger) a vast sea scallop bed was discovered a few years ago, reaching all the way from a few miles off Nantucket to Maine.

Nobody has a bad word to say for the scallop, except perhaps a young woman interviewed by *The New Yorker,* whose job was shucking them. "They don't have much personality," she said.

SCH
stands for

schmaltz, or liquid chicken fat, while

SCI
stands for

scirpus, a tuber eaten by prehistoric man at points as far apart as Denmark and Anatolia, but not by historic man, who has perhaps lost the art of separating it from its toxins.

SCO
stands for

scoke, also known as Virginia poke in defiance of the fact that the places where it was most eaten in the nineteenth century were Philadelphia, Louisiana and the Sandwich Islands; for the **scorpionfish,** whose spines are venomous but whose flesh is not; for **scorzonera,** or black SALSIFY, pretty much abandoned nowadays, but its fleshy roots graced the table of Louis XIV; for the **Scotch bonnet,** the wildly improbable name of a hot CHILI; **Scotch grass,** which is couch grass; **Scotch lovage,** sometimes used instead of the real thing in northern Britain; the **Scotchman,** which in Africa could mean either Dr. Livingstone or the silverfish; and the **Scotch pine,** whose inner bark formed an important part of the diet of eighteenth-century Lapps; for the **scoter duck,** which Louis XI in the fifteenth century seasoned with salt and the Baron Brisse in the nineteenth with chocolate sauce; for the **scourer** or **scourfish,** eaten in the Comoro Islands, whose name is explained by its nickname, the castor-oil fish; and for the **scouring rush** of the Ozarks, so called for the more literal reason that its silica-rich stems are excellent for scrubbing greasy pots and pans, but I have no idea what reactions were produced in the hillbillies who used to eat the plant's cones after treatment which would, or so they hoped, rid them of the nerve poison they contain.

SCR
stands for two specialties of New England:

the **scrod,** which is a young cod when it isn't a young haddock, and **scrunchions,** which are bits of pork fat.

SCU
stands for

scup, a lean food fish of the Atlantic coast of the United States whose name, derived from the Narragansett Indian *mishcup,* describes it as a fish with large, close-set scales; for the **scuppernong,** a native American grape of the southeastern United States which attracted the benevolent attention of Thomas Jefferson; and for **scurvy grass,** a cure for that condition, a fact unknown to Vitus Jonassen Bering in 1744 when he died of scurvy on Bering Island amid thick growths of this plant.

SEA
stands for

the **sea** BASS, or perhaps one should say the sea basses, for the name is given with great freedom to a considerable number of quite different fishes; for the **sea bat,** which when it means the devil ray is applied to a fish which so far as I know is not eaten, but when it means the angelfish of South Africa, it is; for the **sea belt,** *Laminaria saccharina,* alias sugarwrack, sweet wrack, sugar tang, tangle, oarweed or kelp, a chestnut-brown seaweed eaten in Iceland, and the **sea girdle,** *Laminaria digitata,* alias tangle (confusingly), fingered tangle, sea tangle, horsetail kelp or (again confusingly) kelp, an olive-brown seaweed eaten in Ireland; for the **sea blite,** a beach plant which doesn't look edible but it is if you don't mind a heavy dosage of salt; and for **sea blubber,** which you can sample in Hong Kong if your mouth is really made up for jellyfish and you are willing to ignore the fact that "it takes hours to prepare and . . . is too bland to be really worth the effort," as Geri Trotta wrote in *Gourmet* magazine.

SEA
stands for

the **sea bream,** *Pagus pagus,* a rose-colored Mediterranean fish too pretty to eat, but it is eaten all the same; for the **sea buckthorn,** whose acid fruit seems repugnant to most adults, but British children delight in eating it from the plant; for the **sea calf,** the name given in Venice to the dogfish known in English as the smooth hound, and the **sea clam,** the name given in New England to the bivalve known farther south as the surf clam; for **seacoast angelica,** which grows on the Atlantic coast from Labrador to Long Island and tastes like overassertive celery; for the **sea cockle** of California, which isn't a cockle, but tastes just as good as if it were; for the **sea** COCONUT, which grows in the Vallée de Mer of the Seychelles island of Praslin, also referred to as the Garden of Eden; and for the **sea cow,** a northern Pacific relative of the dugong and the manatee, which ran to 10 tons in weight but was so clumsy and so unmissable a target that Russian fur hunters rendered it extinct in the eighteenth century, not for its fur, which was mediocre, but for its flesh, which, they said, tasted as good as beef.

SEA
stands for

the **sea crab,** which means the blue CRAB on America's East Coast and the red crab on the West Coast; for the **sea cradle,** which is a chiton, an unappetizing-looking mollusk armored with overlapping plates which let it curl up like an armadillo, in a vain effort to protect its fleshy foot from the American Indians of the Pacific Northwest, who doted on it; for the **sea crayfish,** which in the southeastern United States is the name given to the SPINY LOBSTER; for the **sea crow,** which is what several Romance languages call a Mediterranean fish akin to a meagre, but I know of no name for it in English; and for the **sea cucumber,** the renowned bêche-de-mer which the Chinese eat enthusiastically, but their enthusiasm was not shared by the scallops shucker interviewed by *The New Yorker,* who said of it: "There is nothing more disgusting. It has no head, no tail, no top, no bottom—no identity at all. Just purple-and-pink mush. You don't know what it is, but you know it's alive!"

SEA
stands for

the **sea date,** a name given to certain mussels because of their shape; for the **sea dog,** a small sea lion eaten in the Middle Ages, at the same period as the **sea dragon,** an unidentified species which could hardly have been the fish known by that name today, the Australian pipefish, since Australia had not yet been discovered; for the **sea ear,** which is the abalone, and the **sea egg,** which is the sea urchin; for the **sea fruit** of Sumatra, "round, hairy and generally much covered with mud," whose seeds "taste like chestnuts soaked in salt water"; and for the **sea grape,** whose flowering plant was used as a fig leaf in the 1880s by Eliza Fraser, wife of the captain of the *Stirling Castle,* when that ship was wrecked on the Australian coast, where the aborigines stripped her of all her clothing except her Easter hat.

SEA
stands for

the **sea grasshopper,** as the Italians call the mantis prawn, which looks like a fat shrimp with an eye on its tail; for the **seagull,** whose flesh was eaten by American Indians and whose eggs were eaten by Gold Rush Alaskans; for the **sea heath,** one of the very few plants native to St. Helena, now suspected of being extinct; and for **sea holm,** the same thing as **sea holly,** of which Gerard reports that "the root is of the bignesse of a man's finger, so very long, as that it cannot be all plucked up but very seldome; set here and there with knots, and of taste sweet and pleasant"; that "the roots, condited or preserved with sugar . . . are exceeding good to be given to old and aged people that are consumed and withered with age, and which want natural moisture; they are also good for other sorts of people, nourishing and restoring the aged, and amending the defects of nature in the yonger"; and that "if one goat take it into her mouth, it causeth her first to stand still, and afterwards the whole flocke, untill such time as the sheepheard take it from her mouth."

SEA
stands for

sea kale, whose nutty, slightly bitter stalks were once, cooked like asparagus, much eaten in Britain but are almost abandoned today, and the **sea-kale beet,** or chard, which, being less acid than spinach, is sometimes preferred to it among leafy green plants; for the **seal,** which appeared on aristocratic London tables in the fifteenth century; for **sea lace,** an edible seaweed which seems to be all twisting, flexible, floating stem, so it is also called the mermaid's fishing line; for the **sea lamprey,** also called seven-eyes or seven-holes, because it does have seven small holes, purpose unknown, behind each eye; for the **sea lettuce,** a seaweed storehouse of proteins, vitamins and minerals, tastiest in early spring but most nutritious in late spring; for the **sea lion,** eaten by Alaskan Indians and Eskimos; for **sea lyme grass,** alias strand wheat or wild rye, eaten in Iceland for the last nine centuries, which according to Euell Gibbons tastes like wild rice; for the **sea nettle,** an anemone eaten in southern France under such improbable names as *pastèque, rastugnat, bilerba* and *orticolu*; for the **sea otter** of the Pacific Northwest, hunted for its fur rather than for its flesh, for the local Indians, though not total abstainers, conceded that it was not particularly good to eat; for the **sea parrot,** whose liver was relished by the ancient Romans; and for the **sea pea,** a sort of medieval manna, by which, John Gerard tells us, "the poore people, at that time there being a great dearth, were miraculously helped. . . . In the month of August . . . in Sussex at a place by the sea side all of hard stone and pibble . . . where nether grew grasse, nor any earth was ever scene, it chanced in this barren place suddenly to spring up without any tillage or sowing, a great abundance of Peason, whereof the poore gathered (as men judged) above an hundred quarters, yet remained some ripe and some blossoming, as many as ever there were before: to the which place rode the Bishop of Norwich and the Lord *Willoughby*, with others in great number, who found nothing but hard rockie shore the space of three yards under the roots of these Peason: which roots were great and long, and very sweet. . . . These Pease, which by their great encrease did such good to the poore that year, without doubt grew there for many yeares before, but were not observed till hunger made them take notice of them, and quickned their invention, which commonly in our people is very dull."

SEA
stands for

the **sea** PERCH, which is the common BASS or the grouper or the viviparous surfperch and no doubt a few other fish, as local whimsy dictates; for the **sea porcupine,** which is the sea urchin, and the **sea robin,** which is the gurnard; for the **sea rocket,** whose flavor is described with relentless precision by Euell Gibbons as "reminiscent of mustard greens and horseradish with a hint of garlic"; for the **sea salmon,** a name sometimes given confusingly to the saltwater BASS because its flesh is pink; for the big (8 inches across) **sea** SCALLOP of New England, whose shell is rose-colored and non-fluted; for the **seaside grape** of India, Africa and the West Indies, where it is sold in the markets but is held in low esteem; for **seaside lamb's-quarters,** which is orach, and **seaside plantain,** which is goosetongue; for the **seaside sword bean,** often described as toxic, but chemical analysis has detected no poisonous elements in its composition and the Japanese eat it and survive; for the **sea slug** of Samoa, there considered a great delicacy, described rather vaguely by Rafael Steinberg as "a small creature of many parts, almost all of them edible, and every one tasting slightly different from the others"; and for the **sea snail,** which was the vehicle for one of the most grotesque misapprehensions in the history of zoology when Magellan's men mistook it for a rook.

SEA
stands for

the **sea spider,** which is the spider crab; for the **sea squab,** the name under which New York and Boston converted into a luxury the after portion of the northern swellfish or blowfish which had formerly been treated as a trash fish and thrown overboard fore and aft; for the **sea stock,** a plant eaten in times of famine; for the **sea tomato,** a name given by the French to a Mediterranean sea anemone with the color and size of a tomato, but not its succulence, so it is often submerged in the other flavors of a variegated bouillabaisse; for the **sea trout,** a European fish which looks and acts very much like a salmon, returning from the sea to spawn in rivers from considerable distances, with the Polish fish holding the record for the longest homing run, more than 600 miles; for the **sea truffle,** the name bestowed by Italians impressed by its fine flavor on the warty Venus, a cousin of the American QUAHOG; for the **sea turtle,** an aliment which in more heroic days was delivered to American housewives alive in 60-pound specimens, so that Mrs. J. Chadwick's *Home Cookery* (Boston, 1853) started its recipe for turtle soup with instructions for cutting off the animal's head; for the **sea urchin,** whose usually delectable flavor became temporarily bitter in Corsica in 1970 because, the locals explained, of an eclipse of the moon; for the **sea wand** or **seaware,** an edible seaweed closely related to the sea belt and the sea girdle mentioned above; for **seaweed** in general, of which an eighteenth-century English visitor to the island of Skye reported with surprise that "the Natives eat it boil'd with Butter, and reckon it very wholesom"; and for the **sea wolf,** which in French designated the delectable sea BASS, but in English the lancet fish, whose delectability I doubt.

SE
stands for

the **sebestan,** also known as the Australian plum, though it isn't a plum but a nut which tastes something like a filbert, eaten in Australia, Africa and tropical Asia; for **seeds of paradise,** identified at one time or another with a bewildering variety of spices, but the name seems now to have settled down to designating cardamom seeds; for the **sego lily,** the Mormon manna, whose roots kept the early settlers of Salt Lake City alive; for the **seim bean,** universally eaten in tropical Africa under so many different names that it would be impracticable to list them all here; for **selu,** which is the sebestan; for **senna,** of which there is a sweet variety whose seeds are much appreciated in Indonesia; and for the **sennep,** or northern barracuda, of which we are told that when it dines on human beings it prefers Englishmen to Frenchmen, and when human beings dine on it, it is nourishing on one side of an island and poisonous on the other.

SE
stands for

the **sephardia,** or buffalo fat, whose berries were eaten by American Indians and whose boiled leaves were applied by the Navahos as a poultice to the eyes of their sheep when they were inflamed by desert sandstorms; for **sepia,** the inkfish, whose discouraging liquid is allowed in Spain to accompany the fish to the table; and for the **sergeant major,** a damselfish eaten in Africa, of which the former name, so out of tune with the latter, is due to an aggressiveness which caused an ichthyologist to write that "these small attractive fishes seem more deserving to be called Amazons than damsels."

SE
stands for

the **serpent eel,** eaten, sparingly, in South and Mediterranean Africa; for the **serrano,** whose bright green color makes it look cool, and so it is—relatively—for a chili; for the **serval cat,** or wildcat, eaten in tropical and South Africa and Madagascar; for the **serviceberry,** alias the grapepear or Juneberry, a favorite fruit of Pacific Northwest Indians, and the **service tree,** whose fruit looks like miniature apples but doesn't taste like them even at its best, that is to say, when it is rotten; for **sesame,** whose seeds are eaten like grain in Asia and Africa, but get into European and American cooking almost exclusively in the form of oil, also used in Japan for deep frying despite the opinion of Isabella L. Bird, who wrote in 1881 that it produces "one of the most horrific smells in Japan"; for **sesbania,** a spiny eastern Asian shrub whose seeds are fed mostly to animals but whose young green pods are eaten by people; for **seventy-four,** a rather scarce South African food fish whose name is a mystery to me; for the **Seville orange,** or bitter ORANGE, which in sixteenth-century England, by virtue of mispronunciation, found itself being referred to as the civil orange; for the **Sevruga,** the smallest sturgeon in the CAVIAR business; and for the **sewin,** only dubiously a separate species of trout.

SHA
stands for

the **shadberry,** which is the serviceberry; for the **shaddock,** a relative of the grapefruit, whose name is attributed, somewhat dubiously, to a certain Captain Shaddock who is supposed to have brought it to America about 1770; for the **shaggy cap** or **shaggy mane,** *Coprinus comatus,* a mushroom classified as of first quality when eaten young, while the **shaggy ink cap,** praised by Pliny, probably its cousin, C. *atramentarius,* the ink coprinus, must be eaten *very* young and immediately after picking on pain of palpitation of the heart, excessive perspiration and chills, which, however, soon pass away; and the **shaggy parasol,** *Lepiota rhacodes,* rated only as second quality, but it is a favorite in Britain all the same; for **shallot,** which is probably *not* simply another name for the SCALLION; for **shamrock,** which in the sixteenth and seventeenth centuries meant watercress; for the **shark,** which tastes like swordfish and has almost certainly been eaten by you, but almost certainly not under its own name; for the **shark eye,** a type of moon shell found from Cape Cod to Texas, and the **shark sucker,** better known as the remora, which attaches itself to sharks by suction, and is eaten, detached from the shark, in Africa; and for the **sharp-nosed eel,** which feeds on smaller prey than the broad-nosed eel, and the **sharp-nosed puffer,** which, I learn from a well-informed fish encyclopedia, is distinguished from other puffers by having a sharper nose.

And **SHA** also stands for

SHAD. One of the cherished memories of my boyhood is of the day each spring when my father would wake me up before dawn "to see the herring run." It was at six A.M., if I remember correctly, that water from behind the dam, which fish bent on spawning had to pass, was diverted into the fish ladder, a stairway of wooden boxes, one above the other, with openings alternatively at right and left to let the water pass, leaving a comparatively quiet pool in a corner of each box where fish exhausted by their efforts could pause to rest before resuming their uphill struggle. When we arrived, the ladder would be dry, and the waiting fish crowded so tightly together that their backs protruded from the water. When the sluices were opened, the flood rushed down and the fish pushed up.

I know today that these fish were not herring, though they looked like them, but were *Pomolobus pseudoharengus*, a name which specifically denies herringhood. The first whites to reach America knew they were not herring too. A member of the Plymouth colony wrote in his diary:

> In April there is a fish much like a herring that comes up into the small brooks to spawn, and when the water is not knee deep they will presse up through your hands, yea, thow you beat at them with cudgels, and in such abundance as is incredible.

They were alewives, which sounds like a good old-fashioned English word, but it is a distortion of the Indian name for this fish, *aloofe*, probably attracted to this form by the existing English word "alewife" which meant only a woman who sold ale. The fish is also called the big-eye by Chesapeake Bay fishermen and is perhaps the same one known elsewhere as the Ohio shad, though the scientific tag of the Ohio shad is usually given as *P. chrysochloris*. The Ohio shad is not a simon-pure shad; indeed, its vigor in fighting its way up fish ladders is most unshadlike. The true shad is a rather passive fish, easily discouraged by man-made barriers like weirs, which it does not often try to pass, and also by pollution. Thoreau noticed this and hoped that the day would come when "Nature will have leveled the Billerica dam and the Lowell factories, and the Grassground River run clear again" to save the shad.

There are other false shads besides *P. pseudoharengus*: the gizzard shad, *Dorosoma cepedianum*, or the fish known variously as the green-tailed shad, the yellow-tailed shad or the hard-head shad, which is the menhaden, probably called a shad because it is, like that fish, entirely too well endowed with bones. (It works the other way around too: the fish called the blueback in Chesapeake Bay, or the glut herring, because it brings so low a price, is actually a shad, *Alosa aestivalis.*) Oddly enough, the one called scientifically and popularly the false shad, *A. fallax* (*fallax* means false), or in French the *alose feinte*, "feigned shad," is a real one—the species known in English as the twaite shad. But the West African shad, *Ethmalosa dorsalis*, is not a genuine shad (but it is at any rate an important commercial fish), nor are the so-called shads of the Black and Caspian seas (the latter has been given the generic name *Caspialosa*, which incorporates that of the shad), nor are the fish called Indian and Chinese shads, probably members of the related *Hilsa* genus.

There seem to be only two countries which appreciate the shad, America (or at least, the East Coast) and France; non-French Europeans, ignorant of the fact that their own waters teem with shad, sometimes think of it as a fish exclusively American. I was not prepared to believe it when I read in an English fish encyclopedia that "most Englishmen today don't even know the name of the fish"; and then I received a letter from an English reader who had eaten shad in France and wanted to know whether the fish existed in the British Isles. I find in *American Cooking: The Eastern Heartland*, whose author, José Wilson, is English-born, evidence that she also had not known of this fish in her own country, for it was apparently new to her when she wrote:

> I arrived in New York in April, the season for shad and shad roe, and got my first taste of it when I was taken out to lunch and told to forget everything else on the menu. Since then the flavor of this incomparable fish that spawns in the Eastern rivers has marked for me that longed-for, imperceptible turning point when winter yields to spring.

The reason why America has paid more attention to the shad than England is perhaps because American shad is better. "The English shad is a coarse and insipid fish," *Harper's Weekly* remarked in 1859, admitting, however, that "there is a particular species caught in Scotland called the Alice shad, which is much esteemed." What *Harper's* meant must have been the allis shad, *A. alosa* or *A. vulgaris*, which is indeed better (and larger) than the twaite shad, *A. finta* or *A. fallax*, which is commoner in England than the allis shad; but the latter does exist there as well as in Scotland, though not until 1803 did the English realize that they possessed two different species. (They could not have been paying much attention to shad even then, for they are not difficult

SHAD. *Drawing by Angel from Louis Roule:* Les poissons et le monde vivant des eaux, *10 volumes, Paris, 1926–1937*

to distinguish one from the other: the twaite shad has a series of dark spots along its flanks, the allis has none.)

The superiority of American shad is implicit in its scientific name, A. *sapidissima,* which is the Eastern shad or white shad, the one you find on the market. It is the largest of the shads, and for that matter, the largest fish of the entire herring family; the female, which is larger than the male (and many think better eating) may run up to twelve pounds. The Eastern shad was successfully implanted in the West after three attempts, first in the Sacramento River in 1871, and is one of the most common fish of the Pacific coast region today, but Westerners do not much care for it. When they catch shad they remove that great delicacy, its roe, and can or freeze it for the East; the fish itself they use for cat food. The East would never do this, except perhaps for A. *mediocris,* the hickory shad, whose scientific name may refer to its size, but it describes its quality too.

Even in the East, the shad is not eaten as commonly as it used to be; but the importance it once had is implicit in the names it has bestowed on other organisms. The shadbush and the shadberry are so named because they blossom at the season when the shad are running, the shad fly and the shad frog because they appear at the same time.

The shad is strictly a seasonal fish, not particularly good during its seafaring stage, when it tends to be salty, scrawny and dry; but it feeds heavily in preparation for spawning, which makes it then fat and succulent. It remains at its best until after it has spawned, when, like many other fish, it becomes exhausted, thin and tasteless.

James Trager has reported that the Dutch of New Amsterdam called it the *elft,* the eleven fish, because they started to fish for it on March 11, which they had decided was the date when its run began. This would seem an interesting tidbit of information, though the date given overestimates the shad's resistance to cold. The female shad lays her eggs only at night and only in warm water, which does not characterize the Hudson in March. Even in Chesapeake Bay shad do not appear until the end of March and sometimes not until early April. Besides, Mr. Trager adds that the spawning season lasts into June; I do not know of any fish which devotes three months to this diversion. One might be inclined to think that Mr. Trager had mixed up his months; after all the shad is the May fish in Holland and Germany (*Meivisch* and *Maifisch* respectively): but the fact is that *elft,* shad, antedates Dutch acquaintance with the Hudson. I am informed by Mr. Hans Koning, the novelist and etymologist, that *elft* means "the white fish," having worked its way into Dutch in this form from the Latin word for white, *alba;* another example is the Old Dutch *elbiz,* swan, which is thus "the white bird." "Swan" has become *zwaan* in modern Dutch, but *elft* has resisted change.

Shad were once very plentiful in the Hudson, where they swam up the river as far as Albany. They are still caught in some unpolluted sections of this river, about 100,000 pounds a year, but this is a tremendous comedown from the nearly 4.5 million pounds taken there in 1889. Some people now hesitate to buy Hudson shad at all, because they sometimes have a peculiar taste from having ventured into impure waters.

The Indians introduced the Pilgrims to shad, and when they found the fish too bony, showed them how to bury a few of them in a circle around each hill of corn as fertilizer. It is less certain that the Indians, though they planked salmon in the West, ever treated shad this way in the East, as has been asserted; the Philadelphia Fish House eating club claims to have invented planked shad. Nowadays the fish are planked for shad bakes, which used to be in the Hudson valley the equivalent of the clambake in New England, but originally they were cooked without benefit of planks. A corresponding celebration on the Potomac sent boatloads of Congressmen, bureaucrats and ordinary citizens down the river to eat freshly netted shad. George Washington liked baked shad, and when they began to run in the James River, Jefferson had them taken by the barrelful and emptied into a pond at Monticello so he could eat them all year round. In the 1880s shad were still so common and so cheap that H. L. Mencken was able to write about his mother's indignation when her fishmonger charged her for shad roe, which previously had been given away with the fish. Today the roe has become a luxury. You should still get it with the fish if you are offered what in trade parlance is called a hen shad, meaning a female complete with eggs; without the roe, it is a cut shad. The male is a buck shad, and nobody cares whether it comes with its milt or not.

It is surprising that the British have been so neglectful of the shad, for the fish must have been well known there long ago: the word entered English no later than the twelfth century, coming from the Old English *sceadd,* whose original meaning is unknown. It was even the English, when they ruled Aquitaine, who gave the French what any Frenchman would probably insist indignantly is a pure French term—*faire chabrot* (or *chabrol*). This is what you do when, in southwestern France, you pour red wine into a little soup left in the bottom of your plate, and down the two together. *Chabrot* is a French corruption of "shad broth," which is what the English called the shad-and-red-wine soup of that part of France.

Shad are no longer exploited commercially in the British Isles, though both allis shad and twaite shad mount such comparatively clean rivers as the Severn and the Shannon; they have given up the Thames, which is too dirty. Allis shad swim farther upstream than twaites, which prefer to spawn in the brackish water just above the reach of the tide. The land-locked shad in the lakes of Killarney, there called the goureen, is apparently a subspecies of the twaite, which seems to form them with particular ease. A variety which swims up the Nile is sufficiently different from the others of its kind in the Mediterranean so that it has been given the name *A. falla nilotica.* The twaite is probably also the father of the land-locked shad, A. *lacustria,* of Italy's Como, Maggiore, Lugano and Garda lakes and of the subspecies in the Rhone, A. *rhodanensis,* which is not land-locked but does not attempt to migrate to the sea.

Shad is sometimes called rock herring in England, or mother of herring, which is explained as being a corruption of "mouther of herring," because when there is a dearth of the small crustaceans which are the shad's favorite food, it eats young herring instead.

Apparently nobody in Europe has ever appreciated the shad as much as the French. The fish was present in the market of Athens in 500 B.C., but does not seem to have been much liked. When Pliny spoke of *clupea,* he was apparently thinking oftenest of shad, though the word covers the whole category of its family, the *Clupeidae.* When the shad acquired its exclusive name in Latin, *alausa,* it was said to have been borrowed from Gallic; this is indeed still the word for "shad" in Occitan today, but there is a theory that Occitan took it from Latin, in which language it may have meant simply "from Gaul." *Alausa* was "the Gallic fish" and it still is—in modern French, *alose.*

In the thirteenth century the *Proverbes* listed Bordeaux shad as one of the favorite sea fish of the times, and in the fourteenth the *Ménagier de Paris* mentioned it several times and listed it among the dishes served at the famous banquet given by the Abbé de Lagny. But it was a little startling to read in an article by a contemporary French gastronomic writer that "Montesquieu ate [shad] between two chapters of *The Spirit of the Laws.* . . . A zealous friend had brought it by airplane." This would have been news to the Wright brothers, but by reading further I discovered that it was not Montesquieu but the writer who had thus received his shad, which must have plunged him into such euphoria that his meanings became entangled in an attempt to write rich beautiful prose. Beautiful prose has been produced on this subject by many of his compatriots, for instance Grimod de la Reynière, who wrote that the shad "reclines on its bed of sorrel like a beauty on the ottoman of her boudoir." Charles Monselet in the last century went overboard when he wrote:

> Let us hail the shad, which arrives just at the moment when we are beginning to have enough of fish. It is the last word of Lent, but a word which triumphs. What a beautiful fish, shining with silver! The banks of the river are all but lighted up by it when the fishing boats are emptied at twilight. It is the aquatic hazelnut!

Brillat-Savarin remarked more soberly: "It is one of the purest and suavest joys of Lent."

If the shad has remained, in Europe, almost exclusively French, it may be because the French discovered what to do about its bones, which may have been the principal deterrent to its being eaten elsewhere. The shad is indeed devilishly protected by them: they are fine, curved, and seem to penetrate the fish everywhere. "The flesh of the shad," wrote James de Coquet, "reposes on a supple skeleton. Its bones are caressing and demand nothing better than to knot themselves like vines about your epiglottis or your tonsils."

The French counter this attack by stuffing shad with purée of sorrel, whose oxalic acid softens, and indeed seems to all but dissolve the bones, so that you eat them embedded in the flesh without being aware of their presence. This property is shared by some other plants as well. Another method for dealing with the bones of the shad is to make several X-shaped incisions along the flanks of the fish and tuck a bay leaf into each one. The city of Saint-Emilion maintains that it was the Latin poet Ausonius, a native of the region, who invented this process, but it sounds unlikely; Ausonius described the shad in one of his poems as a fish fit only for the riffraff. But "without shad," the Marquis de Cussy snarled, "there would be no excuse for sorrel."

Germans must have shared with the French at least a partial liking for shad at the beginning of this century, for W. J. Gordon wrote in 1902 that German fishermen hung bells on their nets to ring under the water and call the fish, which were held to be fond of music. The bells, he wrote, "not only attract the fish, but keep them lost in admiration as the nets are drawn in."

SHE
stands for

the **shea tree,** or butternut tree, from which tropical Africans (who call it meepampa) obtain flower calyces for salads, fruit pulp (which is in short supply), nuts for eating fresh, shea butter (also called bambuck butter or galam butter) made from the nuts, and oil cake made from the butter; for the **shearwater,** a petrel considered such good eating when it is young and fat that in Australia it is called the mutton bird; for the **sheathfish,** the famous naked catfish known reverently in Austria as the wels; for **shedders,** crabs trying to make up their minds to become busters; for **sheefish,** which Alaskan Eskimos net under the ice; for **sheep,** which are being regarded with more respect as meat animals since synthetic fibers have almost put them out of business as wool animals; for the **sheepberry,** black, sweet and flavorful, which, playing no favorites, also allows itself to be called the nannyberry; for the **sheepnose,** a New England apple so dark a red as to be almost black, considered the country's best baking apple in the eighteenth and nineteenth centuries, but almost unfindable in the twentieth; for the **sheepshead bream,** of which as a Mediterranean fish Alan Davidson wrote, "It has many bones; the flesh is not much esteemed," and of which as a Gulf of Mexico fish, Howard Mitcham wrote, "Sheepshead is a delicious fish; its firm white flesh tastes so much like crabmeat that some restaurants have been known to dilute their lump crabmeat cocktails with sheepshead"; for **sheep sorrel,** a close relation of the SORREL eaten by human beings, and indeed it is eaten by humans in South Africa despite a characteristic which has given it the alternative name of sour sorrel; for the **sheldrake,** a member of the duck family much appreciated in medieval France, where poultry breeders tried to domesticate it, but without success; for the **shellbark,** or king nut, eaten by American Indians and recommended for development by the American Pomological Society, but in vain; for **shellfish,** a term often understood to include crustaceans, but I feel that it should be restricted to mollusks, sufficiently glorified by the clam, the oyster and the mussel so that they hardly need the added distinction of the crab, the lobster and the shrimp; for the **shepherd's-clock** or **shepherd's-weatherglass,** the scarlet pimpernel, so called because it predicts bad weather by closing its flowers; for the **shepherd's-club,** our nineteenth name for the mullein; for **shepherd's-joy,** a Pacific Islands substitute for asparagus; for the **shepherd's-needle,** so named for its long fruits, which the mother of Euripides was said by his enemies to have sold in the market at Athens; for **shepherd's-purse,** which an English botanist of the last century wrote was "largely raised about Philadelphia for sale in the markets," but a Philadelphia botanist called it "a worthless little intruder from Europe"; and for **shepherd's-rod,** or small teasel, which Catherine de' Medici was advised to eat to end her sterility, as, finally, either this or something else did.

SHI
stands for

the **shiitake,** perhaps the first MUSHROOM ever cultivated, by the Japanese 2000 years ago; for the **shiner,** a fish too small to bother about when it is a minnow, but not when it is a surfperch; for the **shiny nose,** or, in Yorumba, the efum, a fish widely eaten in West Africa, equatorial Africa and Madagascar; and for the **ship-holder,** a name given to the remora, which attaches itself by its sucker to ships as well as to sharks and stops them in their tracks—according to Montaigne, who wrote: "In the great and last naval engagement, that Anthony lost to Augustus, his admiral galley was stayed in mid-course by the little fish the Latins call Remora."

SHO
stands for

shoat, a pig which is still young, but too big to be conveniently cooked whole; for the **shore crab,** the same animal as the green crab of America's East Coast, which in Venice produces the only European version of the soft-shelled crab known to me; for the **short-billed** (or **short-nosed**) **spearfish,** a marlin more prized as a game fish than a food fish; for the **Shorthorn,** the first BEEF cattle breed for which a herdbook was established, in its native England in 1842, which emigrated to America and became one of the parents of the famous Santa Gertrudis; for the **short-spired purple snail,** a dog whelk found along the Pacific coast from Alaska to Mexico, which is edible if you don't mind doing a lot of chewing; for the **shovelard,** listed among early sixteenth-century game birds, which should be the **shoveler** duck, unless sixteenth-century Englishmen enjoyed eating spoonbills; for the **shovelnose shark,** one of the five species of hammerheads, whose face is shaped less like a shovel or a hammer than like a kidney; and for the **shovelnose cat,** or paddlefish, of the Ohio, the Missouri and the Mississippi, and the **shovelnose sturgeon** of the Don, the Volga and the Dnieper.

SHR
stands for

the **shrew,** eaten by prehistoric man in Borneo; and for the **shrubby capsicum** of Africa which is in reality the cayenne pepper of tropical America.

And **SHR** also stands for

SHRIMP. Worms might seem a rather unsalable foodstuff, much less one on which trade could be developed to such a point as to be basic to an economy, but it has been done—in, of all places, the Sahara Desert.

> Near Mourzouk, in the Fezzan [Lloyd Cabot Briggs wrote in *Tribes of the Sahara*], small "water worms" . . . are collected and pounded together with a little salt until the mixture becomes a black paste, which is then rolled into balls about the size of a big orange and set out in the sun to dry. The finished product is eaten preferably mixed with a greasy sauce used on millet or barley bread [called *bazeen* or *aseeda*]. Captain George Lyon, writing in 1821, said of these "worms" that "They resemble very bad caviar in taste, and the smell is extremely offensive; but habit and necessity overcome all prejudices in this country, and I soon became very partial to them."

The tribe which exploits this article of the diet is called the Dauada, who

> still have a few camels and sheep, together with small though more substantial numbers of goats, donkeys, and chickens. But by far their most important economic resource, both for local consumption and external trade, is [this creature], which flourishes so abundantly in their little lakes that the water actually looks pink at times. Known locally as *dood,* an Arabic word for "worms," these tiny creatures have given their name to the Dauada, a name which means literally "wormers" or "wormermen" (as one would say "fishers" or "fishermen"). [They] are gathered the year around by women, or sometimes men, working usually in groups; but no woman who is menstruating is allowed to take part in this activity. The fishers wade along knee-deep in the water, parallel to the shore, with sleeve-shaped nets made of cheap European cloth which they swing in front of them, much as a farmer swings a scythe when cutting hay.

One gathers that Saharans are not squeamish and so have no objection to describing one of their important foods as worms, although it would be accurate to call it by a more appetizing name. What the Dauada eat, and persuade others to eat, is not a worm at all, but a primitive miniature shrimp, *Artemia salina,* about one-eighth of an inch long.

This shrimp is perhaps the only one ever to have given its name to a tribe, but others have bestowed their titles on a country and on a cooking technique. A Portuguese navigator who discovered an important indentation in the West African coastline, abundantly populated by large luscious shrimp, named it the Rio des Camarões—Shrimp River. Hence the Cameroons.

The cooking technique which is said to owe its name to a shrimp is Japanese deep frying—tempura—variously ascribed to the influence of Jesuit missionaries or Portuguese traders. They were supposed to have explained to the Japanese that they could not eat meat on the fast days described in ecclesiastical Latin as the *quatuor tempora,* the "four times" included in the Ember days, and must have fish. The Japanese thought *tempora* the key word in this context, and are said to have applied it first to shrimp and then to other fish or vegetables cooked in the same fashion. I do not vouch for this story, I simply pass it on.

"Shrimp" is an all-encompassing word standing for any member of the *Decapoda* (ten-legged crustaceans) except the larger long-tailed animals of that order, meaning chiefly lobsters and crawfish. It thus includes prawns, an even vaguer word. Many people understand it to mean large shrimp and others as confined to freshwater shrimp. There are several hundred species of shrimp, found, usually over mud bottoms, in shallow water and in deep, pretty much everywhere in the world, but especially in the Northern Hemisphere. They are often thought of as warm-water animals, but they are plentiful off Norway, Iceland, Greenland and Alaska.

A number of crustaceans regularly referred to as shrimps or prawns are misnamed; the most conspicuous example is the famous Venetian *scampi*, often referred to as shrimps. This error is common even in Italy, where restaurants profit by the prestigious reputation of this crustacean, giving its name to any of its relatives they happen to be serving; most of the impostors are shrimps. Actually, *scampi* are zoologically, though perhaps not quite so gastronomically, the same thing as Dublin Bay prawns, which are not prawns or shrimps either, and Norway lobsters (*Nephrops norvegicus*), which can be described as small spiny lobsters. The mantis shrimp is not only not a shrimp, but not even a decapod; it is a squilla. The crustacean the Peruvians call the *camarón*, Spanish for "shrimp," has lobsterlike claws, as shrimps have not, and is probably a crawfish.

Among genuine shrimp there is tremendous variation. We are apt to think of shrimp as pink, but along the northeastern coast of the United States there are medium-sized white shrimp which are sweeter, other things being equal, than pink ones, for they contain less iodine, which is what gives pink shrimp that color. In some large, very pink shrimps from the Gulf of Mexico the taste becomes almost medicinal; it can be rendered less so by deveining the shrimp (which it is not necessary to do for hygienic reasons, as many think). In Europe, Belgium and England in particular appreciate "gray" shrimp, which are often closer to brown, and tend to run smaller than pink ones. From California to Alaska we find an imaginatively decorated species, the sidestripe shrimp, so called because of the red bands on its body; it runs up to five inches in length and has the disadvantage of being so perishable that it is advisable to cook it as soon as possible after it comes out of the water. It is a conservatively dressed animal in comparison with the giant shrimp of Campeche, Mexico, which is a purplish blue (and was much taken by the shrimping fleets of Texas and Louisiana until Mexico dealt them a serious blow by establishing a 200-mile limit for foreign

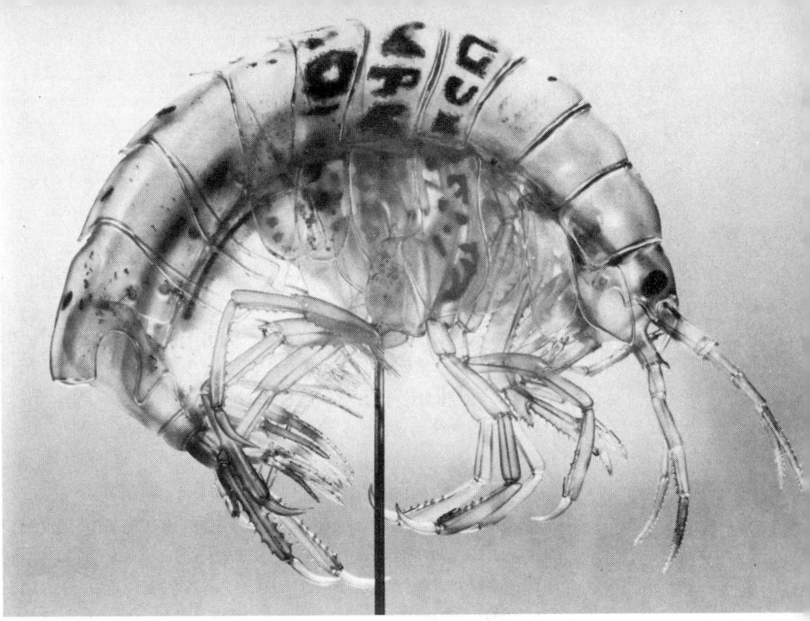

SHRIMP. *Glass model by Herman Mueller, photographed by Lee Boltin, 1950*

fishing in her waters after which Nature dealt them another, the blow-out of the Mexican underwater Iytoc I oil well in June 1979, precisely in this shrimp's waters). The Campeche shrimp is in turn outdone by a Panama variety which is striped like a zebra, but blue on white.

From the fisherman's point of view, the most important variation in shrimp is in their size, for the price paid for them is determined by their "count," meaning the number it takes to make a pound. Classifications vary locally, but in New Orleans, for instance, the categories are: giants, 10 to 12 per pound; jumbos, 15 to 20; large, 20 to 25; medium, 25 to 35; small, 35 to 45; and titi, 75 to 100. American merchants lose interest at this point (the two smallest classes are already considered too small for eating whole, and go into shrimp paste), but Iceland sells midgets which run 150 to the pound, and Holland even tinier ones, 300 to the pound, about the length of the nail on your little finger. I have no weight figures for the tiny tender shrimp of the small Chausey islets off the coast of Normandy, but they are so small that they are eaten shells and all.

One of the pygmy shrimps is A. *salina*, the "water worm" of the Sahara Desert, to which we must now grant wider range, for it is also found in the ocean, though how it got from one to the other is something of a mystery; perhaps it was stranded after the Cretaceous period, when parts of the Sahara were under water. Small as they are, these shrimp are fished commercially, but not for human consumption: they are fed to other shrimp being raised artificially at the experimental hatchery in Brittany, which thus duplicates the processes of nature, for in the sea A. *salina* provides an important proportion of the food of shrimp larvae at one stage of their development.

Humans may be eating shrimp almost as small

as these some day if the scientists who are always seeking new sources of protein succeed in a project of making us eat krill. This is *Euphausia superba*, a shrimp of the South Atlantic, so prolific that it used to provide hundreds of millions of tons for whales, which doted on it. Now that most of the whales have been killed off, their leftovers are available for man. A scientist who sampled krill himself reported, "It's not the best of seafood platters, but it's acceptable."

The largest shrimp in the world seem to be freshwater animals. Some sources call *Macrobrachium carcinus*, of the Philippines, the largest of all shrimps, but a three-pound specimen of *M. jamaicense* taken in Devils River, Texas, should be able to give it a good run for the money. A more modest freshwater shrimp, *M. ohionis*, small, pink and sweet, is found in the Mississippi delta and also in Georgia's Savannah River. River and lake shrimp are eaten to some extent in Louisiana and South Carolina, but otherwise freshwater shrimp are not in much demand in the United States, though they are in Latin America and the Orient.

Among saltwater shrimp, identification of the largest is made difficult by descriptions based more on local pride than on unemotional figures. The northern Pacific coast of North America has a prawn which reaches a length of nine inches, yet China gives the name "giant prawn" to the species it takes from the Gulf of Chihli, which measures only six. Mombasa, Kenya, which claims "the most generously fleshed prawns in the world," contents itself with calling its animal the "king prawn" and dispensing with dull measurements.

It was only in this century that shrimp began to appear commonly on the tables of the world—not that the shrimp wasn't on hand, but it wasn't reaching the tables. Shrimp are highly perishable; they die quickly after being taken from the water and decay quickly after dying. In consequence there was formerly no commercial shrimp fishing, for the catch could not be delivered in edible condition more than a few miles from the place where it was taken, and people who lived that close to shrimp caught their own or bought them from small local fishermen—like the Charleston criers who used to pass through the streets early in the morning with tiny "crick shrimp," still wet and kicking, calling, "Swimpy raw-raw! Swimpy raw-raw!"

Many people tasted shrimp only once a year, on seaside vacations, for which they took along square shrimp nets, held open by wooden (later, metal) bars, of which the lower one scraped the bottom as its wielder waded through shallow water at low tide. In Europe these nets are still occasionally seen for family fishing (though this has now been discouraged by pollution), but more often by small-scale professional fishermen (or fisherwomen, since this is considered women's work) with local clienteles. Mechanization seized upon this home industry in the nineteenth century, when large dragnets were devised, to be pulled through the water by a horse; there are still a few horse-drawn nets operating at Oostduinkerke in Belgium. All this was changed by refrigeration, followed by deep freezing; today shrimp are taken by trawlers (the first offshore shrimp trawlers appeared only about 1917), which may stay out ten days at a time and bring in shrimp by the ton.

There have always been customers for shrimp ready to fall upon them whenever and wherever they could be delivered. In the ancient Mediterranean world, where fishing was on an artisanal scale and almost everybody lived close to the water, the Greeks preferred the larger types of shrimp even to lobster, and cooked them wrapped in fig leaves. The Romans made the finest grade of their all-purpose sauce, *liquamen*, from shrimps. When Apicius heard that there were particularly large, luscious ones in Libya, he chartered a ship to sample them on the spot himself, but he was so much disappointed by the first ones brought to him aboard ship that he sailed home without ever setting foot on shore. As the European world expanded, distances grew longer; a large proportion of the population was out of reach of shrimps, so we hear little about them in the Middle Ages.

Apparently nobody tried to preserve shrimp for the benefit of inlanders except the Chinese. Their know-how was imported into the United States when Lee Yuen, who came to Louisiana from Canton, astonished by the abundance of shrimp on this coast, went into the shrimp-drying business, building a platform on piles for this purpose. The venture was so profitable that he was joined by others of his countrymen, who built similar shrimp-drying structures until they constituted a village which was given the name of Chinamen's Platform. Filipinos then turned up too, and the name became Manila Village. Its products were sold all over the world until refrigeration knocked dried shrimp off the market. There is little demand for them today, though they sometimes serve as an expensive substitute for salted peanuts or potato chips in bars, except in Brazil, where by some mystery of the local drying process a special pungent flavor is communicated to the shrimp.

Americans are the largest producers and consumers of shrimp—a natural development, since the Gulf of Mexico harbors the richest shrimp fisheries of the world and the United States was the first to develop the modern techniques which make it possible today to deliver this perishable animal to every part of its vast market. In the United States, shrimp is the most popular of all crustaceans, followed by crab and lobster; the consumption is on the order of 500 million pounds a year. New York is the biggest shrimp market in the country, eating 1.5 million pounds a week, but that is partly because of its large population; the shrimp city *par excellence* is New Orleans. Most American cities prefer to buy their shrimp minus what they consider its nonedible parts, the head and the thorax; New Orleans insists on receiving its shrimp whole. "The brains are the best part," a native of the city explained to a Yankee reporter, by which he undoubtedly meant the tomalley, which, though it is the liver, is in the head. The Shrimp Boil and Beer Bust, according to Howard Mitcham, New Orleans writer and cook, is the Louisiana equivalent of the New England clambake. It is said that you can tell a native of New Orleans by the speed and dexterity with which he or she peels a shrimp.

There are one or two other places in the world where shrimp have become almost as much of a cult as in New Orleans. In Denmark, white push-carts at street corners offer you, instead of ice cream, slices of buttered bread covered thickly with a multitude of tiny, pink, deliciously sweet shrimp. In Paris you may pass a person eating French-fried potatoes from a sheet of newspaper twisted into a cone, but if you see the same sight in the Saintonge, the coastal region between Bordeaux and Poitiers, the contents of the cone will be shrimp. The Japanese have been accused of eating shrimp alive (as we eat oysters alive), but that depends on whether a decapitated animal can be considered to be alive. This happens at lunch bars, where the counterman beheads the shrimp and strips off its shell in what seems to be a single deft motion. He hands you the animal to hold by the tail and dip into the sauce waiting for it. It is still wriggling, like a chicken which makes convulsive movements after its head has been cut off. You can wait for it to quiet down if you want, but some Japanese insist that it tastes better while it is still squirming.

The Chinese eat a good deal of shrimp too, but if you see "brushwood shrimp" on a Chinese menu, beware: it means grasshoppers.

SH
stands for

shungiku, a chrysanthemum grown for ornament in the West but for food in China and Japan, where the young plants are used as a cooked vegetable, despite a flavor which to Occidentals seems too sharp for comfort; and for the **shy-eye shark** eaten in South Africa, so called because of its coy habit of covering its eyes with its tail when caught and perhaps also because this is easier to pronounce than its popular name "shaamoog," not to mention its scientific one, *Holohalaelurus regani.*

SI
stands for

the **Siberian crab,** which isn't a crab, for the word is a shortening of "crab apple," but it isn't quite a crab apple either; for the **Siberian oilseed,** a noxious weed in northeastern America but a provider of cooking oil in northwestern Europe; for the **Siberian pea tree,** whose seeds can be eaten by human beings, but are generally fed to poultry; for the **sicklefish,** a fairly common food of tropical Africa and Madagascar; for **Sierra Leone butter,** a very common oil extracted from seeds in tropical Africa, and the **sieva bean,** a very common pulse of tropical Africa, Madagascar and Mauritius; for the **silk-cotton tree,** or god-tree, of the West Indies, where the young leaves and buds, as gluey as okra, are boiled as greens in Jamaica, while in China it is its flower petals which are eaten, and in Africa the calyces and the seeds; for the **silkfish,** or wolf herring, of the Red Sea; for **silkweed,** or milkweed, of which Thomas Jeffery in his *Natural History of Canada* (1760) wrote that the flowers "are shaken early in the morning before the dew is off of them when there falls from them with the dew a kind of honey"; for the **silkworm,** which in Marco Polo's time was made into pies in Hangchow; and for **silphium,** a mystery plant which the ancient Romans allowed to die out although it was worth its weight in gold, now believed to have been the laserwort, which Gerard described as "that stinking and loathsome gum called *Asa* and *Affa*"—in other words, a kind of asafoetida.

SI
stands for

silver, of which an edible kind exists in India, where, beaten into paper-thin sheets, it is used on various dishes for decoration rather than for nourishment; for the **silver-bell tree** of the southern United States, whose fruit is known as the wild olive; for the **silverberry** of North America, a floury drupe eaten chiefly around Hudson's Bay; for the **silverfish** of South Africa, otherwise known as the Scotchman; for the **silver HAKE,** the North American Atlantic species of this very useful member of the cod family; for the **silver salmon,** which is the coho SALMON; for the **silversides,** the American name for what the British call the sand smelt, which in both countries is admitted to be really the grunion, also known as the dancing fish because of its wriggling progress out of the water to lay its eggs on the shore; for the **silver smelt** of North Africa, which is not a grunion; for the **silverweed**, whose parsniplike roots were, in the eighteenth century, sometimes virtually the only food available to the inhabitants of the Hebrides Islands for months at a time; and for the **silverwood**, a Brazilian tree whose fruit looks like a black plum and tastes like a rather inferior cherry.

SI
stands for

the **simain**, called the neeno in tropical Africa, whose seeds are not only roasted for munching like peanuts, but are also made into a jelly or pressed for their oil; for **Simmental**, a superior breed of Russian cattle; for **sim-sim oil**, which is what tropical Africans call sesame oil; for the **singhara nut**, a relative of the Chinese water chestnut, scooped up from the bottom of lakes in Kashmir; for the **sitatunga**, an antelope hunted in tropical Africa; for **sive**, the Caribbean word for the SCALLION, an obvious misspelling of the French *cive*; and for **Siwash cheese**, a derisory name given by whites to American Indian preserved SALMON.

SK
stands for

the **skate**, synonymous, in popular terminology at least, with the ray, a fish much eaten by Europeans but abandoned by Americans soon after Captain John Smith had reported that he found so many of them in Virginia that he speared them with his sword and "we tooke more in owne hour than we could eate in a day"; for the **skink**, a sort of lizard sometimes eaten by Saharans, wrote Lloyd Cabot Briggs, "usually when on the trail far from any settlement"; for the **skipjack**, or ocean bonito, a fish which knows its way around in the Pacific, the Atlantic and the Mediterranean but loses its bearings in cans when it is labeled Light Meat TUNA; for the **skipper**, or saury, a fish which looks too thin to have much meat on its bones, but since it may be 16 inches long, still has space to provide a plentiful portion of palatable flesh; for **skirret**, whose tubers, "most commonly not a finger thick," wrote John Gerard, "are sweet, white, good to be eaten, and most pleasant in taste," as they must have seemed to the Emperor Tiberius, who imported them from Germany; for the **skittledog**, a fish often preserved in formaldehyde for dissection by zoology students, but worthy also of dissection with knife and fork, fried, but without formaldehyde; for **skunk**, "one of our greatest delicacies," according to a descendant of the Mashpee Indians of Massachusetts, adding, "White people have an idea that cranberries go best with turkey, but, let me tell you, cranberries were made to go with roast skunk"; for **skunk cabbage**, highly recommended by some writers on wild foods, but of which Euell Gibbons, a man hard to discourage, wrote, "The bruised or cut leaves smell like a skunk, the cut stem smells like a mixture of mustard and rotten, raw onions . . . the flowers smell like carrion [and] it tasted exactly like it smelled"; and the **skunk egg**, which in the language of American cowboys means the onion.

SL
stands for

the **sleeper**, a freshwater fish of tropical Africa and Madagascar, and the **slimy soapy**, a saltwater fish of South Africa and Madagascar; for the **slender foxtail**, a kind of couch grass; for the **slippery elm**, whose boiled inner bark kept American Indians alive in time of famine; for **sloe**, the black sheep among PLUMS; for **slokam** or **sloke**, *Porphyra laciniata*, an edible seaweed much relished in England, which should not be confused with **sloak** or **slook**, *P. umbilicalis*, an edible seaweed much relished in Wales, where you can buy it, cellophane-wrapped, at the corner grocery; for the **sloth**, eaten by prehistoric American Indians about 10,000 B.C.; for the **slow-match tree**, whose fruit is eaten in East India; and for the **slug**, of which that of the maguey was considered a delicacy by the Aztecs, and for that matter is still so considered by their descendants.

SM
stands for

smallage, which is wild celery; for the **small field bean**, which at blossoming time floods the air with a delightful fragrance; for the **smallmouth bass**, a game fish particularly relished in the northwestern United States; for the **smare**, a saltwater fish eaten with slight enthusiasm in Ghana; for the **smelt**, a small, sweet fish which Brillat-Savarin called "the warbler of the waters," and the **smolt**, a SALMON trying to make up its mind to go to sea; for **smilax**, or China-root, a root eaten in China, and **smoke plant**, whose leaves were eaten in China, but apparently not since the fourteenth century; and for the **smooth hound**, which is a dogfish, but not the same kind as the rough hound.

SN
stands for

the **snail,** forbidden to drink beer in Britain at the instigation of the Society for the Prevention of Cruelty to Animals, though snails seem to enjoy it; for **snake,** of which venomous species are held to be in general tastier than others, information which I have at second hand; for the **snake cucumber,** long, thin and sinuous, eaten in Egypt, and the **snake gourd,** long, thin and sinuous, eaten in tropical Africa; for the **snakehead,** one of the few fish which can live for long periods out of water, an important food in parts of Asia and Africa; for **snakeroot,** a North American substitute for ginger, **snakeweed,** a Russian substitute for bread, and **snakewood,** a tropical American substitute for food; for the **snapdragon,** considered a flower elsewhere, but its roots are eaten in Jamaica; for the **snapper,** a fish praised oftenest when it is the red snapper, but there are more than 250 species, most of them edible and some of them important; and for the **snapping turtle,** in little demand except in Philadelphia.

SN
stands for

the **snipe,** a delectable game bird which travels in wisps and takes off upwind; for the **snot-apple,** a name which is no improvement over *mato,* as it is called in Kenya, or even over *caglacagla,* as it is called in Tanzania, and **snoutfish,** which is perhaps preferable to *mdomodomo,* as it is called in Tanzania; for **snow algae,** which grows on glaciers in the Pacific Northwest and tastes a little like watermelon; for the **snow apple,** once known also as the Fameuse, but it is famous no longer, being restricted today to northern Vermont and Quebec; for the **snowball tree,** "a miserable food for savage nations," wrote John Lindley in 1846, having in mind perhaps the Cree Indians, who called it *nipi minam,* or the Narragansett Indians, who called it *wuchipoquamneash* and may have pointed it out to Roger Williams, who said that it was "a kind of sharp fruit like a barberry in taste"; for the **snowberry,** which was eaten by the Indians of Oregon and Washington, unless it was the creeping snowberry, which was eaten by the Indians of Maine; for the **snow crab** of the northern Pacific, hitherto neglected because of the great prestige of the Alaska king crab, which inhabits the same waters, but some connoisseurs think the snow crab is better; for the **snow fungus,** which the Chinese put in soups; for the **snow goose,** which is a vegetarian, and the **snow grouse,** which is a ptarmigan; for the **snow pea** of China, eaten pods and all; and for the **snuffbox tree,** whose fruit pulp is eaten in the Congo.

SOA
stands for

the **soapbark tree** of Malaysia, whose sweet fruit had better not be eaten by those afraid of dysentery; for the **soapberry** of Alaska, where the Indians make cakes from it, "an exceedingly repulsive food to Whites," according to the American naturalist W. H. Dall; for the **soapfish,** so called because when alarmed it excretes a sort of slime and thrashes about in the water, beating it into what looks like soapsuds, a defense which does not save it from being eaten in tropical West Africa; for the **soap-pod,** whose leaves are used in East Indian cooking as a substitute for tamarind and whose beans are roasted for eating in China; and for the **soap plant** of California, with an edible bulb sometimes called the wild potato, and the **soapwood** of tropical America, with an edible berry sometimes called the wild pear.

SOF
stands for

the **soft-shelled clam,** which is the STEAMER, and the **soft-shelled** CRAB, which, caught at the moment of molting, can be eaten with delight, shell and all.

SOL
stands for

the **soldier,** a fish eaten in South Africa; for the **sole,** one of the most widely appreciated of all FLATFISH; and for **Solomon's-seal,** whose roots have been made into bread, but usually only in times of famine.

SOR
stands for

the **sorb apple,** which is the service pear; for the **sorbet,** which is the cornelian cherry, not quite a cherry and so acid that its cultivation has been abandoned; and for the **sordid dragonet,** an ungallant name to give to the female of this species of fish, of which the male is the gemmeous dragonet.

And **SOR** also stands for

SORGHUM. It is in Austria, I think, that there is the saying, "We were better off when we were worse off." In America we could say the same thing about sweeteners. In the mid-nineteenth century, sorghum was called "the sugar of the Plains." It was grown throughout the south-central part of the country, where every locality had its own mill to crush the stalks and produce from them a golden syrup, a little thinner than molasses, which was then the general sweetener; it could be poured over pancakes, used in baking, or serve for making candy and preserves. The Southeast still grows a good deal of sorghum.

By the beginning of this century, sorghum had been replaced by refined granulated sugar, so convenient to use that the per capita sugar consumption of the United States doubled between 1880 and 1915, contributing to make American dentists the best in the world.

The change represented a dietary loss. "White sugar has little nutritive value other than as fuel," Richard Osborn Cummings wrote in *The American and His Food,* "whereas the sweetenings that it displaced . . . retain a significant proportion of the mineral elements of the plant juice." Sorghum has a good deal of protein too, though it is not all utilizable. The plant is short in lysine, an amino acid which is required to enable the human body to absorb the protein; but a Purdue University team working to improve the quality of sorghum discovered two Ethiopian strains which contained a large dose of lysine, and used them, by cross-breeding, to enrich other types. Nature, unfortunately, seems always to demand a quid for a quo; the new strains were more nutritious, but less resistant to drought, thus diminishing an important asset of sorghum, which in Africa and Asia is grown in arid regions where no other cereal can be raised successfully, with the possible exception of millet.

If you were asked to name the three or four most important cereals in the world, it might not occur to you to include sorghum in the list, but it stands fourth, after wheat, rice and maize, according to some authorities, or third, after rice and wheat, according to others. It may be, though complete figures do not seem to exist, second, after rice, in acreage sown to it, for though wheat is produced in greater volume, its yields are higher, so that it requires less acreage to reach a higher figure. Sorghum is in any case one of the fifteen most important food crops of the world, which among them provide between 85 and 95 percent of all human energy.

Most Occidentals would probably be inclined, on first realizing the importance of sorghum, to attribute it to its wide use as forage for livestock. It is indeed largely so used; in Oklahoma, for instance, the sorghum crop is second only to the wheat crop, because sorghum is used for the final fattening of cattle raised in the Panhandle. But sorghum is also a basic food for 300 million of the world's worst-fed people, in Africa, India and China. "Not a very good food—it may fill bellies but does not provide nutritive quality," said one authority less impressed by its merits than Richard Osborn Cummings. Filling bellies in those parts of the world where sorghum is not merely a sweetener but a cereal is an important function; the big sorghum eaters have little opportunity to be choosy about the quality of their nutrition.

It is perhaps more prudent not to generalize too readily about the nutritive merits of sorghum. There are hundreds of species, grown mostly in dry tropical and subtropical climates, and their varying characteristics have been defined only fuzzily by growers, dietitians or taxonomists; the last are not even in agreement on its genus. Some call it *Sorghum,* some *Andropogon,* and some *Holcus. Holcus* might be preferable: it would be consistent with the uncertainty which presides over the sorghum family. It is the Latin name for some sort of grain, but we don't know which one: perhaps it was sorghum, perhaps it wasn't.

The ancient Romans knew sorghum, but not very much about it. Pliny speaks of a black variety, *Sorghum nigrum,* but apparently the Romans made no attempt to cultivate it. They were not very well provided with sweeteners, but perhaps the kind of sorghum they knew was not sweet. If it was not primarily a sweetener but a cereal, they might have been uninterested in it, for they had plenty of superior wheat, millet and barley already. They seem to have learned about sorghum from Egypt, where six varieties are widely grown today, none of them sweet; this may also have been the case in ancient times.

Africa seems to have been the native continent of sorghum; it is still the leading grain there. Some people think it started in Ethiopia, others that it originated just south of the Sahara or even within it; in either case, it would belong to the very rare category of food plants native to Africa south of its Mediterranean littoral countries. In favor of the theory of Ethiopian origin might be the fact that it was in this country that the Purdue University researchers found their superior strains of sorghum (two varieties out of ten thousand examined!). If they did not find it more quickly, this may have been because of secrecy on the part of the few growers who knew its merits. They raised it surreptitiously. The Ethiopian farmers were almost all sharecroppers; their landlords wanted them to grow varieties which would have to be sent to mills to be converted into flour, thus enabling them to check on the size of the crop so the proprietors could get their full share of it. The superior sorghum, however, did not have to be made into flour. The farmers gathered the grains, roasted them, and ate them like peanuts, neglecting to inform the landlords about their own consumption. To get away with this, they grew the best sorghum in small patches in the middle of other stands; and they told nobody they were growing it, not even American researchers.

As for the theory of Saharan origin, there is no evidence against it. It is grown today in almost all the oases, for local consumption, not for sale, and has been cultivated there since Neolithic times. It was also cultivated in China and India early enough so that both countries have developed special types of their own, but not necessarily separate species: many botanists think all of the multitudinous kinds of sorghum are varieties of a single species, of *Sorghum vulgare* or *Holcus sorghum.*

We do not really know what kind of sorghum is grown in the United States—that is, we do not know its origin; we can of course look at it growing in the fields and describe it as it exists now. The first sorghum to reach America seems to have come from the West Coast of Africa, and was probably a non-sweet variety. It was imported first by Jamaica, and from there was transferred to the southern states, where it was last reported growing in Georgia, after which we lose track of it. The second delivery came from France, which had imported seeds from northern China about 1851. Of a shipment of seeds from Shanghai, only one germinated; either it was a prolific ancestor, or France placed other, unrecorded orders, for in 1854 the U.S. Patent Office secured seeds of Chinese origin from France. After that we lose track of them. In 1857 a Mr. Wray, otherwise unidentified, is reported to have brought fifteen varieties of sorghum to the United States, some of them, if not all, sweet sorghums. After that we lose track of them. The sorghums now growing in the United States may have come from one or another or all or none of these imports.

The United States does not use the non-sweet sorghums grown in other parts of the world for their grain as human food, but only to feed animals, especially cattle (this is true of Australia also). Elsewhere in the world, animals usually get only human leftovers—the whole plant in the rare instances when a large crop leaves a surplus, the rest of the plant after humans have taken the grain, or the not-very-rich remains left after the stalks have been crushed for their sweet sap. America raises some forms of sorghum which seem to be cultivated nowhere else, solely for animal food, such as *H. sudanensis,* an African variety which will grow only where the climate is quite warm, and, the best known, *H. halepense,* Johnson grass, also called Aleppo grass or Means grass, widely grown in the South, where it has an unfortunate penchant for turning up in gardens or in stands of other crops, where it becomes a pernicious weed. The United States also grows *H. sorghum* var. *drummondi,* whose use is explained by its popular name, chicken corn.

SORGHUM. *Photograph by Marion Post Wolcott: A. E. Scott and his son, Charles, tying up shocks of sorghum cane for livestock fodder on their farm, Nebraska, September 1941*

Of the grain cereals, one of the oldest favorites is *H. sorghum* var. *durra,* cultivated in ancient times in the valley of the Nile. It was exported early in New World history to Jamaica, where it is called little millet or Guinea corn, and is used in the West Indies to make bread. The scientific label *durra* is echoed in the popular *dari,* Jaffa sorghum, considered the best in the Mediterranean, whence it is exported to foreign countries. *H. sorghum* var. *caffrosum* has white, red and black subvarieties, and is one of the grains used to produce mealie for the blacks of South Africa, where it is called kaffir corn. *H. sorghum* var. *roxburghi* is the *shallu* of India, most eaten in the center and the north. It is also known in different parts of the country as *cholum, jowar* or *jonna.*

In China, sorghum is called *kaoliang,* and is thought by some botanists to be a separate species. It must differ from its fellows at least in hardiness, for instead of growing in the south, as we might expect, it appears in Manchuria and northern China, substituting there for bamboo in several of its uses, since bamboo will not grow north of the Hwai River. When the wheat crop fails in northern China, sorghum takes its place; and even when wheat is available, poor people often eat a rather coarse bread made from sorghum, which is less expensive. Sorghum is also eaten to a lesser extent in Japan.

In Europe, though grain sorghum is grown in Hungary, Yugoslavia, Portugal and Italy, it is not much eaten except in the last, where bread is made from the grain of the black variety. This is the sorghum of which Pliny wrote, so one might wonder if this is not one of the many examples in food history of the triumph of habit over quality. The white-grained varieties, whose flour is also white, are usually preferred for human food, but perhaps the Italians are still eating the black because they are following in the footsteps of their ancestors, who in ancient times would have had to eat it wild. There are also red-grained sorghums, but they have a bitter taste and are used mostly for making beer.

The most important sorghum used as a sweetener, today grown chiefly in South Africa and the United States, is *H. sorghum* var. *saccara*, known variously as sorgho, sorgo, sweet sorghum or sugar sorghum. It may not have been common in ancient times in Africa, or at least in that part of it reachable from Rome, which would account for the neglect by the ancients of a plant which might have appealed to them more strongly as a sweetener. However, sugar sorghum was common there by the nineteenth century, when Dr. Livingstone reported that it was widely cultivated in the part of Africa he visited, where the natives chewed it like sugarcane and grew fat on it. In the south, the Zulus chewed and sucked the stalks of a variety they called *imphee*. To the north, the Tartars of the Crimea raised sweet sorghum also.

In the United States, where it was once so common, sugar sorghum has pretty much disappeared from commercial cultivation, but in the backhills of western North Carolina the Tarheels still grow it on a small scale, mostly for their own use. The stalks are run between rollers to squeeze out the juice, and the thin greenish liquid thus obtained is boiled down in long shallow rectangular pans, like those used for making maple syrup, until it has been reduced to one-tenth of its original volume. It is then called sorghum molasses, though "molasses," strictly speaking, is a word which should be reserved for the product of the sugarcane. It is thinner in consistency than molasses, and lighter in color—an almost transparent golden shade. The discarded grain is of course edible if it is wanted, but, like the leftover foliage, is ordinarily given to animals.

So far as I know, only in the United States is much attention given to *H. sorghum* var. *technicus*, popularly called broomcorn. It has been developed for the stiff bristles which rise from the inflorescences, used for making brooms. It is an endangered species, likely soon to be rendered obsolete by the vacuum cleaner.

466 **SORREL.** "There are few countries where sorrel is as much liked as in France," Georges Gibault wrote in his *Histoire des légumes* (he could have added Belgium). "In England, and in countries where English is spoken, this vegetable does not seem to be popular." The prejudice goes far back; in 1699 the English Dr. Lister, on an official mission to France, was surprised to find how abundantly sorrel, little esteemed in England, was cultivated in the region of Paris. "There is so much taste for sorrel here that I have seen whole acres devoted to it," he wrote. "For that matter, nothing is healthier, and this could very well substitute for the lemon in the treatment of scurvy and its related afflictions."

Yet in the time of Henry VIII, sorrel had been appreciated in Britain, where it was used in salads or as cooking greens, and it was found in most home gardens. All the early English herbalists wrote of it, but later reports are contradictory. One, dated 1807, said sorrel was common in England; another, dated 1874, asserted that it had fallen out of favor many years before. It was remarked somewhat sniffishly that "in Ireland, it is largely consumed by the peasantry" and "seems to be particularly relished by the Hebrideans." In America it seems to have been used more commonly at the beginning of the nineteenth century than it is now. (When I returned to the United States from France in 1940 and wanted sorrel, I had to grow it myself.) Could it be that the great increase in the use of granulated cane sugar which took place in the middle of the nineteenth century, and caused both England and America to make excessive use of sweetness in their foods, modified their cuisines in a direction incompatible with acid tastes like that of sorrel? Sorrel is common enough in countries which do not object to acidity in certain foods, in northern Europe, for instance. Norwegians eat sorrel leaves with milk, or mix it with meal and bake it (the Swedes, however, seem to have put sorrel in bread only during periods of scarcity). Laplanders —who, it is true, are often hard up for vitamin-rich foods—are given to boiling sorrel leaves in water, allowing the resulting juice to cool, and then mixing it with reindeer milk. In the north also, sorrel is relished on the shores of Alaska's Kotzebue Sound, and it is also among the foods of China and Japan. In India it is relished for soups and omelets.

Sorrel is a plant of northern Eurasia, of the genus *Rumex*, which includes about one hundred species of sorrels and docks. There is sometimes disagreement about which is which, and also about which popular names should be attached to which scientific names. The one point of agreement seems to be on *R. acetosa*, which everyone except the *Encyclopaedia Britannica*,

SORREL. *Drawing from Theodore Francis Garrett:* The Encyclopaedia of Practical Cookery, *New York*

which calls it garden sorrel, refers to simply as sorrel, with no restrictive adjective (but it is also sometimes called at the same time "sour dock"). Georges Gibault makes a subtle distinction by remarking that today's common sorrel is "descended" from *R. acetosa,* a name he apparently wants to reserve for wild sorrel. It does not really matter very much. Although botanists have developed many improved varieties of sorrel, there is less difference between wild and cultivated kinds than for almost any other food plant.

Although many gardening books seem to take it for granted that *R. acetosa* is the species still most commonly grown, notably in France, it seems in actuality to have been displaced by improved varieties of other kinds—but the authorities are not agreed as to which ones they are. For Sturtevant (*Edible Plants of the World*), *R. acetosa* has given way to the bitterer *R. scutatus,* which he calls garden sorrel and Gibault calls round sorrel. But Sturtevant may be thinking only of England, where this species appeared in 1596 (John Gerard mentions it in his *Herball,* but does not specify that it was cultivated; it may have been gathered wild). Gibault may have been thinking only of France; he seems to think that improved varieties there stemmed from *R. montanus* (alias *R. arifolius*), which Sturtevant calls French sorrel, known in France since the eighteenth century as virgin sorrel because it does not produce seed and has to be propagated by division. Its failure to produce seed has the advantage that it remains throughout the entire growing season in a condition which permits taking leaves from it as wanted, leaving the rest of the plant in the ground to produce more. This variety is less acid, lighter in color, and produces a thicker growth of leaves than common sorrel; its varieties seem to be the kinds most commonly cultivated in France.

R. acetosella is sheep sorrel, *R. paucifolius* is described by the *Encyclopaedia Britannica* as mountain sorrel, and *R. hastatulus* as heartwing sorrel. *R. abyssinicus,* perhaps developed in the country for which it is named, is called spinach-rhubarb because its leaves are used like the former and its stalks like the latter; it should probably be classed with the docks.

Since the bitterness of sorrel results from its high content of oxalic acid, other plants which share this characteristic are abusively called sorrels also, like *Oxyria digyna,* which Sturtevant calls mountain sorrel, the name the *Britannica* gives to *R. paucifolius* (curiously, nobody seems to call *R. montanus* mountain sorrel). Alaskan Indians are fond of *Oxyria digyna,* chopped up together with scurvy grass or watercress and fermented. Species of the *Oxalis* genus can all be called lady's sorrel or wood sorrel, according to the *Britannica,* but *Oxalis acetosella* is distinguished from the others by being called sheep sorrel in Africa, while in French it is named *alléluia* (hallelujah); the explanation seems to be that it becomes edible about Easter, when a good deal of religious music is trumpeting that word. This plant is eaten in Iceland in spring salads and is gathered wild by French peasants, but is apparently no longer cultivated, though it was in the royal gardens in 1690. A Mexican species is referred to deceptively in French as the oxalis of Dieppe; it has tubers which are edible, but watery and almost tasteless. The farthest remove from the real thing is probably the so-called Indian sorrel, also known as Guinea sorrel, Jamaica sorrel or red sorrel; it is *Hibiscus sabdariffa,* more accurately described as roselle, one of the names given it in the West Indies, along with *rosella* and *flor de Jamaica.* It is also grown in Florida.

R. patientia, the patience or spinach dock, is no doubt not a sorrel but a dock, as the second of these two popular names indicates, but the ancient Romans mixed us up about it by describing it as *lapathum,* a word they used also for genuine sorrels. It seemed to mean *R. patientia* more often than not, but for Plautus and Horace it meant some not-quite-identified type of sorrel, for which Pliny and Virgil used the word *rumex.* It seems to have been sorrel also which Dioscorides meant by *oxalis* and Galen by *oxulapathon.* I do not know what species Gaius Laelius, a friend of Scipio Africanus, had in mind when he praised sorrel for its "philosophic superiority." The ancients used sorrel, but sparingly, and seem not to have cultivated it, contenting themselves with the wild plant as nature gave it to them.

We hear frequently of sorrel in the twelfth century, when it is usually called *acetosa* ("acid"), while the English monk Neckam called it *acidularum*; in Low Latin it was also *surele*, the ancestor of the English word, which was still being used in France as its popular name at the beginning of this century, though officially it had been supplanted by *oseille*, probably derived from *oxalis*. It seems to have been in the fourteenth century that sorrel juice was used for verjuice in sauces. The anonymous *Ménagier de Paris* makes several allusions to it, and it appears often in household accounts of the fourteenth and fifteenth centuries. Curiously, Bruyerin-Champier wrote that it was only beginning to come into general use in his time, the sixteenth century; he must have been as unaware of its role in France as Dr. Lister was of its role in England. In France today, though sorrel remains in favor, its use has declined greatly since the end of the last century, when market gardeners around Paris produced it in great quantity for the capital: in 1895, 20 million kilograms (44 million pounds) of sorrel leaves were delivered to the Paris markets.

In the United States, *R. acetosa* and *R. scutatus* were reported growing in gardens in 1806 and again in 1832. *R. montanus* had joined them at least by 1863. Sorrel is almost non-existent today unless you grow it yourself, which deprives the country of one of the most subtle of all cold soups, *potage Germiny*. (For another important use of sorrel, see SHAD.)

SO
stands for

soump oil, a fat universally used in the Ivory Coast, Chad and East Africa, made from the intensely bitter fruit of the zachun-oil tree, which fails to explain why it is also called heglik oil; for **sour cherries,** of which the best is the morello, *Prunus acida*; for **sour dock,** an inaccurate name for **sour grass,** an alternative name for **sour sorrel,** an inaccurate name for sheep SORREL; for the **soursop,** alias the corossol, alias the prickly custard, a tropical American fruit which has, depending on whom you read, (a) "a biting wild taste," (b) a taste which "much resembles that of the black currant," (c) "a flavor of perfumed cream," or which (d) unripe, "tastes like turnips"; for the **Southdown sheep,** reputed to be particularly flavorful, but I cannot say, though I once owned twenty-five of them myself, for I sold them, idiotically, untasted; for the **southern periwinkle,** which is getting less and less southern as time goes by, for it started out in Florida and has now spread as far north as Massachusetts; for **southernwood,** which seems to be used only in beverages (beer and tea) and should therefore be out of bounds for this book, but I cannot resist informing you that its other names are "old man" and "lad's love"; for the **sow,** which might seem incapable of offering delicacies not obtainable from any kind of pig, but it did for the ancient Romans, who ate its nipples and vulva; for the **sow thistle,** whose milky stem is peeled and eaten raw by Lapps, undeterred by a bitterness which discourages everybody else; and for the **soybean,** the most important BEAN of China, Manchuria, Japan and Malaysia.

SPAD
stands for

spadic, which you know about under the name of its leaves, coca, chewed in South America as a stimulant; and for the **spadefish,** a circular animal just the right shape to fit a frying pan, which it does with excellent results.

SPANISH
stands for

the **Spanish bayonet,** whose figlike fruit is eaten in Mexico and the southwestern United States by Indians and whites alike, but only Indians eat the insipid flower buds; for the **Spanish bean,** which is the scarlet runner, and the **Spanish bream,** which is the bronze bream, a silver-colored fish; for the **Spanish lentil** or **Spanish pea,** or curling vetch, eaten especially in India, in spite of the danger that it may cause lathyrism, which is why it was prohibited by law in Württemberg in the seventeenth century; for the **Spanish mackerel,** which is the chub mackerel of Chesapeake Bay; for the **Spanish nut** of the Mediterranean area, which, John Gerard wrote, was "eaten at the table of rich and delicious persons in sallads or otherwise"; for the **Spanish oyster plant,** or golden thistle, whose root seems to have been eaten more commonly in ancient times than it is today; for the **Spanish potato,** which is what the sweet potato was once called; for **Spanish rhubarb,** eaten everywhere in tropical Africa, which is actually a form of dock or SORREL; and for **Spanish SALSIFY,** also called black salsify, black oyster plant or viper's grass, the last because it was supposed to be an antidote against the bites of venomous snakes.

SPA
stands for

sparrows, eaten by Englishmen in the sixteenth century and by Japanese and tropical Africans in the twentieth; for **spat,** baby oysters still floating free in the water, where they should be allowed to remain and put on weight, but they are improvidently eaten at this stage in Japan; for

spatlum, the butterroot of Northwest Pacific Indians; for **spatterdock**, the yellow pond lily, whose seeds and roots were eaten by American Indians, the first tasting like sorghum seeds and the second like sheep's liver; and for **spawner**, the name given to an Atlantic salmon when it reaches its breeding grounds.

SPE
stands for

the **spearfish**, which is a marlin, and **spearmint**, which is a MINT; for **spelding**, a word used loosely in Scotland for fish of various species when they are salted and sun-dried, but which strictly speaking should be applied only to the whiting; for **spelt**, a sort of WHEAT in which the grain adheres to the chaff, eaten more commonly in ancient times than it is today; and for the **spet**, which is a barracuda.

SPH
stands for

sphagnum, or bog moss, which the English botanist John Lindley characterized in 1849 as "a wretched food in barbarous countries."

SPI
stands for

Spice, which Webster defines as "any of various aromatic vegetable products used in cookery to season food and to flavor foods," which lets in shallots and rules out salt; for the **spicebush**, *Lindera benzoin*, called the benjamin-bush by persons unable to pronounce "benzoin," whose berries were once used as a substitute for allspice, unless it is *Umbellularia californica*, also called balm of heaven, the cajeput tree, the California olive, mountain laurel or sassafras laurel, whose leaves are used by Spanish-Americans as a condiment; for the **spice tree**, which produces what is known variously as Negro pepper, African pepper, Guinea pepper or Ethiopian pepper, widely used in tropical Africa; for the **spider**, which the United Nations Food and Agricultural Organization, in its listing of African foods, describes as "very rarely eaten," a statement which does not strain credibility; for the **spider crab**, which Balzac tells us was in his times more expensive than lobster; for the **spider flower**, whose pungent seeds, suggesting mustard in flavor, are used in East Indian curries; for the **spiderwort**, whose rhizomes are said to be eaten in India, and **spignel**, whose roots are said to be eaten in the Canary Islands; for the **spiky jack**, a dogfish of which Africans partake only sparingly; for the **spinach beet**, which like chard is a beet grown only for its leaves; for the **spindle tree**, whose young leaves are eaten in China; for the **spiny cockle**, an enormous Pacific coast shellfish, whose commodious shell can serve as a decorative dish after you have disposed of its original occupant in the habitual fashion; for the **spiny dogfish**, or spurdog, which you might catch off the Atlantic coast of the United States or off the Mediterranean coast of Africa, where it is called simply the spiny fish, but wherever you catch it, look out for the vicious spike just in front of each of the two dorsal fins; for the **spiny melon**, or jelly melon, of Southwest Africa, which looks like a short fat cucumber studded with spikes like a floating mine; for the **spiny shark** eaten in Algeria, which isn't a shark, but what it really is I have no idea and it doesn't help to know that the French call it a caterpillar; and for the **spiny snapper**, which inhabits the Red Sea.

And **SPI** also stands for

SPINACH. "Italian spinach is as much better than French spinach as French spinach is better than American spinach," I wrote in *The Food of Italy* in 1971. It was a simple observation, tested at the table, which I did not attempt to follow up, except to note that Italians are exceptionally skillful market gardeners. But today I wonder if the reason for the mediocrity of American spinach is not simply that America plants the wrong seed.

There are two main groups of cultivated spinach (both probably varieties of the same species), the prickly-seeded and the smooth-seeded. I have found both kinds registered in an American *botanical* book (one that dates, however, from early in the century), but I have found no inkling in American *gardening* books that their authors know that a smooth-seeded variety exists—with one exception. It is an exception that proves the rule. After describing the fruit of spinach as "an utricle, surrounded by a small, prickly, capsule-like body (commonly, but incorrectly called the seed)," it goes on to remark: "There is also a variety, little known, where the fruit is invested with a covering that is not spiny." It happens that this "little known" variety is the one which is planted in France, Italy and elsewhere in Europe, where the spiny type was given up long ago as inferior. It would have been given up sooner if it had not been believed that it was hardier, and thus preferable for planting late in the year to winter in the ground and be harvested early in the spring. This proved to be untrue, and Europe turned to smooth-seeded spinach even for winter use. America, on the evidence of the garden books, seems still to be wedded to a variety which Europe has abandoned. If so, it is a trifle behind the times. Smooth-seeded spinach has been around at least since the early sixteenth century.

Prickly-seeded spinach (still called winter spinach) seems to be the more primitive variety; smooth-seeded spinach (also called summer spinach, round-seeded spinach or oval-seeded spinach) was an improvement from the start (but there are also improved prickly-seeded varieties). Garden spinach, whatever the shape of its seeds, is *Spinacia oleracea,* which has not been positively identified with any wild form; but it is generally agreed to have been native to Persia, or very near there (the Chinese word for "spinach" means "the Persian herb"). A wild spinach still exists, and is still eaten, in Persia, *S. tetrandra.* It may have been the ancestor of domestic spinach, which possibly never existed in a wild form.

It is curious that we are not better informed about the origin of spinach, for it is apparently quite recent, as a cultivated plant at least, and there should have been knowledgeable witnesses to its beginnings. The ancients apparently did not know it; it may be that it was not cultivated until after the Greco-Roman civilization had collapsed. Affirmations of its existence in earlier times are subject to suspicion; they may result from errors in translation, or, when they get into English, from a tendency in that language to use "spinach" as a generic word which can cover indiscriminately all leafy green plants which in any way resemble it. Thus when Ibn-el-Beithar in the thirteenth century wrote that Nineveh and Babylon made much use of it, he was almost certainly wrong (a telltale indication is that there is no Hebrew word for "spinach"). I have come across two references to a mention of spinach in an alleged Nabataean treatise on agriculture, which seems itself to have disappeared into the mists of time, but they do not inspire confidence. One of them describes this source as a Spanish work of the twelfth century and the other as a Syrian compilation of the fourth century—about two centuries after the Nabataeans had ceased to exist.

We are told that Charlemagne ordered that spinach be planted in his domains, which would have been at the beginning of the ninth century, almost certainly too early. But when de Candolle, whose *Origin of Cultivated Plants* is usually cited with reverence in such matters, tells us that spinach was new to Europe in the sixteenth century, that is almost certainly too late. Georges Gibault, in his *Histoire des légumes,* suggests that de Candolle was misled by badly informed writers, and that his date has to be pushed back by at least three centuries.

As early as 1351, spinach appeared in a list of vegetables recommended for monks on fast days. In England, Turner wrote of spinach in 1568 as "an herbe lately found and not long in use," but a manuscript dated 1440 states that the chief vegetables then eaten in England were cabbage, leeks, radishes and spinach, and it had also been cited in *The Forme of Cury,* a cookbook compiled in 1390 at the court of Richard II. Matthiola and Brassavola said it was new in Italy in the sixteenth century, but Crescenzi, an Italian agronomist, had already written in the thirteenth century that it was better than orach, and was sowed in that country in autumn to be picked for Lent, a calendar which is still followed. Ruellius, in 1536, gave the impression that it was then new in France, but the peasants who grew it had been hawking it in the streets a century earlier, and the French physician Arnauld de Villeneuve had listed it among common foods in the thirteenth century. Albertus Magnus, in Bavaria, had also described the plant in that century, calling particular attention to its prickly seeds. At the very beginning of the fourteenth century it is listed in the household accounts of wealthy families, and at the end of that century the anonymous *Ménagier de Paris* reported that "there is a species of chard called espinoche which is eaten at the beginning of Lent."

It is thus evident that spinach was present in Europe well before the generally accepted date, but it seems nevertheless to have passed eastward into Asia before it passed westward into Europe. The earliest record we have of it comes from China, where we hear that the king of Nepal sent some plants as a present to the Chinese in A.D. 647. We hear of spinach next from the Arabs, first from Abu Bakr Muhammad ibn Zakariyya al-Rhazes (860–923) and in the eleventh century from Avicenna, which is also when Ibn-Had-Jadj, a Spanish Moor, is supposed to have written a treatise on spinach which among other details reported that in the region of Seville an early variety was planted in January; but we know of this work only at second hand, through Ibn-el-Awam (twelfth century); its author seems to have gone overboard when he described spinach as "the prince of vegetables." It was very probably the Arabs who introduced spinach into Europe, as early as 900 according to one writer, which seems unlikely. Most accounts situate it about two centuries later, which ought to be about right, since it seems to have become fairly widespread by the twelfth century. This date also permits the alternative assumption that it was the Crusaders who brought it to Europe from Moslem territory rather than the Moors of Spain (a theory apparently accepted by Tragus, who in 1552 called it *hispanicum olus,* "the Spanish vegetable"). It could have traveled by both routes. "Spinach" is

SPINACH. *Early Italian illumination*

in any case derived from an Arabic word, a little mishandled by confusion with words meaning "thorn"—the prickly seed again.

By the sixteenth century spinach had become a favorite Lenten food, because winter-sown seeds produced plants just right for eating at that period. Catherine de' Medici was so fond of spinach that to this day the description *à la florentine* almost always identifies in France a dish containing spinach, a meaning it does not have in Florence (the word "Viroflay" in the name of a French dish also signals the presence of spinach, for Viroflay, a suburb of Paris, was renowned, before its soil was roofed over with cement, for a particularly large variety of spinach grown there).

It was in the sixteenth century that smooth-seeded spinach made its first appearance. Tragus spoke of it in 1552, Olivier de Serres mentioned it also, and in the following century *Le Jardinier Français*, published in 1651, described it as lighter in color and more delicate in taste than the prickly-seeded variety. It may be that these first smooth-seeded varieties were natural mutants. It was not until the end of the eighteenth century that two new kinds were developed deliberately —English spinach and Holland spinach, of which both probably originated in Holland. English spinach was still prickly-seeded, but Holland spinach had a smooth seed, and seems to have been the point of departure for all the smooth-seeded varieties cultivated today.

La Quintinie planted spinach in the gardens of Louis XIV, but the oft-repeated story that Louis liked it but was forbidden it by his doctor and would send out for it all the same, crying, "What! I am king of France and I cannot eat spinach?" had perhaps better be taken with a pinch of salt. Its source was a jesting poem written by a *chansonnier*, no very great guarantee of historical accuracy.

Spinach seems to have slipped surreptitiously into America. We do not know who brought it there, or when, or where; but in 1806 three varieties were growing in American gardens: one of them was smooth-seeded. Thomas Jefferson grew spinach, but from what sort of seed I do not know. Today California produces 50 percent of all American spinach, which does not prevent Zavala County, in the brash state of Texas, from calling itself "the Spinach Capital of the World."

The present ubiquity and popularity of spinach have naturally caused its name to be usurped by other plants which have little right to it. A fairly close relative is the so-called wild spinach which is the pigweed of Pennsylvania, not bad eating if gathered while it is still young and tender. The wild spinach of England, *Chenopodium bonus-henricus*, also called all-good, fat-hen, Good-King-Henry, goosefoot or mercury, eaten in some parts of the British Isles and even preferred there to genuine spinach, is of the same family as the Pennsylvania plant, and so is Australian spinach, *C. auricomum*. Southwestern France has a family of plants called *sarousses*, described as wild spinach, but I doubt if it is a relative.

We all know that NEW ZEALAND SPINACH, *Tetragonia implexicoma*, is not spinach, and neither are a number of plants which are called "spinach" in Africa. North America's Cuban spinach is *Claytonia perfoliata*, and what is called mountain spinach, *Atriplex hortensis*, is orach. I have no idea what *thovey*, Indian spinach, really is, nor *borenso*, Japanese spinach, nor *hin choy*, Chinese spinach, except that the last-named neither looks nor tastes like the real thing.

And what does the real thing taste like? "Spinach is not worth much essentially," Grimod de la Reynière said. "It is susceptible of receiving all imprints: it is the virgin wax of the kitchen."

SPINY LOBSTER. Flaubert, who never finished collecting the material for his projected *Dictionnaire des Idées Reçues* ("Dictionary of Widespread Popular Errors," shall we translate it?), listed one definition which read: "Spiny lobster: female of the lobster." This might be excusable in English, where the same word appears in the name of both crustaceans, but it is difficult to understand in French, where lobster is *homard* and spiny lobster is *langouste*. Yet I find that even French gastronomic writers do not always seem to realize that they are dealing with two different animals. I suspect that it is because the majority of French gastronomic books are written in the north and the majority of spiny lobsters are taken in the south.

If lobsters read books, the spiny lobster would know that it is supposed to be present from the

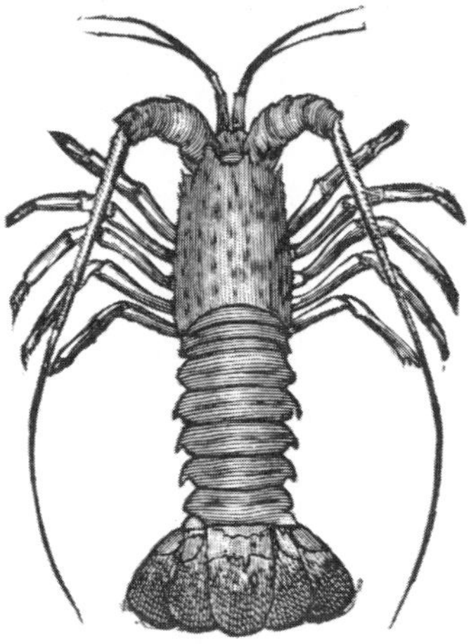

SPINY LOBSTER. *Engraving from Urbain Dubois and Emile Bernard:* La Cuisine Classique, *Paris, 1888*

southern coast of England all the way down the Atlantic coast of Europe, as well as in the Mediterranean and on the African coast, in the warmer waters which it prefers. Being illiterate, spiny lobsters have neglected the northern part of this range, and the human inhabitants of these coasts, who may well be better educated, are not particularly conscious of their presence either. The English are so unaware of the existence of the spiny lobster in their waters that they call it the Cape lobster (when they are not seriously underestimating it by calling it the crawfish); the cape they have in mind is the Cape of Good Hope.

On the French coast, spiny lobsters may have been more plentiful in earlier times than they are now, but I cannot remember ever encountering spiny lobsters in Brittany, or even on the Ile de Ré (at the level of La Rochelle), a place I happen to know very well, which is the farthest point north reached by warm-water fish ordinarily found only in Mediterranean or African waters. (Conversely, though the books locate lobster in the Mediterranean, I do not recall ever having eaten any there, though it appears that they are of excellent quality in Turkey, where the water is colder; as a general rule, lobsters improve in flavor where the water they inhabit is colder, spiny lobsters where the water is warmer.)

In the United States, similarly, the spiny lobster, according to the books, should be found as far north as Cape Cod (its southern side, I presume), but I have never come across one there. It begins to turn up in North Carolina, is found in the Gulf of Mexico, and also in the warmer waters of the Pacific coast, from Santa Barbara south.

At first sight the principal differences between these two crustaceans seem to be that the lobster has two large claws and the spiny lobster none, the latter making up for the lack of claw meat by a more capacious tail, and the fact that the lobster is rather neatly put together, while the spiny lobster, with its long antenna and its straggling feet, looks as if it had not yet been completely packed. Its insect-like appearance accounts for the derivation of *langouste*, its French name, from the Latin *locusta*, "locust"; indeed when Corneille referred to the desert diet of St. John, locusts and honey, he used the word *langouste*, which in his time had not yet become attached exclusively to the spiny lobster. This crustacean is also known in America as the rock lobster; if you want to determine whether "spiny" or "rock" is the better description, just pick one up in an ungloved hand.

Spiny lobsters vary greatly in color, red or even brick-red off Brittany when you can find any there; red or reddish brown, with white and yellow spots, in the Mediterranean; a marbled green down the West African coast as far as Mauritania; midnight blue south of that (but the deep-water spiny lobsters of the Canaries are rose-colored); and red off the Cape of Good Hope. They are light red off Florida, dark blue in the Caribbean, and brown in Brazil, where they caused the "lobster war" between France and Brazil when Breton fishermen began taking them in large quantities from the Brazilian continental shelf, whose spiny lobsters are less flavorful than those of France, but more plentiful. Spiny lobsters are a greenish brown off Ceylon. It may be that some of the differences between spiny lobsters of different habitats depend on the food available in each. Moroccan spiny lobsters are sometimes brought to France and kept in cages in Breton waters to improve their flavor before they are sold.

The ancients do not seem to have been much impressed by the spiny lobster, whose firm white flesh is nevertheless a superb taste treat; I prefer it cold, with mayonnaise. There is little reference to this crustacean in ancient writings, though Athenaeus did write that large shrimp were preferred to spiny lobsters. Nevertheless, a dining room floor uncovered in Pompeii revealed a mosaic representing all kinds of fish, with a large spiny lobster in the center. Mediterranean indifference has persisted to this day in Corsica, where I once spent a month in a hotel whose dining room windows looked out over a sea full of spiny lobsters; but if I wanted one I had to order it the day before and a boy was dispatched by bus to buy one in Bastia, sixty-three miles away. The French mainland was already more appreciative in 1393, when *Le Ménagier de Paris* called the *langouste* alternatively the giant crawfish, the sea crawfish or the spiny sea lobster and opined that in Lent "the flesh of the spiny sea lobster is good instead of meat." The contemporary *Dictionnaire de l'Académie des Gastronomes* writes that its "fine flesh, compact, uniform, white as a camellia and delicate as an almond, has a flavor less pronounced than that of its rival"—the *homard*, of course.

Most people who discuss their respective flavors seem to prefer lobster to spiny lobster, a question which seems to me to make little sense. The two tastes are different; each should be appreciated on its own merits. There is no basis for rating them on grounds of inferiority or superiority.

We need not take with entire seriousness the comment of James de Coquet, gastronomic writer for the Paris *Figaro*: "There are two categories of spiny lobster: that of firm flesh, which comes from rocky bottoms, and the limp spiny lobster which seems to have issued from the brain of Salvador Dali. The latter are generally found at gala banquets."

I have been told what is reputed to be a Cajun legend, which relates how the Acadians, when they were expelled from Canada in the eighteenth century and fled to Louisiana, were followed by their friends, the spiny lobsters, who arrived so thin after their long journey that they became crawfish. One slight flaw in this story is that there have never been any spiny lobsters in Canada, and another is that there has never been any lack of either crawfish or spiny lobsters in Louisiana—no lack for Louisianans, that is. The American South does not fish enough spiny lobsters to export them to the rest of the United States and neither do the Caribbean islands, which cannot keep up with their own demand, not even in Jamaica, where half of the three thousand fishermen specialize in spiny lobster. There is one exception—Cuba, which has the largest spiny lobster fishing industry in Latin America and exports large quantities, but not always to the United States, where politics gets in the way. This obliges Americans to fall back on frozen South African lobster tails, which is the only form in which the spiny lobster is known to the majority of Americans (or Britons either, for that matter), who eat 10 million pounds of them a year, though they are obtainable in a fresher state at home.

"I suspect that the popularity in America of frozen South African lobster tails," wrote Calvin Trillin, "can be accounted for by their being so easy to eat—the only other logical explanation being that Americans, for some reason, are attracted to the taste of unpainted papier-mâché if it is priced high enough."

SPO
stands for

the **sponge tree,** present, though rarely cultivated, in the southern United States, but raised in India for its edible gum; for the **spoonbill,** a wading bird eaten with pleasure in England in the fifteenth century, or a freshwater fish eaten without much pleasure today, for it is only second-rate provender, whether it is taken under the name "spoonbill cat" in the Mississippi or under the name "spoonbill sturgeon" in the Yangtse; for the **spoonwort** of the Arctic area, eaten as a scurvy grass in Alaska and as a salad plant in northern Scotland; for the **spotfin,** a freshwater North American fish which makes a noise like a bell, and the **spotfin croaker,** a saltwater North American fish which makes a noise like a drum; for the **spottail,** a very common freshwater food fish in tropical Africa, sometimes called a sardine or a herring, though it is neither, and also ngara or khula, which doesn't help much in identifying it; for the **spotted cat's-ear,** once cultivated as a potherb in Britain but now abandoned to wild-food fanciers; for the **spotted dogfish,** eaten in North Africa; for the **spotted jewfish,** whose prominent fins and scales make it indubitably kosher, but it is rather poor eating; and for the **spotted triggerfish,** considered a delicacy on some South Pacific islands, preferably eaten young, as the adults have a lamentable habit of secreting poison.

SPR
stands for

the **sprat,** which resembles the anchovy and is accordingly passed off for that fish in Norway and Sweden, though it is much inferior in flavor; for the **spring beauty,** which many Americans know as a pretty rose-colored wild flower in ignorance of the fact that it has edible bulbs which were highly thought of by American Indians; for the **springbok,** perhaps the most graceful of all African antelopes, but also, unfortunately for itself, "by far the most appetizing game to be found in Africa," Laurens van der Post *dixit*; for **spring cress,** which is winter CRESS, and **spring salmon,** which is Chinook SALMON; and for **sprouting** BROCCOLI, which is not only green, but also, on occasion, purple or white.

SPU
stands for

spud, which is not only slang for POTATO but also, usually expanded to "fairy spuds," another name for spring beauties; for **spurge,** including balsam spurge, whose juice is made into jelly in the Canaries, and caper spurge, sometimes used as a substitute for that condiment in southern Europe, though it is acrid; and for **spurry,** whose seeds have been used to make bread in Finland and Scandinavia, but only when times were *very* bad.

SQ
stands for

squab, which Brillat-Savarin told us should be eaten in its early age, superfluous advice since this is, by definition, the only age squab possesses; for the **square nut**, a sort of hickory nut whose prominent angles justify its name, more or less; for the **squashberry**, which is a close relative of the highbush cranberry, while the **squaw bush** *is* the highbush cranberry; and for **squaw honey**, which is extracted directly from the flowers in Alaska without the aid of bees; **squaw** MINT, which is American pennyroyal, the **squaw vine**, which is the partridgeberry (and an "old squaw" is a duck).

And SQ also stands for

SQUASH (with which we will link **pumpkins** and **gourds**). In 1540 or thereabouts, Hernando de Alvarado, acting as a scout for Coronado's penetration of the American Southwest, reported to his chief that the territory which he had explored grew melons. They could not have been melons, Old World fruits which did not exist in America until Europeans brought them there. What were they then? Almost certainly they were the same plants that other early explorers also called melons, for want of a better word: squashes or pumpkins.

In 1584 Jacques Cartier reported from the St. Lawrence region that he had found there *gros melons*, which was translated into English not as "big melons" but as "pompions," pumpkins. As early as 1586, English botanists began writing about "melons" and "millions" as meaning pumpkins. They had picked the word up, perhaps, from Thomas Hariot, who in the same year had reported the presence in Virginia of vegetables "called by us pompions, melons, and gourds, because they are of the like forms as those kinds in England." In 1672 John Josselyn wrote of

> "squashes," but more truly "squoutersquashes," a kind of mellon or rather gourd, for they sometimes degenerate into gourds. Some of them are green, some yellow, some longish, like a gourd, others round, like an apple; all of them are pleasant food boyled and buttered, and seasoned with spice. But the yellow squash—called apple squash (because like an apple) about the bigness of a pomewater—is the best kind.

The Europeans who encountered squashes and pumpkins in America had to compare them to melons or some other European vegetable or fruit because they had never seen anything quite like them before and had no word for them. Despite some assertions that European varieties of squash existed, and despite the caution which persists to this day among botanists, who describe these vegetables as of uncertain origin but probably American, I think we may make bold to assert that squashes and pumpkins are uniquely American and were completely unknown to the Old World before the time of Columbus.

We are told nevertheless that squash was grown in the hanging gardens of Babylon; that Pliny mentioned it; that Apicius gave recipes for it; that Martial gave a dinner composed entirely of different kinds of squash, of which each had a distinctive taste; that they were grown in Gaul; that in the very first post-Roman cookbook, that of Platina, there was a recipe for squash soup; and that squash was on the list of plants which Charlemagne ordered grown on his domains. This last assertion gives us the clue to what the ancient world and medieval Europe had in mind when they used words which we have translated as "squash." Charlemagne's instructions were written in Latin: I have one translation of them in French, and another in English. The French translation of the word Charlemagne used is *courge*, "squash"; but the English translation is "gourd."

It seems likely that all the European pre-Columbian words we have translated as "squash" really meant gourds. But they were described as edible, and we tend to think of gourds as plants which we grow because they are ornamental, but which are not fit to eat. Many kinds of gourds, however, can be eaten, were in fact eaten, and are still eaten. In the thirteenth century Albertus Magnus spoke of edible gourds, and in the seventeenth Bauhin named two species which were eaten. In the time of Louis XV, Pierre Poivre reported that in the gardens of Pondicherry, a French enclave in India, there was every kind of *citrouille*, of which the most curious was what he called the *pipangaya*, "which is shaped like a fat snake." This sounds like the snake gourd, and as *citrouille* in French can mean either pumpkin or gourd, we may suspect that the others were gourds too, especially as some botanists think India is the homeland of *Lagenaria*, the gourd genus. In China today, the fuzzy gourd (*mao gwa*) is preferred to squashes, having a "succulent, sweet, sophisticated flavor" not found in the squash. Not only the young fruits, but also the young leaves and young shoots of *L. sicetraria*, the bottle gourd, there called the white pumpkin, are widely eaten in North Africa, South Africa and Madagascar. The name "white pumpkin" is also given to a gourd of another genus, *Benincasa cerifera*, the wax gourd, whose bloom constitutes so heavy a deposit of this substance that it can be scraped off and made into candles. It is still eaten

SQUASH. *Engraving from Joseph Harris:* Catalogue of Field, Garden and Flower Seeds, *1882*

today in India, China, Japan, Africa, and on many of the Pacific islands.

It seems not unlikely that just as squashes and pumpkins are almost certainly exclusively of the New World, gourds may belong exclusively to the Old, though they were quick to reach America after its discovery. This is sometimes disputed, usually on the theory that since gourds, especially the bottle gourd, serve as vessels to hold liquids, vegetables of this family capable of serving this purpose in the New World as in the Old must be gourds. Hence Amerigo Vespucci in 1489 wrote of the small dried "gourds" the Indians of Trinidad suspended around their necks (did he know that their contents were not liquid, but either a plant they chewed or a sort of flour?), and there are many other references to vessels made of these vegetables, some of enormous size, described alternately as gourds or pumpkins. The ability to hold liquids is not an infallible method of identifying gourds. Latin America still uses hard-shelled squashes or pumpkins not only to hold liquids, but even as cooking vessels: a popular Argentine dish, *carbonada criolla*, is a complicated beef stew baked in a hollowed-out squash, which doubles as an ingredient and a casserole. It was probably such hard-rinded squashes which Vespucci saw.

The case for the exclusively American character of squashes and pumpkins is much less debatable than that of the exclusively Old World character of gourds. No traces of squashes or pumpkins have ever been found in ancient Egypt, but its tombs have yielded water flasks made from gourds. The Bible does not mention them. There is no word for "squash" in Sanskrit, nothing resembling it was described in ancient Chinese writings, and it has never been found in a wild state in Asia. Botanical works contain no references to squash before the discovery of America, but there is a rash of them immediately afterwards, for the very first Europeans, beginning with Columbus, were impressed by this strange new food and hastened to send specimens of it to naturalists. Columbus, in his account of his first voyage, wrote of coming upon a populous village at the eastern end of Cuba where there were great expanses of fields "planted with several native plants and with *calebazzas*"—meaning gourds, but it is practically certain that they were squashes. (His example seems to have been enduring, for in the Caribbean islands large squashes and pumpkins are still called *calabazas.*) Cabeza de Vaca reported pumpkins growing near Florida's Tampa Bay in 1528, and de Soto in western Florida found pumpkins "better and more flavorful than those of Spain"—which once again must have meant the gourds then cultivated in Europe. The botanists now began to describe these plants. Whenever they recorded their origin, they invariably referred to them as American, or gave them American place names. Several botanists described the turban squash, identified as coming from Brazil; a new variety brought to the United States in 1824 was called the Valparaiso because it came from Chile; the Hubbard originated in the West Indies; the seed of the cushaw was obtained from the Seminole Indians of Florida; Gerard (1567) identified the maycock as an import from Virginia; the pineapple squash came originally from Chile.

It is possible that the squash was the very first food to be cultivated by American Indians; it seems at least to have been the first within what has been called the Indian triad—maize, beans and squash—which constituted the basis of the Indian diet in both Americas, North and South, a diet which, W. R. Aykroyd and Joyce Doughty pointed out, "has hardly changed since prehistoric times." Archeological finds in Mexican caves, dated variously from 4000 to 9000 B.C., yielded squash seeds of cultivated varieties, while beans found with them were still from wild plants; as for maize, that did not appear at all until a good deal later. In the burial mounds of the Adana culture, which flourished in an area straddling what is today southern Ohio, northern Kentucky and northwestern Virginia between 1200 and 2000 years ago, squash was found but corn had not yet appeared. Squash was being cultivated by the Pueblo Indians of the southwestern United States at least 2000 years ago, and probably long before.

As soon as we reach historical times in the New World, European explorers begin to report on the importance of squash. Friar Bernardino de Sahagún wrote that squash seeds and squash flowers appeared on the table of Montezuma; both are still eaten today, the first like peanuts or pistachios in, for instance, the Middle East and Russia, the second in various dishes of Zuñi Indian cooking, and in many European and Asian countries in the

SQUASH *by Rev. Jonathan Fisher (1768–1847).* The Latter Harvest, *oil on canvas*

form of deep-fried fritters. John Bartram tells of a meal he ate with the Iroquois in 1743 which did honor to the Indian triad:

> This repast consisted of three great kettles of Indian corn soup, or thin hominy, with dry'd eels and other fish boiled in it, and one kettle full of young squashes and their flowers boiled in water and a little meal mixed . . . last of all was served a great bowl full of Indian dumplings, made of new soft corn, cut or scraped off the ear, then with the addition of some boiled beans, lapped well up in Indian corn leaves, this is good hearty provision.

Some of the early explorers seem to have been more confident that they could distinguish between squashes and pumpkins than we are today. Peter Kalm, in 1772, had them sorted out to his complete satisfaction: he defined squashes as being what we call summer squashes today; winter squashes he named gourds, probably because they tend to develop tougher shells; "pumpkins" meant varieties fed to livestock. But six years later the confusion which exists in our present terminology was prefigured by Jonathan Carter when he referred to "the melon or pumpkin, which by some are called 'squashes.'" Today there seems to be no hard-and-fast distinction between "squash" and "pumpkin," either in popular or in scientific terminology. "Squash" is employed more or less as a generic term to cover all three of the groups we are discussing here, or at least squashes and pumpkins (the French use *courge* in the same fashion), but when a squash has a very hard rind it is sometimes recognized as a gourd, and when it is very large and orange, as a pumpkin. "Squash" is an American term; the English equivalent is "vegetable marrow."

The taxonomists offer us three chief species of squashes: *Cucurbita pepo, C. maxima* and *C. moschata*, but fight shy of reserving any one of them for the pumpkin as distinct from the squash; and when they attempt to do so, each is apt to distinguish them in a different fashion. The official publication of the United Nations Food and Agricultural Organization on African foods defines *C. maxima* indifferently as pumpkin, squash and gourd; *C. moschata* as pumpkin and squash; and *C. pepo* as field pumpkin, gourd and marrow. "Vegetable marrows, as well as many pumpkins and summer squashes are varieties of a single species . . . *Cucurbita pepo*," says *The Oxford Book of Food Plants*, and decides that winter squashes are *C. maxima*; but when it comes to the pumpkin, it cannily refrains from attaching it to any species, except that it calls the cushaw a pumpkin. But the cushaw, whatever it may be, does not belong to any of the three recognized principal species, but to *C. mixta*.

Our difficulty in distinguishing between squashes and pumpkins arises perhaps from the fact that to arrive at the right answers you have to begin by asking the right questions, and we may have been looking at these vegetables from an inverted point of view.

> What is particularly striking in the common differences among the three types of Cucurbita [wrote Naudin] is the prodigious variability of the form, the volume and the color of their fruits, which, real Proteuses, show themselves indifferently sometimes stretched out like clubs, sometimes spherical or completely flattened, some with soft skins, others with hard and woody rinds.

Instead of starting from the premise that they are dealing with a single species and consequently waxing ecstatic on its prodigious versatility, perhaps botanists should have started with the fact of versatility and asked themselves if a single species could account for them all. E. L. Sturtevant dared to hint that his scientific colleagues had been guilty of misnaming when he wrote:

> There seems to exist a permanency of types which is simply marvelous, and which would seem to lend countenance to the belief that there is need of revision of the species and a closer study of the various groups or types which appear to have remained constant during centuries of cultivation.

This was written at the beginning of the century, but no one since has dared plunge into the labyrinth of the squash family to sort out its members. Perhaps if somebody did so, we might be able to decide which varieties are pumpkins.

Despite their speedy entry into botanical literature in the sixteenth and seventeenth centuries, squashes did not reach European tables in any numbers until the nineteenth. There is one reference (in a French source) to the introduction of the vegetable marrow into England about 1700, but the English themselves do not seem to have been aware of it; they begin to talk about squash as a food only about the middle of the nineteenth century. It is true that experimental plantings of the vegetable marrow were made in the gardens of the London Horticultural Society in 1816, but a contemporary naturalist (Sabine), who seems to have been unacquainted with the works of his predecessors, wrote of it:

I have not been able to obtain any but uncertain information concerning this gourd; it is certainly new in this country and I think it was introduced through seeds brought here by a monk of India or probably from Persia, where it is called *cicader*.

The French were even slower to take to squash. Olivier de Serres, who could only have tasted it on its very first appearance in Europe, where it must have reached him from more southerly countries, was hardly bowled over by its excellence: he called it "Naples' and Spain's revenge." To this day squash is little relished in France. It does best in the south, which is more receptive to rustic foods, among which I think we must put the squashes. In the Old World as a whole the squash has been most generally adopted in Africa, which has no prejudice against rusticity either.

Disregarding the subtleties of taxonomy, we may divide squashes from the eaters' point of view between summer and winter varieties (and lament the fact that some of the finest varieties of both have disappeared from our stores). Winter squashes include such familiar varieties as the Hubbard squash, the Canada or winter crookneck, the Boston marrow (probably the oldest North American squash still being grown commercially), the butternut and the buttercup, the acorn squash, and the sugar pumpkin, which is the Halloween jack-o'-lantern. Winter squashes grow slowly, are harvested late, and have tough skins which protect the pulp inside so that they can be stored for three or four months before eating. They are as a rule tastier, sweeter and more nutritious than the summer varieties.

Summer squashes—reservation made for possible errors of nomenclature, such as the disagreement about the turban squashes, which some naturalists put in one category, some in the other—include the familiar yellow or orange crookneck; the yellow straight-neck, which is the same vegetable straightened out into a small warty club; the British custard marrow, which looks like a round, thick, whitish or yellow cushion with scalloped edges (despite nearly four hundred years of continuous cultivation it has never become particularly popular); the oddly shaped and brilliantly colored turban squashes; the pineapple or pattypan squash; the cocozelle; and the internationally popular zucchini. They share a number of characteristics: they grow quickly, must be picked unripe before they have time to harden, and must then be eaten without much delay, for they do not keep well. In some opinions also, they lack taste. "They call for help from without to augment their flavor, for instance from cream, cheese, rice, tomatoes or meat stuffings," says the *Dictionnaire de l'Académie des Gastronomes.*

I shall not concern myself with the crookneck summer squash [wrote Jonathan Norton Leonard, inappropriately in *American Cooking: New England*, for New Englanders eat more squash than any other Americans, with the possible exception of Pueblo Indians]. My only willing contact with it as a child was to look for crookneck squashes that had been allowed to "go by" and had grown hard shells. By attaching stretched rubber bands I made them into guitars of a sort.

SQUASH *by Henri Matisse (1869–1954).* The Green Pumpkin, *oil on canvas*

The French gastronomic writer James de Coquet has come to the defense of the summer crookneck squash (*courgette* in French), explaining that one reason why some people find it lacks taste is that they do not know how to prepare it. The mistake is made, he says, of peeling it completely: only the outer layer of the skin, he maintains, should be cut away, for the inner layer is the tastiest part of the fruit.

Quoting the opinion of the *Dictionnaire de l'Académie des Gastronomes* cited above, M. de Coquet called it "a slanderous charge."

> The summer squash [he argued] is a foundling which is little respected. . . . It is considered as a neutral substance, made to carry flavors which are not directly acceptable on their own, like garlic or onion. . . . The summer squash demands no help from without. . . . We must be living in an epoch in which discretion does not pay, since it is reproached for the subtlety of its taste. To pretend . . . that foods are to be valued in proportion to the intensity of their flavor is to arrive at the conclusion that the finest of all dishes is pickled herring. . . . Summer squash appeals only to connoisseurs, who eat it poached and touched with butter, or chopped and sautéed raw in oil. No help from without, no other ingredients, nothing but this simple little squash. It brings deliciously to the table all the freshness and the charm of your vegetable garden.

SQUI
stands for

the **squid,** which, whether you think of it as a fish or a mollusk, is a much admired food among Asians, Africans and Mediterranean Europeans, but not by Anglo-Saxons, because, as Alan Davidson puts it, it lacks allure; for the **squill,** whose bitter, nauseous and sometimes downright poisonous root was nevertheless recommended by Pliny for cooking in honey, but no one uses it today except in medicine—though, we were told in 1870, "the men of the Moon roast the leaves and stalks and cook them as a spinach," meaning, of course, the inhabitants of the African Mountains of the Moon; for the **squilla,** or mantis shrimp, which, because its pincers are a prolongation of its mouth, has been described as the marine equivalent of the praying mantis, but it tastes better—or so I imagine, for to tell the truth, though I have sampled the mantis shrimp (in Venice) I do not recall ever having tasted the praying mantis, though I was once caught in so thick a cloud of them (in New York) that if I had opened my mouth I would have; for the **squirrel,** which Thomas Jefferson hunted and undoubtedly ate in Brunswick stew, and which Brillat-Savarin cooked in a *court-bouillon* enriched with Madeira wine, but of which Charles Monselet would only say that "it can't be worse than some other foods and it might even turn out to be delicious"; for the **squirrelfish,** an important food fish in Hawaii, so named, apparently, because like the earthbound squirrel it has large eyes; for **squirrel-tail grass,** a wild barley whose grain seems never to have appealed to anybody except the Shoshone Indians of northern Oregon; and for **squitch,** or Quitch, Twitch, Scutch and Couch, which sounds like a firm of brokers, but is only a grass from whose seeds bread has been made in times of need.

STA
stands for

the **staff tree** of Peru whose buds are eaten and whose seeds are pressed for their edible oil; for the **stag,** whose venison is of course as tasty as that of other kinds of deer, but whose choicest cut is the horns, which, powdered, bring fancy prices from Asians who consider them aphrodisiac, and **stag's-horn,** which is not the product cited above but, prosaically, only a sort of sumac whose leaves are edible; for the **stagbush,** or black haw, whose berries at their best were described by Euell Gibbons as "the finest wild fruit I ever tasted"; for **star anise,** the Chinese member of the two kinds of ANISE, which are unrelated; for the **star apple,** a sweet tropical fruit of which one species is found in Asia and another in the West Indies; for the **star flower,** which is borage, and the **star fruit,** which is the carambola; for the **starchroot,** whose many other names include such picturesque labels as cuckoo pint, wake robin, lords-and-ladies and Adam-and-Eve, but all it produces is arrowroot; for the **stargazer,** a Mediterranean fish whose eyes are so placed that it can look only upward, legendarily the Apocryphal animal whose gall restored the sight of Tobias; for **starlings,** "of which I shot some," Boswell wrote from the Isle of Coll, "and found them pretty good eating"; for the **star-of-Bethlehem,** which sounds more appetizing when it is *Ornithogalum pyrenaicum,* of which the stalks are eaten under the name "Prussian asparagus," than when it is *O. umbellatum,* of which the bulbs are eaten under the name "dove's dung," as it is called in the Bible; for **star-of-the-earth,** a kind of plantain which sometimes gets into French salads; for the **starry moray,** a particularly decorative version of a fish of which six thousand were served at a single banquet given by Julius Caesar; for the **star thistle,** whose young stems and leaves were once eaten raw in Egypt, a habit which seems to have been dropped; for the **starwort,** otherwise chickweed, which some people think tastes like spinach when boiled; and for the **Stayman Winesap,** an aromatically flavored American apple best grown in Virginia or thereabouts, since it does not like cold winters.

STE
stands for

steam, not ordinarily rated very high in nutritive value, but we are told in the account of the expedition of the Carpini mission to Central Asia in 1245–47 of a people called the Parossits "who are tall in stature but thin and frail [who] . . . eat nothing at all but live on steam, for instead of a mouth they have a minute orifice, and obtain nourishment by inhaling the steam of meat stewed in a pot"; for the **steelhead trout,** a seagoing variety of the freshwater rainbow TROUT, which spawns in the Pacific Northwest; for the **steenbok** of Africa, a kind of antelope, and the **steenbras** of the same continent, a kind of sea bream; for the **Steinpilz,** the German representative of one of the world's most famous MUSHROOMS, the boletus; and for the **sterlet,** the smallest of the sturgeons, whose most spectacular appearance in history was probably at a banquet given by Grigori Potemkin in the time of Catherine the Great, when it was used to make a soup which cost six thousand roubles, but of course there was a good deal of it, for it completely filled the vessel in which it was served, a bathtub of solid silver.

And **STE** also stands for

STEAMER. Few prejudices are harder to shake off than food prejudices: *Mya arenaria,* the common American steamer clam, and *Mytilus edulis,* the common European mussel, provide an outstanding example of this phenomenon. *Mya* and *Mytilus* exist on both sides of the Atlantic, but while Europeans dote on mussels, few Americans will eat them; and Europeans, in turn, do not eat steamer clams, though their reference books admit that they are edible.

Mya arenaria means sand clam, but it is often called instead the mud clam by hunters accustomed to digging it up from the mud or sand between low- and high-water marks when the tide is out. (Steamers also lie farther out, and along the Middle Atlantic coast are harvested by dredgers from the permanently submerged sea bottom.) The fact that this clam is popularly called the steamer, thus referring to it only after it has reached the kitchen, is a tribute to its succulence. More properly it is the soft clam (as opposed to the hard clam, alias the QUAHOG), but it is also called the soft-shelled clam, the long-neck, the long clam or the nannynose.

The quahog has a hard shell; the steamer's is so brittle that it frequently breaks when the clam is dug up, filling it with sand. The quahog is thick, with a shape which seems to be having difficulty in deciding whether it wants to be round or triangular; the steamer is a thin oval. The quahog is a pronounced gray; the steamer is a chalky white. The quahog shell is clamped tightly shut; the steamer is unable to close completely, one shell being smaller than the other, to leave room for the foot to protrude from one end and the neck from the other.

The siphon, spectacularly long, which accounts for the alternative name "long-neck," is largely responsible for the fact that the steamer is exceptionally ingenious, for a clam. The steamer can reach a maximum length of five inches, though it is so diligently harvested nowadays that few of them succeed in surviving to a size of more than two or three; the siphon is twice as long as the clam, or more. Extremely vulnerable because of its brittle, unclosable shell, the steamer lies at the bottom of a vertical shaft it excavates for itself, six or eight inches below the surface, and delegates to the siphon, extruded upward through the shaft, the task of keeping it in touch with the world above. The siphon is double, as in many clams, with one channel for expelling wastes and the other for sucking in food from the water which fills the shaft—minute bits of animal and vegetable organisms, diatoms, spores, eggs, tiny larvae of shellfish or crustaceans, bits of seaweed—and, incidentally, quite a lot of sand. The end of the siphon is provided with a crown of tentacles, enabling it to sweep these delicacies

STEAMER CLAM. *Postcard map by Robert Brooks, c. 1975*

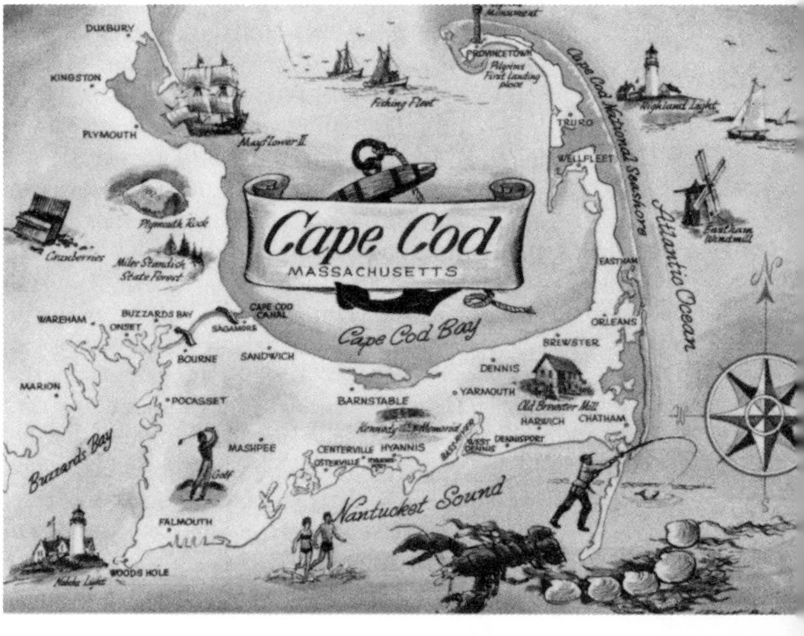

into its mouth; but the most remarkable thing about the siphon is that it can see.

If the clam lifted its siphon above its protective shaft, fish might bite it off if it were underwater, or birds attack it when the tide was out. But it is sensitive to light; so whenever the tip escapes from the shade of its sheath, it senses that fact and withdraws into obscurity again. However, the steamer has not yet had enough time to learn how to conceal itself from a recent enemy, man, who has only been present for a couple of million years; so when you walk across an uncovered tidal beach, steamers lying beneath the surface withdraw their siphons so precipitately that they squeeze the water out of them, squirting it into the air and betraying their whereabouts to the clam digger. The only problem that remains is to get them up without breaking the fragile shell, for if a clam is broken it fills so completely with sand that the attempt to get rid of it is almost hopeless.

Even an undamaged clam contains so much sand that freeing it of this unwelcome addition is not easy. Euell Gibbons, in his *Stalking the Blue-Eyed Scallop*, suggests two methods: one is to pack the clams into a covered hardware-cloth basket and suspend them in the sea for a couple of days; the other, which also takes a couple of days, is to put them into a tub of fresh water and sprinkle a little cornmeal on it, changing the water and sprinkling in more cornmeal twice a day. "Such long soaking in fresh water," Gibbons wrote, "would be fatal to most other clams," but steamers can tolerate a considerable degree of freshness in their water, and often establish themselves on the banks of tidal rivers far enough upstream so that the water in which they find themselves is merely brackish. They can get along for quite a while with no oxygen at all, a gift more useful to the clam than to its buyer. Clams found on the market have sometimes been out of water too long. If you see a clam whose siphon hangs limply at full length from the shell, touch the neck; if it doesn't move, the clam is dead, and the chances are that all the others in the same batch will die before you can get them to the stove, in which case they should not be eaten. It is safer to reject them all.

The steamer clam is firmly established in the memory of my New England childhood, associated with that part of the country, as it is, it seems, for most people. "The steamer is the clam that has been made famous by the renowned New England clambake," Gibbons wrote, but in my family we preferred quahogs for clambakes. I seem to remember that we put steamers in clam chowder, though this is perhaps unorthodox; it is a role often reserved for quahogs which have become too tough to eat raw.

A correspondent from Boston has informed me that "fried clams are advertised up and down the Massachusetts coast," and that "I would guess that 90–95 percent of the steamers used on the Massachusetts coastline are eaten fried." This he attributes to a current belief that they may carry viral hepatitis and that frying kills the villainous virus. "I doubt this," he continues, and goes on: "I never knew anyone to fry clams at home. In restaurants they always come in a thick carapace of greasy batter that completely obscures the flavor of the clam. The only good fried clams I ever had were sold in a little shack on Martha's Vineyard, in 1964. There was little or no batter. The clams, which were shipped out from New Bedford, were plump and tasty." This obviously refers to deep-fried clam fritters, which I do not recall ever eating at home either, though I believe they were sometimes offered with shore dinners. But the best way to eat steamers is undoubtedly in the delectable classic fashion which gave them their name, for the clams are cooked by steaming, after which they are picked up in the fingers by the neck, dipped first into a bowl of clam broth and then into a bowl of melted butter, and popped into the mouth, where the teeth shuck the siphon out of its inedible tough black skin in the same motion in which the rest of the clam is swallowed.

Despite its association with New England, the steamer is by no means confined to this region. Its range on the east coast is from Labrador to North Carolina, and on the west coast, to which it was transplanted toward the end of the last century, it is found from Alaska to Monterey, California. Except for the oyster, it is the most popular shellfish on both the Atlantic and Pacific coasts, outdistancing even the quahog; like the oyster, it is cultivated on both coasts.

Also edible, but much less popular, is *Mya truncata*, a close relative of the soft clam, which also appears on both coasts, but made the connection between them with no help from man. It is one of a few species of mollusks which must have originated in very cold waters, occupying a more or less continuous range across the top of North America, through the Arctic Ocean, and from there spread southward along both coasts to the point where the water became too warm for them. *M. truncata* is also found in Europe, where it is edible but, like *M. arenaria*, is not eaten.

STI
stands for

the **stiff pen shell**, or prickly pen shell, the largest of the three species of this group of sweet, tasty shellfish found on the southeastern coast of the United States; for the **stinging nettle,** whose young tops, cooked like spinach as a purée, may put you off by their earthy flavor, but you can subdue it by making a Scotch nettle pudding, whose leeks and cabbage neutralize the character of the nettles; for the **stingray,** whose spike contains so potent a poison that Pliny said it would cause a tree to wither if driven into its root, but the Bedouins of the Near East eat it and fail to wither; for **stinkgrass,** whose seeds are eaten, without enthusiasm, in the Chad; for the **stinking weed,** with pea-like pods whose young grains are eaten mostly by young boys in a number of tropical countries; and for **stitchwort,** which, C. P. Johnson wrote in 1862, much resembled spinach when boiled, and, John Gerard wrote in 1597, would cure a stitch in the side.

STO
stands for

the **stock,** which is left undisturbed in its function of bearing flowers except in times of famine; for the **stockmelon** of Africans, which is the watermelon for us; for the **stomach,** which, according to Marco Polo, was removed from one of their horses by Tartars on the march when no cooking vessels were available and used as a pot in which most of the rest of the horse was stewed, after which the result was eaten "pot and all"; for the **stompkop** of South Africa, a relatively uncommon fish of uncommon quality; for the **stone** BASS, also called the wreckfish because of its habit of congregating around wrecks on the sea bottom; for the **stone crab** of the southeastern United States and the Gulf of Mexico, from which conscientious CRAB hunters break off one claw and toss the animal back into the water, to grow another claw and propagate the race; for **stonecrop,** a not very well known salad plant, which seems to be eaten commonly only in Holland and Greenland; for the **stone groundnut,** a subterranean legume widely cultivated in tropical Africa, where it was first described by Father Merolla, a missionary, who wrote, "It is like a musquet-ball and very wholesome and well tasted"; for the **stone pine** of the Mediterranean basin, whose soft seeds are versatile in their uses and even lend themselves to vegetarian imitations of meat; for the **stonesucker,** which is the lamprey; for **storax,** which produces gum benzoin, used for flavoring by chocolate manufacturers, who think the best comes from Siam; for the **stork,** eaten by Henry VIII in the sixteenth century and by natives of the Cameroons in the twentieth century, but forbidden to Jews in any century; for **stork's-bill,** which on the Cape of Good Hope is *Pelargonium acetosum,* of which both buds and leaves are eaten despite their acidity, and **storksbill,** which in Europe is *Erodium cicutarinum,* introduced into America, where it became food for American Indians, including the miserable Diggers, whose patronage of a foodstuff is no guarantee of quality; and for the **stout razor,** an Atlantic coast clam of the United States, whose very close relatives on the Pacific coast are usually called jackknives.

STR
stands for

the **strainer vine** of India, a club-shaped gourd much used in curries, whose high seasoning compensates for its own insipid taste; for **strand wheat,** which grows along northern beaches on both sides of the Atlantic and is eaten in Iceland but not in America though it tastes like that gourmets' delight, wild rice; for **straw,** eaten in France in 1709 as an ingredient of bread and in Poland in 1865 chopped together with acorns, the common factor between these times and places having been famine; for the **strawberry guava,** smaller and hardier than the ordinary guava, with the flavor which you divine, the **strawberry tomato,** which is the ground cherry, and the **strawberry tree,** which doesn't bear strawberries, and whatever it is which it does bear seems to be eaten nowhere except in Greece; for the **streaked gurnard,** a fish called in Languedoc *imbriago,* which means "drunkard"; for the **striated mussel** of the Atlantic coast of North America, which doesn't seem to be inedible, as the books say it is, but its taste is not good enough to tempt you to test their opinion; for the **string bean,** which has become stringless; for the **striped bass,** always called the rockfish in Chesapeake Bay, the **striped bream,** which is described as marbled in French, the **striped marlin** of the Pacific, which can reach a length of 14 feet and a weight of 1560 pounds, dwarfing the **striped mullet,** which reaches only 3 feet, but this is 50 percent better than for unstriped mullets, the **striped remora,** only 3 feet long too, but that is more than the other seven species of remoras, and the **striped sailback,** an armored catfish, which may not be big, but it's rare; and for **strychnine,** which may sound to you like the last thing you would eat, but Burmese children dote on the pulp of its fruit.

And **STR** also stands for

STRAWBERRY. It must have been madness which moved me, after having bought a 550-acre farm in Vermont, to move into it in January; but the fact of having taken possession of my property at this inappropriate date reserved for me one of the most delightful surprises of my life. The snow went, the mud came, and after the quivering quagmire of my road had solidified sufficiently to bear the weight of my car, I drove into the village from which I had been temporarily marooned, and there, suddenly, as if somebody had flicked a switch, the first warm air of spring flowed across the land like a wave. I drove back to the farm, and as I reached my mailbox, still a mile short of the house, I sensed a sudden sweetness in the air. It swelled into a heady fragrance as I progressed homeward. The hill across the brook flowing a hundred yards from the house, which I had not yet crossed, for it did not lie in the main axis of movement about the farm, green when I had left in the morning, had turned miraculously white. I crossed the brook to investigate this mystery: the hillside, which from a distance I had thought was covered with grass, lay actually under a thick carpet of wild strawberries. With the first warm breath of spring they had sprung into bloom, all at once: their fragrance was so strong that I had smelled it a mile away.

When the plants fruited, there was no question of picking them and bringing them to the house to eat; they were too small and too juicy. At the end of lunch we would wander onto our hillside to pick and eat our dessert *al fresco*, a very pleasant practice. "Look out!" my wife cried out during our first foray. "You're stepping on them." So I was, but there was nothing else on which to step. The problem was not a new one. "Wee can not sett downe foote but tred on strawberries," wrote one of the first Englishmen to reach Maryland, in wonder at the rich abundance of this fruit.

These deliciously flavorful wild strawberries were *Fragaria virginiana*, the scarlet Virginia strawberry of the east coast of North America, the Indian *wuttahimneash* ("heart-seed berry"), which characteristically takes over as the complete ground cover, leaving space for nothing else. Some botanists think the strawberry is circumpolar, which would account for its presence in the Northern Hemisphere of both Old and New Worlds. It is certainly capable of having spread over the roof of the world: it grows above 70 degrees north latitude, which is level with northernmost Alaska and northernmost Scandinavia.

"Doubtless God could have made a better berry, but doubtless God never did," William Butler wrote circa 1600. This seems to be the general opinion. The strawberry is everywhere one of the most popular fruits in the world; yet it was not until the second half of the last century that it could be found readily on the market. The nature of the plant defeated the nature of the fruit: the problem was perishability.

The rare availability of the strawberry goes back to prehistoric times. Berry seeds of many kinds have been found at Mesolithic sites in Denmark, Neolithic sites in Switzerland and Iron Age sites in England; the scarcest finds are of strawberry seeds. Prehistoric man, more given, we may imagine, to valuing quantity than quality in his food, may have considered strawberries as not worth much trouble: they grew on a plant which hugged the ground, often in the woods half hidden by underbrush, hard to spot and hard to pick; and as the berries of prehistoric Europe were even smaller than the wild strawberries of today, they offered little food in exchange for a good deal of work. Their period of ripeness was short, six weeks at the most, and they did not lend themselves to preservation by any methods then used.

In historic times, it continued to be possible to eat strawberries only at the place where they were picked, at first always wild. There was little incentive to cultivate strawberries, for they were no better cultivated than wild. Even today we would not be far short of the truth if we maintained that in spite of all our skill and of all the work we have done to improve strawberries, the result essentially has been little more than to stabilize the best characteristics of the wild fruit. "The strawberry plant is variable in nature," wrote E. L. Sturtevant, "and it seems probable that the type of all the varieties noted under cultivation may be found in the wild plant, if diligently sought for"—including quality. There is tremendous variation in the size of wild plants, in the size of their berries, in the flavor of the berries and in their appearance, and when they are at their best they are quite as good as our "improved" varieties. "The changes which have been produced, or have appeared, under cultivation seem comparatively few," Sturtevant continued, and in respect to flavor in particular he suggested that modern improvements are of a degree which "does not seem to exceed that which occurs between natural varieties."

In some opinions the domesticated berry does not even equal wild berries at their best. Referring to upstate New York early in the century, Dale Brown wrote, "The best of the berries, by far, were always (and continue to be) the wild strawberries." In luxury restaurants all over the world, gourmets pay premium prices for the subtly scented *fraises des bois*, wood strawberries or wild strawberries (which nowadays are often not genuinely wild, though here again the range for improvement is limited). *The Oxford Book of Food Plants* says that this species, "although cultivated for centuries, did not greatly improve in the size and flavour of its fruits." The chief

OCTO . XVII .
The wordling feedes his shallowe braine
With hoipes of his discourses vaine .
Which are nought els but smooke and wind
That so do him deceive and blinde
And his soule with such shadows hooke .
Then wonder not although he be
So light and voladge , sith you see
Him ever feed of wind and smooke .

STRAWBERRY. *Illuminated manuscript page for Prince Henry, eldest son of James I, by his tutor Esther Inglis:* Octonaries Upon the Vanity and Inconstancy of the World, *London, 1600/1*

gains of cultivation for strawberries in general have been the increase in yields, the lengthening of the season and the production of bigger (not necessarily better) berries—not to mention tougher kinds which will stand up better to the battering of large-scale or mechanized picking, handling and transportation. These are advantages more interesting to merchandisers than to gourmets, but it is difficult to imagine successful commercial exploitation of such small, juicy, fragile fruit as I found on my farm, however remarkable the taste. The complaint that such "improvements" have to be paid for in decreased flavor was uttered as long ago as 1560 by Bruyerin-Champier, physician to Henry II of France, who wrote that wood strawberries had only just been introduced into gardens, "by which they had attained a larger size, though they at the same time lost their quality."

The strawberry was only partially present in the ancient world. It is represented nowhere in the art of Egypt or of Greece. It has been suggested that the Greek word *komaros* should be translated as "strawberry." In reality, it designates the strawberry tree, which bears a fruit resembling the strawberry but much inferior to it in taste; it is not related to the strawberry, which the Greeks apparently never knew. The Romans, who did know the real strawberry, confused it with the strawberry tree all the same. Pliny called the former the ground strawberry ("the only plant which crawls along the ground whose fruit resembles that of bushes") to distinguish it from the tree strawberry, which he called *anedon* ("It is a fruit little esteemed"). Ovid realized that they were different, for in listing the fruits eaten in the Golden Age he mentions both, but separately, recognizing no relationship between them.

None of the ancient Roman writers speaks of the strawberry as cultivated; it was apparently only picked wild. Cato, Varro, Columella and Palladius did not mention it at all, nor did Apicius in his cookbook. Virgil referred to it only to warn young people picking strawberries to beware of serpents lurking in the grass. The fact that he addressed youngsters might imply that he considered strawberries as a fruit eaten only by children; however, adults were taking them seriously at least by the time of Trajan, when the strawberries around Lake Nemi, wild also, were highly praised as the best available (Nemi still raises strawberries and holds a strawberry festival yearly in June). Pliny named as wild plants eaten in his time strawberries, parsnips and hops, "though these different species are rather rustic hors d'oeuvres than foods properly so called." He does not list strawberries with cultivated plants. The slight recourse the Romans had to strawberries was perhaps the result of a certain inaccessibility, for they seem to have originated in the mountainous areas of northern Italy (and perhaps adjacent areas in France, for the ancient Gauls also picked them wild). The ancients at least found a way to preserve strawberries, by pickling them.

Professor Stephen Wilhelm of the University of California at Berkeley has written that the strawberry was mentioned in the sixth century in the *Herbarius* of Apuleius Barbarus, a work unknown to me, and so far as I know, it is not heard of again for seven centuries, when a certain Nicolas Myrepsus, described as an Alexandrian doctor at the Byzantine court of Nicaea in the thirteenth century, also mentioned it. In the meantime, a number of usually exhaustive sources on food fail to mention the strawberry. It is not among the plants Charlemagne ordered grown in his domains in the ninth century, and it is ignored by Ibn-al-Awan in the twelfth, by Albertus Magnus in the thirteenth, by *Ancient Cookery*, published in 1381, by *The Forme of Cury*, compiled by the master cooks of Richard II in 1390, and by the *Ménagier de Paris* in 1393. We hear of strawberries being planted in the royal gardens of the Louvre for the delectation of Charles V in 1368; in the gardens of the Duchess of Burgundy, who doted on them, in 1375; and in the gardens of a hospital in the north of France in 1382. In none of these cases is there any hint of cultivation; wild plants were simply transplanted to a place where they would be handier.

Strawberries became accessible to common folk only in the fifteenth century. They seem to have been hawked in the streets of London during the reign of Henry VI, on the evidence of a poem by John Lidgate, who died in 1483:

Then unto London I dyde me hye,
Of all the land it beareth the pryze;
"Gode pescode," one began to cry—
"Strabery rype, and cherrys in the ryse."

Apparently it was not until a century later that strawberry sellers invaded the streets of Paris, with a chanted formula which included a warning about the fruit's fragility, an example of mercantile candor which it would be difficult to match today. Other countries may have been ahead of France in developing the strawberry: the first known drawing of the plant, a rather crude one, appeared in Germany in the *Herbarius Latinus Moguntiae*, the *Latin Herbal of Mainz*. From this point forward all the herbals took cognizance of the strawberry, but they did not usually present it to the public as a food, but stressed its virtues as a medicine. John Gerard said nothing about its taste, but dwelt upon the efficacy of its boiled leaves as a poultice, and said of the fruit that "the ripe Strawberries quench thirst, and take away, if they be often used, the redness and heate of the face." It was a medicine often taken through the mouth; patients treated with it could hardly have failed to notice that it was a good deal more palatable than most of the preposterous potions proposed to them by the doctors of the times. They not only began to use strawberries for non-medical reasons, they even devised means for making them more agreeable, such as lapping them with wine, for men, or cream, for women. "Rawe crayme undecocted," Andrew Boorde wrote in 1542, "eaten with strawberyes . . . is a rurall mannes banket. I have knowen such bankettes hath put men in jeoperdy of theyr lyves"—from overeating perhaps?

Across the Channel, Bruyerin-Champier remarked in 1560 that ladies enjoyed strawberries and cream as an evening dessert. He recorded their transfer from woods to gardens in the same year, which sounds like cultivation at last, and when it was reported towards the end of the century that Germany was enjoying a variety which produced two crops a year, that sounded also like a result of cultivation (but some wild strawberries do this naturally). Genuine cultivation was at least under way in England in 1608, when Sir Hugh Plat published a book in which he expounded his methods for lengthening the fruiting season and increasing the size of strawberries. One person who became aware of the fruit was Louis XIV, always avid of new and exotic foods, for whom Jean de la Quintinie started forcing strawberries to unseasonable growth. In his time, the Virginia strawberry could have been obtained, for it appeared in the French seed catalog of Jean Robin in 1624. But La Quintinie seems not to have known about this species; at least he did not grow it for the king. Similarly, the herbals of the sixteenth and seventeenth centuries did not mention the American strawberry, though some of them certainly knew about it; Gerard, indeed, grew it in his own garden, but left it out of his *Herball*. So far as Europe was concerned, the strawberry was still the fruit the ancient Romans had known, *F. vesca*, called variously the wood strawberry, the mountain strawberry, the Alpine strawberry or the perpetual strawberry.

F. vesca may well be the original strawberry, from which all the others are derived; it is, with one exception, the only species which breeds true from seed. It was the one Shakespeare had in mind when he wrote

My Lord of Ely, when I was last in Holborn,
I saw good strawberries in your garden there,

and again when he compared Henry V, who grew up to the measure of his responsibilities after a dissolute youth, to a strawberry which had been growing beneath a nettle.

The original *F. vesca* possesses an advantage which will be appreciated by any amateur who has tried to grow strawberries: birds, for some reason, do not touch it. This is true also of the only other strawberry which breeds true to seed, *F. moschata*, also a wild European species rarely seen in gardens, which has a musky scent. It is called the hautboy in English, from the French *hautbois*, "high wood"—high in a more literal sense than when this word means the oboe; the plant grows more or less erect instead of creeping over the ground like other species.

Gerard reported that there were also green and white strawberries; the latter was the one he chose to illustrate his article. The green strawberry, of Europe and northern Asia, is *F. collina*, whose greenish tinge is enlivened with spots of red; it has a rich, musty, pineapple flavor, but is pretty much unfindable nowadays. The present existence of a white strawberry was news to me until I read that it was found in Hawaii, and I commented on this peculiarity in a newspaper article. Readers in Royan and Beauvais, France, in Istanbul, Turkey, and in Litchfield, Connecticut, all wrote to tell me that they had eaten white strawberries and thought them superior to the ordinary kinds. "Flowerlike and more perfumed. They were divine!" one of them wrote. They are described as beautiful—heart-shaped, creamy white with golden seeds, smaller than garden strawberries but larger than wild strawberries. I learned subsequently that this variety, apparently developed from the Alpine strawberry, had been mentioned in 1536; that white strawberries existed in Massachusetts and New York, where they were thought to be varieties of the Virginia berry; and that in Chile (which also has yellow strawberries) they were assumed to be offshoots of the species found there.

The American strawberry astonished its discoverers by its size and its abundance. In 1534 Jacques Cartier recorded in his diary that in Canada he had seen "vast patches of strawberries along the great river [the St. Lawrence] and in the woods." Thomas Hariot wrote in 1588 that in Virginia he had found strawberries "as good and great as those which we have in English gardens." Roger Williams reported in 1643 from Rhode Island: "This berry is the wonder of all the fruits growing naturally in those parts. . . . In some parts where the Indians have planted them, I have many times seen as many as would fill a good ship, within few miles compass. The Indians bruise them in a Morter, and mixe them with meale and make strawberry bread." Farther south, the Natchez Indians called one of the thirteen months into which they divided the year the Strawberry Moon.

F. virginiana in its wild version was smaller than our garden strawberries of today, but larger than European wild strawberries. It may be suspected that all the East Coast American berries were varieties of this species, except the one baptized the Carolina strawberry about 1765; but was this really an East Coast berry? It seems more like an offspring of the Chilean strawberry, for both of them taste a little like pineapple. It may not be American at all, except by ancestry, for it seems to have been noticed first growing either in Chelsea, now part of London, where North American varieties were growing at that time, or in Amsterdam, where Chilean varieties were growing. If it originated in England, it might have been named in honor of Queen Charlotte; if in Holland, some publicity-minded grower may have felt that the name Carolina would create an association with Virginia, and give a new variety some of the prestige already enjoyed by the Virginia strawberry.

The Virginia strawberry, or meadow strawberry or scarlet strawberry, had been growing in Europe since about 1600. It seems to have been first cited in England by John Parkinson in 1629, despite

STRAWBERRY *by Lilly Martin Spencer (1827–1902).* Kiss Me and You'll Kiss the Lasses, *oil on canvas*

the fact that Gerard was already growing it in his own garden. Perhaps Gerard left it out of his *Herball* because he thought it had no future: it was hard to pick, it stayed green on the side turned away from the sun, and in the damp English climate it was subject to mildew and gave poor yields. The first plants to reach England were of course wild, and were soon improved by cultivation; growers persevered with them, despite their defects, because of their sweetness and excellent flavor. (Horace Walpole's estate was named Strawberry Hill because Virginia strawberries were grown there.) The American berry not only triumphed, becoming the favorite English strawberry for the next two centuries, but it entered into a cross with another to produce the garden strawberry which is today the standard fruit of this kind everywhere in the world. The other member of this hybrid was an American species too, but, oddly enough, their union occurred not in America but in France.

In 1712 the French navy dispatched one of its engineers—named, almost unbelievably, Frézier, pronounced like *fraisier*, "strawberry plant"—to the west coast of South America to report on the defensive capacity of the ports of Chile and Peru. History has forgotten what André François Frézier may have written about coastal defense, but it has remembered the result of a private interest of his: an amateur botanist, he was impressed by a plant the Indians called *quelghen,* the Spaniards *frutilla,* and our scientists today call *F. chiloensis,* the Chilean strawberry. The name was an underestimate: the "Chilean" strawberry grows along the Pacific coast from Alaska to Patagonia. Frézier was surprised by the size of the berries, the largest he had ever seen, "as big as a walnut and sometimes as large as a hen's egg." Its firm dark-red flesh had an extremely agreeable pineapple taste, so it was called the pine strawberry, and sometimes also the beach strawberry.

It was not a new discovery. A number of Europeans had reported its presence during the seventeenth century in less ecstatic terms than Frézier, including Alonso de Ovalle in 1646, who said it was the only fruit the Indians cultivated for the market, but none of the others had brought anything back to Europe except the description. Frézier returned with plants, of which two were planted in the royal gardens and five at Plougastel in Brittany, whose seaside climate matched reasonably well that to which *F. chiloensis* had been accustomed. The vines grew splendidly, but set no fruit. This baffled everybody for thirty years, until somebody chanced to plant Virginia strawberries beside the Chilean ones—which promptly began to produce fruit. Frézier had outwitted himself by taking care to select only vigorous plants heavy with fruit for transplanting; what he did not know was that in this species of strawberry the male and female flowers grow on separate plants. He had brought in only females, with no males to pollinate them. The Virginia plants filled the gap, and by pure luck this hybrid between an American east coast strawberry of the Northern Hemisphere and an American west coast strawberry of the Southern Hemisphere, consummated on foreign territory, turned out to produce the world's leading strawberry.

It is probable that this berry was already in the royal gardens of the Petit Trianon at Versailles in the time of Louis XV, who had ordered his gardener, Antoine Nicolas Duchesne (who in 1776 wrote *A Natural History of Strawberries*), to plant every type of strawberry which could be obtained in Europe; three hundred varieties were cultivated there. Yet the fruit was still so far from being common in France that in the mid-nineteenth century Alexandre Dumas' *Grand Dictionnaire de Cuisine* simply named five kinds and said not one word about them.

In the United States, where strawberries were being grown in home gardens for family consumption, they were rare in the markets. The problem was still perishability, which meant that strawberries could only be delivered to markets not far from where they were being grown. Wherever they were available they were quickly snapped up, as in Philadelphia in the early 1800s. The Philadelphia suburbs raised strawberries close to this concentrated market, capable of making it profitable to supply a fruit so vulnerable and so short-lived; it was fashionable to frequent the city's many "strawberry gardens" to eat the delectable berry. Elsewhere, strawberries were still a luxury; in 1840 Martin Van Buren was attacked during his presidential campaign on the ground that he had used public money to raise that suspect rarity for his own table.

But the democratization of the strawberry was on the way. In 1847 the Erie Railroad began to operate, facilitating the delivery of perishable products; in a single night in June 1847 its milk train brought 80,000 baskets of strawberries to New York, which quickly became the largest market for this fruit in the world. In 1851 James Wilson developed a heavy-yield strawberry, which made growing the fruit more profitable, and by 1880 there were 100,000 acres under cultivation in the United States, compared to only 1400 at the beginning of the century. Today no other fruit yields more food per acre in so short a time; and with more robust fruit (a mixed blessing: James de Coquet described one of the new varieties as "hard as a golf ball," but insipid in taste and cottonlike in texture), and with speedy and sometimes refrigerated transportation, strawberries are now within everybody's reach. They are grown in every state in the Union (but California supplies 55 percent of the commercial crop), and the American acreage is 130,000, out of a world total of 300,000.

The most faithful customer for strawberries in history was probably Mme. Tallien, who in Napoleonic times added strawberry juice to her bath water to keep her skin soft and satiny. Every time she took a bath, twenty-two pounds of strawberries were crushed for it. The species she used was *F. ananassa.*

STU
stands for

the **stump tree**, whose pods are edible though aperient and whose seeds served early Kentuckians as a coffee substitute; for the **sturgeon,** which makes good eating, but most people think of it only as the fish which produces CAVIAR; and for the **Sturmer Pippin,** a fine dessert apple created in 1843 at Sturmer, Essex, which is hard by Steeple Bumpstead.

SU
stands for

succory, which sounds like one of those charming old-fashioned English terms for plants more briskly named today (in this case for chicory), but it is actually a variation of the Dutch *suyckereye*; for **suet**, the basis for a New England pudding which was really an old English pudding, known as spotted dick; for the **sugar apple**, or sweetsop, a tropical American fruit which according to one authority tastes like strawberries and according to another like clotted cream mixed with sugar; for the **sugar BEET**, popularized by Andreas Sigismund Marggraf and Napoleon Bonaparte; for the **sugarberry**, which is the ubiquitous hackberry of the Louisiana bayou country; for the **sugarbush**, whose flowers in the region of the Cape of Good Hope yield "bush syrup," a characterless imitation of honey; for the **sugar MAPLE**, a tree which might justifiably be described as having progressed from rags to riches; for the **sugar palm**, which yields sweetness when beaten; for the **sugar PEA**, which in French is the *mangetout*, "eat everything," which is what you do; and for the **sugar plum**, a fruit regarded appreciatively by equatorial Africans.

And **SU** also stands for

SUGARCANE. "Sugar Cane is a pleasant and profitable reed," John Gerard wrote in 1597. "The Cane it selfe, or stalke is not hollow as the other Canes or Reeds are, but full, and stuffed with a spongeous substance in taste exceeding sweet." One might think from this that Gerard thought sugar came from the pith of the plant, but he was not so deceived:

Of the juyce of this Reed [he continues] is made the most pleasant and profitable sweet, called Sugar, whereof is made infinite confections, confectures, Syrups and such like, which still retaine with them the name of Sugar, as Sugar Roset, Sugar Violet, &. The which to write of would require a peculiar volume, and not pertinent unto this historie, for that it is not my purpose to make of this booke a Confectionary, a sugar Bakers furnace, a Gentlewomans preserving pan, nor yet an Apothecaries shop or Dispensatorie; but onely to touch the chiefest matter that I purposed to handle in the beginning, that is, the nature, properties, and descriptions of plants. Notwithstanding I think it not amisse to shew unto you the ordering of these reeds when they be new gathered, as I received it from the mouth of an Indian my servant: he saith, They cut them in small pieces, and put them into a trough made of one whole tree, wherein they put a great stone in manner of a mill-stone, whereunto they tie a horse, buffle, or some other beast which draweth it round: in which trough they put those pieces of Canes, and so crush and grind them as we doe the barkes of trees for Tanners, or apples for Cyder. But in some places they use a great wheele wherein slaves doe tread and walke as dogs do in turning the spit: and some others doe feed as it were the bottoms of the said wheele, wherein are some sharpe or hard things which doe cut and crush the Canes into powder. And some likewise have found the invention to turne the wheele with water works, as we doe our Iron mills. The Canes being thus brought into dust or powder, they put them into great cauldrons with a little water, where they boile untill there be no more sweetnesse left in the crushed reeds. Then doe they straine them through mats or such like things, and put the liquor to boile again unto the consistence of hony, which being cold is like unto sand both in shew and handling, but somewhat softer; and so afterwards it is carried into all parts of Europe, where it is by the Sugar Bakers artificially purged and refined to that whitenesse as we see.

SUGAR. *Silver tea and coffee service with portraits of Russian rulers on enamel medallions by Johann Heinrich Blohm, St. Petersburg, 1773*

Thus does Gerard, in the idiom of his times, used also by Shakespeare and the King James Bible, refute those many writers who tell us that sugar was virtually unknown in Elizabethan times. But we knew that already from the greatest Elizabethan of them all, who wrote: "If sack and sugar be a fault, God help the wicked!" (*King Henry IV, Part I*); "Your fair discourse hath been as sugar, / Making the hard way sweet and delectable" (*King Richard II*); and " 'Tis too much prov'd—that with devotion's visage / And pious action, we do sugar o'er / The Devil himself" (*Hamlet*).

Sugarcane

Not only in Elizabethan times, but from the beginning, sugar has played a game of hide-and-seek with history: now you see it, now you don't. It may be true that sugar was never common, in the Western world at least, until the seventeenth or indeed even the nineteenth century, but it was always there for a privileged few, lurking in the wings, ready to burst forth when conditions became favorable—which generally meant when it became cheap enough, for, as the French put it, "Sugar never hurt anybody, except in the pocketbook."

Sugarcane today is found in the wild state nowhere in the world, depriving us of this clue to its place of origin; indeed, we are short of information about its spread almost up to our own times. Few foods have fuzzier histories. There seems little doubt, however, that it originated on the shores of the Bay of Bengal, spreading rapidly into surrounding territories, especially the islands of Malaysia and Indonesia, Indochina and southern China. A minority opinion that sugarcane is native to China seems to have died out. "The first historic mention of sugar is found in China in the eighth century B.C.," write Helen and Scott Nearing, without identifying the source, "where it is spoken of as a product of India," so it would seem that it was known as a foreign plant in China even before it reached there, which, according to the Nearings, did not happen until three centuries later. Reay Tannahill, in *The Fine Art of Food,* says that by 800 B.C. the Aryans, who may have invaded India as much as seven centuries earlier, had "rediscovered sugarcane," implying that it had already been cultivated, or at least eaten, there before their time but had been neglected during a period when they adjusted slowly to new foods in a new climate. Don and Patricia Brothwell in *Food in Antiquity* wrote that the Dravidians, who preceded the Aryans, grew sugarcane and though they did not make sugar, did know how to make molasses (*guda*) from it, an art which they had themselves learned from the proto-Austronesians (or proto-Malays) who preceded the Dravidians, the prehistoric Indians. By 500 B.C. the Aryans are believed to have devised a machine by which they made "crystal sugar."

The first westward move of sugarcane seems to have been into Persia, but here again our information is vague and conflicting. The Larousse gastronomic encyclopedia suggests that the Persians may have acquired it after an expedition of Darius the Great into India in the fifth century B.C., and some authorities maintain that the Persian emperors were eating sugar in the fifth and fourth centuries. It was imported by caravan from India and was too expensive to be available except to the very rich. According to some others, what the Persians imported was not sugar but cuttings of the cane because it "was more practicable to plant than to import."

The ancient Mediterranean world did not know sugarcane, but it knew about it. There was none in ancient Egypt, though it would be grown there later. "Thou hast bought me no sweet cane with money," the Lord complained in Isaiah 43:24, and again in Jeremiah 6:20, "To what purpose cometh there to me . . . the sweet cane from a far country?" This certainly does not sound as if sugarcane was then growing in the Near East. The first news the Mediterranean had of it came from members of Alexander's army returning from his campaign in India. Nearchus, an officer in that army, wrote an account of the expedition, probably the source of Strabo's report that the army had seen Indian reeds "which produced honey although there were no bees." Theophrastus recorded the existence of a sort of honey which was procured from canes or reeds, and Varro thought that the "exceedingly sweet juice" of the Indian plant came from its root. The Indians near the Ganges, wrote Marcus Annaeus Lucanus, "drink the sweet juices of the tender reed." Dioscorides said, "There is a sort of solidified honey which is called sugar found upon canes in India and Arabia. In consistency it is like salt, and is brittle under the teeth." Pliny reported that "it is a kind of honey which collects in reeds, white like gum and brittle to the teeth; the largest pieces are the size of a filbert. It is used only as a medicine." The ancient Greeks and Romans never used sugar, with one exception, when it was received, rarely, in a form which they perhaps failed to identify. The Greeks imported from the East, along with various exotic spices, a liquid which they used only for medicine. They do not seem to have seen any connection between it and the cane whose existence had been so abundantly reported; but it was in fact sugarcane syrup.

It was the Arabs who first brought sugarcane to the Western world, but, as usual, nobody knows precisely just when or where. You can take your choice, according to the authority you prefer to trust, of any date between the eighth century and the seventeenth, and of any place among Syria, Palestine, Rhodes, Crete, Egypt, Sicily, Libya, Morocco, the Balearic Islands or southern Spain. There is a divergence of opinion also between those who think that Europe had sugar directly from the Arabs, and those who believe that it was brought back by Crusaders who had seen it in Moslem lands. A chronicler of those times reported that in Tripoli the Crusaders saw for

Sugarcane

the first time whole fields of "these honeyed reeds called sugar. . . . When this herb is ripe, the natives crush it in a mortar, catching the sap in vases and letting it coagulate to the consistency of snow or white salt."

Before the period when regular trade in sugar between the East and Europe was established, some of it trickled through to privileged persons, apparently not from Spain, where the Moors were growing it, for there were barriers between Christian and Moslem territories, especially when they adjoined each other, but from more distant sources. When the Venerable Bede died in 735 and left the precious contents of his spice cupboard to be divided among the brethren of his monastery, they were found to include sugar, brought from the East at great expense by caravan, which accounted for the enrichening fragrance which it had acquired en route, that of camel sweat.

When the mists clear, we find Venice in possession of a monopoly over the new "spice," sugar, which it had very probably acquired by its astute practice of ferrying Crusaders to the Holy Land, at a price, and bringing back spices from Alexandria and the Levant on the return voyages. In the thirteenth century Marco Polo, a Venetian, showed himself familiar with sugar, for in China he was not astonished by its nature but only by its abundance. He wrote of Foochow that it "produces sugar, in quantities past all reckoning," and of the province of Manzi that it "produces more sugar than all the rest of the world put together [understatement was not one of his faults], and this . . . is the source of an immense revenue." He tells us further of

> a city called Unken, in which is produced a vast quantity of sugar. From this city the Great Khan derives all the sugar consumed at his court, which is certainly enough to cost a pretty penny. But you must know that in these parts before they came under the rule of the Great Khan the natives did not know how to make and refine sugar as well as it is done in Egypt. They did not know how to solidify it in moulds, but merely boiled and skimmed it so that it remained in the form of a black paste. But certain Egyptians who were at the Khan's court came here and taught them how to refine it with the ashes of certain trees.

Marco Polo's reference to Egypt suggests that in his time Venice was importing sugar from Alexandria in a finished state, but by the fifteenth century at least it was buying raw sugar, or even sugarcane, and treating it in its own refineries before selling it at fancy prices to the rest of Europe. Once it became generally available, Italy went wild over sugar, putting it into everything. Banquets which had previously started with salad now began with sweet hors d'oeuvres; even macaroni was sweetened. It was still expensive, so the rich showed off by making ostentatious use of it, for table decorations as well as for food. Ascancio Sforza, a man with a macabre sense of humor, gave a dinner for his fellow cardinals with drinking cups in the shape of skulls, accompanied by bones fashioned of sugar. A century later "when Henri III visited Venice," Reay Tannahill tells us, "he was entertained at a collation where bread, plates, knives, forks, tablecloths and napkins were made of spun sugar. The napkin broke in the King's hand."

In France as in Italy, sugar, once obtainable, was widely used, though with a little more restraint; but it went into all sauces which were not of the piquant type. In 1333 the household accounts of the Dauphin of the Viennois records the purchase of "white sugar." In 1380 Charles V was one of the few persons in the world to possess a fork; he used it to spear toasted cheese, over which, in conformity with the current idea that sugar was a spice, he sprinkled sugar and cinnamon. In 1393 the anonymous *Ménagier de Paris* made several mentions of sugar, recommended it for putting into decoctions for the sick, and gave a recipe for making *rosat*, a rather complicated combination of sugar with rose water.

It is not certain that France was always obliged to procure its sugar via Venice; some of it may have come directly from Greek islands, especially from Candia in Crete, which could explain why the deluxe sugar sold today in the form of large crystals is called *candi* in French (an alternative explanation says it comes from the Arabic *qandi*, which is supposed to mean "sugarcane"). When the first book on cooking with sugar appeared in Venice in 1541, it was translated and published in Lyons the following year, and in 1555, also in Lyons, the first French book on the subject appeared—by none other than Nostradamus, who devoted only the second part of his work to cooking with sugar; the first part gave recipes for making cosmetics.

The primary function of sugar at this period remained medical. During the reign of Louis XIV it was sold only by apothecaries, who doled it out by the ounce, expensively; it was so important a part of their stock that a French household phrase was born which designated someone who lacked an essential element as, "He's like an apothecary without sugar." It was not universally admired in its healing role. Joseph du Chesne, Henri IV's doctor, wrote in his *Portrait of Health*, "Sugar burns up the blood, impairs and blackens the teeth. . . . Underneath its sweetness, there lurks a very great bitterness." Other critics accused it of causing fever, attacking the lungs, and provoking apoplexy. But in 1542 Andrew Boorde, in his *A Dyetary of Helth*, prescribed "sugar and white wyne" to cure melancholy, though one might be excused for wondering if, in this partnership, the sugar was not superfluous.

As Benjamin Mosely wrote in *A Treatise on Sugar*: "It is not to be supposed that such a delicious and innocent article could longer be subject to the control of the physician and confined to the apothecary's shop." It escaped, inevitably, from the sphere of medicine and even emerged from the restricted role of a spice. The process of promoting it as a full-fledged ingredient in cookery had, indeed, begun long before it emerged from the apothecaries: in 1475 a certain Martino, first name unknown, had inspired what is usually described as the first postclassical cookbook, *De honesta voluptate et valetudine,* for which credit is usually given to Platina. His use of sugar seems to have stemmed from the Arab example. He gave recipes for dishes in which sugar did not appear only as a sort of afterthought, to lend an extra fillip to them, but was their *raison d'être,* like dessert fritters and sweet pastries.

In 1498 Vasco da Gama reached India and the Venetian sugar monopoly was ended. Lisbon imported raw sugar, as Venice had done; refined it on its own territory, as Venice had done; and became the sugar capital of Europe for the sixteenth century. Sugarcane was planted on Madeira and the Cape Verde Islands, and reached the Canaries in 1503 (a fact probably unknown to Charles Edward Carryl [1842–1920] when he observed in "The Plaint of the Camel" that "canary birds feed on sugar and seed"), and the Florentine trader Luca Landucci humiliated Venice by buying, under her nose, sugar from Madeira. But Portugal had arrived on the scene a little late. An event had already occurred which was about to revolutionize the history of sugar: the discovery of America.

"It was in the colonies of the New World that sugar was really born," Brillat-Savarin wrote, with a touch of exaggeration. What was true is that with the planting of sugar in the New World it became for the first time accessible to everybody; and though it had already played an important role in promoting the power of Venice and Portugal, it had been only one among a number of factors which had contributed to their dominance. In the West Indies it would be sugar alone which would shape their economies and accordingly their history. Among the important consequences of the planting of sugar on the islands of the Caribbean would be the cancerous development in the Americas of the "peculiar institution," slavery, which would spread to the United States and provoke the gravest upheaval in its history. "The little plant which had originated in the Bay of Bengal and, in the course of the millennia, had little by little gained strength in its course from east to west," wrote Georges and Germaine Blond, "found in the West Indies its climate of election and bloomed like a happy woman. . . . Its supremacy lasts still."

It was Columbus himself who brought the first sugarcane to the New World, presumably on his second voyage, for it was in 1494 that he reported that the pieces of sugarcane which he planted "germinated in seven days. . . . The small quantity we planted has succeeded very well." The Spaniards swiftly introduced the plant to all their islands. It is said to have been under cultivation on Hispaniola as early as 1506, and to have been planted in Cuba in 1518 by Diego Velasquez, the island's first lieutenant-general. On the mainland the original big grower of sugarcane was Cortez, who a few years earlier had rejected a grant of land with contempt, exclaiming, "I have come to gain gold, not to cultivate the fields like a peasant!" In 1524 he realized that there was gold in the fields as well as in the mines, planted large holdings at Cuernavaca with sugarcane, built his own mills to handle the crop, and became a merchant of sugar.

The Portuguese planted sugarcane from Madeira in Brazil early in the sixteenth century. The Dutch started growing it on their islands (and on a piece of the South American mainland too) at an unrecorded date, but Amsterdam was already receiving large shipments of sugar from the New World about 1600. The French and the English, latecomers, followed suit about 1650, the English on Barbados, the French on Martinique. The French would eventually become the most important sugar suppliers of the world, but the British did not do badly either. George III is reported to have been overcome with astonishment and envy when, driving through London, he passed a carriage more splendid than his own and learned that its owner had made his money in sugar. "Sugar became so important to trade," Reay Tannahill tells us, "that in the 1670s the Dutch yielded New York to England in exchange for the captured sugar lands of Surinam, and in 1763 France was prepared to leave England with the whole of Canada, provided she had Guadeloupe returned to her."

The introduction of slavery into the West Indies was to a considerable extent imposed by the nature of sugarcane, which for successful exploitation required large plantations and an abundance of cheap labor—in the context of the

Sugarcane

times, slaves. The Spaniards began by using the natives to work the plantations but soon ran out of Indians, who had either been massacred or killed by overwork, for we may suppose that their conditions were no better than those of the blacks who followed them, imported from Africa to labor "for half a year together night and day like horses," after which they were fit for the discard. By 1512 slaves were being imported for Hispaniola, and the Portuguese about 1583 brought them into Brazil, where their forced labor made it possible for the five sugar plantations which had existed there in 1550 to increase to 350 by 1623. It was calculated that the smallest sugar plantation capable of making a profit required a working force of 250 slaves; most of them had many times that. In two centuries more than 10 million slaves are estimated to have been brought to the New World from an Africa then so sparsely populated that this constituted a serious drain on the peoples of the West Coast. As early as 1526 this had been pointed out to the king of Portugal by a Congolese ruler converted to Christianity, Mbeba Nzinga, who pleaded with the king to stop the slave traffic; but the Portuguese sovereign allowed it to continue with a tranquil conscience, for Pope Nicholas V had exhorted the Portuguese to "attack, subject, and reduce to perpetual slavery the . . . pagans, and other enemies of Christ southward from Capes Bajador and Non, including all the coast of Guinea."

The sugar economy of the West Indies played an important part in shaping the economy of the North American colonies, especially New England. In 1647 a correspondent wrote from the Caribbean to Governor Winthrop of Massachusetts: "Men are so intent upon planting sugar that they had rather buy foode at very deare rates than produce it by labour, so infinite is the profitt of sugar workes." Massachusetts was not averse to selling foode to the planters, even at very deare rates, and to a considerable extent her economy became complementary to that of the sugar islands. Her most important commodity was salt cod, which was sold to the West Indies to feed the slaves on the plantations; the returning ships brought back sugar and molasses, but more of the latter than the former, for it was more profitable to ship the sugar to Europe and the molasses to New England, which thus absorbed a by-product of which there was a considerable surplus available at an advantageous price. Molasses was then a sweetener much more commonly used in America than sugar, for it was cheaper. A surplus developed in New England too, so the New England rum industry was founded, which was destined to have historical and social consequences. New England shipping and shipbuilding profited from the West Indian trade, and soon American ships were sailing to Africa loaded with salt cod and rum, for which slaves were bought, deliverable to the West Indies—and eventually to America also.

Some of the other colonies established profitable trade relations with the West Indies too, for the planters were interested only in producing sugar. Everything else they needed they preferred to buy, and the nearest sellers were the American colonies. Cheap lumber from their extensive forests built the cabins of the slaves and a better grade of timber the sugar mills, and horses from New England supplied the power to turn the rollers which crushed the cane. Baltimore exported wheat and flour, Pennsylvania maize, New York and the Carolinas livestock and pickled beef and pork, and the Connecticut valley beans, onions and potatoes. The West Indies import most of their food to this day.

It was inevitable that America would be tempted to grow sugarcane herself, but the climate was not propitious to it, though not quite as unfavorable as Thomas Jefferson thought. Asked by one of his agricultural correspondents in France for an opinion on the feasibility of growing cane in that country, Jefferson answered, "I should certainly conjecture that the sugar cane could never become an article of profitable culture in France. We have within the ancient limits of the United States, a great extent of country which brings the orange to advantage, but not a foot in which the sugar cane can be matured."

Yet when Jefferson wrote this letter, sugarcane was already being cultivated on the banks of the Mississippi, where the first sugar mill had been built in 1758. By 1770 locally grown sugar was a common product in the area around New Orleans. In 1841 a particularly successful operation was established by John Hampden Randolph, who bought several thousand acres in Louisiana on which to grow cotton, but soon switched to sugar with success: he owned 195 slaves. (Would it have been at this period that "Turkey in the Straw," an old American song of unknown origin, was born, with its couplet "Sugar in the gourd and honey in the horn, / I never was so happy since the hour I was born"?)

Jefferson was right in the main. Production of sugar on a commercial scale has never been developed very profitably in the United States, despite efforts to encourage it, such as the imposition by Congress of a quota on sugar imports from the Philippines. Before the Civil War, sugar estates of not inconsiderable size existed not only in Louisiana but also in Alabama, Florida, Georgia and Mississippi, but in the more competitive world which emerged after the war, sugar growing in America became non-competitive, not only because more efficient methods of extraction had been developed in countries which had been at it longer, but also because the sugar content of cane grown in the American climate was low; the yield per acre was much higher in Cuba, Java and the Philippines. In 1875 only forty-two refineries remained in the United States, and they were fighting for survival; by 1880 the number had been cut to twenty-seven. Today the extreme southern part of Louisiana is the only place which makes sugar—less than one-half of one percent of the world production.

However, some cane is still grown, on a small scale, or even on a family scale, in Georgia, Alabama, Mississippi and Louisiana, not for sugar, but for sugar syrup. It is a different variety from the kind grown in the West Indies, a soft cane which you may see people chewing in the streets like candy in China, Vietnam or Africa. It is believed to have been developed centuries ago in China from an Indian ancestor.

Before the middle of the nineteenth century cane sugar was not the principal sweetener in the United States; it was too expensive. Molasses was more widely used, and in the Northeast, maple sugar. For the latter, the price differential gradually decreased. In 1860 Catherine P. Traill wrote, "There is little call for maple sugar, Muscovado being quite as cheap." Muscovado was not white sugar. It was an only partially refined brown sugar in which much molasses still remained, a product considerably coarser than our brown sugar of today. It came in large lumps; the standard equipment of the early nineteenth-century grocery store included a portable mill in which muscovado could be ground into a form usable by the customer. In the 1830s it was ten cents a pound cheaper than white sugar, a considerable difference in those days. In the 1880s the tariff on imported sugar was suppressed; maple sugar and cane sugar became equal in price, and indeed by 1885 cane sugar was sometimes cheaper. Today, of course, maple sugar has become a luxury and cane sugar is commonplace.

Meanwhile the Mason jar had been invented, in 1858. Its development was retarded by the Civil War, which caused sugar prices to rise sharply, but after the war they dropped again, white sugar became as cheap as brown, and women used tremendous quantities of it for home canning, for which purpose neither brown sugar nor molasses was suitable. White sugar became king in the United States; consumption doubled between 1880 and 1915. The workers who were building the Union Pacific Railroad sang:

Drill, ye tarriers, drill!
Drill, ye tarriers, drill!
And it's work all day
Without sugar in your tay,
Drill, ye tarriers, drill!

It was fitting for heavy laborers to be aware of sugar: it is high-energy food.

"The articles of sugar and salt," wrote G. Imlay in 1792, "though not absolutely necessary to life, have become from habit so essential, that I doubt if any civilized people would be content to live without them." It is astonishing to find salt being described as non-essential so many centuries after Homer and Herodotus, who already knew better. For that matter, Mr. Imlay was wrong about sugar too, but in this area he has company. "Sugarcane," says *The Oxford Book of Food Plants* (1971), "is useless except as a source of carbohydrate." "Certain foods, such as white flour and sugar, contain few of the essential elements and so are chiefly energy-yielders," wrote Richard Osborn Cummings (1940). "White sugar has little nutritive value other than as fuel."

But are energy foods negligible factors in nutrition? I fear we have become so dazzled by our discovery of vitamins and mineral salts that we tend to conclude that no other elements have any importance. Yet the major constituents of food may be divided into three categories, proteins, fats and glucides—of which the last include sugars, starches and carbohydrates (which work out to much the same thing after digestion has dealt with them). They furnish two-thirds of our food, by bulk. Sugarcane produces more calories per acre than any other common food source. It provides 1794 calories of nourishment per pound, and is the quickest easily available supplier of energy, as soldiers, athletes and English race horses, who are given a lot of it, know. This is because it requires no time for digestion. It does not linger in the stomach, but passes directly into the intestine, to be stocked in the liver and delivered as needed to its chief destination, the muscles.

Sugar is "a food indispensable, excellent and irreplaceable," wrote Rosie Maurel in her *Dictionnaire des aliments*, and as such is more directly comparable than any other food to salt, which it resembles in the relative rigidity with which the body demands that it be supplied. To maintain health, the human body needs to contain 100 grams of salt; much less or much more is undesirable. To maintain health, human blood needs to contain about 1 gram of sugar per liter; much less or much more is undesirable. For salt, the required daily intake must be enough to maintain the 100-gram balance; it is variable, for the body's loss of salt is variable, depending on many uncon-

Sugarcane

trollable factors, such as the temperature; it varies from 5 or 6 grams to 30. For sugar, the optimum intake is steadier: 50 to 60 grams for the average adult. (Children can absorb up to 100 grams, for they burn up more energy, some of it simply by growing.)

Our white sugar of today would be a better food than it is if we had not overreached ourselves in refining it: we remove from what nature gave us not only undesirable trash, but some desirable nutrients as well. Well-educated taste buds know it. In the unexpected context of a *New Yorker* interview with the former head of the Royal Ballet, Frederick Ashton, I happened across an observation which corroborates this fact. Mr. Ashton was deploring the decline in quality of some ballet performances—"as quality has begun to go in almost everything," he continued. "I mean, even *sugar* doesn't taste the way it used to, does it?" Indeed it doesn't. It had more character when it had less refinement, an observation which might be made in other fields as well.

Probably the United States has never had sugar as close to nature as the "black sugar" of South America (it is actually a very dark brown), which keeps almost all its molasses, and is eaten like fudge (so, on the other side of the world, is the very similar Pakistani *gur*, usually homemade, starting with the cane). The sugar eaten in Colonial times and in the earlier days of the Republic was richer than that which we eat now. It was usually brown, not entirely freed from its molasses and its rather limited list of other elements. Brown sugar contains 85 milligrams of calcium per 100 grams, 3.4 milligrams of iron and traces of thiamin, riboflavin and niacin, of the vitamin B family. Modern refined white sugar contains nothing.

The rivalry between white and brown sugar provides a chapter in the history of snobbery. When white sugar first became generally available, it was expensive. Brown sugar was still used in the kitchen, but white sugar appeared on the table, especially when there were guests. It was a symbol of the sound financial standing of the family. Nowadays it is often white sugar which is used in the kitchen and brown sugar which is put on the table. Health-food snobbery and pseudo-gastronomic snobbery have exalted the merits of brown sugar, granting the pleasant feeling of superiority to those who serve it (it also of course has permitted brown sugar to take on the aspect of a luxury item and thus to be sold at luxury prices). Unfortunately, the brown sugar which has now become fashionable is not the brown sugar of our ancestors. It is usually refined white sugar colored with a little refined molasses. You may do a little better, though not much, with turbinado, a beneficiary of the health-food fad too, which has been refined by washing (and has probably had a little refined molasses added to it also). More taste will be found in the brown and yellow sugars refined by evaporation, like Demerara (coffee sugar) or the very dark Barbados sugar, if you can find them.

We . . . have become a bastion of sugar addicts [John and Karen Hess charge in *The Taste of America*]. . . . We give our babies a formula that provides something like two teaspoons of sugar per feeding, wean them on heavily sweetened baby foods, and raise them on double-sweetened frankfurter and hamburger buns, sweet ketchup, candy, and drinks. We consume more of this poor nutrient than any other society ever has . . . and we look for it in everything we eat—bread, meat, even soups, vegetables, and salads.

I had myself never realized how much sugar there was in American food until I moved to Europe, and returned on a visit two years later, bringing along the French wife I had acquired in the meantime. We had lunch at the home of my aunt and uncle, where my wife, in an occasional aside to me delivered in French (the household's knowledge of it was restricted to the first two lines of one of La Fontaine's poems, all that remained of my uncle's linguistic studies at Harvard), complained of the amount of sugar in every dish. The salad appeared. "At last!" she whispered. "A tart taste for a change!" There was sugar in the salad dressing.

I will not enlarge here on America's overconsumption of sugar, for together with my fellow author, Richard de Rochemont, I have already devoted twenty-five pages to this question in the chapter "The Great American Sweet Tooth" in our *Eating in America*. We may console ourselves, if we wish, by reflecting that we do not sin as heavily in this matter as the English, from whom we inherited most of our bad eating habits.

We are . . . eating too much of some things, notably sugar [Elspeth Huxley said for her countrymen in *Brave New Victuals*]. Nutritionally speaking, sugar is little more than potted energy. Of course we need energy, but less of it than we did, now that fewer of us are employed in hewing coal, wielding picks, humping sacks or scrubbing floors, and more in sitting still, and should therefore be eating foods with fewer calories—units of energy—and more vitamins and proteins. But actually we are sopping up many more calories because of our sweet tooth. Today we eat in a fortnight as much sugar as our ancestors, a couple of centuries back, ate in a year. . . . The Americans are being rather more sensible.

A little more sensible, but not much. The comparative figures were given thus in *Eating in America*:

> American sugar consumption is ninety-nine pounds per capita per annum, or a quarter pound a day [about twice the optimum intake], a figure exceeded by the United Kingdom, which eats 111, not the record—Australia, Holland and Ireland eat more, countries of which two . . . share the gastronomic heritage of Great Britain (the third shares its damp climate). France, a country universally conceded to eat well, consumes only seventy-six pounds per capita [about 50 percent too much].

The one factor which affects sugar consumption radically is its price, which has fluctuated violently throughout its history. In the seventeenth century, the development of the West Indian sugar industry caused a tremendous drop in prices and consequently an enormous worldwide increase in consumption. At the end of the eighteenth and the beginning of the nineteenth century, prices skyrocketed in Europe because of the British blockade and consumption accordingly dropped. In 1883, sugar prices reached a record low in the United States, but this time the amount of sugar sold did not increase: its quality did. The American housewife spent just as much money for sugar, but she bought better grades of it; perhaps she had already reached the saturation point from the point of view of quantity. Sugar consumption in America dropped slightly because of shortages and higher prices during World War I, but not as much as might have been expected; the explanation was that civilians bought less, but the Army bought enormously more. Sugar prices rose precipitously in 1974 (a five-pound bag which cost 88 cents in 1973 sold for $2.45 a year later); sugar users cut down their buying and stepped up their stealing. Restaurants had to stop putting sugar bowls on the table and instead doled out individual-sized envelopes of sugar with each cup of coffee, and in supermarkets packaged sugar was moved from the open shelves to the check-out counter, where it could be kept under guard. Sweden cushioned the effect of this rise for its citizens by subsidizing sugar, and found itself involved in a diplomatic squabble with Norway when Norwegians living near the frontier flocked into Sweden in droves and loaded up with sugar at fifteen cents a pound less than it cost in Norway. On December 9, 1974, sugar suddenly and mysteriously returned to normal levels again, and the causes of honesty and good neighborliness were saved.

It would be interesting to know how dear sugar may have been in England on January 4, 1819. We could then gauge more exactly the value John Keats put on the society of the opposite sex. It was on that date that he wrote to his relatives George and Georgiana Keats: "The opinion I have of the generality of women, who appear to me as children to whom I would rather give a sugar plum than my time—forms a barrier against matrimony which I rejoice in."

Tut, tut, Keats! Never use a preposition to end a sentence with.

SUM
stands for

sumac, from which you can make, illogically, elderberry jelly, but be sure to use only the species with red berries, as one which bears white berries is poisonous; for the **summer clam**, which is the horse CLAM, and the **summer flounder**, which is the fluke; and for **summer savory**, a pungent herb called ass's pepper in Provence, and **summer** SQUASH, a pallid vegetable called vegetable marrow in England.

SUN
stands for

the **sunfish**, a name which covers not only the familiar freshwater bluegill of North America (called also the **sun perch**), but also the saltwater fish known alternatively as the opah, kingfish or Jerusalem haddock, and the ocean sunfish or trunkfish, of which both are eaten in Africa; for the **sunflower**, of which Gerard wrote, "We have found by triall, that the buds before they be floured boiled and eaten with butter, vinegar, and pepper, after the manner of Artichokes, are exceeding pleasant meal"; and for **suntwood**, which produces gum arabic of superior quality.

SUR
stands for

the **surf** CLAM, the biggest of its breed on the Atlantic coast of the United States and probably also the toughest, and the **surfperch**, the lustiest of its kind on the Pacific coast of the United States, where about 150 tons a year are taken for American consumption; for the **surgeonfish**, of which some varieties are edible, but as others are poisonous and all of them are armed with viciously sharp lancets, you will be wise to leave them all alone; for the **Surinam cherry** of Brazil, which isn't a cherry and whose fruit, E. L. Sturtevant wrote, "is about the size of a button and is considered agreeable by the natives"; and for the **surmullet**, a name sometimes given to the red MULLET, but never to the gray mullet, which is a different fish for the kettle.

SWA
stands for

swale, a word unknown to the dictionaries, but not to Oregonians, who have bestowed it upon the extra-large huckleberries found in that state; for the **swallow,** eaten in Florence during the siege of 1530; for the **swallowwort,** whose latex is used in West Africa to curdle milk; for the **swamp cabbage** of the southeastern United States, which tastes better when it is called palm hearts, and the **swamp ebony** of tropical Africa, which tastes no better when it is called monkey guava; for the **swamp eel,** which isn't an eel, but this does not discourage the natives of some of its tropical habitats from eating it, especially the variety known as the rice eel, which starts its life male and finishes it female; for the **swamp sugar pear,** sweet and half an inch long, a bit puny for a pear, but it isn't a pear, it's a berry; and for the **swan,** which is still, when white, a "royal fowl" in England, so we must suppose that the permission of the Crown had to be obtained when swans were eaten in England in the fifteenth century, which is perhaps why swans there cost as much as pigs, though they were cheaper in France, where they were raised in great quantities for mass consumption.

SWE
stands for

the **swede,** a Johnny-come-lately to the vegetable family, whose name is deceptive if it is true that this relative of the turnip was developed in Bohemia in the seventeenth century, but its name enshrines the theory that it came from Sweden at the end of the eighteenth; and for the **Swedish river trout,** one of the three European species Linnaeus recognized in 1758, a count which has since been disputed.

SWEET
stands for

sweet, of course, which could be the meadow sweet, whose roots have been eaten as a substitute for bread, or mountain sweet, whose leaves served as a substitute for tea during the American Revolution; for the **sweet berry** of tropical Africa, called the miraculous fruit in French because it sweetens acid fruits and even vinegar; for the **sweet birch** of the United States, which is tapped like the sugar maple for its sap, faintly flavored with wintergreen; for the **sweetbrier,** a relative of the currant, whose berries seem to be eaten only in Norway; for the **sweet elm,** a synonym for the slippery elm, whose inner bark is no longer easy to find in pharmacies; for **sweet flag, sweet grass** or **sweet rush,** whose root was once used to make candy for people addicted to pungent flavors; for the **sweet gale,** of which both leaves and seeds are used for seasoning; for the **sweet-reed** of Africa, which is a sort of sorghum; for the **sweet shrubs,** a group of bushes grown for their fragrant flowers, of which one, the Carolina allspice, has bark which can be substituted for cinnamon; for the **sweetsop,** or sugar apple, a tropical American fruit eaten on its native ground for its pleasant strawberry-like flavor, but, transplanted to India, it has played there the more substantial role of saving whole populations from famine; and for the **sweet yam,** a native of tropical America which is also called the Indian yam, but is eaten oftenest in Africa.

And **SWEET** also stands for

SWEETBREADS. Some time ago I received a telephone call from two friends on the staff of the *International Herald Tribune* who were locked in an argument which was apparently becoming acerbic. One of them was maintaining heatedly that sweetbreads come from the pancreas, the other, with equal fervor, that they come from the thymus. I was able to stave off the rupture of a beautiful friendship by telling them that they were both right.

This was perhaps less true in France than it would have been in America, for while it would be rash to say of any edible that it is not eaten in France, I have never personally encountered pancreatic sweetbreads ("stomach sweetbreads" for butchers) in that country, but only thymus sweetbreads ("neck sweetbreads"). The latter comes in two sections, which has deceived some American writers into identifying one of them with the thymus and the other with the pancreas, but this is an error. The thymus, a gland in the neck, has two parts, connected by a tube which should be cut away in preparing this meat for the customer. The choicer part is round, the *noix* ("nut") in French, the heart sweetbread in English; the other section is long and irregular in shape, the *gorge* ("throat") in French, and the throat sweetbread in English also. When my family buys sweetbreads, which we eat fairly often at home (meaning in Paris), we are never offered anything but the *noix.* I assume that the *gorge* is reserved for restaurants, to be included in the complicated dishes of which sweetbreads are only one ingredient: when you are eating sweetbreads for the sake of sweetbreads alone, you want the best. This is less important when the taste of the sweetbread is submerged in other flavors.

FAMILLE ROYALE DE BELGIQUE

POTAGES.	Bisque aux écrevisses. Consommé printanier.
HORS-D'ŒUVRE	Petites bouchées purée de gibier. Croquettes de volaille.
RELEVÉS.	Turbot à la hollandaise. Filet de bœuf à la financière.
ENTRÉES.	Ris de veau aux petits-pois. Cailles à la bohémienne. Filets de sole à la vénitienne. Mayonnaise de homards.
	PUNCH AU KIRSCH.
LÉGUMES.	Asperges sauce au beurre. Haricots verts à la maître-d'hôtel.
RÔTS.	Selle de sanglier, sauce venaison. Éperlans frits.
PATISSERIE.	Timbale de fruits. Pain d'ananas.
	Glaces aux fraises, et au chocolat.

Diner servi à la cour de Bruxelles, sous la direction de M. Jules Dignimont, avec le concours de MM. Georges Bouzou, etc., etc.

SWEETBREADS. *Entrees:* ris de veau *on menu served at the court of Brussels, 1868*

Similarly, you never see on a French menu any inscription other than *ris de veau,* calf sweetbreads, for those of the calf are held to be the best. Lamb sweetbreads (smaller but less tasty) and even kid sweetbreads exist, but either they also go only into mixed dishes or restaurants do not care to admit that they are serving them. So far as the thymus is concerned, beef sweetbreads, mutton sweetbreads and goat sweetbreads do not exist. The thymus is a mysterious gland whose function is not understood, but it is suspected of having something to do with the development of sexuality, for in the human as in animals it reaches its greatest volume at puberty, and then shrinks gradually until it becomes lost in a mass of fatty tissue. Thus adult animals provide no thymus sweetbreads.

Sweetbreads are soft in texture and delicate in taste. Their blandness, and their reputation in some parts as a luxury food (but they are a well-established bourgeois dish in France), often tempts chefs to employ them as a background for elaborate confections involving expensive ingredients ranging from capers to truffles. I have no particular quarrel with this practice, which has produced some delectable dishes, but if you really want to taste sweetbreads, unobscured by other flavors, you should cook them as simply as possible. We usually eat them at home in the classic form known as *ris de veau Clamart,* meaning with peas, for Clamart, a suburb of Paris which today grows nothing except high-rise jerry-built municipal housing, was once renowned for its delicious sweet *petits pois.* As it happens, we had *ris de veau Clamart* for lunch, by chance, not by design, just before I wrote this page. They had been sautéed in a mixture of half-oil half-butter, with a whisper of chopped shallots and parsley; there was a sprig of thyme in the accompanying peas.

Sweetbreads thus prepared go down easily and seem a light food as you eat them, but this is deceptive. They are rich and filling; a little of them goes a long way. They have a reputation as a fortifying food. The famous French gourmet Curnonsky wrote that when the Marquis de Boufflers returned from an exacting mission as governor-general of Senegal, he restored his strength by eating sweetbreads.

SWEET POTATO. I do not know if Thor Heyerdahl was aware of this when he evolved his theory that navigators from South America had succeeded in crossing the Pacific, but the Maoris of New Zealand have a tradition that the sweet potato, a native of tropical America, reached them from "the country of the ancestors," wherever that may have been, in "canoes made of pieces of wood sewed together" (balsa rafts tied together with cordage or vines, like Heyerdahl's *Kon Tiki?*). This vegetable is known by the same name in New Zealand, the Fiji Islands and Tahiti. If you consult a chart of the currents of the South Pacific, you will see that a raft or canoe drifting from the west coast of South America could pass by Tahiti and the Fijis, and then veer southward toward New Zealand. Did the sweet potato actually reach these islands across the Pacific before it got to Europe across the Atlantic? (It could have done so at the same time, carried, perhaps, by Indians fleeing the Spanish invasion of Peru.) This would account for the reference by Antonio Pigafetta of the Magellan expedition to eating sweet potatoes in the Ladrones (near Guam), which in 1519 would seem highly unlikely if they came from the West.

However, Pigafetta was no botanist. Although he had seen genuine sweet potatoes in Brazil, where he recorded that Magellan's men "made refreshment on *batatas,* which are eaten like

Sweet Potato

chestnuts, and as long as a turnip," he may nevertheless have confused the sweet potato with the yam, a mistake which has often been made in the past and is still being made in the present. The two look alike and even, to a certain extent, taste alike, but they belong to different families—the yam is a member of the *Dioscoreaceae* and the sweet potato of the *Convolvulaceae*. What Pigafetta saw in the Pacific islands, and took for the same vegetable he had seen in Brazil, was in all probability a yam (and so, perhaps, was the vegetable the Maoris had received from the land of the ancestors, even if they identified it later with the sweet potato). Or Pigafetta may have seen a relative of the sweet potato, the water convolvulus, an Old World species which has on occasion been called incorrectly a sweet potato; its difference from that plant is indicated by the fact that the Chinese cultivated it for its leaves, not for its root (but in the Philippines the root was eaten too). Vasco da Gama's "cooked roots that had the flavor of chestnuts" were probably yams also.

In the improbable case that the vegetable of Magellan and the Maoris really was the sweet potato, it certainly did not reach the Asian mainland before Europeans discovered it in the West Indies. If it had previously existed in China, as one French writer has asserted without offering any evidence to back up his opinion, it could hardly have escaped the Arab traders who, during the Middle Ages, delivered so many Far Eastern foods to Europe, or the European travelers who, like Marco Polo, reported fully on other foreign foods. Neither of them knew of the sweet potato's existence. There is no Sanskrit word for this vegetable. It was unknown in the ancient Mediterranean world, and there is no mention of it in the Bible. All its known species are found in the New World; no wild sweet potato has been found elsewhere. It seems to be exclusively an American plant, which originated in the tropics or subtropics, where it is a perennial, though it is sufficiently hardy so that it can be grown as an annual in the warmer parts of the temperate zone.

Its history in America is minutely documented from the time of its first discovery in America by Christopher Columbus, who reported that it existed in many varieties. He was served three or four kinds at a feast given in his honor by the king of the island of Saint Thomas. Columbus likened them to large radishes, which suggests that he was more impressed by their shape than by their taste. He recorded the fact that bread was made from them, which he called *aje* bread, *aje* or *axi* being the local name for the sweet potato. In 1494, Chanca, the physician to Columbus's fleet, mentioned its presence on Hispaniola, where it was called *ages*, but its name was *camote* in Yucatán, where its presence was noted in the account of the fourth voyage of Columbus. In Arawak it was *batatas*, the form which, after a certain amount of confusion, has given us our word "potato." This was also the word used by Pierre Martyr when in 1514 he gave the names of nine varieties cultivated in Honduras; but Garcilaso de la Vega wrote in 1522 that it was called *apichu* in Peru, where, he said, red, yellow, white and brown varieties were being grown.

Peru is where we find the oldest archeological evidence concerning the sweet potato. It was already widely cultivated there in what is known as the Formative Period of Agriculture, from 750 B.C. to the present era; its dried seeds were found in the necropolis of Paracas, which dates from the beginning of this period.

The sweet potato was planted in Spain very soon after the Spaniards first found it in the West Indies—in 1493 according to one authority, in which case it would have had to be from plants brought back by Columbus himself. Oviedo wrote in 1526 that sweet potatoes had often been brought to Spain, and that he himself had carried some which were planted in Avila. The Spaniards liked them better than the white POTATO (which had to endure a long period of probation before it was popularly accepted in Europe). By the second half of the sixteenth century they seem to have been in general cultivation in Spain and Portugal, and perhaps even in Italy. Clusius wrote in 1566 that red (or purple) as well as pale (or white) sweet potatoes were being cultivated in Spain, and later that he had eaten them there himself, in 1601. Spain was presumably their first source for England, where they were often called Spanish potatoes. It was from Spain that Henry VIII obtained them, and ate them in a sweet spiced pie which he is said to have appreciated greatly.

England seems to have first acquired sweet potatoes directly in 1564, when Sir John Hawkins, master of the *Jesus* of Lübeck, returned from what he described as a voyage to "the coast of Guinea, and the Indies of Nova Hispania," with a cargo which included sweet potatoes. Richard Hakluyt sampled some and wrote in 1589, in *The Principall Navigations, Voyages and Discoveries of the English Nation*: "These potatoes be the most delicate rootes that may be eaten, and doe farre exceed our passeneps or carets." By this time the vegetable had become fairly well known, at least to botanists; it appeared in all the books about plants of the last quarter of the sixteenth century, before the white potato. It was *the* potato for John Gerard, in his *Herball* of 1597. The white potato, which sneaked into the *Herball* at the last moment, had to be distinguished from the sweet potato, which was in sole possession of the name, by being called the "Potato of Virginia," which it was not; but this mistake of Gerard's has plagued us ever since with the belief that the white potato, a native of the Andes, came originally from North America.

This Plant (which is called of some Skyrrets of Peru [Gerard wrote of the sweet potato]) is generally called Potatus or Potato's. . . . I had in my garden divers roots that have flourished unto the first approach of Winter, and have growne unto a great length of branches, but they brought forth no floures at all; whether because the Winter caused them to perish before their time of flouring, or that they be of nature barren of floures, I am not certain. [The sweet potato does not produce seed above 30 degrees of latitude and usually does not produce flowers either above 35 degrees: London is at about 51.5 degrees.]

The Potato's grow in India, Barbarie, Spaine, and other hot regions [a list of countries which may seem particularly surprising since Gerard had already mentioned Peru, but perhaps he still believed that Columbus had landed in India]. . . . The Potato roots are among the Spaniards, Italians, Indians, and many other nations, ordinarie and common meat; which no doubt are of mighty and nourishing parts, and doe strengthen and comfort nature; whose nutriment is as it were a mean between flesh and fruit, but somewhat windie; yet being rosted in the embers they lose much of their windinesse. . . . Some when they be so rosted infuse and sop them in wine; and others to give them the greater grace in eating, do boile them with prunes and so eat them: likewise others dresse them (being first rosted) with oile, vinegar, and salt, every man according to his owne taste and liking. Notwithstanding howsoever they be dressed, they comfort, nourish, and strengthen the body.

Gerard was a contemporary of Shakespeare, who used the word "potato" several times in his plays: he meant, as Gerard did, the sweet potato. "Potatoes" still must have meant sweet potatoes in 1656 when Marnette's *The Perfect Cook* gave a recipe for potato pie whose other ingredients included cinnamon, nutmeg, mace, grapes and dates, which would be a little hard to reconcile with white potatoes. The latter did not achieve possession of the name until 1775, when, according to the *Oxford English Dictionary*, the term "sweet potato" entered the English language; thereafter "potato" alone meant the white potato.

The sweet potato's penetration into the Old World was uneven; its success was greatest where indigenous foods of comparable nutritive value were few, which meant Africa and the Pacific islands, and to a lesser degree, parts of Asia. It would seem that it should have been transplanted early in Africa by the slavers who introduced similarly cheap nourishing foods from the New World to the West African coast, to feed their human merchandise waiting there for transport to the transatlantic plantations, but the earliest date I have come across is 1563, when it was planted on the island of São Tomé; it was still flourishing there in 1879, when the Portuguese pilot Ramusio reported: "The root which is called by the Indians of Hispaniola *batata* is named *igname* [which ought to mean "yam"] at São Tomé and is one of the most essential articles of their food." Not only is the tuber widely eaten in Africa today, but also the young leaves.

In many of the Pacific islands the sweet potato, apparently first introduced there by the Spaniards in Manila and then distributed farther by the Portuguese, is now the staple food (which has helped to make it one of the fifteen most important food crops in the world). In New Guinea it is said to account for 90 percent of the total food intake, which sounds incredible, but when Papuans were brought together a few years ago for a two-day "singsing," designed to promote tribal harmony (it didn't), the provisions the participants carried with them consisted almost entirely of sweet potatoes. The date of this vegetable's arrival in Hawaii is unknown to me, but when Charles Wilkes, a United States Navy explorer, visited the islands in 1845, he reported that no less than thirty-three varieties were being cultivated there, nineteen red and fourteen white.

On the mainland of Asia, India, which has had the sweet potato since at least 1616, probably appreciates it the most. It is widely cultivated in all parts of the subcontinent, where many varieties are grown—but the plant called the Pondicherry sweet potato, which is a dull crimson-red outside and has glistening white flesh within, imported into India from the island of Mauritius, is not to be counted among them. It is *Dioscorea purpurea*, and hence a yam.

China is supposed to have received the sweet potato from Spanish traders who brought it from the Philippines; it has been credited with having helped the country to support a larger population than could have been fed on the crops available there before its arrival. The Chinese probably gave it to the Japanese, who make considerable use of it. They grow it not only for direct consumption, but also for drying and for making starch and alcohol.

Except in Russia, where sweet potato production began to be pushed in the 1930s, Europe has not gone overboard for the sweet potato. It is grown scantily in southern Europe, chiefly in Spain and to a lesser extent in France's Provence,

SWEET POTATO. *Photograph by Russell Lee:* Sweet potatoes in a Field, *Laurel, Mississippi, November 1938*

where its complete name, *patate douce*, is often shortened to *patate* and applied also, a little slangily, to the white potato. This usage has now also reached the north, but creates little confusion there because there are not, in the main, two kinds of potatoes there to be mistaken one for the other, but only one, the white potato. Parisians are barely aware of the existence of the sweet potato, though they can buy it if they want it. Most of them don't want it. When I first came to live in Paris, in 1927, the sweet potato was completely unknown there. I suppose it could have been found in luxury shops which dealt in exotic foods, but I never happened to try. Nowadays sweet potatoes occasionally appear in the displays of everyday markets, if they are well-stocked ones; we buy them ourselves from time to time at a nearby department store, but it is one which has a special section for exotic foods.

Among the Frenchmen of the north who do not know what the sweet potato is are some who write books about food. Alexandre Dumas in the nineteenth century could be excused for saying it was a native of India, but it is astonishing to find the Larousse gastronomic encyclopedia presenting the same misinformation in 1960, and the *Dictionnaire de l'Académie des Gastronomes* in 1962. The Larousse gastronomic encyclopedia compares its taste to that of the artichoke and the general Larousse encyclopedia to that of violets.

Yet during two periods sweet potatoes were grown in northern France, though briefly and on a small scale. They did not appeal to the French palate, which is understandable enough, for their sweetness is not in tune with a cuisine which reserves sugary tastes for desserts, so in both cases they disappeared from cultivation when the illustrious persons who had promoted them were no more. The first such champion of sweet potatoes was Louis XV, who was fond of them. One of his gardeners presided over the plants of the Trianon, which about 1750 acquired a reputation for growing foreign and exotic plants. It is a reasonable guess that this was where Louis' sweet potatoes were raised, probably in hothouses, but he appears to have been their only admirer, and after his death the plant was relegated to botanical gardens as a curiosity.

About a century and a half later, the sweet potato became the object of a brief and limited fad when the Empress Josephine, a native of Martinique, sweet potato country, had vines sent to her from the West Indies, to be planted in her gardens at Malmaison.

The sweet potato immediately became fashionable among the courtiers [wrote Georges Gibault in his *Histoire des légumes*]; they had it cultivated for themselves, and many persons were thus able, if not to eat, at least to taste, the sweet potato. Soon restaurant owners, educated about the good qualities of the sweet potato by the gossip of the court, wanted to serve it on their tables and asked gardeners for it. Some of them succeeded in raising it, like melons, with more or less success, and sold a few, at first for five francs a pound. This price quickly dropped to two francs and less; but in spite of this diminution, the restaurants did not use more, so the gardeners, who could not sell all their crops, gave up growing it. After the Empire, no august person was found at the Bourbon court who had a passion for sweet potatoes; and, as courtiers never have any other tastes than those of the sovereign, the sweet potato, little by little, was abandoned.

It never made a comeback in northern France, even after the blight wiped out most of the white potatoes of Europe. It was then proposed as a substitute, unsuccessfully, by several French botanists. For that matter, it had already been touted in the 1780s by several champions of new foods, including Parmentier, who is usually credited with having persuaded France to eat white potatoes; but he got nowhere with sweet ones.

In the New World, where the sweet potato started, we find it still important in Latin America, but almost absent today from the diet of the United States, where not long ago it was of considerable importance. This may be partly because, even several years afterward, sweet potatoes tend to pick up a musty taste from soil which has been treated with pesticides, and it is not easy today to find land which has never been sprayed. In addition, sweet potatoes spoil more quickly than white potatoes, which does not endear them to grocers. Sweet potatoes are even losing ground in their former stronghold, the Southeast, where sweet potato pies and sweet potato biscuits, not to mention candied sweet potatoes, were classed among soul foods. If they could not be saved by George Washington Carver, who found a hundred new uses for them, it is not surprising that the University of Maryland failed too when it tried to aid that state's beleaguered sweet potato growers by creating sweet potato ice cream.

We know more about the early history of the sweet potato in the West Indies than we do about its presumable presence in territory which was to become part of the United States. It would seem highly unlikely that a plant so important in the Caribbean islands should have been absent from Florida, at least, but if anyone reported it from there, I have failed to find the reference. Even if the sweet potato proper, *Ipomoea batatas*, did not grow there in pre-Columbian times, its near relative, *I. macrorhiza*, must have been present, for it is native to Florida and Georgia. Botanists today do not call it a sweet potato, but it could easily have been confused with it; its starchy roots used to be eaten by blacks in the South. The earliest mention I have found of the real sweet potato on the mainland is dated 1648 and reports that it was then being cultivated in Virginia, and may have been raised there as early as 1610. Information about its existence among Indian crops begins more than a century later, when William Bartram reported its presence in Indian villages of the South. By that time it had reached a point in colonists' gardens farther north than the areas in which it could easily be cultivated today; it is said to have been introduced into New England in 1764, and to have come quickly into general cultivation. John Lowell wrote in 1821 that sweet potatoes of excellent quality could be grown in the Boston area, whereas nowadays the farthest north where they can be raised profitably for sale is New Jersey and southern Illinois. Fearing Burr described nine varieties grown in American gardens in 1863, mostly in the South.

In the West there is a plant sometimes called the wild potato vine (but not the sweet potato), *I. leptophylla*, oftener known as the moonflower, the manroot or the man-of-the-earth, the last two because the tuber tends to assume human shape. It was eaten roasted by the Cheyenne, Arapaho and Kiowa Indians, but only when other food was scarce. It was not particularly interesting in taste and was difficult to grub up with the primitive implements of pre-Columbian Indians, for it was very large and deep-buried. It may be that this is the same plant, *I. pandurata*, of which Lewis and Clark made "yellow loaf bread."

Food plants tend to run in families. A family like the *Cruciferae* offers cabbage, cauliflower, collards, broccoli, Brussels sprouts, kale, kohlrabi, mustard, radishes and rutabagas; the *Solanaceae* includes the tomato, eggplant, red peppers (and tobacco); but the sweet potato is exceptional in being the only member of the family *Convolvulaceae* which is raised for human food. (Its dense aboveground foliage, called haulm, is good animal food, and has even been eaten by human beings in times of famine.) The varieties whose flesh is definitely yellow or orange (some kinds are even red or purple) betray by this fact the presence of considerable dosages of carotene, and hence of vitamin A. There is also some vitamin C, a little calcium and iron, and traces of other elements, along with pantothenic acid, which helps in the metabolism of its carbohydrates. Despite its potential perishability, it has the advantage for the amateur gardener that it ripens late, too late to be much subject to wilt or mildew, and can therefore be kept for a reasonable time if protected from frost. Its chief disadvantages are the extreme hardness of its seed coat, which may keep it from germinating for as long as a year unless you nick it or scrape off a little, after which it will reach maturity in four to eight months, depending on the species, and its vulnerability to insect pests. The remedy for the latter, if we may believe Stephen Vincent Benét, is to have a gift for music equal to that of the character in "The Mountain Whippoorwill" who "could fiddle all the bugs off a sweet-potato vine."

SWI
stands for

the **swift**, the bird which provides the raw material for swallows'-nest soup but doesn't get the credit for it; for the **swimming crab**, which is not a tautological name, for not all CRABS swim; and for **Swiss chard**, which so far as I know has no particular association with Switzerland.

SWO
stands for

the **sword bean**, a double-edged name, which may designate either *Entada scandens*, which contains a toxic substance of which its eaters in southwestern Asia and the West Indies manage to free it, or *Canavalia obtusifolia*, which is reported to contain a toxic substance, but its eaters in tropical Asia and Africa can't get rid of it because, so far as chemists can ascertain, it isn't there; for the **swordbill sturgeon**, which is the paddlefish; and for the **swordfish**, a noble dish as cooked at home in New England and an ignoble one as cooked in restaurants in New York, but that seems to be past history, since it isn't being much cooked anywhere in the United States since the Food and Drug Administration (which contradicted itself later) announced that 85 percent of all the specimens it had examined contained dangerous levels of mercury. *Sic transit gloria Friday.*

SY
stands for

the **sycamore**, which deserves a better popular name than asses' fig, for its sweet fruit was believed by the ancient Egyptians to be the special gift of the goddess Netpe to those worthy of admittance to the regions of eternal happiness; for the **Sydney rock oyster**, which isn't raised in Sydney and is a foreigner from New Zealand anyway; for **symrnium**, whose leafy tops used to be boiled in Egypt and whose roots also were eaten by Indians of the western United States; and for the **Syrian bread tree**, whose sweetish yellow cherry-sized fruits are eaten by children though they are said to be poisonous and whose leaves are used in soups and curries in India though they are discouragingly bitter.

THACKERAY: *"No business before breakfast, Glum!" says the King. "Breakfast first, business next."*

THOREAU: *To many creatures there is . . . but one necessary of life, Food.*

THACKERAY: *Everybody has the same dinner in London, and the same soup, and the same saddle of mutton, boiled fowls and tongues, entrées, champagne, and so forth. Who does not know these made dishes, with the universal sauce to each . . . the compound of grease, onions, bad port wine, cayenne pepper, and curry powder.*

TUSSER, THOMAS: *Make hunger thy sauce, as a medicine for health.*

THSENG-TSEU: *The soul not being mistress of herself, one looks, and one does not see; one listens, and one does not hear; one eats, and one does not know the savor of food.*

THOREAU: *He who distinguishes the true savor of his food can never be a glutton; he who does not cannot be otherwise.*

TELECLEIDES (describing the glutton's paradise): *Every torrent ran with wine, and barley-pastes fought with wheaten loaves to be first to men's lips. . . . Fish would come to the house and bake themselves, then serve themselves up at table. A river of broth, swirling along hot pieces of meat, would flow by the couches; conduits full of piquant sauces for the meat were close at hand for the asking. . . . On dishes there would be honey cakes all sprinkled with spices, and roast thrushes served up with milk cakes flew down a man's gullet.*

THOREAU: *Simplify, simplify!*

T

TA
stands for

tacca, a Malayan root from which is made flour so acrid and bitter that "agreeable acids" have to be mixed with it to subdue its own pungency; for the **tacso,** a fruit eaten sparingly in East Africa, described noncommittally as having "a rather agreeable flavor"; for **tadpoles,** eaten by the Aztecs, who enjoyed a plentiful supply from the waters which surrounded their capital city of Tenochtitlán; for **tagart, taheli** and **tahounek,** Saharan plants which provide food for the Tuaregs, of which the first is described as a shrub bearing juicy sweet pods, which sounds as though it might be related to the carob, the second as a reed which grows in shallow water of which the young shoots are eaten in time of famine, and the third as a tree of the Ahaggar Mountains whose bays would seem too small to justify the toll exacted for them by its multitude of thorns.

TA
stands for

the **Tahitian chestnut,** which is not a chestnut, though it tastes a little like it, and is not confined to Tahiti, for it is eaten also in Samoa and the Fiji Islands; for **tails,** which are edible on, or rather, from, among others, the kangaroo, the lobster, the pig and the black deer, the last sought out by the Chinese as a cure for impotence; for the **tailor,** an Australian bluefish favored by surf-casters and gourmets; for the **tala,** a large edible fruit of southern Brazil; for **talewort,** which is nothing other than borage; for the **talha,** a common acacia of the Sahara, whose thorns serve the Tuaregs as toothpicks and whose seeds are ground into a kind of flour, but only as famine food; for the **talking catfish,** which grunts, presumably in protest, when it is taken from the water; and for the **Taliaferro apple,** which seems to have disappeared from our orchards, more's the pity, for Thomas Jefferson wrote that it was "from a seedling tree discovered by a gentleman of that name near Williamsburg, and yields unquestionably the finest cyder we have ever known, and more like wine than any liquor I have ever tasted which was not wine."

TA
stands for

tallow, which in the Faeroe Islands, a seventeenth-century chronicler reported, "was cut in pieces and allowed to rot awhile; it was then rendered, and cut into large pieces, which they dig and put in earth to keep it, it growing the better the longer it is kept, and, when it is old and is cut, it tasteth like old cheese"; for the **tallow bush,** which is the bayberry, of which you can use the leaves for seasoning and the berries for making candles; for the **tallow tree,** which is (a) *Detarium senegalense,* the dattock, of which the pods are eaten in tropical Africa and the seeds pressed for their edible oil; (b) *Pentadesmae butyracea,* the butter tree, of which a greasy yellow juice flows from the cut fruit and is mixed with their food by tropical Africans but not by Europeans, who do not appreciate a strong redolence of turpentine; or (c) *Sapium sebiferum,* a Chinese tree whose seeds are covered with a thick coating of a wax called vegetable tallow which is fine for making candles or soap, but no good for food; and for the **tamarind,** whose name in Arabic means Indian date and covers a number of tropical fruits none of which is anything like a date, including (a) *Tamarindus indica,* the tamarind proper, whose pods contain a bitter but refreshing pulp much appreciated in southern Asia, central Africa and the West Indies; (b) *Leucaena glauca,* the wild tamarind, whose fruit and seeds are both eaten, though some people assert that the latter makes your hair fall out; (c) *Leucaena leucocephala,* the horse tamarind, whose follicles are eaten on the Ivory Coast; (d) *Dialium guineense,* the white or velvet tamarind, whose pulp is agreeably acid and is widely eaten in tropical Africa; or (e) *Vangueria madagascariensis,* the Spanish tamarind or the tamarind of the Indies, an apple-sized fruit eaten in Africa, India and the West Indies, whose taste has been described by one naturalist as "far from palatable," but by another as recalling the European medlar.

TA
stands for

the **tamarillo,** a tart, egg-shaped, red or yellow fruit of New Zealand, which some New Zealanders prefer to call a vegetable; for **tamarisk manna,** which might be described unappetizingly as the liquid from a festering wound of that tree, for it oozes from punctures made in its twigs by insects, and is collected by the natives of India and mixed with sugar before they eat it; for the **tangerine,** which despite being named for the North African city of Tangier has been called "the most delicious of the oranges of China," and its children, the **tangelo,** a cross between the tangerine and the pomelo, a sort of grapefruit, and the **tangor,** a cross between the tangerine and the orange; for the **Tangier oyster,** which in Chesapeake Bay is dying out because of some mysterious disease; for **tangle,** which when it isn't the type of edible seaweed known as the sea girdle is a kind of huckleberry known more completely as the blue tangle, probably a misunderstanding derived from its alternative name, dangleberry; for the **tanner crab,** of which Japanese fishermen when netting pollack take about 100 million a year off Alaska but dump them back into the sea because fishery agreements with the United States do not allow the Japanese to keep them though the Americans don't want them; for the **tanner's tree** of Nepal, whose fruit is eaten there though, unlike most fruits, it causes thirst instead of quenching it; for the **tannia,** a yam related to taro; and for **tansy,** a somewhat bitter, sometimes toxic and now neglected herb which used to be an English favorite after Lent because it was supposed to be an antidote against the evil effects of having eaten too much salt fish and also, as a seventeenth-century writer put it, against "the moist and cold constitution of winter . . . though many understand it not, and some simple people take it for a matter of superstition to do so."

TA
stands for

the **tapa-cloth tree,** or paper mulberry, of the Pacific islands, whose fruit is edible, but the real reason for raising it is to use its inner bark for making cloth or paper; for the **tapir,** which Magellan's men ate in Brazil, but what they thought of it we will never know, for their chronicler wrote that "we will not mention [it] for the sake of brevity"; for the **taraire tree,** whose dark purple fruit is eaten by the Maoris of New Zealand, but only after having been thoroughly boiled, for its seeds are poisonous; for the **tare,** or white vetch, whose seeds are eaten in Asia, North Africa and even Europe, though their attractiveness seems insufficient to encourage this practice; for **taro,** from whose roots is made the paste called *poi,* a staple food of Pacific islanders, chiefly from the species called elephant's-ear, though India prefers another, the dasheen, and both eat a less luscious root which, though unrelated to the first two, is also called taro except in Tahiti, where it is the ape; for the **tarpon,** esteemed more highly as a game fish than as a food fish; for the **tautog**, to which New Englanders are particularly partial, perhaps because it has an obstinate character akin to their own, persisting in inhabiting the cold waters which reach from Labrador to New Jersey, though as a wrasse it ought to prefer tropical seas; and for the **tawa,** a close relative of the taraire tree, which grows in the same place, is eaten by the same people, and exposes them to the same danger of poison.

And **TA** also stands for

TARRAGON. If you happen to be one of those unfortunates condemned by your physician to the mirthless monotony of a saltless diet, you have at hand an easy remedy for your gastronomic deprivation: instead of salt, use tarragon. Again and again, in the less than a thousand years that it has been known to Westerners, food writers have extolled it for its ability to replace salt, pepper and vinegar. (It can also replace garlic for those allergic to this food.) There are no counter-indications. I do not know if tarragon itself has ever been touted as a specific for any of the thousand natural shocks that flesh is heir to, but it comes from a health-giving family. Its scientific name is *Artemisia dracunculus*. Its nearest relatives are A. *abrotanum*, southernwood; A. *absinthium*, wormwood; and A. *vulgaris*, mugwort; all of which have been used in folk medicine. Dietetic rather than strictly medical was the use made of tarragon by the renowned chef Marie Antoine Carême when George IV (at the time still Prince of Wales) was at death's door from indigestion brought on by dissipation. Carême put him on a diet with no seasoning except tarragon, which was credited with having prolonged his life—a dubious desideratum in many opinions, including that of George III, but the Prince of Wales, who thought differently, rewarded Carême with a gold snuffbox.

Tarragon is an herb of moderate height which you can easily grow for yourself even in the city, if you have a wide enough window ledge. William Wallace Irwin, who raised it on the balcony of his Paris apartment, wrote, "We conducted an exhaustive series of agronomic experiments before arriving at the conclusion that, of all pot herbs, only tarragon and chives really enjoy an atmosphere consisting largely of exhaust gas."

Mr. Irwin was only one of a considerable number of people whose acquaintance with tarragon has moved them to superlatives. He called it "the marvelous tarragon"; recommended for a balcony garden like his a half-dozen pots containing various herbs, of which "the sixth and best is the home of the tall tarragon, the undisputed king of salad herbs and prince of digestives"; and for an outdoor herb garden wrote that "the 'musts' are sage, thyme, chervil, chives, pimpernel, parsley, and, above all—tarragon. After garlic, tarragon is the most precious seasoning known to this sinful but interesting world." La Quintinie, Louis XIV's gardener, called it "one of the best furnishers of flavor." "No store-room should be without tarragon vinegar," Colonel Kenney-Herbert wrote in *Culinary Jottings for Madras,* in 1885. "Tarragon is the most palatable of the artemisias," Rosemary Hemphill opined in *Spice and Savour.* Violet Stevenson in *A Modern Herbal* told us that of all the *Compositae* (the daisy family), "the most important is tarragon. . . . This is really a versatile herb, and is almost a necessity in some dishes."

In M. F. K. Fisher's *The Cooking of Provincial France*, tarragon is described as "faintly licorice-like in flavor." I fail to detect any such taste in tarragon myself, and this deficiency is shared by several French friends to whom I put the question, France being the country which uses tarragon more than any other. Tarragon has a tart, subtle but strong (one might even say aggressive) flavor, which is the opposite of the namby-pamby, almost sickly sweetness of the anise-scented licorice. If one dared to say so in these Amazonian days, I would describe tarragon as masculine and licorice as feminine. The error, if it is an error, of discerning a licorice flavor in tarragon might be explained by either one of two possible factors: confusion with tarragon's close relative, wormwood, which does taste like licorice; or by the fact that the essential oil which can be pressed from tarragon *smells* like anise, but it doesn't taste like it. It tastes like terebinth.

When, in a newspaper article, I expressed my surprise that though tarragon was widely used in France, I had never come across it in Italy, a reader wrote:

Artemisia dracuncula is almost completely unknown and unused in Italy except in Siena, where, as *dragoncello*, it is said to grow wild in the dry, steppe-like hills around the Tuscan town.

I have seen a plate of artichokes flavored with tarragon (*carciofi al dragoncello*) offered on a restaurant menu in Siena, but have not, unfortunately, had the opportunity to sample the dish. I have also read of a Sienese *salsa di dragoncello*, to be served with meat or fish, but have never been able to find it, either in restaurants or cookery books.

The most curious part of the story is the legend that when St. Catherine went to Avignon in the mid-14th century to try to persuade Clement VI to return the papacy to Rome, as a skilled healer she took with her a number of plants from her native Siena, including *dragoncello*. The plant was adopted by the cooks of the papal palace in Avignon, and that, say the Sienese, is the origin of French *estragon*.

Tarragon is the only important Old World herb we have today which was unknown to the ancients. Some food writers have tried to establish its presence in ancient Rome, but their efforts seem to me to be unconvincing. It has been suggested that tarragon was the plant Dioscorides called *chrysocoma*, but this was apparently serpentaria, snakeroot. Similarly, it has been suggested that it was the *dragontea* which Charlemagne ordered planted on his lands, but this was serpentaria too. Working backward from the name of Charlemagne's plant, the attempt has been made to associate it with the ancient Greek *drakonteion*, "dragon," and to explain *dragontea* as referring to the long, serpentine principal root of tarragon. It is true that tarragon was sometimes called "the dragon herb" in medieval and Renaissance times, but this seems to have been no more than an attempt to give familiar form to the word which was really the origin of the name "tarragon"—the Arabic *tarkhun*. Linnaeus was under the spell of the hypothetical and probably false derivation from Greek when he gave tarragon its scientific name *Artemisia dracunculus*. It was most commonly called *targon* in the Middle Ages, a form which in English has not changed very much, while in French it seems to have been first modified by gardeners into the present name, *estragon*.

The native land of tarragon has not been identified precisely, but its most probable place of origin seems to be the steppes of Asia. One of the last Old World foods to be introduced to the Western world, it is believed to have reached the West with the invading Mongols. This would coincide well enough with the date at which we find it first mentioned, the mid-twelfth century, by the Byzantine physician whose name has been Anglicized, almost comically, as Simon Seth. He too called it *targon* and failed to ascribe any medicinal virtues to it, an exceptional lack at a time when the arrival of any new food was more apt to be hailed as a medical event than a gastronomic one. Simon Seth nevertheless described tarragon solely as a condiment, which he said was particularly good in salads. In the thirteenth century, Ibn-el-Beithar, remarking that Avicenna and Rhazes had mentioned it before he did, called it a vegetable whose young shoots were eaten "to arouse the appetite and sweeten the breath." It was then, he added, well known in Syria, but rare in Egypt. This is about the total of our information on the early history of tarragon.

If the Mongols moved tarragon toward the Near East, it is the Crusaders who are generally credited with relaying it to Europe. This is likely enough, though the plant went virtually unnoticed there before the sixteenth century. The first

TARRAGON. *Woodcut from John Gerard:* Herball or General Historie of Plantes, *London, 1597*

Western botanist who wrote about it seems to have been Ruellius, who said in 1536 that "it is one of the most agreeable of salads, which requires neither salt nor vinegar, for it possesses the taste of these two condiments." Twenty or thirty years later, Rembert Dodoens gave Ruellius credit for having been the first to discover tarragon. He called it "the dragon herb." "It is still unknown in the cities of this country [Flanders, for he lived in Lille]," he wrote, "except Antwerp, Brussels, Malines and elsewhere where this herb was first brought from France"—but nobody there seems to have written about it before La Quintinie. About 1548 it reached England, where Gerard, in his *Herball* (1597), also cited Ruellius, but rather backhandedly:

> *Ruellius* and such others have reported many strange tales hereof scarce worth the noting, saying, that the seed of flax put into a Raddish root or sea Onion, and so set, doth bring forth this herbe, Tarragon. . . . Tarragon is not to be eaten alone in sallades, but joyned with other herbes, as Lettuce, Purslain, and such like, that it may also temper the coldnesse of them, like as Rockets doth, neither do we know what other use this herbe hath.

It did have other uses in early times, however. The young shoots or tips of the plants were cooked and eaten as a vegetable; they are still so served, cooked or raw, as an appetizer in the Near East. In Syria, during their season, it was deemed essential to serve young tarragon shoots whenever a notable guest was coming to dinner. In the West the use of tarragon has been confined to its leaves, employed as a condiment in a classic version of the bouquet garni (tarragon, chervil and chives); or chopped fine to season sauces (Béarnaise, Hollandaise, tartar, béchamel), soups, stews, salads (where it is particularly successful with Romaine lettuce) and a considerable number of other dishes (fish, some crustaceans and shellfish, chicken, rabbit and veal). It is excellent in pickles, and in France particularly gives us tarragon mustard and tarragon vinegar. "There is no good vinegar without tarragon," Alexandre Dumas wrote, and Mathieu Leclerc du Sablon said that without tarragon, vinegar "withdraws glumly into the monotonous rigidity of a chemical product."

Tarragon is much less used in the United States (where it was first reported in gardens in 1806) than in Europe, perhaps because Americans have been using the wrong kind of tarragon. In the United States anyone who wants tarragon is often obliged to grow his own, indoors or out; but the seeds he buys, though they will come in a packet labeled "tarragon," will in all probability not produce the herb the French use so freely. Its contents are likely to be, not *A. dracunculus*, tarragon, which when it is described more precisely is known as French tarragon, but *A. dracunculoides*, false tarragon or Russian tarragon. French tarragon is looked upon with disfavor by seed sellers, for it rarely produces fertile seeds; it is propagated by division, which is more trouble than simply collecting seeds. If you want to grow French tarragon yourself, buy roots or started plants. Russian tarragon has the advantage of producing viable seeds, but the disadvantage of being almost tasteless.

You can buy tarragon in the form of dried leaves, but you may be disappointed even if they come from French tarragon plants. Most herbs have a stronger flavor dried than fresh (which does not mean that they are better, freshness being a desirable quality in itself); this is because drying diminishes their water content, so the other constituents of the plant are consequently more concentrated. Tarragon is an exception. In its case, drying removes the essential oil, which is the repository of its savor, so dried tarragon has less taste than the fresh variety. Elizabeth David has written that when she has to use dried tarragon instead of fresh, she puts in twice as much.

TE
stands for

the **teaberry**, which is wintergreen; for **teak**, which when it is genuine (*Tectona grandis*) provides no food, but when it is bastard (*Guibourtia coleosperma*) is a fruit eaten in southern Africa; for the **teal**, a duck approved by the Church as proper Lenten food, inspiring medieval artists with a sense of humor to depict it growing on trees; for the **tea-oil plant**, from whose nut the Chinese press oil which they describe as equal in quality to that of the olive; for **teats**, which Martial had detached from a sow so that he could serve them, "swimming in tunny sauce," as an appetizer at what he called with false modesty "my little dinner"; and for the **teborak**, into whose thorny branches the Tuaregs of the Sahara throw stones to drive away demons before profiting by its shade, but the demons have the last word, for the fruit is so bitter that it has to be boiled lengthily before anyone dares eat it.

TE
stands for

teff, an Abyssinian MILLET highly popular among Ethiopians, who make from it a bread of which Mansfield Parkyns wrote in *Life in Abyssinia*, "Fancy yourself chewing a piece of sour sponge and you will have a good idea of what is considered the best bread in Abyssinia"; for the **telefaria nut**, which tropical Africans boil with an effect suggested by its alternative name, the oyster nut; for the **telokat**, a small, red, slightly sweet fruit related to the fig, found in the mountains of the central Sahara, and the **telout**, a small jerboa, or jumping mouse, eaten in the same undernourished region; for the **temple orange**, the North African name for the citrus fruit known also as the clementine; for the **tench**, a carplike fish which the Latin poet Ausonius thought should be reserved for the riffraff; for the **tenrec**, erroneously nicknamed the hedgehog, a small insect-eating mammal of Madagascar, where its flesh is considered a delicacy and its fat is used for cooking; for **teosinte**, a Mexican grass which may be the ancestor, or one of the ancestors, of maize; for the **tepary bean** of Mexico and Arizona, which survives drought and produces a quick crop after the slightest shower, a comportment which endeared it to American Indians; for **terebinth**, a Mediterranean tree which yields turpentine and also an edible nut oilier than the almond, but less alluring; for **termites**, whose large, fat queens are devoured raw by tropical Africans, but when Europeans eat them they coat them with chocolate, thus depriving themselves of its delicate flavor of marrow; for the **tern**, a sort of gull of which a lake-loving species is eaten in Italy's Umbria; for the **terrapin**, which Eliza Leslie advised us judiciously to boil "until they are quite dead" before eating them, while Joseph Mitchell wrote that they are "by far the finest of the North American turtles, and terrapin stew is our costliest native delicacy"; for **testicles**, of which man has eaten at various times and in various places those of the ass, the bull, the bear, the ram, the lamb, the lion, the cock and the halibut; for **teton de Venus,** "nipple of Venus," which turns out to be nothing more esoteric than a French peach; and for **tetra,** a name applied bewilderingly to at least thirty-four species of fish belonging to nine genera, of which many are home-aquarium size, but a few are big enough to eat, like an African variety which it is easier to order by its Ghanian name "prekese" than by the only label Europeans seem to possess for it, *Tetrapleura tetraptera,* which would seem to go better on bongo drums than on a bill of fare.

THI
stands for

the **thickback sole,** seldom eaten because it is relatively rare, the **thick-knee,** the largest bird of the plover-snipe-woodcock family, the **thick-lipped gray mullet,** which is distinguished from the **thin-lipped gray mullet** by the greater thickness of its lips, and the **thick scallop** of the American West Coast, which is distinguished from the scallops of the East Coast by the greater thickness of its shell; for the **thimbleberry,** which on the West Coast is the salmonberry and on the East Coast is the blackcap; and for the **thistle,** which if it is the acanthus-leaved, or carline, thistle has an edible heart like the artichoke, if it is the cotton thistle has an edible stalk like the cardoon, if it is the golden thistle has an edible root like salsify unless it is the golden *spotted* thistle, in which case its young leaves can be eaten like spinach, if it is the holy thistle, or milk thistle, also has young leaves which are boiled and eaten like spinach, if it is the sow thistle has particularly wholesome young leaves which are eaten in salad, and if it is the star thistle allows Egyptians to eat its young leaves and stems raw.

THO
stands for

Thomson's gazelle, whose meat, prepared in the African manner by being marinated in berries and wine before being roasted with a basting of banana gin, is said to be of intoxicating excellence; for **thorn,** an all-embracing term, which includes, no doubt among others: *Zizyphus spina-christi,* Christ's-thorn, of North Africa and the Orient, so called because it is supposed to be the plant which provided the Crown of Thorns, but today offers nothing more sinister than oblong, sloe-sized fruit with a pleasant sub-acid flavor; *Z. lotus,* the Jew thorn, of the Mediterranean region, whose round sweet purplish fruit is the one which is alleged to have seduced Homer's lotus-eaters; *Z. muoronata,* the buffalo thorn or Cape thorn, of East Africa, whose bitter fruit is barely edible; *Balanites aegyptiaca,* the thorn tree, of North, East and West Africa, whose pulpy fruit is eaten fresh or dried; *Acacia royal,* the thirsty thorn, of North Africa, which furnishes the world's best gum arabic; *Citriobatus* plus any number of specific names, the orange thorn of Australia, whose leathery-skinned berries are eaten only by the aborigines; *Lycium europaeum,* the box thorn, of the Mediterranean region, which has tiny red or white fruits, sweet, but without flavor; *L. ruthenicum,* the Russian box thorn, of the Orient, which also has small fruit, sweet and without flavor, and is eaten oftenest in India; *Crataegus clavus,* the yellow-fruited thorn, of North America, which despite its name has red, oval, well-flavored fruit; *C. orientalis,* the eastern thorn, of the Near East, which also has well-flavored fruit, either bright red or golden; *C. oxyacantha,* the white thorn or quickset thorn, of temperate Eurasia, which has dark-red insipid fruit which seems to appeal only to Kamchatkans and Scottish Highlanders; *C. parvifolia,* the dwarf thorn, of North America, which has greenish-yellow fruit, indifferently flavored; and *C. tormentosa,* the black thorn or pear thorn, of the eastern United States, perversely called the white thorn in 1634 by W. Wood, who said it was "esteemed above a cherrie for his goodnesse and pleasantnesse for the taste"; for the **thornback ray,** the source of the leathery-looking capsules called "mermaids' purses" frequently found on the beaches of America, where skates and rays usually go uneaten, but in England they have been appreciated at least since 1552, when they were listed in his household accounts among the fish purchased for Sir William Petre, Secretary of State, and the **thornback shark,** otherwise the common dogfish, also little consumed in the United States except in biological laboratories where an appropriate sauce for it is considered to be formaldehyde, but in England, without benefit of formaldehyde, it is cut into strips, dipped into batter and fried, when, on the authority of Euell Gibbons, it becomes "perfectly delicious, with a flavor reminiscent of lobster"; for the **thorny catfish,** one of whose five species is the talking catfish listed above; for the **thoroughwax,** of which Gerard said, "Hippocrates hath commended it in meats for salads and potherbs," but nobody since has taken these words to heart; and for **thousand-year-eggs,** which should be provided by ducks, and are eaten when six to ten weeks old by Chinese who must be in a thundering hurry.

THR
stands for

the **threadfin,** a fish which is universally eaten in Atlantic Africa when it is the fine-flavored

Galeoides decadactylus, but less widely eaten in equatorial and West Africa when it is *Pentanemus quinquarius*, a dweller in brackish water, and the **threadfin horse mackerel**, *Soyris alexandrinus*, which is not confused with the first two by those who eat it on the Mediterranean and Atlantic coasts of Africa, for the similarity of names exists only in English; for the **threadfish** of tropical waters, otherwise known as the pipefish, of the genera *Nerophis, Phycodurus* or *Syngnathus*, mostly too small to eat except in West Africa and Madagascar, where they belong to the genus *Alectis*; and for the **thrush**, which ancient Romans fattened for the table on millet and modern Romans fatten for the market on juniper berries.

And **THY** stands only for

THYME. Dionysius of Syracuse, a fabulous entertainer, worked out a formula for success at his parties which consisted in strewing his palace beforehand with wild thyme, whose scent was deemed sufficiently strong to carry its alleged aphrodisiac powers into the air about to be breathed by his guests, and always inviting a large proportion of toothsome young ladies. "Thyme, a member of the mint family [of] aphrodisiac virtues . . . was appropriately used in sacrifices to Venus and the nymphs," I find I wrote in my lamentably unpublished *The Food of Ancient Greece and Rome.* "It is under Venus and is excellent for nervous disorders," Nicholas Culpeper reported in the early seventeenth century, by which I assume he meant *against* nervous disorders. But in the case of Venus, an unpredictable goddess, it is rash to assert that her intervention will cure emotional disturbances; it has been known to cause them.

Pliny also found it versatile [I continued]. Boiled in vinegar, he said, it would stop headaches. Burned, it put venomous sea animals to flight. It was effective against snake bite, a danger which loomed large in his world. He advocated laying epileptics on beds of it, so that they might be stimulated by its healthy fragrance. Wild thyme, called *serpyllum*, which means "creeper," referring to the growing habits of this plant, reversed certain qualities of the cultivated herb, Pliny reported: thus the wild variety did not cure snake bite, but its odor drove snakes away. On the contrary, it did not drive venomous sea animals away, but it did cure their bites. It checked colic, angina and vomiting, and when crushed in vinegar and honey was good for disorders of the liver and the spleen. The Romans were acquainted with several varieties of the wild plant, and some of them preferred it to the domesticated variety because of its balmy odor.

Thyme, a native of the Mediterranean basin,

THYME. *Woodcut from Peter Schoffer:* Hortus Sanitatis, *Mainz, 1485*

did not wait for the Romans to enter into history. It was used by the Sumerians, whose civilization dated from about 3500 B.C.

Among the ingredients required for remedies listed on a medical tablet (c. 2750 B.C.) [Reay Tannahill wrote in *The Fine Art of Food*] were thyme, pears and figs. The dry ingredients were to be pulverized, says one prescription, and made into a thick paste. Then "pour beer over it, rub with oil, fasten as a poultice."

The Egyptians, who called it *tham*, included thyme among the herbs and spices used for embalming. Hippocrates listed it among four hundred healing herbs. The Greeks recognized several different varieties, though I fail to identify the kind which Dioscorides, who had nevertheless recommended thyme as a salubrious seasoning, called black thyme, which "corrupted the organism and provoked the secretion of bile." Otherwise nothing but good seems to have been said about this herb. Aristophanes waxed lyrical on a drink made from the unlikely combination of figs and thyme. Virgil included it in *moretum*, a mysterious mixture which different writers have described as a salad, a stew and a cheese; in my opinion it was a bouquet garni. But he differed from those ancient writers who boasted of its invigorating powers by ranking it as inferior to another unidentified food which I shall not attempt to pin down, since John Gerard did not succeed in doing so in his translation:

Thestilis, *for mowers tyr'd with parching heate,*
Garlicke, wilde Time, strong smelling herbes doth
beate.

At least the fact that Virgil thought of thyme in this context confirms its association with energy, activity and courage. The Romans thought eating thyme promoted bravery, and this is said to be also why medieval knights setting out for the wars wore scarves on which their ladies had embroidered sprigs of thyme; another version has it that it was on their pennants that a sprig of thyme was embroidered with a bee above it, to symbolize the fact that the energy demanded of them need not rule out sweetness of character.

Courage in another domain, consistent with

THYME. Spring, *Engraving by Petrus a Merica, after Pieter Brueghel, the Elder*

the harmony between thyme and Venus, is recorded by Euell Gibbons, who wrote:

> According to ancient tradition, if a girl wears a corsage of wild thyme flowers it means that she is looking for a sweetheart, and according to another tradition, if a bashful boy drinks enough wild thyme tea it will give him courage to take her up on it.

Thyme can at least be counted upon to dispel melancholy. The ancient Romans reported this, and so did Aetius of Amida, a physician at the Byzantine court early in the sixth century, who advised its use also by those whose minds were troubled by demons. Demons dote on disturbing dreams, so this is perhaps what Nicholas Culpeper had in mind when he prescribed strong thyme tea as "a certain remedy for that troublesome complaint, the night-mare." Preoccupation with protection may have inspired the addition of thyme straw to the bed on which the Christ Child lay in the manger.

Hostile to demons, thyme is less prejudiced against pleasanter inhabitants of the invisible sphere of our world, and may be used, if you are so minded, to enable you to see elves or fairies. (It was, after all, Oberon, king of the fairies, who confided, "I know a bank where the wild thyme grows," and prophesied, correctly, that Titania would be found there.) Eleanor Sinclair Rohde, who informs us that "wild thyme has always been a favorite with fairies" in *Herbs and Herb Gardening*, a book published no longer ago than 1936 in the fey city of Boston, has been kind enough to give us the formula for viewing fairies. The vial "in which the liquid is made must first be washed with rose-water and marygolde water," she explains, and the thyme seeds must be gathered in an easterly direction from the side of a fairy throne. She does not tell us how to locate a fairy throne before we have concocted the charm which enables us to see fairies.

Considering how conscious of thyme the ancients were, it seems curious that medieval Europe paid little attention to it until the sixteenth century, except occasionally as a medicine: St. Hildegarde thought it could cure leprosy, paralysis and an excessive infestation by body lice, but did not specify the threshold above which the lice population becomes excessive. This neglect of thyme was not an example of the disappearance of a food after classical times because the Roman Empire had collapsed and ceased importing it, for thyme was native to southern Europe and, as it likes to grow on heights, was quite capable of crossing the Alps and the Pyrenees and invading the cooler parts of the temperate zone, where today it grows wild and abundantly from Greece to the British Isles. It is so plentiful in Iceland that one characteristic dish there is sour milk flavored with lemon thyme.

One of the first herbalists to notice thyme was John Gerard, who reported in 1597 that his garden contained wild thyme which "beareth floures of a purple colour, as every body knoweth. Of which kinde I found another sort, with floures as white as snow, and have planted it in my garden, where it becometh an herbe of great beauty." He thought the best wild thyme was that of Crete:

> Wilde Time of Candy is like unto the other wild Times, saving that his leaves are narrower and longer, and more in number at each joynte. The smell is more aromaticall than any of the others, wherein is the difference.

This was also the opinion of Valmont de Bomare, whose *Dictionnaire raisonné d'histoire naturelle* appeared in 1753 under the patronage of Louis XIV. Having sampled it at Candia, he declared that he had never tasted its like. "The thyme of Crete," he wrote, "is the thyme of the ancients. The species of Candia has a savor comparable to no other, a flavor penetrating and warm." The ancients would probably have rated it below that of Mount Hymettus in Greece; but they thought of Mount Hymettus thyme chiefly as the source of the finest honey of the ancient world, the kind eaten by the gods, which did not prevent humans from enjoying it too. The Romans called it *melthyminum*, and could recognize it before it was smelled or tasted, not so much for its clear golden color, but because when it was poured from the jar, it separated into fine threads. Thyme honey, especially wild thyme honey, is indeed highly esteemed to this day everywhere in the world; its taste distinguishes it from all others, for the pungent scent of the herb underlies the honeyed sweetness, as though it were struggling to break through it.

The British have always had a penchant for wild thyme honey, "the mother of thyme," said Culpeper, whose flavor was described by Matthias Hermann as "more concentrated and zestful" than that of the common garden variety, *Thymus vulgaris.* Wild thyme is of a different species, *T. serpyllum*—so different that at least one French herbal does not even call it *thym,* but discusses it in a separate article under the name *serpolet.* It has numerous varieties, many of them grown as much for decorative reasons as for seasoning: *T. serpyllum* var. *coccineus,* which is much like its parent, but a heavier bearer of flowers; *T. serpyllum* var. *lanuginosus,* favored for growing on garden walls, over which it pours a shower of thin silver strands; or *T. serpyllum* var. *albus,* Gerard's white-flowered thyme, which was indeed a rarity in his garden, for that period at least, despite the considerable competition given it by other little-known species among the more than one thousand different plants Gerard grew.

There are numberless varieties of garden thyme, whose popular names you can guess with ease by crushing a few leaves to release their odors—orange thyme, caraway thyme, camphor thyme, turpentine thyme—but there is only one which is deliberately raised and used besides *serpyllum* and *vulgaris*: lemon thyme, *T. citriodorus.* It is of more delicate flavor, with, of course, the hint of lemon its name promises, and is recommended particularly to season veal, poultry and baked fish—it should *always* be used in stuffing pike, one expert insists arbitrarily. It accommodates itself to any dessert where lemon would be acceptable—custards, creams, sherbet; it adds a fillip to stewed rhubarb; and its young leaves can be added to salads, but don't overdo it. Ordinary thyme is better for seasoning heavier dishes—soups, stews, stuffings, sauces, either alone or as part of a bouquet garni (thyme, bay leaf and parsley, for instance). You might even risk a touch of the assertive wild thyme in New England clam chowder.

The creeping varieties of thyme can be used as ground cover, giving you a lawn which, when you walk across it (but not too often), envelops you in the rising scent of the crushed aromatic leaves. "Luxury of luxuries!" wrote Edna Walling. "I've been lying on my own thyme lawn, there was just enough room to turn over without landing on the surrounding rock plants. You haven't lived if you have not lain flat on your middle on a thyme lawn."

The Shropshire Lad seems to have enjoyed the same luxury, for when

Here of a Sunday morning
My love and I would lie,

A. E. Housman makes it plain what their bed was:

And I would turn and answer
Among the springing thyme.

Springing, of course, but perhaps a trifle scratchy?

TI
stands for

ti, a plant whose long shiny leaves are used in the Pacific islands to wrap foods for cooking, and though the leaves themselves are not eaten, the berries are, in New Zealand; for **ti-es,** a tropical American fruit also called the egg-fruit, a small mystery, since it neither looks nor tastes like an egg; for the **tiger,** whose flesh seems to have been consumed regularly by no one since Peking Man, though tiger's claws are still considered a delicacy in Thailand; for the **tigerfish,** which can be either the saltwater fish of the Indian and Pacific oceans eaten in Madagascar and South Africa, called in France, I don't know why, the violin, or the freshwater fish eaten universally in tropical Africa; for the **tiger flower,** whose root was eaten by ancient Mexicans, and the **tiger lily,** whose dried buds are eaten by modern Chinese; for the **tiger nut,** a food for adults in tropical Africa but for children in Europe and America, under the less exciting name "chufa"; for the **tilapia,** a much-eaten fish unable to keep out of Biblical history, for one legend says that when the Red Sea was parted to let the Hebrews pass, the tilapia was split also, into two distinct species, while another attributes the miraculous draught of fishes to the habit this fish displays in Lake Tiberias of gathering in immense schools in the early morning; for the **tilefish,** valuable as food, which first attracted the attention of fishermen at Georges Bank, off the coast of Massachusetts; for **timothy,** a grass considered in most places as food only for livestock, but its seeds are eaten by human beings in Africa's Volta when it is the kind known as Rhodesian timothy; for the **tinamou,** a South American bird which, according to the *Encyclopaedia Britannica,* is "exceedingly stupid and . . . excellent to eat"; for the **tinder plant,** which is our twentieth name for the mullein; and for

tinker mackerel, a species unknown to science, but which for New Englanders identifies the small mackerel which are so voracious that they will snap at anything, even a shiny piece of tin.

TO
stands for

the **toad**, which in the last century was served in a *blanquette* by a zoology professor of Rouen named Pouchet, and in the Volta today is preferred dried and ground; for the **toadfish** of the Adriatic, so ugly that it is offered for sale in fish markets minus its head; for **toadflax**, alias corn spurry, from whose seeds bread has been made in Finland and Scandinavia, but only in times of need; for the **toadstool**, thought of popularly as an inedible MUSHROOM, but scientists (who prefer not to use this term at all) make no distinction between the two on grounds of edibility; for the **tobacco-root**, which for American Indians living on the western side of the Rocky Mountains was once the most important food of this kind despite "a very strong and remarkably peculiar taste and an odor most offensive," but we are told that "from a bitter and somewhat pernicious substance, it is converted by baking into a soft, pulpy mass of sweet taste which is not unwholesome"; for **toba specie**, a trade name for the pichurim bean of Brazil, whose aromatic seed is grated for seasoning like nutmeg; and for the **toheroa**, a rare clamlike mollusk of New Zealand dug up with wooden shovels because the law forbids using metal ones.

TOM
stands for

tomalley, the soft greenish substance found in the heads of certain crustaceans, such as lobster and shrimp, regarded by some with suspicion, but it is the liver of the animal, particularly delicious in taste; for the **tomatillo**, or jamberry, which looks like a yellow cherry inside a paperlike husk, and though virtually flavorless has been transported from its native Mexico to South Africa, where it is commonly eaten; for **Tompkins King**, a fine-scented yellow-fleshed apple more appreciated in the nineteenth century than in the twentieth, but it is still grown in some small orchards in New York and New England which specialize in old-fashioned species; and for the **Tomput**, an apple of this century, whose name preserves that of the otherwise unknown person who produced it, a clergyman of Somerset, England, named Tom Putt.

And **TOM** also stands for

TOMATO. "The whole plant is of a ranke and stinking savour," says Gerard's *Herball* under the heading "Apples of Love," which of course means "tomatoes," in reference to the aphrodisiac reputation they then enjoyed. In his time the tomato was also called the golden apple, for the first to reach Europe were yellow. Gerard also paid his compliments to them under that name:

> The Golden Apple, with the whole herbe it selfe is cold, yet not fully so cold as Mandrake, after the opinion of Dodonaeus. But in my judgement it is very cold, yea perhaps in the highest degree of coldnesse: my reason is, because I have in the hottest time of summer cut away the superfluous branches from the mother root, and cast them carelessly in the allies of my Garden, the which (notwithstanding the extreme heate of the Sun, the hardnesse of the trodden allies, and at that time when no rain at all did fal) have growne as fresh where I cast them, as before I did cut them off; which argueth the great coldnesse contained therein. True it is, that it doth argue also a great moisture wherewith the plant is possessed, but as I have said, not without great cold, which I leave to every mans censure.

But he handled himself the censure of the Spaniards, benighted by definition since they had not the good fortune to be English:

> In Spaine and those hot regions they use to eate the Apples prepared and boiled with pepper, salt, and oyle: but they yeeld very little nourishment to the body, and the same naught and corrupt.

The tomato was not merely "naught and corrupt," it was downright poisonous in the opinion of early botanists, who recognized it as a member of the family *Solanaceae*, along with belladonna, black henbane and deadly nightshade (and also with the potato and the eggplant, both of which have been similarly accused of being poisonous). Foremost among the accusers was a native of the country which, soon after his time, would take the lead in developing the tomato, Italy. The naturalist Pierandrea Mattioli seems to have been the first to write about the tomato. He described it in 1544 as a sort of eggplant, under the name *mala aurea*, "golden apple," which he revised later to *mala insana*, "unhealthy apple." Other writers followed his lead. "This herb," Dalechamps wrote, "is a foreign plant not found at all in this country except in the gardens of a few herbalists. The leaves are like those of the Mandragore, consequently it is dangerous to use them." Had some persons, confronting the unknown tomato for the first time, made the mistake of eating the wrong part of the plant, the leaves instead of the fruit, as had occurred in the case of the POTATO when the leaves were eaten instead of the tubers? If so, the tomato would have earned its evil reputation, for its leaves and stems really are toxic, and have occasionally killed imprudently grazing livestock.

In the latter part of the nineteenth century a new charge was brought against the tomato in England and the United States: that it caused cancer. Even when it was not accused of actual crimes, the tomato was criticized as lacking merit.

The conclusions reached by the early American workers in the field of nutrition [Richard Osborn Cummings wrote in *The American and His Food*] are excellent examples of the fact that a little knowledge may be a dangerous thing. Being ignorant of vitamins and knowing little of minerals, they condemned the use of fruits which today are prized. . . . Canned tomatoes were found to be one of the most costly sources of proteins and energy; they served chiefly as an appetizer and when used by poor and undernourished families simply took the place of other materials which though no more expensive were nutritious and not unpalatable.

As late as the time of World War I, when the United States government was trying to urge its citizens to eat more fresh vegetables, Vernon Kellogg and Alonzo Taylor wrote, "In unit cost, tomatoes almost rank with champagne," without specifying how they managed to establish this curious comparison. Similarly in England, the anthropologist Anne Buckland had written in *Our Viands* (1895) that the tomato was too expensive to be generally popular and was regarded with suspicion by the poor, who "despise and dislike it."

The toxic reputation of the tomato caused it to be approached with caution. We read often in old books that tomatoes were eaten with salt, pepper and oil, which sounds like the salad dressing we now apply to raw sliced tomatoes; but in earlier times, these ingredients were cooked, sometimes along with others, to arrive at a tomato sauce in which it was assumed that the tomato's venom had been neutralized by the cooking. Lengthy cooking seems to have been relied upon in the United States to make the tomato safe for human consumption. In 1860 the bible of the American housewife, *Godey's Lady's Book*, advised that tomatoes should "always be cooked for three hours," though it may be that this counsel was gastronomic as well as hygienic, for it was remarked that if tomatoes were cooked for so short a time as a single hour all one would get would be "a sour porridge"; and in 1848 Eliza Leslie wrote in her *Directions for Cookery* that tomatoes "will not lose their raw taste in less than three hours' cooking," from which we may assume that there was then little appreciation of the flavor of raw tomatoes.

There seems to be no record of the time at which the first hero ventured to eat a tomato raw, but according to James Trager it was in 1840 that a daredevil named Colonel Robert Gibbon Johnson, standing on the steps of the courthouse of Salem, New Jersey, defied death publicly by eating a raw tomato. He survived, but if by an unfortunate coincidence he had suffered a heart attack the following day, we would probably not be eating tomatoes yet.

It is difficult to imagine Italian cooking today without the tomato; and it seems indeed to have been the Italians who, despite the warning of Pierandrea Mattioli, were the quickest to incorporate it into their cuisine after it arrived in Europe from its place of origin, the lower Andes, in an area covering parts of what are today Ecuador, Peru and Bolivia. The Peruvians, so apt at developing other foods, do not seem to have cultivated it. Archeology has produced no information on its early history there, and it is speculated that pre-Columbian Peruvians simply gathered the wild fruit in its season (which was short) and made no attempt to improve it, partly because it was so small (originally about the size of a large cherry) but mostly because it was perishable, unlike most of the food plants they did cultivate—potatoes, beans, maize and even squash. It seems to have spread northward as far as Mexico in pre-Columbian times (and may have been cultivated there) but apparently did not reach the area inhabited by the Pueblo Indians of what is now the southwestern United States, though they received many other foods from pre-Columbian Mexico. Even in Mexico the tomato may have been a late arrival. It was almost certainly not there in 2000 B.C., for no tomato seeds have been found in the caves of that period investigated by archeologists, though they turned up remains of beans, squash and maize in deposits dated several millennia earlier. The tomato had apparently not had time to reach the Caribbean islands before Columbus, for the Spanish discoverers did not report its presence there.

How did the tomato get from its native Peru, where it seems to have been held in slight esteem, to Italy, which was to make so much of it? In Naples it is maintained that the first tomatoes to reach Italy were brought from Peru by Neapolitan sailors, which is possible but unlikely. More plausible is the theory that the Spaniards, who were present at the two points where we know that the tomato was present, Mexico and Peru, brought the first tomato seeds to Spain, which passed them

TOMATO. *Photograph by John Collier:* Seed Catalogs, *Dorchester City, Maryland, January 1942*

on to Italy almost immediately through the kingdom of Naples, which had come under Spanish rule in 1522, just at the right time to receive the tomato.

The Spaniards seem to have accepted the new plant passively, as a gift of God which required no ministrations from man, but the Italians were aggressive about it, both for its cultivation and its expansion. It was natural enough for the tomato to have moved from Italy across the frontier into southern France, but it is a little surprising to hear the French food writer Robert J. Courtine report that the tomato was well known in Poland from Renaissance times, a period when other northern European countries were still suspicious of it. Where it came from is evident from the Polish word for tomato, *pomodory* (Italian *pomodoro*).

Italians were tomato pioneers in the kitchen as well as in the garden. The first cook to use it much as we do today was Francesco Leonardi, probably Roman-born, who worked his way up to the position of cook for Catherine II of Russia. His most fecund period fell between 1750 and 1780, a century before Americans abandoned the practice of three-hour stewing for this distrusted food.

In France, Olivier de Serres, agronomist under Henry IV, wrote that "love apples are marvelous and golden," but his enthusiasm was not necessarily for their qualities as food, for, he continued, "they serve commonly to cover outhouses and arbors." It was indeed true that the tomato was grown in Europe for a long time more as an ornament than as a food, in the north at least, while that part of the south adjacent to Italy was already growing it for the kitchen. The 1760 edition of the Vilmorin seed catalog listed it with ornamental plants; not until 1778 did it admit that it could be used for food.

In 1805 a seed seller named Tollard (who spelled the name of the fruit *thomate*) reported hopefully that "this pulpy fruit, also called the love apple, has multiplied greatly in the last few years," but he was talking about home gardening, not about commercial production. Not until 1830 did growers begin to raise tomatoes for the Paris market, but they did not cut enough ice to impress Alexandre Dumas, whose voluminous *Grand Dictionnaire de Cuisine* devoted just one sentence to this subject: "A fruit which comes to us from southern peoples, among whom it is in great honor; its pulp is eaten in purées and its juice is used for seasoning." He did, at least, append a single recipe to this description, for stuffed tomatoes. We are sometimes informed that it was the Empress Eugénie, the Spanish wife of Napoleon

III, who introduced tomato dishes into France in the 1850s; but the general public does not seem to have been aware of it. For northern France, the tomato was a phenomenon of the twentieth century. In 1912 Georges Gibault reported in his *Histoire des légumes* that the tomato had only begun to be eaten generally within the previous ten years, "for sauces and seasonings. It is also eaten stuffed." Apparently no Frenchman had yet dared bite into a raw tomato. As late as 1927 the Larousse household encyclopedia was still writing that "the consumption of tomatoes continues to increase," which does not sound as though they had yet been completely accepted.

The English were also reticent about the tomato:

> Incredible though it now seems [observed Elizabeth David], the tomato, brought by the Spaniards from Peru to Spain at the close of the sixteenth century and shortly afterwards planted in France, Portugal, Italy and England, was well known to us as an ornamental plant for two hundred years before its culinary properties were perceived.

It had been, in fact, in 1578 that Henry Lyte, who improved a little on the term "love apple" by calling it the "amorous apple," reported that tomatoes were being grown in England only in the private gardens of professional herbalists, and nearly a century later, in 1656, that is where they still were, according to John Parkinson, who wrote that they were being cultivated in such gardens for ornament and as a curiosity. The first English writer willing to admit that tomatoes were being eaten by his countrymen was Philip Miller, in 1752:

> The Italians and Spaniards eat these apples as we do cucumbers, with pepper, oil, and salt, and some eat them in sauces, etc., and in Soups they are now much used in England. . . . This fruit gives an agreeable Acid to the Soup, though there are some persons who think them not wholesome from their great Moisture and Coldness and that the nourishment they afford must be bad.

As in other countries, the English approached the tomato gingerly, using it first in ketchup and other sauces; "presumably the mixture of vinegar and spices was regarded as a safety device against the possibly toxic effects of the fruit," Miss David remarked. In this form it must have been generally known at least by 1836, when Charles Dickens had one of his most famous characters end a letter cryptically: "Chops and Tomata sauce. Yours, Pickwick."

The tomato was slow about infiltrating Asia. It is mentioned in Java in 1658, as the tomata, though we do not know which Europeans brought it there, and this is also true for Malaysia, where it was reported in 1755. But in Thunberg's supposedly complete listing of the food plants of Japan in 1776 it does not appear. Not until the nineteenth century is it on record as being cultivated there.

Africa offers the greatest mystery of tomato history. It was found growing in the interior in 1860, but nobody seems to know how it got there. The best guess would seem to be that it was introduced by slavers, but in that case it seems that it should have been spotted on the coast; and, a greater mystery still, the Africans, who usually seemed ready to eat anything and everything—everything familiar at least—had not realized it was edible. They were astounded when they saw a European eat one. Today it is widely eaten everywhere in Africa, including the Sahara Desert, where it is one of the most important vegetables of that region; it is sometimes mixed with onions and then with dough to make Saharan bread.

One of the first persons to grow tomatoes in the United States was, as one would expect, Thomas Jefferson, but we do not know where he got them. One source suggests that they came from an Italian painter who is known to have attempted to popularize the tomato in Salem, Massachusetts, without success: his neighbors were afraid even to taste it. But this was in 1802, while Jefferson was raising tomatoes by 1781 at the latest (and he wrote that they were common in Virginian private gardens in 1782). The theory sometimes expressed, by Richard Osborn Cummings for instance, that the French encouraged the eating of tomatoes in the United States (at the end of the eighteenth century, when they were still wary of the vegetable themselves!) seems to have been extrapolated from the fact that *one* Frenchman made himself conspicuous in Philadelphia in 1798 by urging the merits of the tomato. He had not come from France, but from Santo Domingo, a refugee from the fighting there; and he was so little successful that the first recorded appearance of tomatoes on the Philadelphia market is dated 1829. Washington, D.C., did better than that, for in the records Jefferson kept of the dates of the appearance of different vegetables on the capital's markets during his Presidency (1801–1809) the tomato is listed, and with a surprisingly long season, from July 16 to November 17.

It may be that American food historians have overemphasized the fact that some Americans shunned tomatoes because it was believed they caused cancer. This is a picturesque detail of the kind which writers like to play up to season their texts, without always feeling it necessary to introduce an anticlimactic element by establishing the just proportion of the phenomenon reported—which in the case of the toxic tomato does not seem to have been very great. Tomato recipes, especially for "tomata catsup," appear in Richard Briggs's *The New Art of Cookery*, 1792; Mary Randolph's *The Virginia Housewife*, 1824; Eliza Leslie's *Directions for Home Cookery*, 1828; Mrs. J. Chadwick's *Home Cookery*, 1853; and E. Hutchinson's *New Family Book*, 1854. None of these authors expressed any misgivings about the tomato (though they were voiced about the potato as late as 1904), nor do they seem to be aware that anyone else had qualms about it. I deduce from this either that the fear of the tomato was less widespread than we are encouraged to believe, or that the cancer fable had not yet appeared in America at the period when these cookbooks were published. If it dated only from the end of the nineteenth century, it was extremely short-lived.

The tomato seems to have been eaten in the United States more generally and at a date earlier than is recorded in most books, whose authors have been led astray by the fact that most available statistics are based on market records, while in the United States, as elsewhere, the tomato was grown in home gardens long before it was cultivated commercially, chiefly because of its perishability. Bernard McMahon, whose *American Gardener's Calendar* made in 1806 a sort of census of the plants being raised in home gardens, reported that at this date the tomato was "much esteemed." Louisiana seems to have been quickest to develop this vegetable; it was being eaten there fairly commonly in 1812, in 1818 we hear of its being pickled, and in 1832 it was going into soups and sauces—but apparently it was not yet being eaten raw. The Thorbun seed catalog gave directions for growing tomatoes in 1817, but offered only one variety; by 1881 it would be selling thirty-one. T. S. Gold, secretary of the Connecticut Board of Agriculture, wrote in a letter to a friend: "We raised our first tomatoes about 1832 as a curiosity, made no use of them though we had heard that the French ate them. They were called love apples." Sturtevant wrote that the tomato was beginning to become popular in 1844; it gained ground as improved transportation permitted carrying it longer distances. In 1835 the northern markets sold tomatoes during only four months of the year; by 1865 they were offering them all year round.

The tomato did not really come into its own in the United States until World War I. It was in 1916 that farm clubs for boys and girls were first organized in the South to encourage the growing of healthier foods. They would interest themselves eventually in the whole gamut of available fruits and vegetables, but they started by concentrating on just one, the tomato. In 1929 the Bureau of Home Economics promoted an ideal diet which postulated the consumption of fifty-five pounds of tomatoes per person per year, at a time when the actual consumption was only thirty-six pounds; as consciousness of the importance of vitamins and minerals grew, this figure increased. Today tomatoes are a major crop in the United States and are grown in every state in the Union except Alaska. More than sixty varieties are offered in the seed catalogs. It is the most popular of all vegetables for home gardeners and the third most popular for consumers of canned vegetables (after sweet corn and green beans).

Botanically, the tomato is a fruit; legally, it is a vegetable—in the United States at least, by decree of the Supreme Court, which in 1893 ruled that because it was used like a vegetable it must be considered one for the purposes of trade.

When the tomato is evoked nowadays, we ordinarily think of a large, red, nearly spherical fruit, usually smooth, but occasionally very slightly fluted; but until 1830 the dominant kind everywhere was deeply ribbed, apparently ready to be separated into triangular segments, like an orange under its peel. This seems to have been the form reached by the best tomatoes after the Italians had bred them away from the small yellow fruit inherited from the Peruvians, which happened about 1570. Not until 1700 do we find a reference, still in Italy, to *Lycopersicum rubeo non striato* (a red tomato not fluted or ribbed). It was being cultivated in Pisa in 1723, but it would take more than a hundred years to become established elsewhere. It is rarely grown nowadays.

In spite of the great variation among tomatoes in growing habits, productivity, hardiness, resistance to disease, color, shape, size, firmness of flesh—and, of course, taste—there are only two species of commercial importance, of which the first, by far, is *Lycopersicum esculentum* (or *Solanum lycopersicum*, if you prefer). With one exception, all our commonly cultivated tomatoes are varieties of this species—the common garden tomato, the large-leaved or potato-leaved tomato, the tiny fig tomato or pear tomato, and the cherry tomato, among others. The last is probably the original tomato, for it is the only one which breeds true from seed, usually the sign of a pure species, as opposed to hybrids, which do not breed true. Yellow, small in size, with dimensions which vary from those of a large cherry to those of a small egg, it fits closely the description we have of the original Peruvian tomato, the *pomo d'oro* of the sixteenth century.

The single exception to the rule that all our commercially important tomatoes are of the same species also breeds true from seed: *L. pimpinelli-*

folium, the currant tomato, grape tomato or cluster tomato, whose red fruits are a trifle larger than those of the common currant. It still grows wild in Peru and Brazil, and was first recorded in American gardens in 1863.

The tree tomato bears fruits which look like small oval tomatoes and taste rather like them, though with more acidity. It is also a member of the *Solanaceae* and also a native of Peru, but it is not a tomato. Botanists seem unable to agree on a name for it; it is labeled variously *Cyphomandra hartwegi, Cyphomandra betacea, Cyphostemma betacea* or *Solanum betacea.*

The tomato is extraordinarily sensitive to the presence of household gas; potted tomatoes are sometimes used in hothouses or florist shops to detect it. A one-millionth part of such gas in the air, a proportion too small to be betrayed by ordinary chemical means, will cause the leaves of tomatoes to wilt, curl up and die.

In the early 1940s, when I was living in Rockport, Massachusetts, we had on our back lawn an arbor over whose trellises rambler roses wove a protective parasol, under which, when the weather was fine, we placed a table for lunching outdoors. The vegetable garden ended beside the arbor. Without rising from my chair I could pick a ripe tomato from the vine, sprinkle salt on the warm spot which an instant before had been gilded by the sun, and bite deep into its juicy, full-flavored succulence. As some other writer has said in some other context, I shall not look upon its like again.

The fate of the tomato—the *fresh* tomato, for I suppose the canned tomato will subsist—seems likely at present to be that of a fruit whose life span, as a mass food and a quality food, will not exceed a century. It did not come into its own until the early 1900s; it seems on its way out in the late 1900s. We deprived ourselves of this splendid food out of fear during the first three or four centuries when we might have been eating it, and we are now succeeding, out of greed, in making it inedible for the future. Once we had improved the tomato in size and lusciousness and, perhaps a little grudgingly, but through a necessity for compromise, to a state of firmness sufficient to get it to market without degenerating into pulp, about the middle of the nineteenth century, we should have stopped, leaving well enough alone. But we kept on improving the tomato until we had improved all the improvement out of it; after all, when the optimum is reached, any change can only be a change for the worse. More exactly, what happened was that we set ourselves to improve those aspects of the tomato which did not appeal to the eater, but only to the seller—the short-sighted seller.

Some years ago, a University of Florida scientist who had participated in producing our new tomatoes found himself confronted on a Washington television program called *Caution* by sharp criticism of the quality of his creations. He defended himself by saying that no thought had been given to the factor of taste in the new tomatoes because it had occurred to nobody that it would differ from those of the varieties from which the plant breeders had started. This was disingenuous, for no botanist could be ignorant of the fact that changing the character of food plants almost invariably alters their flavor. All he succeeded in doing was to confirm the suspicion that in developing new varieties, the scientists have taken neither taste nor nutrition into account. All they wanted to improve was yield and toughness, to permit the fruit to resist the assaults of the steel fingers of mechanical pickers and the bruising of high-speed mass-quantity transport. To this, long shelf life was added by picking tomatoes green and coloring them (not ripening them) by artificial means, for instance by storing them in an atmosphere of ethylene gas. As every home grower knows, a tomato picked at its full size, though still green, will ripen partially if kept indoors at house temperature or placed on a sunny window sill, though it will never attain the full flavor or achieve the total potential nutritiveness of a vine-ripened tomato. But the commercial tomato is often picked before it has even attained full size. Harvested at this stage, it will never become ripe—and this, indeed, is the object of picking it so early: a ripe tomato is vulnerable.

When the Department of Agriculture polled consumers in 1974, it found that the greatest number of protests expressed about the declining quality of uncooked foods concerned the tomato.

> Our tomatoes have become hard, grainy and tasteless because governmental researchers, serving agribusiness rather than the consumer, breed them for toughness rather than quality [wrote William Robbins in *The American Food Scandal*]. . . . In the stores we get the same dry, pulpy, boxed-and-shipped vegetables whatever the season. . . . In their cellophane-windowed cartons, they will be lined up on the counter, having been shipped across country, while nearby farmers may have vines heavy with tomatoes that are juicy and rich in vitamins.

As Calvin Trillin wrote in *Alice, Let's Eat*:

> In the United States these days, some people shop at a market [meaning, of course, not a supermarket, but its antithesis] on the theory that it represents their only hope of coming across fruit and vegetables that have not been bred by the agribusiness Frankensteins to have a shelf life approximately that of a mop handle. They hope, for instance, to find a

tomato that does not have a bright-red skin so hard that anyone who wanted to indulge in the old-fashioned American pleasure of slinging it at a windy political stump speaker would risk being arrested for assault with intent to kill.

And as John and Karen Hess wrote, deadpan, in *The Taste of America*: "A longtime favorite of ours was the tart, juicy Rutgers tomato, whose name honors the university where it was bred. Rutgers' new pride is called the Red Rock."

The American tomato seems to have lost the battle. In Europe, especially in Italy, tasty vine-ripened tomatoes can still be bought; but they face in Europe the same economic pressures as in the United States, mass marketing is developing there in the same fashion, and one may wonder how long the quality of tomatoes can hold out. It is already dropping. In 1975 I received a letter from a reader in Switzerland, a country skilled in producing tasty fruits and vegetables, asking "what they've been doing to tomatoes in recent years."

My complaint about tomatoes [this desperate correspondent wrote] is that the skins are getting tougher . . . I am no longer able to digest tomato skins and must laboriously peel the slices when served outside my own home. This has been going on for about five years, and I had always had a cast-iron stomach until then. There is no . . . problem with my innards . . . but they can't accept tomato skins. . . . Tomatoes will simply have to get along without me.

I have noticed myself that the tomatoes reaching my table (I live in Paris) have lately been tougher-skinned and less tasty. James de Coquet, gastronomic writer for the Paris daily *Le Figaro*, has written, "The tomato is a vegetable which is losing its clientele." It would seem to be normal that as quality declines, demand declines too.

At least the tomato no longer has against it the stigma of being unhealthy—not yet. The use of ethylene gas to turn green tomatoes red does not seem to render them dangerous—after all, this gas is given off in nature by apples and bananas—and though it may be an offense against ethics (since the reason for its use is to deceive consumers about the merchandise) it is not an offense against health, except indirectly in the sense that it persuades us to buy tomatoes whose nutritional value is not what it ought to be. There are other practices which may be more dangerous. We are ill-informed about the possibly deleterious effects of treating growing tomatoes with mercury in England or protecting them against deterioration by radiation in Pakistan, a big producer of tomatoes; and there is a chilling report in the Hesses' book:

Tomatoes . . . have traditionally been safe for home canning because their acid is inhospitable to bacteria, but a recent outbreak of botulism was traced to a variety whose acid is so weak that the botulin is said to thrive in it.

Toxicity: botulism. This seems to be where the tomato came in. In other contexts, the place where one comes in is normally the place where one goes out.

TON
stands for

tongue, a food which in the Sahara is taboo for deaf-and-dumb Jews and, if it comes from a camel, for everybody among the Moslem Chaamba; for the **tonka bean** of South America, which produces coumarin, much used as a vanilla substitute in the United States before the Food and Drug Administration forbade it; and for **tonkin peas**, planted by Thomas Jefferson, which were simply what is now generally known in the southeastern United States as black-eyed peas.

TOO
stands for

toor, a tropical pea which is one of the oldest cultivated plants in the world, as we know from having found it in Egyptian tombs of the Twelfth Dynasty, usually dated at from 2400 to 2200 B.C.; for the **toothache tree**, which I cannot guarantee is edible, though about 1720 it was reported that its "leaves smell like those of Orange; which with the seeds and bark, is aromatic, very hot and astringent, and is used by the people inhabiting the Sea Coasts of Virginia and Carolina for the tooth-ach"; and for the **toothbrush tree**, which I can guarantee is edible, for its sweet fruit is eaten in the Punjab, but why it bears this name is a mystery, unless it is because its leaves are supposed to be an antidote against poison.

TOP
stands for

the **topaz**, which nobody has served as food since Heliogabalus, who mixed topazes with lentils, but in what proportions I do not know; for the **tope**, a kind of shark, and the **topi**, a kind of antelope, both eaten in East Africa; for the **Topinambour**, or Jerusalem artichoke, so named, we are told, because when six Topinambour Indians from Brazil were brought to Paris in 1613 their name was promptly attached to the vegetable Samuel de Champlain had discovered in Canada ten years earlier, in the belief that Brazil and Canada were part of the same territory, a confirmation of the accusation frequently made that the strong point of the French is not knowledge of geography; and for the **top-shell,** a large periwinkle eaten in Europe as an appetizer.

TOR
stands for

torches, our twenty-first name for the mullein; for the **torchwood,** whose fruit is occasionally eaten in South Africa; for the **tormentil,** whose roots, converted by long boiling into a sort of gum, have been consumed, without relish, in Eurasia, but they have generally been more prized as an analgesic against various forms of "torment," hence their name; for **tornillo,** a type of mesquite whose pods are pounded into meal by Indians in California, Texas and Mexico; for the **torpedo ray,** whose habit of delivering electric shocks with its tail does not prevent it from being edible; for the **tortoise,** which Charles Darwin sampled in the Galapagós Islands and described as good eating, particularly if roasted in its shell; and for the **tortoise-shell limpet,** or Atlantic plate limpet, which you can collect, if you are so minded, on the beaches of Maine, but even Euell Gibbons, a man hard to daunt, admitted that "limpets will never make a major contribution to the cuisine of the coast dweller."

TOT
stands for

the **totuava,** a member of the weakfish family found in the Gulf of California, which tastes like striped bass and has been known to reach a weight of three hundred pounds.

TOU
stands for

the **toucan,** the big-billed tropical American bird familiar to many of us in zoos and to Amazonian Indians on the spit; and for **touch-me-not,** a word John Gerard used in 1597 for the Mediterranean squirting cucumber, which is definitely edible, but which today usually means the jewelweed, which is definitely not, in the opinion of some writers, who describe it as poisonous, but Euell Gibbons wrote that he had eaten its young shoots and had found them delicious, adding that its juice is possibly a protection against the effects of poison ivy.

TRA
stands for

Tradescant's heart, a heart-shaped cherry developed early in the seventeenth century by the naturalist John Tradescant the Elder from a variety known as the Noble; for **tragacanth,** whose young leaves are eaten sparingly in Guinea, prized chiefly elsewhere for its gum, used as a thickener in various processed foods; for the **trapa nut,** a sort of water chestnut which somehow managed to make its way from the Far East to the Concord River of Massachusetts, where it became naturalized; for the **travelers' palm** or **travelers' tree,** whose chief asset is the clear pure water which collects in cavities at the base of the leaf stalks, for though the seeds can be eaten, they are scarce, and though the terminal buds can be eaten too, they are of poor quality.

TRE
stands for

treacle, which as everybody knows is the English term for molasses, a processed product which therefore does not belong in this book unless it is clown's treacle, which is garlic, or the **treacle-berry,** which is false spikenard (and tastes like molasses), or **treacle mustard,** which is not mustard, and indeed doesn't even mean what it used to mean in the eighteenth century, penny cress; for the **tread-softly** of the southern United States, a sort of stinging nettle with an edible root; for **tree cranberries,** which Thoreau, deep in the Maine woods, said "were very grateful to us who had been confined to hard bread, pork, and moose meat . . . equal to the common cranberry," but which the English botanist John Lindley in 1846 called "a miserable food for savage nations"; for the **tree ear,** or cloud ear, a gelatinous mushroom much used in Chinese cooking; for the **tree fern,** of which at least two species, the silvery tree fern and the black-stemmed tree fern, yield their pith to New Zealanders, who use it as a sago substitute; for the **tree kangaroo,** whose flesh is considered a delicacy by the aborigines of Queensland, Australia; for the **tree of heaven** of China, whose leaves are used in times of plenty to feed silkworms and in times of want to feed people; for the **tree of life** of tropical America, a palm which is exactly that in times of flood; for the **tree** TOMATO, which is not quite the real thing; for **trefoil,** of which the young pods of bird's-foot trefoil are eaten by the poor on Crete, the bitter rhizomes of marsh trefoil are powdered and made into a sort of bread in Lapland and Finland, and the broad leaves of Shanghai trefoil serve as a winter vegetable in China; and for the **trepang,** the fabled bêche-de-mer, a holothurian which for most of us has to be an acquired taste—or, alternatively, doesn't have to be.

TRI
stands for

Tridacna, the giant clam, of which a single specimen can supply twenty pounds of food; for the

triggerfish, reported to travel in pairs so that if one is hooked the other can bite through the line; and for the **triple-fin,** a fish eaten in Madagascar and the Cameroons, whose French name exemplifies the difference between Latin and Anglo-Saxon points of view, for it translates as "triple-tail."

And **TRI** also stands for

TRIPE. Let us admit that though food is the first necessity of man, writing about food is not necessarily the loftiest form of literature; but if it is to be done at all, it should be done with a reasonable amount of care out of respect for the reader. In my own attempts to unravel fact from fiction in the tangled web of gastronomic history, I frequently feel that I am doing the homework of my predecessors, who seem rarely to have taken the trouble to check a name, verify a date, or ask themselves whether the statements they were copying from *their* predecessors were correct or even credible.

I am moved to these exasperated musings in relation to tripe because both the *Nouveau Larousse Gastronomique* and the *Guide Gourmand de la France* of Henri Gault and Christian Millau have found it pertinent to quote on this subject the prose of one Philéas Gilbert. This could certainly not have been for literary reasons, since Mr. Gilbert's writing is precious and pretentious, apparently inspired by the desire to display his erudition, a dangerous practice. We must suppose therefore that his work has been preserved for the value of its information, of which this is a sample:

> William the Conqueror delighted in primitive [sic] tripe, accompanying it with the juice of Neustrian [!] apples, and history, which, very mistakenly, does not stop to consider small details, has neglected to mention that a question of *gaudebillaux* [Rabelais's word for tripe] was the cause of the quarrel which arose between William the Bastard and the King of France, Philippe Ier—a question which provoked a pleasantry [nature unexplained] of the latter to which the former answered by a promise as historic [?] as it is threatening "that he would come to make his churching [?] at Notre Dame de Paris with ten thousand pikes for candles." And it was thus that, in the tenth century, a gastronomic quarrel led to the invasion of the Norman Vexin.

One wonders how two supposedly carefully edited publications could have invited us to shudder in retrospect at this threat to the magnificence of the cathedral of Paris—or indeed how the original author could have written it—without pausing to reflect that the danger was minimal, since William the Conqueror died in 1087 and the construction of Notre Dame began in 1163.

In more accurately recounted history, tripe does not loom large, but we do glimpse it from time to time. Thus we are told that the reason why the citizens of Porto are called "tripe eaters" in the rest of Portugal is that Prince Henry, who would later be known as Henry the Navigator, had all the cattle of this region slaughtered in 1415 to provision his fleet, which was sailing for the Crusades, leaving to the local citizenry nothing but the entrails, of which they consequently became fond. (One might have expected it to work the other way around.) He was not, as a matter of fact, leaving for the Holy Land, as this account might lead us to believe, but only for the conquest of Ceuta, in Morocco, which would not seem to require such extensive preparation.

Another tripe legend is told in the French town of Olargues, which boasts a dish made from the tripe of castrated kid, whose invention is attributed to the Devil. In the twelfth century, the story goes, he offered to build a bridge overnight in exchange for the delivery to him, body and soul, of the first to cross it. The astute villagers drove a goat onto the bridge, whereupon the Devil, in a rage, disemboweled it and threw its internal organs in the faces of the inhabitants. Bombarding people with tripe seems to fall a trifle short of creating a new dish, but this aspect of the story interests me less than two questions it raises: First, why is the Devil so often cast in the role of a bridge builder? (there is a similar story about the Pont Valentré of Cahors); second, why is he always so easy to outwit? He would seem to be an extremely bad lawyer.

There must be something about tripe which precipitates gastronomic writers into purple prose, or attempts at it. A good deal of highfalutin writing is committed on this subject, probably because

TRIPE. *Etching by Rembrandt (1606–1669). Detail of* The Angel Appearing to the Shepherds

our *arbitri elegantiarum* feel it necessary to display their sophistication to disarm critics who might have at them for dealing with such lowly subject matter. But *is* tripe a lowly food? No doubt if you remarked to any of its pretentious chroniclers that they were writing tripe, they would not feel that you meant to flatter them. Nevertheless, lowly foods, humble foods, simple foods, are not necessarily unworthy foods; they are simply not glamorous. Usually they are not expensive either, which downgrades them in the opinions of those incapable of applying to food any other criteria than its cost; in their eyes what is cheap is vulgar.

The world of tripery is barred to the well-bred, except for occasional exposure to an expurgated version of *tripes à la mode de Caen* [wrote A. J. Liebling in *Between Meals*]. They have never seen *gras-double* (tripe cooked with vegetables, principally onions) or *pieds et paquets* (sheep's tripe and calves' feet with salt pork). In his book [*The Food of France*], Waverley Root dismisses tripe, but he is no plutocrat; his rejection is deliberate, after fair trial. Still, his insensibility to its charms seems to me odd in a New Englander, as he is by origin. Fried pickled honeycomb tripe used to be the most agreeable feature of a winter breakfast in New Hampshire, and Fall River, Root's home town [from the age of seven; I was born in Providence, Rhode Island], is in the same cultural circumscription.

This surprised me a little, for tripe was never served on our family table, though we were not snobs, and as a matter of fact, I don't remember ever knowing anyone who ate it, in my younger days. I turned for enlightenment to Jonathan Norton Leonard's *American Cooking: New England*, one of the best, it seems to me, of the Time-Life Foods of the World series, and found no mention of tripe there either. My curiosity aroused, I consulted the indexes of the other six books of this series which deal with American food, and found that only one listed tripe—in the Mexican dish *menudo*, which had sneaked across the southern border into Texas. Although mention of this proletarian food had been shamefacedly omitted from the index, I did discover one other admission that tripe is eaten in America—in a recipe for Philadelphia pepper pot, which, like *menudo*, seems to be an immigrant, imported by the Pennsylvania Dutch. (The story that this dish was invented to feed Washington's soldiers at Valley Forge strikes me as being in the same category as William the Conqueror's posthumous threat to Notre Dame.) I also found one other reference to a tripe confection in this series, but if the author knew that tripe was involved, he was keeping it in the dark. This was in the case of two Creole sausages made in Louisiana, *chaudin* and *andouille*, which are in fact tripe sausages—foreigners too, from France, which has stamped the *andouille* especially with its characteristic peculiarity: unlike other American sausages, and for that matter most other French sausages too, the meat with which they are stuffed is not ground; the tripe is cut into thin strips and packed into the sausage casing, in Louisiana as in France. I deduce that tripe is not really a popular native food of the United States.

As for myself, I occasionally eat tripe dishes, not for their tripe, but in spite of it. The form in which I have sampled it oftenest is that most famous of tripe dishes (apart from sausages), the *tripes à la mode de Caen* cited by Mr. Liebling, which is flavored with cider and applejack. I recall having once, in Narbonne, deliberately ordered a tripe dish from a menu which offered a considerable choice among other alluring possibilities because I was curious to know what *tripes à la narbonnaise* might be (I still don't know exactly, except that there was an excellent combination of tomato, garlic and certain strongly aromatic herbs which I was unable to identify). It is my theory that the function of tripe is to permit us to taste flavors which we cannot sample on their own because they do not have sufficient substance to be served alone. "Dined with my wife upon a most excellent dish of tripes of my own directing," wrote Samuel Pepys, "covered with mustard as I have seen them at my Lord Crew's." I doubt if it would have occurred to Pepys to eat mustard alone, but he could enjoy its pungent bite when tripe served as its vehicle. Tripe is an ideal carrier for other tastes since it has virtually none of its own to compete with them, once it has been cooked long enough to rid itself of its boiling-laundry odor.

The texture of tripe apparently enchants nobody. Elizabeth David wrote that it has a "repellent slithery consistency" when overcooked; all tripe recipes seem to insist that it be overcooked, from eight hours to as much sometimes as forty-eight. It is "slippery, ivory-white rubber," according to M. F. K. Fisher, who describes herself nevertheless as "a happy, if occasionally frustrated, tripe eater"—frustrated by her family, for instance, for she reports that "not even my children really like it, although studiously conditioned reflexes forced them to taste it in various guises and countries and to give fair judgment, which in their case was No."

This is about my position also, and I find I have support. Alexandre Dumas gave no sign of admiring tripe. Writing of a dish of tripe and beans, whose paternity was disputed between France and Italy, he remarked that if he were not duty bound to defend French claims he would have been content to abandon the credit for this dish to Italy. Elizabeth David, after giving several recipes for outstanding tripe dishes and praising Italian cooks for their skill in handling this food, added, "I do not myself greatly care for tripe," and Calvin Trillin wrote in *Alice, Let's Eat,* "I don't like tripe, but, after many years of research, I have finally decided that its presence on the menu of a Mexican restaurant is a badge representing seriousness of intention."

Tripe is more complicated than you might think. The meaning of this term has been expanded in common usage to cover an area much broader than that to which strict usage would restrict it. In the purest sense it should refer only to the stomach lining of ruminants, and purists would even confine it to the first two of the four with which such animals are provided. However, it is now often used to denote organs other than the stomach, and from animals other than ruminants, chiefly the pig.

In the category of other organs, an unusual example is provided by the famous Milanese *buseca,* a tripe stew which uses two kinds of "tripe"—in the local dialect, *la ciappe* and *la francese,* "the cap" and "the Frenchwoman" (in standard Italian, *cuffia* and *ricciolotta*). The second of this pair is orthodox enough: it is what is called in English "curly tripe," and it gets to be "the Frenchwoman" because the same word also means "curly hair," and curled hair, at the time when this food was named, suggested the elegance of the carefully coiffed *Parisienne.* The "cap," however, is a far cry from the stomach. It is the caul, the membrane which covers the brain.

In the other questionable category, that of non-mammals, not to say non-ruminants, the limit was perhaps reached at the banquet given in 1571 in Paris when that city received Elizabeth of Austria; the menu listed "cods' tripes." In Languedoc today, the fishermen of Palavas-les-Flots make aboard their boats a dish whose composition is supposed to be secret (it isn't), of tuna tripe.

Returning to genuine tripe, we are on our most familiar ground with the first and largest of the ruminant stomachs, the rumen, the one which gives us the familiar honeycomb tripe, so called, of course, because of its appearance. It is the inner lining of the rumen which in French is called *gras-double,* a name found in a number of classic French tripe dishes, of which the most celebrated is probably the *gras-double de Lyon* (with onions, which is the classic English combination also). A French gastronomic writer of the last century with the repetitive name of Robert Robert indulged his sense of humor by asserting solemnly that a dish existed called the *gras-triple à la mode de Caen.* This may have sounded plausible to those who thought that *gras-double* meant something like "doubly fat," but it doesn't. *Double* in this combination is not the adjective which means "twice as much," but a noun which signifies, simply, an animal's stomach.

Gras-double serves as the starting point for *tablier de sapeur,* "sapper's apron," delivered already partly cooked by the butcher, which takes its name from the leather aprons which once covered the uniforms of the engineering detachments of the Foreign Legion, for it comes in large thick sheets.

Also from the first stomach (I think) comes *fraise,* which whatever it means as tripe can hardly be "strawberry," which is its commonest signification. It may have reached this form from *fressure,* illogically, for *fressure* is a blanket term which covers all the major organic meats *except* tripe. *Fraise* also means a ruff, in the sense of the choker-like collar worn in medieval times, which does come from *fraise,* "tripe," because its lacy openings recall the alveoli of honeycomb tripe.

The word "tripe" itself is given by most dictionaries as of unknown origin, but I have found two sources which maintain that it is Arabic, from *therb,* "intestine." If "tripe" came from *therb,* how did it get from Arabic to Gaelic? For the closest approach to *therb* which I have come across in Western writings appears in Robert Burns's poem "To Haggis":

Fair fa' your honest sonsie face,
Great chieftain o' the puddin'-race!
Aboon them a' ye tak your place.
Painch, tripe, or thairm.

TRO
stands for

TROUT. To return to my memory the full fine flavor of trout, I have to go back to the year 1950 when, from time to time, the thought of trout for lunch would assail me suddenly. I would walk a hundred yards or so to the point where one of the two brooks which flowed through my 550-acre Vermont farm fell ever so slightly, not more than a foot or so, over a log which had been wedged across the stream to serve as a rough footbridge. So slight a drop would not seem capable of adding much to the already excellent aeration of the stream, yet there they always were, three good-sized trout, headed upstream, their snouts under the point where the water fell. It was not deep, the water was crystal clear, I could see them perfectly and I suppose they could see me, but I had only to lower a line, one of them would snap at the bait, and I had my lunch.

But did I have a trout? If it was what is ordinarily called a brook trout in New England, I had not: it would have been a CHAR, of the genus *Salvelinus*; trout belong to *Salmo*. I was not much concerned with scientific labels in those circumstances. A char by any other name would taste as sweet, and this fish did all that could be expected of it in the frying pan. But if it was not a genuine trout, then I have to go back another twenty years, to 1930, to recall a comparable taste. This time I was on my way to a snowplow contest in the Pyrenees which had to be postponed because there was too much snow for snowplows: they couldn't get through. Neither could I. The narrow-gauge mountain railway which was to meet the normal-gauge train from which I had planned to shift from plain to heights couldn't make the connection. I found myself stranded for the night, along with three coaches full of passengers bound for the same destination, in a tiny village which did not look as if it could provide even bread and butter for unexpected arrivals; but in the middle of an open field tilted slightly upward stood a country restaurant whose clientele must have been provided by passing motorists. The personnel should have blanched when they saw a trainful of unannounced hungry travelers pour in, but they were prepared for emergencies. Beside the low wooden structure flowed a clear swift brook descending from the Pyrenees. The restaurant owners had broadened it just beside the building and placed a fish trap there. It was jammed with trout, enough to feed all of us, and such trout as I would not taste again until Vermont a score of years later, and since then, never.

I do not remember, at this distance, whether the common European river or brown trout or the spurious American brook trout tasted better, but they were both superb. Indeed today, looking back, I wonder if they were not *both* brown trout. In Vermont in 1950 the fish should have been *Salvelinus alpinus* or *S. fontinalis*, char; but the European brown trout, *Salmo trutta fario*, had been introduced into the United States by game fishermen towards the end of the last century. My brook had been stocked by a previous owner, but with what kind of fish? I wonder about this today because of a detail mentioned above: there were always *three* trout at the same place in my brook. If I returned to the same spot the next day, or sometimes even a few hours after I had removed one of the three, there were *still* three trout. I read recently in a publication issued by the French association of trout raisers: "Adult brown trout do not leave the spot they have chosen. If one is taken, it is quickly replaced by another trout of the same size." Were my fish, then, European brown trout? The same publication, however, describes brown trout as "wary; they take flight at the slightest alarm," whereas the char is of a less suspicious character—like my trout, which let themselves be taken so guilelessly. Perhaps they were hybrids.

Trout, it is true, as the *Encyclopaedia Britannica* points out, "are among the most difficult fishes to classify. Indeed, scarcely two ichthyologists agree as to the number of species that should be recognized." The *Britannica* immediately illustrates its own words by devoting that part of its article subheaded "The Trouts" to *Salmo solar*, which is not a trout, but the Atlantic salmon. The difficulties in sorting out the trouts seem to arise from the tremendous individual variations produced by habitat, available food and other external influences; from the ease with which they hybridize; and perhaps also to readiness to lend themselves to mutation.

Trout seem to have originated in the mountain streams of central and western Europe. Linnaeus, who had to deal only with European trout, decided in 1758 that there were three species—river trout, lake trout and sea trout. In 1880 Dr. Albert Gunther, then a leading authority on fish, demurred. "We know of no other group of fishes which offers so many difficulties . . . to the distinction of species," he wrote, and without even taking the Continent into account, he divided the trout of the British Isles alone into ten distinct species. Present theory seems to have reversed Dr. Gunther's tendency toward diversity with a vengeance, erasing even Linnaeus's three species and deciding that all European trout belong to the same species, *Salmo trutta fario*.

This, the common European brown trout, must be the one I ate in the Pyrenees region, in its river variety—*truite de rivière* or *truite commune* in French, *trutta di fiume* in Italian, *Back Forelle* or *Flussforelle* in German, *forel* in Dutch, *boekørreden* in Danish. Dark in color, with a maximum weight of eighteen pounds, it has been introduced not only into the United States, but also into New Zealand and, strangely for a fish which demands cold water, into Africa. This was the work of British anglers, who wanted their familiar brown trout wherever they happened to be themselves, so they stocked the mountain streams of Kenya, Uganda and Tanzania, where the altitude maintained temperatures at which trout could survive. Altitude, however, does not seem to be sufficient to ensure full flavor despite warm climates, for the ancient Romans, who had plenty of trout in their own mountain streams, nevertheless took the trouble to bring others all the way from the Vosges Mountains of northeastern Gaul, in a cooler climate, urged on, it is true, by a conviction that these northern fish were able to restore ardor to "exhausted matrons."

Salmo trutta fario var. *lacustris* is the European lake trout—*truite de lac* in French (except for the large older fish which have become sterile and are called *truites argentées*), *trota di lago* in Italian, *Seeforelle* in German, *zeeforel* in Dutch, *søereden* in Danish. They are larger than the river trout (up to forty-five pounds in some of the bigger Swiss lakes) and paler in taste as well as in color according to some opinions, but both Gregory of Tours and Voltaire are on record as having paid tribute to the trout of Geneva. But were they talking of trout? If they were thinking of the lake, there *are* trout there, but the fish for which it is most famous, and the one which is universally acclaimed for its flavor, is the *omble-chevalier*, which is a char; after that, for the gourmet, come two closely related fishes, the fera and the lavaret, which are *Coregonidae*, not trouts, though they are also members of the *Salmonidae*. In Lake Geneva the trout ranks only fourth.

Salmo trutta fario var. *marina*, the sea trout (sometimes called by the French, too modestly, the Dieppe trout), is the last of the European triad. It reaches a length of four and a half feet, a weight of thirty pounds, and is migratory, mounting the rivers to spawn at the beginning of winter, whereas other trout spawn in the spring. This is the one the anonymous fourteenth-century *Ménagier de Paris* called the "vermilion" trout, adding that its season begins in May. It is indeed at its best then, after it has had time to recuperate from its winter spawning. At the end of the last century the Ledoyen restaurant in Paris traditionally served it on the day in May when the Salon of paintings opened. It was accompanied by a green sauce supposed to have been created especially for it by Balvay, the proprietor of Ledoyen, when he was chef for Napoleon III. The *Ménagier de Paris* was making a mistake when it took the "vermilion" trout for a special kind, a mistake which is still being repeated to this day when the sea trout (or sometimes the lake trout) is called the salmon trout because of its pink flesh; it is not a separate species, despite this particularity.

This error goes far back. Ausonius, the fourth-century Latin poet of Bordeaux, apostrophized the fish:

And thou, who, between two species, is of neither,
Not yet a salmon, nor not still a trout
Ambiguously placed between the pair,
O salmon trout, taken between two ages!

Apparently Ausonius thought trout became salmon, and the pink-fleshed fish had been caught

TROUT. *Medal designed and executed by Gifford MacGregor Proctor, 1953*

in the middle of its metamorphosis. At the beginning of the nineteenth century it took the authority of Lacépède to scotch the theory that the salmon trout was born either from a trout egg fertilized by a salmon or a salmon egg fertilized by a trout. Today we know that the rosy hue of such fish is simply the result of feeding on small crustaceans, which the sea trout is in a position to eat oftener than the lake trout, and the lake trout oftener than the river trout. If the fish changes diet, its flesh returns to a normal white. Artificially raised trout are often given carotene to produce this color, which seems to be a marketable asset. Apparently it has no effect on the taste.

The European sea trout does not cross the Atlantic to its American shores, though its name does; what are called sea trout in the United States are really weakfish. Since the so-called American sea trout is a weakfish and the so-called Eastern brook trout is a char, this leaves the eastern United States with no native trout at all (though today it does have imported ones). When the Great Lakes are reached, we come upon a fish known as the lake trout, but once again it seems to be a case of a European name applied to an American fish. The Great Lakes "trout" acquired this name in 1687 when Louis Armand de Lom d'Arce, Baron de la Hontan, reported that he had seen, apparently in Lake Michigan, "trout as big as one's thigh." The *Encyclopaedia Britannica* calls this fish *Cristivomer namaycush* (the second word of this tag is Algonquian) and says that specimens of fifty to sixty pounds are occasionally caught and that the largest ever reported weighed one hundred pounds. I do not know what *Cristivomer* signifies except that it isn't a trout; but other authorities call the fish *Salvelinus namaycush,* which would make it a char. It is an important commercial fish, found in lakes all the way from Michigan to Alaska. It makes good eating, but it is less fine than European lake trout, or river trout either.

Apparently the United States has no true trout until we cross the Rockies; its appearance only on the western side of those mountains suggests that it reached the New World from Eurasia via the Bering Strait. What we find there is probably the most celebrated and the most widely eaten trout in the world—the rainbow trout, *Salmo irideus,* whose name has been translated literally into the languages of the many countries where it has been introduced—*truite arc-en-ciel* in French, *trota iridea* in Italian, *trucha arco iris* in Spanish, *Regenbogen Forelle* in German, *regenboogforel* in Dutch, *regnebueørreden* in Danish. As its name indicates, it is a beautiful fish—possibly the one Gerard Manley Hopkins had in mind when he wrote:

Glory be to God for dappled things . . .
For rose-moles all in stipple upon trout that swim.

Just as all the European trout, once dignified by a variety of species names, are now thought to be one species, so one might wonder whether all the West Coast American fish, which have been given a score or more of distinctive species names too, are not really all varieties of the rainbow—whether the steelhead is not a large rainbow trout (six to eighteen pounds) which has decided to visit the sea, the smaller cutthroat (one and a half to five pounds) simply a differently marked rainbow, the golden trout, state fish of California, only a Kerr Plateau rainbow trout, and so on. As for those which are certainly not rainbows, they are not trouts either. The Dolly Varden trout—apparently named by an avid reader who was reminded by its characteristic red spots of the cherry-colored ribbons worn by the Charles Dickens character of that name—is classified as *Salvelinus malma,* which makes it a char. Even farther from troutdom is the fish called the green trout in the northwestern United States: it is a large-mouthed bass.

The reason why the rainbow trout is today probably the best known and certainly the most widely eaten of its family is that it has been exported into practically all the waters of the world—first, probably, to the eastern United States, and then to Europe, South America, Asia, Africa, Australia and New Zealand. It fared badly at first in European waters: *Salmo trutta fario* spawns earlier than the rainbow trout, so European brown trout often devoured all the rainbow alevins before they were big enough to defend themselves.

Even without such fierce enemies, trout have difficulty in maintaining themselves. At the best, they are fussy about reproducing their kind. Although a single male can fertilize the eggs of two or three females, which is not the case for many fish, there must be no hesitation in the process, for trout sperm lives in the water only about thirty seconds. There are many inhibiting factors which can prevent trout from performing their breeding ritual in time, for instance the absence of gravel on the bottom. Normally the female trout, by vigorous agitation of her tail, scoops out a sort of nest in the gravel, called a redd, in which the fertilized eggs, 1000 to 5000 at a time, are deposited and then covered protectively. The absence of gravel seems to afflict the fish with temporary sterility, and no breeding takes place. When streams are stocked artificially, if it is observed that the bottom gravel has been covered with silt, new gravel is often poured in, sometimes to a depth of as much as two feet.

The presence of gravel depends on the speed of the stream, which when it is right for trout washes away everything lighter. Trout are usually not found in brooks or rivers with a drop of less than 4 percent, which assures sufficient oxygenation of the water. Trout do not object to steeper inclines, but they grow more slowly in faster waters. (They also grow more slowly in small streams than in large ones, and in lakes more slowly than in the sea.) This may be because their growth depends largely on the amount of calcium they absorb, which comes from the shells of the minute crustaceans they eat; swift waters sweep the crustaceans by before the trout can get their fill of them. The need for fast-flowing water may explain why, of two brooks on my farm, only the smaller contained trout. The larger one had a beaver dam across it, above which the flow of water was backed up and slowed down. This brook also, though it looked clear enough, may have been slightly polluted, for it crossed a cow pasture before entering my property; the other one rose in springs in the woods above my farm and did not emerge into inhabited territory until it reached me. Trout are extremely sensitive to dirty water, more so, perhaps, than any other freshwater fish except the grayling. In the French city of Nantes, whose drinking water comes from running streams, trout are caged in them to detect pollution: when the water is clear they head upstream; if it becomes less so, they turn downstream, apparently in an effort to escape.

One of the beauties of life among the rapids [for

trout, one gathers] is that the water is usually quite highly saturated with oxygen [wrote Millard C. Davis in *The Near Woods*]. Not only does turbulence drive it in, but cool water holds oxygen . . . better than does warm water. A stream that slows down and bakes in the sun can lose so much oxygen as to asphyxiate many of its larger animals. The heat alone can kill. Heat and lack of oxygen are both aspects of thermal pollution. Floodwater-retarding dams have actually wiped out trout in a stream below by releasing only water that has been drawn from the top of a pond, which is relatively warmer and deficient in oxygen.

Since the rainbow trout in Europe is exposed, like its fellows, to all these difficulties, and in addition to the onslaughts of the brown trout—equaled perhaps only by the pike for cannibalism—it is not surprising that it failed to gain a foothold in open European waters. But it was saved in Europe and elsewhere by the discovery that it adapts itself admirably to artificial raising. Some of the rainbow trout raised artificially are used to stock streams or lakes, but most of them reach maturity in the breeders' tanks and are sold directly to restaurants or fish stores, or frozen. Curiously, many of the rainbow trout frozen in other countries are exported to the United States, the country of its origin. Japan, for instance, produces about 16,500 tons of rainbow trout a year and exports 3000 tons, much of it to America.

The rainbow trout has thus gained a widespread reputation throughout the world as a supplier of food, but a lamentable one as a supplier of flavor. Europeans who have never had an opportunity to taste fresh rainbow trout taken from the streams or lakes of its own country attribute to the nature of the fish a tastelessness which should really be ascribed to the effects of artificial raising. The late French "prince of gourmets," Curnonsky, described the cultivated rainbow trout as "a wet bandage," and the Paris *Monde*'s gastronomic editor, Robert J. Courtine, called it "a cotton-fleshed substitute."

Born from a test-tube, from parents which had never seen each other [wrote Albert Simonin], the trout, once a feast for gourmets, is perhaps the most disinherited [of our fish]. Brought up in a basin where the cubage of water necessary for its survival is measured out for it with parsimony, this free rover of the torrents, whose appetite for savory and varied foods is well known to fishermen, finds itself being fed at fixed hours with bits of spleen or even of spoiled meat unfit for human consumption, the diet least capable of flavoring fish already softened by the absence of the struggle necessary for its subsistence in white water. Such a trout, served up with almonds [a treatment described by Jean Giono as "packaging, not cooking"] in a fallacious hope of distracting the attention of the gourmet, or else served smoked to play the card of Nordic exoticism, can hardly maintain the illusion after the first mouthful.

This from the country which, neck and neck with Japan, produces the largest number of artificially raised trout in the world! Barred from buying wild trout, French restaurants do the best they can with what they can get, keeping their artificially raised trout alive until ordered in tanks into which oxygen bubbles constantly. But picturesque and tempting though they look in their glass prisons, these are listless fish supplied by hatcheries, and the liquid in which they swim is chlorinated city water.

Oxygenation must have brought much better trout to the consumer in the Belgian Ardennes, where I once saw a cistern cart drive up to my hotel; the cart was equipped with great tanks of oxygen, which kept the trout-filled water it was carrying in constant ebullition. The fish had been taken from hill streams a few hours before. I was leaving the hotel at the time, so I had no opportunity to sample the trout, but I should think that this must have represented about the best which could be done in the way of getting quality fish to the table. Alas, this was a quarter-century ago, and I fear that such fish exist no longer where I have seen the once lovely Meuse exchange the greenery along its banks for belching factories.

I doubt if I shall ever again taste trout (or char) like those I took myself from my Vermont brook and ate minutes out of the water. "These kinds of Fish," wrote Izaak Walton, "a trout especially, if he is not eaten within four or five hours after he is taken, is worth nothing."

TRU
stands for

the **trumpeter**, a tropical American bird the size of a large hen, which, according to Alexandre Dumas, who tried it, has "very delicate" flesh; for the **trumpet of death**, a cornucopia-shaped mushroom of an unhealthy purplish color which anyone can see at a glance must be poisonous, but actually it is of agreeable flavor, has a plum-like odor, makes excellent eating, and is especially recommended for drying as a seasoning for various dishes; for the **trumpet tree**, also known as the Indian snakewood, a tropical American plant whose young buds serve as a potherb; for the **truncated borer**, a clam which sounds more interesting under its alternative name "fallen angel"; for the **trunkfish**, of a tropical family of surprising shapes and colors, which when placed in an aquarium with other fish emits a toxic substance which distresses them, but is nevertheless not only edible but is considered a great delicacy in certain South Pacific islands.

And **TRU** also stands for

TRUFFLE. "Lybians, unyoke your oxen!" Juvenal cried. "Keep your grain, but send us your truffles!"

Truffles were already an old story by Juvenal's time. They were being eaten in Mesopotamia at least by 1800 B.C., although I do not know that we are obliged to believe the contemporary French author who tells us that a certain Queen Shibtu of Babylon was fond of truffles wrapped in papyrus and roasted in the ashes of the hearth, the ancient precursor of the French *truffes sous les cendres*. The Romans had truffles from Greece, where they seem to have been appreciated, but less so than by themselves; Coelius Apicius concocted six truffle recipes, but we do not know what kind of truffles they were: one description suggests that they were gray truffles, a sort which has little flavor. The ancient Romans also ate, from their own territory, the truffles of Spoleto, in Umbria, highly thought of still; but whether they discovered them before or after Juvenal appealed to the Libyans I do not know. Apparently they never discovered that in what is now the Piedmont they possessed the tubercle most exclusively associated with Italy today, the white truffle.

Pliny agreed with Juvenal that the best truffles came from Africa; the latter prized them so highly that he advised the well-to-do to prepare them with their own hands, for they were too precious to trust to servants. Yet he did not rank them above what he evidently felt was Italy's best MUSHROOM, putting them only on the same level as *boleti*, while Martial even ranked them a degree lower. *Boleti* did not mean what we might expect it to today—the boletus—but Caesar's mushroom, *Amanita caesarea*. This species does indeed make excellent eating, but today it would generally be considered inferior to the truffle: Is it possible that the ancients did not know our best truffle, probably a native of France, not of Italy, nor of Libya either? Indeed we may wonder whether Martial was talking about truffles at all when, in a burst of unbridled empathy, he cast himself as a truffle and wrote: "We truffles, who burst through the nurturing soil with our soft heads, are of earth's apples second only to *boleti*." The peculiarity of truffles is precisely that they do not burst through the nurturing soil with heads soft or otherwise, but remain buried snugly underground.

Truffles disappear from history after the collapse of the Roman Empire, though they must still have been there, allowed to stay underground by a society which was not characterized by gastronomic finesse. The reference books tell us that they returned about the middle of the fourteenth century, but without offering any specific examples; they are not mentioned in the anonymous *Le Ménagier de Paris* at the end of that century. The first trustworthy reference I have found dates from the fifteenth century, when Platina wrote of truffles that "they must be eaten as the last course, for they help greatly to make meat descend through the opening of the stomach." It is at this period also that we first hear of truffles being sought in France with the aid of pigs carefully muzzled to prevent them from eating the truffles before their masters had time to lay hands on them. They seem at that time almost always to have been pickled, which must have deprived them of much of their natural flavor. The celebrated chef Pierre François de la Varenne rescued them from pickling in the seventeenth century, using them in cooking like other mushrooms. In the eighteenth, truffles were still rare and expensive. "A truffled turkey," Brillat-Savarin wrote, "was a luxury, found only on the tables of the greatest lords and of kept women."

It was in the nineteenth century that truffles reached their apogee. They cannot be said, however, to have penetrated deep into the less privileged layers of society in 1848, when the mob which pillaged the pantries of Louis Philippe's Tuileries palace of its fine foodstuffs left his stock of truffles untouched because nobody knew if they were safe to eat. Yet in 1825 Brillat-Savarin had written, "Nobody dares admit that he has been present at a meal where there was not at least one dish with truffles. However good it may be in itself, an entrée does not appear to advantage unless it has been enriched with truffles." The demand for them trebled, and so did the price. "The Bourbons governed with truffles," Alexandre Dumas wrote, and of the two reigning theatrical queens of the time he ranked Mlle. George above Mlle. Mars because the former served truffles to her guests and the latter did not. Balzac, who mentions truffles often in his works, said of the Comte de Fontaine, one of the characters in his *Le bal de Sceaux*, that "the luxury of his table at his dinners, perfumed with truffles, rivaled the celebrated feasts by which the ministers of the times assured themselves of the votes of their warriors in parliament."

From the beginning the truffle was a mystery, and to a certain extent it still is. Some of the ancients held that it was produced by spontaneous generation, and others improved on that by adding that truffles were formed where lightning had struck. Theophrastus recognized them cor-

Truffle. *Engraving from Urbain Dubois and Emile Bernard:* La Cuisine Classique, *Paris, 1888*

rectly as plants, but Pliny found it difficult to believe that a plant could grow without roots. "We know for a fact," he wrote, "that when Lartius Licinius, an official of praetorian rank, was serving as Minister of Justice at Cartagena in Spain a few years ago, he happened when biting on a truffle to come on a denarius contained inside it which bent his front teeth. This clearly shows that truffles are lumps of earthy substance balled together." To this day there are Spaniards who believe that the truffle is a product of the Devil, partly perhaps because the ground where it is found often presents a devastated appearance, as though it had been scorched by infernal fires. They are "the jewels of poor soils," Colette put it, absolving the Devil. Yet even in this century a malignant power has been attributed to these mushrooms, which, it is held, becomes more potent at night. A French writer advised anyone who discovered that he was traversing truffle territory at night to cross himself quickly three times for protection.

The origin of the truffle is unknown [wrote Brillat-Savarin]. We find it, but we do not know how it is born nor how it grows. The most skillful men have busied themselves with it, they have believed that they had identified its seeds, they have promised that they would sow it at will. Vain efforts! Lying promises! Their plantings have never been followed by crops.

The attempt to grow truffles goes back at least 175 years, during which time triumphant claims of success have been uttered from time to time—followed, invariably, by silence. One of the first came from a French peasant who, early in the nineteenth century, planted acorns from "truffle oaks" (the scrub oaks around which truffles are oftenest found) in truffle territory and attributed truffles found there ten or fifteen years later to his acorns; but nobody else has succeeded in achieving this result since. Strenuous efforts to cultivate truffles were made about 1870, when phylloxera devastated the vineyards of Périgord and the Quercy, forcing landholders to seek other sources of revenue; but an increase of the harvest at this time seems to have been the result of more intensive truffle hunting rather than of any increase in the number of truffles. Seedling oaks have been planted in the hope that they would encourage the development of satellite truffles, without significant success; and pieces of truffles or truffles themselves have been buried in what seemed propitious soil, and the ground has been soaked with water in which truffles had been steeped. "Wasted effort," wrote *Le Monde* in January 1978. "The truffle is a wild and fantastic vegetable, whose underground growth escapes all observation and defies all prediction."

One month after this pessimistic conclusion, the French National Institute for Agronomics announced that it had produced twenty cultivated truffles which had taken three and a half years to grow after a seeding of truffle spores accompanied by the planting of oak saplings. The first, it was reported, weighed 170 grams, nearly six ounces, a good size, quality undescribed. But at the time of writing it is still not possible, and will not be possible for several years, to assert that the problem of cultivating truffles has been solved. The planting, in 1974, had been a large one—150,000 oak seedlings, covering an area of about 7500 acres in a number of plantations on land chosen because it seemed suitable for truffles: who can say that this much land might not have developed twenty truffles in three and a half years even if the oaks had never been planted and the spores never sown?—and three and a half years should theoretically have been too little time to permit a truffle to reach this size and too little time also to permit an oak sapling to contribute to its growth.

The truffle has for centuries been celebrated with extravagant praise. The most common epithet for it is "black diamond," perhaps originated by Brillat-Savarin, who called it "the black diamond of the kitchen"; it has also been called the "black pearl." George Sand, in a kittenish moment, referred to the truffle as "the fairy apple." Alexandre Dumas, who said that it "holds the first place among mushrooms," called it, in bad Latin, the "*sacro sanctorum*" of gourmets. For the Marquis de Cussy it was "the underground empress," for James de Coquet "a fragrant nugget," and for Fulbert-Dumonteil "the divine tuber."

I did not go overboard about the truffle myself in *The Food of France*, where I wrote that "on those rare occasions when truffles are served relatively alone, their own taste can be detected as a rather faint licorice flavor." The fact is that I had not then ever tasted a really first-class truffle, but I didn't know it; and besides, I had been subjected to an experience which should have put me off truffles forever. In an unwary moment I had consented to be filmed eating *truffes sous les cendres* for a television short on Paris restaurants, a process which I had assumed would take about half an hour. I ate truffles-cooked-in-the-ashes for five hours without a break—the same truffles, which by the end of the session had become thoroughly tired, and so had I. I felt that I never wanted to see a truffle again.

Several years later I was invited to the opening of a new Parisian restaurant owned by a man who was a specialist in the foods of the French southwest—truffle country. Truffles were present, beautiful truffles which should have been painted by Van Gogh—as large as tangerines, almost black, with a suggestion of purple, attractively pebbled, and glistening as though they had just been oiled. They were there to admire, not to eat: they were too precious to be lavished, free, on guests. But it happened that I was standing between the Admiral de Toulouse-Lautrec and the restaurant owner when he steeled himself to make the supreme sacrifice. I did not rate such magnificent treatment, but the admiral did—not because he was an admiral, not because he was an authentic member of the famous painter's family, but because his wife was Mapie de Toulouse-Lautrec, the Mary Margaret McBride of France (I purposely avoid comparison with present practitioners of public gastronomy out of cowardice), who was not present. Our host unlocked one of the glass cases behind which his truffles beamed at us, removed one, and handed it to the admiral, who regarded it with misgiving. "Here," he said, thrusting it at me. "*You're* the food expert." I bit full into it and my mouth was flooded with what was probably the most delicious taste I have ever encountered in my entire life, simultaneously rich, subtle and undescribable. I ate it all, while the other guests regarded me with loathing.

"Rather faint licorice flavor" indeed! There was no suggestion of licorice, nor of any other fragrance I could recollect. I find it quite impossible to pass on any idea of its taste. If I say it was as sturdy as meat, I will start you off on a completely wrong track as to its savor. If I say it was as unctuous and aromatic as chocolate, I will do the same. Truffles taste like truffles, and like nothing else whatsoever; and it is a rare, rare privilege to be able to taste a fresh truffle of this quality. I never have since, though I have occasionally come across truffles which redeemed those I had reduced to chewing gum for the television camera—at Rocamadour and Sarlat, in the heart of French truffle country, and in Perugia, in the heart of Umbrian truffle country.

The Umbrian truffles seemed to me quite rich, but they did not match the French samplings, which I assume were Périgord truffles, reputed since the end of the fifteenth century to be the best of the forty-two botanically recognized species. Périgord truffles are not restricted to the Périgord; indeed, almost none of them come from there today, for the truffle fields of that area became exhausted many years ago and were almost unanimously abandoned, as yielding too few truffles to be worth hunting for; but after its long resting period, the Périgord country seems now to be recuperating. Meanwhile the most important truffle region of France has become the Quercy, capital Cahors, just south of Périgord. (Quercy comes from the Latin *quercus*, "oak," the tree with which the truffle is most frequently associated.) The truffles of this province and also of the Vaucluse, good truffle country too, as well as of one or two other minor truffle centers, are authentic Périgord truffles, for this is not a place name, but the popular equivalent of a species name. The Périgord truffle is *Tuber melanosperm*, also called the black truffle—in the Périgord dialect, the *truffaïro* (*negro soumo l'amò d'un domna*, "black as a damned soul"). It is indeed black or a very dark brown on the outside; inside, the flesh (technically the gleba) is whitish to begin with, but as it ripens passes through gray to brown. The mature truffle is a dark brown inside, but not uniformly so; it gives a marbled appearance, and is threaded with very fine white veins.

The second best truffle, in common opinion, is *T. magnatum*, the white truffle of northern Italy, which grows especially in the region of Alba (the Umbrian truffle mentioned above was black, not white). Its flesh is described poetically in the Italian Rinaldi-Tyndalo mushroom encyclopedia as "rosy white, then silver amethystine," and, like the Périgord truffle, it appears to be marbled. The odor is described as like a mixture of garlic and cheese, and almost everybody agrees that it has a faint taste of garlic (there is a good deal of sulfur in truffles, including Périgord truffles, which is principally what accounts for the flavor of garlic). I did not myself note a garlic taste on the only occasion when I have eaten white truffles, and though it is usually reported that their taste is stronger than that of black truffles, it seemed to me to be rather too thin to justify the praise lavished on that species; but after having so badly underestimated the black truffle on the basis of insufficient experience, I am not going to base any opinion on the strength of a single sampling. I shall assume that the white truffles I met were not the best representatives of their type. White truffles, unlike black truffles, are never cooked. They are usually sliced thin and sprinkled over whatever dish they are to adorn; if it is a hot dish, they are added to it at the last moment, after the cooking is over.

In France, where there are between fifteen and twenty thousand professional truffle gatherers, all small operators, there are, besides the Périgord truffle, other black, brown, gray, violet and white truffles of several species, ranging in flavor from "extreme succulence to pale banality"—most of them closer to the banal side. One rarely hears specific mention of the other kinds. I have come across references to an Italian variety, black outside and white inside, described as "without much flavor." Of the gray truffle, Dumas wrote that it was "almost as delicate as the white truffle" of northern Italy, but Colette described it as "almost insipid." I do not know the species of Alsatian truffles, of which there are in any case not many, but an eighteenth-century historian of cooking wrote that though they were inferior to Périgord truffles, "they have nevertheless their own special perfume and their own charm."

The truffle is pretty much unsung in English literature, for it seems to have short-changed English-speaking countries. The only edible variety in the British Isles is *T. aestivus*, the summer truffle, dark brown or black, with an aromatic odor but not much taste. Found oftener in association with beeches than with oaks, it is the best Britain can do. (There is also a winter truffle, *T. brumale*, dark and fragrant, which I suspect may be the kind I encountered in Umbria.) The situation is even sadder in the United States, where there are perhaps as many as thirty varieties of truffles, none of which make particularly good eating. Every once in a while somebody discovers truffles there and glimpses fortune ahead, only to suffer disappointment. This happens oftenest in Oregon and California, but the truffles there are neither numerous enough nor good enough to be worth gathering; they have also appeared occasionally in Tennessee, North Carolina and Vermont.

A number of writers nowadays think Juvenal went overboard in his praise of Libyan truffles. According to Brillat-Savarin, those tubers had whitish or reddish flesh, in contrast to the brownish flesh of all the best truffles of today, with the exception of the Italian white truffle. Was the tuber he was talking about really a truffle? The truffle is normally a mushroom of the temperate zone; there seem to be no truffles in Africa today (there is reported to be a white truffle in Morocco, but I have not been able to pin it down). What does appear in Africa, and specifically in Libya, is a tuber of the genus *Terfezia*, hence not a truffle, though for want of a better name it is sometimes called "truffle" in English, and sometimes the "desert truffle" in French, but usually *terfas*. It looks something like a truffle, and exists in black and red varieties. I suspect that this may also be the "truffle" found in the Kalahari Desert of Botswana. If there is a real truffle in Africa, the United Nations Food and Agricultural Organization has not heard about it.

"How do you prefer your truffles?" an anxious hostess who was preparing to take the risk of inviting him to dinner asked the famous gourmet Curnonsky. "In great quantity, madame," he replied. "In great quantity." This may have taken her aback, but it was the right answer. If you want to be able really to taste a truffle, you need enough of it to provide a fair sample. "Truffles are a luxury," James de Coquet wrote, "and the first requirement of luxury is that you should not have to economize. A capon with no truffles at all is better than one which has been truffled, but not enough." A character in a book of the nineteenth-century gastronomic writer Charles Monselet cried, "I don't want truffles cut into little pieces, so scarce that you have to scrape the insides of your chicken to find a few shavings; no, I want avalanches of truffles, *I want too much of them.*"

Robert J. Courtine, a contemporary French gastronomic writer, inveighs perhaps a little too vehemently against the use of bits and snippets of truffle to ornament various dishes, in which their taste is often imperceptible. He admits the use of small pieces of truffle only for Périgueux sauce, a marvelous confection as made by my mother-in-law, a native of the Périgord, but you are not likely to find its equal in restaurants—she takes two days to produce it. On one occasion Courtine conceded grudgingly that pieces of truffle might be permissible in the classic Lyons specialty, chicken in half-mourning, where the mourning note is provided by black truffles, or in pheasant Suvarov, where they are an essential ingredient of the dish, not a mere decoration; but he continued to object to the classic combination of truffle in foie gras. It may have been his influence which caused a Paris restaurant to serve a slab of pure untruffled foie gras, with a whole fresh truffle on the side, a dish for kings—wealthy kings. In the days of the truffle's glory, the proportion of truffles to foie gras was such that it was remarked that instead of truffled foie gras this preparation should have been called "foie-gras'd truffles." Nowadays such a lavish use of truffles would price this marriage off the menu, for expensive as foie gras may be, truffles, volume for volume or weight for weight, are much more so. Another dish I have not seen on a menu for a long time, even in the most expensive restaurants, is the one Charles Chaplin used as a symbol of snobbery in *A Woman of Paris*—truffles cooked in champagne.

Truffles are never likely to descend to a price within reach of the average consumer, for the demand increases and the supply diminishes each year. In 1892, described as "the year of grace" by Périgord truffle gatherers, 2000 tons of truffles were harvested in France. Just before World War I the figure had dropped to 300 tons, by the 1950s to 100, in 1971 to 85, and it now varies between 25 and 150 tons annually, depending chiefly on the weather. France is the world's most important producer of truffles, and enjoys a virtual monopoly of them, for it buys most of the surplus truffles of Italy and Spain, the only other truffle-exporting countries. The French demand alone is greater than the French supply; but France exports about one-third of her superior truffles, making do herself with the less prestigious varieties she buys from the others. Even if the present attempts at the artificial planting of truffles succeed, their price is not likely to drop very much, for what has always made truffles expensive is the cost of gathering them. It is a hit-or-miss affair at best: "Truffles is not farming, it's luck," one producer told John Hess. Since the truffle grows underground, the first problem is to find it, and the second to ease it up gently in order not to disturb the mycelium and prevent it from giving birth to more truffles. This means expenditure of care and time in an era when time is becoming more and more costly, and the employment of hand labor in an era when hand labor also is becoming more and more costly.

For the detection of the tubers, truffle hunters have used sows, dogs, goats (in Sardinia), bear cubs (in Russia, or so I am told), the water-witch's wand (with indifferent success) and the know-how of the skilled observer. Under the last heading, it is not difficult to recognize probable truffle ground because of its scorched-earth appearance, but as this may cover a circle with a radius of 150 feet or more around the nourishing tree, trying to locate the exact spots at which the tubers, walnut-sized or larger, are hiding remains a puzzle. However, though most truffles grow well below the surface, often as deep as a foot, a large one buried less deeply sometimes cracks the soil, where a trained eye can detect its presence. An easier sign for the experienced truffle hunter to read is the presence of flies, of which several species try to lay their eggs in truffles—particularly one which looks like a small wasp, and another which is blue. If a swarm of them hovers over a certain spot, there is probably a truffle beneath it. Some truffle hunters claim to have a sense of smell sufficiently acute to locate truffles, but it is more common to have recourse to animals better endowed olfactorily by nature; even if a man were their equal he would be handicapped over pigs and dogs by wearing his nose higher from the ground, unless he elected to crawl over the terrain on hands and knees.

Truffles are often sought at night, especially in Italy. It is usually explained that this is because the odor of truffles is stronger then, but it may be suspected that there is another reason: to make it difficult for spies to spot the exact location where a truffle has been found. Another tuber may be expected to form in the same location, and if someone else knows where that is, the landowner may arrive to gather his next truffle only to find that someone has been there before him. Night truffle digging is done with the aid of a small flashlight, which does not illuminate a sufficient area to help a truffle thief to find the right place. Poachers are one of the banes of the truffle-land owner; during the season, about November through February, Sunday promenaders, especially if they are accompanied by dogs, are regarded with suspicion.

As is usually the case with expensive foods, fraud is rampant in the truffle market. At the level of the first sale, by the truffle digger to the wholesaler, tunnels bored into truffles by insects are frequently filled skillfully with clay or even with lead, the latter less commonly, for much of this metal would make the truffle too heavy and the buyer suspicious. For foreign markets, where there is little familiarity with this tuber, gray truffles are often dyed black to make them look like the prized Périgord variety. The limit has been reached in Holland and the United States, where traders offer what they refer to disarmingly as "fantasy truffles"—black balls of blood, starch and egg yolk treated with synthetic truffle flavoring. When truffles enter into other foods—such as foie gras—they may be replaced by the mushrooms which the French have named "death trumpets," possibly to discourage others from finding out how good they are. This is not a very serious fraud, for you do get a substitute of excellent flavor, but you pay truffle prices for it.

Truffles are often credited with aphrodisiac virtues, and though one is tempted to ask what isn't, the report in this case is more insistent than in most others. True or not, Mme. de Pompadour believed it, and stuffed herself with truffles, among other things, to maintain an ardor which was not natural to her, for the benefit of the king. No less an authority than Brillat-Savarin (but he was only relaying what others had said) wrote that eating truffles "permitted the stuttering and underpowered Emperor Claudius not to lose face before his young and impetuous wife, Messalina"; but if Juvenal was right, Messalina had slight need of Claudius, being bountifully busied elsewhere, and when she herself fed him mushrooms, it was not truffles, to invigorate him, but a type of fungus selected to do quite the opposite. I have read in a magazine article that it was to truffles "that Henry IV owed his prowess in the bedroom," but most accounts agree that the gallant French monarch required no other stimulant than the presence of an attractive woman. We are told also that one of Napoleon's generals advised him to eat truffles to increase his potency, but not whether Napoleon took his advice, and I have read also, authority unstated, that Louis XIV ate a pound of them a day. No doubt he did: he was a glutton.

Brillat-Savarin devoted exhaustive research to this question, and while he remarked that truffles provoked dreaming, like many mildly exciting foods, he concluded cautiously that "the truffle is not at all a positive aphrodisiac; but it can, on certain occasions, make women more tender and men more amiable."

Truffles might very well act as a general stimulant to the system, for they contain a not inconsiderable dosage of invigorating mineral salts—iron, for instance. Balzac testified to the help this food gave him in his work of creation. "If one truffle falls on my plate," he wrote, "that will suffice: it is the egg which immediately hatches ten characters for my *Comédie Humaine*."

The worst gastronomic use ever made of the truffle was probably that committed by Delmonico's, the famous New York restaurant, which, attempting to outdo itself for a gala dinner, created ice cream (flavor unspecified) with truffles—"strange to say, very good," said Ward McAllister, who was strange too.

TUB
stands for

tubers, the edible underground growth of many food plants, whose succeeding generations are ordinarily replicas of themselves, except in Uighuristan, where a tuber formed from the sap of *esca* trees gave birth to the area's first king, so Marco Polo tells us; for the **tuber-root** of North America, whose boiled roots used to be eaten by many Indian tribes, whose seed pods were eaten by the Sioux along with sugar made from its flowers, and whose tender shoots were prepared like asparagus by Canadian Indians; and for the **tub-gurnard** or **tub-fish**, the largest of the gurnards and the tastiest in more senses than one, for not only does it make good eating, but it is itself provided with taste buds curiously placed on the spines of its fins.

TUL
stands for

tule, the name given to the bulrush in California, where its roots are eaten by the Sierra Indians, and the **tule perch**, which, since it lives in California's Sacramento River, may be suspected of taking its name from the bulrush; and for **tulips**, whose bulbs are poisonous according to James Trager but not according to John Gerard, who wrote that "the roots preserved with sugar, or otherwise dressed, may be eaten, and are not unpleasant nor any way offensive meat, but rather good and nourishing," as the Dutch discovered when they ate them during food shortages in World War II.

TUN
stands for

tuna, an edible cactus of subtropical America, whose fruit fed the army of Cortez in Mexico in 1519 when there was nothing much else to eat, and today, transplanted to Sicily, is apparently at its best on the slopes of Mount Etna; and also, of course, for

TUNA, the fish. The city of Trapani, on the western coast of Sicily, derives a double revenue from tuna—a name which covers a whole family of fishes, including some of the most important in the world for food. Its primary revenue, of course, is derived from the sale of the fish (Sicily catches one-half of all the tuna taken off Italy, and Trapani alone takes 10,000 fish yearly, average weight 530 pounds). But there is a second revenue derived from the influx of tourists who visit the region each spring to revel in the *mattanza del tonno*, the slaughter of the tuna. It assumes there the aspect of a sacrificial rite, a bloody one, which, it has been asserted, goes back to Phoenician times. We know that the ancient Greeks were acquainted with this fashion of taking tuna, for Aeschylus compared their slaughter with the massacre of the Persians at Salamis. Homer and Oppian both wrote about harpooning tuna with tridents, a method still used by Sardinians in the Gulf of Oristano.

At Trapani, tuna are taken in May or June by means of immense fixed nets called *isole* (islands) from half a mile to three miles long. The capture of the fish is carried out under the direction of an absolute monarch, *il rais* (from the Arabic for "chief," a reminder that Sicily was once ruled by the Saracens). Chosen for his experience and his knowledge of the habits of tuna, the *rais* makes all the decisions. He determines when the nets shall be set, and where, depending on the known paths taken by the migrating fish, the direction of the currents and certain variable factors which point to the direction the great shoals of fish will take. They swim unsuspectingly into the nets, whose dimensions are such that they can hardly realize that they are entering an enclosure. Each *isola* is divided into a series of compartments which the fish can enter, but from which they cannot get out; the pen farthest from the entrance is "the chamber of death." When it is full, a horizontal net stretched along the bottom is raised, bringing the imprisoned tuna within reach of gaffs or boathooks, with whose aid they are hoisted onto the deck of a boat lying parallel to the nets and killed. At some places in the Mediterranean, the fishermen jump directly into the net to stab the fish to death, an even bloodier spectacle, which turns the surrounding sea red.

Tuna react curiously in the face of violent death, according to Dr. Vito Fodera in *The Sicilian Tuna Trap*: "The first tuna of the take are the most difficult to haul aboard; after about ten minutes, the fish which remain in the death chamber either kill each other by fighting, or else, half dead, let themselves be taken easily." This behavior is mysterious to fishermen, especially the sudden passivity of a strong and active fish which resigns itself to being slaughtered without resistance. Perhaps we can explain it by turning from fishermen to biologists.

These exceedingly active fish literally never rest [write John and Mildred Teal in *The Sargasso Sea*]. They swim actively and continuously throughout their lives, a staggering fact from the human viewpoint since our body machinery must idle a number of hours out of every day, if we are to live. The giant tuna . . . could not idle if they wanted to, for they must swim to breathe. [They have no] pumping mechanism and so . . . must swim fast enough to ram water through their open mouths and over their gills.

The behavior of the trapped tuna thus becomes plain: a fish which must move to live is immobilized by the restricted dimensions of the death chamber. The tuna do not attack each other, except accidentally; they are thrashing about, trying to beat water by their gills to renew their supply of oxygen. When they fail, they become passive because they are, indeed, literally half dead, from asphyxiation.

To maintain a sufficient oxygen supply, tuna apparently have to move through the water at a rate of twenty body lengths a second—20 to 30 knots. It is believed that they can reach 45 miles an hour (and perhaps 50 in spurts), which would make them the fastest fish in the ocean with the exception of sailfish. Magellan's men were impressed by the speed of the albacore, a small tuna, when they saw it pursuing flying fish off Patagonia. Despite the resistance of the water, it swam faster than the flying fish could rocket through the air:

When any of these . . . fish encounter any of these flying fish, the flying fish immediately leap out of the water and fly as far as a bowshot without wetting their wings. And the other fish dart under the shadows of the flying fish, and no sooner do they fall into the water, than they are immediately seized and eaten.

The bluefin tuna, the monarch of the family, which "weighs up to sixteen hundred pounds, comparable to a Hereford bull," the Teals put it (Maurice and Robert Burton make it eighteen hundred), is probably the strongest swimmer of the ocean, because of other physical peculiarities, some of them almost too obvious to mention, like its streamlined body; but others are less visible and more complex.

How is it possible for these large fish to maintain such speeds—speeds usually associated with warm-bloodedness [ask the Teals]? . . . Tuna should never have a body temperature different from the water in which they swim, yet they have. Francis Carey, a physiologist at Woods Hole [the Woods Hole Oceanographic Institute of Massachusetts], with John Teal and other colleagues . . . discovered a "countercurrent heat exchanger" within the fish's muscles, similar to the structures used in heating and cooling devices such as refrigerators, in which heat passes between two fluids flowing in opposite directions. . . . In tuna, venous blood leaves the muscles, where most of the heat is produced, and flows back toward the heart and the gills. The cold arterial blood, loaded with oxygen, flows in from the gills. They meet in an intermingling of closely packed vessels where both types of blood flow in opposite directions. . . . By the time the arterial blood reaches the muscles it is nearly as warm as the venous blood leaving it at that point, and by the time the venous blood has left the heat exchanger, it is nearly as cold as the incoming arterial blood: that is, the same temperature as the outside water.

But the fish, internally, is *warmer* than the water in which it swims. (Nature, never willing to squander a good trick on a single organism, uses approximately the same situation to maintain warmth in a cold environment for the benefit of an animal far removed from the tuna—the caribou.)

There are other specializations in the tuna—in the gills, for instance—which account for its being a warm-blooded fish and lend it its endurance and speed. Muscular contractions occur more readily at warm than at cool temperatures. Great muscular effort normally requires a plentiful supply of blood; that is why strong-flying migratory birds have darker meat than barnyard fowls. Similarly, the strongest swimmer among the tunas, the bluefin, has the darkest flesh, deep red (it is sometimes called the red tuna), which apparently frightens Americans and makes them reluctant to eat it.

Despite American misgivings, it may be that the bluefin tuna, *Thunnus thynnus*, is the kind most widely consumed, for it is the one preferred for eating raw by the Japanese, the world's greatest fanciers of seafood. Far from being put off by its dark red color (the lean meat; the fattier parts are pink), the Japanese delight in it, for it promotes the exercise of one of their favorite arts—converting dishes of food into works of nonfigurative art. Large cubes or rectangles of red tuna are assembled together with foods of other colors on the plate; the chunks of tuna resemble raw beef in hue and texture, and indeed its taste has been described as like that of refrigerated raw roast beef. (I find another description of its flavor as falling "somewhere between cold raw beef and raw shellfish," a concept at which my mind boggles.) When they plan to eat tuna raw, usually in spring or early summer, when fresh fish are more plentiful, the Japanese are extremely fussy about the quality of the tuna they buy. Northern Pacific tuna commands the highest price because, fished nearest home, it will be fresher than tuna brought from the Indian or Atlantic Ocean, and also because it contains a larger proportion of the pink fatty *toro,* which they particularly like (tuna as a whole is *maguro*).

Africans are fond of bluefin tuna too, but northern Europeans are apt to find the firm, close-textured flesh rather heavy and oily. Tuna is indeed a fat fish, but there are ways of getting around this. Newfoundlanders, who do not share the American prejudice against red meat, maintain that bluefin is not in demand as a fresh fish in the United States because nobody there knows how to cook it. Their formula is to bake a four-inch slab of it and then cut off the bottom inch, in which the oil will have become concentrated during the cooking.

The best tuna fish I have ever come across [Elizabeth David wrote in *Italian Food*] was in Sardinia. It was *ventresca* (stomach), cut into thin slices, brushed with oil, and breaded. It was tender and delicate, and bore no relation to the boot-like slabs of tuna stewed in tomato sauce which one gets on the south coast of France . . . and in Italy too. To have good tuna fish, it is essential to ask for *ventresca.*

I would suspect this to be bluefin tuna because that is the species Sardinian fishermen usually take; it becomes a certainty a few sentences later when Miss David describes it as "of an appetizing creamy-pink color"—the lighter-colored stomach meat which the Japanese call *toro.*

Canned, bluefin tuna is marketed as Dark Meat Tuna or Tano. Both its roe and milt are excellent.

By official American standards, the choicest tuna is the albacore, *Thunnus alalunga,* alias the long-finned albacore, the white tuna or the germon, the only one which can legally be labeled White Meat Tuna. Abundant in the Pacific, the albacore is fished by fleets from Japan and Hawaii

TUNA. *Photograph by Robert C. Murphy:* Tuna, Yellow-Fin on Deck of Boat

and is the fish which the American tuna fleet based at San Diego takes from California southward down the South American coast at least as far as Ecuador, which has caused some difficulties with that country. It is also important on the eastern side of the Atlantic, where it is taken under the name "germon" from Brittany to Mauritania. The albacore is much smaller than the bluefin, with a top length of about four feet, corresponding to a weight of 65 pounds. It has, of course, lighter-colored flesh. Blander in flavor than the bluefin, it is the variety most prized for eating fresh, but it is not easy to find it fresh. Most of it nowadays is hustled into cans before fanciers of fresh fish can get to it, a process which may have begun aboard the boats before they have even touched port.

It is doubtful whether many people notice the subtle difference between White Meat Tuna and Light Meat Tuna, or if they do, know which is supposed to be the better. The second label is supposed to mark a slightly inferior sort; two species may be so designated, but what is in a can thus marked is something of a gamble. It may be all yellowfin tuna, one of the two permissible species; it may be all skipjack, the other; it may be a mixture of the two; and even, if nobody is looking, some young bluefin, which has not yet acquired the dark color of the adult, may have been slipped in. (Still lower grades are sometimes half fish and half soybean flour, the latter treated with artificial flavoring to make it taste like tuna.)

Yellowfin tuna, *Thunnus albacares*, is also called albacore in tropical Africa, where it is very widely eaten. It is fished particularly in a five-million-square-mile area in the Pacific, where eight nations have agreed to limit the take, and one of them, the United States, makes efforts to do so. Six other nations fish yellowfin in this area too, but break no agreements because they haven't subscribed to any. The yellowfin can reach 45 pounds, but commercial fishermen prefer to take it at 20 to 30 pounds, for as it grows older it becomes not only tougher but also darker, a quality disliked by consumers. Yellowfin are less migratory in their habits than other tunas, preferring to stay in warm water.

The skipjack, *Katsuwonus palamis* (a Japanese name because it is very common in Japanese waters), alias the lostao, the oceanic bonito, or the striped or striped-belly bonito (because of the parallel longitudinal dark-blue stripes on its white stomach), reaches a length of nearly three feet. It prefers wide waters, seldom entering the Mediterranean, for instance, although it is a small fish, for a tuna, usually taken between 6 and 15 pounds. Its meat is darker than that of the yellowfin, but tender and of soft texture.

There is also a small tuna, *Thynnus thunina* or *Euthynnus alletteratus—alletteratus* because it bears marks on the back which look as if someone had been scribbling on it in an unknown language. This accounts also for its popular name *letterato* in Italian, though its proper name there is *tonnetto*, and its Turkish name *yazili orkinos*, which means "writing on the fish." Little or not, it can reach a length of more than three and a half feet. It is more widely eaten than the bluefin in countries which are put off by the latter's dark color, and its firm fat tasty flesh is appreciated by many people who find in its flavor a suggestion of veal. It was probably this species which the nineteenth-century gastronomic writer Grimod de la Reynière called "Charterhouse veal," being the closest approach to meat that the ascetic Carthusians could permit themselves to eat. Alexandre Dumas wrote, "You might say that it is neither meat nor fish."

Man has been eating tuna since prehistoric times. Its bones have been found in kitchen middens dating from Upper Paleolithic to Iron Age times in northern Europe, at the upper limit of its range, though it had formidable competition from the two most important food fishes of that region, the herring and the cod. Neither of these entered the Mediterranean, so the tuna, which is believed to have been taken there in net traps in Neolithic times, may well have been the most important food fish in the classical world, in terms of volume at least. We know from Homer that in his day it was a favorite food of the Greeks, who consecrated it to Diana; it was still much appreciated in Periclean times. The rich ate the fresh fish marinated in liquids rendered aromatic by exotic spices from Asia; salted, it was the mainstay of the poor, the cheapest product of the sea. It was also preserved in oil, as it is today. The Greeks must have consumed more than they could catch themselves, for they imported dried or salted tuna from the Black Sea. Perhaps Greece was less favorably situated for tuna fishing than Sicily or Sardinia, its spawning centers: those of the eastern Mediterranean seem to have spawned in the Black Sea. Pliny suggested that the Golden Horn was so called because its abundance of tuna gave it wealth; many Byzantine coins carried representations of this fish. Archestratus criticized the importation of salt tuna; he wrote that only fresh tuna from Byzantium should be eaten, "in the autumn, what time the Pleiad is setting."

On the opposite shore of the Mediterranean, tuna was served at Carthaginian wedding banquets; on the Roman side it was one of the fish from whose fermented intestines the Romans made their all-purpose seasoning, *garum*. Aristotle thought that the tuna which spawned off the Italian coast came from the Atlantic to breed, a theory which has been disputed by some modern ichthyologists who believe that Mediterranean tuna stay in that sea, but in deep water except at the spawning season. Aristotle still has some support, however. The fact is that among the many things we do not know about tuna are the itineraries of their migrations.

We do not hear much about tuna during the Middle Ages, probably because herring and cod were more important. One of the rare reports was brought back from Hormuz by Marco Polo: "The natives do not eat our sort of food, because a diet of wheaten bread and meat would make them ill. To keep well, they eat dates and salt fish, that is, tunny; and on this diet they thrive." The anonymous *Ménagier de Paris* (1393) does not mention tuna, unless it is hiding under some Old French word unknown to me. In Renaissance times it was marinated; eating it thus treated offered the closest approach to fresh fish when tuna were out of season, preferable to the same fish salted or dried.

Since then tuna has seemed to be losing favor, most recently, perhaps, because of increased avoidance of fat or oily foods, and fewer fish have been taken. The number of fixed net-traps has been slowly diminishing for centuries, until only about a hundred remain, along the coasts of Sicily, Sardinia, other places in Italy, Yugoslavia, Turkey and Libya, and in the Atlantic a few off France and Portugal. The Portuguese traps used to net about 20,000 fish a year. In 1972 they took two. Nobody bothered to set them again in 1973. Up to the 1950s as many as 150,000 fish a year were being taken in the North Atlantic; in 1973 the number had dwindled to 2100. The Norwegians, who had been accustomed to catching over 10,000 tons of tuna in the 1950s, took only 100 fish in 1973. Tuna accounted for only 3 percent of the total world catch of food fish.

But then herring, probably the world's number one food fish, unless it was the cod, became increasingly scarce, the victim of enormous bottom-scraping fishing boats. Cod, if it was not already number one, succeeded to that rank, and is now disappearing under the onslaughts of enormous bottom-scraping fishing boats. Tuna, suddenly viewed as number three, became number one, and is now under attack from enormous bottom-scraping fishing boats. Tuna ships use enormous seines covering 25 acres, capable of sinking 6500 feet and bringing up a ton of fish at each haul. Once these fish were taken only when they came inshore to spawn, spotted from towers on the shore or from the crows'-nests of ships. Today they are sought in deep waters, detected by infrared rays, helicopters, planes and even satellites. Tuna are even more vulnerable to these tactics than were herring or cod, because of their growth pattern.

Bluefins weigh between 55 and 60 pounds at four years, well worth taking, and they are. But a four-year-old bluefin is not adult. It does not begin to reproduce until the age of five, and it starts slowly; it reaches full fecundity only when it is ten years old and weighs about 320 pounds. Its prime occurs at thirteen or fourteen years, when it weighs from 440 to 660 pounds, and is eight or nine feet long. Who can wait fourteen years for a tuna to grow, with the demand constantly increasing? In the last fifteen years, world consumption has almost doubled, to 1.5 million tons a year. Nobody waits any longer for 500-pounders, or even for 300-pounders. As the demand increases, the take increases, and it is made up of ever smaller fish, for there are few big ones left. The point is being approached where all the tuna big enough to reproduce will have been taken; and then, suddenly, there will be no more tuna.

TUR

stands for

the **turban shell**, a marine snail plentiful on the Pacific coast of the United States, edible though small, but the Atlantic coast species is not big enough to bother with; for the **turbot**, best of the FLATFISH, which one fussy expert has included in his list of the only five food fish worth eating; for the **turkey berry**, which grows on the banks of the Orinoco; for the **turkeyfish**, one of the showiest of the scorpionfishes; for the **Turkish fish**, a category unknown to ichthyologists, which for Italians means any fat fish, especially if it is blue; for the **Turkish gram**, a sort of bean which in India serves oftener to feed animals than man; for **Turkish wheat**, one of the many names given to maize when Europeans first became conscious of it; for the **Turk's-cap**, a sort of lily whose bulb is or was eaten by the Cossacks of the Volga, which had better not be confused with another plant of the same name, for the latter is poisonous; for the **turnip bean**, whose young pods are eaten in tropical countries, but the ripe grains are avoided because they are toxic; for **turnip-rooted parsley**, grown, unlike most PARSLEY, for its roots more than for its leaves; for the **turnstone**, an edible shore bird whose name comes from its habit of looking under stones for food, a process in which it shows great ingenuity, allowing itself a running start to upset a stone a little too large for it to lift and enlisting the help of several of its fellows to unbalance even larger ones; for **turpentine**, which when it is the Cyprus variety is identical with terebinth; for the **turtle**, which is less eaten now than in the early nineteenth century, when valiant American housewives bought live 60-pound sea turtles and began by cutting off their heads to make turtle soup, a dish disdained in Madagascar, where they pen and force-feed turtles like geese, and for the same purpose, to obtain foie gras; and for the **turtledove**, whose destruction distressed Darwin in the Galápagos Islands.

And **TUR** also stands for

TURKEY. "I wish the eagle had not been chosen as the representative of our country," Benjamin Franklin wrote to his daughter, Sarah Bache, on January 26, 1784. "He is a bird of bad moral character; like those among men who live by sharping and robbing, he is generally poor, and often very lousy. The turkey is a much more respectable bird, and withal a true original native of America."

We may suspect that Franklin wrote this with tongue in cheek, as would have been the case also when, it is said, he advocated putting the turkey on the American flag. However, the turkey was indeed "a true original native of America," provided "America" is taken in its broader sense as referring to the New World as a whole, not solely to the United States. Although the colonizing Europeans found the turkey ubiquitous in North America, it was in all probability not a native of any territory now included within the United States, but of Mexico.

Alexandre Dumas did his best, which turned out to be his worst, to prove Franklin wrong, with the obstinacy and bad faith of a man harboring a personal grudge. Could he have taken for himself the acerbic observation of Brillat-Savarin (though he was only twenty-four when Brillat-Savarin died)? "Those who always want to know more than anybody else," Brillat-Savarin had written, "have said that the turkey was known to the Romans, that it was served at the marriage of Charlemagne"; and he gave his reasons for believing that it was not. Undeterred, Dumas argued that the turkey had been present in the Old World fifteen hundred years before it was found in the New, with a vehemence which did nothing for his reputation as a stickler for historical accuracy, which was in any case virtually non-existent.

Turkeys were known to the Greeks, who called them *Meleagrides* [he wrote] because it was Meleager, king of Macedonia, who brought them to Greece [from where? he doesn't say] in the year of the world 3,559. Some scholars have contested this fact, and have said that they were guinea-fowl; but Pliny describes the turkey in unmistakable fashion. Sophocles, in one of his lost tragedies, introduced a chorus of turkeys who wept on the death of Meleager. . . .

The Romans professed a particular esteem for the turkey. They raised it on their farms. How did they disappear? What epidemic wiped them out? That is something history does not tell us at all. But they became so rare that in the end they were put into cages, like parrots today. . . .

In 1432, the ships of Jacques Coeur brought the first turkeys back from India. . . . Our opinion is therefore not that of most scholars, who say that the turkey comes from America.

Thus Dumas the historian. His account requires, perhaps, a little annotation. For instance:

1. It may be supposed that Sophocles, in his conveniently lost tragedy, told the Meleager story in the same terms as Homer. According to Homer the Meleagrides were the sisters of Meleager, who wept inconsolably at his death and were finally turned into guinea hens, whose plumage was spotted by their teardrops—which conforms with the markings of guinea hens, but not with those of turkeys.

2. Pliny's description of an imperfectly identified ancient bird may have been unmistakably a turkey for Dumas; for others it was a guinea fowl.

3. Dumas gives no sources for his account of the sojourn of the turkey in ancient Rome. I have come across his details nowhere else.

4. His information about Jacques Coeur's sailors importing the turkey from India seems to be exclusive to him. No one had ever reported the presence of turkeys in India before they arrived from the New World, introduced, it is thought, by the Portuguese through their trading counter at Goa. Having no word for it, the Indians called it the *peru*, from the place they thought it came from—not a very near miss, for though the potato and the tomato had arrived from Peru, there were probably no turkeys in South America at that time. When the Mogul emperor Jahangir (1569–1627) received a gift of three turkey cocks, he had great difficulty locating hens to mate with them.

Dumas was ignorant of a fact which might have given him a potent argument for the existence of the turkey in Europe, and so was I until an alert reader in Athens wrote me about it in 1976. "The turkey," he informed me, "appears in the marginal decorations of the Bayeux Tapestry. . . . The tapestry dates from about 1087 if my memory is good. [His memory was excellent.] As for the turkey which appears there it is unmistakable both by its tail and its wattles." The Bayeux Tapestry is, as everybody knows, Norman: the

Norsemen maintained settlements in North America, within the turkey's range, from 985 to 1121, dates which straddle that of the tapestry. They may have brought back drawings of this strange and unknown fowl (Dumas' alleged ancient turkey fanciers never achieved a picture of it), or they may even have imported a few birds as a curiosity. If so, they left no progeny.

Brillat-Savarin gave a number of reasons for believing that the turkey was a native of the New World, one of which had been cited by Dumas as evidence to the contrary—the fact that the bird was known in France as the *poule d'inde* (today *dinde*), "hen of India." Brillat-Savarin pointed out that this referred, not to the East Indies, but to the West Indies; the writings of several sixteenth-century chroniclers confirm that the term was so understood at the time. Brillat-Savarin pointed out also that the turkey is found wild nowhere else in the world except in America. He added that, at a time when the fauna of Europe, Asia and Africa were all relatively familiar, the fact that the turkey belonged to the unknown New World was evident because all the Europeans who had come upon it were struck by its foreign appearance, unlike anything they had seen before. At first they could find no name for it, and had to fall back on description. When Bernal Diaz, chronicler of Cortez's conquest of Mexico, visited the Tlatelolco market he reported that "they were selling fowls and birds with great dewlaps." Bartolome de Las Casas wrote that during the Córdoba expedition the Indians brought to them large roasted *gallinas* (hens), as big as peacocks but better eating, whose distinctive feature was a large dewlap. Coronado wrote from the American Southwest that "in this country . . . there are a quantity of native fowls and cocks with great hanging dewlaps."

We do not know who sent, or carried, the first turkey to Europe, but it was certainly not Columbus, who so far as we know never saw one. There were none on the Caribbean islands, understandably enough, for the turkey, a heavy bird, is not a long-distance flyer. It can stay in the air for about a mile, but after that it has to touch ground. Hence the Spaniards did not meet it until they reached the mainland. The earliest date mentioned seems to be 1511, when it is reported, a little dubiously, that Miguel de Passamonte was instructed by the Bishop of Valencia to bring turkeys to Spain, and returned from America with ten birds. Ponce de León, who landed in 1513 in Florida, where turkeys were plentiful, could have collected some, but there is no record that he did: he was not looking for food, he was looking for a mirage. Francisco Fernández de Córdoba saw turkeys in Yucatán in 1517 and Cortez in Mexico in 1519; either could have dispatched birds to Spain. Coronado, a chaser of mirages too (the Seven Cities of Cibola), would have been too late. He apparently did not see a turkey until 1540 or 1541, in the Indian pueblos; by then they were already gracing the tables of Europe.

Cortez would have been a very likely dispatcher of turkeys to Europe; he was familiar enough with them. Bernal Diaz reported that pre-prepared turkey dishes (already!) could be bought in the Mexican markets, including the characteristic dish of turkey with chocolate *molé* sauce, still popular today. For Montezuma's table, he wrote, "they daily cooked turkeys." The Spanish friar Bernardino de Sahagún, shortly after the Spanish conquest of Mexico, confirmed the fact that roast turkey was one of the most important Aztec foods.

Benjamin Franklin was right. The turkey is "a true original native of America." Thomas Haliburton was guilty of an anachronism when, in the nineteenth century, he wrote "as poor [feeble] as Job's turkey, that had to lean against the barn to gobble." Job had no turkey. They are not mentioned in the Bible. There were none in the ancient world.

When the strange foods of the New World began to reach Europe at the turn of the century (the fifteenth to the sixteenth, of course), they were, as a rule, received with suspicion. The tomato and the potato were regarded as potentially

TURKEY *by Claude Monet (1840–1926).* The Turkeys, *oil on canvas*

poisonous, and it took a century or two before anyone ate them with less concern than is given nowadays to testing a new and unknown variety of mushroom. The turkey was an exception. As soon as it arrived it was embraced. This was perhaps because it did not seem entirely strange. Europe knew large birds already, though not quite as large as the turkey. The great bustard, the largest, could reach thirty-two pounds. The wild turkey nearly doubled that, but the first birds brought to Europe were not necessarily record breakers. Indeed, their importers may well have chosen smaller birds deliberately, because they would have been easier to handle than bigger ones—meaning also older ones, less desirable because they were tougher on the plate and weaker in the breeding pen. It is probable that Europe's first turkeys were indeed about bustard size, not large enough to frighten anybody, especially on a platter.

They were already tame birds. The turkeys the Spaniards discovered in Mexico had been domesticated by the Aztecs. Some of the priests who accompanied the soldiers began to raise them on their own farms in the New World and are credited with having transferred them to monastic establishments in the Old—where in Spain, presumably their first stop, is not known, but in France they seem to have been raised first in monasteries in Bourges, and from there spread to the rest of the country.

Just when they first arrived in Europe is not on record, unless you accept the somewhat shaky story that Miguel de Passamonte imported them in 1511. Most historians think that the Spaniards (or somebody else) brought the first turkeys to Europe in 1523 or 1524. This would be consistent with the old English ditty:

Turkey, carp, hops, pickerel and beer
Came into England all in one year.

In France, it has been asserted, the first turkeys were imported during the reign of Francis I by Admiral Philippe de Chabot, which seems to be in conflict with the Bourges story, but Bruyerin-Champier wrote that they did not arrive until later. It could not have been much later, since Bruyerin-Champier was the physician of Francis I, who died in 1547. "A few years ago," Bruyerin-Champier wrote, "certain strange birds reached us, called Indian hens, a name which was given them, I believe, because they were transported into our climate for the first time from the Indian islands [i.e., the West Indies] discovered not long ago by the Portuguese and the Spaniards. Their size is not much different from that of peacocks."

Another clue to the time when turkeys reached France is offered us by the fact that Rabelais mentioned them—but not in the first edition of his works, only in the 1542 edition, which justifies us in assuming that they were then comparatively new. Shakespeare was aware of the turkey too, and must have known what it looked like: "Contemplation makes a rare turkey-cock of him; how he jets under his advanced plumes!" he wrote in *Twelfth Night*; but the turkey would have been an old story in England by then, for *Twelfth Night* was probably written in 1599 or 1600. There is a much earlier reference to this bird, in 1541, when prelates were enjoined from being served more than one of these "greater fowles" at a single meal.

Turkeys, on their arrival, were not appreciated by everybody.

This bird [Charles Estienne wrote in 1564] is a bin of oats, a gulf for victuals, from which no other pleasure can be derived than noise and fury from the adults and a continual chirping from the chicks. The flesh is delicate, but tasteless and hard to digest. That is why it has to be sprinkled [with spices], heavily larded and seasoned. These Indian hens eat as much as mules.

This unfavorable opinion did not prevent turkeys from being served at Mézières on November 26, 1570, at the banquet which marked the marriage of Charles IX of France and Elizabeth of Austria, where it made enough of an impression to decide the lords of Biron and Mesmes to raise turkeys on their estates.

In those days turkeys, when roasted for a ceremonious repast, were brought to the table in full plumage like peacocks, a festive fowl which had been important in Italy until the turkey, better eating whatever Charles Estienne thought, drove it off Italian tables. In England (and in France too), the bird displaced by the turkey as holiday fare was not the peacock, but the goose. As early as 1570, Thomas Tusser had written that the turkey furnished the farmer's Christmas dinner—the "Christmas husbandlie fare."

By the end of the sixteenth century, the turkey was well installed: a German cookbook of that period recorded twenty different ways of serving it. Brillat-Savarin did not tell us how Henri IV preferred it, but he did inform us that "the supper even of kings was sometimes subject to hazard. . . . Henri IV would have had a very frugal repast one evening if he had not had the ingenious idea of inviting to his table the citizen whom he knew was the lucky owner of the only turkey which existed in the city where the king had to spend the night."

In France the bird was so popular in the

Middle Ages that Privat d'Eglemont listed among the little known professions of Paris that of "varnisher of turkey legs"—with the intention of deceiving the customers about the quality of the merchandise, one supposes: aging in turkeys is quickly recognizable from the legs, which in young birds are smooth and black, but later become white and peeled.

In the eighteenth century, France was swept by a wave of turkeymania, intensified by the American Revolution, which impelled Frenchmen sympathetic to it to eat this thoroughly American bird as a symbol of solidarity. A favorite stuffing for the roast bird became truffles. One reads with wonder today of turkeys being stuffed with a dozen or two dozen truffles; they were left in the body cavity overnight to impart their fragrance to the bird and were then thrown away! At today's prices it would be more economical to throw away the turkey and eat the truffles.

I wonder if France was the place of origin of an admonition which I find in Eliza Leslie's 1848 *Directions for Cookery in Its Various Branches.* "Do not help any one to the legs, or drum-sticks as they are called," she writes, but does not explain why. At the height of its popularity in France, roast turkey was often the *pièce de résistance* when there was company for dinner. The guests were served slices from the breast, for the white meat was considered the choicest (erroneously, in my opinion). The legs were usually left over, and kitchen economics ruled that the family, sans guests, would make a meal of them the next day. Aware of this, guests did not ask for dark meat and refused it if it were offered, in order to leave their hosts' next lunch intact. It gradually became polite not to offer it at all.

"The turkey," wrote Brillat-Savarin, "is certainly one of the handsomest gifts the New World made to the Old World. . . . [It] is the largest and, if not the most subtle, at least the most tasty of our domestic birds." He tasted it, it is true, under the best of circumstances. He had cooked it himself after having also shot it himself in the wilderness near Hartford, Connecticut, so that it was not even the domestic bird he sampled, but the wild fowl, which, he explained, was better than the tame bird. He called himself a *dindonophile*, a turkey lover.

"I am as much a turkey hater as Brillat-Savarin proclaimed himself to be a turkey lover," wrote Robert J. Courtine, gastronomic critic of the Paris *Monde*. "The turkey and I do not fraternize," he added in one of his books, and in another: "I have on one occasion remarked that it tastes like an old zouave (with a little bad faith, it is true, for I have never sampled one of those forgotten warriors)."

It would seem that unanimity is lacking on the succulence of the turkey.

In the ranks of the turkey lovers we can enlist Alexandre Dumas: "The flesh, especially cold, is excellent, full-flavored, and preferable to that of chicken." James de Coquet, gastronomic writer for the Paris *Figaro*, falls into line too: "Our forebears, who baptized it 'Saint Martin's bird,' ate it by preference in the first half of November. [St. Martin's Day is November 11.] It is then that it is at its best age and that its flesh is pearly and melting. . . . Even if the flesh is a little too solid and the fat a little too yellow, everybody feasts on it." Virginia Pasley must be a turkey lover too, for in her *In Celebration of Food* she wrote: "We used to have turkeys . . . like those the Pilgrims ate. They were farm grown, but still wild turkeys, not penned or fed in factory-like buildings. They had a gamy taste, which I miss, but on the other hand, the legs were often stringy, the breasts were tough and had not nearly as much meat on them as today's turkeys." This does not constitute pure unmitigated praise, but Virginia Pasley gives herself away as a turkey lover a little further along in this passage when she adds, "White meat is most prized (except by me)." By me, too. I consider this a test.

Among turkey haters we must list Adrian Bailey, who in *The Cooking of the British Isles* wrote: "Turkey, to my mind, is one of the least interesting exports from the New World to the Old, and should come last on any listing of Christmas favorites. . . . For my taste, the turkey is too tough for roasting." With surprise, I find in the late A. J. Liebling's *Between Meals*: "A tough old turkey with plenty of character makes the best civet, and only in a civet is turkey good enough to eat." I shared many excellent meals with Mr. Liebling, whose competence in matters of food is therefore well known to me, but I find it hard to reconcile this estimate with my boyhood memories of the magnificent roast turkeys which appeared ritually on our table at Thanksgiving and Christmas. It is true that I am a New Englander, while Mr. Liebling was brought up, I believe, in Brooklyn, not noted for its turkeys. But I find in this passage a possible clue to the denigration of turkeys, which in many cases, I suspect, is the result either of eating the wrong kind of turkey, or turkey badly cooked.

"Young turkey," Liebling wrote, "is a pale preliminary phase of its species," and in this he was right. Yet we find everywhere recommendations that turkeys should be eaten young. "To be tender," I read in one article, "it must be young (six to eight months)." "A young bird hatched that year," says another, "well fattened, bears on breast and back patches of exquisite tender meat." "Too much weight does it no good at all," opines James de Coquet, which is exactly contrary to my own opinion. Turkey, like wine, should be served in magnums.

The magazine *Gourmet*, it seems to me, hit it just right when it wrote:

> The more the turkey weighs, the less dry and the meatier it will be. The ideal turkey, the juiciest and the best, weighs about 30 pounds. Too many chefs seem to have the idea that a 12-pound turkey is better than one weighing 25 pounds, when just the reverse is true. The size does make a difference in the flavor. The larger, the better.

The marvelous turkeys of my youth were large. Our family, in peacetime strength, mustered seven; but at Thanksgiving and Christmas we were apt to be joined by any number of grandparents, aunts, uncles and cousins, some of them honorary. For us the turkey started at twenty-two pounds and ranged upward.

Even more important than size is the quality of the bird. Wild turkey "has much more taste than its barnyard counterpart," wrote James de Coquet, thus redeeming himself for his position on size. "Fed on berries and small invertebrates, it has ivory flesh which guards all the perfumes of the forest." There seems to be no dissent on this point:

> The flesh of the wild turkey is more highly colored and more flavorful than that of the domestic turkey [Brillat-Savarin observed]. I learned with pleasure that my esteemed colleague, Monsieur Bosc [otherwise unknown to fame], had in the Carolinas killed some which he found excellent and especially much better than those we raise in Europe. So he advises those who raise them to give them as much freedom as possible, to take them into the fields and even the woods to increase their flavor and bring them as close as possible to the original species.

Even though they were not wild, the turkeys of my youth still retained a hint of gamy flavor, a reminiscence of their former freedom never present in European birds, which were domesticated from the start. This loss of flavor in the exiled bird may account for the prejudice some Europeans feel about it. It may have been an attempt to recover some of the flavor lost through domestication and expatriation which accounted for a practice I reported in *The Food of Italy* at a time when it had impressed me only by its cruelty:

> The favorite bird of the province of Vicenza is the turkey. A turkey contest which used to be held at Montebello during the three-day festival of Santa Maria Assunta, beginning the first Sunday in May, has now, happily, been forbidden. Blindfolded contestants armed with long rods tried to knock off the heads of the unfortunate birds.

Some years later I came across this account of the way in which turkeys are killed in Oberbetschdorf, Alsace:

> The turkey is kept without food or drink for a whole day. It is then driven all around the farmyard to anger it. When it has become furious and terrified, it is forced to drink salted ginger-flavored vinegar, and then strangled.

The similarity between these customs in two fairly widely spaced localities reminded me that the ancient Romans used to badger animals before slaughtering them to enhance their flavor. This effect will be understood by hunters, who know that the meat of a wounded deer killed after a long, exhausting chase has a bitterer taste than one felled instantaneously by a single shot, because of the secretions discharged into the muscles during agony. Such treatment of the turkey might give it more taste, but that it would be a better taste seems unlikely, unless it produces an atavistic whiff of the wilderness.

Turkey boiled is turkey spoiled
And turkey roast is turkey lost
But for turkey braised
The Lord be praised,

runs an old ditty with which I am in disagreement. For the sort of turkeys we used to have in my boyhood it seems to me that the ideal method is roasting, which brings out the bird's flavor better than any other (braising? well, yes, perhaps). Roasting a turkey properly demands a good deal of skill for a number of reasons, of which the two most important are probably that turkey, unlike goose, is not fat meat and one method or another must be employed to keep it from coming out of the oven (or off the spit) too dry, and that the drumsticks take longer to cook through than the white meat. This problem exists even when you start with an old-fashioned turkey full of flavor, but such birds are becoming daily more rare.

> Our forefathers would never recognize the taste of most of what is sold as turkey nowadays [Karen Hess wrote]. You cannot expect old-fashioned flavor from birds that have been frozen, injected with nameless oils (guilefully called "butter ball"), boned

Turkey

and treated with sodium tripolphate or other allowable chemicals.

Better meat markets will be able to furnish quality birds that were decently fed and freshly killed. These command a somewhat higher price . . . but they may well be a better buy because they are not full of water and injected fats. They also tend to be meatier as well as far tastier.

A few years ago a university professor defied tradition and, perhaps incidentally, made headlines, by asserting that despite the strong tradition to the contrary, turkey was not eaten at the first Thanksgiving. This information, it was explained, was based on the menu for the meal drawn up by William Bradford, then governor of the Plymouth Colony, which the iconoclastic professor had found among the governor's notes. Tradition is frequently as valid as written documentation, but never mind that. I find it quite as easy to believe that Governor Bradford, in the heat of composition, forgot to inscribe one important item on his menu (to tell the truth, it surprises me a little, given the circumstances, that he ever prepared a menu at all) as to believe that the most festive, the most obvious and the most easily hunted game of the place could possibly have been omitted. It occurs to me also that the Indians—ninety of them, surprise guests who accompanied their chief, Massasoit, who had really been invited—thoughtfully brought food along with them, and it is hard also to believe that the contribution of men who lived largely by hunting would not have included turkeys, even if they had failed to inquire beforehand if this was compatible with Governor Bradford's menu. Musing on this improbability, I started hunting through reference books and discovered that Roger Tory Peterson had written that the Indians did indeed bring turkeys with them. I also learned that Edward Winslow, one of the original *Mayflower* passengers, who later became governor of the colony himself, had written that turkeys had been hunted, successfully, for that first dinner.

Our harvest being gotten in [he reported] our governor sent four men on fowling, that so we might, after a special manner, rejoice together after we had gathered the fruit of our labors. They four in one day killed as much fowl as, with a little help beside [from the Indians?], served the company almost a week.

The Pilgrims had no hesitation about eating turkey, as they had in the case of the strange, and consequently suspect, foods of the New World. The turkey was not strange food for them, since it had reached Europe a century earlier and was already being eaten there commonly. In the New World turkeys were plentiful and easy to take—indeed, too easy: as early as 1672, only half a century after the Pilgrims' arrival, John Josselyn complained of how "the English and the Indians having destroyed the breed . . . 'tis very rare to meet with a wild turkie in the woods." Some counties in New York declared a closed season on turkeys in 1708. Yet for those not in a position to shoot their own, a small turkey could still be bought in northeastern markets for a shilling. In 1837 Frederick Marryat reported that wild turkeys were still plentiful in New York markets and that their quality was excellent.

In the South, the story was the same: the first arrivals found the land teeming with turkeys. (The Natchez Indians had named the eighth month of their thirteen-month year "the Moon of the Turkey.") Captain John Smith told of the Indians bringing him turkeys when he first arrived at Jamestown. William Byrd described the sharp hissing of their wings when a large flock took off, and in Florida William Bartram complained of being wakened too early by "wild turkeycocks saluting each other from the sun-brightened tops of the lofty cypresses and magnolias." In the spring (the mating season), he wrote, the cocks "begin to crow at dawn and continue until sunrise from March . . . to April . . . the watch word being caught and repeated from one to another for hundreds of miles around; the whole country is for an hour or more in a universal shout." About 1737, according to William Byrd, "a large fat turkey-hen which weighs from thirty to forty and even more pounds" could be had in Virginia for 24 to 30 pence. When Chateaubriand visited the United States he reported that he had seen turkeys on the banks of the Meschacébé (Mississippi). In Kentucky in 1820 wild turkeys were still so plentiful that farm chickens cost more.

For a considerable time after the colonists arrived in the East, all the turkeys were wild; the Indians had never bothered to domesticate a bird which was always harvestable by bow and arrow and in the meantime took care of its own food and shelter. In the Southwest, when Coronado saw them they were already domesticated—the only domesticated animal the Indians possessed except the dog. Their domestication in this part of the country though not elsewhere can be explained by the fact that the Pueblo Indians were sedentary, whereas most of the eastern and Plains Indians were nomadic or semi-nomadic, and that in this arid region there was not enough natural food available to maintain an abundant population of wild turkeys if they had to fend for themselves (aridity also meant that men and turkeys had to live in close propinquity at the rare places where there was water). There were probably less than 250,000 turkeys in a territory which corresponds today to the states of Colorado, New Mexico and Arizona, and even these numbers were apparently possible only because the Indians fed the turkeys. But did they start to do so deliberately to assure a supply of meat, or was it the turkeys which realized that the pickings were better around the Indian fields than in the comparatively barren woods? Was man the noblest conquest of the turkey?

Who Domesticated Whom? Jean M. Pinkley inquired in the title of a 1965 publication, which answered the question: "To say that the Indian domesticated the turkey is to put the cart before the horse. He had no choice: it was the turkey which domesticated him." When the Indians began to plant grain in what archeologists call the Basket Maker II period, the turkeys flocked enthusiastically to the source of food provided by their fields; it was necessary to post sentinels in the plantations to chase the birds away. Frustrated in the open, the turkeys became expert at getting into the granaries. Unable to shut up the grain tightly enough to preserve it from the birds, the Indians hit upon the opposite solution: they shut up the birds, and thereafter had to provide them with food and living quarters.

As an ever larger proportion of Americans began to reduce the size of their families and to move into small city apartments, breeders had to concentrate on turkeys small enough to fit into kitchenette ovens. The 30-pound birds of earlier times had high breastbones, which refused to bow to modern stoves, so a flat-chested breed had to be developed—whereupon the reproductive rate of the streamlined turkeys promptly declined. The male turkey, it was discovered, could no longer mount the female to impregnate her; the hens had to be fitted with canvas saddles for the convenience of the cocks. I am told that breeders are now showing interest in large birds again, but not for family feasting, for processors.

Curiously enough, the American turkey-raising industry started less for the production of meat than for the production of feathers. Some Indian tribes raised turkeys primarily for their plumes, which they valued for ornamental reasons; and whites were still following their example as recently as 1935, when turkeys were being judged at agricultural fairs on the perfection of their plumage. A little more than half a century ago, the quality of the meat at last became the dominant factor in turkey breeding, one may suppose because of the development of new varieties like the heavily fleshed Broad-Breasted Bronze turkey, which became the leading type about 1945.

The turkey as a feather producer founded the chief industry of Monticello, Iowa, where William Hoag (pronounced Hoig) invented the turkey-feather duster in 1872. "As long as there is dust, there will be a demand for feather dusters," a member of the Hoag family asserted as recently as 1951; he had under-estimated the virtues of the vacuum cleaner and modern furniture polish. For nearly a century, Monticello provided half the world's feather dusters, the dark-bronze striped feathers being in greatest demand. But in the 1970s turkey feathers, once fifteen cents a pound, reached a price of three dollars: the feather duster was no longer competitive. In 1974 Mrs. Shirley Hoag Eden, great-granddaughter of the founder, closed the factory and, according to her own words as quoted in the press, "went home and had two Bourbons and cried for hours." The factory was converted to make computer circuit boards.

TURNIP. The turnip is a capricious vegetable, which seems reluctant to show itself at its best. Protean by nature, it exists in innumerable varieties, and the search for excellence has to begin by finding the right variety; to continue by finding the right variety in the right place, for turnips are greatly affected by local and temporary conditions; and to end by finding the right variety in the right place at the right time. Its season is brief. The Paris restaurant where I used to eat that classic dish, duck with turnips (*canard aux navets*), when the management would permit it, served it only during six weeks in April and May. For the rest of the year turnips were deemed unfit to eat.

Contempt for the turnip as a lowly vegetable reaches far back. When the Aryans established their dominion over India, they gave sumptuary legislation a curious twist. Such laws have often prohibited poor or despised classes from eating the fine foods of their betters, but the Aryans turned it the other way around. They forbade members of their own race to demean its reputation by partaking of the foods of common people —beans, garlic, onions, mushrooms (hardly humble food nowadays) and turnips.

It did not necessarily express dislike of the turnip but only recognition of its humble nature when the ancient Romans told how in the third century B.C. a Samnite delegation waited on that early military genius Curius Dentatus to bribe him to lead their army against his fellow-countrymen and gave up the idea when they found him cooking his own frugal meal of

Turnip. *Porcelain dishes, Edo Period, Japan, 17th century*

turnips in the ashes of his hearth; they realized that so simple a man was impervious to the lure of gold. Later it became common to pelt unpopular persons with turnips (tomatoes being not yet available), which would seem to indicate scant esteem for the turnip, though it was perhaps more respected than its target. Columella seems to have felt it necessary to apologize for stooping to give recipes for pickling this vegetable, for he wrote that it could not be disregarded since it provided filling food for country people. The turnip does, of course, have a rustic character; but rusticity has its charms.

"Turnips are hard and cook badly," wrote the anonymous author of *Le Ménagier de Paris* in 1393, but with the reservation "until they have been in the cold and the frost," so his turnips were a late-ripening variety. Gerard in 1597 remarked that "the bulbous or knobbed root . . . is many times eaten raw, especially of the poore people in Wales, but most commonly boiled." One may suspect, without wishing to exaggerate the merits of a vegetable whose gastronomic gamut is obviously limited, that one reason why the turnip was looked down upon was that it was so often a food of the poor. It has usually been cheap; it grows in poor, ungrateful soils (which also produce poverty); it ripens quickly, a merit for those who have no margin of time to permit them to wait for harvests; and it keeps relatively well. It was with no intention of complimenting the people of France's Limousin region that Rabelais called them "turnip chewers," nor would it seem that William Wallace Irwin was demonstrating esteem either for the turnip or the English when he described the latter as "a hardy race that considers plain boiled turnips to be food." The contemporary French historian André Castelot wrote that "turnips are sad, insipid, pale and stringy out of season." (The remedy, of course, is to respect their season.) The French use the word *navet*, "turnip," to designate an artistic flop: a bad book, the sort of play we call a turkey or, in the precise definition of the Larousse encyclopedia, "a bad painting, particularly one in which the nude limbs have no muscles."

When the United States Department of Agriculture conducted a survey in 1974 on national preferences in vegetables, half of the children polled named as their most disliked vegetables asparagus, Brussels sprouts, eggplant and turnips; their parents voted against okra, eggplant and turnips.

The condemnation of turnips is far from unanimous. The Romans may have thought them lowly, but they ate a good many of them. Since Columella's reference to them sounds like an apology, we might consider the message Martial sent with a gift of turnips as an apology too, but if so, it was one full of effrontery—a quality which, of course, he did not lack: "I give you these roots, friends of winter and of rime; Romulus ate of them at the table of the Gods." The fact that Apicius gave several turnip recipes, including duck with turnips, indicates that they were not entirely contemptible, or Apicius, a snob, would have disdained them. At times the Romans took a great deal of trouble with turnips. They managed to prepare them in ways which presented them in sixteen different colors, of which the favorite was purple; Pliny said it was the only foodstuff which was dyed. Imitation anchovies are said to have been made from pickled turnips, and they were added to sauces of insipid flavor to perk them up.

Le Ménagier de Paris, Rabelais and Gerard to the contrary, the Middle Ages and the Renaissance paid tribute to the turnip with the teeth. In the sixteenth century, Bruyerin-Champier praised the turnips of Orléans, but it was from Saulieu in Burgundy that they were sent to the king's table. Charles Estienne wrote that Parisians were very fond of them: "This vegetable is to them what large radishes are to the Limousins," he said; but it is not certain that what he called large radishes were not in fact turnips. There has always been a good deal of confusion about the identity of edible roots. Alexandre Dumas lumped turnips together with radishes and horseradishes, and Pliny before him not only thoroughly mixed up different types of turnips but seemed to feel that they included the black radish, the horseradish and even the beet.

There is a fact about the turnip which might have been seized upon by its detractors, but none of them seem to have known it: it is the only common food except the cabbage (a member of the same genus) which contains arsenic. This need not work you into a tizzy if you are confronted inescapably with turnips: there is so little that it can do you no harm, and it may, indeed, do you some good. A trace of arsenic is desirable to keep the human body functioning properly, but so small a trace that Nature in her wisdom has confined it to these two vegetables and (sometimes) water. Despite this element the turnip is inoffensive (except that it also contains sulfur, which accounts for its pungent taste, an element which does not suit every digestion). It has been given a clean bill of health by (perhaps) Henry Wadsworth Longfellow, though he denied authorship of the testimonial attributed to him—understandably, for its quality is definitely lower than that of the turnip:

Mr. Finney had a turnip,
And it grew behind the barn.
And it grew, and it grew.
And the turnip did no harm.

There be sundry sorts of Turneps [wrote John Gerard], some wild, some of the garden; some with round roots globe fashion, others ovall or peare-fashion; and another sort longish or somewhat like a Radish; and of all these there are sundry varieties, some being great, and some of a smaller sort. . . .

The small Turnep is like unto the first described, saving that it is lesser. The root is much sweeter in taste, as my selfe have often proved. . . .

They floure and seed the second yeare after they are sowne: for those that floure the same years that they are sowne, are a degenerat kind, called in Cheshire . . . Madneps, of their evill qualitie in causing frensie and giddiness of the brain for a season.

Aside from the pleasure which may be derived from its Elizabethan language, there might seem to be little point in quoting a work published in 1597 on the nature of the turnip; but to tell the truth, we do not know much more about it now than Gerard did. His "Turnep" includes the varieties in whose scientific names today some form of the Latin *rapus* is found. His "small Turnep" covers those described by the word *napa*. As for his "Madnep," I wonder if it could be bryony, *Bryonia dioica*, whose large root is strongly cathartic; it is sometimes called the devil's turnip. Gerard did not have to take the rutabaga into account; in his time it had not yet put in an appearance.

The classical world knew both of the two main families of turnips, but, wrote Georges Gibault, "were no better at telling them apart than we are." Strictly speaking, *goggullo* in Greek and *rapum* in Latin should correspond with Gerard's "Turnep" and our ordinary turnips; *bunias* in Greek and *napus* in Latin with Gerard's "small Turnep," our French turnip today, or even, in

English, the navet, its French name. But the ancients often used these terms very loosely, even interchangeably, and also confused them with roots which were not turnips at all—or their translators did. Thus when the Emperor Diocletian imposed a price ceiling on *radices* (literally, "roots"), English texts tell us that he was regulating the cost of radishes; actually he meant turnips, as we know from the Greek text of his edict, which uses the more precise word, *gogguloi.*

Brassica rapa, our common turnip, is typically spherical and white-fleshed (it is sometimes called the white turnip), and the varieties grown in the United States are almost always white; but today it is found also in yellow-fleshed varieties. The upper part of the root, which often bulges slightly from the ground, may be white, yellow, green, red, purple or black. It has also assumed all the shapes known to turnipdom, which remain stable generation after generation, so they have been gratified with individual subspecies names—*B. rapa oblonga* for the tapering sort (which is at least as old as classical times) or *B. rapa depressa* for certain flattened varieties (already described by sixteenth-century botanists). The French call turnips of this kind *raves,* which means simply "roots," and is also used for other roots (*betterave,* beet, *celeri-rave,* celeriac). Charles Estienne wrote that *raves* "are much larger and of a more agreeable taste than *navets.*" He seems to be the only one who ever thought so.

B. napa, the French turnip or *navet,* has indeed been considered almost universally as superior in flavor to its fellow, which is why it is also labeled *B. napus esculenta.* It is sometimes held to be a comparatively recent development by the French, but while present varieties have been improved over the centuries, this turnip basically seems quite as old as the other. It is probably what Pliny called the Amiternum turnip and described as the kind most appreciated by the Romans. It was the *napa* of Columella, who emphasized its importance in Gaul. In later times its quality occasionally surprised individual Englishmen, but did not move their countrymen, great turnip eaters, to switch to the French variety. Visiting France on an official mission in the sixteenth century, Martin Lister wrote:

> The roots of this country differ much from ours. Here there are no round turnips, but they are long and thin and moreover of excellent flavor, good to season soups and stews, for which ours are too strong. This species has recently been introduced into England, but our gardeners do not know how to manage them. . . . After having advanced into France for the distance covered in two or three days, we no longer found any other turnips except navets; and they became better as we approached Paris. They are no thicker than a knife handle, and excellent, as I have just said, either in soup or with mutton.

Like its fellow, the common turnip, the French turnip, typically white and carrot-shaped, has developed other forms and colors (principally yellow and black), which, however, have retained the particular finesse of this variety. France has also produced a small, round, spring-ripening form which is the one served in *canard aux navets,* and is also described as *sec* (dry) because it remains firm when cooked in soup, a particular merit when it gives pot-au-feu its characteristic spiciness.

Both the common white turnip and the French navet offer a second food in their leaves, a common ingredient in the mixed greens of the southern United States (not to mention the *pote gallego* of northwestern Spain). There are varieties of turnips which have been developed solely for their tops, in which the root has been allowed to shrink into insignificance in favor of concentrating all the turnip's nourishment in its leaves. (The ancient Romans ate the leaves too, but it is hard to agree with Pliny when he says that they are best when yellow and half dead.) Turnip greens are becoming increasingly hard to get unless you live in the country and can raise them yourself or get them from a neighbor; supermarkets are not enthusiastic about handling them. This is a pity, for, as Joan M. Jungfleish points out, "Turnip tops or greens . . . are richer in vitamins and minerals than almost all other vegetables, including the turnip itself. . . . They aid digestion by absorbing fat in the stomach."

The greens of the rutabaga are not eaten. This root, otherwise known as the Swedish turnip, or simply the swede, is a recent arrival in the world of foods. Its existence is reported nowhere before the seventeenth century, when it is supposed to have first appeared in Bohemia. It is almost certainly a mutant, not a hybrid, for it has thirty-eight chromosomes while the common turnip has twenty. It is generally thought of as yellow, both within and without, large, and of coarser flavor than the *navet* or even the common white turnip, but it also has a white-fleshed form. Many people, especially outside of Scandinavia, think the proper vocation of the rutabaga is to serve as fodder for animals, but others actually prefer it for their own eating to the smaller garden turnips precisely because it is more assertive in taste. There have been persons who thought all turnips were fit only for fodder, and at least one who turned this around, denigrating simultaneously both men and turnips: the author of the sixteenth-century *Haven in Heaven,* who remarked that "although men do love to eat Turneps, yet do swine abhor them." His swine must have been of a different breed from mine.

Man's use of the turnip [wrote Georges Gibault in his *Histoire des légumes*] must go back to prehistoric times. These roots, cooked in the ashes, seem to have played a large part in the nourishment of the inhabitants of northern Europe. Natives of the seashore, they acquired their qualities only in cold or temperate-cold countries, under clouded skies. In Belgium, their vegetation becomes more and more handsome as one approaches the sea. The south produces only mediocre turnips.

This affinity with the sea and the cold has guided savants in their search, still unrewarded, for the original wild turnip. I wonder if they have not been looking for the ancestor of turnips one generation too late. No original wild cabbage has been found either, but it has been suggested that it arose from sea kale, *Crambe maritima*; if so, perhaps sea kale gave birth to the turnip too, or to some intermediate form, a missing link, from which both turnip and cabbage arose. *B. oleracea* embraces the whole cabbage family, *B. campestris* perhaps embraces the whole turnip family. This would make both of them natives of northern European coasts, which is what they seem to be.

It has been suggested that the turnip was first cultivated by ancient Celts and Germans, who would have been in the right part of the world for it, but the first written evidence of its cultivation comes from what ought to be rather far from the turnip's best territory, Babylon, which we may suppose was reached from the Caucasus, sometimes described as the southernmost limit of its original range. It was no doubt from Asia Minor that the turnip spread into Greece, where Theophrastus recorded several varieties, while Roman listings of different kinds frequently refer them to Greece, an indication that they entered the Mediterranean from the east.

Greeks and Romans, despite Apicius, both seem to have thought of turnips primarily as food for the poor and for country folk, which may be why they were little honored in art. They are not represented in any Pompeiian paintings or mosaics yet uncovered, though this city was given to picturing fruit and vegetables, especially on dining-room walls. About all we have is a silver vase in the Louvre, recovered from the ashes near Vesuvius, on which turnips are shown, and a Roman painting discovered in 1783. Nevertheless, Pliny said turnips constituted the third most important product north of the Po, after wine and wheat. He also tells us that the turnip in his time could reach a weight of 40 pounds, which would make it about equal to what the English botanist John Martyn in 1792 said was the greatest weight he had heard of in England, 36 pounds; but these weights have been dwarfed elsewhere—50 to 60 pounds reported by Amatus Lusitania in 1524, 100 pounds by Matthiolus in 1558 (and the same in California about 1850). John McPhee gives no weight for those he encountered in Alaska, but he described them as "blood-red turnips a foot in diameter that resemble the hearts of bulls."

In the Middle Ages the turnip was one of the commonest of vegetables; it was not yet subject to the competition of the potato. It did not always get into the records as soon as it got into the kitchens; it was probably too commonplace to serve as a subject for literature. Besides, it was a food of the poor, who were not considered an appropriate subject for literature either. The chronicles and poems of the times dealt with lords and their ladies, who did not eat vegetables: they ate game. However, it is on record that turnips were one of the principal foods of the Flemish in the fifteenth century, and the first turnips to be sent to England, in the first half of the fifteenth, came from Holland, with no applause from such Britons as the one who wrote that "the poore Dutch men, like swine, digge up the rootes!" Nevertheless, during this half-century, the time of Henry VIII, Britons were eating turnips baked or roasted, and enjoying the greens, raw in salads or cooked like spinach. They were importing turnips grown elsewhere, however; probably almost no one was actually growing them on English soil earlier than John Gerard, who in 1597 described the plants he was raising in his own garden. We do not hear of turnips as a field crop in Britain until 1645 (and the French navet was not cultivated until 1683), but forty years later they were being grown everywhere, though not in vast quantity according to Philippa Pullar, who wrote in *Consuming Passions*:

Much has been written of the improvements in husbandry at this time. Of the introduction of clover and turnips—a magic root, sovereign for cattle, swine, poultry and hunting dogs, producing "very good syder," exceeding "good oyl." Some progressive and interested men did plant them, and write agricultural tracts on their findings, but in the main the new crops were not generally known until the last part of the next century.

In Germany turnips had already become a field crop in the sixteenth century, when the average burgher, who ate simply, devoured considerable quantities of beans, cabbage and turnips.

Turnips appeared in the markets of medieval Paris, but only in their season; there seems to have been little interest in storing them. Nicolas de

Bonnefons, a preacher of the virtues of vegetables, recommended turnips in 1654; he suggested cooking them with leeks, and peeling them only after they had been cooked.

The first description of the rutabaga seems to have been that of the Swiss naturalist Jean Bauhin, in his *Prodomus,* published posthumously in 1620, and three years later in his *Pinax,* but it was not discussed by a French botanist until 1700, which is no guarantee that it was already being grown in France. Rutabagas were planted in the English royal gardens in 1699, also no guarantee that they were reaching the public. The *Gardeners' Chronicle* reported that the rutabaga was introduced into non-regal circles in England only in 1790, in which case Scotland had them first, since they appeared there in 1781 or 1782.

Meanwhile the ordinary turnip was consolidating its territory. Its intensive cultivation as fodder for sheep and cattle began in England about 1724, but the dissident Philippa Pullar is still of the opinion that it flourished more slowly in the fields than in the libraries:

> The eighteenth century was the wondrous climax of English cooking and it was possible because of the improved methods of agriculture. The meat was now good, they say, the beasts were bred especially for the plate and not the plough; they were larger and more succulent and they were stored through the winter in the new fertile enclosures, fattened on juicy turnips and clover and served up steaming with new potatoes. This is not strictly true . . . it was not until the end of the century that the old leisurely pace of the country changed . . . there is a hole in the eighteenth-century agricultural argument: during a large part of it *the improvements did not exist.* It was men like Turnip Townshend . . . who introduced the changes. [Lord Townshend won his nickname for his zeal in introducing improved varieties of turnips from Holland as livestock fodder; his grandson was the author of the Townshend Acts which contributed so largely to losing a large portion of His Majesty's colonies in North America.] . . . But Townshend did not devote himself to his estates, his theories and his turnips until 1730. . . . The country farmers . . . were slow to adopt newfangled ways. It was the amateurs, the gentleman farmers who took them up. But roads were appalling, communications dreadful, and by 1768 turnips and clover were still generally unknown.

The turnip was already rooting itself solidly in the New World. Sir Francis Bacon, who had never been there, said nevertheless that turnips "grow speedily, and within the year" in America. Francis Higginson, who was on the spot, wrote in 1630, "Our turnips are here both bigger and sweeter than is ordinarily to be found in England." Both men may have been reporting simply on the success of this vegetable in a new climate, or they may have thought it was native there, though of course it was not; but by the time English-speaking colonists began to settle in America the turnip already had an eighty-year history there.

Jacques Cartier had planted turnip seeds in Canada in 1540, at the time of his third voyage, and French Jesuit missionaries followed suit by raising them along the banks of the St. Lawrence and carrying them into New York, where Father Paul Le Jeune, in a letter home, reported that they grew splendidly. The Virginia colonists must have brought seeds with them, for turnips are said to have grown there in 1609. Massachusetts seems to have been twenty years behind; it was only in 1629 that Francis Higginson and William Wood reported turnip cultivation there. They were plentiful in the neighborhood of Philadelphia in 1707, appeared in Connecticut by 1747 at least, in Florida in 1775 and in South Carolina in 1779. The Indians took to them at once, for they were much superior to the wild roots they had been grubbing from the ground, and were growing fields of turnips around Geneva, New York, which in 1779 were extensive enough to make it worthwhile for General John Sullivan to destroy them during a punitive raid into Indian country. As the white man moved west, taking turnips with him, they were received with enthusiasm all the way to the Northwest. Indian women baked or roasted them whole in their skins, as they had done with camass roots and similar foods, a method which brought out their full flavor.

The white man's turnip replaced what had been called the Indian turnip, *Arisaema dracontium,* known also as the dragonroot or green dragon, and *A. triphyllum,* alias the brown dragon, the bog onion or starchwort—which is our familiar jack-in-the-pulpit. The Indians ate its roots, but whites were defeated by its many needlelike crystals of oxalate of lime; unlike the Indians, they lacked the skill or the patience to eradicate them. Was this what George Catlin, who has left us so many remarkable paintings of Indians, was offered at a Mandan feast? One of the dishes, he wrote, was "a kind of paste or pudding, made of the flour of the 'pomme blanche,' as the French call it, a delicious turnip of the prairie, finely flavored with . . . buffalo berries."

U

UDE, LOUIS EUSTACHE (famous nineteenth-century chef, quoted by Anne Villan): *The habit of limiting children to plain food "so that they are not introduced to their parents' table till their palates have been completely benumbed by the strict diet observed in the Nursery and Boarding-Schools" was responsible for the generally abysmal standards of English cooking.*

UNIDENTIFIED: *They came as a boon and a blessing to men, / The Pickwick, the Owl, and the Waverley pen.* (Advertisement explains *The Oxford Dictionary of Quotations,* from which this gem is culled. So be it.)

U
stands for

udders, removed from the cow and attributed to the goose when they go into what is labeled, unblushingly, *mousse de foie gras;* for **udo,** a Japanese plant whose roots are eaten like salsify and its young stalks like asparagus; for the **ugli,** a hybrid between the grapefruit and the tangerine; for the **ulloco,** or melloco, a small pink starchy mucilaginous tuber eaten only on its native territory, western South America; for the **umber,** a fish which is the European version of the grayling; for **umbles,** the heart, liver, tongue, feet, palate, kidneys, brain and ears, preferably of deer, which is what we get when we eat 'umble pie; for the **umbrella tree,** or corkwood, whose succulent fruit is eaten only in the Congo, and **um khirr,** whose crisp seed is eaten only in the Sudan; for the **umkokolo,** or key (for kei) apple, a fruit found frequently in California; for the **undercut,** which is the Queen's English for tenderloin; for the **unicorn,** which Julius Caesar reported lived in the forests of Gaul, where it must have made fabulous eating, the **unicorn fish** of the Red Sea, the **unicorn plant,** or martynia, of southwestern North America, whose pods are pickled, and the **unicorn root,** one of the bitterest foods known, but American Indians used to eat it; for **upland cress,** which is winter CRESS; for the **upside-down catfish** of tropical Africa, which does indeed swim upside down whenever it tires of swimming right side up; for the **urhur,** a pea of many aliases, which in the twenty-fourth century B.C. was placed in Egyptian tombs and in the nineteenth century A.D. produced 4000 pounds of peas per acre in Egyptian fields; and for **utility meats,** which is a Nice Nelly term for organic meats.

VIRGIL: *The Sire of gods and man, with hard decrees, forbids our plenty to be born with ease.*

VOLTAIRE: *Thought depends absolutely on the stomach, but in spite of that, those who have the best stomachs are not the best thinkers.*

VOLTAIRE: *As for cooks, I cannot tolerate essence of ham, nor excess of morels, of mushrooms, of pepper and of nutmeg, with which they disguise foods which are very good on their own.*

V

VOLTAIRE: *In England there are sixty different religions, but only one sauce.*

VOLNEY, COMTE DE: *I will venture to say that if a prize were proposed for the scheme of a regimen most calculated to injure the stomach, the teeth, and the health in general, no better could be invented than that of the Americans.*

VA
stands for

the **Valencia orange**, the variety most widely grown everywhere in the world except Valencia; for **valerian,** whose uses are mainly medicinal, but red valerian is used as a salad in Italy, long-spurred valerian is used as a salad in France, African valerian began to be used as a salad in Europe about 1840, the valerian known as horn-of-plenty is reported to have been grown as a salad in France in the nineteenth century, but the valerian known as the tobacco root is eaten only by Indians of the rainbow TROUT country, although it has "an odor most offensive" and has been called "a bitter and somewhat pernicious substance"; for the **valley quail,** state bird of California; for the **varan,** or monitor, a large, repugnant-looking lizard which is universally eaten by the dauntless natives of tropical Africa; for the **variable wedge,** another name for the coquina, a clam of Florida and adjacent territories, very small but very tasty in soup or chowder; for **variety meats,** an evasion resorted to by squeamish persons unwilling to face the fact that there are mortals sufficiently benighted to eat the internal organs of animals; and for the **varnish tree,** which if it is the marking-nut tree bears fruit which is tolerable if roasted or dried, or if it is the tree of heaven bears leaves which in time of plenty nourish silkworms and in times of famine, men.

And **VA** also stands for

VANILLA. Marco Polo, Marthe de Fels tells us in her biography of Pierre Poivre, encountered vanilla somewhere during his travels. He didn't. It was the French who discovered it in the sixteenth century, she continues. It wasn't. She follows this up in the same sentence by stating that Clusius made the first study of it, implying that it was those French discoverers who passed it on to him. It wasn't, and he didn't. "And from where did this beautiful emigrant reach us?" she asks, and answers her own question by listing, among other places, Gabon and Madagascar. If she meant its place of origin, as her text seems to imply, it didn't. "It is a native of . . . Africa and Asia," says the ten-volume Larousse encyclopedia. It isn't. "Like cacao, it was first cultivated by the Indians, who, however, never combined the two to make sweet chocolate," says the *Encyclopaedia Britannica.* They did. If you have a toothache, advises *The Foxfire Book,* put a few drops of vanilla extract on the sore tooth and it will relieve the pain. It won't.

Marco Polo never saw vanilla, and it did not originate either in Africa or in Asia, because it is a native of Central America (of southeastern Mexico, the *Britannica* specifies daringly) and was unknown on any other continent before the Spaniards (not the French) discovered it there.

Of the statements above, the least reprehensible is perhaps that about toothache. It may have been true when it was first made, but those were the days when there was vanilla in vanilla extract; nowadays you are likely to be treating your sore tooth with hydroxy-4 methoxy-3 benzaldehyde, the formula the chemists have compounded in their magic test tubes to make us think we are getting vanilla.

Many authors have asserted that the Aztecs did not combine vanilla with chocolate; yet William Prescott wrote in his classic *Conquest of Mexico*: "The Emperor [Montezuma] took no other beverage than *chocolatl,* a potation of chocolate, flavored with vanilla and other spices, and so prepared as to be reduced to a froth of the consistency of honey, which gradually dissolved in the mouth." Prescott, of course, was not there; but Bernardino de Sahagún was. A Franciscan missionary in Mexico, he was the first to instruct Europe about *tlixochitl* (the Aztec word for vanilla), in his *General History of the Things of New Spain,* published in 1560 (forty-two years before Clusius). He reported that the Aztecs mixed vanilla with chocolate, which they used habitually as an after-dinner drink.

Elizabeth David, who sagely restricts herself to reporting the facts, does remark that:

> It is odd . . . that when the Spaniards took chocolate . . . to Spain in the sixteenth century, they appear not to have known about vanilla, for until the eighteenth century and even after cinnamon was the common flavouring for both drinking chocolate and chocolate as a sweetmeat. Indeed cinnamon complements chocolate more suitably than does vanilla which is overpowered by the heavy cocoa taste, although the synthetic vanilla of commerce has such a coarse aroma that it surmounts any such consideration. Plain chocolate, so the manufacturers declare, is today scarcely acceptable without a vanilla flavoring.

I fear I do not agree that chocolate with cinnamon is better than chocolate with vanilla. Two such warm spicy lush fragrances as cinnamon and chocolate used together seem to me to produce an effect cloying to excess; but, of course, excess is not incompatible with the Spanish temperament.

I suspect that the reason why the Spaniards did not import vanilla at the same time as chocolate was that they did not know about its flavor. They could have found out, of course, from the Aztecs, but their soldiers were concentrating on finding gold, their priests were concentrating on saving souls, and neither spent very much time investigating Aztec food. Vanilla does not flaunt its merits. In nature it is virtually odorless; one would not suspect that it is capable of exuding so much flavor. Not only is what is passed off on us as vanilla nowadays usually artificial, but *natural* vanilla is artificial too—in the sense that its potential flavor does not become active until it is released by man.

"Vanilla," wrote Louis Lagriffe in *Le Livre des épices, des condiments et des aromates,* "is not, strictly speaking, either a spice or a seasoner; it would seem more exact to call it a perfume." It has, indeed, nothing to contribute except flavor. That has proved enough to keep it in demand throughout the world ever since peoples more modern than the Aztecs learned how to draw the flavor out of it.

The vanilla plant, *Vanilla planifolia,* V. *fragrans* or V. *aromatica,* is an orchid, a giant vine which demands a trellis or a tree up which it can climb; it is capable of reaching a length of 350 feet. Its fruit is a long thin pod filled with a pulpy substance in which are embedded a multitude of all but invisible black seeds—the tiny specks you may see in, for instance, vanilla ice cream. (In less sophisticated days, they guaranteed the authenticity of the flavoring; but modern technology has now proved equal to the challenge of providing the specks without the aid of vanilla.) The pods, green at first, become a golden yellow and reach a length of between four and twelve inches by the time they are ready to be picked, which must be done just before the moment when, thoroughly ripened, they would split open by themselves. This means that they must be picked individually, by hand, as each reaches the precise stage, and so the same plant must be gone over daily until all of its forty to fifty pods, or beans, have been gathered. This is only one of the painstaking processes which have always made vanilla expensive. Picking is followed by others, which, over a period of several weeks, produce the long thin very dark chocolate-brown or almost black vanilla bean.

Among these processes, fermentation is perhaps the most important in converting the potential flavor of vanilla into actual flavor. There appears on the outside of the pod a sort of rime, known in the trade as givre, the French word for frost. It is formed by concentrated crystals of vanillin, sometimes individually perceptible; at others the bean may look somewhat fuzzy. Vanillin is the element chiefly responsible for the vanilla flavor (of secondary importance is the heliotrope-scented piperonal). If you buy natural vanilla beans, look for pods covered with givre.

Three grades are distinguished in the trade. The best is what is called in French fine vanilla and in English legitimate vanilla. The pods are thin, eight to twelve inches long, almost dead black, with a shiny surface covered with givre. Next comes woody vanilla (in French) or bastard vanilla (in English)—pods five to eight inches long, reddish-brown, with a dull surface and not much givre. Bringing up the rear is vanillon, the same word in both languages, with thick flattened short (four to five inches) soft brown pods. They are often partly open and rarely show visible signs of givre. Although the odor of vanillon is stronger than that of the two others, it is sharp and coarse, giving the impression of being, may we put it, unfinished, as though it had attempted to reach the smooth perfectly blended fragrance of fine vanilla and had been unable to achieve it, leaving the separate elements of its flavor unintegrated and dissonant.

There is not enough natural vanilla in the world to supply even the American demand alone, which intensified during the last decades of the nineteenth century because of the growing popularity of vanilla ice cream. Vanilla accounts for 51 percent of all the ice cream sales in the United States, and vanilla is also a constituent of many other flavors of ice cream of mixed ingredients. The country imports 100,000 pounds of vanilla annually from Mexico, which produces the best, and enough from several other small tropical American countries to exercise an appreciable effect on their economies.

That part of the demand which genuine vanilla cannot meet is furnished by substitutes. Connoisseurs maintain that there is no substitute for vanilla, but not everybody is endowed with well-educated taste buds, and we may suspect that a large proportion of vanilla consumers could not tell the difference between the genuine article and most of the substitutes for it. Several other plants contain vanillin, though not as abundantly as vanilla does. In the southwestern United States, hikers or campers entering a stand of ponderosa pine are often struck by an odor of vanilla in the air. The tree's bark smells of it, and it probably does contain vanillin, but nobody has been tempted to try to extract it, for ponderosa is too valuable for other purposes. A pine tree would be a likely host for vanillin, for we know that it can be derived from coniferin, found in the sapwood of fir trees, and from lignin, removed from wood pulp (which comes mostly from conifers) in the process of papermaking. There is vanillin also in Siam benzoin and even in asafoetida.

Coumarin, obtained from the tonka bean (tropical South American too) and also from sweet clover and woodruff, apparently contains no vanillin, but it provides a flavor close enough to fool most people (in countries which permit its use; it has sometimes been banned as a vanilla substitute, for reasons of health). What seems to have been the first vanilla substitute was developed in Germany in 1876, from eugenol, contained in essence of clove (and also in the guaiacol, a tree which, once again, is native to tropical South America). Germany manufactures much of the artificial vanilla used in Europe, but it is very strong in flavor, has to be used cautiously, and is coarse and much inferior to the real thing.

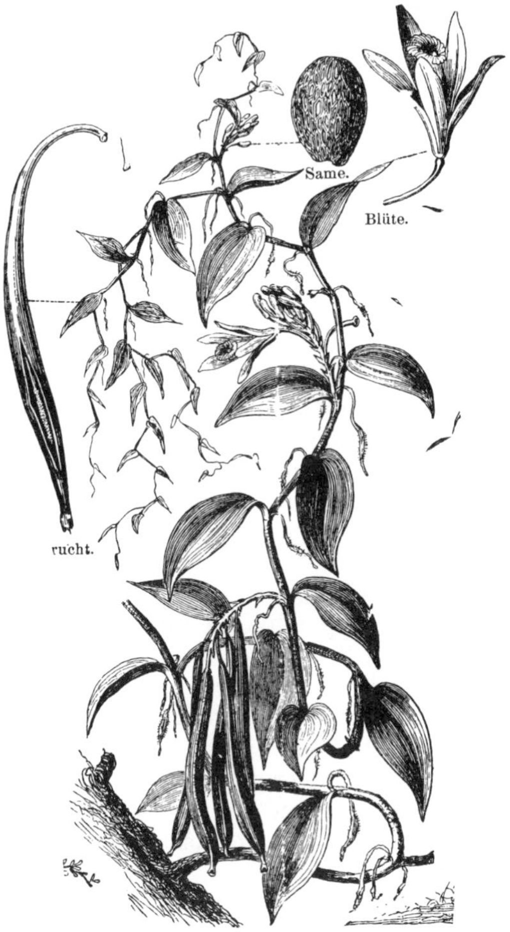

VANILLA. *Engraving from Meyers:* Lexikon, *Bibliographisches Institut, Leipzig, 1897*

All these substitutes, though they start from natural products containing vanillin, fail to measure up to vanilla itself because they lack some of the other constituents of the genuine article, first of all piperonal. In recent years, chemists have learned how to produce completely synthetic vanilla, made from pure molecules undefiled by contact with Nature the Cultivator. Fabricators of artificial flavors claim that they can produce a product undistinguishable from real vanilla, and perhaps they can, but they do not choose to do so. They seem unable to avoid the temptation of exaggerating the taste, probably to persuade the public that they have really succeeded. What is missing is nature's subtlety, a result of nature's irregularity. Only synthetic products can be perfect, and perfection seems to be an uninteresting quality, in taste as elsewhere, because it is without individuality. However, our present synthetic-vanilla makers probably do better than the manipulators of food who produced what Balzac referred to in *La Rabouilleuse* as "little pots of cream in which the vanilla had been replaced by burnt oats, as much like vanilla as chicory is like coffee."

The United States has long been in the habit of using vanilla in liquid form. Extract of vanilla is convenient to use, and recommendable enough when it is really extracted from vanilla; but this is becoming increasingly rare. It requires great faith in human nature and the integrity of merchants to believe that you are likely to get real vanilla if you buy it in powdered form. In my home we use vanilla in the form of beans: put a pod in your cake or custard and remove it after cooking; it can be reused a good many times before its flavor begins to fade. But even with vanilla beans, you are not always safe from the ingenuity of sellers—bastard vanilla or even vanillon is sometimes rolled in benzoic acid crystals, thus producing an excellent simulation of the givre, which makes the inferior bean look like the best grade.

The worldwide use of the French word *givre* for the white deposit on the vanilla bean tips us off to the fact that France was the chief supplier of Europe when vanilla became commercialized; the fact that the word "vanilla" is not on record in English before the seventeenth century tips us off to the time when it began to be generally known in Europe; and the fact that its name is vanilla tips us off to the original source of supply—Spanish-speaking territory, either Spain itself, or Spanish possessions in the New World. The very first European to use this name seems to have been Piso, in 1658. It was then taken up by Charles Plumier, botanist to the king of France, who made several voyages to tropical America. It was then adopted everywhere. Most writers on this subject explain that *vanilla* in Spanish is a diminutive of *vaina*, "sheath" or "pod," but frequently refrain from delving deeper into etymology to give the derivation of the Spanish word, which comes from the Latin *vagina*. This was what the shape of the bean suggested to a number of people, giving it, in accord with the medieval Doctrine of Signatures, an aphrodisiac reputation.

Vanilla was known to botanists before it had acquired that name. It was in 1602 that Clusius received some pods, not from the French, but from Queen Elizabeth's apothecary. They had probably started to decompose and ferment, for they gave off more odor than would be normal for untreated beans; Clusius wrote that they smelled like benzoin, strongly enough to provoke headaches. He gave the plant the name *Lobus oblongus aromaticus*.

In the same century, vanilla vines are reported to have been grown in France in the royal hothouses, purely as a curiosity; at that period, Europe had not even begun to consume vanilla imported from the New World. The earliest mention of its use in cookery known to me dates from 1756, when it appeared in Hannah Glasse's *Art of Cookery*. Vanilla had indeed become generally available both in England and in France during the eighteenth century, at which period it was probably being imported directly from the New World, where both countries had colonies in the right places. Beginning in that century, Louis Lagriffe wrote, "vanilla became associated with chocolate, the vanilla being held to increase the aphrodisiac and anti-venereal-disease properties of the chocolate"—a practical combination.

Although chocolate itself was by no means cheap, vanilla seems to have been the element in this mixture which determined its price. A French advertisement of 1776 offered "health chocolate" for sale at a price of "three pounds containing half a vanilla bean, four pounds with a whole vanilla bean, and five pounds with two vanilla beans." The combination remains popular. Brillat-Savarin said that chocolate without vanilla was only "cocoa paste," but "when to the sugar, the cinnamon and the cacao you add the delicious aroma of vanilla, you attain the nec plus ultra of the perfection to which this preparation can be brought."

It was in France that Thomas Jefferson made the acquaintance of vanilla, and when he returned to the United States in 1789 to establish himself as Secretary of State in Philadelphia, then the national capital, he missed it. He sent his French maître d'hôtel, Adrien Petit, to the market to get him some vanilla beans, and Petit returned to report that vanilla was unknown in Philadelphia. Jefferson accordingly wrote to William Short, the American chargé d'affaires in Paris, "to send me a packet of 50 pods (batons) which may come very well in the middle of a packet of newspapers." I do not know whether the combination of Jefferson, vanilla and Philadelphia was responsible for it, but Philadelphia long enjoyed the reputation of having the best vanilla ice cream in the world.

In England vanilla must have gained considerable popularity by 1845, the year of Sydney Smith's death, to have given meaning to a compliment of his, reported by his daughter, Lady Holland: "Ah, you flavor everything; you are the vanilla of society."

Meanwhile an important development had occurred in France. Vanilla was still growing in Paris in what had been the royal hothouses and had become those of the Natural History Museum, in what is now the Jardin des Plantes. Slips were taken from it and planted on the Ile de Bourbon (rebaptized Réunion when the French Revolution rendered Bourbons unpopular). The plants flourished, but produced no pods. In 1841 a Creole named Edmond Albius found out why and remedied the situation. Vanilla is one of those plants for which nature, in its zeal to ensure reproduction, has overshot the mark and cursed them with over-specialization. The inconspicuous flower of the vanilla plant is hermaphroditic; presumably to prevent it from fertilizing itself and becoming weakened by inbreeding, a little tongue-like process separates anthers from stigmas. To perform the pollination the plant could not manage by itself, nature provided the melipona bee, the one insect which can get to the pollen, and then deposit it in another flower, thus assuring cross-pollination. (There is also a small hummingbird which can do this, but it has had less importance as a pollinator of vanilla.) There were no meliponas on the Ile de Bourbon.

Albius simply lifted the inhibiting partition with a little stick, and, lo and behold—vanilla beans! This operation alone would have defeated nature's purpose of preventing self-pollination, so artificial cross-pollination had to be instituted, a delicate operation performed by hand, another process which has helped keep vanilla expensive. (Hand pollination is now necessary in Mexico too, for pesticides have killed the melipona bees.) The principal crop of the Ile de Bourbon had been sugarcane, but the introduction of vanilla gave the island an important secondary source of revenue. According to a nineteenth-century handbook, there was hardly a sugar plantation which had not "more or less land under vanilla," and even on tiny holdings "the occupants of almost every hut cover their yards, courts, and plots with vanilla creepers."

From the Ile de Bourbon, France planted vanilla on some of her other tropical islands—Tahiti, where it has developed a local species, *V. tahitiensis*, Mauritius, the Comores, Madagascar. Nearly all the vanilla sold in France (and in most of Europe) was Bourbon vanilla, the name under which it is still marketed today. It remains important, but in Europe, even including France, most of the vanilla now comes from Madagascar, the world's largest producer. According to a 1972 advertisement published on behalf of the government of Madagascar, the island was then producing more than 90 percent of the total world crop. Since it came from two of the least trustworthy sources of information in the modern world—advertisers and governments—it is easier to believe the figure given in a contemporary encyclopedia, 65 percent.

Though vanilla is now one of the most popular flavors in the world, Brillat-Savarin seems to have gone off the deep end when he delivered himself, in his *Elégies Historiques*, of a piece of prose perfumed even more headily than vanilla:

> Aspasia, Chloe, and all those of whom the chisels of the Greeks immortalized the forms to the despair of the beauties of today, never did your charming lips breathe such suavity as that of a vanilla meringue; you hardly rise to the level of gingerbread. How I pity you!

The vanilla added to some American cigarettes in the process known as "saucing" is not vanilla. It is vanilla leaf, also called Carolina vanilla or deer's-tongue, *Trilisa odoratissima*, which exudes a vanilla-like fragrance when the leaf is crushed. It would be a reasonable guess that it contains vanillin.

VEA
stands for

VEAL. The world's greatest eaters of veal are the Italians. Varro, indeed, expressed the theory that the name Italy came from the word for veal (*vitulus*, or its diminutive, *vitellus*), and some modern scholars, out of respect, I suppose, for the most erudite Roman of his times (though one misled, occasionally, by superficial resemblances), have followed him. "The name seems to be a Graecized form of an Italic Vitelia, from the stem vitlo-, 'calf,' and perhaps meant 'calf land,' 'grazing land,'" says the *Encyclopaedia Britannica*. Perhaps; but if Varro (116–27 B.C.) had been born a century earlier, this idea might never have occurred to him. Veal does not seem to have been much eaten by the ancient Romans before the second century B.C., when "Italy" was already an old word. Originally it had not been applied to Varro's part of the peninsula, but only to its two southernmost provinces, whose poor soil was better suited for raising goats, or at the best, sheep, than cattle. It is difficult to imagine anyone describing that area as "calf land." It would be my guess that the similarity between the name Italy and the name of the calf is mere coincidence.

Even by the time of Trajan (A.D. 52–117), when Rome was probably better provided with food than it ever had been before, veal was only fourth in Roman preferences: the meat most widely eaten was pork, followed by lamb, preferably in the form of mutton (after all, the early Latins had been shepherds), and goat, preferably in the form of kid. Veal did take precedence over beef, very rare because very dear, but not until the reign of Alexander Severus (208–235) would Varro have found much support for his theory. At that period Rome was seized by a mania for young meat—not only from cattle, but also from pigs, sheep and goats—to such an extent that there was danger that the herds and flocks would disappear, wiped out by the practice of killing off virtually all domesticated animals before they reached reproductive age. By imperial decree the slaughter of young animals was forbidden, after which matters returned to normal and meat prices dropped by one-half to three-quarters of the levels which they had reached before the prohibition.

Modern Italians eat 15.4 pounds of veal per person per year, as compared with 4 pounds for Americans and 2.3 pounds for Britons. Most writers explain that this is because Italian pasturage is poor and limited, making it economically unsound to bring animals to maturity. It is true that all over the world beef is usually preferred to veal (even in Italy, where the annual per capita consumption of beef is 48.4 pounds, more than three times as much as for veal), and therefore veal production everywhere usually trails well behind beef production except when economic circumstances make it more profitable to slaughter animals young than to continue to feed them.

But Italy has at least two regions where there is excellent pasturage for cattle—in the Po valley, where meat is a by-product of milk (so veal comes from young males and is called *vitello*), and in Tuscany, where meat is a by-product of work (so veal comes from the less strong young females and is called *vitella*). The Tuscan area produces a third type of "veal," *vitellone* ("big veal"), which by analogy with American "baby beef" might perhaps be called "adult veal." Although it is not slaughtered before the age of fifteen to seventeen months, its flesh is still called *vitellone* and not *manzo*, "beef," and continues to be so called up to the age of three years, provided it is not put to work as a draft animal. It is fitting it with a yoke which produces the magic change. This curious terminology results from the existence in Italy of the Chianina, the world's heaviest cow and Italy's best meat animal, in which it is difficult to draw a line where veal ends and beef begins. It is precocious in weight (more than a thousand pounds at one year, often two thousand at two years) and in nature, producing red meat from the age of six months, and is virtually the same animal the Etruscans were raising on the same territory in Varro's time. They were seldom slaughtered young for veal, for they were primarily draft animals, which seems to have been the rule in antiquity. In the oldest civilization where we hear of veal—the Sumerian, about 2500 B.C.—cattle were worked until they became too old for labor before being killed for beef, so the only Sumerians who tasted veal were those wealthy enough to pay for the loss of the services of a valuable worker.

Italians do not eat veal because it is cheaper than beef, they eat it whenever it is in season and pay a premium price for it, 15 to 20 percent more than they pay for beef; if it were not for this price differential they would undoubtedly eat even more than they do. They like veal more than do consumers of other nationalities, and what seems to me the explanation for this I have already given in *The Food of Italy*:

Most persons think of the French as the great sauce makers; but it was Italians who first developed this art. . . . It is a giveaway that in large French kitchens making the sauces is a job entrusted to a specialist, the *saucier*. In Italy every cook must be able to concoct sauces or he could hardly cook at all. In France, a sauce is an adornment, even a disguise, added to a dish more or less as an afterthought. In Italy, it *is* the dish, its soul, its *raison d'être*, the element which gives it character and flavor. The most widespread Italian foods are bland, neutral; they would produce little impact on the taste buds unassisted. Pasta unadorned could quickly become monotonous. The whole point of *tagliatelle alla bolognese* or *spaghetti con le vongole* is the sauce. Rice, so common in Italy that the Italian word risotto has become naturalized in most countries, is not only a wonderful carrier of sauces, it can hardly get along without them. Even the favorite meat of Italy is the most neutral of all—veal.

The charm of veal for the Italians is the opportunity it gives them to utilize their culinary artistry to the full. Meats with more individualistic flavors refuse to enter with becoming modesty into the harmonious blends which are the triumph of Italian cooking. The neutrality of veal is the secret of its often-remarked versatility—"the chameleon of the kitchen," the nineteenth-century gourmand Grimod de la Reynière called it, a phrase he must have liked, for he applied it also to sole. "There are few animals, the pig excepted," Charles Monselet wrote in the same century, "which lend themselves to as many metamorphoses as the calf." It lends itself, indeed, even to disguise, not to say deception, possible only because its own flavor does not get in the way of others. Consider, for instance, the famous dish known as *vitello tonnato*, veal with tuna-fish sauce. Food writers tend to become dithyrambic about the genius of cooks who conceived a combination which at first blush seems so strange and yet turns out so successfully. This is not quite the angle from which the creation of this dish was approached. At a period when tuna failed to turn up in their normal profusion, cooks sought a way to counterfeit this fish for the benefit of its aficionados, disappointed at being deprived of the real thing. Veal was chosen as the best basis for an imitation. In the Middle Ages a similar subterfuge was practiced in France. In the anonymous *Ménagier de Paris* (1393), I find a recipe for "counterfeit sturgeon"; it is made from veal, from the calf's head. The sort of veal we get today is even better for dupery, probably its only claim to superiority:

Before the war [John and Karen Hess wrote in *The Taste of America*] unscrupulous purveyors would use cheap veal in place of expensive chicken in Chicken à la King. Today, veal is so dear, and chicken so relatively cheap, that we have met chicken labeled as veal. No matter—they're both fed the same and look the same, and would taste the same if they had any taste at all.

This decline in taste since the mass producers laid their hands on the calf probably explains why American consumption of veal has been more than halved since the late 1940s, when it was 9.7 pounds per capita per annum instead of today's 4 pounds. Italian veal may be modest and retiring by nature, but it is flavorful in its subtle way, and so is French veal, from the country probably second only to Italy in consumption of veal. Oddly enough, Joan M. Jungfleisch mentions neither Italy nor France specifically in her *For Innocents Abroad*:

The best veal in the world is Continental, especially that from Holland, and it is known in the trade as "fed veal" or "milk-fed veal." It is generally 2½ to 3½ months old when slaughtered and has spent its short life being fattened on milk and eggs which keep the flesh its characteristic pale pink color. American veal does not have the same quality as Continental. While a small amount is of the tender and succulent milk-fed quality and slaughtered at 3 months, most American veal is slaughtered only between 3 and 8 months and has been fattened on solid foods for some of that period.

English veal is the poorest [so no wonder English consumption is the lowest]. This is because veal in England is a by-product of the dairy industry, and the baby calves are slaughtered as early as possible, at two to four weeks. The resulting veal is thin and tasteless. There is traditionally little demand for veal in England, beef, lamb and pork being preferred, and thus little incentive to increase the quantity or quality.

Did Italy serve as the focal point from which the cult of the calf was transmitted to her neighbors to the north? Austria is a country dedicated to veal, from the point of view of quality rather than quantity, for almost 60 percent of all the meat eaten in Austria is pork, and 25 percent beef; veal accounts for only 10 percent. It is true that veal is expensive there. Nevertheless, Austrians swear by Wiener schnitzel (breaded veal scallops, Vienna style), but is it Viennese? In Lombardy they will tell you that the Austrians picked up this dish from that province when they were its governors. As early as 1528, the Venetian ambassador at Vienna reported that Austrian veal was

VEAL *by Jean-Baptiste Oudry (1686–1755).* Still Life with a Quarter of Veal, *oil on canvas*

excellent, but the Milanese claim to having originated the most famous Austrian veal dish dates much farther back, to 1134, when a banquet was given for the canon of Milan's ancient Church of Sant' Ambrogio, whose menu included *lombolos cum panitio*, breaded veal scallop, today *costoletta alla milanese*. In the nineteenth century the Austrian general Joseph Radetz told in a letter which has been preserved to our day how he encountered this dish in Milan and introduced it into Vienna.

The Italians are also sometimes reported to have introduced veal into France via Catherine de' Medici, whom historians like to credit with having brought into that country any food they have not been able to account for otherwise. It appears that she did like veal, as was natural for anyone who came from Florence, where we may deduce that it was considered particularly luxurious from the fact that during one of Florence's intermittent attacks of bad conscience expressed in sumptuary legislation, it was decreed that if veal were served at a wedding dinner, no other meat could appear on the same menu. But the *Ménagier de Paris,* a comfortable century and a half before Catherine appeared on the French scene, gave not only a recipe for "counterfeit sturgeon," but several others as well. It reported also that 19,604 calves had been sold on the Paris market during the year, about 60 percent of the total for steers (the comparison, note, is between numbers of animals, not by weight). In the sixteenth century Bruyerin-Champier reported that veal was then considered the best kind of butchers' meat, and when raised for the tables of the upper classes was entirely milk-fed for six months or even a year (too long in most opinions) to keep the flesh tender and delicate. Cardinal Mazarin is said to have eaten veal from calves fed only on milk, egg yolks and biscuits.

In England as in France, veal seems to have been present earlier than some writers are willing to admit. A recent book on food history tells us that "to the Saxons, killing veal calves was a Norman act of wantonness; eating veal was not sanctioned in any English cookbook until 1658." This seemed to stigmatize the Normans as more lackadaisical than they are shown to be in history, if it took them six centuries to introduce veal into England; but in fact veal, though then as now it was not much liked in that country, had been eaten much earlier than the seventeenth century. English yeomen are known to have fed on it in the sixteenth century; at least two fifteenth-century English cookbooks give a number of recipes for veal dishes; and one for a veal pasty appeared in *The Forme of Cury,* whose date is 1378.

> I never have figured out anything interesting to do with veal [Richard Gehman wrote in *The Haphazard Gourmet*]. Sometimes I stuff a veal roast with a pocket in it, using ordinary chicken stuffing, a little heavier on the sage than usual. . . . But don't cook veal at home. Go to an Italian restaurant. They know more about it than you and I do.

This is probably not bad advice provided you have access to an Italian restaurant which has not slipped into unimaginative routine and decided that the beginning and end of veal cookery is tired scallopini. There are any number of great veal dishes, most of them Italian, and many of them within reach of an average cook. Perhaps you had better not try the delicious but elaborate *cima alla genovese,* a complicated form of stuffed breast of veal destined to be eaten cold, which sits on the sideboard cut open so that the hard-boiled egg at its center fixes you with its yellow stare, but ordinary stuffed breast of veal is easy enough to make. We have it often at my home, where we do not attempt culinary exploits but fix a stuffing of breadcrumbs mixed with chopped York ham, bacon, an egg for a binder and a judicious selection of whatever herbs happen to be handy. This mixture is sewn into the enveloping breast of veal and put into already boiling water, otherwise it would disintegrate when it cooled—a pity, for this dish is even better cold than hot.

Everybody knows the Milanese *osso buco,* a cut of veal shank including the marrow bone, which we also make at home, complete with the traditional *gramolada* sauce which goes with it. Easy to make also is the Roman *saltimbocca* (the name means "jump into the mouth"), a slice of ham on a slice of veal, seasoned with sage, sautéed in butter, and braised in white wine (it has infinite variations, including some in which you roll it around various sorts of stuffing). What some connoisseurs consider the finest cut of veal is the boned rolled section of loin to which the kidneys, left on, are attached; I have never encountered this in the United States, but it is prized in France under the name *rognonnade de veau* and in Germany as *Kalbsnierenbraten.* Shifting to the opposite extreme, among homely honest French family dishes, we have the unassuming stew called *blanquette de veau* and the venerable classic *tête de veau en tortue,* calf's head (the muscles around the eye are the tenderest part) in a rich sauce.

There is also, of course, the limitless family of schnitzels—not only Wiener schnitzel (which in Vienna is particularly esteemed when made from the *Kaiserteil,* "emperor's cut"), but also *Naturschnitzel, Pariserschnitzel,* Cordon Bleu schnitzel (rumored to have originated in Switzerland), Prague schnitzel, *Sardellenschnitzel,* Parma schnitzel (with grated cheese of course), *Paprikaschnitzel, Rahmschnitzel, Jägerschnitzel.* Or, if you plan to indulge in *Holsteinerschnitzel,* which may or may not have been named for Baron Friedrich von Holstein, a diplomat of the imperial period, I would advise sticking to its simplest form—breaded, under a fried egg with a pair of anchovy fillets crossed on top—and avoiding its pretentious ambassadorial garnish of smoked salmon, caviar, mushrooms, truffles and crawfish tails. Neither the veal nor the luxury foods are at their best in this shotgun marriage of irreconcilable incompatibilities.

Skipping such peripheral manifestations as *ghiveciu,* Rumanian veal stew, and the jellied veal loaf which is a fixture of Swedish smorgasbord, I may point out that there is nothing wrong with simple roast veal, perhaps surrounded by tiny sweet boiled onions or accompanied by the French vegetable stew *ratatouille*; cold, with mayonnaise, roast veal has always been a standard dish on the menus of the no-nonsense all-hours bourgeois French *brasseries.* For the sake of completeness it may be added that calves provide organic meats usually superior to the same delicacies from other animals—tongue, brains, liver, sweetbreads, kidneys; that their feet produce excellent jelly; and that rich fattening sauces can be avoided by using *blond de veau*, obtained by boiling veal shanks in water with carrots, onions, celery and a chicken carcass. "Come to Citey [where he was living]," Voltaire wrote to his friend Saint-Lambert, "where Madame du Châtelet [his cook] will not let you be poisoned. There is not a spoonful of gravy in her cooking: everything is made with *blond de veau*. We will live one hundred years [he was cut off at eighty-four, Mme. du Châtelet must have returned to gravy] and you will never die."

VEGETABLE
stands for

vegetables, of which Joseph Mitchell's Old Mr. Flood said, "Vegetables have been improved until they're downright poisonous"; for the **vegetable hummingbird**, which is not a bird but an East Indian leguminous plant with a beautiful white or red flower which serves alternatively as a decoration or a salad, depending on the whim of the moment; for the **vegetable marrow**, a name applied confusingly either to the AVOCADO or, in England, to certain types of SQUASH; for the **vegetable oyster**, which is SALSIFY; for the **vegetable pear**, a versatile Central American plant whose fruit is a sort of squash, whose root is a sort of yam, whose young shoots and leaves are a sort of salad, and whose seeds are a sort of nut; and for the **vegetable sponge**, or smooth loofah, whose leaves and fruit are both eaten universally in West Africa when young and abandoned unanimously when mature.

VELVET
stands for

the **velvet apple**, or mangosteen, an agreeably flavored fruit native to the Philippines, now planted widely throughout the tropics, and particularly popular in Africa; for the **velvet bean**, alias the Florida velvet bean, the Georgia velvet bean, the Bengal velvet bean, the Mauritius bean, the *pois mascate*, the *frijol terciopelo*, the *mucuma arra*, the cowitch, the cowhage and the cowage, cultivated as green manure in the United States but as human food in tropical Asia and Africa despite its tendency to become slightly poisonous around the edges; and for **velvet dock**, our twenty-second name for the mullein, and **velvet plant**, the twenty-third.

VEN
stands for

the **vendace**, a fish much appreciated in Finland (it exists also in Scotland, but there they make less to-do about it), usually eaten sardine-sized (or even smaller in the form of roe), a far-north version of the famous fera and lavaret of the Swiss lakes, all members of the genus *Coregonus*, related to the salmon; and for **venison**, which makes most of us think automatically of DEER, but actually it applies to mammalian game of any kind.

VENUS
stands for

Venus, a family of clams, notably the quahog, eaten with gusto in New England, and the warty Venus, eaten with gusto in Africa; for the **Venus comb**, the plant which the mother of Euripides was accused of selling in the market of Athens, a slanderous allegation, since only women of the lowest social status hawked merchandise in the markets; for **Venus's looking-glass**, a European-Mediterranean plant nowadays grown mostly in French flower gardens, but once used in salads; and for **Venus's navelwort**, whose seeds and flowers by their shape give it a name so picturesque that I wish I could pass it on to you, but as there is no indication that it is edible, I am unable to mention it.

VER
stands for

verbascum, our twenty-fourth name for the mullein; for **verjuice**, thought of oftenest as the juice of unripe grapes used as a condiment or as an ingredient for lean sauces, but it may mean any tart juice, such as that of crab apples, gooseberries, sorrel or cress, sometimes fermented; for **vermin**, a little-admired category of human food, though it has been eaten during periods of dearth at many times in many places by many peoples, like the seventeenth-century American Indians of the Pacific Northwest who used to throw sea-otter pelts over kettles of boiling water and feast on the fleas driven out by the steam; for **veronica**, or speedwell, reputed capable of staving off scurvy; and for the **vers-palmiste**, or palm-tree caterpillar, of the Caribbean, where it is considered a dainty tidbit when well roasted.

VET
stands for

the **vetch**, which American writers are likely to

tell you is a legume fit only for fodder, but men have been cultivating it for their own use since Neolithic times and are still doing so in South America, India, North Africa, the Near East and even to a limited extent in southern Europe under such diverse names as the bard vetch, bitter vetch, chickling vetch, milk vetch, monantha vetch and the grass pea.

VI
stands for

viburnum, a term which covers, among others, the maple-leaved viburnum, the sweet viburnum or nannyberry, the highbush cranberry or witch hobble, and the naked viburnum or withe rod, which Thoreau found "rather insipid and seedy"; for the **Victoria plum,** so named because it turned up in Sussex, apparently a mutant, three years after Queen Victoria ascended the throne, which "enshrines the taste of bad Victorian cooking," according to Geoffrey Grigson, who doesn't explain how; for the **vicuña,** a wild member of the South American llama family, valued for its meat and even more so for its wool, which cannot be domesticated because it refuses to perform its elaborate courtship ritual to work up interest in the next generation except in the privacy of freedom; for the **vigna** of tropical and subtropical Australia, which gives its name to the genus which also includes the familiar cowpea; for **vinegar,** which can fabricate itself naturally, but since virtually all the vinegar used nowadays is manufactured by man, it is automatically ruled out of this dictionary of non-manhandled foods; for the **vinegar tree,** or scarlet sumac, whose acid sour berries are pressed to produce a substitute for lemon juice; for the **violet,** whose petals were added to Louis XIV's salad; for the **violet wood,** which yields an edible gum for Australians; for the **viper,** which the Chinese preferred to eat under the name "white flower snake"; for the **Virginia DEER,** a prized game animal in, of all places, Finland, where they were imported in 1930 from, of all places, Minnesota; for the **virgin's-bower,** so named I don't know why, a Mediterranean plant whose young shoots are eaten boiled; and for the **viscacha,** a large South American rodent, which when Pizarro's men arrived was being eaten by Peruvians, and for all I know, still is.

VO
stands for

the **voandzeia,** alias the Bambara groundnut, the Congo goober, the earth pea, the kaffir pea, the ground bean, the jugo bean, the Madagascar groundnut and the stone groundnut, Africa's reply to the peanut, widely cultivated from Guinea southward, which came to European notice in 1682 when Father Merolla described it as "like a musquet-ball and very wholesome and well tasted"; for the **vole,** a mouselike creature of neat habits eaten in Russia in Mousterian times, but so far as I know, nowhere now; and for **volvaria,** a group of mushrooms of which the silky volvaria is classed among those of the top quality, despite its woody smell, which, however, disappears when it is cooked.

VU
stands for

the **vulture,** which Jews (and no doubt Moslems also) are forbidden to eat, but everyone else can indulge to his heart's content; and for the **vulva,** which for ancient Roman gourmets was the most interesting part of the sow.

W

WALTON, IZAAK: *This dish of meat [meaning fish] is too good for any but anglers or very honest men.*

WELBY, THOMAS EARLE: *"Turbot, Sir," said the waiter, placing before me two fishbones, two eyeballs, and a bit of black mackintosh.*

WA
stands for

the **wadalee-gum tree** of the East Indies, whose wood yields the extract called catechu, one of the ingredients of the betel-leaf package chewed incessantly in India and contiguous territories; for the **wafer ash**, whose bitter seed has been used as a substitute for hops; for the **wahoo,** which when it is a fish provides food for East Africa and some Indian Ocean islands, but when it is a tree has, so far as I know, no palatable parts; and for **wake-robin,** also known, among other names, as Adam-and-Eve, lords-and-ladies, cuckoopint and starch-root, of which the root is the part usually eaten, but in ancient times, wrote John Gerard, "Dioscorides showeth that the leaves also are prescribed to be eaten and that they must be eaten after they be dried and boyled"—not the same plant as the Virginia wake-robin, whose roots were held to be poisonous but were eaten by American Indians all the same.

WAL
stands for

the **waller,** another name for the famous European catfish more commonly called the wels, which bestowed its name on a Danubian city in Austria unless it was the other way around; for the **walleye,** a pickerel or pike particularly praised by sports fishermen in the Pacific Northwest, where it is also known as the jack or jackfish; and the **walleye surfperch,** which employs the kelp surfperch as a barber; and for the **walrus,** which has been called "the Eskimos' grocery store."

And **WAL** also stands for

WALNUT. For the ancient Romans, the walnut was a portrait of the human brain. The outer green husk (which many walnut eaters have never seen) was the scalp. The hard shell of the kernel was the protective skull. The thin envelope inside, with its paperlike partitions between the two halves of the nut, was the membrane. And the convoluted nut itself represented the two hemispheres of the brain. Presented with such promising material for a start, the myth-making ancients pursued the subject no further, though they had produced complicated legends about some other foods which offered much scantier opportunity (the CABBAGE, for instance). They contented themselves with naming the walnut *juglans,* Jupiter's acorn, and concluding that it cured headaches. This was in tune with the medieval Doctrine of Signatures, the theory that the shape of a plant, or part of a plant, was a signal from nature to man of the purpose it could serve. When the Middle Ages arrived, however, the signal was interpreted the other way around. The anonymous *Ménagier de Paris* (1393) said that walnuts *caused* headaches.

The history of the walnut goes back so far that nobody knows where it originated. We often read that it is a native of Persia, an assumption based on the fact that Pliny called it the Persian nut and said it had been introduced into Italy from that country. If so, it was before his time, for Varro, who antedated him by nearly a century and a half, recorded its presence in Italy then; and the Greek philosopher Theophrastus, nearly two and a half centuries before Varro, wrote of it under the name *karuon*—or at least, we are told that it was the walnut which he had in mind. Actually *karuon* meant a nut in general; the walnut, strictly speaking, was *karuon basilikon,* "kingly nut."

Just as the ancient Romans called *Juglans regia* the Persian nut because they got it from Persia, either directly or via Greece or Asia Minor, so Americans call the same species the English walnut because they got it from England, though it was certainly not a native of the British Isles.

The majority opinion today seems to be that while Persia does fall within the oldest area to which it has been possible to attribute the walnut, it covered a great deal more ground, ranging from southeastern Europe and/or Asia Minor to the Himalayas, where it grows up to 8000 feet. Wild walnuts are found throughout this region. If this was indeed the original habitat of the walnut, it had already spread beyond it in prehistoric times. The oldest find of walnuts, in the Shanidar caves of northern Iraq, falls within the right area, but the next oldest are in Mesolithic middens and the Neolithic remains of lake settlements in Switzerland, a considerable distance farther west.

The first historic mention of walnuts tells us that they were grown in Babylon. The ancient Greeks pressed them for their oil; they seem to have been using them nearly a hundred years before the Romans, about the beginning of the fourth century B.C., whereas the Romans apparently inherited them only toward the end of the century. The Romans proved they considered them a luxury by paying high prices for them; they were often eaten along with fruit as a dessert. The priests of the Temple of Isis at Pompeii had perhaps reached the last stage of the meal to which they sat down on the perfect bright sunny day of August 24, A.D. 79, for there were nuts on the table. They never got around to eating them.

Meanwhile on the other side of the world, China, despite one minority opinion that this was the original home of the walnut, seems to have made its acquaintance only a short time before 100 B.C., during the reign of the Emperor Wu Ti. It could have come from India, where walnuts were particularly important in Kashmir, within what is believed by the majority to have been their original habitat.

The Romans are often credited with having carried the walnut to the rest of Europe, but there are at least three reasons for doubting this: the fact that walnuts were being eaten in Switzerland in the Stone Age, before there were any Romans; a report that the ancient Gauls used them before the Romans came; and the circumstance that, though the agency of the Romans in spreading the walnut is almost always alleged in connection with the introduction of this nut into England, there is no evidence that there were any walnuts in the British Isles until a thousand years after the Romans had gone home. Geoffrey Grigson, in *A Dictionary of English Plant Names,* says the walnut was grown in Roman Britain, but, though he ordinarily gives both the date for the introduction of a plant name into the English language and the date when the plant itself reached the British Isles, he is in this case unable to give either. He does say that "walnut" comes from the Old English *walh-hnuta,* meaning "foreign nut," but foreign from where? From Germany, perhaps, for he says that the word entered English "late"—how late is not specified—from Low German. *The Oxford Book of Food Plants* suggests that the time of the walnut's arrival in England "may have been" the fifteenth century, but does not explain why it thinks so. The earliest actual record of its existence in the British Isles, according to the *Encyclopaedia Britannica,* is dated 1567.

Evidence in the case of Britain may be so scanty because, "English" walnut though it may be called, it does not seem to have stirred much interest among the English. Except for certain specific restricted uses (walnuts and port with Stilton cheese as the traditional ending for a meal, or walnuts, pickled shells and all—"looking like something out of the compost heap," writes a correspondent—on the counters of English country pubs), the walnut played only a very limited role in Britain until after World War I, when its commercial production became important for the first time.

Early French history affords us more frequent glimpses of this food. Historian André Castelot says that intensive cultivation of walnuts in France was undertaken as early as the fourth century in the region of Grenoble, which still produces the best walnuts in France and possibly in the world. Charlemagne had walnut trees planted in his domains, at a time when walnuts were used rather like spices, to season other foods. Church records of the Dordogne region in the eleventh century list walnuts among the crops on which the peasants paid tithes in kind, so they must have been the object of systematic cultivation. In the twelfth and thirteenth centuries, walnuts were shipped from the nut-producing centers of France to Paris, where their oil was used as a flavoring. It was later replaced for that purpose by poppyseed oil, in an apparent whim of fashion, for walnut oil was cheaper. However, the whole walnut remained popular, creating a new minor profession, that of "measurer of walnuts"—an official whose function it was to make sure that the medieval consumer was not cheated on quantity.

Fourteenth-century menus list walnuts among the desserts served at important banquets. At the end of this century the *Ménagier de Paris* confirmed the esteem in which they were held by describing the pains taken to preserve them, in spiced honey, by a process which required a month for the initial preparation (after which no time limit was prescribed for finishing the job, except that the direction to stir them once a week indicated that it was lengthy). It was during the Middle Ages that Europeans learned from the Arabs, who had learned it from the Persians, a technique of making a sort of paste out of ground nuts, which was then used as a basis for sauces or to thicken stews and soups. Anyone who has given much attention to medieval cooking must have been struck by the lavish use of almond-flavored sauces during the Middle Ages, but there were walnut-flavored sauces too.

Cultivated walnuts pleased the palates of the rich, and wild walnuts, free for foragers in the forests, filled the bellies of the poor—and in times of famine, fed everybody. Castelot wrote that in the Dordogne during medieval times walnuts were the principal food of the very poor. In mid-fifteenth-century Paris, during the reign of Charles VII, there were times when the only food on the market was walnuts. During the last quarter of the seventeenth century, chestnuts and walnuts were among the most important foods of many families in central and southern France, and in the famine year of 1663 peasants in the Dauphiné, after eating their walnuts, ground up the shells together with acorns to make what could not have been particularly palatable bread. "In Europe," Reay Tannahill wrote in her *Food in History*, "walnuts . . . blanched, pulverized and soaked in water, provided the staple milk of many households until at least the end of the eighteenth century." A record of sorts must have been achieved by the Cathar "Perfect" (meaning a member of that heretical medieval sect who had attained its highest level by the practice of extreme asceticism) who disciplined himself for his imagined sins by living for days at a stretch on the warm water in which he had boiled a walnut.

Up to now we have been looking at only one of the at least seventeen separate species of the walnut genus, *J. regia*, the so-called Persian walnut (or English walnut), but there is one other of commercial importance, the Eastern black walnut, *J. nigra*, native to North America, the largest of the family, which reaches a height of 150 feet, while trunks 6 feet in diameter are not unusual. Its magnificent dimensions make it a conspicuous landmark of fertility, for where it grows well there is a promise of limestone in the soil. When the Pennsylvania Dutch were choosing their land, they picked areas where they found stands of black walnut, while the early settlers of Illinois looked for tall sycamores near the streams and sturdy black walnuts away from them as a guarantee of fertility. Indians had been eating black walnuts at least since 2000 B.C., the date of archeological finds made in the upper Great Lakes area. They used both the nut and the tree's sap in their cooking.

The early colonists had to depend on the native nut too, for the first Persian walnuts, planted in Virginia and Massachusetts from the seeds of English trees, proved inadaptable to the new environment; some individual trees lived, but most of them died before reaching bearing age. No region propitious to the Persian nut was found until the Pacific coast was reached, where it flourished in Oregon and California. California today produces 98.4 percent of all the walnuts grown commercially for food in the United States, and since 1973 has been causing concern to the Grenoble growers of Europe's best walnuts, underselling them in their formerly secure markets of Scandinavia, encroaching on that of Germany, and even making inroads in parts of France itself. In 1975 Grenoble walnut growers staged demonstrations to bring pressure to bear on the French government to come to their aid: road signs reading "Grenoble" were painted over with "San Francisco, Walnut Capital." One of their complaints was that the government was hampering

WALNUT. *Gelatin silver print:* Walnuts—types of, variety, *photographer unknown, date unknown. Records of the Bureau of Plant Industry, Soils, and Agricultural Engineering*

their sales by too great a concern for quality, expressed in such regulations as the one which denied the Grenoble label to nuts not of the current year's crop.

The reason why California grows Persian walnuts despite the availability of an American nut is that the Persian species is held almost unanimously to be finer in flavor. The black walnut is sweet and oily, but stronger in taste ("richer" say the few who prefer it, "coarser" say those who do not). It has the advantage of retaining more of its flavor when cooked, but the disadvantage of having both an outer husk and an inner shell thicker and tougher than that of the Persian walnut, making it really difficult to reach its edible portion. For the task of opening the inner shell, two techniques have been developed, from opposite approaches to the problem. One technique increases the power available to vanquish the resistance of the nut, the other weakens the resistance of the nut to the power exerted upon it: concretely, utensil manufacturers have made a stronger nutcracker specifically for the black walnut, while at the same time horticulturists have been working to produce varieties with thinner shells. (Euell Gibbons, a no-nonsense type, advised attacking the black walnut with a heavy hammer and a nutpick.)

The husk is an even harder problem. Gibbons wrote that the easiest method was to wear heavy shoes and grind the walnuts under the heel. He also advised wearing gloves, for "if the freshly hulled nut is handled with bare hands, it will leave a brown stain that it is almost impossible to remove." Another black-walnut fan suggested placing the unhusked nuts on a driveway and running a car back and forth over them, but warned that if the driveway were of white cement an unsightly blotch would be left on it. The most long-lasting walnut-juice stain (from Persian walnuts) seems to be that on the discolored cliffs of La Barre, near La Malène, in the department of the Lozère. They are supposed to have been marked by the oil-charged smoke from a warehouse full of walnuts which was burned down during the French Revolution; their signature is still there, after nearly two centuries' exposure to wind and water.

Despite the secondary rating accorded the black walnut, it has its champions for certain purposes. It is superb as a flavoring for ice cream and combines so well with chocolate that many people find it superior for fudge and other chocolate confections. It is used for these purposes in Great Britain, where it was transplanted in the seventeenth century, but perhaps less for its nuts than its timber. Both species provide excellent wood, but black walnut is perhaps handsomer, and is considered sturdier, which explains why it was used for airplane propellers during World War I and is today the favorite wood for gunstocks. Both species are extensively used for furniture and wall paneling.

As a food, walnuts are today peripheral—they are nibbled with before-dinner drinks or go into confectionery or pastry. In earlier times, however, they often constituted a full-fledged ingredient in cooking (they were a basic element in the cuisine of France's Quercy), and in some parts of the world, notably the Middle East, they still do. One of Iran's national dishes is *fesenjan*, a duck or chicken stew simmered with walnuts and pomegranate juice, seasoned with cardamom, and served with chopped walnuts sprinkled over it. Bulgaria's *tarator* is a walnut and cucumber soup. Soviet Georgia makes two traditional sauces from pounded walnuts, which recall those the Arabs had from Persia in medieval times. A similar walnut-cream sauce exists in Turkey, while Elizabeth David gives the recipe for an Italian version in which walnuts are combined with breadcrumbs, olive oil, butter, cream and parsley, which she describes as "bizarre." Walnut-stuffed chicken is also an Italian dish, while finely ground walnut *shells* are sometimes used in the stuffing of the ring-shaped pasta called *agnolotti.* In the United States the walnut is returning to the role of a full-fledged food in vegetarian dishes. It is perhaps the vegetable product oftenest used to counterfeit meat, for its proteins (20.5 grams per 100 grams of shelled nuts) are perhaps the closest in the vegetable kingdom to animal proteins, except for those of the soybean.

The jingle

A woman, a dog, and a walnut-tree,
The more you beat 'em the better they be

has been traced back, through varying forms, to 1560. While the motivation can be understood, without necessarily being approved, in the first two cases, it is difficult to discern in the third. Thomas Fuller in the seventeenth century did write that "a nut-tree must be manured [in his day, "manured" meant "cultivated"] by beating, or else would never bear fruit"; this falls a little short of complete explanation. Could it be that pounding on the tree dislodges the pollen and helps fertilization? Another possible explanation is provided by Dorothy Hartley, who, in *Food in England*, says that the beating was done with a billhook in early March while the sap was rising, to encourage it to step lively. Another suggestion transfers the beating to harvest time, when its object is supposed to be to knock out of the trees unripe nuts which remain clinging obstinately to their branches.

If you plan to raise walnut trees by this or any other method of encouragement, be careful what you plant near them. The roots secrete juglone, poisonous to many flowers and vegetables, notably rhododendrons, azaleas and tomatoes.

WAP
stands for

the **wapatoo**, also called arrowhead, arrowleaf or duck potato, possibly the favorite tuber of North American Indians, who harvested it by wading through the marshes, ponds and streams where it grows and picking the tubers with their toes; and for the **wapiti**, or elk, the largest land mammal of the Pacific Northwest (up to half a ton) and the second-largest member of the DEER family, in which it is exceeded only by the moose.

WAR
stands for

the **warbler**, whose diminutive size and sympathetic appearance disqualify it as food in Anglo-Saxon eyes, but Continental Europeans have been eating it with untroubled consciences at least since the time of the ancient Romans, who called it the Cyprus bird; for the **warden pear**, bright green with black splotches, shaped like an acorn squash and much esteemed in England in the Middle Ages and in modern times on certain Greek islands, which may be where it started; for the **wart hog**, so universally eaten in tropical Africa that it must taste better than it looks; and for the **warty venus**, a bivalve whose name might lead us to expect that it is studded with protuberances, but it isn't, it only has the concentric growth ridges common to many clams more deeply scored than is usual.

WATER
stands for

the **water apple** of Burma, producer of small white or rosy fruits which look appetizing but, despite a faint aromatic flavor, are barely eatable; for the **water berry** of Africa, of which one species appeals mildly to East Africans and South Africans and another widely to tropical Africans; for **water-betony**, called siege grass in French because its roots were eaten by the famished garrison at La Rochelle during the siege of 1628; for the **waterbuck**, an African antelope which has been deemed worthy food by tropical Africans since prehistoric times; for the **water buffalo**, which supplies the milk for Italy's mozzarella cheese; for the **water chestnut**, which, as you may be surprised to learn if you have classified it in your mind as Chinese, grows so profusely in the Potomac as to form in some spots impassable barriers for boats; for the **water chinquapin**, a pale yellow water lily whose beauty for American Indians lay chiefly in its farinaceous seeds and edible tubers; and for **watercress**, which John Gerard calls cuckow-floure, lady-smock and even impatient lady-smock, but is discussed less picturesquely in this book in the entry on CRESS.

WATER
stands for

the **water deer**, a species of this eminently edible family which lives beside large Chinese rivers and spends much of its time wading or swimming; for the **water-dragon**, or water arum, whose starch is edible once you rid it of its acrid taste; for the **water-filter nut**, eaten in the East Indies, with what effect on the human digestive system I do not know, but its seeds will clarify muddy water; for **waterleaf**, which may mean either the tropical African plant whose leaves are eaten universally like spinach or the North American plant otherwise known as woolen-breeches whose young shoots used to be eaten in Kentucky as a salad; for **water lettuce**, whose greenery is eaten in the Sudan, but it is scarce; and for **water lilies**, a popular term which is the despair of botanists who cannot divine from it whether the speaker has in mind *Victoria regia*, the giant South American water lily whose seeds are edible; or *Euryale ferox*, the prickly water lily of East India and China, whose starch-rich seeds, rhizomes and stalks are all eaten; or *Nelumbium nuciferum*, the **water lotus**, whose rhizomes, eaten chiefly in southeastern Asia, a taste which reminds some people of artichokes; or some member of the genus *Nymphaea*, whose rhizomes, flower receptacles and, more rarely, stems are eaten in West Africa and North Africa, and whose seeds are eaten in tropical Africa but are considered as famine food in India; or some member of the genus *Nuphar*, of which the roots and leafstalks of the yellow water lily are eaten by Finns and Russians; the seed stalks and tubers of the Australian water lily are eaten by the natives of that continent, who report that the tubers, toasted, taste like potatoes; and the roots of the yellow pond lily or spatterdock were eaten by American Indians, who said that they tasted like liver. I do not know the exact nature of the water lily from whose leaves Pauline Bonaparte brewed a tea which she thought was a cure for syphilis.

WATER
stands for

the **watermelon**, concerning which you are not

obliged to believe the story that when half a MELON was thrown at Demosthenes during a political debate he clapped it on his head and thanked the thrower for providing him with a helmet to wear while fighting against Philip of Macedonia; for the **watermelon berry**, which is the fruit of the wild cucumber; for **water-mint**, in form, flavor and fragrance much like land-bound MINT; for **water pimpernel**, or brooklime, of which John Lightfoot wrote in 1789 that "it is esteemed an anti-scorbutic and is eaten by some in the spring as a sallet, but it is more bitter and not so agreeable to the palate as watercresses"; for the **water purslane**, a salad plant of ancient Greece and Rome, not, so far as I know, used today; for the **water shield**, whose tuberous rootstock used to be eaten by California Indians; for the **water worm**, eaten in the Sahara, which, fortunately for Saharans, is not a worm but a SHRIMP; and for the **water yam**, which as botanists see it is not really a YAM, but the natives of Madagascar, who eat the fleshy root, are willing to give it the benefit of the doubt.

WA
(from this point on)
stands for

the **wattle** of Australia, which when it is the black wattle, the green wattle or the silver wattle yields nothing but a gum similar to gum arabic, but when it is the Sydney golden wattle provides Tasmanians with starchy seeds and roastable pods; for the **wattle tree** of Jamaica, which produces edible fruit, but what it tastes like deponent knoweth not; for the **waved whelk**, a shellfish which is sold by the ton in the British Isles but disdained in the United States, though it is the same animal on both sides of the ocean, and the **wavy turban**, also a shellfish, which is eaten on the Pacific coast from California to Mexico, but not by everybody; for the **wavy**, which when it is the scabby-nosed wavy is Ross's goose, nearly wiped out in California by taste-conscious hunters until it was accorded the protection of the law, despite the suspicious fact that instead of honking as any conscientious goose should, it goes "luk-luk"; for the **wax myrtle**, also known as the bayberry, the candleberry and the tallow bush, the last two because in the gentle simple days of the last century its berries were used to make candles, but the leaves can be used as seasoning, like bay leaves, though, wrote Euell Gibbons, "the flavor . . . is quite different . . . and in my opinion much better"; and for the **waxwork**, also known as the bittersweet and the staff vine, from whose tender young branches Chippewa Indians used to derive nourishment, for, I read, they have "a thick bark which is sweetish and palatable when boiled," but as I have never sampled it myself I do not know whether my idea of palatability is up to the standard of the Chippewas.

WE
stands for

the **weakfish**, whose mellifluous talents, it has been suggested, may have been responsible for the ancient legend about the song of the sirens; for the **Wealthy**, an American apple bred deliberately to resist cold about 1865 by Peter Gideon, who named it for his wife, née Wealthy Hull; for the **weasel**, eaten entire, or almost, by Alaskan Indians but recommended only in part to Catherine de' Medici when she was told to stew the left hind foot of a weasel in strong vinegar and to drink the vinegar before having intercourse with the crown prince in order to assure the birth of a male heir; for the **wedge shell**, a clam, or more exactly a family of clams, whose members are tiny but also tasty, so their small size fails to deter gourmets; for the **weever**, a fish Alan Davidson admits to the table though Maurice and Robert Burton say it is poisonous, but this apparently applies only to its spines, not to its flesh; for the **weevil**, whose larva has a taste even more exquisite than that of the beetle, according to the Reverend Father Labbat, a French Jesuit missionary who enlarged his gastronomic scope in Africa; for the **wels**, the European catfish, which can reach a length of nine feet and has been accused of swallowing children; and for the **Welsh blackfinned trout**, which in 1880 was too hastily promoted to specieshood under this name, but has since been relegated to *Salmo trutta*, a label it shares with all other European river trouts.

WHA
stands for

whale, eaten with relish by Eskimos, Japanese and some Scandinavians, but I was derelict to duty when a friend brought me a chunk from Norway, the size of a rectangular bathroom sponge, blood colored, with a forbidding dark-brown crust, and, without tasting it, I invited him to take it away, while my wife hastily lit incense sticks throughout the apartment to clear the air; for the **whale shark**, a gentle giant which in theory should be more orthodox eating than whale, but as it runs to 70 tons very few fishermen have ever ventured to take one, and so far as I know, of the few who have no one has tasted it, though somebody somehow did find out that its liver is devoid of vitamin A; and for the **whample**, an acorn-sized fruit of the East Indies which is mostly seeds but does contain a small ration of pulp with a taste like anise-flavored grapes.

WHE
stands for

whelks, tasty marine gastropods (the Florida conch is one), of which some are left-handed; and for **whey,** which Miss Patience Muffet, daughter of the sixteenth-century entomologist Dr. Thomas Muffet, was consuming with her curd when interrupted by a stray from her father's collection of *Arachnidae.*

And **WHE** also stands for

WHEAT. "Wheat," wrote Henry Linguet, an intemperate Frenchman of the eighteenth century, "is an unfortunate little product which causes hunger instead of appeasing it and seems, from its baleful qualities, to have been a gift made by Nature in anger, for its ear contains more evils than kernels. . . . Bread is a murderous drug whose primary ingredient is corruption. We are obliged to adulterate it with a poison [he meant yeast] to make it less unhealthy."

Wheat has managed to survive despite the disapproval of Linguet, who may be suspected of having been less interested in attacking wheat than in attacking his mortal political enemy, Anne Robert Jacques Turgot, minister of Louis XVI, who had issued an edict establishing free trade in that grain. Linguet could have looked back a couple of centuries for an authoritative statement on the already unassailable position of wheat, in the *Herball* of John Gerard, who wrote that "wheat . . . is preferred before all other corne. . . . The plant is so well knowne to many, and so profitable to all, that the meanest and most ignorant need no larger description to know the same by"—a deft way to duck a job; Gerard in fact all but ignored wheat as a food for the rest of his article, concentrating instead on its medicinal virtues.

Hardly anyone else has had a derogatory word to say about wheat unless you so class the observation of Sir William Osler: "Wheat and pork, though useful and necessary, are but dross in comparison with those intellectual products which alone are imperishable." Without pausing to examine the question of whether or not intellectual products are perishable (which works of Sir William Osler have you re-read recently?), we may note that men are perishable, that the food which for several millennia has often saved them from perishing is wheat, and that millions are in danger of perishing today for lack of it. For those who are at grips with the problem of surviving, wheat is far from being dross, and the question of comparing it with undoubtedly loftier intellectual products does not even arise in a world which has not attained Sir William Osler's well-fed detachment.

If it is possible to describe any one food as the most important in the world, it would be wheat or rice. Everywhere the staple food, the irreplaceable food, the one food eaten by those who may have nothing else, is some form of cereal. About one-half of all the cultivated land in the world is sown to cereals, which provide 80 percent of all the calories consumed by mankind. Three cereals alone supply 66 percent of the world's seed crops, wheat, rice and maize. Maize is consumed in a large proportion by livestock; wheat and rice are eaten oftener by human beings. More people eat rice as their primary grain, but wheat leads rice both in the amount produced and the acreage sown to it (about two-fifths of all the land devoted to cereals), which is another way of saying that in general people living in the wheat-growing areas of the world get more to eat than those living in the rice-growing areas.

Wheat is important even in the two largest overpopulated and undernourished countries which we are accustomed to think of as dominated by rice—India and China. Wheat is second to rice among Indian staples, but not much so: in the northern and western parts of the subcontinent wheaten bread, made in a large variety of classic forms, is the mainstay of the meal. Similarly in China the three most important food crops are all cereals—rice, wheat and millet—occupying about 54 percent of all the cultivated land. Rice is far ahead when the country is viewed as a whole, covering 28 percent of the land (and getting the best soil); but in northern China, where rice will not grow, as much as 40 percent of the cultivated area is devoted to wheat in some districts, and wheat, not rice, is the staple—eaten usually in the form of noodles, though bread is also important.

In the temperate regions of the earth, wheat is king.

> Wheat bread is more than the staff of life [in the Middle East, Harry G. Nickles wrote in *Middle Eastern Cooking*]. It is so holy that a piece of it dropped on the floor must be picked up and kissed in atonement. . . . A meal without bread is unthinkable, and if the bread is not homemade, it is bought fresh and warm, sometimes twice a day.

This is the part of the world where wheat was probably born, but it has since spread almost limitlessly in every direction—first, presumably, to the rest of the Mediterranean basin, where for centuries the three dominant crops have been grain (first of all wheat), olives and grapes, of which only the first, obviously, is capable of serving as a staple food.

France has long been considered a country of bread eaters. Frenchmen have preferred wheaten bread at least since the Middle Ages, when the habit of eating bread of mixed wheat and RYE began to dwindle. The economist Jean Fourastié calculated that until well into the nineteenth century a modest French family spent three-quarters of its budget on food, and that half of this was for bread. French bread consumption has been diminishing since the beginning of this century—the average Frenchman today eats less than half as much as in 1900—but this is not so much a sign of disaffection with bread as a measure of the rising standard of living; it is true everywhere that cereal consumption drops and meat consumption rises as soon as a population can afford meat (which is cereal in a more expensive form).

Half of all the land sown to food crops in Australia is devoted to wheat, which has been the dominant crop of that continent ever since it was first settled by Europeans, whether measured by acreage or by value. It is a witness to the universality of wheat that the great producers and exporters of this grain today are countries to which it was originally foreign—Australia, the United States, Canada and Argentina, on continents where wheat was non-existent five hundred years ago. Even the biggest European producer, Russia, though it may have dipped its southernmost toe into the original wheat-growing area (in the Caucasus perhaps), grows most of its wheat on territory which lies outside the original habitat of this grain.

Wheat will grow, after a fashion at least, almost everywhere. Its altitude range is described as running from below sea level (Jericho, 825 feet below, was reputed to produce the best wheat of ancient times) to 10,000 feet above. The ideal territory for it is described as between 30 and 60 degrees of latitude wherever the annual rainfall is between 12 and 35 inches; this describes the situation of the great grasslands of the world, like the prairies of the United States and the pampas of Argentina. (Wheat is, of course, a grass.)

But wheat is tolerant and adaptable (and modern seed developers have made it even more so). It would be difficult for it to exceed its altitude limit on the low end of the scale, but on the upper end it is grown in Colombia at 13,000 feet. The latitude limits are broken at both ends, for wheat can be grown from the Arctic Circle (Iceland was good wheat country until about 1000 B.C.) to the equator. More tolerant of heat than most temperate-zone plants, wheat provides excellent harvests in Egypt, North Africa, Cuba and northeastern Mexico. As for rainfall, it will grow even where the annual precipitation is well below 12 inches (in the Sahara Desert, though yields there are expectably low) and in some areas where it is as high as 70. The one combination which defeats it is too much heat combined with too much humidity, not because this inhibits its growth but because it grows too well. In the moister parts of Mexico it throws itself so unreservedly into the proliferation of luxuriant greenery that it never gets around to forming ears.

Wheat had spread over so much territory by the Stone Age (when it was already being cultivated) that it is difficult to tell where it started; but most of the evidence points to Asia Minor, in a belt which may have extended northeast to Afghanistan and southwest to Ethiopia. This is the area within which wheat is still found growing wild today.

> The varieties of wheat are almost endless, and their characteristics vary widely under the influence of cultivation and climate [E. L. Sturtevant wrote, about the end of the last century]. There are 180 distinct sorts in the museum of Cornell University; Darwin says Dalbret cultivated during 30 years from 150 to 160 kinds; Colonel Le Conteur possessed upwards of 150; and Philippar, 132 varieties.

What would Sturtevant have said if he had known about the 12,000 varieties listed by the German botanist Pelshenke or the 30,000 enumerated by the Soviet scientist N. I. Vazilov?

Despite this multiplicity of varieties, basically only two kinds of wheat are cultivated on a large scale today—hard wheat, *Triticum durum*, and common (or bread) wheat, *T. vulgare*. There are so many variations of the latter that taxonomists have abandoned the attempt to be precise in their nomenclature: their names are usually written as though they were full-fledged species, though they are in fact subspecies, varieties or subvarieties. Whatever names they may bear, they are all *T. vulgare*, and one among them should be the original, the pure species, the ancestor of all the others, but nobody knows which it is. It has been lost in the crowd.

In the attempt to impose order on chaos, botanists have divided all wheats into three categories on the basis of the number of chromosomes in their reproductive cells—seven, fourteen or twenty-one pairs. This leads us back to the time when we must assume that there was only one kind of wheat in the world. In most opinions, this original wild ancestor of all wheat no longer exists, though some see it in an Abyssinian plant which bears a single grain on each fruiting spike; it has seven pairs of chromosomes. This, or some other un-

WHEAT *by Pieter Brueghel the Elder (active by 1551–1569).* The Harvesters, *oil on wood*

known species, seems to have split into three genera: *Triticum*, which in turn separated into a few species; *Agropyron*, which divided into a large number of species; and *Aegilops*, which did the same. One of the species of *Triticum* (probably *T. boeoticum*) is thought next to have combined with one of the species of *Aegilops* (probably *A. speltoides*), producing wild emmer; later another species of *Aegilops* (probably *A. squarrosa*) combined with wild emmer to produce our common wheat, *T. vulgare*. The first cross was produced by nature; wild emmer still grows today in Syria. It is possible that the second was the work of man, for *T. vulgare* has never been found wild.

T. vulgare was already sophisticated wheat—fourteen pairs of chromosomes. It is a reasonable assumption that wheat with only seven pairs is earlier and more primitive. This exists in einkorn, meaning "one grain," and why it is identified the world over by a German name I don't know. Wild einkorn is *Triticum* (or *Crithodium*) *aegilopoides*, cultivated einkorn is *T. monococcum*. This is probably the Kussemeth of the Bible. It has been found in one of the oldest excavations of civilization—at Jarmo, in northeastern Iraq, whose lowest excavated level is dated at 6700 B.C.—and also at Chatal Huyuk, in Anatolia, of the third millennium B.C. It did not spread very far from its place of origin in Asia Minor (for instance, it seems never to have been cultivated in Greece, Egypt or India), no doubt because it failed to entice farmers; its small yields make it unprofitable except on soils so poor that superior strains would do no better. Nevertheless, it is still raised, under the name "lesser spelt" or "small spelt," in Syria and Turkey, chiefly for fodder, though bread is sometimes made from it. It is still found growing wild in Turkey.

Emmer, one step up from einkorn, is *T. dicoccoides* when wild, *T. dicoccum* when cultivated, and is known popularly also as German wheat or two-grained wheat. It has also been found at Jarmo, where its kernels, though they come from cultivated strains, are so close to the wild form as to suggest that in them we are witnessing the very beginnings of agriculture. Emmer probably remained the dominant species in Egypt up to Roman times. It has been found in many ancient sites in Asia Minor and was probably the grain which Dioscorides called *zeia dipokpos*. It moved westward early enough to be found in the Swiss lake settlements and at other Neolithic sites in Europe, where, as in Egypt, it seems to have been the dominant grain until well into the Christian era.

Emmer is usually classified into eight basic species, two wild, six cultivated, including hard wheat, *T. durum*, the second most important kind raised today; it is often called macaroni wheat, since its chief use is for noodles. It is grown extensively around the Mediterranean, especially in Italy, southeastern France and North Africa, where it occupies more acreage than any other type of wheat, and in the north-central United States and Canada. The other species, though they are still grown here and there, chiefly for fodder, are of little importance.

One more step up, and we come to wheat with twenty-one pairs of chromosomes, *T. aestivum*, "soft wheat," from which is derived our common bread wheat, *T. vulgare*. This species accounts for 90 percent of all the wheat cultivated in the world today; but before it reached this exalted situation, it existed in various forms which have since been more or less abandoned. One was club wheat, *T. compactum*, which appeared in the third millennium B.C., probably first in Egypt, though it has also been found in Mesopotamia and Kurdistan in sites almost as old as the Egyptian ones. Discovered in association with einkorn and emmer as early as 2700 B.C., it absorbed much of the land formerly given over to emmer towards the end of the first millennium A.D.

Also among the 21-chromosome wheats is spelt, which should mean those types in which the grain adheres to the chaff and is freed from it only with difficulty; but here we run into an area of nomenclatural confusion which I am not going to be foolhardy enough to attempt to clarify. *T. spelta* sounds as if it should be spelt, and Sturtevant gives its popular name as spelt, but then adds in the same breath: "This is the species which includes all the true wheats [did he mean 21-chromosome wheats?] *excepting the spelts*" (italics mine), which leaves one a little fearful for the sanity of taxonomy. *T. spelta* seems to have been first recognized on the shore of the Black Sea by the army of Alexander the Great; it may have been the plant called variously *olura, zeia* or *zea* by the Greeks. What Sturtevant seems to regard as undisputed spelt is *T. binorne*, little grown except at the eastern end of the Mediterranean. In theory, spelt should have originated in or near Asia Minor, but it was already present in Europe on both sides of the Alps early in the second millennium B.C.

The earlier varieties of soft wheat were all but driven out by bread wheat, especially the kind which the French call *froment*, but which in English we can only distinguish by describing it as the finest quality of common wheat, the kind which makes the best bread. Bread wheat (not necessarily *froment*) is what we all eat most of the time today; but it is far from being uniform.

It is presumably because all the wheat we plant today has such a multiplicity of ancestors that the wheat grower, when he plants his seed, can never be quite sure what will come up. What he hopes for in major portion is hard winter wheat, a confusing name because it reminds us of "hard wheat" meaning *T. durum*, while "hard" in "hard winter wheat" simply describes a characteristic of one strain or another of *T. vulgare*. The grower plants his seed, apparently all of the same kind, and what he gets is likely to be a mixed stand of dark red grain and yellow grain. The proportions vary widely. In the great wheat-growing regions of the United States in 1974, 19 percent of the early harvest was yellow grain; in the following year 95 percent was yellow.

What most buyers prefer is the kind sold as "hard winter wheat," which means that between 40 and 75 percent is red grain. Wheat which contains more than 75 percent red is sold as "dark red winter wheat." Wheat which contains less than 40 percent is marketed as "yellow wheat." Yellow wheat usually contains less protein than red wheat, but not always.

No wonder we lose our way when dealing with wheat: among those who have done so was Linnaeus himself. He classed winter wheat and spring wheat as two different species. They aren't. They are simply what we untutored duffers would expect—wheat planted at the onset of winter, or wheat planted at the onset of summer. The species is irrelevant.

Wheat may be credited with having played an important role in the creation of civilization, or at least of urban civilization. The earliest settlements we know about arose where wheat grew wild; it is probable that they were established there *because* of the presence of wheat.

There are many bases on which one could justify describing the Neolithic era as marking the beginning of civilization; one of them is that it was then that men seem to have begun to cultivate wheat. Paleolithic man was eating wheat in the ninth millennium B.C. in the upper Tigris valley, where flint sickles with stone mortars and pestles have been found, but it seems to have been wild wheat. When one of the small bands (families, really) of Paleolithic men came upon a stand of wild wheat, they stopped long enough to eat it, and then, following their wanderers' bent, moved on. The crucial change came when men halted beside the stand and instead of eating all of the grain planted some of it (and presumably put aside enough of this easily preservable food to carry them through until the next crop could ripen). They were thus anchored to the spot, obliged to remain there until the new grain became edible. Nomadism was abandoned, fixed settlements were born.

The cultivation of grain (wheat and barley probably both at the same time, but wheat was usually the more important)—or, if you prefer, the beginning of agriculture, for these cereals were probably the first crops deliberately planted by men—is thought to have begun in the seventh millennium B.C., when wheat had already spread so far from its presumed place of origin in or near Asia Minor that it existed in the Mesolithic site at Mas d'Azil in the French Pyrenees. By the sixth millennium its culture was in full swing. In Halicar, Turkey, it has been possible by carbon dating to situate the time of the cultivated wheat kernels found there at 5500 B.C. In the Neolithic Swiss lake settlements, wheat has been found which does not differ in form or size from what we have now. Even in the Sahara Desert, hard wheat was being cultivated in Neolithic times.

When the invention of the art of writing lifted the veil of darkness which up to then had obscured our view of ancient times, wheat was found to have already established itself on the scene. The oldest written language of which we have knowledge, Sumerian, dating from about 3100 B.C., informs us rather light-heartedly that the Sumerians were already using wheat to make eight different kinds of beer; it was also employed, of course, for making bread. In the process of raising wheat, the Sumerians learned something which would only be perceived in the southwestern United States five thousand years later: that irrigation, a short-term boon, can become a long-term calamity unless it is skillfully controlled. Irrigation was introduced into Sumeria shortly after 5000 B.C.; in a few centuries it had leached most of the nutritive elements from the soil. Yields decreased, and some of the land deteriorated into desert. It is regrettable that farmers in the American Southwest were not much given to reading Sumerian.

The second oldest language of man, Akkadian, reports that wheat was grown in Babylonia. In Mesopotamia, wheat and barley are the grains found oftenest in archeological sites. This is true also in Egypt, where the first written document of any length is dated at about 2650 B.C. It is in Egypt likewise that we find early pictorial representations of wheat. The Phoenicians, a nonliterary people little given to producing written records, have not given us much information, and it is possible that they had little to give: the coastal strip they inhabited contained so little cultivatable land that they had to import wheat from Egypt. We are all familiar with the many references to wheat in the Bible (in sections believed to have been written about the first millennium B.C.), often intertwined with Egyptian history—for instance, the story of Joseph, who, in the service of Egypt, built up a reserve of wheat in the good years as a precaution against bad years.

Wheat was being eaten by the peoples of the Indus valley at least by 2500 B.C.; wheat kernels have been found in tombs of that date. The diet of these early Indians seems indeed to have been based on grain, barley as well as wheat. When the conquering Aryans arrived in the second millennium B.C. they disdained many of the foods being eaten there by peoples they considered inferior; they do not seem to have taken to wheat until about 800 B.C. (The Sanskrit word for wheat means "food of the barbarians," which was the status attributed to the original Indians by the Aryans, who by this name described themselves as "the nobles.")

In China, legend attributed the introduction of wheat, about 2800 B.C., to the Emperor Shen Nung, who is also credited with having initiated the use of agricultural implements. In his time the five sacred crops of China were the soybean, rice, wheat, barley and millet. At the earliest period for which we have documentation in China, we find that the planting of cereals, including wheat, was attended with elaborate ceremonies in which the superstitious and the religious were mingled. It was only natural that a food so important should be associated with religion in a world where crops were considered to be gifts from the gods.

In Egypt, which became the greatest wheat-growing country of ancient times after the yields of Asia Minor began to diminish, the goddess Isis was believed to have discovered the grain in Phoenicia and bestowed it on the Nile about the third millennium B.C. Wheat was an ideal crop for Egypt, since it had a growing time which accorded with the periodic rising and falling of the Nile. Planted in time to take advantage of the yearly flooding, which gave a powerful start to its growth, it would be ready for harvesting after the ground had again become firm and the air dry.

We know from Egyptian art how wheat was harvested. It was cut knee-high with short-handled copper sickles, then the grain was trodden by buffaloes and subsequently winnowed by farm workers. In their midst was an idol made of unleavened wheaten dough, in the form of a crescent swollen at its center. This was obviously a fertility symbol, whose name in Egyptian was *arouseh*. (Is it only a coincidence that in southern France small buns of barely leavened bread, shaped like crescents with swollen centers, are made today and called *raousels?*)

Wheat became the basis of the Egyptian economy; the yields achieved in the Nile valley in ancient times were as high as those attained nowadays on the same terrain with the best improved seed and the most modern machinery and methods. The quasi-sacred nature of wheat made it appropriate for offerings to the gods and donations to their temples: Ramses III, in his thirty-year reign, dowered the temples with six million sacks of wheat and seven million sacks of bread. It was of course also one of the foods placed in the tombs of the Pharaohs to sustain them in the afterworld; but the often repeated story that grains of wheat taken from those tombs have been planted in our time and have flourished is a fable. I do not know how long wheat properly stored may remain fit for human consumption; but the maximum life for wheat as a *seed* is about ten years. Grains older than that are dead and will not grow.

It was almost certainly the Egyptians who discovered how to make raised bread, no doubt by accident. In warm temperatures, yeast spores are always present in the air: exposed dough provides an excellent medium for them and may therefore rise spontaneously. The Egyptians were not likely to have understood the process by which this happens, for they failed to develop yeast; but, observing this phenomenon, they tried to reproduce it by mixing with the next batch some of the dough which had risen naturally, and found that it worked. They had, in fact, discovered what we now call sourdough bread.

Curiously enough, the Greeks, who imported wheat from Egypt, do not seem to have had risen bread before the fourth century B.C.; they must have failed to import with it the secret of leavening. Yet in Egypt leavened bread had been common enough at the time of the Exodus (as early as 5000 B.C. or as late as 500) to give unleavened bread, by contrast with it, the particularly sacred character it acquired for the Hebrews. The Jews fled from Egypt so precipitately, the story goes, that they hastily scooped up batches of dough to which they had not yet added the leavening mixture and therefore ate unleavened bread in their flight: hence the commemorative practice still honored today of eating matzoh at Passover.

The ancient Israelites seem to have grown yeast, and to spare. Hiram, king of Tyre, supplied Solomon with timber from the cedars of Lebanon; Solomon in turn sent 20,000 measures of wheat annually to the Phoenicians.

The Phoenicians may have been short of wheat, but they had a wheat god nevertheless, Dagon, borrowed from the Philistines. (The Hebrew word *dagan* means "wheat" or "grain.") Dagon was the father of another grain god, Aleyan Baal; when the Phoenicians settled Carthage, taking their gods with them, it seems reasonable to believe that Dagon and Aleyan Baal would have been among them, but I have not come across references to them in Carthage. Perhaps they were eclipsed by the feminine counterpart of Dagon, the goddess Danit, whose symbol was the crescent (*crescere*, "to grow"); goddesses have usually seemed more apt representatives of fertility than gods. Whether a male or female divinity sponsored grain growing in Carthage, the benediction of godhead there was remarkably effective. Carthage became one of the richest wheat-growing countries of the Mediterranean; we are told about it by the considerable number of agricultural writers, of whom Mago is the best known, spawned by this nation of husbandmen. What is now central Tunisia and the Medjerda valley possessed some of the best soil for cereal in all of the then known world. The Carthaginians produced much more wheat than they needed for their own use; the surplus was stored in sealed underground silos, like those still found in Malta and some other Mediterranean regions, until they wanted it—or somebody else did. "Somebody else" usually meant the Romans. Carthaginian wheat became Roman wheat by force of conquest, and on an enormous scale. The peace terms proposed by Scipio Africanus in 203 B.C. included tribute from Carthage to the extent of 500,000 bushels of wheat and 300,000 of barley.

On the other side of the Mediterranean, where Theophrastus reported that the Greeks of his time knew eight different kinds of wheat, this cereal was playing its customary role as a shaper of history. If Athens became the dominating maritime power of the Mediterranean, it was because of wheat. The mountainous ungrateful soil of Greece was not particularly propitious to the growing of grain. The best place for it seems to have been on the plains of Boeotia, but even there the crops sufficed only for the Boeotians themselves, sparing the Athenians the indignity of having to beg wheat from a people they considered coarse and uncultured. Sparta seems to have devoted something like three-quarters of its tillable land to wheat and barley (but half of it lay fallow each year), providing enough grain to give everyone his normal quota of one dry quart per day, eaten in the form of porridge or hearth-cakes. (The state-raised Spartan youths under Lycurgus were given only wheat gruel to eat, but were encouraged to steal whatever else they might desire, to develop in them courage and cunning.)

Attica was peculiarly poor in suitable soil for grain, yet grain was so essential for Athens that its adoration, whether in the form of wheat or barley, seems to have been central to the Eleusinian mysteries and other rites dedicated to Demeter. A fertility goddess in general at the beginning, Demeter became associated particularly with grain, and was equated by Herodotus with Isis. Just as Isis was credited with having brought wheat to Egypt, so Demeter was credited with having brought it to Greece. The importance of grain for Athens was such that the first item on the agenda of each meeting of the Assembly, held ten times a year, was to hear a report on the stocks of grain in the wheat hall at Piraeus, which was required always to contain enough wheat for the needs of the civilian population and the army should supplies from abroad be cut off by war.

Reserves so important could not be provided by the niggardly soil of Attica, especially since agricultural techniques were primitive: the plow of Pericles' time (the fifth century B.C.) was no improvement over the plow of Hesiod's (the eighth century B.C.). Drawn by oxen (rarely) or by mules (usually), it barely scratched the soil, which after the plowing still had to be worked over with pick and hoe. The solution was to import wheat, almost necessarily by sea. It could have been had from Thrace, overland, but at a prohibitive price. Oxen could haul a ton of grain one hundred miles in a week, but a ship could carry ten times as much three times as far in half the time. Hence Athens imported its wheat from overseas (it was cheaper than wheat grown at home) and was thus obliged to build a merchant marine of heavy, lumbering cargo carriers to transport it from Sicily, Egypt or the shores of the Black Sea, and a navy of fast fighting ships to protect them. For at least a century and a half after the time of Solon (c. 638–c. 558 B.C.) grain virtually disappeared from the soil of Attica, which was taken over by the crops it could grow best, olives and grapes.

One of Athens' chief sources of wheat was eastern Sicily, peopled by Greeks too, who were pretentious enough to claim that the grain had originated on their island. They called the inland city of Enna, center of their wheat-growing territory and of the cult of Demeter, the navel of the world. The Sicilians put an end to this profitable trade when they took the liberty of destroying the Athenian fleet at Syracuse in 413 B.C., thus restricting Athenian naval power to the eastern end of the Mediterranean, and when unfortunate military adventures against Egypt deprived Athens of wheat from the Nile in the same century, it became dependent on the Black Sea territories for its grain. Athens' foreign and military policies were shaped almost entirely by the imperative necessity of safeguarding the route to this last source of its basic food. Attica had returned to growing what wheat it could at least by the end of the Periclean age, but this did not suffice, as was evident from a speech delivered by Demosthenes in 354 B.C. before a tribunal in Athens on the importance of maintaining the Pontine supply (Pontine, because the Black Sea was the Pontus Euxinus).

> More than any other country in the world [Demosthenes pointed out] we are importers of wheat. The quantity of wheat which the Pontus sends us is roughly equal to that which comes from all other sources combined. . . . [Pontus] has given a franchise to the merchants who import it to Athens and . . . vessels leaving for our country are authorized to load first. . . . Even more, two years ago, when there was a universal famine, it sent us a quantity of wheat not only sufficient for our needs, but so great that we reaped a profit of fifteen talents.

The eloquence of Demosthenes did not suffice to preserve the wheat supplies of Greece. The replacement of Athens by Rome as the dominant city of the Mediterranean may justifiably be attributed in some part to Athens' loss of control over its most important food, and in assuming the succession, Rome too was to find its destinies being shaped by wheat. "Wheat was a factor in the imperial expansion of Rome," Reay Tannahill wrote in *Food in History*. "The imperial frontiers, along most of their length, came to be closely aligned with the borders of the wheat-growing regions of the classical world."

On the Italian peninsula, the great wheat growers were not the Romans, but the Etruscans.

> Titus Livy [I wrote in my still unpublished *The Food of Ancient Greece and Rome*] . . . saluted "the rich Etruscan plains" (*opulenta arva Etruriae*) "fecund in wheat, in cattle and in everything." What the Romans of his time thought of when they spoke of the *Etrusci campi*, the Etruscan plains, was above

all the area between Fiesole and Arezzo, Tuscan cities today, Etruscan cities then, producers then as now of the great white cattle known as Chianinas, but not now as then of the high quality wheat prized for making fine pastry and pasta. . . .

Etruria became a great granary; it evolved varieties of wheat which produced fifteen times what had been sown. Hard wheat from Clusium (today Chiusi) weighed 26 pounds per bushel, and its flour was so white and fine that Roman women used it for face powder. Both Clusium and Arezzo grew soft wheat (*siligo*) . . . Pisa produced a sort of semolina flour . . . which was sometimes mixed with honeyed wine to produce a sweet dish. Etruria grew more wheat than it needed for itself and consequently had a surplus for export, a circumstance of which the Romans took advantage several times in the fifth century B.C., when they suffered periods of famine.

The Etruscans also sometimes supplied the Greeks with grain. Thanks to the network of canals and irrigation ditches which their engineers constructed in the Paduan plain, they produced crops so abundant that ships from Athens put in at upper Adriatic ports (including Adria, which gave its name to the sea, but is now inland) to pick up wheat for Attica. Later Rome proved able to absorb all the wheat Etruria could grow, and more. In 205 B.C., when Scipio set out for Africa, a list of the supplies contributed by various parts of the country included great quantities of wheat from Etruria.

The Romans themselves had only a mediocre record as wheat growers, largely because of unfavorable economic and political circumstances created by themselves. Wheat nevertheless enjoyed their respect and shaped their history. The equivalent of Demeter in the Roman pantheon was Ceres (who gives us, of course, our word "cereal"), but the Romans went the Greeks one better by endowing themselves with a god in charge of wheat rust—Robigus, who ravaged the crops of the wicked. (Not until 1800 would it be discovered that wheat rust is a fungus disease.) Near divinity was even attributed to the dole (the *annona*), distributed chiefly in the form of wheat. The administrative headquarters of the *annona* at Ostia, where half a million tons of imported wheat a year arrived, mostly from Africa, was barely distinguishable from a temple.

The need for cheap corn in ever-increasing quantities [wrote Colin McEvedy] can be accepted as an important factor in Rome's overseas aggressions. First Sicily and Sardinia, then Carthaginian Africa and finally Egypt: a bigger granary was needed with each century. (It has been calculated that Sicily was able to export three million bushels, Africa ten million and Egypt twenty million.) . . . The importation of cheap corn, depriving the mid-Italian farmer of his market and his profit, drove him from his village into the city, where he completed the vicious circle by adding his voice to the demand for cheap corn.

Not simply cheap corn (meaning wheat): *free* corn. It is not surprising that the small landholders who tried to live by growing wheat could not compete with the grain which poured into Rome as tribute, and preferred to move into the cities to live like everybody else on the free wheat of the dole. Wheat growing was virtually abandoned on the Italian peninsula, and a large percentage of the Roman population found its food in free government grain, opening the way for the emperors to govern by bread and circuses.

The quantities of wheat required to feed the people of Rome were considerable [wrote Reay Tannahill in *Food in History*]. It has been estimated that in the time of Augustus it was necessary to import fourteen million bushels of grain a year—the produce of several hundred square miles of wheatfields—to secure supplies for the city alone.

In the time of Trajan the amount of grain, chiefly wheat, which the city of Rome had to keep on hand to feed its citizens was used to arrive at an estimate of its population: 1.2 million. Rome was probably the only city of the ancient world ever to pass the million mark except Alexandria—which, perhaps not entirely by coincidence, was the port from which Egyptian wheat (one-third of the entire North African total) was shipped to Ostia.

How many Romans were eating free foreign wheat?

From one-third to one-half of the population, according to different estimates (one-half seems to have been more likely) were on the dole [if I may be permitted to quote myself again]. Drawing free grain must have been something of a racket, especially as at least two-fifths of the population (this is probably also a serious underestimate) was slave and should have been fed by its masters. Perhaps the masters had means of acquiring government grain for their slaves, so that in the long run they were being maintained partly by the state.

After Trajan, according to Jérôme Carcopino, "the entire urban proletariat—that is to say, all Romans who were neither senators nor knights—were listed on the rolls of the Public Assistance Board," which gave them the right to draw five pecks of wheat a month, plus some other foods, depending on the varying largesse of the emperors. With virtually the entire population getting its grain free, one might think there would be little room left for private enterprise, but this was not the case. If you happen to drive from

Rome's airport into the city, your eye may be caught, at the point where you pass through the ancient walls, by an impressive pyramid which might cause you to wonder whether one of the last Egyptians had not chosen to be entombed in Rome. The pyramid, however, is not Egyptian; but it is a tomb—the tomb of Caius Sextius, who amassed a fortune as a wheat importer and wholesaler. He had to do so at a low price level, since he was competing with a product which could be had free, but wheat obviously was still profitable.

Perhaps the low price was the reason for Caius's success: wheat was within everybody's reach, making the market limitless—or at least it was within the reach of everybody in Pompeii. Excavators found from two to twenty sesterces on the bodies of the Pompeiians preserved under the ashes which had stifled them; most of the private homes contained about two hundred sesterces. As a *modius* (14⅓ pounds) of run-of-the-mill wheat cost three sesterces, almost every Pompeiian had with him enough to buy this much wheat, and most of them enough to buy a *modius* of luxury wheat of the finest quality, which cost seven sesterces. Even those who had the least money could command their fill of bread at an *as* a pound (an *as* was one-fourth of a sesterce). It is true that Pompeii was a rich city.

When the dole was paid in unground wheat, the recipient had to convert it into flour himself (unless he chose to eat it in some form other than bread or porridge, which was of course possible). This may not always have been done with consummate skill. "Pound the wheat grains with sand to remove the husks," Pliny advised, "the grain then being but one-half its former measure. Then 25 percent gypsum is added to 75 percent of this meal and mixed, and the flour is bolted."

One wonders [Don and Patricia Brothwell comment] . . . to what extent fine sand particles remained in the flour, and indeed it is possible that some stone dust from querns was also regularly incorporated in the bread. It has been suggested that the severe wear found on the teeth of some earlier populations may have resulted from the abrasive properties of this intrusive powder, but in fact this can only be one of a number of contributory factors.

A somewhat different point of view on the presence of stone in flour was expressed in the nineteenth century by the not necessarily infallible French historian Jules Michelet, who expressed the opinion that the solidity of the French people came from the pebbles which they swallowed in their bread.

In Rome as in Greece, the end of power coincided with the end of control over the supply of wheat, whether there was a relation of cause and effect or not. When the empire split into western and eastern fractions, the wheat of Egypt was diverted to Byzantium (and in the seventh century, when the power of Byzantium dwindled too, Egyptian wheat would be shipped to the holy cities of Islam; there was always a market for it). In 428, wrote Colin McEvedy, "Africa was invaded by the Asding Vandals, who blackmailed the best provinces from the Romans, anxious to preserve the African corn supply for Italy." Ceding to blackmail failed, as it usually does, and the grain of Africa was lost. Rome became a city of secondary importance.

The ancient Gauls seem to have been ahead of the Romans in their handling of wheat. Wheat grew everywhere in Gaul, abundantly, including all the varieties then known, even our bread wheat of today, which would not become generally common in Europe until some ten centuries later. Gaul had a plow which really turned the soil instead of simply opening it, like those used by the Greeks and Romans. The Gauls had invented a two-handed scythe like the one used for hand mowing today; and their grain was sifted through a sieve made of horsehairs. What astonished the Romans most was the mechanical harvester which the Gauls had devised: an ox pushed before it a cart equipped with metallic teeth which mowed the grain at ground level; the slow forward movement of the cart tipped the heavy ripe ears into its waiting cavity.

The wealth of wheat in Gaul had its disadvantages. One of the great difficulties of Vercingetorix was his inability to destroy all the warehouses choked with grain and the crops in the fields before the Romans could seize them. "We had everything in abundance, nourished by those we were fighting," wrote Julius Caesar.

In the time of Charlemagne, wheat was still the most prized grain of France. In a decree which fixed cereal prices, Charlemagne valued a bushel of oats at one denier, of barley at two, rye at three and wheat at four. Across the Channel it was less appreciated. I find one English author asserting that wheat was introduced into Britain about 3000 B.C. and that in 330 B.C. "a Roman visitor" saw wheat being threshed in covered barns. (What in the world was a Roman visitor doing in Britain in 330 B.C.; had he traveled by misprint?) No source is given for either of these statements, and I myself find no reference to British wheat before the seventh century A.D. It could have been present earlier but allowed to die out because of conditions unfavorable to it. Ancient Britain was heavily wooded; that part of its soil which was free of trees was mostly undrained;

and the climate was wet, and severe in winter. Even in the seventh century, when it is the Venerable Bede who tells us of its presence, it was not sown at the onset of winter to be harvested in the spring, as was the case for the best wheat almost everywhere else; it was not planted until spring.

Wheat seems to have remained a comparative luxury in England almost until the seventeenth century. It was an unimportant crop during the reign of Elizabeth I (though Shakespeare mentions it). Still, it was always there for those who could afford it, and it must have been a little more widespread than the official chroniclers tell us, for we catch telltale glimpses of it from time to time. The first Corn Laws in England were enacted in 1177; true, "corn" covered all grains, and though it usually means wheat in England nowadays, it may have covered more ground in the twelfth century. That it had a certain importance as food may be divined from the edicts passed now and then in times of bad harvests prohibiting the use of wheat for making beer. (In the sixteenth century the same prohibition had to be applied in Bavaria, where the population was showing an improvident tendency to drink its wheat instead of eating it.) In 1266, Henry III decreed that "one English penny, called a stirling, round and without any clipping, shall weigh twenty-two well-dried wheat corns gathered out of the midst of the ear." Somewhere far back in feudal times the Dame of Sark acquired the right to be paid a few pennies for every bushel of wheat grown on the island, a privilege which I believe her descendants still enjoy.

By the thirteenth century, the Baltic region had become great wheat-growing country (but southern Germany has always preferred rye). As a result, wrote Colin McEvedy, "the Grand Master [of the Teutonic Order], himself a member of the Hanse, became the greatest corn merchant of the world. From 1280 on, his grain reached the West in increasing quantity and caused a significant lowering of price." (But in England the cost of wheat nearly tripled between the late twelfth and early fourteenth century.)

Medieval Europe seems often to have preferred other grains to wheat—barley, rye and even millet. Perhaps the Arabs discouraged wheat growing in Europe. When they flowed into the south, one of the plants they brought with them was the barberry; they could hardly have known that it was an intermediate host for the parasite which produces black stem rust in wheat. This was a scourge which had never been seen in Europe before the tenth century, when Spain, where the Arabs had recently settled down, suffered an almost complete loss of its wheat crop from this malady and was prostrated by famine.

Another sort of invasion occurred in the great wheat-growing country of France (still the largest European producer of this grain, except Russia). The invader was RYE, which overran the wheat fields. The French willy-nilly were obliged to accept the fact of mixed stands of wheat and rye (*méteil* in French, maslin in English), which were harvested together and, the next year, resown together, while the grains were ground into flour together and baked into bread together. This situation persisted into the nineteenth century, permitting Daniel Defoe to claim in 1721 that England was the supplier of wheat for all Europe. England had begun to push wheat production after the War of the Roses had left the nation short of food; by 1590 it had turned the tables on France and was exporting wheat to the country from which it had formerly imported it. England suffered a brief setback in 1596, when failure of the harvest threatened to throw the population into famine; but it was able to buy wheat from Russia, already a great wheat-growing country, which was also exporting its grain to Holland in exchange for cloth. If Russia today is in some years unable to grow enough wheat to feed its population, the causes are perhaps not to be found exclusively in the eccentricities of nature.

The first wheat in the New World seems to have been planted at Isabela, Puerto Rico, at the order of no less a personage than Christopher Columbus, who registered with surprise that on "March 30, a laborer harvested spikes of wheat which had been planted at the end of January." He was right to be surprised, for wheat grows fast, but not that fast: somebody, perhaps the anonymous laborer, must have applied a bit of imagination to the dating of this miraculous harvest. (In Canada the pilot John Alphonse wrote that in the region of Montreal, "I have told [counted] in one ear of corn 120 grains, like the corn of France, and you need not to sow your wheat until March and it will be ripe in the midst of August.")

There seems to have been no important sequel to the planting of Spanish wheat in the Caribbean islands, which were hardly propitious to this crop; it did better on the mainland. The first Mexican wheat is said to have been sown in 1530 from a few grains which an African slave of Cortez found in a sack of rice which had been sent from Spain to feed the troops. According to Humboldt, the first wheat in Ecuador was raised by a Franciscan monk on the grounds of his monastery, and according to Prescott, the first in Peru by an anonymous woman who imported it and encouraged the Spanish colonists to grow it (but Garcilaso de la Vega reported that in Cuzco wheaten bread was still unknown in 1547). The Spaniards also planted wheat in what would become the southwestern United States; the wheat Father Baegert reported as flourishing in California in 1751 had probably been sown by them.

It was in the Southwest that Indians first began to grow wheat, probably for climatic reasons; the Pimas of the Gila valley were raising it as early as 1799. In the East, though the Indians took quickly to many of the new foods brought in by the Europeans, they showed little interest in wheat, which competed for the same role in their diet as their familiar maize, which they preferred. Indeed, the incoming Europeans also tended to eat maize rather than wheat as soon as they learned how to cope with it, for wheat was not at first particularly successful in its new habitat. The Dutch of the Hudson valley perhaps did best with it at the beginning, on farms whose status recalled feudal times: their occupants did not own the land, but held perpetual leases on it and paid token rents for its use—ten bushels of wheat, for instance, on one hundred acres of land. Their wheat was of sufficiently good quality so that specimens were sent to Holland for exhibition.

The first wheat in New England seems to have been sown by that forgotten man of early exploration, Bartholomew Gosnold, who did almost everything before the Pilgrims who were credited with it—for instance, giving its name to Cape Cod. Gosnold planted wheat in the Elizabeth Islands—very probably on Cuttyhunk, where he also built, in 1602, the first permanent structure erected by a speaker of English on American soil. Like Columbus, he was surprised by the speed with which the wheat grew: it "sprang up eight or nine inches in fourteen days."

The Pilgrims brought seed wheat with them, but they were not practiced farmers, and found the grain difficult to grow on land which had been wooded and whose fields were still studded with stumps even after they had cut down the trees. Was it because of total failure of their first plantings that they were obliged, in 1629, to order more seed from England? In its unaccustomed environment New England wheat was frequently attacked by what was called "the blast," possibly again black stem rust. For this and other reasons it remained too expensive throughout the eighteenth century for the average pocketbook (an unskilled laborer would have had to pay more than four days' wages for a bushel of wheat), so that, though the basic food of the landless was bread, it was not wheaten bread.

In Virginia, the first wheat seems to have been sown in 1611. The trouble there was that the big money crop was tobacco. Planters were loath to waste land on wheat. There was nevertheless enough grown in the mid-eighteenth century so that wheat and wheat flour were shipped to the West Indies from the port of Baltimore (but Maryland depended less on tobacco and more on wheat than did Virginia, and had waterpower available in the Chesapeake Bay region to mill it). Both North and South made their first substantial exports of wheat and flour to England in 1767, when Britain abolished the import duty on these products, and in 1773, when grain crops failed in Europe, English specie had to be sent to America for the first time to pay for the wheat the colonies were able to furnish to the mother country.

When some far-sighted citizens of Virginia, George Washington and Thomas Jefferson among them, reflected that however profitable tobacco might be, food after all was more essential, and that there was an advantage, as the ancient Romans had so disastrously failed to realize, in maintaining a domestic source of one's basic food, they often found themselves obliged to plant wheat on ground which had formerly been devoted to tobacco, a notoriously soil-depleting crop. The result was poor yields. "An English farmer must entertain a contemptible opinion of our husbandry, or a horrid idea of our lands," Washington wrote, "when he shall be informed that not more than eight or ten bushels of wheat is the yield of an acre." (Today wheat can produce as much as one hundred bushels an acre.) Nevertheless, the flour from Mount Vernon was famous for its quality.

At Monticello, Jefferson stimulated the production of wheat by putting his overseers against one another: the man who produced the best crop was awarded an extra barrel of flour among the payments in kind which he received for his work. There were difficulties which even the most skillful overseers could not surmount. "We, of this state," Jefferson wrote to his friend William Johnson on May 10, 1817, "must make bread, and be contented with so much of that as a miserable insect will leave us; this remnant will scarcely feed us the present years, for such swarms of the Wheat-fly were never before seen in this country." This was probably the Hessian fly, so called because it was said to have been brought into the country in the straw bedding of the Hessian mercenaries who fought in the Revolution.

The development of wheat in the United States to the point at which it would play an important role in the national history began with its progress westward, where a soil and climate which seemed to have been prepared for it by destiny were waiting. This began in 1718, with the planting of wheat in the Mississippi valley by the Company of the West. When wheat first crossed the Mississippi into Kansas, the early settlers could not produce enough for their own needs; but then hard red winter wheat was introduced, and today the Kansas farmer produces three hundred calories of nourishment for each calorie of energy which he expends.

The Civil War played an important part in stimulating the development of wheat cultivation in the American Midwest; and wheat played a great role in winning the victory for the North. This part of the country had land to spare, into which farmers streamed to till the hitherto empty acres with the passage of the Homestead Act in 1862. This gave the North an advantage in feeding its armies over the South, which was often hard put to it to produce enough food for its troops, or at least to get it to the points where it was needed.

The *Encyclopaedia Britannica* was perhaps overdramatizing the situation when it wrote:

> The evolution of wheat production occurred very slowly and a farmer of about 4000 B.C. moved forward to any year prior to A.D. 1800 probably could have continued wheat production without any appreciable change. All that was needed or used was a few seeds, a pointed stick, some type of sickle and perhaps a beast of burden. There are still areas in the world where wheat production remains as primitive as it was 6000 years ago. [There also remain areas in the world where fields of wild grain are as dense as those of cultivated grain.] After 1800 many remarkable changes occurred. Improvement of machinery, relieving man as the source of power, resulted in increased wheat production.

Too strongly stated or not, this factor also gave the North an important advantage over the South. Largely industrialized, the North was able to develop agricultural machinery quickly, particularly efficient on the vast flat grasslands of the Middle West. The South was hampered by a slave economy, in which a plenitude of cheap hand labor had made it seem unnecessary to develop tools more complicated than the shovel and the hoe. The South found itself pitting men with sickles against mechanical harvesters which worked at least five times as fast as hand labor.

The North profited also by an element of luck. During the Civil War period, Europe was afflicted by a series of poor harvests. England, which might have been tempted to aid the South, the provider of cotton for its textile industries, found it more urgent not to offend the North, which could supply wheat for its most dire need of all, food. In 1862 the North exported over 400 million bushels of wheat and flour to Europe, chiefly to England, as compared with less than 100,000 which both North and South together had exported in 1859. The British did not miss the point. "Old King Cotton's dead and buried," ran a popular song of the period. "Brave young corn is King." The outcome of the war would probably have been the same in any case, but it remains at least arguable that wheat played a more or less decisive role in determining the issue.

It is hardly necessary to belabor the point of the importance of wheat in our own time. Possession of wheat or lack of it sways the destinies of nations; nor is it rare to find wheat being used as a political weapon. It may be definitely surpassed one of these days by rice, but it is difficult to foresee any future in which it will not still exert a powerful influence on human history. "The corn was oriental and immortal wheat," wrote Thomas Traherne in the seventeenth century, "which never should be reaped, nor was ever sown. I thought it had stood from everlasting to everlasting."

WHI
stands for

the **whimbrel,** a shore bird whose name comes from "whimpernel" because it is credited with uttering houndlike whimperings, and is thought in the north of England, where it is called "Gabriel's hound," to be a harbinger of death; for the **whimberry,** which the *Encyclopaedia Britannica* says is another name for the cowberry, mountain cranberry, partridgeberry or foxberry, *Vaccinium vitis-idaea,* and the **whinberry,** which E. L. Sturtevant says is another name for the bilberry, blaeberry or whortleberry, *V. myrtillus*; for the **whippoorwill,** which in the realm of eatables is not a bird, but another name for the field pea, cowpea, Jerusalem pea, Tonkin pea or black-eyed pea, *Vigna catjang*; for the **whiskery batfish,** which lures smaller fish into biting distance by disguising itself as edible seaweed; for the **whistling swan,** which the ear can confuse with a dog, as in the case of the whimbrel, cited above, for when a flock of these birds, in tight V-formation, flies overhead, their calls sound like the mournful baying of hounds; and for the **whistling tree,** producer of what is considered to be the world's best gum arabic, which must be the opinion of the gnats which infest it and riddle it with tiny holes through which the wind whistles.

WHITE
stands for

white ant, a misleading name for the termite, a

tasty tidbit if you like termites; for **whitebait,** probably the tiniest (except roe) and among the tastiest forms of fish eaten by man, described by Théophile Gautier as "a fish fry reduced to the scale of Lilliput, a miraculous draft of fishes for Tom Thumb"; for the **white bass,** which, properly speaking, is not a BASS but a sunfish; for the **white crappie,** otherwise known as the bachelor perch or the papermouth; for the **whitefish,** which provides black eggs, after they have been properly dyed to simulate caviar; for the **white** MULBERRY, which is the one silkworms appreciate, but humans find its fruit insipid; for the **white salmon,** a name given to a controversially classified sea bass; for the **white sand clam** of the American Pacific coast, which looks like a bent-nosed clam without the bent nose; for the **white sapote,** or Mexican apple, whose fruit is tastiest when it is about to rot, said by the ancient Aztecs to be soporific, which modern observers attribute to a toxin in its seeds; for the **white shark,** the species oftenest accused of being a man-eater, but if so, man reciprocates; for the **white sturgeon,** which lives off the Pacific coast of North America; for the **whitethorn,** a variety of hawthorn which seems to be little appreciated except in India; for the **white walnut,** a name sometimes given to the BUTTERNUT; and for the **whiteweed,** which is nothing other than our well-known ox-eye daisy, whose leaves, it appears, can be eaten in salads, though I have never known anyone who did so.

WH
(from this point on)
stands for

the **whiting,** a fish related to the cod which has little taste but is easy to digest, provided it is very fresh and happens to be the *blue* whiting; for the **Whitstable oyster,** a small but delicious English variety, which has become regrettably rare since a shellfish disease invaded its beds; for the **whitten tree,** or *wuchipoquameneash* if you speak Narragansett, whose cranberry-like fruit has been described as "a miserable food for savage nations," but Thoreau ate it; for the **whooping crane,** presumably as good eating as any other crane, but since it enjoys maximum protection to save it from the menace of imminent extinction, none of us is likely to be afforded an opportunity to find out; and for the **whortleberry,** which we met just above disguised as the whinberry.

WID
stands uniquely for

the **widgeon,** or baldpate, a chunkily built duck whose tastiness is the product of its characteristics: it is a powerful flyer, so that its flesh is enriched by the plentiful flow of blood which this exercise requires, and a fussy feeder, sticking to a diet which is 85 percent grass, grain and plant roots.

WILD
stands for

the **wild banana,** which is not a banana but what they call the inkamangu in Swaziland, where its seeds are eaten sparingly, but what it is I don't know except that it belongs to the same genus as the bird-of-paradise flower, of which it is also the seeds which are eaten, by the blacks of South Africa; for the **wild beet,** which is not a beet but the green amaranth, whose seeds are said to have been ground into flour by pre-Columbian American Indians and whose leaves are sometimes eaten as greens by wild-food enthusiasts today despite their regrettable lack of flavor; for the **wild boar,** of which the adult male, before it becomes the richest kind of PORK, roams the forest accompanied by a younger male called its "page," whose function is to run ahead when hunters are about and get itself killed to give its master time to escape; for the **wild carrot,** which I find an English writer describing as a medieval food whose roots were "more delicious and greater than domestic ones grown in the garden," which seems a trifle exaggerated when you consider that the wild carrot is nothing other than our familiar field weed Queen Anne's lace; for the **wildcat,** eaten commonly by Africans a thousand years ago but apparently not now; for the **wild climber,** a vine which seems to provide food not only for Africans but also for Alaskans, if the watermelon berry, also called the wild cucumber, is the same plant; for the **wild date palm,** still so called though it is planted by man in India for its sugar; for the **wildebeest,** a gnu, a plentiful provider of meat in those parts of East and South Africa where it may still be hunted; for **wild ginger,** which is not ginger but Canadian snakeroot or colicroot; for the **wild gobo,** on sale as a Japanese specialty in exotic food shops in Chicago, where it is not recognized as the root of our common weed, the great burdock; for **wild iris,** alias calamus, sweet flag, myrtle sedge, sweet grass, sweet rush, and so on and on, whose candied roots are appreciated by some but make others gag; and for the **wild leek,** which when I first discovered it growing on my Vermont farm I ate with delight in its unfamiliar pungency, but which quickly fatigued my taste buds, causing me to return to the tame variety with the reflection that civilization is less picturesque than savagery, but more comfortable.

WILD stands for

the **wild lemon,** also known as the raccoon berry, the hog apple or the American mandrake, but more properly as the May apple, whose exotically flavored fruit is relished by many, but its leaves and roots can be toxic; for **wild LETTUCE,** of which *Lactuca scariola,* one of the two species found in the United States, is called the compass plant because of its habit of turning its leaves edgewise toward the sun; for the **wild mango,** a name given to two different fruits in Africa, neither of them a mango; for **wild musk,** which, though it originated in Europe, seems to have been relished by nobody except the Blackfeet, Shoshone and Digger Indians, the least choosy of their race; for the **wild plum,** a name given to a disconcerting number of different fruits in Africa, of which few are plums; for the **wild potato,** a term I have found in the writings of American wild-food enthusiasts without explanation of what it is, but I would guess that it is the Indian potato, or groundnut, *Apios americana,* whose tuber looks a little like a small POTATO but tastes, faintly, more like a turnip; for the **wild raisin,** *Viburnum lentago,* otherwise known as the nannyberry, sheepberry or wild viburnum, which implies a certain amount of confusion in berryland, for in other contexts both nannyberry and sheepberry are equated with the highbush cranberry, which ought to be *V. opulus,* which in turn ought to be the whitten tree, cited just above; for **wild rice,** which is not RICE, but what we are told is a grain unique to America, though there is a Chinese species, kawsun; for **wild rye,** which is not rye but strand wheat, which is not wheat and tastes more like wild rice; and for **wild tobacco,** which is not tobacco, but our twenty-fifth name for the mullein.

WILL
stands for

the **willet,** an only moderately edible shore bird known in less matter-of-fact times as the humility; for the **Williams' Bon Chrétien,** a PEAR renowned throughout Europe by that name because of its quality, but no stranger to America, where it is called the Bartlett; for the **willow,** whose inner bark has been made into bitter bread in times of scarcity; and for the **willow herb,** whose young shoots and young leaves are, or were, eaten in some northern countries, from Iceland to Kamchatka.

WIN
stands for

the **Windsor bean,** which under many other names—the broad bean, the horse bean, the fava, the haba—was the only BEAN the Old World possessed before the discovery of America endowed it with the haricot bean; for the **wineberry,** a Far Eastern member of the widespread blackberry-raspberry family; for the **Winesap,** an eccentric apple which insists on showing pink blossoms instead of white and since 1950 has been losing its market in spite of its fine flavor, for nowadays we buy only what is big and the Winesap is small; for the **winged bean,** so called because its foot-long pods are decked out with ruffles, eaten in warm countries, pods and all, under the name of the Goa bean or the asparagus pea, titles sometimes distributed among other vegetables of this type with little regard for precision; for the **winkle,** appreciated on the Scottish island of Ulva under the name of "buckies" by Boswell and Dr. Johnson, who were undoubtedly ignorant of the fact that no other food is richer in nitrogen except the cacao bean; and for the **Winnipeg goldeye,** a southwestern Canada specialty, where a fish of little flavor is elevated to supreme succulence by first soaking it in brine and then smoking it into a delicious nutty sweetness.

WINTER
stands for

the **winter cherry,** also called the strawberry tomato or Chinese lantern, the familiar wild fruit often found in fields whose cherry-sized berry is enclosed in a little box which looks as if it had been made from very thin parchment; for **winter cress,** less widely grown than watercress or ordinary CRESS; for **wintergreen,** used chiefly for flavoring, but wintergreen flavor usually doesn't come from wintergreen, since it can be obtained more easily from the sweet birch and even more easily from a chemical retort; for the **winter melon** of China, which looks like a honeydew melon but whose translucent white flesh is not sweet, like a fruit, but vegetable-like, resembling zucchini; for **winter savory,** an herb of southern Europe and North Africa which savantly seasons sausages, stuffings, meat pies and various vegetables; and for **winter's bark,** whose only use, according to the *Encyclopaedia Britannica,* is medical, but in Brazil it is used as a spice.

WIR
stands only for

wire grass, which doesn't sound enticing and probably isn't, for it is eaten only in Tanzania, and not often there.

WIS
stands for

wisteria, which is not only a flower but also a food, at least in China; and for the **wistful squirrelfish,** of a genus which is an important provider of food in Hawaii and makes so much noise under the surface that it can be heard above it; but why it is called wistful is a mystery to me.

WIT
stands for

witches' butter, a sort of fungus which grows on decaying or dead branches, for instance *Tremellodon gelatinosum,* which is edible, but is likely to taste like resin; for **witchetty grub,** a term loosely employed to cover various larvae eaten, or formerly eaten, by the aboriginal Australians; for **witch grass,** ordinarily considered a troublesome weed, but bread has been made from its roots in times of famine, notably by the ancient Aztecs; for **witch hazel,** whose seeds, according to some authors, are edible, but there seems to be a certain amount of doubt as to its usefulness other than as medicine or as a cosmetic; for **witch hobble,** a popular name for the highbush cranberry; for the **witch's candle,** our twenty-sixth name for the mullein; for the **withe rod,** found from Newfoundland to Georgia, whose fruit, Euell Gibbons wrote, "is more a nibble than a solid food, for the berries are about the size of small raisins and the stone is large [but] the thin pulp is very sweet and quite good-flavored, what there is of it"; and for **witloof,** a large-rooted variety of ENDIVE which is subjected to forced growth in the dark.

WO
stands for

woad, whose leaves are eaten in China, of which it is reported to be a native, but if so, how in the world did the ancient Britons manage to get hold of it to dye themselves blue?; for **wokas,** the American Indian name for the yellow pond lily, whose roots were eaten in pre-Columbian times and even after; for the **wolf,** which John McPhee tells us reminded an Alaskan woman he interviewed of canned beef; for the **wolf bean,** or field lupine, eaten by the ancient Romans as a vegetable, but now cultivated chiefly as green manure, though in some parts of Italy the seeds, boiled to reduce their bitterness, still serve as human food; for the **wolf fish,** the largest of the blennies, appreciated particularly in Scandinavia; for **wolfsbane,** which in principle should be poisonous, but its roots are boiled and eaten in Lapland; for **wong bok,** which, as a member of the *Brassica* genus, may be described as Chinese cabbage as aptly as by any other name, though it is eaten more like lettuce, as greens, in autumn and winter rather than in spring; and for **wonderboom,** a name which seems to promise something special, but all it means is a South African version of the fig.

WOO
stands for

the **woodbine,** a YAM which is perhaps really a sweet potato; for the **woodchuck,** which, "though it afforded me a momentary enjoyment, notwithstanding a musky flavor," wrote Thoreau, "I saw that the longest use would not make that a good practice"; for the **woodcock,** a game bird worthy of the gourmet's attention whether or not he believes that it was hunted especially by a type of dog which for this reason was named the cocker spaniel, and the **woodpecker,** not usually considered a game bird, but worthy of a gourmand's attention in the opinion of the ancients of Greece and the Indians of Maine; for **woodwaxen,** also known as the dyer's-broom, whose buds are pickled in the Caucasus region and used as a substitute for capers in sauces; for **woolen breeches,** which, believe it or not, serve as a salad in Kentucky; and for the **woolly pyrol,** the name given in the West Indies to the black gram.

WOR
stands for

Worcesterberry, the name given in the United States to a species of small black gooseberry, and the **Worcester Pearmain,** which in medieval times would have been a winter pear, but in 1873, when this fruit was developed in Worcester, England, meant an apple; for **worms,** eaten under many forms, not all genuine, and in varying circumstances by, for instance, prehistoric man, who seems to have preferred them, as we do oysters, alive; by the ancient Sumerians, who nevertheless did not lack more appetizing food; by the Aztecs, at the end of the 85-day siege of Tenochtitlán by Cortez, with less relish than that with which modern Mexicans devour the agave worm, more accurately named when it is called the maguey slug; by the Caribbean Indians, who, Columbus reported, ate "white worms that breed in rotten wood," not to mention those which were encouraged to infest zamia cakes and were eaten alive with them, as some modern gourmets refrain from eating certain types of cheese until it is crawling with maggots; by Columbus's sailors themselves, but only because they got into the sea biscuit; by the Maoris of New Zealand, who considered them a delicacy, though they were not aware of their richness in provitamin D, and by Australians, not always aborigines, who eat the bardi worm, but it is really a slug; by Africans, who eat palm worms and mealie worms; by American gourmets of the nineteenth century, who prized the worms found in the stomachs of woodcocks under the name "trail" (from "entrail"), and German gourmets of the twentieth century, who indulge in the undigested contents of the stomachs of snipes under the name *Schnepfendreck*; and by the customers of World Wide Worms, an Illinois company which touts the common earthworm as containing 80 percent protein, amino acids to assimilate it, and little cholesterol; and for **wormseed**, genus *Artemisia*, whose bitterness was disguised in former times when it was preserved in sugar in the Caucasus region, and **wormwood**, genus *Artemisia* also, which has been used to season sauces but is oftenest employed to flavor absinthe and vermouth.

And **WR** stands only for things marine, for instance:

wrack, a term which includes many seaweeds, such as *Ascophyllum mackaii*, eaten in Massachusetts in late winter and early spring; *Fuscus vesiculosis*, bladderwrack, which in western Europe produces what might be called a marine potlikker from the juice boiled out of algae not themselves eaten; *Laminaria saccharin*, sugarwrack, used to make bread in Normandy and Brittany; and *Chondrus crispus*, white wrack, which you probably know as Irish moss, a classic ingredient of blancmange; for **wrasse**, a group of ill-defined fish which are usually best in chowders since most of them are not particularly tasty, like the one called in English the cuckoo wrasse and in French the old flirt; and for the **wreckfish**, which is the stone bass, thus nicknamed because it swims along with flotsam on the surface and congregates around wrecks on the sea bottom.

X

XENOPHON: *He was right, who said that agriculture is the mother and the wet-nurse of the other arts. When all goes well for agriculture, all the others prosper.*

XENOPHON: *Nature supplies good things in abundance, yet she suffers them not to be won without toil.*

X
stands for

Xanthocephalus xanthocephalus, only relatively edible, since it is the yellow-headed blackbird, and **Xanthosoma sagittifolium,** which does a little better, since it is closely related to taro, but both may be considered as examples of foods which by any other name would taste as sweet, and in all probability sweeter.

YUAN WEI (eighteenth century): *In no department of life, in no place, should indifference be allowed to creep; into none less than the domain of cookery.*

Y

YEATS: *I will arise and go now,*
and go to Innisfree,
And a small cabin build there, of
clay and wattles made;
Nine bean-rows will I have there,
a hive for the honey-bee,
And live alone in the bee-loud glade.

YA
stands for

the **yabby**, an Australian crawfish which delights in burrowing in the mud; for the **yak**, the main source for meat and milk in Tibet, which Marco Polo described as "wild cattle . . . as big as elephants . . . so handsome that they are a wonder to behold," which must have been the opinion also of Genghis Khan when he designed his first standard, a white banner with nine yak tails; for the **yallah-oil plant** of the East Indies, whose sickish-sweet flowers, picked up from the ground when they fall from the tree, and dried, are there considered an important food; for the **yam bean**, a name given to two different genera of plants, neither of which is a yam or a bean, but they have been given this compound name because both produce edible tubers and edible seed-filled pods (the latter are only eaten young since they become poisonous with age); for the **yapock**, an aquatic opossum found from Guatemala to southern Brazil; for the **yard-long bean**, which is just that, an overweening development of the cowpea cultivated in China and by Chinese farmers in California; and for the **yautia**, a root which resembles the taro and is almost as important in tropical Africa and tropical America as the taro in the South Seas.

And **YA** also stands for

YAM. "As soon as the natives had cast off their fear," wrote Christopher Columbus, "they all went to the houses and each one brought what he had to eat, consisting of yams, which are roots like large radishes, which they sow and cultivate in all their lands, and is their staple food. They make bread of it and roast it."

"This offering of yams," adds *The Horizon Cookbook*, "was perhaps man's first important encounter with the fare of the New World." Uh-huh; but the yam is a native of the Old World. *The Horizon Cookbook* is nevertheless right despite itself, for it was almost certainly not yams which the natives of Hispaniola offered to Columbus, but sweet potatoes, native to the New World.

On another page the same book salutes "the appearance in England of the first yam from the New World in 1564." Uh-huh; but Geoffrey Grigson, a careful researcher, while agreeing that yams first reached England in the sixteenth century, says that they came from Africa.

Finally the same publication, this time going far out on the limb, reports in a third passage that "when Senegalese slaves first discovered the strange sweet tuber growing in the West Indies, they named it *nyami*, their word for 'to eat.' Yams were soon brought to West Africa where they thrived in the subtropical soil, became staples of the native diet, and inspired much tribal ritual." Uh-huh; but the majority of experts who relate the movement of West Africans from the Old World to the New with the movement of yams between these two hemispheres think that both traveled in the same direction: it was the enslaved Africans who carried yams, already a staple in their country, to the Caribbean, along with their word for it.

The Horizon Cookbook may be presumed to have been led astray by the general confusion between the yam and the sweet potato, concerning which only the primitive Papuans of New Guinea seem to be able to make a clear distinction. They know that the sweet potato is the tuber-producing plant cultivated by women while the yam is the tuber-producing plant cultivated by men, because the root resembles the male member.

You need not feel ashamed if you are less well informed about the yam than Papuan savages, for you are in good company. Most of the distinguished sixteenth-century botanists, Dalechamp and Clusius among them, took the sweet potato for a sort of yam, or vice versa. One excuse for this confusion in their time, in addition to the fact that the two look alike and taste alike, is that Europe became acquainted with both at about the same period, though they probably (but not necessarily) arrived from different directions. An excuse for continued confusion in our time is the looseness of popular usage. In the United States, Southerners often refer to the sweet potato as a yam, including even those who organize "yam" festivals at which it is the sweet potato which is served. The situation is hardly clarified by the fact that genuine yams and sweet potatoes are both grown in the same region.

It is not impossible that the yam did reach the New World before Columbus—carried not by slaves, but by the African Equatorial Current. If it crossed the Atlantic by drifting, its likeliest landfall would have been somewhere in the region of the Guianas. It happens that this is precisely the area where New World yams today are the most abundant, which is why the French call the starch extracted from yams "Guiana arrowroot." Amerigo Vespucci is supposed to have heard the word *nyami,* or something which sounded like it, on the Brazilian seacoast. If so, it could hardly have been introduced by African slaves, unless they were singularly mobile in those days. The first slaves to reach America were landed on Hispaniola in 1503; Vespucci's last contact with Brazil occurred in 1505. It seems unlikely that Brazil had ever seen an African at that time. However, all the early explorers of Brazil report that the staple there was cassava; none of them mention the yam. There is perhaps another explanation for the Vespucci story, assuming that he heard aright and that he has been quoted aright: I have read that there was a somewhat similar Brazilian Indian word, unfortunately not specified by the source of this information, applied to a food from which bread could be made, probably cassava. May it be suggested that *nyami* seems to be a primitive word, one of those almost animal-like noises produced instinctively and spontaneously by human beings of different races in response to simple situations? Young children of many countries make a similar noise to express pleasure with food (in English "yum-yum").

The word "yam" does not appear in English until the seventeenth century, which would have been late enough for it to be picked up from American blacks (it was preceded by the form "iniamo"). However, it seems likelier that it reached English (and French, where the word for yam is *igname*) from the Portuguese *inhame* (or the Spanish *iñame,* pronounced exactly like today's French word). The Portuguese or the Spaniards would, of course, have picked it up in Africa, where they were the first to reach the areas where the yam is supposed to have originated.

It seems likeliest that Columbus spoke of the natives offering him "yams" because the sweet potato was unknown to him and he tried to pass on an idea of what it was like by using the name of a food which resembled it, just as Coronado, when he came upon American squashes in the Southwest, called them melons. I do not know when the word for yam (not to mention the thing itself) first appeared in Portuguese, but it seems to have become common in Spanish towards the beginning of the sixteenth century. This would have been about half a century after Europe could have learned of the yam, if it was first found in Africa, as seems probable, for the yam is believed to be one of the very few foods which originated on that continent south of the Sahara. Portuguese navigators, exploring the African west coast, reached yam territory at Guinea in 1441, fifty-one years before Columbus found sweet potatoes in America; Vasco da Gama rounded the Cape of Good Hope five years after Columbus discovered America. There was a sort of leapfrog progression between the discoverers of the yam and the discoverers of the sweet potato. No wonder contemporary botanists were confused.

It seems reasonable to believe that the birthplace of the yam was West Africa. This is one of the two regions of the earth where it is found wild and abundant, and in many sections is the staple food. The other is a large area of Asia which includes India; but as there was no Sanskrit word for "yam," it may be suspected that at the period when Sanskrit was evolving there were no yams in Asia. The earliest reference to yams anywhere on that continent which I know about goes back only to the third century B.C., when there was a reference to roast kid with yam sauce in a Chinese poem called "The Summons of the Soul."

"The only indigenous European species [of yam] is *D. pyrenaica,* a native of the Pyrenees, a remarkable instance of a species growing at a long distance from all its congeners," says the *Encyclopaedia Britannica.* It is so remarkable that we are perhaps not required to believe it, especially as we do not hear of its presence there before the sixteenth century, when it could have been introduced from Africa, the Pyrenees being a region accessible to at least one, and perhaps both, of the first European countries to have investigated West Africa. The *Britannica* does not observe that on this basis it would be even more remarkable to find yams native to America: it is, on the contrary, one of a number of reference books which assert that native yams exist in the New World as well as in the Old. Most such sources add that there is only one American species; unfortunately for credibility, they do not agree on which one it is.

Yams, according to Don and Patricia Brothwell, are "probably the best known edible root plants today in the modern civilized world." One's first reaction is likely to be: "Did they forget the potato?" On second thought, it seems probable that they did not. The areas where yams are most eaten—subtropical America, West Africa, the Pacific islands, India, Malaysia, Indochina, China—include some of the most densely populated regions of the world, regions, moreover, where the potato enjoys little favor.

What is a yam? First of all, definitely not a sweet potato. However much the two resemble one another, they are botanically very far apart. The sweet potato belongs to the *Convolvulaceae,* the morning glory family; the yam is the typical genus of the *Dioscoraceae,* a group of tropical and subtropical herbs and shrubs. For all practical purposes, we may define the yam as a member of the genus *Dioscorea,* named perversely for Dioscorides, the ancient Greek physician and naturalist, who in all probability did not even know that it existed. There is no trace of it in ancient writings or inscriptions, neither in Egypt (it grew too far west) nor in classical Mediterranean literature (it grew too far south).

To the confusion of the yam with the sweet potato has been added a series of misapplications of its name, of which the most justifiable is with the cultivated genus *Rajania,* which counts more than two hundred species, for *Rajania* belongs to the *Dioscoraceae* too. We stray farther afield with, for instance, the coco yam or yautia, universally eaten in Africa and Madagascar, or the frankly named false yam, only slightly less popular in tropical Africa. But that primitive key word, *nyami,* gives us license to spread the name widely, for it evolved from its first meaning of something, or anything, to eat, to the more specific sense of a large root, and then of a nutritious root, which covers a great deal of ground—enough to take in the popular understanding of the term as being applicable to almost any fleshy root, especially if it is sweet.

Dioscorea hardly needs to have its meaning extended, for it covers all by itself an almost unbelievable variety of plants, whose number is usually underestimated by standard reference books. The *Encyclopaedia Britannica* says that "several" species are cultivated for food, and so does the Larousse encyclopedia. *The Oxford Book of Food Plants* thinks that about ten species are important for food. Georges Gibault's *Histoire des légumes* calls fifteen to twenty species edible, while *The Practical Encyclopedia of Gardening* admits that there are about two hundred species, but makes no estimate of the number which are edible and names only four, of which one, it is explained, is cultivated only for ornament, while another is not much cultivated at all. I have no idea how many kinds of yams are eaten throughout the world, but I find that in the Fiji Islands alone more than fifty varieties of yams are grown (though I do not know how many *species* this represents), and that the island of Madagascar eats about thirty different species. In addition to the Madagascar yams, the United Nations Food and Agricultural Organization lists thirty-one species, some wild, some cultivated, which serve as food plants on the continent of Africa. There is no indication that the list is exhaustive, and when Sturtevant, in *Edible Plants of the World,* describes twenty-five edible species, this list is not presented as exhaustive either.

There is great variety among different kinds of yams, but the one quality which they share oftenest is toxicity. This is manifested mildly in some species by an acrid taste and violently in others, which can make their eaters ill. The natives of the countries where yams are important have developed different techniques for getting rid of the poison; but in running down the list of African yams I notice that the kinds which are most popular are also the kinds which are most toxic—without much surprise, for I have observed that in a number of other foods with toxic and nontoxic varieties (cassava, almonds, arrowroot, even lima beans) the toxic versions seem to be preferred, a tribute to the tastiness of poison.

Among the variable characteristics of yams, the least variable is perhaps color, the most variable, size. Yams are usually brownish, whitish, yellowish or a dull red outside, while the flesh is white or yellow; but that of some varieties becomes purple when cooked. In size, the average yam, if there is any such thing, weighs somewhere between two and eight pounds, but *Dioscorea nummularia,* the tivolo yam of the Moluccas, has a tuber as thick as a man's arm, and D. *alata*, the white yam, has been known to reach one hundred pounds. Near the other end of the scale is D. *triloba*, which in Jamaica (where it is probably an immigrant from Guiana) seldom exceeds eight or nine inches in length and two or three in diameter; it is pleasantly sweet.

Yams do not vary much in shape, but on the rare occasions when they do, it is extravagantly. A case in point is D. *bulbifera*, whose tuber is edible, in a pinch, though rather unpalatable; but naturalists who have described it as inferior in taste were eating the wrong part of the plant. In this yam, the best eating is provided by what are inaccurately called its aerial tubers ("tubers" is not a very accurate term for yams in general, for that matter, for they are actually underground swellings of the stem). D. *bulbifera*'s "aerial tubers" might better be called bulbils. In size and shape rather like Brazil nuts, they grow from the axils of the leaves, accounting for this yam's alternative popular names of air potato, aerial yam or bulb-bearing yam. The bulbils are excellent boiled, and this species has therefore achieved a wide distribution. Found in central Africa, which seems to be where it started, D. *bulbifera* is also much cultivated in tropical Asia and in the Caribbean; William Bartram reported seeing one growing in a garden in Mobile, Alabama, in 1733. There are several other species of yams which produce edible bulbils, but the only true yam I know about which offers a third part of the plant to eat is D. *pentaphylla*, of which the male flowers are eaten as a salad plant in India.

Opinions as to the taste of different yams vary widely. When Georges Gibault writes, apropos of the Chinese yam, that "its flesh is superior to that of the potato," it must be the taste he has in mind, for from any other point of view it would be untrue. Not only the potato, but even the sweet potato, is nutritionally far superior to yams in general, which have very little to offer except starch. In countries where they provide the staple food, widespread protein deficiency might be expected, but it happens that most of them have access to a source of proteins which is cheap for anyone with a line or a net: fish. Where fish complements yams, a reasonably balanced diet is assured.

Among the innumerable species of yams, D. *esculenta*, as one might expect from its name, is considered to be among the best, a fact less evident when it is referred to as D. *aculeata*, which seems to be another name for the same species, or at least a variety of it; in the vast confusion which attends the yams, it is hard to be sure. Those who prefer to use the term D. *aculeata* are apt to associate it with the popular names birch-rind yam and Goa potato; those who prefer D. *esculenta* equate it with the Chinese yam, the Chinese potato or the lesser yam. But D. *divaricata* is also called the Chinese yam, the Chinese potato or the cinnamon yam (because its flowers smell like cinnamon), and the attempt to find out which yam is which is not facilitated by the fact that the *Encyclopaedia Britannica* calls D. *batatas* the Chinese yam or the cinnamon vine, and *The Practical Encyclopedia of Gardening* calls it the Chinese yam, the Chinese potato or the cinnamon vine; both say it is cultivated only for ornament. This should infuriate Georges Gibault, who makes it plain when he exalts the merits of the Chinese yam that he is talking about D. *batatas*, which he also calls the cinnamon vine, adding that it is the same thing as D. *divaricata*. At this point, the layman is about ready to throw in the towel.

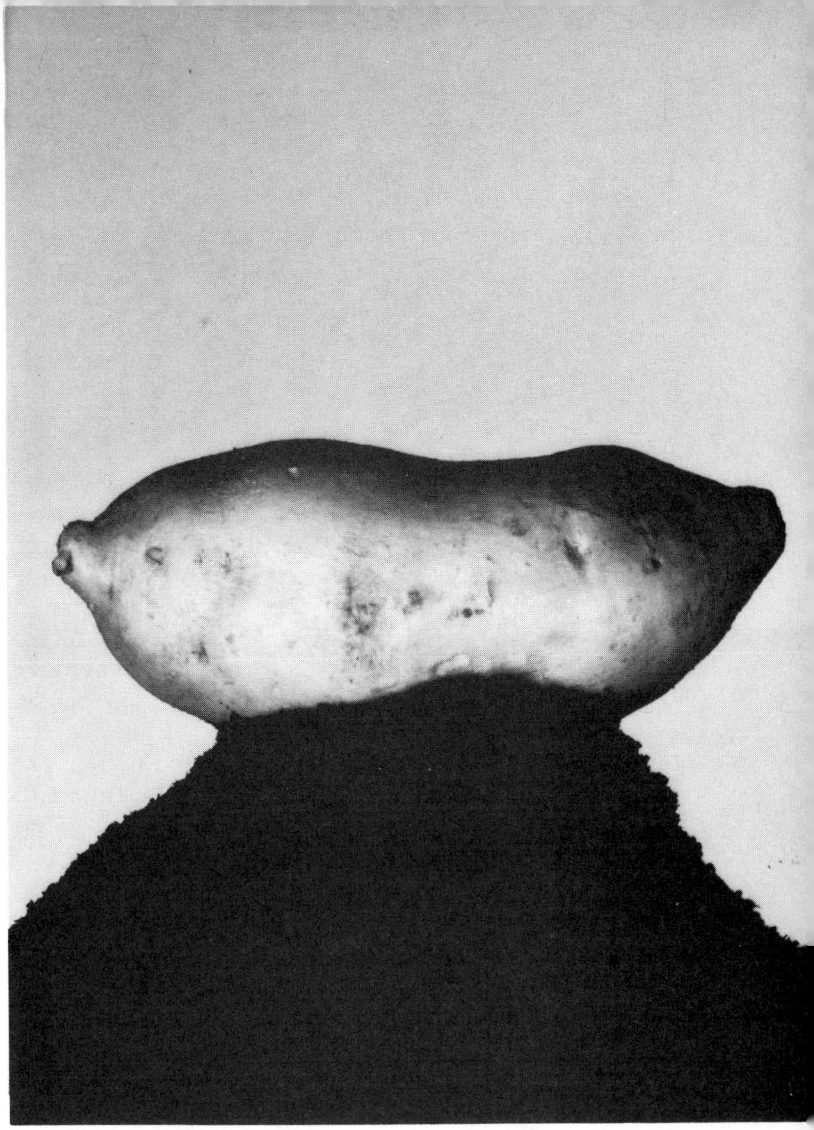

YAM. *Photograph by Ralf Manstein, 1980*

Pursuing our way doggedly nonetheless, we discover that the white yam, D. *alata*, is one of the most widespread; but there is a catch here too, or even catches: different authors ascribe the name white yam to D. *rotundata*, or to D. *cayenensis* (also referred to broad-mindedly as the yellow yam or yellow Guinea yam), or to *D. praehensilis*, which is also known as the bush yam and seems to be the same thing as *D. abyssinica*. When the white yam stays put as *D. alata*, it is popularly dubbed the winged yam, the water yam or the greater yam. It is cultivated all over the world, notably in southern India, on the islands of the South Pacific, on both east and west coasts of Africa and in the Caribbean.

The *Britannica* cites *D. sativa* as a widespread variety, which seems somewhat of an overestimate: though it is grown in the Old World, where it seems to be most popular in the Malay Peninsula, it is cultivated especially in the Orinoco delta, and is the species oftenest found in the United States. This would seem to qualify it for nomination as the one native American yam, assuming that there really is one, but nobody cites it for this honor; that would be too simple. The one oftenest named is *D. trifida*, the yampee or cush-cush yam, which instead of growing one large tuber produces a cluster of small ones, of excellent flavor. It can be grown only in the extreme south of the United States, and is apparently the same species as the Mexican *barbasco*, which serves various pharmaceutical uses, including the manufacture of contraceptive pills. The *Britannica* offers as the only native North American yam *D. villosa*, found wild from Rhode Island to Ontario and Minnesota in one direction and to Florida and Texas in another; so far as I know, nobody has ever bothered to cultivate it. One or two other minor species have also been attributed dubiously to America, notably *D. cayenensis* and *D. piperifolia*. Similarly dubious is the attribution of a single species, *D. hastifolia*, to Australia, where we are told that it was the only plant cultivated by the aborigines; but *The Oxford Book of Food Plants* asserts that no crops at all were ever cultivated by Australian natives before the settlement of the continent in 1788 by Europeans, who brought in all the foods cultivated later, including the yam.

Of the many other yams eaten in one part of the world or another, one worth noting is *D. fasciculata*, because its tubers are the size, shape and color of large kidney potatoes and its flesh, when thoroughly cooked, comes closer to resembling the white potato in taste and mealiness than any other. It is widely cultivated and much liked in the Philippines, while in the Calcutta area starch is made from it. *D. globosa*, common in the East Indies and India, is described as one of the tastiest yams, "much esteemed by both Europeans and natives"; according to one botanist it is the species most liked in Bengal and according to another, the best of the white-fleshed varieties. *D. rubella*, much grown in the East Indies and one of the most common species in India, is said by Sturtevant to be "as good perhaps as any other in cultivation," and he writes also that *D. aculeata* has a tuber "of sweetish taste, regarded as one of the finest esculent roots of the globe." But when he goes on to remark that it is particularly delicious as grown in Caracas, he has to report the opinion of another botanist that in Jamaica it is bitter. Dissent seems to be the rule in the case of yams. Thus the Malayan *keladi*, whose scientific name I do not know, is much liked by the natives, but Europeans think it tastes like soap. One botanist refers approvingly to *D. pentaphylla* as "a good yam," but another describes it as "dreadfully nauseous and intensely bitter." Species which are popular in some parts of Africa are considered in others as famine food.

According to Georges Gibault, the yam barely missed becoming an important European food in the nineteenth century. He reports that what he calls the Chinese yam was first brought into France in 1846, when it was planted in the hothouses of the Paris Natural History Museum and promptly forgotten. It got a second chance in 1850 when French Consul de Montigny sent some plants from Shanghai together with a report pointing out that the yam was as important in China as the potato in Europe. This was at the time when the blight had destroyed virtually all the potatoes of Europe, so seed sellers tried to promote yams as a potato substitute. The effort failed, Gibault explained, because of the difficulty of harvesting yams: the tubers often formed three feet or more beneath the surface and they broke easily. De Montigny had apparently neglected to explain how the Chinese got around this difficulty—they plowed three-foot-deep furrows in their fields and planted the yams in the ridges between them. Perhaps the French did not try very hard. After all, there was one other difficulty which Gibault did not mention: the climate. Besides, the potato recovered.

This left the yam to the tropical and subtropical regions where it is really at home; it is within such climatic areas that it has become the staple food of many populations. The most important among them is probably the place where it started, West Africa, where today as yesterday "the family yam patch is the mainstay of the family diet," James Trager tells us.

Along much of the west coast the yam is not only a food of vast importance but also a kind of symbol [Laurens van der Post wrote in *African Cooking*]. The yam has helped many West Africans to survive.

Accordingly, his gratitude is so great that eating it is almost a religious exercise. Yam feast days are common; they are celebrated at their best, I think, among the Ashanti of Ghana, where yam dishes figure in the ceremonies that accompany birth, death, marriage and recovery from accidents or disease.

Another place where the yam is the staple food is the Trobriand Islands of New Guinea, and there the importance of yams in a social order which is matrilineal, not to say matriarchal, has promoted it to an instrument of power. As Marvin Harris tells the story:

In recognition of the existence of matrilineal descent, at harvest time brothers acknowledged that a portion of the produce of the matrilineal lands was owed to their sisters and sent them presents of baskets filled with yams, their staple crop. The Trobriand chief relied on this custom to maintain his political and economic base. He married the sisters of the headmen of a large number of sublineages. Some chiefs acquired as many as two dozen wives, each of whom was entitled to an obligatory gift of yams from her brothers. These yams were delivered to the chief's village and displayed on special yam racks. Some of the yams were then redistributed in elaborate feasts in which the chief validated his position as a "great provider," while the remainder were used to feed the canoe-building specialists, artisans, magicians, and family servants who thereby fell under the chief's control and enhanced his power.

This passage comes from Harris's *Cannibals and Kings*. The Trobriand Islanders and the Papuans both lived in cannibal country: Could there be a culinary kinship between cannibalism and yams? Reay Tannahill, in her *Flesh and Blood*, told the story of the British consul general Sir Spenser St. John, who in Haiti attended the trial of voodoo ritual murderers who had killed a twelve-year-old girl, and wrote an account of it:

The child was thrown to the ground and ceremonially strangled by one of the "papaloi" (priests), Floréal. "Then Jeanne handed him a large knife, with which he cut off Claircine's head, the assistants catching the blood in a jar . . . the flesh was cut from the bones, and placed in large wooden dishes. . . . The whole party then started for Floréal's house, carrying the remains of their victim with them. . . ."

Peering through some chinks in the wall, a woman and girl sleeping next door saw what happened next, and watched "Jeanne cooking the flesh with congo beans, small and rather bitter, whilst Floréal put the head into a pot with yams to make some soup . . ."

For years after, remarked Spenser St. John laconically, "congo beans were forbidden at our table."

Congo beans are, after all, "small and rather bitter." Yams are larger and luscious. The consul general did not report that this experience deterred him from eating yams.

YE
stands for

yeast, of which biochemist George Wald remarked that "as living creatures we are more like yeast than unlike it. Yeast and man had a common ancestor. Some of the ancestor's progeny became yeasts and some went another way and became men, and these two journeys resulted in a change of only 53 nucleotides out of 312"; and for the **yebb**, also called the yebbnut in Ethiopia and Somalia, though it is not a nut but a pulse with only one seed to the pod.

YELLOW
stands for

the **yellow bell flower**, an APPLE which would have been forgotten by now if it had not thrown off a mutant seed which produced America's most widely eaten variety, the Delicious; for the **yellow belly**, a freshwater fish eaten occasionally in Tanzania; for the **yellowberry**, a cold-loving member of the blackberry family which provides winter food for Eskimos and Indians in Alaska and ripens so late in Lapland that it is preserved by the uncomplicated method of burying it in the snow; for the **Yellow Delicious**, an APPLE now more esteemed than it deserves to be, but I am so old that I can remember the time when commercialism had not yet reduced its flavor to insipidity; for the saltwater **yellowfin**, or albacore, which is a TUNA, the widely eaten freshwater **yellowfish** of south and tropical Africa, which is a barbel, and the saltwater **yellow gurnard**, which is a sea robin; for the **Yellow Ingestrie**, an English apple named after Ingestre [sic] Hall in Staffordshire in honor of William, Lord Talbot, who had distinguished himself by his progressive agricultural methods; for the **yellowjack**, a sort of scad of the Indian and Pacific oceans; for the **yellowlegs**, a shore bird also known as the telltale tattler because it never stops chattering, which would be more appreciated as food if it ate less fish; for the **yellow lily**, whose bulbous roots, according to Thoreau, look and taste "somewhat like raw green corn on the ear"; for the **yellow perch**, which for ichthyologists means exclusively an American PERCH, though European perches are yellow too, and the **yellow pickerel**, which is perhaps the same fish, though it is oftener called the walleye in the northwestern United States; for the **yellow rocket**, which is winter CRESS; for the **yellowtail**, edible whether it is a snapper (for biologists), a flounder (in New England) or an

I-don't-know-what in Japan; for the **yellow tang,** *Ascophyllum nodosum,* the seaweed otherwise known as knotted wrack; and for the **Yellow Transparent**, an apple better for cooking than eating fresh, since it is only moderately tasty, but since it originated in Russia and is resistant to cold, it has been crossed with many superior apples to make them hardy too.

Y
(from this point on)
stands for

yerba buena, an aromatic herb which gave its name to San Francisco before it was San Francisco because it grew so abundantly there; for the **yew**, whose berries are eaten by children and Himalayans and whose nuts contain a kernel with a taste of pine, unless it is the plum-fruited yew of Japan, which, as you might suspect, bears fruit resembling plums, sweet, but with a slight taste of pine also; for the **York Imperial**, an American apple which, like several others which subsequently rose to fame, began as an accidental mutant, on a farm near York, Pennsylvania; for the **youngberry,** one of the many improvements on the blackberry developed at a time when variety was an asset, but more or less abandoned when uniformity became the ideal, except in Africa, where it is still cultivated in both north and south; for the **yucca** of Central America, Mexico and the southwestern United States, of which several species bear edible fruit or flowers which can be used in mixed salads if their hard bitter centers are first pinched out; for the **yuka,** a root which is the staple summer food of the inhabitants of Ecuador's Vilcabamba valley, noted for its large proportion of centenarians; for the **yulan,** whose buds are pickled in China and used to flavor rice; and for the **yuzu,** a Japanese citrus fruit much like a lime.

ZEUXIS: *Criticism comes easier than craftsmanship.*

ZINSSER, HANS: *How sweet*
the Summer! and the Autumn
shone
Like warmth within our hearts
as in the sky,
Ripening rich harvests that
our love had sown,
How good that ere the Winter
comes, I die!

Z

ZA
stands for

the **zachun-oil tree,** whose fruit tastes like a date so bitter that it would seem to induce sneezing, if we may judge from its name in equatorial Africa, *m'choonchoo,* and for the **zahidi,** a real DATE which is all sweetness and is one of the varieties grown in California; for the **zamang,** a Mexican tree with edible pods; and for **zamia,** whose starchy roots contain, inconveniently, an alkaloid poison, of which Caribbean Indians disembarrassed themselves by giving worms, apparently poison-proof, first crack at the roots, a method considered of scant appeal in Florida, whose species of zamia are known as coontie and comfortroot.

ZE
stands for

the **zebra,** counted among the game animals of Africa, but two friends of mine who have tasted it are of the opinion that zebra is more palatable on the plains than on the plate; for **zebrafish,** of which there are so many kinds, some eaten and some not, that I shall make no attempt to examine them here; for the **zebrawood,** whose fruit is eaten in the West Indies; for the **zebu,** the humpbacked cattle which probably originated in India but were already being raised as early as the third millennium B.C. in Asia Minor (where Marco Polo saw white ones and exclaimed, "They are the loveliest things in the world to look at") and today are eaten everywhere in Africa; for the **zedoary,** a plant native to the Himalayas which has somehow worked its way to Madagascar, whose rhizome yields a seasoning which substitutes acceptably for turmeric; and for the **zerba,** a fish of the sargo family which is universally eaten on all Africa's shores, except on the northern part of the east coast.

ZI
stands for

zigzag scallops, found on the East Coast south of Cape Hatteras, whose maximum width is two inches, but they are tasty enough to be worth gathering for yourself: you won't find them on the market.

ZU
stands for

the **zucca,** an extravagantly spectacular Italian squash from whose orange hemisphere knobs and bumps of various bright colors bubble from the surface as though the interior were volcanic; for **zucchini,** originally an Italian squash too, of the summer variety, though it has now become cosmopolitan, which is a conservative dark green, the size and shape of a bludgeon; and for the **Zulu nut,** which is not a nut but a tuber, the one known in Europe and the United States (where it is found wild on the banks of the Delaware and neighboring streams) as the chufa or earth almond, neglected today but esteemed in ancient Egypt, where it has been discovered in tombs of Pharaohs of the XII dynasty, 2400 to 2200 B.C.

AMEN

Works Consulted

Works Consulted

ABBEY, EDWARD. *Cactus Country*. American Wilderness series. New York: Time-Life, 1973.
ALIBERT, LOUIS. *Dictionnaire Occitan-Français*. Toulouse: Institut d'Etudes Occitans, 1965.
ALLAN, DONALD ASPINWALL. "Flavors of Lebanon." *Gourmet*, August 1974.
ALLEN, MYRTLE. "Irish Cookery." *Gourmet*, June 1975.
AMBROISE-RENDU, MARC. *Prehistoire des Français*. Paris: Presses de la Cité, 1967.
AMORY, CLEVELAND. "The Bunny Bop." *Esquire*, December 1969.
ANDOH, ELIZABETH. "The Seasonal Japanese Kitchen." *Gourmet*, January, March, May, July, August and September 1975.
ANDOQUE, PIERRE. *Conseiller du Roy au Séneschal et Siège Prèsidial de Béziers*. Catalogue des Evesques de Béziers, Jean Martel, Béziers, 1650.
ANDRIEUX, MAURICE. *La vie quotidienne dans la Rome pontificale au 18e siècle*. Paris: Hachette, 1962.
ANDROUET, PIERRE. *Guide du Fromage*. Paris: Stock, 1962.
ANONYMOUS. *Le Ménagier de Paris*. Paris: Société des Bibliophiles Français, undated, from edition of c. 1393.
APICIUS, COELIUS. *De obsonii et condiments sive arte coquinaria*. Venice: Giuseppe Antonelli, 1852.
ARESTY, ESTHER. *The Delectable Past*. New York: Simon and Schuster, 1969.
ASHER, GERALD. "Wine Journal." *Gourmet*, February 1977.
——— "Anjou and Maine." *Gourmet*, July 1978.
ATWOOD, MARY S. *A Taste of India*. Boston: Houghton Mifflin, 1969.
AVERY, PETER. *Muslim India, Persia and Turkey. In the Age of Expansion*. New York: McGraw-Hill, 1968.
AYKROYD, W. R., AND JOYCE DOUGHTY. *Les graines de légumineuses et l'alimentation humaine*. United Nations Food and Agricultural Organization, Rome, 1964.
BAILEY, ADRIAN. *The Cooking of the British Isles*. Foods of the World series. New York: Time-Life, 1969.
BAINBRIDGE, JOHN. "London Journal." *Gourmet*, June 1975, March 1977.
BARBER, RICHARD. *Cooking and Recipes from Rome to the Renaissance*. London: Allen Lane, 1973.
BARKAS, JANET. *The Vegetable Passion*. New York: Scribner's, 1975.
BARRY, JOSEPH. *Passion and Politics: A Biography of Versailles*. New York: Doubleday, 1972.
BARRY, NAOMI. Numerous articles in the *International Herald Tribune*, Paris.
BARZINI, LUIGI. *The Italians*. New York: Atheneum, 1965.
BATES, CAROLINE. Articles in *Gourmet* magazine:
"Pueblo Indian Breads," November 1977.
"Strawberries," July 1978.
"San Francisco Sourdough," November 1978.
"Oranges," January 1979.
And fifteen articles in her California restaurants department.
BEAL, DOONE. Articles in *Gourmet* magazine:
"Brittany," May 1974.
"Turkey's Aegean Coast," February 1976.
"Exploring Northern Holland," June 1976.
"Djerba," December 1976.
"Belgian Flanders," June 1978.
"Poros, Hydra, and Spetsai," August 1978.
"A Sussex Sojourn," September 1978.
BEAR, JAMES A., JR. *Jefferson at Monticello*. Charlottesville, Va. University of Virginia Press, 1967.
BEARD, JAMES. *Beard on Bread*. New York: Alfred A. Knopf, 1973.
BENNETT, WENDY. See Condon, Richard.
BENSON, SARAH S. "Buckwheat." *Gourmet*, December 1978.
BERNAL, IGNACIO. *Mexico-Tenochtitlán*. In *Cities of Destiny*. New York: McGraw-Hill, 1967.
BICKERDYKE, JOHN. *The Curiosities of Ale and Beer*. London: Spring Books, 1965.
BIELENSTEIN, HANS. See Morris, Ivan.
BINFORD, LAURENCE C. *Birds of Western North America*. New York: Macmillan, 1974.
BLOND, GEORGES AND GERMAINE. *Histoire pittoresque de notre alimentation*. Paris: Fayard, 1960.
BLOOMFIELD, ARTHUR. *Guide to San Francisco Res-*

Works Consulted

taurants. New York: Ballantine Books, 1975.
BLUME, MARY. Numerous articles in the *International Herald Tribune*, Paris.
BOORSTIN, DANIEL J. *The Americans: The Colonial Experience.* New York: Random House, 1958.
——— *The Americans: The National Experience.* New York: Random House, 1965.
——— *The Americans: The Democratic Experience.* New York: Random House, 1973.
BOURLIERE, FRANÇOIS. *Paysages et Nature en Eurasie.* Monde Vivant series. New York: Time-Life, 1964.
BOWRA, SIR MAURICE. *Athens in the Age of Pericles.* In *Cities of Destiny.* New York: McGraw-Hill, 1967.
BOZZI, OTTERINA PERNA. *Vechhia Milano in Cucina.* Milan: Aldo Martello Editore, 1965.
BRETON, GUY. *Les Nuits secretes de Paris.* Paris: Editions Noir et Blanc, 1963.
BRIGGS, LLOYD CABOT. *The Living Races of the Sahara Desert.* Cambridge, Mass.: Peabody Museum, 1958.
——— *Tribes of the Sahara.* Cambridge, Mass.: Harvard University Press, 1967.
BRILLAT-SAVARIN, ANTHELME. *Physiologie du goût.* Belley, France: Librairie Gustave Adam, 1948.
BROTHWELL, DON AND PATRICIA. *Food in Antiquity.* London: Thames & Hudson, 1919.
BROWN, DALE. *American Cooking.* Foods of the World series. New York: Time-Life, 1968.
——— *The Cooking of Scandinavia.* Foods of the World series. New York: Time-Life, 1968.
——— *American Cooking: The Northwest.* Foods of the World series. New York: Time-Life, 1970.
——— *Wild Alaska.* American Wilderness series. New York: Time-Life, 1972.
BRUZEK, MAURICE. See La Prairie, Yyes.
BUCKLEY, PETER. *Eat It Raw.* New York: Dodd, Mead, 1978.
BURTON, MAURICE AND ROBERT. *Encyclopedia of Fish.* London: Octopus Books, 1975.
CAESAR, JULIUS. *La Guerre des Gaules.* Paris: Garnier-Flammarion, 1964.
CALKINS, CARROL C., AND JEROME A. EATON. "The Vegetable Garden." *Gourmet*, April and May 1975.
CALLVERT, Isabel E. "Historic Charleston." *Gourmet*, April 1976.
CAMINITI, MARCELLO, LUIGI PASQUINI, AND GIANNI QUONDAMATTEO. *Mangieri di Romagna.* Bologna: Edizioni Alfa, 1964.
CARCOPINO, JÉRÔME. *La vie quotidienne à Rome à l'apogée de l'Empire.* Paris: Hachette, 1932.
——— *The Rome of the Antonines.* In *Cities of Destiny.* New York: McGraw-Hill, 1967.
CARRINGTON, RICHARD. *Les Mammifères.* Le Monde Vivant series. New York: Time-Life, 1968.
CARSON, RACHEL. *Silent Spring.* Boston: Houghton Mifflin, 1962.
CASTELOT, ANDRÉ. *L'histoire à table.* Paris: Plon, 1972.
CAVALLERO, GENE, AND TED JAMES. *The Colony Cookbook.* New York: Bobbs-Merrill, 1972.
CERAM, C. W. *Le premier américain.* Paris: Fayard, 1972.
CHADWICK, MRS. J. *Home Cookery: A Collection of Tried Recipes, Both Foreign and Domestic.* Boston, 1853. Facsimile reprint edition, Arno Press, New York, 1973.
CHALAIS, FRANÇOISE. *L'atterrisage.* Paris: Stock, 1974.
CHEKHOV, ANTON. "At the Call of the Siren." *Gourmet*, October 1978.
CHENG, F. T. "Try the Beautiful Simplicity of Chinese Cooking." *House Beautiful*, March 1959.
——— "Cooking by Steam — A Chinese Art." *House Beautiful*, September 1959.
CHILDRESS, WILLIAM. "Fishing in the Ozarks." *Gourmet*, August 1977.
CHRISTENSEN, BJARNE. "Herring Tidbits." *Gourmet*, June 1979.
CHUDWIN, CARYL. "Manitoba Memories." *Gourmet*, July 1977.
CLAIBORNE, CRAIG. "Poor Man's Oysters." *New York Times*, November 22, 1961.
——— *Dining Out in New York.* New York: Atheneum, 1968.
——— AND PIERRE S. FRANEY. *Classic French Cooking.* Foods of the World series. New York: Time-Life, 1970.
CLARK, ELEANOR. *The Oysters of Locmariaquer.* New York: Pantheon Books, 1959.
CLASEN, CLAUS-PETER. *Peace in Germany.* In *The Age of Expansion.* New York: McGraw-Hill, 1968.
CLIFFORD, WILLIAM. "It May Be Offal to Some, but to Others It's Sweetbreads, Kidney Pie, and Calf's Liver." *Holiday*, New York.
CLOS-JOUVE, HENRY, AND JEAN DESMUR. *La Cuisine de Bacchus.* Paris: Solar, 1974.
COLCHIE, ELIZABETH SCHNEIDER. "Cornmeal." *Gourmet*, October 1977.
COLLIER, JOHN. *Indians of the Americas.* New York: New American Library, 1948.
COLLINS, JOSEPH. See Lappe, Frances Moore.
CONDON, RICHARD. "Eating in Hongkong." *Gourmet*, January 1979.
——— AND WENDY BENNETT. "Mexican Fruit and Vegetable Cookery." *Gourmet*, April 1975.
COQUET, JAMES DE. *Propos de Table.* Paris: Hachette, 1964.
——— Numerous articles in *Le Figaro*, Paris.
CORRIGAN, ANNE W. "Capital Markets." *Gourmet*, October 1974.
CORTI, EGAN CAESER. *Vie, mort et résurrection d'Herculaneum et de Pompéii.* Paris: Plon, 1953.
COSTAIN, THOMAS B. *The Conquering Family.* New York: Doubleday, 1962.
COURTINE, ROBERT J. *L'assassin est à votre table.* Paris: La Table Ronde, 1969.
——— (signed La Reynière). *Cent merveilles de la Cuisine Française.* Paris: Seuil, 1971.
——— *Mes repas les plus étonnants.* Paris: Robert Laffont, 1973.
——— *Balzac à table.* Paris: Robert Laffont, 1976.
——— Numerous articles in *Le Monde, Paris Match, Jours de France*, etc.

Works Consulted

Cox, Leyland. "German Christmas Baking." *Gourmet*, December 1978.

Crockett, James Underwood. *Vegetables and Fruits*. Foods of the World series. New York: Time-Life, 1972.

Cummings, Richard Osborn. *The American and His Food*. Chicago: University of Chicago Press, 1940. Facsimile reprint edition, Arno Press, New York, 1970.

Daniel, Charles. See Smith, Page.

David, Elizabeth. *Italian Food*. New York: Alfred A. Knopf, 1958.

——— *Spices, Salt and Aromatics in the English Kitchen*. Harmondsworth, England: Penguin Books, 1971.

——— *English Bread and Yeast Cookery*. Harmondsworth, England: Penguin Books, 1977.

Davidson, Alan. *Le monde merveilleux des poissons de la Méditerranée*. Paris: Solar, 1973.

——— *Fish and Fish Dishes of Laos*. Rutland, Vt.: Charles E. Tuttle Company, 1975.

Davis, Millar C. *The Near Woods*. New York: Alfred A. Knopf, 1974.

Day, Beth. "Philippine Fare." *Gourmet*, June 1974.

Decaux, Alain. *Histoire des Françaises: La Soumission*. Paris: Librairie Académique, 1972.

——— *Histoire des Françaises: La Revolte*. Paris: Librairie Académique, 1972.

de Rochemont, Richard. See Root, Waverley.

Desmur, Jean. See Clos-Jouvé, Henry.

Diaz, Bernal. *The Conquest of New Spain*. Harmondsworth, England: Penguin Books, 1963.

Dickens, Charles. *American Notes*. London: Thomas Nelson and Sons, 1900.

Dickson, Paul. *The Great American Ice Cream Book*. New York: Atheneum, 1973.

Dictionnaire de l'Académie des Gastronomes. Paris: Editions Prisma, 1962.

Dietzel, Dr. Karl. *Eine culinarische Symphonie in zehn Satzen*. Privately published, Krefeld, Germany, 1978.

Donovan, Maria Kezslik. Articles in *Gourmet* magazine, New York.
"The Far Side of the Tiber," October 1974.
"Adelaide," February 1976.
"Palermo," May 1976.
"Lake Balaton," October 1977.

Doolittle, Jerome. *Canyons and Mesas*. American Wilderness series. New York: Time-Life, 1974.

Dorsey, Deborah. "The Eastern Shore of Maryland." *Gourmet*, April 1974.

——— "East Coast Bread." *Gourmet*, November 1974.

Doughty, Joyce. See Aykroyd, W. R.

Douglas, James Sholto. "Forest-farming: An Ecological Approach to Increase Nature's Food Productivity." *Impact of Science on Society*, XXIIII, 1 (1973).

Dumas, Alexandre. *Le Grand Dictionnaire de Cuisine*. Paris: Tchou, 1965.

Eaton, Jerome A. See Calkins, Carroll C.

Elbert, Virginia and George. "Growing Herbs Indoors." *Gourmet*, November 1978.

Elder, Mimi. "Maple Sugaring." *Gourmet*, March 1975.

——— "Sailing the British Virgin Islands." *Gourmet*, April 1976.

Encyclopaedia Britannica. edition of, 1962.

Encyclopédie des dates et des évènements. Paris: Editions de la Courtille, 1968.

Engel, Leonard. *La Mer*. Le Monde Vivant series. New York: Time-Life, 1962.

Etienne, Robert. *La vie quotidienne à Pompéii*. Paris: Hachette, 1966.

Eustis, Celestine. *Cooking in Old Creole Days*. New York, 1904. Facsimile reprint edition, Arno Press, New York, 1973.

Farb, Peter. *Les Insectes*. Le Monde Vivant series. New York: Time-Life, 1964.

——— *L'écologie*. Le Monde Vivant series. New York: Time-Life, 1968.

——— *Man's Rise to Civilization as Shown by the Indians of North America from Primeval Times to the Coming of the Industrialist State*. New York: E. P. Dutton, 1968.

Feibleman, Peter S. *The Cooking of Spain and Portugal*. Foods of the World series. New York: Time-Life, 1969.

——— *American Cooking: Creole and Acadian*. Foods of the World series. New York: Time-Life, 1971.

——— *The Bayous*. American Wilderness series. New York: Time-Life, 1973.

Fels, Marthe de. *Pierre Poivre, ou l'amour des épices*. Paris: Hachette, 1968.

Ferber, Ellen. "Potluck of the Irish." *Gourmet*, March 1968.

Field, Michael. "The Egg." *McCall's*, April 1966.

——— "All About Garlic." *Esquire*.

——— and Frances Field. *A Quintet of Cuisines*. Foods of the World series. New York: Time-Life, 1970.

Fisher, M. F. *The Cooking of Provincial France*. Foods of the World series. New York: Time-Life, 1968.

——— "The Trouble with Tripe." *The New Yorker*, November 2, 1968.

Flaceliere, Robert. *La vie quotidienne en Grece au siècle de Périclès*. Paris: Hachette, 1959.

"Food in the Middle East." *Aramco World Magazine*, The Hague, November-December, 1955.

Forcat, L. *Mollusques, terrestres et d'eau douce*. Lausanne, Switzerland: Librairie Payot, undated.

Franey, Pierre S. See Claiborne, Craig.

Frazier, Greg and Beverly. *Aphrodisiac Cookery, Ancient and Modern*. San Francisco: Troubadour Press, 1970.

Gade, Daniel W. "Horsemeat as Human Food in France." *Ecology of Food and Nutrition*, Vol. 8, London, 1976.

Galland, E. M. See Habersaat, E.

Garvey, William. "La Nouvelle Cuisine." *Johns Hopkins Magazine*, June 1978.

Gault, Henri, and Christian Millau. *Guide de New York, Boston, Chicago, Los Angeles, New Orleans, San Francisco et Montréal*. Paris: Julliard, 1967.

——— *Guide Gourmand de la France*. Paris: Hachette, 1970.

Works Consulted

——— Numerous articles in *Nouveau Guide*, Paris.
GAY, RUTH. "Fear of Food." *American Scholar*, c. 1976.
GEHMAN, RICHARD. *The Haphazard Gourmet*. New York: Scribner's, 1966.
GERARD, JOHN. *Gerard's Herball*. From the edition of Th. Johnson, 1636. London: Minerva, 1974.
GIBAULT, GEORGES. *Histoire des légumes*. Paris: Librairie Horticole, 1912.
GIBBONS, EUELL. *Stalking the Wild Asparagus*. New York: David McKay, 1962.
——— *Stalking the Blue-Eyed Scallop*. New York: David McKay, 1964.
——— *Stalking the Healthful Herbs*. New York: David McKay, 1966.
GIUSTI-LANHAM, HEDY. "Noontime in Venice." *Gourmet*, May 1977.
Grand Atlas Historique. Paris: Librairie Stock, 1968.
Grand Larousse Encyclopédique. Paris: Larousse, 1960.
GRASS, GÜNTER. *Der Butt*. Darmstadt and Neuwied: Hermann Luchterhand Verlag, 1974.
——— *Le Turbot*. Translated by Jean Amsler. Paris: Editions du Seuil, 1979.
GREENE, GRAHAM. *Lord Rochester's Monkey*. London: Bodley Head, 1974.
GRIGSON, GEOFFREY. *A Dictionary of English Plant Names (and Some Products of Plants)*. London: Allen Lane, 1974.
GRUB, CLEO. "Green Peppercorns." *Gourmet*, October 1974.
GUINAUDEAU, MME. Z. *Moroccan Gastronomy*. Rabat, Morocco: Moroccan National Tourist Office, undated.
GUY, CHRISTIAN. *Une Histoire de la cuisine française*. Paris: Les Productions de Paris, 1962.
HABERSAAT, E., AND E. M. GALLAND. *Nos Champignons*. Lausanne, Switzerland: Librairie Payot, undated.
HAHN, EMILY. *The Cooking of China*. Foods of the World series. New York: Time-Life, 1968.
HALE, WILLIAM HARLAN. *Horizon Cookbook*. New York: American Heritage, 1968.
HARDEN, DONALD. *The Phoenicians*. Harmondsworth, England: Penguin Books, 1971.
HARRIS, MARVIN. *Cannibals and Kings*. New York: Random House, 1977.
HARRISON, S. G. See Masefield, G. B.
HAWKES, ALEX D. Articles in *Gourmet*, New York.
"Banana Bounty," April 1974.
"The Illustrious Avocado," September 1974.
"Tropical American Soups," February 1977.
HAZLETON, NIKA STANDEN. *The Cooking of Germany*. Foods of the World series. New York: Time-Life, 1969.
HEMPHILL, ROSEMARY. *Spice and Savour*. Sydney, Australia: Angus and Robertson, 1964.
——— *Fragrance and Flavor*. Sydney, Australia: Angus and Robertson, 1973.
Herbs and Other Medicinal Plants. London: Orbis Publishing, 1972.
HERMANN, MATTHIAS. *Herbs and Medicinal Flowers*. New York: Galahad Books, 1973.
HESS, JOHN L. *Vanishing France*. New York: Quadrangle, 1975.
——— AND KAREN. *The Taste of America*. New York: Viking, 1977.
——— "Pity the Poor Patat." *Viva*, September 1978.
HESS, KAREN. "Recipe for a Cookbook: Scissors and Paste." *Harper's*, October 1975.
HEURGON, JACQUES. *La vie quotidienne chez les Etrusques*. Paris: Hachette, 1961.
HILL, ROWLAND G. P. *A Guide to Life in Finland*. Helsinki: Otave Publishing Company, 1952.
HODGSON, MOIRA. "Dutch Cookery." *Gourmet*, December 1974.
HORN, YVONNE. "The Call of the San Juan Islands." *Gourmet*, September 1974.
HUTCHINSON, E. *The New Family Book, or Ladies' Indispensable Companion and Housekeeper's Guide: Addressed to Sister, Mother, and Wife*. New York, 1854. Facsimile reprint edition, Arno Press, New York, 1973.
HUXLEY, ALDOUS. *The Devils of London*. London: Chatto & Windus, 1952.
HUXLEY, ELSPETH. *Brave New Victuals*. London: Chatto & Windus, 1965.
IRWIN, WILLIAM WALLACE. *The Garrulous Gourmet*. New York: McBride, 1952.
IZZO, E. C. *La Cuisine exotique, insolite, érotique*. Paris: Laffont, 1965.
JACKSON, MICHAEL. *The English Pub*. New York: Harper & Row, 1975.
JACOBS, JAY. Articles in *Gourmet* magazine:
"Capital Dining," August 1976.
"The Butcher's Art," February 1977.
"Memories of Málaga," February 1978.
And twenty-one articles in his New York restaurants department.
JAFFREY, MADHUR. "The Spicy Eats of India." *Holiday*, December 1969. And articles in *Gourmet* magazine:
"An Indian Reminiscence," October 1974.
"Goa," October 1976.
"Delhi—Old and New," January 1978.
"Tastes of Thailand," October 1978.
JAMES, TED. See Cavallero, Gene.
JARDIN, CLAUDE. *List of Foods Used in Africa*. United Nations Food and Agricultural Organization, Rome, 1967.
JOHNSON, DIANE. *Lesser Lives*. New York: Alfred A. Knopf, 1972.
JOHNSON, WILLIAM WEBER. *Baja California*. American Wilderness series. New York: Time-Life, 1972.
JONES, EVAN. *American Food: The Gastronomic Story*. New York: E. P. Dutton, 1975.
——— "Garden Sass." *Gourmet*, August 1976.
——— *A Food Lover's Companion*. New York: Harper & Row, 1976.
JOYCE, ALLEN. *The Duck Press*. Newsletter, Berkeley, Calif.
JOYCE, JAMES. *Ulysses*. New York: Random House, 1946.
JUNGFLEISCH, JOAN M. *For Innocents Abroad*. Washington, D.C.: Hardley Company, 1971.
KATZ, MARTHA, AND ROBIN WHYATT. "Sprouts." *Gourmet*, June 1978.
KENYON, MICHAEL. Articles in *Gourmet* magazine:

Works Consulted

"Truffling in the Lot," October 1974.
"Two Bicycles in Normandy," June 1975.
"The Channel Islands," July and August 1975.

KIMBALL, YAFFE, AND JEAN ANDERSON. *The Art of American Indian Cooking*. New York: Doubleday, 1965.

KINARD, EPSIE. "The Bean Sprout." *House Beautiful*, May 1959.

——— "Ancient Chinese Way." *House Beautiful*, June 1959.

KINKEAD, EUGENE. "The Squirrels of Central Park." *The New Yorker*, September 9, 1974.

KLUGER, MARILYN. Articles in *Gourmet*, New York:
"Freezing Vegetables and Fruit," July 1975.
"The Wilding Apple," October 1976.
"Gathering Wild Persimmons," October 1978.

KNAUTH, PERCY. *The North Woods*. American Wilderness series. New York: Time-Life, 1972.

KOBLER, JOHN. *Ardent Spirits: The Rise and Fall of Prohibition*. New York: G. P. Putnam's Sons, 1973.

KOEHLER, MARGARET HUDSON. "The Merits of Mussels." *Gourmet*, June 1978.

LACROIX, PAUL. *France in the Middle Ages*. New York: Frederick Unger, 1963.

LADURIE, EMMANUEL LE ROY. *Histoire du climat depuis l'an mil*. Paris: Flammarion, 1967.

LAGRIFFE, LOUIS. *Le livre des épices, des condiments et des aromates*. Paris: Robert Morel, 1966.

LANGSETH-CHRISTENSEN, LILLIAN. Articles in *Gourmet*, New York.
"Switzerland Rhine Country," July 1974.
"Lingering Charms at Lübeck," September 1974.
"Madrid's Lhardy," October 1974.
"Skiing in Val Gardena," December 1974.
"Chocolate in England," June 1975.
"Longleat Kitchen," September 1975.
"Helsinki," May 1976.
"Shopping in Dublin," March 1977.
"Horseradish," April 1978.

LAPPE, FRANCES MOORE, AND JOSEPH COLLINS. *Food First*. Boston: Houghton Mifflin, 1977.

LA PRAIRIE, YVES, WITH MAURICE BRUZEK. *Le nouvel homme et la mer*. Paris: Editions Mènges, 1977.

Larousse des Citations. Paris: Larousse, 1976.

Larousse Gastronomique. Paris: Larousse, 1938. Revised edition, 1960.

LAWRENCE, R. DE TREVILLE, SR., ed. *Jefferson and Wine*. The Plains, Va.: Vinifera Wine Growers Association, 1974.

LE BRETON, AUGUSTE. *Langue Verte et Noirs Desseins*. Paris: Presses de la Cité, 1960.

Le chant du riz pilé. Paris: Editeurs Français Réunis, 1974.

LEONARD, JONATHAN NORTON. *Latin American Cooking*. Foods of the World series. New York: Time-Life, 1968.

——— *American Cooking: New England*. Foods of the World series. New York: Time-Life, 1971.

——— *American Cooking: The Great West*. Foods of the World series. New York: Time-Life, 1971.

——— *Atlantic Beaches*. American Wilderness series. New York: Time-Life, 1972.

LEOPOLD, A. STARKER. *Le Desert*. American Wilderness series. New York: Time-Life, 1962.

LESLIE, ELIZA. *Directions for Cookery*. Philadelphia, 1848. Facsimile reprint edition, Arno Press, New York, 1973.

LEWIS, EDNA. "The Taste of Country Cooking." *Gourmet*, May 1976.

LHOTE, HENRI. *Dans les campements Touaregs*. Paris: Amiot et Dumont, 1951.

LIANIDES, LEON. "Easter in Greece." *Gourmet*, April 1974.

LIDDELL, HENRY GEORGE, AND ROBERT SCOTT. *A Greek-English Lexicon*. Revised by Sir Henry Stuart Jones with the assistance of Roderick McKenzie. London: Oxford University Press, 1973.

LIEBLING, A. J. *Between Meals*. New York: Simon and Schuster, 1962.

——— "Memoirs of a Feeder in France." *The New Yorker*, April 11, April 18, April 25 and May 2, 1959.

——— "The Soul of Bouillabaisse." *The New Yorker*, October 27, 1962.

LIEUTAGHI, PIERRE. *Le livre des bonnes herbes*. Paris: Robert Morel, 1966.

LIMBURG, PETER R. *The Story of Corn*. New York: Julian Messner, 1971.

LINK, DAVID. "Early American Kitchens." *Gourmet*, November 1969.

LO, KENNETH H. C. *Peking Cooking*. London: Faber & Faber, 1971.

LO RUSSO, R. See Pierotti, D.

LUCAS-DUBRETON, J. *La vie quotidienne à Florence au temps des Médicis*. Paris: Hachette, 1958.

LYON, NINETTE. *Le guide culinaire des poissons, crustacés et mollusques*. Verviers, Belgium: Marabout, 1979.

MAAS, CARL. "Beyond the Tagus." *Gourmet*, April 1974.

——— "New York's Chinatown." *Gourmet*, July 1974.

MACLEAN, VIRGINIA. *Much Entertainment*. London: J. M. Dent, 1973.

MADLENER, JUDITH COOPER. *The Seavegetable Book*. New York: Clarkson N. Potter, 1977.

MALLERET, LOUIS. *Pierre Poivre*. Paris: École Français d'Extreme-Orient, 1974.

MANÇERON, CLAUDE. *Les vingt ans du roi*. Paris: Laffont, 1972.

——— *Le Vent d'Amerique*. Paris: Laffont, 1974.

——— *Le bon plaisir*. Paris: Laffont, 1976.

MARCHANT, PIERRE. "The Pig Behind the Pork." *Réalités*, English-language edition, April 1974.

MARGOLIUS, SIDNEY. *Health Foods: Facts and Fakes*. New York: Walker, 1973.

MARSTON, THOMAS E. See Skelton, R. A.

MARTIN, ALICE A. *All About Apples*. Boston: Houghton Mifflin, 1976.

MASEFIELD, G. B., M. WALLIS, S. G. HARRISON, AND B. E. NICHOLSON. *The Oxford Book of Food Plants*. London: Oxford University Press, 1973.

MATTHIESSEN, PETER. "The Wind Birds." *The New Yorker*, May 27 and June 3, 1967.

Works Consulted

——— "The Snow Leopard." *The New Yorker*, March 27 and April 3, 1972.
MAUREL, ROSIE. *Dictionnaire des Aliments*. Paris: La Table Ronde, 1960.
McDOUGAL, MENAKKA. "Sri Lanka." *Gourmet*, September 1977.
McEVEDY, COLIN. *The Penguin Atlas of Medieval History*. Harmondsworth, England: Penguin Books, 1961.
——— *The Penguin Atlas of Ancient History*. Harmondsworth, England: Penguin Books, 1967.
McKENDRY, MAXIME. *Seven Centuries of English Cooking*. London: Weidenfeld and Nicholson, 1973.
McLEOD, CATHERINE. "The Salt of the Earth." *Réalités*, English-language edition, September 1972.
McPHEE, JOHN. *Oranges*. New York: Farrar, Straus & Giroux, 1967.
——— "A Forager." *The New Yorker*, April 6, 1968.
——— *Coming Into the Country*. New York: Farrar, Straus & Giroux, 1977.
——— "Brigade de Cuisine." *The New Yorker*, February 19, 1979.
MESSEGUE, MAURICE. *Votre poison quotidien*. Paris: Jacques Lanore, 1961.
MILLAU, CHRISTIAN. See Gault, Henri.
MILLER, GLORIA BLEY. "Techniques of Chinese Cooking." *Gourmet*, May and July 1974.
MIREAUX, EMILE. *La vie quotidienne au Temps d'Homère*. Paris: Hachette, 1954.
MITCHAM, HOWARD. *Creole Gumbo and All That Jazz*. Reading, Mass.: Addison-Wesley, 1978.
MITCHELL, FANNY TODD. "Brussels." *Gourmet*, May 1975.
——— "A Forgotten Corner of France." *Gourmet*, October 1975.
MITCHELL, JOSEPH. *McSorley's Wonderful Saloon*. New York: Duell, Sloane and Pearce, 1943.
——— *Old Mr. Flood*. New York: Duell, Sloane and Pearce, 1948.
MONSELET, CHARLES. *La cuisinière poétique*. Paris: Michel Lévy Frères, undated, c. 1850.
——— *Lettres gourmandes*. Paris: Editions Rabelais, 1974.
MOOREHEAD, ALAN. *Darwin and the Beagle*. New York: Harper & Row, 1969.
MORISON, SAMUEL ELIOT. *The Oxford History of the American People*. New York: Oxford University Press, 1965.
Moroccan Gastronomy. Rabat, Morocco: Moroccan National Tourist Office, undated.
MORRIS, IVAN, AND HANS BIELENSTEIN. *Ming China and the Unification of Japan*. In *The Age of Expansion*. New York: McGraw-Hill, 1968.
MUSCATINE, DORIS. *A Cook's Tour of Rome*. New York: Scribner's, 1964.
NEARING, HELEN AND SCOTT. *The Maple Sugar Book*. New York: Galahad Books, 1970.
NELLI, RENÉ. *La vie quotidienne des Cathares de Languedoc au XIIIe siècle*. Paris: Hachette, 1969.
NELSON, KAY SHAW. "Philadelphia's Culinary Heritage." *Gourmet*, March 1976.
——— "Down East Country." *Gourmet*, December 1976.
NICKLES, HARRY G. *Middle Eastern Cooking*. Foods of the World series. New York: Time-Life, 1962.
NUTTING, WALLACE. *Beautiful Vermont*. New York: Bonanza Books, 1922.
OGRIZEK, DORÉ. *Le Monde à Table*. Paris: Odé, 1952.
OJAKANGAS, BEATRICE. Articles in *Gourmet* magazine:
"European Entrée Pies," January 1975.
"Worldly Rye Bread," February 1976.
"Phyllo Fare," April 1977.
"Twice-Baked Breads," February 1978.
"Vegetables with Nuts," March 1978.
OLIVER, RAYMOND. *Recettes pour un ami*. Paris: Galerie Jean Giraudoux, 1964.
OMMANNEY, F. D. *Les Poissons*. Le Monde Vivant series. New York: Time-Life, 1964.
ORTIZ, ELISABETH LAMBERT. Articles in *Gourmet* magazine:
"Yogurt," November 1974.
"Cuernavaca and Acapulco," December 1974.
"Shopping in Bermuda," September 1975.
"The Cookery of Brazil," October 1975.
"Bath and Wells," April 1977.
"Okra," June 1977.
"Oaxaca," December 1977.
"Exploring Winchester," March 1978.
PAINTER, GEORGE D. See Skelton, R. A.
PALOMBI, ARTURO, AND MARIO SANTARELLI. *Gli animali commestibili dei mari d'Italia*. Milan: Editore Urico Hoepli, 1969.
PAPASHVILI, HELEN AND GEORGE. *Russian Cooking*. Foods of the World series. New York: Time-Life, 1969.
PASLEY, VIRGINIA. *In Celebration of Food*. New York: Simon and Schuster, 1974.
PASQUELOT, MAURICE. *La Terre Chauve*. Paris: La Table Ronde, 1971.
PASQUINI, LUIGI. See Caminiti, Marcello.
PATTERSON, SUZANNE. "French Country Cooking with Pork." *Réalités*, English-language edition, April 1974.
PECH, J. L. *Espoirs de longue vie*. Paris: Gallimard, 1965.
PETERSON, ROGER TORY. *Les Oiseaux*. Le Monde Vivant series. New York: Time-Life, 1965.
PIEROTTI, D., R. LO RUSSO, AND S. SILVIERI-BUGGIANI. *Il dattero di mare, Lithodomus lithophagus, nel golfo di Spezia*. Pisa: Arti Grafiche Pacini Mariotti, 1966.
PIGAFETTA, ANTONIO. *The Voyage of Magellan*. Translated by Paula Spurlin. Englewood Cliffs, N. J.: Prentice-Hall, 1973.
POLO, MARCO. *The Travels*. Translated by Ronald Latham. Harmondsworth, England: Penguin Books, 1958.
POLVAY, MARINA. Articles in *Gourmet* magazine:
"Watercress," June 1976.
"Hungarian Cookery," June 1977.
"Cooking with Rice," August 1978.
"The Magical Mushroom," June 1979.
Practical Encyclopedia of Gardening. Edited by Norman Taylor. Garden City, N. Y.: Garden City Publishing Co., 1936.
PRESTWICH, MENNA. *France's Monarchy and People*,

Works Consulted

From Henri III to Louis XIV. In *The Age of Expansion*. New York: McGraw-Hill, 1968.

PULLAR, PHILLIPA. *Consuming Passions*. Boston: Little, Brown, 1970.

Pyrenées. Paris: Michelin, 1952.

QUONDAMATTEO, GIANNI. See Caminiti, Marcello.

RAU, SANTHA RAMA. *The Cooking of India*. Foods of the World series. New York: Time-Life, 1969.

Reader's Encyclopedia. New York: Thomas Y. Crowell, 1925.

REYNOLDS, C. P. "Oxford." *Gourmet*, June 1977.

RHODES, RICHARD. *The Ozarks*. American Wilderness series. New York: Time-Life, 1974.

RINALDI, AUGUSTO, AND VASSILI TYNDALO. *The Compete Book of Mushrooms*. New York: Crown, 1974.

RIPLEY, S. DILLON. *Asie Tropicale*. Le Monde Vivant series. New York: Time-Life, 1969.

ROBBINS, WILLIAM. *The American Food Scandal. Why You Can't Eat Well on What You Earn*. New York: William Morrow, 1974.

RODEN, CLAUDIA. "Sephardic Cookery." *Gourmet*, April 1977.

RODGERS, MARY AUGUSTA. Articles in *Gourmet* magazine:
"Derby Day Breakfast," May 1974.
"New Orleans," September 1976.
"Louisiana's Acadia Country," October 1976.
"Savannah," March 1977.

ROOT, WAVERLEY. *The Food of France*. New York: Alfred A. Knopf, 1958.

——— *Italian Cooking*. Foods of the World series. New York: Time-Life, 1968.

——— *Paris Dining Guide*. New York: Atheneum, 1969.

——— *The Food of Italy*. New York: Atheneum, 1971.

——— *The Food of Ancient Greece and Rome*. Unpublished.

——— AND RICHARD DE ROCHEMONT. *Contemporary French Cooking*. New York: Random House, 1962.

——— *American Eating*. New York: William Morrow, 1976.

ROUECHE, BERTON. Articles in *The New Yorker* magazine:
"Ricing," December 25, 1967.
"The Humblest Fruit," October 1, 1973.
"A Friend in Disguise," October 28, 1974.

RUSSELL, FRANKLIN. *The Okefenokee Swamp*. American Wilderness series. New York: Time-Life, 1973.

SANTARELLI, MARIO. See Palombi, Arturo.

SASS, LORNA J. "A Medieval Feast." *Gourmet*, April 1976.

SCHAPIRA, JOEL, DAVID, AND KARL. *The Book of Coffee and Tea*. New York: St. Martin's Press, 1975.

SCHEFFEL, RICHARD L. "A Weed Indeed." *Gourmet*, May 1975.

SCOTT, ROBERT. See Liddell, Henry George.

SHAKESPEARE, WILLIAM. The Yale Shakespeare, Yale University Press, New Haven, Conn. 1926.

SILVIERI-BUGGIANI, S. See Pierotti, D.

SIMONS, NINA. Articles in *Gourmet* magazine:
"Chinese Cuisine: Seasonings," January and February 1979.
"Chinese Cuisine: Rice," March 1979.
"Chinese Cuisine: Noodles," April and May 1979.
"Chinese Cuisine: Breads," June 1979.
"Chinese Cuisine: Dumplings," July 1979.

SJOBY, JAN. "A Kingdom for a Bivalve." *International Herald Tribune*, Paris, November 19, 1974. And numerous other articles in the *International Herald Tribune*.

SKELTON, R. A., THOMAS E. MARSTON, AND GEORGE D. PAINTER. *The Vinland Map and the Tartar Relation*. New Haven, Conn.: Yale University Press, 1965.

SMITH, JOHN. *The General Historie of Virginia, New-England and the Summer Isles with the names of the Adventurers, Planters, and Governors from their first Beginning An 1584 to their present 1626*. London, 1626.

SMITH, LEONA WOODRING. *The Forgotten Art of Flower Cookery*. New York: Harper & Row, 1973.

SMITH, PAGE, AND CHARLES DANIEL. *The Chicken Book*. Boston: Little, Brown, 1975.

STEINBERG, RAFAEL. *The Cooking of Japan*. Foods of the World series. New York: Time-Life, 1969.

——— *Pacific and Southwest Asian Cooking*. Foods of the World series. New York: Time-Life, 1970.

STEVENSON, JAMES. "Scalloping." *The New Yorker*, August 15, 1977.

STEVENSON, VIOLET, ed. *A Modern Herbal*. London: Crown, 1974.

STOKES, STEPHANIE. "Bhutan—A Realm of Shangri-La." *Gourmet*, August 1976.

STURTEVANT, DR. E. LEWIS. *Edible Plants of the World*. Edited by V. P. Hedrick. New York: Dover Publications, 1976.

TANGYE, JEAN NICOL. "Simpson's-on-the-Strand." *Gourmet*, October 1978.

TANNAHILL, REAY. *The Fine Art of Food*. New York: A. S. Barnes, 1968.

——— *Food in History*. New York: Stein and Day, 1973.

——— *Flesh and Blood. A History of the Cannibal Complex*. London: Hamish Hamilton, 1976.

TANTTU, ANNA-MAIJE AND JUHA. See Viherjuuri, Matti.

TEAL, JOHN AND MILDRED. *The Sargasso Sea*. Boston: Little, Brown, 1975.

THOMAS, VERONICA. Articles in *Gourmet* magazine:
"The Lowlands of Scotland," January 1975.
"Vancouver," September 1975.
"Southern British Columbia," September 1975.
"Alaska," July 1976.
"Prince Edward Island," May 1977.

THOMPSON, DANIEL V. "Chronicle of a Sweetmeat." *Gourmet*, January 1978.

THOMPSON, SYLVIA VAUGHN. "The Magnificent Mussel." *Holiday*, December 1970.

Works Consulted

——— "The Venerable Quince." *Gourmet*, October 1974.

THOREAU, HENRY DAVID. *The Maine Woods*. New York: Bramhall House, 1950.

——— *Walden*. New York: Bramhall House, 1951.

TRAGER, JAMES. *The Enriched, Fortified, Concentrated, Country-Fresh, Lip-Smacking, Finger-Licking, International, Unexpurgated Foodbook*. New York: Grossman Publishers, 1970.

TREVOR-ROPER, HUGH. *The Age of Expansion*. New York: McGraw-Hill, 1968.

TRILLIN, CALVIN. *American Fried: Adventures of a Happy Eeater*. New York: Doubleday, 1974.

——— *Alice, Let's Eat*. New York: Random House, 1978.

——— "U.S. Journal." *The New Yorker*, February 7, 1977.

TROTTA, GERI. Articles in *Gourmet* magazine:
"Intriguing India," May 1974.
"Madrid's Café Gijón," December 1974.
"The Spell of Hongkong," June 1975.
"Treasures of Taipei," September 1975.
"Iran Beyond Teheran," March 1977.
"Seychelles," February 1978.
"Guadalajara," October 1978.
"Bermuda," March 1979.

TYNDALO, VASSILI. See Rinaldi, Augusto.

TZABAR, NAOMI AND SHIMON. *Yemenite and Sabra Cookery*. Tel Aviv: Sadan Publishing House, 1966.

VAN DER POST, LAURENS. *African Cooking*. Foods of the World series. New York: Time-Life, 1970.

VELIKOVSKY, IMMANUEL. *Worlds in Collision*. London: Victor Gollancz, 1950.

VETTER, ERNEST G. *Death Was Our Escort*. New York: Prentice-Hall, 1944.

VIHERJUURI, MATTI, ANNA-MAIJE TANTTU AND JUHA TANTTU. *Finlandia Gastronomica*. Helsinki: Otava, 1974.

VIRGIL. *The Pastoral Poems*. Harmondsworth, England: Penguin Books, 1949.

WALDO, MYRA. *The Complete Book of Oriental Cooking*. New York: David McKay, 1960.

WALLACE, ROBERT. *Hawaii*. American Wilderness series. New York: Time-Life, 1973.

WALLIS, M. See Masefield, G. B.

WALTER, EUGENE. *American Cooking: Southern Style*. Foods of the World series. New York: Time-Life, 1968.

WARNER, WILLIAM W. *Beautiful Swimmers*. Boston: Little, Brown, 1976.

WASSON, R. GORDON. *Soma: Divine Mushroom of Immortality*. New York: Harcourt Brace Jovanovich, 1968.

WAUGH, ALEC. *Wines and Spirits*. Foods of the World series. New York: Time-Life, 1968.

WEBSTER, MOLLIE C. Articles in *Gourmet* magazine:
"A Suffolk Childhood: Early Summer," May 1974.
"A Suffolk Childhood: Spring," March 1976.
"A Suffolk Childhood: Autumn," October 1978.
"Scalloping on Pleasant Bay," October 1978.
"Autumn in Vermont," October 1976.
"The Aldeburgh Festival," May 1977.
"A Hungarian Riding Tour," June 1977.
"A Chinese Vegetable Garden," June 1978.

WECHSBERG, JOSEPH. *The Cooking of Vienna's Empire*. Foods of the World series. New York: Time-Life, 1968.

——— "La Nature des Choses." *The New Yorker*, July 28, 1975.

——— Articles in *Gourmet* magazine:
"Turin," May 1974.
"Bread and Cheese," November 1974.
"Paris Journal," January 1975.
"The Bois de Boulogne," May 1975.
"Two Pilgrims in Périgord," February 1976.
"Cipriani of Venice," March 1976.
"All About Truffles," November 1976.
"Venice Pharmacies," September 1977.

WEDECK, HARRY E. *Dictionary of Aphrodisiacs*. New York: Philosophical Library, 1961.

WENT, FRITZ. *Les Plants*. Le Monde Vivant series. New York: Time-Life, 1968.

WHYATT, ROBIN. See Katz, Martha.

WIGGINTON, ELIOT, ed. *The Foxfire Book*. New York: Anchor Books, 1972.

WILDMAN, FREDERICK S., JR. *A Wine Tour of France*. New York: William Morrow, 1967.

WILHELM, STEPHEN. "The Garden Strawberry: A Study of Its Origin." *American Scientist*, May-June 1974.

WILLAN, ANNE. *Great Cooks and Their Recipes, from Taillevent to Escoffier*. New York: McGraw-Hill, 1977.

WILLIAMS, RICHARD L. *The Northwest Coast*. American Wilderness series. New York: Time-Life, 1973.

WILSON, JOSÉ. *American Cooking: The Eastern Heartland*. Foods of the World series. New York: Time-Life, 1971.

WITTY, HELEN. Articles in *Gourmet* magazine:
"Dill," August 1976.
"Rosemary," December 1976.
"Bay Leaves," January 1977.
"Garlic Chives," May 1977.

WOLFE, LINDA. *The Cooking of the Caribbean Islands*. Foods of the World series. New York: Time-Life, 1969.

WOODHAM-SMITH, CECIL. *The Great Hunger*. New York: Harper & Row, 1962.

WYNNE, PETER. *Apples*. New York: Hawthorne Books, 1975.

Acknowledgments

Acknowledgments

This book has benefited by a considerable amount of information gained from sources not generally available—the testimony of individual informants knowledgeable about various sorts of food who have been kind enough to share their knowledge with the author. For eight years while this book was in preparation, I contributed articles on various foods to several daily newspapers, whose readers frequently wrote to me, either to do me the service of correcting errors, or to report an interesting or curious item which had come to their attention.

Most of my correspondents fell into one of four categories: they were living, or had lived, in parts of the world relatively inaccessible to Westerners and were acquainted with their esoteric foods; or they raised food, animal or vegetable, themselves; or they were naturalists or scientists; and a few of them were etymologists. I checked their reports, of course, against standard reference books. Most of my correspondents stood the test of comparison better than the reference books did. I had already discovered that even the best of the standard works were lamentably inaccurate on questions of food. By supplying a missing link or revealing where a mistake had worked its way in, my private informants often clarified for me problems which the reference books had posed by providing incomplete, contradictory, misleading or even downright false data.

Some of the persons who wrote to me developed into dependable, more or less permanent informants. Thus I found myself benefiting from the backstopping provided by a naturalist in France, a botanist in California, an ichthyologist in Germany and an anthropologist in Africa. Some of them overawed me by their erudition. Several elucidated the popular names of foods by adding in parentheses the equivalent in Greek, which, after a fashion, I could handle; but two did the same thing with Chinese ideograms, which I could not; and I even had one correspondent who elucidated his meaning with Egyptian hieroglyphics. My correspondents surprised me also by the nature of the subjects which stirred their interest. Who would have anticipated that four of them, writing from four different countries, would have been inspired to dwell upon the edibility of worms?

I wish to express my thanks to the persons listed below for their contributions on the subjects coupled with their names, and to excuse myself to those (I know there are some) whom I have failed to mention because my filing system is less than perfect.

Acevedo, Mrs. Raymond, Malibu, California, CHILIES.
Arthur, Allen A., Sherman Oaks, California, LOBSTER, PASSION FRUIT.
Asch, Claude, Strasbourg, France, LETTUCE.
Baier, Willard E., Ontario, Canada, ORANGE.
Bates, Betsy Buffington, Paris, France, CONCH.
Bauman, Mark P., Munich, Germany, BROCCIU.
Behrens, Helen Kindler, Rabat, Morocco, BASIL, CORIANDER, CUMIN, PARSLEY, RAS EL HAOUT.
Berger, Kay S., Los Angeles, California, AVOCADO.
Beslop, R. A., North Witham, Essex, England, ORANGE.
Bingo, David G., Paris, France, OYSTERS.
Blixt, Stig, Landskrona, Sweden, PEA.
Bocca, Andrée, La Colle sur Loup, France, EDIBLE FLOWERS.
Bondi, Henry S., Maennedorf, Switzerland, DURIAN.
Brennan, Dan, Anaheim, California, PHEASANT.
Briggs, Dr. Lloyd Cabot, Hancock, New Hampshire, ASS, CAMEL, GHEE, GOAT, HORSE, MULE, MUTTON.
Bryan, J., Albufera, Portugal, CAPERS.
Bryson, Mrs. David, Labadie, France, BLOOD.
Bull, Michael, Vienna, Austria, WORMS.
Burdet, Michèle, Chesières, Switzerland, HORSERADISH, RADISH, SALSIFY, SCORZONERA, TOMATO.
Cadgene, Henri M., Athens, Greece, TURKEY.
Campbell, John M., Preuilly sur Claise, France, SQUASH FLOWERS.
Carlbom, Arthur, Fuengirola, Spain, BARLEY.
Carpenter, Malcolm and Kiki, no address, MAIZE.
Carter, Michele, Chesières, Switzerland, ARTICHOKE, SAXIFRAGE.
Chenier, Dorothy, Paris, France, MELON, PEANUT.
Chiu, Miss Lihbut, no address, GALINGALE.
Chown, Dr. Bruce, Victoria, B.C., Canada, JERUSALEM ARTICHOKE.
Crawford, Geoffrey, New Haven, Connecticut, COMICE PEAR.

Acknowledgments

CROWTHER, A. W., Reading, England, OYSTER.
CUTTAT, ALFRED, no address, CRAB APPLE, CURRANTS, TERMITES.
DAHART, BROOKE, Oslo, Norway, PEAR.
DARCY, A., Fontainebleau, France, SWEETBREADS.
DAVIS, MRS. BILL, Málaga, Spain, BUCKWHEAT.
DAVISON, ROBERT, Paris, France, CERVELAS SAUSAGE.
DELS PRATS, ALFONO TORRENTS, Geneva, Switzerland, QUINCE.
DENES, N., Zurich, Switzerland, STRAWBERRY.
DIETZEL, DR. KARL, Krefeld, Germany, FISH, HERBS.
DILLI, A., Zurich, Switzerland, MANGO.
DIXON, J. C., Paris, France, HANGOVERS.
DORRANCE, MRS. DONALD ROSS, St Vincent de Cosse, France, SEAWEED.
DOWNIE, MRS. JUDITH, London, England, CANDY, LEEKS.
DUCLOS, DANIEL, Queens, New York, OCCITAN LANGUAGE.
DUERR, CARL F., Starnberg, Germany, COWSLIP, SWEETBREADS.
DURHAM, JIMMIE, Geneva, Switzerland, PORK.
EMIL, CHRIS, Granada, Spain, AVOCADO.
ENGELSBY, MARY, Isfahan, Iran, LENTILS.
FEDDERSEN, LEE, Elkhart, Indiana, GARDENING.
FERRARY, JEANETTE, Belmont, Colorado, PARSLEY.
FIELDING, NANCY and TEMPLE, Mallorca, Spain, DURIAN.
FISH, CLIFFORD J., Villajoyesca, Spain, MAN.
FORGUE, GUY JEAN, Montmorency, France, BALONEY.
FOWKER, GLEN R., Terra Bella, California, PISTACHIO.
FOX, CHARLES, Davis, California, TRIPE.
FRANZ, CAROL, San Francisco, California, PINEAPPLE.
FRAZIER, DR. CLAUDE A., no address, HANGOVERS.
FRIENDLICH, MRS. RICHARD J., San Francisco, California, OYSTER.
GARDNER, DORIAN, Paris, France, STRAWBERRY.
GLASER, MORRIS, Pistoia, Italy, CARROT.
GRAHAM, RICHARD, no address, SNAKE.
GRANDJOUAN, MOUGINS, France, ALBERGE, ARROWROOT, BAOBAB, BARLEY, BARNACLE, BASIL, BEANS, BREADFRUIT, CARAWAY, CHAR, CHUFA, GOOSE, INJERA, JACK FRUIT, JORDAN ALMOND, LIMPET, MILLET, MUSHROOM, SALMON, TEFF, TROUT, WATT.
GROSJEAN, MRS. CHARLES A., Overijse, Belgium, ABSINTHE, BROCCOLI.
GUERRERO, MRS. ANTONIO PERAL, Sardinero, Spain, CELERY.
GUSEN, BILL, Decca, Bangladesh, KIWI FRUIT.
HANNA, MRS. W. A., St. Dye sur Loire, France, CHRYSANTHEMUM, CRAB.
HARDY, NOAH, Paris, France, CRANBERRY, PUFFIN, WHALE.
HARTMAN, CARL, Brussels, Belgium, LAMB'S LETTUCE.
HAWKINS, FREDDIE, Paris, France, CAMEL.
HAYES, MARY ANNE, Paris, France, OKRA, POTATO.
HAYNA, MRS. LOIS, Wheat Ridge, Colorado, CATNIP, CARAWAY, CUMIN.
HEIMLICH, MYRIAM, Borex, Switzerland, CHESTNUT, LYCHEE NUT, MACE.
HIX, AL, St. Valéry en Caux, France, ARTICHOKE, ASPARAGUS, CHEESE, CUCUMBER, MEAT, MILK, ONION, PIGEON, POTATO.
HOLLAND, PHILIP, Brussels, Belgium, CARP, LOBSTER, MELON.
HOLLOME, BENJAMIN S., Los Angeles, California, KIWI FRUIT.
HOLMES, ALBERT, Lugano, Switzerland, CLOVER.
HOLZMAN, DONALD, Triel sur Seine, France, GINSENG, MILLET.
HUTCHINSON, GREGORY L., Washington, D.C., BRIE.
HYMAN, PHILIP, Paris, France, HERBS, SILPHIUM.
INGRAHAM, SUSAN, Singapore, PAPAYA.
JACKSON, COLONEL ALLEN, Annapolis, Maryland, CAMEL.
JASON, RICK, Sherman Oaks, California, QUAIL.
JEFFRIES, JOHN, Amsterdam, the Netherlands, MAIZE.
JENKINS, NANCY, Rome, Italy, TARRAGON.
JOHNSON, BETSEY, Paris, France, CARP.
JOHNSON, DANIEL, Posio, Finland, BUCKWHEAT.
JOHNSON, OWEN DENIS, Paris, France, CRAWFISH.
JONES, COLONEL WILLIAM P., Falls Church, Virginia, MANGO.
JONES, WARREN H., Heidelberg, Germany, PIG.
KESEND, MICHAEL, New York, New York, GRAY MULLET ROE.
KIETZMAN, LEROY R., Lausanne, Switzerland, LOBSTER, SHRIMP.
KING, NICHOLAS, Paris, France, CROCODILE.
KOBB, Heidelberg, Germany, CATNIP.
KONINE, HANS, London, England, SHAD.
KORN, CARL G., London, England, WORMS.
KUHL, JEROME M., Rabat, Morocco, GINGER.
LAMBERT, REGINALD F., Nice, France, LAMPREY.
LANG, GEORGE, New York, New York, PEPPERS.
LATTIMORE, OWEN, Leeds, England, CLAMS, CUCUMBER, MUSSELS, PORK.
LESSONA, CONTESSA, Rome, Italy, CHIVES, LIME, MINT.
LEVENE, MRS. SAM, Lausanne, Switzerland, RICE.
LONG, GERALD, London, England, COCKLES.
LORTHIOR, PH., no address, BURDOCK, CAPON, COMICE PEAR.
LYALL, GAVIN, London, England, WALNUT.
MACDOUGALL, HUGH C., Lourenço Marques, Mozambique, CASHEW.
MANASSEER, F., Palma de Mallorca, Spain, DATE.
MAURI, GERALD, Florence, Italy, CARDOON, CITRON, FENNEL.
MCQUIGG, MRS. RUTH, Monrovia, California, DUCKS.
MEDLICOTT, GRACE GIFFEN, Florence, Italy, STRAWBERRY.
MELLON, DORRIE, Ghent, Belgium, HORSE.
MELLON, MRS. J. W., St. Mitre les Remparts, France, BREADFRUIT.
MELO, ANNE MARIE CUNHA, Lisbon, Portugal, ALBERGE.
MERKENS, MRS. W. H., Masy, Belgium, OKRA.
MOISO, MR. AND MRS. JAMES ROBERT, Sinaio, Mexico, DOGFISH.
MOORE, MRS. FRANCES O., Uwchland, Pennsylvania, MUSHROOMS.
MOORE, VIOLET, Macon, Georgia, COLLARDS.
MOWRER, MICHAEL S., Heidelberg, Germany, RADISH.
NOLAN, KATHERINE, Big Sur, California, MUSHROOMS.
NORBOM, ELLEN, Commugny, Vaud, Switzerland, CLOUDBERRY, COD, SALMON, SHRIMP, TROUT.

Acknowledgments

NORMAN, JAMES, San Miguel Allende, Mexico, CACTUS.
OBERMANN, ANTON P. R., Les Issambres, France, CHICKEN.
OLDENHEIMER, W. L., Brussels, Belgium, WORMS.
OPITZ, KURT, Hamburg, Germany, CABBAGE, COLLARDS, KALE, MUSTARD, ORACH, SPINACH.
PALMER, MRS. MARTHA, Paris, France, CAPERS, CLAMS, HERBS.
PELTON, RUSSELL M., Brussels, Belgium, CLAMS.
PERRY, CHARLES, Los Angeles, California, ALMOND, CLOVES, GUAVA, OLIVE, PEA, PEANUT, PEPPER, PERSIMMON.
PINEO, RONN, Orange, California, CRAB APPLE.
POLAK, H. JOOST, Manila, Philippine Islands, CHAYOTE.
POLLOCK, SYLVIA, Paris, France, SWEETBREADS.
PONS, ROBERT W., El Biar, Algeria, MEDLAR.
PROBYN, E. M., Richmond, Surrey, England, CARP.
PUTNAM, M. W., Paris, France, OKRA.
RANKIN, MARK, London, England, COTTON.
REWALD, JOHN, Menerbes, France, WORMS.
RHODES, LYMAN P., Torremolinos, Málaga, Spain, CRAWFISH, MAIZE.
RICHARDSON, J. C., UNESCO, Paris, France, CAROB.
ROBINSON, PRESTON, Williamstown, Massachusetts, ASPARAGUS.
ROOT, Winifred, Rockport, Massachusetts, CLOVES, SEA COCONUT.
ROSENBERG, FRED, St. Sulpice, Switzerland, PLUMS.
RUSSELL, FRANCES S., Burbank, California, FENUGREEK.
SALMON FAMILY, Wayside Farm, Boonton, New Jersey, APPLES.
SANTREY, LAURENCE, Paris, France, WORMS.
SAROYAN, WILLIAM, Paris, France, GARLIC.
SCHLIGT, ADRIENNE, Le Chesnay, France, TRIPE.
SCHLOSS, EDITH, Rome, Italy, MUSHROOMS.
SCHNUR, DR. HARRY C., St. Gall, Switzerland, CITRON.
SCHRIBER, H. J., Sacramento, California, ALMOND.
SCHROEDER, PROF. C. A., Los Angeles, California, CITRON, CITRUS FRUITS, EXOTIC FRUITS, GRAPEFRUIT, KUMQUAT, SHADDOCK.
SCHWARZ, DR. KLAUS, Long Beach, California, ARSENIC.
SCHWOBE, CALVIN U., Cambridge University, England, BARNACLE, LIMPET.
SEARS, DR. BERNARD, Brookline, Massachusetts, STEAMER CLAMS.
SENVER, JOHN, San Diego, California, OSAGE ORANGE.
SHIMIROV, I., Turku, Finland, CAVIAR.
SIMONS, A. D., Pany, Switzerland, BULLACE, PLUMS, SILPHIUM.
SIMPLICH, FREDERICK, JR., Kula, Maui, Hawaii, GRAVEY, KUKUS NUT, MAUI ONION, MOUNTAIN APPLE, O'HIA APPLE, RED SALT.
SINSHEIMER, BERNARD, Wiesbaden, Germany, PHEASANT.
SJÖBY, JAN, Brussels, Belgium, DILL.
SMITH, CHARLES H., JR., Orléans, France, ACORN.
SMITH, T., Ferney-Voltaire, France, HERRING.
SMITS-CHIANG, KATHRYN, Paris, France, PEACH.
SMYTH, W. F., Tel Aviv, Israel, WATERCRESS.
STAGG, F. L., Paris, France, PLANTAIN.
STANFORD, DONALD KENT, Ontario, Canada, CUBEB.
STEINGUT, STEPHEN S., London, England, BEAR.
STEVENS, PROF. HALSEY, Los Angeles, California, ORANGE.
STONEMAN, WILLIAM H., La Celle St. Cloud, France, SALMON.
TEMPLE, WILLARD, Santa Barbara, California, CUBEB.
TIMMERMAN, MRS. E. H. L., Terveruren, Belgium, SORREL.
TURKER, MRS. MARION, no address, BURDOCK.
TUTTLE, M. A., Cape Town, South Africa, CARP, CASSAVA, MAIZE.
UNREADABLE, various addresses, BLOOD, CLEAVERS, COCKSCOMBS.
VAJDA, NIKLÓS, Budapest, Hungary, BAY LEAF.
VAN VOORTHUISEN, E. G., Onagadoungo, Upper Volta, Africa, YAM.
VERGOTTIS, P., Monte Carlo, SQUASH FLOWERS.
VOGEL, THERESA, Los Angeles, California, WALNUTS.
VOMWO, MS. BRENDA, Paris, France, OKRA.
WAIN, WILLIAM, Canoga Park, California, WALNUTS.
WALLACE, MRS. PAT, Beverly Hills, California, CARIBOU.
WARREN, BROOKS, Brussels, Belgium, KALE.
WATSON, LUCIA H., Waterville, Ireland, CURDS.
WEISER, HUBERT H., Los Angeles, California, CHILIES.
WHITBREAD, R. L., no address, BLACK-EYED PEA, YOGURT.
WISE, R. G., Ramatuelle, France, CAMEL, POTATO.
WRIGHT, JOHN S., Santa Barbara, California, CRAWFISH.

Picture Credits

Picture Credits

Abbreviations:
AMNH—American Museum of Natural History, New York
BLSI—Botany Library, Smithsonian Institution
BM—Brooklyn Museum
LC—Library of Congress
MMA—Metropolitan Museum of Art, New York
MOMA—Museum of Modern Art, New York
NGA—National Gallery of Art
NYPL—New York Public Library
OHS—Oregon Historical Society

Abalone—p. 1. AMNH
Allspice—p. 3. BLSI
Almond—p. 4. LC
Anchovy—p. 5. NYPL
Angelica—p. 6. LC
Anise—p. 6. LC
Apple—p. 7. Cliché des Musees Nationaux—Paris
Apple—p. 8. MMA, Bequest of Samuel A. Lewisohn, 1951
Apple—p. 9. BM, Dick S. Ramsay Fund
Apple—p. 11. NYPL
Apricot—p. 13. Art Gallery of Ontario, Toronto
Artichoke—p. 13. MMA, Bequest of Emma A. Sheafer, 1974
Asparagus—p. 15. BLSI
Avocado—p. 17. Cliché des Musées Nationaux—Paris

Banana—p. 20. Petersburg Press
Barley—p. 21. The Pierpont-Morgan Library
Basil—p. 23. NYPL
Bass—p. 23. MMA, George A. Hearn Fund, 1952
Bay Leaf—p. 24. NYPL
Bean—p. 27. British Library
Beef—p. 29. MMA
Beet—p. 30. Mondadori
Bison—p. 32. Dunbarton Oaks Garden Library
Blackberry—p. 34. Private Collection
Blueberry—p. 35. BLSI
Breadfruit—p. 36. The Hermitage
Broccoli—p. 37. Felipe Rojas-Lombardi
Brussels Sprouts—p. 38. Felipe Rojas-Lombardi
Buckwheat—p. 40. NGA, Chester Dale Collection, 1962
Bustard—p. 41. From *Bird Life*, published in the United States by Harry N. Abrams, Inc., New York, © Mr. Ad Cameron/Elsevier Publishing Projects Lausanne.
Butternut—p. 41. BLSI

Cabbage—p. 43. MMA, Maria de Witt Jesup Fund, 1939
Camel—p. 45. National Gallery of Canada, Ottawa, Gift of Allan Bronfman, Montreal
Capercaillie—p. 46. NYPL
Capers—p. 47. BLSI
Caraway—p. 48. NYPL
Carp—p. 49. MMA, The Cloisters Collection
Carrot—p. 51. MMA
Cassava—p. 52. BLSI
Catfish—p. 53. NYPL
Cauliflower—p. 54. Felipe Rojas-Lombardi
Caviar—p. 55. AMNH
Celery—p. 57. NYPL
Char—p. 59. BM, Dick S. Ramsay Fund
Chard—p. 60. NYPL
Cherry—p. 61. MMA, Sansbury Mills Fund, 1974
Chervil—p. 63. LC
Chestnut—p. 64. Felipe Rojas-Lombardi
Chicken—p. 67. MMA, Fletcher Fund, 1947, The A. W. Pahr Collection
Chick Pea—p. 69. BLSI
Chili—p. 69. NYPL
Chives—p. 70. BLSI
Chocolate—p. 71. The Lester Glassner Collection
Cicely—p. 73. BLSI
Cinnamon—p. 75. NYPL
Citron—p. 76. Felipe Rojas-Lombardi
Clam—p. 78. NYPL
Clove—p. 79. LC
Cockle—p. 81. NYPL
Coconut—p. 82. MMA, Amelia B. Lazarus Fund, 1910
Cod—p. 85. New Hampshire Historical Society
Collards—p. 87. Joseph Harris Company, Rochester, NY
Coriander—p. 89. LC
Corn—p. 90. MMA
Cowpea—p. 91. BLSI
Crab—p. 92. MMA, Bequest of Joseph Durkee, Gift of Darius Ogden Mills, and Gift of Ruxton Love, by Exchange, 1972
Cranberry—p. 93. Will Bradley, Nostalgia Inc. Collection
Cress—p. 97. Felipe Rojas-Lombardi
Cucumber—p. 99. The Frick Collection
Currant—p. 101. The Chrysler Museum, Gift of Walter P. Chrysler, Jr.

Dandelion—p. 103. AMNH
Date—p. 105. BLSI
Deer—p. 107. MMA, Fletcher Fund, 1946
Dill—p. 109. British Library
Duck—p. 111. MMA, Gift of Mrs. W. Bayard Cutting, 1932
Durian—p. 113. BLSI

Eel—p. 115. NYPL
Egg—p. 119. The *Forbes* Magazine Collection, New York
Eggplant—p. 121. MOMA, The Philip L. Goodwin Collection
Endive—p. 123. Mondadori

Fennel—p. 127. Mondadori
Fenugreek—p. 128. LC
Fig—p. 129. Naples Museum
Filbert—p. 131. BLSI
Fish—p. 132. MMA, The Henry L. Phillips Collection, Bequest of Henry L. Phillips, 1940
Fish—p. 133. MMA, The Fletcher Fund, 1925
Flatfish—p. 136. MMA, Harris Brisbane Dick Fund, 1953
Flatfish—p. 137. Rosalie Stambler Nadeau, photo by Andrew DeLory

Garlic—p. 143. LC
Gelatin—p. 145. Philadelphia Museum of Art, Bequest of Mr. and Mrs. William M. Elkins
Ginger—p. 147. LC
Goose—p. 151. MMA
Gooseberry—p. 153. MOMA
Grape—p. 154. Lester Glassner Collection
Grape—p. 155. Elvehjem Museum of Art, Max W. Zabel Fund Purchase
Grapefruit—p. 157. Joanne Klein
Grouse—p. 159. Wallace Collection
Grouse—p. 161. NYPL
Guava—p. 163. BLSI
Guinea Fowl—p. 164. NYPL
Guinea Pig—p. 165. AMNH

Haddock—p. 168. NYPL
Hake—p. 170. NYPL
Hare—p. 173. Albertina Museum, Vienna
Herring—p. 175. Archives of the City of Prague
Honey—p. 179. MMA, Egyptian Expedition
Hops—p. 181. NYPL
Horse—p. 183. MMA, Rogers Fund, 1921
Horseradish—p. 185. MMA, Bequest of A. T. Clearwater, 1933
Huckleberry—p. 187. NYPL
Hyssop—p. 188. LC

Jerusalem Artichoke—p. 193. NYPL
John Dory—p. 195. LC
Jujube—p. 197. New-York Historical Society

Kale—p. 199. OHS
Kelp—p. 201. BLSI
Kid—p. 203. MMA
Kidney—p. 205. Cliché des Musées Nationaux—Paris
King Crab—p. 207. AMNH
Kiwi Fruit—p. 207. Ralf Manstein
Kohlrabi—p. 209. NYPL
Kumquat—p. 210. BLSI

Lamb—p. 213. MMA, Gift of J. Pierpont Morgan, 1917
Land Crab—p. 215. NYPL
Leek—p. 217. Mr. Millar
Lemon—p. 220. Kunstmuseum, Basel
Lentil—p. 223. NYPL
Lettuce—p. 225. LC
Liver—p. 228. Felipe Rojas-Lombardi
Lobster—p. 231. The Houghton Library, Harvard University

Picture Credits

Mackerel—p. 234. AMNH
Maize—p. 237. LC
Mango—p. 241. MMA, Gift of William Church Osborn, 1949
Maple—p. 243. The Phillips Collection, Washington
Marjoram—p. 247. NYPL
Meat—p. 249. MMA, The Elisha Whittelsey Collection, The Elisha Whittelsey Fund, 1964
Medlar—p. 251. LC
Melon—p. 253. LC
Milk—p. 259. Rijksmuseum, Amsterdam
Milk—p. 261. MMA
Millet—p. 263. MMA, Purchase, Joseph Pulitzer Bequest
Mint—p. 264. LC
Mulberry—p. 269. The Folger Shakespeare Library, Washington
Mullet—p. 271. Alfred A. Knopf
Mushroom—p. 273. Union House and Millville Public Library, photo courtesy New Jersey State Museum
Mushroom—p. 274. LC
Mussel—p. 275. The Pierpont Morgan Library
Mustard—p. 278. LC
Mutton—p. 280. The *Forbes* Magazine Collection, New York, photo by O. E. Nelson

New Zealand Spinach—p. 283. NYPL
Nut—p. 286. Private collection, London
Nutmeg—p. 289. NYPL

Oats—p. 293. NYPL
Okra—p. 294. Joseph Harris Company, Rochester, NY
Olive—p. 297. NGA, Chester Dale Collection, 1962
Onion—p. 301. Cliché des Musées Nationaux—Paris
Orange—p. 305. NGA, Chester Dale Collection, 1962
Oregano—p. 306. The Pierpont Morgan Library
Oyster—p. 309. NGA, Adele R. Levy Fund, Inc., 1962

Papaya—p. 314. NYPL
Parsley—p. 317. NYPL
Parsnip—p. 319. OHS
Partridge—p. 321. NYPL
Pea—p. 325. Murray Alcosser
Peach—p. 327. BM
Peach—p. 329. MMA
Peanut—p. 331. NYPL
Pear—p. 333. MOMA, Gift of Archibald Macleish
Pecan—p. 337. BLSI
Pepper—p. 339. O. K. Harris
Perch—p. 343. NYPL
Persimmon—p. 345. MMA, Rogers Fund, 1957
Pheasant—p. 349. MMA, The Cloisters Collection, Gift of John D. Rockefeller, Jr., 1937
Pike—p. 352. NYPL
Pineapple—p. 355. MMA, George A. Hearn Fund, 1931
Pistachio—p. 359. BLSI
Plum—p. 361. LC
Pomegranate—p. 367. MMA, Gift of W. R. Valentiner, 1908
Pork—p. 371. MMA, Harris Brisbane Dick Fund, 1928
Pork—p. 374. MMA
Potato—p. 379. MMA, Robert Lehman Collection, 1975
Potato—p. 383. Vincent Virga

Quahog—p. 389. Bromley and Company, Boston
Quail—p. 391. NYPL
Quince—p. 395. LC

Rabbit—p. 399. MMA, Gift of Horace Havemeyer, 1929, The H. C. Havemeyer Collection
Radish—p. 401. MOMA, Gift of the Artist
Raspberry—p. 405. OHS
Rhubarb—p. 409. British Library
Rice—p. 413. Eve and Frank Metz
Rosemary—p. 419. Thomas C. Crowell/Harper & Row
Rye—p. 421. Allen Art Museum, Oberlin

Saffron—p. 426. LC
Sage—p. 429. LC
Salmon—p. 431. OHS
Salsify—p. 437. LC
Salt—p. 439. MMA, Gift of Frederick Ashton de Peyster (Sr.), 1946
Scallion—p. 447. Julie Metz
Scallop—p. 449. NGA, Samuel H. Kress Collection, 1952
Shad—p. 445. NYPL
Shrimp—p. 459. AMNH
Sorghum—p. 465. LC
Sorrel—p. 467. Felipe Rojas-Lombardi
Spinach—p. 471. NYPL
Spiny Lobster—p. 472. Felipe Rojas-Lombardi
Squash—p. 475. Joseph Harris Company, Rochester
Squash—p. 476. Farnsworth Art Museum, Rockland, Maine, photo by Roy M. Elkind
Squash—p. 477. Museum of Art, Rhode Island School of Design
Steamer clam—p. 479. Bromley & Company, Inc.
Strawberry—p. 483. The Folger Shakespeare Library
Strawberry—p. 485. The Brooklyn Museum, A. Augustus
Sugar—p. 487. MMA, Rogers Fund, 1947
Sweetbreads—p. 496. Felipe Rojas-Lombardi
Sweet potato—p. 499. LC

Tarragon—p. 505. LC
Thyme—p. 508. LC
Thyme—p. 509. MMA
Tomato—p. 513. LC
Tripe—p. 519. MMA, Gift of George Coe Graves, The Sylmaris Collection, 1920
Trout—p. 523. MMA, Gift of the Society of Medalists, 1953
Truffle—p. 527. Felipe Rojas-Lombardi
Tuna—p. 533. AMNH
Turkey—p. 537. Cliché des Musées Nationaux—Paris
Turnip—p. 543. MMA, The Harry G. C. Packard Collection of Asian Art, Gift of Harry G. C. Packard and Purchase, Fletcher, Rogers, Harris Brisbane Dick and Louis V. Bell Funds, Joseph Pulitzer Bequest and The Annenberg Fund, Inc., Gift 1975

Vanilla—p. 551. NYPL
Veal—p. 555. The Hermitage, Acquired from the State Museum Fund, 1923

Walnut—p. 561. National Archives
Wheat—p. 567. MMA, Rogers Fund, 1919

Yam—p. 585. Ralf Manstein

Color Photos

A. *Apricot—Art Gallery of Ontario, Toronto*
B. *Beef—MMA*
C. *Cherry—MMA, Sansbury Mills Fund, 1974*
C. *Cucumber—MMA, The Jules S. Bache Collection, 1949*
D. *Duck—MMA, Gift of Mrs. W. Bayard Cutting, 1932*
E. *Egg—The* Forbes *Magazine Collection, New York*
F. *Fig—Jarry Lang*
G. *Goose—MMA*
H. *Horse—MMA, Rogers Fund, 1921*
J. *Jerusalem Artichoke—BLSI*
K. *Kiwi Fruit—Ralf Manstein*
L. *Leek—Petersburg Press*
M. *Maple—The Phillips Collection, Washington*
M. *Millet—MMA, Purchase, Joseph Pulitzer Bequest*
M. *Mutton—The* Forbes *Magazine Collection, New York, photo by O. E. Nelson*
N. *Nutmeg—BLSI*
O. *Oyster—NGA, Adele R. Levy Fund, Inc., 1962*
P. *Peach—MMA*
P. *Pheasant—MMA, The Cloisters Collection, Gift of John D. Rockefeller, Jr., 1937*
P. *Plum—The Pierpont Morgan Library*
Q. *Quahog—Emerick Bronson*
Q. *Quince—LC*
R. *Rabbit—MMA, Gift of Horace Havemeyer, 1929, The H. C. Havemeyer Collection*
S. *Salt—O. K. Harris*
S. *Squash—Farnsworth Art Museum, Rockland, Maine*
T. *Turkey—NA*
V. *Venison—MMA, Fletcher Fund, 1946*
W. *Wheat—MMA, Rogers Fund, 1919*